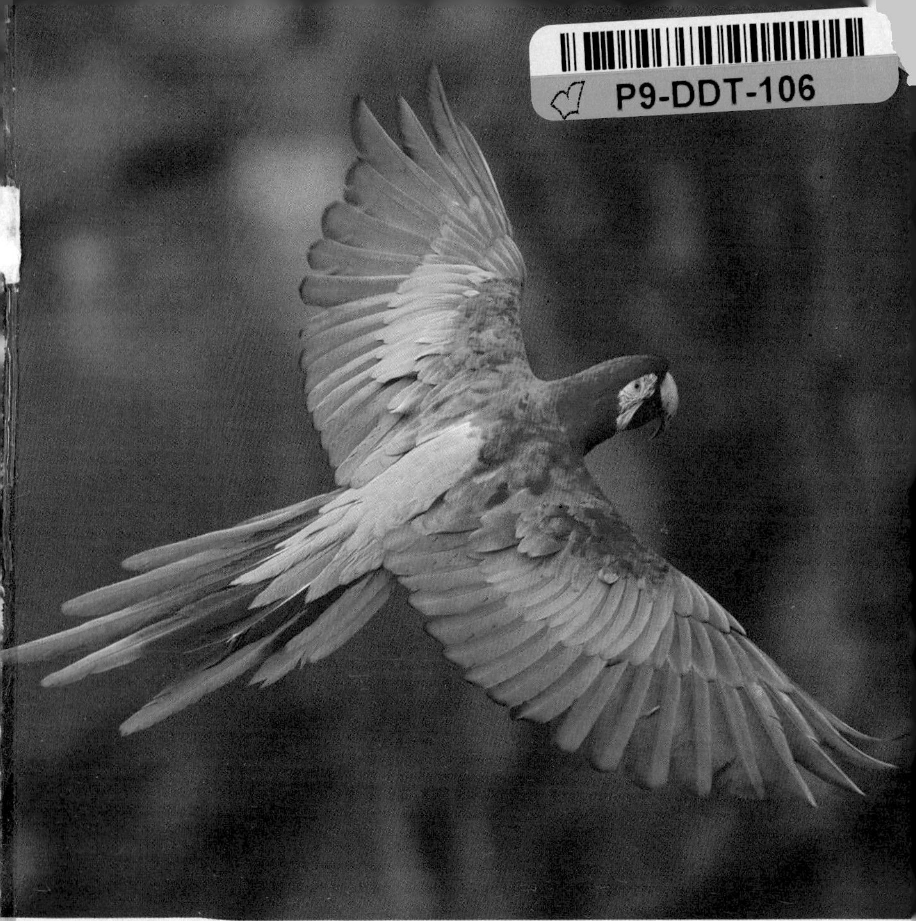

THE ROUGH GUIDE TO

Peru

written and researched by

Dilwyn Jenkins

roughguides.com

TAXI
CARGA
CANTER
PZ 5432

Contents

OPPOSITE BUS TRAVEL, PERUVIAN ANDES **PREVIOUS PAGE** PARROT, AMAZON JUNGLE

Introduction to
Peru

From exotic jungle to coastal desert via the breathtaking peaks of the Andes, Peru's staggering variety of landscapes means the potential for adventure is boundless. Whether you want to trek the hallowed Inca Trail, drink pisco sours in a sleepy colonial town, swim with pink dolphins or paddle your way down the Amazon in a dugout canoe – or all of the above – this is a country that's ripe for exploring. Wherever you go, Peru's vibrant Andean culture, one of the most exciting in the Americas, will brighten your travels: tucked-away highland towns explode into colour on market day, and local fiestas are celebrated with unbridled enthusiasm.

This immense wealth of sights and experiences has its roots in one of the world's richest heritages, topped by the **Inca Empire** and its fabulous **archeological gems**, not to mention the monumental adobe temples and pre-Inca ruins along the desert coast. Magical Machu Picchu may be the big gun in Peru's archeological arsenal, but there are plenty of other fascinating sites too – and important new discoveries are constantly being unearthed.

Boasting access to the highest tropical mountain range in the world as well as one of the best preserved areas of virgin Amazon rainforest, Peru's **wildlife** is as diverse as you'd expect, and sights such as jaguars slinking through the jungle, caimans sunning themselves on riverbanks and dazzling macaws gathering at Amazon clay licks are all within the visitor's grasp. For those looking for adrenaline-fuelled fun, a host of **outdoor activities** are on offer, from trekking ancient trails and whitewater rafting to paragliding and hurtling through the desert on dune-buggy rides.

Equally, a trip to Peru could focus on more restful pursuits. Widely touted as one of the world's **culinary hotspots**, the country – and Lima in particular – offers an array of exotic tastes to appeal to curious palates, as well as a laidback, vibrant dining scene, ranging from backstreet cevicherías to gourmet restaurants. And in the big cities, you can expect buzzing **nightlife** too.

ABOVE RESERVA NACIONAL PARACAS **OPPOSITE** CANOPY WALKWAY, AMAZON JUNGLE

Despite it all, simple, unaffected pleasures remain in place. The country's prevailing attitude is that there is always enough time for a chat, a ceviche, or another drink. Peru is accepting of its visitors – it's a place where the resourceful and open-minded traveller can break through barriers of class, race and language far more easily than most of its inhabitants can. Even the Amazon jungle region – nearly two-thirds of the country's landmass, but home to a mere fraction of its population – is accessible for the most part, with countless tour operators on hand to organize trips to even the furthest-flung corners. Now all you have to do is figure out where to start.

Where to go

You're most likely to arrive in the buzzing and at least fitfully elegant capital, **Lima**; a modern city, it manages to effortlessly blend traditional Peruvian heritage with twenty-first-century glitz. **Cusco** is perhaps the most obvious place to head from here. A beautiful and bustling colonial city, it was once the ancient heart of the Inca Empire, and is surrounded by some of the most spectacular mountain landscapes and palatial ruins in Peru, and by magnificent hiking country. The world-famous **Inca Trail**, which culminates at the lofty, fog-shrouded Inca citadel of **Machu Picchu**, is just one of several equally scenic and challenging treks in this region of Peru alone.

Along the **coast**, there are more fascinating archeological sites as well as glorious beaches and sparky towns. South of Lima are the bizarre **Nasca Lines**, which have mystified since their discovery some seventy years ago, as well as the vast **Reserva**

Metres
5000
4000
3000
2000
1000
500
200
100
0
QUITO
ECUADOR
COLOMBIA
N
Guayaquil
Río Pastaza
Río Putumayo
Río Napo
Río Morona
Tumbes
TUMBES
RESERVED ZONE
Mancora
CERRO DE
AMOTAPE
NATIONAL PARK
Talara
Piura
Catacaos
Sechura
Olmos
Lambayeque
Chiclayo
Pacasmayo
San Pedro de Lloc
Trujillo
Huamachuco
Cajamarca
Celendín
Leymebamba
Tingo
Chachapoyas
Jaen
Bagua Grande
Río Marañón
Orellana
Borja
Barranca
Puerto América
Lagunas
Santa Cruz
Yurimaguas
Rioja
Moyobamba
Lamas
Tarapoto
Juanjui
Río Huallaga
DANGEROUS ROUTE
JUANJUI - TINGO MARIA
PACAYA-
SAMIRIA
NATIONAL
RESERVE
Iquitos
Nauta
Requena
Río Ucayali
Pucallpa
Pevas
Río Amazonas
Caballococha
Leticia
Tabatinga
Ramon
Castilla
BRAZIL
Manaus, Belém & the Atlantic

PACIFIC OCEAN
BOLIVIA
CHILE
LA PAZ
Chimbote
Caraz
Casma
Huaraz
HUASCARÁN NATIONAL PARK
Tingo Maria
Huánuco
Pozuzo
Oxapampa
Cerro de Pasco
La Merced
Canta
Satipo
La Oroya
Tarma
LIMA
Huancayo
Huancavelica
Ayacucho
Cañete
Pisco
Peninsula de Paracas
Ica
Nasca
Chala
Camana
Mollendo
Ilo
Tacna
Arica
Moquegua
Arequipa
Cotahuasi
Chivay
COLCA CANYON
Juliaca
Puno
Juli
Yunguyo
Lake Titicaca
Sicuini
Urcos
Cusco
Abancay
Urubamba
Machu Picchu
Quillabamba
Kiteni
PONGO DE MAINIQUE
Paucartambo
Pillcopata
Shintuya
MANU NATIONAL PARK
Boca Manu
Boca Colorado
Río Ucayali
Atalaya
R. Tambo
Río Ene
Río Urubamba
Sepahua
Río de las Piedras
Iñapari
Iberia
Puerto Maldonado
Puerto Heath
TAMBOPATA-CANDAMO RESERVED ZONE
BAHUAJA-SONENE NATIONAL PARK
R. Tambopata
Río Inambari
0
250
kilometres

BEST OF THE FIESTAS

Peruvians love any excuse for a celebration. In Andean towns and villages, especially, communities host a huge number of **festivals**. Most of these have some link to the religious calendar, and the major Christian holidays of Christmas and Easter – infused with indigenous elements – still provide the basis for the biggest festivities. **Cusco** in particular is a great place for holidays that involve some sort of Inca ritual, **Puno** is renowned as the capital of Andean music and folkloric tradition, and in the hills around **Huaraz**, it's common to stumble across a village fiesta, with its explosion of human energy and noise, bright colours and a mixture of pagan and Catholic symbolism. Costumed processions, eating and drinking are the core activities of village celebrations, and gatherings are an excuse for locals to show off their musical talents and dance moves.

Carnival For a grand old time just about anywhere, you can't go wrong during **Carnival** (generally late February), a wholesale licence to throw water at everyone and generally go crazy.

Corpus Christi About two months after Easter Sunday, Peruvians celebrate Corpus Christi, honouring the saints. Processions are the most vibrant in Cusco, where church officials carry ornate sacred icons through the streets.

Fiesta de la Virgen del Carmen At this festival, which takes place in the pueblo of Paucartambo near Cusco (see box, p.272), usually the second or third weekend in July, the villagers enact symbolic dramas, dressing up as Spanish colonists and wearing hideous blue-eyed masks with long hairy beards.

Inti Raymi At the end of June, Inti Raymi (see p.219) – Quechua for "resurrection of the sun" – is one of the largest festivals in South America, drawing visitors from all over the world for a lavish and theatrical week-long presentation of Peru's Inca roots. Based on the Inca ritual of the same name (held on the winter – June – solstice to honour and welcome the sun god and request his return), the festival is celebrated in the fortress of Sacsayhuaman.

Qoyllur Rit'i Just before Corpus Christi, the festival of Qoyllur Rit'i (see p.219) is held on a full moon and blends Catholic and indigenous traditions. Pilgrims trek to the foot of a glacier – considered an *apu*, or mountain god – to recharge their spirits.

Nacional Paracas, dense with wildlife, and the oasis resort of **Huacachina**, which offers both relaxation and white-knuckle thrills. If that all sounds too active, you could always duck away to spend a day lazily sipping wine at the many **Ica Valley bodegas**.

North of Lima lie the great adobe city of **Chan Chan** and the **Valley of the Pyramids**. The surfing hangouts of **Puerto Chicama** and trendy **Máncora** beach are big draws along this stretch, but almost all of the coastal towns come replete with superb beaches, plentiful nightlife and great food.

For high mountains and long-distance treks, head for the stunning glacial lakes, snowy peaks and little-known ruins of the **sierra** north of Lima, particularly the ice-capped mountains and their valleys around **Huaraz**, but also the more gentle hills, attractive villages and ancient sites in the regions of **Cajamarca and Chachapoyas**. The central sierra is crammed with tradition and stunning colonial architecture, at its peak in **Ayacucho** and **Huancayo**; the region around **Tarma** is also worth exploring, offering a variety of landscapes, from jungles and caves to waterfalls and stupendous terraced valleys.

If it's wildlife you're interested in, there's plenty to see almost everywhere, but **the jungle** provides startling opportunities for close and exotic encounters. From the comfort of tourist lodges in **Iquitos** to river excursions around **Puerto Maldonado**, the fauna and flora of the world's largest tropical forest can be experienced first-hand here more easily

CLOCKWISE FROM TOP LEFT FIESTA DE LA VIRGEN DE CARMEN, PAUCARTAMBO; LLAMA, MACHU PICCHU; HUANCAYO CATHEDRAL

PERUVIAN CUISINE

Peru's astonishing ecological diversity has helped to produce an exciting **cuisine**. The national dish – **ceviche** – is made from fresh seafood marinated in lime juice and chillies, then served with sweet potato, a cob of corn and salad. Washed down at Sunday lunchtime with a cool Cusqueña beer, it's an experience not to be missed.

Cuy (roast guinea pig), an exotic local speciality, is also worth a try, even if the thought may be off-putting. **Street snacks** are tasty and good value – grilled meats and *empanadas* are available almost anywhere, alongside delicious tropical produce. Finally, don't leave without sampling the national tipple, **pisco sour**: a mix of Peruvian pisco, lime, syrup, egg white and bitters – delicious and surprisingly potent.

than in any other Amazon-rim country. Not far from Iquitos, the **Reserva Nacional Pacaya-Samiria** is a remote and stunningly beautiful, though little-visited region; while close to Cusco, just below the cloud forest, the Manu Biosphere Reserve is another wildlife hotspot. Further towards the Bolivian and Brazilian jungle frontier, the **Reserva Nacional Tambopata** holds some of the most exciting jungle and varied wildlife in the world.

When to go

Picking the best time to visit Peru's various regions is complicated by the country's physical characteristics; temperatures can vary hugely across the country (see box, p.45). Summer along the **desert coast** more or less fits the expected image of the southern hemisphere – extremely hot and sunny between December and March (especially in the north), cooler and with a frequent hazy mist between April and November – although only in the polluted environs of **Lima** does the coastal winter ever get cold enough to necessitate a sweater. Swimming is possible all year round, though the water itself (thanks to the Humboldt Current) is cool-to-cold at the best of times. To swim or surf for any length of time you'd need to follow local custom and wear a wetsuit. Apart from the occasional shower over Lima it hardly ever rains in the desert. The freak exception, every ten years or so, is when the shift in ocean currents of **El Niño** causes torrential downpours, devastating crops, roads and communities all down the coast. The last really heavy one was in 1983, though there have been several El Niños since then.

In **the Andes**, the seasons are more clearly marked, with heavy rains from December to March and a warm, relatively dry period from June to September. Inevitably, though, there are always some sunny weeks in the rainy season and wet ones in the dry. A similar pattern dominates **the jungle**, though rainfall here is heavier and more frequent, and it's hot and humid all year round.

Taking all of this into account, the **best time to visit** the coast is around January while it's hot, and the mountains and jungle are at their best after the rains, from May until September. Since this is unlikely to be possible on a single trip there's little point in worrying about it – the country's attractions are invariably enough to override the need for guarantees of good weather.

OPPOSITE FROM TOP POISON DART FROG; CORDILLERA BLANCA MOUNTAINS; MÁNCORA BEACH

Author picks

After 35 years of exploring every corner of Peru, author Dilwyn Jenkins has selected a few experiences he considers essential for a true taste of this richly diverse country.

Peruvian cuisine Try traditional favourites like seafood ceviche at *Caplina* in Lima (p.89) or *Restaurant Big Ben* in Huanchaco (p.367), as well as *novoandino* fusion cuisine at *Astrid y Gastón* in Lima (p.89) and *Fallen Angel* in Cusco (p.228).

Music Andean tribal fusion is at its best in Cusco; try *The Muse* (p.230). Traditional folk can be enjoyed at *La Quinta Jerusalen* in Arequipa (p.169). For twenty-first-century sounds, head for lively *Deja-vu* in Lima (p.92) or *Forum Rock Café* in Arequipa (p.169).

Inca citadels Machu Picchu (p.257) is justifiably Peru's greatest attraction, but the country abounds in strikingly perpendicular sites such as Choquequirao (p.267) and Pisac (p.239).

Beach life Around 2000km long, Peru's desert coastline is one very big beach. Of the resorts, Máncora (p.414) is the most popular, but other hotspots include Puerto Chicama (p.372) and Huanchaco (p.365).

Trekking in the Andes The Inca Trail (see p.252) remains the most popular trek, but the hike to Choquequirao (p.267) or one of the glacial landscapes around Cusco are equally inspiring. The Cordillera Blanca mountains around Huaraz (p.314) are renowned for their hiking and climbing, or head for scenic Chachapoyas (p.385) and Kuelap (p.389).

Ancient mysteries The lure of ancient mysteries has drawn millions to Peru over the years. Most of these cultural puzzles – like the Nasca Lines (p.129), the Valley of the Pyramids (p.404) and Temple of the Moon (p.236) – are along the desert coastal strip.

The jungle In the south, the Río Tambopata (p.443) and Manu (p.446) are best for spotting wildlife, while the central (p.453) and northern selva (p.465) also offer excellent tours into the unspoilt Amazon and its communities.

Our author recommendations don't end here. We've flagged up our favourite places – a perfectly sited hotel, an atmospheric café, a special restaurant – throughout the Guide, highlighted with the ★ symbol.

28

things not to miss

It's not possible to see everything that Peru has to offer in one trip – and we don't suggest you try. What follows, in no particular order, is a selective taste of the country's highlights: colourful towns, awe-inspiring ruins, spectacular hikes and exotic wildlife. Each highlight has a page reference to take you straight into the Guide, where you can find out more.

1

1 PISAC MARKET

Page 240

Andean markets serve as true community hubs – not to mention excellent places to sample local goods and produce – and Pisac's thriving morning market is one of the best.

2 PERUVIAN WILDLIFE

Page 514

Whether spotting a three-toed sloth in the Amazon treetops or crossing paths with a *vicuña* while hiking in the Andes, Peru's sheer variety of flora and fauna never fails to amaze.

3 TRADITIONAL HEALING

Page 479

Alternative medicine, using herbs sold in markets and practised by shamans and other healers, has a long and respected history in Peru.

4 HIKING THE INCA TRAIL

Page 252

Culminating at Machu Picchu, this is one of the most popular and eye-opening trails in the world.

5 LAGUNAS DE LLANGANUCO

Page 330

The deep blue of these lakes in the Cordillera Blanca changes with the weather.

6 HUACACHINA

Page 128

This sacred healing lagoon, ringed by palm trees and hidden among massive sand dunes, draws sandboarders and dune-buggy riders from all over the world.

7 KUELAP

Page 389

The ruined citadel of Kuelap is one of the most fascinating archeological sites in the Andes.

8 UROS ISLANDS

Page 194

One of Lake Titicaca's many treasures, these man-and-woman-made floating villages have existed in the lake since Inca times.

9 PISCO SOUR

Page 88

Deservedly the national drink of Peru, the pisco sour refreshes thanks to its limes with crushed ice – and can also have the kick of a mule.

10 ANDEAN AGRICULTURAL TERRACES

Pages 184 &178

These mountainside terraces in the magnificent Cotahuasi and Colca canyons give evidence of the impressive organization of pre-Conquest native societies.

8
9
10

11
12
13
14

11 TRUJILLO

Page 354

Though it doesn't attract the hype of Lima or Cusco, Peru's third city charms with its colonial architecture and cosmopolitan atmosphere.

12 BALLESTAS ISLANDS

Page 116

Often called the Peruvian Galapagos, these islands located off the coast of Pisco are teeming with bird and marine life.

13 CEVICHE

Page 34

Peru's national dish is a refreshing treat – fresh fish soaked in lime juice and chillies.

14 SHIPIBO TRIBAL ARTS AND CRAFTS

Page 464

Dressed in traditional skirts and colourful seed jewellery, the women of this tribe travel all over Peru to sell their craft goods.

15 RAINFOREST CANOPY WALKWAY

Page 478

Peru's jungle can be viewed at its best from the Amazon's longest tree-top canopy walkway, reaching 35m above ground at the Amazon Explorama Field Station.

16 RESERVA NACIONAL PARACAS

Page 116

Just a few hours out of Lima, Paracas is a coastal wildlife haven, boasting some fantastic beaches alongside archeological sites.

17
18
19

CORDILLERA BLANCA

Page 325

The glacial scenery of the Cordillera Blanca mountain range is among the finest and most accessible on the planet.

AREQUIPA

Page 152

This white stone city, beautiful and intriguing, is watched over by the awesome, ice-capped volcano of El Misti.

AYACUCHO

Page 296

Bustling streets, impressive churches, passionate religious processions and unique artesanía make this Andean city a standout.

SACSAYHUAMAN

Page 234

The zigzag megalithic defensive walls of this Inca temple-fortress are home to the annual Inti Raymi Festival of the Sun.

CHAVÍN DE HUANTAR

Page 337

Dating back over 2500 years, this large temple has many striking stone carvings and gargoyles, both externally and within its subterranean chambers.

PUERTO BELÉN

Page 470

A frenetic, floating jungle port that has been called the Venice of the Peruvian jungle.

22

23 TEXTILES

Page 231

Peru has been producing fine cotton textiles for over three thousand years.

24 MÁNCORA

Page 414

Peru's most popular surfer hangout features gorgeous beaches and buzzing nightlife.

25 VALLEY OF THE PYRAMIDS

Page 404

Over twenty adobe pyramids built by a pre-Inca civilization surround a sacred mountain at Túcume in the northern deserts.

26 NASCA LINES

Page 129

Take a helicopter tour to get the full impact of these intricate symbols, etched into the deserts of southern Peru.

27 COLCA CANYON

Page 178

Twice the size of the Grand Canyon, the enormous Colca, one of the deepest canyons in the world, is also one of Peru's biggest destinations.

28 MACHU PICCHU

Page 257

With mysterious temples and palaces nestling among hundreds of terraces, this fabulous Inca citadel is awe-inspiring.

26
27
28

Itineraries

First-time visitors will inevitably try to fit in most of the major sites of the south; for those with ample time on their hands, the northern circuit offers an offbeat array of tastes and destinations. You could also take an adventurous trip into the Amazon rainforest, staying at one of its many eco-lodges.

THE GRAND TOUR

Taking in the main attractions of the south of Peru, this tour can be covered in a couple of weeks, but could very easily absorb an extra week or two.

❶ **Paracas and the Ballestas Islands** A few hours south of Lima, this beachside area offers boat trips to islands of penguins and sea lions, great beaches, desert scenery, a scattering of pre-Inca sites and fine seafood. **See p.115**

❷ **Huacachina** At this desert oasis, its lagoon ringed by palm trees, you can relax and enjoy the scenery, or hit the dunes on a sandboard or dune buggy. **See p.128**

❸ **Nasca** Located in an attractive desert valley, Nasca sits next to a huge plain on which an ancient civilization etched enormous animal figures, as well as geometric shapes and perfectly straight lines. **See p.131**

❹ **Arequipa and canyon country** Arequipa is a stunning city with a colonial heart, built on white volcanic stone. The rugged regions around the city offer access to two of the world's deepest canyons – Colca and Cotahuasi. **See p.152**

❺ **Puno and Lake Titicaca** One of the most desolate yet scenic corners of Peru, Puno sits at the edge of the enormous Lake Titicaca. Take in its lively and vibrant music and festivals scene, and visit its peaceful islands. **See p.186**

❻ **Cusco** Capital of the Inca Empire, Cusco today embodies outdoor activities, lively nightlife and craft-shopping as much as it does ancient history. **See p.206**

❼ **Machu Picchu** Easily accessible from Cusco, this magnificent Inca citadel makes a fitting culmination to any trip. **See p.257**

THE NORTHERN CIRCUIT

The main focus of the little-visited north is beaches and surfing, coastal archeology and a chain of ancient mountain citadels and tombs, with the option of a jungle trip tagged on for those with more than two weeks to spare.

❶ **The Mochica Trail** Stretching from the desert valley where Trujillo now stands, the ancient Mochica civilization developed an important centre around the Huacas del Sol y de la Luna. Mochica dominance is also in evidence at the richly endowed tombs of El Señor de Sipán and the Valley of the Pyramids. **See p.362, p.401 & p.404**

❷ **Máncora and the beaches** Máncora is the trendy focus of several stunning sandy beaches – all good for surfing, fishing and diving. Further south, Cabo Blanco has been popular since Hemingway gave it his seal of approval; closer to Trujillo are the surfers' paradise of Chicama and the more traditional Huanchaco. **See p.414, p.372 & p.365**

ABOVE IQUITOS STREET LIFE

❸ **Chachapoyas and Kuelap** Inland and high up in the northern Andes, the Chachapoyas region competes pretty well with Cusco. Instead of Machu Picchu, it offers Kuelap, a mountain citadel with 20m-high walls. The area abounds in waterfalls, cliff-bound mausoleums and little-explored trails. **See p.385 & p.389**

❹ **Tarapoto and the jungle** Those with more time can head from Chachapoyas down into the Amazon region around the busy little jungle frontier city of Tarapoto. From here you can travel by river as far as the Reserva Nacional Pacaya-Samiria or Iquitos, for a taste of Peru's rainforest. **See p.392**

AMAZON HIGHLIGHTS

To get the most out of a jungle visit, allow at least four days (three nights), otherwise you're likely to spend most of the time in a bus, plane and/or boat.

Tambopata A wide selection of lodges lies along the Río Tambopata and nearby Río Madre de Dios, offering access to luxuriant jungle and unrivalled wildlife-spotting in the Reserva Nacional Tambopata. **See p.443**

Manu The Manu Biosphere Reserve ranges from lowland tropical rainforest to cloud forest, teeming with monkeys, jaguars, giant otters, deer and wild boar. **See p.446**

Pampa Hermosa Located in stunning cloud forest, this national reserve boasts a well-populated lek, where Peru's national bird, the cock-of-the-rock, can be seen dancing every morning. Impressive waterfalls dissect the reserve's unusually rich vegetation, which includes orchids, royal palms, lianas and giant ferns. **See p.455**

Iquitos and around Peru's liveliest jungle town, accessible only by air or riverboat, friendly Iquitos offers so much more than wildlife safaris and ecotourism. Clubs, bars and restaurants keep you busy in town, while the many eco-lodges nearby offer access to pink river dolphins, wild tapirs and jaguars. **See p.466 & p.473**

Riverboat trips Iquitos is the obvious starting point for riverboat trips. Some boats simply head for the frontier with Brazil, but many are dedicated to ecotourism, with cabins, hammock areas, decks and restaurant-bars, and some offer positively five-star luxury as you float along the Amazon. **See p.434**

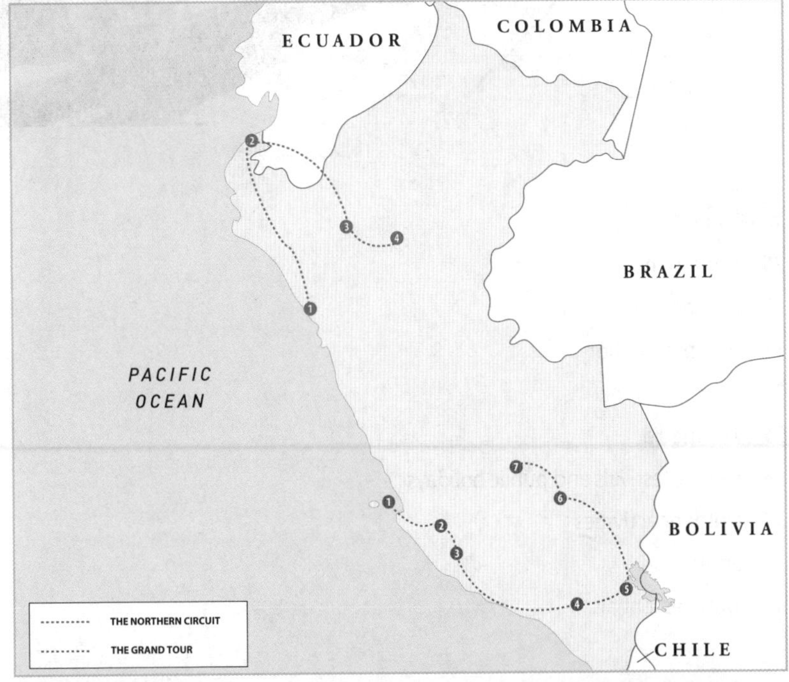

TRAIN TO MACHU PICCHU

Basics

Getting there

Unless you're travelling overland through South America, you'll need to fly to reach Peru. Although prices vary depending on the time of year, how far in advance you buy and the type of ticket, the main airlines seem to hold fares fairly steady and tickets can easily be bought online. Outside of Christmas and to a lesser extent Easter, high season is roughly from late May to early October.

You can sometimes cut costs by going through a specialist **flight or travel agent**, who, in addition to dealing with discounted flights, occasionally also offer special student and youth fares and a range of other travel-related services such as insurance, car rental, tours and the like.

Most people arrive at Jorge Chavez airport in Lima (see p.79). There's an airport hotel (ⓦramada.com), but it's a fair distance to downtown areas of Lima – Miraflores, San Isidro, Barranco – or even the old Lima Centro. A taxi to downtown Lima takes 35 to 55 minutes (S/45–S/55).

Flights from the UK

As there are no **direct flights** from the UK to Peru, getting there always involves switching planes somewhere in Europe or America. From Heathrow you can expect the journey to take anywhere between 16 and 22 hours, depending on the routing and stopovers. The permutations are endless, but the most common routes are **via Amsterdam** on KLM (ⓦklm.com), **via Madrid** on Iberia (ⓦiberia.com), **via Frankfurt** on Lufthansa (ⓦlufthansa.com) or **via Miami, Atlanta, New York and Houston** on one of the US airlines.

Fares (usually £750–£1200) vary almost as much as route options, and the closer to departure you buy, the higher the price is likely to be, so it is worth **booking in advance**. KLM, Iberia and Continental airlines (ⓦcontinental.com) tend to offer the most competitive rates.

There's also a wide range of **limitations** on the tickets (fixed-date returns within three months etc), and options such as "open-jaw" flights are available (flying into Lima and home from Rio, for example). Having established the going rate, you can always check these prices against those on offer at **discount flight outlets** and other travel agents listed in the press.

It's best to avoid buying international air tickets in Peru, where prices are inflated by a **high tax** (and are not cheap to begin with). If you're uncertain of your return date, it will probably still work out cheaper to pay the extra for an **open-ended return** than to buy a single back from Peru.

Flights from the US and Canada

With the exception of Continental's frequent nonstop service **from Newark** to Lima ($900–1500 return), nearly all flights to Peru from the US go **via Miami, Houston or Atlanta**. Delta (ⓦdelta.com), Continental (ⓦcontinental.com) and American airlines (ⓦaa.com) are the traditional carriers serving Peru from the US. Most airlines can book connecting flights to Miami, Houston or Atlanta from a range of cities throughout the US. A number of airlines fly Miami-to-Lima, including American, Copa (ⓦcopaair.com) and LAN (ⓦlan.com); the fare is usually $1000–1500 return. Fares **from New York** (via Miami) cost no more than fares from Miami.

Flights **from Toronto** straight to Lima start at about Can$900 with LAN (ⓦlan.com); it costs around the same price when flying from Montréal via Toronto.

There are a huge variety of **tours and packages** on offer from the US and Canada to Peru, starting from around $1500 for a two- to three-day package and ranging up to $4000–5000. You'll also find a number of packages that include Peru on their itineraries as part of a longer **South American tour**.

Flights from Australia, New Zealand and South Africa

Scheduled flights to Peru from Australia and New Zealand are rather limited and tend to involve changing planes, usually in the US. **High season** is December to February; low season is the rest of the

A BETTER KIND OF TRAVEL

At Rough Guides we are passionately committed to travel. We believe it helps us understand the world we live in and the people we share it with – and of course tourism is vital to many developing economies. But the scale of modern tourism has also damaged some places irreparably, and climate change is accelerated by most forms of transport, especially flying. All Rough Guides' flights are carbon-offset, and every year we donate money to a variety of environmental charities.

year, but prices also vary depending on how long you stay (between a minimum of 21 days and a maximum of a year).

Aerolineas Argentinas (Ⓦ aerolineas.com) fly **from Sydney** via Auckland and Buenos Aires, with connecting flights to Lima; fares start at Aus$1875. LAN (Ⓦ lan.com), in combination with Delta (Ⓦ delta.com) and Air Canada (Ⓦ aircanada.com), also fly from Sydney to Lima via the US; their cheapest tickets are 45-day returns at Aus$2500. Continental (Ⓦ continental.com) and American airlines (Ⓦ aa.com) fly regularly **from Melbourne** via Sydney, Auckland and the US (stopovers available) with fares that start at Aus$2800/NZ$3600 and range up to Aus$4000/NZ$5160 for a six-month return in high season, including connecting flights to Lima.

Air New Zealand (Ⓦ airnewzealand.com) fly to LA **from Auckland and Wellington** but have no specific connections to Peru. Qantas (Ⓦ qantas.com.au) have flights from Auckland to LA via Sydney or Melbourne and also fly to Dallas and New York from Sydney, from where there are connecting flights to Lima; prices start from about NZ$1300. **Round-the-world (RTW)** tickets including Peru are usually a good investment.

All flights from South Africa to Lima involve making connecting flights. British Airways (Ⓦ britishairways.com) fly **from Johannesburg** to Heathrow and Toronto, which gives the option of flying Heathrow-to-Madrid (to connect with Iberia flights for Lima) or connecting with Air Canada flights to Lima. Lufthansa also fly from Johannesburg to Frankfurt where there's a change for Lima flights via Caracas (ZAR18,500). South African Airways (Ⓦ flysaa.com) fly to Lima from Johannesburg, with a changeover in either Buenos Aires (ZAR12,000–15,000) or Sao Paulo (ZAR11,000–16,000) and also fly **from Cape Town** via the US.

Buses from neighbouring countries

Peru neighbours five other South American countries: Brazil, Ecuador, Colombia, Bolivia and Chile. **From Brazil**, you can now drive directly into Peru via Puerto Maldonado on the new Transoceanic Highway; Puerto Maldonado is just two to three hours from Peru's side of the frontier.

Arriving in southern Peru **from Bolivia** requires catching a bus, either directly or in stages, from La Paz across the altiplano to Copacabana or Desaguaderos, both near Lake Titicaca, and on to Puno, or even straight to Cusco. **From Chile** it's a similarly easy bus ride, across the southern border from Arica to Tacna, which has good connections with Lima and Arequipa.

From Ecuador, there are two routes, the most popular being a scenic coastal trip, starting by road from Huaquillas, crossing the border at Aguas Verdes and then taking a short bus or taxi ride on to Tumbes, from where there are daily buses and flights to Chiclayo, Trujillo and Lima. An alternative – and also rather scenic – crossing comes into Peru from Macará in Ecuador over the frontier to La Tina, from where there are daily buses to Peru's coast.

Boats from neighbouring countries

It's possible to take a boat ride up the Amazon from the **three-way frontier** between Brazil, Colombia and Peru (see p.480) to Iquitos. This is a 12-hour to 3-day ride depending on the type of boat. **From Leticia**, just over on the Colombian side of the three-way frontier (see p.480), there are speedboats up the Río Amazonas more or less daily to Iquitos. Taking the slow boat is usually a memorable experience – you'll need a hammock (unless you book one of the few cabins) and plenty of reading material.

AGENTS AND OPERATORS

Adventure tours or customized packages are often good value, but always check in advance exactly what's included in the price. Other specialist companies organize **treks** and **overland travel**, often based around some special interest, such as the rainforest, twitching, native culture or Inca sites.

Abercrombie & Kent US Ⓣ 1 800 554 7016 or for direct Ⓣ 630 954 2944, Ⓦ **abercrombiekent.com.** Offers luxury itineraries across the globe, including in Peru.

Adventure Associates Australia Ⓣ **02 8916 3000,** Ⓦ **adventureassociates.com.** Tours and cruises to Central and South America, including Peru and the Amazon.

Adventure Center US Ⓣ **1 800 228 8747** or Ⓣ **510 654 1879,** Ⓦ **adventurecenter.com.** Hiking and "soft adventure" specialists with some tours in Peru.

Adventure Travel Company New Zealand Ⓣ **03 364 3400** or Ⓣ **04 494 7180,** Ⓦ **adventuretravel.co.nz.** New Zealand agent for Peregrine Adventures (see opposite).

Adventure World Australia Ⓣ **1 300 295 049,** Ⓦ **adventureworld.com.au.** Agents for a vast array of international adventure travel companies that operate trips to every continent, with several options for Peru.

Austral Tours Australia Ⓣ **03 9370 6621,** Ⓦ **australtours.com.** A Central and South American specialist, mainly covering the region from Ecuador to Easter Island and Tierra del Fuego, with special tours to Machu Picchu and the Amazon.

Australian Andean Adventures Australia Ⓣ 02 9299 9973, Ⓦ **andeanadventures.com.au.** Trekking specialist for Argentina, Peru, Bolivia and Chile.

Backroads US Ⓣ **1 800 462 2848 or** Ⓣ **510 527 1555,** Ⓦ **backroads.com.** Cycling, hiking and multi-sport tour offerings including Peru.

Classic Journeys US Ⓣ **1 800 200 3887 or** Ⓣ **858 454 5004,** Ⓦ **classicjourneys.com.** Offers tours to Machu Picchu from Cusco by train.

Dragoman UK Ⓣ **01728 861133,** Ⓦ **dragoman.com.** Extended overland journeys in expedition vehicles through the Americas, covering Machu Picchu, Titicaca, Arequipa, Colca, Nasca and other sites in Peru. Offers shorter camping and hotel-based safaris, too.

ebookers UK Ⓣ **0800 082 3000,** Ⓦ **ebookers.com; Republic of Ireland** Ⓣ **01 488 3507,** Ⓦ **ebookers.ie.** Low fares on an extensive selection of scheduled flights and package deals.

eXito US Ⓣ **1 800 655 4053,** Ⓦ **exitotravel.com.** Latin American specialists in cut-rate fares, student tickets, year-long tickets and tours, with savings of up to forty percent off regular fares. Good for travel advice.

Exodus UK Ⓣ **208772 3936,** Ⓦ **exodus.co.uk.** Adventure-tour operators taking small groups on tours to South America, usually incorporating Peru's main destinations. They also provide specialist programmes including walking, biking, overland, adventure and cultural trips.

Explore Worldwide UK Ⓣ **0845 154 7960 or** Ⓣ **020 86 75 5550,** Ⓦ **explore.co.uk.** Big range of small-group tours, treks, expeditions and safaris on all continents, including the Cusco and Arequipa areas of Peru.

Mountain Travel Sobek US Ⓣ **1 888 831 7526 or** Ⓣ **1 510 594 6000,** Ⓦ **mtsobek.com.** Hiking, river rafting and trekking in Peru.

Nature Expeditions International Ⓣ **1 800 385 8489 or** Ⓣ **954 693 8852,** Ⓦ **naturexp.com.** Offers luxury wildlife and adventure tours in 25 countries around the world.

North South Travel UK Ⓣ **01245 608 291,** Ⓦ **northsouthtravel .co.uk.** Friendly, competitive travel agency, offering discounted fares worldwide. Profits are used to support projects in the developing world, especially the promotion of sustainable tourism.

On the Go Tours UK Ⓣ **020 7371 1113,** Ⓦ **onthegotours.com.** Runs group and tailor-made tours to Egypt, India, Sri Lanka, Africa, Jordan, Russia, China and Turkey.

Overseas Adventure Travel US Ⓣ **1 800 995 1925,** Ⓦ **oattravel .com.** Offers a wide variety of adventure trips around the planet, including some South American combinations, like Machu Picchu and the Galapagos.

Peregrine Adventures Australia Ⓦ **peregrineadventures.com.** Adventure tours in South America, which aim to explore the Inca heartlands as well as the Amazon rainforest.

STA Travel UK Ⓣ **0871 2300 040, US** Ⓣ **1 800 781 4040, Australia** Ⓣ **134 782, New Zealand** Ⓣ **0800 474 400, South Africa** Ⓣ **0861 781 781;** Ⓦ **statravel.co.uk.** Worldwide specialists in independent travel; also student IDs, travel insurance, car rental, rail passes and more. Good discounts for students and under-26s.

The Surf Travel Co Australia Ⓣ **02 9222 8870, New Zealand** Ⓣ **09 473 8388;** Ⓦ **surftravel.com.au.** Packages and advice for catching the waves (or snow) in the Pacific region, including main sites on the Peruvian coastline such as Chicama and Máncora.

Trailfinders UK Ⓣ **0845 054 6060, Republic of Ireland** Ⓣ **021 464 8800, Australia** Ⓣ **1300 780 212;** Ⓦ **trailfinders.com.** One of the best-informed and most efficient agents for independent travellers.

Travel CUTS Canada Ⓣ **1 800 667 2887, US** Ⓣ **1 800 592 2887;** Ⓦ **travelcuts.com.** Canadian youth and student travel firm.

USIT Republic of Ireland Ⓣ **01 602 1906, Northern Ireland** Ⓣ **028 9032 7111;** Ⓦ **usit.ie.** Ireland's main student and youth travel specialists.

Wilderness Travel US Ⓣ **1 800 368 2794 or** Ⓣ **510 558 2488,** Ⓦ **wildernesstravel.com.** A variety of programmes in Peru, from nine-day hotel-based holidays to 24-day camping and trekking trips, some of which include Bolivia in the itinerary. Also runs Inca Trail tours culminating in the Inti Raymi festival in Cusco during the summer solstice in June.

World Expeditions UK Ⓣ **020 8543 8316,** Ⓦ **worldexpeditions .com.** Australian-owned adventure company offering more than just Antipodean expeditions, with several programmes focused on the Peruvian jungle.

Getting around

With distances in Peru being so vast, many Peruvians and other travellers are increasingly flying to their destinations, as all Peruvian cities are within a two-hour flight of Lima. Most Peruvians, however, still get around the country by bus, a cheap way to travel with routes to almost everywhere. In a few cases, it's possible to arrive by train – an interesting and sought-after experience itself – though these trips are considerably slower than the equivalent bus journeys.

By plane

There's a good **domestic air service** in Peru these days. Some places in the jungle can only sensibly be reached by plane and Peru is so vast that the odd flight can save a lot of time. There are three main established airline companies: LAN, a Chilean-owned company, who fly to all of the main cities and many smaller destinations; StarPerú, a Peruvian airline that began operating in 2005; and TACA, which initially grew out of a military-operated internal domestic service. More recently, Peruvian Airlines has set up to compete with these three.

Most tickets for all these domestic airlines can be booked and bought online as well as from travel agents or airline offices in all major towns. The jungle towns, such as Pucallpa, Tarapoto, Puerto Maldonado and Iquitos, also tend to have small **air colectivo** companies operating scheduled services carrying missionaries and hospital patients between larger settlements in the region, at quite reasonable rates. If there's space you pay your share; for example a place on a 30min four-seater flight would cost S/200 to S/400 ($75 to $150) per person.

The most popular domestic routes cost upwards of S/215 ($80) and are generally cheaper if booked well in advance. In high season some Lima–Cusco flights are fully booked months in advance. Less busy routes tend to be less expensive per air mile and can be booked the day before. On all flights it's important to **confirm your booking** two days before departure.

Flights are often cancelled or delayed, and sometimes they even leave earlier than scheduled – especially in the jungle where the weather can be a problem. If a passenger hasn't shown up **an hour before the flight**, the company may give the seat to someone on the waiting list, so it's best to be on time whether you're booked or are merely hopeful. The luggage allowance on internal flights is generally 16kg, not including hand luggage.

Unscheduled services

There are also **small planes** (four- and ten-seaters) serving the jungle and certain parts of the coast. A number of small companies fly out of Jorge Chavez Airport in Lima most days (their counters are between the international check-in counters and the domestic departure area), but these have few fixed schedules as well as a reputation for being dangerous and poorly maintained.

For an *expreso* **air taxi**, which will take you to any landing strip in the country whenever you want, you'll pay $600 per hour (which can be shared between up to four passengers); this price is based on a half-hour flight and is calculated to include the return journey with the pilot in an empty plane.

ADDRESSES

Addresses are frequently written with just the street name and number: for example, Pizarro 135. Officially, though, they're usually prefixed by Calle, Jirón or Avenida. The **first digit** of any street number (or sometimes the first two digits) represents the block number within the street as a whole. Note too that many of the major streets in Lima and also in Cusco have **two names** – in Lima this is a relic of the military governments of the 1970s, in Cusco it's more to do with a revival of the Inca past.

PERUVIAN AIRLINES

LAN Av José Pardo 513, Miraflores, Lima T 01 213 8200, W lan.com. To call collect (reverse charge) from outside Lima ring T 0801 11234.

StarPerú Av Comandante Espinar 331, Miraflores, Lima T 01 705 9000, W starperu.com.

TACA José Pardo 811, Miraflores, Lima T 01 511 8222, W taca.com.

Peruvian Airlines Av José Pardo 495, Miraflores, Lima T 01 716 6000, W peruvian.pe.

By bus

Peru's **buses** are run by a variety of private companies, all of which offer remarkably low fares, making it possible to travel from one end of the country to the other (over 2000km) for under $35. Long-distance bus journeys cost from around $1.75 per hour on the fast coastal highway, and are even cheaper on the slower mountain and jungle routes. The condition of the buses ranges from the efficient and relatively luxurious Cruz del Sur fleet that runs along the coast, to the older, more battered buses used on local runs throughout the country. Some of the better bus companies, including Cruz del Sur (W cruzdelsur.com.pe) and Ormeño (W grupo-ormeno.com.pe), offer excellent onboard facilities including sandwich bars and video entertainment. The major companies generally offer two or three levels of service, and many companies run the longer journeys by night with a **bus-cama** (comfortable deeply reclining seat) option. Cruz del Sur now operates an excellent website with timetables and ticket purchase option (credit cards accepted).

As the only means of transport available to most of the population, buses run with surprising regularity, and the coastal Panamerican Highway and many of the main routes into the mountains have now been paved (one of ex-President Fujimori's better legacies), so on such routes services are generally **punctual**. On some of the rougher mountainous routes, punctures, arguments over rights of way and, during the rainy season, landslides may delay the arrival time by several hours.

At least one **bus depot**, or stopping area, can be found in the centre of any town. Peru is investing in a series of **terminal terrestres**, or *terrapuertos*, centralizing the departure and arrival of the manifold operators. Lima does not have this facility and, in any case, it's always a good idea to double-check where the bus is leaving from, since in some cities, notably Arequipa, bus offices are in different locations to the bus terminal. If you can't get to a bus depot or *terminal terrestre*, you can try to catch a bus from the exit roads or **police checkpoints** on the outskirts of most Peruvian cities, though there's no guarantee of getting a ride or a seat.

For intercity rides, it's best to **buy tickets in advance** direct from the bus company offices; for local trips, you can buy tickets on the bus itself. On long-distance journeys, try to avoid getting seats right over the jarring wheels, especially if the bus is tackling mountain or jungle roads.

By taxi

Taxis can be found anywhere at any time in almost every town. Any car can become a taxi simply by sticking a taxi sign up in the front window; a lot of people, especially in Lima, take advantage of this to supplement their income. Whenever you get into a taxi, always fix the price in advance (in nuevo soles rather than in US dollars) since few of them have **meters**. Taxi drivers in Peru do not expect tips.

Relatively short journeys in **Lima** generally cost around S/5–10 (US$2–4), but it's cheaper elsewhere in the country. Radio taxis, minicabs and airport taxis tend to cost more. Even relatively long taxi rides in Lima are likely to cost less than S/15 (US$6), except to and from the airport, which ranges from S/30–60 (US$11–22); prices depend on how far across the city you're going, how bad the traffic is and how much you're prepared to pay for a more official or stylish vehicle.

By mototaxi

In many rural towns, you'll find small cars – mainly Korean Ticos and motorcycle rickshaws, known variously as **mototaxis**, or *motokars*, all competing for customers. The latter are always cheaper (starting at S/1 for short rides), if slightly more dangerous and not that comfortable, especially if there's more than two of you or if you've got a lot of luggage. In a rural town, you might find normal car taxis (eg Toyotas), Tico taxis and mototaxis competing for business; a ride across town might cost S/5–8 in a normal taxi, S/3–5 in a Tico or S/2–3 in a mototaxi.

By colectivo

Colectivos (shared taxis) are a very useful way of getting around that's peculiar to Peru. They connect all the coastal towns, and many of the larger centres in the mountains. Like the buses, many are ageing imports from the US – huge old Dodge Coronets – though, increasingly, fast new Japanese and Korean minibuses run between the cities.

Colectivos tend to be faster than the bus, though they are often as much as twice the price. Most **colectivo cars** manage to squeeze in about seven people including the driver (three in the front and four in the back), and can be found in the centre of a town or at major stopping places along the main roads. If more than one is ready to leave it's worth bargaining a little, as the price is often negotiable. **Colectivo minibuses**, also known as combis, can squeeze in twice as many people, or often more.

In the cities, colectivos have an appalling reputation for **safety**. There are crashes reported in the Lima press every week, mostly caused by the highly competitive nature of the business. There are so many combis covering the same major arterial routes in Lima that they literally race each other to be the first to the next street corner. They frequently crash, turn over and knock down pedestrians. Equally dangerous is the fact that the driver is in such a hurry that he does not always wait for you to get in. If you're not careful he'll pull away while you've still got a foot on the pavement, putting you in serious danger of breaking a leg.

By train

Peru's spectacular **train journeys** are in themselves a major attraction, and you should aim to take at least one long-distance train ride during your trip, especially as the trains connect some of Peru's major tourist sights. At the time of writing, the **Central Railway**, which climbs and switchbacks its way up from Lima into the Andes as far as Huancayo on the world's highest standard-gauge tracks, only runs about once a month for passengers (see p.284).

There are three rail companies operating out of Cusco. PeruRail (Ⓦ perurail.com) offers passenger services inland from Puno on Lake Titicaca north to Cusco, from where another line heads out down the magnificent Urubamba Valley as far as Machu Picchu. On the Cusco-to-Machu Picchu line there are two new competitor companies – Inca Rail (Ⓦ incarail.com) and Machu Picchu Train (Ⓦ machupicchutrain.com).

The trains move slowly, allowing ample time to observe what's going on outside. For all train journeys, it's advisable to buy **tickets** a week or two before travelling and even further in advance during high season.

By car

Driving around Peru is generally not a problem outside of Lima, and allows you to see some out-of-the-way places that you may otherwise miss. However, road traffic in Lima is abominable, both in terms of its recklessness and the sheer volume. Traffic jams are ubiquitous between 8 and 10am and again between 4 and 7pm every weekday, while air pollution from old and poorly maintained vehicles is a real health risk, particularly in Lima and Arequipa.

If you bring a car into Peru that is not registered there, you will need to show (and keep with you at all times) a **libreta de pago por la aduana** (proof of customs payment) normally provided by the relevant automobile association of the country you are coming from. **Spare parts**, particularly tyres, should be carried along with a tent, emergency water and food. The chance of **theft** is quite high – the vehicle, your baggage and accessories are all vulnerable when parked.

International driving licences are technically only valid for thirty days in Peru, after which a permit is required from the Touring y Automóvil Club del Perú, Av Trinidad Moran 698, Lince, Lima (Mon–Fri 9am–4.45pm; T 01 614 9999, W touringperu.com.pe); in practice, however, a US or European photo licence is generally accepted without question.

Renting a car costs much the same as in Europe and North America. The major rental firms all have offices in Lima, but outside the capital you'll generally find only local companies are represented. You may find it more convenient to rent a car in advance online – expect to pay from around $40 a day, or $200 a week for the smallest car. In jungle cities it's usually possible to rent **motorbikes** or **mopeds** by the hour or by the day: this is a good way of getting to know a town or to be able to shoot off into the jungle for a day.

By boat

There are no coastal **boat services** in Peru, but in many areas – on Lake Titicaca and especially in the jungle regions – water is the obvious means of getting around. From Puno, on Lake Titicaca, there are currently no regular services to Bolivia by ship or hydrofoil – though check with the tour agencies in Puno (see p.191) – but there are plenty of smaller boats that will take visitors out to the various islands in the lake. These aren't expensive and a price can usually be negotiated down at the port.

In the jungle areas **motorized canoes** come in two basic forms: those with a large outboard motor and those with a Briggs and Stratton **peque-peque** engine; the outboard is faster and more manoeuvrable, but they cost a lot more to run. Your best option is to **hire a canoe** along with its guide/driver for a few days. This means searching around in the port and negotiating, but you can often get a *peque-peque* canoe from around S/135–216 ($50–80) per day, which will invariably work out cheaper than taking an organized tour, as well as giving you a choice of guide and companions. Obviously, the more people you can get together, the cheaper it will be per person.

On foot

Even if you've no intention of doing any serious hiking, there's a good deal of walking involved in checking out many of the most enjoyable Peruvian attractions. Climbing from Cusco up to the fortress of Sacsayhuaman, for example, or wandering around at Machu Picchu, involves more than an average Sunday afternoon stroll. Bearing in mind the rugged terrain throughout Peru, the absolute minimum **footwear** is a strong pair of running shoes. Much better is a pair of hiking boots with good ankle support.

Hiking – whether in the desert, mountains or jungle – can be an enormously rewarding experience, but you should go properly equipped and bear in mind a few of the **potential hazards**. Never stray too far without food and water, something warm and something waterproof to wear. The weather is renowned for its dramatic changeability, especially in the mountains, where there is always the additional danger of altitude sickness (see p.45). In the jungle the biggest danger is getting lost (see p.434).

In the mountains it's often a good idea to hire a **pack animal** to carry your gear. Llamas can only carry about 25–30kg and move slowly; a *burro* (donkey) carries around 80kg and a mule – the most common and the best pack animal – will shift 150kg with relative ease. Mules can be hired from upwards of $5 a day, and they normally come with an *arriero*, a muleteer who'll double as a guide. It is also possible to hire mules or horses for **riding** but this costs a little more. With a guide and beast of burden it's quite simple to reach even the most remote valleys, ruins and mountain passes, travelling in much the same way as Pizarro and his men did over four hundred years ago.

Hitching

Hitching in Peru usually means catching a ride with a truck driver, who will almost always expect payment. Always agree on a price before getting in as there are stories of drivers stopping in the middle of nowhere and demanding unreasonably high amounts (from foreigners and Peruvians alike) before going any further. Hitching isn't considered dangerous in Peru, but having said that, few people, even Peruvians, actually hitch. Trucks can be flagged down anywhere but there is greater choice around markets, and at police controls or petrol stations on the outskirts of towns. Trucks tend to be the only form of public transport in some less accessible regions, travelling the roads that buses won't touch and serving remote communities, so you may end up having to sit on top of a pile of potatoes or bananas.

Hitchhiking in **private cars** is not recommended, and, in any case, it's very rare that one will stop to pick you up.

Organized tours

There are hundreds of **travel agents** and **tour operators** in Peru, and reps hunt out customers at bus terminals, train stations and in city centres. While they can be expensive, **organized excursions** can be a quick and relatively effortless way to see some of the popular attractions and the more remote sites, while a prearranged trek of something like the Inca Trail can take much of the worry out of camping preparations and ensure that you get decent campsites, a sound meal and help with carrying your equipment in what can be difficult walking conditions.

Many **adventure tour companies** offer excellent and increasingly exciting packages and itineraries – ranging from mountain biking, whitewater rafting, jungle photo-safaris, mountain trekking and climbing, to more comfortable and gentler city and countryside tours. Tours cost $45–300 a day and, in Cusco and Huaraz in particular, there's an enormous selection of operators to choose from. **Cusco** is a pretty good base for hiking, whitewater rafting, canoeing, horseback riding or going on an expedition into the Amazonian jungle with an adventure tour company; **Arequipa** and the **Colca Canyon** offer superb hiking; **Huaraz** is also a good base for trekking and mountaineering; **Iquitos**, on the Amazon River, is one of the best places for adventure trips into the jungle and has a reasonable range of tour operators. Several of these companies have branches in Lima, if you want to book a tour in advance. Reliable tour operators are listed in the relevant sections throughout the Guide.

Accommodation

Peru has the typical range of Latin American accommodation, from top-class international hotels at prices to compare with any Western capital down to basic rooms or shared dorms in hostels. The biggest development over the last ten years has been the rise of the mid-range option, reflecting the growth of both domestic and international tourism. Camping is frequently possible, sometimes free and perfectly acceptable in most rural parts of Peru, though there are very few formal campsites.

Accommodation denominations of *hotel*, *hostal*, *residencial*, *pensión* or *hospedaje* are almost meaningless in terms of what you'll find inside. Virtually all upmarket accommodation will call itself a **hotel** or, in the countryside regions, a **posada**. In the jungle, **tambo lodges** can be anything from somewhere quite luxurious to an open-sided, palm-thatched hut with space for slinging a hammock. Technically speaking, somewhere that calls itself a **pensión** or **residencial** ought to specialize in longer-term accommodation, and while they may well offer discounts for stays of a week or more, they are just as geared up for short stays. There's no standard or widely used **rating system**, so, apart from the information given in this book, the only way to tell whether a place is suitable or not is to walk in and take a look around – the proprietors won't mind this, and you'll soon get used to spotting places with promise.

Many of the major hotels will request a **credit card number** to reserve rooms in advance; be careful, since if you fail to turn up they may consider this a "no-show" and charge you for the room anyhow. Always check beforehand whether the quoted price includes **IGV tax** (as a tourist, if you register your passport and tourist card with the hotel, they don't usually charge you this tax, which is currently nineteen percent and any service extras). It's not advisable to pay **travel agents** in one city for accommodation required in the next town; by all means ask agents to make reservations but do not ask them to send payments as it is always simpler and safer to do that yourself.

The **prices** quoted for accommodation throughout the Guide are for the **cheapest double room in high season**, except where noted.

Hotels

Peru's cheaper **hotels** are generally old – sometimes beautifully so, converted from colonial mansions with rooms grouped around a courtyard. They tend to be within a few blocks of a town's central plaza, general market or bus or train station. For a night in a no-frills place, expect to pay S/60.

You can find a good, clean single or double room in a **mid-range hotel** (generally three-star), with a private bathroom, towels and hot water, for S/55–160 ($20–60). Quality hotels, not necessarily 5-star, but with good service, truly comfortable rooms and maybe a pool or some other additional facility, can be found in all the larger Peruvian resorts as well as some surprisingly offbeat ones. Out of season some are relatively inexpensive, at S/55–120.

There are quite a few **five-star hotels** in Peru (usually costing upwards of S/600/$225 for a double room), nearly all in Lima, Arequipa, Cusco, Trujillo and Iquitos. Even **four-star hotels** (S/300–500/$112–225) offer excellent service, some fine restaurants and very comfortable rooms with well-stocked minibars.

A little haggling is often worth a try, and if you find one room too pricey, another, perhaps very similar, can often be found for less: the phrase "Tiene un cuarto más barato?" ("Do you have a cheaper room?") is useful. Savings can invariably be made, too, by **sharing rooms** – many have two, three, even four or five beds. A double-bedded room ("con cama matrimonial") is usually cheaper than a twin ("con dos camas").

Hostels

Called *hostals* in Peru, most of Peru's **hostels** are unaffiliated to Hostelling International, though there are over forty that are (see ⓦhihostels.com and ⓦrepaj.org), spread throughout Peru and located in Arequipa, Cusco, Huaraz, Ica, Iquitos, Lima, Máncora and Tarma. Most of the hostels that are linked to Hostelling International don't bother to check that you are a member, but if you want to be on the safe side, you can join up at the Asociación Peruana de Albergues Turísticos Juveniles, Casimiro Ulloa 328, Miraflores, Lima (ⓣ01 2423068, ⓦlimahostell.com.pe).

While not the standardized institution found in Europe, Peru's hostels are relatively cheap and reliable; expect to pay S/15–25 ($6–9) for a bed (the most expensive ones are in Lima). All hostels are theoretically open 24 hours a day and most have cheap cafeterias attached. They are always great places to meet up with other travellers and tend to have a party scene of their own.

YOUTH HOSTEL ASSOCIATIONS

US AND CANADA

Hostelling International–American Youth Hostels US ⓣ1 301 495 1240, ⓦhiusa.org.

Hostelling International Canada Canada ⓣ1 800 663 5777, ⓦhihostels.ca.

UK AND IRELAND

Youth Hostel Association (YHA) UK ⓣ0800 019 1700, ⓦyha.org.uk.

Scottish Youth Hostel Association UK ⓣ0845 293 7373, ⓦsyha.org.uk.

Irish Youth Hostel Association Ireland ⓣ01 830 4555, ⓦanoige.ie.

Hostelling International Northern Ireland Northern Ireland ⓣ028 9032 4733, ⓦhini.org.uk.

AUSTRALIA, NEW ZEALAND AND SOUTH AFRICA

Australian Youth Hostels Association Australia ⓣ02 9565 1699, ⓦyha.com.au.

Youth Hostelling Association New Zealand New Zealand ⓣ0800 278 299 or ⓣ03 379 9970, ⓦyha.co.nz.

Hostelling International South Africa South Africa ⓣ021 424 2511, ⓦhisa.org.za.

Camping

Camping is possible almost everywhere in Peru, and it's rarely difficult to find space for a tent; since there are only one or two organized campsites in the whole country (costing between S/10–15/person), it's also largely free. Moreover, camping is the most satisfactory way of seeing Peru, as some of the country's most fantastic destinations are well off the beaten track: with a tent – or a hammock – it's possible to go all over without worrying if you'll make it to a hostel.

It's usually okay to set up camp in the fields or forest beyond the outskirts of settlements, but ask **permission** and advice from the nearest farm or house first. Apart from a few restricted areas, Peru's enormous sandy coastline is open territory, the real problem not being so much where to camp as how to get there; some of the most stunning areas are very remote. The same can be said of both the mountains and the jungle – camp anywhere, but ask first, if you can find anyone to ask.

> **ACCOMMODATION ALTERNATIVES**
>
> These useful websites provide some interesting alternatives to standard hotel and hostel accommodation:
> **CouchSurfing** couchsurfing.org.
> **Vacation Rentals by Owner** vrbo.com.
> **Airbnb** airbnb.com.
> **Crashpadder** crashpadder.com.

Reports of **robberies**, particularly along such popular routes as the Inca Trail, are not uncommon, so travelling with someone else or in groups is always a good idea. There are a few basic precautions that you can take: let someone know where you intend to go; be respectful, and try to communicate with any locals you may meet or who you are camping near (but be careful who you make friends with en route).

Camping equipment is easy to find in Peru, but good-quality gear is hard to obtain. Several places sell, rent or buy secondhand gear, mainly in Cusco, Arequipa and Huaraz, and there are some reasonably good, if quite expensive, shops in Lima. It's also worth checking the notice boards in the popular travellers' hotels and bars for equipment that is no longer needed or for people seeking trekking companions. Camping Gaz butane canisters are available from most of the above shops and from some *ferreterías* (hardware stores) in the major resorts. A couple of essential things you'll need when camping in Peru are a mosquito net and repellent, and some sort of water treatment system.

Food and drink

Peruvian cuisine is rated among the best in the world and is currently experiencing a period of flourishing self-confidence and great popularity overseas. The country's chefs are adept at creating innovative new fusions with its fantastic wealth of food products, most of which are indigenous.

As with almost every activity, the style and pattern of eating and drinking varies considerably between the three main regions of Peru. The food in each area, though it varies depending on the availability of different regional ingredients, is essentially a *mestizo* creation, combining indigenous cooking with four hundred years of European – mostly Spanish – influence.

Guinea pig (*cuy*) is the traditional dish most associated with Peru, and you can find it in many parts of the country, especially in the mountain regions, where it is likely to be roasted in an oven and served with chips. It's likely however, that you may encounter more burgers and pizza than guinea pig, given that fast food has spread quickly in Peru over the past two decades.

Snacks and light meals

All over Peru, but particularly in the large towns and cities, you'll find a wide variety of traditional **fast foods** and snacks such as *salchipapas* (chips with sliced sausage covered in various sauces), *anticuchos* (a shish kebab made from marinated lamb or beef heart) and *empanadas* (meat- or cheese-filled pies). These are all sold on street corners until late at night. Even in Peru's villages you'll find cafés and restaurants that double as bars, staying open all day and serving anything from coffee and bread to steak and chips, or even lobster. The most popular sweets in Peru are made from either *manjar blanco* (sweetened condensed milk) or fresh fruits.

In general, the **market** is always a good place to stock up – you can buy food ready to eat on the spot or to take away and prepare – and the range and prices are better than in any shop. Most food prices are fixed, but the vendor may throw in an orange, a bit of garlic or some coriander leaves for good measure. Smoked meat, which can be sliced up and used like salami, is normally a good buy.

Restaurants

All larger towns in Peru have a fair choice of **restaurants**, most of which offer a varied menu. Among them there are usually a few **Chinese** (*chifa*) places, and nowadays a fair number of **vegetarian** restaurants too. Most establishments in larger towns stay open daily from around 11am until 11pm, though in smaller settlements they may close one day a week, usually Sunday. Often they will offer a **set menu**, from morning through to lunchtime, and another in the evening. Ranging in price from S/6 to S/25, these most commonly consist of three or four courses: soup or other starter, a main dish (usually hot and with rice or salad), a small sweet or fruit-based third plate, plus tea or coffee to follow. Every town, too, seems now to have at least one restaurant that specializes in *pollos a la brasa* – spit-roasted chickens.

Seafood

Along the coast, not surprisingly, **seafood** is the speciality; the Humboldt Current keeps the Pacific Ocean off Peru extremely rich in plankton and other microscopic life forms, which attract a wide variety of fish. **Ceviche** is the classic Peruvian seafood dish and has been eaten by locals for over two thousand years. It consists of fish, shrimp, scallops or squid, or a mixture of all four, marinated in lime juice and chilli peppers, then served "raw" with corn, sweet potato and onions. *Ceviche de lenguado* (sole) and *ceviche de corvina* (sea bass) are among the most common, but there are plenty of other fish and a wide range of seafood is utilized on most menus. You can find ceviche, along with fried fish and fish soups, in most restaurants along the coast from S/15–25.

Escabeche is another tasty fish-based appetizer, this time incorporating peppers and finely chopped onions. The coast is also an excellent place for eating **scallops** – known here as *conchitas* – which grow particularly well close to the Peruvian shoreline; *conchitas negras* (black scallops) are a delicacy in the northern tip of Peru. Excellent **salads** are also widely available, such as *huevos a la rusa* (egg salad), *palta rellena* (stuffed avocado), or a straight tomato salad, while *papas a la Huancaina* (a cold appetizer of potatoes covered in a spicy light cheese sauce) is great too.

Mountain food

Mountain food is fairly basic – a staple of potatoes and rice with the meat stretched as far as it will go. *Lomo saltado*, or diced prime beef sautéed with onions and peppers, is served anywhere at any time, accompanied by rice and a few French fries. A delicious snack from street vendors and cafés is *papa rellena*, a potato stuffed with vegetables and fried. **Trout** is also widely available, as are cheese, ham and egg sandwiches. *Chicha*, a **corn beer** drunk throughout the sierra region and on the coast in rural areas, is very cheap with a pleasantly tangy taste. Another Peruvian speciality is the **pachamanca**, a roast prepared mainly in the mountains but also on the coast by digging a large hole, filling it with stones and lighting a fire over them, then using the hot stones to cook a wide variety of tasty meats and vegetables.

Jungle food

Jungle food is quite different to the rest of the country. **Bananas** and **plantains** figure highly, along with *yuca* (a manioc rather like a yam), rice and plenty of fish. There is **meat** as well – mostly chicken supplemented occasionally by **game** (deer, wild pig or even monkey). Every settlement big enough to get on the map has its own bar or café, but in remote areas it's a matter of eating what's available and drinking coffee or bottled drinks if you don't relish the home-made *masato* (cassava beer).

> ### TIPPING
>
> In budget or average restaurants **tipping** is normal, though not obligatory and you should rarely expect to give more than about ten percent. In fancier places you may well find a **service charge** of at least ten percent as well as a **tax** of nineteen percent (IGV) added to the bill. In restaurants and *peñas* where there's live music or performances a **cover charge** is generally also applied and can be as high as $5 a head. Even without a performance, additional cover charges of around $1 are sometimes levied in the flashier restaurants in major town centres.

Drinking

Beer, wines and spirits are served in almost every bar, café or restaurant at any time, but there is a **deposit** on taking beer bottles away from a shop (canned beer is one of the worst inventions to hit Peru this century – some of the finest beaches are littered with empty cans).

Nonalcoholic drinks

Soft drinks range from mineral water, through the ubiquitous Coca-Cola and Fanta, to home-produced favourites like the gold-coloured Inka Cola, with rather a home-made taste, and the very sweet Cola Inglesa. **Fruit juices** (*jugos*), most commonly papaya or orange, are delicious and prepared fresh in most places (the best selection and cheapest prices are generally available in a town's main market), and you can get **coffee** and a wide variety of herb and leaf **teas** almost anywhere. Surprisingly, for a good coffee-growing country, the coffee in cafés outside of Lima, Cusco and Arequipa leaves much to be desired, commonly prepared from either *café pasado* (previously percolated coffee mixed with hot water to serve) or simple powdered Nescafé. Increasingly it's possible to find great coffee in larger towns where certain cafés prepare good fresh espresso, cappuccino or filtered coffee. *Starbucks* (complete with wi-fi) has arrived in several of Peru's cities and is everywhere you turn in Lima.

Beer and wine

Most **Peruvian beer** – except for *cerveza malta* (black malt beer) – is bottled lager almost exclusively brewed to five percent alcohol content, and extremely good. Traditional Peruvian beers include Cristal, Pilsen and Cusqueña (the latter, originating from Cusco, is generally preferred, and has even reached some UK supermarkets in recent years). In Trujillo on the north coast, they drink Trujillana beer, again quite similar; and in Arequipa they tend to drink Arequipeña beer. There are several new lager beers now on the market, including the Brazilian brand Brahma. Peru has been producing **wine** (*vino*) for over four hundred years, but with one or two exceptions it is not that good. Among the better ones are Vista Alegre (the Tipo Familiar label is generally OK) – not entirely reliable but only around S/8 a bottle – and, much better, Tabernero or Tacama Gran Vino Reserva (white or red) from about S/25–45 a bottle. A good Argentinian or Chilean wine will cost from $10 upwards.

Spirits

As for **spirits**, Peru's main claim to fame is **pisco**. This is a white-grape brandy with a unique, powerful and very palatable flavour – the closest equivalent elsewhere is probably tequila. Almost anything else is available as an import – Scotch **whisky** is cheaper here than in the UK, but beware of the really cheap whisky imitations or blends bottled outside of Scotland which can remove the roof of your mouth with ease. The jungle regions produce a sugar-cane rum, **cashassa** (basically the Peruvian equivalent of Brazilian *cachaça*), also called *aguardiente*, which has a distinctive taste and is occasionally mixed with different herbs, some medicinal. While it goes down easily, it's incredibly strong stuff and is sure to leave you with a hangover the next morning if you drink too much.

The media

English language, or non-Spanish, magazines and newspapers are hard to find in Peru; there are some sold around *El Haiti Café* in Miraflores, Lima, and they can occasionally be found in airports or bookshops in Cusco. BBC World Service and VOA can be picked up if you have the right receiver.

There are many poor-quality newspapers and magazines available on the streets of Lima and throughout the rest of Peru. Many of the **newspapers** stick mainly to sex and sport, while **magazines** tend to focus on terrorism, violence and the frequent deaths caused by major traffic accidents. Meanwhile, many get their news and information from **television** and **radio**, where you also have to wade through the panoply of entertainment-orientated options.

Newspapers and magazines

The two most established (and establishment) **daily newspapers** are *El Comercio* (Ⓦelcomercio.com.pe) and *Expreso* (Ⓦexpreso.com.pe), the latter having traditionally devoted vast amounts of space to anti-Communist propaganda. *El Comercio* is much more balanced but still tends to toe the political party of the day's line. *El Comercio*'s daily *Seccion C* also has the most comprehensive cultural listings of any paper – good for just about everything going on in Lima. In addition, there's the sensationalist tabloid *La República* (Ⓦlarepublica.com.pe), which takes a middle-of-the-road to liberal approach to politics; and *Diario Ojo*, which provides interesting tabloid reading.

International newspapers are fairly hard to come by; your best bet for English papers is to go to the British Embassy in Lima (see p.96), which has a selection of one- to two-week-old papers, such as *The Times* and *The Independent*, for reference only. US papers are easier to find; the bookstalls around Plaza San Martín in Lima Centro and those along Avenida Larco and Diagonal in Miraflores sell *The Miami Herald*, the *International Herald Tribune*, and *Newsweek* and *Time* magazines, but even these are likely to be four or five days old.

One of the better weekly **magazines** is the fairly liberal *Caretas*, generally offering mildly critical support to whichever government happens to be in power. There's one environmental and travel magazine – *Rumbos* (Ⓦrumbosperu.com) – which publishes articles in both Spanish and English and has excellent photographic features.

Television and radio

Peruvians watch a lot of **television** – mostly football and soap operas, though TV is also a main source of news. Many programmes come from Mexico, Brazil and the US, with occasional eccentric selections from elsewhere and a growing presence of manga-style cartoons. There are nine main terrestrial channels, of which channels 7 and 13 show marginally better quality programmes. **Cable and satellite TV** is increasingly forming an important part of

Peru's media, partly due to the fact that it can be received in even the remotest of settlements.

Alternatively, you can tune in to **Peruvian radio stations**, nearly all of which play music and are crammed with adverts. International pop, salsa and other Latin pop can be picked up most times of the day and night all along the FM wave band, while traditional Peruvian and Andean folk music can usually be found all over the AM dial. Radio Miraflores (96FM) is one of the best stations, playing mainly disco and new US/British rock, though also with a good jazz programme on Sunday evenings and an excellent news summary every morning (7–9am).

Fiestas, festivals and public holidays

Public holidays, Carnival and local fiestas are all big events in Peru, celebrated with an openness and gusto that gives them enormous appeal for visitors; note that everything shuts down, including banks, post offices, information offices, tourist sites and museums. The main national holidays take place over Easter, Christmas and during the month of October, in that order of importance. It is worth planning a little in advance to make sure that you don't get caught out.

In addition to the major regional and national celebrations, nearly every community has its own saint or patron figure to worship at town or **village fiestas**. These celebrations often mean a great deal to local people, and can be much more fun to visit than the larger countrywide events. Processions, music, dancing in costumes and eating and drinking form the core activities of these parties. In some cases the villagers will enact **symbolic dramas** with Indians dressed up as Spanish colonists, wearing hideous blue-eyed masks with long hairy beards. In the hills around towns like Huaraz and Cusco, especially, it's quite common to stumble into a village fiesta, with its explosion of human energy and noise, bright colours, and a mixture of pagan and Catholic symbolism.

Such celebrations are very much **local affairs**, and while the occasional traveller will almost certainly be welcomed with great warmth, none of these remote communities would want to be invaded by tourists waving cameras and expecting to be feasted for free. The dates given below are therefore only for established events that are already on the tourist map, and for those that take place all over the country.

TOP 5 FESTIVALS

Yawar fiesta See p.219
Qoyllur Rit'i See p.219
Fiesta de la Virgen de Carmen See p.272
Inti Raymi See p.219
Easter processions in Cusco See p.219

FESTIVALS AND PUBLIC HOLIDAYS

JANUARY

1 New Year's Day. Public holiday.

FEBRUARY

2 Candlemas. Folklore music and dancing throughout Peru, but especially lively in Puno at the Fiesta de la Virgen de la Candelaria and in the mountain regions.

Date varies Carnival. Wildly celebrated immediately prior to Lent, throughout the whole country.

MARCH/APRIL

Date varies Semana Santa (Easter/Holy Week). Superb processions all over Peru (the best are in Cusco and Ayacucho); the biggest is on Good Friday and in the evening on Easter Saturday, which is a public holiday.

MAY

1 Labour Day. Public holiday.

2–3 Fiesta de la Cruz (Festival of the Cross). Celebrated all over Peru in commemoration of ancient Peruvian agro-astronomical rituals and the Catholic annual calendar.

JUNE

Beginning of the month Corpus Christi. This takes places exactly nine weeks after Maundy Thursday, and usually falls in the first half of June. It's much celebrated, with fascinating processions and feasting all over Peru, but is particularly lively in Cusco.

24 Inti Raymi. Cusco's main Inca festival (see p.219).

29 St Peter's Day. A public holiday all over Peru, but mainly celebrated with fiestas in all the fishing villages along the coast.

JULY

15–17 Virgen de Carmen. Dance and music festivals at Pisac (see p.240) and Paucartambo (see p.272).

28–29 National Independence Day. Public holiday with military and school processions.

AUGUST

13–19 Arequipa Week. Processions, firework displays, plenty of folklore dancing and craft markets take place throughout Peru's second city.

30 Santa Rosa de Lima. Public holiday.

SEPTEMBER

End of the month Festival of Spring. Trujillo festival involving dancing – especially the local Marinera dance and popular Peruvian waltzes (see p.359).

OCTOBER

8 Public holiday to commemorate the Battle of Angamos.

18–28 Lord of Miracles. Festival featuring large and solemn processions (the main ones take place on October 18, 19 and 28); many women wear purple for the whole month, particularly in Lima, where bullfights and other celebrations continue throughout the month.

NOVEMBER

1 Fiesta de Todos los Santos (All Saints Day). Public holiday.

2 Día de los Muertos (All Souls Day). A festive remembrance of dead friends and relatives that is taken very seriously by most Peruvians and a popular time for baptisms and roast pork meals.

1–7 Puno Festival. One of the mainstays of Andean culture, celebrating the founding of Puno by the Spanish conquistadors and also the founding of the Inca Empire by the legendary Manco Capac and his sister Mama Ocllo, who are said to have emerged from Lake Titicaca. October 5 is marked by vigorous, colourful, community dancing.

1–30 International Bullfighting Competitions. Bullfights take place throughout the month, and are particularly spectacular at the Plaza de Acho in Lima.

12–28 Pacific Fair. One of the largest international trade fairs in South America – a huge, biennial event, which takes place on a permanent site on Av La Marina between Callao and Lima Centro.

DECEMBER

8 Feast of the Immaculate Conception. Public holiday.

25 Christmas Day. Public holiday.

Outdoor activities

Few of the world's countries can offer anything remotely as varied, rugged and stunningly beautiful as Peru when it comes to ecotourism, trekking, mountain biking and river rafting. Apart from possessing extensive areas of wilderness, Peru has the highest tropical mountain range in the world, plus the Amazon rainforest and a long Pacific coastline, all offering different opportunities for outdoor activities and adventure.

Trekking and climbing

The most popular areas for **trekking and climbing** are: north and south of Cusco; the Colca Canyon; and the Cordillera Blanca. But there are many other equally biodiverse and culturally rich trekking routes in other *departamentos*: Cajamarca and Chachapoyas both possess challenging but rewarding mountain trekking, and the desert coast, too, has exceptional and unique eco-niches that are most easily explored from Lima, Trujillo, Chiclayo, Nasca, Pisco, Ica and Arequipa, where there is some tourism infrastructure to support visits.

The main tours, treks and climbs have been listed throughout the Guide in their appropriate geographical context. Chapter Six, which includes Huaraz and the Cordillera Blanca, contains further information on climbing, mountaineering and trekking in the Andes, or **Andinismo**, as it's long been known (see p.326). The Cusco and Arequipa chapters also contain extensive listings of tour and trek operators as well as camping and climbing equipment rental.

TREKKING AND CLIMBING INFORMATION

Regional trekking resources can also be found in the relevant chapters of the Guide.

Casa de Guías Parque Ginebra 28-G, Huaraz (Mon–Fri 9am–1pm & 4–8pm, Sat 9am–1pm; **T 044 421811, W casadeguias.com.pe**). Base for the Huaraz and Cordillera Blanca mountain guides association (see p.329).

Club de Andinismo de la Universidad de Lima Av Javier Prado Este, Lima 33 **T 01 4376767 ext 30775.** Peru's leading mountaineering club.

Club Andino Peruano Av Dos de Mayo 1545, Oficina 216, Lima 27 **E info@clubandinoperuano.org.** Established over 50 years ago, this mountaineering club has a membership base and links with equipment suppliers.

Club de Montañismo Américo Tordoya Tarapacá 384, Lima **T 01 4606101 or T 01 4311305.** An association of six different clubs with climbing and backpacking interests.

Federación Peruana de Andinismo y Deportes de Invierno Block 3 of José Díaz, Lima Centro **T 01 4240063.** Peruvian Federation of Mountaineering and Sport.

Canoeing and whitewater rafting

Peru is hard to beat for **canoeing** and **whitewater rafting**. The rivers around Cusco and the Colca Canyon, as well as Huaraz and, nearer to Lima, at Lunahuana, can be exciting and demanding,

TOP 5 TREKS

Ausangate See p.270
The Chiquián Loop See p.342
Choquequirao See p.267
The Inca Trail See p.252
The Llanganuco to Santa Cruz Loop See p.332

NATIONAL PARKS AND RESERVES

Almost ten percent of Peru is incorporated into some form of **protected area**, including seven national parks, eight national reserves, seven national sanctuaries, three historical sanctuaries, five reserved zones, six buffer forests, two hunting reserves and an assortment of communal reserves and national forests.

The largest of these protected areas is the **Reserva Nacional Pacaya-Samiria**, an incredible tropical forest region in northern Peru. This is closely followed in size by the **Manu Biosphere Reserve**, another vast and stunning jungle area, and the **Reserva Nacional Tambopata and Parque Nacional Bahuaja-Sonene**, again an Amazon area, with possibly the richest flora and fauna of any region on the planet. Smaller but just as fascinating to visit are the **Parque Nacional Huascarán** in the high Andes near Huaraz, a popular trekking and climbing region, and the lesser-visited **Reserva Nacional Pampas Galeras**, close to Nasca, which was established mainly to protect the dwindling but precious herds of *vicuña*, the smallest and most beautiful member of the South American cameloid family.

Bear in mind that the parks and reserves are enormous zones, within which there is hardly any attempt to control or organize nature. The term "park" probably conveys the wrong impression about these huge, virtually untouched areas, which were designated by the **National System for Conservation Units (SNCU)**, with the aim of combining conservation, research and, in some cases (such as the Inca Trail) recreational tourism.

In December 1992, the **Peruvian National Trust Fund for Parks and Protected Areas (PROFONANPE)** was established as a trust fund managed by the private sector to provide funding for Peru's main protected areas. It has assistance from the Peruvian government, national and international nongovernmental organizations, the World Bank Global Environment Facility and the United Nations Environment Program.

VISITING THE PARKS

There's usually a small **charge** (usually around S/30 a day) to visit the national parks or nature reserves; this is normally levied at a reception hut on entry to the particular protected area. Sometimes, as at the Parque Nacional Huascarán, the cost is a simple daily rate; at others, like the Reserva Nacional Paracas on the coast south of Pisco, you pay a fixed sum to enter, regardless of how many days you might stay. For really remote protected areas, like Pacaya-Samiria, or if for some reason you enter an area via an unusual route, it is best to check on permissions – for Pacaya-Samiria you would need to contact the SERNANP office in Iquitos (see p.471). Most frequently visited National Parks will have an official hit for registration and paying of entry fees (which range from S/4 up to S/30 a day). For details check with the protected areas national agency **SERNANP** at Calle Diecisiete 355, Urb. El Palomar, San Isidro, Lima (T 01 7177500, W sernanp.gob.pe), the South American Explorers' Club in Lima (see p.81) or at the local tourist office.

though there are always sections ideal for beginners. **Cusco** is one of the top rafting and canoeing centres in South America (see box, p.224), with easy access to a whole range of river grades, from 2 to 5 on the Río Urubamba (shifting up grades in the rainy season) to the most dangerous whitewater on the Río Apurimac (level 6). On the Río Vilcanota, some 90km south of Cusco, at Chukikahuana, there's a 5km section of river that, between December and April, offers constant level-5 rapids. One of the most amazing trips from Cusco goes right down into the **Amazon Basin**. It should be noted that these rivers can be very wild and the best canoeing spots are often very remote, so you should only attempt river running with reputable companies and knowledgeable local guides.

The main companies operating in this field are listed in the relevant chapters. Trips range from half-day trips to several days of river adventure, sometimes encompassing both mountain and jungle terrain. **Transport, food and accommodation** are generally included in the price where relevant; but the costs also depend on levels of service and whether overnight accommodation required.

Cycling

In Peru, **cycling** is a major national sport, as well as one of the most ubiquitous forms of transport available to all classes in towns and rural areas virtually everywhere. Consequently, there are bike shops and bicycle-repair workshops in all major cities and larger towns. Perhaps more importantly, a number of tour companies offer **guided cycling tours** which can be an excellent way to see the best of Peru. Huaraz and Cusco are both popular destinations for bikers. For further information check the relevant chapter sections or contact the Federación Peruana de Ciclismo, Estadio Nacional, Lima Centro (Mon–Fri 9am–1pm & 2–5pm; ⓣ01 4336646, ⓦfedepeci.org).

Surfing

People have been **surfing** the waves off the coast of Peru for thousands of years and the traditional *caballitos de totora* (cigar-shaped ocean-going reed rafts) from the Huanchaco (p.365) and Chiclayo (p.395) beach areas of Peru are still used by fishermen who ride the surf daily. Every year around twelve thousand surfers come to Peru whose best beaches – Chicama, Cabo Blanco, Punta Rocas – rival those of Hawaii and Brazil. Good websites to find out more about the scene include: ⓦperusurfguides.com, ⓦperuecosurf.com and ⓦvivamancora.com/english/surf.htm.

Diving and fishing

For information on **diving** and **fishing** contact the Federación Peruana de Caza Submarina y Actividades Acuaticas, Estadio Nacional, Lima Centro (ⓣ01 4336626, ⓔdidimar@mail.cosapidata.com.pe). The private company Aquasport, Av Conquistadores 645, San Isidro, Lima (ⓣ01 2211548), is worth contacting.

Sport

Football is Peru's sport of passion, closely followed by women's volleyball, at which they are remarkably good, often contending at the very top international levels. After roughly 30 years of disappointment, Peru has hopes that its young new football team might make it through to the finals of the 2014 World Cup in Brazil. Bullfighting has a strong heritage both in Lima and small Andean villages.

Football

Peru's major sport is **football** and you'll find men and boys playing it in the streets of every city, town and settlement in the country down to the remotest of jungle outposts. The big teams are **Cristal**, **Alianza** and **El U** in Lima and **Ciencianco** from Cusco. The "Classic" game is between Alianza, the poor man's team from the La Victoria suburb of Lima, and El U ("U" from "Universitario"), generally supported by the middle class. To get a flavour for just how popular football is in Peru try a visit to the *Estadio Restaurant* in Lima (p.88), which has great murals, classic team shirts and life-size models of the world's top players.

Volleyball

Volleyball (*vóley*) is a very popular sport in Peru, particularly for women. The national team frequently reach World Cup and Olympic finals, and they are followed avidly on TV. Even in remote villages, most schools have girls' volleyball teams. For more information, check out ⓦvivevoley.com.

A WALK ON THE WILD SIDE: ECOTOURISM IN PERU

Ecotourism is most developed in the Amazon rainforest region of Peru, particularly around Manu, which is considered one of the most biodiverse regions on Earth; Iquitos in the northern jungle and the Tambopata region around Puerto Maldonado are similar ecotourism hotspots. These areas, and others in Peru's extensive rainforest, all offer a wide choice of operators leading tours up rivers to **jungle lodges**, which themselves function as bases from which to explore the forest on foot and in smaller, quieter canoes. Naturally, the focus is on wildlife and flora; but there are often **cultural elements** to tours, including short visits to riverside communities and indigenous villages, and sometimes even mystical or healing work with jungle shamans. Prices vary and so does the level of service and accommodation, as well as the degree of sustainability of the operation.

Ecotourism is very much alive in the Peruvian **Andes** too, with several tour operators offering expeditions on foot or on horseback into some of the more exotic high-Andes and cloudforest regions.

Bullfighting

Although **bullfighting** is under threat from the pro-animal lobby, and has diminished significantly in popularity in the twenty-first century, in many coastal and mountain haciendas (estates), bullfights are still often held at fiesta times. In a less organized way they happen at many of the village fiestas, too – often with the bull being left to run through the village until it's eventually caught and mutilated by one of the men. This is not just a sad sight, it can also be dangerous for unsuspecting tourists who happen to wander into a seemingly evacuated village. The Lima bullfights in October (see box, p.68), in contrast, are a very serious business; even Hemingway was impressed.

Travel essentials

Costs

Peru is certainly a much **cheaper** place to visit than Europe or the US, but how much so will depend on where you are and when. As a general rule low-budget travellers should, with care, be able to get by on around S/40–80/$15–30/£10–20/€11–22 per day, including transport, board and lodging. If you intend on staying in mid-range hotels, eating in reasonable restaurants and taking the odd taxi, S/135–245/$50–90/£32–60/€38–72 a day should be adequate, while S/270–540/$100–200/£63–125/€76–150 a day will allow you to stay in comfort and sample some of Peru's best cuisine.

In most places in Peru, a good **meal** can still be found for under S/27 ($10), **transport** is very reasonable, a comfortable **double room** costs $20–60 a night and **camping** is usually free, or under S/13/$5 per person. Expect to pay a little more than usual in the larger towns and cities, and also in the jungle, as many supplies have to be imported by truck. In the villages and rural towns, on the other hand, some basic commodities are far cheaper and it's always possible to buy food at a reasonable price from local villages or markets.

In the more popular parts of Peru, costs vary considerably with the **seasons**. Cusco, for instance, has its best weather from June to August, when many of its hotel prices go up by around 25–50 percent. The same thing happens at **fiesta** times – although on such occasions you're unlikely to resent it too much. As always, if you're travelling alone you'll end up spending considerably more than you would in a group of two or more people.

Tipping is expected in restaurants (10 per cent) and upmarket hotels, but not in taxis.

BARGAINING

You are generally expected to **bargain** in markets and with taxi drivers (before getting in). Nevertheless, it's worth bearing in mind that travellers from Europe, North America and Australasia are generally much wealthier than Peruvians, so for every penny or cent you knock them down they stand to lose plenty of nuevo soles. It's also sometimes possible to haggle over the price of hotel rooms, especially if you're travelling in a group. Food and shop prices, however, tend to be fixed.

Student and youth discounts

It's also worth taking along an international **youth/student ID card**, if you have one, for the occasional reduction (up to fifty percent at some museums and sites). Cards generally cost from $20–25; but, once obtained, they soon pay for themselves in savings. Full-time students are eligible for the International Student ID Card (ISIC) or ITIC, Youth, VIP, YHA or Nomads card, most of which entitle the bearer to special air, rail and bus fares and discounts at museums, theatres and other attractions. For US citizens there's also a **health benefit**, providing emergency medical and hospital coverage, plus a 24-hour hotline to call in the event of a medical, legal or financial emergency.

You only have to be 26 or younger to qualify for the International Youth Travel Card, which carries the same benefits. Teachers qualify for the International Teacher Card, offering similar discounts. All these cards are available in the UK, US, Canada and South Africa from STA (Ⓦstatravel.com) and from Hostelling International (Ⓦhihostels.com) in Australia and New Zealand. Several other travel organizations and accommodation groups also sell their own cards, good for various discounts.

Crime and personal safety

The biggest problem for travellers in Peru is arguably **theft**, for which the country once had a bad reputation. While pickpockets are remarkably ingenious in Peru, as far as violent attacks go, you're probably safer here than in the backstreets of New York,

Sydney, Durban or London; nevertheless, muggings do happen in certain parts of Lima (eg in the Centro main shopping areas, La Victoria district, Barranco late at night and even in the parks of Miraflores), Cusco, Arequipa and, to a lesser extent, Trujillo.

Theft

While the overall situation has improved, **robbery** and **pickpocketing** are still real dangers; although you don't need to be in a permanent state of paranoia and watchfulness in busy public situations, common sense and general alertness are still recommended. Generally speaking, **thieves** (*ladrones*) work in teams of often **smartly dressed** young men and women, in crowded markets, bus depots and train stations, targeting anyone who looks like they've got money. One of them will distract your attention (an old woman falling over in front of you or someone splattering an ice cream down your jacket) while another picks your pocket, cuts open your bag with a razor or simply runs off with it. Peruvians and tourists alike have even had earrings ripped out on the street.

Bank **ATMs** are a target for **muggers** in cities, particularly after dark, so visit them with a friend or two during daylight hours or make sure there's a policeman within visual contact. **Armed mugging** is rare but does happen in Lima, and it's best not to resist. The horrific practice of "strangle mugging" has been a bit of a problem in Cusco and Arequipa, usually involving night attacks when the perpetrator tries to strangle the victim into unconsciousness. Again, be careful not to walk down badly lit streets alone in the early hours.

Theft from cars and even more so, theft of car parts, is rife, particularly in Lima. Also, in some of the more popular **hotels** in the large cities, especially Lima, bandits masquerading as policemen break into rooms and steal the guests' most valuable possessions while holding the hotel staff at gunpoint. Objects left on restaurant floors in busy parts of town, or in unlocked hotel rooms, are obviously liable to take a walk.

Precautions

You'd need to spend the whole time visibly guarding your luggage to be sure of keeping hold of it; even then, though, a determined team of thieves will stand a chance. However, a few simple **precautions** can make life a lot easier. The most important is to keep your ticket, passport (and tourist card), money and travellers' cheques on your person at all times (under your pillow while sleeping and on your person when washing in communal hotel bathrooms). **Money belts** are a good idea for travellers' cheques and tickets, or a holder for your passport and money can be hung either under a shirt or from a belt under trousers or skirts. Some people go as far as lining their bags with chicken wire (called *maya* in Peru) to make them knife-proof, and wrapping wire around camera straps for the same reason (putting their necks in danger to save their cameras).

Cities are most dangerous in the early hours of the morning and at **bus or train stations** where there's lots of anonymous activity. In rural areas robberies tend to be linked to the most popular towns (again, be most careful at the bus depot) and treks (the Inca Trail for instance). Beyond that, **rural areas** are generally safe. If you're camping near a remote community, though, it's a good idea to ask permission and make friendly contact with some of the locals; letting them know what you are up to will usually dissolve any local paranoia about tomb-robbers or kidnappers.

The only certain precaution you can take is to **insure** your gear and cash before you go (see p.46). Take refundable travellers' cheques, register your passport at your embassy in Lima on arrival (this doesn't take long and can save days should you lose it) and keep your eyes open at all times. If you do have something stolen, report it to the tourist police in larger towns, or the local police in more remote places, and ask them for a certified **denuncia** – this can take a couple of days. Many insurance companies will require a copy of the police *denuncia* in order to reimburse you. Bear in mind that the police in popular tourist spots, such as Cusco, have become much stricter about investigating reported thefts, after a spate of false claims by dishonest tourists. This means that genuine victims may be grilled more severely than expected, and the police may even come and search your hotel room for the "stolen" items.

Terrorism

You can get up-to-date information on the **terrorism** situation in each region from the South American Explorers' Club (see p.50), Peruvian embassies abroad (see p.43) or your embassy in Lima (see p.96). Essentially, though, **terrorism** is not the problem it was during the 1980s and 1990s when the two main **terrorist groups** active in Peru were the Sendero Luminoso (the Shining Path) and Tupac Amaru (MRTA).

The police

Most of your contact with the **police** will, with any luck, be at frontiers and controls. Depending on your personal appearance and the prevailing political climate, the police at these posts (Guardia Nacional and Aduanas) may want to **search your luggage**. This happens rarely, but when it does, it can be very thorough. Occasionally, you may have to get off buses and **register documents** at the police controls which regulate the traffic of goods and people from one *departamento* of Peru to another. The controls are usually situated on the outskirts of large towns on the main roads, but you sometimes come across a control in the middle of nowhere. Always stop, and be scrupulously polite – even if it seems that they're trying to make things difficult for you.

In general the police rarely bother travellers but there are certain sore points. The possession of (let alone trafficking of) either soft or hard **drugs** (basically marijuana or cocaine) is considered an extremely serious offence in Peru – usually leading to at least a ten-year jail sentence. There are many foreigners languishing in Peruvian jails after being charged with possession, some of whom have been waiting two years for a trial – there is no bail for serious charges.

Drugs aside, the police tend to follow the media in suspecting all foreigners of being **political subversives** and even gun-runners or terrorists; it's more than a little unwise to carry any Maoist or **radical literature**. If you find yourself in a tight spot, don't make a statement before seeing someone from your embassy, and don't say anything without the services of a reliable translator. It's not unusual to be given the opportunity to pay a **bribe** to the police (or any other official for that matter), even if you've done nothing wrong. You'll have to weigh up this situation as it arises – but remember, in South America bribery is seen as an age-old custom, very much part of the culture rather than a nasty form of corruption, and it can work to the advantage of both parties, however irritating it might seem. It's also worth noting that all police are **armed** with either a revolver or a submachine gun and will shoot at anyone who runs.

Tourist Police

It's often quite hard to spot the difference between **Tourist Police** and the normal police. Both are wings of the Guardia Civil, though the tourist police sometimes wear white hats rather than the standard green. Increasingly, the Tourist Police have taken on the function of informing and assisting tourists (eg in preparing a robbery report or *denuncia*) in city centres.

If you feel you've been ripped off or are unhappy about your treatment by a tour agent, hotel, restaurant, transport company, customs, immigration or even the police, you can call the 24-hour **Tourist Protection Service** hotline for the Tourist Police in Lima (Lima North ⓣ51 1 423 3500; Lima South ⓣ51 1 243 2190). There are also Tourist Police offices in 15 other cities, including all major tourist destinations, such as Cusco, Arequipa and Puno.

Customs and etiquette

The most obvious cultural idiosyncrasy of Peruvians is that they **kiss** on one cheek at virtually every meeting between friends or acquaintances. In rural areas (as opposed to trendy beaches) the local tradition in most places is for people, particularly women, to **dress modestly** and cover themselves (eg longish skirts and T-shirts or blouses, or maybe traditional robes). In some hot places men may do manual labour in shorts, but they, too, are generally covered from shoulder to foot. Travellers sometimes suffer **insults** from Peruvians who begrudge the apparent relative wealth and freedom of tourists. Remember, however, that the terms "gringo" or "mister" are not generally meant in an offensive way in Peru.

Punctuality has improved in Peru in the last 20 years or so, but for social happenings can still be very lax. While buses, trains or planes won't wait a minute beyond their scheduled departure time, people almost expect friends to be an hour or more late for an appointment (don't arrange to meet a Peruvian on the street – make it a bar or café). Peruvians stipulate that an engagement is *a la hora inglesa* ("by English time") if they genuinely want people to arrive on time, or, more realistically, within half an hour of the time they fix.

Try to be aware of the strength of **religious belief** in Peru, particularly in the Andes, where churches have a rather heavy, sad atmosphere. You can enter and quietly look around all churches, but in the Andes especially you should refrain from taking photographs.

Electricity

220 volt/60 cycles AC is the standard **electrical current** all over Peru, except in Arequipa where it is 220 volt/50 cycles. In some of Lima's better hotels you may also find 110 volt sockets to use with standard electric shavers. Don't count on any Peruvian power supply being one hundred percent reliable and, particularly in cheap hostels and hotels, be very wary of the wiring (especially in electric shower fittings).

Entry requirements

Currently, EU, US, Canadian, Australian, New Zealand and South African citizens can all stay in Peru as tourists for up to ninety days without a visa. However, the situation does change periodically, so always check with your local Peruvian embassy some weeks before departure. All nationalities need a **tourist/embarkation card** *(tarjeta de embarque)* to enter Peru, issued at the frontiers or on the plane before landing in Lima. Tourist cards are usually valid for between sixty and ninety days. Unless you specifically ask for ninety days when being issued a Tourist Card on arrival, you may only receive sixty. For your own safety and freedom of movement a copy of the tourist card should be kept on you, with your passport, at all times – particularly when travelling away from the main towns.

Should you want to **extend your visa** (between thirty and sixty additional days), there are two basic options: either cross one of the borders and get a new tourist card when you come back in; or go through the bureaucratic rigmarole at a Migraciones office, which involves form filling, taking a photocopy of your passport and visa (or tourist card) and a visit to the Banco de la Nación to pay the required fee ($20) to the State, where you get issued an official receipt (*recibo de pago*). This process is easiest in Lima, where it can be all be done in the same building, but even there it can take a couple of hours or more. A further $4.50 is needed for legalizing the Migraciones form (usually issued at reception), and you may also be asked to provide evidence of a valid exit ticket from Peru. Migraciones is also the place to sort out new visas if you've **lost your passport** (having visited your embassy first) and to get passports re-stamped.

Student visas (which last twelve months) are best organized as far in advance as possible through your country's embassy in Lima, your nearest Peruvian embassy or the relevant educational institution. **Business visas** only become necessary if you are to be paid by a Peruvian organization, in which case ask your Peruvian employers to get this for you.

PERUVIAN EMBASSIES AND CONSULATES

An up-to-date list of Peruvian diplomatic missions can be accessed in Spanish on Ⓦ rree.gob.pe.

AUSTRALIA

Peruvian Embassy Canberra Ⓣ 02 6286 9507.

Peruvian Consulate 157 Main St, Croydon, Melbourne Ⓣ 03 9725 4655.

Peruvian Consulate Level Three, 30 Clarence St, Sydney Ⓣ 02 9262 6464.

CANADA

Peruvian Embassy Ottawa Ⓣ 613 238 1777.

NEW ZEALAND

Peruvian Embassy Level Eight, Cigna House, 40 Mercer St, Wellington Ⓣ 04 499 8087.

SOUTH AFRICA

Peruvian Consulate Brooklyn Gardens Building Block A, 1st Floor 235 Veale and Middle Street, Nieuw Muckleneuk, 0181 Pretoria. Ⓣ 0027 1234 68744.

UNITED KINGDOM

Peruvian Embassy 52 Sloane St, London SW1X 9SP Ⓣ 020 7838 9223.

US

Peruvian Embassy 1625 Massachusetts Ave NW, Suite 605, Washington, DC 20036 Ⓣ 202 462 1081.

Gay and lesbian travellers

Homosexuality is pretty much kept underground in what is still a very macho society, though in recent years Lima has seen a liberating advance and transvestites can walk the streets in relative freedom from abuse. However, there is little or no organized gay scene. **The Peruvian Homosexual and Lesbian Movement** can be contacted at C Mariscal Miller 828, Jesús María (Ⓣ 01 4335519). There are few specialist gay organizations, hotel facilities, restaurants or even clubs (where they exist they are listed in the relevant sections of the Guide). Further information can be accessed at the following websites: Ⓦ lima.queercity.info, Ⓦ deambiente.com, Ⓦ peruesgay.com and Ⓦ gayperu.com.

Health

No inoculations are currently required for Peru, but a **yellow fever vaccination** is sometimes needed to enter the jungle, as well as being generally recommended. It's always a good idea to check with the embassy or a reliable travel agent before you go. Your doctor will probably advise you to have some **inoculations** anyway: typhoid, cholera, rabies and, again, yellow fever shots are all sensible precautions, and it's well worth ensuring that your polio and tetanus-diphtheria boosters are still effective. Immunization against hepatitis A is also usually recommended.

In case you don't get your shots before you leave for Peru, there is a useful 24-hour vaccination service at the International Health Department in Lima's airport (Ⓣ 01 517 1845), and also a vaccination centre in the Lima suburb of Jesús María at C Capac Yupanqui 1400 (Mon–Fri 8am–1pm & 2–5pm; ⓣ01 471 9920).

Yellow fever

Yellow fever breaks out now and again in some of the jungle areas of Peru; it is frequently obligatory to show an inoculation certificate when entering the Amazon region – if you can't show proof of immunization you'll be jabbed on the spot. This viral disease is transmitted by mosquitoes and can be fatal. Symptoms are headache, fever, abdominal pain and vomiting, and though victims may appear to recover, without medical help, they may suffer from bleeding, shock, and kidney and liver failure. The only treatment is to keep the patient's fever as low as possible and prevent dehydration.

Malaria

Malaria is quite common in Peru these days, particularly in the Amazon regions to the east of the country, and it's very easy to catch without prophylactics. If you intend to go into the jungle regions, malaria tablets should be taken – starting a few weeks before you arrive and continuing for some time after. Make sure you get a supply of these, or whatever is recommended by your doctor in advance of the trip. There are several commonly recommended malarial **prophylactics** recommended for the Peruvian jungle regions; some are more expensive than others and some are not recommended for prolonged periods. You should investigate your options with your GP, ideally more than a month prior to your departure for Peru. To avoid getting bitten in the rainforest wear long sleeves, long trousers, socks and a mosquito-proof net hat and sleep under good mosquito netting or in well-proofed quarters. For more information check out ⓦcdc.gov/travel/regionalmalaria.

Dengue fever

Like malaria, **dengue fever** is another illness spread by mosquito bites; the symptoms are similar, plus aching bones. Dengue-carrying mosquitoes are particularly prevalent during the rainy season, with urban jungle areas often the worst affected; they fly during the day, so wear insect repellent in the daytime if mosquitoes are around. The only treatment is complete rest, with drugs to assuage the fever – unfortunately, a second infection can be fatal.

Diarrhoea

Diarrhoea is something everybody gets at some stage, and there's little to be done except to drink a lot of water and bide your time. You should also replace salts either by taking oral rehydration salts or by mixing a teaspoon of salt and eight teaspoons of sugar in a litre of purified water. You can minimize the risk by being sensible about what you eat, and by not drinking **tap water** anywhere (see below). Peruvians are great believers in herbal teas, which often help alleviate cramps.

Dysentery and giardia

If your diarrhoea contains blood or mucus, the cause may be dysentery (one of either two strains; see below) or giardia. Combined with a fever, these symptoms could well be caused by **bacillic dysentery** and may clear up without treatment. If you're sure you need it, a course of antibiotics such as tetracyclin or ampicillin (travel with a supply if you are going off the beaten track for a while) should sort you out, but they also destroy "gut flora" which help protect you, so should only be used if properly diagnosed or in a desperate situation. Similar symptoms without fever indicate **amoebic dysentery**, which is much more serious, and can damage your gut if untreated. The usual cure is a course of metronidazole (Flagyl), an antibiotic which may itself make you feel ill, and should not be taken with alcohol.

Similar symptoms, plus rotten-egg-smelling belches and gas, indicate **giardia**, for which the treatment is again metronidazole. If you suspect you have any of these illnesses, seek medical help, and only start on the metronidazole (250mg three times daily for a week for adults) if there is definitely blood in your diarrhoea and it is impossible to see a doctor.

Water and food

Water in Peru is better than it used to be, but it can still trouble non-Peruvian (and even Peruvian) stomachs, so it's a good idea to only drink **bottled water** (*agua mineral*), available in various sizes, including litre and two-litre bottles from most corner shops or food stores. Stick with known brands, even if they are more expensive, and always check that the seal on the bottle is intact, since the sale of bottles refilled with local water is not uncommon. Carbonated water is generally safer as it is more likely to be the genuine stuff. You should also clean your teeth using bottled water and avoid raw foods washed in local water.

Apart from bottled water, there are various methods of **treating water** while you are travelling, whether your source is tap water or natural groundwater such as a river or stream. **Boiling** is the time-honoured method, which is an effective way to sterilize water, although it will not remove any unpleasant tastes. A minimum boiling time of five minutes (longer at higher altitudes) is sufficient to kill microorganisms. In remote jungle areas, **sterilizing tablets** are a better idea, although they leave a rather bad taste in the mouth. Pregnant women or people with thyroid problems should consult their doctor before using iodine sterilizing tablets or iodine-based purifiers. There also several portable **water filters** on the market. In emergencies and remote areas in particular, always check with locals to see whether the tap water is okay (*es potable?*) before drinking it.

Peruvian **food** cooked on the street has been frequently condemned as a health hazard, particularly during rare but recurrent **cholera outbreaks**. Be careful about anything bought from street stalls, particularly seafood, which may not be that fresh. **Salads** should be avoided, especially in small settlements where they may have been washed in river water or fertilized by local sewage waters.

The sun

The sun can be deceptively hot, particularly on the coast or when travelling in boats on jungle rivers when the hazy weather or cool breezes can put visitors off their guard; remember, **sunstroke** can make you very sick as well as burnt. Wide-brimmed hats, sunscreen lotions (factor 60 advisable since the sun high up in the Andes is deceptively strong) and staying in the shade whenever possible are all good precautions. Note that suntan lotion and sunblock are more expensive in Peru than they are at home, so take a good supply with you. If you do run out, you can buy Western brands at most *farmacias*, though you won't find a very wide choice available, especially in the higher factors. Also make sure that you increase your water intake, in order to prevent **dehydration**.

Altitude sickness

Altitude sickness – known as *soroche* (see box, p.210) in Peru – is a common problem for visitors, especially if you are travelling quickly between the coast or jungle regions and the high Andes. The best way to prevent it is to eat light meals, drink lots of coca tea and spend as long as possible acclimatizing to high altitudes (over 2500m) before carrying out any strenuous activity. Anyone who suffers from headaches or nausea should rest; more seriously, a sudden bad cough could be a sign of **pulmonary edema** and demands an immediate descent and medical attention – altitude sickness can kill. People often suffer from altitude sickness on trains crossing high passes; if this happens, don't panic, just rest and stay on the train until it descends. Most trains are equipped with oxygen bags or cylinders that are brought around by the conductor for anyone in need. **Diamox** is used by many from the US to counter the effects of *soroche*. It's best to bring this with you from home since it's rarely available in Peruvian pharmacies.

Insects

Insects are more of an irritation than a serious problem, but on the coast, in the jungle and to a lesser extent in the mountains, the **common fly** is a definite pest. Although flies can carry typhoid, there is little one can do; you might spend mealtimes swatting flies away from your plate but even in expensive restaurants it's difficult to monitor hygiene in the kitchens.

A more obvious problem is the **mosquito**, which in some parts of the lowland jungle carries malaria. Repellents are of limited value – it's better to cover your arms, legs and feet with a good layer of clothing. Mosquitoes tend to emerge after dark, but the daytime holds even worse biting insects in the jungle regions, among them the **manta blanca** (or white blanket), so called because they swarm as a blanket of tiny flying insects. Their bites don't hurt at the time but itch like crazy for a few days afterwards. **Antihistamine creams** or tablets can reduce the sting or itchiness of most insect bites, but try not to scratch them – if it gets unbearable go to the nearest *farmacia* for advice. To keep hotel rooms relatively insect-free, buy some of the spirals of incense-like **pyrethrin**, available cheaply everywhere.

AVERAGE TEMPERATURES AND RAINFALL

	Oct–April	May–Sept	Temp. range (approx) °C/°F	Annual rainfall mm/in
COAST	Sunny season	Some coastal cloud	13–30/55–86	0.55/0.02
ANDES	Rainy season	Dry season	0–18/32–64	400–1000/16–39
JUNGLE	Rainy season	Dry season	20–35/68–95	2000–3900/79–154

HIV and AIDS

While Peru does not have as bad a reputation for **HIV** and **AIDS** (also known as **SIDA** in Latin America) as neighbouring Brazil, they are a growing problem in South America and you should still take care. Although all hospitals and clinics in Peru are supposed to use only sterilized equipment, many travellers prefer to take their own sealed hypodermic syringes in case of emergencies.

Contraception

Condoms (*profilacticos*) are available from street vendors and some *farmacias*. However, they tend to be expensive and often poor quality, so bring an adequate supply with you. **The Pill** is also available from *farmacias*, officially on prescription only, but frequently sold over the counter. You're unlikely to be able to match your brand, however, so it's far better to bring your own supply. It's worth remembering that if you suffer from moderately severe **diarrhoea** on your trip the Pill (or any other drug) may not be in your system long enough to take effect.

Pharmacies

For **minor ailments** you can buy most drugs at a pharmacy (*farmacia* or *botica)* without a prescription. Antibiotics and malaria pills can be bought over the counter (it is important to know the correct dosage), as can antihistamines (for bite allergies) or medication for an upset stomach (try Lomotil or Streptotriad). You can also buy Western-brand **tampons** at a *farmacia*, though they are expensive, so it's better to bring a good supply. For any serious illnesses, you should go to a doctor or hospital; these are listed throughout the Guide, or you can try the local phone book.

Alternative medicines

Alternative medicines have a popular history going back at least two thousand years in Peru and the traditional practitioners – *herbaleros*, *hueseros* and *curanderos* (see p.507) – are still commonplace. **Herbaleros** sell curative plants, herbs and charms in the streets and markets of most towns. They lay out a selection of ground roots, liquid tree barks, flowers, leaves and creams – all with specific medicinal functions and sold at much lower prices than in the *farmacias*. If told the symptoms, a *herbalero* can select remedies for most minor (and apparently some major) ailments. **Hueseros** are consultants who treat diseases and injuries by bone manipulation; while **curanderos** claim diagnostic, divinatory and healing powers, and have existed in Peru since pre-Inca days.

MEDICAL RESOURCES

UK AND IRELAND

Hospital for Tropical Diseases Travel Clinic thehtd.org.
MASTA (Medical Advisory Service for Travellers Abroad) masta.org for the nearest clinic.
Tropical Medical Bureau Ireland 1850 487 674, tmb.ie.

US AND CANADA

Canadian Society for International Health 613 241 5785, **csih.org.** Extensive list of travel health centres.
CDC 1 800 232 4636, **cdc.gov/travel.** Official US government travel health site.
International Society for Travel Medicine 1 404 373 8282, **istm.org.** Has a full list of travel health clinics.

AUSTRALIA, NEW ZEALAND AND SOUTH AFRICA

The Travel Doctor – TMVC 1300 658 844, **tmvc.com.au.** Lists travel clinics in Australia, New Zealand and South Africa.

Insurance

Insurance (see box opposite) is definitely a good idea for a destination like Peru. Most worldwide policies offer a range of options to cover different levels of adventurous activities. Some of the extreme sports, including kayaking and bungee jumping, may not be covered by standard policies.

Internet

Peru has good **internet** connections, with cyber-cafés and internet cabins in the most unlikely of small towns. Lima and Cusco have abundant internet cafés, closely followed by Arequipa, Huaraz, Puno, Iquitos and Trujillo. The general rate is 50¢ to $1 an hour, though thirty- and fifteen-minute options are often available.

Language lessons

You can learn **Peruvian Spanish** all over Peru, but the best range of schools is in Lima, Cusco, Arequipa and Huancayo. Check the relevant Directory sections in the Guide.

Laundry

Mid- to high-end hotels frequently offer a **laundry** service and some basic hotels have communal washrooms where you can do your own washing. It's no great expense to get your clothes washed by a *lavandería* (laundry) on the street.

Living and working in Peru

There is a certain amount of **bureaucracy** involved if you want to work (or live) officially in Peru. Your only real chance of **earning money** here is by teaching English in Lima, or, with luck, teaching English or working in an expat bar in Arequipa or Cusco. In the more remote parts of the country it may sometimes be possible to find board and lodging in return for a little building work or general labour.

For biology, geography or environmental science graduates there's the chance of free board and lodging, and maybe a small salary, if you're willing to work very hard for at least three months as a **tour guide** in a jungle lodge, under the Resident Naturalist schemes. One or two lodges along the **Río Tambopata** offer such schemes and other research opportunities. For more details, it's best to contact lodges such as the *Tambopata Research Centre* (see p.446) directly; for independent, up-to-date advice contact the Tambopata Reserve Society (Ⓦ wtsonline.co.uk/treesnewweb/home2.shtml). Arrangements need to be made at least six months in advance. Based in Arequipa, the relatively new **Traveller Not Tourist** organization (Ⓦ travellernottourist.com) is not-for-profit and helps volunteers work directly to support children in poverty.

Teaching English

There are two options if you'd like to teach English in Peru: find work before you go, or just wing it and see what you come up with while you're out there, particularly if you already have a degree, teaching experience or a relevant ELT or TEFL qualification. The British Council's website (Ⓦ britishcouncil.org) has a list of English-teaching vacancies and Overseas Jobs Express (Ⓦ overseasjobs.com) also lists jobs.

STUDY AND WORK PROGRAMMES

AFS Intercultural Programs US Ⓣ 1 800 237 4636, Canada Ⓣ 1 800 361 7248, Australia Ⓣ 02 9215 0077, NZ Ⓣ 0800 600 300, SA Ⓣ 11 447 2673; Ⓦ afs.org. Intercultural exchange organization with programmes in over 50 countries.

American Institute for Foreign Study US Ⓣ 1 866 906 2437, UK Ⓣ 020 7581 7300, Australia Ⓣ 02 8235 7000; Ⓦ aifs.com. Language study and cultural immersion, as well as au pair and Camp America programmes.

BUNAC US Ⓣ 1 800 462 8622, UK Ⓣ 020 7251 3472, Australia Ⓣ 03 9329 3866; Ⓦ bunac.org. Organizes working holidays in a range of destinations for students.

BTCV (British Trust for Conservation Volunteers) UK Ⓣ 01302 388 883, Ⓦ btcv.org.uk. One of the largest environmental charities in Britain, with a programme of national and international working holidays (as a paying volunteer).

Council on International Educational Exchange (CIEE) US Ⓣ 1 207 553 4000, Ⓦ ciee.org. Leading NGO offering study programmes and volunteer projects around the world.

Earthwatch Institute UK Ⓣ 01865 318 838, US Ⓣ 978 461 0081, Australia Ⓣ 03 9682 6828; Ⓦ earthwatch.org. Scientific expedition project that spans over 50 countries, with environmental and archeological ventures worldwide.

Mail

The Peruvian **postal service** – branded as Serpost – is reasonably efficient, if slightly irregular and a little expensive. Letters from Europe and the US generally take around one or two weeks to arrive – occasionally less – while outbound letters to Europe or the US seem to take between ten days and three weeks. Stamps for postcards and airmail letters to the UK, the US and to Australia, New Zealand and South Africa cost around S/3–7.

Be aware that **parcels** take about one month to arrive and are particularly vulnerable to being opened en route – in either direction – and expensive souvenirs can't be sure of leaving the building where you mail them. Never send money through the Peruvian post!

Maps

Maps of Peru fall into three basic categories. A standard **road map** should be available from good map-sellers just about anywhere in the world or in Peru itself from street vendors or *librerías*; the Touring y Automóvil Club de Perú, Av César Vallejo 699, Lince, Lima (01 6149999, touringperu.com.pe), is worth visiting for its good route maps. **Departmental maps**, covering each *departamento* (Peruvian state) in greater detail, albeit often very out of date, are also fairly widely available. **Topographic maps** (usually 1:100,000) cover the entire coastal area and most of the mountainous regions of Peru. In Lima, they can be bought from the Instituto Geográfico Nacional (www.ign.gab.pe), and they're also available at the South American Explorers' Club (see p.81), along with a wide variety of hiking maps and guidebooks for all the most popular hiking zones, and quite a few others.

Money

The **currency** in Peru is the **nuevo sol**, still simply called a "sol" on the streets, and whose symbol is S/. The sol remains relatively steady against the US dollar, though the dollar has weakened slightly since 2009, and at time of writing, the exchange rate for the nuevo sol was roughly $1 = S/2.7, £1 = S/4.3, Aus$1 = S/2.9, NZ$1 = S/2.3, ZAR1 = 35¢.

Dollars are also accepted in many places, including smart hotels, tour companies, railway companies and classy restaurants. The main supermarkets in Lima also take dollars, as do some taxi drivers (especially those picking up from airports).

ATMs are common in all of Peru's cities and main towns, with the BCP (Banco de Credito del Peru) probably being the most common, but all the main banks' ATMs seem to work well with standard credit and debit cards. Travellers' cheques and cash dollars or euros can be cashed at **casas de cambio**. Cash can be changed on the street, sometimes at a slightly better rate than the banks or casas de cambio, but with a greater risk of being short-changed.

Opening hours

Most **shops** and **services** in Peru open Monday to Saturday 9am to 5pm, or 6pm. Many are open on Sunday as well, if for more limited hours. Of Peru's **museums**, some belong to the state, others to institutions, and a few to individuals. Most charge a small admission fee and are open Monday to Saturday 9am to noon and 3 to 6pm.

Peru's more important **ancient sites** and ruins usually have opening hours that coincide with daylight – from around 7am until 5pm or 6pm daily. Smaller sites are rarely fenced off, and are nearly always accessible 24 hours a day. For larger sites, you normally pay a small admission fee to the local guardian – who may then walk around with you, pointing out features of interest. Only Machu Picchu charges more than a few dollars' entrance fee – this is one site where you may find it worth presenting an ISIC or FIYTO student card (which generally gets you in for half-price).

Churches open in the mornings for Mass (usually around 6am), after which the smaller ones close. Those which are most interesting to tourists, however, tend to stay open all day, while others open again in the afternoon from 3 to 6pm. Very occasionally there's an admission charge to churches, and more regularly to monasteries (*monasterios*).

Phones

It's easy to make **international calls** from just about any town in the country, either with a pre-paid phonecard or via a telephone cabin, which can be found in all town centres. **Mobiles** are expensive to use, but almost everyone seems to have one these days. Using your own mobile almost always works out to be the most expensive form of telephone communication, but it may be worth checking with your provider before departure. It is certainly cheaper to buy a local mobile phone and sim card (available in shops everywhere from around S/94–121/$35–45) and use this for in-Peru calls. Probably the most popular mobile company is Claró.

Phonecards (eg Telefónica Tarjeta 147) are the cheapest way to communciate by phone either domestically or internationally; indeed, international calls from a fixed phone often work out cheaper than ones to Peruvian mobiles or between Peruvian cities. Each card has directions for use (in Spanish) on the reverse and most are based on a scratch-card numeral basis. You can buy phonecards from corner shops, *farmacias* or on the street from cigarette stalls in the centres of most towns and cities.

Most shops, restaurants or corner shops in Peru have a **phone** available for public use, which you can use for calls within Peru only.

Photography

The light in Peru is very bright, with a strong contrast between shade and sun. This can produce a nice effect and generally speaking it's easy to take good

DIALLING CODES AND USEFUL NUMBERS

USEFUL TELEPHONE NUMBERS

Directory enquiries ☎ 103
Operator ☎ 100
Emergency services ☎ 105
International operator ☎ 108

CALLING HOME FROM ABROAD

Note that the initial zero is omitted from the area code when dialling Australia, New Zealand, the Republic of Ireland, the UK, US, Canada and South Africa.
Australia international access code + 61 + area code.
New Zealand international access code + 64 + area code.
Republic of Ireland international access code + 353 + area code.
UK international access code + 44 + area code.
US and Canada international access code + 1 + area code.
South Africa international access code + 27 + area code.

CALLING PERU FROM ABROAD

Dial the international access code + 51 (country code for Peru) + area code in Peru (minus intitial zero; see below) + number.

PERUVIAN TOWN AND CITY CODES

Amazonas 41
Ancash 43
Apurimac 83
Arequipa 54
Ayacucho 66
Cajamarca 76
Cusco 84
Huancavelica 67
Huánuco 62
Ica 56
Junín 64
Lima and Callao 01
La Libertad 44
Lambayeque 74
Loreto 65
Madre de Dios 82
Moquegua 53
Pasco 63
Piura 73
Puno 51
San Martín 42
Tacna 52
Tumbes 72
Ucayali 61

photographs. One of the more complex problems is how to take photos of people without upsetting them. You should always talk to a prospective subject first, and ask if she/he minds if you take a quick photo (*"una fotito, por favor?"* – "a little photo please"); most people react favourably to this approach even if all the communication is in sign language.

Digital photography is by far the most common format for Peruvians and travellers alike. Digital cameras, memory cards, batteries and accessories are now widely available pretty much everywhere in Peru. Most internet cafés can also help download memory cards. Camera film is expensive to buy, and not readily available outside of the main cities; colour Kodak and Fuji films are easier to find, but black-and-white film is rare. If you can bear the suspense it's best to save getting films developed until you're home – you'll probably get better results.

Senior travellers

Senior travellers in reasonable health should have no problems in Peru. Anyone taking medication should obviously bring enough supplies for the duration of the trip, though most drugs are available over the counter in Lima and other cities. The altitude is likely to be the most serious concern, so careful reading of our section on altitude sickness (see p.45) becomes even more crucial; so does taking great care with what food you eat (see p.44).

As far as accommodation for senior travellers goes, most middle- to top-range hotels are clean and comfortable; it's mostly a matter of clearly asking for what you need when booking or on arrival at the hotel. This is particularly true if you have special requirements such as a ground-floor room.

Shopping

Peru is one of those places where you want to buy something from virtually every street corner. Apart from all the fine alpaca sweaters and blankets, there are baskets, musical instruments, paintings and a whole raft of quite well known **artesanía** (craft goods).

Of course, most Peruvians live in cities with massive supermarkets and a pharmacy on each street corner. **Shopping centres** are springing up all over Lima, each more or less a replica of the other. Traditional craft goods from most regions of

Peru can be found in **markets** and independent shops in Lima. Woollen and alpaca products, though, are usually cheaper and often better quality in the mountains – particularly in Cusco, Juliaca and Puno; carved gourds are imported from around Huancayo; the best places to buy ceramic replicas are Trujillo, Huaraz, Ica and Nasca; and the best jungle crafts are from Pucallpa and Iquitos.

If you get offered an "ancient" pot or necklace, remember that **Peruvian law** stipulates that no items of archeological or historical value or interest may be removed from the country. Many of the **jungle crafts** which incorporate feathers, skins or shells of rare Amazonian animals are also banned for export – it's best not to buy these if you are in any doubt about their scarcity. If you do try to export anything of archeological or biological value, and get caught, you'll have the goods confiscated at the very least, and may find yourself in a Peruvian court.

Time

Peru keeps the same hours as **Eastern Standard Time**, which is five hours behind GMT.

Tourist information

These days, **i-Peru** (T 01 574 8000, W peru.info) is the key government source of tourist information. They have offices in most major cities, often operating in parallel with a local municipal service. They will provide information by email and their website is useful.

The **South American Explorers' Club** is also a great source of relevant and up-to-date travel information both before you leave home and when you arrive in Lima. It is a nonprofit organization that was founded in 1977 to support scientific and adventure expeditions and to provide services to travellers. In return for membership (from $50 a year) you get four copies of the magazine *South American Explorer* a year, and you can use the club's facilities, which in Lima include an excellent library, a map collection, trip reports, listings, a postal address and storage space. The club also provides discounts on maps and guidebooks, information on visas, doctors and dentists, and access to a network of experts with specialist information. Some trip reports are now also available online. They have clubhouses in Lima (see p.81), and Cusco (see p.222), and their main office is in the US, at 126 Indiana Creek Rd, Ithaca, NY 14850 (T 607 277 0488, F 277 6122, W saexplorers.org), plus there is a clubhouse in Ecuador and one in Argentina.

GOVERNMENT WEBSITES

Asociación Peruano de Tursimo Receptivo e Interno W apoturperu.org.
Australian Department of Foreign Affairs W dfat.gov.au.
British Foreign & Commonwealth Office W fco.gov.uk.
Canadian Department of Foreign Affairs W international.gc.ca.
Instituto Geográfico Nacional W ign.gob.pe.
Instituto Nacional de Cultura W inc.gob.pe.
Irish Department of Foreign Affairs W foreignaffairs.gov.ie.
New Zealand Ministry of Foreign Affairs W mfat.govt.nz.
US State Department W state.gov.
South African Department of Foreign Affairs W dfa.gov.za.

Travelling with children

South Americans hold the family unit in high regard and **children** are central to this. Prices can often be cheaper for children; tours to attractions can occasionally be negotiated on a **family-rate** basis and entry to sites is often half-price or less (and always free for infants). Children under 10 generally get half-fare on local (but not inter-regional) buses, while trains and boats generally charge full fare if a seat is required. Infants who don't need a seat often travel free on all transport except planes, when you pay around ten percent of the usual fare.

Travelling around the country is perhaps the most difficult activity with children. **Bus and train journeys** are generally long (twelve hours or more). Crossing international borders is a potential hassle; although Peru officially accepts children under 16 on their parents' **passports**, it is a good idea for them to have their own to minimize problems. For more information you can try *The Rough Guide to Travel with Babies and Young Children*.

Health

Most types of nappies, creams, wet-wipes and childrens' medication can be bought easily in main **chemists** and larger supermarkets in Lima, Arequipa and Cusco, but outside of these places it's wise to arrive prepared. Consult your doctor before leaving home regarding health matters. **Sunscreen** is important, as are sun hats (cheap and readily available), and you might consider a parasol for very small children. Conversely, it can get cold at night in the Andes, so take plenty of **warm clothing**. In the mountains, the **altitude** doesn't seem to cause children as many problems as it does their elders, but they shouldn't walk too strenuously above 2000m without full acclimatization.

The major risk around the regions is a bad stomach and **diarrhoea** (see p.44) from water or food; you should be ready to act sooner than usual when treating children under 10 with rehydration salts. In **Lima**, where the water is just about good enough to clean your teeth, but not to drink, the issues for local children are mainly bronchial or asthmatic, with humid weather and high pollution levels causing many long-lasting chest ailments. This shouldn't be a problem for any visiting children unless they already have difficulties.

Food and drink

The **food and drink** in Peru is varied enough to appeal to most kids. Pizzas are available almost everywhere, as are good fish, red meats, fried chicken, chips, corn on the cob, and nutritious soups, and vitamin supplements are always a good idea. There's also a wide range of **soft drinks**, from the ubiquitous Coca-Cola and Sprite to Inka Cola (now owned by Coca-Cola). Recognizable, commercial **baby food** (and nappy brands) is available in all large supermarkets. **Restaurants** in Peru cater well to children and some offer smaller, cheaper portions; if they don't publicize it, it's worth asking.

Hotels

Like restaurants, **hotels** are used to handling kids; they will sometimes offer discounts, especially if children share rooms or beds. Lower- to mid-range accommodation is the most flexible in this regard, but even the expensive ones can be helpful. Many hotels and hostels have collective rooms, large enough for families to share at reasonable rates.

Travellers with disabilities

Peru is not well set up in terms of access infrastructure for welcoming **travellers with disabilities** (even the best buses have mostly ordinary steps), but nevertheless, in the moment many Peruvians will support and help. **Airlines** have facilities and will assist in most of Peru's airports.

While there are still few hotels or resorts that are well designed enough to ensure access for all, Peru, and Lima in particular, has made progress in recent years. The hotel chain Posadas del Inca (Ⓦ sonesta.com) caters well for disabilities and has places in Lima, Cusco, Puno and the Sacred Valley; other pioneers in Peru include the travel agency Apumayo Expediciones (Ⓦ apumayo.com), Rainforest Expeditions (Ⓦ perunature.com) and InkaNatura Travel (Ⓦ inkanatura.com). Accessible Journeys (Ⓦ disabilitytravel.com), meanwhile, offer tours specifically designed for travellers with physical disabilities, including a ten-day trip to Lima, Paracas, Cusco, the Sacred Valley and Machu Picchu. Additional information on access for travellers in Peru with disabilities can be obtained from the South American Explorers' Club (see opposite).

Women travellers

Machismo is well ingrained in the Peruvian male mentality, particularly in the towns, and female foreigners are almost universally seen as liberated and therefore sexually available. On the whole, the situations female travellers will encounter are more annoying than dangerous, with frequent comments such as *que guapa* ("how pretty"), intrusive and prolonged stares, plus whistling and hissing in the **cities**. Worse still are the occasional rude comments and groping, particularly in crowded situations such as on buses or trains. Blonde and fair-skinned women are likely to suffer much more of this behaviour than darker, Latin-looking women.

Mostly these are situations you'd deal with routinely at home but they can seem threatening without a clear understanding of Peruvian Spanish and slang. To avoid getting caught up in something you can't control, any provocation is best ignored. In a public situation, however, any real harassment is often best dealt with by loudly drawing attention to the miscreant.

In the predominantly Indian, **remote areas** there is less of an overt problem, though surprisingly this is where physical assaults are more likely to take place. They are not common, however – you're probably safer hiking in the Andes than walking at night in most British or North American inner cities.

Personal safety

Two obvious, but enduring, pieces of advice are to **travel with friends** (being on your own makes you most vulnerable), and if you're **camping**, it's a good idea to get to know the locals, which can give a kind of acceptance and insurance, and may even lead to the offer of a room – Peruvians, particularly those in rural areas, can be incredibly kind and hospitable. It's also sensible to check with the South American Explorers' Club (see opposite), particularly in Cusco, for information.

Lima and around

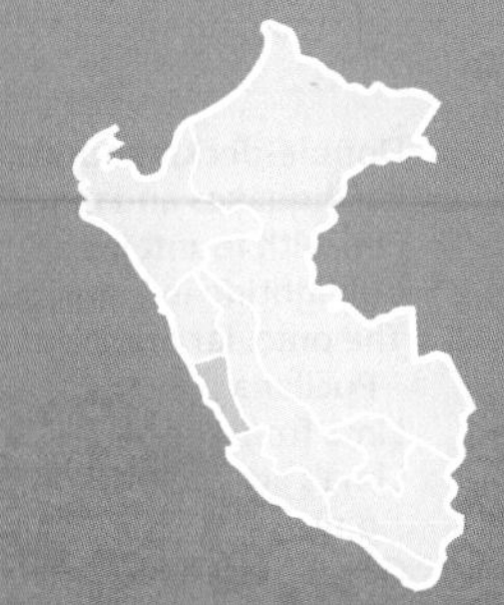

PLAZA DE ARMAS, LIMA

1

Lima and around

Crowded into the mouth of the arid Rimac river valley, with low sandy mountains closing in around its outer fringes, Lima is a boisterous, macho sprawl of a city, full of beaten-up cars chasing Mercedes and 4WDs: this is a place where money rules, with an irresistible, underlying energy. A large part of the city's appeal is its fascinating mix of lifestyles and cultures: from the snappy, sassy, cocaine-influenced criolla style to the easy-going, happy-go-lucky attitude of Lima's poorer citizens. Somehow, though, it still manages to appear relaxed and laidback in the barrios and off the beaten track, and the noisy, frenetic craziness of it all is mellowed somewhat by the presence of the sea and beaches. Even if you choose not to spend much time here, you can get a good sense of it all in just a few days: Limeño hospitality and kindness are almost boundless once you've established an initial rapport.

Considered the most beautiful city in Spanish America during the sixteenth and seventeenth centuries and long established as Peru's seat of government, Lima retains a certain elegance, particularly in colonial Lima Centro. The city still brims with culture and history, though it may not be obvious at first. Top of its attractions are some excellent **museums** – the best of which should definitely be visited before setting off for Machu Picchu or any of Peru's other great Inca ruins – as well as fine Spanish **churches** in the centre, and some distinguished **mansions** in the wealthy suburbs of Barranco and Miraflores. Add to this some outstanding **restaurants** and hedonistic **nightlife**, and you'll find there's plenty to explore in Peru's distinctive capital.

As a transport and communications hub, Lima also makes a good base for exploring the surrounding region, and the immediate area offers plenty of reasons to delay your progress on towards Arequipa or Cusco. Within an hour's bus ride south is the coastline – often deserted – lined by a series of attractive **beaches**. Above them, the imposing fortress-temple complex of **Pachacamac** sits on a sandstone cliff, near the edge of the ocean. In the neighbouring **Rimac Valley** you can visit the pre-Inca sites of **Puruchuco** and **Cajamarquilla**, and, in the foothills above Lima, intriguingly eroded rock outcrops and megalithic monuments surround the natural amphitheatre of **Marcahuasi** (see p.285). To the north, meanwhile, the oldest stone pyramids in the world sit abandoned in the desert of **Caral**.

GOLDEN ARTEFACT, MUSEO ARQUEOLÓGICO LARCO HERRERA

Highlights

❶ **Huaca Pucllana** A vast pre-Inca adobe pyramid mound in the middle of suburban Miraflores, this is a good place to get your bearings and a taste of ancient Lima. **See p.69**

❷ **Parque Kennedy** The central park in downtown Lima's Miraflores district draws locals and tourists alike to its small craft market every evening, and there are some fun cafés and restaurants located along its edges too. **See p.71**

❸ **Fishermen's Wharf** At the southern end of Lima's cliff-hemmed beaches, a small wooden jetty is home to the fishermen of Chorrillos, whose morning catch is landed just in time for the ceviche kiosks next door to prepare inexpensive, but fantastically fresh, fish lunches. **See p.75**

❹ **Museo Arqueológico Larco Herrera** One of the city's most unusual museums, and the largest private collection of Peruvian archeology, containing more than 400,000 excellently preserved ancient ceramics, including an extensive erotic section. **See p.76**

❺ **El Cordano** One of Lima's last surviving traditional bar/restaurants, bustling with locals. **See p.87**

❻ **Lima restaurants** Enjoy a lazy lunch in one of Lima's excellent restaurants – you can't go wrong with the ceviche served up by seafood specialists, *Caplina*. **See p.89**

HIGHLIGHTS ARE MARKED ON THE MAP ON PP.58–59

Lima

Laid out across a wide, flat, alluvial plain, Lima's buildings fan out like a concrete phoenix in long, straight avenues and roads from its centre. The old colonial heart, **Lima Centro**, is of both architectural and cultural interest as well as being the seat of government and religion. South of here, along and just inland from the ocean cliff top, the modern centre of **Miraflores**, where most tourists stay, buzzes with shoppers by day and partiers by night. East along the coast a few kilometres, what was once a separate seaside suburb and artists' quarter, **Barranco**, still boasts both tradition and a vibrant atmosphere. Between Miraflores and Lima Centro, jammed between the Paseo de la República and the Avenida Arequipa main roads that connect them, rise the skyscraping banks of **San Isidro**, Lima's heaving commercial centre.

To the west, the city reaches a fine finger of low-lying land pointing into the Pacific; this is **Callao**, the rather down-at-heel port area, close to the airport. The **shantytowns** that line the highways, meanwhile, continue to swell with new arrivals from the high Andes, responsible in large part for the dramatic surge in Lima's population in recent years.

Lima's **climate** seems to set the city's mood: in the height of summer (December to March) it fizzes with energy and excitement, though during the winter months (June to September) a low mist descends over the arid valley in which the city sits, forming a solid grey blanket – what Limeños call **garua** – from the beaches almost up to Chosica in the foothills of the Andes; it's a phenomenon made worse by traffic-related air pollution, which dampens the city's spirit, if only slightly.

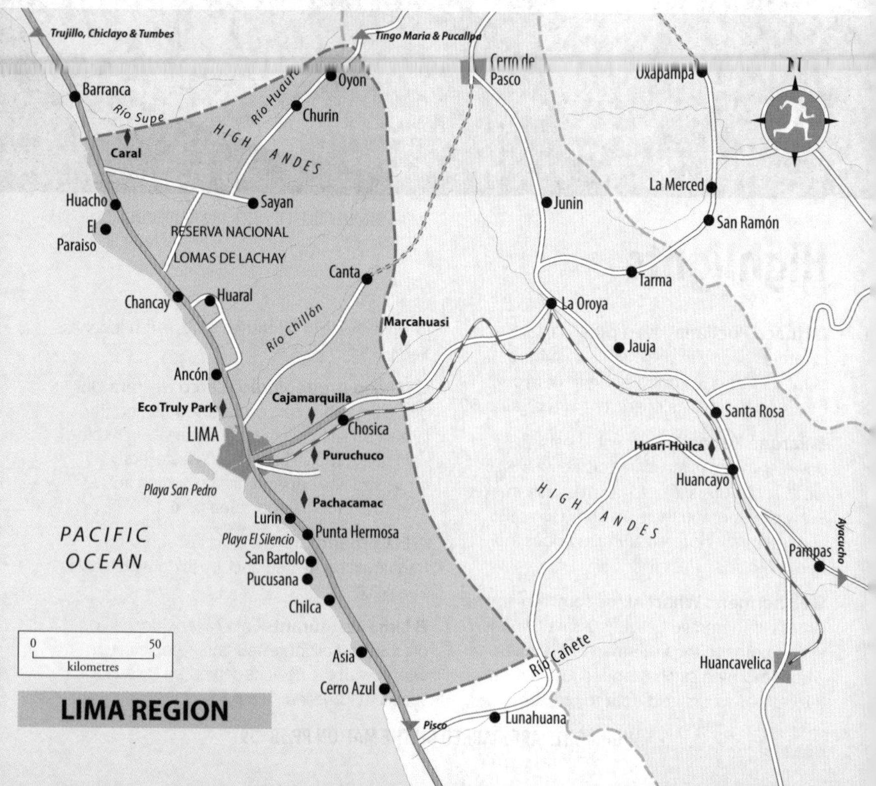

Brief history

When the Spanish first arrived here in 1533, the valley was dominated by three important **Inca**-controlled urban complexes: **Carabayllo**, to the north near Chillón; **Maranga**, now partly destroyed, by the Avenida La Marina, between the modern city and the Port of Callao; and **Surco**, now a suburb within the confines of greater Lima but where, until the mid-seventeenth century, the adobe houses of ancient chiefs lay empty yet painted in a variety of colourful images. Now these structures have faded back into the sandy desert terrain, and only the larger pyramids remain, protruding here and there amid the modern concrete urbanization.

The sixteenth century

Francisco Pizarro founded **Spanish Lima**, nicknamed the "City of the Kings", in 1535. The name is thought to derive from a mispronunciation of Río Rimac, while others suggest that the name "Lima" is an ancient word that described the lands of Taulichusco, the chief who ruled this area when the Spanish arrived. Evidently recommended by mountain Indians as a site for a potential capital, it proved a good choice – apart perhaps from the winter coastal fog – offering a natural harbour nearby, a large well-watered river valley and relatively easy access up into the Andes.

Since the very beginning, Lima was different from the more popular image of Peru in which Andean peasants are pictured toiling on Inca-built mountain terraces. By the 1550s, the town had developed around a large **plaza** with wide streets leading through a fine collection of elegant mansions and well-stocked shops run by wealthy merchants, rapidly developing into the capital of a Spanish viceroyalty which encompassed not only Peru but also Ecuador, Bolivia and Chile. The **University of San Marcos**, founded in 1551, is the oldest on the continent, and Lima housed the Western Hemisphere's headquarters of the Spanish Inquisition from 1570 until 1820. It remained the most important, the richest, and – hardly believable today – the most alluring city in South America, until the early nineteenth century.

The seventeenth century

Perhaps the most prosperous era for Lima was the **seventeenth century**. By 1610 its **population** had reached a manageable 26,000, made up of forty percent black people (mostly slaves); thirty-eight percent Spanish people; no more than eight percent pure Indian; another eight percent (of unspecified ethnic origin) living under religious orders; and less than six percent *mestizo*, today probably the largest proportion of inhabitants. The centre of Lima was crowded with shops and stalls selling silks and fancy furniture from as far afield as China. Rimac, a suburb just over the river from the Plaza Mayor, and the port area of Callao, both grew up as satellite settlements – initially catering to the very rich, though they are now fairly run down.

The eighteenth century

The **eighteenth century**, a period of relative stagnation for Lima, was dramatically punctuated by the tremendous **earthquake of 1746**, which left only twenty houses standing in the whole city and killed some five thousand residents – nearly ten percent of the population. From 1761 to 1776 Lima and Peru were governed by **Viceroy Amat**, who, although more renowned for his relationship with the famous Peruvian actress **La Perricholi**, is also remembered for spearheading Lima's rebirth. Under his rule, the city lost its cloistered atmosphere, and opened out with broad avenues, striking gardens, Rococo mansions and palatial salons. Influenced by the Bourbons, Amat's designs for the city's architecture arrived hand in hand with other transatlantic reverberations of the Enlightenment, such as the new anti-imperialist vision of an independent Peru.

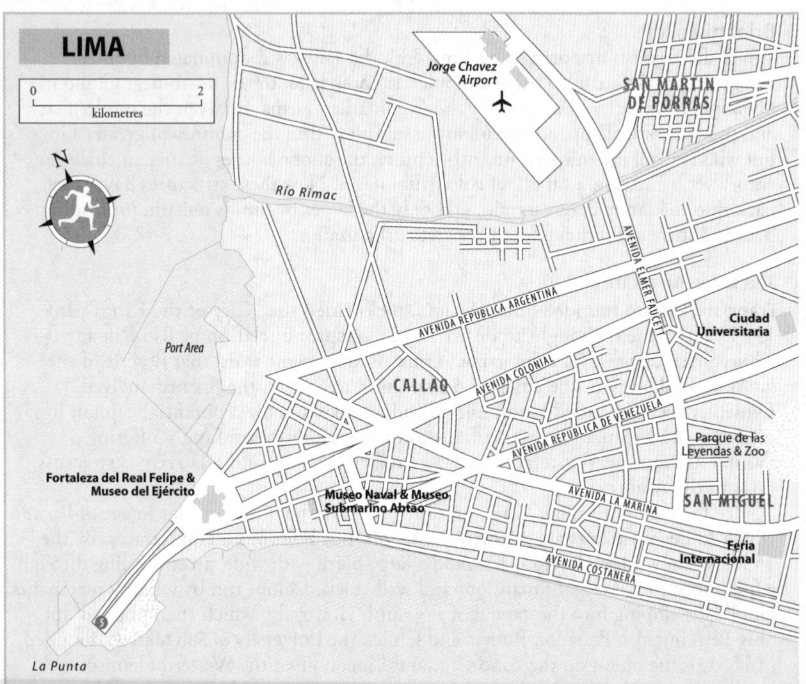

P A C I F I C O C E A N

HIGHLIGHTS

1. Huaca Pucllana
2. Parque Kennedy
3. Fisherman's Wharf
4. Museo Arqueológico Larco Herrera
5. El Cordano
6. Lima restaurants

RESTAURANTS & CAFÉS	
La Carreta	4
Caplina	9
Centro Turistico Perco's Restaurant	6
Cevichería Mi Barunto	1
Cevichería El Rey Marino	8
Guru	10
El Italiano Trattoria Pizzeria	2
Manolo	5
Punto Azul	3
Siam Thai Cuisine	7
Sushi Ito	11

CLUBS & LIVE MUSIC VENUES	
CC Club Delfus Taberna	4
Karamba	1
Kimbara	5

GAY CLUBS	
La Cueva	3
Sagitario Disco	2

ACCOMMODATION	
Casa Bella Peru	5
Hostal Mami Panchita	3
Hotel Libertador	6
Malka Youth Hostal	1
Suites del Bosque	2
Swissotel Lima	4

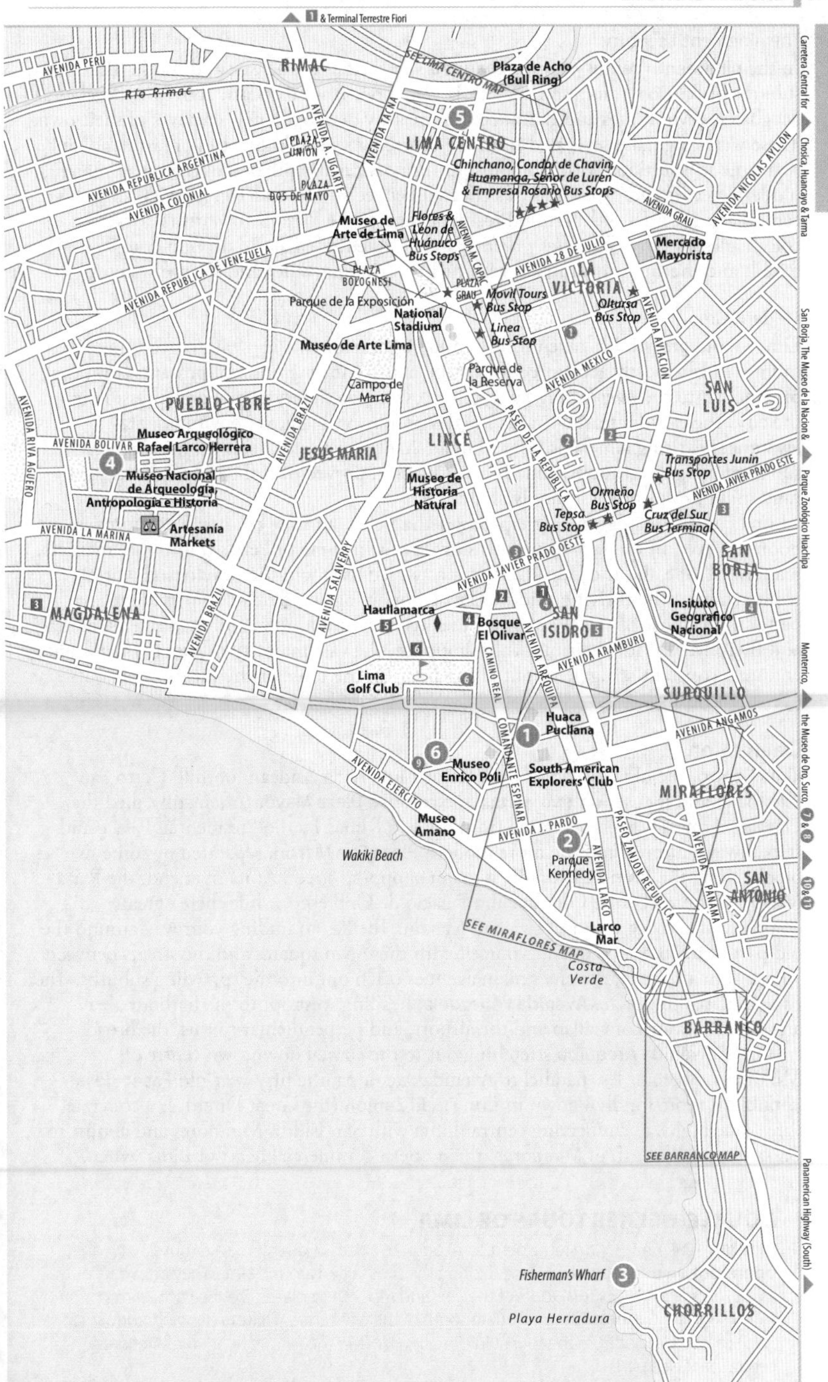
1 & Terminal Terrestre Fiori
RIMAC
AVENIDA PERU
Rio Rimac
SEE LIMA CENTRO MAP
Plaza de Acho (Bull Ring)
LIMA CENTRO
AVENIDA TACNA
AVENIDA A. UGARTE
PLAZA UNION
AVENIDA REPUBLICA ARGENTINA
AVENIDA COLONIAL
PLAZA DOS DE MAYO
Chinchano, Condor de Chavin, Huamanga, Señor de Luren & Empresa Rosario Bus Stops
AVENIDA GRAU
AVENIDA NICOLAS AYLLON
Museo de Arte de Lima
Flores & Leon de Huánuco Bus Stops
AVENIDA M. CAPAC
AVENIDA 28 DE JULIO
Mercado Mayorista
AVENIDA REPUBLICA DE VENEZUELA
PLAZA BOLOGNESI
PLAZA GRAU
LA VICTORIA
Movil Tours Bus Stop
Oltursa Bus Stop
Parque de la Exposición
National Stadium
Linea Bus Stop
Museo de Arte Lima
Parque de la Reserva
AVENIDA MEXICO
AVENIDA AVIACION
Campo de Marte
SAN LUIS
PUEBLO LIBRE
AVENIDA BRAZIL
PASEO DE LA REPUBLICA
Museo Arqueológico Rafael Larco Herrera
AVENIDA BOLIVAR
LINCE
JESUS MARIA
AVENIDA RIVA AGUERO
Museo Nacional de Arqueología, Antropologia e Historia
Museo de Historia Natural
Transportes Junin Bus Stop
Ormeño Bus Stop
AVENIDA JAVIER PRADO ESTE
Tepsa Bus Stop
Cruz del Sur Bus Terminal
AVENIDA LA MARINA
Artesanía Markets
AVENIDA SALAVERRY
SAN BORJA
AVENIDA JAVIER PRADO OESTE
MAGDALENA
Haullamarca
Bosque El Olivar
SAN ISIDRO
Insituto Geografico Nacional
AVENIDA AREQUIPA
CAMINO REAL
AVENIDA ARAMBURU
Lima Golf Club
SURQUILLO
Huaca Pucllana
AVENIDA ANGAMOS
COMANDANTE ESPINAR
Museo Enrico Poli
South American Explorers' Club
AVENIDA EJERCITO
MIRAFLORES
Museo Amano
AVENIDA J. PARDO
Wakiki Beach
Parque Kennedy
AVENIDA LARCO
PASEO ZANJON REPUBLICA
AVENIDA PANAMA
SAN ANTONIO
SEE MIRAFLORES MAP
Larco Mar
Costa Verde
BARRANCO
SEE BARRANCO MAP
Fisherman's Wharf
Playa Herradura
CHORRILLOS
Carretera Central for Chosica, Huancayo & Tarma
San Borja, The Museo de la Nacion & Parque Zoologico Huachipa
Monterrico, the Museo de Oro, Surco, 7 & 8
10 & 11
Panamerican Highway (South)

1

The nineteenth century

In the **nineteenth century** Lima **expanded** still further to the east and south. The suburbs of Barrios Altos and La Victoria were poor from the start; above the beaches at Magdalena, Miraflores and Barranco, the wealthy developed new enclaves of their own. These were originally separated from the centre by several kilometres of farmland, at that time still studded with fabulous pre-Inca *huacas* and other adobe ruins. Lima's first modern facelift and expansion was effected between 1919 and 1930, revitalizing the central areas. Under orders from **President Leguia**, the Plaza San Martín's attractive colonnades and the *Gran Hotel Bolívar* were erected, the Palacio de Gobierno was rebuilt and the city was supplied with its first drinking-water and sewage systems.

Modern Lima

Lima's rapid **growth** has taken it from 300,000 inhabitants in 1930 to over nine million today, mostly accounted for by the massive immigration of peasants from the provinces into the *pueblos jovenes* ("young towns", or **shantytowns**) now pressing in on the city. The ever-increasing traffic is a day-to-day problem, yet **environmental awareness** is rising almost as fast as Lima's shantytowns and neon-lit, middle-class suburban neighbourhoods, and air quality has improved over the last ten years for the nine-million-plus people who live here.

Lima continues to grow, perhaps faster than ever, and the country's **economy** is booming even in the face of serious slowdowns in some of Peru's traditional markets, namely Europe and the US. The city is as varied as any in the developing world: while many of the thriving middle class enjoy living standards comparable to, or better than, those of the West, and the elite ride around in chauffeur-driven Cadillacs and fly to Miami for their monthly shopping, the vast majority of Lima's inhabitants endure a constant struggle to put either food on the table or the flimsiest of roofs over their heads.

Orientation

Lima Centro, the old city, sits at the base of a low-lying Andean foothill, Cerro San Cristóbal, and focuses on two plazas: the colonial **Plaza Mayor** (often still called the Plaza de Armas) – itself separated from the Río Rimac by the Presidential Palace and the railway station – and the more modern **Plaza San Martín**, separated by some five blocks along the **Jirón de la Unión**, a major shopping street. At its river end, the Plaza Mayor is fronted by the Catedral and Palacio de Gobierno, while there's greater commercial activity around Plaza San Martín. The key to finding your way around the old part of town is to acquaint yourself with these two squares and the streets between.

From Lima Centro, the city's main avenues reach out into the sprawling suburbs. The two principal routes are **Avenida Venezuela**, heading west out to the harbour area around the suburb of Callao and the airport, and perpendicular to this, the broad, tree-lined **Avenida Arequipa** stretching out to the coastal downtown centre of Miraflores. More or less parallel to Avenida Arequipa, the fifty-year-old **Paseo de la República**, more fondly known in Lima as **El Zanjón** (the Great Ditch), is a concrete, three-lane highway connecting central Lima with San Isidro, Miraflores and almost to Barranco. The suburb of **Miraflores**, the modern commercial heart of Lima, where

DOUBLE-DECKER TOURS OF LIMA

Mirabus (T 4764213, W mirabusperu.com) operate a fleet of double-decker buses, with an **open roof** on the upper deck, for exploring the sites in and around Lima. They offer day- or night-tours of Lima, colonial tours of the city, and trips out to places like the Pachacamac archeological site (see p.97) some 30km south of the city centre. **Tickets** (ranging from S/8 to S/65) can be bought from the tourist information kiosk in the Parque Kennedy, Miraflores' central park (see p.81).

much of the city's businesses have moved over the last forty years, is located 7 or 8km down Avenida Arequipa and El Zanjón, by the ocean.

Lima Centro

With all its splendid architectural attractions, **Lima Centro** might well be expected to have a more tourist-focused vibe than it does. In reality, though, the neighbourhood is very much a centre of Limeños' daily life. The main axis is formed by the parallel streets – Jirón de la Unión and Jirón V Carabaya – connecting the grand squares of the **Plaza San Martín** and **Plaza Mayor**. Here the roads are narrow and busy, bringing together many of the city's office workers with street workers and slightly downmarket shops. There are many fine buildings from the colonial and Republican eras, overhung with ornate balconies, yet apart from a few – notably the **Presidential Palace** and **Torre Tagle** – these are in a poor state of repair. To the north you'll find the slightly run down, but fascinating **Rimac suburb**, home to the city's bullring. South of the two main plazas, some lavish parks and galleries are within walking distance.

Plaza Mayor

The heart of the old town is **Plaza Mayor** – also known as the Plaza de Armas, or Plaza Armada as the early conquistadors called it. There are no remains of any Indian heritage in or around the square; standing on the original site of the palace of Tauri Chusko (Lima's indigenous chieftain at the time the Spanish arrived) is the relatively modern Palacio de Gobierno, while the cathedral occupies the site of an Inca temple once dedicated to the puma deity, and the Palacio Municipal lies on what was originally an Inca envoy's mansion.

Palacio de Gobierno

Plaza Mayor • Changing of the guard Mon–Sat warm-up at 11.45am, start at noon; tours daily 9.30am–noon; pre-register at Departamento de Actividades, office 201, Jr de la Unión, block 2, Plaza Peru (also known as Plaza Pizarro) • Tours free • T 4267020 or T 3113908 ext 378, W presidencia.gob.pe

The **Palacio de Gobierno** – also known as the Presidential Palace – was the site of the house of **Francisco Pizarro** (see p.490) long before the present building was conceived. It was here that he spent the last few years of his life, until his assassination in 1541. As he died, his jugular severed by the assassin's rapier, Pizarro fell to the floor, drew a cross, then kissed it; even today some believe this ground to be sacred.

The **changing of the guard** takes place outside the palace – it's not a particularly spectacular sight, though the soldiers look splendid in their scarlet-and-blue uniforms. There are free guided **tours** in English and Spanish, which include watching the changing of the guard; to go on a tour you have to register with the Departamento de Actividades at least 24 hours in advance. The tour also takes in the imitation Baroque **interior** of the palace and its rather dull collection of colonial and reproduction furniture.

La Catedral and Museum of Religious Art and Treasures

Plaza Mayor • **Catedral** Mon–Fri 10am–4pm, Sat 10am–1pm • Free • T 4279647 • **Museum** Daily 10am–4pm • S/5

Southeast across the square, less than 50m away from the Palacio de Gobierno, the squat and austere **Catedral**, designed by Francisco Becerra, was modelled on a church from Seville, and has three aisles in a Renaissance style. When Becerra died in 1605, the cathedral was far from completion, with the towers alone taking another forty years to finish. In 1746, further frustration arrived in the guise of a devastating **earthquake**, which destroyed much of the building. Successive restorations over the centuries have resulted in an eclectic style; the current version, which is essentially a reconstruction of Becerra's design, was rebuilt throughout the eighteenth and nineteenth centuries, then remodelled once again after another quake in 1940.

Convento de los Descalzos, Plaza de Acho & 1
1
LIMA CENTRO
RIMAC
JULIAN PINÉYRO
Colectivo for Av Arequipa to Miraflores
Puente de Piedra
Río Rimac
ALMEDA CHABUCA GRANDE
Train Station
Iglesia de San Francisco
JIRÓN AYACUCHO
Casa Aliaga
JIRÓN ANCASH
Casa Pilatos
Iglesia de Santo Domingo
Palacio de Gobierno
Casa de Osambela
JIRÓN JUNÍN
JIRÓN LIMA (CONDE DE SUPERUNDA)
Museo de la Inquisición
Sanctuario de Santa Rosa de Lima
Palacio Municipal
PLAZA MAYOR
Catedral
Barrio Chino & Central Market
JIRÓN HUALLAGA
JIRÓN CALLAO
JIRÓN CAYLLOMA
Palacio Torre Tagle
Muncipal Etnográfico José Pia Asa
JIRÓN DE LA UNION
JIRÓN CARABAYA
JIRÓN LAMPA
Centro Cultural Inca Garcilaso
JIRÓN UCAYALI
AVENIDA TACNA
JIRÓN ICA
JIRÓN CAMANÁ
Teatro Municipal
Iglesia de San Agustín
Casa de Riva-Aguero
Museo del Banco Central
Iglesia de San Pedro
AVENIDA ABANCAY
JIRÓN MIRO QUESADA
HUANCAVELICA
Iglesia de La Merced
Iglesia de Las Nazarenas
AVENIDA EMANCIPACION
AVENIDA CUSCO
JIRÓN UFINO TORRICO
IRÓN AZÁNGARO
MOQUEGUA
JIRÓN PUNO
Iglesia de Jesus Maria y Jose
Plaza Dos de Mayo
JIRÓN OCOÑA
Lan Peru
PLAZA SAN MARTÍN
AVENIDA NICOLAS DE PIEROLA (LA COLMENA)
AVENIDA NICOLAS DE PIEROLA
Parque Universitario
Buses to Pachachamac & Lurin
AVENIDA GARCILASO DE LA VEGA
Tans
MONZON
Casona de San Marcos
Tourist Police
JR. RUFINO TORRICO
BELÉN
PACHITEA
Buses & Colectivos to Miraflores
JIRÓN QUILCA
PLAZA FRANCIA
AVENIDA ROOSEVELT
COTABAMBAS
N
JIRÓN WASHINGTON
Ormeno & Mariscal Caceres buses
AVENIDA BOLIVIA
0
200
metres
Parque Neptuno
Museo de Arte Italiano
CHOTA
PLAZA GRAU
Museo de Arte de Lima
AVENIDA ESPAÑA
PASEO COLÓN
9 DE DICIEMBRE
Parque de la Exposicion
Avenida Arequipa, Casa Museo José Carlos Mariátegui, Parque de la Reserva & 12
RESTAURANTS & CAFÉS
Bar/Restaurant Machu Picchu 2
Chifa Capon 5
El Cordano 1
De Cesar 2
Don Lucho's Restaurant 4
El Estadio Restaurant Bar 7
L'Eau Vive 6
El Paraiso de la Salud Restaurant Vegetariano 3
Queirolo Café Bar Restaurant 8
BAR & CLUB
Las Brisas del Titicaca 1
Rincon Cervecero 2
ACCOMMODATION
Gran Hotel Bolívar 8
Hostal de Las Artes 11
Hostal Granada 5
Hostal Roma 4
Hostal Wiracocha 3
Hotel España 2
Hotel Europa 1
Hotel Kamana 6
Inka Path 7
Lima Sheraton 10
Pensión Rodriguez 9
La Pousada del Parque 12

The building is primarily of interest for its **Museum of Religious Art and Treasures**, which contains seventeenth- and eighteenth-century paintings and some superb **choir stalls** – exquisitely carved in the early seventeenth century by Catalan artist Pedro Noguero. Its other highlight is a collection of human remains thought to be **Pizarro's body** (quite fitting since he placed the first stone shortly before his death), which lie in the first chapel on the right. Although gloomy, the interior retains some of its appealing Churrigueresque (or highly elaborate Baroque) decor.

Palacio Municipal

Plaza Mayor • Mon–Fri 9am–1pm • Free

The square-set edifice directly across the square from the cathedral is the **Palacio Municipal**, usually lined with heavily armed guards and the occasional armoured car, though actual civil unrest is fairly uncommon. Built on the site of the original sixteenth-century city hall and inaugurated in 1944, it's a typical example of a half-hearted twentieth-century attempt at Neocolonial architecture, designed by Alvarez Emilio Harth Terré and Ricardo de Jara Malachowski, and fronted by grand wooden balconies.

The elegant **interior** is home to the **Pinacoteca Ignacio Merino Museum**, which exhibits a selection of Peruvian paintings, notably those of Ignacio Merino from the nineteenth century. For those with an interest in Peruvian constitutional history, the library displays the city's **Act of Foundation and Declaration of Independence**.

Iglesia de San Francisco

Jr Ancash • Daily 9.30am–5pm; tours at least hourly • S/5, including tour

Jirón Ancash leads east from the Palacio de Gobierno towards one of Lima's most attractive churches, **San Francisco**, a majestic building that has withstood the passage of time and the devastation of successive earth tremors. A large seventeenth-century construction with an engaging stone facade and towers, San Francisco's vaults and columns are elaborately decorated with Mudéjar (Moorish-style) plaster relief.

The **Convento de San Francisco**, part of the same architectural complex and a museum in its own right, contains a superb library and a room of **paintings** by (or finished by) Zurbarán, Rubens, Jordaens and Van Dyck. You can take a forty-minute guided tour of the monastery and its **subterranean crypt**, both of which are worth a visit. The museum is inside the monastery's vast crypts, which were only discovered in 1951 and contain the skulls and bones of some seventy thousand people.

Casa Pilatos

Jr Ancash 390 • Mon–Fri 11am–1.30pm • Free, but advance booking necessary • T 4275814

Opposite San Francisco is the **Casa Pilatos**, today home to the constitutional courts; although you can't enter the building, you can get as far as the central courtyard. Quite a simple building, and no competition for Torre Tagle (see p.64), it is nevertheless a fine, early sixteenth-century mansion with an attractive courtyard and a stone staircase leading up from the middle of the patio. The wooden carving of the patio's balustrades adds to the general picture of opulent colonialism.

Museo de la Inquisición

Jr Junín 548 • Daily 9am–5pm, by guided tour only • Free • T 3117777

Behind a facade of Greek-style classical columns, the **Museo de la Inquisición** was the **headquarters of the Inquisition** for the whole of Spanish-dominated America from 1570 until 1820, and contains the original tribunal room with its beautifully carved mahogany ceiling. Beneath the building, you can look round the **dungeons** and torture chambers, which contain a few gory, life-sized human models, each being put through unbearably painful looking, antique contraptions, mainly involving stretching or mutilating.

Mercado Central and Barrio Chino

The few blocks east of Avenida Abancay are taken over by the **Mercado Central** (Central Market) and **Barrio Chino** (Chinatown). Perhaps one of the most fascinating sectors of Lima Centro, the Barrio Chino (which can be entered by an ornate Chinese **gateway**, at the crossing of Jirón Ucayali with Capon) houses Lima's best and cheapest *chifa* (Chinese) **restaurants**. Many Chinese came to Peru in the late nineteenth century to work as labourers on railway construction; many others came here in the 1930s and 40s to escape cultural persecution in their homeland. The shops and street stalls in this sector are full of all sorts of inexpensive goods, from shoes to glass beads, though there is little of genuine quality.

Iglesia de San Pedro

Jr Ucayali and Jr Azángaro • Mon–Sat 7am–12.30pm & 5–8pm • Free

At the corner of Jirón Ucayali, the **Iglesia de San Pedro** was built and occupied by the Jesuits until their expulsion in 1767. This richly decorated colonial church is home to several religious art treasures, including paintings from the Colonial and Republican periods, and a superb main altar which was built in the late nineteenth century after the Jesuits returned; definitely worth a look around.

Palacio Torre Tagle

Jr Ucayali 323 • Mon–Fri 9am–5pm; book two days in advance • Free • T 3112400

The spectacular **Palacio Torre Tagle** is the pride and joy of the old city. A beautifully maintained mansion, it was built in the 1730s and is embellished with a decorative facade and two elegant, dark-wood balconies, typical of Lima architecture in that one is larger than the other. The **porch and patio** are distinctly Andalucian, with their strong Spanish colonial style, although some of the intricate **woodcarvings** on pillars and across ceilings display a native influence; the *azulejos*, or **tiles**, also show a combination of Moorish and Limeño tastes. In the left-hand corner of the patio you can see a set of **scales** like those used to weigh merchandise during colonial times, and the house also contains a magnificent sixteenth-century **carriage** (complete with mobile toilet). Originally, mansions such as Torre Tagle served as refuges for outlaws, the authorities being unable to enter without written and stamped permission – now anyone can go in (afternoons are the quietest times to visit).

Museo del Banco Central de Reserva del Peru

Jr Lampa and Jr Ucayali • Tues–Fri 10am–4.30pm, Sat & Sun 10am–1pm • Free • T 6132000 ext 2655

The **Museo del Banco Central de Reserva del Peru** holds many antique and modern **Peruvian paintings**, as well as a good collection of **pre-Inca artefacts**, including some ancient objects crafted in gold; most of the exhibits on display come from grave robberies and have been returned to Peru only recently. The museum also has a numismatic display and sometimes shows related short films for kids.

Centro Cultural Inca Garcilaso

Jr Ucayali 391 • Tues–Sun 11am–7pm • Free • T 3112756

By Torre Tagle, you'll find the **Centro Cultural Inca Garcilaso**, built in 1685 as the Casa Aspillaga but restored during the late nineteenth century and again in 2003. It contains an art gallery (mainly temporary photographic or sculpture exhibtions) but is most interesting for its Neoclassical Republican-style architecture.

Casa Aliaga

Jr de la Unión 224 • Tours S/5 • Book tours through Lima Tours at T 6195000 or T 6196911

Heading north from the Plaza Mayor you pass the **Casa Aliaga**, an unusual mansion, reputed to be the oldest in South America, and occupied by the same family since 1535, making it the oldest colonial house still standing in the Americas. It's also one of the most elaborate mansions in the country, with sumptuous reception rooms full of Louis XIV mirrors, furniture and doors. It was built on top of an Inca palace and is largely made of wood divided stylishly into various salons.

Iglesia de Santo Domingo

Mon–Sat 9am–noon & 3–6pm, Sun & holidays 9am–1pm • S/3 • ⓣ 4276793

Just off the main square, a block behind the Palacio Municipal, is the church and monastery of **Santo Domingo**. Completed in 1549, Santo Domingo was presented by the pope, a century or so later, with an alabaster statue of Santa Rosa de Lima. The **tombs** of Santa Rosa, San Martín de Porres and San Juan Masias (a Spaniard who was canonized in Peru) are the building's great attractions, and much revered. Otherwise the church is not of huge interest or architectural merit, although it is one of the oldest religious structures in Lima, built on a site granted to the Dominicans by Pizarro in 1535.

Casa de Osambela

Jr Conde de Superunda 298 • Mon–Fri 9am–4pm • Free; guided tours donation appreciated

The early nineteenth-century **Casa de Osambela** has five balconies on its facade and a lookout point from which boats arriving at the port of Callao could be spotted by the first owner, Martín de Osambela. This mansion is home to the Centro Cultural Inca Garcilaso de la Vega, which offers **guided tours** of the building.

Sanctuario de Santa Rosa de Lima

First block of Avenida Tacna • Mon–Sat 9am–1pm & 3–6pm • Free

Two traditional sanctuaries (see box below) can be found on the western edge of old Lima, along Avenida Tacna. Completed in 1728, the **Sanctuario de Santa Rosa de Lima** is a fairly plain church named in honour of the first saint canonized in the Americas. The construction of Avenida Tacna destroyed a section of the already small church, but in the patio next door you can visit the saint's **hermitage**, a small adobe cell; there's also a twenty-metre-deep well where devotees drop written requests.

Museo Etnográfico José Pia Asa

Jr Callao 562, at the corner with Avenida Tacna • Mon–Sat 10am–5pm • S/3 • ⓣ 4310771

A short stroll down Avenida Tacna from the Sanctuario de Santa Rosa takes you to the fascinating **Museo Etnográfico José Pia Asa**, containing crafts, tools, jewellery and weapons from jungle tribes, as well as some photographs of early missionaries.

Iglesia de San Agustín

Jr Ica and Camana • Daily 8.30am–noon & 3.30–7pm • Free

The southern stretch between the Plaza Mayor and Plaza San Martín is the largest area of Old Lima, home to several important churches, including **San Agustín**, founded in 1592. Although severely damaged by earthquakes (only the small side-chapel can be

EARTHQUAKES AND MIRACLES

Despite its small size and undistinguished appearance, the **Iglesia de las Nazarenas** (daily 7am–noon & 4–8pm; free; ⓣ 4235718), on the corner of Avenida Tacna and Huancavelica, has an unusual history. After the severe **1655 earthquake**, a mural of the Crucifixion, painted by an Angolan slave on the wall of his hut and originally titled *Cristo de Pachacamilla*, was the only object left standing in the district. Its survival was deemed a miracle – the cause and focus of popular processions ever since – and it was on this site that the church was founded in the eighteenth century. The widespread and popular **processions for the Lord of Miracles**, to save Lima from another earthquake, take place every spring (October 18, 19, 28 & November 1), and focus on a silver litter, which carries the original mural. **Purple** is the colour of the procession and many women in Lima wear it for the entire month.

1

visited nowadays), the church retains a glorious **facade**, one of the most complicated examples of Churrigueresque–Mestizo architecture in Peru; it originally had a Renaissance doorway, signs of which can be seen from Calle Camana.

Casa de Riva-Aguero

Jr Camaná 459 • Daily 10am–1pm & 2–8pm • S/3 • ⓣ 4279275

Across the road from San Agustín, the **Casa de Riva-Aguero** is a typical colonial house, built in the mid-eighteenth century by a wealthy businessman and later sold to the Aguero family. Its patio has been laid out as a **Museo de Arte y Tradiciones Populares**, displaying crafts and contemporary paintings from all over Peru.

Iglesia de la Merced

Jr de la Unión 621 at Av Miro Quesada • Mon–Sat 8am–12.45pm & 4–8pm, Sun 7am–1pm & 4–8pm; cloisters daily 8am–noon & 5–6pm • Free • Cloisters ⓣ 4235718, guided visits ⓣ 4278199

Perhaps the most noted of all religious buildings in Lima is the **Iglesia de la Merced**, two blocks south of the Plaza Mayor. Built on the site where the first Latin Mass in Lima was celebrated, the original sixteenth-century church was demolished in 1628 to make way for the present building whose ornate granite facade, dating back to 1687, has been adapted and rebuilt several times – as have the broad columns of the nave – to protect the church against tremors.

By far the most lasting impression is made by the **Cross of the Venerable Padre Urraca** (La Cruz de Padre Urraca El Venerable), whose silver staff is witness to the fervent prayers of a constantly shifting congregation, smothered by hundreds of kisses every hour. If you've just arrived in Lima, a few minutes by this cross may give you an insight into the depth of Peruvian belief in miraculous power. Be careful if you get surrounded by the ubiquitous sellers of candles and religious icons around the entrance – **pick-pockets** are at work here. The attached **cloisters** are less spectacular, though they do offer a historical curiosity: it was here that the Patriots of Independence declared the Virgin of La Merced their military marshal.

Iglesia de Jesus María y José

Jr Camaná and Jr Moquegua • Daily 7am–1pm & 3–7pm • Free

Close to the Plaza San Martín stands the **Iglesia de Jesus María y José**, home of Capuchin nuns from Madrid in the early eighteenth century; its particularly outstanding interior contains sparkling Baroque gilt altars and pulpits.

Plaza San Martín

A large, grand square with fountains at its centre, the **Plaza San Martín** is almost always busy by day, with traffic tooting its way around the perimeter. Nevertheless, it's a place where you can sit down for a few minutes – at least until hassled by street sellers or shoeshine boys.

Ideologically, the Plaza San Martín represents the sophisticated, egalitarian and European spirit of intellectual liberators like San Martín himself, while remaining well and truly within the commercial world. The plaza has attracted most of Lima's major **political rallies** over the past hundred years, and rioting students, teachers or workers and attendant police with water cannons and tear gas are always a possibility here.

Plaza Dos de Mayo

The city's main rallying point for political protests is **Plaza Dos de Mayo**, linked to the Plaza San Martín by the wide Avenida Nicolas de Pierola (also known as La Colmena). Built to commemorate the repulse of the Spanish fleet in 1866 – Spain's last attempt to regain a foothold in South America – the plaza is markedly busier and less visitor friendly than Plaza San Martín. It sits on the site of an old gate dividing Lima from the road to Callao.

Casona de San Marcos

Av Nicolás de Piérola 1222 • Mon–Sat 9am–6pm • S/5 • ⓣ 6197000, ⓦ ccsm-unmsm.edu.pe

East of Plaza San Martín, Avenida Nicolás de Piérola runs towards the **Parque Universitario**, site of South America's first university. Right on the park itself, the **Casona de San Marcos** is home to the Centro Cultural de San Marcos and the Ballet de San Marcos. Once lodgings for the Jesuit novitiate San Antonio Abad (patron saint of everything from animals to skin complaints), it's a pleasant seventeenth-century complex with some fine architectural features including colonial cloisters, a Baroque chapel, a small **art and archeology museum**, exhibitions and a great café. The **amphitheatre** in the park is sometimes used for free public performances by musicians and artists.

Museo de Arte Italiano

Paseo de la República 250 • Parque Neptuno • Tues–Fri 9am–5pm, Sat 11am–3pm • S/3.5 • ⓣ 4239932

South of Plaza San Martín, Jirón Belén leads down to the Paseo de la República and the shady **Parque Neptuno**, home to the pleasant **Museo de Arte Italiano**. Located inside a relatively small and highly ornate Neoclassical building that's unusual for Lima, built by the Italian architect Gaetano Moretti, the museum exhibits oils, bronzes and ceramics by Italian artists, and offers a welcome respite from the hectic city outside.

Parque de la Cultura Peruana

Tues–Sun 10am–8pm

The Museo de Arte is at the city end of the extensive, leafy **Parque de la Cultura Peruana**, originally created for the International Exhibition of Agricultural Machines in 1872. Conspicuously green for Lima, the park is where lovers meet at weekends and students hang out amid greenery, pagodas, an amphitheatre, a small lake, and organized music and dance performances at fiesta times. The park stretches a couple of hundred yards down to Avenida 28 de Julio, from where it's just a few blocks to the Estadio Nacional and **Parque de la Reserva** (see below).

Museo de Arte de Lima

Paseo Colón 125 • Mon–Fri & Sun 10am–8pm, Sat 10am–5pm • S/12 • ⓣ 2040000, ⓦ mali.pe

A couple of minutes' walk south of the Museo de Arte Italiano is the commanding **Museo de Arte**, housed in the former International Exhibition Palace, built in 1868. The museum holds interesting permanent collections of colonial art, as well as many fine crafts from pre-Columbian times, and also hosts frequent international exhibitions of modern photography and video as well as contemporary Peruvian art. Film shows and lectures are offered on some weekday evenings (check the website, *El Comercio* newspaper listings or posters in the lobby).

Casa Museo José Carlos Mariátegui

Jr Washington 1946 • Mon–Fri 9am–1pm & 2–6pm, Sat 9am–1pm • Free

Not far from the Parque de la Cultura Peruana is the **Casa Museo José Carlos Mariátegui**, an early twentieth-century one-storey house – home for the last few years of his life to the famous Peruvian political figure, ideologist and writer Mariátegui – which has been restored by the Instituto Nacional de Cultura. The period furnishings reveal less about this man than his writings, but the house is kept alive in honour of one of Peru's greatest twentieth-century political writers.

Parque de la Reserva

Between the Paseo de la República and Av Arequipa, beside the Estadio Nacional • Wed–Sun and hols 4–10pm; fountains go off at 7.15pm, 8.15pm & 9.30pm • S/4

The **Parque de la Reserva**, next to the Estadio Nacional, was superbly and imaginatively refurbished in 2007 to create the **circuito mágico del agua** (see box, p.68), a splendid array of fountains, each with a different theme, set to go off at specific times.

1

FUN WITH FOUNTAINS

A popular haunt, the **circuito mágico del agua** (or "magical water circuit"; Wed–Sun 4–10pm; S/5), in the Parque de la Reserva near blocks 5–8 of Avenida Arequipa, boasts fifteen colourful and well-lit **fountains**, some of which spurt some eighty metres into the air. Watch out for the Fuente de Fantasía, which moves to music, and the Cupula Visitable, which you can get drenched climbing inside, as well as the beautiful water pyramid and the Tunel de Sorpresas (Tunnel of Surprises), which you can walk through; it all makes for one of Lima's most memorable evening attractions.

Puente de Piedra

It's a short walk north up Jirón de la Unión from the Plaza Mayor to the **Puente de Piedra**, the stone bridge that arches over the Río Rimac – usually no more than a miserable trickle – behind the Palacio de Gobierno. Initially a wooden construction, the current brick structure was built in the seventeenth century, using egg whites with sand and lime to improve the consistency of its mortar.

Rimac

The function of the Puente de Piedra was to provide a permanent link between the centre of town and the Barrio of San Lázaro, known these days as **Rimac**, or, more popularly, as **Bajo El Puente** ("below the bridge"). This district was first populated in the sixteenth century by African slaves, newly imported and awaiting purchase by big plantation owners; a few years later Rimac was beleaguered by outbreaks of leprosy. Although these days its status is much improved, Rimac is still one of the most run-down areas of Lima. It can be quite an aggressive place after dark, when drug addicts and thieves abound, and it's **dangerous** to walk this area alone at any time of day. Take a taxi direct to where you want to go.

Museo Taurino de Acho

Jr Hualgayoc 332 • Mon–Sat 9am–6pm • S/5 • ☎ 4813433

Rimac is home to the **Plaza de Acho**, Lima's most important **bullring** (see box below), which also houses the **Museo Taurino de Acho**, or Bullfight Museum, containing some original **Goya engravings**, several related paintings and a few relics of bullfighting contests.

The Alameda de los Descalzos and Paseo de Aguas

A few blocks to the right of the bridge, you can stroll up the **Alameda de los Descalzos** (though best not to do so alone, even in daylight), a fine tree-lined walk designed for courtship, and an afternoon meeting place for the early seventeenth- to nineteenth-century elite (the railings were added in 1853). Along the way stands the **Paseo de Aguas**,

BULLFIGHTING IN LIMA

Bullfighting has been a popular pastime among a relatively small, wealthy elite from the Spanish Conquest to the present day, despite some 185 years of independence from Spain. Pizarro himself brought out the first *lidia* bull for fighting in Lima, and there is an enduring tradition between the controlling families of Peru – the same families who breed bulls on their haciendas – to hold fights in Lima during October and November. They invite some of the world's best bullfighters from Spain, Mexico and Venezuela, offering them significant sums for an afternoon's sport at the prestigious **Plaza de Acho** in Rimac. **Tickets** can be bought in advance from major shops such as the Wong and Metro chain of superstores throughout the city. Fights take place most Saturday and Sunday afternoons throughout the year, but the best time to catch a fight – and see one of the international bullfighters in action – is in October or November.

built by Viceroy Amat in the eighteenth century. It leads past the foot of a distinctive hill, the **Cerro San Cristóbal**, and, although in desperate need of renovation, it still possesses twelve appealing marble **statues** brought from Italy in 1856, each one representing a different sign of the zodiac.

At the far end of the Alameda is a fine Franciscan monastery, **Convento de los Descalzos** (Mon & Wed–Sun 10am–1pm & 3–6pm; S/3, usually including a forty-minute tour; ⊕4810441 or 4813433), dating from 1592 and housing a collection of colonial and Republican paintings from Peru and Ecuador; its chapel – **La Capilla El Carmen** – possesses a beautiful Baroque gold-leaf altar. The monastery was built in what was then a secluded spot beyond the town, originally a retreat from the busy heart of the city at the base of Cerro San Cristóbal. Now, of course, the city runs all around it and way beyond.

Lima's suburbs

The old centre of Lima is surrounded by a number of sprawling **suburbs**, or *distritos*, which spread across the desert between the foothills of the Andes and the coast. Just south of Lima Centro lies the lively suburb of **Miraflores**, a slick, fast-moving and very ostentatious mini-metropolis, which has become Lima's business and shopping zone. South of Miraflores begins the oceanside suburb of **Barranco**, one of the oldest and most attractive parts of Lima, above the steep sandy cliffs of the **Costa Verde**, hosting a small nightlife enclave. Sandwiched between Lima Centro and Miraflores is the plush suburb of **San Isidro**, boasting both the city's main commercial and banking sector and a golf course surrounded by sky-scraping apartment buildings. West of here, **Pueblo Libre** is older, an established home to several good museums. To the east lies **San Borja**, a more recently constructed district with another fine museum, the Museo de la Nación. The city's port area, **Callao**, is an atmospheric, if rather old and insalubrious zone tapering into the western peninsula of **La Punta**, with its air of slightly decayed grandeur. The suburb of **La Victoria**, on the other side of central Lima from Callao, contains some once-fine plazas and buildings, but is better known these days for its bus depots and pickpockets. Lima city's sprawl means that there are massive urbanizations to the north, the south, and into the western foothills, where the upmarket suburb of **Monterrico** is found.

Most of Lima's popular city **beaches**, like the surfers' hangout of **Playa Wakiki**, are directly below the sea-facing cliffs of Miraflores, visible from the Larco Mar commercial complex and accessible on foot from Parque Kennedy.

Miraflores

As far as Lima's inhabitants are concerned, **Miraflores** is the major focus of the city's action and nightlife, its streets lined with cafés and the capital's flashiest shops. **Larco Mar**, a modern entertainment district built into the cliffside at the bottom of Miraflores' main street, adds to its swanky appeal. Although still connected to Lima Centro by the long-established Avenida Arequipa, which is served by frequent colectivos, another generally faster road – Paseo de la República (also known as the Vía Expressa and El Zanjón) – provides the suburb with an alternative route for cars and buses.

Huaca Pucllana

General Borgoño 800 • Wed–Mon 9am–4.30pm • S/10 • ⊕6177138 • 5min walk from Av Arequipa, on the right as you come from Lima Centro at block 44

A good place to make for first is the **Huaca Pucllana**, a temple, pre-Columbian tomb and administrative centre in the middle of suburban Miraflores. This vast pre-Inca adobe mound continues to dwarf most of the houses around and has a small site museum, craft shop and very good restaurant (see p.89). From the top of the *huaca* you

1

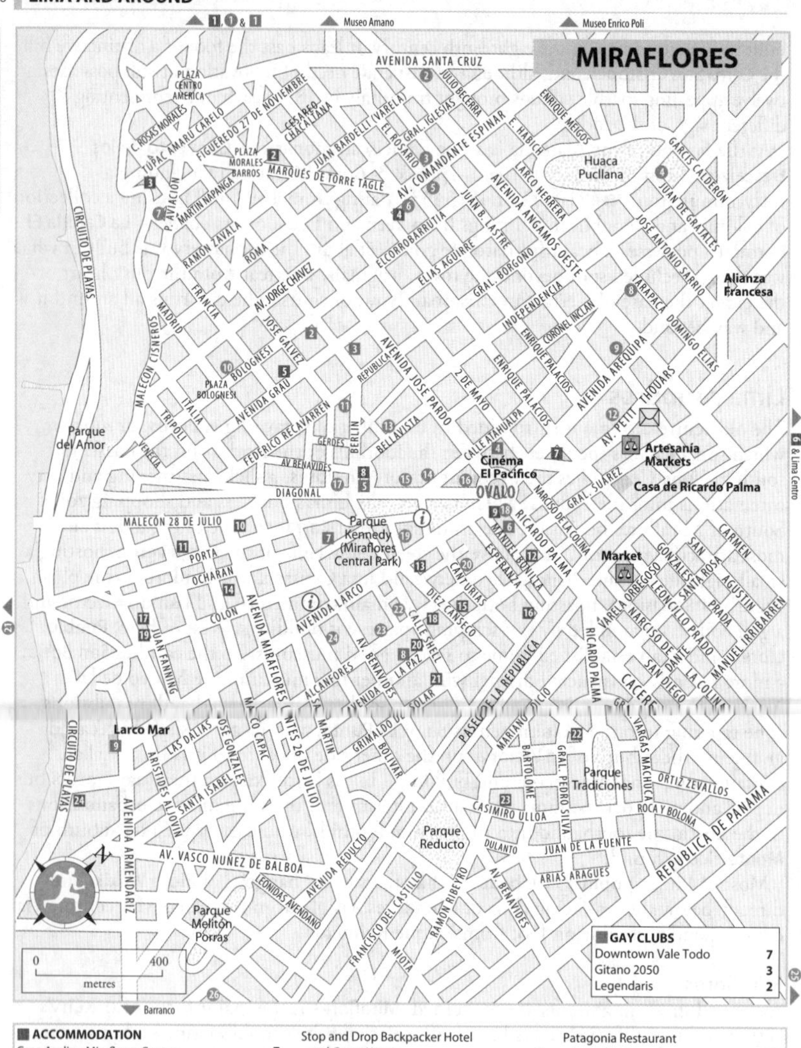

ACCOMMODATION

Casa Andina Miraflores Centro	7
Casa de Baraybar	1
Casa del Mochilero	2
Colonial Inn	4
Embajadores Hotel	17
Faraoña Grande Hotel	12
Friends House	14
Hospedaje Flying Dog	13
Hostal Antigua Miraflores	5
Hostal Buena Vista	21
Hostal Martinika	6
Hostal Pariwana	9
Hostal El Patio	15
HI Hostel Lima	23
Lex Luthor's House	11
Marieta Bed & Breakfast Inn	3
Miraflores Colon Inn	19
Miraflores Park Hotel	16
Pension Jose Luis	24
Radisson	10
Sonesta Posada del Inca – Miraflores	18
Stop and Drop Backpacker Hotel and Guest House	8
Tinkus Hostel	20
El Zaguan Lodging	22

RESTAURANTS & CAFÉS

Arabica Espreso Bar	11
Astrid y Gastón	20
El Bodegon	8
Las Brujas de Cachiche	10
Café Café	14
Café Haiti	16
Club Suizo	25
Café Verde	2
Café Z	17
Dinnos Pizza	5
La Divina Comida	6
La Hamaca	9
El Kapallaq	26
Madre Natura	3
Mama Lola	19
La Mar	1
Patagonia Restaurant Arte y Diseno	24
Restaurant Huaca Pucllana	4
Restaurant Naturista El Paraiso	23
Restaurant Tai-i Vegetariano	12
La Rosa Nautica	21
Scena Restaurant Bar	13
El Senorio de Sulco	7
Starbucks	15
La Tiendacita Blanca	18
Urban Tea	22

BARS, CLUBS & LIVE MUSIC VENUES

Aura	9
Brenchley Arms	4
Gotica	9
Habana Café Bar	6
Jazz Zone	8
The Old Pub	5
Peña Sachúm	1
Satchmo	8

THE ORACULAR ORIGINS OF THE HUACA PUCLLANA

One of a large number of *huacas* and palaces that formerly stretched across this part of the valley, little is known about the **Huaca Pucllana**, though it seems likely that it was originally named after a pre-Inca chief of the area. It has a hollow core running through its cross section and is believed to have been constructed in the shape of an enormous **frog**, symbol of the rain god, who spoke to priests through a tube connected to the cavern at its heart. This site may well have been the mysteriously unknown **oracle** after which the Rimac (meaning "he who speaks") Valley was named; a curious document from 1560 affirms that the "devil" spoke at this mound.

can see over the office buildings and across the flat roofs of the multicoloured houses in the heart of Miraflores.

Parque Kennedy

Av Arequipa • Market daily 6–9pm

Miraflores' central area focuses on the attractive, almost triangular **Parque Kennedy** (or Miraflores Central Park) at the end of Avenida Arequipa. Neatly grassed and with some attractive flowerbeds, the park divides into four areas of activity: at the top end is the pedestrian junction where the shoeshiners hang out; further down there's a small amphitheatre, which often has mime acts or music; next you come to a raised and walled, circular concrete area, which has a good **craft and antiques market** set up on stalls every evening; and just down from here is a small section of gardens and a children's play area. Painters sell their artwork in and around the edges of the park, particularly on Sundays – some quite good, though it's aimed at the tourist market. The streets around the park are lined with smart cafés and bars, and crowded with shoppers, flower-sellers and car-washers.

Larco Mar

The flash development at the bottom of Avenida Larco, **Larco Mar**, has done an excellent job of integrating the park end of Miraflores with what was previously a rather desolate clifftop area. Essentially a shopping zone with patios and walkways open to the sky, sea and cliffs, Larco Mar is also home to several bars, ice-cream parlours, reasonably good restaurants, a host of cinema screens and a couple of trendy clubs.

Parque del Amor

From the end of Avenida Arequipa, Avenida Larco and Diagonal fan out along the park en route to the ocean about a kilometre away. Near where the continuation of Diagonal reaches the clifftop, the small but vibrant **Parque del Amor** sits on the clifftop above the Costa Verde and celebrates the fact that for decades this area has been a favourite haunt of young lovers, particularly poorer Limeños who have no privacy in their often overcrowded homes. A huge sculpture of a loving Andean couple clasping each other rapturously is usually surrounded by pairs of real-life lovers walking hand-in-hand or cuddling on the clifftop, especially on Sunday afternoons. In recent years there have been reports of muggings around here, but it's become relatively safe again.

Casa de Ricardo Palma

General Suarez 189 • Mon–Fri 10am–1pm & 3–5pm • S/6 • ⓣ 6177115 and ⓣ 4455836

Miraflores' only important mansion open to the public is the **Casa de Ricardo Palma**, where Palma, Peru's greatest historian, lived for most of his life. Located between Avenida Arequipa and the Paseo de la República, just behind the artesanía markets on Petit Thouars (see p.95), the ninteenth-century house has some architectural merit, but is mostly visited for an insight into Palma's lifestyle through household furnishings, and mind, through some first editions of his written works and some diary extracts. The set

1

LIMA FROM THE AIR

To see Lima from a completely different perspective, jump off the coastal cliffs in Miraflores on a tandem **paragliding flight**. Flights take around ten to fifteen minutes, and you're in the safe hands of expert guides and teachers Mike Fernandez, from Aeroextreme (Tripoli 350, Dpto 302, Miraflores; T 2425125 or T 99480954, E 2mike@aeroextreme.com), and Marco Mercado of Tandem Flights (Tripoli 340, Dpto 402, Miraflores; T 2417370 or T 994 092537, W tandemperu.com) throughout. No previous experience is necessary, and prices start at around $45. Call T 997 375317 or see W paraglidingtours.pe for information.

of spacious rooms includes a music room, bedrooms, patio and bathroom, all of which can be explored.

Museo Enrico Poli

Lord Cochrane 466 • $20 per person; minimum five people • By appointment only; call T 4222437

Within a few blocks of the Ovalo Gutierrez in Miraflores, the **Museo Enrico Poli** contains some of the finest pre-Inca archeological treasures in Lima, including ceramics, gold and silver. The highlight of this private collection is the treasure found at **Sipán** in northern Peru, in particular four golden trumpets, each over a metre long and over a thousand years old.

Museo Amano

C Retiro 160, by block 11 of Av Angamos Oeste • Mon–Fri, opening and tours by appointment but usually 3 or 4pm • Entry by donation • T 4412909

The private **Museo Amano**, off block 11 of Angamos Oeste, merits a visit for its fabulous exhibition of beautifully displayed **textiles**, mainly Chancay weavings (among the best of pre-Columbian textiles), as well as some beautiful **ceramics**

Parque Reducto

Av Benavides, by Paseo de la República

The greatest attraction of the **Parque Reducto** is arguably its Saturday-morning organic food and sustainable products **market** (8am–noon), which takes place along the southern edge of the park. There's also a good kids' play area, and a **museum** (Mon–Sat 7am–5pm; free) dedicated to the Municipality of Miraflores and the Peruvian army, in particular to their battle against invading forces from Chile – the 1881 Battle of Miraflores. Exhibits include war memorabilia, photographs, small cannons and guns.

Barranco

Some 3km south of Larco Mar and quieter than Miraflores, **Barranco** overlooks the ocean and is scattered with old mansions, including fine colonial and Republican edifices, many beginning to crumble through lack of care. This was the capital's seaside resort during the nineteenth century and is now a kind of Limeño Left Bank, with young artists, writers, musicians and intellectuals taking over some of the older properties. Only covering three square kilometres, Barranco is quite densely populated, with some 40,000 inhabitants living in its delicately coloured houses. The area's primary attractions are its **bars, clubs and cafés**, and there's little else in the way of specific sights, though you may want to take a look at the clifftop remains of a **funicular rail-line**, which used to carry aristocratic families from the summer resort down to the beach.

Plaza Municipal de Barranco and south

The small but busy and well-kept **Plaza Municipal de Barranco** is the hub of the area's **nightlife**: the bars, clubs and cafés clustered around the square buzz with frenetic energy after dark, while retaining much of the area's charm and character. A couple of museums

FROM TOP BARRANCO NIGHTLIFE (P.91); LA CATEDRAL (P.61) >

1 near here are worth a browse: the **Museo de Electricidad**, Pedro de Osma 105 (daily 9am–5pm; free; phone in advance for tours on ⓣ4776577), displays a wide range of early electrical appliances and generating techniques; and just down the road, at Pedro de Osma 421, the **Museo de Arte Colonial Pedro de Osma** (daily 10am–1.30pm & 2.30–6pm; S/10; ⓣ4670063, ⓦmuseopedrodeosma.org) holds a number of treasures and antiques such as oil paintings, colonial sculptures and silverware.

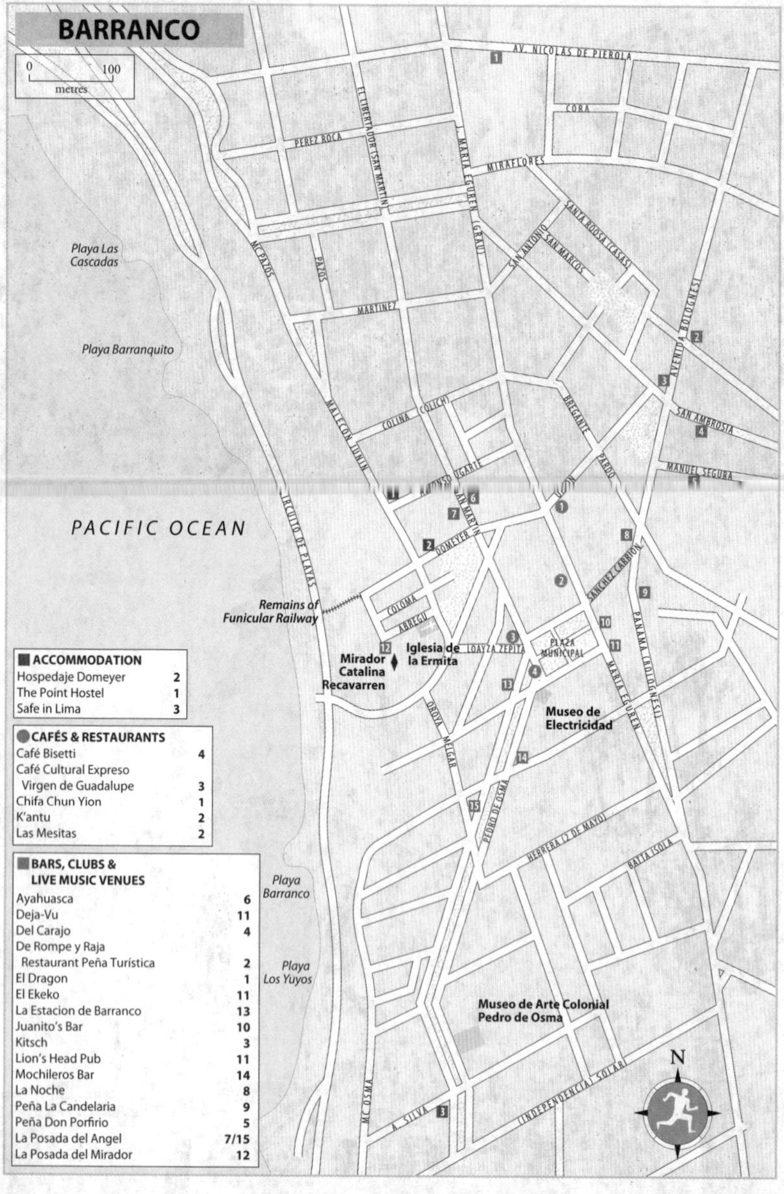

LIMA'S ART AND PHOTOGRAPHY GALLERIES

Lima's progressive culture of **art and photography** is deeply rooted in the Latin American tradition, combining indigenous ethnic realism with a political edge. The city boasts a few permanent galleries – all free – with temporary exhibitions on display in many of the main museums.

Artco C Rouad y Paz Soldan 325, San Isidro ⓣ 2213579. One of the most happening painters' galleries in Lima, usually well worth checking out. Mon–Fri 11am–8pm, Sat 10.30am–1.30pm & 3.30–7.30pm.

Centro Cultural de la Municipalidad de Miraflores Av Larco and Diez Canseco, Miraflores ⓣ 6177266. Hosts a series of innovative photography exhibitions. Daily 10am–10pm.

Centro Cultural Ricardo Palma Av Larco 770, Miraflores ⓣ 6177263. Hosts fixed and changing exhibitions of paintings, photographs and sculpture. Daily 10am–9pm.

Centro Cultural de la Universidad Católica Av Camino Real 1075, San Isidro ⓣ 6161616. Art gallery hosting visiting exhibitions by foreign artists. Daily 10am–10pm.

Corriente Alterna Las Dalias 381, Miraflores ⓣ 2428482. Often presents shows by non-Peruvian painters. Mon–Fri 10am–8pm.

Galeria L'Imaginaire Av Arequipa 4595, Miraflores ⓣ 6108000. Usually exhibits Latin American painters and sculptors. Mon–Sat 5–9pm.

Sala Cultural del Banco Wiese Av Larco 1101, Miraflores ⓣ 4465240. A contemporary, international art gallery in the Banco Weise in the heart of downtown Miraflores. Mon–Sat 10am–2pm & 5–9pm.

Trapecio Av Larco 743, Miraflores ⓣ 4440842. Specializes in oils and sculpture. Mon–Sat 5–9pm.

Iglesia de la Ermita and around

One block inland of the funicular, the impressive **Iglesia de la Ermita** (Church of the Hermit) sits on the cliff, with gardens to its front. Local legend says that the church was built here after a miraculous vision of a glowing Christ figure on this very spot. Beside the church is the **Puente de los Suspiros**, a pretty wooden bridge crossing a gully – the Bajada de Baños – which leads steeply down to the ocean, passing exotic dwellings lining the crumbling gully sides. A path leads beside the church along the top edge of the gully to the **Mirador Catalina Recavarren**, boasting lovely sea views. There's a uniquely situated pub, *La Posada del Mirador*, at the end of the path, as well as some other pleasant cafés and bars, buzzing on weekend evenings.

Costa Verde

Down beside the pounding rollers lies the **Costa Verde** beach area, so named because of vegetation clinging to the steep sandy cliffs. A bumpy road follows the shore from an exclusive yacht club and the Chorrillos Fishermen's Wharf northwest past both Barranco and Miraflores, almost to the suburb of Magdalena. The sea is cold here, but the surfers still brave it. The **Fishermen's Wharf** (around S/1) is always an interesting place for a stroll, surrounded by pelicans and, early in the day, fishermen unloading their catch, which is delivered immediately to the neighbouring market. The outdoor restaurants here compete vigorously for customers; all of them are pretty good and, not surprisingly, have a reputation for serving the freshest **ceviche** in Lima.

San Isidro

Unless you're shopping, banking or looking for a sauna or disco, there are few reasons to stop off in **San Isidro**. The exception is to take a stroll through the **Bosque El Olivar**, 150m west from block 34 of Avenida Arequipa: one of Lima's relatively few large, open, green spaces. A charming grove first planted in 1560, it's now rather depleted in olive trees but you can still see the old press and millstone, and the grove has developed its own **ecosystem**, which is home to over thirty different **bird species** including doves, flycatchers and hummingbirds. There's also a stage where concerts and cultural events are often held.

Huallamarca

Nicolas de Rivera 201, just off Av El Rosario • Tues–Sun 9am–5pm • S/5

A few blocks northwest of the Bosque El Olivar and a few north of Lima Golf Club, the impressive reconstructed adobe *huaca*, **Huallamarca**, is now surrounded by wealthy suburbs. Like Pucllana (see p.69), this dates from pre-Inca days and has a small **museum** displaying the archeological remains of ancient Lima culture, such as funerary masks and artwork found in the *huaca* – including textiles oddly reminiscent of Scottish tartans.

Jesús María

The workaday suburb of **Jesús María**, west of San Isidro and Lince, south of Lima Centro, has only one real attraction: the little-visited, but quite fascinating, **Museo de Historia Natural Jesús María**, Av Arenales 1256 (Mon–Fri 9am–3pm, Sat 9am–4.30pm, Sun 9am–12.30pm; S/10, tours S/30 per group; ☎4710117). The museum presents a comprehensive if dusty overview of Peruvian wildlife and botany. One highlight is the sun fish: one of only three known examples of this colourful fish that can be found in the American coastal waters. There are also great **gardens** with botany displays, as well as a **geology** section.

Pueblo Libre

The quiet backstreets of **Pueblo Libre**, a relatively insalubrious suburb lying between San Isidro and Callao, on the western edge of Lima, is now home to a trio of Lima's major **museums**. These are quite tucked away, so it may be worth taking a taxi.

Museo Nacional de Arqueología, Antropología e Historia del Peru

Plaza Bolívar, cnr San Martín and Antonio Pola • Tues–Fri & Sun 10am–8pm, Sat 10am–5pm • S/12; tours S/10 • Phone in advance for tours on ☎4635070 • Take a taxi, or one of the microbuses that run along Av Brasil or Av Sucre

Primary among Pueblo Libre's attractions is the **Museo Nacional de Arqueología, Antropología e Historia del Peru**, which possesses a varied collection of pre-Inca artefacts and a number of historical exhibits relating mainly to the Republican period (1821 until the late nineteenth century). The liberators San Martín and Bolívar both lived here for a while. Although there's plenty to see, even more of the museum's immense collection is in storage, though some has permanently shifted to the Museo de la Nación (see p.78).

Renovated displays give a detailed and accurate perspective on Peru's prehistory, a vision that comes as a surprise if you'd previously thought of Peru simply in terms of Incas and conquistadors. The galleries are set around two colonial-style courtyards, with exhibits including stone **tools** some eight thousand years old, Chavin-era **carved stones** engraved with felines and serpents, and the Manos Cruzados or Crossed Hands stone from Kotosh, evidence of a mysterious cult from some five thousand years ago. From the Paracas culture there are sumptuous **weavings** and many excellent examples of deformed heads and trepanned **skulls**: one shows post-operative growth, and a male mummy, "frozen" at the age of 30 to 35, has fingernails still visible and a creepy, sideways glance fixed on his misshapen head. From Nasca there are incredible **ceramics** representing marine life, agriculture, flora, sexuality, wildlife, trophy-heads and scenes from mythology and everyday life. The **Mochica** and **Chimu cultures** (see pp.486–487) are represented, too, and there are also exhibits devoted to the **Incas**. The national history section shows off some dazzling antique clothing, extravagant furnishings and other period pieces, complemented by early Republican paintings.

Museo Arqueológico Larco Herrera

Av Bolívar 1515 • Daily 9am–6pm • S/30 • ☎461312, Ⓦmuseolarco.org • Take a taxi or bus #23 (passes Av Abancay in Lima Centro) • From the Museo Nacional de Historia, follow the blue path painted on the pavement north up Avenida Sucre, then west for ten blocks

Within a fifteen-minute walk from the district's two other museums is one of Lima's most unusual attractions, the **Museo Arqueológico Rafael Larco Herrera**, which contains hundreds of thousands of excellently preserved **ceramics**, many of them Chiclin or Mochica pottery from around Trujillo. The mansion itself is noteworthy as a stylish *casa Trujillana*, in the style of the northern city where this collection was originally kept. The museum houses the largest collection of Peruvian antiquities in the world and is divided into three sections: the **main museum**, which contains an incredible range of household and funerary ceramics; the **warehouse museum**, with shelf after shelf stacked with ceramics; and the **erotic art museum**, holding a wide selection of sexually themed pre-Inca artefacts – mainly from the explicit Mochica culture – which tends to attract the most interest.

Parque de las Leyendas and the zoo

Av Las Leyendas 580, San Miguel • Daily 9am–6pm • S/9, students S/4.50 • ☎ 7177456 • Take yellow bus #48 from the Plaza Mayor or a taxi

Located in a deserted spot on the sacred site of the ancient Maranga culture, but close to block 24 of Avenida La Marina, the **Parque de las Leyendas** is laid out according to the three regions of Peru – *costa*, *sierra* and *selva*. The park and **zoo** have been much improved in recent years, though there's little attempt to create the appropriate habitats and the animals are caged. Nevertheless, it does offer a glimpse of many of Peru's animal and bird species: condors, jaguars, sea lions, snakes, pumas, king vultures, bears and other exotica. It's also a fine spot for a picnic and there's an interesting **botanical garden**. Just outside there are often some interesting **artesanía** stalls selling cases of dead insects, including colourful Amazonian butterflies and tarantulas.

Callao and La Punta

Isolated on a narrow, boot-shaped peninsula, **Callao** and **La Punta** (The Point) form a natural annexe to Lima, looking out towards the ocean. Originally founded in 1537 and quite separate from the rest of the city, Callao was destined to become Peru's principal treasure-fleet port before eventually being engulfed by Lima's other suburbs during the course of the twentieth century. These days it's a crumbling but attractive and atmospheric area full of restaurants and once-splendid houses. The land is very low-lying and, at La Punta itself, the surf feels as though it could at any moment rise up and swallow the small rowing-boat-dotted beach and nearby houses.

Still the country's main commercial harbour, and one of the most modern ports in South America, Callao lies about 14km west of Lima Centro. The suburb also has its slum zones, nameless areas located in the backstreets infamous for prostitution and gangland assassins, considered virtually **no-go areas** for visitors – but if you keep to the main streets, you will find some of the best **ceviche restaurants** anywhere on the continent.

Fortaleza del Real Felipe

Av Saenz Peña, 1st block, Plaza Independencia • Daily 9.30am–3.30pm; museum Mon–Fri 9.30am–4pm • S/8 • ☎ 4658394

Away from Callao's rougher quarters and dominating the entire peninsula is the great **Fortaleza del Real Felipe**, built after the devastating earthquake of 1764, which washed ships ashore and killed nearly the entire population of Callao. This is a superb example of the military architecture of its age, designed in the shape of a pentagon. Although built too late to protect the Spanish treasure-fleets from European pirates like Francis Drake, it was to play a critical role in the **battles for independence**. Its firepower repulsed both Admiral Brown (1816) and Lord Cochrane (1818), though many

GETTING TO CALLAO AND LA PUNTA

To reach Callao, take **bus #25** from Plaza San Martín, which runs all the way here – and beyond to La Punta – or take a bus marked "La Punta" from Avenida Arequipa west along either Avenida Angamos or Avenida Javier Prado.

1

Royalists (Peruvians loyal to the Spanish Crown) starved to death here when the stronghold was besieged by the Patriots (those patriotic to Peru but keen to devolve power from the Spanish colonial authorities) in 1821, just prior to the Royalist surrender. The fort's grandeur is marred only by a number of storehouses, built during the late nineteenth century when it was used as a customs house. Inside, the **Museo del Ejercito** (Military Museum) houses a good collection of eighteenth- and nineteenth-century arms, and has various rooms dedicated to Peruvian war heroes.

Museo Naval

Av Jorge Chavez 123, off Plaza Grau • Mon–Fri 9.30am–2.30pm • S/5 • T 4294793 ext 6794

If your interest in military matters has been piqued by the Fortaleza, head for the **Museo Naval**, displaying the usual military paraphernalia, uniforms, paintings, photographs and replica ships. Outside is the **Canon del Pueblo**, a large gun installed in a day and a night on May 2, 1866, during a battle against a Spanish fleet; it is also claimed to have deterred the Chilean fleet from entering Lima during the War of the Pacific in 1880.

Museo Submarino Abtao

Av Jorge Chavez, 1st block, waterside • Tues–Sun 9am–5pm • S/8 • T 7956900, W submarinoabtao.com

From the same building as the Naval Museum, there's also access to the nearby **Museo Submarino Abtao**, or Submarine Museum, actually a real sub that literally opened its hatches in 2004 to allow public access for thirty-minute guided tours, including a simulated attack by enemy submarine. A Sierra-type vessel, this torpedo-firing battle sub was built in Connecticut, US, between 1952 and 1954, when it first arrived in Peru. You can touch the periscope, visit the dorms and enter the engine and control rooms, which were responsible for over five thousand submersions during 48 years of service.

La Punta

Out at the end of the peninsula, what was once the fashionable beach resort of **La Punta** is now overshadowed by the Naval College and Yacht Club. Many of its old mansions, slowly crumbling, are very elegant, though others are extravagant monstrosities. Right at the peninsula's tip, an open and pleasant **promenade** offers glorious views and sunsets over the Pacific and the nearby offshore islands such as **Fronton** (with its small, isolated prison), **San Lorenzo** (with evidence of human occupation, fishing, and the use of both cotton and maize going back to 2500 BC) and **Isla Palomino** (with a colony of sea lions). Meanwhile, at the back of the strand, there are some excellent **restaurants** serving traditional food (many are difficult to find, so ask locally).

Museo de la Nación

Javier Prado Este 2465, San Borja • Tues–Sun 9am–5pm • Free • T 4769878 • Take a colectivo along Av Javier Prado east from Av Arequipa; after 10min, you'll see the vast, concrete building on the left

The **Museo de la Nación**, situated in the suburb of **San Borja** just east of San Isidro, is Lima's largest modern museum, with exhibitions covering most of the important aspects of Peruvian archeology, art and culture, including regional peasant costumes from around the country, and life-sized and miniature models depicting life in pre-Conquest times. Frequent high-profile temporary exhibits, displayed in vast salons, are usually worth the trek out of town.

Museo de Oro

Av Alonso de Molina 1100, Monterrico • Daily 11.30am–7pm • S/35 • T 3451292 • Taxi from Miraflores or Lima Centro S/12–15 one way

Housed in a small, fortress-like building set back in the shade of tall trees and owned by the high-society Mujica family, the **Museo de Oro** is located along Javier Prado Este, in the suburb of **Monterrico**. As it's difficult to find and quite far from Miraflores and Lima Centro, it's best to take a taxi.

The upper floor holds some excellent **tapestry** displays, while the ground level boasts a vast display of **arms and uniforms**, which bring to life some of Peru's bloodier historical episodes. The real gem, however, is the basement, crammed with original and replica pieces from **pre-Columbian** times. The pre-Inca weapons and wooden staffs and the astounding Nasca yellow-feathered poncho designed for a noble's child or child high-priest are especially fine. Look out for the **skull** with a full set of pink quartz teeth.

Parque Zoológico Huachipa

Av Las Torres, Vitarte • Daily 9.30am–5.30pm • S/10 • ⓣ 3563666, ⓦ zoohuachipa.com.pe • Take a taxi (S/20–25) or any bus going west from Lima Centro marked "Vitarte"

Much newer and more appealing than the Parque de las Leyendas zoo, if a long way out to the east of Lima in the Vitarte district, the **Parque Zoológico Huachipa** offers a diverse, man-made habitat with lakes and rides, and plenty of animals and birds. There's an African savanna section, another dedicated to carnivores (including tigers), a kangaroo enclosure and an aquatic area.

ARRIVAL AND DEPARTURE — LIMA

Most visitors arrive in Lima by **plane**, landing at the Jorge Chavez airport, or by **bus**, concluding their long journeys either in the older, central areas of the city, or in one of the modern terminals en route to the busy commercial suburb of San Isidro, or close to the Avenida Javier Prado Este. **Driving** into the city is only for the truly adventurous: the roads are highly congested and the driving of a generally poor standard.

BY AIR

Jorge Chavez airport is 7km northwest of the centre (ⓣ 5116055, ⓦ lap.com.pe). Many hotels, even mid-range ones, will arrange for free or relatively inexpensive airport pick-up; otherwise, the best way into town is to take a taxi.

Facilities There's an ATM at the top of the stairs by the internet cabins at the north end of the building. 24hr exchange counters with reasonably competitive rates are located in both the arrivals baggage reclaim area and near the departure gates, but you'll get slightly better rates in the centre of Lima or Miraflores.

Official taxis The quickest way into the city is by taxi, which will take around 45min to Lima Centro or downtown Miraflores. The simplest way is to book or find on arrival an official taxi from the Taxi Green kiosk (ⓣ 484 2734), or official drivers with laminated badges inside the terminal. To most parts of Lima the cost is S/55.

Non official taxis It is possible, though not easy without good Spanish, to negotiate with nonofficial taxi drivers outside the terminal building and agree a price as low as S/35; however the streets here are quite rough and have a reputation for theft. If you don't use the official service, it's very important to fix the price in Peruvian soles with the driver before getting in. It can be in US$, if required, but the important thing is to be clear both about the amount and the currency. Take extra care when looking for a taxi outside the perimeter at the roundabout or on the road into Lima, as there are often thefts in these areas.

Domestic airline contacts Aeroica (ⓣ 4443026, ⓦ aeroica.net); Aeroparacas, Santa Fe 270, Higuereta, Surco (ⓣ 4494768, ⓦ aeroparacas.com); Lan, at Jr de la Unión 958, Lima Centro (ⓣ 2138200), also at C Las Begonias 780, San Isidro, Tienda 102, Centro Comercial, Jockey Plaza, Surco, and Av José Pardo 513, Miraflores (ⓣ 2138200 or ⓣ 080011234, ⓦ lan.com); Star Peru, Av Comandante Espinar 331, Miraflores (ⓣ 7059000, ⓦ starperu.com); TACA Peru (ⓣ 2136060, ⓦ taca.com); TANS, Av Arequipa 5200, Miraflores (ⓣ 2418510).

International airline contacts Aerolineas Argentinas, Carnaval y Moreyra 370 (ⓣ 080052200, ⓦ aerolineas.com); Air Canada (ⓣ 080052073, ⓦ aircanada.com); Air France, Av Alvarez Calderon 185, 6th floor, San Isidro (ⓣ 2130200, ⓦ airfrance.com); American Airlines, Jr Juan de Arona 830, 14th floor, San Isidro (ⓣ 2117000 or ⓣ 080040350, ⓦ americanairlines.com); Avianca, Av Paz Soldan 225, Oficina C-5, Los Olivos, San Isidro (ⓣ 4440747, ⓣ 4440748 or ⓣ 080051936, ⓦ avianca.com); Continental Airlines, Victor Andrés Belaunde 147, Oficina 101, Edificio Real, San Isidro (ⓣ 2214340 or ⓣ 080070030, ⓦ continentalairlines .com); Delta Airlines (ⓣ 2119211, ⓦ delta.com); Iberia, Av Camino Real 390, Oficina 902, San Isidro (ⓣ 4417801, ⓦ iberia.com); KLM, Av Alvarez Calderon 185, sixth floor, San Isidro (ⓣ 2130200, ⓦ klm.com); Japan Airlines (ⓣ 2217501, ⓦ jal.com); Lan Chile, Av José Pardo 269, Miraflores (ⓣ 2138200 or ⓣ 08011 1234, ⓦ lan.com).

Destinations Arequipa (1 daily; 1hr 20min); Chiclayo (1 daily; 1hr 40min); Cusco (several daily; 1hr); Iquitos (2 daily; 2hr); Jauja for Huancayo (1 weekly; 30min); Juliaca for Puno (1 daily; 2hr); Piura (1 daily; 2hr); Pucallpa (1 daily; 1hr); Rioja/Moyabamba (1 weekly; 2hr); Tacna (1

1

weekly; 2hr 30min); Tarapoto (1 weekly; 1hr 30min); Trujillo (1 daily; 1hr); Tumbes (1 daily; 2hr 30min).

BY BUS

Lima doesn't have any bus terminals, but a mass of individual private bus companies with their own offices and depots (see box below). Whichever terminal you arrive at, your best bet, particularly if you have luggage, is to hail a taxi and fix a price – about S/8–20 to pretty well anywhere in Lima.

Long-distance and inter-regional buses The bus terminals of the main operators – Cruz del Sur, Ormeño and Tepsa – are on Av Javier Prado Este. Plenty of buses and

LIMA BUS COMPANIES

The best and most reliable **bus companies** – Cruz del Sur, Ormeño, Tepsa and Oltursa – can deliver you to most of the popular destinations up and down the coast, and to Arequipa or Cusco. Cruz del Sur is the best choice – if not the cheapest – for the big destinations.

Below is a list of bus companies and the destinations they serve. Note that the addresses given below are of the **companies' offices**, and buses often depart from elsewhere: always check which **terminal** your bus is departing from when you buy your ticket.

Chanchamayo Manco Capac 1052, La Victoria ⓣ4701189. Tarma, La Oroya, San Ramon and La Merced.

Chinchano Av Carlos Zavala 171, La Victoria ⓣ275679. The coast as far as Cañete, Chincha and Pisco.

Cial Av Abancay 947 and Av República de Panamá 2469–2485, Santa Catalina, La Victoria ⓣ2076900, ⓦexpresocial.com. North coast including Mancora, Cajamarca and Huaraz.

El Condor Av Carlos Zavala 101, Lima Centro ⓣ4270286. Trujillo and Huancayo.

Condor de Chavín Montevideo 1039, La Victoria ⓣ4288122. Callejón de Huaylas, Huaraz and Chavín.

Cruz del Sur Av Javier Prado Este 1109, at the corner with Nicolas Arriola, on the border of San Isidro and La Victoria ⓣ3115050, ⓦcruzdelsur.com.pe. Chiclayo, Trujillo, Mancora, Piura, Tumbes, Ica, Nasca, Tacna, Arequipa, Puno, Cusco, Huaraz, Huancayo and Ayacucho.

Empresa Huaral 131 Av Abancay, Lima Centro ⓣ4282254. Huaral, Ancon and Chancay.

Empresa Rosario Jr Ayacucho, La Victoria 942 ⓣ5342685. Huánuco and La Unión.

Flores Buses C Paseo de la República and C 28 de Julio, La Victoria ⓣ4243278 or ⓣ4310485. Arequipa and south coast.

Huamanga Jr Montevideo 619 and Luna Pizarro 455, La Victoria ⓣ3302206. Ayacucho, Chiclayo, Moyobamba, Yurimaguas and Tarapoto; you'll probably need to change bus at Pedro Ruiz for Chachapoyas.

León de Huánuco Av 28 de Julio 1520, La Victoria ⓣ43290880. Cerro de Pasco, Huánuco, Tarma and La Merced.

Libertadores Av Grau 491, Lima Centro ⓣ4268067. Ayacucho, Satipo and Huanta.

Linea Paseo de la República 979, La Victoria ⓣ4240836. Buses to all north coast as far as Piura, plus Huaraz and Cajamarca.

Lobato Buses 28 de Julio 2101–2107, La Victoria ⓣ4749411. Tarma, La Merced and Satipo.

Mariscal Caceres Av 28 de Julio 2195, La Victoria ⓣ4747850. The coast and some other sectors, including Huancayo.

Movil Tours Paseo de la República, opposite the Estadio Nacional, La Victoria ⓣ7168000 or ⓣ3329000; other depot at Av Carlos Izaguirre 535, Los Olivos. Huaraz, Tarapoto and Chachapoyas.

Oltursa Av Aramburu 1160, La Victoria ⓣ7085000. Mancora and Tumbes, down south all the way to Arequipa, as well as to Cusco, Huancayo and Huaraz.

Ormeño Av Javier Prado Este 1059, on the border of San Isidro and La Victoria ⓣ4721710; some buses also pass through the depot at Carlos Zavala 177, Lima Centro ⓣ4275679, ⓦgrupo-ormeno.com.pe. Good for big national and international services along the north coast, south coast to Tacna and Arequipa and Puno, and also Cusco and into Ecuador, Bolivia, Brazil, Argentina and Chile.

Palomino Av 28 de Julio 1750, La Victoria ⓣ4286356. Cusco via Nasca and Abancay.

Señor de Luren Manco Capac 611, La Victoria ⓣ4798415. Nasca.

Soyuz/Peru Bus Av Carlos Zavala y Loyaza 221 and Av Mexico 333, La Victoria ⓣ4276310 or ⓣ2661515. Nasca, Ica and the coastal towns en route.

Tepsa Av Javier Prado Este 1091, on the border of San Isidro and La Victoria ⓣ6179000. Good buses serving the whole coast, north and south (Tacna to Tumbes) as well as Cajamarca, Huancayo, Abancay, Cusco and Arequipa.

Transportes Junin Av Nicolás Arriola 240, C Av Javier Prado, La Victoria ⓣ3266136. Tarma, San Ramon, La Merced and the Selva Central.

Transportes Rodríguez Av Paseo de la República 749, La Victoria ⓣ4280506. Huaraz, Caraz and Chimbote.

colectivos pass by here (those marked Todo Javier Prado), and can be picked up on Av Javier Prado or where Av Arequipa crosses this road. Many operators have alternative depots in the suburbs, to avoid the worst of Lima Centro's traffic.

Local and intercity buses Some of the smaller buses serving the area north of Lima depart from the Terminal Terrestre Fiori, block 15 of Avenida Alfredo Mendiola in San Martín de Porres; other companies arrive at small depots in the district of La Victoria, including those that connect with the Central Sierra and jungle regions; some arrive on the Paseo de la República, opposite the Estadio Nacional. Other common arrival points nearby include Jirón García Naranjo, Calle Carlos Zavala (in the Cercado district) and Avenida Luna Pizarro.

Destinations Arequipa (12 daily; 14–16hr); Chincha (8 daily; 2–3hr); Cusco (10 daily, some change in Arequipa; 30–40hr); Huacho (12 daily; 2–3hr); Huancayo (12 daily; 6–8hr); Huaraz (10 daily; 9–10hr); Ica (every 15min; 3–4hr); La Merced (8 daily; 7–8hr); Nasca (10 daily; 6hr); Satipo (2 daily; 12–14hr); Pisco (6 daily; 3hr–3hr 30min); Tacna (6 daily; 18–20hr); Tarma (8 daily; 6–7hr); Trujillo (10 daily; 8–9hr).

INFORMATION

TOURIST INFORMATION

Some of the commercial tour companies (see below) are also geared up for offering good tourist information, notably Fertur Peru and Lima Vision. The South American Explorers' Club at Calle Piura 135, Miraflores (T 4442150, W saexplorers.org) has good information, including maps, listings and travel reports, available to its members.

Airport Información y Asistencia al Turista, run by i-peru, has a kiosk at the airport (T 5748000).

Lima Centro The main public municipal office of Información Turística is hidden away in a small office behind the Palacio Municipal on the Plaza Mayor at C Los Escribanos 145 (daily 9am–5pm; T 3151505 or T 3151300 ext 1542).

Miraflores There's a small tourist information kiosk in the central Parque Kennedy (daily 9am–2pm & 2.30–7pm). Maps, leaflets and information can also be obtained from the Central de Información y Promoción Turística, Av Larco 770 (Mon–Fri 9am–1pm & 2–5pm; T 4463959 ext 114, W miraflores.gob.pe and W regionlima.gob.pe). There are other kiosks on the corner of Av Petit Thouars and Enrique Palacios, close to the craft stores – the Petit Thoars Mercado Indio – and also in Larco Mar (T 4459400, E iperuLarcoMar@promperu.gob.pe).

San Isidro The office of Información y Asistencia al Turista is run by i-peru from Jorge Basadre 610 in San Isidro (Mon–Fri 8.30am–6pm; T 4211627, W peruinfo.org).

LISTINGS

Published monthly in Peru, the *Peru Guide* gives up-to-date information on Lima, from tours and treks to hotels, shopping, events and practical advice; it's readily available in hotels, tour and travel agents, and information offices.

MAPS

Buy city maps from kiosks in Lima Centro or the better bookshops in Miraflores; the best is the *Lima Guía "Inca" de Lima Metropolitan* ($15).

TRAVEL AGENTS AND TOURS

For standard tours, tickets, flights and hotel bookings, the best agencies are below. A number of companies also organize specialist outdoor activities in and around Lima (see box, p.82).

Class Adventure Travel San Martín 800, Miralores T 4441652, W cat-travel.com. Organizes excellent tours and packages including Lima culinary tours, Nasca, and desert experiences.

Fertur Peru Jr Junín 211, Lima Centro T 4272626, W fertur-travel.com; or in Miraflores at Schell 485 T 2421900. Top service in tailor-made visits around Peru, as well as overland, air or other travel needs and accommodation.

Highland Tours Av Pardo 231, Oficina 401, Miraflores T 2426292, W highlandperu.com. Offer tours and will arrange travel around Peru plus accommodation when required.

Lima Tours Jr de la Unión (ex-Belén) 1040, near Plaza San Martín T 6196900, W limatours.com.pe. One of the more upmarket companies, with an excellent reputation.

Lima Vision Jr Chiclayo 444, Miraflores T 4477710, W limavision.com. A variety of city tours, plus a range of archeological ones: Pachacamac, Nasca and Cusco.

Marilí Tours Av Primavera 120, Oficina. 306, Chacarilla T 2410142, W marilitours.com.pe. Tours to most of Peru, including Cusco, Madre de Dios, Puno and the northern desert region.

New Planet Travel Genaro Castro Iglesias 795, Urb. La Aurora, Miraflores T 4455052, W newplanettravel.net. This company has a passion for Lima and offers everything from fast-driving tours to pisco-drinking packages and horseriding (not simultaneously), as well as trips to the beach; they also run, and can customize, tours to Cusco, the rainforest and the high Andes.

Overland Expeditions Jr Emilio Fernández 640, Santa Beatrice T 4247762. Specialize in the Lachay Reserve.

Paracas Tours Av Rivera Navarette 723, San Isidro T 2222621, E paracas@paracastours.com.pe. A small office with a very professional air-ticketing service.

1

ADVENTURE TRIPS AND TOURS AROUND LIMA

Many of Lima's travel agents (see p.81) can organize trips to the most popular destinations; the operators below specialize in adventure tours. There are a huge range of trips on offer, from paragliding above the city (see box, p.72) to trekking and mountain biking.

TREKKING

For advice on **trekking and mountain climbing** and trail maps, visit the Trekking and Backpacking Club, Jirón Huascar 1152, Jesús María (☎4232515), the Asociación de Andinismo de la Universidad de Lima, based at the university on Javier Prado Este (☎4376767; meets Wed evenings), or the South American Explorers' Club (see p.81).

Most trekking companies run trips to the Cordillera Blanca and Colca, as well as around the Cusco area and along the Inca Trail.

Incatrek Av Pardo 620, Oficina 11, Miraflores ☎2427843, Ⓦincatrekperu.com. This outfit sometimes runs tours to Lima's Museo de Oro, the ancient site of Caral, Ica and Paracas, Tarma, Oxapampa, Pozuzo and Satipo.

Peru Expeditions C Colina 151, Miraflores ☎4472057, Ⓦperu-expeditions.com. A professional, helpful company specializing in adventure travel, particularly on the coast (Paracas and Ballestas, Nasca), Arequipa and Colca areas. They offer trekking, mountain-biking and 4WD tours.

Rainforest Expeditions Av Larco 1116, Dep-S, Miraflores ☎7196422, Ⓦperunature.com. Arguably Peru's best eco tourism operator, with three lodges in the Peruvian Amazon; check website for toll-free telephone details.

WHITEWATER RAFTING

For **whitewater rafting** around Cusco and Huaraz, contact Explorandes or Mayuc (see below) or check for other operators in Cusco, Lunahuana or Huaraz (see relevant chapter listings).

Explorandes San Fernando 320, Miraflores ☎4450532, Ⓦexplorandes.com. Offering itineraries to most areas of Peru, this company tailors trips to individual interests as well as pre-packaged expeditions.

Mayuc Portal Confituras, Cusco ☎084 2425824. One of Peru's best and longest-established operators; while specializing in rafting, they also operate tours to Nasca, Colca and Titicaca.

DIVING AND BOAT TRIPS

Motor Yachts Contact through Ecocruceros, Av Arequipa 4960, of 202, Miraflores ☎2268530, Ⓦislaspalomino.com. Offer trips from Lima to the nearby islands, Islas Palomino, to see marine mammals, including a sea lion colony; a pleasant trip in clear weather.

Nature Expeditions ☎94104206, Ⓦnature-expeditions-peru.com. Diving and scuba are popular sports in Peru – this is the best operator for trips.

GETTING AROUND

BY COLECTIVO

Colectivos vary in appearance, but are usually either microbuses (small buses) or combis (minibuses); both tend to be crowded and have flat rates (from around S/1). Quickest of all Lima transport, combi-colectivos race from one street corner to another along all the major arterial city roads; microbuses generally follow the same routes, albeit usually in a more sedate fashion.

Avenida Arequipa colectivos The Av Arequipa colectivos start their route at Puente Rosa in Rimac, running along Tacna and Garcilaso de La Vega (formerly Av Wilson) in the centre, before picking up on the Av Arequipa which will take you all the way down to Miraflores, passing the Ovalo (a large roundabout), going down Diagonal to Calle José González before starting the route back to the centre, up Larco, then via Avenida Arequipa.

Barranco colectivos To reach Barranco from Miraflores, pick up one of the many colectivos or buses (marked Barranco or Chorrillos) travelling along Diagonal (which is one-way, from the central park towards Larco Mar and the ocean).

BY BUS

The new Lima Metropolitana bus system (☎2039000, Ⓦmetropolitano.com.pe) is an attempt to speed up Lima's traffic, connects Chorrillos and Barranco in the south with Independencia to the north of the city. Much of the route follows a dedicated track in the centre of the Paseo de la República, and the bus track can be accessed via the road bridges acros the multi-lane freeway. There are "regular" and "expreso" buses (every 10min; daily 6am–9.50pm), the former stopping at all stations, the latter at certain set

1

CATCH A COLECTIVO

Almost every corner of Lima is linked by the ubiquitous, regular and privately owned **colectivos**. Generally speaking, colectivos chalk up their **destinations or routes** on the windscreen and shout it out as they pull to a stop. So, for instance, you'll see "Todo–Arequipa" or "Tacna–Arequipa" chalked up on their windscreens, which indicates that the colectivo runs the whole length of Avenida Arequipa, connecting Lima Centro with downtown Miraflores. The driver will call out the destination sing-song style, competing with market-stall holders and the like for the attention of prospective passengers.

ones. Tickets (*tarjeta inteligente*) can be bought at the station entry points, mainly from machines. You can catch other (non-Lima Metropolitana) buses to most parts of the city from Av Abancay in the centre; to catch a bus to a destination covered in this chapter look for the suburb name (written on the front of all buses).

BY TAXI

Taxis are a fast and cheap way to get around Lima, and can be hailed pretty well anywhere on any street at any time.

Official taxis Official taxis are based at taxi ranks and licensed by the city authorities (most but not all their cars have taxi signs on the roof; some of the larger taxi companies are radio-controlled). Short rides cost S/5–10 for 10 blocks or so, say from Parque Kennedy in Miraflores to Barranco, while longer rides will set you back S/10–25, for example from Miraflores to Lima Centro or the Museo de Oro in Monterrico. Taxis can be rented for the day from about S/150. You should always fix the price to your destination in soles before getting in, and pay in soles only at the end of your journey. Reliable 24hr taxi companies include: Taxi Seguro ⓣ 22419292 or 2752020; Taxi Amigo ⓣ 3490177; and Taxi Movil ⓣ 4226890.

Unofficial taxis Unofficial taxis abound in the streets of Lima; they're basically ordinary cars with temporary plastic "taxi" stickers on their front windows, and are cheaper than official taxis.

BY CAR

Driving in Lima is incredibly anarchic. It's not too fast, but it is assertive, with drivers, especially *taxistas*, often finding gaps in traffic that don't appear to exist – as such, you have to be brave as a visitor to take the wheel. Given the city's size and spread, however, this is still an option, particularly if you want to visit sites just north or south of the city (such as Caral, Pachacamac or the beaches).

Car rental Budget, Av Larco 998, Miraflores (ⓣ 4444546, ⓦ budgetperu.com); Hertz, Cantuarias 160, Miraflores (ⓣ 4472129, ⓦ hertzperu.com.pe).

Van and driver hire Backpacker Van Express, Av Comandante Espinar 611, Miraflores (ⓣ 4477748); Transporte Manchego Turismo (ⓣ 4201289 ⓦ manchegoturismo .com.pe); LAC Dolar, Av La Paz, Miraflores (ⓣ 7173588).

BY BIKE

Bike Tours of Lima C Bolívar 150, Miraflores ⓣ 4453172 ⓦ biketoursoflima.com. Bilingual themed bike tours, as well as bike rentals, from S/20 for 2hr to S/50 for a full day.

Rentabike Alcanfores 132, Miraflores ⓣ 6921082. Bike tours and rentals.

ACCOMMODATION

There are three main areas in which to stay. Most travellers on a budget end up in **Lima Centro**, in one of the traditional gringo dives around the Plaza Mayor or the San Francisco church. These are mainly old buildings and tend to be full of backpackers, but they aren't necessarily the best choices in the old centre, even in their price range, as most of them are poorly maintained. If you can spend a little bit more and opt for mid-range, you'll find some interesting old buildings bursting with atmosphere and style. If you're into nightlife and want to stay somewhere with a downtown feel, with access to the sea, opt for a hotel further out of the city in **Miraflores**, which is still close to the seafront as well as home to most of Lima's nightlife, culture and shops. However, most hostels here start at around S/50 per person, and quite a few hotels go above S/350. The trendy ocean-clifftop suburb of **Barranco** is increasingly the place of choice for the younger traveller. Apart from the artists'-quarter vibe and the clubs and restaurants, though, the area has little to offer in the way of sights. Other suburban options include **San Isidro**, mainly residential but close to some of the main bus terminals; and **San Miguel**, a mostly rather down-at heel suburb, close to the clifftop and extending from Miraflores towards La Perla and Callao.

LIMA CENTRO

★ **Gran Hotel Bolívar** Jr de la Unión 958 ⓣ 6197171, toll free ⓣ 1 888 790 5264, ⓦ granhotelbolivar.com.pe; map p.62. This old, elegant and luxurious hotel is well located and full of old-fashioned charm, dominating the northwest corner of the Plaza San Martín. Even if you don't stay here, you should check out the cocktail lounge (famous for its Pisco Sour Cathedral) and restaurant, which host live

1

piano music most nights (8–11pm). Great-value online deals. S/200

Hostal de Las Artes Chota 1460 ⓣ4330031; map p.62. At the southern end of Lima Centro, this clean, gay-friendly place is popular with travellers, located as it is in a large, attractive house. Some rooms have private bathroom, and there's also a dorm with shared bathroom; avoid the downstairs rooms, which can be a little gloomy. English is spoken and there's a book exchange, as well as a nice patio. Dorms S/30, doubles S/70

Hostal Granada Huancavelica 323 ⓣ4287338; map p.62. This place could be more welcoming, but it's in a great location and the service is efficient. It has small but tidy rooms, private bathrooms and cordial service. Breakfast is included. S/100

Hostal Roma Jr Ica 326 ⓣ4277576 or 4277572, ⓦhostalroma.8m.com; map p.62. A pleasant, safe and gay-friendly place, always popular so book online in advance. It's conveniently located a few blocks from the Plaza Mayor, offers a choice of private or communal bathrooms (but only one shower for women) and a reliable luggage storage service. There's a TV room and a café in the entrance area. S/60

Hostal Wiracocha Jr Junín 284 ⓣ4271178; map p.62. Run by the same owners since 1975, it's located on the second level of this building, a couple of blocks from the Plaza Mayor. Rooms are quite spacious, if simply furnished, fairly clean and with a choice of shared or private bathroom. S/75

Hotel España Jr Azángaro 105 ⓣ4285546, ⓦhotelespanaperu.com; map p.62. A converted nineteenth-century Republican-style house very popular with backpackers, this secure hostel has rooms available with or without private bathroom. There's also a dorm with shared bathroom. Amenities include a nice courtyard and rooftop patio, internet connection, book exchange and safe. S/120

★ **Hotel Europa** Jr Ancash 376 ⓣ4273351; map p.62. One of the best-value budget pads, conveniently located opposite the San Francisco church, with a lovely courtyard. It's a good place to meet fellow travellers and as such is very popular and fills up quickly. Dorms S/35, doubles S/60

★ **Hotel Kamana** Jr Cámana 547 ⓣ4267204, ⓦhotelkamana.com; map p.62. An adequate, small hotel in the heart of Lima Centro, with friendly staff and TVs and showers in all of the nicely furnished rooms. Facilities include a 24hr café, room service, wi-fi and money exchange. S/140

Inka Path Jr de La Unión 654 ⓣ4261919, ⓦhotelinkapath.com; map p.62. About as central as you could wish for, *Inka Path* is newly refurbished, with very comfortable rooms. Beds are queen size and bathrooms private, with 24hr hot water. Price includes breakfast and internet. S/120

Lima Sheraton Paseo de la República 170 ⓣ3155000, ⓦsheraton.com.pe; map p.62. A top-class, modern international hotel – concrete, tall and blandly elegant, though past its heyday. It also boasts a casino, a spa and a good restaurant. S/350

Pensión Rodríguez Av Nicolás de Piérola 730 ⓣ4236465, ⓔjotajot@terra.com.pe; map p.62. Excellent value but often crowded, with shared rooms and bathrooms, and prone to noise from the road outside. The pension staff will organize airport pick-up if required. Dorms S/35, doubles S/55

★ **La Pousada del Parque** Parque Hernan Velarde 60, Santa Beatriz ⓣ4332412, ⓦincacountry.com; map p.62. A wonderful boutique hotel in a large, quiet and stylish house close to Lima Centro and the Parque de La Exposición, but just south of the centre's busy sectors. The rooms are excellently kept and well furnished, and there are good breakfasts. Internet access available. S/150

MIRAFLORES

★ **Casa Andina Miraflores Centro** Av Petit Thouars 5444 ⓣ2139700 or ⓣ21397309, ⓦcasa-andina.com; map p.70. Occupying five floors, this popular, well-appointed place is close to most of Miraflores' shops and nightlife, though rooms are neither spacious nor grand. It's hard to beat for value at the top end; all rooms have private bathrooms and TV, and the price includes an exceptional buffet breakfast. S/500

Casa de Baraybar C Toribio Pacheco 216 ⓣ4412160, ⓦcasadebaraybar.com; map p.70. Located between blocks 5 and 6 of Av El Ejercito, this hotel has ten spacious rooms available, all with comfortable beds, private bathroom, 24hr hot water and cable TV. Continental breakfast is included, and there's a a 10–20 percent daily discount if you stay for a few nights. S/180

Casa del Mochilero Jr Cesareo Chacaltaña 130a, second floor ⓣ4449089, ⓔpilaryv@hotmail.com; map p.70. Within walking distance of central Miraflores, this place has bunk-bed rooms. Though none too big, rooms do come with hot water and cable TV, and there are kitchen facilities too. The very friendly and helpful staff will arrange airport pick-up. Dorms S/35

Colonial Inn Av Comandante Espinar 310 ⓣ2032840 or ⓣ2417471; map p.70. Great service and exceptionally clean, if slightly away from the fray of Miraflores. It also has a lunchtime restaurant with surprisingly good Peruvian cuisine. S/290

Embajadores Hotel Juan Fanning 320 ⓣ2429127, ⓦembajadoreshotel.com; map p.70. Part of the Best Western chain, this is located in a quiet area of Miraflores, just a few blocks from Larco Mar and the seafront. Small but pleasant, the hotel has comfortable rooms and access to a mini-gym, small rooftop pool and restaurant. S/380

Faraoña Grande Hotel C Manuel Bonilla 185 ⓣ4469414, ⓦfaraonagrandhotel.com; map p.70. A plush, secure, quite modern hotel in a central part of this busy suburb; there's a rooftop pool and a pretty good restaurant with Peruvian, international and vegetarian dishes. Live piano music performed daily in the bar 7–10pm. S/400

Friends House Jr Manco Capac 368 ⓣ4466248, ⓔfriendshouse_peru@yahoo.com.mx; map p.70. Located on the second level of this building, this is a small but well-maintained and popular hostel in a superb Miraflores location; comfortable and clean rooms, hot water, cable TV and open kitchen. Dorms S/40, doubles S/75

HI Hostel Lima Casimiro Ulloa 328 ⓣ4465488, ⓦlimahostell.com.pe; map p.70. A great deal, this hostel is a base for International Youth Hostals in Peru. It's located just over the Paseo de la República highway from Miraflores in the relatively peaceful suburb of San Antonio, in a big, fairly modern and stylish house with a pool. There's also a restaurant and bar with views to the garden, and they'll pick up from the airport. Dorms S/40, doubles S/100

★ **Hospedaje Flying Dog** Jr Diez Canseco 117 ⓣ4450940, ⓦflyingdogperu.com; map p.70. A clean and homely backpackers B&B-style hostel right in the middle of Miraflores. Most rooms are shared but the maximum size is four beds; you also have the option of a double with private bathroom. There's an open kitchen facility and cable TV lounge, as well as internet access. Price includes breakfast. It has an annexe over the road at Lima 457 (ⓣ4445753). Dorms S/30, doubles S/90

Hostal Antigua Miraflores Av Grau 350 ⓣ2416116, ⓦperu-hotels-inns.com; map p.70. Within walking distance of downtown Miraflores, the *Antigua* is an expanding mock mansion with professional and helpful service, and spacious, well-appointed and very quiet rooms. There's also a small restaurant with reasonable food. Good breakfast included. S/250

Hostal Buena Vista Av Grimaldo del Solar 202 ⓣ4473178, ⓦhostalbuenavista.com; map p.70. Located in a distinctive house in downtown Miraflores, the *Buena Vista* offers large rooms with private bathroom, and there's also outside space in the form of gardens and rooftop patios. Staff are friendly and helpful, and a buffet breakfast is included in the price. S/50

Hostal Martinika Av Arequipa 3701 ⓣ4223094, ⓔmartinika@terra.com.pe; map p.70. Very reasonably priced and centrally located within the greater city area – it's close to the boundary of Miraflores and San Isidro – if a little noisy in the mornings. It's also comfortable and friendly, offering fairly large rooms with private bathroom. Airport pick-up available. S/150

★ **Hostal Pariwana** Av Larco 189 ⓣ2424350, ⓦpariwana-hostel.com; map p.70. With a wide, grand stairway entrance including spectacular stained-glass window, this converted mansion is a veritable backpackers' haven and a great meeting place for young travellers. It's also in a lovely location, overlooking the main park in Miraflores. There are dorms (including a women-only option) as well as private rooms, mainly with shared bathroom, as well as games, free internet, kitchen access, rooftop terrace and a good bar and café, which serves very tasty late breakfasts. Dorms S/27, doubles S/85

★ **Hostal El Patio** Diez Canseco 341 ⓣ4442107, ⓦhostalelpatio.net; map p.70. A very agreeable, gay-friendly and secure little place right in the heart of Miraflores, with comfy beds and private – albeit small – bathrooms. More expensive mini-suites and full suites are also available, and it's often fully booked, so reserve in advance. S/141

Lex Luthor's House Jr Porta 550 ⓣ2427059, ⓔluthorshouse@hotmail.com; map p.70. Within an easy stroll from the ocean, this hostel (named after the owner's childhood nickname) offers excellent value with hot water, kitchen facilities, cable TV in all rooms, and table games. The rooms are basic but clean and comfortable. S/70

Marieta Bed & Breakfast Inn Malecón Cisneros 840 ⓣ4469028, ⓔgato@amauta.rcp.net.pe; map p.70. A small but spotless B&B in a lovely house in one of Lima's more exclusive locations overlooking the ocean, with private bathrooms and a terrace. The family that runs the B&B also operate a number of tours in and around Lima and will pick guests up from the airport for a reasonable fee. Advance bookings only. S/115

Miraflores Colón Inn Colón 600 ⓣ6100900, ⓦmirafalorescolonhotel.com; map p.70. Located near the corner of Juan Fanning. Rooms are spacious, clean and equipped with bathtubs, while rooms equipped with jacuzzi and hydro-massage baths are also available. Breakfast included. S/400

Miraflores Park Av Malecón de la Reserva 1035 ⓣ2423000, ⓦorientexpress.com; map p.70. Conspicuously modern hotel belonging to the Orient Express chain, with a great restaurant, pub-style bar and lovely views over Miraflores, the city and the Pacific. In short, total luxury. S/480

Pensión José Luís Francisco de Paula de Ugarriza 727 ⓣ4441015; map p.70. Comfortable, modern house, in a good location, within walking distance of central Miraflores and the ocean, and popular with English-speaking travellers. All rooms come with private bathroom, and internet access is available. S/130

Radisson Av 28 de Julio 151 ⓣ6251241, ⓦradisson .com/miraflores.pe; map p.70. Entering the *Radisson* resembles boarding a spaceship: lobby and bars alike have a sci-fi ambience. The rooms are as modern and luxurious as you'd expect from this famous chain. S/440

Sonesta Posada del Inca – Miraflores Alcanfores 329 ⓣ2417688, ⓔreservas@sonestaperu.com; map p.70.

1

This very plush, excellently run and modern downtown hotel offers cable TV, a/c and a decent 24hr restaurant. There's a ten percent discount and complimentary breakfast for guests who show a copy of this book. Airport pick-up is available. S/450

Stop and Drop Backpacker Hotel and Guest House Berlin 168, 2nd floor ☎2433101, Ⓦstopandrop.com; map p.70. Located in the heart of the action just behind Pizza Alley and near an English pub, this is a friendly and pretty safe place. Dorms are available, as well as private doubles with TV and internet. Surfing lessons are organized just two blocks from the hostel ($25/2hr). Dorms S/30, doubles S/110

Tinkus Hostel Av La Paz 608 ☎2420131, Ⓦhoteltinkus.com; map p.70. Well located just a few blocks from Avenida Larco in central Miraflores, *Tinkus* is a good-value option. The lobby is larger and more salubrious-looking than the rooms, though the larger ones aren't too bad. Service is friendly, although the breakfast of instant coffee, bread and jam is rather insubstantial. S/140

El Zaguan Lodging Av Diez Canseco 736 ☎4469356, Ⓦelzaguanlodging.com; map p.70. Located in a relatively tranquil street near the Parque Tradiciones, yet within a stone's throw of the heart of the district, *El Zaguan* offers eminently accommodating rooms with or without private bathroom. Generous breakfasts. S/120

BARRANCO

Hospedaje Domeyer Domeyer 296 ☎2471413, Ⓦdomeyerhostel.net; map p.74. Close to the Plaza Municipal and nightlife of Barranco, this is a beautiful old mansion from the outside, though not particularly elegant or well maintained internally. Shared and private rooms available, and most are small but comfortable, with hot water and cable TV; price includes breakfast. Dorms S/40, doubles S/110

The Point Hostel Malecón Junín 300 ☎2477997, Ⓦthepointhostels.com; map p.74. A B&B hostel with twelve rooms created by two *mochilleros* (backpackers) in a colonial house with relaxing gardens; the shared kitchen and billiard room are further bonuses. There's often music playing, sometimes live jams among travellers, sometimes rock and reggae CDs, but rarely so loud it interferes with others' sleep. The managers are helpful and offer sensible travel information. Dorms S/27, doubles S/70

Safe in Lima Alfredo Silva 150 ☎2527330, Ⓦsafeinlima.com; map p.74. This Belgian-run guesthouse offers a quiet bolt-hole in Barranco, just off block 5 of Pedro de Osma, not far from the action. Pleasant rooms and good service; there's airport pick-up (S/51) and tours within the city and the country as a whole on offer. A simple but ample breakfast is included in the price. S/55

SAN ISIDRO

Casa Bella Las Flores 459 ☎4217354, Ⓦcasabellaperu.net; map pp.58–59. A modern hotel located one block from the Country Club and Golf Club in San Isidro (behind *Los Delfines Hotel*), offering exceptionally pristine rooms with state-of-the-art finishing in a re-designed mansion from the early 1930s. Staff can help with tours and tickets. S/170

Hotel Libertador Los Eucaliptos 550 ☎5186300, Ⓦlibertador.com.pe; map pp.58–59. A top-class hotel with a convenient location in this well-to-do Lima suburb. The service and room standards are excellent. S/400

Malka Youth Hostal Los Lirios 165 ☎4420162, Ⓦyouthhostelperu.com; map pp.58–59. Well located, *Malka* is cheerful and intimate as well as being good value for this part of the city. There are several airy rooms, one with views over the garden, but most bathrooms are shared. Dorms S/27, doubles S/60

Suites del Bosque Av Paz Soldan 165 ☎6162121, Ⓦsuitesdelbosque.com; map pp.58–59. Though essentially a business hotel with conference centre, the suites themselves are smartly furnished, complete with dining/living room, cable TV, internet access, heating and a/c. There's also a restaurant and bar, a jacuzzi and great buffet breakfasts. S/700

Swissotel Lima Vía Central 150, Centro Empresarial Real ☎4214400, Ⓦswissotel.com; map pp.58–59. Conveniently located near banks, bus depots and some department stores and supermarkets, this is luxurious accommodation with all the modern conveniences you'd expect, aimed largely at the business traveller. S/550

SAN MIGUEL

Hostal Mami Panchita Av Federico Gallesi 198 ☎2637203, Ⓦmamipanchita.com; map pp.58–59. Located in the suburb of San Miguel, this is a very approachable hostel in lovely gardens with a well-appointed, shared dining room, TV lounge and bar. Both English and Dutch are spoken, and they also offer airport pick-up (just 20min away). Price includes breakfast. S/100

EATING

Lima boasts some of the best **restaurants** in the country, serving not only traditional Peruvian dishes (see box opposite), but cuisines from all over the world. Many of the more upmarket places fill up very quickly, so it's advisable to **reserve in advance**. In recent years a large number of **cafés** have sprung up around Miraflores and Barranco, many offering free wi-fi and providing snacks as well as coffee. Lima Centro is less well served by cafés, though there are a few appealing options.

LIMA ON A PLATE

Among South American capitals, Lima ranks alongside Rio and Buenos Aires for its selection of places to eat and drink, with **restaurants, bars and cafés** of every type and size crowding every corner of the city, from expensive hotel dining rooms to tiny, set-meal street stalls. What makes the local cuisine so special is a combination of diverse **cultural ingredients** (Andean, Spanish, Italian, African and Chinese in particular) alongside perhaps the world's greatest store of indigenous **edible plants**, a by-product of Peru's great biodiversity and range of ecosystems. Having the world's largest forest and source of plants just on the other side of the Andes, in the Amazon Basin, and a good range of climates, Peru can boast that a lot of its food originated here. This ready availability has helped shape the culinary habits of the modern city, whose citizens take for granted fresh and varied food of great quality. Regardless of class or status, virtually all Limeños **eat out** regularly – and a meal out usually ends up as an evening's entertainment in itself.

CAFÉS

LIMA CENTRO

Bar/Restaurant Machu Picchu Jr Ancash 318; map p.62. A busy place opposite San Francisco church, serving inexpensive snacks such as omelettes and sandwiches or even *cuy picante* (spicy guinea pig); they offer cheap, set-menu lunches and it's a good spot for meeting up with other travellers. Daily 11am–10pm.

★ **El Cordano** Jr Ancash 202 ☎4270181; map p.62. Across the street from the Palacio de Gobierno, this is one of the city's last surviving traditional bar/restaurants with mirrored walls, racks of bottles and old-style waiters, who are curt but efficient, even charming in an old-fashioned way. Worth visiting if only to soak up the atmosphere, sample the excellent ham sandwiches and see first-hand the exquisite late nineteenth- and early twentieth-century decor. Mon–Sat 8am–9pm.

El Paraiso de la Salud Restaurant Vegetariano Jr Cámana 344 ☎3475112; map p.62. Offering a delivery service, this vegetarian option offers good breakfasts, as well as yoghurt, juice, salads, wholemeal breads and smoothies. It's a large space but gets busy at lunch, when it serves delicous plates like steamed broccoli and lentil tortillas. Mon–Sat 11am–5pm.

Queirolo Café Bar Restaurant Corner of Cámana 900 with Quilca; map p.62. This is a classic meeting place for poets, writers and painters, and is worth a visit just for the splendour of its old Lima Cason-style architecture and bohemian atmosphere. They serve comida criolla, sandwiches, beer and pisco; great for inexpensive but good-quality set lunches. Mon–Sat 9am–2am.

MIRAFLORES

Arabica Espreso Bar General Recavarren 269 ☎7152152; map p.70. A narrow space with small patio and coffee-roasting equipment out back, this place serves arguably the best coffee in Lima. There are great cakes, too, as well as free wi-fi. Mon–Sat 8am–7pm.

Café Café Martir Olaya 250 ☎4451165; map p.70. Located just off Diagonal in downtown Miraflores, this is a hip, gay-friendly coffee shop that plays good rock music and serves a variety of sandwiches, salads, paellas, pastas and Peruvian dishes, as well as a selection of cocktails. Daily 10am–midnight.

Café Haiti Diagonal 160 ☎4463816; map p.70. The most popular meeting place for upper-middle-class Limeños, based near the Cinema El Pacífico in the heart of Miraflores. It offers excellent snacks, such as stuffed avocado or *ají de gallina*, and a decent range of soft and alcoholic drinks, although it's not cheap. Daily 8am–2am.

Café Verde Av Santa Cruz 1305 ☎6527682; map p.70. One of the best places for coffee in Lima is this small café, which roasts on site. Mon–Sat 8am–7pm.

Café Z Corner of José Galvez with Diagonal ☎4445579; map p.70. Very pleasant ambience, with plenty of glass, a wooden interior balcony and two floors crowded with small round tables. Rock is usually on the stereo, and the staff are young and cool; good coffee, salads and bar food are their specialities. Daily 7am–11pm.

Starbucks Diagonal 314; map p.70. Just another strategically located *Starbucks* (there are several around Lima), with good wi-fi, and tables both inside and out. Usually very busy. Daily 8am–9pm.

La Tiendacita Blanca Av Larco 111 ☎4451412; map p.70. Located right on the busiest junction in Miraflores, this is a popular meeting place, with a superb range of Peruvian and Swiss foods, plus cakes and pastries, though they are pricey. Live piano music Mon–Fri 7–8pm. Daily 7am–7pm.

Urban Tea Boulevard Tarata 256 ☎2433812; map p.70. Just off Av Larco in Miraflores, this new teashop sells and serves a wide range of brews. The environment is a bit plastic, but the service is friendly. Mon–Sat 9am–8pm.

BARRANCO

Café Bisetti Av Pedro de Osma 116 ☎7139565; map p.74. On the Plaza Municipal, this place serves really excellent coffees and very good snacks. It's a large space

1

with plenty of tables and a pleasant garden, and it also roasts coffee on the premises. Occasional live music on Saturdays. Daily 8am–10pm.

K'antu Av Grau 323 ☎992681419; map p.74. Both a café and a centre for fairtrade, handmade craft goods. It serves good organic coffee and tasty cakes, and is linked to the Inter-regional Centre for Artesans of Peru. Mon–Thurs 10am–10pm, Fri & Sat 9am–11pm.

Las Mesitas Av Grau 341 ☎4774199; map p.74. A tasteful café serving delicious snacks, meals and scrumptious sweets including excellent *humitas*, tamales, juices and sandwiches. Daily noon–2am.

RESTAURANTS

LIMA CENTRO

Chifa Capon Ucayali 774; map p.62. ☎4272969. An excellent and traditional Limeño-Chinese fusion restaurant, the best in this block of Chinatown. It offers a range of authentic, moderately priced *chifa* dishes. Daily noon–2/3am.

De Cesar Ancash 300 ☎4288740; map p.62. Great little café/restaurant and bar right in the heart of old Lima, with a buzzing atmosphere. The spacious interior is sometimes a bit dark but the food is fine and cheap, the service very friendly and the range of breakfasts and juices endless. Daily 7.30am–10pm.

Don Lucho's Restaurant Jr Carabaya 346; map p.62. Just off the Plaza Mayor, this is a busy lunchtime spot with a cool interior, popular with local office workers and offering fast service and decent set-menu meals for less than S/10. Mon–Sat 8am–10pm.

El Estadio Restaurant Bar Nicolás de Piérola 926, Plaza San Martín ☎4288866, Ⓦestadio.com.pe; map p.62. A restaurant with a strong football theme, and walls covered in murals and sports paraphernalia: fascinating even for those only remotely interested in the sport. You can even have your picture taken next to a life-size bust of Pele while you're here. Both the food and bar are excellent and sometimes there are club nights in the basement. There's also a Peruvian food festival every Fri and Sat. Mon & Tues noon–6pm, Wed & Thurs noon–11pm, Fri & Sat noon–4am.

L'Eau Vive Ucayali 370 ☎4275612; map p.62. Opposite the Palacio Torre Tagle, this interesting restaurant serves superb French and Peruvian dishes cooked by nuns. It offers a reasonable set menu at lunch and dinner, and closes after

LIMA SPECIALITIES

Widely acclaimed as one of the world's great culinary destinations, Lima is a paradise for food enthusiasts. As well as a wide array of delicious meat-, rice- and vegetable-based **criolla dishes**, you'll come across the highly creative **novo andino cuisine**, often pairing alpaca steaks with berries or cheese sauces from lush Andean farms, and best appreciated in Lima's finest restaurants. Below are a few specialities that your taste buds will thank you for trying.

Ceviche Seafood is particularly good in Lima, with ceviche – raw fish or seafood marinated in lime juice and served in dozens of possible formulas with onions, chillis, sweetcorn and sweet potatoes – a must-try.

Chorros a la Chalaca These spicy mussels are best sampled near the port area of Callao.

Cabrito a la Norteña This traditional goat feast has made its way to Lima from the northern coast of Peru; as well as tender goat meat, the dish incorporates a sauce made with *chicha de jorra* (rustic maize beer), yellow chillis, *zapallo* squash, onions and garlic, plus *yuca* and lots of fresh coriander, served with rice.

Arroz con Pato a la Chiclayana From northern Peru, this is a dish of duck and rice prepared as in the city of Chiclayo, with oranges, spices, beer, brandy, peas and peppers. It's such a popular dish you'll probably come across it in all regions of the country.

Asado A good cut of beef roasted in a red sauce, ususally served with *pure de papas* (smooth, garlic-flavoured mashed potatoes).

Chicken broaster The staple at the thousands of broaster restaurants found in every corner of Peru: essentially, spit- or oven-roasted chicken with chips, and often a very meagre salad on the side.

Cuy This is the Inca word for guinea pig, one of the most common foods for Andean country folk, but also something of a delicacy which can be found everywhere from backstreet cafés to the best restaurants in Lima, Cusco and Arequipa. There are various ways to prepare *cuy* for the plate, but *cuy chactado* (deep-fried) is one of the most common.

Pisco Sour Pisco is Peru's clear, grape-based brandy, which forms the heart of the national drink – pisco sour. The pisco, crushed ice, fresh lime juice, plus a sweetener and egg white, are whisked together with a bitter added at the end. It's refreshing and sometimes surprisingly potent.

a chorus of *Ave Maria* most evenings. Mon–Sat 12.30–3pm & 7.30–9.30pm.

MIRAFLORES

★ **Astrid y Gastón** Cantuarias 175 ⓣ2425387, ⓦastridygaston.com; map p.70. A trendy, colonial-style signature restaurant run by the world-renowned Peruvian chef Gastón Acurio. Possibly the best in Lima, and voted one of the world's top 50 restaurants, it is stylish and expensive (expect to spend from around S/70), with a menu blending Peruvian criolla and Mediterranean-style cooking. Acurio has opened restautants in six other Latin American countries, plus Spain, flying the flag for Peruvian cuisine. Daily 12.30–11.30pm.

El Bodegon Tarapaca 197–199 ⓣ4456222; map p.70. This place serves up Mediterranean, vegetarian and *novo andino* cuisine in pleasant surroundings, with creative alpaca dishes, among others, with French or European influence, and a good selection of wines and piscos. Mon–Sat 11am–11pm.

Las Brujas de Cachiche Av Bolognesi 460 ⓣ4771883 or ⓣ4471133; map p.70. Very trendy and expensive, this top-class restaurant and bar serves mainstream Peruvian dishes as well as a range of pre-Columbian and *novo andino* meals, such as seafood ceviche and maize-based dishes made using only ingredients available more than a thousand years ago. Daily noon–11pm.

★ **Caplina** Mendiburu 793 ⓣ4753404; map pp.58–59. A good cevichería on the outskirts of Miraflores, serving tasty, classic ceviche as well as a range of other seafood dishes, around an attractive, almost Japanese, pebble pond. They also prepare seafood *a la Chalaca* (traditional Callao-style, often spicy hot and one of the best) and *a la Chiclayana*, as well as meat and Italian pasta dishes. Daily 9am–5pm.

Club Suizo Genaro Iglesias 550, La Aurora, Miraflores ⓣ4459230; map p.70. Located level with block 17 of Avenida Benavides, this fine place offers exquisite Swiss cuisine, including extravagant fondues combining four cheeses, in a very pleasant environment. Tues–Sat 11am–11pm, Sun 11am–4pm.

Dinnos Pizza Comandante Espinar 408 ⓣ2190909; map p.70. This flashy, brightly lit restaurant offers some of the best pizza in Lima, as well as relatively fast service and delivery. Daily noon–midnight.

La Divina Comida Av Comandante Espinar 300, in the *Hotel Colonial Inn*; map p.70. A fine restaurant for a lunchtime set menu ($3–5 with a choice of main course); not to be missed if you're in this part of Miraflores. Mon–Sat 11am–10pm.

La Hamaca Av Arequipa 4698 ⓣ2427978; map p.70. This Lima stalwart serves quality criollo meals. Their *ají de gallina* (a chillied chicken dish with ancient roots) is spectacular, and the colonial museum-mansion it's based in is almost as good. Daily 6–10.30pm.

El Kapallaq Av El Reducto 1505 ⓣ4444149; map p.70. Recently opened in a new, 1950s-style renovated house on the border between Miraflores and Barranco, this excellent restaurant focuses on a fusion of north-coast and Lima seafood cuisine. Service and food are both excellent. Advance booking necessary. Mon–Sat 11am–5pm.

Madre Natura Chiclayo 815; map p.70. Located by block 4 of Av Comandante Espinar, this cafetería serves tasty but healthy snacks and meals. It's in the Madre Natura complex, with an organic and health products store, an eco gifts centre and a wholemeal bakery. Mon–Sat 8am–9pm, Sun 9am–2pm.

Mama Lola Diez Canseco 119 ⓣ42416335; map p.70. Right in the heart of Miraflores, near the bottom end of the park, this welcoming trattoria and pizzeria buzzes at night with locals and tour groups. *Mama Lola* serves great Italian dishes such as onion soup and spinach ravioli with ricotta, as well as Peruvian dishes like *tacu tacu*, black beans and seafood. Daily 11.30am–11pm.

La Mar Av La Mar 770 ⓣ4213365, ⓦlamarcebicheria.com; map p.70. Easily Lima's trendiest and lively cevichería, *La Mar* is stylish, swanky and very, very busy. Noisy but with great salsa music and strong pisco sours, the restaurant serves a wide range of ceviche in all sorts of regional styles, such as *tiraditos* (thin slivers of fish in sweet sauces) in innovative combinations such as the *tiradito poderoso* with sea urchin and black scallops in a lemon and olive oil vinagrette. Get there before 12.30pm to avoid the queues. Tues–Sun noon–7pm.

Patagonia Restaurant Arte y Diseno C Bolívar 164 ⓣ4468705; map p.70. With walls full of photos and paintings, plus a space for theatre and music performances, this place offers a slightly different dining experience. Specialities include Italian–Argentine cuisine, and the *pasta fresca* is excellent. Good wines available. Mon–Sat 6pm–2am.

Restaurant Huaca Pucllana General Borgoño, block 8 ⓣ4454042; map p.70. Tasty, international cuisine with a French flavour and quality Peruvian dishes, including *novo andino* and excellent traditional *cuy*, *cabrito* (goat) and various fish offerings. The service is outstanding, and the restaurant has an elegant terrace that looks out onto the ancient monument of the Huaca Pucllana (see p.69). Mon–Sat 12.30pm–midnight, Sun 12.30–4pm.

Restaurant Naturista El Paraiso C Alcanfores 416–453; map p.70. A great vegetarian restaurant, and a cheerful place to shelter from the hustle and bustle of the Miraflores streets. Daily 8am–10pm.

Restaurant Tai-i Vegetariano Av Petit Thouars 5232 ⓣ2426654; map p.70. Handily located opposite the artesanía markets, this veggie standby offers simple, inexpensive and satisfying food in the shape of set-lunch

1

menu meals, plus a range of great Asian dishes. Daily 8am–8pm.

La Rosa Nautica Espigon 4, Costa Verde ⓣ4475450; map p.70. With excellent ocean views thanks to its pier location, this is one of Lima's more expensive seafood restaurants. The menu offers a wide range of Latin American and European dishes. Jazz performances every Thurs eve. Daily 12.30pm–12.30am.

Scena Restaurant Bar C San Francisco de Paula Camino 280 ⓣ2418181; map p.70. Ultra modern in design, this restaurant's dishes are a fusion of flavours based on the chef's own interpretation of *cocina Peruana*, with good meat and fish. Mon–Fri 12.30–4pm, Sat 7.30pm–12.30am.

El Señorio de Sulco Malecón Cisneros 1470 ⓣ4410183; map p.70. Specializing in Peruvian cuisine, including *novo andino*, this restaurant uses the finest ingredients to prepare mainly traditional dishes, many cooked in earthen pots. This type of meal can be found on street stalls all over Peru, but here the chef is top quality – and this is reflected in the prices. Mon–Sat noon–midnight.

BARRANCO

★ **Café Cultural Expreso Virgen de Guadalupe** Av Prol San Martín 15a ⓣ2528907; map p.74. A unique, atmospheric restaurant and bar situated right beside the Puente de los Suspiros, serving typical international and Peruvian fare inside an ornate nineteenth-century railway carriage. Live music at weekends. Daily 5pm–midnight.

Chifa Chun Yion C Unión 126, Barranco ⓣ4770550; map p.74. An excellent and very busy traditional Chinese restaurant, with some private booths in the back room. The quality isn't high, but it's very reasonably priced. Daily noon–3pm & 7pm–midnight.

SAN ISIDRO

La Carreta Av Rivera Navarrete 740 ⓣ4422690; map pp.58–59. One of Lima's best *churrascarías* (Brazilian-style steakhouses), close to San Isidro's Centro Comercial. Designed to resemble an old hacienda, this place serves dishes that are mainly Peruvian or international, and there's a spectacular bar with quality wines. Daily noon–midnight.

Centro Turístico Perco's Restaurant C Elias Aguirre 166 ⓣ4456697; map pp.58–59. Don't be put off by the name: this is Lima's one and only restaurant specializing in the cuisine of the jungle region. They offer venison, wild pig, *paiche* fish and many other tasty and reasonably priced dishes. Daily 8am–11pm.

Punto Azul Corner of Javier Prado with Av Petit Thouars ⓣ2213747; map pp.58–59. One of a chain of excellent and unpretentious cevicherías, this one is unusual in that you eat outside at tables overlooking one of Lima's busiest junctions. Mon–Sat 11.30am–6pm.

LA VICTORIA

Cevichería Mi Barunto Jr Sebastián Barranca 935 ⓣ4272066; map pp.58–59. Close to the Alianza football stadium, this popular cevichería is full of club regalia and has a great atmosphere. It's a large space but often full. Daily 11am–6pm.

El Italiano Trattoria Pizzeria C Enrique León García 376 ⓣ4721281; map pp.58–59. A locals' place, not at all touristy. Unlike most pizzerias or Italian restaurants in Peru, all food is freshly prepared on the premises. Tues–Sun 1–4pm & 6–11pm.

SURQUILLO

Cevichería El Rey Marino Clara Barton Lte. 10, La Calera, Surquillo ⓣ4488667; map pp.58–59. Located close to block 43 of Av Aviación, this is a brilliant and unpretentious cevichería with very friendly service and good Peruvian music. Best at lunch. Daily 11am–6pm.

SURCO AND MONTERRICO

Guru Av Benavides 3796, Monterrico ⓣ2735658; map pp.58–59. If you like spice, this is the place. A small but

SELF-CATERING

Lima offers plenty of options for DIY lunches. **Surquillo market** (daily 6.30am–5.30pm), a couple of blocks from Miraflores over the Av Angamos road bridge, on the eastern side of the Paseo de la República freeway, is a colourful place fully stocked with a wonderful variety of breads, fruits, cheeses and meats. Pickpockets are at work here, though, so keep your wallet and passport close.

Of Lima's **supermarkets**, Metro has the best range at reasonable prices. You'll find this chain across the city, notably at the San Isidro Comercial Centre, the Ovalo Gutierrez in Miraflores and next to Ripley's on Calle Schell in the centre of Miraflores. All branches accept and change US dollars. **Bakeries and delicatessens** can be found in most urban districts – try Avenida Larco in Miraflores, within a few blocks of Larco Mar. *Madre Natura*, Jirón Chiclayo 815, off Avenida Comandante Espinar, in Miraflores, stocks a wide range of **health foods** and ecological products, as well as having its own café and wholemeal bakery.

excellent curry and kebab house, located in the district of Surco, but easily accessible by taxi from Miraflores. The owner is an English-speaking African-Asian. Daily noon–10pm.

Siam Thai Cuisine Av Caminos del Inca 467, Surco ⓣ720680; map pp.58–59. Superb Thai food in a delightful, tranquil environment with small indoor gardens and very reasonable service and prices. Best to take a taxi (S/12 from Miraflores). Daily 11.30am–10.30pm.

Sushi Ito Av El Polo 740, Monterrico ⓣ4355817; map pp.58–59. Located in the Centro Comercial El Polo, this is an excellent, posh sushi restaurant serving *sashimi* and *maki-temaki*, among other dishes. Mon–Sat noon–4pm & 7pm–midnight.

CALLAO

Manolo Malecon Pardo, block 1, La Punta ⓣ4531380; map pp.58–59. A fine seafood restaurant and bar on the seafront (best sampled when sunny rather than windy). The food is very fresh; try the *chicharones de pulpo* (battered and fried octopus nuggets) or the *ceviche de pescado*. Daily 11am–4pm.

DRINKING AND NIGHTLIFE

Lima's nightlife is more urban, modern and less traditional than in cities such as Cusco and Arequipa; **Barranco** is the trendiest and liveliest place to hang out. The city has an exciting **club** scene, with the majority of its popular **bars** and discos located out in the suburbs of San Isidro and Miraflores. In the summer months (Jan–March) the party sometimes carries on down the coast to the resort of **Asia**, 110km south (see p.100), where there are some surprisingly sophisticated nightclubs.

As far as the **live music scene** goes, the great variety of traditional and hybrid sounds is one of the best reasons for visiting the capital, with folk group *peñas*, Latin jazz, rock, reggae and reggaeton all popular. All forms of **Peruvian music** can be found here, some – like **salsa** and **Afro-Peruvian** (see p.511) – better than anywhere else in the country. Even Andean folk music can be close to its best here (though Puno, Cusco and Arequipa are all more probable contenders).

Entrance charges and policies Most clubs charge an entrance fee of around S/20–50, which often includes a drink and/or a meal. Many clubs have a members-only policy, though if you can provide proof of tourist status, such as a passport, you usually have no problem getting in.

Listings The daily *El Comercio* provides the best information about music events, and its Friday edition carries a comprehensive nightlife supplement – easy to understand even if your Spanish is limited. Things are at their liveliest on Friday and Saturday nights.

BARS

Ayahuasca Av Prol. San Martín 130, Barranco ⓣ4459680; map p.74. A fantastic venue, this place is based in a lovingly restored mansion with several interesting bar areas; it's not cheap but the drinks are inventive and there are great snacks too. Very busy after 10pm at weekends. Mon–Sat 8pm–2am.

Brenchley Arms Atahualpa 174, Miraflores ⓣ4459680; map p.70. An attempt to replicate an English pub, *Brenchley Arms* has a pleasant atmosphere and three bars stocked with good beer. Rock music is occasionally performed live. Thurs–Sun 6.30pm–late.

El Dragon Nicolás de Piérola 168, Barranco ⓣ7155043, ⓦeldragon.com.pe; map p.74. A dark, often packed out and fun cultural bar, *El Dragon* almost always has live music, frequently good Latin rock and jazz. Tues–Sat 8pm–2am.

Habana Café Bar Av Manuel Bonilla 107, Miraflores ⓣ4463511; map p.70. Live music Fri and Sat 10pm–1am, particularly Cuban, but also great jazz and nostalgic rock. Serves an excellent range of rum and cocktails. Tues–Sun 6pm–late.

Juanito's Bar Av Grau 274, Barranco; map p.74. Probably the most traditional of the neighbourhood's bars; facing onto the Parque Municipal, it's small and basic and offers an excellent taste of Peru as it used to be. The music policy is strictly criolla and traditional Peruvian folk, and the front bar open until very late. Closed during World Cup finals, when the owners travel to watch the games. Mon–Sat 4pm–2am.

Lion's Head Pub Av Grau 268, Barranco; map p.74. Located on the second floor of the building is this British-style pub with dartboard, pool table, newspapers, sports TV and, of course, English beers. Daily 5pm–late.

Mochileros Bar Av Pedro de Osma 135, Barranco ⓣ2471225; map p.74. Located in a fine old Barranco mansion, now converted into an *albergue* and live music bar. It has outside tables and good cocktails (the house speciality is El Beso del Diablo, consisting of pisco, tequila and grenadilla). Tues–Sat 8am–11pm.

La Posada del Mirador On the cliff top point behind the Puente de Suspiros and church, Barranco; map p.74. A popular evening bar with great views and a lively atmosphere. Daily 10am–10pm.

Rincon Cervecero Jr de la Unión 1045, Lima Centro ⓣ4288866; map p.62. An original Lima bar but in Germanic style, with satisfyingly large pitchers of draught beer and shots, and a buzzing atmosphere. The kitchen serves original recipes, and there's a beer festival in Oct. Mon–Sat 10am–midnight.

The Old Pub San Ramón 295, Miraflores ⓣ2428155; map p.70. The most authentic of the English-style pubs in

Lima – it's run by an Englishman – and easy to find, just a block or two from the park in Miraflores, at the far end of Little Italy (San Ramón). There's good music and a dartboard, and sandwiches, salads, chips and roast-beef meals are available. Daily noon–1am.

CLUBS

Aura Larco Mar, Miraflores ⓣ2425516, ⓦaura.com.pe; map p.70. Well respected for its weekend shows and electronica prowess; now and then international DJs make an appearance. Special events are generally Thurs–Sat. Tues–Sat 10pm–3am.

Deja-Vu Av Grau 294, Barranco ⓣ2476989; map p.74. A heaving dance club from Monday through to Saturday night. Music mainly ranges from trance to techno, but also live music, mainly rock, sessions at weekends. Best Thurs–Sat. Mon–Sat 10pm–3am.

Gotica Larco Mar, Miraflores ⓣ6283033, ⓦgotica.com.pe; map p.70. A fairly exclusive but popular disco with excellent music and an even better sound system: expect anything from hip-hop and punk to Latin rock, salsa and reggaeton, as well as occasional live bands at weekends. Tues–Sun 9pm–2am.

Karamba Jr Manuel Asencio Segura, Boulevard Los Olivos, Los Olivos, north Lima ⓣ2080920, ⓦboulevardlosolivos.com; map pp.58–59. This is a hectic *salsódromo* based north of Lima Centro in the district of Los Olivos. Split into two levels with its walls painted in coconuts, the club has a hot, tropical feel and plays heavy electronica as well as salsa. Nearby, also on the Boulevard, is another popular club, *Kokos*. Thurs–Sun 9pm–3am.

Kitsch Av Bolognesi 743, Barranco; map p.74. A funky and gay-friendly disco-bar with weird decor, known for playing lots of 70s and 80s tunes; it gets hotter later on. Tues–Sun 9pm–2am.

PEÑAS AND SALSÓDROMOS

Lima's **peñas** – some of which only open at weekends and nearly all located in Barranco – are the surest bet for listening to authentic **Andean folk**, although some of them also specialize in **Peruvian criolla**, which brings together a unique and very vigorous blend of Afro-Peruvian, Spanish and, to a lesser extent, Andean music. These days it's not uncommon for some of Lima's best *peñas* to feature a fusion of criolla and Latin jazz. Generally speaking, *peñas* don't get going until after 10pm and usually the bands play through to 3 or 4am, if not until first light.

Lima is also an excellent place to experience the Latin American **salsa** scene, and there are *salsódromos* scattered around many of the suburbs. They play a mix of tropical music, salsa, merengue and technocumbia. Most are open Friday and Saturday 10pm–3am.

★ **Las Brisas del Titicaca** Jr Wakulski 168, Lima Centro ⓣ3321901, ⓦbrisasdeltiticaca.com; map p.62. One of the busiest and most popular venues for tourists in the know and locals alike; excellent bands and yet this is one of the cheapest of the city's *peñas*. Thurs–Sat 8.30pm–5am (shows 10.30pm–2.30am).

★ **Del Carajo** San Ambrosia 328, Barranco ⓣ2418904, ⓦdelcarajo.com.pe; map p.74. A lively and popular *peña* playing a range of criolla, Andean and coastal traditional and modern music. Some of Latin America's top criolla muscians play here. Thurs–Sat 10pm–3am.

La Estación de Barranco Av Pedro de Osma 112, Barranco ⓣ2470344; map p.74. Just across the road from the suburb's main plaza, this established *peña* regularly varies its flavour between folklore, criolla and even Latin jazz or rock at times, with a lively atmosphere most Fridays and Saturdays. Tues–Sat 9pm–3am.

Kimbara Paseo de la República 1401, La Victoria ⓣ2655831; map pp.58–59. This is a sprawling, unpretentious choice, with vibrant salsa music, sometimes performed live at weekends. Top Peruvian criolla musicians sometimes play here. Thurs–Sat 9pm–2am.

Peña La Candelaria Av Bolognesi 292, Barranco ⓣ2471314, ⓦlacandelariaperu.com; map pp.74. An enormous venue presenting live music and dance from the three regions (coast, Andes and Amazon). Thurs, Fri & Sat 9pm–3am.

Peña Don Porfirio C Manuel Segura 115, Barranco ⓣ4773119; map p.74. Possibly the only traditional-style *peña* left in Lima. Offers dance lessons during the week. Fri from 10pm.

Peña Sachún Av del Ejercito 657, Miraflores ⓣ4410123; map p.70. Very lively and popular tourist restaurant with a good reputation for live folkloric music and criolla dancing. Tues–Sat 8.30pm–3am.

De Rompe y Raja Restaurant Peña Turística C Manuel Segura 127, Barranco ⓣ2473271, ⓦderompeyraja.pe; map p.74. Located between blocks 5 and 6 of Avenida Bolognesi, this *peña* presents live Peruvian music from 10pm. Ideal for groups, with big tables and entertainment into the small hours. Thurs–Sat 9pm–midnight.

JAZZ, ROCK AND LATIN JAZZ

CC Club Delfus Taberna San Martín 587, San Borja ⓣ9431211; map pp.58–59. Live rock music every Friday and Saturday night, with open jam sessions on Tuesday and Thursday. Wed–Sat 9pm–2am.

El Ekeko Av Grau 266, by the Plaza Municipal, Barranco ⓣ2473148; map p.74. Often has Latin jazz at weekends, though also hosts Peruvian Andean and coastal music, mainly criolla. It's best to call first to make sure there's live music on when you go. Wed–Sun 9pm–late.

CLOCKWISE FROM TOP LEFT CEVICHE AT *ASTRID Y GASTÓN* (P.89); PARAGLIDING ABOVE MIRAFLORES (P.72); LIMA BEACH >

Jazz Zone Av La Paz 656, Miraflores ☎2418139; map p.70. Located in the Pasaje El Suche, *Jazz Zone* offers cutting-edge live Latin or Brazilian rock, salsa and jazz, as well as fine examples of avant-garde Andean folk and occasionally Peruvian ballad singers. Daily 8pm–2am.

La Noche Av Bolognesi 307, El Boulevard Pazos, Barranco ☎2472186, Ⓦlanoche.com.pe; map p.74. Don't let the slightly risqué website put you off: this is a top club located at the top end of the Boulevard, and is arguably the best venue in Barranco for meeting people; it gets really packed at weekends. Musically, it specializes in Latin rock and electronica, with free jazz sessions on Mon evenings. Live music (Fri & Sat 10pm–2am) comes with a small entry fee. Daily 9pm–2am.

★ **La Posada del Angel III** Av Prol San Martín 157, Barranco ☎2475544; map p.74. This is the largest of three *Posada del Angel* venues, all within a stone's throw of each other in Barranco. Well known for its Trova and Latino live music sessions, it has a great bar and also serves snacks and meals. All three locations are richly – and kitschly – decorated; the other two are at Pedro de Osma 164 & 218. Tues–Sat 6.30pm–midnight.

Satchmo Av La Paz 538, Miraflores ☎4428425; map p.70. A large, traditional indoor live venue, best at weekends when performances range from Latino and Peruvian criolla music to jazz and blues. It's reasonably priced and food is also available. Fri–Sun 8pm–late.

GAY AND LESBIAN LIMA

Since the **gay and lesbian scene** is relatively small, there are few gay meeting places, though the main park and **Larco Mar** centre in Miraflores (see p.71) can be cruisey in the evenings. Lima society has begun to grow more tolerant, but this does depend on which area you're in. The male culture, however, is still primarily macho, so as a visitor, keeping a relatively low profile makes for an easier time.

GAY BARS AND CLUBS

La Cueva Av Aviación 2514, San Borja ☎97888044; map pp.58–59. A simple gay and lesbian disco, mostly popular with under-40s. Great shows on Friday and Saturday, usually peaking around 3am. Thurs–Sun 10.30pm–late.

Downtown Vale Todo Pasaje Los Pinos 160, Miraflores ☎4446433; map p.70. Arguably the best gay club in Lima; now and then there are caged go-go dancing boys, occasional striptease acts and a cruise bar. Mon–Sat 8pm–3am.

Gitano 2050 Berlin 231, Miraflores; map p.70. Well-known as a Lima gay club, this place is divided into various levels, with cruising above the dancing. Wed–Sun 9.30pm–late.

Legendaris C Berlin 363, Miraflores ☎4463435; map p.70. Fashionable *Legendaris* is a large, comfortable club with personalized service, good drinks and shows, particularly on Saturday night. Wed–Sun 10pm–late.

Sagitario Disco Av Wilson 869, Lima Centro ☎4244383; map pp.58–59. The longest-established gay club, in the heart of Lima, has cruising balconies filled with young people – a large number of them gay – and dancing through the night, often until 11am the next day. Daily 8pm–late.

ARTS AND ENTERTAINMENT

Going to the **cinema** and **theatre** is an important part of life in Lima. Peruvians are a well-cultured people with a passion and intuitive understanding of everything from Latin music and fine arts to ancient textiles and traditional Andean dance forms. **Peruvian culture** is very much alive and most locals know dozens of songs and several folk dances, as well as being able to dance salsa with the best of them. Lima's **cultural centres**, often associated with one of the local universities, are often the best place to catch innovative films, music shows and drama. The best source of **information** about film, theatre, sporting events and exhibitions is the daily *El Comercio*, especially its Friday supplement.

CINEMAS

There are clusters of cinemas around the Plaza San Martín, Jirón de la Unión and Avenida Nicolas de Pierola in Lima Centro, on the fringes of the park in Miraflores, at Larco Mar and in some of the suburban shopping malls.

Cinemark Peru Jockey Plaza 12, Av Javier Prado, Surco ☎4370222.

Cinemark Plaza Lima Sur 7 Av Prol Paseo de la República, Chorrillos ☎4370222.

Cineplanet Alcazar 1–8 Santa Cruz 814, Miraflores ☎4527000.

Cineplanet Centro Jr de la Unión, Lima Centro ☎4527000.

Cineplanet Primavera Av Angamas Este 2684, San Borja ☎4527000.

Cinerama El Pacífico Av Pardo 121, Miraflores ☎2430541.

UVK Multicines Larco Mar 1–12 Parque Salazar, Larco Mar, Miraflores ☎4467336.

CULTURAL CENTRES

Centro Cultural de la PUCP (Universidad La Católica) Av Camino Real 1075, San Isidro ☎6161616. One of the most active cultural centres in Lima, with innovative theatre, cinema and video, as well as art exhibitions, a library and cafeteria.

Centro Cultural de la UNMSM (Universidad de San Marcos) Av Nicolás de Piérola 1222, Parque Universitario, Lima Centro ☎4280052. Often presents folk music and dance performances. The centre is run by the Universitario de San Marcos (see p.67), on the Parque Universitario, and performances are publicized on the noticeboard at the entrance.

Centro Cultural Ricardo Palma Av Larco 770, Miraflores ☎4466164 or ☎4463959. Often hosts excellent concerts of Andean music, but doesn't have the same participatory feel of the *peñas* (see p.92). It does, however, boast a library, two exhibition rooms and occasional cinema festivals, plus jazz, dance and theatre performances.

THEATRE, BALLET AND CLASSICAL MUSIC

Lima possesses a prolific and extremely talented **theatre** circuit, with many of its best venues based in Miraflores. In addition to the major theatres, short performances sometimes take place in the bars of the capital's top theatres. The country's major prestige companies, however, are the **National Ballet Company** and the **National Symphony**, both based seasonally at the Teatro Municipal (see below).

Teatro Britianico Jr Bellavista 527, Miraflores ☎4471135.

Teatro Larco Larco 1036, Miraflores ☎3300979.

Teatro Municipal Block 3 of Jr Ica, Lima Centro ☎4282302.

Satchmo Av La Paz 526, Miraflores ☎4444957.

SHOPPING

When it comes to **shopping** in Peru's towns and cities, Lima is the most likely to have what you're looking for. It's certainly your best bet for **shoes and clothing**, particularly if you want a large selection to choose from. The same is true of **electronic goods**, **stationery** and **music**, though bear in mind that most Limeños who can afford it do their main shopping in Miami. Lima also has a good selection of reasonably priced **arts and crafts** markets and shops.

Shopping hours The usual shopping hours are Mon–Sat 10am–7pm, though in Miraflores, the main commercial area, many shops and artesanía markets stay open until 8pm and sometimes later. Some shops, but by no means all, shut for a two-hour lunch break, usually 1–3pm, and most shops shut on Sundays, though the artesanía markets on avenidas La Marina and Petit Thouars tend to stay open all week until 7pm.

ANTIQUES

Collacocha C Colón 534, Miraflores ☎4474422. Parallel to block 11 of Avenida Larco, this place has good-quality antiques, as well as arts and crafts.

Rafo Martinez de Pinillos 1055, Barranco ☎2470679. Quality antiques and a good lunchtime restaurant too.

ARTS AND CRAFTS

Agua y Tierra Diez Canseco 298, Miraflores ☎4446980. A wide range of ethnic and traditional healing or *curanderos'* artefacts.

Artesanías Huayruro and Killapura Diez Canseco 392 and 378, Miraflores. These adjacent stores sell crafts and some edible produce from the Andes and Peru's Amazon tribes.

Artesanía Santo Domingo Jr Conde de Superunda 221–223, Lima Centro. This little square pavement area, just a stone's throw from the Correo Central in Lima Centro, is good for beads, threads and other artesanía items.

La Casa de Alpaca Av La Paz 665, Miraflores. Good but expensive alpaca clothing.

CRAFT-SHOPPING IN LIMA

Lima is a treasure-trove of **Peruvian artesanía**, with woollen goods, crafts and gemstones among the best souvenirs. Artesanía shops tend to cluster in particular areas, and there are some dedicated craft markets too. **Avenida La Paz** in Miraflores boasts several shops selling precious metals, gemstones and antiques shops, with many places devoted to silverwork and other jewellery. Some of the cheapest traditional crafts in Peru can be found in an artesanía market area en route to Callao (or the Parque de Las Leyendas), located by the roadside blocks 6–8 of **Avenida La Marina**, in Pueblo Libre. The **Mercado Indio**, on Avenida Petit Thouars between blocks 48 and 54 (between Av Ricardo Palma and Av Angamos) is much more central, reasonably priced and home to the best craft and souvenir stalls and shops, all well within walking distance of Miraflores centre. **Artesanía Gran Chimu**, Av Petit Thouars 5495, has a wide range of jewellery and carved wooden items, as does **Mercado Artesanal**, Av Petit Thouars 5321. At La Rotunda, the small circular area towards the bottom (ocean) end of Parque Kennedy in Miraflores, a small selection of reasonable-quality crafts and antiques are displayed every evening (6–9pm).

1

Cuy Arts and Crafts Av Larco 1175 & 874, Miraflores. Handmade crafts of all kinds.
Las Pallas Cajamarca 212, Barranco ⊕4774629. A fascinating, veritable museum of artesanía, run by a British woman who has spent most of her life collecting fine works and who may be able to show you the rest of her collection (ring for an appointment).
Santos Alpaca 859 Av Larco 859, Miraflores. Excellent-quality pima cotton and alpaca products at quite reasonable prices.

BOOKS

ABC Bookstore Colmena 689, Lima Centro. Well supplied with all kinds of works in English. Also in Lima Centro, Av Nicolas de Pierola has a few shops which stock English-language books (try the store at no. 689).
Librería Ibero Larco 199, Av Oscar Benavides 500 & Comandante Espinar, by the Ovalo Gutierrez, Miraflores. The best bookshops are in Miraflores.This bookshop has three branches, which generally have a wide range of books and magazines in English.
Zeta Books Comandante Espinar 219, Miraflores. Has a small selection of new English paperbacks.

CAMPING, SURF AND SPORTS EQUIPMENT

Altamira Arica 800, Miraflores. A block from the Ovalo Gutierrez roundabout, this shop sells a good range of quality camping equipment.
Alta Montana Av Julio Bailetti 610, San Borja ⊕3463010. Probably the best place for climbing gear.
Big Head Larco Mar, Miraflores. Good surf store. There's a second branch in the Jockey Plaza Shopping Centre (see opposite).
Boz Av Angamos Oeste 1130, between Miraflores and San Isidro ⊕4401033. Specializes in surfing equipment.
Camping Centre Av Benavides 1620, Miraflores ⊕2421779. Has a a good range of tents and other equiopment in a small space.
Klimax José González 488, Miraflores ⊕4421685. Good for surf gear.
Peru Bike Parque Nueva Castilla, Calle A, d-7, Surco ⊕4498435. Good range of bikes and related accessories.
Surf n Soul Av San Martín 564, Barranco ⊕2494383. A new surf shop and small café; good equipment and lots of information on surfing in Peru.
Todo Camping Av Angamos Oeste 350, Miraflores. Has a range of tents and other equipment.

JEWELLERY

Arte y Canela Larco Mar, Miraflores. Stocks fine silver jewellery.
Casa Wako Jr de la Unión 841, Lima Centro. Probably the best place in Lima Centro for jewellery, specializing in reasonably priced Peruvian designs in gold and silver.
Nasca Av La Paz 522, Miraflores. Has a nice range of less expensive jewellery, particularly silverware.

PHOTOGRAPHIC EQUIPMENT

Renato Service 28 Julio 442, Miraflores. For excellent camera and video equipment.
Foto Digital Av Larco 1005, Miraflores ⊕4479398. Good for fast developing.

SHOPPING MALLS

Jockey Plaza Av Javier Prado Este 4200, Surco. The largest of the shopping malls, with over two hundred shops including two massive department stores (Saga and Ripley), a bowling alley, twelve cinema screens and dozens of restaurant-cafés. Take any colectivo or bus marked "Todo Javier Prado" heading east from the junction of Av Javier Prado with Av Arequipa.
Centro Comercial Larco Mar At the clifftop end of Av Larco, Miraflores. This centre only has forty shops but they are complemented by thirty restaurant-cafés, cinema screens, two nightclubs and three bars.

DIRECTORY

Embassies and consulates Australia, Av Victor Belaunde 147, Office 1301, Torre Real 3, San Isidro (⊕2228281); Bolivia, Los Castaños 235, San Isidro (⊕4402095 or ⊕4428231); Brazil, Av José Pardo 850, Miraflores (⊕4215660); Canada, C Bolognesi 228, Miraflores (⊕3193200); Chile, Javier Prado Oeste 790, San Isidro (⊕7102211); Ecuador, Las Palmeras 356, San Isidro (⊕4217050); Ireland, Paseo de la República 5353B, San Antonio, Miraflores (⊕2429516); New Zealand, Los Nogales 510, Piso 3, San Isidro (⊕4227491); South Africa, Victor Andres Belaunde 147 (office 801), Edificio Real Tres, San Isidro (⊕4409996); UK, Torre Parque Mar, Av Larco 1301, 22nd floor, Miraflores (⊕6173000); US, La Encalada, block 17, Monterrico (⊕4343000).

Health For an ambulance call ⊕4400200 or ⊕3726080, but if you can, take a taxi – it'll be much quicker. The following hospitals are well equipped, with emergency departments which you can use as an outpatient, or which you can phone for a house call: Clínica Anglo Americana, Av Salazar, San Isidro (⊕2213656); Clínica Internacional, Washington 1475, Lima Centro (⊕4288060); Clínica Ricardo Palma, Av Javier Prado Este 1066, San Isidro (⊕2248027 or ⊕2222224); and Clínica San Borja, Av Guardia Civil 337, San Borja (⊕4753141). For anti-rabies vaccinations and emergency treatment contact Antirabico (⊕4256313). If you just need to see a doctor, try one of the following: Dr Bazan works as a "backpackers medic" (⊕97352668, ⊕backpackersdr@yahoo.com); Dr Aste,

Antero Aspillaga 415, Oficina 101, San Isidro (T 4417502), speaks English; Dr Alicia Garcia, Instituto de Ginecología, Av Monterrico 1045, Surco (T 4342650); or Dr Raul Morales, Clínica Padre Luis Tezza, Av del Polo 570, Monterrico (T 4346990), speaks good English. The best pharmacy is Boticas Fasa, Av Benavides 847, Miraflores (T 6190000), with 24hr delivery; they accept major credit cards. There's a comprehensive Mifarma pharmacy in Lima Centro at Av Abancay 601. Inka Farma (T 6198000) is a delivery service.

Internet You can find internet cafés virtually anywhere in Lima, particularly in Miraflores, where Dragonfans, Tarata 230, and Larconet, Av Larco 675, are the best. Wi-fi is available in many cafés.

Language Schools Hispana Spanish School, C San Martín 377, Miraflores (T 4463045, W hispanaidiomas.com); Ecela, Gen Recavarres 542, Miraflores (T 4442279); Lima School of Languages, Av Grimaldo del Solar 469, Miraflores (T 2427763, W elsol.idiomasperu.com), where you can start any Monday for small-group or private tuition, full- or part-time; El Tulipán, José Galvez 426, Miraflores (T 64477403 W eltulipanperu.com), which offers a good Spanish survival course.

Laundry Many hotels will do this cheaply, but there are numerous *lavanderías* in most areas; the Lavandería Saori, Grimaldi del Solar 175, Miraflores (Mon–Sat 8am–7pm; T 4443830), is fast; LavaQueen, Av Larco 1158, Miraflores, does washing by the kilo at reasonable prices.

Money and exchange Banco de la Nación, Av NicolΣas de Piérola 1065 and Av Abancay 491; Banco de Credito, Jr Lampa 499, Av Larco 1099, Miraflores (well run and with small queues) and Juan de Arona, San Isidro; Banco Continental, Av Larco, Miraflores. Casa de Cambios sometimes offer better rates and are often the only places where travellers' cheques will be accepted. Try Casa de Cambio, Ocoña 211a; LAC Dollar, Camana 779, second floor; and another office in Miraflores at La Paz 211.

Police Peru's Tourist Police are based at Jr Colón 246, Miraflores (T 2258698 or T 4233500), and in the Museo de La Nación at Javier Prado Este 2465 (T 2258698).

Post office The main post office is at Pasaje Piura, Jr Lima, block 1 near the Plaza Mayor (Mon–Sat 8am–8pm, Sun 8am–2pm), with other branches in Miraflores, at Petit Thouars 5201, a block from the corner of Angamos (Mon–Fri 8am–8pm). The best bet for sending large parcels is to use KLM (Av Elmer Faucett 2823, Oficina 404, Lima Cargo City, Callao; T 5755270) who charge about $12/kilo to Europe. Concas Travel, Alcanfores 345, Oficina 101, Miraflores (T 2417516), can arrange larger shipments.

The coast around Lima

Stretching out along the coast in both directions, the **Panamerican Highway** runs the entire 2600-kilometre length of Peru, with Lima more or less at its centre. Towns along the sometimes arid coastline immediately north and south of the capital are of minor interest to most travellers, though there are some glorious **beaches**, mostly to the south, with next to no restrictions on beach camping. The best of the beaches begin about 30km out, at the impressively hulking pre-Inca ruins of **Pachacamac**, a sacred citadel that still dominates this stretch of coastline.

Pachacamac

Daily 9am–5pm • S/10, guides S/20 for a small group • T 4300168

Originally one of the most important centres of pilgrimage on the Peruvian coast, **PACHACAMAC** functioned from around the time of Christ as a very sacred location that, even in pre-Inca days, housed a miraculous wooden idol (see box, p.99). It's by far the most interesting of the Rimac Valley's ancient sites, and well worth making time for even if you're planning to head out to Cusco and Machu Picchu; allow a good two hours to wander around the full extent of the ruins. The site can easily be combined with a day at one or other of the beaches, and it's little problem to get out there from the capital.

The museum

The entry fee for the citadel includes admission to the site **museum**, which merits a quick browse on the way in, if only to get a look at the wooden idol of Pachacamac (see box, p.99) and a 3D site model; there are nice gardens attached, and a café serving snacks.

The ruins

Entering the ruins, after passing the restored sectors, which include the **Templo de la**

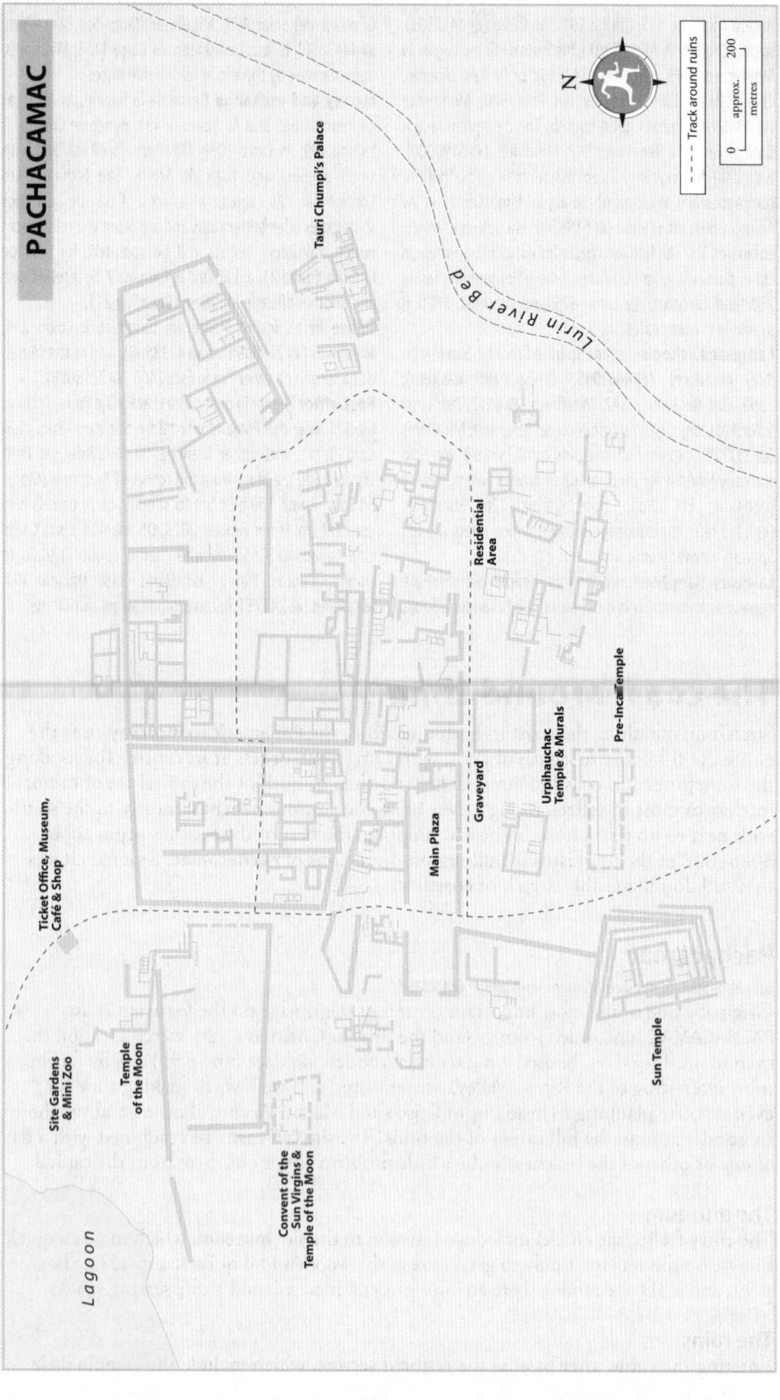

PACHACAMAC

Tauri Chumpi's Palace
Lurin River Bed
Residential Area
Pre-Inca Temple
Urpihuachac Temple & Murals
Graveyard
Main Plaza
Ticket Office, Museum, Café & Shop
Site Gardens & Mini Zoo
Temple of the Moon
Convent of the Sun Virgins & Temple of the Moon
Sun Temple
Lagoon
N
- - - - Track around ruins
0 approx. 200 metres

IDOLS AND ORACLES

Pachacamac means (more or less) "Earth's Creator", and the site was certainly occupied by 500 AD and probably for a long time before that. When other *huacas* were being constructed in the lower Rimac Valley, Pachacamac was already a temple-citadel and centre for mass pilgrimages. The god-image of Pachacamac was believed to express his or her anger through **tremors and earthquakes**, and was an **oracle** used for important matters affecting the State: the health of the ruler, the outcome of a war and so on. Later this became one of the most famous **shrines** in the Inca Empire, with Pachacamac himself worshipped along with the sun. The Incas built their Sun Temple on the crest of the hill above Pachacamac's own sacred precinct.

In 1533, **Francisco Pizarro** sent his brother Hernando to seize Pachacamac's treasure, but was disappointed by the spoils, which consisted of little more than a **wooden idol** representing, through intricate carvings, a two-faced humanoid. This wooden representation of Pachacamac may well have been the oracle itself: it was kept hidden inside a labyrinth and behind guarded doors – only the high priests could communicate with it face to face. When Hernando Pizarro and his troops arrived they had to pass through many doors to arrive at the main idol site, which was raised up on a "snail-shaped" (or spiralling) platform, with the wooden carving stuck into the earth inside a dark room, separated from the world by a jewelled curtain. Pizarro ended up burning the complex to the ground, dissatisfied with the relatively small amounts of gold on offer.

As well as earthquakes, Pachacamac's powers extended to the absence or presence of **disease and pestilence**. His wife, or female counterpart, was believed to dominate **plant and fish life**.

Luna (Temple of the Moon) and the **Convento de las Virgenes del Sol** (Convent of the Sun Virgins, or *Mamaconas*), you can see the later Inca construction of the **Sun Temple** directly ahead. Constructed on the top level of a series of pyramidical platforms, it was built tightly onto the hill with plastered adobe bricks, its walls originally painted in gloriously bright colours. From the very top of the Sun Temple there's a magnificent **view** west beyond the Panamerican Highway to the beach (Playa San Pedro) and across the sea to a sizeable yet uninhabited island, which resembles like a huge whale approaching the shore. Below the Sun Temple is the **main plaza**, once covered with a thatched roof supported on stilts, and thought to have been the area where pilgrims assembled in adoration. The rest of the ruins, visible though barely distinguishable, were once dwellings, storehouses and palaces.

ARRIVAL AND DEPARTURE — PACHACAMAC

By bus Buses leave every 2hr for Pachacamac from Av Abancay in Lima Centro and around the Parque Universitario on Jr Montevideo at the corner with Jr Ayacucho. Buses can also be picked up from one of the bus-stop lay-bys on the Panamericana Sur (south direction); the spot where Avenida Angamos Este crosses the Panamericana is a good bet.

By taxi A taxi to Pachacamac and back from Miraflores can be found from around S/100.

By tour Many of the tour agencies in Lima offer half-day tours to the site (see p.81).

Lomas de Lucumo

Taxi from Lima (S/120–180) or Pachacamac (S/15)

Going away from the Pachacamac site via the pueblo of the same name you pick up a hard road heading for the Quebrada Verde area. Within a few kilometres you come across the **Lomas de Lucumo**, a beautiful natural ecosystem at the edge of the desert replete with shrubs and the odd flower thriving on little more than seasonal coastal fog.

Southern beach towns

South from Pachacamac lie some of Lima's most attractive **beaches**. Closest to the ruins, just a couple of kilometres away, is **Playa San Pedro**, a vast and usually deserted strip of sand. Constantly pounded by rollers, however, it can be quite dangerous for swimming. Though much more sheltered, the bay of **El Silencio**, 6km to the south, occasionally suffers from low-level pollution that can appear here from the local beachside developments. You may be better off heading to one of the excellent **seafood restaurants** on the cliff above, or to the smaller, more secluded bays a short drive further down the coast.

Santa María and San Bartolo

At **Punta Hermosa**, about ten minutes on the bus beyond El Silencio, you come to an attractive cliff top settlement and, down below, what's becoming Lima's leading surf resort, **Santa María**, a great family haunt, with plenty of hotels and a reasonable beach. Just south of here the surf and beach resort of **San Bartolo** offers hostels, restaurants and reasonably good waves.

Pucusana, Chilca and around

South of San Bartolo lies the fishing village of **Pucusana**, clustered on the side of a small hilly peninsula, which is now perhaps the most fashionable of the beaches – a holiday resort where Limeños actually stay rather than just driving out for a swim.

Continuing south, the road cruises along the coast, passing the long beach and salt pools of **Chilca** after 5km, and the curious lion-shaped rock of **León Dormido** (Sleeping Lion) after another 15km or so.

Asia and further south

Spread out along the roadside from Km 95 to 103, **Asia** has turned from a small agricultural town, producing cotton, bananas and corn, to a modern, trendy resort with hotels and fashionable **clubs** alongside its long **beach**. Archeological finds in local graveyards have revealed that this site was occupied from around 2500 BC by a pre-ceramic agricultural community associated also with the earliest examples of a trophy-head cult (many of the mummies were decapitated). About 20km on from Asia is the growing surfers' resort of **Cerro Azul**.

ARRIVAL AND GETTING AROUND — SOUTHERN BEACH TOWNS

By bus Buses to San Bartolo and Pucusana can be picked up in Lima from one of the bus-stop lay-bys on the Panamericana Sur (south direction); wait at the spot where Av Angamos Este crosses the Panamericana. Some buses start from the corner of Jr Montevideo and Jr Ayacucho every 2hr, passing Pachacamac, San Pedro, El Silencio, Punta Hermosa and Santa María on the 65km journey. For Asia and Cerro Azul take the Peru Bus (Av Mexico 280, La Victoria; ⓣ2052370, ⓦperubus.com.pe).

ACCOMMODATION AND EATING

Doña Paulina About 20km south of Chilca on the highway, where it bypasses the town of Malfa. At this cafetería, you can sample the best *chicharones* (chunks of deep-fried pork) in the region. Daily 9am–7pm.

Penascal Surf Hotel Av Las Palmeras 258, San Bartolo ⓣ4307436, ⓦsurfpenascal.com. These apartments with oceanfront views are part of a surfing school (also offering Spanish lessons). Rates include breakfast, lunch, parking and laundry. S/240

Inland from Lima: into the foothills

Several destinations in the **foothills of the Andes** are within relatively easy reach of Lima. The most spectacular is the mystical plateau of **Marcahuasi** (see p.285), a weekend trip from the city; much closer to Lima are the impressive sites of **Puruchuco** and **Cajamarquilla**, which are typical of ruins all over Peru and make a good introduction to the country's archeology. The attractive mountain towns of **Huancayo**,

Huancavelica and **Tarma**, all interesting destinations, are within a day's easy travelling of the capital (see Chapter Five).

Puruchuco and around

Between Km 4 and Km 5 of the Carretera Central • Daily 9am–5pm • S/5 • Ⓣ 4942641 • Take any bus marked Vitarte or Chaclacayo and get off in Villa Vitarte, where the entrance is signposted from the Carretera Central (quite close to the football stadium)

An 800-year-old, pre-Inca settlement, **PURUCHUCO** is a labyrinthine villa. Nearby is the small but interesting **Museo de Sito Puruchuco**, containing a complete collection of artefacts and attire found at the site (all of which bears a remarkable similarity to what Amazon Indian communities still use today). The name itself means "feathered hat or helmet", and recent building work in the locality discovered that the Puruchuco site was also a massive **graveyard**, revealing greater quantities of buried pre-Incas than most other sites in Peru. The villa's original adobe structure was apparently rebuilt and adapted by the Incas shortly before the Spanish arrival: it's a fascinating ruin, superbly restored in a way which vividly captures what life was like before the Conquest.

Very close by, in the Parque Fernando Carozi (ask the site guard for directions), two other ruins – **Huaquerones** and **Catalina Huaca** – are being restored, and at **Chivateros** there's a quarry dating back some twelve thousand years.

Cajamarquilla

Huachipa, Carretera Central • Daily 9am–5pm • S/50 • Take any bus marked Chaclacayo and get off at Santa Clara junction; cross over the river from here and turn right along the signposted road, from where it's 3km to the site

First occupied in the Huari era (600–1000 AD), **CAJAMARQUILLA** flourished under the **Cuismancu culture**, a city-building state contemporary with the better-known Chimu in northern Peru. It was an enclosed city containing thousands of small, complex dwellings clustered around a higher section, probably nobles' quarters, and numerous small plazas. The site was apparently abandoned before the Incas arrived in 1470, possibly after being devastated by an earthquake. Pottery found here in the 1960s by a group of Italian archeologists suggests habitation over 1300 years ago.

Today the site is a vast and almost overwhelming labyrinth of cracked and weathered adobe-built corridors, rooms and small plazas, and feels almost as if it was only recently deserted after a massive earthquake.

ARRIVAL AND DEPARTURE — PURUCHUCO AND CAJAMARQUILLA

Both Puruchuco and Cajamarquilla lie near the beginning of the Central Highway, the road that climbs up behind Lima towards Chosica, La Oroya and the Andes. The two sites are only 6km apart.

By tour The sites are most easily visited on a half-day guided tour from Lima (see p.81).

By colectivo You could take a colectivo from Calle Montevideo, La Victoria (daily from 7am; S/8), and return by waving down passing buses on the main Carretera Central; the Chosica-to-Lima bus will be the most likely to have spare seats. For Cajamarquilla, the colectivo will drop you off at the refinery turn-off before Km10 of the Carretera Central; then it's about 4km, or an hour's walk to the ruins, which are well hidden next to an old hacienda.

Parque Zoológico Huachipa

Av Las Torres, Vitarte; close to the Cajamarquilla turn-off • Daily 9am–5.30pm • S/10 • Ⓣ 3563141, Ⓦ zoohuachipa.com.pe • Take any bus marked Chaclacayo and get off at Santa Clara junction; it's on the right and well signposted before you reach the river and bridge, just a short walk along Av Las Torres

The **Parque Zoológico Huachipa**, a theme park and zoo, is fun for kids. There's a walk-on pirate boat, a waterworld area, an imaginative play area and a zone full of exotic animals, including zebras, tigers and giraffes, not to mention an array of brightly coloured reptiles.

San Juan de Pariachi

Km 12.5 of the Carretera Central

A few kilometres east of the Parque Zoológico Huachipa is an archeological site on the right bank of the Río Rimac: the Inca administrative centre now known as **San Juan de Pariachi**, dating from at least a thousand years ago.

Chosica and around

Into the foothills through sprawling developments, the road comes to the town of **Chosica**, a narrow settlement squeezed between the steepening dry and rocky foothills and the turbulent river below. Just 35km from Lima, Chosica has long been a traditional weekend escape from the city, particularly during winter, when it provides some respite from Lima's mist and smog. There's not much to visit here, just some country clubs, mostly private, in the valley below. Above Chosica the road starts to climb fast, winding its way past some impressive-looking hydro power stations into the Andes towards Ticlio and way beyond to the beautiful **Mantaro Valley**.

ARRIVAL AND DEPARTURE — CHOSICA

By bus Catching a bus from Chosica to Huancayo, Tarma or Huánuco can be tricky: although they pass through here, they may well be full already. Colectivos or shared taxis may be an easier solution. Buses from Lima to Chosica will usually drop passengers off and pick them up around the Parque Central.

By colectivo There are plenty of minibus colectivos connecting Lima with Chosica for around S/10 (45min–1hr 10min); in San Isidro, they leave from behind the Cine Orantia; in Lima Centro they depart from the corner of Jr Ayacucho with Av Nicolás de Piérola.

ACCOMMODATION AND EATING

Hospedaje Chosica Av 28 de Julio 134 ⊕3610841. Pleasant and good value, this is a family-run place. They have four rooms with baths and six without. S/80

Restaurant Liluzca Jr Chiclayo 250. It's difficult to do better than this place, in a small side-street off the main road by the plaza; it has outside seating and serves decent food, though it usually closes before 7pm.

North of Lima

To the north of Lima, the desert stretches up between the Pacific Ocean and the foothills of the Andes. A couple of short trips north of Lima are becoming increasingly popular as long-weekend breaks. One of these is a horseshoe loop connecting the **Chillón and Chancay valleys** via the beautiful town and region of Canta in the foothills of the Andes. Another route, further out from Lima, heads up the Huara Valley from Huacho; although the road can be traced all the way to Huánuco, most people only get as far up into the Andes as **Churin** where their efforts are pleasantly rewarded with a visit to the hot springs. Futher north again, yet still feasible as a day-trip from Lima, the recently discovered pyramids of **Caral** are considered to be the most ancient ruins in the Americas.

The Chillón and Chancay valleys

Leaving Lima and heading north, the Panamerican Highway passes through the **Chillón Valley**, dotted with ancient **ruins**, of which the most important are on the south side of the Río Chillón within 3 or 4km of the Ventanilla road. The most impressive is the 2000–3000-year-old **Temple El Paraiso**, which was built by a sedentary farming community of probably no more than 1500 inhabitants and consists of three main pyramids built of rustic stones.

From here, the Panamerican Highway passes the yacht and tennis clubs that make up the fashionable beach resort of **Ancón**, about 30km from Lima, then crosses a high, often foggy, plateau from the Chillón to the **Chancay Valley**. Still covered by sparse vegetation, this was a relatively fertile *lomas* area (where plants grow from moisture in the air rather than rainwater or irrigation) in pre-Inca days, and evidence of winter camps from five thousand years ago has been found. The highway bypasses the market town of Huaral and runs through **Chancay**, some 65km north of Lima.

Eco Truly Park

Km 63 on the Panamerican Highway • Lima contact: Av Javier Prado Este 185, San Isidro • ⓣ 4210016, ⓦ ecotrulypark.org • Coastal buses headed for Chancay, Barranca or Chimbote can drop off here

The unique domes of **Eco Truly Park** appear along the beach at Km 63 on the Panamerican Highway, by Chacra y Mar beach. Set at the foot of desert cliffs and close to the pounding ocean, this ashram offers guided tours of their adobe huts and organic gardens, plus yoga and meditation, hikes and workshops on ecology. Always book visits in advance.

Reserva Nacional Lomas de Lachay

Signposted off the Panamerican Highway between Chancay and Huacho, before the police controls at Doña María • Daily 7am–7pm

North of Chancay, the road passes through stark desert for 20km until at Km105 you reach the **Reserva Nacional Lomas de Lachay**, a protected area of unique *lomas* habitat some 5000 hectares in extent and around 600m above sea-level. Run by the Ministry of Agriculture, the centre maintains the footpaths that thread through the reserve's beautiful scenery. Formed by granite and diorite rocky intrusions some seventy million years ago, the **lomas** – at its best between June and December when it is in full bloom – is home to more than forty types of **bird**, including hummingbird, parrot, partridge, peregrine and even condor; you may also spot various species of reptile and native deer.

ARRIVAL AND DEPARTURE — RESERVA LOMAS DE LACHAY

By tour The easiest way to get to the reserve is with an organized tour from Lima (see p.81).

By car or taxi In a car or taxi from Chancay (S/20 each way; 45min), continue up the Panamerican Highway for about 6km beyond the turning for Sayan and Churin. The turn-off to the reserve is signposted at the top of a hill, but from the road it's still an hour's walk along a sandy track to the interpretive centre at the entrance to the reserve.

El Paraíso and Huacho

A little north of the Reserva Nacional Lomas de Lachay, at Km133 of the Panamerican Highway, a track turns off onto a small peninsula and leads to the secluded bay of **El Paraíso** – a magical beach perfect for camping, swimming and scuba diving. Crossing bleaker sands, the Panamerican Highway next passes through **Huacho**, an unusual place with some interesting colonial architecture and a ruined church in the upper part of town, but mostly made up of recent concrete constructions. As it's so close to Lima, it was one of the first towns to be hit by expanding and migratory populations, as well as wealthy Lima families taking on a second home or farmstead.

Into the Huara Valley

Just beyond Huacho a side road turns east into the **Huara Valley** and the foothills of the Andes to reach **Sayan**, a small farming town where little has changed for decades – the church here has a very attractive colonial interior.

1

Churin

Further up the valley from Sayan lies **CHURIN**, a small thermal spa town popular with Limeños during holidays, located in the district of Pachangara 210km from Lima. Most of the farmland on the valley floor and the Sayan-to-Churin road was washed away in the 1998 El Niño, and a new, rough road has been carved out between the boulders littering the valley floor. There are two spas in town, both fairly cool, with private and communal baths; the **El Fierro spa** (all baths cost S/1–2) is the hottest and reputed to be the most curative. It's a ten-minute ride by colectivo from town (S/1.50).

Churin is also a good base from which to explore a number of traditional communities as well as archeological **ruins**, such as Ninash, Kutun, Antasway and Kuray. For climbers, there are also some challenging **peaks** in the Cordillera Raura (up to 5700m). The main **festival** here is San Juan, between June 23 and 25, which includes a ritual procession to the river for a cleansing bath, to ensure health in the coming year.

Huancahuasi

Baths S/5

An excellent day-trip from Churin can be made to more thermal baths at **Huancahuasi**. There are two sets of hot baths here, and traditional snacks such as *pachamanca* (meat and vegetables on pre-heated rocks covered with earth and left for a few hours) are prepared outside them. En route to Huancahuasi you'll spot a remarkable, early colonial, carved facade on the tiny church at **Picoy**.

ARRIVAL AND DEPARTURE — INTO THE HUARA VALLEY

By bus There are several buses to Sayan and Churin from Lima daily (6–7hr), the best run by Transportes Estrella Polar, Av Luna Pizarro 330–338, La Victoria (☎ 3328182; expect to pay around S/12).

By colectivo Colectivos run between Sayan and Huacho every thirty minutes. Colectivos to Huancahuasi leave from Churin church at around 8am (S/12 return), returning mid-afternoon.

ACCOMMODATION AND EATING

There are many places to stay in Churin, but they all get packed out in the main holiday periods, when prices double. All of the **hotels** are within a couple of blocks of each other in the town centre. Churin has some good restaurants and cafés too, mostly around the main plaza. Local specialities include honey, *alfajores*, *manjar blanca* and cheeses.

Hotel Las Termas Av Larco Herrera 411, Churin ☎ 2373094. This well-located place has pleasant rooms, good service and a pool. S/100

Caral

Supe Valley, accessed via Carretera Caral-Las Minas Ambar from Supe Town • Daily 7am–5.30pm • S/10 • ☎ 4312235, caralperu.gob.pe

North up the coast from Huacho, only the town and port of Supe breaks the monotonous beauty of desert and ocean, until you reach Barranca and the labyrinthine ruins of the Fortress of Paramonga (see p.343). Inland from Supe, however, along the desert coast in a landscape that looks more lunar than agricultural, archeologists have uncovered one of the most important finds of the past century. Thought to be the oldest city in the Americas at around five thousand years old, the **ancient pyramids of Caral** are now a UNESCO World Heritage Site.

Brief history

From humble beginnings (see box opposite), Caral developed into one of the earliest metropolises, representing human achievements that took place four thousand years earlier than the Incas: the stone ceremonial structures here were flourishing a hundred years before the Great Pyramid at Giza was even built.

THE ORIGINS OF CARAL

Before the advent of urban living and stone ceremonial pyramids here, the region was only populated by a few **coastal villages**, each with around a hundred inhabitants. Around 2700 BC it appears that a number of larger villages emerged, principally, it seems, based around the successful domestication and early cultivation of the cotton-bush plant. The early use of **cotton** was nothing short of a bio-technological revolution, not only providing cloth for garments but more importantly permitting the fabrication of nets for fishing in the rich coastal waters, as well as net or woven bags for carrying produce and fish back home to their settlements. The introduction of cotton fishing nets transformed the lives of coastal communities, giving them sufficient protein, more spare time to evolve social and religious practices, and surplus food to trade with neighbouring communities, laying the groundwork for what was to become a thriving urban centre.

Archeologists have studied its temples, houses and plazas, and the artefacts unearthed here, to form a picture of the ancient Caral culture, which focused heavily on agriculture and construction. There's evidence of ceremonial functions, too, and music was also important: a collection of coronets and flutes have been found on site.

The site

The heart of the site covers about 150 acres. There are two large, sunken circular plazas, the base of the tallest mound measurimg 154m by 138m, making it the largest pyramid yet found in Peru. Excavations have revealed that this **Piramide Mayor** (main pyramid) was terraced, with a staircase leading up to an atrium-like platform, culminating in a flattened top housing enclosed rooms and a ceremonial fire pit. Some of the best artefacts discovered here include 32 **flutes** made from pelican and animal bones and engraved with the figures of birds and even monkeys, demonstrating a connection with the Amazon region.

The six mounds, or pyramids, are arranged together around a large plaza. Archeologists believe that the pyramids were constructed in a maximum of two phases, which suggests a need for particularly complex social structures for planning, decision-making and the mobilization of a large sector of the population to provide sufficient labour as and when it was required. Around the pyramids is evidence of many residential structures.

ARRIVAL AND DEPARTURE — CARAL

By bus and colectivo Transportes Paramonga (Av Luna Pizarro 251, La Victoria; ⓣ 4236338, ⓦ turismoparamonga.com.pe) run buses every day to Supe, usually leaving around 6.20am. From here, if unguided, you'd need to take a colectivo (S/6; 45min), which leave regularly from near the market in Supe centre.

By car Easier to reach with your own car, Caral is connected to the Panamerican Highway by a badly rutted dirt-track road that starts at Km 184 of the Pamerican Highway and continues for 23km to the site.

By tour Fertur Peru (see p.81) offer a day-trip from around $80 per person, including guide, bus and taxi to the site.

Nasca and the south coast

PARACAS NATIONAL RESERVE

2

Nasca and the south coast

South of Lima, a beautiful dry desert stretches the entire 1330km to Chile. In places just a narrow strip of desert squashed between Andes and Pacific, it is followed diligently by the Panamerican Highway. The region harbours one of South America's greatest archeological mysteries – the famous Nasca Lines – as well as offering access to coastal wildlife and stunning landscapes. Once home to at least three major pre-Inca cultures – the Paracas (500 BC–400 AD), the influential Nasca (500–800 AD) and the Ica culture – this region of Peru was eventually taken over by the Incas. Today, Nasca and Paracas are very much part of the tourist trail and are often visited en route between Lima and Cusco.

Once beyond Lima's beaches, the first significant town is **Cañete**, which is of little interest itself, but is a gateway to the attractive **Lunahuana** valley, well known as a river-rafting centre as well as for its vineyards. Just south of here, near the town of **Pisco** and the emerging coastal resort of **Paracas** (previously known as El Chaco), **Paracas National Reserve** and the offshore **Islas Ballestas** take a couple of days out of most travellers' time, offering an exciting mix of wildlife – including sea lions, dolphins and sharks – boat trips and ancient archeology.

Just inland from Pisco, the adobe Inca remains of **Tambo Colorado** are an interesting diversion, perhaps rounded off by a great seafood dinner at the fisherman's wharf in **San Andrés**. Hidden in sand dunes just outside the city of **Ica**, the resort of **Huacachina** combines peaceful desert oasis with sandboarding. A couple of hours' drive south, the geometric shapes and giant figures of the **Nasca Lines** are etched over almost 500 square kilometres of bleak pampa. Nasca also offers access to the outstanding, rare *vicuña* reserve of **Pampa Galeras** (in the Andes above Nasca).

Further south, just before the town of Chala, **Puerto Inca** is a stunning but still relatively undeveloped beach resort, at one time a coastal port for the nobles of Inca Cusco. Once past the town of Camaná, south of Chala, the **Panamericana Sur highway** runs inland to within almost 40km of Arequipa (see Chapter Three), where there's a fast road connection into the city. From here the highway cuts south across undulating desert to the calm colonial town of **Moquegua**, a springboard for the region's archeological heritage, before heading south another 150km to **Tacna**, the last pit-stop before the **frontier with Chile**.

GETTING AROUND — THE SOUTH COAST

Transport is not usually a problem along the south coast, with local buses connecting all the towns with each other and with Lima, and express buses ploughing along the coastal road between Lima and Arequipa day and night.

By bus The best bus company serving the south coast is Cruz del Sur (01 3246332, cruzdelsur.com). A more frequent service from Lima to all towns as far south as Ica, is the Peru Bus Soyuz/Peru Bus, Av México 333, La Victoria

SANDBUGGY, HUACACHINA

Highlights

❶ **Lunahuana** This beautiful coastal valley is almost always sunny, and a focus for whitewater rafting and mountain biking as well as good local wines and piscos. **See p.111**

❷ **Ballestas Islands** Within a morning's boat ride from the town of Pisco, these are guano islands covered in bird and mammalian marine life. **See p.116**

❸ **Paracas National Reserve** A beautiful peninsula with stunning desert landscapes touching the Pacific Ocean; both beaches and sea are a haven for wildlife, and there is a museum dedicated to the ancient Paracas culture. **See p.116**

❹ **Huacachina** A magical oasis surrounded by some of the most arid sand-dune desert landscapes in the Americas, Huacachina is both a leisure resort and a healing spa. **See p.128**

❺ **Nasca Lines** The world-famous Nasca Lines, including stylized geometric and animal figures, were etched, seemingly impossibly, into a massive desert pampa. **See p.129**

❻ **Puerto Inca** This small but secluded resort lies in an area of coast teeming with rare Inca remains as well as offering great access to beaches, coves, fishing and excellent diving. **See p.140**

HIGHLIGHTS ARE MARKED ON THE MAP ON P.110

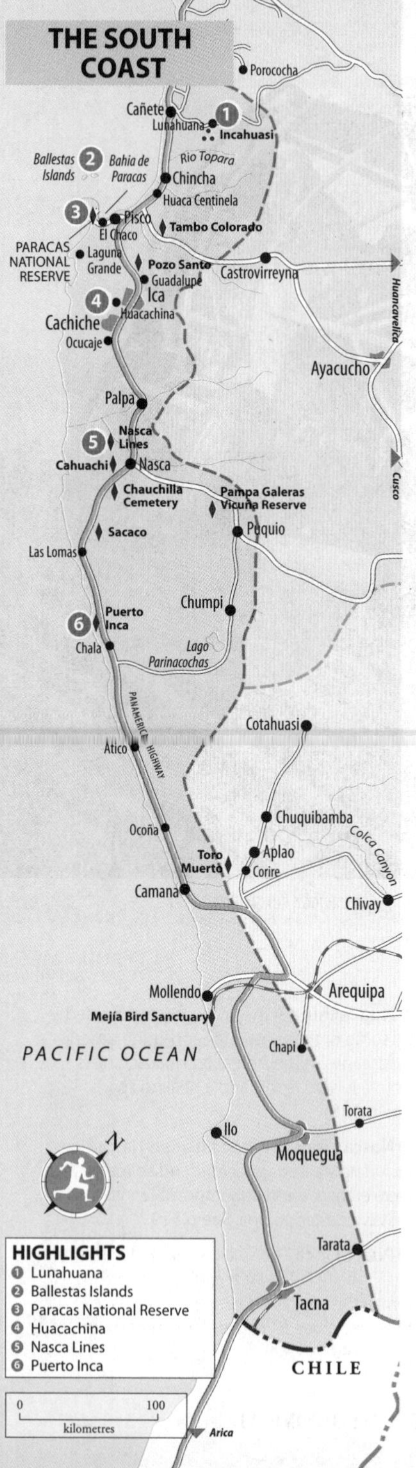

(☎01 4276310, 🌐soyuz.com.pe); these buses leave every 10min during the day (every 30min at night) and can also be picked up from obvious bus stops along the Panamericana Sur in Lima (ie where the highway is crossed by either Av Javier Prado Este or Av Benavides Este).

By colectivo from Ica From Ica, it's fun to travel on to Nasca with one of the last Peruvian road routes still connected by large 1970s colectivo cars, mainly Dodge Coronets, allowing anyone who fancies doing this segment of the coast a trip – of three hours or so – through glorious desert scenery in relative style and comfort.

Cañete

Around two hours' or so drive from Lima brings you to the busy market town of **CAÑETE**. This is not an obviously attractive town in itself, despite some colonial flavour, but the surrounding marigold and cotton fields and easy access to the nearby district and small town of Lunahuana (see opposite) grant it a certain appeal. In many ways, Cañete and its surrounding area is the nearest place from Lima where you can get a feel for the rural desert coast and there is almost constant sunshine year round. New roads extend nearly all the way from Lima, but this particular valley has not yet been overdeveloped or populated with factories or *pueblos jovenes* (shanties).

ARRIVAL CAÑETE

BY BUS

Most buses on the south-coast road pass through Cañete and stop briefly but you should check this with the bus company before buying your ticket if you need to get off, since there's a new stretch of Panamericana which now bypasses Cañete, taking a route between the town and the ocean.

Bus companies Peru Soyuz Bus (Jr Unanue 20; ☎01 5811391, 🌐soyuz.com.pe) connects with Paracas, Ica and Nasca as well as north with Lima. Cruz del Sur usually stops on Dos de Mayo. For Lunahuana take a bus for Yauyos (usually leaves daily around 3pm), which departs from Dos de Mayo. ETAS buses run once or twice a week from Cañete to Huancayo via Lunahuana.

Destinations Huancayo (weekly; 10–15hr); Ica (every 20min; 2hr 30min); Lima (hourly; 2–3hr); Lunahuana (several daily; 1hr); Nasca (every 20min; 4hr 15min); Paracas (every 20min; 2hr); Yauyos (weekly; 5–8hr).

BY COLECTIVO

Colectivos all arrive on the old Panamericana in town, opposite the intersection with Dos de Mayo or on Dos de Mayo itself. As with most colectivos, these are informal operators with no specific depot. Colectivos generally leave for Lunahuana from Dos de Mayo during the day (first block coming from the Old Panamericana.)

Lunahuana

2

Just 35km east of Cañete, the pleasant river-based resort of **LUNAHUANA** is home to several hotels and a wide variety of tour agencies offering trekking, mountain biking, valley tours, whitewater rafting or canoeing. The place varies in feel considerably depending whether it is the busy time (mainly Dec–March, plus one week either side of the national holiday on July 28) – when there are festivals for the grape harvest combined with rafting competitions. Outside these, it's empty and laidback. Few foreign visitors come here; it mainly sees a young and sporty crowd from Lima.

Lunahuana and the surrounding area consists of beautifully sculpted, dusty mountainsides surrounding a narrow, irrigated and fertile green valley floor. As well as abundant vineyards, some of which can be visited on tours (see below), the valley is also dedicated to cultivating maize, cotton, rice, avocados, chillies, limes, papayas and bananas. And as well as adventure sports, Lunahuana is a great base for exploring the local Inca archeological complex of **Incahuasi**.

On the plaza there's a fine colonial church with a cool interior and a sky-blue wooden vaulted ceiling. Within easy striking distance there's a horse dressage (*caballos de paso*) centre, a traditional hanging bridge, plus rustic **pisco haciendas**, such as the *Bodega Fidelina Candela*, Anexo Jita, at Km 37 (Lima ⊕0128 41030).

Incahuasi

Incahuasi was established by the Inca Emperor Pachacuti (1438–71), who created his empire by expanding the territorial base out of the Cusco Valley; this was one of his coastal palaces, hunting lodge and optimum spot for his administrators and soldiers to control the flow of goods and people in and out of the Andes. What remains are scattered low stone and mud walls in a dominant position overlooking the northern section of Lunahuana Town and the cemetery.

ARRIVAL AND DEPARTURE — LUNAHUANA

By bus Buses stop on Jr Grau, within walking distance of the Plaza de Armas.

By colectivo Colectivos drop you on Jr Grau or the Plaza de Armas. The far end of Jr Grau is close to the river and *Camping Lunahuana*.

By taxi Taxis to Lunahuana from Cañete (S/30) are usually available in the town centre, around the bus stops on the main through-road.

TOURS

Cicloturismo Peru ⊕4337981, ⊛cicloturismoperu.com. An online source of information about cycling tours, bike rentals and events.

Hemiriver Adventures Jr Grau 255 ⊕01 5347342, ⊛hemiriver.com. Short city tours (from $10 depending on size of group). Their offices are located 2 or 3 blocks from the Plaza de Armas.

Lunahuana Adventure Tours Jr Grau ⊕96143873. Tours for trekking and adventure action; rafting usually costs $20–35 for about an hour on the river – including guide, transport and training – depending on the season (cheapest in low season, May–Oct).

Peru Cycling ⊕1 990 128105, ⊛perucycling.com. Offers 2-day cycle tours into and around Lunahuana; check website for prices.

Popy Tours Jr Grau 380 ⊕2841162. Minibus tours to the main valley sights, including vineyards.

Rio Cañete Expediciones Jr Grau 284 ⊕1 2841271 or ⊕96353921, ⊛riocanete.com. A 9km river-run from Lunahuana, taking around 1hr 30min, but also offer shorter runs. From $35 a person, depending on size of group.

2

ACCOMMODATION

Camping Lunahuana Entry at the opposite end of Jr Grau to the Plaza de Armas. Usually has space available. Prices are likely to rise in high season. S/15

Camping El Tambo Annexo Condoray ⊤5318413. Carmen Hererra runs a good campsite with toilets at Km 41.2, some 10km up the valley from town. S/15

La Fortaleza del Inca Carretera Central Km 31.5 ⊤99411864, ⓦfortalezainca.com. Located a few kilometres before the main Lunahuana settlement and Plaza de Armas, *La Fortaleza* has pleasant, well-equipped rooms with private showers based around a courtyard dominated by a swimming pool; breakfast around the pool is included. S/80

Hostal Casurinas Jr Grau 295 ⊤2841045. Cheap option with clean, hot showers and basic rooms, located near the action within the main Lunahuana settlement and near the Plaza de Armas. Rooms are more expensive during busy weekends and national fiestas. S/40

Hotel Embassy ⊤2841194, ⓦhotelesembassy.com. A large, concrete, modern resort hotel, this place has much less style and comfort, though it does offer a riverside location, reasonably big pool and bar/disco. Rooms S/75

Refugio de Santiago C Real 33, Paullo, Lunahuana Km 31 ⊤991991259 or ⊤01 4362717, ⓦrefugiodesantiago.com. A fascinating and beautifully furnished hostel inside a colonial-style house, with an internal courtyard bar and a few acres of gardens with outside tables, this is one of the finest restaurants (dishes based around indigenous and ancient fruits, herbs and vegetables) south of Lima. They also offer camping in the garden, and run walking and minibus tours to interesting sites around the valley. Book well in advance. Camping S/10, doubles S/70

EATING

El Refugio C Real 33, Paullo, Lunahuana Km 31. This place provides undoubtedly the best cuisine in the valley, served out in the gardens in fine weather. The owner-chef takes great pride in cooking fresh home-grown herbs and vegetables; unfortunately, it is not always open to day-visitors. It is very important to call in advance and check opening times outside of high season. Daily noon–6pm.

Restaurant Antojitos Plaza de Armas. Serves freshly cooked meals, from breakfast through to late-evening snacks and meals; they also stock some local wines and brandy and offer a genuine local atmosphere. Daily 8am–9pm.

DIRECTORY

Internet Available in the major hotels and also in cabins close to the main Plaza, at Jr Grau 311.

Money and exchange Banco de la Nación, Jr Grau 398. It's best to bring enough soles with you as the rate may be poor and there are no other options.

Chincha

Languishing at the top of a cliff, **CHINCHA** is a relatively rich oasis that appears after a stretch of almost Saharan landscape – and a mightily impressive sand dune. A busy little coastal centre renowned for its cheap wines and variety of **piscos** (brandies), Chincha is a strong cultural hub for **Afro-Peruvian culture**; the town was developed during the early colonial period when Africans (mainly from Guinea) were brought over as slaves to work on the cotton plantations. Chincha is dominated by two roads running north to south; most hotels and restaurants are on the main Panamericana itself.

Archeological sites

A taxi from Chincha will take you to the sites for S/40–50, depending on how long you want the driver to wait

The Chincha area has a number of **ruins**, with numerous *huacas* lying scattered about the oasis. Dominated in pre-Inca days by the Cuismancu (or Chincha) state, activity focused around what were probably ceremonial pyramids. One of these, the majestic **Huaca Centinela** – also known as the little city of Chinchacamac – sits in the valley below the Chincha tableland and the ocean, around thirty minutes' walk from the town, some 8km off the Panamericana. Not far from Chincha, 40km up the Castrovireyna road (which leaves the Panamerican Highway at Km 230) is another impressive Cuismancu ruin, Tambo Colorado (see p.120).

CHINCHA'S FESTIVALS

The main local festival – **National Pisco Day** – takes place on the third Saturday in September, when things really get lively along this section of the coast. The area is also well-known for its traditionally rhythmic music and annual, athletic dance festival, **Verano Negro**, which happens at the end of February. In November, the **Festival de Danzas Negras** is an excellent spectacle, a vibrant dance event based on Afro-Peruvian traditions; in both cases the celebrations are liveliest in El Carmen, 10km southeast of Chincha.

2

Hacienda San José

Pueblo San José • Daily 9am–6pm • Free • Catacomb tours 45min; $3 • ⓣ 056 221458

Don't miss the **Hacienda San José** – now converted into a hotel (see below) – based 9km southeast of Chincha in an extensive plantation. Its colourful history includes the tale of an owner murdered on the house's main steps by his slaves, and it still sports impressive Churrigueresque-domed towers built in the 1680s. Note that you don't necessarily have to take a room: non-guests can use the pool and watch local folklore shows, and there are **tours** around the labyrinthine **catacombs**, themselves containing prison cells still clearly showing the poor conditions in which slaves were once shackled.

ARRIVAL AND DEPARTURE — CHINCHA

By bus Most bus connections to and from Chincha are at the Terminal Terrestre, Avenida Benavides, close to the big bend in the Panamerican Highway as it enters the urban areas of town from the north. Peru Soyuz Bus (Av. Benavides 704; ⓣ 056 269239, ⓦ soyuz.com.pe) connects every 20min south with Paracas, Ica and Nasca as well as north with Lima.

By colectivo Colectivos and taxis drop off and pick up on main Panamericana Sur, as well as around the big bend in the Panamerican Highway as it enters town from the north and crosses over Jr Santo Domingo.

BODEGA TOURS

Bodega Naldo Navarro Pasaje Santa Rosa, Sunampe ⓣ 056 271356, ⓦ vinosnaldonavarro.com. A 100-year-old bodega that's one of the best places for pisco and local wine (*vino dulce*). Based 1km north of Chincha, it offers free guided tours and samples; call to check opening times and when there are special music events.

ACCOMMODATION

Hacienda San José Not operational at the time of writing – ask for an update at *Hotel Casa Andina Classic* (see below).

Hostal El Condado Km 195 on the Panamerican Highway ⓣ 056 261424, ⓔ hostalcondado@terra.com. A rather elegant and upmarket hostel with a pool and reasonable restaurant at the northern entry to Chincha. S/200

Hotel Casa Andina Classic Km 197.5 on the Panamerican Highway ⓣ 01 2139739, ⓦ casa-andina.com. This plush, hacienda-style hotel has its own pool and football pitch. S/350

Hotel El Valle Panamerican Highway (no number) ⓣ 056 262556. A smart place, which offers good rooms at reasonable prices. If these are booked, you can try any one of the several hotels located on the main street. S/65

EATING

Palacio de Mariscos *Hotel El Valle* (see above). Serves good local cuisine and seafood in a pleasant environment; it's best for lunches. Non-residents 11am–9pm.

Restaurant El Fogon Plaza Bolognesi. Pretty standard Peruvian food on offer here with acceptable service and a generally busy, brisk ambience; if you want a full meal the *lomo saltado* (S/14) is a decent enough choice. Daily 8am–8pm.

Pisco and around

Less than three hours by bus from Lima, the old port town of **PISCO** has long been a rewarding stop en route to Nasca, Arequipa or the frontier with Chile. Along with the neighbouring town, **Paracas** – 12km away and previously known as **El Chaco** – Pisco makes a handy base for visiting the **Paracas National Reserve**, **Ballestas Islands** and the well-preserved Inca coastal outpost of **Tambo Colorado**. The two towns, with good facilities and plenty of tour operators, restaurants and hostels, are also decent stop-offs before heading up into the Andes: you can take roads from here to Huancavelica and Huancayo, as well as to Ayacucho and Cusco.

The region's past has been far from uneventful. An earthquake hit in the evening of August 15, 2007, and, measuring 8.0 on the Richter Scale, devastated Pisco and the entire surrounding area – and it's still reeling from the aftermath. Hundreds of people were killed and over 15,000 made homeless. Pisco, which remains one of the most active seismic spots on earth, is still complaining that little of the promises made for rapid redevelopment have thus far materialized.

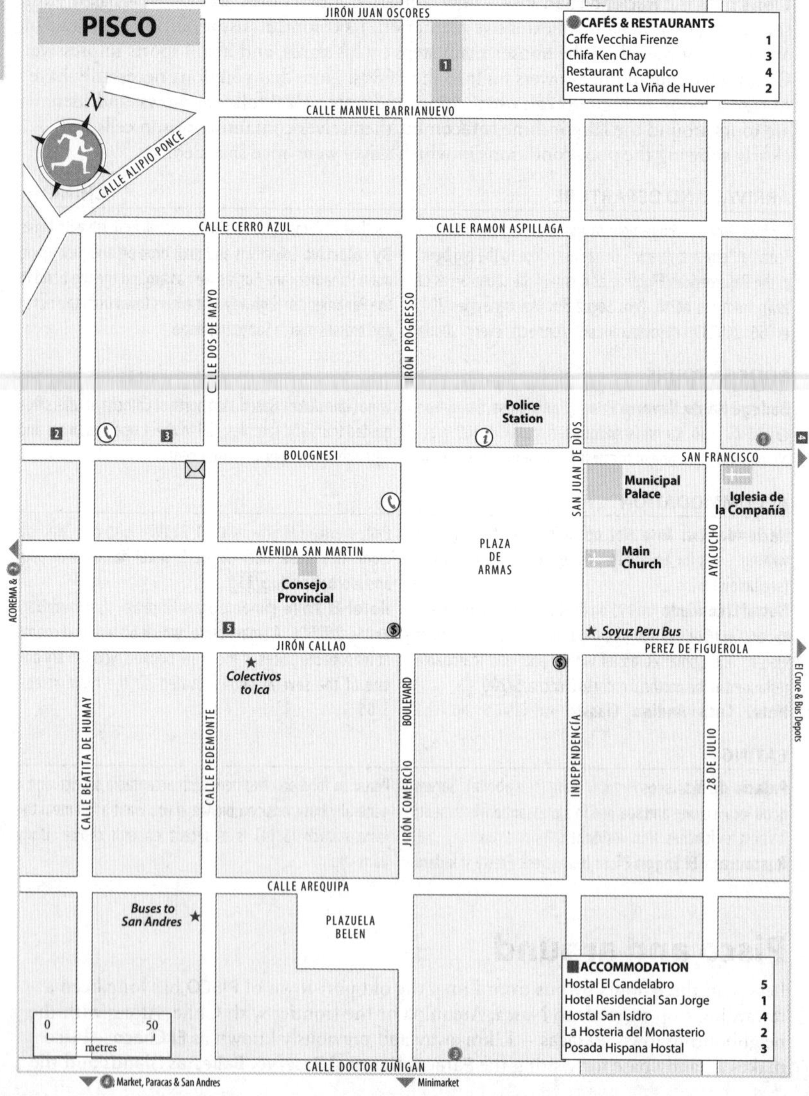

Plaza de Armas

Pisco's focus of activity is the **Plaza de Armas** and adjoining **Jirón Comercio**; every evening the plaza is crowded with people walking and talking, buying *tejas* (small sweets made from pecan nuts) from street sellers, or chatting in one of several laidback cafés and bars around the square. Clustered about the plaza, with its statue of liberator San Martín poised in the shade of ancient ficus trees, are a few fine colonial showpieces, including the mansion where San Martín stayed on his arrival in Peru, half a block west of the plaza. Unusual in its Moorish style, the **Consejo Provincial** (or Municipal Palace), just to the left if you're facing the earthquake-destroyed church on the Plaza de Armas, is painted in striking blue and white in memory of the liberator San Martín's own colours.

Iglesia de la Compañía

Calle San Francisco • Mon–Sat 8am–6pm • Free

One block from the Plaza de Armas, the heavy Baroque **Iglesia de la Compañía**, built in 1689, originally boasted a superb carved pulpit and gold-leaf altarpiece, plus some crypts with subterranean galleries; however, it was all but destroyed by the big 2007 earthquake. A temporary looking anti-seismic bamboo-and-concrete construction has taken its place with no attempt at repeating the original Baroque style.

Avenida San Martín

If you have an hour or so to spare, it's worth exploring **Avenida San Martín** from the plaza west (fifteen to twenty minutes' walking to the sea), but beware – there have been tourist muggings here in recent years, so go in a group. Here you can see the decaying remains of the old pier, second in size only to the Muelle de Pacasmayo in the north of Peru, and notice just how much further out the sea edge is today than it clearly was a hundred or so years ago.

The ACOREMA Centre

Av San Martín 1471 • Daily 10am–1pm & 2–6pm • S/4 (half-price with student card) • T 056 532046, W acorema.org.pe

The Avenida San Martín is also traditional home to many of Pisco's finest mansions, one of which was converted into the **ACOREMA Centre**, a small maritime ecology museum with varied and fascinating collections of shells, interpretative displays, bones of a five-metre humpback whale and the skeleton of a Gray's beaked whale.

San Andrés

Reached via taxi from Pisco (S/10) • Moving on, there are usually at least two buses hourly on to the El Chaco wharf in El Balneario, where boats leave for the Ballestas Islands (see p.116)

South along the shore from Pisco Town towards Paracas, the road keeps close to the shoreline and there's a fisherman's jetty at **SAN ANDRÉS**, where fresh fish is received and taken straight to the nearby restaurants or to Pisco market. This is a great place to enjoy a fish dinner.

Paracas

Paracas, lying on the road from San Andrés past the Pisco air force base, is arguably a more scenic place to base yourself than Pisco. The resort (also known as El Baneario or El Chaco) was once a spot for wealthy Limeños, whose expensive resort hotels and large bungalows line the beach close to the entrance to the reserve, but now reasonably priced hostels and restaurants dominate the scene. It's also possible to **camp** on the

2

SEA TURTLES, DOLPHINS AND WHALES

San Andrés is still known for its **sea turtle** dishes, even though it is now **illegal** to serve them due to the danger of extinction. Warm turtle blood is occasionally drunk in the region, reputedly as a cure for bronchial problems. These days, in order to save these endangered turtles from extinction, it's recommended that visitors avoid turtle dishes and perhaps even consider the merits of reporting any restaurant which offers it, to a turtle conservation group. The seas around here are traditionally rich in fish life, and **dolphins** are often spotted. The abundant plankton in the ocean around Pisco and Paracas attracts five species of **whale**, and in 1988 a new, small species – the *Mesoplodon peruvianus*, which can be up to 4m long – was discovered after being caught accidentally in fishermen's nets.

sand, though the nearby Paracas Reserve (see below) is a much nicer place to pitch a tent. The wharf here, surrounded by pelicans, is the place to board **speedboats** (*lanchas*), for a quick zip across the sea, circling one or two of the islands and passing close to the famous Paracas Trident (see p.118).

Ballestas Islands

The **Ballestas Islands** (often called the Guano Islands, as every centimetre is covered in bird droppings), are similar to the Galapagos but on a smaller scale and lie off the coast due west from Pisco. They seem to be alive and moving with a mass of flapping, noisy pelicans, penguins, terns, boobies and Guanay cormorants. The name *Ballesta* is Spanish for crossbow, and may derive from times when marine mammals and larger fish were hunted with mechanical crossbow-style harpoons. There are scores of islands, many of them relatively small and none larger than a couple of football pitches together. The waters are generally rough but modern boats can get close to the rocks and beaches where abundant wildlife sleep, feed and mate. The waters around the islands are equally full of life, sometimes sparkling black with the shiny dark bodies of sea lions and the occasional killer whale. It's best to take a **tour** (see p.119) to visit these islands; guides on the boats vary in ability, but most are knowledgeable and informative about marine and bird life.

Paracas National Reserve

Reserve 6am–6pm • S/5; pay at guard booth, located on the entrance road to the reserve • **Paracas Visitor Centre** Lies 2km beyond guard booth • Daily 7am–6pm • Free • To get to the reserve, take a taxi from Paracas (from S/20/hr) or join a tour organized with one of the local agents (see p.119) or hotels

Of greater wildlife interest than the Ballestas Islands (see above), the **Paracas National Reserve**, a few kilometres south of Paracas, was established in 1975, mainly to protect the marine wildlife. Its bleak 117,000 hectares of pampa are frequently lashed by strong winds and sandstorms (*paracas* means "raining sand" in Quechua). Home to some of the world's richest seas (a couple of hundred hectares of ocean is included within the reserve's borders), an abundance of marine plankton gives nourishment to a vast array of fish and various marine species including octopus, squid, whale, shark, dolphin, bass, plaice and marlin. This unique desert is also a staging point for a host of migratory birds and acts as a sanctuary for many endangered species. Schools of dolphin play in the waves offshore; condors scour the peninsula for food; small desert foxes come down to the beaches looking for birds and dead sea lions; and lizards scrabble across the hot sands. People have also been active here – predecessors of the pre-Inca Paracas culture arrived here some 9000 years ago, reaching their peak between 2000 and 500 BC.

On the way from Pisco to the reserve, the road passes some unpleasant-smelling fish-meal-processing factories, which are causing environmental concern due to spillages of fish oil that pollute the bay, endangering bird and sea-mammal life. Just before the entrance to the reserve, you'll pass a bleak but unmistakeable concrete obelisk vaguely shaped like a nineteenth-century sailing boat, built in 1970 to commemorate the landing of San Martín here on September 8, 1820, on his mission to liberate Peru from the Spanish stranglehold.

Cycling is encouraged in the reserve, though there are no rental facilities and, if you do enter on a bike, keep on the main tracks because the tyre marks will damage the surface of the desert.

Museo de Sitio Julio Tello

Tues–Sun 9am–3pm • S/20

Located 2km beyond the reserve entrance and park office at Km 27, right between the two major Paracas archeological sites – Cerro Colorado and Cabeza Largas – this

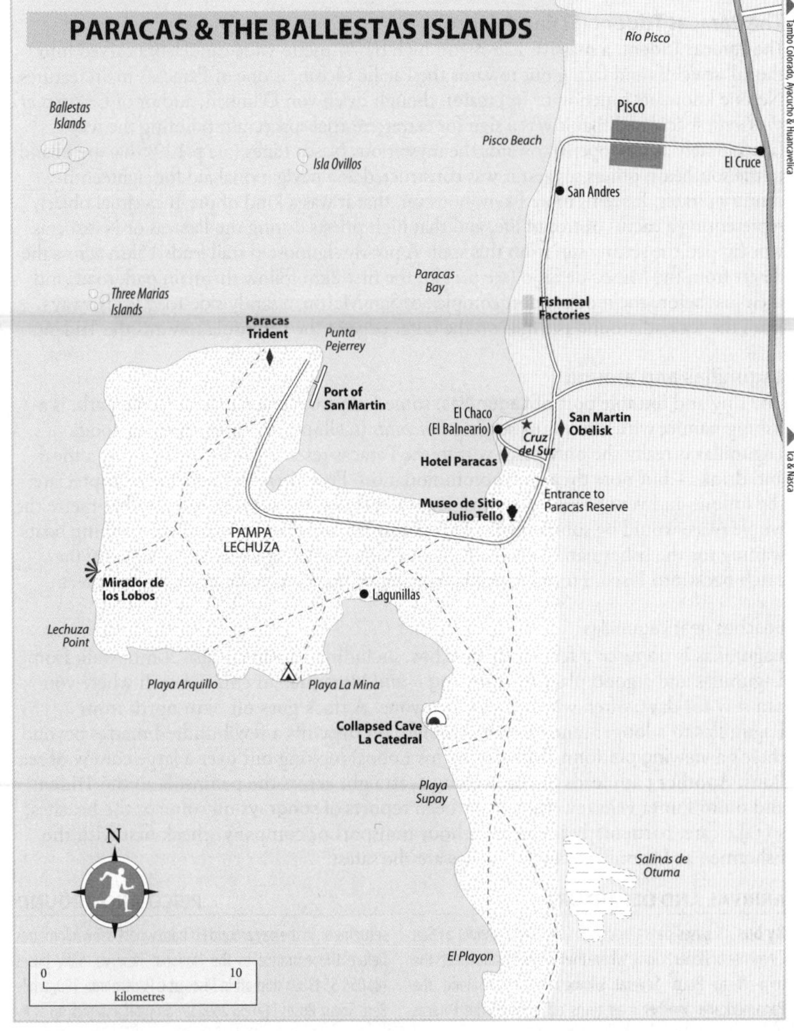

2

museum depicts human life here over the last 9000 years, with interpretative exhibits relating to the national park and a wide range of Paracas artefacts – mummies, ceramics, funerary cloths and a reconstructed dwelling.

Necropolis of Cabeza Largas

The oldest discovered archeological site in the region, the 5000-year-old **Necropolis of Cabeza Largas**, once containing up to sixty mummies in one grave, is located just outside the Museo de Siteo at Km 27. Most mummies were wrapped in *vicuña* skins or rush matting, and buried along with personal objects like shell beads, bone necklaces, lances, net bags and cactus-spine needles. A little further on, near the beach where dozens of pink flamingoes gather between July and November (they return to the high Andean lakes for breeding from December to May), are the remains of a Chavín-related settlement, known as **Disco Verde**, though all there is left to see now are a few adobe walls.

The Paracas Trident (El Candelabro)

The Paracas Trident, a massive 128-metre-high by 74-metre-wide candelabra carved into the tall sea cliffs and facing out towards the Pacific Ocean, is one of Paracas's main features. No one knows its function or its creator, though Erich von Däniken, author of *Chariots of the Gods*, speculated that it was a sign for extraterrestrial spacecraft, pointing the way (inaccurately as it happens) towards the mysterious Nasca Lines (see p.129) that are inland to the southeast; others suggest it was constructed as a navigational aid for eighteenth-century pirates. It seems more likely, however, that it was a kind of pre-Inca ritual object, representing a cactus or tree of life, and that high priests during the Paracas or Nasca eras worshipped the setting sun from this spot. A poorly signposted trail leads 15km across the desert from the Museo de Sitio (see p.117); the first 2km follow the main park road, and then just before the modern port complex of San Martín, a sandy side-road leads away from the sea and around the hills on the outer edge of the peninsula towards the Trident.

Lagunillas and around

The tiny and likeable port of **Lagunillas**, some 6km from the entrance to the park, is a fishing hamlet with a few huts serving *conchitas* (scallops) and other great seafood. Lagunillas is really the only place within the Paracas reserve where you can buy a meal and drinks – but note there's no accommodation. From here, it's possible to appreciate the unique and very beautiful peninsula, so flat that if the sea rose just another metre the whole place would be submerged. Pelicans and sea lions hang around the bobbing boats waiting for the fisherman to drop a fish, and little trucks regularly arrive to carry the catch back into Pisco. From Lagunillas the rest of the Paracas Reserve is at your feet.

Beaches near Lagunillas

Lagunillas is home to a few lovely **beaches**, including **La Mina** – just 20min walk from Lagunillas and a good place for **camping** – and **Yimaque**, an empty beach where you can stay for days, often without seeing anyone. A track goes off 5km north from Lagunillas to a longer sandy beach, **Arquillo**; on the cliffs a few hundred metres beyond there's a **viewing platform** (Mirador de los Lobos) looking out over a large colony of sea lions. Another path leads north from here, straight across the peninsula to the Trident and on to Punta Pejerrey. There have been **reports of stingrays** on some of the beaches, so take care, particularly if you're without transport or company; check first with the fishermen at Lagunillas which beaches are the safest.

ARRIVAL AND DEPARTURE — PISCO AND AROUND

By bus All buses pass through El Cruce (also known as San Clemente or Repartición), where the Panamericana meets the turn-off to Pisco. Several kilometres further along the Panamericana another road turns off right to the Paracas settlement, in the bay around El Chaco wharf, a few kilometres before the entrance to the National Reserve. Saky buses (☎ 056 554309) stop off in Pisco at C Pedemonte 190, while Peru Soyuz Buses (☎ 056 269239) drop off and pick up at Av

Ernesto Diez Canseco 41. Cruz del Sur (☎056 536636) go direct to Paracas, where they have a depot at C Independencia, Mz A, Lot 20. The Oltursa bus from Lima (☎994 616492) also stops in Paracas, outside the *Hotel Double Tree* by the *Hilton Paracas* in El Chaco. If for some reason you end up alighting at El Cruz, there are regular colectivos from here to both Pisco (S/2; 10min) and Paracas (S/5; 25min); all south-coastal buses also pass through El Cruz, so it has some potential as a place to pick up buses back to Lima or further south.

Destinations Ica (several daily; 1hr); Lima (several daily; 3hr); Nasca (several daily; 3hr).

2

GETTING AROUND

Most travellers use one of the local tour companies (see below) located in town or affiliated to hostels to get the most out of their time in and around Pisco and Paracas.

On foot Pisco is small enough to walk around the main attractions.

By taxi A taxi anywhere in the central area should cost less than S/3–4.

INFORMATION AND TOURS

Tourist information Available from the regional tourism directorate (Mon–Fri 8am–7pm; ⓦpisco.info) in the Subprefectura's office next to the police station on the Plaza de Armas; they also have a list of official guides in the area and sometimes maps or photocopied information on the town, islands and local beaches. A somewhat better information service is offered by the staff at the *Posada Hispana Hostal*, Bolognesi 222 (☎056 536363, ⓦposadahispana.com), who provide informed details about most of the local sites of interest and worthwhile places to eat.

Tours The companies below operate package excursions to the Islas Ballestas (see p.116) and Paracas National Reserve (see p.116) with good guides and a reliable service. A speedboat takes you out to the Ballestas Islands; after this most people continue on the tour from the Playa El Chaco wharf (Paracas Bay) to the main sights in the Paracas National Reserve. It's a standard package costing S/40 (2–3hr) for the islands morning trip and a further S/40 for the afternoon tour of the reserve. Most of these companies also organize tours to Tambo Colorado (see p.120) and offer a discount for ten or more people. Choose from: Paracas Overland, C San Francisco 111 (☎056 533855, ⓦparacasoverland.com.pe); Paracas Explorer, Av Paracas Mz D Lote 5 (*Hostal Los Frayles*), El Chaco, Paracas (☎056 545141 or ☎056 531487); Zarcillo Connections, C Independencia A20, Pisco (☎056 536636, ⓦzarcilloconnections.com); Paracas Inca Tour, Av Manco Capac Mz 32, Lot 1, El Chaco, Paracas (☎056 532466).

ACCOMMODATION

Most of the accommodation options below are located 12km south along the seafront and by Paracas Bay, pleasantly away from noisy Pisco town centre; Paracas is quickly being developed as a resort.

PISCO

Hostal El Candelabro Jr Callao 190–198 ☎056 532620, ⓦhoteleselcandelabro.com. A luxurious, stone-and-concrete modern building, it lacks local style, but nevertheless has excellent service; all rooms are equipped with minibar, TV and bath. S/85

Hostal San Isidro San Clemente 103 ☎056 536471, ⓦsanisidrohostal.com. In a relatively peaceful and safe area of Pisco, this place is friendly and clean. Tours can be arranged via staff. S/50

La Hostería del Monasterio Av Bolognesi 326 ☎056 531383, ⓦlahosteriadelmonasterio.com. Close to and under same ownership as the *Posada Hispana* (see opposite), this is well kept, with reliable hot water and TVs in every room. S/90

Hotel Residencial San Jorge Barrio Nuevo 133 ☎056 532885, ⓦhotelsanjorgeresidebcial.com. A modern hotel, three short blocks north of the town centre, and with two entrances: one on the Barrio Nuevo road, one block nearer the plaza than the Jr Juan Oscores entrance. Rooms are clean and well-furnished with private bath, and there's a bit of a garden with ample parking. S/120

Posada Hispana Hostal Av Bolognesi 222 ☎056 536363, ⓦposadahispana.com. One of the best choices in Pisco – very safe and well decorated with friendly and helpful staff who are always happy to provide good tourist information. All rooms are clean and equipped with a TV, telephone, private bath and reliable hot water. Laundry facilities are available, and breakfast is served on the rooftop patio. S/75

PARACAS

Hostal El Mirador El Chaco ☎056 545086, ⓦelmiradorhotel.com. A popular place close to the ocean which has a pool, games room and serves meals; they can also help organize tours; best to make reservations in advance. S/190

Hostal Los Zarcillos Av Paracas Lote 106, Urb. El Golf ☎056 545082, ⓕ056 545082. Modern and comfortable, this hostel is fairly close to the beach area in Paracas (close to El Chaco); it offers excellent value with small but pleasant rooms and a pool. S/50

Hotel Paracas Av 173, Ribera del Mar, El Balneario, El Chaco ⓣ056 545100. A luxurious option worth the money, with pool, excellent bar and restaurant (open to non-residents) right on the ocean and the edge of Paracas Reserve, close to Playa El Chaco wharf. It's very popular as a weekend retreat for wealthy Limeños, and quite good as a base for fishing trips and watersports. S/300

Refugio del Pirata Av Paracas D-6, El Balneario, El Chaco ⓣ056 545054, ⓦrefugiodelpirata.com. Some of the tidy rooms have sea views; there is a parking area, wi-fi and cable TV. S/120

PARACAS NATIONAL RESERVE

Camping The reserve's natural attractions include plenty of superb, deserted beaches where you can camp for days without seeing anything except the lizards and birdlife, and maybe a couple of fishing boats. Free

EATING AND NIGHTLIFE

Most Pisco restaurants specialize in a wide range of locally caught fish and seafood. Nightlife is restricted to the lively pubs and bars, on or within a block or two of the main plaza, as well as on the beach and in hotels out in the Paracas area.

PISCO

Caffé Vecchia Firenze San Francisco 327. A great little snack bar with the best coffee in town; they also serve cakes, local sweets (*tejas*) made from pecan nuts with sugar coating, and sandwiches. Daily 8am–9pm.

Chifa Ken Chay C Doctor Zunigan 131. Just two blocks south of the plaza, this Chinese restaurant serves surprisingly good-quality *chifa* dishes for a relatively small town; good food and great value. Daily 11am–9pm.

Restaurant Acapulco Av Genaro Medrano 620. Located just fifty yards or so from the main fisherman's wharf at San Andrés, this is one of the more traditional and popular seafood restaurants in the region, serving massive fish dishes at reasonable prices. Daily 11.30am–8.30pm.

Restaurant La Viña de Huver Prolongación Cerro Azul, next to the Parque Zonal. Just a little way from the centre of town, this is easily the busiest lunch spot in Pisco serving excellent, huge and relatively inexpensive ceviche and other seafood dishes in a bustling and appealing environment. Daily 11am–4pm.

PARACAS

Restaurant La Brisa Marina, El Malecon ⓣ056 545125. Open for lunch only, this is a very tasty seafood restaurant out at Paracas; on the promenade close to El Chaco wharf and San Andrés, it has access to excellent fresh fish and clams. Daily 11am–3pm.

DIRECTORY

Health The hospital is at C San Juan de Dios 350.

Money and exchange Banco de Credito, Perez de Figuerola 162, and Banco Continental, next door on the corner of the Plaza and Independencia. Most hotels and the tour companies (see p.119) will change dollars for cash. The best rates are from the *cambistas* on the corner of the pedestrian boulevard between Comercio and Progreso and Plaza de Armas.

Police Plaza de Armas, C San Francisco ⓣ034 532165.

Post office Bolognesi 173 (Mon–Sat 8am–7pm).

Telephones Locutorio Telefónico, C Progreso 123a, Plaza de Armas (daily 7am–11pm).

Tambo Colorado

Some 48km northeast of Pisco, and 327km south of Lima, the ruins at **TAMBO COLORADO** were originally a fortified administrative centre, probably built by the Chincha before being adapted and used as an Inca coastal outpost. Its position at the base of steep foothills in the Pisco river valley was perfect for controlling the flow of people and produce along the ancient road down from the Andes. You can still see dwellings, offices, storehouses and row upon row of barracks and outer walls, some of them even retaining traces of coloured paints. The rains have taken their toll, but even so this is considered one of the best-preserved **adobe ruins** in Peru – roofless, but otherwise virtually intact. Though in an odd way reminiscent of a fort from some low-budget Western flick, it is an adobe complex with everything noticeably in its place – autocratic by intention, oppressive in function and rather stiff in style.

ARRIVAL AND DEPARTURE **TAMBO COLORADO**

By bus It's best to visit Tambo Colorado with one of the local tour agents (see p.119) but you can also travel there independently from Pisco: take the Ormeño bus from Jirón San Francisco or the Oropesa bus from Calle Comercio (both leave most mornings, but check first with the bus company as departure times and frequencies vary from day to day; approximately S/12 each way). The bus takes the surfaced Ayacucho road, which runs straight through the site, and the ruins are around twenty minutes beyond the village of Humay.

2

South from Pisco

South from Pisco, the Panamerican Highway sweeps some 70km inland to reach the fertile wine-producing Ica Valley, a virtual oasis in this stretch of bleak desert. **Pozo Santo**, the only real landmark en route, is distinguished by a small, towered and whitewashed chapel, built on the site of an underground well. Legend has it that when Padre Guatemala, the friar Ramón Rojas, died on this spot, water miraculously began to flow from the sands. Now there's a restaurant here where colectivo drivers sometimes stop for a snack, but little else.

Beyond Pozo Santo, the Panamerican Highway crosses the Pampa de Villacuri and further down the highway, the pretty roadside village of **Guadalupe** (at Km 293) signals the beginning of the Ica oasis.

Ica and around

An old but busy city with around 170,000 inhabitants, **ICA** sits in a fecund valley, close to enormous sand dunes some 400m above sea level and around 50km from the ocean. It's one of the first places south of Lima where you can virtually guarantee **sunny weather** most of the year.

The surrounding region is famous throughout Peru for its wine and pisco production. The city's very foundation (1563) went hand in hand with the introduction of grapevines to South America, and for most Peruvian visitors it is the **bodegas**, or wineries, that are the town's biggest draw. However, the **Museo Regional**'s superb collections of pre-Columbian ceramics and Paracas, Ica and Nasca cultural artefacts would alone make the city worth an excursion, despite some damage by the 2007 quake.

Ica's streets and plazas are crowded with hundreds of little *tico* taxis, all beeping their horns to catch potential passengers' attention and making crossing the streets a dangerous affair. Aside from the traffic and the occasional pickpocket – particularly round the market area – Ica is a pleasant place with a friendly and curious population. After a day or less, though, most visitors are ready to head for the relaxing desert oasis resort of **Huacachina**, a few kilometres to the southwest, a much more exotic and restful haven to pass the hot, sunny afternoons. On the edge of town is the rather ramshackle suburb of **Cachiche**, known throughout Peru as a traditional sanctuary for white witches (see box, p.127).

Brief history

Founded in 1563, and originally called Villa de Valverde de Ica, the settlement was moved (due to regional earthquake activity) after only five years, and renamed **San Jerónimo de Ica**. It was subsequently moved several times until finding itself in its present position in a relatively sheltered river valley protected slightly from the coastal weather (especially the mists) by large sand dunes, but still quite a way from the foothills of the Andes to the east.

The Plaza de Armas

Ica's colonial heart – the inevitable **Plaza de Armas**, site of the 1820 declaration of independence from Spain – remains its modern centre, smart and friendly, with the inclusion of an obelisk and fountains. The **cathedral** on the plaza was first constructed in the eighteenth century then remodelled in 1814 with a Neoclassical exterior and a Baroque altar and pulpit. Running east from the plaza, the modern commercial spine is the busy Avenida Grau with the market area parallel, a couple of blocks to the north. Walking alone east of this area is not recommended, as **muggings** are not unheard of.

Ica's churches

Apart from the cathedral, Ica's important churches are within a few blocks of the plaza. The church of **La Merced**, southwest of the plaza, contains Padre Guatemala's tomb – said to give immense good fortune if touched on New Year's Day. Around the corner on Avenida Municipalidad is the more recent, grander **San Francisco** church, whose stained-glass windows dazzle against the strong sunlight. Quite a stroll south of the plaza, down Jirón Lima, then left along Prolongación Ayabaca, stands a third major church, **El Santuario de Luren**. Built on the site of a hermitage founded in 1556, the present construction, Neoclassical in style and with three brick-built *portales*, houses the Imagen del Señor de Luren, a statue of the patron saint of the town, something of a national shrine and centre for procession and pilgrimage at Easter as well as on the third Sunday October.

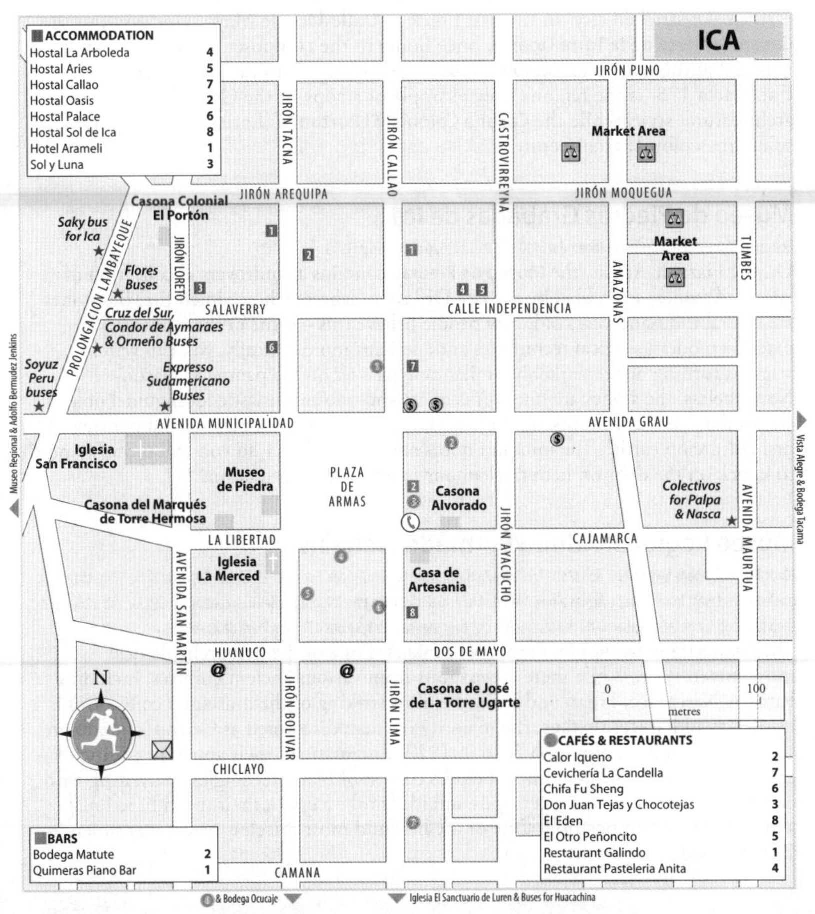

FIESTAS IN ICA

There are several important **fiestas** in Ica throughout the year. The most enjoyable time to be in town is in **March** after the grape harvest has been brought in, when there are open-air concerts, fairs, handicraft markets, cockfighting and *caballo de paso* (horse dressage – where horses are trained by riders to dance and prance for events or competitions) meetings. Over the **Semana de Ica** (June 12–19), based around the colonial founding of Ica, there are more festivities, including religious processions and fireworks, and again in the last week of September for the **Semana Turística**. On July 25, there's the nationwide **Día Nacional de Pisco**, essentially a big celebration for the national brandy (rather than the town of the same name), mostly held in the bodegas south of Lima, particularly around Ica. As in Lima, **October** is the main month for religious celebrations, with the focus being the ceremony and procession at the church of El Santuario de Luren (main processions on the third Sunday and following Monday of October).

Ica's mansions

There are a few **mansions** of note near the plaza, including the **Casona del Marqués de Torre Hermosa**, block 1 of Calle Libertad. Now belonging to the Banco Continental, it is one of the few examples of colonial architecture to survive in this earthquake-stricken city. In the first block of Calle Dos de Mayo, you can find the **Casona de José de la Torre Ugarte**, once home to the composer of the Peruvian national anthem. The **Casona Alvorado**, now belonging to the Banco Latino, at Cajamarca 178, is the region's only example of a copy of the Greco-Roman architectural style, while the **Casona Colonial El Porton**, C Loreto 233, conserves some fine colonial architecture.

Museo de Piedras Grabadas de Ica

Bolívar 178b • Guided tours by arrangement S/10 • ⓣ 056 213026 or ⓣ 056 231933

On the Plaza de Armas, the **Museo de Piedras** contains a controversial collection of engraved stones, assembled by the late Dr Javier Cabrera who claimed that the stones are several thousand years old. Few people believe this – some of the stones depict patently modern surgical techniques and, perhaps more critically, you can watch artesans turning out remarkably similar designs over on the pampa at Nasca. Nevertheless, the stones are fine works of art and one enthusiastic local guidebook claims that "dinosaur hunts are portrayed, suggesting that Ica may have supported the first culture on earth". The museum doors are usually closed, so you will probably need to knock on the door or, better, telephone in advance for attention.

Museo Regional Adolfo Bermúdez Jenkins

Block 8 of Av Ayabaca ⓣ 034 234383 • Mon–Fri 8am–7pm, Sat & fiestas 9am–6pm, Sun 9am–1.30pm • $4, extra if you want to take photos • Head west from Plaza de Armas along Avenida Municipalidad, then turn left onto Calle Elias; continue south for half a kilometre, then turn right onto Calle Ayabaca and the museum is just over the road. Or take bus #17 from Plaza de Armas

The **Museo Regional Adolfo Bermúdez Jenkins** is one of the best archeological museums in Peru. While there are exhibits from various ancient cultures, including Paracas, Nasca, Ica, Huari and Inca, the most striking of the museum's collections is its display of **Paracas textiles**, the majority of them discovered at Cerro Colorado on the Paracas Peninsula by Julio Tello in 1927. Enigmatic in their apparent coding of colours and patterns, these funeral cloths consist of blank rectangles alternating with elaborately woven ones – repetitious and identical except in their multidirectional shifts of colour and position. One of the best and most priceless pieces was stolen in October 2004, so security is tight.

The first room to the right off the main foyer contains a fairly gruesome display of **mummies**, **trepanned skulls**, **grave artefacts** and **trophy heads**. It seems very likely that the taking of trophy heads in this region was related to specific religious beliefs – as it was until quite recently among the head-hunting Jivaro of the Amazon Basin. The earliest of these skulls, presumably hunted and collected by the victor in battle, come from the Asia Valley (north of Ica) and date from around 2000 BC.

The main room

The museum's main room is almost entirely devoted to pre-Columbian **ceramics and textiles**, possibly the finest collection outside Lima. There are some spectacular Paracas urns – one is particularly outstanding, with an owl and serpent design painted on one side, and a human face with arms, legs and a navel on the other. The room boasts some exquisite Nasca pottery, too, undoubtedly the most colourful and abstractly imaginative designs found on any ancient Peruvian ceramics. The last wall consists mainly of artefacts from the Ica-Chincha culture – note the beautiful **feather cape**, with multicoloured plumes in almost perfect condition. Displayed also in the main room are several **quipus**, ancient calculators using bundles of knotted strings as mnemonic aids, also used for the recitation of ancient legends, genealogies and ballads. Due to the dryness of the desert climate, they have survived better here on the coast than in the mountains and the Ica collection remains one of the best in the country. Behind the museo there's an excellent large-scale model of the Nasca Lines.

ARRIVAL AND DEPARTURE — ICA AND AROUND

By bus Ormeño, Cruz del Sur, or Saky buses (056 213143) from Pisco arrive at Prolongación Lambayeque 217, a few blocks west of Plaza de Armas. Soyuz Peru Bus fast services from Lima arrive close by on Av Matías Manzanilla 130 (056 224138); Expresso Sudamericano arrive at Av Municipalidad 336; and Flores come in at

ICA'S BODEGAS

The best way to escape Ica's hot desert afternoons is to wander around the cool chambers and vaults, and sample the wines at one of the town's **bodegas** or wineries. Many of the region's best wine and piscos can be sampled from stores in and around the Plaza de Armas in Ica, but if you have the time, it's well worth visiting the producer haciendas located outside the town centre.

Vista Alegre Daily 9am–4.30pm; 056 222919. Orange microbus #8 from Avenida Grau or the market. This well-known bodega, one of Peru's best, is based in an old hacienda still chugging happily along in a forgotten world of its own. There's usually a guide who'll show you around free of charge, then arrange for a wine- and pisco-tasting session at the shop. You don't have to buy anything, but you're expected to tip (around $2–5 a person or small group).

Bodega Tacama Daily 9am–5pm; 056 228395, tacama.com. Follow the road beyond Vista Alegre (see above) for another 6km. Some microbuses pass this way; a taxi is likely to cost from S/15 each way. Bodega Tacama is a large and successful wine producer located about 3km from the centre of Ica. The vineyards here are still irrigated by the Achirana Canal, which was built by the Inca Pachacutec (or his brother Capac Yupanqui) as a gift to Princess Tate, daughter of a local chieftain. Apparently it took 40,000 men just ten days to complete this astonishing canal, which brings cold, pure water down 4000m from the Andes to transform what was once an arid desert into a startlingly fertile oasis. Clearly a romantic at heart, Pachacutec named it Achirana – "that which flows cleanly towards that which is beautiful". Guided tours and tastings are available.

Bodega Ocucaje Mon–Fri 9am–noon & 2–5pm, Sat 9am–noon; 056 408011. Any bus or colectivo heading south will get you to within a few kilometres of the bodega (within view). Alternatively a taxi from Ica should cost around S/30 one way. About 35km further south of Ica, the oasis of Bodega Ocucaje is one of Peru's finest vineyards. You can stay here at the *Hotel Ocucaje* and explore the surrounding desert, particularly the Cerro Blanco site where whalebone remains have been found.

Salaverry 396, on the corner with Lambayeque. Orange buses to Huacachina (see p.128) leave from outside the Santuario de Luren (every 20min or so).

Destinations Lima (several buses daily; 3–4hr); Nasca (several buses daily; 2–3hr).

By colectivo Colectivos from Nasca drop you off within 2 or 3 blocks of the Plaza de Armas, the same small depots from where they depart back to Nasca.

By taxi Taxis to Huacachina cost $3–5; mototaxis cost $1–2.

GETTING AROUND

By taxi and mototaxi Most people take taxis, generally small, flimsy and dangerous *tico* cars (try to use one of the rarer, but larger and more solid vehicles), with journeys within town rarely costing more than S/5. Cheaper still (S/2–3 for anywhere in town and under S/10 to Huacachina) are the mototaxis (motorcycle rickshaw taxis) which can be hailed anywhere in town.

By microbus For longer journeys to the outlying parts of town, take one of the microbuses, which leave from Jr Lima or Prolongación Lambayeque and have their destinations chalked up on their windscreens.

INFORMATION AND TOURS

Tourist information Available from some of the bodegas (see box, p.125) and tour offices on the Jr Lima side of the Plaza de Armas or at the Automóvil Club at Manzanilla 523.

Tour operators There are several tour operators in town offering excursions such as Ica City Tour (including Huacachina, wine bodegas, the Museo Regional and the barrio of Cachiche), buggy rides in the desert and also trips to the Palpa Valley, various Nasca archeological attractions, the Ballestas Islands and Paracas; most have shop fronts on the Plaza de Armas and all can arrange for flights over the Nasca Lines: Colibri Tours, Lima 121 056 214406; Huacachina Tours, Av Angostura 355, L-47, close to *Hotel las Dunas* entrance 056 256582, huacachinatours.com; Las Brujas de Cachiche, C Cajamarca 100 056 211237, lasbrujasdecachiche.com; Desert Travel and Service, Lima 171 (in Tejas Don Juan shop) 056 234127; and Diplomatic Travel, Av Municipalidad 132, Oficina 13 056 237187.

ACCOMMODATION

Finding somewhere to stay in Ica is rarely a problem, though there's very little of particular quality or note in the town itself. For style or range of choice, most people go to Huacachina (see p.128) or one of the other out-of-town places.

Hostal La Arboleda C Independencia 165 056 234597. Very cheap yet basic rooms available in this stylish old building. Reasonable service but no hot water. S/30

Hostal Aries C Independencia 181 056 235367. The best of Ica's budget hostels, with clean rooms, though bathrooms are communal. There's also a pleasant patio with room for bikes or motorbikes, and service is OK. S/30

Hostal Callao Jr Callao 128 056 235976. Very central – just a few metres from the Plaza de Armas – small, simple but clean rooms, some with private shower. S/40

Hostal Oasis Jr Tacna 216 056 234767. Hot water and some private bathrooms are available in this rather basic place. S/45

Hostal Palace Jr Tacna 185 056 211655. Modern building with its own café next door; it has private bathrooms but no single rooms. S/50

Hostal Sol de Ica Jr Lima 265 056 236168, hotelsoldeica.com. Located between the town centre, Huacachina and the Museo Regional, the *Sol de Ica* is quite modern and clean, with a nice swimming pool, though the building has suffered some earthquake damage and no longer looks its best. S/140

Hotel Arameli Jr Tacna 239 056 239107. A modern-style hotel, all rooms are plain but have private bath and hot water; it's clean, central and very friendly. S/60

Sol y Luna Salaverry 292 056 227241. A modern, very clean hotel. Service and facilities such as a laundry, cafeteria and room service are superior to others of a similar price. S/60

EATING

Most of the restaurants in Ica are within a block or two of the Plaza de Armas. Their quality in terms of food and general ambience varies enormously, but there is ample choice from breakfast to the evening meal. Ica is famous for its sweets, too, and this is reflected in several of the shops around and near to the Plaza de Armas.

Calor Iqueno Av Grau 103. Small and fairly quiet, this snack bar/coffee shop has great hot drinks, yoghurt and local *empanadas* (pasties filled with meat, onions and olives). Daily 8am–8pm.

Cevichería La Candella Block 4 of Jr Lima. Decent food and affordable prices, plus a lively atmosphere and a bar that's open in the evenings. Mon–Fri 11am–5pm, bar 7–11pm.

Chifa Fu Sheng Jr Lima 243. A budget Chinese restaurant, packed with locals in the evenings; nothing special but reasonable standard rice and noodle dishes plus some inexpensive set meals at lunch time. Daily10am–9pm.

Don Juan Tejas y Chocotejas Jr Lima 171, Plaza de Armas. Some of the best local *dulces* in town, including traditional *tejas* sweets made from *manjar blanco* and pecan nuts. Daily 7.30am–9pm.

El Eden C Andaguayllas 204. A popular vegetarian restaurant making good use of local ingredients like avocados, rice and potatoes; nice juices and barley drinks. Mon–Sat 8am–8pm.

El Otro Peñoncito Jr Bolívar 255 ⓣ056 233921. Less than a block from the plaza, this stylish restaurant has walls tastefully adorned with artwork from Andean cosmology by an Iqueño artist; their speciality is *pollo iqueño* – chicken stuffed with spinach and pecan nuts topped with a pisco sauce. Daily 7pm–midnight.

Restaurant Galindo Jr Callao 145, just off the Plaza de Armas. A popular locals' dive serving big portions and sometimes the Ica speciality *carapulchra* (pork, chicken and potato casserole). A busy atmosphere with a loud TV. Daily 7am–9pm.

Restaurant Pastelería Anita C Libertad 137, Plaza de Armas. This is Ica's slightly upmarket downtown eating and meeting place serving pretty fine traditional cuisine, including excellent *lomo saltado* (see p.34) and lots of sweets and pastries for eating in or out. Has a relatively inexpensive set-lunch menu. Daily 10am–10pm.

2

DRINKING AND NIGHTLIFE

Not surprisingly, Ica wines are very much a part of the town's life, and locals pop into a bodega for a quick glass of pisco at just about any time of the day; most are open 9am–9pm.

Bodega Matute Jr Lima 143, Plaza de Armas. This place has a good range of piscos, wines, *tejas* and juices; you can not sit down and eat here as such, it's a case of sampling the drinks and sweets then buying them to take away. Daily 9am–10pm.

Quimeras Piano Bar Jr Callao 224 ⓣ056 213186. This café-bar sometimes offers live performances by local musicians of criollo, Mexican and Cuban music, open 8pm until late at weekends.

DIRECTORY

Internet Space Net, Huánuco 177, one block from plaza (daily 9am–10pm; ⓣ056 217033) or De Cajon.com, Huánuco 201 (daily 9am–midnight; ⓣ056 237396).

Money and exchange Banco de Credito, Av Grau 109 (Mon–Fri 8am–5pm), has an ATM; Caja Municipal, Av Municipalidad 148 (Mon–Fri 8.30am–6pm); and the Banco de la Nación, Av Matías Manzanilla (Mon–Fri 9am–6pm). For dollars cash try any of the *cambistas* on the corners of the Plaza de Armas.

Police The Tourist Police are on block 1 of Prolongación Lambayeque (ⓣ056 233632 or ⓣ056 235421).

Post office San Martín 156, not far from the Plaza de Armas (Mon–Sat 8am–7pm).

Shopping Casa de Artesanía, on Calle Cajamarca just a few metres from the plaza, is a small but often busy place that sells artesanía, including local leather craft. They serve drinks and sell bottles as well.

Telephones Telefónica Locutorio, Lima 149, Plaza de Armas (daily 8am–8pm).

THE WITCHES OF CACHICHE

In the down-at-heel suburb of Cachiche, history and mythology have merged into a legend of a local group of **witches**. The story dates back to the seventeenth century, when Spanish witches were persecuted for their pagan beliefs during the Inquisition. Seeking religious refuge, the witches emigrated to Lima, where they were also persecuted for their beliefs before finally settling in the countryside in particular the Ica Valley, in a village called Cachiche. For hundreds of years, the Cachiche witches operated in secret until the 1980s, when there was a renewed interest in alternative health practices and even the Peruvian presidents of the 80s and 90s openly consulted them about health matters. The popularity of Cachiche healing methods grew even more when a powerful congressman was dramatically cured of a terminal illness on TV by a Cachiche witch. Similar to witchcraft and shamanism along the Peruvian coast, Cachiche practices involve the use of San Pedro (see p.507), a psychedelic cactus containing mescaline.

2

Huacachina

According to myth, the lagoon at **HUACACHINA**, about 5km southwest of Ica, was created when a princess stripped off her clothes to bathe. When she looked into a mirror and saw that a male hunter was watching her she dropped the mirror, which then became the lagoon. More prosaically, during the late 1940s, the **lagoon** became one of Peru's most elegant and exclusive resorts, surrounded by palm trees, sand dunes and waters famed for their curative powers, and with a delightfully old-world atmosphere. Since then the lagoon's subterranean source has grown erratic and it is supplemented by water pumped up from artesian wells, making it less of a red-coloured, viscous syrup and more like a green, salty swimmable lagoon; it retains considerable mystique, making it a quiet, secluded spot to relax. The **curative powers** of the lagoon attract people from all over: mud from the lake is reputed to cure arthritis and rheumatism if you plaster yourself all over with it; and the sand around the lagoon is also supposed to benefit people with respiratory problems, so it's not uncommon to see locals buried up to the neck in the dunes.

The settlement, still little more than twenty houses or so, is growing very slowly, but one end of the lagoon has been left fairly clear of construction. Climb the dunes at the end of the lake and take in the views from the top early in the morning, before it gets too hot and prior to the noisy dune-buggy runs. On the Salvaterra side of the lake there's a great little library – Biblioteca Abraham Valdelomar – with a strong ecological focus.

ARRIVAL AND INFORMATION — HUACACHINA

By mototaxi or taxi All taxis drop off and pick up passengers at the top end of the lagoon, within 100m of the lake edge. On arrival, you'll find a small wooden kiosk, frequently staffed by the local tourist police; they have information sheets and rather poor maps, and will also direct you to accommodation or other services.

ACTIVITIES

The tour operators in Ica (see p.126) can also help organize the following activities:

Sand-dune surfing On the higher slopes, sand-dune surfing is all the rage and you can rent wooden boards or foot-skis for around S/10 per hour from the cafés and hotels along the shoreline.

Dune buggies Adrenaline rides are offered at some of the cafés, hotels and independent kiosks and shops.

Boating You can rent boats for rowing or peddling on the lagoon.

ACCOMMODATION

Camping It's possible to camp in the sand dunes around the lagoon – it's rarely cold enough to need more than a blanket. Free

Hostería Suiza Balconario de Huacachina 264 T 056 238762, E hostesuiza@terra.com.pe. Comfortable, cosy, quiet and located at the far end of the lake. S/320

Hospedaje Titanic T 056 229003. This small hostel above the left end of the *malecón* is notable for having a pool. S/60

Hotel Mossone Nicolás Ariola, block 4, Santa Catalina T 056 213630. The most stylish accommodation around: this large place is luxurious and exceptionally elegant, once the haunt of politicians and diplomats, who listened to concerts while sitting on the colonial-style veranda overlooking the lagoon. Outside high season it is sometimes possible to get very reasonable deals. S/300

Hotel Salvatierra Malecón de Huacachina T 056 232352, W salvaturgroup.galeon.com. Excellent value, with an enormous amount of character; its splendid dining room holds a number of important murals by the Ica artist Sérvulo Gutiérrez (1914–61), who evidently drank his way through a massive number of pisco bottles in his time here. Most rooms have private baths, there's a good swimming pool and internet connections, and the owner's family offers transport to and from Ica whenever possible. S/50

EATING

Hotel Mossone Nicolás Ariola, block 4, Santa Catalina T 056 213630. This very plush hotel has a stylish and wonderful restaurant serving a wide range of Peruvian and international cuisine, but it's very pricey. Daily lunch & dinner.

Restaurant Trattoria Novaro A stone's throw from the lake, and close to the *Mossone* (see opposite), it's very popular in the evenings with its wide range of Italian and

Peruvian dishes. Daily 11.30am–9/10pm.

Restaurante Moron Under the bandstand beside the lake. An informal restaurant that serves lunch right beside the lake; ceviche (from S/22) and other fish dishes are their mainstay. Daily noon–4pm.

La Sirena On the opposite lakeside to the bandstand. A small place with some outside tables, they serve pastas, brilliant fish dishes, wine and beer. Daily 11am–9.30pm.

The Nasca Lines

One of the great mysteries of South America, the **NASCA LINES** are a series of animal figures and geometric shapes, some up to 200m in length, drawn across some five hundred square kilometres of the bleak, stony **Pampa de San José** or, as more simply referred to, the Nasca Plain. If you plan to visit the lines by air or on foot, you'll have to spend at least one night in Nasca, more to do it justice. If you're staying over, base yourself in either the small town of **Palpa** or larger **Nasca Town**. When it comes to visiting the Lines, by far the best way is by **air** (see box, p.132). If you're keen to keep your feet on the ground, though, make for the **mirador** (viewpoint), 2km north of Palpa.

The Lines are a combination of straight lines continuing for many kilometres in some cases across the sandy, stone-strewn plateau; others look like trapezoidal plazas, perfectly created by clearing the stones from the surface for the required pattern. Around seventy other "lines" are actually stylized line drawings of birds and animals (some over fifty metres wide), believed to symbolize both astrological phases and possible ancient Nasca clan divisions, with each figure representing, perhaps, the totem of a particular sub group of this pre-Inca society and that clan's animal ally in the spirit world. Theories discussing their purpose and origin are as varied as the patterns themselves (see box, pp.130–131).

GETTING THERE **NASCA LINES**

Approaching from Ica in the North, you first have to cross a wide desert plain and pass through a couple of valleys, including Palpa, before arriving at the Pampa de San José and the Nasca Lines proper. The Lines themselves begin on the tableland above the small town of Palpa, about 90km south of Ica on the Panamerican Highway.

By bus It's best to visit the Lines with a tour (see p.136), but if you want to travel independently, take a local bus from Nasca (S/2) or one of the intercity buses for Ica and Lima, which leave every couple of hours from the corner of the Panamerican Highway and Jirón Lima on the outskirts of Nasca and let you off at the main *mirador* on the road between Palpa and Nasca. It's usually easy enough to get a lift with a bus back to town. Buses leave every hour for the Nasca airstrip, from the corner of Grau with Jirón Bolognesi and are normally marked "B-Vista Alegre".

By colectivo/taxi A taxi to the Lines from Nasca Town costs S/30, and it will wait and bring you back again. Colectivos link the airstrip with Jirón Bolognesi and Av Grau in town. It's also fairly easy to get a colectivo back from the Nasca lines.

Palpa

Palpa is a one-street town, but there are a few archeological sites in the area and incipient signs of tourism infrastructure are beginning to emerge.

Just 2km to the north of town there's a *mirador*, or viewing tower, from which geometric lines forming a pattern known locally as a Solar Clock, or **Reloj Solar**, can be seen on the lower valley slopes. It's said that during the equinox seers can tell from the Reloj Solar what kind of harvest there will be. Some 8km by navigable dirt track from Palpa it's possible to see the **petroglyfos de Casa Blanca**, where stone human figures and cubic shapes have been etched on one sunken but upright stone. Roughly 4km further on is a series of petroglyphs on the scattered volcanic boulders, known as the **petroglyfos de Chicchictara**. The images depict two-headed snakes, a sunburst, a moon and various animals.

If you happen to be in town around August 15, your visit will coincide with the annual Fiesta de la Naranja (Orange Festival), which sees a few days of processions, dancing, singing and drinking; the main street usually has plenty of stalls selling fruit, nuts and other local produce.

The mirador and museum

Mirador S/1 • **Museum** Mon–Sat 9am–5pm • $1 • A tour with an operator (see p.136) to the *mirador* on the Palpa road and the Casa Museo Maria Reiche takes 2hr 30min and costs from $12

2

At Km 420 of the Panamerican Highway, a tall metal **mirador** (viewing tower) has been built above the plain. Unless you've got the time to climb up onto one of the hills behind, or take a flight over the Lines (see box, p.132), this is the best view of the Lines you'll get.

The rather underdeveloped **Casa Museo y Mausoleo Maria Reiche**, about 1km beyond the *mirador*, consists of three main rooms containing displays of photos, drawings and ceramics relating to the Nasca Lines and the studies of **Maria Reiche**, a premier Nasca Lines researcher (see box below). Housed in her old adobe home in the shadow of the pampa, the museum includes one room dedicated solely to Reiche's personal possessions, showing the spartan reality of her daily life here, right down to her flip-flops.

THEORIES ABOUT THE NASCA LINES

The Lines are undoubtedly one of the world's biggest archeological mysteries and bring many thousands of visitors every year to Peru's south coast. Theories abound as to their purpose and creation.

MARIA REICHE

The greatest expert on these mammoth desert designs was **Maria Reiche**, who escaped from Nazi Germany to Peru in the 1930s and worked at Nasca almost continuously from 1946 until her death in 1998. Standing on the shoulders of US scientist Paul Kosok, a colleague of hers, she believed that the Lines were an astronomical calendar linked to the rising and setting points of celestial bodies on the east and west horizons. The whole complex, according to her theory, was designed to help organize planting and harvesting around seasonal changes rather than the fickle shifts of weather. When certain stars lined up with specific lines, shapes or animals, it would signal a time for planting, the coming of the rains, the beginning or end of summer, the growing season or the time for harvesting. It also gave the elite high priests, who possessed this knowledge, a large element of control over the actions of the populace. In a desert area like Nasca, where the coastal fog never reaches up to obscure the night sky over the pampa, there was a strong emphasis on relating earthly matters to the movements of the heavens and on knowledge of the night skies and how they relate to nature's cycles. Reiche's theories, after sixty years of research, are thought to have established some alignments, many of which were confirmed by the computer analysis (particularly those for the solar solstices) of astronomer Gerald Hawkins (world famous for "decoding" Stonehenge in England), who himself spent much of the 1960s working on the Nasca Lines. Much, however, was left unexplained, and this has allowed more recent theorists to fill out the picture.

THEORIES OF RITUALS

Regarding social aspects of the Lines, Toribio Mejía Xesspe, a Peruvian archeologist, actually "discovered" the site in 1927 and believed that they were made for walking or dancing along, probably for ritual purposes. The archeologist Johan Reinhard, meanwhile, has drawn on present-day anthropological studies from the Peruvian Andes to understand the meaning of similar lines today. His research has shown how mountain people still worship mountains and river sources as important gods.

In 2000, Dr Anthony Aveni, a leading archeoastronomer, agreed that at least some of the Nasca Lines were **pathways** meant to be walked in rituals, perhaps consciousness-changing like labyrinths, but also relating to the acquisition of water. A statistically significant number of

2

Nasca and around

The colonial town of **NASCA** spreads along the margin of a small coastal valley some 20km south of the viewing tower (see opposite). The river is invariably dry, but Nasca's valley remains green and fertile through the continued use of an Inca subterranean aqueduct, and though it was badly affected by an earthquake in 1996, necessitating the rebuilding of half the town, it's still an interesting and enjoyable place to stay.

There are plenty of fascinating local sites, some within walking distance like the pre-Inca and Inca remains of **Paredones** and the Inca aqueducts or canals of **Cantayoc**. Others, like the ancient Nasca ceremonial and urban centre of **Cahuachi** and the early Nasca graveyard at **Chauchilla** lie a little further away in the desert. They can only be reached by car or with a tour bus, and are poorly signposted so you will need a guide.

Museo Antonini

Av de la Cultura 600 • Daily 9am–7pm • $1.50 • ⓣ 056 523444

Walking east across Nasca's main plaza and heading along Avenida de la Cultura you soon come to the town's best museum – the fascinating **Museo Antonini**, an Italian pre-Columbian archeological research and study centre. Opened in 1999, the museum stretches for six long blocks from the Plaza de Armas along Bolognesi and presents

the Lines point towards a section of the horizon where the sun used to rise at the beginning of the rainy season, suggesting that perhaps they were created to help worship or invoke their gods, particularly those related to rain. According to Aveni, air and ground surveys revealed that "most of the straight lines on the pampa are tied to water sources". This certainly fits the anthropological evidence from annual Andean pilgrimages which continue to this day in some parts of Peru.

IT'S IN THE WATER

In 2003, David Johnson (University of Massachusetts) put forward evidence that the ancient Nascans mapped the desert to mark the surface where aquifers appeared. His work suggested that large underground rivers run under the pampa and many of the figures are connected to this, in some ways creating a giant map of what's happening under the earth. Zigzag lines are linked to a lack of underground water, while trapezoids point towards the source of it. Archeological research also suggests that Nasca experienced a serious drought around 550 AD, at the same time as the ancient Nasca's main ceremonial centre – Cahuachi – was abandoned on the plain, and more or less contemporaneous with the construction of the trapezoid spaces where evidence of ritual offerings has been found.

MORE IDEAS...

Further thoughts about why the lines and figures were drawn by the ancient Nasca include the concept of shamanic flight or out-of-the-body experience, with the symbolic "flight path" already mapped out across the region. Such an experience is induced by some of the "teacher plants", such as the mescaline cactus San Pedro, which are still used by traditional healers in Peru (see p.507). Visually, there are clear links and similarities between the animal figures found on the plain and those elaborately painted onto Nasca's fine pre-Inca ceramics. Animal totems or spirit helpers are commonly used, even today, by traditional Peruvian healers to communicate with the "other world".

Most of the above theories are fairly compatible; taken together, they form a matrix of interrelated explanations – agro-astonomical, environmental, spiritual and ritual. However, just how the ancient Nasca people ever constructed the Lines is possibly the biggest mystery of all – not least since they can't even be seen from the ground. In the early 1970s the populist writer Erich von Däniken claimed that the Lines were built as runways for alien space ships. Less controversially, perhaps, in the 1980s a local school in Nasca tried building its own line and from its efforts calculated that a thousand patient and inspired workers could have made them all in less than a month.

excellent interpretative exhibits covering the evolution of Nasca culture, a good audio visual show and scale-model reconstructions of local remains such as the Templo del Escalonado at Cahuachi. The museum complex extends to almost ten thousand square metres and includes an archeological park that contains the Bisambra aqueduct (fed by the reservoir higher up the valley) and some burial reconstructions.

The market and Barrio San Carlos

2

South along Calle Arica from the Plaza de Armas, the town's **main market**, offering the usual food and electronic goods, is based in a ramshackle collection of huts and stalls on the left just before the river bridge on Calle Arica.

Slightly further afield, the **Taller Artesanía**, Pasaje Torrico 240, over the river in the **Barrio San Carlos**, a short walk south of the plaza over the bridge, is worth a visit for its wonderful ceramics produced by the maestro Andrés Calle Flores for over twenty years; as long as there are a few customers, they are more than happy to demonstrate the ceramic-making process from moulding to polishing. San Carlos also boasts the **Taller de Cerámica Juan José**, at Pasaje López 400, and a **gold processing** operation, both located on the right-hand side about 500m down Avenida San Carlos from the market bridge. Don't be put off by the fact that they're in someone's back garden – it's fascinating to watch them grind rocks into powder and then extract gold dust from it.

Los Paredones

Once an Inca trade centre where wool from the mountains was exchanged for cotton grown along the coast, **Los Paredones** can be reached easily on foot from Nasca Town. Simply follow Calle Arica from the Plaza de Armas, cross the bridge, and keep going straight (off the main road which curves to the right). At the end you reach a road which passes below the ruins, following the same route to Puquio as the Inca road from Nasca to Cusco, at the foot of a sandy hillside.

The adobe buildings at Los Paredones are in a bad state of repair and the site is dotted with *huaqueros*' (grave robbers) pits, but if you follow the path to the prominent central sector you can get a good idea of what the town must have been like. Overlooking the valley and roads, it's in a commanding position – a fact recognized and taken advantage of by local cultures long before the Incas arrived. At the foot of the ruins, you can usually look round a collection of funereal pieces collected and displayed by the Pomez family in their adobe home adjacent to the site.

FLYING OVER THE NASCA LINES

A pricey but spectacular way of seeing the Lines – and arguably the only way to fully appreciate them – is to **fly** over them. Flights can be arranged with **tour companies** in Nasca (see p.136) or directly at the Nasca airstrip (where they depart), about 3km south of Nasca (at Km 447 on the Panamericana highway), and **cost** from $45–250 a person depending on the season, the size of the group, how long you want to spend buzzing around (eg if you want to include Palpa lines as well) and how much demand there is on the day. Flights can last from ten minutes to a couple of hours, with the **duration** of the average package being 30–45 minutes. Bear in mind that the planes are small and bounce around in the changeable air currents, which can cause airsickness, and that you'll get a better **view** on an early morning trip, since the air gets hazier as the day progresses. There have been fatal accidents in recent years, so prices and regulations continue to increase. Many hotels and tour agencies (see p.136) will book a flight for you and arrange transport to the airport from your hotel.

Aeroica Best booked from the *Hotel La Maison Suisse*, opposite the airport outside Nasca (T 01 445 0859 or T 034 522434, W aeroica.net).

Alas Peruana Based at the airport (T/F 056 522444 or in US +1 800 548 5486, W alasperuanas.com). They can also fly in from Ica or Lima.

Nasca graveyard

Just 2km up the Puquio road from Los Paradones (with Nasca in front of you, turn right leaving Paradones) there's a **Nasca graveyard**, its pits open and burial remains spread around. Though much less extensive than the cemetery at Chauchilla (see below), it is still of interest – there's an abundance of subterranean galleries, but they're rather hard to find unless you're travelling with a local guide.

The Inca canal

A half-hour walk up the valley from the graveyard through the cotton fields and along a track will bring you to the former hacienda of **Cantayo** (see p.137), now a converted spa hotel resort with a fabulous restaurant. Just a little further above the hotel, you can make out a series of inverted conical dips, like swallow-holes, in the fields. These are the air vents for a vast underground **canal** system that siphons desperately needed water from the Bisambra reservoir; designed and constructed by the Incas, it is even more essential today. You can get right down into the openings and poke your head or feet into the canals – they usually give off a pleasant warm breeze and you can see small fish swimming in the flowing water.

Chauchilla Cemetery

Tours need to be arranged in advance • 2hr 30min • $12–15 per person

Some 27km southeast of Nasca along the Panamerican Highway to Km 464.20, then out along a dirt road beside the Poroma riverbed, **Chauchilla Cemetery** certainly rewards the effort it takes to visit. Once you reach the atmospheric site you realize how considerable a civilization the riverbanks must have maintained in the time of the Nasca culture. The desert landscape rolls gently down towards a small river and copses of *huarango* trees on the northern side. To the south are several rain destroyed adobe pyramids, difficult to discern against the sand. Scattered about the dusty ground are thousands of graves, most of which have been opened by grave robbers, leaving the skulls and skeletons exposed to the elements, along with broken pieces of pottery, bits of shroud and lengths of braided hair, as yet unbleached by the desert sun. Further up the track, near Trancas, there's a small ceremonial **temple** – Huaca del Loro – and beyond this at Los Incas you can find Quemazon **petroglyphs**. These last two are not usually included in the standard tour, but if you hire your own guide, you can negotiate with him to take you there – expect to pay $5 extra.

Cahuachi

Tours need to be arranged in advance • 4hr • Approx $50–75 for 4 or 5 people

The ancient centre of Nasca culture, **Cahuachi** lies to the west of the Nasca Lines, about 30km from Nasca and some 20km from the Pacific. Cahuachi is typical of a Nasca ceremonial centre in its use of natural features to form an integral part of the structure. The places where the Nasca lived their everyday lives showed no such architectural aspirations – indeed there are no major towns associated with the Nasca, who tended to live in small clusters of adobe huts, villages at best.

All of the landscape between Nasca Town and the distant coastline is a massive, very barren desertscape – almost always hot, dry and sunny. In many ways it's hard to imagine how ancient peoples managed to sustain such an advanced civilization here; but, as in northern Peru, it had much to do with a close religious and technical relationship with natural water sources, all the more important because of their scarcity. The site consists of a religious citadel split in half by the river, with its main temple (one of a set of six) constructed around a small natural hillock. Adobe platforms step the sides of this twenty-metre mound and although they're badly weathered today, you can still make out the general form. Separate courtyards attached to each of the six pyramids can be distinguished, but their exact purpose is unknown.

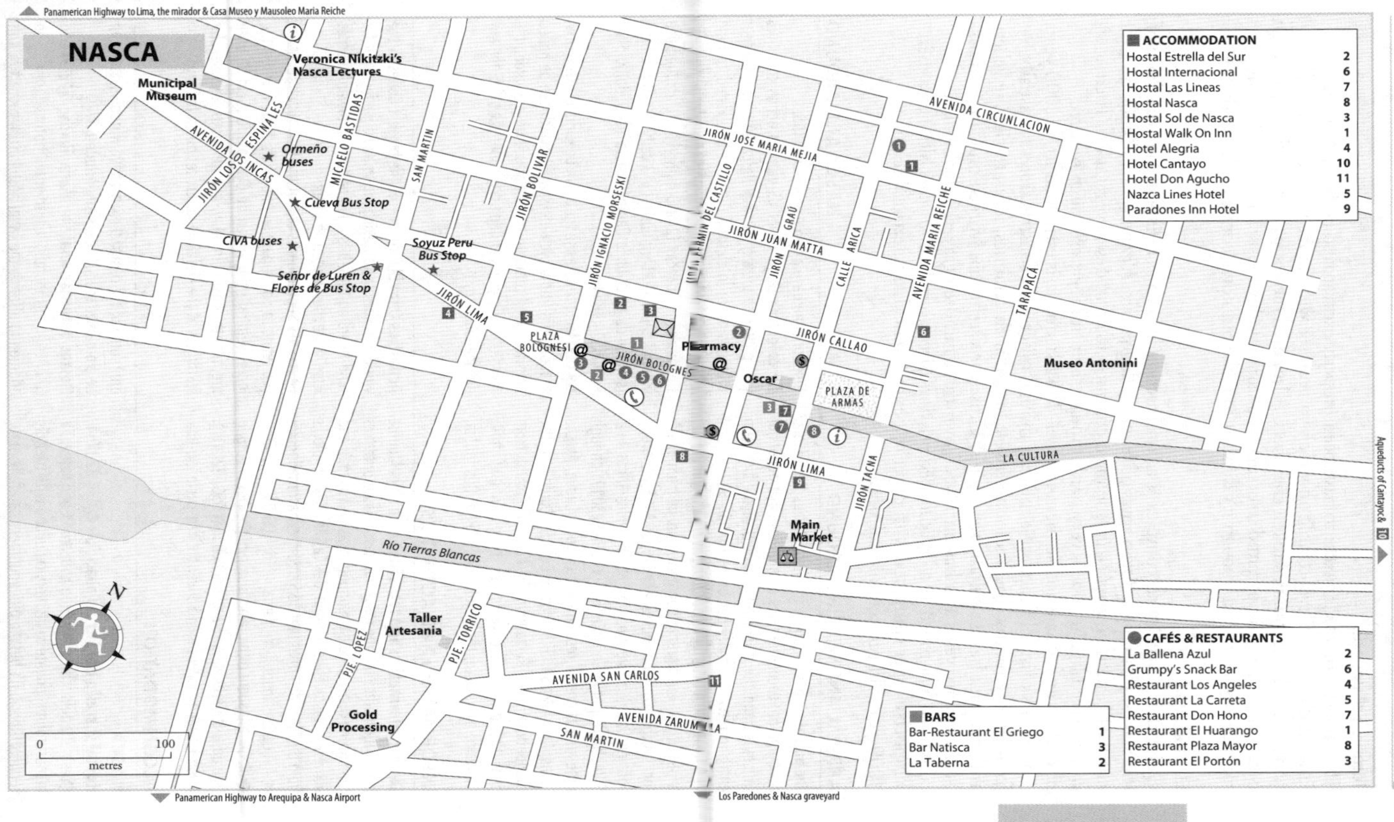
NASCA
Panamerican Highway to Lima, the mirador & Casa Museo y Mausoleo Maria Reiche
Panamerican Highway to Arequipa & Nasca Airport
Los Paredones & Nasca graveyard
Aqueducts of Cantayoc & 10
ACCOMMODATION
Hostal Estrella del Sur 2
Hostal Internacional 6
Hostal Las Lineas 7
Hostal Nasca 8
Hostal Sol de Nasca 3
Hostal Walk On Inn 1
Hotel Alegria 4
Hotel Cantayo 10
Hotel Don Agucho 11
Nazca Lines Hotel 5
Paradones Inn Hotel 9
CAFÉS & RESTAURANTS
La Ballena Azul 2
Grumpy's Snack Bar 6
Restaurant Los Angeles 4
Restaurant La Carreta 5
Restaurant Don Hono 7
Restaurant El Huarango 1
Restaurant Plaza Mayor 8
Restaurant El Portón 3
BARS
Bar-Restaurant El Griego 1
Bar Natisca 3
La Taberna 2
Municipal Museum
Veronica Nikitzki's Nasca Lectures
Ormeño buses
Cueva Bus Stop
CIVA buses
Señor de Luren & Flores de Bus Stop
Soyuz Peru Bus Stop
Museo Antonini
Pharmacy
Oscar
Main Market
Taller Artesania
Gold Processing
PLAZA DE ARMAS
PLAZA BOLOGNESI
AVENIDA CIRCUNLACION
AVENIDA MARIA REICHE
TARAPACÁ
LA CULTURA
CALLE ARICA
JIRÓN CALLAO
JIRÓN TACNA
JIRÓN LIMA
JIRÓN GRAÚ
JIRÓN JUAN MATTA
JIRÓN JOSÉ MARIA MEJIA
JIRÓN FERMIN DEL CASTILLO
JIRÓN BOLOGNES
JIRÓN IGNACIO MORSESKI
JIRÓN BOLIVAR
SAN MARTIN
MICAELO BASTIDAS
ESPINALES
AVENIDA LOS INCAS
JIRÓN LOS INCAS
Río Tierras Blancas
PJE. TORRICO
PJE. LOPEZ
AVENIDA SAN CARLOS
AVENIDA ZARUMILLA
N
0 100
metres

2

Templo Escalonado

The only section of Cahuachi to have been properly excavated so far is the **Templo Escalonado**, a multilevel temple on which you can see wide adobe walls and, on the temple site, some round, sunken chambers. A hundred metres away, from the top of what is known as the main pyramid structure, you can look down over what was once the main ceremonial plaza, though it's difficult to make out now because of the sands.

2

El Estaquería

Quite close to the main complex is a construction known as **El Estaquería**, The Place of the Stakes, retaining a dozen rows of *huarango* log pillars. *Huarango* trees (known in the north of Peru as *algarrobo*) are the most common form of desert vegetation. Their wood, baked by the sun, is very hard, though their numbers are much reduced nowadays by locals who use them for fuel. The Estaquería is estimated to be 2000 years old, but its original function is unclear, though other such constructions are usually found above tombs. The bodies here were buried with ceramics, food, textiles, jewellery and chaquira beads. Italian archeologist Giuseppe Orefici has worked on Cahuachi for nearly twenty years and has uncovered over three hundred graves, one of which contained a tattooed and dreadlocked warrior. Also around 2000 years old, he's a mere whippersnapper compared with other evidence Orefici has unearthed relating to 4000-year-old pre-ceramic cultures.

ARRIVAL AND GETTING AROUND

NASCA AND AROUND

By bus Most people arrive in Nasca by bus from Lima, Arequipa or Cusco. Most bus companies have depots or offices around the *ovalo* (roundabout) at the northern entry to town. Cruz del Sur buses (056 522495 and 056 522712) drop off close to the *ovalo* on Avenida Los Incas at the entrance to town coming in from north (or south). Ormeño buses (056 522058, grupo-ormeno.com) arrive close by at Av de los Incas 112; CIVA, block 1 of Av Guardia Civil (056 523019), though note that there's a restaurant out front; Cueva, Av Los Incas 106 (056 523061); Señor de Luren, at the roundabout near *Restaurant La Kañada*; Flores, from near the *ovalo*, have Mercedes buses to and from Arequipa and Cusco; the regular Soyuz Perú Bus for Ica, Pisco or Lima have a depot at Av Lima 155.

By colectivo Large 1970s US vehicles act as colectivos (see p.29), connecting Ica with Nasca (leaving from near CIVA bus office in Nasca); they can be spotted cruising along in patched-up Dodge Coronets or similar.

Destinations Abancay (2 or 3 daily; 10–11hr); Arequipa (several daily; 9–11hr); Cusco (2–3 daily; 14–16hr); Lima (several daily; 5–6hr); Pampa Galera (2–3 daily; 5hr); Puquio (2–3 daily; 5–6hr).

By taxi Most people use the noisy, beeping little *tico* taxis or mototaxis (motorcycle-rickshaws), which can be hailed anywhere and compete to take you into – or around – town cheaply; you shouldn't pay more than S/5 for any destination in town.

INFORMATION AND ACTIVITIES

Tourist information and tours There is no official tourist information office but the following Nasca-based operators can provide general tourist information, as well as tours and activities: Nasca Trails, Fermin del Castillo 637, 4 blocks from the Plaza de Armas (056 522858, nascatrails.com) or Alegria Tours, Jr Lima 168 (056 523775, alegriatoursperu.com), who also run the *Hostal Alegria* (see opposite); Huarango Travel Arica 602 (056 5221410). If you're after a minibus with a driver, try Transporte Turístico.

Activities Cerro Blanco, one of the biggest dunes in the world, provides breathtaking views and a perfect spot for sand-boarding trips. It is a 1–2hr drive up towards Puquio from Nasca, best visited on a tour.

Festivals September is one of the best times to visit if you want to participate in one of its fiestas, when the locals venerate the Virgen de Guadalupe (Sept 8) with great enthusiasm. In May, the religious and secular festivities of the Fiesta de las Cruces go on for days.

ACCOMMODATION

NASCA

Hostal Estrella del Sur Jr Callao 568 056 522764, estrelladelsurhotel@yahoo.com.mx. Good value, TV in most rooms, private baths, very clean and with friendly service; though it's best to pick your room carefully, since only some of the compact rooms have windows. Staff can help organize tours. Breakfasts included. **S/70**

Hostal Internacional Av Maria Reiche 112 056 522744, hostalinternacional@hotmail.com. In addition to offering the usual hostel accommodation, this place has some quieter and more spacious bungalows out back. Most rooms have private bath, some have TV and all have hot water. S/60

Hostal Las Lineas Jr Arica 299 T 056 522488, E lineas@terra.com.pe. This modern, affordable hotel overlooks the Plaza de Armas and has its own decent restaurant. All rooms come with private bath and hot water. S/90

Hostal Nasca Jr Lima 438 T 056 522085, E marionasca13@hotmail.com. Friendly, basic hostel with shared bathrooms, very clean, airy and popular. It also has a pleasant restaurant and they can exchange dollars and organize taxis, tours and good-value flights over the Lines. S/50

Hostal Sol de Nasca Jr Callao 586 T/F 056 522730, E reservasnazca@hotmail.com. Located just a couple of blocks from the Plaza de Armas, this hostel is clean and contemporary with TVs, private bath and a rooftop breakfast space. Excellent value with all-day hot water and very friendly service. S/55

Hostal Walk On Inn (ex Via Morburg) Jr José María Mejía 108 T 056 522566, W walkoninn.com. An up-to-date, secure place offering very good value and in a quiet part of town, with comfortable rooms with private bath and constant hot water. There's also a small pool and a rooftop terrace where breakfast can be enjoyed. S/50

Hotel Alegria Jr Lima 166 T 056 522283, W hostalalegriacom. This popular hotel has rooms with private baths set around an attractive garden with a fine pool; it also runs a café that serves tasty, affordable meals and their travel agency can arrange tours and bus connections to Lima or Arequipa. Spacious parking area at back. S/120

★ **Hotel Cantayo** T 056 522345, W hotelcantayo.com. Located 15min from the town centre in an old hacienda, this is a stylish luxury spa and hotel resort with pools, helipad, fine gardens, gym, sauna, martial arts *dojo* and a yoga programme; lovely if you can afford it. Service is good, and there's also an excellent restaurant serving organic dishes. S/450

Hotel Don Agucho Av Paredones, at corner with Av San Carlos 100 T/F 056 522048. One of the nicest options in and around Nasca, this hacienda-style place has comfortable rooms, with bath and TV, entered via cactus-filled passages. There's also a pool and a bar-restaurant; breakfast included in the price. S/100

★ **Nazca Lines Hotel** Jr Bolognesi 147 T 056 522293, E reservas@derramajae.org.pe. Luxurious hotel, with its own well-kept pool (which non-residents can use for approximately $5 a day) and an excellent restaurant. S/400

Paradones Inn Hotel Jr Lima 600 T 056 522181, W paredonesinn.com. A modern and yet stylish hotel in the heart of Nasca's small commercial area, the *Paradones* is smart and clean, with TVs, private bathrooms and hot water. Some rooms have jacuzzis. S/120 per person

2

AROUND NASCA

★ **Hostal Wasipunko** Km 462, Panamerican Highway, Pajonal T 056 523212, W nascawasipunko.com. A delightful, rustic country hostel, with its own small ecological and archeological museum. There's no electricity, but it's very clean and rooms (some with private bath) are set around a lovely courtyard, while the restaurant specializes in tasty pre-Inca dishes utilizing guinea pigs and local vegetables. It's signposted on the right of the highway some 15km south of Nasca; a taxi from town will cost around $5, or take one of the local buses or colectivos heading south from Nasca's main *ovalo*. S/150

Hotel de la Borda Km 447, Panamerican Highway T 056 522750. A once-luxurious hacienda hotel set in an oasis just 2km off the highway close to the Nasca airstrip, it's certainly not as well kept as it once was, but still has charm and is a comfortable place to stay. The hotel also runs tours, including some to wildlife havens on the nearby coast. S/300

Nido del Condor Km 447, Panamerican Highway T 056 522424, E contanas@terra.com.pe. A modern hotel with pools and a camping area, with good deals which sometimes include a flight over the Lines. This hotel offers the closest camping spot to the airstrip (tent prices from S/10 a person). S/350

Pampa Galera Vicuña Reserve The reserve has a shelter, but it's a very basic concrete shack with no beds, and you need written permission from the Ministry of Agriculture and Fauna in Lima (Av La Universidad 200, La Molina, Lima T 01/613 5800, W minag.gob.pe; S/15), which is not easy, so it is best to take an organized tour with one of the Nasca companies (see opposite). However, you can camp here without a permit. Camping S/5

EATING

Eating in Nasca offers more variety than you might imagine given the town's small size. Most places are in or around Jirón Bolognesi and Jirón Lima, where, for vegetarians, there are a number of pizza, pasta and snack places worth trying out. There's also a small market on Jr Lima, opposite the Banco de la Nación as well as the Panificadora La Esperanza bakery at Jr Bolognesi 389.

La Ballena Azul Jr Grau and Jr Callao 698. Considering there's no ocean in sight, this is a surprisingly decent cevichería, serving up very tasty seafood; popular as a lunch venue for local business people. Mon–Sat noon–6pm.

Grumpy's Snack Bar Jr Bolognesi 282. All earthen floor

and bamboo walls, this little establishment serves cool drinks and good breakfasts in a friendly atmosphere; they also serve sandwiches, cakes and other snacks. Mon–Sat 7.30am–10pm.

Restaurant Los Angeles Bolognesi 266 ⓣ056 522294. A very nice family-run restaurant with a wide range of freshly cooked foods, from burgers and omelettes to pizza, French fries and more traditional Peruvian food like *lomo saltado*. Mon–Sat 9.30am–9pm.

Restaurant La Carreta Bolognesi 270 ⓣ056 521286. Decent food and reasonable pisco sours; this restaurant dedicates much of its service to the large groups of tourists who hurtle through Nasca every day; there are great cakes and coffee as well as a la carte menus. They have live music at fiesta times and often host discos at weekends. Daily 11am–late.

Restaurant Don Hono C Arica 251 ⓣ056 523066. Opposite the *Restaurant Plaza Mayor* (see opposite), by the Plaza de Armas, this place is small and relatively inexpensive, with excellent local, national and international cuisine. With the kitchen near the tables, you can have a glimpse of the chef preparing your meal. Daily lunch–11pm.

NASCA CERAMICS

In 1901, when Max Uhle "discovered" the Nasca culture, it suddenly became possible to associate a certain batch of beautiful **ceramics** that had previously been unclassifiable in terms of their cultural background: the importance of Nasca pottery in the overall picture of Peru's pre-history asserted itself overnight. Many of the best pieces were found in Cahuachi (see p.134).

Unlike contemporaneous Mochica ware, Nasca ceramics rarely attempt any realistic imagery. The majority – painted in three or four earthy colours and given a resinous surface glaze – are relatively stylized or even completely abstract. Nevertheless, two main categories of subject matter recur: naturalistic designs of bird, animal and plant life, and motifs of mythological monsters and bizarre deities. In later works it was common to mould effigies to the pots. During Nasca's decline under the Huari-Tiahuanaco cultural influence (see p.487), the workmanship and designs were less inspired. The style and content of the early pottery, however, show remarkable similarities to the symbols depicted in the **Nasca Lines**, and although not enough is known about the Nasca culture to be certain, it seems reasonable to assume that the early Nasca people were also responsible for the drawings on the Pampa de San José. With most of the evidence coming from their graveyards, though, and that so dependent upon conjecture, there is actually little to characterize the Nasca and not much known of them beyond the fact that they collected heads as trophies, that they built a ceremonial complex in the desert at Cahuachi, and that they scraped a living from the Nasca, Ica and Pisco valleys from around 200–600 AD.

★ **Restaurant El Huarango** C Arica 602 ⓣ056 521287. Offering a fine rooftop patio and a great ambience, this place serves delicious food, mostly traditional coastal Peruvian dishes such as *aji de gallena* (chilli chicken) but also including some more international cuisine. Daily 11am–11pm.

Restaurant Plaza Mayor C Arica and Jr Bolognesi, on main plaza ⓣ056 523548. A large, popular central restaurant on three levels, the *Plaza Mayor* serves plenty of meat dishes, mainly *parrillas*, amid interesting decor, with Andean godlike figurines on the walls and the feel of a large, chunky, wooden structure. Daily lunch–11pm.

★ **Restaurant El Portón** Jr Ignacio Moreski 120 ⓣ056 523490. A lively hangout at night, especially at weekends with frequent live folk music, a dancefloor and bar. Pastas, meat and seafood dishes are complemented by the colonial mansion-style decor. Best espresso in town. Daily 8am–10pm.

2

DRINKING

What little nightlife exists is mainly based around restaurants and bars, particularly on Jr Lima, Plaza de Armas and Jr Bolognesi.

For an alcohol fix try the Licoria liquor store at C Arica 401.

Bar Natisca Jr Bolognesi 484. A small but lively bar which plays a mix of modern music (reggae, salsa, rock) and serves a variety of snacks and bar food; a good place to meet other travellers as well as local young people. Daily noon–midnight.

Bar-Restaurant El Griego Jr Bolognesi 287 ⓣ056 521480. A friendly local eating-house with fine food and decent drinks at reasonable prices. Good breakfasts and can be fun in the evening when it functions less as a restaurant and more as a bar. Daily 10.30am–midnight.

La Taberna Jr Lima 321. Serves a good selection of local and international dishes, plus a variety of drinks; its walls are covered with graffiti scrawled over the years by passing groups of travellers. Live folk music plays until around midnight most evenings. Daily 11am–12pm.

DIRECTORY

Health Pharmacies include Botica Central, Jr Bolognesi 355 at corner with Jr Fermin del Castillo; Botica Alejandra, C Arica 407.

Internet Available all over Nasca, but in particular next door to the *Restaurant El Portón*. Also at Fox Internet, Jr Bolognesi block 1; Mundo Virtual, Jr Bolognesi 395 and Jr Bolognesi 225.

Money and exchange Banco de Credito, Jr Lima 495; Interbanc, C Arica 363; and Banco de la Nación, Jr Lima 463. The best rates for dollars cash are with the *cambistas* in the small park outside the *Hotel Nasca*, where Jr Bolognesi and Jr Lima merge, or outside the Banco de Credito.

Police Block 5, Jr Lima ⓣ056 522442 or ⓣ056 522105.

Post office Jr Fermin del Castillo 379; Mon–Sat 8am–8pm.

Shopping Oscar, Jr Bolognesi 465, sells local artesanía.

Telephones Jr Lima 525; daily 7am–11pm.

Pampa Galeras Vicuña Reserve

Get off one of the main daily Nasca–Cusco buses, for example Tour Huari runs to Puquio at around 4pm; ask the driver to tell you where to get off

Some 90km inland from Nasca, and well signposted at Km 89 of the Nasca–Cusco road, the **Pampa Galeras Vicuña Reserve** is one of the best places in Peru to see the **vicuña**, a llama-like animal with very fine wool. The *vicuña* have lived for centuries in the area of reserve, which is now maintained as their natural habitat and contains more than five thousand of the creatures.

The *vicuña* themselves are not easy to spot. When you do notice a herd, you'll see it move as if it were a single organism. They flock together and move swiftly in a tight wave, bounding gracefully across the hills. The males are strictly territorial, protecting their patches of scrubby grass by day, then returning to the rockier heights as darkness falls.

Puquio, Chumpi and Lago Parinacochas

Chumpi and Lago Parinacochas can only be accessed by private car, tour groups (see p.136) or irregular local buses and colectivos from or via Puquio

Located east of the Pampa Galeras Vicuña Reserve along the Cusco road, **PUQUIO** is a quiet, relatively uninteresting stop-off, but if you have to break your journey, there's a choice of several hostels, most within a block or two of the plaza, none of them particularly enticing. As soon as you cross over the metal bridge at the entrance to the village, you get a real sense that the desert coast is left behind and the Andean ecology and landscapes abruptly take over. In fact, Puquio was an isolated community until 1926, when the townspeople built their own road link between the coast and the sierra.

The road divides at Puquio, with the main route continuing over the Andes to Cusco via Abancay. A side road goes south for about 140km along the mountains to Lago Parinacochas; although frequently destroyed by mudslides in the rainy season, the road always seems full of passing trucks, which will usually take passengers there for a small price. Continuing to **Chumpi**, an ideal place to camp, there is some exceptionally stunning sierra scenery. Within a few hours' walk of the town is the beautiful lake, **Lago Parinacochas**, named after the many flamingoes that live there and probably one of the best unofficial nature reserves in Peru. If you're not up to the walk, you could take a day-trip from Nasca for about $40; try Alegria Tours (see p.136). From Chumpi you can either backtrack to Puquio, or continue down the road past the lake, before curving another 130km back down to the coast at Chala.

The Panamerican Highway

From Nasca, the **Panamerican Highway** continues for about 1000km to the border with Chile. Apart from Chala and Camaná, the road only passes the occasional fishing village or squatter settlement until it reaches the Arequipa turn-off; from there, it's straight south across the northern altiplano desert to Tacna. The desert landscape immediately south of Nasca is stunningly bleak and there's relatively little of specific interest in the 170km of desert between Nasca and Chala.

Sacaco

Ask at the house in daylight hours for the guardian to open the museum, which is a few hundred metres further • Voluntary payment ($2–3 per person recommended)

The remarkable paleontological site of **Sacaco** gives access to fossilized whale remains sitting in the desert near a small museum about 96km south of Nasca. One fossilized whale skeleton is housed within the museum building itself with some interpretative material about the geology and paleontology of the region on the walls. It can be reached on some tours and also by hopping off one of the Nasca-to-Chala (or Lima-to-Arequipa) buses. The site is well hidden to the left of the road going south along the Panamericana Sur, some 11 or 12km after the Las Lomas turn-off (which goes to the right). Look out for a small sign on the left and ask the driver where to disembark. From here it's a thirty-minute walk along a sand track for 1 or 2km into the desert, away from the road, coming eventually to a house and cultivated area.

Las Lomas

Las Lomas is a remote fishing village with a **beach** that's especially good for spotting pelicans, about 90km to the south of Nasca and off the Panamerican Highway. It can only be reached in private car or with a tour group from Nasca.

Puerto Inca

Open access • Free • To get to the ruins, take a taxi from Chala (about $10), or catch an Arequipa-bound bus along the Panamerican Highway and ask to be dropped off at Km 610. It's an easy 2–3km walk from here along a rustic but passable road following a narrow gully to the beach

The ruins of **Puerto Inca**, the Incas' main port for Cusco, stand 10km before Chala. There's an excellent **beach**, and fine diving and fishing here. The ruins are close to *Puerto Inka Hotel* (see opposite) and beach, while within a half-day's walk there are caves, grottos, hidden coves, rock formations and plenty of opportunity for getting lost in the desert coastline, birdwatching or even spotting Humboldt penguins if you're patient and lucky enough.

Chala

A small, quietish town, **Chala** was the main port for Cusco until the construction of the Cusco–Arequipa rail line. Now, it's a more or less agreeable little fishing town, where you can overindulge in fresh seafood, the best of which is found along the sea front at the southern edge of town.

Camaná

About 200km south from Chala, **CAMANÁ** is a popular Arequipeño beach resort from December to March, when the weather is hot, dry and relatively windless, although outside high season it has little to offer. The most popular **beach** is at **La Punta**, around 5km along the Arequipa road.

Continuing toward Arequipa (see p.152), the sealed road keeps close to the coast wherever possible, passing through a few small fishing villages and over monotonous, arid plains before eventually turning inland for the final uphill stretch into the land of volcanoes and Peru's second largest city. At Km 916 of the Panamerican Highway, a road leads off into the Maches Canyon towards the Toro Muerto petroglyphs, the Valley of the Volcanoes and **Cotahuasi Canyon** (see p.184). At Rapartición, the road splits: east to Arequipa and south towards Mollendo, Moquegua, Tacna and Chile.

ACCOMMODATION — THE PANAMERICAN HIGHWAY

PUERTO INCA

Puerto Inka Km 610, Panamericana Sur ☎054 692596, @puertoinka.com.pe; or contact in Arequipa at C Arica 406a, Yanahuara ☎054 252588. This hotel is spread out across several bungalows overlooking the sea; it offers a reasonable restaurant, big parking area, campsite and quick access to the beach. Check the website for deals. Camping $10, doubles S/190

CHALA

Hotel Grau A basic place to rest your head, but situated in a nice position, right next to the beach. S/50

Hotel de Turistas ☎054 551111, ☎501110 or ☎555111. Old-fashioned but comfortable hotel. S/120

CAMANÁ

Hotel de Turistas Av Lima 138, Km 841 ☎054 571113 or ☎054 571608. A charming spot, with adequate rooms. Service is good and the large building has gardens, terraces, good restaurant, a swimming pool and plenty of decent showers. S/90

Mollendo and Mejía

Serving as a coastal resort for Arequipa and home of the **Reserva Nacional de Mejía**, a marvellous lagoon-based bird sanctuary, **MOLLENDO** is a pleasant old port with a decent stretch of sand and a laidback atmosphere. This is a relaxed spot to spend a couple of days chilling out on the **beach** and makes a good base from which to visit the nearby nature reserve lagoons at **MEJÍA**, also known as the **Reserva Nacional de Mejía bird sanctuary**, just south of town.

The National Sanctuary and Lakes of Mejía

Daily 7am–5pm • $2 • Take an Empresa Aragon bus from Arequipa (see p.164); you'll see the lagoons just before you get to Tambo Valley; alternatively, get a colectivo (every 10min) from the top end of Calle Castilla in Mollendo

The **National Sanctuary and Lakes of Mejía**, 7km south of Mollendo, is an unusual ecological niche consisting of almost 700 hectares of lakes separated from the Pacific

Ocean by just a sand bar, and providing an important habitat for many thousands of migratory birds. Of the 157 species, such as blue-footed boobies, pelicans, penguins and Inca terns, sighted at Mejía, around 72 are permanent residents; the best time for sightings is early in the morning.

ARRIVAL AND DEPARTURE — MOLLENDO AND MEJÍA

By bus Empresa Aragon buses from Arequipa, Moquegua and Tacna stop and start in or close to the Terminal Terrestre, four blocks north of Plaza de Armas; Tepsa buses stop at Alfonso Ugarte 320 (☎054 532872); and Cruz del Sur (☎054 253156) also stop nearby on Alfonso Ugarte.

Destinations Arequipa (several daily; 2–3hr); Moquegua (several daily; 2hr); Tacna (several daily; 4hr).

ACCOMMODATION AND EATING

Cevichería Alejo Panamerican Highway South, Miramar. This great little restaurant is a little out of town, but well worth the 20min walk (or 5min taxi ride) for its excellent, reasonably priced seafood dishes, in particular their *fuentes de pescado* (literally, large serving bowls of freshly cooked fish). Daily 11am–7pm.

Hostal Cabaña Comercio 240 ☎054 534571 and ☎054 533833. Inexpensive rooms in a slighty down-at-heel but lovely wooden building with verandas and patio; all rooms have private bath and hot water 24hr, with good service. S/75

Hostal El Muelle Arica 144 ☎054 533680. Clean and friendly with pleasant views from some of the rooms; service is fine, rooms have TV and 24hr hot water with private baths. S/90

Pizzeria Golosa Plaza de Armas. Pizzas and pasta dishes galore, although the place itself is and feels like part of a plastic-looking regional restaurant chain. The upside is that service is fast and the food is predictably edible. Daily 11am–10pm.

DIRECTORY

Money and exchange If you need to change money, you'll get the best rates for dollars cash from the *cambistas* on Plaza Bolognesi; ATMs available at the Banco de la Nación, Arequpa 243 and the Banco de Credito, Comercio 323.

Moquegua

Situated on the northern edge of the Atacama Desert, most of which lies over the border in Chile, the **MOQUEGUA** region is traditionally and culturally linked to the Andean region around Lake Titicaca, and many ethnic Colla and Lupaca from the mountains live here. The local economy today is based on copper mining, fruit plantations and wine. More interestingly, for those partial to spirits, Moquegua has a reputation for producing Peru's best **pisco**. Historically, this area is an annexe of the altiplano, which was used as a major thoroughfare first by the Tiahuanacu and later the Huari peoples. In the future it may well be the main route for the gas pipeline out of Peru's eastern rainforest regions to the coast. Right now, though, located in a relatively narrow valley, the colonial town of Moquegua has winding streets, an attractive plaza and many of adobe houses roofed in thatch and clay.

Few non-Peruvians come to Moquegua to visit the local attractions, as most are in a hurry to get in or out of Chile. That said, the area has plenty of little-visited but interesting sites, from wine and pisco bodegas and volcanoes to petroglyphs and archeological remains. All of these require personal car transport, or, better, going with a local tour company (see p.144).

Catedral de Santo Domingo

C Tacna and C Ayacucho • Mon–Sat 7am–noon & 4–7pm • Free

Standing close to the plaza – which has an ornate metal fountain designed in 1877 by Gustave Eiffel – the **Catedral de Santo Domingo** was restored after an earthquake in 1868 and now contains a large single nave, two finely worked *retablos*, and, in one of its towers, the first clock to arrive in Moquegua from London in 1798. The cathedral

2

MOQUEGUA'S BODEGAS

Initially established during the colonial era, Moquegua's bodegas have various lines in piscos (including *italia* and *mosto verde*), cognacs, aniseed liqueurs and wines. The below are two excellent options you can visit:

Bodega Villegas e Hijos C Ayacucho 1370 ☎053 461229; Mon–Sat 8am–noon & 2–5pm. Welcoming bodega run by Alberto Villegas Vargas, grandson of the original founder Norberto Villegas Talavera, one of the town's benefactors.

Bodega Zapata Km 1142 of the Panamericana Sur ☎053 461164; Mon–Sat 10am–5pm. Produces fine piscos from *quebranta* and *italia* grapes.

also houses the relics of Santa Fortunata whose remains were excavated from their original resting place in Spain and brought to Peru in the nineteenth century.

Museo Contisuyo

C Tacna 294 • Daily 9am–1pm & 2.30–5.30pm • S/2

On the western side of town, just half a block from the main plaza, there's the **Museo Contisuyo**, an archeological museum that exhibits relics from the region including stone arrow points, ceramics, textiles, gold and silver objects and specimens from the Tiahuanuco and Huari cultures as well as the local ancient coastal Chiribaya and Tumilaca cultures. There's also a permanent geographical exhibition room.

Torata

Bus from Carretera Binacional ($1; 30min)

About 24km away from Moquegua on the main road to Puno, **TORATA** is a picturesque district and settlement of country homes made with traditional *mojinete* (slanted and gable ended) roofs. There's also an imposing church and old stone mill, both from the colonial period, as well as some (more contemporary) restaurants. The **petroglyphs of Torata**, which depict llamas, geometric shapes and what look like maps and water symbols, are within relatively easy reach of Moquegua by following the small *quebrada*, a dry canyon which runs east 200m from the bridge at Km 120.45 of the Carretera Binacional.

Cerro Baúl

Before you hit the bodegas (see box above), it's advisable to check out some of the ancient sites in the region; that way you'll have the opportunity to work up a justifiable thirst. One of the bigger sites around is the archeological remnant of a Huari (600–1100 AD) citadel that is easily visited by taxi from Moquegua. Sitting atop a truncated hill – **Cerro Baúl**, after which the ruins are named – some 17km northeast of the town, this commanding site once offered its ancient inhabitants a wide view around the Moquegua Valley, allowing them to control the flow of goods and people at this strategic point.

The volcanoes and Omate

Within striking distance of Moquegua are the majestic Ubinas (5673m, with a 350m crater) and Huaynaputina (4800m) **volcanoes**. Visiting these is an adventurous operation that demands 4WD support from one of the local travel agencies (see p.144). Also in the sierra is the remote town of **Omate**, 130km (3hr) from Moquegua on the back mountain road to Arequipa. Surrounded by unique and impressive terrain formed by rock, volcanic ash and sands, it's also famous for its crayfish. Check out the natural **thermal baths** of Ulucan (3100m; daily 8am–5.30pm; S/2), just 10km from Omate.

2

Toquepala

Into the hills southeast of Moquegua, the town of **Toquepala** and nearby mysterious **caves** (2500m) can be visited in a day. The caves – occupied by a group of hunter-gatherers from the Archaic era around nine thousand years ago – are fascinating but rarely visited. Close to the mine of the same name, these caves contain roughly drawn pictures of cameloid animals, hunting scenes and Andean religious symbols. Again, the best way to find this site is by taking a short tour with a local travel agency (see below).

The Chen Chen geoglyphs

The little-seen **geoglyphs of Chen Chen** can be accessed by car from Moquegua, by taking the track towards Toquepala which leaves the Panamericana Sur between Km 98 and 97; the track passes along the base of some hills where the geoglyphs, mainly large Nasca-like representations of llamas, are scattered around, some hidden from the road.

ARRIVAL GETTING AROUND — MOQUEGUA

Moquegua is a busy nodal point for two important roads into the Andes: the Carretera Transoceanica connecting Ilo on the coast to Puno and Juliaca, and the Carretera Binacional to Desaguadero, which shears off from it some distance after Torata.

BY BUS

Most people arrive in town by bus, either at blocks 2 and 3 of Av Ejercito or Avenida La Paz, both several long blocks from the heart of town and worth the S3–5 taxi ride.

Bus companies Cruz del Sur, Av La Paz 296 (T 053 462005) serves Lima, Tacna, Arequipa and Desaguadero; as does Tepsa, at Av del Ejercito 33b (T 053 461171); and Flores, Avenida del Ejercito, at the corner with Calle Andres A. Caceres (T 053 462181, E florbus@terra.com.pe). Empresa Aragon have offices on Calle Balta, four blocks southwest of the Plaza de Armas and serve Arequipa, Mollendo and Tacna. Civa, at Av del Ejercito 32b, serves most destinations in Peru. Altiplano, Av Ejercito 444 (T 053 426672), runs direct services to Puno. Transportes Korimayo, Av del Ejercito, also run buses to Desaguadero and Puno. Similarly, Expreso Turismo San Martín, Av del Ejercito 19, runs buses all the way to Desaguadero, Puno and Juliaca.

Destinations There are several buses daily to: Arequipa (2hr); Desaguadero (5hr); Lima (18hr); Mollendo (2hr); Puno (6hr); Tacna (2hr).

BY COLECTIVO

Colectivos run much the same routes as buses (see above), though without set itineraries. They all leave from Av Ejercito by the corner with C Cáceres. Mili Tours run several cars daily to Desaguadero (5–6hr), as well as two or three cars a day to Arequipa (3–4hr). Comite 1, Comite 11 and El Buen Samaritano each serve Tacna, each taking four or five passengers daily. El Buen Samaritano, Av del Ejercito, also serves Desaguadero and offers *expresso* services to take passengers anywhere they like.

BY CAR

For car rental, try Mili Tours, Av del Ejercito 32 (T 053 464000), from around $45/day.

INFORMATION AND TOURS

Tourist information Camara de Turismo, Jr Ayacucho 625 (T 053 462008 or T 053 462342), the Regional Tourism Directorate at Jr Ayacucho 1060 (T 053 462236), and Ledelca Tours, Jr Ayacucho 625 (T/F 053 462342, E ledelca@viabcp.com), provide information; also, some historical information is available from the Museo Contisuyo, in the Plaza de Armas.

Tour operators Ledelca Tours, Jr Ayacucho 625 (T/F 053 462953), sell airline tickets and are the local representatives for DHL. They offer city tours (3hr) and countryside tours (3hr), which generally includes a visit to a bodega, or a longer tour to the Chen Chen geoglyphs, the archeological site of Cerro Baúl (4hr) and, if requested, Ubinas and other local volcanoes (4–6hr) in 4WDs.

ACCOMMODATION

Alameda Hotel Jr Junín 322 T 053 463971. This is friendly, well-run and has a great little café; all rooms have private bathrooms, some with TV. S/90

Hostal Adrianela Miguel Grau 239 T 053 463469. Rooms all have private baths, colour TVs and hot water, but it's located in the busy and sometimes noisy commercial sector of town close to the market. S/60

Hostal Arequipa C Arequipa 360 T 053 461338. Basic yet fairly comfortable and good-value hostel with private bathrooms. S/75

Hostal Carrera Jr Lima 320 ⓣ053 462113. A basic but clean hostel, just one block parallel to Plaza de Armas; appeals to backpackers, not least because of its low price. S/40

Hostal Limoñeros Jr Lima 441 ⓣ053 461649. Just one and a half blocks northwest of the plaza, with constant hot water, cable TV, attractive gardens, semi-rustic atmosphere and a small pool. S/50

Hotel El Mirador Alto de Villa ⓣ053 424193, ⓦdematourshoteles.com. One of the smartest options in town with swimming pool and all mod-cons. S/250

EATING AND DRINKING

Bandido Pub C Moquegua 333 ⓣ053 461676. One of the few bars in town and a place where they play good music and serve pizzas cooked in wood-fired earth ovens, as well as reasonably priced drinks. Mon–Sat 6pm–midnight.

Restaurante Moraly C Lima and C Libertad ⓣ053 463084. This is a traditional and stylish restaurant in the town centre with a reputation for great breakfasts and good service. Daily 7am–7pm.

Restaurante Palmero C Moquegua 644. Just half a block from the plaza, this typical Peruvian restaurant serves mouthwatering comida criolla and some local specialities in an open and friendly space. Daily 8.30am–8.30pm.

Restaurante Recreo Turístico Las Glorietas Calle Antigua de Samegua. Located on the outskirts of town, this is a relatively large restaurant which serves good local food in a traditional atmosphere. Daily 10.30am–7pm.

Restaurante El Totoral Calle Antigua de Samegua ⓣ053 461862. On the edge of town, this place serves tasty, mainly meat, dishes in a pleasant setting. Mon–Sat 11am–7pm.

Trattoria La Toscana C Tacna 505 ⓣ053 461043. Good quality Italian restaurant serving the usual pizzas, some pasta dishes and, being close to Chile, a range of quite good wines as well as cool beer. Daily noon–9pm.

DIRECTORY

Internet Sybernet, Jr Moquegua 434, half a block from the plaza (daily 8am–11pm), and Café Internet, Jr Moquegua 418, which serves drinks (daily 8am–10pm).

Money and exchange Cash can be changed at the Banco de la Nación, Jr Lima 616; the Banco de Credito has an ATM on the corner at Moquegua 861; or there are the *cambistas* outside Plaza Bolívar.

Post office C Ayacucho 560, Plaza de Armas (Mon–Sat 8am–8pm).

Telephones Locutorio Público, C Moquegua 617 (Mon–Sat 7am–10pm, Sun 7am–1pm & 4–10pm).

Ilo

About 95km southeast of Moquegua, **ILO** is a busy port on the Peruvian Atacama Desert coastline, with a population of over 65,000 inhabitants and an economy based around fishing and mining. The most strategically, and economically, important port in Peru, in itself Ilo doesn't offer visitors very much, but it does have one or two interesting features.

Templo de San Geronimo

Plaza de Armas • Daily 6am–6pm

The Plaza de Armas is the civic heart of the city, dominated by the **Templo de San Geronimo**. The temple was built originally in 1871 and contains an antique font created with a seashell and brought here from Paris. It has a single rectangular nave and central tower, while one of the three church bells was crafted in 1647.

Malecón costero

Museo Naval Daily 9am–6pm • $1.50

The *malecón costero* (seaside promenade) and the seafront developments lie two blocks away from the Templo. The *malecón* boasts La Glorieta, an iron bandstand structure built onto a huge boulder overlooking the sea. Ilo's promenade has had the reputation as the most modern in Peru, since its installation in 2002. In the Capitano del Puerto's offices, there's a small **Museo Naval** with documents and artefacts relating to the maritime past including manuscripts pertaining to Admiral Miguel Grau. Next to the nineteenth-century iron pier, you can find a busy wharf used by artisan fishermen who use small boats and simple nets, and a seafood market.

Ilo's beaches

Ilo is known for its fifteen or so **beaches** spreading out both north and south of the town. The nearest and most popular is the **Playa Pozo de Lisas**, close to the airport; it's extensive and usually empty except weekends in December and January when it's invariably crowded. At the other end of town, to the north, the **Playa Boca del Río** has fine sand and good views back to the city. About 20km further north, the **Playa Pocoma** is ideal for camping; the nicer **Playa Waikiki** is another 4km further north.

Museo de Sitio El Algarrobal

Municipalidad El Algarrobal • Daily 7am–5pm • T 053 761844 • Free

Arguably the most interesting local attraction is the **Museo de Sitio El Algarrobal**, about 15km east of town. The museum presents exhibits from the pre-Hispanic cultures of the Ilo region, including textiles from the local Chiribaya culture and mummies, and offers views over the valley of Algarrobal and the old hacienda Chiribaya (1000–1350 AD).

ARRIVAL AND DEPARTURE — ILO

BY BUS

Arriving at Ilo, most buses come in on or close to C Matara. Buses to Bolivia leave from nearby at the corner of Matara and Junín.

Bus companies Cruz del Sur (T 053 782206) serves Lima and Arequipa, and set off from the corner of Matara with Jr Moquegua. Buses for Chile and Arica leave daily with Flores Hnos (T 053 482512) from the corner of Jr Ilo with Matara.

ACCOMMODATION AND EATING

Calienta Negros Costanera Sur Km 02 T 053 782839 or T 053 785184. One of the better and most popular restaurants for most types of Peruvian and standard international dishes; can also cater for vegetarians. Daily 10.30am–8.30pm.

Gran Hotel Ilo Av Cáceres T 053 782411. Arguably the most comfortable hotel in town, it has over 60 well-kept rooms, a private beach, pool, car park and restaurant. The service is also good. **S/200**

Hotel Vip Jr Dos de Mayo 608 T 053 481492, W viphotelito.com. This is a very modern five-storey hotel whose bar and restaurant area has good views over the nearby port; rooms are carpeted and well equipped with TV, fridge-bar and good bathrooms. **S/156**

Los Cangrejos 28 de Julio 362 T 053 784324. Offers seafood, including its specialities – crab, clams and mussels – and comida criolla in a pleasing environment at very reasonable prices. Daily 11am–7pm.

DIRECTORY

Money and exchange Banco de Credito, Jr Zepita 402, has an ATM; and there's the Casa de Cambio Dolares Vilca, 28 de Julio 331 T 053 782728.

Post office Av Mariano Urqueta, block 3 (Mon–Sat 8am–7.30pm).

Tour agencies Tropical Travel, Jr Moquegua 608 (T 053 483865), offer local travel and tour packages as well as car hire services; Romes Tours, Calle Zepita 526 (T 053 485292), also provide local tours and travel tickets.

Tacna

Over three hours south of Moquegua and five times larger, **TACNA**, at 552m above sea level, is the last stop in Peru. The only reason to stay here is if you're coming from or going over the border into **Chile** (see box, p.148) and the border-crossing timing demands you stop, or if you feel like a break in your overland journey. Tacna is designated a **Zona Franca** (a tax- or duty-free zone) where visitors can spend up to $1000 in any one trip (with a limit of $3000 in a year) on a range of tax-free electronic, sports and other luxury items. Tacna is also a centre for **cyclists**, particularly in August when there's usually a bicycle festival attracting competitors and enthusiasts from Bolivia and Chile as well as Peru.

Brief history

Founded as San Pedro de Tacna in 1535, just three years after the Spanish first arrived in Peru, Tacna was established by Viceroy Toledo as a *reducción de indigenas*, a forced concentration of normally scattered coastal communities, making them easier to tax and use as labour. Almost three hundred years later, in 1811, Francisco Antonio de Zela began the first struggle for independence from Spanish colonialism here. The people of Tacna suffered Chilean occupation from May 1880 until the Treaty of Ancón was signed in August 1929, after a local referendum. Tacna, in fact, has long been noted for its loyalty to Peru and was also highly active in Peruvian emancipation from Spain, though nowadays it's better known as an expensive city, infamous for both its contraband and its pickpockets. The reputation is worse than the reality: the usual precautions (see p.40) are generally adequate and it's not a violent place.

Plaza de Armas

The main focus of activity in this sprawling city is around the **Plaza de Armas** and along the Alameda Bolognesi. At the centre of the plaza, the ornamental *pileta*, designed by Gustave Eiffel, has a Neoclassical base depicting the four seasons, while on top of the main fountain are four children holding hands. The nearby Arco Parabólico was erected in honour of the Peruvian dead from the War of the Pacific. Fronting the plaza is the **Catedral**, designed by Eiffel in 1870 (though not completed until 1955) and built from *cantera* stones quarried from the hills of Intiorko and Arunta. The **Alameda Bolognesi**, located in the civic centre near the *Hotel de Turistas*, is an attractive, palm-lined avenue constructed in 1840; it's dotted with busts of local dignitaries and also one in fine marble of Christopher Columbus.

Some 8km north of Tacna (10–15min by taxi; S/8 one way), on Cerro Intiorko, the eight steel sculptures of **Campo de Alianza** stand in memory of the war heroes; there's also a small Museo de Sitio (daily 8am–5pm; free) which houses some old uniforms, arms and missiles left over from the historic battles.

Tacna's museums

There are a few museums in town. The **Museo Histórico Regional de Tacna** (Jr Apurímac 202; Mon–Sat 9am–6pm; free) combines ceramics and textiles from ancient cultures with exhibitions related to the nineteenth-century wars with Chile. The **Casa de Zela** (C Zela 542; Mon–Fri 8am–noon & 3–7pm) houses a small archeological museum exhibiting ceramics largely discovered in the region; the building itself has been a recognized historic monument since 1961. There is also the **Museo Ferroviario** on the corner of Calle Albarracin and Avenida Dos de Mayo (daily 8am–5.30pm; $1), which is a must for rail enthusiasts; just five minutes' walk from the plaza, containing locomotives, machinery and documents mainly relating to the now defunct Tacna–Arica line, but also a collection of train-related stamps from around the world. On Avenida Grau, there's also a **Parque de la Locomotora**, built in 1977, dedicated exclusively to housing the antique Locomotive No. 3, which carried troops to the historic battle of Morro de Arica in 1879.

ARRIVAL AND GETTING AROUND — TACNA

BY BUS

You'll most likely alight at one of the Terminal Terrestres. It's easy enough to walk to the centre of town from the Manuel Odria Terminal, but better to take a taxi from the Bolognesi Terminal, where they are easy enough to find.

Most buses leave from outside the train station on Av 2 de Mayo, or from the Manuel Odria Terminal; buses for the interior of the region leave from the Bolognesi Terminal (T 052 411786).

Destinations Arequipa (3 weekly; 6hr); Arica (3 weekly; 1–2hr); Cusco (3 weekly; 12–14hr); Desaguadero (3 weekly; 6hr); La Paz (3 weekly; 10–12hr); Lima (3 weekly; 20hr); Moquegua (3 weekly; 2hr); Puno (3 weekly; 8hr).

BY PLANE

The airport, Aeropuerto Carlos Ciriani Santa Rosa, is out on the Panamericana Sur at Km 5 (T 052 844503). The main airline office is Lan Perú, Apurimac 107 (T 052 443252).

Destinations Lima (several weekly; 2hr).

BY TAXI

Can be stopped anywhere in the centre with ease at any time of day and the fare for destinations within the city should not be any more than S/5–7.

INFORMATION

Tourist information Available from the tourist office at Av San Martín 405 (Mon–Fri 9am–6pm & Sat 9am–1pm; T 052 415352), the Plaza de Armas offices at Av Bolognesi 2088 (Mon–Sat 8am–3pm; T 052 413501 or 413778), or the Regional Tourism Directorate, Blondell 50 (T 052 422784). Failing that, try the Dirección Regional de Industria y Turismo, Jr Blondell 506, or check out W hellotacna.com.

CROSSING THE CHILEAN BORDER

The border with Chile (daily 9am–10pm) is about 40km south of Tacna. Arica, the first town in Chile, lies 25km beyond the border. There are a couple of hotels and plenty of restaurants. Bus and air services from here to the rest of Chile are excellent.

PERU–CHILE

By bus and colectivo Regular buses and colectivos to Arica leave from the modern bus terminal, on Hipolito Unanue, in Tacna. Tepsa (Leguis 981) and Ormeño (Araguex 698) buses leave the bus terminal every couple of hours or so for the one- to two-hour journey to Arica ($4). Colectivos (normally around $7) are quicker and slightly more expensive than the bus, but well worth it given the hassle saved, as they'll wait at the border controls while you get your Peruvian exit stamp and Chilean tourist card.

By train Three trains a day depart from the station, on Calle Coronel Albarracin (at 7am, 8.30am & 3pm). At around S/15, the train is the cheapest option, but it's slow and you'll have to visit the Oficina de Migraciones, Avenida Circunvalación (Mon–Fri 8am–4pm; T 052 443231; no entry fee), and the Chilean Consulate (Mon–Sat 8am–5.30pm; T 052 423063 or T 052 721846) on Presbitero Andia, just off Coronel Albarracin, beforehand.

Customs You clear Peruvian customs control on your way into Tacna, along the Panamerican Highway.

CHILE–PERU

Coming into Peru from Arica is as simple as getting there. Colectivos run throughout the day and the train leaves at the same times as the one from Tacna. Night travellers, however, might be required to have a *salvoconducto militar* (safe-conduct card), particularly in times of tension between the two countries; if so, your driver will likely organize it. If you intend to travel at night, check first with the tourist office in Arica, C Prat 305, on the second floor.

ACCOMMODATION IN ARICA

Hotel Avenida Diego Portales 2422, Arica T 056 585 83656, W hotelavenida.cl. A modern three-storey hotel with lovely gardens, a large pool and ample-sized bedrooms, some with kitchenette; wi-fi and cable TV available throughout. Doubles US$32

Hotel El Paso Av G Velásquez 1109 T 056 582 30808, W hotelelpaso.cl. Swish suites and smaller standard rooms, some ground-floor ones with access to pleasant gardens. Standard rooms smaller but still comfortable. TV and wi-fi available. Doubles US$85

ACCOMMODATION

Gran Hotel Central Av San Martín 561 ⓣ052 415051, ⓦhotelcentralperu.net. Close by the Plaza de Armas, a modern building and with many rooms which are not exactly large but all well appointed and with private baths and hot water; there's a bar-cafetería and parking. S/145

Hostal Hogar 28 de Julio 146 ⓣ052 426811, ⓦhostalhogartacna.com. Good value in a secure hostel which has nice rooms with private baths, cable TV and also internet service; it is centrally located just half a block from the Plaza de Armas. S/90

Hotel Alcazar Bolívar 295 ⓣ052 424991. Good value but one of the more basic pads in the city; rooms are clean, service is friendly enough and the place seems secure. S/40

Hotel Las Lido Av San Martín 876 ⓣ052 577001. Comfortable rooms in a well-looked-after, basic hotel; centrally located in the *cercado* area of town, just off the Plaza de Armas. S/50

2

EATING

El Caquique C José Rosa Ara 1903. The local *picantería* (traditional eating place specializing in spicy comestibles), and probably the best place to try guinea pig. Daily 11am–5pm.

Comedor Mercado Central, Zona Monumental. The central market is the best place for a tasty and very cheap meal; also excellent juice-stands where you can select your own mix. Busiest between 7 and 11am. Daily 7am–6pm.

Genova Av San Martín 649 ⓣ052 244809. Serves good grills and a wide range of the usual international dishes as well as specializing in seafoods, particularly grilled fish and ceviche. Daily 11.30am–9pm.

Gerolamo Ristorante Di Mare Av San Martín 981. Fine seafood and great, fast service. Daily 10.30am–4pm.

La Olla de Barro Billinghurst 951. Prides itself on Peruvian dishes typical of the region, such as the delicious *choclo con queso* (sweetcorn and cheese) or the spicy *picante de Tacnena* (duck in a chili and oregano sauce). Daily 11am–9pm.

DIRECTORY

Money and exchange Cash and travellers' cheques can be changed at the Banco de la Nación, San Martín 320, on the Plaza de Armas; Banco del Sur, Apurimac 245; Banco Continental, San Martín 665; Banco de Wiese, Av San Martín 476; Banco de Credito, San Martín 574; and the Banco Latino, San Martín 507. *Cambistas* hang around in avenidas Bolognesi and Mendoza. It's a good idea to get rid of your extra nuevo soles before going into Chile (exchange them for US dollars or, if not, Chilean pesos), and the *cambistas* in Tacna usually offer better rates than those in Santiago or Arica anyway.

Post office Av Bolognesi 361 (Mon–Sat 8am–8pm).

Arequipa and Lake Titicaca

COLCA CANYON

Arequipa and Lake Titicaca

While the southern coast of Peru boasts all manner of intriguing cultural sites, the adjacent interior of the south is much better known for its extremely beautiful geographical features. The Andes take hold here, punctuated by spectacular lakes, towering volcanoes and deep, stark canyons – a landscape well suited to adventurous outdoor pursuits like trekking, canoeing, climbing or mountain biking. The region has two distinct areas: one focused around Arequipa, not far removed from the coast though high above sea level; the other, the Titicaca Basin, high in the east at the northern end of the immense Altiplano, which stretches deep into Bolivia. Both are detached from the rest of the country, something reflected as much in political leanings as their landscapes, themselves unique in Peru.

3

Arequipa, second city of Peru and a day's journey from Lima, sits poised against an extraordinary backdrop of volcanic peaks. Located 2335m above sea level, the city enjoys a distinctly poetic appearance. If you're coming from the north, it's one of the last places to really merit a stop before continuing on south to the **Chilean border** (see p.148). White local stone from the surrounding mountains has been heavily incorporated into the city's buildings and was a major factor in Arequipa being designated a UNESCO World Heritage site. Trekkers from across the world are attracted by the startlingly varied countryside within the city's reach: from the gorges of both the **Colca Canyon** – massive but dwarfed by the glaciers and volcanoes on either side of the valley – and the more distant **Cotahuasi Canyon**, to the unsettling isolation of the **Valley of the Volcanoes**.

Further inland from Arequipa, you'll probably want to spend time at the world's highest lake, **Lake Titicaca**. The surrounding area is renowned for its folk dances and Andean music and this is an obvious place to break a journey from Arequipa to Cusco or into **Bolivia**. Visit and stay on one of the huge lake's islands to experience life in a very traditional Andean household or get to know its main town and port – **Puno**, a high, quite austere city with a cold climate and incredibly rarefied air. **Juliaca**, to the north of Puno, makes an alternative, if dull and unattractive, base for exploring the lake, or the countryside of this poor, largely peasant area.

Arequipa

A wealthy city with a population of almost 800,000, **AREQUIPA** maintains a rather aloof attitude towards the rest of Peru. Most Arequipans feel themselves distinct, if not culturally superior, and resent the idea of the nation revolving around Lima. This confident image arose in the nineteenth century when the city found itself wealthy on the back of the wool trade with England.

TAQUILE

Highlights

❶ **Monasterio Santa Catalina** Exploring the labyrinthine, sunlit streets of this Arequipa convent is a calming, even spiritual, experience in its own right. **See p.158**

❷ **Tradición Arequipeña** This usually full and always full-on restaurant, close to downtown Arequipa, bustles with people enjoying unique local delicacies like *cuy* or *rocoto relleno*. **See p.169**

❸ **La Calera** Wallow, swim and relax in the fantastic hot springs of La Calera, a short distance from Chivay at the head of Colca Canyon. **See p.175**

❹ **Mirador Cruz del Condor** A breathtaking viewpoint on the rim of Colca Canyon, offering daily sightings of wild condors swooping above and below. **See p.180**

❺ **Cotahuasi Canyon** Not only one of the deepest canyons in the world, this is also one of the most remote valleys that can be reached relatively easily by bus in the Peruvian Andes. **See p.184**

❻ **Sillustani** The ring of tower-like *chullpa* tombs at this ancient temple/cemetery overlooks Titicaca from a little peninsula in Lake Umayo. **See p.193**

❼ **Taquile and Amantani islands** These Lake Titicaca islands offer a genuinely fascinating glimpse of what life must have been like five hundred years ago. **See p.195**

HIGHLIGHTS ARE MARKED ON THE MAP ON P.154

Situated at the foot of an ice-capped volcano – **El Misti** (5821m) – and close to four other prominent volcanoes, Arequipa has long been famous for having one of the most beautiful settings and pleasant climates of all Peru's cities. Despite a disastrous earthquake in 1687, it's still endowed with some of the country's finest colonial **churches** and **mansions**, many of which were constructed from white volcanic *sillar*, cut from the surrounding mountains and often flecked with black ash.

Characterized by arched interior ceilings, Arequipa's architectural beauty comes mainly from the colonial period. In general, the style is stark and almost clinical, except where Baroque and *mestizo* influences combine, as seen on many of the fine sixteenth- to eighteenth-century facades. A huge number of religious buildings are spread about the old colonial centre. The architectural design of the **Monasterio de Santa Catalina**, a convent complex enclosing a complete world within its thick walls, constitutes perhaps the city's main appeal to travellers. Further out, but still within walking distance, you can visit the attractive suburbs of **San Lázaro**, **Yanahuara** and **Cayma**, the latter being particularly renowned for its dramatic views of the valley.

3

Brief history

Arrowheads and rock art have proven human occupation around Arequipa for over ten thousand years. This began with early groups of hunter-gatherers arriving here on a seasonal basis for several millennia from 8000 BC to around 1000 BC when horticulture and ceramic technology began to appear in small settlements along streams

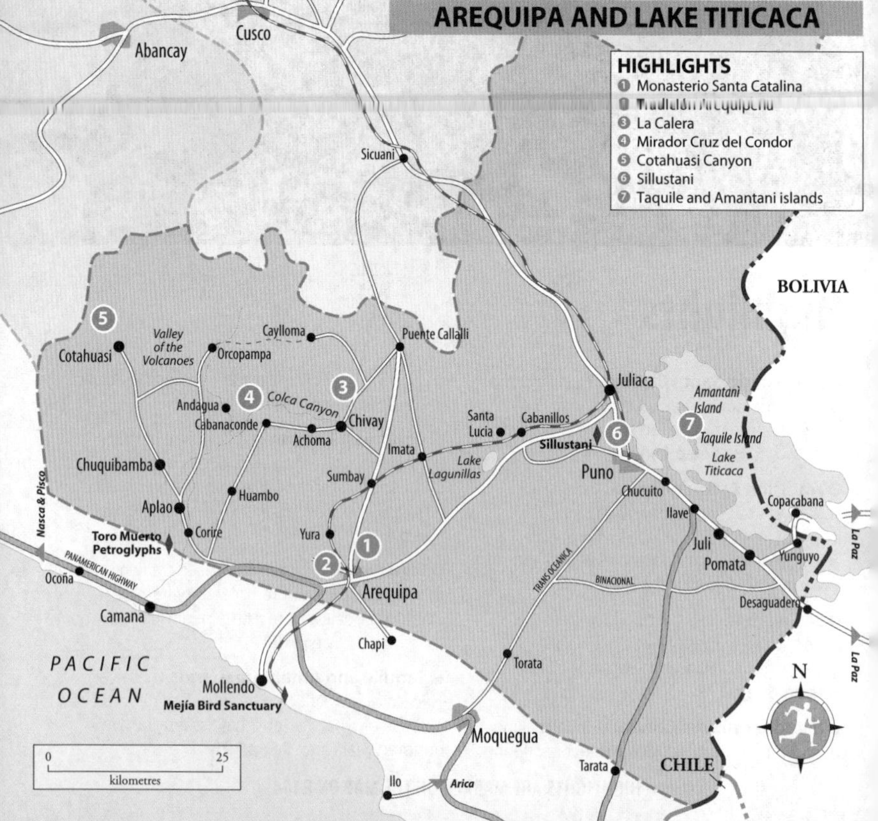

and rivers. Initially influenced by the Paracas culture and later by the Tiahuanaco-Huari, two major local tribes emerged sharing the area: the **Churajone** living in the far northwest section of the Arequipa region, and the **Chuquibamba** who thrived higher up in the Andean plateaus above Arequipa until the arrival of the Incas.

The name Arequipa is derived from the **Quechua** phrase "*ari quepay*", meaning "let's stop here", which, according to local legend, is exactly what the fourth Inca emperor, **Mayta Capac**, said to his generals on the way through the area following one of his conquest trips.

Colonial development

The Incas were not alone in finding Arequipa to their liking. When **Pizarro** officially "founded" the city in 1540, he was moved enough to call it Villa Hermosa, or Beautiful Town, and *Don Quixote* author Miguel de Cervantes extolled the city's virtues, saying that it enjoyed an eternal springtime. The lovely white stone lent itself to extravagant buildings and attracted master architects to the city.

3

The wool trade

During the eighteenth and nineteenth centuries, this mountainous region became an important source of sheep and alpaca **wool exports**, largely to the UK. Connected to the rest of Peru only by mule track until 1870, Arequipa was slow to become the provincial capital it is today. Money made mainly from exports kept the economy growing enough to establish an electric urban tramway in 1913 and then a road up to Puno in 1928.

Political upheaval

Having acquired a reputation as *the* centre of **right-wing political power**, while populist movements have tended to emerge around Trujillo in the north, Arequipa has traditionally represented the solid interests of the oligarchy. Important politicos, like Francisco Javier de Luna Pizarro, who was president of Congress on many occasions in the nineteenth century, came from Arequipa. Sanchez Cerro and Odria both began their **coups** here, in 1930 and 1948 respectively, and Belaunde, one of the most important presidents in pre- and post-military coup years, sprang into politics from one of the wealthy Arequipa families. By 1972 the city's population had reached 350,000. Twenty years later it passed half a million, with many people arriving from the Andean hinterland to escape the violence of Peru's civil war.

The **social extremes** are quite clear today; despite the tastefully ostentatious architecture and generally well-heeled appearance of most townsfolk, there is much poverty in the region and there's been a huge increase in the number of street beggars in Arequipa. Social polarization came to a head in 2002, when the city's streets were ripped up in political protest against President Toledo's plans to sell off the local electric utility.

Plaza de Armas

The **Plaza de Armas**, one of South America's grandest, is very much the focus of the city's social activity in the early evenings, dotted with palms, flowers and gardens. At its heart sits a newly renovated bronze fountain, topped by an angel fondly known as *turututu* because of the trumpet it carries. The east and west sides of the plaza are dominated by fine granite portals and colonial-style wooden balconies, while the southern edge is taken up by a municipal building.

La Catedral

North side of Plaza de Armas • Mon–Sat 7–11.30am & 5–7.30pm, Sun 7am–1pm & 5–7pm • Free

The arcades and elegant white facade of Arequipa's seventeenth-century **Catedral**

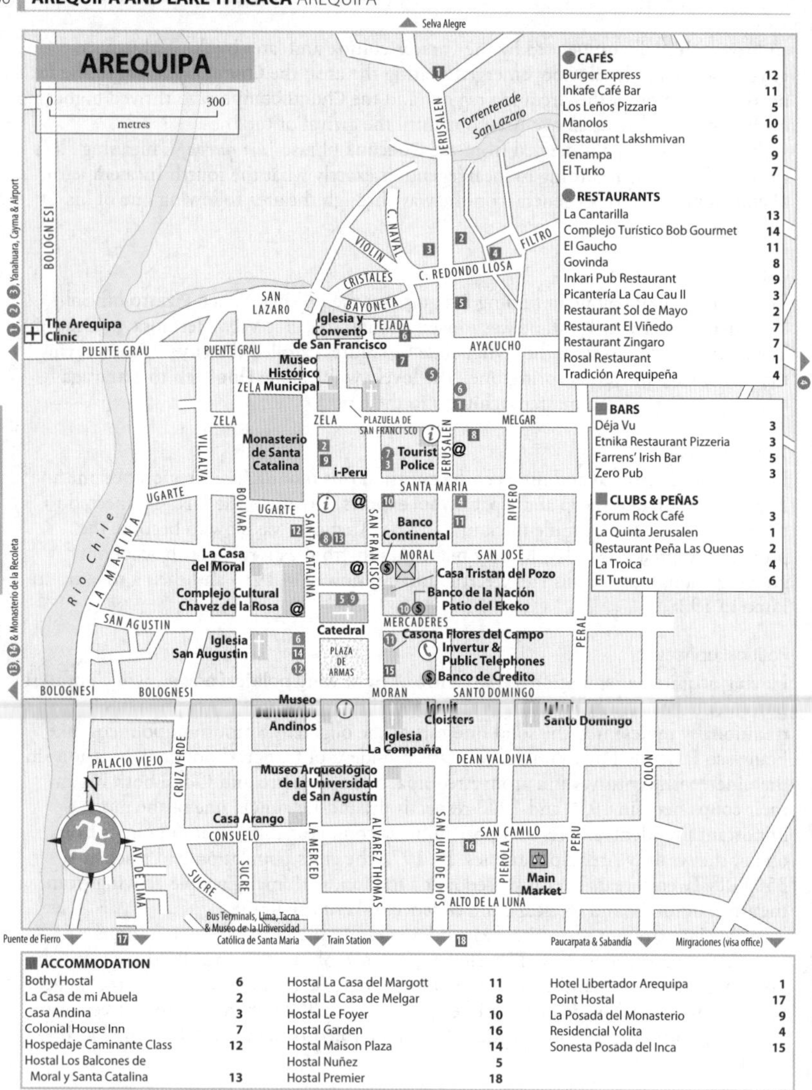

demand attention, even drawing your sight away from El Misti towering behind. Displaying some French influence in its Neo-Renaissance style, it looks particularly beautiful when lit up in the evenings. Consecrated in 1556, the cathedral building was subsequently gutted by fire in 1844 and restored in 1868 by Lucas Poblete, before coming to grief again in 2001 when its impressive Neoclassical towers were seriously damaged in an earthquake.

Apart from the massive Belgian-built organ, said to be one of the largest in South America, a beautiful French-made pulpit and a marble altar created by Felippo Moratillo, the vast interior is actually rather disappointing in its generally bland and austere design.

Iglesia La Compañía

C General Moran and C Alvarez Thomas • Daily 10am–1pm & 3.30–7pm • Free

On the southeast corner of the Plaza de Armas, opposite the Catedral, and more exciting architecturally, sits the elaborate **Iglesia La Compañía**. The original church, built in 1573, was destroyed eleven years later by an earthquake. The present structure was completed in 1660, when the magnificently sculpted **doorway**, with a locally inspired zigzagging *mestizo*-Baroque stone relief, was crafted using only shadow to outline the figures of the frieze. Inside, by the main altar hangs a *Virgin and Child* by Bernardo Bitto, which arrived from Italy in 1575. In what used to be the sacristy (now the Chapel of San Ignacio), the polychrome cupola depicts images of jungle alongside warriors, angels and the Evangelists.

Jesuit Cloisters

Plaza de Armas • Mon–Sat 8am–10pm, Sun noon–8pm • S/2

Next door to the Iglesia La Compañía are the **Jesuit Cloisters**, superbly carved back in the early eighteenth century. In the first cloister, squared pillars support white stone arches and are covered with intricate reliefs showing angels, local fruits and vegetables, seashells and stylized puma heads. The second cloister is, in contrast, rather austere.

3

Casona Flores del Campo

Portal de Flores 136 • Daily 10am–5pm • S/2

Dating back to the sixteenth century (it was apparently once used by Fernando Pizarro), but not completed until 1779 by one Coronel Manuel Flores del Campo, the **Casona Flores del Campo** is older than most houses in Arequipa. It's quite easy to distinguish different stages in the construction of this *casona* (colonial mansion): most notably the double arch and balcony date from the late eighteenth century. These days the building is home to a reasonably wide-ranging exhibition of artesanía.

Iglesia Santo Domingo

C Santo Domingo and C Rivero • Mon–Fri 7am–noon & 3–7.30pm, Sat 7–9am & 3–7.30pm, Sun 5.30am–12.30pm • Free

East of the Iglesia La Compañía and the plaza you'll find the exquisitely restored **Iglesia Santo Domingo**, originally built in 1553 by Gaspar Baez, the first master architect to arrive in Arequipa. Most of what you see today was built between 1650 and 1698, but suffered major damage during the earthquakes of 1958 and 1960. The large main door represents an interesting example of Arequipa's *mestizo* craftsmanship – an Indian face amid a bunch of grapes, leaves and cacti – and the side door is said to be the oldest in the city.

Casa Arango

The **Casa Arango** sits two blocks down from the Plaza de Armas at the corner of calles La Merced and Consuelo. Built in the late seventeenth century in what was then the city's most important street, it brings together a number of architectural styles, including both *mestizo*-Baroque and nineteenth-century Neoclassical.

Casa de Tristan del Pozo

C San Francisco 108 • Mon–Fri 9am–1pm & 3.45–6pm, Sat 9am–1pm • Free • T 054 212209

Opposite the northeast corner of the Catedral stands a particularly impressive colonial mansion, **Casa de Tristan del Pozo**, also known as La Casa Rickets. Built in 1737 as a seminary, it later became the splendid residence of the Rickets family, who made their fortune from the wool trade in the late nineteenth century. The building boasts an extremely attractive traditional facade and courtyard. The stonework above the main door depicts Christ's genealogy, with highly stylized plants supporting five discs, or

Jesuit medallions, with JHS (the abbreviation for Jesus) at the centre, María and José to the side of this, and Joaquin and Ana on the extremes. Now owned and lavishly restored by the Banco Continental, the mansion houses a small museum and art gallery.

Complejo Cultural Chavez de la Rosa

C Santa Catalina 101 • Mon–Sat 10am–6pm • free **Art store** Mon–Sat 10am–1pm & 4–8pm • Free

North of the Plaza de Armas, the Casa Arróspide (also known as the Casa Iriberry) is home to the **Complejo Cultural Chavez de la Rosa**. This attractive 1743 colonial building belongs to the law faculty of the University of San Agustín and hosts changing selections of modern works by artists (mostly Peruvian). It possesses three main galleries as well as an art store with local art and crafts for sale.

La Casa del Moral

3

C Moral 318 • Mon–Sat 9am–5pm, Sun 9am–1pm • S/5

Around the corner from the Casa Arróspide sits the seventeenth-century **La Casa del Moral** (literally meaning "Mulberry House"), lovingly restored and refurbished with period pieces. Its most engaging feature is a superb stone gateway, carved with motifs that are similar to those on Nasca ceramics – puma heads with snakes growing from their mouths – surrounding a Spanish coat of arms. The mansion's name comes from an ancient *mora* tree, still thriving in the central patio.

Iglesia San Agustín

C Bolívar and C San Agustín • Mon–Sun 8am–12.30pm & 5–8pm • Free

One block from the Casa del Moral, the elegant 1575 **Iglesia San Agustín** has one of the city's finest Baroque facades, added later in the late eighteenth century. Its old convent cloisters are now attached to the university, while inside only the unique octagonal sacristy survived the 1868 earthquake.

Monasterio de Santa Catalina

C Santa Catalina 301 • Mon–Sat 9am–5pm (from 8am April to end Sept); occasionally open till 8pm • S/30; guides are optional at around S/10–15 • Ⓦ santacatalina.org.pe

Two blocks north of the Plaza de Armas the vast walls of the **Monasterio de Santa Catalina** shelter a convent that housed almost two hundred secluded nuns and three hundred servants from the late sixteenth century until 1970, when it opened some of its outer doors to the public. The most important and prestigious religious building in Peru, its enormous complex of rooms, cloisters and tiny plazas takes an hour or two to explore. Some thirty nuns who still live here today, worship in the main chapel only outside of opening hours.

Originally the concept of Gaspar Baez in 1570, though only granted official licence five years later, the convent was funded by the Viceroy Toledo and the wealthy María de Guzmán, who later entered the convent with one of her sisters and donated all her riches to the community. The most striking feature is its predominantly Mudéjar style, adapted by the Spanish from the Moors, but which rarely found its way into their colonial buildings. The quality of the design is emphasized and harmonized by a superb interplay between the white stone and brilliant colours in the ceilings, the strong sunlight and deep-blue sky above the maze of narrow interior streets.

Los locutorios

Once you enter, you file left along the first corridor to a high vaulted room with a ceiling of opaque *huamanga* stone imported from the Ayacucho Valley. Beside here are **los locutorios** – little cells where on holy days the nuns could talk, unseen, to visitors.

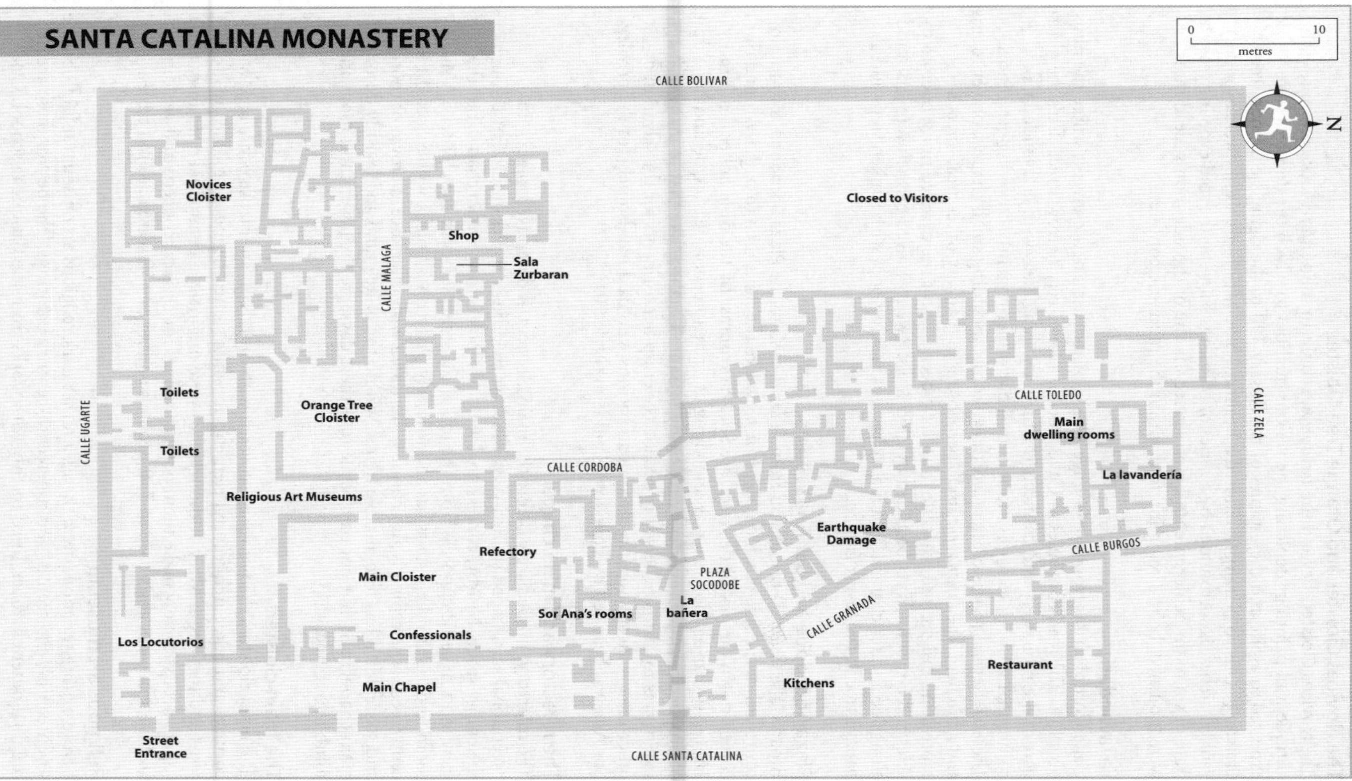
SANTA CATALINA MONASTERY
0
10
metres
N
CALLE BOLIVAR
Novices Cloister
Shop
Sala Zurbaran
CALLE MALAGA
Closed to Visitors
CALLE UGARTE
Toilets
Toilets
Orange Tree Cloister
CALLE TOLEDO
CALLE ZELA
Main dwelling rooms
La lavandería
CALLE CORDOBA
Religious Art Museums
Earthquake Damage
Refectory
CALLE BURGOS
Main Cloister
PLAZA SOCODOBE
Sor Ana's rooms
La bañera
CALLE GRANADA
Los Locutorios
Confessionals
Restaurant
Kitchens
Main Chapel
Street Entrance
CALLE SANTA CATALINA

The Novices Cloister and Orange Tree Cloister

The **Novices Cloister**, beyond the *locutorios*, is built in solid *sillar*-block columns, with antique wall paintings depicting the various qualities to which the devotees were expected to aspire and the Litanies of the Rosary. Off to the right, the **Orange Tree Cloister** (Claustro Naranjal), painted a beautiful blue with birds and flowers over the vaulted arches, is surrounded by a series of paintings showing the soul evolving from a state of sin to the achievement of God's grace. In one of the side rooms, dead nuns were mourned, before being interred within the monastic confines.

La lavandería

Calle Cordoba runs from the Orange Tree Cloister past a new convent, where the nuns now live. The road continues as Calle Toledo, a long, very narrow street that's the oldest part of the monastery and connects the main dwelling areas with **la lavandería**, or communal washing sector, is brought to life with permanently flowering geraniums. There are several rooms off here worth exploring, including small chapels, prayer rooms and a kitchen. The *lavandería* itself, perhaps more than any other area, offers a captivating insight into what life must have been like for the closeted nuns; open to the skies and city sounds yet bounded by high walls. Twenty halved earthenware jars stand alongside a water channel, and it also has a swimming pool with sunken steps and a papaya tree in the lovely garden.

Plaza Socodobe and Sor Ana's rooms

Broad Calle Granada brings you from *la lavandería* to the **Plaza Socodobe**, a fountain courtyard to the side of which is *la bañera*, where the nuns used to bathe. Around the corner, down the next little street, are **Sor Ana's rooms**. By the time of her death in 1686, 90-year-old Sor Ana was something of a phenomenon, leaving behind her a trail of prophecies and cures. Her own destiny in Santa Catalina, like that of many of her sisters, was to castigate herself in order to offer up her torments for the salvation of other souls – mostly wealthy Arequipan patrons who paid handsomely for the privilege. Sor Ana was beatified by Pope John Paul II in the 1990s.

The refectory and main chapel

The **refectory**, immediately before the main cloisters, is deceptively plain – its exceptional star-shaped stained-glass windows shedding dapples of sunlight through the empty space. Nearby, confessional windows look into the **main chapel**, but the best view of its majestic cupola is from the top of the staircase beside the cloisters. A small room underneath these stairs has an intricately painted wall niche with a Sacred Heart centrepiece. The ceiling is also curious, illustrated with three dice, a crown of thorns and some other, less recognizable items. Within the quite grand and lavishly decorated **main chapel** itself, but not part of the tour these days, are the lower choir room and the tomb of Sor Ana.

The main cloisters

The **main cloisters** themselves are covered with murals on an intense ochre base with cornices and other architectural elements in white stone; the murals follow the life of Jesus and the Virgin Mary. Although they were originally a communal dormitory, their superb acoustics now make them popular venues for classical concerts and weddings and the space can absorb up to 750 people standing or 350 seated around tables.

Religious art museum

Before exiting the monastery, there's a rather dark **religious art museum** full of obscure seventeenth-, eighteenth- and nineteenth-century paintings. The best of these are in the final outer chamber, lined mainly with works from the Cusqueña school. One

FROM TOP PLAZA DE ARMAS, AREQUIPA (P.155); COLCA CANYON, NEAR CABANACONDE (P.178) >

eye-catching canvas, the first on the left as you enter this room, is of Mary Magdalene. Painted by an anonymous nineteenth-century Arequipan, it's remarkably modern in its treatment of Mary and the near-Cubist style of its rocky background.

Museo Histórico Municipal

Plazuela de San Francisco • Tues–Sun 9am–5pm • S/2, students with international student card 50¢

Just above Santa Catalina, the small, leafy Plazuela de San Francisco, usually buzzing with students and townspeople, is where you'll find Arequipa's city museum, the **Museo Histórico Municipal**, which devotes itself principally to local heroes – army chiefs, revolutionary leaders, presidents and poets (including the renowned Mariano Melgar). It's rather a dull collection of memorabilia, though some rooms have interesting photographs of the city. There are also displays of artefacts from the colonial period and the war with Chile. The university's museums, located on the outskirts of the city, are of greater interest (see opposite).

3

Iglesia y Convento de San Francisco

Plazuela de San Francisco • Church Mon–Sat 4–8pm, Sun 6am–8pm, convent Mon–Sat 9am–noon and 3–5pm • Church free, convent S/5

The Plazuela de San Francisco is home to a striking Franciscan complex, dominated by a convent and the **Iglesia de San Francisco**. Yet another of Gaspar Baez's projects, this one dating back to 1569, it shows an interesting mix of brick and *sillar* work both inside and on the facade. Original paintings by Baltazar de Prado once covered the central nave, but the earthquake of 1604 destroyed these. However, the nave retains its most impressive feature – a pure-silver altar. Adjoining the church are rather austere convent cloisters and the very simple **Capila del Tercera Orden**, its entrance decorated with modest *mestizo* carvings of St Francis and St Clare, founders of the first and second orders.

Monasterio de Santa Teresa

C Melgar 303 • Mon–Sat 9am–5pm, Sun 9am–1pm • S/10 • T 054 281188

Close to the centre of town, **Monasterio de Santa Teresa** is smaller than Santa Catalina but has astonishingly beautiful colonial patios set around a large open courtyard. Internally it has a colonial art museum which displays some fine religious artwork and murals, as well as twelve exhibition spaces and over three hundred works of art.

Monasterio de La Recoleta

C La Recoleta 117 • Mon–Sat 10am–noon & 3–5pm • S/5 • T 054 270996

The **Monasterio de La Recoleta** is located on the western side of the Río Chili, which runs its generally torrential course through Arequipa from Selva Alegre, dividing the old heart of the city from what has become a more modern downtown sector, including Yanahuara (see opposite) and Cayma (see p.164). This large Franciscan monastery stands conspicuously alone on Callejón de La Recoleta, just ten to fifteen minutes' walk east of the Plaza de Armas.

The stunning major and minor cloisters were built in 1651; in 1869 it was converted to an Apostolic Mission school administered by the Barefoot Franciscans. It is the archeology and natural history **museums** that really draw people here though. Open to the public since 1978, they house: two rooms of pre-Columbian artefacts including textiles and ceramics; an Amazon room showing artefacts from jungle Indian tribes and examples of forest flora and fauna; a religious and modern art gallery displaying both Cusqueña and Arequipeña classical works; plus a renowned historic library with some 25,000 sixteenth- and seventeenth-century volumes.

Museo Santuarios Andinos

C La Merced 110 • Mon–Sat 9am–6pm, Sun 9am–3pm • S/15 • T 054 200345

The **Museo Santuarios Andinos**, part of the Universidad Católica de Santa María, is arguably the most important museum in Arequipa today, with displays of some nineteen Inca mummies and a range of archeological remains; guides are obligatory but their fee, which is additional, is negotiable. The main exhibit is Juanita, the ancient 13-year-old "princess" uncovered in her icy ritual grave on September 8, 1995, by an expedition that included the archeologists Johan Reinhard and José Chavez, along with the well-known *Andinista* Miguel Zarate. Her gravesite, located at the incredible altitude of 6380m on Ampato Volcano, is estimated to be about 500 years old. It is thought that Juanita was sacrified to the Apu Ampato and killed, after a time of fasting and herbal sedation, with a blow to the head by a five-pointed granite mace. The museum also contains fine examples of associated grave goods like textiles, precious metals and Inca ceramics.

3

Museo de Arqueología de la Universidad Católica de Santa Maria

C Cruz Verde 303 • Mon–Fri 9am–12 and 2–5pm • Free, includes a video and guided tour • T 054 959636

Distinct from Santuarios Andinos, but also a Univeristy affiliate, is the **Museo de Arqueología de la Universidad Católica de Santa Maria**. This museum has seven rooms concentrating on items from pre-Conquest cultures such as the Huari, Tiahuanuco, Chancay and Inca, and boasts around a thousand different pieces such as stone weapons, ceramics, textiles, grave goods, as well as other worked and ancient stone, wood and metal objects.

Museo Arqueológico de la Universidad de San Agustín

C Alvarez Thomas with C Palacio Viejo • Mon–Fri 8.15am–4.15pm • S/5 • Call for an appointment T 054 288881

The largest of Arequipa's museums, the **Museo Arqueológico de la Universidad de San Agustín**, has good collections of everything from mummies and replicas of Chavín stones to Nasca, Huari and Inca ceramics, as well as colonial paintings and furniture. There are over eight thousand pieces held here at the university campus.

San Lázaro

The oldest quarter of Arequipa – and the first place the Spaniards settled in this valley – is the barrio of **San Lázaro**, an uncharacteristic zone of tiny, curving streets stretching around the hillside at the top end of Calle Jerusalen, all an easy stroll north from the plaza. If you feel like a walk, and some good views of El Misti, you can walk down to the river from here and cross over Puente Grau towards Yanahuara suburb (ten minutes away) where there's a superb vantage point.

Yanahuara

Until the railway boom of the late nineteenth century, which brought peasant-migrants to Arequipa from as far away as Cusco, **Yanahuara** was a distinct village. It is now built up, though it still commands stunning views across the valley, above all from its **churches**. There are also one or two fine **restaurants** in this sector. The municipal plaza possesses a beautiful **viewing point** (*mirador*), which has been made famous by postcards.

To get here, buses and colectivos can be caught from the corner of Grau with Santa Catalina, or from Puente Grau, or it's a fifteen-minute walk from Puente Grau (1–2km), between blocks 2 and 3 of Avenida Ejercito.

Iglesia Yanahuara

Yanahuara Plaza • Daily 9am–5pm • Free

The small **Iglesia Yanahuara** on the tranquil main plaza dates to the middle of the eighteenth century, and its Baroque facade is particularly fine, with a stone relief of the tree of life incorporating angels, flowers, saints, lions and hidden Indian faces.

Cayma

From Puente Grau, a longish stroll takes you across to the west bank of the Chili, along Avenida Ejercito and out to the suburb of **Cayma** (3–4km); there are also buses available (see below). Another kilometre or so further out than Yanahuara, the area was once a small suburb with views over the city, but now reflects the commercial, even flashy side of Arequipa, with large shops and even one or two nightclubs. The suburb also offers good views of the Chachani Volcano.

Iglesia de San Miguel

Main plaza • Daily 9am–4pm • Free

The **Iglesia de San Miguel**, built in the early eighteenth century, houses an image of the Virgen de la Candelaria, donated to the city by King Carlos V. It's possible to climb up to the roof of the church which offers great views across Yanahuara and towards the volcanoes to the north.

Puente de Fierro

South of the city centre, Arequipa's very impressive black-iron viaduct, or **Puente de Fierro**, provides a great vantage point for views over the city to El Misti. Although spanning half a kilometre, it was well-designed by Gustave Eiffel and built to such high standards by the railway baron Henry May that it has successfully vaulted the city's bubbling **Río Chili**, and withstood the test of Arequipa's severe earthquakes and tremors, for over a hundred years.

ARRIVAL AND DEPARTURE — AREQUIPA

Arequipa is a popular stopping-off point between Lima and the Titicaca, Cusco and Tacna regions, and is a hub for most journeys in the southern half of Peru. From Arequipa you can continue to Cusco, or Titicaca by bus or plane. There's no passenger train between Arequipa and Puno or Cusco; but it is easy enough to travel by bus. **Bolivia** is also within a day's bus journey, while Tacna and the **Chilean frontier** (see p.148) are even more accessible from Arequipa by road.

BY PLANE

Flights land at Arequipa airport (Aeropuerto Rodríguez Ballón; 054 443464), 7km northwest of town. A shuttle bus meets most planes and will take you to any hotel in the town centre for S/5; alternatively, a taxi will cost S/15–20. There's a departure tax of about S/12 on all inter-city domestic flights.

Airline offices All of the airline offices are central: LAN's main office is at C Santa Catalina 118c (054 201224), but you can also buy air tickets for their flights from Portal San Agustín 135 (054 203637) and for Star Peru, from C Santa Catalina 105a (054 221896). The Trotomundo office at Portal San Agustín 121 (trotamundosaqp.com) sells tickets for both these airlines.

Destinations Cusco (4 daily; 1hr); Juliaca, for Puno (2 daily; 40min); Lima (at least 2 daily; 1hr).

BY BUS

Most long-distance buses arrive at the modern, concrete Terminal Terrestre bus station (054 427797) about 4km south from the centre of town, or at the newer Terrapuerto (054 422277), next door; a taxi to the Plaza de Armas should cost no more than S/10–15. It's worth noting, too, that when leaving these terminals by bus, there's a S/1 charge per head.

Local buses Local buses (S/1) and colectivos (S1.50) to and from the suburbs of Yanahuara (see p.163) and Cayma (see above) leave from avenidas Ayacucho and Puente Grau.

Destinations Cabanaconde (4 daily; 6–8hr); Chivay (8 daily; 4hr); Cusco (several daily; 9–12hr); Desaguadero (2 daily; 7–9hr); Lima (10 daily; 14–18hr); Moquegua (4 daily; 3–4hr); Paucarpata (every 30min; 15min); Puno (6 daily; 6hr); Tacna (2–3 daily; 5hr).

BUS OPERATORS

Angelitos Negros C San Juan de Dios 510 (054 213094). Services to Chapi, Moquegua, Ilo and Tacna.

CRIME IN AREQUIPA

Crime in Arequipa is largely confined to **pickpocketing**, most likely in busy central areas (bus stations, markets etc). If you have anything stolen, report it to the **Tourist Police** (see below). You can also ask for assistance and advice at the **i-Peru Tourist Office** (see below), or contact your consulate (see p.171).

CIVA Terminal Terrestre or Av Salaverry (054 426563). Services to Cusco, Puno, Lima and Tacna.

Cristo Rey C San Juan de Dios 510 (054 213094 or 054 259848). Services to Chivay and Cabanaconde.

Cromotex Terminal Terrestre (054 421555). Services to Chuquibamba, Cotahuasi and Alcha.

Cruz del Sur Terrapuerto (054/427728 or 054 216625, crusdelsur.com.pe). Services to Lima, Cusco, Tacna and Puno.

Del Carpio Terminal Terrapuerto (054 427049 or 054 430941). Services to the Majes Valley, Aplao and Pampacolca.

Jacantay Terminal Terrestre. Services to Juliaca, Puno, Desaguadero and La Paz.

Ormeño Terminal Terrestre (054 218885 or 054 424187). Services to the coast.

San Cristóbal Terminal Terrestre (054 422068). Services to Lima, Cusco, Puno and Juliaca.

Sur Express C San Juan de Dios 537 (054 213335). Services to Chapi, Chivay and Cabanaconde.

Tepsa Terminals Terrestre and Terrapuerto (054 212451). International services.

Reyna Terminal Terrestre (054 430612). The best services to Cotahuasi, Colca, Chivay (several departures daily), Cabanaconde, Andagua in the Valley of the Volcanoes and Cusco.

Turismo Alex Av Olímpico 203 (054 202863). Services to Andaray, Chuquibamba, Cotahuasi (all departing from Terminal Terrestre).

TZ Turismo Terminal Terrestre (054 421949). Services to Corire and Aplao.

Ultra Tours C San Juan de Dios 510 (054 452742). Services to Chapi.

Zeballos Av Salaverry 107 (054 201013). Services to Lima, Corire, Aplao and Ilo.

3

GETTING AROUND

On foot It's easy enough to walk around the city centre, but we've detailed available city and bus tours (see p.166), should you want to give your feet a rest.

By taxi If you want a taxi it's easy to hail one anywhere in the city; rides within the centre cost about S/4–5. To call a taxi, there's Taxi Seguro, Pasaje 7 de Junio 200, Mariano Melgar (054 450250), or Taxi Sur (054 465656).

By car Given the number of nearby attractions accessible by road, renting a car (with or without *chófer*) can work out well. Aerotur and B&G, C Santa Catalina 213 (054 219291, busgom@terra.com.pe), is a reliable company that rents out 4WD vehicles with or without driver and/or guide, and also rents out satellite phones. There is an Avis office at Palacio Viejo 214 (054 282519) and at the airport (054 653346). Servitours, at C Jerusalen 400 (054 202856 or 054 201636, servitours@hotmail.com), also rent 4WD vehicles.

INFORMATION

Municipal tourist office Portal de la Municipalidad 110-i, Plaza de Armas (daily 8.30am–7.30pm; 054 221228, regionarequipa.gob.pe). It's often worth asking here if there are any hotels with current special offers.

i-Peru Promperu Office of Tourist Information and Assistance *La Casona de Santa Catalina*, C Santa Catalina 210 (daily 7am–6pm; 054 444564). Directly opposite the entrance to the Monasterio de Santa Catalina, among the smart shops set around the mansion's inner courtyard. There's also an i-Peru information office at the airport (daily 8.30am–7.30pm; 054 444564), where they have maps of the city, information on sights and cultural event, and can recommend guides, tour companies and hotels.

Tourist Police C Jerusalen 315 (054 201258). The tourist police are particularly helpful, offering maps, information and assistance with safety precautions.

Terminal Terrestre Many people arrive here by bus, where there is an information kiosk with details of hotels and tour companies, and sometimes maps.

TOURS AND ACTIVITIES

Taking a **guided tour** is the easiest way to get around the otherwise quite difficult region around Arequipa. It's tricky to get around here in a number of ways – the sheer terrain is inhospitable, massive and wild, and the altitude changes between Arequipa City and, say, Chivay, can affect you for a couple of days (mountain sickness with headaches), which makes driving your own rented car tricky until you're properly adjusted.

CITY TOURS

All operators tend to offer similar packages, with city tours lasting around three hours ($10–20) and usually including the Monasterio de Santa Catalina, La Compañía, La Catedral, Iglesia San Agustín and the Yanahuara *mirador*.

Bustour Portal San Agustín 111 054 203434, bustour.com.pe. Half-day bus tours of the city and its outskirts – it starts at the Plaza de Armas and includes other stops such as Puente Grau, Yanahuara and Carmen Alto. The tour takes a circular route ($10) and you can hop on and off along the way so it can be a good way to get your bearings and see some major sites on arrival. Daily 9.15am and 2pm.

COUNTRYSIDE TOURS

Countryside tours (*tur de campiña*) usually consist of a roughly three-hour trip to the rural churches of Cayma and Sachaca, the old mill at Sabandia, Tingo lagoon and local *miradors* ($10–30). Most companies also offer one- to three-day trips out to the Colca Canyon ($25–100; sometimes with very early morning starts) or to the petroglyphs at Toro Muerto ($25–50). Trips to the Valley of the Volcanoes and the Cotahuasi Canyon are only offered by a few companies (from $100 upwards). Specialist adventure activities, such as rafting in the Colca Canyon, mountaineering or serious trekking can cost anything from $120–1000 for a three- to six-day outing. Of course, all prices vary according to the season, the quality you demand (in terms of food, transport to start point and whether you have *arrieros* with mules to carry your gear) and the size of the group. Mountain-bike rental ranges from S/40–100/day depending on the type of bike required, size of group, whether or not a guide is needed and which route is selected.

★ **Campamento Base and Colca Trek** C Jerusalen 401b 054 206217 or 054 9600170, colcatrek.com.pe. An excellent all-round outdoor adventure company, specializing in customized tours with a mix of trekking, mountain biking, canoeing and climbing. They operate a well-stocked camping shop and employ excellent guides for the Colca Canyon and more adventurous treks, including the Cabanaconde, Tapay and Cotahuasi areas. They're also a good source of information on trekking and climbing equipment and the wider region, and will help organize transport.

Giardino Agencia de Viajes C Jerusalen 606a 054 200100 or 054 221345, giardinotours.com. A well-organized outfit with excellent two-day tours to the Colca Canyon, trekking and climbing trips, plus the usual city and countryside tours. Also offers a very reliable air- and bus-ticket buying service.

Illary Tour C Santa Catalina 205 054 220844, illarytour@hotmail.com. A friendly and professional outfit with English-speaking guides who lead enjoyable trips of two days and more in the Colca Canyon. They provide oxygen, accommodation, transport and even live, private-performance folk music.

Naturaleza Activa C Santa Catalina 211 054 695793, naturactiva@yahoo.com. This company specializes in trekking, mountain-bike tours and equipment rental.

Pablo Tour C Jerusalen 400a 054 203737, pablotour.com. Specialists in adventure tourism, with great links to hostels and local guides in Cabanaconde and the *Oasis tambo* in the Colca Canyon.

Peru Adventure (and Biking) Tours Hotel & Adventure Centre: C El Milagro 114, El Cerrillo, Characato 973 842 688 or 054 221658, peruadventurestours.com. A highly professional team, Peru Adventure Tours specialize in offering tours all over Peru, including the Colca Canyon and Cotahuasi. They also organize mountain-biking tours in the region as well as climbing, trekking and luxury tours.

Zarate Adventures C Santa Catalina 204, Oficina 3 054 202461, zarateadventures.com. A good expedition outfitter as well as a leading trekking and climbing company with over 28 years' experience. They use only professional and qualified guides such as Carlos Zarate, the internationally renowned founder. Treks include rock climbing and canoeing in the usual places such as Colca, El Misti and Cotahuasi, but they also offer more adventurous routes including a trip from Colca to the Valley of the Volcanoes, and another to the Mismi Nevado (see p.178).

ACCOMMODATION

Arequipa has a good selection of accommodation in all price ranges, with most of the better options mainly within a few blocks of the **Plaza de Armas** or along **Calle Jerusalen**. For ease of reference, they are divided below into three sections: the pleasant area north of Calle Melgar, the central area between Melgar and the main plaza, and the area around the plaza and to the south, all within walking distance of the Plaza de Armas.

NORTH OF MELGAR AND SANTA CATALINA

★ **Bothy Hostal** Puente Grau 306 054 282438, bothyhostel.com. Rightly describing itself as the friendliest hostel in town and and arguably the funkiest, *Bothy* is comfortable, cheap and central, and has a communal area that includes a DVD/TV room, free wif-fi, a kitchen and a great rooftop terrace. Shared, single and double rooms all available with shared bathroom. Dorms S/27; doubles with shared bathroom S/60; doubles with private bathroom S/70

Casa Andina C Jerusalen 603 054 202070, casa-andina.com. Luxurious and reasonably good value option, with TVs and minibars in the carpeted rooms that have private bathrooms. Also has a pleasant dining room and bar. S/250

Colonial House Inn Puente Grau 114 ⓣ054 223533, ⓦcolonialhouseinn-arequipa.com. Agreeable place with a pretty covered courtyard, electric heated showers, private bathrooms and access to TV and internet facilities. Well worth it, not least for the nice rooftop continental breakfast option (included in room rate). S/56

★ **La Casa de Mi Abuela** C Jerusalen 606 ⓣ054 241206, ⓦlacasademiabuela.com. Innovative family-run hostel, whose name translates as "My Grandma's House", combining elegance, comfort and great value. Rooms are set in a variety of garden environments; there are spacious colonial quarters, chalets, family apartments and a fine swimming pool. It's very secure, has a good library and an excellent cafeteria offering a fantastic buffet breakfast outside under the shady trees. Reserve well in advance during high season. S/165

Hostal Nuñez C Jerusalen 528 ⓣ054 233268 or ⓣ054 218648, ⓦhotel-nunez.de. A friendly, family-run place with attractive patios, constant hot water, laundry and telephone service plus secure luggage deposit. A few rooms have private bathrooms, and you can have breakfast (not included) on the terrace. Shared bathroom S/50; private bathroom S/70

Hotel Libertador Arequipa Plaza Bolívar, Selva Alegre ⓣ054 215110 or ⓣ054 282550, ⓦlibertador.com.pe. Quite a few blocks from downtown but located in a beautiful setting on the spur above the Barrio San Lázaro, this spacious, luxurious hotel is surrounded by the eucalyptus trees of Selva Alegre Park. The price includes a pool and sports facilities, and they serve excellent breakfasts (not included). S/400

Residencial Yolita Pasaje Velez 204 ⓣ054 226505. A comfortable lodging, close to *La Casa de Mi Abuela*, so a possible alternative if *La Casa* is full. Very friendly, and some upstairs rooms have good views. S/40

CENTRAL AREQUIPA

Hospedaje Caminante Class C Santa Catalina 207a ⓣ054 203444, ⓦelcaminanteclass.com. Very clean and pleasant, six-room family-run pad that's also safe and well managed. Extras include a laundry facility and a rooftop terrace with breathtaking views of the city. Shared bathroom S/35; private bathroom S/50

Hostal Los Balcones de Moral y Santa Catalina C Moral 217 ⓣ054 201292, ⓦbalconeshotel.com. A conveniently located and child-friendly place, where rooms abut each other on the second floor and have private bathrooms, 24hr hot water and a sun terrace (albeit not with street views). There's also a cafetería, laundry service and luggage deposit, and breakfast is included in the price. S/135

Hostal La Casa del Margott C Jerusalen 304 ⓣ054 229517, ⓦlacasademargott.com. Based around a colonial courtyard, itself slightly crowded by a massive palm tree, this hostel comprises several rooms (all downstairs) with *sillar* walls and ceilings. All rooms come with good mattresses, cable TV and private bathroom. Don't miss the tiny bar. S/168

Hostal La Casa de Melgar C Melgar 108b ⓣ054 222459, ⓦlacasademelgar.com. An eighteenth-century mansion with stylish tiled floors and exquisite vaulted *sillar* ceilings. Once home to the Bishop of Arequipa, *La Casa de Melgar* is a nice old place, spacious and stylish, with a friendly atmosphere. The best rooms are those with views over the street, and there's also a small cafetería. S/40.

Hostal Le Foyer C Ugarte 114 ⓣ054 286473, ⓦhlefoyer.com. The sign outside says "La Villa Real", which is the name of the mansion in which this popular backpackers' hostel is located, just two blocks from the main plaza; you'll need to ring the bell to get in. The hostel itself is clean and friendly, right at the heart of the action, and has a spacious first-floor patio as well as a small, useful book exchange. S/65

3

★ **La Posada del Monasterio** C Santa Catalina 300 ⓣ054 405728 or ⓣ054 206565, ⓔlaposadadelmonasterio@star.com.pe. An early eighteenth-century building where families of the nuns at Santa Catalina once stayed when visiting them; it has a fine *sillar* courtyard but much of the hotel has been modernized, creating a labyrinthine but plush and pretty environment with a view from many rooms, an inner garden area and a bar. S/140

PLAZA DE ARMAS AND SOUTH

Hostal Garden San Camilo 116 ⓣ054 237440. A misleading name but still excellent value, with solar-heated communal showers and lovely, old-fashioned, clean rooms with or without private bathroom. Located very close to the central market. Shared bathroom S/35; private bathroom S/50

Hostal Maison Plaza Portal San Agustín 143 ⓣ054 218929, ⓦmaisonplaza.com. This hotel is well located on the Plaza de Armas and fairly plush, with a lovely *sillar*-domed reception area. Unusually for Peru the price includes a decent breakfast. S/110

Hostal Premier Av Quiroz 100, Cercado ⓣ054 227821, ⓦhostalpremier.com. Associated with Youth Hostelling International, this hostel lacks any architectural merit, but it's clean, safe and friendly. It also runs a travel agency. S/55

★ **Point Hostal** Av Lima 515, Vallecito ⓣ054 286920, ⓦthepointhostels.com. Located in an attractive villa in the suburb of Vallecito, this hostel offers dormitories, a bar, restaurant, travel centre, book exchange and laundry service. Airport pick-up costs extra. Dorms S/18

★ **Sonesta Posada del Inca** Portal de Flores 116 ⓣ054 215530, ⓦsonesta.com/arequipa. Very well appointed and central hotel, with a top-class restaurant and, more importantly, a rooftop pool and patio, with superb views across the city to the southeastern mountains. This is also the only hotel in Arequipa with the dubious advantage of dehumidifiers in all rooms. Rooms also boast cable TV, a minibar and an internet connection. S/200

EATING

As it's not too far from the Pacific, the town's better restaurants are also renowned for their excellent fresh seafood. **Picanterías** – traditional Peruvian eating houses serving spicy seafood – are particularly well established here. There are also a number of non-*picantería* restaurants on the plaza, many of them with fine views to the Catedral and square below. Some also offer **live music**, especially on weekend evenings.

CAFÉS

Burger Express Portal San Agustín 123. This fairly standard Italian-style café nonetheless serves some of the best and strongest coffee in Arequipa. The menu includes sandwiches, burgers and other fast foods, as well as full meals. Daily 8am–10pm.

Inkafe Café Bar Portal de Flores, Plaza de Armas. Upstairs and to the right of Cinesur, and linked to the luxurious *Sonesta Posada del Inca*, this café is located on one of only two sunny terraces on the east side of the plaza and serves fine sandwiches, pastas and main dishes. An expensive place to dine, but worth it, not least for the high-quality service. Daily 7am–9pm.

Los Leños Pizzaria C Jerusalen 407. Just below the corner of Jerusalen and Puente Grau, this café serves a large range of delicious pizzas, pastas and some meat dishes, all very good value. The walls are covered with the graffiti of travellers from every continent. Daily 11am–11pm.

Manolos C Mercaderes 113. One of Arequipa's longest-established snack bars, offering good service and a delectable selection of meals, cakes and sweets, as well as excellent coffee. Portions are big and prices similar. There's another *Manolos*, newer but almost identical, just a couple of doors away on the same street at number 117. Daily 7am–9pm.

Restaurant Lakshmivan C Jerusalen 402. A very popular lunchtime vegetarian cafetería at the back of a small patio, with a background soundtrack of classical music and a tranquil ambience. There's also a range of health-food products, yoghurts and wholemeal bread for sale. Mon–Sat 11am–3pm.

Tenampa Pasaje Catedral 108. A small vegetarian snack bar in the lane behind the Catedral with good set-menus, great yoghurt and scrumptious Mexican tacos. Prices are very reasonable, even if portions aren't overly generous. Daily 10am–10pm.

El Turko San Francisco 216. Central, vaguely Middle-Eastern-themed place with excellent coffee plus crêpes, sandwiches, sweets and probably the best falafel in Peru; the space is popular and busy into the early hours. Thurs–Sat 24hr, Mon–Wed & Sun 7am–midnight.

RESTAURANTS

★ **La Cantarilla** C Tahuaycani 106, Sachaca. A notable, modern *picantería* located in a suburban district to the south of Yanahuara. Best at lunchtime when you can enjoy the shaded, spacious patios; everything is cooked over wood fires. Main-course prices start at S/20 per dish. Daily noon–5pm.

Complejo Turístico Bob Gourmet Alameda Pardo 123 ⓣ054 270528. Combining two of the finest restaurants in the city, this complex is based in the old Club Alemán, overlooking the city from the western banks of the Río Chili, with shady pagodas and a kids' play area. *El Montonero* is its excellent lunchtime restaurant, which is attempting to rescue some traditional regional dishes such

AREQUIPEÑA DELICACIES

Arequipa's restaurants are famous across Peru for a range of delicious dishes that make use of local food resources such as *rocoto* (an indigenous type of pepper), guinea pig, peanuts, maize, potatoes, chillis and river shrimps. The city is particularly well known for the following dishes:

Adobo Typically eaten for breakfast In Arequipa. This is a pork dish where the meat and bones are soaked and cooked in maize-beer sediment or vinegar, onions, garlic, boiled small *rocotos* and chillis.

Cuy chactado The name comes from the flat, round stone – or *chaqueria* – which is placed on top of a gutted and hung guinea pig to splay it out flat in a large frying pan, while cooking it in ample olive oil; it is usually served with toasted maize and a sauce made from chillis and the herb *huacatay* (black Andean mint)

Chupe de camarones River shrimp casserole incorporating squashes, cheeses, chillis and potatoes.

Ocopa A cold appetizer that originated in this city but can be found on menus across Peru. ilt is made with potatoes, eggs, olives and a fairly spicy yellow chilli sauce, usually with ground peanuts added.

Rocoto relleno A spicy Andean pepper usually stuffed with minced pork meat and blended with garlic, tomato paste, eggs and mozarella.

as *senca* meatballs and *pesque*, which is made from *quinoa* with a cheese and steak topping. *Che Carlitos* is a relatively fancy Argentine grill and bar, serving excellent beef and alpaca cuts, but also offering fine salads and roast vegetables. Best at lunchtime.

El Gaucho Portal de Flores 112. On the plaza but below ground level, this is one of the best meat restaurants in town with quite reasonable prices; try the grills or the *lomo gaucho*. Daily 10.30am–10pm.

Govinda C Santa Catalina 120a ⓣ 054 229523. A highly recommended veggie restaurant with a distinctive atmosphere, serving excellent breakfasts, natural yoghurt, juices and mueslis plus very good and inexpensive vegetarian set meals. The restaurant is associated with the Centro Cultural Bhakti Yoga (in the same building), which offers daily classes. Mon–Sat 6am–8pm.

Inkari Pub Restaurant Pasaje Catedral 113. Half-bar, half-restaurant, this serves good pizzas as well as other food (beef, chicken, pasta) in an often lively environment. There's also a dartboard (dangerously close to the front entrance), tables outside and just about enough room for musicians at weekends. Tues–Sat 4pm–midnight.

Picantería La Cau Cau II C Tronchadero 404, Yanahuara ⓣ 054 254496. One of Arequipa's best-value *picantería* restaurants, specializing in traditional foods like guinea pigs and *ricotto relleno* and with fine views towards El Misti and the city from its patio garden. Daily 11am–5pm.

★ **Restaurant Sol de Mayo** C Jerusalen 207, Yanahuara ⓣ 054 254148, ⓦ restaurantsoldemayo.com. Located in a different Calle Jerusalen (in the suburb of Yanahuara) to the one which bisects Arequipa's centre, this place has tables set within and around attractive gardens, live music and superbly prepared, traditional Peruvian dishes, all enjoyed in a convivial atmosphere. It's quite expensive, with main dishes starting at around S/28, but worth the S/5 taxi ride out there; alternatively it's a 15min walk over Puente Grau, then a few blocks up Av Ejercito. Call to reserve a table, since it's very popular. Daily 11.45am–5.30pm.

Restaurant El Viñedo San Francisco 319 ⓣ 054 205053. Quite a large, posh restaurant; pricey, but worth it for arguably the best Argentine-style steaks and grills in southern Peru, as well as the quality service. Daily 10.45am–10pm.

Restaurant Zingaro San Francisco 309 ⓣ 054 217662. A modern re-fit of an attractive *sillar*-vaulted space, this restaurant offers good Mediterranean-style food at average prices, with equally good service. Best appreciated in the early evening. Mon–Sat noon–10pm.

Rosal Restaurant Prolongación Av Bolognesi 264, Yanahuara ⓣ 054 256336. This is an ecological restaurant run by environmentalists and situated in lovely gardens by the river. All the food is delicious and organic, and their avocado stuffed with vegetables is exceptional. Tues–Sat 11am–4pm.

★ **Tradición Arequipeña** Av Dolores 111 ⓣ 054 426467. Probably the best *picantería* in town, this is the place to try your first *cuy chactado* or *rocoto relleno*. Opened in 1991 several blocks east of the city centre, it has a pleasant garden and is usually bustling with locals enjoying the extremely fresh and tasty food. Mon–Thurs & Sun noon–7pm, Fri & Sat noon–10pm.

3

DRINKING AND NIGHTLIFE

It's often hard to distinguish between bars, restaurants and nightclubs (or discos, as most are referred to), as many restaurants have a bar and live music, while many bars and clubs also serve food. Welcoming **peña** restaurants concentrated along the streets between calles Santa Catalina and Jerusalen, specialize in more traditional music than either bars or clubs. Most *peñas* open Thurs–Sat 8.30pm–midnight, while discos and nightclubs, many just a couple of blocks from the Plaza de Armas, open nightly till 3 or 4am, and usually charge a small entrance fee (around S/10).

BARS

★ **Déja Vu** C San Francisco 319. This small, popular place serves seafood, spaghetti and meat dishes, plus, of course, drinks. There's also a big video screen and a nice rooftop patio, which can get crowded at weekends.

Etnika Restaurant Pizzeria C San Francisco 317 ⓣ 054 202697. A popular restaurant in the Casona Forum complex, with reasonably tasty pizzas accompanied by good table service; the place usually gets very busy later on in the evenings.

Farrens' Irish Bar Pasaje Catedral 107. A tidy Irish pub-type bar with a wide range of cocktails and whiskies, good rock music and outside tables. Food also served. Mon–Sat noon–11pm.

Zero Pub C San Francisco 317. Popular with young locals and calling itself a "temple to rock'n'roll", this bar has a couple of decent pool tables and is decorated with posters of rock icons. Tues–Sat 6.30pm till late.

CLUBS AND PEÑAS

Forum Rock Café C San Francisco 317 ⓦ forumrockcafe.com. The liveliest and funkiest spot in the city, with live rock-centric music on Fri and Sat. This massive venue boasts a concert hall and disco as well as a café, decent bars and snacks. Tues–Sat 10pm–4am.

La Quinta Jerusalen C Jerusalen 522 ⓣ 054 200964. Comes to life at night when excellent food is served amid live local folk music. Sometimes traditional folk-dancing at weekends too. Entrance usually S/5. Mon–Sat 6.30pm–midnight.

TRADITIONAL FOLK MUSIC IN AREQUIPA

Arequipa has a very strong tradition of **folk singing** and **poetry**, and folk musicians will wander from *peña* to *peña*. They often perform the region's most authentic music, *yaraví*, which involves lamenting vocalists accompanied by a guitar. In recent years the youth of Arequipa have developed a preference for Latin- and Cuban-style **ballads** (troubador singing) accompanied by electric guitars, drums and sometimes keyboards, so the choice at weekends can be quite extensive.

3

★ **Restaurant Peña Las Quenas** C Santa Catalina 302 ⓣ 054 281115. One of the larger and better venues in town, *Las Quenas* dishes out authentic Andean music, food (including breakfast) and good pisco sours. Live folk music most weekends (S/10 entrance), and also during the week from June to Sept. Mon–Sat 10am–1am.

La Troica C Jerusalen 522a. One of the main folk venues with music almost every night in high season (S/6 entrance). Also features traditional Afro-Peruvian music. Well frequented by tour groups.

El Tuturutu Portal San Agustín 105. Right on the Plaza de Armas and overlooking the angel fountain of the same name, this restaurant and *peña* has a great atmosphere when busy at weekends. Mon–Sat 8am till late.

ENTERTAINMENT

The **cultural institutes** put on occasional programmes, especially the Instituto Cultural Peruano-Aleman, C Ugarte 207, which has a cultural events notice board, shows good films in Spanish and German and sometimes has children's theatre. Also worth a try are the **Alianza Francesa**, at C Santa Catalina 208, where there's a gallery displaying local artists' work, and the **Instituto Cultural Peruano Norte Americano** at C Melgar 109.

SHOPPING

CENTRAL MARKET

Arequipa's central market is one of the biggest and liveliest in Peru, though it's also a prime spot for pickpockets. Located a couple of blocks down from Iglesia Santo Domingo, it sells all sorts of food, leather work, musical instruments, inexpensive artesanía and even llama and alpaca meat, while offering an excellent range of hats, herbs and even cheap shoe repairs. You can also get a selection of fruit juices, including some combined with eggs and dark, sweet, stout beer.

ARTESANEÍA

Artesanía, alpaca goods and silver jewellery can be found in a number of places, but mainly in shops along the Pasaje Catedral, close to the main plaza, and the stalls and shops around the courtyard at Centro Artesanal Fundo El Fierro, on the second block of Grau.

Patio del Ekeko C Mercaderes 141, near the corner with Calle Jerusalen. A very plush, new shopping mall with a difference: quite upmarket in appearance, the products – silverware, artesanía, clothing, quality food – are surprisingly inexpensive. On the second floor there's a very good internet service, cafetería and bar; on the third floor there's a museum of textiles from southern Peru.

ANTIQUES

For collections of colonial (and older) antiques, including some interesting pre-Columbian ceramics, the antiques and art shops at Puente Grau 314b and along blocks 1 to 4 of C Santa Catalina are excellent. Of the latter the best is Arte Colonial, where there are several jam-packed rooms to explore.

BAKERIES

La Cañasta C Jerusalen 120. The best baker in town, located at the back of a patio, where you can also sit down and eat breakfasts or snack. It also has a small delicatessen counter.

BOOKSTORES

Librería El Lecto C San Francisco 133. Sells a number of books in English and also has the best book-exchange service in Arequipa and a cultural events notice board.

Librería San Francisco C San Francisco 221. Stocks a wide range of English-language books, including many on the history and wildlife of Peru.

CAMPING EQUIPMENT

Campamento Base C Jerusalen 401b. Otherwise known as "Colca Trek" this shop offers camping equipment and maps plus a good range of tents, sleeping bags and all other essentials. It is also a good place to enquire about expert guides.

Zarate Adventures C Santa Catalina 204. Has a significant range of camping and climbing equipment. There are other tour companies that rent out equipment, but not all are of the same quality (see p.166).

DIRECTORY

Consulates Bolivia, Av Ejercito 710 ☎ 054 285508; Chile, C Mercaderes 212, Emergency Medical Attention and Ambulance, ☎ 054 608080; Galerias Gamesa, IV Floor, Oficina 400-402 ☎ 054 226787.

DHL and Western Union Their combined offices are at C Santa Catalina 115 (Mon–Fri 9am–7pm, Sat 9am–1pm; ☎ 054 234288).

Health For hospital treatment, try the Arequipa Clinic, corner of Bolognesi and Puente Grau bridge (24 hr; ☎ 054 253416). If you need a pharmacy, try Inkafarma, Santo Domingo 113 (24hr), or Farmacia Americana, on the plaza at Portal San Agustín 103.

Immigration Migraciones, Urb. Quinta Tristan, 2nd park, Distrito José Bustamante y Rivero ☎ 054 421759.

Internet La Red, Jerusalen 306b (the best in town); C CHIPS Internet, San Francisco 202a (also pretty good); ONLINE, C Jerusalen 412a (offer international calling through their server). There's also a nameless cybercafé on the plaza at Portal San Agustín 105. Close to the plaza there's Catedral Internet, Pasaje Catedral 101 (Mon–Sun 8am–11pm). All stay open seven days a week, some until 8pm or later.

Language schools Rocio Language Classes, C Ayacucho 208, Oficina 22 (☎ 054224568, Ⓦ spanish-peru.com), offers a range of Spanish courses from beginner to technical. Centro de Idiomas Europeos, José Santos Chocano 249, Umacollo, in front of the Parque Libertad de Expresión (☎ 054 252619), runs courses in Spanish and Portuguese.

Laundry Fairy Laundry, C Jerusalen 528 ☎ 054 218648; Lavandería Rapida, C Jerusalen 404b; Magic Laundry, C Jerusalen 404b.

Money and exchange Banco de Credito, C San Juan de Dios 125 (ATM); Banco Continental, Block 1 of C San Francisco; Banco de la Nación, C Mercaderes 127. It's usually quicker to change money at a *casa de cambio* like the one at C San Juan de Dios 120, opposite Banco de Credito, and the rates are generally as good.

Police Tourist Police, C Jerusalen 315 (24hr; ☎ 054 201258).

Post office C Moral 118 (Mon–Sat 8am–8pm, Sun 9am–2pm).

Volunteering Traveller Not Tourist 118b, 2nd Floor, C Santa Catalina (☎ 958 842453 or ☎ 054 214304; Ⓦ travellernottourist.com and Ⓦ pachawawas.com). Offers volunteering opportunies with various community projects.

3

Around Arequipa

The spectacular countryside around Arequipa rewards a few days' exploration, with some exciting and adventurous possibilities for trips from the city. Most people visit these sites on an **organized trip** with one of the tour companies in Arequipa (see p.166). If you are prepared to put up with the extra hassle, you can visit many of the sites by much cheaper **public transport**.

The attractive village of **Sabandia** and the historic **Casa del Fundador** are both within 20km of the city centre; further afield the Inca ruins of **Paucarpata** at the foot of El Misti volcano offer excellent scenery, great views and a fine place for a picnic. Climbing **El Misti** is a very demanding but rewarding trek, but should not be attempted without a professional guide. The attractive village of **Chapi** makes a good day-trip, while the **Cuevas de Sumbay**, just a few hours' drive from Arequipa on the road towards Caylloma, contain hundreds of unique prehistoric paintings.

Yet the greatest attraction here is easily the **Colca Canyon**, some 200km to the north of Arequipa, usually accessed via the quaint town of **Chivay** and second only to Machu Picchu in its ability to attract tourists, it is developing fast as a trekking and canoeing destination (best in the dry season, May–Sept). On route to Colca, the road passes through the **Reserva Nacional de Aguada Blanca**, a good place for wildlife. One of the canyon's pulls is the **Mirador Cruz del Condor**, where several condors, symbols of the Andes, can be seen flying most days. Called the "Valley of Marvels" by the Peruvian novelist Mario Vargas Llosa, it is in places nearly twice the depth of Arizona's Grand Canyon and one of the country's most extraordinary natural sights.

Around 120km west of Arequipa, you can also see the amazing **Toro Muerto petroglyphs** and perhaps go on to hike amid the craters and cones of the **Valley of the Volcanoes**, roughly 25km to the northeast. A little further north is the **Cotahuasi Canyon**, which some people believe could usurp Colca's claim to being the deepest canyon in the world.

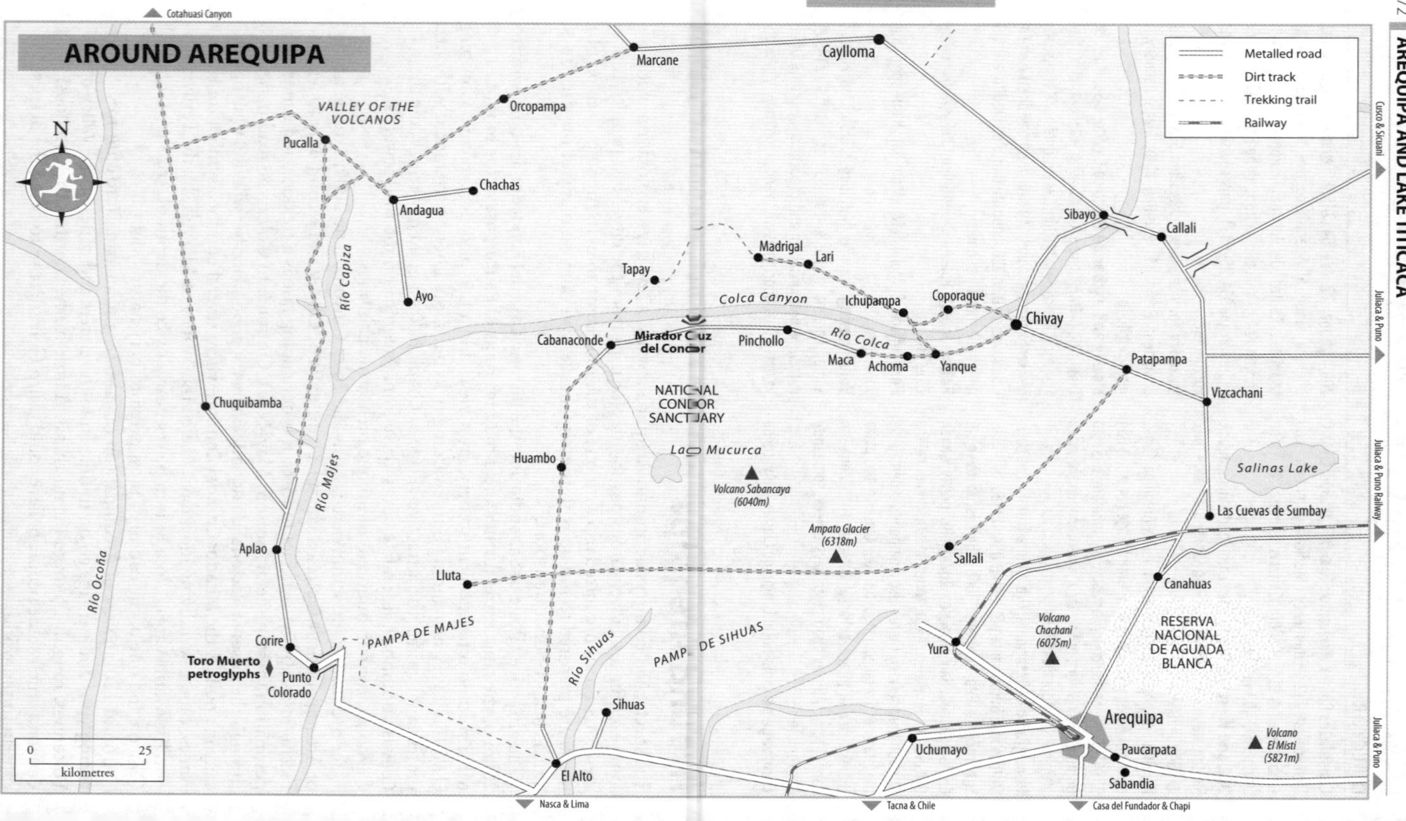

AROUND AREQUIPA
Metalled road
Dirt track
Trekking trail
Railway
Cotahuasi Canyon
Cusco & Sicuani
Juliaca & Puno
Juliaca & Puno Railway
Juliaca & Puno
Nasca & Lima
Tacna & Chile
Casa del Fundador & Chapi
N
Marcane
Caylloma
VALLEY OF THE VOLCANOS
Orcopampa
Pucalla
Chachas
Andagua
Ayo
Río Capiza
Sibayo
Callali
Madrigal
Lari
Tapay
Colca Canyon
Ichupampa
Coporaque
Chivay
Cabanaconde
Mirador Cruz del Condor
Pinchollo
Río Colca
Maca
Achoma
Yanque
Patapampa
Vizcachani
NATIONAL CONDOR SANCTUARY
Chuquibamba
Lago Mucurca
Huambo
Volcano Sabancaya (6040m)
Salinas Lake
Río Majes
Las Cuevas de Sumbay
Ampato Glacier (6318m)
Aplao
Sallali
Lluta
Canahuas
Río Ocoña
PAMPA DE MAJES
Corire
Toro Muerto petroglyphs
Punto Colorado
Río Sihuas
PAMPA DE SIHUAS
Volcano Chachani (6075m)
RESERVA NACIONAL DE AGUADA BLANCA
Yura
Sihuas
Arequipa
Uchumayo
Paucarpata
Volcano El Misti (5821m)
Sabandia
El Alto
0 25 kilometres

3

Paucarpata

Colectivos leave every 30min from the corner of Av Salverry and C San Juan de Dios in Arequipa to Paucarpata (around S/2); otherwise it's a 2hr stroll

Set against the backdrop of El Misti, **PAUCARPATA** is a fine place to while away an afternoon with some wine and a picnic lunch. About 7km out of central Arequipa, this large village is surrounded by farmland based on perfectly regular pre-Inca terraces, or *paucarpata* – the Quechua word from which it takes its name. There's a small colonial church on the southwestern edge of the suburb that contains a few Cusqueña-school paintings.

Sabandia

Mill Daily 9am–5pm • S/5, children S/2 • A return taxi trip from Arequipa costs S/25–30; colectivos cost S/3/person

Another 2–3km beyond Paucarpata lies **SABANDIA**, where you'll find a reconstructed colonial **mill** fronted by lawns with alpacas and llamas, and an attractive riverbank nearby. Built in 1661 to supply the city, along with three others in the region, the mill operated continuously for some three hundred years and was capable of milling 800kg of grain in one eight-hour shift with a single operator; it was only abandoned when industrial milling took root. The surrounding scenery, characterized by Inca terracing and broad vistas of surrounding mountains, is also home to a restored seventeenth-century **windmill**, which makes for an interesting visit.

Casa del Fundador

Daily 10am–5pm • Free • Return taxi from Arequipa S/30–35

Ten kilometres beyond Sabandia, through the fertile Socabaya Valley, the **Casa del Fundador** houses a colonial museum with period furnishings and attractive gardens. Once owned by Garcia Manuel de Carbajal, the original founder of Arequipa, it became the property of the Jesuits, who built a small chapel within the mansion. The mansion was restored in 1821 by the Archbishop José Sebastián de Goyeneche y Barreda, one of Arequipa's greatest nineteenth-century benefactors, who converted the building into a country estate and rural palace for ecclesiastical and civil dignitaries. After the Jesuits were expelled from Peru, the building was bought at auction then resold to the Goyeneche family, who kept it until 1947 when the estate was sold off. It was lovingly restored once again in the late 1980s by some local architectural enthusiasts.

Chapi

Angelitos Negros buses (3hr; S/10 one way) leave from C San Juan de Dios in Arequipa for Chapi at 6 & 7am

CHAPI, 45km southeast of Arequipa, is easily manageable as a day's excursion. Though less dramatic than the Colca Canyon, the landscape here is still magnificent, surrounded as it is by mining territory but few peaks much over 5000m. Chapi itself is famous for its white church, the **Santuario de la Virgen de Chapi**, set high above the village at the foot of a valley, which itself is the source of a natural spring. Thousands of pilgrims come here annually on May 1 to revere the image of the Virgin – a marvellous burst of processions and fiesta fever. There's no hotel, so if you intend to stay overnight you'll need a **tent**, but there are several basic places to eat.

El Misti

Buses (marked "Chiguata"; 1hr; S/10) leave from Av Sepulveda in Arequipa and will drop you at the trailhead

If you feel compelled to climb **EL MISTI** (5821m), 20km northeast of Arequipa, bear in mind that it's considerably further away and higher than it looks from Arequipa.

That said, it's a perfectly feasible hike if you allow two days for the ascent and another to get back down. Buses will drop you at the trailhead, from where there's a seven- to eight-hour hike to **base camp**. To spend the night here you'll need at the very least food, drink, warm clothing, boots and a good sleeping bag. Your main enemies will be the altitude and the cold night air, and during the day you'll need to wear some kind of hat or sun block as the sunlight is particularly strong. Note that the climate is changeable and that water is scarce. From the base camp it's another breathless seven hours to the summit, with its excellent panoramic **views** across the whole range of accompanying volcanoes. Any of the tour companies listed (see p.166) can drop walkers off at a higher starting point than Chiguata, cutting a few hours off the first day.

Reserva Nacional de Aguada Blanca

Covering some 300,000 hectares of plateau behind El Misti is the **Reserva Nacional de Aguada Blanca**, the largest protected area in this region, located at 4000m above sea level. A cold and dry *puna* (a high Andean ecological zone located above the treeline), it's a great place to spot groups of wild *vicuñas*, while its reservoirs – El Farile and Aguada Blanca – are known for their excellent trout fishing. This reserve is crossed by vehicles during the first hour on the Chivay and Colca road from Arequipa as it climbs high above Arequipa's valley floor.

Las Cuevas de Sumbay

Las Cuevas de Sumbay • S/5 • It is only possible to stop here with a private tour group or in your own vehicle

There are signposts showing the entrance to **las Cuevas de Sumbay** from the main road that continues towards Chivay and also Cusco. To stay at Sumbay you'll have to **camp**, but if you have a vehicle it's easy enough to stop for an hour or so en-route, following the signpost (at Km 103 from Arequipa) down a bad track to the village of Sumbay (4532m), about 1.5km away. At this point you'll need to find the guardian of the cave (often just a small shepherd child) who can open the gate for your car to continue another kilometre to a parking area.

From the gate it's a ten-minute walk to the caves, down into a small canyon just before the bridge. The guardian will have to unlock another gate to give you access to the site. Although small, the main Sumbay cave contains a series of 8000-year-old rock paintings representing shamans, llamas, deer, pumas and *vicuñas*. The surrounding countryside is amazing in itself: herds of alpacas roam gracefully around the plain looking for *ichu* grass to munch, and vast sculpted rock strata of varying colours mix smoothly together with crudely hewn gullies.

Chivay and around

Surrounded by some of the most impressive and intensive ancient terracing in South America, **CHIVAY**, 163km north of Arequipa and just four hours by bus from there, lies at the heart of fantastic hiking/mountain-biking country. Although notable as a market town, it is not actually a good place from which to observe the canyon. Chivay is nevertheless bustling with gringos using the town as a base for exploring the Colca Canyon region.

The **market** itself is located along Avenida Salaverry, where you'll also find a slew of artesanía shops. The town has a growing range of accommodation, restaurants and bus services for these visitors, making it a reasonable place to stay while you acclimatize to the high altitude. Serious trekkers will soon want to move on to one of the other canyon towns, likely **Cabanaconde** (see p.181).

3

La Calera

Hot springs Daily 5am–7pm • S/10; museum free • Colectivos (S/1) leave approx every 20min from the church-side corner of Plaza de Armas in Chivay; walking takes under an hour

Just 5km east of Chivay, slightly further up the Colca Canyon, the road passes mainly through cultivated fields until it reaches the tiny settlement of **LA CALERA**, which boasts one of Chivay's main attractions – a wonderful series of **hot spring pools**, fed by the bubbling, boiling brooks that emerge from the mountain sides all around at an average natural temperature of 85°C. Said to be good for curing arthritis and rheumatism these clean and well-kept thermal baths are not to be missed. There's also a **small museum** on site with models and artefacts demonstrating local customs, such as making an offering to the *pacha mama*, Mother Earth.

ARRIVAL AND DEPARTURE

CHIVAY AND AROUND

By bus Buses to and from Arequipa and Cabanaconde (see p.181) all stop at the bus terminal in Chivay, a 10min stroll from the main plaza, where bus departure times (usually 5–6am) are sometimes displayed if you can't find any in the terminal itself. There are three main companies – Reyna (054 531143), Andalucía (054 445089) and Turismo Milagros (054 708090) all of which travel two or three times daily to Arequipa (S/10; 3–4hr) and Cabanaconde (S/4; 2hr).

INFORMATION

Tourist information Turismo Milagros, Av Salaverry 106 (variable hours, but generally 2–8pm). The Municipality (Mon–Sat 8am–1pm & 2.30–5.30pm) and Colca Authority offices (Mon–Sat 8am–1pm & 2.30–6pm; 054 203010, colcaperu.gob.pe), both on the Plaza de Armas, also offer information.

ACCOMMODATION

Despite the town's periodic problems with **water** and **electricity**, Chivay boasts a surprising choice of reasonably comfortable accommodation, as well as a surfeit of atmospheric, thatched-roof lodgings in the immediate vicinity.

3

La Calera Hot Springs La Calera. Camping is sometimes permitted by pool 5 at La Calera hot springs, just 2km from Chivay. Availability and permission needs to be negotiated with the official at the reception hut on arrival. S/10/person

Casa Andina Huayna Capac (no number), Chivay 054 531020, casa-andina.com. For top-quality accommodation in Chivay this is arguably the place to choose. The well-equipped rooms are based mostly in independent, thatched bungalows with scenic views, and evening events such as music and dance take place in the communal spaces. S/250

Estancia Pozo del Cielo 054 531020 or Arequipa 054 205838, pozodelcielo.com.pe. Sited just over the Puente del Inca from Chivay, next to terraces topped by pre-Inca towers, *Estancia Pozo del Cielo* is the most luxurious option in town. Very nice, if rustic in style, with an open fire in the reception area, the hotel offers warm, very comfortable rooms, as well as homely service. S/250

Hostal la Casa de Lucila C Miguel Grau 131 054 60086 or 054 511109, viatours@star.com.pe. Reservations can be made in advance in Arequipa at C Jerusalen 302 054 224526. This small but homely house in Chivay lies within a stone's throw of the plaza. Tastefully decorated rooms – from singles to triples – are available, and a continental breakfast is included. The owners also run tours to most of the valley sites. S/60

Hostal Colca Inn Av Salaverry 307 054 531111 or 054 531088, hotelcolcainn.com. Probably the best mid-range hotel in Chivay. Clean and modern with private bathrooms, hot water and a pretty good restaurant. S/140

Hostal La Pascana Plaza de Armas at the corner of Puente Inca with C Siglo XX 054 531001 or 054 531190, hrlapascana@hotmail.com. Rooms are mostly large and very clean with their own showers, set around a small, attractive and flower-adorned courtyard. A simple breakfast is included in the price. S/60

EATING

Casa Blanca On the main plaza under *Hostal Plaza*. Specializes in local set menus as well as *caldos* (soups and broths) and chicken dishes. This warm space has a great atmosphere and an occasional fire in the evenings. Daily 8am–10pm.

Cuyeria El Chactao Av Salaverry 107. Just around the corner from the main plaza. Specializes in *cuy* (guinea pig), soups and other local dishes. Mon–Sat 7am–6pm.

Inka's Café-Bar Plaza de Armas 205 054 531209. Another popular dive on the main plaza; great for breakfasts and full meals. Daily 8am–10.30pm.

La Pascana Corner of Arco Puente Inca with Siglo XX 054 531 190. Attached to the hotel of the same name, this place serves up some of the best-priced and best-prepared dishes in Chivay; particularly proud of its pork and guinea pig cuisine. Daily 7am–8pm.

Restaurante El Balcon de Don Zacarias Av 22 de Agosto 102 054 531108. Almost fronting the plaza, this pleasantly decorated and friendly restaurant offers high-quality dishes, including an Andean buffet, *novo andino* cuisine plus breakfasts and good coffee. Mon–Sat 7am–8pm.

Restaurante Los Sismos. By the petrol station on the road in from Arequipa. Frequently stages folklore *peñas* as well as serving good alpaca steaks, tasty *quinoa*, carrot juice and sometimes even the local cactus drink, *sancayo*. Tues–Sat 10am–9pm.

DRINKING AND NIGHTLIFE

Lobos Pizzeria and Bar On the plaza 054 531081. This bar boasts a pool table, internet service and a happy hour (6–8pm). It is also a contact point for tourist information, though not the official office. Daily 8am–10pm.

McElroy's Irish Pub Opposite the church on the plaza. Popular for its rock music, bar food and decent range of cocktails; lively at weekends. Daily 11am–11pm.

DIRECTORY

Health MediSur medical centre (24hr), Salaverry 123.

Money and exchange For money changing in Chivay, the fastest option is the shop next door to Turismo Milagros on the plaza. Banco de la Nación is also on the plaza.

Telephones Available in the Turismo Milagros office.

ALPACAS GRAZE NEAR THE COLCA CANYON (P.178) >

Colca Canyon

Claimed to be the deepest canyon in the world at more than 1km from cliff-edge to river bottom, the **COLCA CANYON** may be an impressive sight but is actually estimated to be 170m less deep than its more remote rival, the Cotahuasi Canyon (see p.184). Both of these canyons are among several in the world that claim to be the biggest or deepest on the planet, depending on exactly how you measure them. In places the canyon's sides are so steep that it is impossible to see the valley bottom, while the higher edges of Colca are punctuated with some of the finest examples of pre-Inca terracing in Peru, attributed in the main to the Huari cultural era. Craggy mountains, huge herds of llamas and traditionally dressed Andean peasants complete the picture.

The canyon was formed by a massive geological fault between the two enormous volcanoes of Coropuna (6425m) and Ampato (6318m): the Río Colca forms part of a gigantic watershed that empties into the Pacific near Camana. Despite being one of Peru's most popular tourist attractions, the area's sharp terraces are still home to more-or-less traditional Indian villages. To the north of Colca, meanwhile, sits the majestic **Mismi Nevado**, a snow-capped peak that belongs to the Chila mountain range, and which, according to *National Geographic*, is the official source of the Amazon River; long the subject of argument and speculation, the precise location of the source was finally pinpointed in 2000 by a five-nation National Geographic Society expedition using cutting-edge GPS navigational equipment. The team, headed by 46-year-old maths teacher Andrew Pietowski, identified a spot on Nevado Mismi – a 5597m-high mountain in southern Peru.

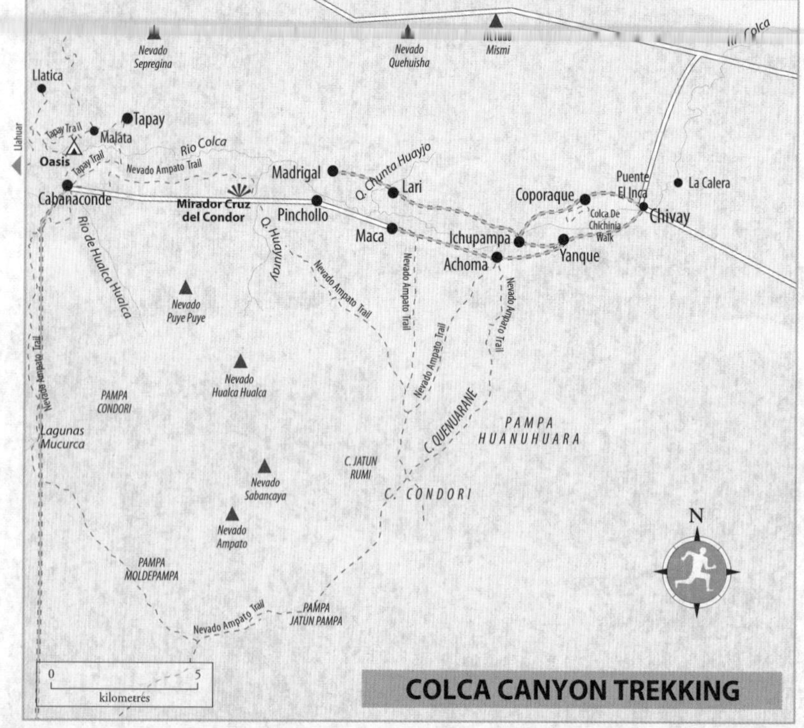

TREKKING IN AND AROUND THE COLCA CANYON

There are dozens of trekking routes in the Colca Canyon, but if you're planning on descending to the **canyon floor**, even if just for the day, it's best to be fit and prepared for the altitude – it's tough going and becomes quite dangerous in sections. Make sure to check whether **oxygen** is provided by your tour operator – even a bus trip to Chivay can bring on mountain sickness (see p.45) if you've only recently arrived from sea level. If you start trekking from Cabanaconde, or visit this town beforehand, it is worth visiting the tourist information centre (see p.181) and also checking out the cost of guides, *arrieros* (muleteers) and mules.

TREKS FROM CABANACONDE

Mirador Achachina Walk A fifteen-minute stroll from the plaza in Cabanaconde takes you past the bullring to the Mirador Achachina, a good spot for spotting condors and viewing the western end of the valley from above.

Basic Colca Trek The start of the classic route from Cabanaconde to the bottom of the Colca Canyon can be reached just ten minutes' walk along a fairly clear track beyond the newly constructed *Casa de Pablo* hostel, itself a five-minute walk from the plaza. The descent from here follows an incredibly steep path, quite dangerous in parts, down to the *Oasis* (see p.182), a rustic lodge and campsite right in the bottom of the canyon; it takes one and a half to two hours to descend and four or five to get back up. Many people stay the night.

The Tapay Trail This well-used trekking route connects Cabanaconde with the small settlement of Tapay via the *Oasis* (see p.182). It is a two- to four-day return hike through fine scenery, immense canyons, tiny hamlets like Cosñirhua (2350m) and Malata as well as various Inca and pre-Inca ruins. Save for the aforementioned campsite – which you'll pass on the first morning – there are no facilities at all in the area.

Cabanaconde to Lake Mucurca There is a popular eight-hour hike from Cabanaconde that culminates at Lake Mucurca (4000m). At its end point the astonishingly beautiful Ampato volcano is reflected in the lake's crystalline waters.

The Ampato Trail From Lake Mucurca the adventurous, fully acclimatized and well prepared can trek all the way around snowcapped Ampato (four to six days). The Ampato Trail has one very high pass – around 4850m at the crossing of two trails on Cerro Quenahuane, above the Quebrada Condori – and most of the walking is at over 4200m. Local guides are a good idea and you will need food and camping equipment. Be prepared for snow and ice; the weather can change very fast. On the last downhill leg of the trek you can choose to follow trails back to Achoma, Maca or Cabanaconde.

THE COLCAS DE CHICHINIA TREK

A relatively easy two-hour walk from the village of **Corporaque** (15min by car or bus from Chivay, on the opposite side of the Colca Canyon to Maca and the Mirador Cruz del Condor), takes in the **Colcas de Chichinia**, a semi-intact set of pre-Inca Huari tombs; today they lie today exposed at the foot of the cliffs on Cerro Yurac Ccacca (also known as Cerro San Antonio). A path leads out a couple of blocks just below the plaza in Corporaque, crossing the stream as you leave the settlement behind and climbing steadily towards a prominent, pink rocky outcrop. Because it's little visited, the entry path to the site isn't marked and more or less leaves you to find your own route; given this, it's important to take care not to damage the stone walls and agricultural plots you have to find your way through.

The tombs are just below the 4000m contour line where several overhangs have been partially filled in with stone as permanent thrones for pre-Inca **mummies**, placed here ceremoniously to spend eternity watching over the valley and gazing east towards several sacred mountain peaks. These days, after the ravages of time and grave-robbers, all that is left of the mummies are skulls and skeletons, some with hair and a few with remnants of the rope and cloth they were originally wrapped in.

To the southwest, a partly tumbled down, but still impressive **Huari village** can be clearly seen stretching from the tombs down to a major *tambo*-style (Quechua for house or resting-place) building on the bottom corner, which commands views around the valley. To get back to Corporaque, you can either drop down to the road and trace this back up to the settlement, or go along the small aqueduct that follows the contour of the hill from the *tambo* back to where you started.

3

COLCA CANYON TOURIST TICKETS

Arriving at Chivay by road, a tourism checkpoint issues standard, mandatory **Colca Boleto Turísticos** (general tourist tickets), which cost S/70 and offer "free" entry to the Mirador Cruz del Condor, other main *miradors* and all the major churches in the valley. These tickets are required just for entry to the Colca National Park area, essentially most of the valley, regardless of whether or not you visit the Mirador Cruz del Condor. The ticket is sold in three places: checkpoints on the road at **Chivay** (see p.174), at **Pinchollo** (see opposite) and also in the tourist office at **Cabanaconde** (see opposite).

Brief history

3

Francisco Pizarro's brother, Gonzalo, was given this region in the 1530s as his own private *encomienda* (colonial Spanish landholding) to exploit for economic tribute. In the seventeenth century, however, the Viceroy Toledo split the area into *corregimientos* that concentrated the previously quite dispersed local populations into villages. This had the effect of a decline in the use of the valley's agricultural terracing, as the locals switched to farming the land nearer their new homes.

The *corregimientos* created the fourteen main settlements that still exist in the valley today, including Chivay, Yanque, Maca, Cabanaconde, Corporaque, Lari and Madrigal. Most of the towns still boast unusually grand, Baroque-fronted **churches**, underlining the importance of this region's silver mines during the seventeenth and eighteenth centuries. During the Republican era, Colca's importance dwindled substantially and interest in the zone was only rekindled in 1931 when aerial photography revealed the astonishing natural and man-made landscape of this valley to the outside world – particularly the exceptionally elaborate terracing on the northern sides of bordering mountains.

Yanque

From Chivay, the first village the road winds through is **YANQUE**. The mountains to the southwest are dominated by the glaciers of Ampato and Hualca, and sometimes the volcano Sabancaya can be seen smoking away in the distance. Yanque boasts a fine white church, a small archeology museum, thermal baths down by the river, horseriding facilities, mountain-bike rental and, after Maca, some of the area's best-preserved pre-Inca ruins. The town lies directly on a fault line and is subject to frequent tremors: the visible effects can be seen in various land movements, abandoned houses and deep fissures around the area.

Maca

The road from Yanque continues on through a very dark tunnel until just beyond **MACA**, a small community which sits on the lower skirts of the volcano Sabancaya and the Nevado Hualca Hualca, some 23km west of Chivay. Immediately after this tunnel, a number of hanging pre-Inca tombs – *las chullpas colgantes* – can be seen high up in seemingly impossible cliff-edge locations, facing perhaps the best example of agricultural terracing in Peru across the valley.

Mirador Cruz del Condor

Pinchollo tourist office Daily 6am–6pm • Colca Canyon tourist tickets S/70 (see box above); all tours come here and public buses will stop briefly

The **Mirador Cruz del Condor** is the most popular point for viewing the canyon – it's around 1200m deep here – and you can almost guarantee seeing several condors circling up from the depths against the breathtaking scenery. The condors are best spotted from 7 to 9am; the earlier you get there the more likely you are to have fewer other spectators around. These days it's a popular spot, and most mornings there will actually be more tourists here than in the Plaza de Armas in Arequipa. For safety's sake, stand well back from the edge.

The gateway to the Mirador, the settlement of **Pinchollo** has a small museum and a tourist information office with photos and a model representing the canyon.

Cabanaconde

The small but growing town of **CABANACONDE** (3300m), 10km on from Pinchollo, is a good base from which to descend into the canyon. An impressive high wall and painted gateway mark the town's eighteenth-century cemetery. The town is also home to several semi-destroyed stone buildings and doorways from the late colonial (or Viceregal) era. If you can make it for the **Fiesta de la Virgen del Carmen** (usually between 14–18 July), you'll see the bullring in action and the town in the throes of a major religious festival and party.

ARRIVAL AND DEPARTURE — COLCA CANYON

By bus Most people arrive and leave the Colca Canyon by bus from Arequipa via Chivay, getting off at their particular village: Yanque, Maca or Cabanaconde. For destinations like Corporaque, on the other side of the canyon, a local bus or taxi needs to be picked up in Chivay (see p.175).

GETTING AROUND

By bus The plaza in Cabanaconde is the drop-off and pick-up point for buses, where you can find the offices of the four main bus companies connecting this settlement with Arequipa and Chivay. Andalucía, Reyna, Turismo Milagros and El Cristo Rey run buses from the Terminal Terrestre in Arequipa daily via Chivay (3–4hr; S/10) and down along the Colca Canyon to Cabanaconde (6hr; S/12); these return from Cabanaconde two or three times a day (check the times on arrival). Transportes Colca run similar itineraries, as do Turismo Milagros and Andalucía. From Cabanaconde the road from Arequipa and Chivay becomes a little-used dirt track continuing down the valley via Huambo and Sihuas to the coastal Panamerican Highway; best avoided unless you have your own 4WD vehicle.

INFORMATION AND TOURS

Tourist information Main plaza, Cabanaconde (T 054 280212). Has very little in the way of printed information, but the staff are very friendly. A good contact point for finding local trekking guides and *arrieros* (men with mules). Guides for the region generally cost S/50–85/day (one guide per two people) plus S/80–85 or more for two mules and an *arriero* (15–20 percent more if going over 4000m).

ACCOMMODATION

Colca Lodge A few kilometres beyond Corporaque, just before the river bridge back south to the village of Yanque T 054 531191 or T 054 202587, W colca-lodge.com. This luxury lodge has its own thermal-spring swimming pool and offers horseriding, mountain biking, short treks and tours to local sites of interest. Part of the big Libertadores hotel chain, it also has great inclusive buffet breakfasts. It is best to book well ahead. S/300

Hospedaje Villa Pastor Plaza de Armas, Cabanaconde T 054 630171, Lima T 01 5672318 or T 993 3750497. Fairly basic but cheap lodging with cable TV and internet access, plus comfortable-enough rooms. S/55

Hostal Valle del Fuego C Grau and C Bolívar, Cabanaconde T 054 830032 or T 054 203737, W pablotour.com. This great backpackers' pad is rightly popular. It offers a range of inexpensive accommodation, help with trips down into the canyon, mountain-bike rental and serves great hot breakfasts. Dorms S/25; doubles S/55

Hotel Kuntur Wassi On the hill above the plaza, Cabanaconde T 054 812166 or T 054 252989, Lima T 01 4951639, E kunturwassi@terra.com.pe. An

HATS IN THE COLCA CANYON

The indigenous communities of the Colca Canyon form two distinct ethnic groups: the Aymara-speaking **Collaguas** and the Quechua-speaking **Cabanas**. Traditionally, both groups used different techniques for deforming the heads of their children. The Collaguas elongated them and the Cabanas flattened them – each trying to emulate the shape of their respective principal *apu* (mountain god). Today it is the shape of their **hats** (taller for the Collaguas and round, flat ones for the Cabanas), rather than heads, which mainly distinguishes the two groups.

interesting and very comfortable hotel some 80m above the plaza. It has fine views right across the canyon to the Huaro waterfall, and the attractive rooms are laid out in an unusual way, clinging to the hill and incorporating some natural rock features and unusual domed roofs. It also has a restaurant and bar as well as solar-heated water. S/120

Mamma Yacchi Hotel Close to the village of Corporaque 054 241206, lacasademamayacchi.com. Out in the countryside on the north side of the canyon, just 20min by car or colectivo, *Mamma Yacchi* is a lovely thatched hotel offering that little bit extra compared with most accommodation in the region. The highlights include great food, lovely architecture, very comfortable rooms, excellent service (including hot-water bottles at bedtime) and music and dancing in the spacious restaurant area with local staff after dinner. S/200

3

El Mirador de los Collaguas C Lima 513, Yanque 054 203966 or 054 521015. Three blocks from the main square in Yanque and some 45min from the Cruz del Condor, this is a pleasant *pousada*, consisting of adobe-look bungalows and boasting stupendous views across the valley. S/182

Oasis Paradise Sangalle, bottom of Colca Canyon, 3–4hr walk from Cabanaconde. A rustic but extremely pleasant lodging and campsite right in the bottom of the canyon; run by the same local family who operate *Hostal Valle del Fuego*. Camping S/15/person; doubles S/50

Tradición Colca Carretera Principal, C Argentina 108 – just a 10min walk from the plaza in Yanque; Arequipa 054 424926, tradicioncolca.com. A beautifully decorated hostel that caters to backpackers (discounts for students or visitors who arrive with the Reyna bus company) and offers bike and horseriding tours, lovely rooms (some with wood-stove heating), excellent food, nice gardens, a book exchange and games room. S/80

Corire

A small town located 160km northwest of Arequipa, **CORIRE** is a small town of around two thousand people. Of very little interest to tourists in its own right, it is a primarily agricultural settlement based on rice and wheat production. Corire's claim to fame is really its proximity to the **Toro Muerto petroglyphs.**

Toro Muerto petroglyphs

Reached by bus or car from Arequipa, the **Toro Muerto petroglyphs** consist of carved boulders strewn over a kilometre or two of hot desert. More than a thousand rocks of all sizes and shapes have been crudely, yet strikingly, engraved with a wide variety of distinct representations. No archeological remains have been directly associated with these images but it is thought that they date from between 1000 and 1500 years ago; they are largely attributed to the **Wari culture**, though with probable additions during subsequent Chuquibamba and Inca periods of domination in the region. The engravings include images of humans, snakes, llamas, deer, parrots, sun discs and simple geometric motifs. Some of the figures appear to be dancing, others with large round helmets look like spacemen – obvious material for the author Erich Von Däniken's extraterrestrial musings (he based his book *Chariots of the Gods* on several archeological sites in Peru). Some of the more abstract geometric designs are very similar to those of the Huari culture, which may well have sent an expeditionary force in this direction, across the Andes from the Ayacucho basin, around 800 AD.

The route to the **petroglyphs** is signalled by a small site museum, but it is a good thirty-minute walk from the road, and at least 500m above it. What you're looking for is a vast row of **white rocks**, believed to have been scattered across the sandy desert slopes by a prehistoric volcanic eruption – the natural setting is almost as magnificent as the hundreds of petroglyphs.

ARRIVAL AND DEPARTURE — CORIRE

By bus There are fairly regular daily buses to Corire from Arequipa. Operating from early morning to early evening, the most regular are with Transportes Zeballos, with others run by TZ Turismo and Del Carpio (see p.165). Buses to Arequipa run from the Plaza de Armas in Corire and, unless full, can be flagged down on the main road at the Toro Muerto turn-off.

TORO MUERTO PETROGLYPHS

By car From the main metal road bridge that crosses the Majes River the site is 3km on, marked by a large sign on the left, "Petroglifos de Torro Muerto", close to the chapel and before the petrol station; buses between Arequipa and Corire will drop people here (Corire is 2 miles further down the road).

ACCOMMODATION AND EATING

Hostal El Molino Progreso 121 ⓣ054 472056, ⓣ054 472002, Arequipa ⓣ054 449298. An agreeable enough choice that also provides good contacts for canoeing, 4WD tours in the valley and visits to the local pisco-producing hacienda. S/35

Hostal Willy Av Progreso 400 ⓣ054 472180, ⓣ054 472046, Arequipa ⓣ054 251711. This is a reasonable-value hostel, most rooms having private bathrooms and a few also have a TV. S/35

Snack-Bar Pollería El Molino Plaza de Armas. While central and often busy, this café is nothing special and has quite a plastic ambience, but it does serve good and fresh chicken and chips all day long. Daily 8.30am–9pm.

DIRECTORY

Money and exchange Banco de Credito, block 1, 28 de Julio. Casa de cambio, Don Rufo.

Telephones There are public telephones at Av Progreso 121.

Valley of the Volcanoes

Following some 65km of the Río Andagua's course, the **VALLEY OF THE VOLCANOES** (Valle de los Volcanoes) skirts along the presently dormant volcano Mount Coropuna, the highest volcano in Peru (6425m) and the highest peak in southern Peru. At first sight just a pleasant Andean valley, this is in fact one of the strangest geological formations you're ever likely to see. A stunning lunar landscape, the valley is studded with extinct craters varying in size and height from 200 to 300m. About 200,000 years ago, these small volcanoes erupted when the lava fields were degassed (a natural release of volcanic gas through soil, volcanic lakes and volcanoes) – at the time of one of Coropuna's major eruptions.

The best overall view of the valley can be had from Anaro Mountain (4800m), looking southeast towards the Chipchane and Puca Maura cones. The highest of the volcanoes, known as Los Gemelos (The Twins), are about 10km from Andagua. To the south, the Andomarca volcano has a pre-Inca ruined settlement around its base.

ARRIVAL AND INFORMATION — VALLEY OF THE VOLCANOES

By bus From Toro Muerto, buses and colectivos to the Valley of the Volcanoes wind uphill, tracing around Mount Coropuna for 7–10 hours before arriving in the little town of Andagua (3450m). Buses continue to Orcopampa, from where serious hikers who don't mind the heat can walk the whole 60km or so down the valley. Most passengers base themselves at Andagua; from here there are 2–3 buses/week that make the 6hr journey to Cotahausi. From Orcopampa there are infrequent buses and occasional slow trucks that climb up the rough track to Caylloma, from where there's a bus service to Chivay and Arequipa (though it is quicker to backtrack to Arequipa via Toro Muerto due to the appalling state of the roads).

Maps The main section of the valley is about 65km long; to explore it in any detail you'll need to get maps (two adjacent ones are required) from the South American Explorers' Club in Lima and Cusco (see pp.81 & 222), the Instituto Geográfico (ⓦwww.ign.gab.pe) or from the Ministerio de Cultura in Arequipa (Alameda San Lázaro 120, Cercado; ⓣ054 213171).

ACCOMMODATION AND EATING

If you plan to camp here you'll need good supplies, especially water and a sunhat; the sun beating down on the black ash can get unbelievably **hot** at noon. Because this is a rarely visited region, where most of the people are pretty well self-sufficient, there are only the most basic of **shops** – usually set up in homes. Local people are also generally very hospitable, often inviting strangers they find **camping** in the fields to sleep in their houses.

La Casona Plaza de Armas, Andagua. Single and double rooms are available in this large old house set around a courtyard and with a balcony overlooking the square. The accommodation is pretty basic but the owners are very friendly. There are no private bathrooms. S/25

Majes River Lodge Aplao ⓣ054 660219, ⓦmajesriver.com. Specializing in river rafting, this place is a S/10 taxi ride from the village of Aplao. It offers beds, comfortable rooms with solar-heated water, a dining room, outdoor fire, rafting and even shamanic sessions. S/60

Cotahuasi Canyon

First navigated by a Polish expedition in 1981 and declared a Zona de Reserva Turística Nacional in 1988, the magnificent **COTAHUASI CANYON** (Cañon de Cotahuasi), 378km from Arequipa, has since opened up to visits that don't involve major rafting trips. However, getting to this wild and remote place is even more adventurous and less frequently attempted than the trip to the Valley of the Volcanoes. One of the world's deepest canyons, along with nearby Colca and the Grand Canyon in the US, it is around 3400m deep and over 100km long.

Arriving from the south along the difficult road from Arequipa (some 375km long) the route passes along the bottom part of the canyon, where the main settlement, **Cotahuasi** (2684m), can be found. This remote and attractive settlemenet boasts quaint narrow streets and a small seventeenth-century church. It has a variable climate but isn't particularly cold and is rapidly developing a name as an adventure travel destination, offering by far the best local facilities.

Continuing north to the village of **Alca** (near the hot springs of Luicho), the road forks. To the right, it heads into the deeper part of the canyon where you'll find the village of **Pucya**; further up the valley, heading pretty well northwest you end up at the astonishingly beautiful plateau of Lauripampa, from where you can walk down into the canyon or explore the massive Puya raymondi cacti hereabouts. The left fork continues to the pueblo of **Pampamarca**, where the locals weave lovely woollen blankets. Above the pueblo there is a fabulous trail that leads to the Uscuni waterfalls on one side of the valley and the natural rock formations of the Bosque de Piedras on the other. A little further on you'll find the thermal springs of Josla, an ancient spa that's a joy for tired legs after a long hike.

About 40km from Cotahuasi, the Wari ruins of **Marpa** can be seen straddling both sides of the river, but another hour away is the larger and better-preserved Wari city of **Maucallacta**.

ARRIVAL AND TOURS — COTAHUASI CANYON

By bus Reyna and Turismo Alex buses run the 12hr route to get here from Arequipa. Reyna has an office on the plaza in Cotahuasi, at Av Arequipa 201 (T 054 581017).

Tours The easiest way to get to Cotahuasi is by taking a guided tour from Arequipa (see p.166).

ACCOMMODATION

COTAHUASI

Hatunhuasi Hotel Centenario 307–309 T 054 581803, W hatunhuasi.com. A small hotel whose six bedrooms, based around a garden courtyard, all have private bathrooms. The restaurant serves great food and the staff can help with guides and trekking. S/60

Hotel Valle Hermosa C Tacna 108 T 054 581057, W hotelvallehermoso.com. With over twenty rooms in a beautiful setting and on two levels, there is hot water and also 24hr room service. This very pleasant pad has elegant rooms and the restaurant serves food mostly grown in its gardens. S/90

ALCA

Hostal Alcalá T 054 280224 and T 054 452258. This very friendly hostel offers exceptional value and has some rooms with private bathrooms, great hot showers and hearty breakfasts in a decent restaurant. Shared bathroom S/40; private bathroom S/55

Lake Titicaca

An undeniably calming and majestic sight, **LAKE TITICACA** is the world's largest high-altitude body of water. At 284m deep and more than 8300 square kilometres in area, it is fifteen times the size of Lake Geneva in Switzerland and higher and slightly bigger than Lake Tahoe in the US. An immense region both in terms of its history and the breadth of its magical landscape, the **Titicaca Basin** makes most people feel like they are on top of the world. Usually placid and mirror-like, the deep blue water reflects the vast sky back on itself. All along the horizon – which appears to bend away from you – the green Andean mountains can be seen raising their ancient backs towards the sun; over on the Bolivian side it's sometimes possible to make out the icecaps of the Cordillera Real mountain chain. The **high altitude** (3827m above sea level) means that recent arrivals from the coast should take it easy for a day or two, though those coming from Cusco will already have acclimatized.

A **National Reserve** since 1978, the lake has over sixty varieties of bird, fourteen species of native fish and eighteen types of amphibian. It's often seen as three separate regions: Lago Mayor, the main, deep part of the lake; Wiñaymarka, the area incorporating various archipelagos that include both Peruvian and Bolivian Titicaca; and the Golfo de Puno, essentially the bay encompassed by the peninsulas of Capachica and Chucuito. The villages that line its shores depend mainly on grazing livestock for their livelihood, since the altitude limits the growth potential of most crops. These days, **Puno** is the largest settlement and port in the whole of Lake Titicaca. Densely populated well before the arrival of the Incas, the lakeside Titicaca region is also home to the curious and ancient tower-tombs known locally as **chullpas**: rings of tall, cylindrical stone burial chambers, often standing in battlement-like formations.

There are more than seventy islands in the lake, the largest and most sacred being the **Isla del Sol** (Island of the Sun), an ancient Inca temple site on the Bolivian side of the border; Titicaca is an Aymara word meaning "Puma's Rock", which refers to an unusual boulder on the island. The island is best visited from Copacabana in Bolivia (see p.200), or trips can be arranged through one of the tour companies in Puno (see p.191).

On the Peruvian side of the lake you can visit the unusual **Uros islands**. These floating platform islands are built out of reeds – weird to walk over and even

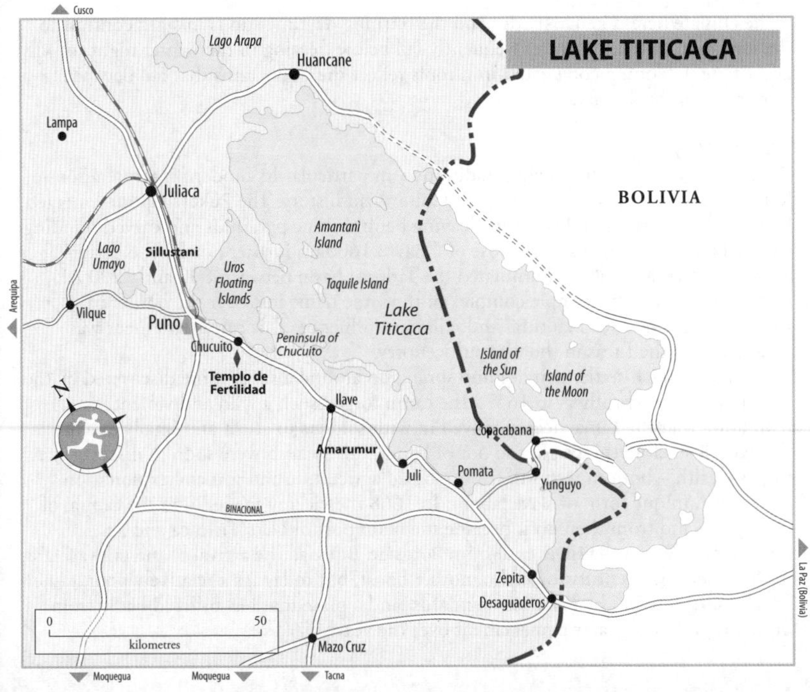

stranger to live on, they are now a major tourist attraction. More spectacular by far are two of the populated, fixed islands, **Amantani** and **Taquile**, where the traditional lifestyles of these powerful communities give visitors a genuine taste of pre-Conquest Andean Peru.

Brief history

The scattered population of the region is descended from two very ancient Andean ethnic groups or tribes – the **Aymara** and the **Quechua**. The Aymara's Tiahuanaco culture predates the Quechua's Inca civilization by over three hundred years and this region is thought to be the original home for the domestication of a number of very important plants, not least the potato, tomato and the common pepper.

Puno

A crossroads for most travellers en route to Bolivia or Chile, **PUNO** lacks the colonial style of Cusco or the bright glamour of Arequipa's *sillar* stone architecture, but it's a friendly place and one of the few Peruvian towns where the motorized traffic seems to respect pedestrians. Busy as it is, there is less of a sense of manic rush here than in most coastal or mountain cities. On the edge of the town spreads vast **Lake Titicaca** – some 8400 square kilometres of shimmering blue water enclosed by white peaks. Puno's port is a vital staging-point for exploring the northern end of Lake Titicaca, with its floating islands just a few hours away by boat.

There are three main points of reference in Puno: the spacious **Plaza de Armas**, the **train station** several blocks north, and the vast, strung-out area of old, semi-abandoned docks at the ever-shifting **Titicaca lakeside port**. It all looks impressive from a distance, but, in fact, the real town-based attractions are few and quickly visited.

The climate here is generally dry and the burning daytime sun is in stark contrast to the icy evenings (temperatures frequently fall below freezing in the winter nights of July and August). Sloping corrugated-iron roofs reflect the heavy rains that fall between November and February.

Brief history

Puno is immensely rich in living traditions – in particular its modern interpretations of folk dances – as well as fascinating pre-Columbian history. The **Pukara culture** emerged here some three thousand years ago leaving behind stone pyramids and carved standing stones, contemporaneous with those of Chavín 1600km further north. The better-known **Tiahuanaco culture** dominated the Titicaca basin between 800 and 1200 AD, leaving in its wake the temple complex of the same name just over the border in Bolivia, plus widespread cultural and religious influence. This early settlement was conquered by the Incas in the fifteenth century.

The first Spanish settlement at **Puno** sprang up around a silver mine discovered by the infamous Salcedo brothers in 1657. The camp forged such a wild and violent reputation that the Lima viceroy moved in with soldiers to crush and finally execute the Salcedos before things got too out of hand. The Spanish were soon to discover the town's wealth – both in terms of tribute-based agriculture and mineral exploitation based on a unique form of slave labour. In 1668 the viceroy made Puno the capital of the region, and from then on it became the main port of Lake Titicaca and an important town on the silver trail from **Potosí** in Bolivia. The arrival of the railway, late in the nineteenth century, brought another boost, but today it's a relatively poor, rather grubby sort of town, by Peruvian standards, and a place that has suffered badly from droughts and poor water management over the years.

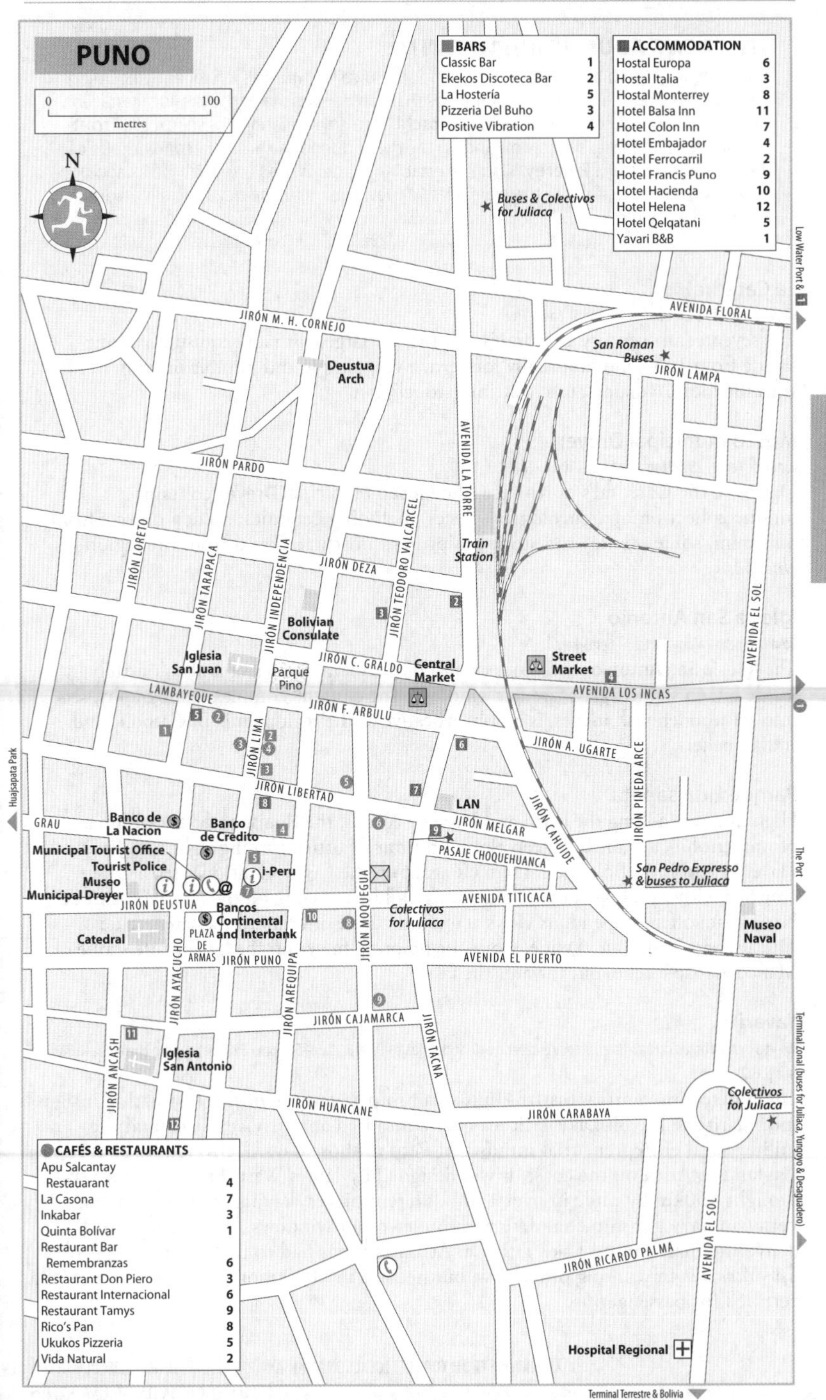
PUNO
0 100
metres
N
BARS
Classic Bar 1
Ekekos Discoteca Bar 2
La Hostería 5
Pizzeria Del Buho 3
Positive Vibration 4
ACCOMMODATION
Hostal Europa 6
Hostal Italia 3
Hostal Monterrey 8
Hotel Balsa Inn 11
Hotel Colon Inn 7
Hotel Embajador 4
Hotel Ferrocarril 2
Hotel Francis Puno 9
Hotel Hacienda 10
Hotel Helena 12
Hotel Qelqatani 5
Yavari B&B 1
CAFÉS & RESTAURANTS
Apu Salcantay Restauarant 4
La Casona 7
Inkabar 3
Quinta Bolívar 1
Restaurant Bar Remembranzas 6
Restaurant Don Piero 3
Restaurant Internacional 6
Restaurant Tamys 9
Rico's Pan 8
Ukukos Pizzeria 5
Vida Natural 2
Buses & Colectivos for Juliaca
JIRÓN M. H. CORNEJO
AVENIDA FLORAL
San Roman Buses
JIRÓN LAMPA
Deustua Arch
AVENIDA LA TORRE
JIRÓN PARDO
JIRÓN LORETO
JIRÓN TARAPACA
JIRÓN INDEPENDENCIA
JIRÓN TEODORO VALCARCEL
JIRÓN DEZA
Train Station
Bolivian Consulate
AVENIDA EL SOL
Iglesia San Juan
Parque Pino
JIRÓN C. GRALDO
Central Market
Street Market
LAMBAYEQUE
JIRÓN F. ARBULU
AVENIDA LOS INCAS
JIRÓN A. UGARTE
JIRÓN LIMA
JIRÓN LIBERTAD
JIRÓN PINEDA ARCE
LAN
JIRÓN CAHUIDE
GRAU
Banco de La Nacion
Banco de Credito
JIRÓN MELGAR
PASAJE CHOQUEHUANCA
Municipal Tourist Office
Tourist Police
Museo Municipal Dreyer
i-Peru
San Pedro Expresso & buses to Juliaca
JIRÓN DEUSTUA
AVENIDA TITICACA
Bancos Continental and Interbank
Colectivos for Juliaca
Museo Naval
Catedral
PLAZA DE ARMAS
JIRÓN PUNO
JIRÓN MOQUEGUA
AVENIDA EL PUERTO
JIRÓN AYACUCHO
JIRÓN AREQUIPA
JIRÓN CAJAMARCA
JIRÓN TACNA
Iglesia San Antonio
JIRÓN ANCASH
JIRÓN HUANCANE
JIRÓN CARABAYA
Colectivos for Juliaca
AVENIDA EL SOL
JIRÓN RICARDO PALMA
Hospital Regional
Low Water Port & 1
Huajsapata Park
The Port
Terminal Zonal (buses for Juliaca, Yungoyo & Desaguadero)
Terminal Terrestre & Bolivia

3

TITICACA'S AQUATIC INHABITANTS

Not surprisingly, **fish** are still an important food source for Titicaca's inhabitants, including the islanders, and the ibises and flamingoes that can be seen along the pre-Inca terraced shoreline. The most common fish – the **carachi** – is a small piranha-like specimen. **Trout** also arrived in the lake, after swimming up the rivers, during the first or second decade of the twentieth century. **Pejerey** (kingfish) established themselves only thirty years ago but have been so successful that there are relatively few trout left – *pejerey* fishing is an option for visitors.

La Catedral

Plaza de Armas • Daily 8am–noon and 3–6pm • Free

The seventeenth-century **Catedral** is surprisingly large, with an exquisite Baroque facade from 1657 and, unusually for Peru, a very simple and humble interior, in line with the local Aymaras' austere attitude to religion.

Museo Municipal Dreyer

Conde de Lemos 289 • Mon–Sat 11am–10pm • S/15

Opposite the Catedral's north face, the **Museo Municipal Dreyer** contains a unique collection of archeological pieces, including ceramics, golden objects from Sillustani, some textiles and stone sculptures, mostly removed from the region's *chullpas*.

Iglesia San Antonio

Jirón Ayacucho • Mon–Sat 8am–6pm • Free

The **Iglesia San Antonio**, two blocks south of the plaza, is smaller and colourfully lit inside by ten stained-glass circular windows. The church's complex iconography, set into six wooden wall niches, is highly evocative of the region's mix of Catholic and Indian beliefs.

Parque Huajsapata

High up, overlooking the town and Plaza de Armas, the **Huajsapata Park** sits on a prominent hill, a short but steep climb up Jirón Deustua, turning right into Jirón Llave, left up Jirón Bolognesi, then left again up the Pasaje Contique steps. Often crowded with cuddling couples and young children playing on the natural rockslides, Huajsapata offers stupendous views across the bustle of Puno to the serene blue of Titicaca and its unique skyline, while the pointing finger on the large white statue of Manco Capac reaches out towards the lake.

Yavari

Moored by the *Posada del Inca Hotel*, Sesquicentenario 610, Sector Huaje • Daily 8.15am–5.15pm • By donation; also operates as a B&B (see p.192)

The nineteenth-century British-built steamship **Yavari** provides a fascinating insight into maritime life on Lake Titicaca over a hundred and fifty years ago and the military and entrepreneurial mindset of Peru in those days. Delivered by boat from England to Arica on the coast, it was designed by James Watt. From Arica it was brought 560km by mule in over 1300 different pieces, having started life as a Peruvian navy gunship complete with bullet-proof windows, but ending up delivering mail around Lake Titicaca. At times it has had to use llama dung as fuel. The *Yavari* is in working order now, but needs $559,000 more work before it can be certified for passenger use.

CLOCKWISE FROM TOP LEFT LOCALS ON AMANTANI (P.197); EL MISTI, NEAR AREQUIPA (P.173); MONASTERIO DE SANTA CATALINA (P.212) >

PUNO FESTIVALS

Famed as the **folklore capital** of Peru, Puno is renowned throughout the Andes for its music and dance. The best time to experience this wealth of traditional cultural expression is during the first two weeks of February for the **Fiesta de la Candelaria**, a great folklore dance festival, boasting incredible dancers wearing devil masks; the festival climaxes on the second Sunday of February. If you're in Puno at this time, it's a good idea to reserve hotels in advance (hotel prices can double).

The **Festival de Tinajani**, usually around June 27, is set in the bleak altiplano against the backdrop of a huge wind-eroded rock in the Canyon of Tinajani. Off the beaten trail, it's well worth checking out for its raw Andean music and dance, plus its large sound systems; ask at the tourist offices in Puno or Cusco for details.

Just as spectacular, the **Semana Jubilar** (Jubilee Festival) occurs in the first week of November, partly on the Isla Esteves, and celebrates the Spanish founding of the city and the Incas' origins, which legend says are from Lake Titicaca itself. Even if you miss the festivals, you can find a group of musicians playing brilliant and highly evocative music somewhere in the labyrinthine town centre on most nights of the year.

ARRIVAL AND DEPARTURE — PUNO

BY PLANE

Flights arrive and depart most days for Lima and Cusco. Colectivos connect the airport (Aeropuerto Manco Capac, near Juliaca; ☎051 328974 or ☎051 322905) and Jirón Tacna in Puno; taxis are a bit costly. Some of the more upmarket hotels will arrange for airport pickup. Offices for LAN Peru are at Jr Tacna 299 in Puno (☎051 367227), or Jr San Ramón 125 in Juliaca (☎051 322228). For Star Peru flights, go to Jr San Roman 175 in Juliaca (☎051 327478).

BY TRAIN

If you're coming in from Cusco by train, you'll arrive at the station at Av la Torre 224 (☎051 351041). Taxis and motorcycle rickshaws leave from immediately outside the station and will cost less than S/4–5 to anywhere in the centre of town. There are some rather luxurious trains running up to 3 or 4 times a week in high season, leaving at 8am and arriving in Cusco at 6pm; tickets are available from agents or direct from PeruRail, Av La Torre Puno 224, (☎051 351041), or Plaza Bolognesi 303, Juliaca (☎051 321036, Ⓦperurail.com). Check at the office or online for special deals plus departure dates and times of the trains for Cusco. It's best to buy your seats some weeks in advance.

BY BUS

Buses, combis and cars arriving from local provincial destinations like Juliaca or along the edge of Lake Titicaca come in at the Terminal Zonal, Av Bolívar, block 9. Most inter-regional and international buses arrive at the Terminal Terrestre, Av Primero de Mayo 703 (☎051 364733). From either terminal it's preferable to take a taxi to town. Ignore anyone who offers you help, unless you have already booked with them (there are thieves operating as touts for hotels or tours).

Destinations Arequipa (several daily; 6hr); Copacabana (several daily; 2–3hr); Cusco (several daily; 6hr); Desaguadero (several daily; 2–3hr); La Paz (daily; 5–6hr); Lima (daily via Arequipa; 20hr); Tacna (daily; 10hr); Puerto Maldonado (daily; 20hr).

TO AREQUIPA/LIMA

Alas del Sur (☎051 9660436); Sur Oriente (☎051 368133); Cruz del Sur (☎051 368524); Ormeño (☎051 368176); CIAL (☎051 367821); CIVA (☎051 365882).

TO CUSCO

Inka Express (Empresa de Transportes), Jr Tacna 336 (☎051/365654, Ⓦinkaexpress.com) offers visits to archeological attractions en route. Also CIVA (☎051 365882); Turismo San Luís del Sur (☎051 705955); Cruz del Sur, Av Circunvalación Este 801 (☎051 322011).

TO DESAGUADERO

Alas del Sur (☎051 9660436); Sagitario (☎051 9676743); CIVA (☎051 365882); CIAL (☎051 367821).

TO LA PAZ

Ormeño (☎051 368176); Panamericano (via Copacabana) Jr Tacna 245 (☎051 354001); Tour Peru, Jr Tacna 282 (☎051 352991 or ☎051 368176), runs buses to La Paz via Copacabana from outside the Terminal.

TO PUERTO MALDONADO

Expreso Sagitario (20hr; ☎051 9676743).

TO TACNA

Direct (many stop off at Moquegua): Turismo San Martín (☎051 363631); Expreso Internacional Roel Bus (☎051 369996).

BY COLECTIVO

For Yunguyo, Pomata, Copacabana and Desaguadero there are combis hourly. Some combis and colectivos to Juliaca don't leave from the Terminal, but from Jr Tacna (corner with Pasaje Choquehuanca), and also from Av La Torre, near the exit from Puno to Juliaca, as well as from Jirón Carabaya, near the Ovalo with Av El Sol. Colectur, Jr Tacna 221 (T 051 352302), run to La Paz via Copacabana daily for around S/18.

BY BOAT

The main port, used by boats from Bolivia as well as the Uros islands, Taquile and Amantani, is a 15–20min ride from the Plaza de Armas, straight up Avenida El Puerto, crossing over Jirón Tacna, then up Jirón Puno. It's generally best to take a taxi or mototaxi to and from the port.

INFORMATION

Dirección Regional de Industria and Turismo Jr Ayacucho 682 (Mon–Fri 9am–5pm; T 051 364976).

i-peru Puno Plaza de Armas, Jirón Lima and Jirón Deustua (daily 8.30am–7.30pm; T 051 365088, E iperupuno@promperu.gob.pe).

Tourist police Jr Deustua 538 (daily, 24hr; T 051 353988). Very helpful and also give out free maps.

TOURS

The streets of Puno are full of touts selling guided tours and trips, but don't be swayed – always go to a respected, established **tour company**, such as one of those listed below. There are four main local tours on offer in Puno, all of which will reward you with views of abundant bird and animal life, immense landscapes and genuine living traditions. The trip to **Sillustani** normally involves a 3–4hr tour by minibus and costs $5–8 depending on whether or not entrance and guide costs are included. Most other tours involve a combination of visits to the nearby **Uros Floating Islands** (half-day tour; $8–15), **Taquile and the Uros islands** (full day from $10, or $15 overnight), and **Amantani** (2–5 days from around $10/day, including transport and food).

All Ways Travel Deustua 576 and Tacna 281 T 051 353979 and T 051 355552, W titicacaperu.com. The most progressive, friendly and helpful of all the tour companies in Puno and the Titicaca region, running most of the usual tours but also offering trips to the wildlife haven of Anapia, close to the Bolivian border, where they work with locals on a sustainable tourism project. They have *semi-rapida* ($20) and *rapida* ($45) boats for their full-day trips to the Uros and Taquile. This company is involved in social tourism in the Capachica Peninsula and the three islands of Anapia where they help with educational projects in the community (the island of Yuspique can be visited in small sailing boats for its *vicuña* nursery).

Cusi Expeditions Teodoro Valcarcel 164 T 051 369072 or T 051 9590673. A reliable company offering all the usual tours at reasonable prices: Sillustani, Uros, Taquile and Amantani. Also offers trips to Anapia.

Edgar Adventures Jr Lima 328 T 051 353444, W edgaradventures.com. Edgar leads island tours at average prices, but more interestingly they also offer kayaking, horseback trips and visits to Chucuito and the Templo de Fertilidad from about $12/person, as long as there are four or more in the group.

Leon Tours Jr Libertad 176 T 051 352771, W peru-titicaca.com. A recommended travel agent specializing in catamaran trips to Bolivia (full day by bus to Copacabana, catamaran to Isla del Sol, then bus to La Paz). They also run tours to Sillustani, Uros, Amantani, Taquile and Tinajani, *turismo rustico* with local shaman either on Amantani or near Juli, and adventure tourism, mainly in the Cordillera Carabaya (around 5000m) and down to the rainforest along the Inambari with boats and 4WD vehicles.

ACCOMMODATION

There is no shortage of **accommodation** in Puno for any budget, but most of it is bland compared with Arequipa or Cusco. The town's busy and narrow streets also make places hard to locate, so you may want to make use of a taxi or mototaxi (motorcycle rickshaw).

CENTRAL PUNO

Hostal Europa Jr Alfonso Ugarte 112 T 051 353026, E heuropa@terratmail.com.pe. Somewhat poorly maintained, but nevertheless offering good rates, this is a very secure hostel with safe luggage store and constant hot water, although few private bathrooms. Shared bathroom S/40; private bathroom S/55

Hostal Monterrey Jr Lima 441 T 051 351691, E monterreytours@hotmail.com. Quiet, central and pretty basic but nevertheless comfortable, this classic backpackers dive offers rooms with or without bathroom. Shared bathroom S/70; private bathroom S/90

★ **Hotel Colon Inn** Jr Tacna 290 051 351432, coloninn.com. Converted into the style of a small colonial mansion and very plush, with carpets, private bathrooms and constant hot water. There's also an excellent restaurant/bar and good (albeit non-inclusive) breakfasts; very good value overall. S/110

Hotel Embajador Av Los Incas 289 051 352072, hotelembajadorpuno.com. Plenty of modern rooms, carpeted and warm, with 24hr hot water. There's also a cafeteria with good views over the lake, serving excellent *novo andino* cuisine. S/60

★ **Hotel Francis Puno** Jr Tacna 305 051 364228 and 051 363297, francispuno.com. Modern and spacious hotel with a restaurant, bar, artesanía shop, laundry, safe box, money changing, tourist information and luggage deposit. All rooms are comfortable and with good showers. Constant hot water and buffet breakfast included. S/110

3

Hotel Hacienda Jr Deustua 297 051 356109 or 051 365134, lahaciendapuno.com. This very stylish, renovated mansion is plush and quaint with finely decorated rooms, hot water, TV, private bathrooms, internet and luggage-storage facilities. S/200

WEST OF JIRÓN LIMA

Hotel Balsa Inn Jr Cajamarca 555 051 363144, hotelbalsainn.com. A fine modern hotel conveniently located about one block from the plaza, comprising some twenty well-fitted rooms, most with cable TV, all with private bathrooms and heating. S/180

Hotel Helena Jr Ayacucho 609 051 352108. A very quiet, friendly and clean place that can also help with local tour arrangements. Its best feature would have to be the fabulous views over town and towards the lake from the breakfast room. S/80

Hotel Qelqatani Jr Tarapaca 355 051 366172, qelqatani.com. Modern and very smart, the rooms in this attractive new hotel have TV and private bathrooms, and there's a bar and restaurant. Security is excellent, plus there are internet facilities. S/200

Yavari B&B Moored by the *Posada del Inca Hotel*, Sesquicentenario 610, Sector Huaje 051 369329, yavari.org. A unique opportunity to spend the night on a British-built boat and get a porthole view of Puno from a freshly varnished wooden cabin. Hearty Andean breakfast included in the price. Dorms S/105

EAST OF JIRÓN LIMA

Hostal Italia Jr Teodoro Valcarcel 122 051 367706, hotelitaliaperu.com. A tastefully furnished, warm and stylish haven, if slightly overpriced and not particularly friendly. All rooms have private bathrooms and 24hr hot water. S/120

Hotel Ferrocarril Av la Torre 185 051 352011. Very close to the station and reasonably priced with good, old-fashioned service and an excellent restaurant. Rooms have private bathrooms and central heating. S/120

EATING

Puno's restaurant scene is fairly busy and revolves mainly around Jirón Lima, but bear in mind that places here shut relatively **early** – not much happens after 11pm on a weekday. The food in Puno is generally nothing to write home about, but the local delicacies of trout and kingfish (*pejerey*) are worth trying and are available in most restaurants. The best local fare can be found in small traditional restaurants in the **Huaije zone**, en route to the Isla Esteves; here you'll find various *picanterías*, many with convivial atmospheres and good views.

Apu Salcantay Restauarant Jr Lima 425 051 363955. Offers pizzas and pastas, as well as alpaca and a range of wines, *cuy* and a variety of vegetarian dishes; main meals start at around S/18. Daily noon–10.30pm.

La Casona Jr Lima 517 051 351108. The best restaurant in town, particularly for evening meals, serving excellent criolla dishes in an attractive traditional environment with lace tablecloths. It is also something of a museum, with antiques everywhere, and is very popular with locals. Daily 11.30am–10pm.

Inkabar Jr Lima 348 051 368031. A groovy restaurant-bar in the heart of town, serving a wide range of inventive meals, including great alpaca steaks, lakefish, stir-fries, even curry; good-value set menus and breakfasts. Daily 8am–11pm or later.

Quinta Bolívar Av Simon Bolívar 401, Barrio Bellavista. Quite far from the centre, but worth the trip for its wide range of quality local foods in a traditional setting; the barrio is a bit dodgy after dark, so it's advisable to arrive, and depart, with friends and take a taxi.

Restaurant Bar Remembranzas Jr Moquegua 200. Open from breakfast till late, this place specializes in pizzas, but also serves, alpaca and trout among other delicacies. Daily 7am–10pm.

Restaurant Don Piero Jr Lima 364. A favourite with travellers and relatively inexpensive, *Don Piero* has good breakfasts, a fine selection of cakes and a rack of magazines for customer browsing. Daily 7am–9pm.

★ **Restaurant Internacional** Jr Moquegua 201 051 352502. A classic Puno restaurant, popular with locals for lunch and supper, with a good range of reasonably priced meals. Go upstairs for the best atmosphere. Daily 7am–10pm.

Restaurant Tamys Jr Moquegua 431 051 363638. This restaurant specializes in broasted chicken meals (basically roast chicken and chips) in a well-preserved colonial mansion, where the poet Carlos Oquendo y Amat was born in 1905. Daily 10am–10pm.

Rico's Pan Jr Moquegua 326. A delightful bakery with freshly baked bread, cakes, pies and pasties. Also serves reasonable coffee, herb teas and cold drinks. Mon–Sat 6–10pm.

★ **Ukukos Pizzeria** Pasaje Grau 172 ⊕051 367373. Very nice ambience and varied cuisine, including pizzas, Chinese, local, *novo andino* and vegetarian. Good service. Daily early afternoon–10.30pm.

★ **Vida Natural** Jr Lambayeque 141 ⊕051 366386. Serves probably the best vegetarian food in town including salad, set lunches and yoghurt. The place is family run and very clean and the service is friendly. Mon–Fri & Sun 11am–8pm.

DRINKING AND NIGHTLIFE

The city's strong tradition as one of the major Andean folklore centres in South America means that you're almost certain to be exposed to at least one live band an evening. **Musicians** tend to visit the main restaurants in town most evenings from around 9pm, playing a few folk numbers in each, usually featuring music from the altiplano – drums, panpipes, flutes and occasional dancers. **Nightlife** centres around Jirón Lima, a pedestrian precinct where the locals, young and old alike, hang out, parading up and down past the hawkers selling woollen sweaters, craft goods, cigarettes and sweets. Most **bars** are open Monday to Friday 8 to 11pm or midnight, but keep going until 2am at the weekends.

3

Classic Bar Jr Tarapaca 330-a ⊕051 363596. Well-stocked bar with good service, ambience and decor, and a variable music policy according to clientele; it's a large friendly space which rarely gets too crowded.

Ekekos Discoteca Bar Jr Lima 355, 2nd floor. *Ekekos* offers snacks, drinks, cable TV, books and games; also shows films and favours a soundtrack of rock, salsa, reggae, trance and techno music. Daily 5pm–4am.

La Hostería Jr Lima 501 ⊕051 365406. A smart pizzeria and bar, busy in the evenings and a good meeting place; also serves steaks, including alpaca. Daily noon–11pm.

Pizzeria Del Buho Lima 349 ⊕051 363955 or ⊕051 356223. A warm, genial environment, crowded with travellers on Puno's cold, dark evenings. Serves delicious mulled wines and often has good music. Daily midday–11pm.

Positive Vibration Jr Lima 355. A decent, trendy bar, popular with young locals and travellers alike; also serves decent breakfasts and plays rock and reggae music. Daily 9pm until late.

Teatro Municipal Block 1 of Arequipa. Hosts folklore music, dance and other cultural events. For details of what's on, check at the tourist information office or the box office.

SHOPPING

Artesanía Jirón Lima is the best street for craft goods; try the Asociacion de Artesanos "La Cholita", Jr Lima 550, 2nd floor (daily 8am–7pm).

Ceramics For original Andean handmade ceramics and to see artesans at work, there's the Ceramica Titikaka, Jr Tarapaca 341 (⊕051 363955).

Musical instruments The unnamed shop at Jr Arbulu 231 sells most traditional Andean musical instruments (though fairly similar ones can be bought cheaply in the street market, on Av Los Incas).

DIRECTORY

Consulate Bolivia, Jr Arequipa 136 ⊕051 351251 (Mon–Fri 8.30am–2pm).

Health Clinica Los Pinos (⊕051 351071) or the Hospital Regional, Av El Sol 1022 (⊕051 351020).

Immigration Jr Ayacucho 280 ⊕051 357103 or ⊕051 352801 (Mon–Fri 8am–1pm and 3–5pm).

Internet Internet cafés on Jr Lima blocks 3 and 4 offer the best speed and prices.

Money and exchange Banco Continental, Jr Lima 400; Banco de la Nación, Ayacucho 215; Banco de Credito, Jr Lima 510 with corner of Grau; Interbank, Jr Lima 444. *Cambistas* hang out on the corner of Jr Tacna near the central market. There are casas de cambio at Jr Tacna 232 and 255, as well as at Jr Lima 440.

Police The Tourist Police are at Jr Deustua 538 (⊕051 353988) and the Policia Nacional's Comisaria can be found at Jr Ramón Castilla 722 (⊕051 321591).

Post office Jr Moquegua 269 (Mon–Sat 8am–8pm).

Taxis ⊕051 351616 or ⊕051 332020.

Telephones Public cabinas for telephone access are very common; one central one can be found at Jr Lima 439 (daily 7am–10pm).

Sillustani

Scattered all around Lake Titicaca you'll find *chullpas*, gargantuan white-stone towers up to 10m in height in which the ancient Colla tribe, who dominated the region before the Incas, buried their dead. Some of the most spectacular are at **SILLUSTANI**, set on a little peninsula in Lake Umayo overlooking Titicaca, 30km northwest of Puno. This ancient temple/cemetery consists of a ring of stones more than five hundred years old – some of which have been tumbled by earthquakes or, more recently, by tomb robbers intent on stealing the rich goods (ceramics, jewellery and a few weapons) buried with important mummies. Two styles predominate at this site: the honeycomb *chullpas* and those whose superb stonework was influenced by the advance of the Inca Empire. The former are set aside from the rest and characterized by large stone slabs around a central core; some of them are carved, but most are simply plastered with white mud and small stones. The later, Inca-type stonework is more complicated and in some cases you can see the elaborate corner-jointing typical of Cusco masonry.

ARRIVAL AND DEPARTURE — SILLUSTANI

By colectivo The easiest way to get here is on a guided tour from Puno (see p.191); alternatively, you can take a colectivo from Avenida Tacna most afternoons from 2–2.30pm, for under S/20.

3

ACCOMMODATION

If you want to **camp** overnight at Sillustani (though remember how cold it can be), the site guard will show you where to pitch your tent. It's a magnificent place to wake up, with the morning sun rising over the snowcapped Cordillera Real on the Bolivian side of Titicaca.

AROUND SILLUSTANI

Eco Inn Av Chulluni 195 ⊕051 365525, ⊕ecoinnhotels.com. Located out of town, more or less opposite the Isla Esteves, *Eco Inn* has lovely rooms with great views, as well as an astronomical observatory and splendid breakfasts. S/400

Hotel Puno (Libertador) ⊕051 367780, ⊕libertador.com.pe. A renovated and really special former *Hotel de Turistas* located on an island out to the north of town, with a top-notch restaurant, magnificent views from floor-to-ceiling windows and full spa facilities. A really long way from the fray of Puno's daily life. S/400

★ **Hotel Sonesta Posada del Inca** Sesquicentenario 610, Sector Huaje ⊕051/36411, ⊕sonesta.com. A very plush hotel bang on the side of the lake between the University of Puno and the Isla Esteves, with over sixty rooms, a gift shop, business centre, good heating and carpets. It has its own exclusive train-station stop as well as a private jetty on the lake. S/400

Hotel Taypikala Chucuito ⊕051/356042, ⊕taypikala.com. A rather fantastic and stylish New Age-style hotel, built next to the Templo de la Fertilidad (see p.198), with superb rooms, a spa and even meditation suites. They also now have the associated *Taypikala Lago* hotel at Chucuito, close by. It is best to book your room in advance online. S/350

Uros islands

The man-made floating **UROS ISLANDS** have been inhabited since their construction centuries ago by Uros Indians retreating from more powerful neighbours like the Incas. They are now home to a dwindling and much-abused Indian population. Although there are about 48 of these islands, most guided tours limit themselves to the largest, **Huacavacani**, where several families live alongside a floating Seventh-Day Adventist missionary school.

The islands are made from layer upon layer of **totora reeds**, the dominant plant in the shallows of Titicaca and a source of food (the inner juicy bits near the roots), as well as the basic material for roofing, walling and fishing rafts. During the rainy season months of November to February it's not unusual for some of the islands to move about the surface of the lake.

ARRIVAL AND TOURS — UROS ISLANDS

By boat You can visit independently with the skipper of one of the many launches that leave from the port in Puno about every thirty minutes (S/10 one way), or take the daily public transport boat leaving at 9am (S/7 one way), usually getting back between noon and 1pm (always check with the captain for the time they plan to depart the islands).

Tours The easiest way to get to the islands is on a short two- to three-hour trip (from S/25) with one of the tour agencies in Puno (see p.191).

Taquile

One of Titicaca's non-floating islands, **TAQUILE** is a peaceful place that sees fewer tourists than the Uros. Located 25–30km across the water from Puno it lies just beyond the outer edge of the Gulf of Chucuito. Taquile is arguably the most attractive of the islands hereabouts, measuring about 1km by 7km, and looking from some angles like a huge ribbed whale, large and bulbous to the east, tapering to its western tail end. The horizontal striations are produced by significant amounts of ancient terracing along the steep-sided shores. Such terraces are at an even greater premium here in the middle of the lake where soil erosion would otherwise slowly kill the island's largely self-sufficient agricultural economy, of which potatoes, corn, broad beans and hardy *quinoa* are the main crops. Without good soil Taquile could become like the main floating islands, depending almost exclusively on tourism for

THE UROS

There are only six hundred **Uros** people living on the islands these days and a lot of the population is mixed-race, with Quechua and Aymara blood. When the Incas controlled the region, they considered the Uros so poor – almost subhuman – that the only tribute required of them was a section of hollow cane filled with lice.

Life on the islands has certainly never been easy: the inhabitants have to go some distance to find **fresh water**, and the bottoms of the reed islands rot so rapidly that fresh matting has to be constantly added above. Islands last around twelve to fifteen years and it takes two months of communal work to start a new one.

More than half the islanders have converted to **Catholicism** and the largest community is very much dominated by its evangelical school. Forty years ago the Uros were a proud **fishing tribe**, in many ways the guardians of Titicaca, but the 1980s, particularly, saw a rapid devastation of their traditional values. However, things have improved over recent years and you do get a glimpse of a very unusual way of life. Note that lots of the people you may meet actually live on the mainland, only travelling out to sell their wares to tourists.

3

its income. Today, the island is still very traditional. There is no grid-connected electricity on the island, though there is a solar-powered community loudspeaker and a growing number of individual houses with solar lighting; it's therefore a good idea to take a torch, matches and candles.

The island has two main ports: **Puerto Chilcano Doc** (on the west or Puno side of the island) and **El Otro Puerto** (on the north side, used mostly by tour boats of tour agents because it has an easier and equally panoramic access climb). Arriving via Puerto Chilcano Doc, the main heart of the island is reached via 525 gruelling steps up a steep hill from the small stone harbour; this can easily take an hour of slow walking. When you've recovered your breath, you will eventually appreciate the spectacular view of the southeast of the island where you can see the hilltop ruins of **Uray K'ari**, built of stone in the Tiahuanaco era around 800 AD; looking to the west you may glimpse the larger, slightly higher ruins of **Hanan K'ari**. On arrival, before climbing the stairs, you'll be met by a committee of locals who delegate various native families to look after particular travellers – be aware that your family may live in basic conditions and speak no Spanish, let alone English (Quechua being the first language).

Brief history

The island has been inhabited for over ten thousand years, with agriculture being introduced around 4000 BC. Some three thousand years ago it was inhabited by the Pukara culture and the first stone terraces were built here. It was dominated by the Aymara-speaking Tiahuanaco culture until the thirteenth century, when the Incas conquered it and introduced the Quechua language. In 1580, the island was bought by Pedro Gonzalez de Taquile and so came under Spanish influence.

During the 1930s the island was used as a safe place of exile/prison for troublesome characters like former president Sánchez Cerro, and it wasn't until 1937 that the residents – the local descendants of the original tribe – regained legal ownership by buying it back.

ARRIVAL AND TOURS — TAQUILE

By boat The Comunidad Campesina de Taquile has at least eight wooden boats of its own and sells tickets for rides to the island directly from the port in Puno (daily from 7am, returning by around 5.30 or 6pm; S/15 one way); although most passengers are locals, tourists are very welcome. Daily boats for Taquile leave Puno at 7am. You can go on an organized trip with one of the tour companies listed (see p.191), but the agencies use the same boats and charge at least twice the going rate (around $25). The sun's rays reflected off the lake are strong, so it's a good idea to protect your head and shoulders during this voyage. Most boats return some time after lunch the same day.

Tour guides There are around thirty indigenous Taquileño tourist guides, many who now speak English, so it's not essential to book a visit to Taquile via a travel agent in Puno. The quality can be just as good or even better by arranging a visit to Taquile directly with the islanders: this way you can help keep the economic benefit of tourism on the island itself.

ACCOMMODATION

Homestays Many visitors choose to stay a night or two in bed and breakfast accommodation (from around S/14) in islanders' homes. The only way to guarantee a place to stay is to book in advance through one of Puno's tour agencies (see p.191); if you arrive on spec, you can ask the relevant island authorities or talk to the boat's captain and you may be lucky, but don't bank on it. Sleeping bags and toilet paper are recommended, and fresh fruit and vegetables are appreciated by the host islanders.

EATING AND SHOPPING

Restaurants Away from the plaza there are over twenty restaurants, or eating houses, dotted around the island, most serving the classic local dish of *sopa de quinoa* or *pejerey* fish with French fries.

Shops There are a few small stores that sell artesanía, mostly weavings and a couple of places to eat around the small plaza.

Amantani

Like nearby Taquile, **AMANTANI**, a basket-weavers' island and the largest on the lake, has managed to retain some degree of cultural isolation and autonomous control over the tourist trade. Amantani is the least visited of these two islands and consequently has fewer facilities and costs slightly more to reach by boat. Of course, tourism has had its effect on the local population, so it's not uncommon to be offered drinks, then charged later, or for the children to sing you songs without being asked, expecting to be paid. The ancient **agricultural terraces** are excellently maintained, and traditional stone masonry is still practised, as are the old Inca systems of agriculture, labour and ritual trade. The islanders eat mainly vegetables, with meat and fruit being rare commodities, and the women dress in colourful clothes, very distinctly woven.

The island is dominated by two small hills: one is the **Temple of Pachamama** (Mother Earth) and the other the **Temple of Pachatata** (Father Earth). Around February 20, the islanders celebrate their main festival with half the 5000-strong population going to one hill, the other half gathering at the other. Following ancient ceremonies, the two halves then gather together to celebrate their origins with traditional and colourful music and dance.

3

ARRIVAL AND DEPARTURE — AMANTANI

By boat Boats for Amantani usually leave Puno daily at 9am, returning between 4 and 4.30pm; as usual, check with the captain for the time they plan to depart the islands. You can go on an organized trip with one of the tour companies listed (see p.191), but the agencies are at least twice as expensive. It's a good idea to protect your head and shoulders from the sun on the journey over.

ACCOMMODATION AND EATING

Homestays Currently the only accommodation is in islanders' houses though there are plans to build a hostel. These can be booked in advance (S/84/$30/ person, including boat and accommodation) via most Puno-based tour companies (see p.191).

Food shops There are no restaurants, but you can buy basic supplies at the artesanía trading post in the heart of the island.

Juliaca

There's no particular reason to stop in **JULIACA**, in many ways an uninspiring and geographically very flat settlement, but at the same time it's hard to avoid. This is the first town out of Puno towards Cusco, less than an hour away across a grassy pampa. The wild, flat and relatively barren terrain here makes it easy to imagine a straggling column of Spanish cavalry and foot soldiers followed by a thousand Inca warriors – Diego de Almagro's fated expedition to Chile in the 1530s. Today, much as it always was, the plain is scattered with tiny isolated communities, many of them with conical kilns, self-sufficient even down to kitchenware.

WEAVING AND KNITTING ON TAQUILE

Although they grow abundant maize, potatoes, wheat and barley, most of Taquile's population of 1200 people are also weavers and knitters of fine **alpaca wool**, renowned for their excellent cloth. You can still watch the locals drop-spin, a common form of hand-spinning that produces incredibly fine thread for their special cloth. The men sport black woollen trousers fastened with elaborate waistbands woven in pinks, reds and greens, while the women wear beautiful black headscarves, sweaters, dark shawls and up to eight skirts at the same time, trimmed usually with shocking-pink or bright-red tassels and fringes. You can tell if a man is married or single by the colour of his **woollen hat**, or *chullo*, the former's being all red and the latter's also having white; single men usually weave their own *chullos*. The community authorities or officials wear black sombreros on top off their red *chullos* and carry a staff of office.

Inland from the lakeside, this is not an inviting town, looking like a large but down-at-heel, desert-bound work camp. There are some good **artesanía** stalls and shops on the Plaza Bolognesi, and excellent woollen goods can be purchased extremely cheaply, especially at the **Monday market**. The daily market around the train station is worth a browse and sells just about everything – from stuffed iguanas to second hand bikes.

ARRIVAL AND DEPARTURE — JULIACA

By plane If you come by air to Titicaca, it's Aeropuerto Manco Capac you'll arrive at. Flights leave daily from the airport, 2km north of Juliaca, for Cusco (40min), Arequipa (40min) and Lima (2hr). Taxis and colectivos leave from Plaza Bolognesi for the airport (shouldn't cost more than S/12–15). There's an airport departure tax (S/25).

3

By train If you're going by rail to Cusco from Puno, you have to pass through Juliaca en route; no one really gets off here though.

By bus Cruz del Sur buses leave from Huancane 443 (T 054 322011) twice a day for Arequipa and Lima; Empresa San Martín operate from Jr Tumbes 920 to Puno and Moquegua; San Ramón, for Arequipa, are next door at 918 (T 051 324583).

By colectivo Frequent colectivos to Puno (45–60min; S/6) and Lake Titicaca leave from Plaza Bolognesi and from the petrol station Grifo Los Tres Marías, off Avenida Noriega, two blocks from the plaza.

By taxi A taxi to Puno will set you back around $12.

ACCOMMODATION

Royal Inn Hotel San Román 158 T 054 321561, W royalinnhoteles.com. A surprisingly classy hotel with heating, carpets, private bathrooms and reasonably good service. This is the best place to sleep if you get stranded here and need to sample one of Juliaca's several bland establishments. S/300

DIRECTORY

Money and exchange Though rates tend to be better in Puno, you can change money with the street dealers on Plaza Bolognesi, with the casa de cambio J.J. Perú on Mariano Núñez or with the money-changing shops on block 1 of San Martín. Alternatively, banks include the Banco de la Nación, Lima 147; Banco Continental, San Román 441; and the Banco de Credito, Mariano Núñez 136.

South to Bolivia

The most popular routes to Bolivia involve overland road travel, crossing the frontier either at **Yunguyo** or at **Desaguadero**. En route to either you'll pass by some of Titicaca's more interesting colonial settlements, each with its own individual style of architecture. The lakeside stretch between Puno and the Bolivian frontier at Desaguadero is known – also for linguistic reasons – as the **Corredor Aymara**. This sector is full of fascinating but unfortunately slowly decaying colonial relics, particularly the fine churches of Chucuito, Acora, Ilave, Juli, Pomata and Zepita. The most commonly used of the two frontier crossings is Yunguyo.

Chucuito

CHUCUITO, 20km south of Puno, is dwarfed by its intensive hillside terracing and the huge igneous boulders poised behind the brick and adobe houses. It was once a colonial town and the main plaza retains the **pillory** (*picota*) where the severed heads of executed criminals were displayed. Close to this there's a **sundial**, erected in 1831 to help the local Aymara people regulate to an 8am–5pm work day. The base is made from stones taken from the Inca Templo de Fertilidad. Also on the plaza is the **Iglesia Santo Domingo**, constructed in 1780 and displaying a very poor image of a puma.

Templo de Fertilidad

Located behind the *Hotel Taypikala* (see p.194), the **Templo de Fertilidad** remains Chucuito's greatest treasure. Inside the temple's main stone walls are around a hundred stone phalluses, row upon row jammed within the temple space, ranged like seats in a

THE GATEWAY OF AMARU MURU

Coming from Puno, beyond the bridge over the Río Ilave, the road cuts 60km across the plain towards Juli, passing by some unusual rock formations scattered across the altiplano of the Titicaca basin, many of which have ritual significance for the local Aymara population. The most important of these is the **Gateway of Amaru Muru**, a doorway-like alcove carved into the rock and said by indigenous mystics to serve as a dimensional link to the ancestors, a belief shared by new agers, who view it as the Andean "star gate", a kind of link to non-Earthly beings and other worlds; it is very hard to find, without a local guide or tour leader.

theatre. Some of the larger ones may have had particular ritual significance, and locals say that women who have difficulty getting pregnant still come here to pray for help on the giant phalluses.

ARRIVAL AND DEPARTURE — CHUCUITO

By bus/colectivo Chucuito is a small settlement and both buses and colectivos between Puno and the frontier (at Yunguyo and Desaguadero) drop off and pick up on the main street, one block from the Templo de Fertilidad.

3

Ilave

About two-thirds of the way between Puno and Juli you pass through the village of **ILAVE**, where a major side-road heads off directly down to the coast for Tacna (320km) and Moquegua (231km). Ilave is quite an important market town and has a large **Sunday market** selling colourful clothing and coca leaves, and also hosts a few shamanic fortune-tellers. The large Plaza de Armas hosts a statue to Coronel Francisco Bolognesi, hero of the Arica battles between Peru and Chile, while half a block to the south, the ancient and crumbling **Iglesia de San Miguel** has an impressive cupola and belfry.

ARRIVAL AND DEPARTURE — ILAVE

By bus The town has a surprisingly large and modern Terminal Terrestre, where all the buses from Puno stop and from where it's possible to catch services to Tacna and Moquegua on the coast.

Juli

A few kilometres on from the Amaru Muru rock (see box above) is the relatively large town of **JULI**, now bypassed by a new road, but nestling attractively between gigantic round-topped and terraced hills. Juli is also known as Pequeña Roma (Little Rome) because of the seven prominent mountains immediately surrounding it, each one of them of spiritual significance to the indigenous inhabitants in terms of magic, healing and fertility. Perhaps because of this, the **Jesuits** chose Juli as the site for a major missionary training centre, which prepared missionaries for trips to the remoter regions of Bolivia and Paraguay. The concept they developed, a form of community evangelization, was at least partly inspired by the Inca organizational system and was extremely influential throughout the seventeenth and eighteenth centuries. The Jesuits' political and religious power is reflected in the almost surreal extravagance of the church architecture.

Iglesia de San Pedro

Plaza de Armas • Mon–Sat 6.30–11.30am and 2–4pm • Free

Fronting the town's large, open plaza is the stone-built parish church of **San Pedro**, marked by its intricately carved Plateresque side-altars. Constructed in 1560, it has an impressive cupola, and the cool, serene interior, awash with gold-leaf, is home to many superb examples of Cusqueña-school artwork. Behind the altar there's a wealth of silver and gold, and the patterned woodwork drips with seashells, fruits and angels. In front of this church you'll often see local shamanic fortune-tellers.

Iglesia San Juan

Plazuela de San Juan • Mon–Sat 8am–4pm • S/5

Juli's numerous other churches display superb examples of Indian influence, particularly the huge brick and adobe **Iglesia San Juan**, with its *mestizo* stonework on some of the doors and windows. Cold and musty but with a rather surreal interior, due in part to the play of light through its few high windows, this church was founded in 1775 but is now an excellent **museum of religious art and architecture**, which handsomely rewards the inquisitive visitor.

Pomata

Twenty kilometres on from Juli lies the historic town of **POMATA**, with its pink granite church of **Santiago Apóstol**, built in 1763. Outside the church, in a prominent location overlooking the lake, is a circular stone construction known as **La Glorieta**; crumbling today, it's still the site where local authorities meet for ceremonial purposes. Pomata's name is derived from the Aymara word for "puma", and you'll see the puma symbol all over the fountain in the Plaza de Armas and outside the church. If you happen to be around the area in October, try to get to Pomata for the **Fiesta de la Virgen de Rosaria** on the first Sunday of the month, a splendid celebration with processions, music and folk dancing, as well as the usual drinking and feasting.

3

CROSSING THE BOLIVIAN BORDER

SOUTH TO BOLIVIA

BY HYDROFOIL

Expensive, irregular hydrofoils from Juli to La Paz (and vice versa) are run along with cultural tours by Crillon Tours (US ⓣ 305 3585353, ⓦ titicaca.com), bookable through the tourist office or tour operators in Puno (see p.191) and their own office in La Paz (Av Camacho 1223 ⓣ 00591 2 2337533), but you need to book well in advance in all cases; note that parts of the journey are made by bus. A similarly upmarket catamaran service runs on demand; contact Transturin (Av Ayacucho 148 ⓣ 051 352771, ⓦ transturin.com) for details.

VIA YUNGUYO–COPACABANA

The Yunguyo–Copacabana crossing is slightly less direct than travelling via Desaguadero but is arguably a more enjoyable route into Bolivia. Unless you intend staying overnight in Copacabana (or take the 3hr Puno–Copacabana minibus) you'll need to set out quite early from Puno. The actual border (8am–6pm) is a 2km walk from Yunguyo, although there are usually taxis available, which only take 5min. The Bolivian passport control, where there's usually a bus for the 10km or so to Copacabana, is just a hundred metres on from the Peruvian border post (8am–7pm Peruvian time) where you need to get an exit stamp and surrender your tourist card. From the border and passport controls at Yunguyo some buses connect with a minibus service to Copacabana, then a Bolivian bus on to La Paz.

Copacabana to La Paz The cheap afternoon bus service from Copacabana to La Paz takes you through some of the basin's most exciting scenery. At Tiquina you leave the bus briefly to take a passenger ferry across the narrowest point of the lake, the bus rejoining you on the other side from its own individual ferry. Once across the lake it's a 4–5hr haul on to La Paz.

Changing money You can change money at the Banco de la Nación at Triunfo 219 and 20 de Julio, but there are several casas de cambio and street *cambistas* nearby, usually offering better rates and dealing in a greater variety of currencies, though even then you should change only enough to get you to La Paz, as the rate is not good.

VIA DESAGUADERO

With a newly paved road, the Desaguadero crossing is the most popular way to make the Peru–Bolivia border crossing, although it is not a very friendly town and there's a conspicuous abundance of rubbish on some streets. It offers the advantage of passing the ruined temple complex of Tiahuanaco over on the Bolivian side. If you do want to travel this route, take one of the early morning colectivos (6–9am) from Jr Tacna in Puno to Desaguadero ($2; 3–4hr). You'll need to get a stamp in your passport from the Peruvian control (daily 7am–8pm Peruvian time) by the bridge and the Bolivian one just across the other side of the bridge (same hours). If you arrive here by bus, it's a short walk across the border and you can pick up a bus on to La Paz more or less hourly ($3; 3–4hr), which goes via Tiahuanaco.

Changing money Money can be changed on the bridge approach but the rates are poor, so buy only as much as you'll need to get you to La Paz.

ACCOMMODATION AND EATING

YUNGUYO

Hostal Residencial Isabel San Francisco 110 ⓣ 014 856084. The best hotel in Yunguyo is the *Hostal Residencial Isabel*, which has hot water but only communal bathrooms, and friendly staff who can advise on border crossing if required. S/50

DESAGUADERO

Pollería El Rico Riko Close to the border crossing. Few of the restaurants here can really be recommended, but this is not too bad.

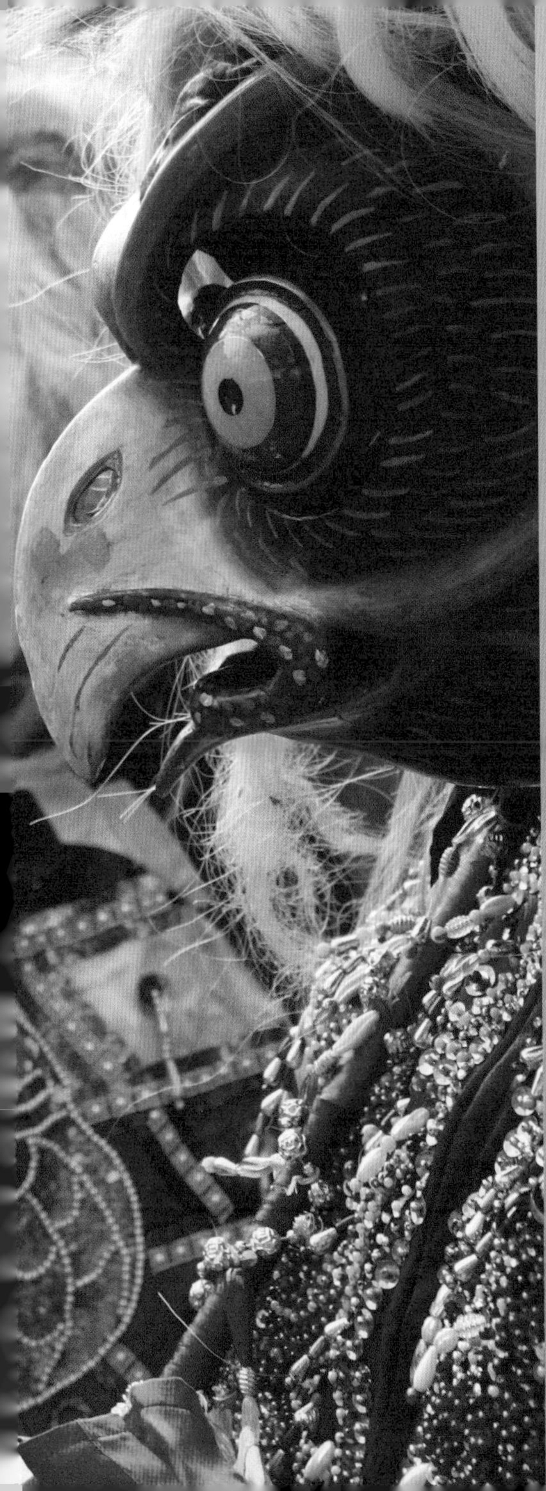

Cusco and around

FIESTA DE LA VIRGEN DELCARMEN, PAUCARTAMBO

Cusco and around

Known to the Incas as the "navel of the world", colourful Cusco was built by the Spanish on the remains of Inca temples and palaces, and is as rich in human activity today as it must have been at the height of the empire. One of South America's biggest tourist destinations, the city boasts a thriving Andean culture, and Inca architecture and colonial treasures galore, not to mention exclusive access to the mighty Machu Picchu, an unmissable highlight to any trip to Peru. In high season – June to September – the entire Sacred Valley swarms with visitors. It may be difficult to avoid the crowds, but Cusco's magnificent history and ancient feel may well tempt you to consider extending your stay.

Enclosed between high hills, Cusco's heart is the **Plaza de Armas**. Directly above it, the imposing ceremonial centre and fortress of **Sacsayhuaman** dominates the hillscape. Once the Incas' capital, it is now home to a rich mix of traditional culture, lively nightlife and an endless variety of museums, walks and tours.

4

The wider region of Cusco is mainly mountainous, with several peaks over 6000m, all of them considered sacred. The entire region is **high altitude** and even the city of Cusco sits at 3399m, an altitude which needs to be treated with respect, particularly if arriving by air from sea level (see box, p.210). Within easy access of the city, there are dozens of enticing destinations. The **Sacred Valley** of the **Río Urubamba** is the obvious first choice, with the citadel of **Machu Picchu** as the ultimate goal, but there are hundreds of other magnificent Inca ruins – **Pisac** and **Ollantaytambo** in particular – set against glorious Andean panoramas.

The Cusco mountain region boasts some of the country's finest **trekking**. The **Inca Trail** to Machu Picchu is by far the best known and most popular, but there are excellent **alternative trails** all starting less than a day's overland travel from Cusco. The stunning Inca remains of **Choquequirao**, in the Río Apurímac area, arguably provides the best alternative archeological destination, with tours leaving from Cusco more or less daily. **Salcantay** to the north, and **Ausangate**, visible on the city's southern horizon, are also appealing options.

East of Cusco, the Andean mountains slope steeply down into the lowland **Amazon rainforest**, where protected areas are helping to maintain some of the world's most

MACHU PICCHU

Highlights

❶ **San Blas** Take in the scene of Cusco's vibrant artists' quarter from a bench beside the church in Plazoleta San Blas. **See p.218**

❷ **Whitewater rafting** A fast rafting trip down one of Cusco's whitewater rivers draws many thousands of outdoor adventure seekers here every year. **See p.224**

❸ **Pisac** Standing at this Inca citadel offers one of Peru's most amazing panoramas, along the Sacred Valley and down onto the beautiful little market town of the same name. **See p.239**

❹ **Trekking in the footsteps of the Incas** The Inca Trail – a tourist hotspot now becoming a victim of its own success – is just one of many breathtaking paths in the Andes around Cusco. **See p.252**

❺ **Machu Picchu** Words never adequately describe this awe-inspiring Inca citadel; magically set against forested mountain peaks and distant glacial summits, it's dwarfed only by the sky. **See p.257**

❻ **Paucartambo festival** During the Fiesta de la Virgen del Carmen this normally quiet town changes into a colourful, haunting display of music and surreal outfits. **See p.272**

HIGHLIGHTS ARE MARKED ON THE MAP ON P.206

biodiverse wilderness areas. In particular, the Tambopata–Candamo Reserved Zone (see p.443), or the slightly nearer Manu Reserved Zone (see p.446), are among the best and most accessible ecotourism destinations. South of Cusco are the pre-Inca sites at **Tipón** and **Pikillacta**, nearly as spectacular as those in the Sacred Valley but far less visited. The luxurious **train journey** to Puno and Lake Titicaca passes through scenery as dramatic as any in the country.

The **best time to visit** Cusco and the surrounding area is during the dry season (May–Sept), when it's warm with clear skies during the day but relatively cold at night. During the wet season (Oct–April) it doesn't rain every day, but when it does, downpours are heavy.

Cusco

Nestling majestically in the belly of a highland valley and fed by two rivers, **CUSCO**'s unique layout was designed by the Incas in the form of a puma. Many of the city's finest Inca architectural treasures were so masterfully constructed out of local stone that they are still in great shape today, and the city is ripe for exploring: one minute you're walking down a shadowy, stone-walled alley, the next you burst onto a plaza full of brightly dressed dancers from the countryside, joining in what, at times, seems like the endless carnival and religious **festival celebrations** for which Cusco is famous (see box, p.219).

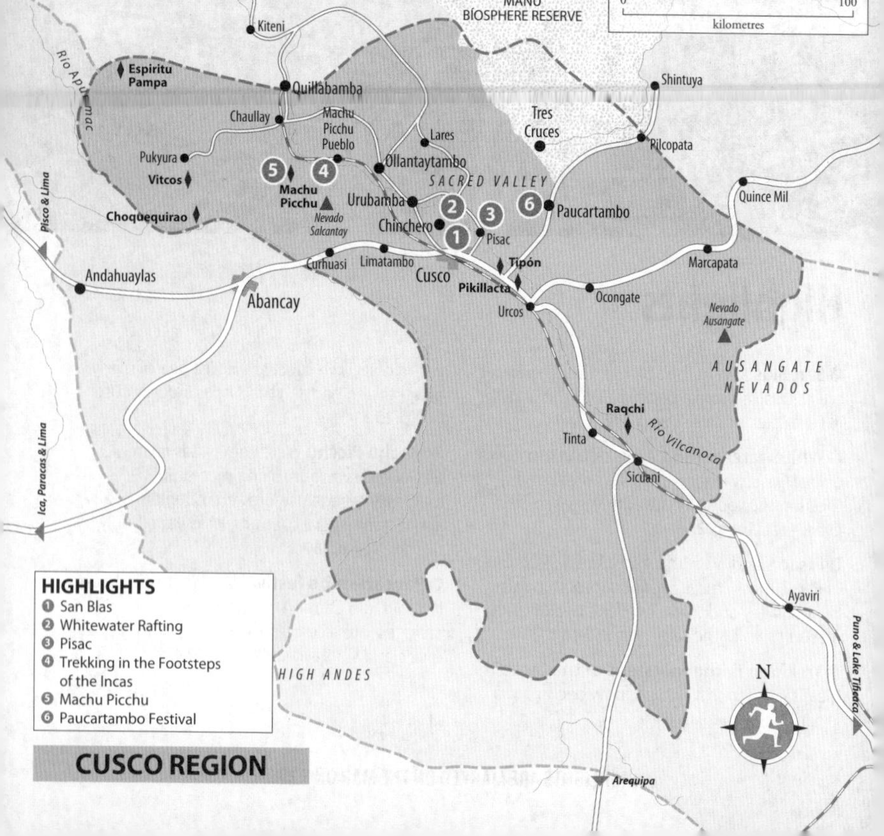

Nearly every site you'll want to visit is within walking distance of the main Plaza de Armas, and you can easily cover the main features of each quarter of the city in half a day. You should be able to cover most of Cusco Town in two or three active days, perhaps allowing a little extra time for hanging out in the bars and shops en route.

Brief history

The Cusco Valley and the Incas are synonymous in many people's minds, but the area was populated well before the Incas arrived on the scene and built their empire on the toil and ingenuity of previous peoples.

Founding Cusco

The **Killki**, who dominated the region from around 700–800 AD, while primarily agrarian, also built temple structures from the hard local diorite and andesite stones. Some of these structures still survive, while others were incorporated into later Inca constructions – the sun temple of Q'orikancha, for example, was built on the foundations of a Killki sun temple.

According to Inca legend, Cusco was founded by **Manco Capac** and his sister Mama Occlo around 1200 AD. Over the next two hundred years the valley was home to the Inca tribe, one of many localized groups then dominating the Peruvian sierra.

Building Cusco

It wasn't until **Pachacuti** assumed leadership of the Incas in 1438 that Cusco became the centre of an expanding empire and, with the Inca army, took religious and political control of the surrounding valleys and regions. As Pachacuti pushed the frontier of Inca territory outwards, he also masterminded the design of imperial Cusco, canalizing the Saphi and the Tullumayo, two rivers that ran down the valley, and built the centre of the city between them. Cusco's city plan was conceived in the form of a puma, a sacred animal: **Sacsayhuaman**, an important ritual centre and citadel, is the jagged, tooth-packed head; **Pumachupan**, the sacred cat's tail, lies at the junction of the city's two rivers; between these two sites lies **Q'orikancha**, the **Temple of the Sun**, reproductive centre of the Inca universe, the loins of this sacred beast; the heart of the puma was **Huacapata**, a ceremonial square approximate in both size and position to the present-day **Plaza de Armas.** Four main roads radiated from the square, one to each corner of the empire.

The overall achievement was remarkable, a planned city without rival, at the centre of a huge empire; and in building their capital the Incas endowed Cusco with some of its finest structures. Stone palaces and houses lined streets which ran straight and narrow, with water channels to drain off the heavy rains. It was so solidly built that much of ancient Cusco is still visible today, particularly in the stone walls of what were once palaces and temples.

The Spanish Conquest

In 1532, when the Spanish arrived in Peru, Cusco was a thriving city, and capital of one of the world's biggest empires. The Spaniards were astonished: the city's beauty surpassed anything they had seen before in the New World; the stonework was better than any in Spain; and precious metals, used in a sacred context across the city, were in abundance throughout Q'orikancha. They lost no time in plundering its fantastic wealth. **Atahualpa**, the emperor at the time, was captured by Spanish conquistadors in Cajamarca while en route to Cusco, returning from bloody battles in the northern extremity of the empire. Hearing from the Emperor Atahualpa himself of Cusco's great wealth as the centre of Inca religious and political power, **Francisco Pizarro** reached the native capital on November 15, 1533.

The Spanish city was officially founded on March 23, 1534. Cusco was divided up among 88 of Pizarro's men who chose to remain there as settlers. **Manco Inca**, a blood relative of Atahualpa – who was murdered by Pizarro (see p.490) – was set up as a

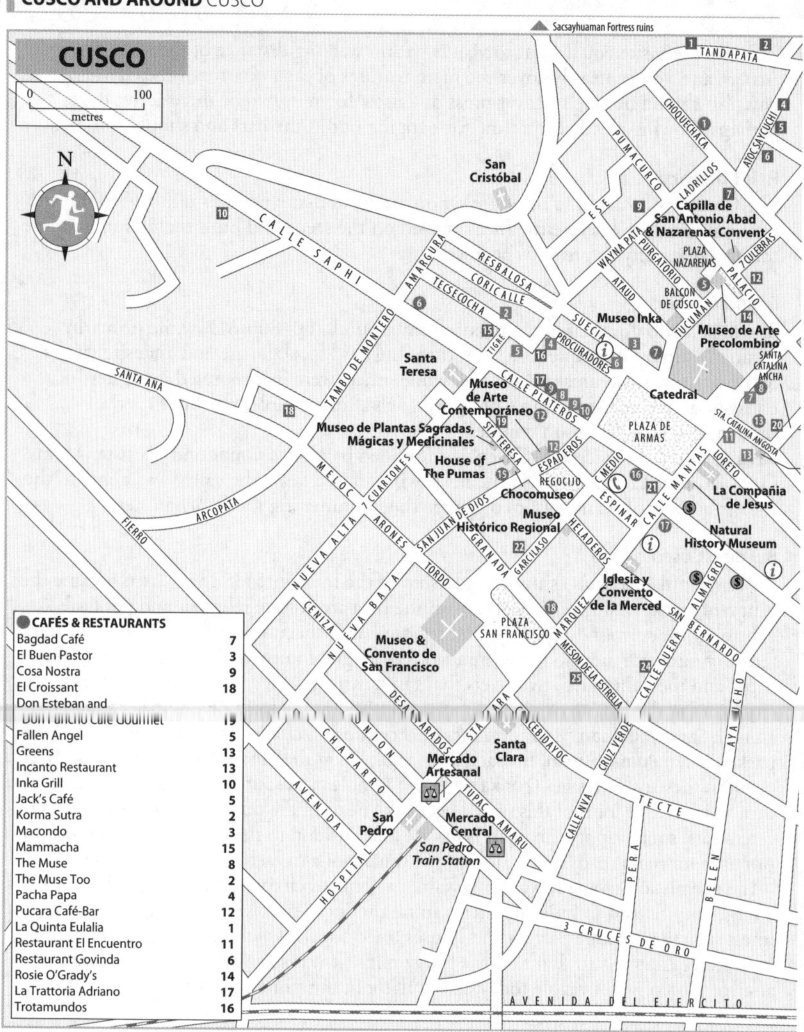

4

puppet ruler, governing from a new palace on the hill just below Sacsayhuaman. After Pizarro's departure, and following twelve months of power struggles, his sons Juan and Gonzalo came out on top and were then free to abuse Manco and his subjects, which eventually provoked the Incas to open resistance. In April 1536 Manco fled to Yucay, in the Sacred Valley, to gather forces for the **Great Rebellion**.

Within days, the two hundred Spanish defenders, with only eighty horses, were surrounded in Cusco by over 100,000 rebel Inca warriors. On May 6, Manco's men laid siege to the city. After a week, a few hundred mounted Spanish soldiers launched a desperate counterattack on the Inca base in Sacsayhuaman and, incredibly, defeated the native stronghold, putting some 1500 warriors to the sword as they took it.

Spanish-controlled Cusco never again came under such serious threat from its indigenous population, but its battles were far from over. By the end of the rains the following year, a rival conquistador, Almagro, had seized Cusco for himself until

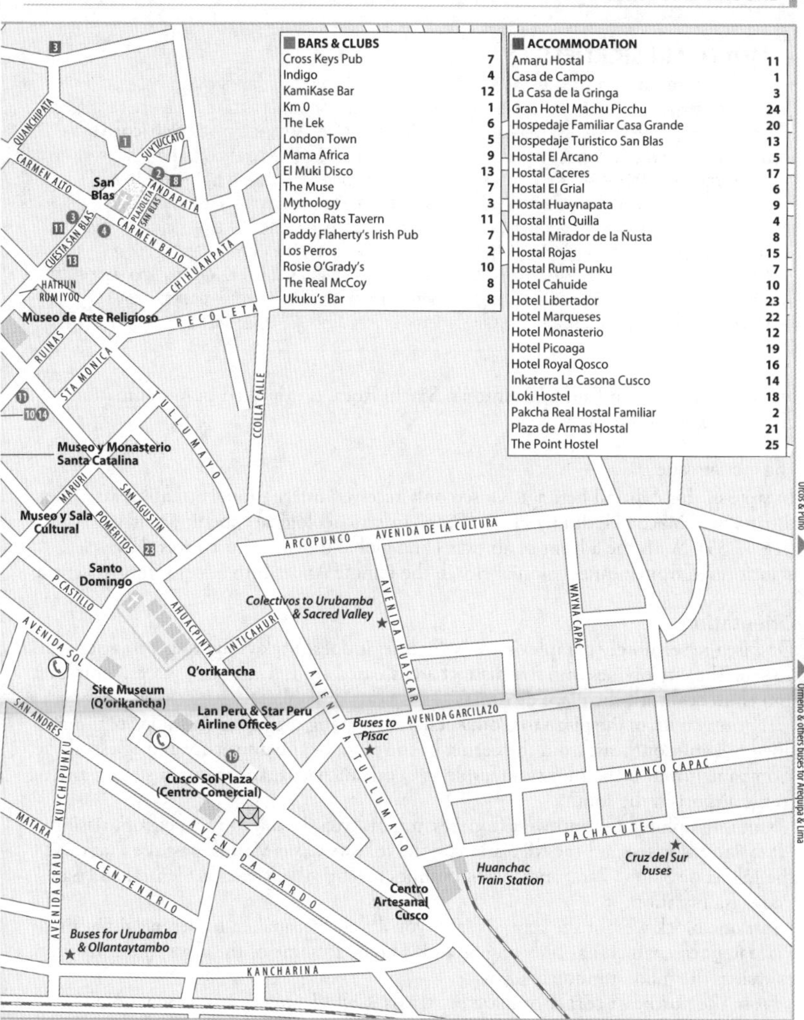

4

Francisco Pizarro defeated the rebel Spanish troops a few months later, and had Almagro garrotted in the main plaza. Around the same time, a diehard group of rebel Incas held out in Vilcabamba until 1572, when the Spanish colonial viceroy, Toledo, captured the leader **Tupac Amaru** and had him beheaded in the Plaza de Armas.

Post-Conquest Cusco

From then on the city was left in relative peace, ravaged only by the great **earthquake** of 1650. After this dramatic tremor, remarkably illustrated on a huge canvas in La Catedral de Cusco, **Bishop Mollinedo** was largely responsible for the reconstruction of the city, and his influence is also closely associated with Cusco's most creative years of art. The **Cusqueña school** (see box, p.213), which emerged from his patronage, flourished for the next two hundred years, and much of its finer work, produced by native Quechua and *mestizo* artists such as Diego Quispe Tito Inca, Juan Espinosa de

MOUNTAIN SICKNESS

Soroche, or **mountain sickness** (see p.45), is a reality for most people arriving in Cusco by plane from sea level and needs to be treated with respect. It's vital to take it easy, not eating or drinking much on arrival, even sleeping a whole day just to assist acclimatization (**coca tea** is a good local remedy). After three days at this height most people have adjusted sufficiently to tackle moderate hikes at similar or lesser altitudes. Anyone considering hiking the major mountains around Cusco will need time to adjust again to their higher base camps.

If you do encounter altitude-related health problems, many hotels and restaurants have **oxygen cylinders** to help; alternatively, for serious cases, try the Clinica Peruano Suiza (English spoken) at Calle Meson de la Estrella 168 (open 24hr; T 237009, W clinicaperuanosuiza .com), which also has a dedicated medical network whose details can be accessed at W o2medicalnetwork.com, and the Clinica Cima at Av Pardo 978 (T 255550).

los Monteros, Fabian Ruiz and Antonio Sinchi Roca, is exhibited in museums and churches around the city.

The modern age

In spite of this cultural heritage, Cusco only received international attention after the discovery of **Machu Picchu** by Hiram Bingham's archeological expedition in 1911 (see p.239). With the advent of air travel and global tourism, Cusco was slowly transformed from a quiet colonial city in the remote Andes into a major tourist centre.

Orientation

Despite the seemingly complex street structure, it doesn't take long to get to grips with Cusco. The city divides into **five distinct areas** based around various squares, temples and churches, with the **Plaza de Armas** at the heart of it all.

The area **south of the plaza to Q'orikancha** starts along the broad **Avenida Sol** running downhill and southeast from the corner of the plaza by the university and Iglesia de la Compañía towards the Inca sun temple at Q'orikancha, Huanchac train station and on to the airport in the south.

Running uphill and southwest from the top of Avenida Sol, the area encompassing **Plaza San Francisco** and the Mercado Central follows Calle Mantas past the Plaza and the Iglesia de Santa Clara, and then continues towards the Mercado Central and San Pedro train station.

Just one block west of the central plaza, you'll find the smaller, leafier, neighbouring **Plaza Regocijo**, which has Inca origins and is home to some of the city's finest mansions as well as the modest municipal palace.

From the northeast corner of Plaza de Armas, Calle Triunfo leads steeply uphill through a classic Inca stone-walled alley before leading through cobbled streets towards the artesan barrio of **San Blas**. One route here from the Plaza de Armas takes you via the tiny but elegant **Plaza Nazarenas**.

Heading northwest along **Calle Plateros**, uphill from Plaza de Armas, you'll pass through some really charming streets that lead toward the fortress of Sacsayhuaman above the city.

Plaza de Armas

Cusco's modern and ancient centre, the **Plaza de Armas** – whose location corresponds roughly to that of the ceremonial *huacapata*, the Incas' ancient central plaza – is the most obvious place to get your bearings. With the unmistakeable ruins of **Sacsayhuaman** towering above, you can always find your way back to the plaza simply by locating the fortress or, at night, the illuminated white figure of Christ that stands beside it on the horizon. The plaza is always busy, its northern and western sides filled with shops and restaurants.

The plaza's exposed northeastern edge is dominated by the squat **Catedral** while the smaller **Iglesia de la Compañía de Jesus**, with its impressive pair of belfries, sits at the southeastern end.

Portal de Panes

Plaza de Armas

Circling the plaza, the **Portal de Panes** is a covered cloister pavement, like those frequently found around Spanish colonial squares, where the buildings tend to have an upper-storey overhang, supported by stone pillars or arches, creating rain-free and sun-shaded walking space virtually all the way around. Usually the *portales* host processions of boys trying their best to sell postcards, and waiters and waitresses attempting to drag passing tourists into their particular dive. Recent restrictions have relegated stalls and shoeshine boys to the hinterland of backstreets emanating from the plaza, particularly the area facing onto the Plaza Regocijo, behind the Plaza de Armas.

The Portal de Panes used to be part of the palace of Pachacuti, the ancient walls of which can still be seen from inside the *Roma Restaurant* close to the corner of the plaza and Calle Plateros.

La Catedral

Plaza de Armas • Daily 10am–6pm • S/25, S/12.50 with ISIC card

La Catedral sits solidly on the foundations of the Inca Viracocha palace, its massive lines looking fortress-like in comparison with the delicate form of the nearby La Compañía. Construction began in 1560; the cathedral was built in the shape of a Latin cross with a three-aisled nave supported by only fourteen pillars. There are two entrances, one via the main, central cathedral doors; the other, more usual, way is through the **Triunfo Chapel**, the first Spanish church to be built in Cusco. Check out its finely carved granite altar and the huge canvas depicting the terrible 1650 earthquake, before moving into the main cathedral to see the intricately carved pulpit, beautiful cedar-wood seats and Neoclassical high altar, made entirely of finely beaten embossed silver, as well as some of the finest paintings of the **Cusqueña school**.

4

In the **Sacristy**, on the right of the nave, there's a large, dark painting of the Crucifixion attributed to Van Dyck. Ten smaller chapels surround the nave, including the **Capilla de la Concepción Inmaculada** (Chapel of the Immaculate Conception), and the **Capilla del Señor de los Temblores** (the Lord of Earthquakes), the latter housing a 26-kilogram crucifix made of solid gold and encrusted with precious stones. To the left of the cathedral is the adjoining eighteenth-century **Iglesia de Jesús María**, a relatively small extension to the main church; here you'll find a sombre collection of murals and a lavish main altar.

Templo de la Compañía de Jesús

Plaza de Armas • Daily 9am–5pm • S/10, S/5 with ISIC card

Looking downhill from the centre of the plaza, the **Templo de la Compañía de Jesus** dominates the Cusco skyline. First built over the foundations of Amara Cancha – originally Huayna Capac's Palace of the Serpents – in the late 1570s, it was resurrected over fifteen years after the earthquake of 1650, which largely destroyed the original

ICONS AND FOLKLORE

The cathedral's appeal lies as much in its **folklore and legends** as in its tangible sights. Local myth claims that an Indian chief is still imprisoned in the right-hand tower, awaiting the day when he can restore the glory of the Inca Empire. The building also houses the huge, miraculous gold and bronze **bell of María Angola**, named after a freed African slave girl and reputed to be one of the largest church bells in the world. And on the cathedral's massive main doors, native craftsmen have left their own pagan adornment – a carved puma's head – representing one of the most important religious motifs and gods found throughout ancient Peru.

version, itself constructed in a Latin cross shape with two belfries. The **interior** is cool and dark, with a grand gold-leaf altarpiece; a fine wooden pulpit displaying a relief of Christ, high vaulting and numerous paintings of the Cusqueña school; and a transept ending in a stylish Baroque cupola. The gilded altarpieces are made of fine cedarwood and the church contains interesting oil paintings of the Peruvian Princess Isabel Ñusta. Its most impressive features, though, are the two majestic **towers** of the main facade, a superb example of Spanish-colonial Baroque design which has often been described in more glowing terms than the cathedral itself. On the right-hand side of the church, the **Lourdes Chapel**, restored in 1894, is used mostly as an exhibition centre for local crafts.

Museo de Historia Natural

Paraninfo Universitario, Plaza de Armas • Mon–Fri 9am–noon & 3–6pm • S/2

Alongside La Compañía, an early Jesuit university building houses the **Museo de Historia Natural**. The entrance is off an inner courtyard, up a small flight of stairs to the left. The exhibits cover Peru's coast, the Andes and the Amazon jungle, with a particularly good selection of stuffed mammals, reptiles and birds. For a small tip, the doorman outside the university building sometimes allows visitors upstairs to the top of the **cupola** to admire the view across the plaza.

Balcon de Cusco

4

Immediately north of the Plaza de Armas, the **Balcon de Cusco**, a small square outside the Museo Inka, affords great views over the plaza and is where dances and firework celebrations tend to happen during festivals. There's also a **panoramic walkway** leading off the square, following the rooftops up to the cobbled backstreets of upper Cusco, directly beneath the ruins of Sacsayhuaman.

Museo Inka

Cuesta del Almirante 103, C Ataúd and C Córdoba del Tucumán • Mon–Fri 8am–6pm, Sat & hols 9am–4pm • S/10

North of the cathedral, slightly uphill beside the Balcon de Cusco, you'll find one of the city's most beautiful colonial mansions, **El Palacio del Almirante** (The Admiral's Palace). This palace now houses the **Museo Inka**, which boasts 10,000 catalogued specimens, and features excellent exhibits of mummies, trepanned skulls, Inca textiles, a set of forty green-turquoise figurines from the Huari settlement of Pikillacta and a range of Inca wooden *quero* vases (slightly tapering drinking vessels). There are also displays of ceramics, early silver metalwork and gold figurines, but it's the spacious, organized layout and the imaginative, well-interpreted presentation that make this one of the best museums in Cusco for understanding the development of civilization in the Andes. Frequent temporary exhibitions are held here, too, including live alpaca spinning and weaving by local women.

Constructed on Inca foundations – this time the Waypar stronghold, where the Spanish were besieged by Manco's forces in 1536 – the **building** itself is noteworthy for its simple but well-executed Plateresque facade, surmounted by two imposing Spanish coats of arms and a mullioned external balcony.

Monasterio de Santa Catalina de Sena

Leading southeast from the Plaza de Armas, Callejón Loreto separates La Compañía church from the tall, stone walls of the ancient Acclahuasi, or **Temple of the Sun Virgins**, where the Sun Virgins used to make *chicha* beer for the Lord Inca. Today, the Acclahuasi building is occupied by the **Convent of Santa Catalina**, built in 1610, with its small but grand side entrance half a short block down Calle Santa Catalina Angosta; just under thirty sisters still live and worship here in isolation.

Museo de Arte y Monasterio de Santa Catalina

C Santa Catalina Angosta • Mon–Sat 8.30am–5.30pm, Sun & hols 2–5pm • S/8, S/4 with student card

Inside the convent, the **Museo de Arte y Monasterio de Santa Catalina** features a splendid collection of paintings from the **Cusqueña school** (see box below), as well as an impressive Renaissance altarpiece and several gigantic seventeenth-century tapestries depicting the union of Indian and Spanish cultures. The blending of cultures is a theme that runs throughout much of the museum's fascinating artwork and is particularly evident in the Cusqueña paintings. Another common feature of much of the Cusqueña art here is the disproportionate, downward-looking, blood-covered head, body and limbs of the seventeenth-century depictions of Christ, which represent the suffering and low social position of the Andean Indians and originate from early colonial days when Indians were not permitted to look Spaniards in the eyes.

Another highlight of the museum, on the first floor at the top of the stairs, is a large fold-up box containing miniature three-dimensional religious and mythological images depicting everything from the Garden of Eden to an image of God with a red flowing cape and dark beard, and a white dove and angels playing drums, Andean flutes and pianos.

Museo y Sala Cultural

C Maruri and C Q'aphchik'ijllu • Mon–Fri 9am–1pm & 4–6pm • Free

On the way from Santa Catalina towards Q'orikancha is the **Museo y Sala Cultural** at the Banco Wiese, where displays include historical documents and archeological and architectural exhibits; displays vary throughout the year. The focus is often on the

THE CUSQUEÑA SCHOOL

Colonial Cusco evolved into an exceptional centre for architecture and art. The era's paintings in particular are curious for the way they adorn human and angelic figures in elaborate lacy garments and blend traditional and ancient with colonial and Spanish elements. They are frequently brooding and quite bloody, and by the mid-seventeenth-century had evolved into a recognizable school of painting.

The **Cusqueña art movement** dedicated itself to beautifying church and convent walls with fantastic and highly moralistic painting, mainly using oils. The Cusqueña school is best known for portraits or religious scenes with dark backgrounds, serious (even tortured-looking) subjects and a profusion of gold-leaf decoration. Influences came from European émigrés – mainly Spainish and Italian – notably Juan de Illescas, Bernardo Bitti and Mateo Perez de Alessio. At the close of the seventeenth century, the school came under the direction of **Bishop Manuel Mollinedo**. Bringing a number of original paintings (including some by El Greco) with him from his parish in Spain, the Bishop was responsible for commissioning **Basilio Santa Cruz**'s fine 1698 reproduction of the *Virgen de la Almudena*, which still hangs behind the choir in Cusco's Catedral. He also commissioned the extraordinarily carved cedarwood pulpit in the church at San Blas.

The top Cusqueña artists were **Bernardo Bitti** (1548–1610), an Italian who is often considered the "father of Cusqueña art" and who introduced the Mannerist style to Peru, and **Diego Quispe Tito Inca** (1611–81), a *mestizo* painter who was influenced by the Spanish Flamenco school and whose paintings were vital tools of communication for priests attempting to convert Indians to Catholicism. Bitti's work is on display in the Museo Historico Regional, while some of Quispe's works can be seen in rooms off the second courtyard in the Religious Art Museum at the Archbishop's Palace in Cusco. The equally renowned **Mauricio García** (painting until the mid-eighteenth century) helped spur the form into a fuller *mestizo* synthesis, mixing Spanish and Indian artistic forms. Many of the eighteenth- and nineteenth-century Cusqueña-*mestizo* works display bold compositions and colours.

By the eighteenth century the style had been disseminated as far afield as Quito in Ecuador, Santiago in Chile and even into Argentina, making it a truly South American art form and one of the most distinctive indigenous arts in the Americas.

restoration work of the Banco Wiese's own premises, an attractive mansion that was once part of the Tupac Inca Yupangui's Pucamarca palace.

The Q'orikancha complex

C Av Sol and C Santo Domingo • Mon–Sat 8.30am–5pm, Sun 2–5pm • S/10, S/5 with student card

The main Inca temple for worship of major deities and a supreme example of Inca stonework underlying colonial buildings can be found just a short walk from the Plaza de Armas, through the Inca walls of Callejón Loreto, then along the busy Pampa del Castillo. You can't miss the **Q'orikancha complex**, with the Convento de Santo Domingo rising imposingly from its impressive walls, which the conquistadores laid lower to make way for their uninspiring seventeenth-century Baroque church – a poor contrast to the still-imposing Inca masonry evident in the foundations and chambers of the Sun Temple.

Brief history

Prior to the Incas, the Wari culture had already dedicated the site with its own sun temple, known as Inticancha (*inti* meaning "sun" and *cancha* meaning "enclosure"). Before the conquistadors set their gold-hungry eyes on it, Q'orikancha must have been even more breathtaking, consisting as it did of four small sanctuaries and a larger temple set around a central courtyard. This whole complex was encircled on the inside walls by a cornice of gold, hence the temple's name (Q'orikancha means "golden enclosure").

4

Q'orikancha's position in the Cusco Valley was carefully planned. Dozens of *ceques* (power lines, in many ways similar to ley lines, though in Cusco they appear to have been related to imperial genealogy) radiate from the temple towards more than 350 sacred *huacas*, special stones, springs, tombs and ancient quarries. In addition, during every summer solstice, the sun's rays shine directly into a niche – the **tabernacle** – in which only the Inca emperor (often referred to as *the* Inca) was permitted to sit. Mummies of dead Inca rulers were seated in niches at eye level along the walls of the actual temple, the principal idols from every conquered province were held "hostage" here, and every emperor married his wives in the temple before assuming the throne. The niches no longer exist, though there are some in the walls of the nearby Temple of the Moon, where mummies of the emperor's concubines were kept in a foetal position.

Punchau golden sun disc

Still visible today, there's a large, slightly trapezoidal niche on the inside of the curved section of the retaining wall, close to the chamber identified as the Temple of the Sun, where there once stood a huge, gold disc in the shape of the sun, **Punchau**, which was worshipped by the Incas. Punchau had two companions in the temple: a golden image of creator god **Viracocha**, on the right; and another, representing **Illapa**, god of thunder, to the left. Below the temple was an artificial garden in which everything was made of gold or silver and encrusted with precious jewels, from depictions of llamas and shepherds to the tiniest details of clumps of earth and weeds, including snails and butterflies. Not surprisingly, none of this survived the arrival of the Spanish.

Chapel of Santo Domingo

Q'orikancha complex • Mon–Sat 8.30am–6.30pm, Sun 2–5pm

The **Chapel of Santo Domingo** is accessed via the complex reception desk, or by walking past the Temple of the Moon and the Catholic Sacristy to a tiny section of the inner edge of the vast curved wall, which, from the outside, seems to support the chapel. Returning from here via the sacristy you'll see a display of the Catholic priest's vestments, some boasting gold thread and jewels.

Q'orikancha site museum

Av Sol • Daily 9am–5pm • Entry by Cusco Tourist Ticket (see box, p.222) • It's a two-minute walk downhill from the complex reception to the underground museum entrance on block 3 of Avenida Sol

Though one of Cusco's smaller and less interesting museums, the **Q'oricancha site museum**, or Museo Arqueológico de Q'orikancha, does contain a number of interesting pieces. The first section is pre-Inca, mainly stone and ceramic exhibits; the second is Inca, with wooden, ceramic and some metallurgic crafts; in the third, archeological excavations are illustrated and interpreted; and the fourth houses a mummy and some bi-chrome ceramics of the Killki era (around 800 AD), which reflect the art of the pre-Inca Wari culture.

From the museum you can access the **garden**, which, though little more than a green, open, grassy space just outside the main walls of Q'orikancha, has a particularly beautiful pre-Inca spring and bath that dates to the Wari period, providing evidence of the importance of Q'orikancha before the Incas arrived on the Andean scene.

Iglesia y Convento de la Merced

C Mantas • Mon–Sat 8am–noon & 2–5pm • S/8

Ten minutes' walk southwest of the Plaza de Armas is the **Iglesia y Convento de la Merced**, which sits peacefully amid the bustle of one of Cusco's more interesting quarters. First raised with Pizarro's financial assistance on top of the Inca site Limipata in 1536, it was rebuilt some 25 years after the 1650 earthquake in a rich combination of Baroque and Renaissance styles by such native artesans as Alonso Casay and Francisco Monya.

The facade is exceptionally ornate and the roof is endowed with an unusual Baroque spire, while **inside** there's a beautiful star-studded ceiling and a huge silver cross, which is adored and kissed by a shuffling crowd. The monastery's highlight, however, is a breathtaking 1720s **monstrance** standing a metre high and crafted by Spanish jeweller Juan de Olmos, who used over 600 pearls, more than 1500 diamonds and upwards of 22kg of solid gold. The monastery also possesses a fine collection of **Cusqueña paintings**, particularly in the cloisters and vestry, and an exceptionally gorgeous white-stone cloister.

Museo y Convento de San Francisco

Plaza San Francisco • Mon–Sat 9am–5.30pm • S/3 • ⓣ 221361

A block south of the Iglesia y Convento de la Merced is the **Plaza San Francisco**, frequently filled with food stalls that couldn't be squeezed into the central market or along Calle Santa Clara. The square's southwestern side is dominated by the simply adorned **Museo y Convento de San Francisco**, built between 1645 and 1652. Inside, two large cloisters boast some of the better colonial paintings by local masters such as Diego Quispe Tito, Marcos Zapata and Juan Espinosa de los Monteros, the latter being celebrated for his massive works on canvas, one or two of which are on display here.

Iglesia de Santa Clara

C Santa Clara • Daily 6am–6pm • Free

Passing under a crumbling archway to the left of the Museo y Convento de San Francisco, follow the flow of people along Calle Santa Clara towards the central market and you'll come across the small but beautiful **Iglesia de Santa Clara**. Originally built around a single nave in 1558 by *mestizo* and indigenous craftsmen under the guidance of the architect Brother Manuel Pablo, and partly restored in 2005, it contains a gold-laminated altar, small mirrors covering most of the interior, and a few canvases. The **outside walls**, however, show more interesting details: finely cut Inca blocks support the upper, cruder stonework, and four andesite columns, much cracked over the centuries, complete the doorway. The belfry is so time-worn that weeds and wildflowers have taken permanent root.

Iglesia de San Pedro

C Santa Clara and C Chaparro • Mon–Sat 10am–noon & 2–5pm • Free

In the busy market area next to San Pedro train station stands the sixteenth-century colonial **Iglesia de San Pedro**, whose steps are normally crowded with Quechua market traders. The interior is decorated with paintings, sculptures, gold leaf and wooden carvings, and an elaborate, carved pulpit. Relatively austere, with only a single nave, the church's main claim to fame is that somewhere among the stones of its twin towers are ancient blocks dragged here from the small Inca fort of Picchu.

Mercado Central

C Santa Clara and C Calle Chaparro • Daily 6am–6pm

Stalls selling every imaginable practical item line the streets below the market building; inside the market you can find plentiful and exotic foodstuffs, as well as some herbalist kiosks that stock everything from lucky charms to jungle medicines. The food stalls at the bottom end of the indoor market offer some of the best and cheapest **street meals** in Peru, while the juice stalls at the top end serve up a delicious range of tropical smoothies.

Plaza Regocijo

A block southwest of the Plaza de Armas, **Plaza Regocijo**, today a pleasant garden square sheltering a statue of Colonel Francisco Bolognesi, a famous Peruvian war martyr, was originally the Inca *cusipata*, an area cleared for dancing and festivities beside the Incas' ancient central plaza. Regocijo is dominated on its northwestern side by an attractively arched municipal building housing the Museo de Arte Contemporáneo, with a traditional Inca rainbow flag flying from its roof. Opposite this is the venerable old *Hotel Cusco*, under refurbishment but formerly the grand, state-run *Hotel de Turistas*, while on the southwest corner of the plaza lies an impressive mansion where more Inca stones mingle with colonial construction, home to the Museo Histórico Regional y Casa Garcilaso.

Museo Histórico Regional y Casa Garcilaso

Plaza Regocijo and C Calle Heladeros • Daily 8am–6pm • Entry by Cusco Tourist Ticket (see box, p.222) • ⓣ 223245

Once the residence of **Garcilaso de la Vega**, a prolific half-Inca (his mother may have been an Inca princess), half-Spanish poet and author, the mansion now known as the **Museo Histórico Regional y Casa Garcilaso** is home to significant regional archeological finds and much of Cusco's historic art.

Fascinating **pre-Inca ceramics** from all over Peru are displayed here, as well as a **Nasca mummy** in a foetal position with typically long (1.5m) hair, embalming herbs and unctures, black ceramics with incised designs from the early Cusco culture (1000–200 BC) and a number of **Inca artefacts** such as *bolas*, maces, architects' plumb-lines and square water-dishes used for finding horizontal levels on buildings. The museum also displays gold bracelets discovered at Machu Picchu in 1995, some gold and silver llama statuettes found in 1996 in the Plaza de Armas when reconstructing the central fountain, and golden pumas and figurines from Sacsayhuaman. From the **colonial era** there are some weavings, wooden *quero* drinking vessels and dancing masks.

The main exhibition rooms upstairs house mainly period furniture and a multitude of **Cusqueña paintings**, which cross the range from the rather dull (religious adorations) to the more spectacular (like the famous eighteenth-century *Jacob's Ladder*). As you progress through the works you'll notice the rapid intrusion of cannons, gunpowder and proliferation of violence appearing throughout the eighteenth century, something which was reflected in Cusco art as a microcosm of what happened across the colonial world – emanating from Europe as part of the general march of technological "progress".

Museo de Arte Contemporáneo

Plaza Regocijo • Mon–Sat 9.30am–5.30pm • Entry by Cusco Tourist Ticket (see box, p.222) • T 233210

The **Museo de Arte Contemporáneo**, in the Municipality building on Plaza Regocijo, is a welcome and relatively new feature in Cusco, and an outlet for the many talented local artists. **Sala 1** displays images of Cusco, mainly paintings but occasional photos of subjects like Inca dancers as well as abstract features and some sculpture. **Sala 2** is dedicated to non-Cusco-inspired contemporary art, some of it very abstract but with exhibits changing quite regularly; the *sala* leads off into a large courtyard with a typically attractive colonial fountain; here you'll find glass cases with dolls in traditional costumes, some regional variations of dance masks (from Paucartambo dance groups, for example) and models of buildings in different Cusco styles. The upstairs **Sala 3** houses more images of Cusco, both ancient and modern.

Museo de Plantas Sagradas, Mágicas y Medicinales

C Santa Teresa 351 • Mon, Wed, Fri & Sat 11am–9pm, Tues & Thurs 10am–9pm, Sun noon–6pm • S/15, S/7.50 with student card • T 222214, W museoplantascusco.org

One of the newest and most thought provoking of Cusco's museums, the **Museo de Plantas Sagradas, Mágicas y Medicinales** specializes in sacred, magical and medicinal plants used in the Andean and Amazon region of the Americas. In many ways, these special plants are fundamental to the Andean-Amazon view of the world, and an understanding of their uses complements visits to archeological sites.

Since the Amazon is the richest source anywhere of **medicinal and sacred plants**, the museum – the only one of its kind in the world – illustrates a surprising range of subjects, many of which have changed the world over the last few centuries. Nine rooms, dedicated to different themes and some with vivid accompanying audio visuals, cover everything from the hallucinogenic teacher plants like the rainforest Ayahuasca vine and the coastal desert cactus San Pedro to the superfood quinoa and the all-important potato. There's also a shop and a good little café, the latter based in the rear patio.

House of the Pumas

C Santa Teresa 385

Along the street from the Museo de Plantas Sagradas, Mágicas y Medicinales, the **House of the Pumas** isn't as grand as it sounds, but is worth a moment or two to admire the six carved stone pumas above its entrance, created during the Spanish rebuilding of Cusco.

Chocomuseo

C Garcilaso 210, 2nd floor • Daily 10.30am–6.30pm • Free; workshops S/70 for 2hr; tours from $230 per person • T 244765, W peru.chocomuseo.com

A few steps from Plaza Regocijo, the **Chocomuseo** has a range of interpretative displays on the history of cacao, starting with the Maya's love of this plant in Central America. The museum also organizes **workshops** on chocolate making and tours to cacao plantations in the Cusco region, and provides the opportunity to see artisanal chocolate production first-hand in the **factory**, from cacao bean to chocolate bar.

Iglesia de Santa Teresa

C Siete Cuartones • Daily 6am–6pm • Free

From the top of Regocijo, Calle Santa Teresa leads to Calle Siete Cuartones and the **Iglesia de Santa Teresa**, an attractive but neglected church with stone walls, the upper half of which have paintings featuring St Teresa. Inside, the small brick ceiling has a beautifully crafted dome and there's a gold-leaf altar inset with paintings. The small

chapel next door is worth a look for its intricately painted walls (featuring yet more images of St Teresa), usually beautifully candlelit.

Museo de Arte Precolombino (MAP)

Plaza las Nazarenas • Daily 9am–10pm • S/15, S/7.50 with student card • ⓣ 233210

Calle Córdoba del Tucuman runs northeast from Plaza de Armas along the northern edge of the cathedral, past the Museo Inka (see p.212) and up to the small, quiet **Plaza Nazarenas**. The unmistakeable **Casa Cabrera**, an eighteenth-century mansion built on top of a ninth-century temple pyramid, has been transformed into the **Museo de Arte Precolombino** at the top end of this small square. The recently remodelled museum boasts many masterpieces dating from 1250 BC to 1532 AD, including gold and other precious metals and jewellery, displayed in chronological order. Some of the new exhibits, the Larco Collection, have come from the Larco Herrera Museum in Lima (see p.76). There's an interesting exhibit exploring the history of urban architecture in this Inca imperial capital city. Frequent temporary exhibitions are also held here.

Capilla de San Antonio Abad and Nazarenas Convent

Plaza Nazarenas

On the northeastern side of Plaza Nazarenas, the ancient, subtly ornate **Capilla de San Antonio Abad** was connected to a religious school before becoming part of the university in the seventeenth century. It's not open to the public, but you can usually look around the courtyard of the **Nazarenas Convent**, virtually next door and now home to the plush *Hotel Monasterio* (see p.226). Nuns lived here until the 1950 earthquake damaged the building so badly that they had to leave; the central courtyard has since been sensitively rebuilt and meals are served in its attractive garden. Beside the convent, the Inca passage of Siete Culebras (Seven Snakes) leads onto Choquechaca.

Barrio San Blas

Originally known as T'oqokachi ("salty hole"), the **San Blas** barrio was the first parish to be established by the Spanish in Cusco and one of twelve administrative sectors in the Inca capital. After the Conquest it became the residence for many defeated Inca leaders. It rapidly grew into one of the more attractive districts in the city, reflecting strong *mestizo* and colonial influences in its architecture and high-quality **artesanía** – even today it's known as the *barrio de los artesanos* (artesans' quarter). Hit hard by the 1950 earthquake, it has been substantially restored, and in 1993 was given a major face-lift that returned it to its former glory. The process of rebuilding continues, with many old houses being converted to hostels, shops and restaurants.

Templo de San Blas

Cuesta de San Blas • Daily 8am–6pm • S/15, S/7.50 with student card

From Choquechaca, turn left into Cuesta de San Blas and after one and a half blocks you'll come to the tiny chapel **Templo de San Blas**. The highlight here is an incredibly intricate pulpit, carved from a block of cedarwood in a complicated Churrigueresque style; its detail includes a cherub, a sun disc, faces and bunches of grapes, believed to have been carved by native craftsman Tomas Tuyro Tupa in the seventeenth century.

Calle Suytuccato

Outside the Templo de San Blas, along **Calle Suytuccato** (the continuation of Cuesta San Blas), there are a few art workshops and galleries, the most notable of which is **Galería Olave**, at no. 651 (Mon–Sat 10.30am–7pm). The **Museo de Cerámica** (daily 10am–6pm), Carmen Alto 133, is worth checking out for its pottery.

Plazoleta San Blas

At the barrio's centre, on the southeast side of the Iglesia San Blas, lies the **Plazoleta San Blas**, with 49 gargoyles set on a fountain that's laid out in the form of a *chakana*, or Inca cross, with four corners and a hole at its centre. On the *plazoleta*, the **Museo Taller Hilario Mendivil** (Mon–Sat 10am–6pm) contains a number of Cusqueña paintings, as well as some interesting murals and religious icons.

FIESTAS IN THE CUSCO REGION

As the imperial capital during Inca times, Cusco was the most important place of pilgrimage in South America, a status it retains today. During Easter, June and Christmas, the city centre becomes the focus for relentless **fiestas and carnivals** celebrated with extravagant processions blending pagan pre-Columbian and Catholic colonial cultures.

Around Jan 20 Adoración de los Reyes (Adoration of the Kings). Ornate and elaborate processions leave from San Blas church and parade through Cusco.

Last week of Jan Pera Chapch'y (Festival of the Pear). A harvest festival in San Sebastián, 4km southeast of Cusco, with lively street stalls and processions.

First week of March Festival de Durasno (Festival of the Peach). Food stalls and folk dancing in Yanahuara and Urubamba.

Easter Week Semana Santa. On Easter Monday there's a particularly splendid procession through Cusco, with a rich and evocative mix of Indian and Catholic iconography. The following Thursday a second procession celebrates the city's patron saint, El Señor de los Temblores (Lord of Earthquakes), and on Easter Friday, street stalls sell many different traditional dishes.

May 2–3 Cruz Velacuy, or Fiesta de las Cruces (Festival of the Cross). All church and sanctuary crosses in Cusco and the provinces are veiled for a day, followed by traditional festivities with dancing and feasting in most communities. Particularly splendid in Ollantaytambo.

Weekend before Corpus Christi Qoyllur Rit'i (Snow Star, or Ice Festival). Held on the full-moon weekend prior to Corpus Christi (see below) in an isolated valley above the road from Cusco via Urcos and Ocongate to the Amazon town of Puerto Maldonado. The festival site lies at the foot of a glacier, considered an *apu*, or mountain god. Close by, and visible during the climb to the festival, is the sacred snowcapped peak – Ausangate. This is one of the most exciting festivals in the Americas, with live music that continues for days, several processions, and bands and dancers from various communities who make an annual pilgrimage to recharge spiritually at a time when the mountain is said to be blossoming in a metaphysical rather than botanical sense. As it involves camping at around 4600m at the foot of a glacier, it's only for the adventurous; some tour operators organize trips, but it's primarily a Quechua festival, with villagers arriving in their thousands in the weeks running up to it.

Corpus Christi (always nine weeks after Easter). Imposed by the Spanish to replace the Inca tradition of parading ancestral mummies, saints' effigies are carried through the streets of Cusco, even as the local *mayordomos* (ritual community leaders) throw parties and feasts combining elements of religiosity with outright hedonism. The effigies are then left inside the cathedral for eight days, after which they are taken back to their respective churches, accompanied by musicians, dancers and exploding firecrackers.

Second week of June Cusqueña International Beer and Music Festival. Lively, with big Latin pop and jazz names, at its best from Thursday to Sunday.

June 16–22 Traditional folk festivals in Raqchi and Sicuani.

June 20–30 Fiesta de Huancaro. An agricultural show packed with locals and good fun, based in the Huancaro sector of Cusco (S/5 taxi ride from Plaza de Armas, or go down Avenida Sol and turn right at the roundabout before the airport).

Last week of June Cusco Carnival. Daily processions and folk dancers, plus lively music on the streets throughout the day and night, peaking with Inti Raymi (see below).

June 24 Inti Raymi. Popular, commercial fiesta re-enacting the Inca Festival of the Sun in the grounds of Sacsayhuaman.

July 15–17 Virgen del Carmen. Dance and music festival celebrated all over the highlands, but at its best in Paucartambo.

July 28 Peruvian Independence Day. Festivities nationwide, not least in Cusco.

Sept 14–18 Señor de Huanca. Music, dancing, pilgrimages and processions take place all over the region but are especially lively in Calca, with a fair in the Sacred Valley.

First week of Dec Yawar Fiesta. A vibrant, uncommercial *corrida de toros* (bull fight) at the end of the week in Paruro, Cotabambas and Chumbivilcas. A condor, captured by hand, is tied to the back of a bull that battles to the death.

4

Hathun Rumiyoq

Go down the Cuesta de San Blas and continue over the intersection with Choquechaca, then head straight on until you come to the narrow alley

One of the main streets in ancient Cusco, **Hathun Rumiyoq** provides classic examples of superb Inca **stonework**: the large cut boulders on the museum side, about halfway along, boast one that has twelve angles in its jointing with the stones around it. Not just earthquake-resistant, it is both a highly photographed ruin and a work of art in its own right.

Museo de Arte Religioso del Arzobispado

C Triunfo and Palacio • Daily 8am–6pm • S/15, S/7.50 with student card • ⓣ 246799

At the end of Hathun Rumiyoq, and just one block from the Plaza de Armas, along Calle Triunfo, you'll find the broad doors of the **Museo de Arte Religioso del Arzobispado**, housed in a superb Arabesque-style mansion built on the impressive foundations of Hathun Rumiyoq palace. Once home to Brother Vicente de Valarde and the Marquises of Rocafuert, and later the archbishop's residence, the museum now contains a significant collection of **paintings**, mostly from the Cusqueña school. There are stunning mosaics in some of the period rooms, and other significant features include the elaborate gateway and the gold-leaf craftsmanship on the chapel's altar.

ARRIVAL AND DEPARTURE CUSCO

Arriving in Cusco is always an exhilarating experience. If coming straight from sea level, there's the physical effect of the **altitude** (see box, p.210), but, more than that, there's a sense of historic imperial glory reflected in people and architecture alike from the moment you step into the city. By far the majority of visitors arrive by plane from Lima or by bus from Lima, Arequipa or Puno. The **airport and main bus station** (Terminal Terrestre) are both located in the very southwest of the city, downhill from the Plaza de Armas and Cusco's bustling heart. Buses, colectivos and taxis are readily available to connect with hotels.

BY PLANE

Aeropuerto Internacional Velasco Astete ⓣ 222611. The airport is 4km southwest of the city centre. It has ATMs and tourist information as well as a reasonable café in the departures area. It's easy enough to find a taxi from outside the baggage collection hall (from S/15 to the city centre) or a colectivo combi from outside the airport car park (frequent departures S/1.5), which goes to Plaza San Francisco via Avenida Sol and Plaza de Armas. Note that the airport is full of tour touts, who should be avoided.

Destinations Arequipa (2 or more daily; 1hr 30min); Juliaca (2 daily; 50min); La Paz (2 weekly; 1hr 30min); Lima (8–12 daily; 1hr); Puerto Maldonado (at least 2 daily; 40min).

Airline offices Lan Peru, Av Sol 627b (ⓣ 255552 in Cusco, or via Lima ⓣ 01 213 8200, ⓦ lan.com), for Lima, Puerto Maldonado and Arequipa; TACA Peru, Av Sol 602 (ⓣ 246858, ⓦ taca.com), for Lima, Puerto Maldonado and Arequipa; Star Peru, Av Sol 627, office 101 (ⓣ 262768 or 253791, via Lima 24hr call centre ⓣ 01 705 9000, ⓦ starperu.com), for Lima and Puerto Maldonado only; Aerosur, Av Sol 574 (ⓣ 254691 and ⓣ 90110 555, ⓦ aerosur.com), for international flights to La Paz, Bolivia.

BY TRAIN

Huanchac station If you're coming in by train from Puno, you'll arrive at the Huanchac train station in the southeast of the city; you can hail a taxi on the street outside (around S/3 to the centre), or turn left out of the station and walk about a hundred metres to Avenida Sol, from where you can walk the eight or nine blocks up a gentle hill to the Plaza de Armas, essentially the city centre.

Trains to Machu Picchu All Machu Picchu trains (see box, p.256) start and finish outside of Cusco city, either from Poroy station (15min by taxi from Cusco), Ollantaytambo (2–3hr by car or colectivo from Cusco) or Urubamba (1hr 30min–2hr from Cusco). There are three competing rail companies that offer the Machu Picchu service: Perurail, Inca Rail and Machu Picchu Train. The latter two only arrive and depart from Ollantaytambo in the Sacred Valley (see p.250).

Train tickets Perurail has a ticket office on the Plaza de Armas at Portal de Carnes 244 (Mon–Fri 10am–10pm, Sat, Sun & hols 2–11pm) and also at Av Pachacutec, Wanchaq (Mon–Fri 7am–5pm, Sat, Sun & hols 7am–noon; ⓣ 238722 or 221992 for reservations, ⓦ perurail.com), selling Puno and Machu Picchu tickets. To travel to either Puno or Machu Picchu with Perurail (see box, p.256) it's best to buy well in advance.

CUSCO BUS COMPANIES AND DESTINATIONS

Abancay BREDDE (T 243278) and Turismo Ampay (T 227541).
Andahuaylas Molina Union (T 236144).
Arequipa and Tacna El Chasqui (T 249961), Pony Express and Turismo Universal (T 243540), and Cruz del Sur (T 243261, W cruzdelsur.com.pe).
Ayacucho Los Chankas (T 242249).
Buenos Aires, Argentina Cruz del Sur (T 243261, W cruzdelsur.com.pe).
Copacabana and La Paz, Bolivia Ormeño (T 227501, W grupo-ormeno.com.pe).
Curahuasi, Sahuite and Lima Tambo Curahuasi (T 227074).
Juliaca, Puno and Desaguadero CIVA (T 249961, W civa.com.pe), Cruz del Sur, Libertad (T 432955) and Urkupiña (T 229962).
Lima CIAL (T 633608, W expresocial.com), CIVA (T 249961, W civa.com.pe), Flores (T 236099) and Ormeño (T 227501).
Puerto Maldonado Movil (T 633608, W moviltours.com.pe).
Quillabamba Selva Tour (T 247975); also for Quillabamba, the Kamisea bus (T 246071) departs from the corner of Santiago and Juan Antonio Manya.
Santiago, Chile Cruz del Sur (T 243261, W cruzdelsur.com.pe).

Destinations: Machu Picchu Pueblo (6–12 daily; 3–5hr); Puno (1 daily: April–Oct Mon, Wed, Fri & Sat; Nov–March Mon, Wed & Sat; 10hr).

BY BUS

Inter-regional and international buses With the exception of Cruz del Sur (see below), all inter-regional and international buses arrive at and depart from the rather scruffy Terminal Terrestre at Av Vallegos Santoni, block 2 (T 224471), southeast of the centre, close to the Pachacutec monument and roundabout (*ovalo*) and roughly halfway between the Plaza de Armas and the airport. Taxis from here to the city centre cost S/5, or you can walk to the Pachacutec *ovalo* and catch a colectivo uphill to either the Plaza San Francisco or the Plaza de Armas – otherwise, it's about a 30min walk. At the Terminal Terrestre there is an embarcation tax of S/1, which you pay before boarding.

Cruz del Sur buses operate both from the Terminal Terrestre and from their own independent depot at Av Pachacutec 510 (T 720444), in Cusco's Huancaro suburb. It's not far from Huanchac station, but it's best to take a taxi (S/3–5).

Sacred Valley buses For Urubamba the best company is Sumay Wayna whose depot can be found on the first block of Av Huascar, with minibuses leaving every 15min or so; for Pisac, independent minibus colectivos leave from Av Tullumayo 207 and also from a depot at the corner of Puputi and Abel Landeo, one block below Recoleta and two blocks up from Avenida La Cultura at the junction with Ejercicios, just beyond the Estadio Universitario; for Chinchero and Ollantaytambo you can take the Urubamba bus or colectivos from a depot near Puente Grau.

Sicuani, Urcos and Paucartambo buses Buses from these areas stop around blocks 15 and 16 of Av de la Cultura, from where it's a bit of a hike to the centre, so you'll almost certainly want to take a taxi (S/5), bus or combi colectivo (S/1.50).

Destinations Abancay (6 daily; 6hr); Arequipa (10 daily; 8hr); Ayacucho (3 daily; 18hr); Buenos Aires, Argentina (3–4 weekly; 3 days); Chinchero (many daily; 40min); Curahuasi (several daily; 2hr); Juliaca (3 daily; 7hr); La Paz, Bolivia (5 weekly; 20hr); Lima via Nasca (2 daily; 20hr), via Pisco and Ayacucho (2 weekly; 30–45hr); Ollantaytambo (many daily; 2hr); Paucartambo (1 daily; 6hr); Pisac (many daily; 40min); Puerto Maldonado (2 daily; 15hr); Puno (3 daily; 8hr); Quillabamba (several daily; 6hr); Santiago, Chile (2 weekly; 50hr); Sicuani (several daily; 3–4hr); Tacna (2 daily; 12hr); Urcos (several daily; 1hr); Urubamba (many daily;1hr 20min).

4

GETTING AROUND

On foot Cusco's centre is small enough to walk around. Although it is well spread out down the valley and might take more than an hour to get from one end to the other, most of the interesting sights are within a 10- to 15-minute walk of the Plaza de Armas.

By taxi Taxis can be waved down on any street, particularly on the Plaza de Armas, Avenida Sol and around the market end of Plaza San Francisco; rides within Cusco centre cost S/3, slightly more for outlying suburbs and around S/20–30 to Sacsayhuaman, Quenko and Tambo Machay (some *taxistas* may prefer to do a round trip, charging double but waiting there for you; in this case give them half in advance and the remainder at the end of the journey). A taxi to Pisac can be found from around S/45–60. To call a taxi, try Alo Cusco (T 222222); Llama taxi (T 222000); or Central 239 (T 239969).

CUSCO TOURIST TICKET

The **Cusco Tourist Ticket**, or **Boleto Turístico General – Cusco** (S/130 for ten days, students S/70), is a vital purchase for most visitors. In some ways it's a bit of a rip-off, but it's the only way to get into many of the city's and region's main attractions, covering some sixteen destinations including the **archeological sites** of the Sacred Valley (Pisca and Ollantaytambo) as well as Sacsayhuaman, Qenko, Tambo Machay, Puca Pucara, Chinchero, Moray and Tipón. The ticket also affords free entry to **museums** including the Museo de Arte Popular, Museo de Sitio Q'orikancha, the municipal Museo de Arte Contemporáneo, the Museo Histórico Regional, Pikillacta and Tipón. It does not, however, give entry to the cathedral, or Q'orikancha main temple site. It comes with useful **maps** and other information, including opening times. In theory, it's available from all of the sites included in the ticket, but in practice it's best to buy from the tourist information office on Portal de Mantas or the i-Peru office on the Plaza de Armas (see below).

A **partial Tourist Ticket** (Boleto Turístico) is also available, costing S/70 and offering access to all the city-centre sights mentioned above, plus Tipón and Pikillacta.

By bus and colectivo The city bus network is incredibly difficult to fathom, though it's cheap, fast and has several networks extending across the entire city. Largely unregulated, the buses are mainly minibuses chalking up their destinations on the front windscreens. Most useful are the buses and colectivos that run up and down Avenida Sol every couple of minutes during daylight hours, stopping at street corners if they have any seats left; these charge a flat fare (about S/1.50) and can be hailed on virtually any corner along the route.

By bike Eric Adventures (see opposite) rent out bikes from $25/day; you can also rent out mountain bikes for trips to the Sacred Valley and around from a range of other outfits, mainly based in Procuradores or Plateros (some outfits arrange guided bike tours). Renny Gamarra Loaiza is a good biking guide (t 231300).

By car and motorbike Some of the more remote and scenic valleys can be reached by car or motorbike with a map rather than a guide. The following organize car and motorbike rental: Manu, Av El Sol 520 (t 233382, w manurentacar.com); ATV Adventures, C Plateros 324 (t 252762, w atv-adventureperu.com); Peru Moto Tours, C Saphy 578 (t 232742, w perumototours.com).

INFORMATION

Apart from the places below, other sources of information are **tour agencies** around the Plaza de Armas or along calles Plateros and Procuradores, running uphill from the plaza. They provide leaflets promoting their own tours, but many also offer customized generic plans of the city and simple maps of the Sacred Valley and nearby regions. The Cuscoperu **website** is another good source of information: w cuscoperu.com.

Dirección Regional de Industria y Turismo (DRIT) Portal de Mantas 117a (Mon–Sat 8am–8pm, Sun 9am–2pm; t 222032). The main tourist office is a short block from the Plaza de Armas; it's possible to buy tickets for Machu Picchu here.

i-Peru In the BCP (Banco de Crédito) tourist centre on the Plaza de Armas at the corner of Portal de Harinas with Procuradores. The best source of tourist information is this kiosk (daily 9am–9pm), offering a friendly service with sound advice on where to go and how to get there, as well as maps and brochures. There are also information kiosks at the airport (daily 6.30am–4.30pm; t 237364) and the Terminal Terrestre (Mon–Fri 7am–6.30pm, Sat 7–11am; t 234498). Another small municipal tourist-information kiosk is sometimes open in the park located between Av Sol and the Centro Artesenal Cusco, or Cusco Handicraft Centre (see box, p.231).

Manu park office Parque Nacional del Manu, Av Micaela Bastidas 310, Wanchaq, Cusco (Mon–Fri 9am–6pm; t 240898). Most travellers are unlikely to need to visit this office, since any organized tour to the Manu Biosphere Reserve will have already obtained permission for you.

South American Explorers' Club Atoqsaycuchi 670 (Mon–Fri 9.30am–5pm, Sat 9.30am–1pm; t 245484, w saexplorers.org). Offers good information sheets, trip reports and files on virtually everything about Cusco and Peru, including transport, trekking, hotels, internet cafés and tour companies. Membership fees would be covered by the discount SE Club members get with some companies on just one tour to the Manu Biosphere Reserve.

TOUR OPERATORS AND TRAVEL AGENTS

Tours in and around Cusco range from a half-day city tour to an expedition by light aircraft or a full-on adventure down to the Amazon. **Prices** range from $30 to over $200 a day, and service and facilities vary considerably, so check exactly what's provided, whether **insurance** is included and whether the guide speaks English. The majority of operators and agents are strung along three sides of the Plaza de Armas, along Portal de Panes, Portal de Confiturias and Portal Comercio, up Procuradores and along calles Plateros and Suecia. Although prices vary, many are selling places on the same tours and treks, so always hunt around. Avoid the **tour touts** at the airport or in the plaza at Cusco, and check out the operators in advance at the South American Explorers' Club (see opposite); members of the club also receive a discount with some outfits. For popular treks you need to **book well in advance** (at least six months ahead – nine months is preferable – for the **Inca Trail**). The companies listed below have been around for some time; there are also a few Lima-based operators in this area (see p.81).

America Tours Portal de Harinas 175 ⊕227208, ⊛americatours.org. This travel agency mostly books and sells air tickets but also arranges packages within Peru and the Cusco region.

Andean Life Santa Teresa 381 and C Plateros 368 (inside the Hospedaje Caceres, on 2nd floor) ⊕221491, ⊛andeanlifeperu.com. Strong on the Inca Trail but generally specialists in small-group treks including Choquequirao (5 days), Salcantay (4–5 days), Lares (4 days) and Ausangate (6 days), as well as whitewater rafting and jungle trips. Inca Trail Classic four-day packages from $480.

Andina Travel Plazoleta Santa Catalina 219 ⊕251892, ⊛andinatravel.com. Reputable agents Andina organize mountain biking as well as alternative treks to the Inca Trail, such as Choquequirao, the Lares Valley, Salcantay and Ausangate. Inca Trail packages from $530 ($40 less with student card).

Apumayo Jr Ricardo Palma 11, Urb. Santa Monica, Wanchaq ⊕246018, ⊛apumayo.com. Expert operators offering trekking in the Sacred Valley region, mountain biking around Cusco and the Sacred Valley, historic and archeological tours, tours for disabled people (with wheelchair support for visiting major sites), horseriding, and rafting on the ríos Urubamba and Apurimac. They can customize their trips to suit your agenda, though note that they usually only work with pre-booked groups.

Colibri Tour C Garcilaso 210 Of. 210–B Casa del Abuelo ⊕255579, ⊛colibritour.com. Specialists on the Inca Trail and will arrange transport and collection from hotel. Also offer treks to Salcantay, Ausangate, Choquequirao and Vilcabamba.

Eric Adventures Urb. Santa María A1-6, San Sebastián ⊕272862, ⊛ericadventures.com. A good selection of tours, from the Inca Trail to trekking, kayaking, paragliding and mountain biking. They also rent out bikes, camping equipment and 4WDs, and have a good reputation for rafting. A day on the Urubamba river can cost as little as $40–50.

Expediciones Vilca C Plateros 359 ⊕244751, ⊛manuvilcaperu.com. A well-established trekking company with a variety of treks, albeit specializing in expeditions to the Manu Biosphere Reserve (see p.446). They can rent you any camping gear you need.

Explorandes Paseo Zarzuela Q-2 Huancaro ⊕238380, ⊛explorandes.com; or Arístides Aljovín 484, Miraflores, Lima ⊕01 7152323. Operating since 1975, award-winning Explorandes are very professional and offer a range of tours and treks across Peru's most fascinating landscapes. In the Cusco area, these are the Inca Trail (5 days from $813), Salcantay (5 days) and Choquequirao (5 days). They also offer jungle rafting expeditions (see box, p.82).

Kantu Portal Carrizos 258, Plaza de Armas ⊕243673. Good for budget rafting, but they also offer motorbike tours and 4WD journeys. Prices include food and somewhere to sleep overnight (usually a tent).

Manu Expeditions C Clorinda Matto de Turner 330, Urb. Magisterial Primero Etapa ⊕225990, ⊛manuexpeditions.com, ⊛manuwildlifecenter.com and ⊛birding-in-peru.com. Run, like the *Cross Keys Pub*, by the enigmatic local British consul and well-known twitcher, Barry Walker, this company specializes in both trips to Manu in the rainforest (see p.446) and birding expeditions, as well as horseriding and mountain adventure tours, including trips to Espíritu Pampa, the Inca site of Choquequirao through the Vilcabamba mountains, to Machu Picchu from Ollantaytambo via Anacachcocha and the Huaynay peaks, as well as more traditional treks like the Inca Trail.

Manu Nature Tours Av Pardo 1046 ⊕252721, ⊛manuperu.com. An award-winning, nature-based adventure travel company, running tours to the jungle, particularly Manu (see p.446), plus mountain biking, birdwatching and rafting. They also operate a garden café next to their offices.

MAYUC Portal Confiturias 211 ⊕242824 (or toll free from US and Canada ⊕1 855 819 5899), ⊛mayuc.com. Highly reliable outfit with the experience to organize any tour or trek of your choice, from the Inca Trail to visiting the Tambopata-Candamo area in the jungle of Madre de Dios. Whitewater rafting is their speciality, with standard scheduled 3-day/2-night excursions involving grade 2 to 5 rapids from about $390.

Milla Turismo Av Pardo 689 ⊕231710, ⊛millaturismo.com. Will organize travel arrangements, tours, study tours, visits to a nearby planetarium and cultural tourist-related activities.

Naty's Travel Agency Triunfo 342 ⊕261811, ⊛natysperutours.com. Travel agent selling plane and bus tickets as well as local tours.

Orellana Tours C Garcilaso 206 ⊕221544. Offering national and international air and bus tickets as well as a range of local tours.

4

Peru Planet C Garcilaso 210, Office 201 ⓣ251145, ⓦperu-planet.net. A well-respected Belgian-Peruvian travel agency offering the usual city tours as well as a wide range of trek options around the Sacred Valley, Salcantay, Lares, Choquequirao, Machu Picchu, Inca Trail, horseriding and rafting.

Peruvian Andean Treks Av Pardo 705 ⓣ225701, ⓦandeantreks.com. Expensive, but top-quality options for the Inca Trail (5 days/4 nights from $375), this US-based company also operates other treks in the Cusco region, including Choquequirao and Ausangante, and other regions of the Peruvian Andes. Worth contacting in advance for their brochure.

SAS Travel C Garcilaso 270, just below Plaza San Francisco ⓣ249194, ⓦsastravelperu.com. One of the most reliable and professional tour and trek operators in Cusco, SAS specialize in the Inca Trail (4 days from $580), but also visit Salcantay, Choquequirao, Ausangate and Vilcabamba, as well as the main jungle destinations. All good value.

ACTIVITIES AROUND CUSCO

The Cusco region and nearby cloudforest and lowland Amazon provide a fantastic range of **activities**, from river-based ecotourism and whitewater kayaking to mountain biking, hiking and horseriding, not to mention white-knuckle experiences of the spiritual variety.

HIKING AND HORSERIDING

The mountains to the south and the north of Cusco are full of amazing **trekking trails**, some of them little touched, most of them still rarely walked (see p.267). Less adventurous **walks** or **horse rides** are possible to Qenko, Tambo Machay, Puca Pucara and Chacan, in the hills above Cusco and in the nearby Sacred Valley. Many **jungle trip operators** are based in Cusco (see p.223).

4

WHITEWATER RAFTING

Cusco is also a great **whitewater rafting** centre, with easy access to classes 2 to 5 (rivers are generally rated from class 1 – very easy – to class 5 – very difficult/borderline dangerous) around Ollantaytambo on the Río Urubamba and classes 1 to 3 between Huambutio and Pisac, on the Río Vilcanota. From Calca to Urubamba the river runs classes 2 to 3, but this rises to 5 in the rainy season. Calca to Pisac (Huaran) and Ollantaytambo to Chilca are among the most popular routes, while the most dangerous are further afield on the Río Apurimac. The easiest stretch is from Echarate to San Baray, which passes by Quillabamba. Costs range from around $40 to about $200 a day, with price usually reflecting quality, but it's always recommended to use a reputable and well-established rafting company such as Mayuc (see p.223). Remember that most **travel insurance policies** exclude this kind of adventure activity, and always ensure that you are fully equipped with a safety kayak, helmets and lifejackets.

BUNGEE JUMPING AND HOT-AIR BALLOON TRIPS

Bungee jumping is big in Cusco. The tallest bungee jump facility in the Americas (122m) is offered by Action Valley Cusco, Santa Teresa 325 (ⓣ240835, ⓦactionvalley.com), just a fifteen-minute walk from the plaza in Poroy (buses run here from block 8 of Avenida Sol). Equally breathtaking but slightly less scary is the option of a **hot-air balloon** adventure (from $400, shared between groups of 5 to 10 people) in the Cusco or Sacred Valley areas; contact Globos de los Andes, C Arequipa 271 (ⓣ232352, ⓦglobosperu.com).

PSYCHEDELIC TOURISM

Psychedelic tourism is popular in Cusco these days, though not as developed as in Iquitos (see box, p.479.). This doesn't involve taking drugs and wandering around the Andes: essentially, psychedelic tourism is based on traditional healing techniques that tend to focus on inner consciousness and well-being through often highly ritualized ceremonies. San Pedro and ayahuasca, the two principal indigenous **psychedelic plants** that have been used ceremonially in Peru for over 3500 years (see p.507), can be experienced with the assistance of **Etnikas Travel and Shamanic Healing** (C Herrajes 148; ⓣ244516) or **Another Planet** (Triunfo 120; ⓣ2445168, ⓦanotherplanetperu.net), who also lead organized spiritual tours. The Shaman Shop, C Triunfo 393, is a good place for contacts; and there's also the Casa de la Serenidad, Tandapata 296a (ⓣ222851), which, besides assisting with altitude problems, offers coca-leaf readings, Reiki, flower and herb baths, and ayahuasca or San Pedro ceremonies.

United Mice C Plateros 351 ⓣ221139, ⓦunitedmice.com. Specializing in guided tours of the Inca Trail, this company is reasonably priced (some discounts for students), with good guides, many of whom speak English. Food is of a high standard and their camping equipment is fine. Tours which avoid the Inca Trail tax include an excellent 5-day trek approaching Machu Picchu via either Salcantay or Choquequirao. They also offer a 6-day trek to Ausangate.

ACCOMMODATION

While there are relatively inexpensive and reasonable mid-range hostels and hotels in most corners of the city, Cusco's accommodation is centred in three main zones: east, west and south of the Plaza de Armas. To the west of the Plaza along calles Plateros, Procuradores and Saphi (Procuradores and Plateros are particularly noisy at night) there are plenty of busy budget hostels. You can find slightly pricier and more luxurious places in the area east of the Plaza around San Blas and Choquechaca in the artists' quarter. To the south of the Plaza, the San Pedro region around the central market and near to the train station for Machu Picchu has improved its facilities in recent years, now offering comfortable and safe accommodation. Closer to the Plaza, along Calle Quera and around Avenida Sol, more varied accommodation can be found.

WEST OF PLAZA DE ARMAS

Hostal Caceres C Plateros 368 ⓣ232616. A popular travellers' hangout, half a block from the Plaza de Armas. It has a courtyard and is within a stone's throw of most of Cusco's best bars and cafés. Rooms are simple and unpretentious, many being shared dorms. Some rooms have hot water and own bathroom. **S/35**

Hostal Rojas C Tigre 129 ⓣ228184, ⓦhostalrojas.com. Located very centrally in a congenial old mansion with many rooms based around a lovely courtyard. Spaces are large, safe, airy and clean. All rooms with own bath; simple breakfasts included in the price. **S/150**

Hotel Cahuide C Saphi 845 ⓣ222771, ⓦhotelcahuide-cusco.com. Located a few blocks uphill from the Plaza de Armas, this is a nice place to stay with clean, modern rooms and a useful message board. Quite pricey but better value in low season. **S/200**

Hotel Marqueses C Garcilaso 256 ⓣ257819, ⓦhotelmarqueses.com. A splendid and sumptuous boutique-style hotel, in an ornate colonial-style building with fine period furnishings. Wi-fi and laundry are available. **S/336**

Hotel Picoaga Santa Teresa 334 ⓣ227691, in Lima ⓣ01 7112000, ⓦpicoagahotel.com. A first-class hotel in one of Cusco's finest colonial mansions, close to the heart of the city, that was originally the old mansion of the Spanish noble, the Marquis of Picoaga (century XVII). It has now been converted, with intimate and public areas beautifully decorated in colonial style. Service is excellent, and the hotel also has a bar and quality restaurant. **S/390**

Hotel Royal Qosqo Tecsecocha 2 ⓣ226221, ⓦhotelesroyalqosqo.com. Based around a small colonial courtyard, this lovely refurbished hostel is right at the heart of the action. Rooms are small but the beds are really comfortable and the showers hot, and they're available with or without bath and TV; breakfast included. **S/115**

★ **Loki Hostel** Cuesta Santa Ana 601 ⓣ243705, ⓦlokihostel.com. Four longish blocks from the main plaza, *Loki* offers backpackers a great space to hang out in Cusco; it has dormitories and some private rooms. One of a small chain of hostels in Peru (also found in Mancora and Lima), this has the usual *Loki* bar and cafeteria. Very popular with younger travellers. Dorms **S/25**, doubles **S/85**

Plaza de Armas Hostal Portal Mantas 114, Plaza de Armas ⓣ231709, ⓔhostal_plaza@terra.com.pe. As central as can be, on the corner of the plaza, this friendly hotel has main doors opening onto the square. Rooms facing the plaza obviously have the best views, but they all feature private bath and cable TV. Price includes breakfast. **S/150**

EAST OF PLAZA DE ARMAS

Amaru Hostal Cuesta San Blas 541 ⓣ225933, ⓦamaruhostal.com. There's a rustic colonial feel at this hostel, based in a republican mansion with lovely garden patio at its centre and another out back with views over town. Some rooms are old and stylish, while those in the back by the patio are newer but less interesting, most with private bath. Service is very good, and facilities include laundry, safety deposit and left-luggage, plus bottled oxygen. **S/140**

Casa de Campo Tandapata 298 ⓣ244404, ⓦhotelcasadecampo.com. In a quiet, uplifting location on the upper edge of Cusco are these attractive rooms and cabins, all with private bath. Rooms come with an ecological and meditation theme, and there are great views of the city from the large patio-garden. As it's relatively high above the centre, it is a good idea to take a taxi to avoid exhaustion or altitude sickness on the first couple of days. They offer combined accommodation and language-school courses. Best booked in advance. **S/130**

La Casa de la Gringa Tandapata 148 ⓣ241168, ⓦcasadelagringa.com. A funky and enjoyably bohemian place that was once used by monks. The South African owner has lovingly restored the yards and rooms in amazing colours, and can organize connections for jungle trips, mystical tours and San Pedro journeys (see box opposite). There is wi-fi and cable TV; shared bathrooms only. **S/85**

4

Hospedaje Familiar Casa Grande Santa Catalina Ancha 353 ⓣ224907, ⓦcasagrandelodging.com.pe. Large, centrally located hotel with an open courtyard. There are some well-furbished rooms as well as more basic ones, with or without bath. S/140

★ **Hospedaje Turístico San Blas** Cuesta San Blas 326 ⓣ225781, ⓦsanblashostal.com. Located in San Blas, this friendly place features a glass-covered courtyard. Most rooms have private bath and a safe deposit is available. The owners also organize tours to the Inca Trail and river rafting on the Vilcanota. A good lower-to-mid-range option. S/110

Hostal El Arcano Carmen Alto 288 ⓣ232703, ⓦcuzco.com/hostal-el-arcano-cuzco.com. A slightly disorganized but otherwise friendly and amenable hostel on the edge of the attractive San Blas area with a reliable hot-water system, laundry, family-sized rooms (accommodating 4–5) and a comfortable lounge. Rooms come with or without private bath. S/60

★ **Hostal El Grial** Carmen Alto 112, San Blas ⓣ223012, ⓦhotelelgrial.com. A relaxed hostal offering very professional and secure service in a central but quiet corner of San Blas. Nicely furnished, the rooms are modernized in tasteful Cusco style and spotlessly maintained, all with private bath and wi-fi access. Spanish lessons can be arranged at a reasonable cost, and breakfast is served on the pleasant communal downstairs patio. S/90

Hostal Huaynapata Wayna Pata 369 ⓣ228034, ⓦhuaynapata.com. This modernized hostel is safe and friendly, with 1970s-style decor and café. Most rooms are ample and offer heating and wi-fi. It's not that far from the main plaza, and the covered roof terrace has splendid views across to the cathedral and, on a clear day, down the valley to Ausangate. Price includes breakfast. S/90

Hostal Inti Quilla Atocsaycuchi 281 ⓣ252659. Small and cheerful hostel, quite a few steps up from the main square, but great value with cosy but relatively spartan rooms, with or without bath. There's also a pretty little courtyard with a massive Andean pine tree, a nice place to read or just relax. S/85

★ **Hostal Mirador de la Ñusta** Tandapata 682 ⓣ248039, ⓔelmiradordelanusta@hotmail.com. An intimate, warm and superbly located place directly overlooking the Plazoleta San Blas in the artists' quarter. It has ten nice rooms, a pretty little yard, breakfast, laundry service and reliable hot water. S/50

★ **Hostal Rumi Punku** Choquechaca 339 ⓣ221102, ⓦrumipunku.com. A welcoming establishment built on an old Inca temple site in one of Cusco's most attractive streets. Entered through an ancient stone doorway and arranged around an inner courtyard, the rooms are really stylish (some lit by resplendent chandeliers) for the price, with private showers and hot water. There's access to a kitchen, a patio, a *comedor* (dining room) and a small sitting room with a fireplace. Best booked in advance at any time of year. Price includes breakfast. S/280

★ **Hotel Monasterio** C Palacio 136, Plazoleta Nazarenas ⓣ241777, ⓦmonasteriohotel.com. One of Cusco's newest luxury establishments, this is a fantastic place, set around massive sixteenth-century monastery cloisters; it may cost a mint, but the rooms are top class and all are large enough for up to three people. There are also tables in the courtyard where you can soak up the atmosphere while sipping drinks and eating delicious food from the plush bar and restaurant. S/1460

Inkaterra La Casona Cusco Plaza Las Nazarenas 113 ⓣ234010, ⓦinkaterra.com. A newly refurbished, top-notch boutique hotel right in the centre of Cusco, and one of its finest places to stay. Although hard to tell from the outside, internally the decor is meticulous in combining style, ethnicity and comfort. A colonial manor house – one of the first Spanish constructions in Cusco – it has eleven suites around a sumptuous courtyard. Offers a great range of excursions in Cusco and the Sacred Valley. S/1200

Pakcha Real Hostal Familiar Tandapata 300, San Blas ⓣ237484, ⓦhostalpakchareal.com. An excellent family-run hostel in San Blas, this fun, modern place has a shared kitchen, a TV room and patio, constant hot water and reasonable security. Rooms are available with or without bath. The location high above the city centre, however, four steep blocks from Plaza de Armas, is a bit of a hike, and can be testing on arrival from sea level. S/70

SOUTH OF PLAZA DE ARMAS

Gran Hotel Machu Picchu C Quera 282 ⓣ231111, ⓦgranhotelmachupicchu.org. About two blocks from the Plaza de Armas, this hostel is hard to beat for friendly atmosphere and value in one package. Prices start low since some rooms are available without private bath; all are set around a verdant colonial courtyard, and there's free internet access too. S/90

★ **Hotel Libertador** Plazoleta Santo Domingo 259 ⓣ231961, ⓦlibertador.com.pe. One of the most expensive and exclusive hotels in Peru, set in a thoroughly renovated mansion close to Q'orikancha, just a few blocks from the Plaza de Armas. Rooms are stylish and luxurious but it's the spacious lobby with knobbly, genuine Inca stonework that is the real treasure. S/1200

The Point Hostel Meson de la Estrella 172 ⓣ252266, ⓦthepointhostels.com. This fun hostel, part of Peru's "The Point" hostel chain (the others are in Lima, Puno, Arequipa and Mancora), is just two blocks from the main plaza and close to Plaza San Francisco. Well known for partying, it has over seventy beds in a modernized colonial mansion with a pleasant garden, laundry, kitchen and book exchange. Dorms S/22, doubles S/80

CLOCKWISE FROM TOP CUSCO CAFÉ LIFE (P.228); GALERÍA OLAVE (P.218); WOMAN WITH LLAMA >

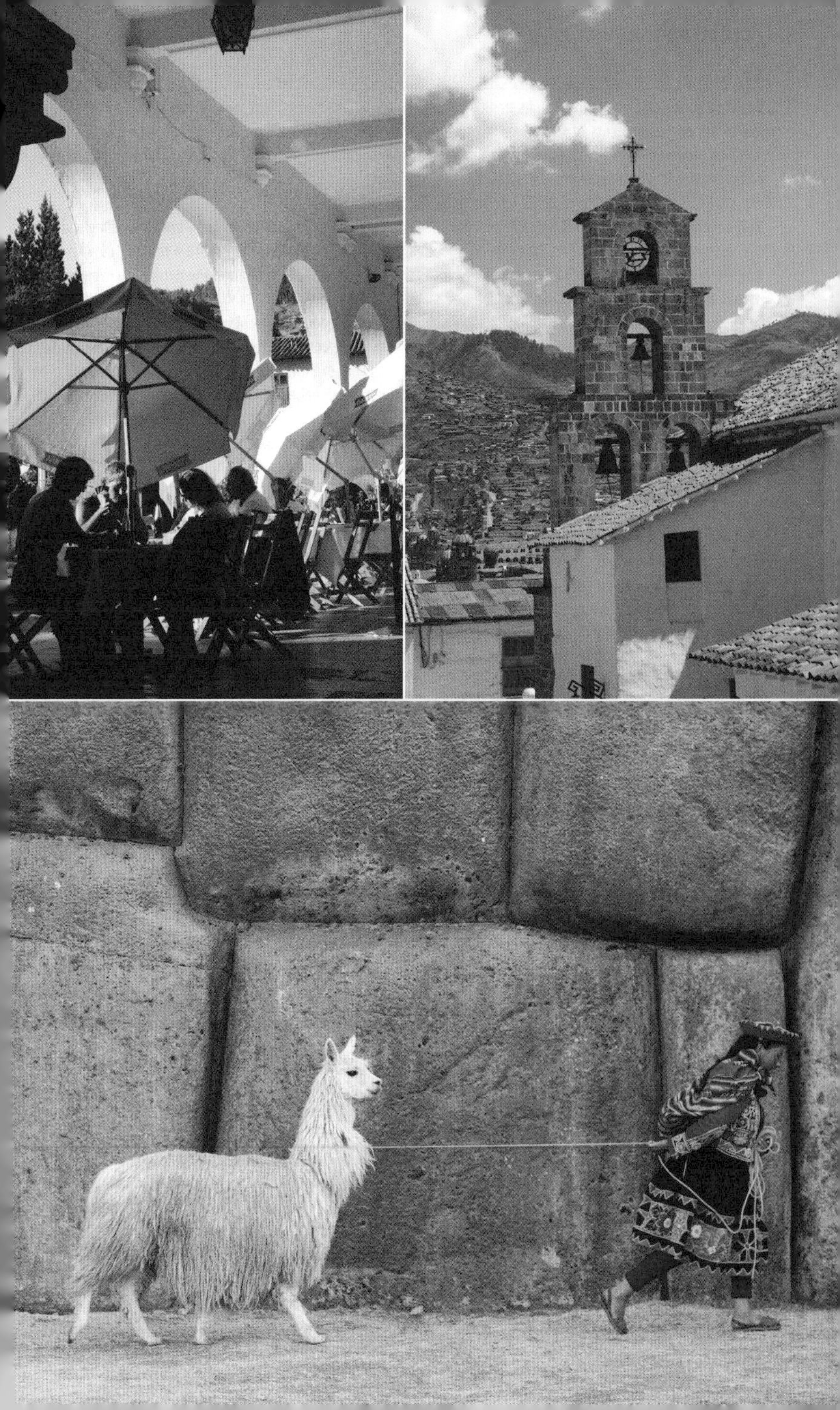

EATING

Local cuisine Cusco prides itself on its traditional dishes, which have evolved this century into a *novo andino* cuisine, fusing the best ingredients of the Andes with exquisite Mediterranean and even Argentinian influences. Generally speaking, trout is plentiful, reasonably priced and often excellent, and roast guinea pig (*cuy*) can usually be ordered – but pizza seems to lead in the popularity stakes.

Self-catering The central market by San Pedro train station sells a wonderful variety of meats, tropical and imported fruits, local vegetables, Andean cheeses and other basics. The market also has a wide range of daytime hot-food stalls where you can get superb, freshly squeezed juices.

Where to eat Eating out in Cusco is enjoyable, and restaurants range from cheap-and-cheerful pizza joints to exceptionally fine gourmet establishments. Many of the best restaurants and bars are within a block or two of the Plaza de Armas and uphill towards San Blas; the more central places serve anything from a toasted cheese sandwich to authentic Andean or criolla dishes. *Quintas* – basic local eating houses – serve mostly traditional Peruvian food, full of spice and character. It's difficult, if not impossible, to categorize some of the establishments in Cusco as distinctly cafés, restaurants or bars since many fulfil all three functions, occasionally simultaneously, sometimes varying between different hours of the day. *The Muse* (see opposite), for instance, is a café-bar in the daytime and a nightlife venue from about 9.30pm, particularly at weekends.

CAFÉS AND RESTAURANTS

Bagdad Café Portal de Carnes 216, Plaza de Armas ☎254504. Located upstairs, the *Bagdad Café* is a popular spot, not least because it has tables on a colonial balcony overlooking the plaza. Serves good pizzas, breakfasts, sandwiches, some pasta dishes and cool drinks. Daily 11am–11pm.

El Buen Pastor Cuesta San Blas 579. One of the best in Cusco, this exceptional bakery has a huge array of sweet and savoury home-made pastries and fine cakes. Mon–Sat 8am–6pm.

Cosa Nostra C Plateros 358a, 2nd floor ☎232992. This stylish and very well appointed restaurant produces the best Italian cuisine in the city. Excellent service in a refined ambience, with black-and-white classic photos decorating the walls; main dishes from around S/30. Mon–Sat 12.30–3.30pm & 6.30–10.30pm.

El Croissant Plaza San Francisco 134. Good French bakery – ideal for croissants, French bread and, best of all, delicious cream pastries. Mon–Sat 7.30am–7pm.

Don Esteban and Don Pancho Café Gourmet Av Sol, opposite and a little uphill from the post office. Excellent coffee and cakes served here all day in a pleasant, Euro-deli atmosphere. Also good for breakfasts, sandwiches and quiche. Mon–Sat 8am–8pm.

★ **Fallen Angel** Plazoleta Nazarenas 221 ☎258184, Ⓦfallenangelincusco.com. A gay-friendly restaurant with games suspended on stools from the ceiling and fake leopard-skin trunks. There's also a resident DJ who plays vibrant trip-hop and trance. The decor is an experience in its own right: arty, wicked and inspired, while the garden art is as good as many of Cusco's art museums – and much more twenty-first-century. The food and cocktails are equally exquisite. Try the Andean tenderloin steak with port and balsamic topping (S/35), the Andean ravioli stuffed with local sweet potato, the wild mushrooms or the warm salad. Book in advance. Daily 7pm–midnight.

★ **Greens** Santa Catalina Angosta 135 ☎243379 or 254753. This brilliantly run restaurant serves superb innovative dishes, both *novo andino* and Mediterranean, using as many organic and green ingredients as possible. Highly recommended and pretty reasonably priced, with main dishes starting around S/25. Reservations are advised. Daily noon–9.30pm.

Incanto Restaurant Santa Catalina Angosta 135 ☎254753. Based in a large space below *Greens* restaurant, this place nevertheless fills up quickly in the evenings because of its reputation for good service and quality pizza. Also serves fine Peruvian dishes like *aji de gallina*, *lomo saltado* and *locro de zapallo* from around S/28. Daily noon–11pm (limited service 4–6pm).

Inka Grill Portal de Panes 115 ☎262992. A grill-based restaurant near a busy corner of Plaza de Armas, with stones from the Inca Pachacuti's palace lining the walls, and both *comida tipica* and *internacional* on the menu. Main dishes start at around S/30. With folklore shows at weekends and evenings from 8pm, it's worth the extra few *soles*. Daily 11.15am–11pm (last orders 10pm).

★ **Jack's Café** Corner of Choquechaca and Cuesta San Blas ☎254606. A popular gringo place, this pleasant café serves very creative all-day breakfasts, burgers, pancakes and a whole host of other very tasty plates. Great coffee and very good service. When busy you may have to queue. Daily 7am–midnight (food served 7.30am–11pm).

Korma Sutra Tandapata 909 ☎233023. Cusco's main curry house, this fine restaurant with unique ambience serves everything from crispy tandoori guinea pig to alpaca curries. Other dishes include bhajis, samosas, chicken korma (S/28), tofu vindaloo and bean rogan josh. Tues–Sat 1–10pm.

Macondo Cuesta San Blas 571 ☎229415. A cosy and homely gay-friendly restaurant with wacky decor, serving some of the best *novo andino* and Amazonian cuisine you'll find anywhere; try the *yuquitas* (fried slices of manioc) stuffed with *chimbivalcano* (from Chimbivalca) cheese, the vegetarian curry or the *alpaca mignon a la parmesana*. Main dishes start at around S/28. Best in evenings (book in advance), but serves a full menu during the day. Daily 11am–midnight.

Mammacha C San Juan de Dios 250, inside the courtyard on the 2nd floor ⓣ984758362. Located inside the beautifully restored Casa Qoriq'ente, a late colonial, early republican mansion with stunning courtyard and working central fountain, *Mammacha* serves quality lunchtime menus and fine evening gourmet meals: a fusion of pastas with traditional Peruvian cuisine in a stylish interior or on the terrace tables; main dishes from around S/28. Daily 11am–3pm & 6–10pm.

The Muse C Triunfo 338, 2nd floor ⓣ242030. During the day this place serves excellent coffee, snacks such as apple pie and cheesecake, and full meals, including all-day breakfasts and excellent soups (like pumpkin and leek and potato, both ideal for adjusting to the altitude). The main room is a large and comfortable space, with a stage for live music in the evenings (see p.230). Out back, there's a more formal restaurant room with a wonderful stone fireplace, ideal for groups. Daily 8am–3/4am.

The Muse Too Tambopata 917, San Blas. A great little place for snacking at any time of day, this sister café to *The Muse* (above) has good coffee, fresh juices and tasty food for meat eaters and vegetarians. It serves breakfast all day and has a large screen for sports and movies, the latter shown daily from around 4pm. In the evenings there's often live music. Wi-fi available. Daily 8am–2am.

Pacha Papa Plaza San Blas 120 ⓣ241318. A great, inexpensive restaurant set around an attractive courtyard, serving a range of hard-to-find Andean dishes (from around S/26), from *gulash de alpaca* to the highly nutritious *sopa de quinoa*, and good wines, both Peruvian and Chilean. Often has wonderful Andean live harp music. Reservations recommended. Daily noon–11pm.

Pucara Café-Bar C Plateros 309 ⓣ222027. Popular with tourists, this pleasant restaurant offers inexpensive set menus, fine salads and well-prepared Peruvian cuisine (main dishes from S/24). There's occasional music in the evenings. Daily 11am–11pm.

La Quinta Eulalia C Choquechaca 384 ⓣ241380. One of the very best and most traditional local eating houses, in a backstreet a few blocks above the Plaza de Armas. Plays fine criolla music and is good for *cuy chactado* (guinea pig fried with potatoes, tamales and *rocoto*, a pepper-like vegetable which is occasionally spicy). Daily 11.30am–4.30pm.

Restaurant El Encuentro Santa Catalina Ancha 384 ⓣ247977. A simple vegetarian café which serves set menus as well as incredibly good value meals a la carte (from around S/15), including delicious omelettes, soups and salads, as well as health drinks. Mon–Sat 9am–9pm.

Restaurant Govinda C Saphy 584 ⓣ221227 or 790687. The original vegetarian eating house in Cusco. You can enjoy simple, healthy food – fruit-and-yoghurt breakfasts and excellent-value set lunches – under the jungle-style *tortora* reed ceiling amid bamboo posts, with a soundtrack of new-age spiritual ambient tunes. Based in two ample spaces, though the tables are a bit tight. Daily 8am–10pm.

Rosie O'Grady's Santa Catalina 360 ⓣ243514. Find good beer and even better full meals at this swish Irish pub and restaurant: the beef steak (S/30-plus) is among the best in Peru. In the evenings, there's a great atmosphere, and major sports games are shown on a big screen. Wi-fi. Happy hour 1–3pm & 8–10pm. Daily 11am–11pm.

La Trattoria Adriano C Mantas 105, corner of Av Sol ⓣ253641. This restaurant serves reasonably good quality Italian cuisine, especially the pasta dishes. Main meals start at S/24 and there's a fine selection of good South American and European wines. Service is fast and the place is popular with both tourists and locals. Daily 10am–midnight.

Trotamundos Portal de Comercio 177, Plaza de Armas ⓣ239590. A welcoming café warmed by an open log fire and serving a mix of local and international food. An internet section is partitioned off from the café itself, with views over the plaza, a notice board and games. Daily 8am–11pm.

4

DRINKING, NIGHTLIFE AND ENTERTAINMENT

Apart from Lima, no Peruvian town has as varied a nightlife as Cusco. The Plaza de Armas is a hive of activity until the early hours, even during the week. Most venues in the city are simply **bars** with a dancefloor and sometimes a stage, but their styles vary enormously, from Andean folk spots with panpipe music to reggae or jazz joints, as well as more conventional **clubs**. Most places are within staggering distance of each other, and sampling them is an important part of any stay in Cusco. Most really get going between 10 and 11pm, then keep on going until 2 or 3am.

PUBS AND BARS

★ **Cross Keys Pub** C Triunfo 350, 2nd floor ⓣ229227, ⓦcross-keys-pub-cusco-peru.com. One of the hubs of Cusco's nightlife, this classic dive has the feel of a London pub, with good music, football scarves adorning the walls, pool tables and decent beers. Wi-fi and tasty food is available and there are often English-language newspapers and magazines – not surprisingly, since it's owned by the British consul. Daily 10am–1/2am (food served until 10pm).

Indigo Tecsecocha 2 ⓣ260271. An atmospheric bar justly famous for its Thai cuisine and cocktails. It's best in the evenings when you can warm up by the fireplace, and there are comfortable seats, sofas and swings, games, books, sports TV, wi-fi and hookahs. Daily 4pm–3am.

Km 0 Tandapata 100, San Blas 236009. This bar and café is small and nearly always busy with a very international mix of musicians and drinkers; there's live music at weekends and sometimes during the week. The music lounge and bar area downstairs can get a bit cramped, but there are restaurant tables upstairs. Tues–Sat 11am–2/3am, Sun & Mon 5pm–4am.

★ **The Muse** C Triunfo 338, 2nd floor 242030. This popular café and restaurant (see p.229) is also one of the most vibrant live music venues in town, with performances mainly Thurs–Sat from 10.30pm. Daily 8am–3/4am.

Norton Rats Tavern Santa Catalina 116, 2nd floor 246204. Just off the Plaza de Armas, with great views over the square, *Norton Rats* is best known as a bar, serving special jungle cocktails and a couple of decent English ales in its spacious interior. It plays rock, blues, jazz and Latin music, and has a pool table and dartboard, plus satellite TV for sports. There's also a café menu of grills and sandwiches. Daily 11am–midnight.

Paddy Flaherty's Irish Pub C Triunfo 124 247719, paddysirishbarcusco.com. Much like a British pub, though its wood-panelled walls are garlanded with Irish artefacts and a working model train, which circulates the room continuously. The atmosphere is pleasant and generally very busy, particularly at weekends, when they often have live Irish music and the Guinness is flowing. There's a sports screen too. Daily 11am–midnight or later.

4

★ **Los Perros** Tecsecocha 436 241447. Billing itself as "the original wine and couch bar", *Los Perros* is a trendy hangout where travellers snack, drink and play board games, or read from the wide-ranging library of books and magazines (books can be exchanged – give two, take one). It serves some of the biggest hamburgers on the planet, plus there's a notice board, good music and often live modern jazz at weekends. Daily 11am–midnight.

Rosie O'Grady's Santa Catalina 360 247935. A capacious Irish pub and great restaurant (see p.229) with a range of beers, Guinness included. There's great live music on Thurs and Fri, plus a popular Friday evening "boat race" drinking competition; satellite TV for sports. Daily 10am–11pm.

CLUBS AND DANCE BARS

★ **KamiKase Bar** Portal Cabildo 274, Plaza Regocijo 233865. One of Cusco's best-established venues, with modern Andean rock-art decor and basic furnishings. Drinks are quite cheap, though when it hosts live music (most weekends), there's usually a small entrance fee – worth it if you're into rock and Andean folk. Happy hour 8–10pm; live music usually starts around 10.45pm, but get there earlier for a good seat. Fri–Sun 8pm–1/2am.

The Lek Portal de Harinas 195 255577. One of Cusco's most popular dance bars, playing a wide range of music, from Latin and Europop to reggae. Sports TV and movies during the day. Happy hour all night. Daily 2pm–3am.

London Town Tecsecocha 415 223082. One of the newest Brit-style lounge bars with wi-fi, good atmosphere and great food. There is usually live music Thurs–Sat, and there's a good vibe even when full. Daily 4pm–3am.

Mama Africa Portal Harinas 109, 3rd floor, Plaza de Armas mamaafricaclub.com. A good, buzzing dance bar with a small entrance fee, playing reggae on Fri and Sat, electronica on Sun, and mixed disco and hip-hop during the week. It regularly presents live shows with fire-dancing, African rhythm, and Latin and Brazilian artists, plus occasional dance classes in salsa and samba. Other pluses are the great view over the Plaza and the good food. Happy hour 4–11pm. Daily 4pm–4am, sometimes later.

El Muki Disco Santa Catalina Angosta 110 227797. Near the Plaza de Armas, *El Muki* has been pumping out pop every night for over twenty years. With its atmospheric catacomb-like dancefloors, it's a safe space for late-night grooving, charging S/8 entrance. Thurs–Sat 9pm–3am.

Mythology Portal de Carnes 298, second floor 255770. Comfortable and chilled, but also good for a dance, *Mythology* has two bars, mainly spinning funk, hip-hop and reggae. Very lively most nights of the week, but really heaving at weekends. Daily 8pm–4am.

The Real McCoy C Plateros 326, 2nd floor [illegible], therealmccoycusco.com. A very British bar and restaurant offering wi-fi, English breakfasts, fish and chips, and pie and mash, as well as imported teas during the day. At night it comes to life with happy hour from 5–8pm, curry nights on Thurs, and regular pub quizzes. Daily 7.30am–2/3am.

Ukuku's Bar C Plateros 316, down the alley and upstairs 254911. A highly popular venue with one of the best atmospheres in Cusco, teeming with energetic revellers most nights by around 11pm, when the music gets going. There's a small dancefloor, a seating area and a long bar, with music ranging from live Andean folk with panpipes, drums and *charangos* (small Andean stringed instruments) to DJs or taped rock. They have a small cafeteria to the side. There's sometimes an entrance charge – usually less than S/8. Daily 8pm–6am.

OTHER ENTERTAINMENT VENUES

Alliance Française Av de la Cultura 804 223755. Runs a full programme of events including music, films, exhibitions, theatre and music.

Dance Performances Centro Qosqo de Arte Nativo, Av Sol 812 227901. During major fiestas you'll encounter colourfully costumed folk-dancing groups in the streets; at other times, Dance Performances is the only group that offers regular shows. Entrance with Cusco Tourist Ticket. Daily 6–10pm.

SHOPPING

Areas Most of the touristy artesanía and jewellery shops are concentrated in streets like Plateros around the Plaza de Armas and up Triunfo, though calles Herraje (first right as you head towards San Blas) and San Agustín have slightly cheaper but decent shops with leather and alpaca work. It's worth heading off the beaten track, particularly around San Blas or the upper end of Tullumayo, to find outlets hidden in the backstreets.

Markets The main street-market day for artesanía is Sat (10am–6pm). The central market, selling fresh produce, is at San Pedro (see p.232). Out of town there are good markets for artesanía at Pisac and Chinchero, market days being Sun and Thurs, respectively (see p.240 and p.246).

Opening hours Cusco opening hours are generally Mon–Sat 10am–6pm, though some of the central gift stores open on Sundays and don't close until well into the evening.

Prices and haggling In the markets and at street stalls you can often get up to twenty percent off, and even in the smarter shops it's quite acceptable to bargain a little. If you're worried about carrying an expensive purchase around town, it's fine to ask the shopkeeper to bring the goods to your hotel so that the transaction can take place in relative safety.

BOOKS AND MUSIC

Genesis Bookstore Santa Catalina Ancha, at corner with Santa Catalina Angosta ⓣ234073 and 241016. One of the best places to find books in English, particularly guides, history books and material on birds or wildlife; it's also a post office agent and sells stationery. Mon–Sat 9am–9pm, Sun 9am–noon & 4–9pm.

Kuskan Bookstore C San Juan de Dios 250, inside the courtyard ⓣ254135. This store has some fascinating books in English, particularly focusing on travel, culture and biodiversity. Mon–Sat 9am–9pm.

Music Centre Av Sol 230. The best range of Andean and Peruvian cassettes and CDs in Cusco. Daily 9am–9pm.

CAMPING EQUIPMENT

Rental or purchase of camping equipment is easy in Cusco, but you may be asked to leave your passport as a deposit on more expensive items; always get a proper receipt. For basics such as pots, pans, plates and so on, try the stalls in Monjaspata, less than half a block from the bottom end of San Pedro market, while others such as buckets, bowls and sheets are sold in various shops along Calle Concebidayoq, close to the San Pedro market area.

Andean Life Santa Teresa 381 and Calle Plateros 372, Plaza de Armas ⓣ261269, ⓦandeanlifeperu.com. An adventure-tour operator with a whole range of camping equipment for rent or sale. Mon–Sat 9am–7pm.

Cordillera C Garcilaso 210. A smart outdoor equipment shop with lots of well-known brands, including North Face clothing. Mon–Sat 8.30am–11.15pm.

Eric Adventures Urb Velasco Astete B-8-B ⓣ234764, ⓦericadventures.com. A selection of camping equipment, new and old. Mon–Sat 8.30am–6pm.

Inkas Trek C Medio 114 ⓣ260747. All the gear you'll need, and all available to rent. Mon–Sat 10am–8pm.

X-Treme Tourbulencia Expeditions C Plateros 358 ⓣ224362, ⓦx-tremetourbulencia.com. A decent range of used mountain camping equipment. Daily 10am–8pm.

CRAFTS, ARTESANÍA AND JEWELLERY

Agua y Tierra Cuesta San Blas 595 ⓣ226951. Some excellent jungle textiles, ceramics, jewellery and *cushma* robes. Mon–Sat 9am–7pm.

Allyu Ecologicos Av Tullumayo 280 ⓣ240509. Sells

CRAFT-SHOPPING IN CUSCO

Crafts and artesanía are Cusco's stock in trade, with the best value and range of **alpaca clothing** in Peru, apart perhaps from Puno. It's an ideal place to pick up **weavings** or **antique cloths**, traditional **musical instruments** like panpipes, and colourful bags and **leather crafts**. There are artesanía (craft shops) all over the centre, but the best prices and fullest range are found at the **Centro Artesanal Cusco** (Mon–Sat 8am–10pm, with most stalls open 9am–6pm, Sun 9am–5pm) at the corner of Huanchac and Tullumayo, close to the huge sun-disc fountain on Avenida Sol. This large building brings together arguably the largest and best-value collection of artesanía under one roof in Peru; it's a nice, clean and relatively hassle-free shopping environment very close to the train ticket office at Huanchac station.

Another good part of town for quality artesanía is the barrio of **San Blas**. This is the traditional artisan area of Cusco, home to a number of jewellers and art and antique shops. The Cuesta San Blas itself contains some of the finest artesanía, selling new and old oil paintings, while Hathun Rumiyoq has more good shops at its bottom end. There are some funky shops around the San Blas *plazoleta* too. The main street-market day for artesanía is Saturday (10am–6pm).

4

handmade textiles of pure alpaca dyed with local plants, as well as natural local herbal remedies. Money goes directly to the craft producers. Mon–Sat 8.30am–6pm.

Alpaca 3 Plaza Regocijo 202 243233. Good alpaca fabrics, yarns, jumpers and scarves. Mon–Sat 9am–9pm.

Joyeria Oropesa Portal de Carrizos, corner of Calle Loreto 231127. Jewellery for fat wallets: these sizeable pieces of fine silverwork start in the hundreds of dollars range. Daily 10am–8pm.

Peru Gifts Santa Catalina Angosta 160 261509. This spacious shop has a smart range of classy crafts, from ceramics to alpaca and a lot more, including gold and silver work – and alcoholic beverages. Daily 9am–10pm.

Shaman Shop C Triunfo 393, interior space 107. A small but well-stocked mystical store selling everything from candles and incense to magical talismans and shamanic music. It's also a good place to find contacts for ayahuasca and San Pedro ceremonies (see box, p.224). Daily 10am–6pm.

Werner and Ana Plaza San Francisco 295a 231076. This clothing boutique is owned by some of Peru's top fashion designers. Mon–Sat 9am–7pm.

FOOD

Calle Plateros minimarkets C Plateros nos. 392, 352 & 355. These minimarket shops are small but packed to the rafters with food for trekking expeditions – cheese, biscuits, tins of tuna, nuts, chocolate, raisins and dried bananas. Daily 8am–10pm.

El Chinito Grande Matará 271. A large, Chinese-run supermarket with good prices and selection, offering an array of Chinese food, as well as other international produce. Mon–Sat 8am–8pm.

Mercado Central San Pedro. The best place for generally excellent and very cheap food – including all the main typical Peruvian dishes like *cau cau* (tripe), rice with meat and veg, and *papas a la huancaina* (see p.34). Daily 6am–4pm.

Union Supermarket C Union, opposite the main San Pedro market at the corner with C Santa Clara. Quite a large supermarket, selling more stuff and at lower prices than the more tourist-oriented ones nearer the Plaza de Armas. Daily 8am–8pm.

DIRECTORY

4

Consulates Bolivia, Av Pardo, Pasaje Espinar (231412); Netherlands, José G. Cosio 307, Urb. Magisterial (261517); UK, Calle Clorinda Matto de Turner 330 first floor, Urbanización Magisterial ([illegible]); US, Av Pardo 845 (231474).

Health If you need a hospital, go to the Hospital Regional, Av de la Cultura (231455, 223030 or 223691), which also offers free yellow-fever inoculations Sat 11am–1pm; the Clinica Pardo, Av de la Cultura 710, Wanchaq (249999); or the Clinica Laboratorio Louis Pasteur, Tullumayo 768 (234727), which has a gynecologist. For high-altitude health matters contact CIMA (see box, p.210). To see a doctor, try one of the following: Dr Oscar Tejada (233836; 24hr), a member of International Association for Medical Assistance to Travellers; Dr Dante Valdivia (231390, 620588 or 252166; speaks English and German); and Dr María Helena (650122 or 227385; will visit your hotel). If you need a dentist, try Dr Virginia Valcarcel Velarde, upstairs at Portal de Panes 123, Plaza de Armas (231558); or Consultorio Dental, Av Los Incas 900 (431569).

Immigration Migraciones, Av Sol, block 620 (Mon–Fri 8am–1pm; 222741).

Internet Wi-fi internet access and internet cafés are ubiquitous. Expect to pay around S/1–3/hr to log on.

Language schools Amigos Spanish School, Zaguan del Cielo B-23 (242292, spanishcusco.com), is a not-for-profit institution which funds education and food for local young people through its teaching of Spanish; family stays can also be organized if required. Staff speak English, Dutch, German, French and Japanese; extracurricular activities include salsa and merengue dance lessons, cooking classes and aerobics at 3400m. The South American Spanish School based at Carmen Alto 112, San Blas ([illegible], sasschool.org), provides excellent teaching along with hostel or family-home-based accommodation where required. Amauta Spanish (amautaspanish.com) also offer group and individual Spanish lessons.

Laundry Lavandería Louis at Choquechaca 264 is very fast; Lavamachine is at both Santa Teresa 383 and Procuradores 50; Laundry, Teqsecocha 428.

Left luggage The South American Explorers' Club (see p.222) has a luggage deposit service.

Money and exchange For ATMs,try the 24hr Scotiabank ATM at the top of Av Sol (no. 104); the BCP tourist centre on Plaza de Armas has several machines at the corner of Portal de Harinas with Procuradores (daily 8am–6pm); Global Net ATMs at Portal de Panes 115 and Portal Comercio 117, both at Plaza de Armas. For banks, try Interbanc, Av Sol 380 (also has ATM at airport) – good for travellers' cheques, exchange and credit card extraction, and has an ATM; Banco de Credito, Av Sol 189 (has ATMs); Banco Continental, Av Sol 366, changes cash and most travellers' cheques. For faster service on cash and travellers' cheque exchange, try hotels or casas de cambio. There are several casas de cambio along Portal Comercio at the Plaza de Armas; Money Money Corner, Calle del Medio with the corner of Portal de Confituia; LAC Dollar, Av El Sol 150, and the Casa de Cambio, Oficina 1, Av Sol 345. Lastly, street *cambistas* can be found on blocks 2 and 3 of Av Sol, around the main banks, but take great care here.

Police The tourist police are at C Saphi 581 (☎249654) and also Monumento Pachacutec (☎211961). The tourist protection service is at Servicio de Protección al Turista, Portal Carrizos 250, Plaza de Armas (daily 8am–8pm; ☎252974, ⓔiperucusco@promperu.gob.pe).

Post office The main office, at Av Sol 800 (Mon–Sat 7.30am–8pm, Sun 7.30am–2.30pm; ☎225232), operates a quick and reliable poste restante system. For courier services, try DHL, Av Sol 608 (☎244167).

Telephones Like internet access, and often in the same places, public telephones can be found very cheaply all over the city. The right phonecard can get you cheap calls in Peru and internationally (see p.48).

Inca sites near Cusco

The megalithic fortress of **Sacsayhuaman**, which looks down onto the red-tiled roofs of Cusco from high above the city, is the closest and most impressive of several historic sites scattered around the Cusco hills. However, there are four other major Inca sites in the area. Not much more than a stone's throw beyond Sacsayhuaman lie the great *huaca* of **Qenko** and the less-visited **Salumpuncu**, thought by some to be a moon temple. A few kilometres further on, at what almost certainly formed the outer limits of the Inca's home estate, you come to the small, fortified hunting lodge of **Puca Pucara** and the stunning imperial baths of **Tambo Machay**.

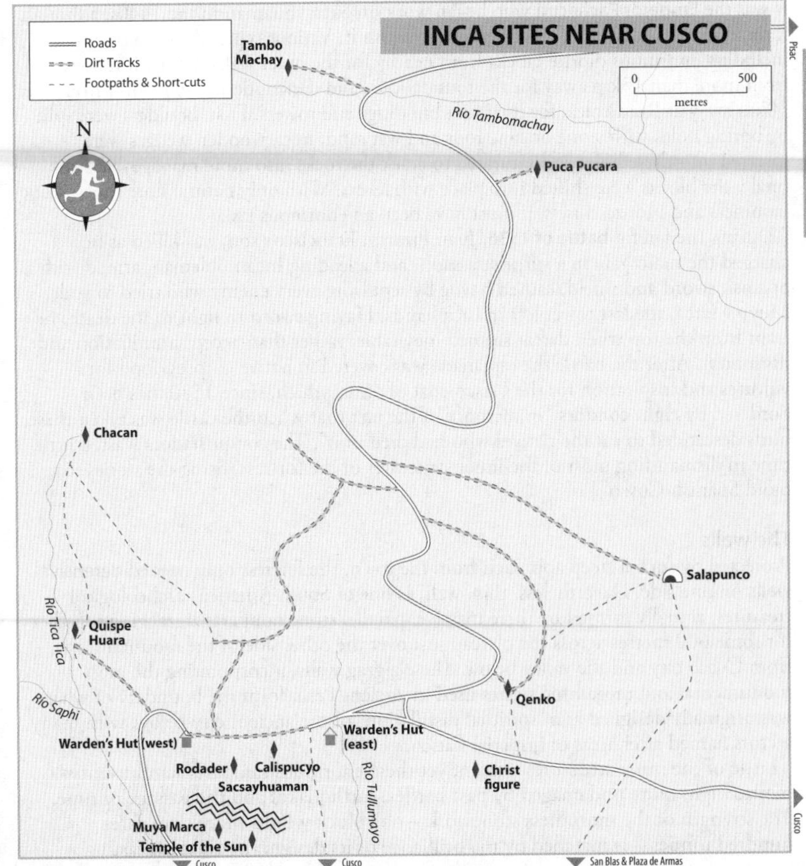

4

SACSAYHUAMAN IN NUMBERS

The chronicler Cieza de León, writing in the 1550s, estimated that some twenty thousand men had been involved in Sacsayhuaman's construction: **four thousand** cutting blocks from quarries; **six thousand** dragging them on rollers to the site; and another **ten thousand** working on finishing and fitting the blocks into position. According to legend, some **three thousand** lives were lost while dragging just one huge stone.

Sacsayhuaman

Daily 7am–5.30pm • Entry by Cusco Tourist Ticket (see p.222)

The walled complex of **SACSAYHUAMAN** forms the head of Cusco's ethereal puma, whose fierce-looking teeth point away from the city. The name Sacsayhuaman is of disputed origin, with different groups holding that it means either "satiated falcon", "speckled head" or "city of stone".

Once the site of a bloody battle between Inca leaders and the Spanish conquistadores, today the most dramatic event to take place at Sacsayhuaman is the colourful – if overly commercial – **Inti Raymi festival** in June (see box, p.219). However, throughout the year, you may stumble across various **sun ceremonies** being performed here by local mystics.

Brief history

It was the **Emperor Pachacuti** who began work on Sacsayhuaman in the 1440s, although it took nearly a century of creative work to finish it. Various types of rock were used, including enormous diorite blocks from nearby for the outer walls, Yucay limestone from more than 15km away for the foundations, and dark andesite, some of it from over 30km away at Rumicolca, for the inner buildings and towers. First, boulders were split by boring holes with stone or cane rods and wet sand; next, wooden wedges were inserted into these holes and saturated to crack the rocks into more manageable sizes, finally the blocks were shifted into place with levers. With only natural fibre ropes, stone hammers and bronze chisels, it must have been an enormous task.

During the fateful **battle of 1536**, Juan Pizarro, Francisco's son, was killed as he charged the main gate in a surprise assault, and a leading Inca nobleman, armed with a Spanish sword and shield, caused havoc by repulsing every enemy who tried to scale Muyu Marca, the last tower left in Inca hands. Having sworn to fight to the death, he leapt from the top when defeat seemed inevitable, rather than accept humiliation and dishonour. After the battle the esplanade was covered in native corpses: food for vultures and inspiration for the Cusco coat of arms, which, since 1540, has been bordered by eight **condors** "in memory of the fact that when the castle was taken these birds descended to eat the natives who had died in it". The conquistadors wasted little time in dismantling most of the inner structures of the fortress, using the stones to build Spanish Cusco.

The walls

Protected by such a steep approach from the town, the fortress only needed **defensive walls** on one side. Nevertheless, this "wall" is one of South America's archeological treasures, actually formed by three massive, parallel stone ramparts zigzagging together for some 600 metres across the plateau just over the other side of the mountaintop from Cusco city and the valley below. These zigzag walls, incorporating the most monumental and megalithic stones used in ancient Peru, form the boundary of what was originally designed as a "spiritual distillation" of the ancient city below, with many sectors named after areas of imperial Cusco.

Little of the inner structures remain, yet these enormous ramparts stand twenty metres high, quite undamaged by past battles, earthquakes and the passage of time. The strength of the mortarless stonework – one block weighs more than three hundred tonnes – is matched by the brilliance of its design: the **zigzags**, casting shadows in the afternoon sun, not only look like jagged cats' teeth, but also seem to have been cleverly designed to expose the flanks of any attacking force. Recently, however, many sacred and ritual objects excavated here have caused archeologists to consider Sacsayhuaman as more of a **ceremonial centre** than a fortress, the distinctive, jagged form of these outer walls possibly symbolizing the important deity of lightning.

The towers and temple

Originally, the inner "fort" was covered in buildings, a maze of tiny streets dominated by three major towers. The tower of **Muyu Marca**, whose foundations can still be seen clearly, was round, over 30m tall and with three concentric circles of wall, the outer one roughly 24m in diameter. An imperial residence, it apparently had lavish inner chambers and a constant supply of fresh water, carried up through subterranean channels. The other two towers – **Salla Marca** and **Paunca Marca** – had rectangular bases about 20m long and were essentially warriors' barracks, and all three were painted in vivid colours, had thatched roofs and were interconnected by underground passages: in its entirety, the inner fortress could have housed as many as ten thousand people under siege. At the rear of this sector, looking directly down into Cusco and the valley, was a **temple dedicated to the sun**, reckoned by some to be the most important shrine in the entire Inca Empire and the most sacred sector of Sacsayhuaman. Excavation of these sites continues, but it's still very difficult to make out anything but the circular tower base.

The Rodadero, Qocha Chincanas and Calispucyo

In front of the main defensive walls, a flat expanse of grassy ground – the esplanade – divides the fortress from a large outcrop of volcanic diorite. Intricately carved in places, and scarred with deep glacial striations, this rock, called the **Rodadero** ("sliding place"), was the site of an Inca throne. Originally there was a stone parapet surrounding this important *huaca*, and it's thought that the emperor would have sat here to oversee ceremonial gatherings at fiesta times, when there would have been processions, wrestling matches and running competitions. On the far side of this huge outcrop are larger recreational sliding areas, smoothed by the many centuries of Inca – and now tourists' – backsides.

From here you can see another large circular space called **Qocha Chincanas**, possibly an Inca graveyard, and on its far side the sacred spring of **Calispucyo**, where ceremonies to initiate boys into manhood were held. Excavations here have uncovered crystals and shells (some of the latter all the way from Ecuador), a sign usually associated with water veneration.

Qenko

Daily 7am–5.30pm • Entry by Cusco Tourist Ticket (see p.222)

The large limestone outcrop of **QENKO** was another important Inca *huaca*. This great stone, carved with a complex pattern of steps, seats, geometric reliefs and puma designs, illustrates the critical role of the Rock Cult in the realm of Inca cosmological beliefs (the surrounding foothills are dotted with carved rocks and elaborate stone terraces). The name of this *huaca* derives from the Quechua word *quenqo*, meaning "labyrinth" or "zigzag", and refers to the patterns laboriously carved into the upper, western edge of the stone. At an annual festival priests would pour sacrificial llama blood into a bowl at the serpent-like top of the main zigzag channel; if it flowed out through the left-hand bifurcation, this was a bad omen for the fertility of the year to come. If, on the other hand, it continued the full length of the channel and poured onto the rocks below, this was a good omen.

The stone may also be associated with solstice and equinox ceremonies, fertility rites and even marriage rituals (there's a twin seat close to the top of Qenko which looks very much like a lovers' kissing bench). Right on top of the stone two prominent round

4

nodules are carved onto a plinth. These appear to be mini versions of **intihuatanas** ("hitching posts" of the sun), found at many Inca sacred sites – local guides claim that on the **summer solstice**, at around 8am, the nodules' shadow looks like a puma's face and a condor with wings outstretched at the same time. Along with the serpent-like divinatory channels, this would complete the three main layers of the Inca cosmos: sky (condor), earth (puma) and the underworld (snake).

The tunnels and caves

Beneath Qenko are several **tunnels and caves**, replete with impressive carved niches and steps, which may have been places for spiritual contemplation and communication with the forces of life and earth. It's been suggested that some of the niches may have been where the **mummies** of lesser nobles were kept.

The amphitheatre

At the top end of the *huaca*, behind the channelled section, the Incas constructed an impressive, if relatively small, semicircular **amphitheatre** with nineteen vaulted niches (probably seats for priests or nobles) facing in towards the impressive limestone. At the heart of the amphitheatre rises a natural **standing stone**, which from some angles looks like a frog (representative of the life-giving and cleansing power of rain) and from others like a puma, both creatures of great importance to pre-Conquest Peru.

4

Salapunco and around

Daily 24hr • Free

Yet another sacred *huaca*, though off the beaten track, the large rock outcrop of **SALAPUNCO** – also known as the Temple of the Moon and locally called Laqo – contains a number of small caves where the rock has been painstakingly carved. At the time of writing an archeological dig was taking place here. You can see worn relief work with puma and snake motifs on the external rock faces, while the caves hold altar-like platforms and niches that were probably used to house mummies. The largest of the caves is thought to have been a venue for ceremonies celebrating the full moon, as it sometimes is today, when an eerie silver light filters into the usually dark interior. Close to Salapunco there's another site, **K'usilluchayoq**, which has some more rock carvings.

Chacan and Quispe Huara

Daily 24hr • Free

An important but little-visited Inca site, **CHACAN** lies about 5km from Sacsayhuaman on the opposite side of the fortress from Qenko and the road to Tambo Machay. Chacan itself was a revered spring, and you can see a fair amount of terracing, some carved rocks and a few buildings in the immediate vicinity; like Tambo Machay, it demonstrates the importance of water as an ever-changing, life-giving force in Inca religion. A pleasant but more difficult walk leads down the Tica Tica stream to **Quispe Huara** ("crystal loincloth"), where a two- to three-metre-high pyramid shape has been cut into the rock. Close by are some Inca stone walls, probably once part of a ritual bathing location.

Puca Pucara

Daily 7am–5.30pm • Entry by Cusco Tourist Ticket (see p.222)

A relatively small ruin, **PUCA PUCARA**, meaning "Red Fort", is around 11km from the city, impressively situated overlooking the Cusco Valley, right beside the main Cusco–Pisac road. A good example of how the Incas combined recreation and spirituality along with social control and military defence, Puca Pucara is well worth the trip.

Although in many ways reminiscent of a small European castle, with a commanding **esplanade** topping its semicircle of protective wall, Puca Pucara is more likely to have been a hunting lodge for the emperor than simply a defensive position. Thought to have been built by the Emperor Pachacutec, it commands views towards glaciers to the south of the Cusco Valley. Easily defended on three sides, it could have contained only a relatively small garrison and may have been a guard post between Cusco and the Sacred Valley, which lies to the northeast; it could also have had a sacred function, as it has excellent **views** towards the *apu* of Ausangate and is ideally placed to keep tabs on the flow of people and produce from the Sacred Valley to Cusco.

Tambo Machay

Daily 7am–5.30pm • Entry by Cusco Tourist Ticket (see p.222)

One of the more impressive Inca baths, **TAMBO MACHAY**, or Temple of the Waters, was evidently a place for ritual as well as physical cleansing and purification. Situated at a spring near the Incas' hunting lodge, its main construction lies in a sheltered gully where some superb Inca masonry again emphasizes their fascination with water.

The ruins basically consist of three tiered **platforms**. The top one holds four trapezoidal niches that may have been used as seats; on the next level, underground water emerges directly from a hole at the base of the stonework, and from here cascades down to the bottom platform, creating a cold shower just high enough for an Inca to stand under. On this platform the spring water splits into two channels, both pouring the last metre down to ground level. Clearly a site for **ritual bathing**, the quality of the stonework suggests that its use was restricted to the higher nobility, who perhaps used the baths only on ceremonial occasions.

About 1km further up the gully, you'll come to a small **grotto** where there's a pool large enough for bathing, even in the dry season. While it shows no sign of Inca stonework, the hills to either side of the stream are dotted with stone terraces and caves, one or two of which still have remnants of walls at their entrance. In Inca, *machay* means "cave", suggesting that these were an important local feature, perhaps as sources of water for Tambo Machay and Puca Pucara.

ARRIVAL AND DEPARTURE — INCA SITES NEAR CUSCO

ON FOOT

These sites are an energetic day's walk from Cusco, but you'll probably want to devote a whole day to Sacsayhuaman and leave the others until you're more adjusted to the rarefied air.

Sacsayhuaman Although it looks relatively close to central Cusco, it's quite a steep forty-minute, two-kilometre climb up to the ruins of Sacsayhuaman from the Plaza de Armas. The simplest route is up Calle Suecia, then right along the narrow cobbled street of Wayna Pata to Pumacurco, which heads steeply up to a small café-bar with a balcony that commands superb views over the city. It's only another ten minutes from the café, following the signposted steps all the way up to the ruins. By now you're beyond Cusco's built-up areas and walking in countryside, and there's a well-worn path and a crude stairway that takes you right up to the heart of the fortress.

Quenko An easy twenty-minute walk from Sacsayhuaman. Head towards the Cusco–Pisac road along a track from the warden's hut on the northeastern edge of Sacsayhuaman, and Qenko is just over the other side of the main road; the route is straightforward but poorly signposted.

Salapunco Walk for 20min uphill and through the trees above Qenko, to the right of the small hill, along the path (keeping the houses to your right), then come out onto the fields and turn right. It's also possible to walk down to the Plaza de Armas from nearby K'usilluchayoq via interconnecting trails that initially go through some new barrios above the main Cusco–Pisac road, then down to San Blas.

Chacan Chacan can be safely, though not easily, reached in the dry season (May–Sept) by following the rather indistinct footpaths directly north from the Rodadero at Sacsayhuaman. When you hit the gully coming from the west, follow this up to the site; if you've been walking for ninety minutes or more and haven't found it, the chances are you've already passed it.

Quispe Huara A difficult walk leads from Chacan down the Tica Tica stream (keep to the right-hand side of the stream and stay well above it) to Quispe Huara. You really need a local map to find your way with any certainty.

Puca Pucara Between one and two hours' cross-country walk, uphill from Sacsayhuaman and Qenko (longer if you keep to the sinuous main road).

Tambo Machay Walk for less than 15min along a signposted track that leads off the main road just north of Puca Pucara.

BY BUS

If you'd rather start from the top and work your way downhill, it's possible to take one of the regular buses from Cusco to Pisac and Urubamba. Empresa Clorinda buses leave from C Puputi 208, one block below Recoleta and two blocks up from Avenida de la Cultura at the junction with Ejercicios, just beyond the Estadio Universitario. Other regular buses depart from Tullumayo 207. Ask to be dropped off at the highest of the sites, Tambo Machay, from where it's a relatively easy two-hour walk back into the centre of Cusco, or at Qenko, which is closer to Sacsayhuaman and the city.

BY TRANVÍA

A wooden bus which resembles a tram car – Tranvía de Cusco (Mon–Sat 8.30am, 10am, 11.30am, 2pm, 3.30pm, 5pm & 6.30pm; S/20, students with ISIC card S/10; ⓣ612388) – takes a scenic ride from the Plaza de Armas up through the historic centre to Sacsayhuaman and back most days (a good option to avoid the tiring experience of walking up there before you've really acclimatized to the altitude), visiting as many as forty other places in Cusco on route. It's usually found parked outside the *Hostal Familiar* on Calle Saphi, but generally leaves from the Plaza de Armas.

BY HORSEBACK TOUR

You could also take a horseback tour (around S/40–50 for a couple of hours), incorporating most of these sites. Tours usually start and finish at Sacsayhuaman or Qenko ($3–5 taxi ride from the centre of Cusco).

The Sacred Valley

The **SACRED VALLEY**, or Vilcamayo to the Incas, about 30km northwest of Cusco, traces its winding, astonishingly beautiful course from here down towards Urubamba, Ollantaytambo and eventually **Machu Picchu** (see p.257): the most famous ruin in South America and a place that – no matter how jaded you are or how commercial it seems – is never anything short of awe-inspiring. The steep-sided river valley opens out into a narrow but very fertile alluvial plain, which was well exploited agriculturally by the Incas. Even within 30km or so of the valley, there are several microclimates allowing specializations in different fruits, maizes and local plants. The **river** itself starts in the high Andes south of Cusco and is called the Vilcanota river until it reaches the Sacred Valley; from here on downriver it's known as the Río Urubamba, a magnificent and energetic torrent which flows on right down into the jungle to merge with other major headwaters of the Amazon.

Standing guard over the two extremes of the Sacred Valley, the ancient **Inca citadels** of Pisac and Ollantaytambo perch high above the stunning Río Vilcanota–Urubamba and are among the most evocative ruins in Peru. **Pisac** itself is a small, pretty town with one of Peru's best artesanía markets, just 30km northeast of Cusco, close to the end of the Río Vilcanota's wild run from Urcos. Further downstream are the ancient villages of **Calca**, **Yucay** and **Urubamba**, the last of which has the most visitors' facilities and a

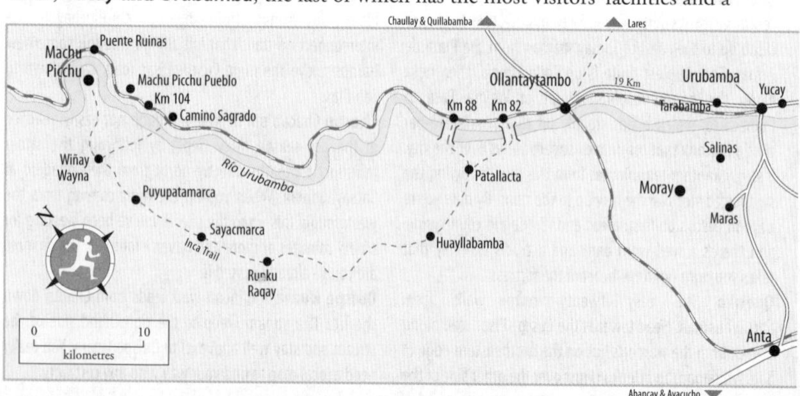

GETTING TO AND AROUND THE SACRED VALLEY

The Sacred Valley and Machu Picchu need to be approached differently, though it is quite possible, even logical, to start in one and then move on to the other. There are three main **transport hubs** in the Sacred Valley – **Pisac, Urubamba and Ollantaytambo** – all best reached by colectivo minibuses or taxis from Cusco. Travelling up and down the valley between them is simple enough, by picking up a colectivo, taxi or local bus, which follow the one main road that hugs the valley floor, keeping fairly close to the Río Urubamba. **Machu Picchu** (see p.257) is further down the valley and is almost exclusively accessible on foot – typically the Inca Trail hike – or by rail.

developing reputation as a spiritual and meditation centre, yet somehow still retains its traditional Andean charm.

At the far northern end of the Sacred Valley, even the magnificent ancient town of **Ollantaytambo** is overwhelmed by the astounding temple-fortress clinging to the sheer cliffs beside it. The town is a very pleasant place to spend some time, with good restaurants and a convenient location in the heart of great trekking country. It makes an ideal base from which to take a tent and trek above one of the Urubamba's minor tributaries, or else tackle one of the **Salcantay** trails.

Beyond Ollantaytambo the route becomes too tortuous for any road to follow. Here, the valley closes in around the rail tracks, and the Río Urubamba begins to race and twist below **Machu Picchu** itself (see p.257).

4

Awana Kancha

Awana Kancha, Corao • Daily 9am–5.30pm • ☎ 9740797

About 23km from Cusco and 7km before you reach Pisac, where the road starts steeply down into the Sacred Valley, **Awana Kancha** offers a rare opportunity to see alpacas and llamas close at hand, as well as traditional weaving in practice. Quality alpaca and wool products are for sale too.

Pisac

A vital Inca road once snaked its way up the canyon that enters the Sacred Valley at **PISAC**, and the ruined **citadel**, which sits at the entrance to the gorge, controlled a strategic route connecting the Inca Empire with Paucartambo, on the borders of the eastern jungle. Less than an hour from Cusco by bus, the town is now most commonly visited – apart from a look at the citadel – for its morning **market**, which takes place three times a week.

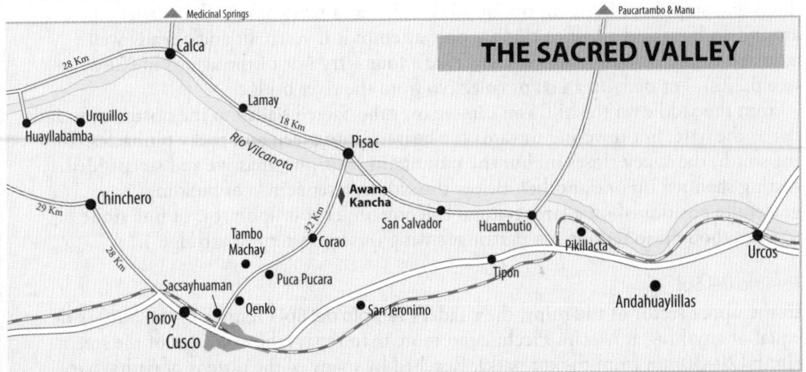

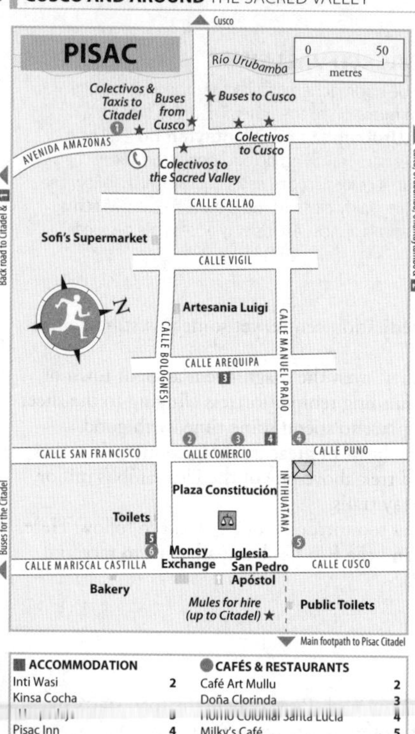

ACCOMMODATION		CAFÉS & RESTAURANTS	
Inti Wasi	2	Café Art Mullu	2
Kinsa Cocha		Doña Clorinda	3
[illegible]	[illegible]	Horno Colonial Santa Lucia	4
Pisac Inn	4	Milky's Café	5
Royal Inca	1	Restaurant Pisac	1
Samana Wasi	5	Restaurant Samana Wasi	6

In addition, the main local **fiesta** – Virgen del Carmen (July 16–18) – is a good alternative to the simultaneous but more remote Paucartambo festival of the same name (see box, p.272), with processions, music, dance groups, the usual firecracker celebrations, and food stalls around the plaza.

Plaza Constitución

Apart from the road and river bridge, the hub of Pisca activity is around **Plaza Constitución**, where you'll find most of the restaurants and the few hotels that exist, as well as the popular market and the town's quaint church.

Iglesia San Pedro Apóstol

Plaza Constitución

Commerce bustles around the **Iglesia San Pedro Apóstol**, an unusually narrow concrete church located in Pisac's central market plaza, which is dominated by an ancient and massive *pisonay* tree.

Pisac market

Plaza Constitución • Tues, Thurs & Sun 8am–3pm

The thriving **market** is held in the town's main square, where you can buy hand-painted ceramic beads and pick up the occasional bargain. Even if the market's not on, there are still a number of excellent artesanía shops, particularly along **Calle Bolognesi** (try Walter's or Luigi), which connects the Sacred Valley road and river bridge with the plaza.

Pisac's citadel

Daily 7am–5.30pm • Entry by Cusco Tourist Ticket (see box, p.222)

Set high above a valley floor patchworked by patterned fields and rimmed by centuries of terracing amid giant landslides, the **citadel** displays magnificent stonework – water ducts and steps have been cut out of solid rock – and **panoramas**. The citadel takes around an hour and a half to **climb** – only attempt it if you're fit and already well adjusted to the altitude. Alternatively, take a **tour** – try one of the agents in Cusco (see p.222) – or pick up a taxi or colectivo from the river bridge.

From the saddle on the hill, you can see over the Sacred Valley to the north: wide and flat at the base, but towering towards the heavens into green and rocky pinnacles. To the south, the valley closes in, but the mountains continue, massive and steep-sided, casting shadows on one another. Below the saddle, a semicircle of buildings is gracefully positioned on a large natural balcony under row upon row of fine stone terraces thought to represent a partridge's wing (*pisac* meaning "partridge").

Templo del Sol

In the upper sector of the ruins, the citadel's **Templo del Sol** (Temple of the Sun) is the equal of anything at Machu Picchu, and more than repays the exertions of the steep climb (20–30min from the car park). Reached by many of the dozens of paths that crisscross their way up through the citadel, it's poised in a flattish saddle on a great spur protruding north–south into the Sacred Valley. The temple was built around an outcrop of volcanic rock, its peak carved into a **"hitching post"** for the sun. The hitching post alone is intriguing: the angles of its base suggest that it may have been used for keeping track of important stars, or for calculating the changing seasons with the accuracy so critical to the smooth running of the Inca Empire. Above the temple lie still more ruins, largely unexcavated, and among the higher crevices and rocky overhangs several ancient burial sites are hidden.

ARRIVAL AND GETTING AROUND — PISAC

By colectivo Colectivo minibuses leave from both Puputi 208 and Tullumayo 207 in Cusco most mornings, less frequently in the afternoons, costing S/3.5–4. For the town, the hopping-off point is the small river bridge; from here to the Plaza Constitución it's just a few short blocks. If you're going to the citadel, take a taxi or colectivo from near the river bridge up to the site car park, just below the main ruins. Leaving Pisac for Cusco or going on down the valley to Calca and Urubamba, if you haven't got a taxi or tour bus organized, wait on the main road by the river bridge and pick up a colectivo, bus or taxi as they pass.

On foot If you want to walk up to the citadel from the village (2hr or more), start on the path that leads off, uphill from Plaza Constitución, along the left flank of Iglesia San Pedro Apósto.

By taxi Taxis cost S/45–60 one-way from Cusco. In Pisac, taxis wait on Av Amazonas, near the river bridge.

By tour Many people arrive in Pisac with an organized tour from Cusco (see p.222).

ACCOMMODATION

The only time when accommodation in Pisac may be hard to find is in **September**, when the village fills up with pilgrims heading to the nearby sanctuary of Huanca, home of a small shrine which is very sacred to local inhabitants. In Pisac itself there's a surprising selection of places to stay. Alternatively, you can usually **rent rooms** at low prices from villagers – ask for details at the *Restaurant Samana Wasi* (see below) – or there is a **campsite** (ask at the *Kinsa Cocha Hospedaje* for details).

Inti Wasi Located about 2.5km down the valley from Pisac on the main road towards Urubamba ⊕203047. Bungalow-style accommodation with an on-site restaurant and swimming pool. **S/150**

Kinsa Cocha Hospedaje Plaza Constitución and C Bolognesi ⊕203101. Small, rustic rooms in a house attached to a restaurant on the main square; although the actual accommodation entrance is a block back on Calle Arequipa, reception is via the restaurant. **S/55**

Pisac Inn Plaza Constitución 333, reservations Casilla Postal 1179, Cusco ⊕203062, ⓦpisacinn.com. Very pleasant hotel with lavishly decorated bedrooms (with or without private bath) and a rock-heated sauna, plus good breakfasts and lunches, including vegetarian options (the fabulous restaurant – *Cuchara de Palo* – is open to non-residents). They also change money, rent out mountain bikes and can book tours to nearby ruins. **S/150**

Royal Inca 2km out of the village ⊕203064, ⓦbooking.com. The most luxurious place to stay in Pisac, with a pool and all modern conveniences, though it's on the long road out of the village that winds up towards the ruins. **S/200**

Samana Wasi Plaza Constitución 509 ⊕203133. This place is better known as a restaurant, but its rooms are simple and clean, all with shared bathrooms arrayed around the upstairs balcony of a very pleasant courtyard (also part of the restaurant). **S/50**

EATING

There are a few decent **restaurants** in Pisac, but they can all get busy on market days, and a traditional **bakery** with an adobe oven on a corner of the plaza. **Sofi's Supermarket**, which stocks most of the usual basics, is halfway up Bolognesi, between Av Amazonas by the river bridge and the main plaza. Addresses aren't displayed on buildings, but the following places are all clustered together and relatively easy to find.

Café Art Mullu Plaza Constitución, by the corner with C Bolognesi. This is a fun little place offering meals, snacks – including particularly fine pizzas – and drinks. Daily 8am–6pm.

Doña Clorinda C Bolognesi 592, on the corner of Plaza Constitución. This shop sells great cakes and is good for cheap lunches, mostly traditional Peruvian dishes. In good weather, you can relax at one of the tables outside. Daily 7am–6pm.

Horno Colonial Santa Lucía On the corners of Plaza

Constitución, C Puno and C Manuel Prado. A bakery with arched adobe ovens which also serves good meals of *roccoto relleno* and *cuy* (roast guinea pig) dishes. Daily 8am–7pm.

Milkys' Café C Manuel Prado and Plaza Constitución. A lovely café serving good coffee, amazing cakes and a range of snacks, pizzas and vegetarian meals in a large cultural-café space with books, magazines and games. Daily 8am–6pm.

Restaurant Pisac Av Amazonas 147. A dingy yet friendly place down on the main road by the taxis, which serves generous portions of basic Peruvian fare. Daily 7am–8pm.

Restaurant Samana Wasi Plaza Constitución 509 ⓣ203018. This restaurant has a pleasant little courtyard out the back and very tasty trout, salad and fried potatoes. They also have decent coffee and a postbox. Daily 8am–8pm.

DIRECTORY

Money and exchange To change dollars, try the jeweller's shop on the corner of the plaza close to *Restaurant Samana Wasi*. There's an ATM outside *Milky's Café*.

Post office On the corner of the plaza where Intihuatana meets Calle Comercio. There's also a postbox in the courtyard of *Restaurant Samana Wasi*.

Lamay and Calca

Take any colectivo (S/1), minibus (S/1) or bus (S/0.50) heading down the valley from the town side of the Pisac river bridge

Known for its medicinal springs, the first significant village between Pisac and Urubamba is **Lamay**, just 3km away. High above this village, on the other side of the Río Vilcanota and just out of sight, are the beautiful Inca terraces of Huchiq'osqo. A little further down the road you come to the larger village of **Calca**. Moving down the valley from here the climate improves and you see pears, peaches and cherries growing in abundance. In July and August vast piles of maize sit beside the road waiting to be used as cattle feed.

4

Machacanca

Combi colectivos (15min; S/1) run quite frequently from Calca, particularly on Sun

The popular **thermal baths** of **Machacanca** are within an hour and a half's walk of Calca, signposted from the town. Situated under the hanging glaciers of Mount Sahuasiray, this place was favoured by the Incas for the fertility of its soil, and you can still see plenty of maize cultivation here.

Yucay

The next major settlement before you get to Urubamba, **Yucay** had its moment in Peruvian history when, under the Incas, Huayna Capac, father of Huascar and Atahualpa, had his palace here. You can admire the ruined but finely dressed stone walls of another **Inca palace** (probably the country home of Sayri Tupac, though also associated with an Inca princess) on the Plaza Manco II.

INCA FIESTAS

Around the end of September and start of October every year local **fiestas** and celebrations take place around Lamay and Calca, which date back at least to early Inca times. The main local ritual theme for the festival is **water**, and there are strong links to a mythic experience high in the hills and tied to the moving shadows of **Mount Pitusiray**: every year around the beginning of October, the mountain casts shadows over neighbouring peaks and cliffs. Over several days the shadow of Pitusiray, considered to be a solar clock, moves in a dynamic and very clear representation of a prostrate Inca being leapt upon and transformed by a black puma or jaguar; it has to be seen to be believed. With this visual effect on the landscape in mind, a festival is now held on the first Sunday in October and based at the **Inca ruins of Urco**, also dedicated to water, which are located a 2km walk above the village of Calca. For information on the festival ask at the Cusco tourist information offices (see p.222).

FROM TOP DOLLS, PISAC MARKET (P.240); TREKKING IN THE CUSCO REGION (P.224) >

ARRIVAL AND GETTING AROUND — YUCAY

By colectivo or bus Take any colectivo (S/1.50), minibus (S/1.50) or bus (S/1) heading down the valley from the town side of the Pisac river bridge.

By bike There's bike rental at *Casa Luna* (see below).

ACCOMMODATION AND EATING

Casa Luna Plaza Manco II 107, right next to the *Libertador*. Offers great pizzas, sandwiches and drinks in a relaxing environment with internet and fax services, bike rental, 4WD tours, and also house and bungalow accommodation (rooms from around S/70). Daily 10am–9pm.

Hostal Yíllary Plaza Manco II 107 Ⓣ226607 or Ⓣ201112. Very friendly, comfortable and excellent value, with a well-tended garden and large rooms with private bath in an attractive old building. **S/120**

Posada del Libertador Plaza Manco II 104 Ⓣ201115, Ⓕ201116. Another fine colonial mansion noted for accommodating Simón Bolívar when he was in the region, this is a lovely boutique-style hotel with great bar and restaurant. **S/300**

Sonesta Posada del Inca Plaza Manco II 134 Ⓣ201107 or Ⓣ01 4219667, Ⓦsonesta.com. Based in a beautifully converted eighteenth-century monastery that houses a small museum (open to non-residents) of fine precious metal objects and ceramics. Rooms are in mostly two-storey buildings accessed by wooden stairways and verandas from lovely, well-kept gardens. **S/400**

Urubamba

About 80km from Cusco via Pisac or around 60km via Chinchero, **URUBAMBA** is only a short way down the main road from Yucay's Plaza Manco II, and it is here that the Río Vilcanota becomes the Río Urubamba (though many people still refer to this stretch as the Vilcanota). Although it has little in the way of obvious historic interest, the town has good **facilities** and is situated in the shadow of the beautiful Chicon and Pumahuanca glaciers. At weekends there's a large **market** on Jirón Palacio, while at the large **ceramic workshops** set around a lovely garden at Av Berriozabal 111 (Ⓣ201002), new and ancient techniques are used to produce colourful, Amerindian-inspired items for sale.

Plaza de Armas

The laid back and attractive **Plaza de Armas** has palm trees and pines surrounded by interesting topiary. At the heart of the plaza is a small fountain topped by a maize plant sculpture, but everything stands in deference to the red sandstone **Iglesia San Pedro**, with its stacked columns below two small belfries. The church's cool interior has a vast, three-tier gold-leaf altar, and at midday light streams through the glass-topped cupola.

ARRIVAL AND INFORMATION — URUBAMBA

By bus Regular buses from Av Grau 525 in Cusco run to Urubamba (S/4–5) daily every 15min, usually from about 5am until early afternoon. Buses also connect Urubamba with Pisac, Calca and Ollantaytambo. Buses for Ollantaytambo, Cusco and Chinchero leave at least once an hour from Terminal Terrestre, on the main road more or less opposite the *Hotel Tambo del Inka*. Other buses leave from the other side of the road, outside *Hotel Tambo del Inka*.

By train Perurail trains – Autowagon or Railcar – depart to Machu Picchu from the *Tambo del Inka* hotel in Urubamba several times a week, taking roughly 2hr 30min each way (S/180–260 return).

By colectivo Near the Puente Grau, on the 5th block of Av Grau in Cusco, you find car or minibus colectivos to Urubamba (1hr–1hr 30min; S/6–8), from around 6am until mid-afternoon.

By taxi Taxis from Cusco to Urubamba charge around S/60.

Tourist information The *Neuvo Mundo Café* (see opposite) sometimes has some local tourist information.

ACCOMMODATION

Camping Los Cedros On the Pumahuanca road, a few blocks beyond Iglesia Torrechayoc, a medium-sized church on the northern edge of town. Signposted just as the road leaves the built-up area of Urubamba, this is a pleasant rustic campsite. Tents **S/10**

Los Girasoles On the Pumahuanca road. Offers camping and accommodation in private bungalows with shower facilities. Camping **S/8**, bungalows **S/80**

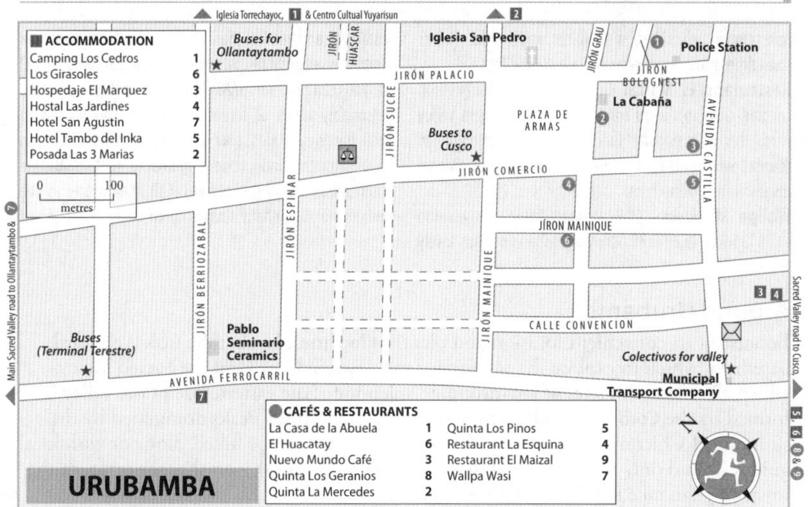

Hospedaje El Marquez C Convención 429 ⓣ201304. A clean, family-run hostel, with a small garden and a couple of rooms with private bath. S/60

Hostal Las Jardines Jr Convención 459 ⓣ201331. *Las Jardines* offers better rooms than most of the other budget places in Urubamba, offering more space and light, and also comprises an appealing garden. S/60

Hotel San Agustin Km 69, Panamerican Highway ⓣ231232, ⓦhotelessanagustin.com.pe. Some twenty minutes' walk down the main road towards Cusco, just beyond the bridge over the Río Urubamba, *Hotel San Agustin* is a plush place to stay, boasting a small pool, spa and a popular restaurant (delicious buffet lunches served Tues, Thurs & Sun). S/248

Hotel Tambo del Inka Av Ferrocarril ⓣ201071 or ⓣ201126, ⓦhotelsone.com. A large resort hotel with over 100 rooms, mainly well-appointed bungalows, and a conference centre with internet access, a pool and tennis courts. S/900

Posada Las 3 Marias Jr Zavala 307 ⓣ201006, Cusco ⓣ225252. A friendly, family-run place offering very clean and intimate accommodation, with a capacity for up to sixteen people over several rooms. S/140

4

EATING

Urubamba isn't home to particularly fine cuisine but it does offer a wide variety of cafés, bars and *quinta* catering (traditional Andean-Peruvian restaurant, usually with tables in a garden, fast service and a limited menu).

La Casa de la Abuela Jr Bolognesi 272 ⓣ622975, to the left of the church and one block up on the left. A very friendly restaurant with a beautiful courtyard full of flowers and trees, and serving excellent pizzas and very good lasagna. Daily 11am–7pm.

★ **El Huacatay** Jr Arica 620 ⓣ201790, ⓦelhuacatay.com. The best of Urubamba's top restaurants by a long way, this place serves up Andean cuisine in a very appealing environment. Best for lunch; reserve in advance if you can. Daily 11am–9pm.

Nuevo Mundo Café Av Castilla and Jr Comercio (four blocks up from the Texaco petrol station). Wholesome vegetarian meals are served all day on the patio here. They also operate a book exchange and stock trekking food. Daily 8am–10pm.

Quinta Los Geranios A ten-minute walk along the main Sacred Valley road towards Cusco, on Avenida Conchatupa. A nicer spot and better food than *El Maizal* (see p.246), *Los Geranios* serves excellent dishes such as *rocoto relleno* (stuffed *rocoto*, a pepper-like vegetable), *chupe de quinoa* (quinoa stew) and *asado a la olla* (pot roast), in a splendid, but usually busy, garden environment. Daily noon–7pm.

Quinta La Mercedes Comercio 445, Plaza de Armas. A rustic place with cheap set menus at lunch. Daily noon–6pm.

Quinta Los Pinos Av Castilla 812. Serving excellent food and specializing in local dishes in an atmospheric little courtyard. Daily noon–7pm.

Restaurant La Esquina Plaza de Armas at the corner of Jr Comercio and Jr Grau. A great meeting place for travellers, serving alpaca steaks, *ponche de leche* (a hot milk punch), pancakes, pies, juices and drinks. There's sometimes music at weekends. Daily 8am–7pm.

Restaurant El Maizal Urb La Cantuta ⓣ201054. Located close to *Quinta Los Geranios* on the main valley road, this is a popular lunchtime spot with Peruvian tourists, who come for the interesting menu of traditional dishes. Daily noon–7pm.

Wallpa Wasi Km 74.2 Urubamba–Ollantaytambo ⓣ201356 or ⓣ201379, ⓦwallpawasi.com. This lovely restaurant and bar, less than 10min by taxi from Urubamba centre, serves great piscos, wine, and as much chicken meal as you can eat for S/28. The food is first-class and reasonably priced, all served in a friendly country setting with gardens, a kids' play area and parking. They also have attractive independent rooms to rent, B&B-style (from around S/80 per person). Call in advance, as the owners are occasionally away in Cusco. Daily 11am–7pm.

Around Urubamba

Because of its convenient location and plentiful facilities, Urubamba makes an ideal base from which to explore the mountains and lower hills around the Sacred Valley, which are filled with sites of jaw-dropping splendour. The eastern side of the valley is formed by the **Cordillera Urubamba**, a range of snowcapped peaks dominated by the summits of Chicon and Veronica. Many of the ravines can be hiked, alone or with local guides (found only through the main hotels and hospedajes) – on the trek up from the town you can take in stupendous views of Chicon.

Moray

Daily 7am–5.30pm • Entry by Cusco Tourist Ticket (see box, p.222) • 2- to 3-hr walk from Urubamba

A stunning Inca site, part agricultural centre and part ceremonial, **Moray** lies about 6km north of Maras village on the Chinchero side of the river, within a two- to three-hour walk from Urubamba. The ruins are deep, bowl-like depressions in the earth, the largest comprising seven concentric circular stone terraces, facing inward and diminishing in radius like a multi-layered roulette wheel.

Salinas

4km walk from Moray

The **salt pans** of **Salinas**, still in use after more than four hundred years, are situated 4km on from the village of Maras, and a similar distance from Moray. Cross the river by the footbridge in the village, turn right, then after a little over 100m downstream along the riverbank, turn left past the cemetery and up the canyon along the salty creek. After this you cross the stream and follow the path cut into the cliffside to reach the salt pans, which are soon visible if still a considerable uphill hike away. The trail offers spectacular views of the valley and mountains, while the Inca salt pans themselves are set gracefully against an imposing mountain backdrop. A **scenic trail** (about an hour's walk) leads down through the salt pans and on to the Urubamba river below, where there's a footbridge across to the village of Tarabamba, which is on the road for Urubamba (6km) or Ollantaytambo; colectivos pass every twenty minutes or so in both directions.

Chinchero

CHINCHERO ("Village of the Rainbow"), an old colonial settlement with a great market, lies 3762m above sea level, 28km (40min) northwest of Cusco and off the main road, overlooking the Sacred Valley, with the Vilcabamba range and the snowcapped peak of Salcantay dominating the horizon to the west. The bus ride here takes you up to the Pampa de Anta, once a huge lake but now relatively dry pasture, surrounded by snowcapped *nevadas*. The town itself is a small, rustic place, where the local women, who crowd the main plaza during the market, still wear traditional dress. Largely built of stone and adobe, the town blends perfectly with the magnificent display of Inca architecture, ruins and megalithic carved rocks, relics of the Inca veneration of nature deities. The best time to visit is on September 8 for the lively traditional **fiesta**. Failing that, the Sunday-morning **market** in the lower part of town, reached along Calle Manco II, is smaller and less touristy than Pisac's but has attractive local craftwork for sale.

Plaza Principal

Uphill from the market, along the cobbled steps and streets, you'll find a vast **plaza**, which may have been the original Inca marketplace. It's bounded on one side by an impressive wall reminiscent of Sacsayhuaman's ramparts, though not as massive – it too was constructed on three levels, and ten classical Inca trapezoidal niches can be seen along its surface. On the western perimeter of the plaza, the raised Inca stonework is dominated by a carved **stone throne**, near which are puma and monkey formations.

Iglesia de Chinchero

Daily 7am–5.30pm • Entry by Cusco Tourist Ticket, available here or in Cusco (see box, p.222)

The plaza is also home to a superb colonial adobe **iglesia**. Dating from the early seventeenth century, it was built on top of an Inca temple or palace, perhaps belonging to the Inca emperor **Tupac Yupanqui**, who particularly favoured Chinchero as an out-of-town resort – most of the area's aqueducts and terraces, many of which are still in use today, were built at his command. The church itself boasts frescoes and **paintings**, which, though decaying, are still very beautiful and evocative of the town's colonial past. Many pertain to the **Cusqueña school** and celebrated local artist Mateo Cuihuanito, the most interesting depicting the forces led by local chief Pumacahua against the rebel Tupac Amaru II in the late eighteenth century (see box, p.444).

4

ARRIVAL AND DEPARTURE — CHINCHERO

By bus Buses leave Cusco from Av Grau 525 (T 805639) for Urubamba via Chinchero (S/2–3) daily every 15min, usually from about 5am until early afternoon. You'll need to keep an eye out for the town or ask the driver to let you know when to get off because the road only passes the outskirts of Chinchero (with a 250m walk into the village).

By colectivo Near the Puente Grau, on the 5th block of Av Grau in Cusco, you'll find car or minibus colectivos to Chinchero (45min; S/4–5), from around 6am until mid-afternoon.

By taxi Taxis from Cusco to Chinchero charge around S/50.

ACCOMMODATION AND EATING

It's possible to **camp** below the terraces in the open fields beyond the village, but, as always, it's best to ask someone local for permission or advice on this.

Camucha Av Mateo Pumacahua 168. At the junction of Calle Manco Capac II and the main road to Cusco, this is one of the few eating places in Chinchero and has a particularly good set lunch.

La Casa de Barro Lodge Calle Miraflores 147 T 84 306031, W lacasadebarro.com. This is the most comfortable and interesting accommodation in town with lovely airy rooms, room service and tourist information; there's also a small bar and restaurant area. S/168

Ollantaytambo and around

OLLANTAYTAMBO has one of the most Inca-looking of the Sacred Valley's settlements. Coming down the valley from Urubamba the river runs smoothly between a series of impressive Inca terraces that gradually diminish in size. Just before the town, the railway tracks reappear and the road climbs a small hill to an ancient **plaza**. The useful **Ollantaytambo Heritage Trail** guides you to most of the important sites with a series of blue plaques around town.

As one of the region's hotspots, and a popular overnight stop en route to Machu Picchu (see p.257), Ollantaytambo can get very busy in high season, making it hard to escape the scores of other travellers. At heart, though, it's a small but still very traditional settlement, worth enjoying over a few days, particularly during its highly colourful **fiestas** (see box opposite), when local folk-dancing takes place in the main plaza. Many women still wear traditional clothing, and it's common to see them gather in the plaza with their intricately woven *manta* shawls, black-and-red skirts with colourful zigzag patterns, and inverted red and black hats.

Beyond Ollantaytambo, the Sacred Valley becomes a subtropical, raging river course, surrounded by towering mountains and dominated by the snowcapped peak of Salcantay; the town is a popular base for **rafting** trips (see box, p.251).

Brief history

The valley here was occupied by a number of pre-Inca cultures, notably the Chanapata (800–300 BC), the Qotacalla (500–900 AD) and the Killki (900–1420 AD), after which the Incas dominated only until the 1530s, when the Spanish arrived.

The legend of Ollantay

Legend has it that **Ollantay** was a rebel Inca general who took arms against Pachacutec over the affections of the Lord Inca's daughter, the Nusta Cusi Collyu. However, historical evidence shows that a fourteen-kilometre canal, that still feeds the town today, was built to bring water here from the Laguna de Yanacocha, which was probably Pachacutec's private estate. The later Inca Huayna Capac is thought to have been responsible for the trapezoidal Plaza Maynyaraqui and the largely unfinished but impressive and megalithic temples.

4

OLLANTAYTAMBO'S FIESTAS

Ollantaytambo's vibrant **fiestas** are a sight to behold, particularly the Festival of the Cross, Corpus Christi and Ollantaytambo Raymi (generally on the Sunday after Cusco's Inti Raymi), and at Christmas, when locals wear flowers and decorative grasses in their hats. On the **Fiesta de Reyes**, around January 6, there's a solemn procession around town of the three *Niños Reyes* (Child Kings), sacred effigies, one of which is brought down from the sacred site of Marcaquocha, about 10km away in the Patacancha Valley, the day before.

A strategic location

Ollantaytambo was built as an Inca **administrative centre** rather than a town and is laid out in the form of a maize corn cob: it's one of the few surviving examples of an **Inca grid system**, with a plan that can be seen from vantage points high above it, especially from the hill opposite the fortress. An incredibly fertile sector of the Urubamba Valley, at 2800m above sea level and with comfortable temperatures of 11–23°C (52–73°F), good alluvial soils and water resources, this area was also the gateway to the **Antisuyo** (the Amazon corner of the Inca Empire) and a centre for tribute-gathering from the surrounding valleys.

As strategic protection for the entrance to the lower Urubamba Valley and an alternative gateway into the Amazon via the Pantiacolla Pass, this was the only Inca stronghold to have successfully resisted persistent Spanish attacks.

Rebel Inca Manco

4

After the unsuccessful siege of Cusco in 1536–37 (see p.208), the rebel Inca **Manco** and his die-hard force withdrew here, with **Hernando Pizarro** (Francisco's brother), some seventy horsemen, thirty foot-soldiers and a large contingent of native forces in hot pursuit. As they approached, they found that not only had the Incas diverted the Río Patacancha, making the valley below the fortress impassable, but they had also joined forces with neighbouring jungle tribes forming a massive army. After several desperate attempts to storm the stronghold, Pizarro and his men uncharacteristically slunk away under cover of darkness, leaving much of their equipment behind. However, the Spanish came back with reinforcements, and in 1537 Manco retreated further down the valley to Vitcos and Vilcabamba. In 1540, Ollantaytambo was entrusted to **Hernando Pizarro**, brother of the conquistador leader.

The Plaza de Armas

The **Plaza de Armas** is the centre of civic life. Backstreets radiating from here are littered with stone water channels, which still come in very handy during the rainy season, carrying the gushing streams tidily away from the town and down to the Urubamba river.

CATCCO Museo

El Parador, Casa del Horno, C Vetidero • Tues–Sun 10am–1pm & 2–4pm • S/5 • ☎ 204024 or ☎ 223637

Close to the central plaza is the **CATCCO Museo**, which contains interpretative exhibits in Spanish and English about local history, culture, archeology and natural history. It also has a **ceramic workshop** where you can buy attractive pottery.

Plaza Mañya Raquy

Downhill from the plaza, just across the Río Patacancha, is the old Inca **Plaza Mañya Raquy**, dominated by the fortress. There are market stalls in the plaza plus a few artesanía shops and cafés nearby, mainly opposite the attractive small church, the **Templo de Santiago Apóstol**. Built in 1620, it has an almost Inca-style stone belfry containing two great bells supported on an ancient timber. The church's front entrance is surrounded by a simple yet appealing *mestizo* floral relief painted in red and cream.

The fortress

Daily 7am–5.30pm • Entry with Cusco Tourist Ticket (see box, p.222)

Climbing up through the **fortress**, the solid stone terraces and the natural contours of the cliff remain frighteningly impressive. Above them, huge red granite blocks mark the unfinished sun temple near the top, where, according to legend, the internal organs of mummified Incas were buried. A dangerous path leads from this upper level around the cliff towards a large sector of agricultural terracing which follows the Río Patacancha uphill. From up above you can see down to the large Inca plaza and the impressive stone aqueducts which carried the water supply. Between here and the river you see the **Andenes de Mollequasa terraces** which, when viewed from the other side of the Urubamba Valley (a 20min walk up the track from the train station), look like a pyramid.

Around Ollantaytambo

High up over the other side of the Río Patacancha, behind Ollantaytambo, are rows of **ruined buildings** originally thought to have been prisons but now considered likely to have been granaries. In front of these, it's quite easy to make out a gigantic, rather grumpy-looking **profile of a face** carved out of the rock, possibly an Inca sculpture of Wiraccochan, the mythical messenger from **Viraccocha**, the major creator-god of Peru (see p.506). According to sixteenth- and seventeeth-century histories, such an image was indeed once carved, representing him as a man of great authority; this particular image's frown certainly implies presence, and this part of the mountain was also known as Wiraccochan Orcco ("peak of Viraccocha's messenger"). From here, looking back towards the main Ollantaytambo fortress, it's possible to see the mountain, rocks and terracing forming the **image of a mother llama** with a young llama, apparently representing the myth of Catachillay, which relates to the water cycle and the Milky Way. *The Sacred Valley of the Incas – Myths and Symbols* (available in most Cusco bookshops), written by archeologists Fernando and Edgar Salazar, is a useful companion for interpreting the sites in this part of the valley.

ARRIVAL AND DEPARTURE — OLLANTAYTAMBO AND AROUND

BY TRAIN

The trains connecting Cusco with Ollantaytambo and Machu Picchu start at Poroy, 20–30min by taxi from Cusco. Ollantaytambo's train station is a few hundred metres down Avenida Estación (also known as Avenida Ferrocarril), on the left after the *Hostal Sauce* as you come down from the plaza towards (but well before) the cathedral or Templo de Santiago Apóstol.

Companies All three of the train companies above offer the Ollantaytambo–Machu Picchu route (roughly 2hr 20min), with slight variations in prices and timings, depending on the company, service level, season and day of the week. Each offers online booking, though they also have ticket offices in central Cusco: Perurail, Portal de Carnes 214, Plaza de Armas (daily 8am–10pm; ⓣ581414, ⓦperurail.com); Inca Rail, Portal de Panes 105, Plaza de Armas (Mon–Fri 8am–6pm, Sat, Sun & hols 9am–6pm; ⓣ233030, ⓦincarail.com); and Machu Picchu Train, Av Sol 576 (Mon–Fri 8am–6pm, Sat & Sun 9am–5pm; ⓣ221199, ⓦmachupicchutrain.com).

Tickets To be on the safe side, it's important to buy tickets well in advance (weeks ahead during high season) online – from a tour agency (see p.222) or direct from one of the three railway companies above – since carriages are often fully booked in high season. Perurail offers the most varied service: Vistadome (large panoramic windows to help see and photograph the scenic route, seats facing forward; S/174 return), Autowagon (panoramic windows, but is an exclusive service that operates only from *Tambo del Inca Hotel* in Urubamba; S/174 return); Expedition (panoramic windows but with seats facing each other and racks for rucksacks; S/95–125 return), and occasionally a more costly Special Service, such as the plush Hiram Bingham carriage (up to S/882); check current timings and costs online. Return or one-way tickets are available, giving visitors the opportunity to stay overnight or longer in Machu Picchu or Aguas Calientes (see p.262).

BY BUS

Afternoon buses (S/8) to Cusco leave regularly from the small yard just outside the train station, often coinciding with the train timetable. In the mornings the buses depart mainly from Ollantaytambo's main plaza.

BY COLECTIVO

At the Puente Grau, on the 5th block of Av Grau in Cusco,

ACTIVITIES AROUND OLLANTAYTAMBO

Ollantaytambo is surrounded by stunning countryside and skyscraping mountain peaks, and offers a wealth of interesting **day-trip** options.

WALKING

It's easy enough just to choose a path leading up into the hills to the east and see where you get to, remembering, of course, that you will need a tent or have to get back to town by nightfall. Any route will provide a good **hike**, bringing you into close contact with local people in their gardens. There are also a number of organized **tours**, available from Ollantaytambo (see below) as well as from agents in Cusco. The local Museo CATCCO (T 204024 or T 204034, E otikary@hotmail.com) provide information on the **Rutas Ancestrales de Ollantaytambo** – Ancestral Routes of Ollantaytambo. This is an entire list of walking circuits that link important points relating to the archeology or history of the area (a large map of this route can also be found at the entry to the Inca fortress).

TREKKING

The area around Ollantaytambo is an excellent spot to begin **trekking** into the hills. One possibility is to head along the main down-valley road to Km 82, where a bridge over the Río Urubamba is becoming an increasingly popular starting point for both the **Inca Trail** and **Salcantay**. Alternatives are the hard-going two-day trail to the beautiful and remote lake of **Yanacocha**, or travel up the Río Patacancha to the little-visited Inca ruins of **Pumamarca**, on the left of the river where the Río Yuramayu merges with the Patacancha under the shadows of the Nevada Helancoma. From here the main track carries on along the right bank of the Río Patacancha through various small peasant hamlets – Pullata, Colqueracay, Maracocha and Huilloc – before crossing the pass, with the Nevada Colque Cruz on the right-hand side. It then follows the ríos Huacahuasi and Tropoche down to the valley and community of **Lares**, just before which are some Inca baths. Beyond the village are several more ruins en route to Ampares, from where you can either walk back to Urubamba, travel by road back to Cusco, or head down towards Quillabamba. It's at least a two-day walk one way, and you'll need camping equipment and food, as there are no facilities at all on the route.

HORSERIDING

The Inca **quarries of Cachiqata** can be reached in four hours on horseback with a Cusco or Ollantaytambo tour company (see p.222 & below). It's also possible to camp here and visit the site of an **Inca gateway** or **Intihuatana**. There are also the nearer ruins of **Pinkuylluna**, less than an hour away by horse, or the **Pumamarca** Inca ruins about half a day away.

RIVER RAFTING

Ollantaytambo is a centre for **river rafting**, organized largely by KB Tours on the main plaza (T 204133, W kbperu.com), who also offer lodging, mountain-biking and trekking tours; all activities start from around $45/day. Alternatively, arrange a rafting trip with one of the Cusco-based tour companies (see p.222). The river around Ollantaytambo is class 2–3 in the dry season and 3–4 during the rainy period (Nov–March).

you find car or minibus colectivos to Ollantaytambo (2hr–2hr 30min; S/8–10), from around 6am until mid-afternoon.

BY TAXI

Taxis from Cusco to Ollantaytambo charge S/70–80. You can pick up a taxi in Ollantaytambo outside the train station.

INFORMATION AND TOURS

Tourist information Try Museo CATCCO (daily 10am–1pm and 3–6pm; T 204024 or T 204034, E otikary@hotmail.com), one block from the plaza in Casa Horno.

Tour operator KB Tambo Tours, C Ventedeirio (T 204091, W kbperu.com).

ACCOMMODATION

El Albergue Ollantaytambo Casilla 784 T 204014, W elalbergue.com. Right next to the river and the train station at the bottom end of town (the entrance is on the station platform), this *albergue* offers discounts to families, although it's advisable to contact them well in advance during the high season. The spacious rooms are rustic but arty, and very attractive and comfortable. There's also a great sauna and very tasty meals, including breakfast. For full meals (also available to non-guests) you need to book in advance. S/200

Hospedaje Los Andes C Ventiderio ☎204095. A small, cosy hostel with traditional patio in the heart of town, offering hot water and private bath in some of the simple yet well furnished rooms. S/100

Hospedaje Las Portadas C Principal ☎204008. A small hostel on the main road into town, with good views from one or two of the rooms, although baths are shared and, unfortunately, the yard is concreted. S/70

Hostal La Ñusta Carretera Ocobamba ☎204035. Very hospitable but basic, this place has simply furnished rooms with shared bath, as well as a patio offering excellent views across to the mountains and the Wiraccochan face (see p.250). S/70

Hostal Ollanta Main Plaza ☎204116. Close to the little market and chapel on the main plaza, *Ollanta* is a refurbished and well-run hostel. Very clean but can be noisy at weekends. S/70

Hostal Las Orquídeas Av Estación ☎204032. Further up the track from the train station to the town, this pleasant place offers small rooms set around a courtyard, with breakfasts available. S/100

Hostal Sauce C Ventiderio 248 ☎204044, Ⓦhostalsauce.com.pe. A modern and safe, if not particularly friendly hostel with elegant rooms and fine views. There's also a reasonable restaurant, only open to residents. S/280

Hotel Pakaritampu Av Estación ☎204020, Ⓦpakaritampu.com. Within a few minutes' walk of the station and set in pleasant gardens, this is a safe and plush hotel. Price includes an excellent buffet breakfast. S/438

EATING AND DRINKING

There are several good **cafés** in town, particularly around the bridge at the top of Avenida Estación (also known as Ferrocarril) and in the main plaza. If you want to try the local *chicha* **maize beer**, pop into any of the private houses displaying a red plastic bag on a pole outside the door – the beer is cheap and the hosts usually very friendly and fun. The red markers date from a time when red flowers were used to indicate which family in the village had enough *chicha* beer to share with friends and neighbours.

El Albergue Ollantaytambo Casilla 784 ☎204014, Ⓦelalbergue.com. It's hard to beat this place, which is open to non-residents by prior reservation; they have a great cook whose food betrays a North American influence. Daily 7am–7pm.

Alcázar C del Medio. A well-used and attractively laid out space just a stone's throw from the Plaza de Armas, *Alcázar* serves great breakfasts, snacks, pancakes and good local meat or veggie meals. Daily 7.30am–9pm.

Café Restaurant Fortaleza Plaza de Armas. A popular place with gringo travellers, serving good pancakes and tasty but relatively inexpensive pizzas. Daily 7am–8pm.

Mayupata Restaurant Bar Jr Convención, opposite the Templo de Santiago Apóstol ☎204009. The fanciest big restaurant in town, serving pizzas and other Italian dishes, and international cuisine. It's not cheap, but has a fine setting by the river bridge. Daily 10am–9pm.

Pachamama Pizzeria Plaza de Armas ☎204168. This place serves up some of the best food in Ollantaytambo, and is particularly strong on meat dishes (try the *lomo saltado*), pizzas and grills. You'll need to arrive before 8pm to be sure of a table. Daily 8am–10pm.

Restaurant La Ñusta Plaza de Armas. A very friendly café and shop with excellent breakfasts, snacks and soups made from fresh vegetables (unusual for this region, despite the fertility of the soil). They also have tables outside, facing the plaza. Daily 7.30am–8pm.

DIRECTORY

Internet Try Cyberpath, opposite the cathedral on the plaza.

Money and exchange Exchange is available in the small shop on the corner of the plaza with Calle Ventiderio.

Post office On the main plaza.

Telephones On the main plaza.

The Inca Trail

Even though it's just one among a multitude of paths across the Andes, the fabulous treasure of Machu Picchu (see p.257) at the end of its 43km path makes the **INCA TRAIL** the world's most famous trek. Most people visit the site on a day-tour by train from Cusco, Ollantaytambo or Urubamba (see box, p.256), but if you're reasonably fit and can dedicate at least four days to the experience, arriving along the Inca Trail offers the most atmospheric and rewarding option.

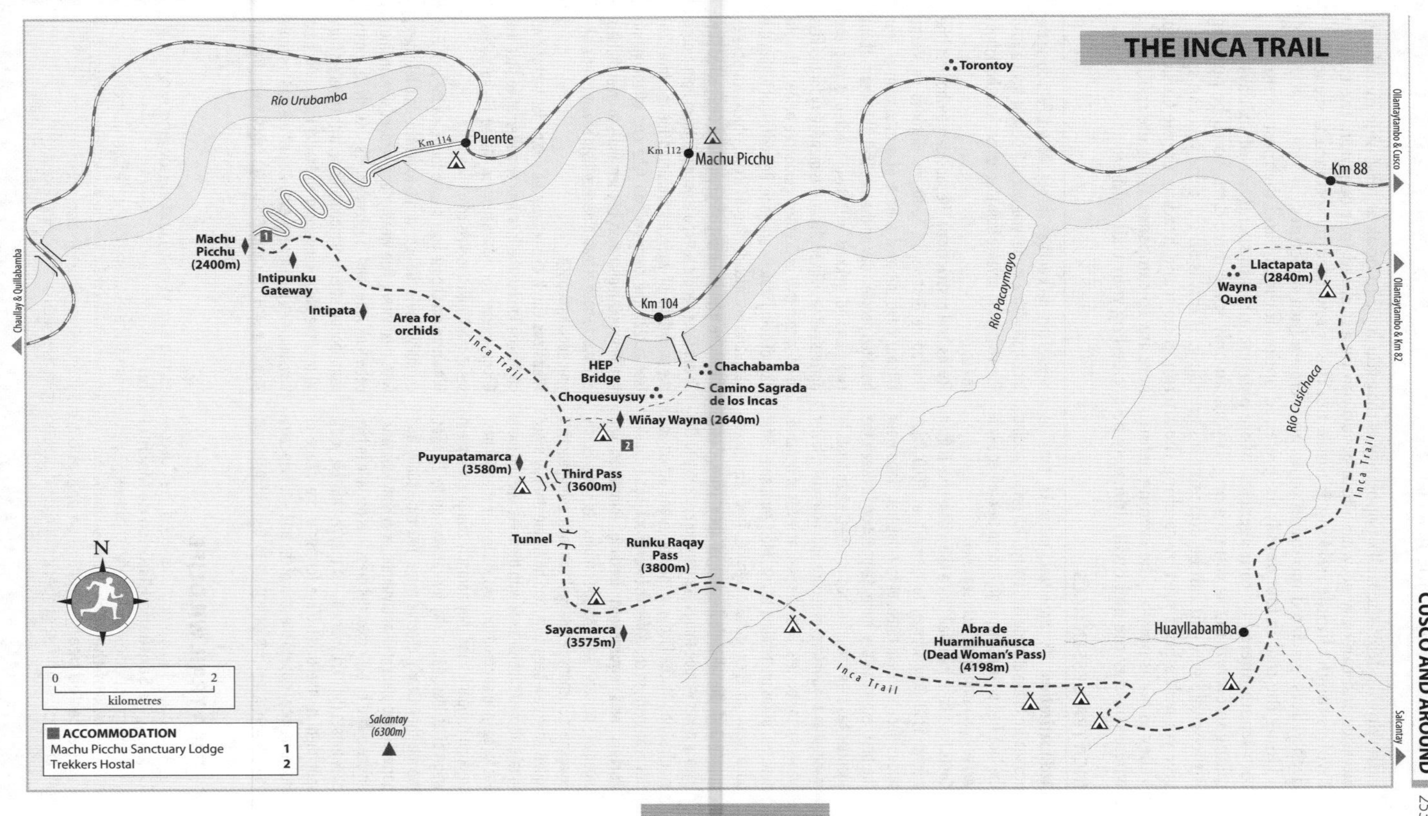
THE INCA TRAIL
Torontoy
Río Urubamba
Km 114
Puente
Km 112
Machu Picchu
Km 88
Ollantaytambo & Cusco
Ollantaytambo & Km 82
Chaullay & Quillabamba
Machu Picchu (2400m)
Intipunku Gateway
Intipata
Area for orchids
Inca Trail
Km 104
Río Pacaymayo
Llactapata (2840m)
Wayna Quent
HEP Bridge
Chachabamba
Camino Sagrada de los Incas
Choquesuysuy
Wiñay Wayna (2640m)
Río Cusichaca
Inca Trail
Puyupatamarca (3580m)
Third Pass (3600m)
Tunnel
Runku Raqay Pass (3800m)
N
Sayacmarca (3575m)
Abra de Huarmihuañusca (Dead Woman's Pass) (4198m)
Huayllabamba
Inca Trail
0 2 kilometres
Salcantay (6300m)
Salcantay
ACCOMMODATION
Machu Picchu Sanctuary Lodge 1
Trekkers Hostal 2

4

The downside of the trail's popularity is that you have to **book** at least nine months in advance and can only go with a **tour group** run by a licensed tour operator. The trail involves tough altitude trekking at times, but this is rewarded by spectacular scenery, deep valleys, glaciated mountain peaks and remote Inca structures.

Doing the trail in **four days** is the preferred option for most, and the most common tour length offered by tour agencies. More pleasant still is to spend five or six days, taking in everything as you go along. If you can only spare three days, you'll be pushing it the whole way – it can be done but it's gruelling. If this is all the time you can spare, give yourself a head start by catching the afternoon train and heading up the Cusichaca Valley as far as possible the evening before. There are 16 **campsites** along the trail; where you stay the night will ultimately be decided by your trail guide.

INCA TRAIL ESSENTIALS

Acclimatization It's important to make time to acclimatize to the altitude (see box, p.210) before tackling the Inca Trail or any other high Andean trek, especially if you've flown straight up from sea level.

Costs For a basic Inca Trail tour a reasonable price is from around $350 (low season) to as much as $600 (high season) for a standard three- or four-day trek. If you want the best, expect to pay more. Competition between the agencies has seen the price drop at times, which tends to manifest as a lower level of service and, potentially, lower wages for the porters. With the present levels of demand, however, prices are tending to rise. Most companies offer good value in their guiding service, food, equipment quality and the all-inclusiveness of their price. Some agency prices include things like transport or entry to the Inca Trail and Machu Picchu in their price, and others add this as an extra, so check details before booking.

Porters and equipment Trekking companies will organize porters and maybe mules to help carry equipment. So many people walk this route every year that toilets have now been built, and hikers are strongly urged to take all their rubbish away with them – there's no room left for burying any more tin cans. Porters are used by most trekking companies and they normally charge a minimum wage of at least $10 a day for carrying up to 25 kilos, though they clearly deserve more. You can usually find porters in the plaza at Ollantaytambo, or in Huayllabamba, distinguished by their colourful dress. It is possible to hire pack horses ($8–12) yourself – if they're available you'll spot them by the ticket office (or ask in the village of Huayllabamba) close to the start of the trail – to help carry your rucksacks and equipment up to the first pass, but beyond this, pack animals are not allowed. Even doing the Inca Trail with a guide, you will still benefit from a map (best bought in advance from tour companies or bookshops in Cusco).

Rules and restrictions The sanctuary authorities (the Unidad de Gestión del Santuario Histórico de Machu Picchu) have imposed a limit of a maximum of four hundred people a day on the Inca Trail (this means about two hundred trekkers with two hundred guides and porters per day). In addition, it is mandatory for trekkers to go with a tour or licensed guide (see below): the old days of going it alone are gone. Be aware that within the Santuario Histórico de Machu Picchu, which incorporates the entire trail, you must only camp at a designated site.

Tours Most people select a tour to suit them from among the multitude of agencies registered for the Inca Trail (see p.222); the company will take care of everything including your registration, but demand is so great that it is essential to book at least nine months in advance and make your booking deposit.

Websites Check machupicchu.gob.pe for background on Machu Picchu, the Inca Trail and alternative sites like Choquequirao. For information on Machu Picchu tickets, see machupicchutickets.com.

When to go Choose your season for hiking the Inca Trail carefully. May is the best month to venture on a hike here, with clear views, fine weather and verdant surroundings. Between June and September it's usually a pretty cosmopolitan stretch of mountainside, with travellers from all over the globe converging on Machu Picchu the hard way, but from mid-June to early August the trail is simply very busy (and the campsites noisy), especially on the last

INCA TRAIL WILDLIFE

Acting as a bio-corridor between the Cusco Andes, the Sacred Valley and the lowland Amazon forest, the **Santuario Histórico de Machu Picchu** possesses over 370 species of bird, 47 mammal species and over 700 butterfly species. Some of the more notable residents include the **cock-of-the-rock** (*Rupicola peruviana*, known as *tunkis* in the Quechua-speaking Andes), **spectacled bear** (*Tremarctos ornatus*) and condor (*Vultur gryphus*). In addition, there are around 300 different species of orchid hidden up in the trees of the cloud forest.

stretch. From October until April, in the rainy season, it's less crowded but also, naturally, quite a bit wetter. Locals will tell you that the best time to hike the trail is during a full moon, and it certainly adds a more romantic, even mystical feeling to your journey.

The main trail

The usual **starting point** for the Inca Trail is a small station at the hamlet and bridge at Q'orihuayrachina, at **Km 88** on the railway from Ollantaytambo and Poroy. Some tours arrive here by car and start at Km 82, where the road stops. The railway stop is hailed by the guards and a small footbridge sees you across the tumbling Río Urubamba. Once over the bridge, the main path leads to the left through a small eucalyptus wood, then around the base of the Inca ruins of Llactapata – worth a visit for archeology enthusiasts, though most people save their energy for the trail and other archeological remains ahead – before crossing and then following the Río Cusichaca upstream along its left bank.

It's a good two hours' steep climb to **Huayllabamba**, the only inhabited village on the route and the best place to hire horses or mules for the most difficult climb on the whole trail, the nearby **Dead Woman's Pass**. This section of the valley is rich in Inca terracing, from which rises an occasional ancient stone building. To reach Huayllabamba you have to cross a well-marked bridge onto the right bank of the Cusichaca.

Many groups spend their first night at Huayllabamba campsite, but if you want to gain distance and time for the second day, there are three commonly used **campsites**: one at Llulluchayoc, also known as **Three White Stones**, where the trail crosses the Río Huayruro, just half a kilometre above its confluence with the Llullucha stream; another slightly higher site, just below Llulluchpampa, where there are toilets and space for several tents; or, slightly higher again, actually on the pampa where there's plenty more camping space – a good spot for seeing rabbit-like *viscachas* playing among the rocks. All of these campsites are on the trail towards the first and highest pass, but only the top one is within sight of it.

4

The first pass

It takes five hours or so to get from Huayllabamba to the Abra de Huarmihuañusca, **the first pass** (4200m) and the highest point on the trail. This is the hardest part of the walk – leave it (or at least some of it) for the second day, especially if you're feeling the effects of the altitude. The views from the pass itself are stupendous, but if you're tempted to hang around savouring them, it's a good idea to sit well out of the cutting wind (many a trekker has caught a bad chill here). From here the trail drops steeply down, keeping to the left of the stream into the Pacamayo Valley where, by the river, there's an attractive spot to **camp**, and where you can see playful **spectacled bears** if you're very lucky, or take a break before continuing.

The second pass

A winding, tiring track up from the Pacamayo Valley takes you to the **second pass** – Abra de Runkuracay – just above the interesting circular ruins of the same name. About an hour beyond the second pass, a flight of stone steps leads up to the Inca ruins of **Sayacmarca**. This is an impressive spot to **camp**, near the remains of a stone aqueduct that supplied water to the ancient settlement (the best spots are by the stream just below the ruins).

The third pass

From Sayacmarca, make your way gently down into increasingly dense cloud forest where delicate orchids and other exotic flora begin to appear among the trees. By the time you get to the **third pass** – which, compared with the previous two, has very little

THE TRAIN JOURNEY TO MACHU PICCHU

The competitive services offered by the three Cusco-based train operators – **Perurail, Inca Rail** and **Machu Picchu Train** (see p.220) – between Cusco and Machu Picchu provide one of the finest mountain train journeys in the world, with all the thrills and vistas associated with riding tracks through fantastic scenery, along with very good service and comfortable, well-kept carriages.

The longest of the train options (the others leave from Ollantaytambo and Urubamba), only offered by Perurail, rumbles out of **Poroy station**, 15–20 minutes by taxi from Cusco centre. The wagons zigzag their way through the backstreets, where little houses cling to the steep valley slopes. It takes a while to rise out of the teacup-like valley, but once it reaches the high plateau above, the train rolls through fields and past highland villages before eventually dropping rapidly down into the **Urubamba Valley** via several major track switchbacks, which means you get to see some of the same scenery twice.

The train reaches the Sacred Valley floor just before getting into **Ollantaytambo**, where from the windows you can already see scores of impressively terraced fields and, in the distance, more Inca temple and storehouse constructions. Ollantaytambo's pretty railway station is right next to the river, and here you can expect to be greeted by a handful of Quechua women selling woollen crafts. The train continues down the valley, stopping briefly at Km 88, where the **Inca Trail** starts (see p.255), then follows the Urubamba River as the valley gets tighter (which is why there's no road) and the mountain becomes more and more forested, as well as steeper and seemingly taller. The end of the line is the new station at **Machu Picchu Pueblo** (also known as **Aguas Calientes**), a busy little town crowded into the valley just a short bus ride from the ruins themselves (see p.259). From Cusco (Poroy Station) the journey takes 4 hours; it's 2 hours from Ollantaytambo and 3 hours from Urubamba. Whichever route you're taking, buy **tickets** well in advance online.

incline – you're following a fine, smoothly worn flagstone path where at one point an astonishing tunnel, carved through solid rock by the Incas, lets you sidetrack an otherwise impossible climb.

The trail winds down to the impressive ruin of **Puyupatamarca** – "Town Above the Clouds" – where there are five small stone baths and, in the wet season, constant fresh running water. There are places to **camp** actually on the pass (above the ruins), commanding stunning views across the Urubamba Valley and, in the other direction, towards the snowcaps of Salcantay (Wild Mountain): this is probably one of the most magical camps on the trail, given good weather, and it's not unusual to see deer feeding here.

Wiñay Wayna

It's a very rough, two- or three-hour descent along a non-Inca track to the next ruin, a citadel almost as impressive as Machu Picchu, **Wiñay Wayna** – "Forever Young" – another place with fresh water, as well as the official *Trekkers Hostal* (see opposite).

Consisting of only two major groups of architectural structures – a lower and an upper sector – Wiñay Wayna's most visible features are **stone baths** with apparently as many as nineteen springs feeding them, all set amid several layers of fine Inca terracing. Nearby there's also a small waterfall created by streams coming down from the heights of Puyupatamarca. Much like today, it is believed that Wiñay Wayna was used by Incas as a washing, cleansing and resting point before arriving at the grand Machu Picchu citadel.

This is usually the spot for the **last night of camping**, and, especially in high season, the crowds mean that it's a good idea to pitch your tent soon after lunch, but don't be surprised if someone pitches theirs right across your doorway. To reach Machu Picchu for sunrise the next day you'll have to get up very early with a torch to avoid the rush.

Intipunku to Machu Picchu

A well-marked track from Wiñay Wayna takes a right fork for about two more hours through sumptuous vegetated slopes to the stone archway entrance called **Intipunku** (Gateway of the Sun), from where you get your first sight of Machu Picchu – a stupendous moment, however exhausted you might be. Aim to get to Machu Picchu well before 9.30am, when the first hordes arrive off the train from Cusco, if possible.

ARRIVAL AND DEPARTURE

THE INCA TRAIL

By tour Organized tours (see p.222) usually approach the trail by road via Ollantaytambo and then take a dirt track from there to a footbridge over the Río Urubamba at Km 82 of the railway line. This adds a few hours to the overall trek but forms the road trailhead.

By bus Minibuses from Ollantaytambo to Km 82 of the railway line cost S/10.

By train For groups arriving by train, the conventional rail trailhead is at Km 88 along the tracks from Cusco, at a barely noticeable stop announced by the train guard generally as "Km 88", though the stop is also called Q'orihuayrachina. Have your gear ready to throw off the steps, since the train pulls up only for a few brief seconds and you'll have to fight your way past sacks of grain, flapping chickens, men in ponchos and women in voluminous skirts. A third entry to a shortened version of the Inca Trail, known as the Camino Sagrado de los Incas, begins at Km 104 (see box, p.267), which is also on the train line and within easy walking distance of Pueblo Machu Picchu (see p.262).

ACCOMMODATION

In the main, travellers tend to stay at **Machu Picchu Pueblo** (see p.262) at the end of the trek. Despite its exciting buzz, charm and stunning location – enclosed by rocky and forested tall mountains – it's little more than a booming concrete conglomeration of restaurants, shops and hotels.

4

Trekkers Hostal Wiñay Wayna. The name Wiñay Wayna means "Forever Young" in the Inca language (Quechua), and this is another spot on the trail with fresh water canalized by the Incas. An official and basic hostel with associated campsite, it's filled on a first-come, first-served basis (there's no phone). It has a restaurant too – nothing amazing, but with a welcome supply of cool drinks. It costs S/5 for a hot shower. Floor space **S/10**, dorm beds **S/35**

Machu Picchu

Daily 6am–5pm • S/126, or S/63 for students with student ISIC card; S/148 including Machu Picchu Museum; S/150 including climb of Huayna Picchu • Ⓦ machupicchu.gob.pe

MACHU PICCHU is one of the greatest of all South American tourist attractions: beautiful stone architecture enhanced by the Incas' exploitation of local 250-million-year-old rocks of grey-white granite with a high content of quartz, silica and feldspar, set against a vast, scenic backdrop of dark-green forested mountains that spike up from the deep valleys of the Urubamba and its tributaries. The distant glacial summits are dwarfed only by the huge sky. The site's mysterious origins are central to its enduring appeal, but even without knowing too much about its history or archeology, or the specifics of each feature, it's quite possible to enjoy a visit to Machu Picchu: for many, it's enough just to absorb the mystical atmosphere.

MACHU PICCHU TICKETS

In spite of the huge numbers of visitors – over 3000 a day in high season – Machu Picchu is large enough to absorb its visitors without it being a scrum. Due to its popularity and attempts to limit visitor numbers because of the potential environmental impact, however, **booking ahead** is a good idea. If you're visiting as part of a tour, the entrance tickets should be sorted out for you; if you're visiting independently the most reliable way to book is via the official website Ⓦ machupicchu.gob.pe. For comprehensive and regularly updated information on tickets and booking, see Ⓦ machupicchutickets.com.

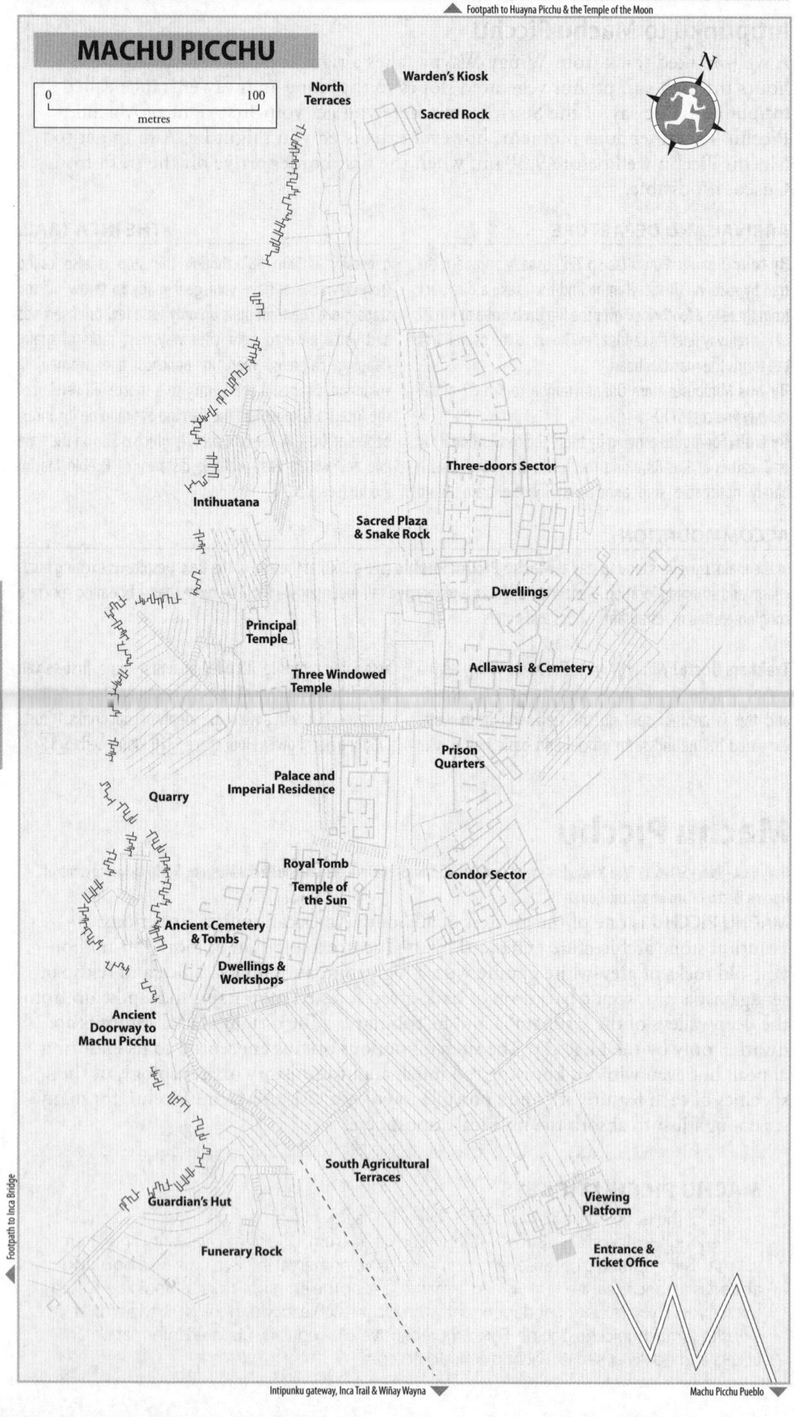

Footpath to Huayna Picchu & the Temple of the Moon

MACHU PICCHU

0 100
metres

N

North Terraces
Warden's Kiosk
Sacred Rock
Three-doors Sector
Intihuatana
Sacred Plaza & Snake Rock
Dwellings
Principal Temple
Three Windowed Temple
Acllawasi & Cemetery
Prison Quarters
Palace and Imperial Residence
Quarry
Royal Tomb
Temple of the Sun
Condor Sector
Ancient Cemetery & Tombs
Dwellings & Workshops
Ancient Doorway to Machu Picchu
South Agricultural Terraces
Viewing Platform
Guardian's Hut
Entrance & Ticket Office
Funerary Rock
Footpath to Inca Bridge

Intipunku gateway, Inca Trail & Wiñay Wayna
Machu Picchu Pueblo

4

Brief history

The name Machu Picchu apparently means simply Old or Ancient Mountain. With many legends and theories surrounding the position of the site, most archeologists agree that its **sacred geography and astronomy** were auspicious factors in helping the Inca Pachacuti decide where to build this citadel here at 2492m. It's thought that agricultural influences as well as geo-sacred indicators prevailed, and that the site secured a decent supply of sacred coca and maize for the Inca nobles and priests in Cusco.

The discovery of Machu Picchu

Never discovered by the Spanish conquerors, for many centuries the site of Machu Picchu lay forgotten, except by local Indians and settlers, until it was found on July 24, 1911 by the US explorer **Hiram Bingham**. It was a fantastic find, not least because the site was still relatively intact, without the usual ravages of either Spanish conquistadores or tomb robbers. Accompanied only by two locals, Bingham left his base camp around 10am and crossed a bridge so dodgy that he crawled over it on his hands and knees before climbing a precipitous slope until they reached the ridge at around midday. After resting at a small hut, he received hospitality from a local peasant who described an extensive system of terraces where they had found good fertile soil for their crops. Bingham was led to the site by an 11-year-old local boy, Pablito Alvarez, but it didn't take him long to see that he had come across some important ancient Inca terraces – over a hundred of which had recently been cleared of forest for subsistence crops. After a little more exploration Bingham found the fine white stonework and began to realize that this might be the place he was looking for.

4

Origins of Machu Picchu

Bingham first theorized that Machu Picchu was the lost city of **Vilcabamba**, the site of the Incas' last refuge from the Spanish conquistadors. Not until another American expedition surveyed the ruins around Machu Picchu in the 1940s did serious doubts begin to arise over this assertion, and more recently the site of the Incas' final stronghold has been shown to be Espíritu Pampa in the Amazon jungle (see p.274).

Meanwhile, it was speculated that Machu Picchu was perhaps the best preserved of a series of **agricultural centres** that served Cusco in its prime. The city was conceived and built in the mid-fifteenth century by **Emperor Pachacuti**, the first to expand the empire beyond the Sacred Valley towards the forested gold-lands. With crop fertility, mountains and nature so sacred to the Incas, an agricultural centre as important as Machu Picchu would easily have merited the site's fine stonework and temple precincts. It was clearly also a **ritual centre**, given the layout and quantity of temples; but for the Incas it was usual not to separate things we consider economic tasks from more conventional religious activities. So, Machu Picchu represents to many archeologists the most classical and best-preserved remains in existence of a citadel used by the Incas as both a religious temple site and an agricultural (perhaps experimental) centre.

The ruins

Though more than 1000m lower than Cusco, Machu Picchu seems much higher, constructed as it is on dizzying slopes overlooking a U-curve in the Río Urubamba. More than a hundred flights of steep stone steps interconnect its palaces, temples, storehouses and terraces, and the outstanding views command not only the valley below in both directions but also extend to the snowy peaks around Salcantay. Wherever you stand in the ruins, you can see spectacular **terraces** (some of which are once again being cultivated) slicing across ridiculously steep cliffs, transforming mountains into suspended gardens.

Though it would take a lot to detract from Machu Picchu's incredible beauty and unsurpassed location, it is a zealously supervised place, with the site guards frequently

THREATS TO MACHU PICCHU

This most dramatic and enchanting of Inca citadels, suspended on an extravagantly terraced saddle between two prominent peaks, is believed to be in danger of **collapse**. The original Inca inhabitants temporarily stabilized the mountainside, transforming some of the geological faults into **drainage channels**. They also joined many of the construction stones together, using elaborate multi-angled techniques, making them more resistant to both tremors and landslides. Nevertheless, these spots remain weak and significant damage can be seen on nearby buildings. The National Institute of Culture, which administers Machu Picchu, acknowledges the problems, but correcting them is an ongoing process.

blowing whistles at visitors who have deviated from the main pathways. The best way to enjoy the ruins – while avoiding the ire of the guards – is to hire a **guide** (see p.254) at the entrance to the site, or buy the **map** from the ticket office and stick to its routes.

The Temple of the Sun

The **Temple of the Sun**, also known as the Torreon, is a wonderful, semicircular, walled, tower-like temple displaying some of Machu Picchu's finest granite stonework. Constructed to incorporate polyhedrons and trapezoidal window niches, the temple's carved steps and smoothly joined stone blocks fit neatly into the existing relief of a natural boulder that served as some kind of altar and also marks the entrance to a small cave. A window off this temple provides views of both the June solstice sunrise and the constellation of the Pleiades, which rises from here over the nearby peak of Huayna Picchu. The Pleiades are still a very important astronomical Andean symbol relating to crop fertility: locals use the constellation as a kind of annual signpost in the agricultural calendar, giving information about when to plant crops and when the rains will come.

4

The Royal Tomb

Below the Temple of the Sun is a cave known as the **Royal Tomb**, despite the fact that no graves or human remains have ever been found there. In fact, it probably represented access to the spiritual heart of the mountains, like the cave at the Temple of the Moon (see opposite).

The funerary rock

Retracing your steps 20m or so back from the Temple of the Sun and following a flight of stone stairs directly uphill, then left along the track towards Intipunku (see p.262), brings you to a path on the right, which climbs up to the thatched **guardian's hut**. This hut is associated with a modestly carved rock known as the **funerary rock** and a nearby graveyard where Hiram Bingham (see p.259) found evidence of many burials, some of which were obviously royal.

The Sacred Plaza

Arguably the most enthralling sector of the ruins, the **Three-Windowed Temple** (Templo de Tres Ventanas), part of the complex based around the **Sacred Plaza** (Plaza Sagrada), is located back down in the centre of the site, the next major Inca construction after the Temple of the Sun. Dominating the southeastern edge of the plaza, the attractive Three-Windowed Temple has unusually large windows looking east towards the mountains beyond the Urubamba River valley. From here it's a short stroll to the **Principal Temple** (Templo Principal), so called because of the fine stonework of its three high main walls, the most easterly of which looks onto the Sacred Plaza. Unusually (as most ancient temples in the Americas face east), the main opening of this temple faces south, and white sand, often thought to represent the ocean, has been found on the temple floor, suggesting that it may have been allied symbolically to the Río Urubamba: water and the sea.

The Intihuatana

A minute or so uphill from the Principal Temple along an elaborately carved stone stairway brings you to one of the jewels of the site, the **Intihuatana**, also known as the **"hitching post of the sun"**. This fascinating carved rock, built on a rise above the Sacred Plaza, is similar to those created by the Incas in all their important ritual centres, but is one of the very few not to have been discovered and destroyed by the conquistadores. This unique and very beautiful survivor, set in a tower-like position, overlooks the Sacred Plaza, the Río Urubamba and the sacred peak of Huayna Picchu.

The Intihuatana's base is said to have been carved in the shape of a map of the Inca Empire, though few archeologists agree with this. Its main purpose was as an **astro-agricultural clock** for viewing the complex interrelationships between the movements of the stars and constellations. It is also thought by some to be a symbolic representation of the spirit of the mountain on which Machu Picchu was built – by all accounts a very powerful spot both in terms of sacred geography and its astrological function. The Intihuatana appears to be aligned with four important **mountains**: the snowcapped mountain range of La Verónica lies directly to the east, with the sun rising behind its main summit during the equinoxes; directly south, though not actually visible from here, sits the father of all mountains in this part of Peru, Salcantay, a few days' walk away; to the west, the sun sets behind the important peak of Pumasillo during the December solstice; and due north stands the majestic peak of Huayna Picchu. The rock evidently kept track of the annual cycles, with its basic orientation northwest to southeast, plus four vertices pointing to the four directions.

4

The Sacred Rock

Following the steps down from the Intihuatana and passing through the Sacred Plaza towards the northern terraces brings you in a few minutes to the **Sacred Rock** (Piedra Sagrado), below the access point to Huayna Picchu. A 3m high and 7m wide lozenge of rock sticking out of the earth like a sculptured wall, little is known for sure about the Sacred Rock, but it is thought to have had a ritual function; its outline is strikingly similar to the Incas' sacred mountain of Putukusi, which towers behind it in the east.

Huayna Picchu

The prominent peak of **Huayna Picchu** juts out over the Urubamba Valley at the northern end of the Machu Picchu site, and is easily scaled by any reasonably energetic person. The record for this vigorous and rewarding climb is 22 minutes, but most people take at least an hour. Access to this sacred mountain is restricted to four hundred people a day (the first two hundred are expected to get back down by 10am so that the second two hundred can then go up); register for the climb with the guardian in the hut just behind the Sacred Rock. From the summit, there's an awe-inspiring **panorama**, and it's a great place from which to get an overview of the ruins suspended between the mountains among stupendous forested Andean scenery.

The Temple of the Moon

Accessed in the same way as Huayna Picchu, but about one-third of the way up, another little track leads to the left and down to the stunning **Temple of the Moon** (Templo de la Luna), hidden in a grotto hanging magically above the Río Urubamba, some 400m beneath the pinnacle of Huayna Picchu. Not many visitors make it this far

SUNRISE OVER MACHU PICCHU

It's easy enough to get into the site before **sunrise**, since the sun rarely rises over the mountains to shed its rays over Machu Picchu before 7am. Make your way to the "hitching post" of the sun before dawn for an unforgettable sunrise that will quickly make you forget the hike through the pre-dawn gloom – bring a torch if you plan to try it.

and it's probably wise to have a **guide** (and if you've already walked up Huayna Picchu, you might want to save this for another day: it's at least another 45 minutes each way and not that easy-going at times). The guardian by the Sacred Rock will often take people for a small fee (around $1 per person, provided there are two or more). Once you reach the temple, you'll be rewarded by some of the best stonework in the entire complex, the level of craftsmanship hinting at the site's importance to the Inca.

The temple's name comes from the fact that it is often lit up by the moonlight, but some archeologists believe the structure was probably dedicated to the spirit of the mountain. The main sector of the temple is in the mouth of a natural **cave**, where there are five niches set into an elaborate white-granite stone wall. There's usually evidence – small piles of maize, coca leaves and tobacco – that people are still making offerings at these niches. In the centre of the cave there's a rock carved like a throne, beside which are five cut steps leading into the darker recesses, where you can see more carved rocks and stone walls, nowadays inaccessible. Immediately to the front of the cave is a small **plaza** with another cut-stone throne and an altar. Outside, steps either side of the massive boulder lead above the cave, from where you can see a broad, stone-walled **room** running along one side of the cave boulder. There are more buildings and beautiful little stone sanctuaries just down a flight of steps from this part of the complex.

Intipunku

If you don't have the time or energy to climb Huayna Picchu or visit the Temple of the Moon, head back to the guardian's hut on the other side of the site and take the path below it, which climbs gently for thirty minutes or so, up to **Intipunku**, the main entrance to Machu Picchu from the Inca Trail. This offers an incredible view over the entire site, with the unmistakeable shape of Huayna Picchu in the background.

Machu Picchu Pueblo

Many people base themselves at the settlement of **MACHU PICCHU PUEBLO** (previously known as **Aguas Calientes**), connected to Machu Picchu by bus, in order to visit the ruins at a more leisurely pace or in more depth. Its warm, humid climate and surrounding landscape of towering mountains covered in cloud forest make it a welcome change from Cusco. The town's explosive growth has pretty well reached the limits of the valley here; there's very little flat land that hasn't been built on or covered in concrete. Not surprisingly, this boom town has a lively, bustling feel and enough restaurants and bars to satisfy a small army.

The thermal baths

Av Pachacutec • Daily 6am–8.30pm • S/10

The main attraction in these parts – apart from Machu Picchu itself – is the natural **thermal bath**, which is particularly enjoyable after a few days on the Inca Trail or a hot afternoon up at Machu Picchu. You can find several communal baths of varying temperatures right at the end of the main drag of Avenida Pachacutec, around 750m uphill from the town's small plaza.

Machu Picchu Museum

In the old station at Km112, by the road bridge Puente Ruinas (1.7km from Machu Picchu Pueblo) • Mon–Sat 10am–4pm • S/20

The **Machu Picchu Museum** is close to the municipal campsite, at the start of the climb and bus route up to the main ruins. The museum displays exhibits previously on show in Cusco's museums, including copper and bronze building tools, multimedia and photographs, as well as displays on Inca metallurgy and on the local flora and fauna.

FROM TOP TRAIN TO MACHU PICCHU (P.256); SALINAS SALT PANS (P.246) >

1641

Trail to Putukusi

A **trail** up the sacred mountain of **Putukusi** starts just outside town, a couple of hundred yards down on the left if you follow the rail track towards the ruins. The walk offers stupendous views of the town and across to Machu Picchu; allow an hour and a half each way.

ARRIVAL AND GETTING AROUND

MACHU PICCHU

BY TRAIN

If travelling all the way to Machu Pichu from Poroy near Cusco, Ollantaytambo or Urubamba by train you'll get off at Machu Picchu Pueblo station, located in the nearest town to the ruins, which has experienced explosive growth over the last decade or so. You walk through a craft market area from the station and over a footbridge; below the bridge you'll see the ticket office and buses. It's from here that you can catch one of the buses to the ruins. When departing, if you don't already have a ticket, buy one from the railway station ticket office, open from around 5am.

Destinations Ollantaytambo (6–12 daily; 2hr–2hr 30min); Poroy (3–6 daily; 3–4hr); Urubamba (occasionally scheduled; 2–3hr).

BY BUS

From Machu Picchu Pueblo The office selling bus tickets to Machu Picchu is within a few minutes' walk of the railway station; just go through the market stalls and cross the Río Aguas Calientes by a footbridge. Tickets can be bought just below this from a small window, where there's usually a queue to help identify it, and from where buses usually depart. The first buses leave at 5.20am and continue every 10min or so according to demand until about 4pm, returning continuously until the last bus at 5.30pm (S/25 one way, S/50 return, children under 4 half-price). Tickets are stamped with the date, so you have to return the same day.

From Cusco An alternative option to the train to Machu Picchu is to take the Turismo Ampay bus from Cusco (Urb.

4

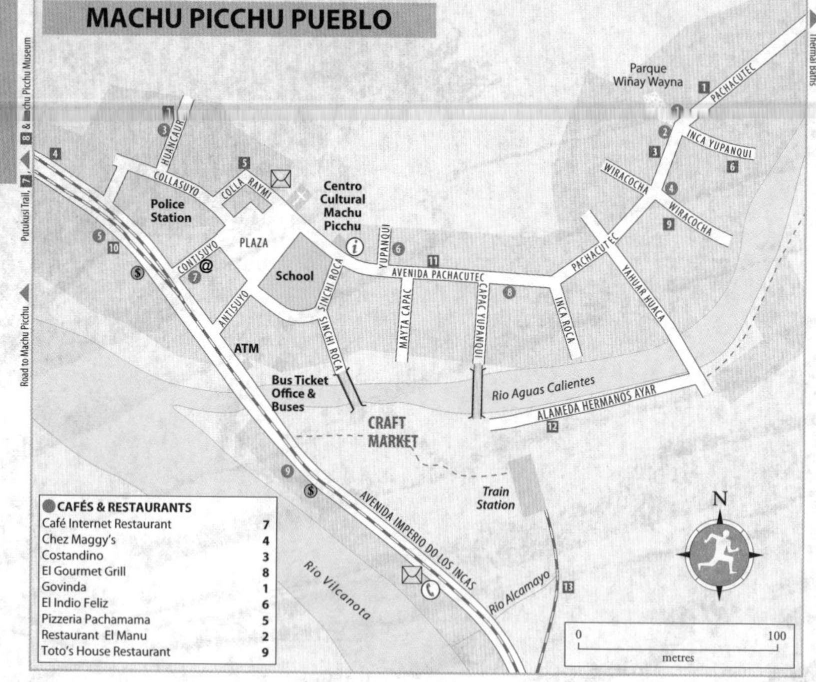

ACCOMMODATION

Chaska	12	Hostal Los Caminantes	4	Machu Picchu Hostal	10
Gringo Bill's	5	Hostal Quilla	3	Machu Picchu Inn	11
Hospedaje Rupa Wasi	2	Inkaterra Machu Picchu	13	Machu Picchu Sanctuary Lodge	8
Hospedaje Samana Wasi	6	Machu Picchu Consejo Campsite	7	Wiracocha Inn	9
Hostal La Cabaña	1				

Pucutupampa B-11, Santiago; ⓣ2457344; S/15) to Santa María (5 daily; 6–9hr), which goes via Ollantaytambo before crossing the mountains east of the Urubamba Valley. From the high pass at Abra Malaga, the bus drops down to Santa María. From here there are colectivos (1hr; S/10) to the larger settlement of Santa Teresa, from where it is possible to walk to Machu Picchu (see below).

ON FOOT

From Machu Picchu Pueblo It's possible to walk from Machu Picchu Pueblo to the ruins, but it'll take one and a half to three hours, depending on how fit you are and whether you take the very steep direct path or follow the more roundabout paved road.

From Santa Teresa If you've taken the bus from Cusco to Santa Teresa (see opposite), you can do the rest of the journey to Machu Picchu on foot. From Santa Teresa you follow the Río Urubamba upstream for 8km (1hr 30min–2hr) to a hydroelectric power station. Colectivos sometimes follow this route (20min; S/3), though the road is frequently washed away in the height of the rainy season (Dec–March/April). Continue upriver from here to an INC hut where you need to register, then follow the path along the railway line a further 10–11km (2–3hr) gently uphill to the site of Machu Picchu and, after another 2km, to Machu Picchu Pueblo (Aguas Calientes).

INFORMATION AND TOURS

Tourist information There's a municipal information office next to the INC (Instituto Nacional de Cultura) office just off Machu Picchu Pueblo's main square on Avenida Pachacutec, which also sells tickets for Machu Picchu entry. If you stay overnight in Machu Picchu Pueblo before visiting the site, this could save time in the morning. i-Peru have an office in the first block of Avenida Pachacutec near the Centro Cultural (9am–8pm daily; ⓣ211104, ⓔiperumachupicchu@promperu.gob.pe). INRENA, the Instituto Nacional de Cultura offices, responsible for management of the national sanctuary of Machu Picchu, are on the rail line, just past the post office, towards the *Inkaterra Machu Picchu* hotel end.

Tour operators Numerous companies offer tours covering Machu Picchu and the Inca Trail (see p.222). Most of the hotels also organize tours or have links with operators.

Website ⓦmachu-picchu-peru.info.

4

ACCOMMODATION

MACHU PICCHU PUEBLO

Although there is an overwhelming choice of places to stay in Machu Picchu Pueblo, there can be a lot of competition for lodgings during the high season (June–Sept), when large groups of travellers often turn up and take over entire hotels. Coming to town on an early train will give you some increased choice in where to stay, but for the better places try and book at least a week or two, if not months, in advance.

Chaska Alameda Hermanos Ayar ⓣ211045, Cusco ⓣ272448, ⓔchaska_machupicchu@hot. Located close to the craft market on the station side of the Río Aguas Calientes, this is a new hostel with comfortable beds, plain rooms (some with views over the river and town), laundry and cafeteria. **S/170**

Gringo Bill's Colla Raymi 104 ⓣ211046, Cusco ⓣ223663, ⓦgringobills.com. Also known as the *Hostal Q'oni Unu*, this is one of the most interesting choices in town, with bar, restaurant and rooms, some painted with attractive and rather cosmic murals, forming an appealing complex built into the lower hillside. It offers money-changing facilities, a book exchange, laundry, sauna, lunch packs, ample hot water and a relaxed environment. Breakfasts are included, and grilled meats are served in the evening. **S/220**

Hospedaje Rupa Wasi C Huanacaure 180 ⓣ211101, ⓦrupawasi.net. This very homely place is something of an eco-spiritual centre as well as a hostel, built onto the valley side but less than 4min walk from the plaza and church. Describing itself as an eco-lodge, making building bricks for the walls with non-degradable rubbish, it has a range of attractive wooden cabins, with simple but elegantly ethnic decor. Some cabins come with balconies and the only view to Machu Picchu available from this part of the valley. There's also a gourmet restaurant – the best in town – on site, and a massage facility. **S/160**

Hospedaje Samana Wasi Inca Yupanqui ⓣ211170. Also known as *Nusta Wasi*, this is a reasonably priced place that has hot water and some rooms with private bath, TV and good views across the Río Aguas Calientes. Price includes breakfast. **S/120**

Hostal La Cabaña Av Pachacutec M20–Lot 3 ⓣ211048, ⓦlacabanamachupicchu.com. The comfy, stylish rooms come with fresh flowers in this safe and friendly boutique-style hotel. Other features include open lounge areas, a laundry and library, and one of the owners is also a local guide. Price includes a great buffet breakfast. A deposit is sometimes required to secure bookings. **S/300**

Hostal Los Caminantes Av Imperio de los Incas 138 ⓣ211007. An older, rambling building, located by the railway at the eastern edge of town, this place has rooms with or without bath and hot water, but not much else. **S/80**

Hostal Quilla Av Pachacutec ⓣ211009, Cusco ⓣ256568, ⓔmariaquilla6@hotmail.com. A very friendly hostel offering rooms with private bath, breakfasts (included) and good tourist information; they can organize guided tours locally. There's a restaurant serving Peruvian dishes and pizzas. **S/140**

Inkaterra Machu Picchu Km110 by the rail line on the western edge of the settlement 211122, Lima 01 6100404, inkaterra.com. Together with its sister hotels in Cusco and the Sacred Valley, this is one of the most elegant and interesting boutique-style hotels in Peru, accessed by an almost hidden entrance just beyond the edge of town as you walk up the rail track towards Cusco. Both the rooms and communal areas are beautiful, and it has its own swimming pool, as well as stunning gardens replete with an amazing variety of fearless hummingbirds, and five hectares of its own protected cloud forest. S/800

Machu Picchu Hostal Av Imperio de los Incas 244598. A clean and smart place, located right beside the old station platform on the river side of the tracks; most rooms are based around a small garden, and all have good showers. S/240

Machu Picchu Inn Av Pachacutec 109 211011, elmapihotel.com. A plain but comfortable hotel with a nice geranium garden, pool room and fine restaurant. S/700

Wiracocha Inn C Wiracocha 211088, wiracochainn.com. A really engaging hotel located down a lane about halfway up Avenida Pachacutec, with a pretty lobby, very colourful and clean bedrooms and a dining room terrace shaded by trees. S/400

AROUND MACHU PICCHU

Machu Picchu Consejo campsite Close to the site. This campsite is just over the Río Urubamba on the railway side of the bridge at the bottom of the hill from Machu Picchu, from where the buses start their climb up to the ruins.

Machu Picchu Sanctuary Lodge By the entrance to the ruins 01 6108300 or 084 9848 16953, sanctuarylodgehotel.com. The only hotel actually up by the entrance to the ruins themselves is this very expensive place. It's something of a concrete block, but it's comfortable and has a restaurant. Staying here allows you to explore the site early in the morning or in the afternoons and evenings when most other visitors have gone. S/2590

EATING AND DRINKING

Café Internet Restaurant Corner of Contisuyo. Serves coffee, omelettes, pizzas, trout and spaghetti, among other dishes, and has fast internet access. Daily 7am–9pm.

Chez Maggy's Av Pachacutec 156 211006. A chain restaurant serving reasonable meals (their speciality being pizzas) and sometimes playing rock music. Daily 10am–10pm.

Costandino C Huancaure 180 211101. By far the best restaurant in town, *Costandino* combines the best of Andean, Italian, Thai and Argentinian cooking. Both main dishes and sweets (try the passion fruit pudding) are exceptional, all made with as many local fresh ingredients as possible, and worth every calorie. Good wines and breakfasts, too. Daily 5am–3pm & 6–9pm.

El Gourmet Grill Av Pachacutec 138. A rather pretentious name for a pizzeria, though the service is good and they have a range of cocktails, as well as international dishes. Daily 10.30am–11pm.

Govinda Av Pachacutec 20 794841. The Machu Picchu outpost of this well-known chain serves up good veggie meals such as plain salads, squash and quinoa soup. Daily 8am–8pm.

★ El Indio Feliz Lloque Yupanqui Lote 4m-12 211090, indiofeliz.com. This place serves exceptional three- or four-course meals of French and local dishes at remarkably inexpensive prices; try to reserve a table as far in advance as possible. Daily noon–11pm.

Pizzeria Pachamama Imperio de los Incas 143 212231. Opposite the small market, this place specializes in pizza, pancakes, breakfasts and *lomo* steak in mushroom sauce. Daily 7am–9pm.

Restaurant El Manu Av Pachacutec. This restaurant has a nice open dining area (sometimes doubling up as a dance space which gets quite lively at night), and specializes in trout and pizza. Daily 10am–10pm.

Toto's House Restaurant Av Imperio de los Incas 211020. A vast restaurant with great views and some tables out front by the rail tracks; they offer an expensive but quite good buffet lunch every day ($10). Daily 8am–9pm.

DIRECTORY

Internet *Café Internet Restaurant*, at the corner of Avenida Imperio de los Incas next to the old train station, has decent access (S/8/hr), plus cakes, snacks and drinks; there are plenty of others along Avenida Pachacutec.

Laundry Most hostels and hotels will offer this, but there are some laundries dotted around, particularly on the station side of Río Aguas Calientes.

Left luggage Next to the entrance to the ruins (no backpacks or camping equipment are allowed inside; price per item S/5).

Money and exchange There's an ATM by the municipal building, just down from the bus ticket office, and also at the Banco de Credito next to *Toto's House Restaurant*.

Photography Kodak shop with digital products and some film on Av Imperio de los Incas, on the same block as the *Café Internet Restaurant*.

Police Avenida Imperio de los Incas, just down from the old train station (211178).

Post office On the rail tracks, some 100m or so west beyond the Banco de Credito.

Telephones Centro Telefónica, Av Imperio de los Incas 132 (211091).

Alternative treks to the Inca Trail

There are **three main trekking routes** that have been developed by Cusco-based adventure tour operators (see p.222) in response to the desperate over-demand for the Inca Trail. The most popular of these is **Choquequirao**, and like the Inca Trail, this trek ends at a fabulous ancient citadel. Treks around the sacred glaciated mountain of **Salcantay** are also well-developed and, to some extent, overlap with and link to the Inca Trail itself. Much less walked, but equally breathtaking, is **Ausangate**, another sacred snow-covered peak (with a convenient looping trail) that on a clear day can be seen from Cusco dominating the southern horizon. Another popular trek is the route from Ollantaytambo to **Lares** (see box, p.251). As for **cost**, these treks are similar in price to the Inca Trail, ranging from about $60 to $100 a day.

Choquequirao

An increasingly popular alternative to the Inca Trail, the hike to **Choquequirao** can be made with a trekking tour of **three to four days**; these leave Cusco on demand and pretty much daily during tourist season. Not quite as spectacular as Machu Picchu, this is still an impressive Inca citadel whose name in Quechua means "Cradle of Gold". Sitting among fine terraces under a glaciated peak of the Salcantay range, less than half the original remains have been uncovered from centuries of vegetation, making a visit here similar to what Hiram Bingham may have experienced at Machu Picchu when he discovered the site back in 1911 (see p.259).

Brief history

Located 1750m above the Apurimac River and 3104m above sea level in the district of Vilcabamba, Choquequirao is thought to have been a **rural retreat** for the Inca emperor as well as a **ceremonial centre**. It was built in the late fifteenth century and almost certainly had an important political, military and economic role, controlling people and produce between the rainforest communities of the Ashaninka (see p.524), who still live further down the Apurimac River, and the Andean towns and villages of the Incas. It's easy to imagine coca, macaw feathers, manioc, salt and other Ashaninka products making their way to Cusco via Choquequirao.

Hiram Bingham came to Choquequirao in 1910 on his search for lost Inca cities. Regardless of the exquisite stonework of the ceremonial complex and the megalithic agricultural terracing, Bingham – as have many archeologists since – failed to see just how important a citadel Choquequirao actually was. Evidence from digs here suggest that a large population continuously inhabited Choquequirao and nearby settlements, even after the Spanish Conquest.

The trek to Choquequirao

The most **direct route** up is along the Abancay road from Cusco – about four hours – to Cachora in Apurímac, over 100km from Cusco and some 93km north of Abancay; from here it's a further 30km (15–20 hours) of heavy but stunningly beautiful trekking to the remains of the Choquequirao citadel. A longer and even more **scenic route**

CAMINO SAGRADO DE LOS INCAS

The **Camino Sagrado de los Incas**, a truncated Inca Trail, starts at Km 104 of the Panamerican Highway, 8km from Machu Picchu. The footbridge here (roughly $50 entry, $25 for students, free for children under 12; includes entry to Machu Picchu) leads to a steep climb (4–6hr) past Chachabamba to reach Wiñay Wayna (see p.256), where most people camp. From here the route joins the remainder of the Inca Trail, which can be reached easily in another 2 to 4 hours.

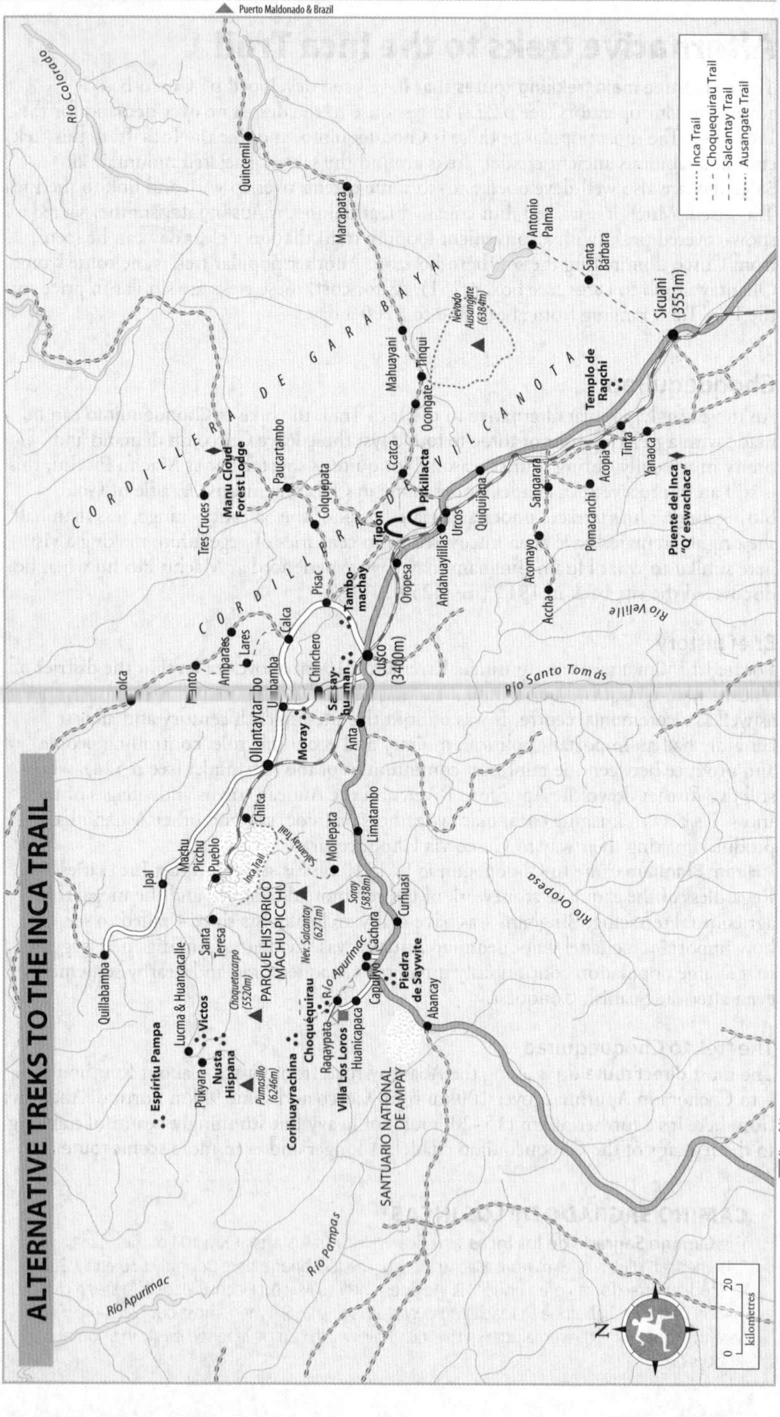

4

ALTERNATIVE TREKS TO THE INCA TRAIL

Inca Trail
Choquequirau Trail
Salcantay Trail
Ausangate Trail

Puerto Maldonado & Brazil
Nazca & Lima
0 20 kilometres
N

CORDILLERA DE GARABAYA
CORDILLERA DE VILCANOTA
Río Colorado
Río Apurímac
Río Pampas
Río Oropesa
Río Santo Tomás
Río Velille

Quincemil
Marcapata
Antonio Palma
Santa Bárbara
Sicuani (3551m)
Nevado Ausangate (6384m)
Mahuayani
Tinqui
Ocongate
Ccatca
Templo de Raqchi
Tinta
Yanaoca
Acopia
Pomacanchi
Sangarara
Quiquijana
Puente del Inca "Q' eswachaca"
Pikillacta
Tipón
Urcos
Andahuayllillas
Oropesa
Acomayo
Accha
Tres Cruces
Manu Cloud Forest Lodge
Paucartambo
Colquepata
Pisac
Tambo-machay
Calca
Lares
Amparaes
Pianto
Colca
Cusco (3400m)
Chinchero
Sacsay-huaman
Urubamba
Ollantaytambo
Moray
Anta
Limatambo
Chilca
Mollepata
Salcantay Trail
Inca Trail
Machu Picchu
Pueblo
Ipal
PARQUE HISTORICO MACHU PICCHU
Nev. Salcantay (6271m)
Soray (5838m)
Curhuasi
Cachora
Piedra de Saywite
Capuliyoc
Abancay
SANTUARIO NATIONAL DE AMPAY
Huanicapaca
Villa Los Loros
Raqaypata
Choquequirau
Corihuayrachina
Santa Teresa
Choquetacarpo (5520m)
Quillabamba
Lucma & Huancacalle
Victos
Nusta Hispana
Pukyara
Pumasillo (6246m)
Espíritu Pampa

involves taking a twelve-day hike from Huancacalle and Pukyura and then over the Pumasillo range, through Yanama, Minas Victoria, Choquequirao and across the Apurímac ending in Cachora.

Taking the direct route, the first two hours are spent hiking to Capuliyo, where, at 2915m, there are fantastic panoramas over the Apurímac Valley. The trail descends almost 1500m from here to Playa Rosalina on the banks of the Río Apurímac, where it's possible to camp the first night. The second day has the most gruelling uphill walking – about five hours as far as Raqaypata and a further two or three to Choquequirao itself.

The site

Daily 6am–6pm • S/35

Consisting of nine main sectors, the **site** was a political and religious centre, well served by a complex system of aqueducts, canals and springs. Most of the buildings are set around the main ceremonial courtyard or plaza and are surrounded by well-preserved and stylish Inca agricultural terracing.

The return journey

You can go in and come out the same way in three to four days, or as an alternative, leave Choquequirao via a different, more or less circular, route following the path straight down from the ruins to the river bridge at San Ignacio. From here it's a two-hour hike up the valley to the *Villa Los Loros* Lodge (see below). The small town of **Huanipaca**, with colectivos for Abancay, is a further two to three hours' steep uphill walk from here (or you can call a taxi from the lodge's phone). Alternatively, Choquequirao can be approached this way (it's a faster route than via Cachora) and, in a reverse circular route, you can then exit via Cachora.

4

ACCOMMODATION AND EATING — CHOQUEQUIRAO

Villa Los Loros Choquequirao Lodge Carretera Al Carmen Km 17,500, Tambobamba ☎83 816053, choquequiraolodge.com. A plush and stylish hotel 5–6 hours' walk from Choquequirao. There are luxury two-person bungalows, as well as superb Italian and Peruvian food served in a swish hacienda-style lounge-bar-cum-restaurant. **S/250**

Salcantay

Colectivos connect Mollepata with Cusco daily (3–4hr); you can take a ride in a truck from Mollepata as far as Soraypampa, cutting out the first 8hr of the usual trek, for around S/15, but trucks arrive irregularly

The **SALCANTAY** mountain (6271m) is one of the Cusco region's main *apus*, or gods. Its splendid snowcapped peak dominates the landscape to the northwest of Cusco and it makes for relatively peaceful trekking territory. The main route joins the Machu Picchu railway line and the Urubamba Valley with the lesser-visited village of Mollepata in the Río Apurímac watershed. The trek usually takes from **five to seven days** and offers greater contact with local people, a wider range of ecological niches to pass through and higher paths than the Inca Trail: a good option for more adventurous trekkers who have already acclimatized.

The trail

Most people start on the Urubamba side of Machu Picchu at Km 82, where the Inca Trail also starts (see p.252). From here you can follow the **Inca Trail path** up the Cusichaca Valley, continuing straight uphill from the hamlet of Huayllabamba (**mules** and muleteers can be hired here, when available, from around S/30 and S/40 a day, respectively), ignoring the main Inca Trail that turns west and right here, up towards Dead Woman's Pass – La Abra de Huarmihuañusca. Throughout the trail, the landscape and scenery are very similar to the Inca Trail, though this route brings you much closer to the edge of the glaciers. The trail is steep and hard, up to the high pass at 5000m, which takes you around the southern edge of **Salcantay glacier**, before descending directly south to the village of **Mollepata**.

The trek is increasingly approached **in reverse**, with guides and mules hired at Mollepata where there is less competition for them than there is on the Huayllabamba side; this route means you finish up in the Urubamba Valley, between Machu Picchu and Ollantaytambo. There are no official **camping** sites en route, but plenty of good tent sites and several traditional stopping-off spots.

Ausangate

The start point of the trail, Tinqui, is reached by a 3–4hr drive from Cusco via Urcos

An important mountain god for the Incas, **AUSANGATE** is still revered daily by locals. One of the most challenging and exciting treks in southern Peru, this **five-day trail** is also relatively quiet: you'll see very few people, apart from the occasional animal herder, once you leave the start and end point for this trail at the village of **Tinqui** at 3800m.

The **Ausangate Circuit** explores the Cordillera Vilcanota, weaving around many peaks over 6000m. Ausangate, the highest peak at 6384m, remains at the hub of the standard trail. Many of the camps are over 4600m and there are two passes over 5000m to be tackled. A good **map** is essential – the best is the *PERU Topographic Survey 1:100,000 – 28-T*, available from the South American Explorers' Club (see p.222) – and a local **guide** strongly recommended. The management at Tinque's *Hostal Ausangate* can arrange guides, mules and a muleteer (*arriero*). Some **supplies** are now available at the trailhead, but it's still safer to bring everything you need with you; there's more choice in Cusco, but some food and cooking utensils could be purchased en route in Urcos.

The trail

The **first day's** uphill walking from Tinqui brings you to a natural campsite on a valley floor almost 4500m above sea level close to the hot springs near Upis with tremendous views of Nevado Ausangate. **Day two** requires about six hours of walking, following the valley up and over into the next valley through the high pass of Arapa (4800m) heading for the camping area at the red-coloured lake of Laguna Jatun Pucacocha; from here you can see and hear the Nevado Ausangate's western ice-falls against a backdrop of alpaca herds.

Day three tackles the highest of all the passes – Palomani (5170m) – early on. From here there are views over Laguna Ausangatecocha, and the walking continues up and down, passing the Ausangate base camp en route. From Palomani it is three or four hours' walk to the next campsite, offering some of the best views towards the glaciated peak itself.

Day four continues downhill towards the Pitumarca Valley, which you follow left uphill to a campsite beyond Jampa, a remote settlement way beyond the electricity grid, but just this side of the magical Campa Pass (5050m), where centuries' worth of stone piles or cairns left by locals and travellers adorn the landscape honouring the mountain god. From here there are spectacular views towards the snowcapped peaks of Puka Punta and Tres Picos.

Day five takes you uphill again through the pass and down beside Lake Minaparayoc. From here it's a three- or four-hour descent to the campsite at Pacchanta where there are some welcoming hot springs, traditionally enjoyed by trekkers as they near the end of this trail. Beyond Pacchanta, it's another three-hour walk back to Tinqui for road transport to Cusco.

Towards the jungle

The two major places to visit **northeast of Cusco** are **Paucartambo**, 112km from Cusco, and **Tres Cruces**, another 50km beyond Paucartambo. The road between the two follows the **Kosnipata Valley** ("Valley of Smoke"), then continues through cloudy

NEW DISCOVERIES

Major Inca sites are still being discovered in this jungle region. In April 2002 British explorer **Hugh Thomson** – author of *The White Rock* (see p.531) – and American archeologist **Gary Ziegler**, following rumours of a **lost city**, led an expedition, which discovered an Inca city in the virtually inaccessible valley bottom at the confluence of the ríos Yanama and Blanco in the Vilcabamba region. Apparently seen briefly by **Hiram Bingham** nearly a hundred years ago, the coordinates were never recorded and this settlement of forty main buildings set around a central plaza hadn't been spotted since. Although very difficult to access – due to river erosion – there appears to have been an Inca road running through the valley, probably connecting this site to the great Inca citadel of **Choquequirao** (see p.267). This settlement is believed to have been Manco Inca's hideout during his rebellion against the conquistadors, which lasted until his execution in Cusco in 1572 (see p.209).

tropical mountain scenery to the mission of Shintuya on the edge of the **Manu National Park** (see p.446). Legend has it that the Kosnipata enchants anyone who drinks from its waters at Paucartambo, drawing them to return again and again.

The area along the Río Urubamba from Machu Picchu onwards, to the **north**, is a quiet, relatively accessible corner of the Peruvian wilderness. As you descend from Ollantaytambo, the vegetation along the valley turns gradually into **jungle**, thickening and getting greener by the kilometre, as the air gets steadily warmer and more humid. Most people heading down here get as far as the town of **Quillabamba**, but the road continues deeper into the rainforest where it meets the navigable jungle river at **Ivochote** (see p.453). Many come to this region to explore its mountains, cloud forest and rainforest areas, either to check out known Inca ruins or to search out some new ones. It's relatively easy to visit the hilltop ruins of the palace at **Vitcos**, a site of Inca blood sacrifices, and possible – though an expedition of six days or more – to explore the more remote ruins at **Espíritu Pampa**, now thought to be the site of the legendary lost city of Vilcabamba.

4

Paucartambo

Eternally spring-like because of the combination of altitude and proximity to tropical forest, the pretty village of **PAUCARTAMBO** ("Village of the Flowers") is located some 110km from Cusco in a wild and remote Andean region, and guards a major entrance to the **jungle zone of Manu**. A silver-mining colony, run by slave labour during the seventeenth and eighteenth centuries, it's now a popular destination that is at its best in the dry season between May and September, particularly in mid-July when the annual **Fiesta de la Virgen del Carmen** takes place (see box, p.272); visitors arrive in their thousands and the village is transformed from a peaceful habitation into a huge mass of frenzied, costumed dancers. Even if you don't make it to Paucartambo for the festival, you can still see the ruined *chullpa* burial towers at **Machu Cruz**, an hour's walk from Paucartambo; ask in the village for directions. Travellers rarely make it here outside of festival time, unless en route to the rainforest by road.

Plaza Principal

The beautiful main **plaza**, with its white buildings and traditional blue balconies, holds concrete **monuments** depicting the characters who perform at the fiesta – demon-masked dancers, malaria victims, lawyers, tourists and just about anything that grabs the imagination of the local communities. Also on the plaza is the rather austere **iglesia**, restored in 1998 and splendid in its own way, simple yet full of large Cusqueña paintings. It's also the residence of the sacred **image of the Virgen del Carmen**, unusual in its Indian (rather than European) appearance. When the pope visited Peru in the mid-1980s, it was loaded onto a truck and driven to within 30km of Cusco, then paraded on foot to the city centre so that the pope could bless the image.

FIESTA DE LA VIRGEN DEL CARMEN

Paucartambo spends the first six months of every year gearing up for the **Fiesta de la Virgen del Carmen**. It's an essentially female festival: tradition has it that a wealthy young woman, who had been on her way to Paucartambo to trade a silver dish, found a beautiful (if body-less) head that spoke to her once she'd placed it on the dish. Arriving in the town, people gathered around her and witnessed rays of light shining from the head, and henceforth it was honoured with prayer, incense and a wooden body for it to sit on.

The energetic, hypnotic **festival** lasts three or four days – usually July 16–19, but check with the tourist office in Cusco (see p.222) – and features throngs of locals in distinctive **traditional costumes**, with **market stalls** and a small **fair** springing up near the church. Clamouring down the streets are throngs of intricately costumed and masked **dancers and musicians**, the best known of whom are the black-masked **Capaq Negro**, recalling the African slaves who once worked the nearby silver mines. Note the grotesque blue-eyed masks and outlandish costumes acting out a parody of the white man's powers – **malaria**, a post-Conquest problem, tends to be a central theme – in which an old man suffers terrible agonies until a Western medic appears on the scene, with the inevitable hypodermic in his hand. If he manages to save the old man (a rare occurrence) it's usually due to a dramatic muddling of prescriptions by his dancing assistants – and thus does Andean fate triumph over science.

On Saturday afternoon there's a **procession of the Virgen del Carmen** itself, with a brass band playing mournful melodies as petals and emotion are showered on the icon of the Virgin – which symbolizes worship of Pachamama as much as devotion to Christianity. The whole event culminates on Sunday afternoon with the **dances of the guerreros** (warriors), during which good triumphs over evil for another year.

4

ARRIVAL AND INFORMATION — PAUCARTAMBO

By bus Transportes Gallitos de las Rocas buses leave from their Cusco office (Av Diagonal Angamos 1952; ⊙ 226095) daily to Paucartambo (4–5hr; $2.50) and three times a week to Pilcopata (see p.448), the first major settlement (6–8hr on from Paucartambo) as you go down into the jungle. Buses generally stop off in Paucartambo's marketplace.

By truck Trucks, which leave from the end of Avenida Garcilaso in Cusco, beyond the Ormeño office, are slightly cheaper but slower and far less comfortable.

Tourist information During festival times, a tourist information point can usually be found near the stone bridge which leads over the river into the main part of town, en route to the plaza.

ACCOMMODATION AND EATING

When the Fiesta de la Virgen del Carmen is on, both of the places below are always fully booked (and their prices hiked), but it's possible to rent out spaces in local residents' homes or find a site to **camp**. It is always best to take a tent, in case all rooms are full. There's a good **restaurant** on the south side of the upper stone river bridge.

Albergue Municipal Near the lower bridge; no phone. A central, no-frills option. S/70

Hotel Quinta Rosa Marina Near the lower bridge; no phone. Central and very basic. S/70

Tres Cruces

The natural special effects during sunrise at **TRES CRUCES** are in their own way as magnificent a spectacle as the Fiesta de la Virgen del Carmen (see box above). At 3739m above sea level, on the last mountain ridge before the eastern edge of the Amazon forest, the **view** is a marvel at any time: by day a vast panorama over the start of a massive cloud forest with all its weird and wonderful vegetation; by night an enormous star-studded jewel. Seen from the highest edge of the **Manu Biosphere Reserve**, the **sunrise** is spectacular, particularly around the southern hemisphere's winter solstice in June: multicoloured, with multiple suns, it's an incredible light show that lasts for hours. The only **accommodation** in Tres Cruces is an empty house that's used as a visitors' shelter, which fills up very fast at Paucartambo and

solstice festival times, when **camping** is the only real option, so take a warm sleeping bag, a tent and enough food.

ARRIVAL AND DEPARTURE — TRES CRUCES

By bus Transport to Tres Cruces can be a problem, except during the Paucartambo fiesta in July; however, on Mon, Wed and Fri, Transportes Gallinos de las Rocas buses to Paucartambo (see p.271) continue on to Pilcopata or Salvación; beyond Paucartambo, you can disembark at the Tres Cruces turn-off (about 8hr from Cusco; $3), but be prepared to walk the remaining 14km into Tres Cruces itself, though you may get a lift with a passing vehicle (especially early in the day from late June to mid-July).

By colectivo Check the notice boards in the main cafés and backpacker joints in Cusco for people trying to gather together groups to share the cost of a colectivo and driver for the two- to three-day trip – usually S/100 to 150 a day, plus food and drink for the driver – or post a notice yourself.

By tour/colectivo Cusco tour operators (see p.222) can organize a trip.

Vitcos and Espíritu Pampa

The easiest way to see the **Vitcos and Espíritu Pampa ruins** is on a guided tour with an adventure tour company (see p.222). If you'd rather travel more independently, expedition-type preparation is required: you should hire a local **guide** (best done through Cusco tour agents) and possibly even mules. You'll need **a week or more** to cover both sites. There are no services or facilities as such at either location, and neither is staffed by permanent on-site guardians; the sites are free and accessible as long as you have **permission** from the Instituto Nacional de Cultura (see p.265).

Vitcos

Daily 24hr • Free, but permission from Instituto Nacional de Cultura required (see p.265)

In 1911, after discovering Machu Picchu, **Hiram Bingham** set out down the Urubamba Valley to Chaullay, then up the Vilcabamba Valley to Pukyura, where he expected to find more Inca ruins. What he found – **VITCOS** (known locally as Rosapata) – was a relatively small but clearly palatial ruin, based around a trapezoidal plaza spread across a flat-topped spur. Down below the ruins, Bingham was shown by local guides a spring flowing from beneath a vast, **white granite boulder** intricately carved in typical Inca style and surrounded by the remains of an impressive Inca temple. This fifteen-metre-long and eight-metre-high sacred white rock – called Chuquipalta by the Incas – was a great oracle where **blood sacrifices** and other religious rituals took place. According to early historical chronicles, these rituals had so infuriated two Spanish priests who witnessed them that they exorcized the rock and set its temple sanctuary on fire.

Espíritu Pampa

Daily 24hr • Free, but permission from Instituto Nacional de Cultura required (see p.265)

Within two weeks of the discovery of Vitcos, Bingham had followed a path from Pukyura into the jungle as far as the Condevidayoc plantation, where he found some more "undiscovered" ruins at **ESPÍRITU PAMPA** – "Plain of the Spirits". After briefly exploring some of the outer ruins at Espíritu Pampa, Bingham decided they must have been built by Manco Inca's followers and deduced that they were post-Conquest Inca constructions since many of the roofs were Spanish-tiled. Believing that he had already found the lost city of **Vilcabamba** he was searching for at Machu Picchu, Bingham paid little attention to these newer discoveries.

Consequently, as the site was accessible only by mule, Espíritu Pampa remained covered in thick jungle vegetation until 1964, when serious exploration was undertaken by US archeological explorer **Gene Savoy**. He found a massive ruined complex with over sixty main buildings and some three hundred houses, along with temples, plazas, wells and a main street. Clearly this was the largest Inca refuge in the Vilcabamba area, and Savoy rapidly became convinced of its identity as the true site of the last Inca stronghold. More conclusive evidence has since been provided by the English geographer and historian

John Hemming who, using the chronicles, was able to match descriptions of Vilcabamba, its climate and altitude, precisely with those of Espíritu Pampa.

ARRIVAL AND DEPARTURE **VITCOS AND ESPÍRITU PAMPA**

By tour Tours are best arranged through one of the companies in Cusco (see p.222).
By truck You can get to the ruins at Vitcos or Espíritu Pampa independently via the villages of Pukyura and Huancacalle, in the Vilcabamba River valley. These settlements are reached in 6hr by trucks which are usually easily picked up (small fee charged) at Chaullay on the Ollantaytambo–Quillabamba road.

South from Cusco

The first 150km of the road (and rail) south from Cusco towards Lake Titicaca (see p.184) passes through the beautiful valleys of Huatanay and Vilcanota, from where the legendary founders of the Inca Empire are said to have emerged. A region outstanding for its natural beauty and rich in magnificent archeological sites, it's easily accessible from Cusco and offers endless possibilities for exploration or random wandering. The whole area is ideal for **camping and trekking**, and in any case, only the rustic towns of **Urcos** and **Sicuani** are large enough to provide reasonable accommodation (see p.278 and p.279).

A few kilometres further up the valley, the superb Inca remains of **Tipón** lie high above the road, little visited but extensive and evocative. Closer to the road, the Huari city of **Pikillacta** is easier to find and worthy of an hour or two. Beyond Urcos but before Sicuani, a rather dull transport hub of a town, the great **Temple of Raqchi** still stands unusually high as a monument to Inca architectural abilities.

4

ARRIVAL AND GETTING AROUND **SOUTH FROM CUSCO**

BY BUS

As the trains are slow, infrequent and don't stop at all towns, most people travel on one of the frequent, and cheaper, buses or minibuses. Many of the bus options are inter-regional carriers (see box, p.221).

Inka Express The best option is offered by Inka Express, Urb. El Ovalo, Av La Paz C-32 (T 247887, W inkaexpress.com), which has quality buses linking Cusco with Puno, but also offers opportunities to stop off at some of the tourist sites below, including Tipón and Raqchi (see p.276 and p.278), en route, with a bilingual tour guide.

El Zorro, Sol Andino & Oriental These companies run daily services (daily from 3.40am until early afternoon; every 20min; T 240406) from Av de la Cultura 1624 as far as Urcos and Sicuani, passing all the sites covered below except La Raya.

Empresa Vilcanota Buses to Sicuani leave to Urcos (S/3) from Av de la Cultura 13230 or the depot behind a *churrascaria* at the end of block 13 of Avenida de la Cultura (opposite the Hospital Regional).

Destinations San Sebastián (many daily; 10–15min); Oropesa (many daily; 25–30min); Tipón (many daily; 30–35min).

San Sebastián

Heading south from Cusco by road, after about 5km you pass through the little pueblo of **San Sebastián**. Originally a small, separate village, it has now become a suburb of the city. It has an impressive **church**, ornamented with Baroque stonework, six Neo classical columns and two squat belfries. It was apparently built on the site of a chapel erected by the Pizarros in memory of their victory over Almagro. These days San Sebastián is celebrated with processions and prayers through the month of Jaunuary, often providing a colourful spectacle.

Oropesa

The next place of any interest beyond San Sebastián is picturesque **Oropesa**, some 25km on, traditionally a town of bakers, whose adobe **church**, boasting a uniquely attractive

SCENIC ROUTES TO PUNO AND LIMA

Even if you aren't planning to spend time around Lake Titicaca, the rail journey south to **Puno** (see p.186) is worth taking. The journey starts in the Cusco region and takes around twelve hours, covering a soul-stirring route that climbs slowly through stunning green river valleys to a desolate landscape to the pass, beyond the town of Sicuani. From here it rolls down onto the altiplano, a flat high plain studded wih adobe houses and large herds of llama and alpaca, before reaching Lake Titicaca and the port city of Puno.

If **Lima** is your destination, consider the 20-hour direct highland route northwest from Cusco through Abancay and then down to the coast at Nasca. Known as the Nasca-Cusco Corridor, it offers access to a range of potential stop-overs on the way: the archeological sites of Choquequirao and Sahuite; the city of Abancay and protected mountain forest area of Ampay; the thermal baths at Chaullanca and the alpaca and vicuña centre at Puquio; and, of course, the mysterious archeological sites around Nasca itself.

three-tiered belfry with cacti growing out of it, is notable for its intricately carved pulpit and the beautiful, Cusqueña-esque interior murals which look to have been painted between 1580 and 1630. On the left side of the church there's a pretty little chapel, the Capilla de Jesús. In early Inca days Oropesa was home to a well-known rebel clan, the Pinaguas, who had to be subdued by Pachacutec before he could safely build his country residence at Tipón (see below).

The Tipón temples and aqueducts

Daily 7am–5.30pm • Entry by Cusco Tourist Ticket (see box, p.222)

Both in setting and architectural design, the **TIPÓN RUINS** are one of the most impressive Inca sites. With no village or habitation in sight, and fresh running water, it's also a breathtaking place to **camp**.

The lower ruins

Well hidden in a natural shelf high above the Huatanay Valley, the **lower sector** of the ruins is a stunning sight: a series of neat agricultural terraces, watered by stone-lined channels, all astonishingly preserved and many still in use. The impressive stone terracing reeks of the Incas' domination over an obviously massive and subservient labour pool; yet at the same time it's clearly little more than an elaborate attempt to increase crop yield. At the back of the lower ruins, water flows from a stone-faced "mouth" around a **spring** – probably an aqueduct subterraneously diverted from above. The entire complex is designed around this spring, reached by a path from the last terrace.

The reservoir and temple block

Another sector of the ruins contains a **reservoir** and **temple block** centred on a large, exploded volcanic rock – presumably some kind of *huaca*. Although the stonework in the temple seems cruder than that of the agricultural terracing, its location is still beneficial. By contrast, the construction of the reservoir is sophisticated, as it was originally built to hold nine hundred cubic metres of water which gradually dispersed along stone channels to the Inca "farm" directly below.

The upper ruins

Coming off the back of the reservoir, a large, tapering stone **aqueduct** crosses a small gully before continuing uphill – about thirty minutes' walk – to a vast zone of **unexcavated terraces** and dwellings. Beyond these, over the lip of the hill, you come to another level of the upper valley literally covered in Inca terracing, dwellings and large stone storehouses. Equivalent in size to the lower ruins, these are still used by locals who have built their own houses among the ruins. So impressive is the terracing at

Tipón that some archeologists believe it was an Inca **experimental agricultural centre**, much like Moray (see p.246), as well as a citadel.

ARRIVAL AND DEPARTURE — THE TIPÓN TEMPLES

On foot From Oropesa (see p.275), the simplest way to reach the ruins is by backtracking down the main Cusco road some 2km to a sign posted track. Follow this up through a small village, once based around the now crumbling and deserted hacienda Quispicanchi, and continue along the gully straight ahead. Once on the path above the village, it's about an hour's climb to the first ruins. Once you've visited the ruins, there's a splendid stroll back down to the main road – take the path through the locals' huts in the upper sector over to the other side of the stream, and follow it down the hillside opposite Tipón. This route offers an excellent perspective on the ruins, as well as vistas towards Cusco in the north and over the Huatanay/Vilcanota valleys to the south.

By bus If you've taken a bus, get off about 5min beyond Oropesa (you can also flag buses down in Oropesa, but many will be full), then walk east towards the entrance to the site, sign posted from the main road, but higher up the hillside with a reception hut.

Pikillacta and Rumicolca

Pikillacta Daily 7am–5.30pm • Entry by Cusco Tourist Ticket (see box, p.222) **Rumicolca** Daily 24hr • Free • Both sites are right beside the main road (ask the bus driver to drop you off)

About 7km south of Oropesa, the neighbouring pre-Inca ruins of Pikillacta and Rumicolca can be seen alongside the road. After passing the Paucartambo turn-off, near the ruins of an ancient storehouse and the small red-roofed pueblo of **Huacarpay**, the road climbs to a ledge overlooking a wide alluvial plain and **Lucre Lake** (now a weekend resort for Cusco's workers). At this point the road traces the margin of a stone wall defending the pre-Inca settlement of Pikillacta.

Spread over an area of at least fifty hectares, **PIKILLACTA**, or "The Place of the Flea", was built by the Huari culture around 800 AD, before the rise of the Incas. Its unique, geometrically designed **terraces** surround a group of bulky two-storey constructions: apparently these were entered by ladders reaching up to doorways set well off the ground in the first storey – very unusual in ancient Peru. Many of the walls are built of small cut stones joined with mud mortar, and among the most interesting finds here were several round turquoise **statuettes**. These days the city is in ruins but it seems evident still that much of the site was taken up by barrack-like quarters. When the Incas arrived early in the fifteenth century they modified the site to suit their own purposes, possibly even building the aqueduct that once connected Pikillacta with the ruined gateway of Rumicolca, which straddles a narrow pass by the road, fifteen minutes' walk further south.

This massive defensive passage, **RUMICOLCA**, was also initially constructed by the Huari people and served as a southern entrance to – and frontier of – their empire. Later it became an **Inca checkpoint**, regulating the flow of people and goods into the Cusco Valley: no one was permitted to enter or leave the valley via Rumicolca between sunset and sunrise. The Incas improved on the rather crude Huari stonework of the original **gateway**, using regular blocks of polished andesite from a local quarry. The gateway still stands, rearing up to twelve solid metres above the ground, and is one of the most impressive of all Inca constructions.

Andahuaylillas and Huaro

Take the same bus as for all the previous sites along this route (see p.275) and ask the driver to drop you off; the roadside restaurant at which buses and minibuses drop off and pick up is a ten-minute walk from Andahuaylillas' plaza

About halfway between Rumicolca and Urcos, the otherwise insignificant villages of Andahuaylillas and Huaro hide deceptively interesting **colonial churches**. In the tranquil and well-preserved village of **ANDAHUAYLILLAS**, the adobe-towered church sits above an attractive **plaza**, fronted by colonial houses. Built in the early seventeenth century on the site of an Inca temple, the **church** has an exterior balcony from which the priests would deliver sermons. While it's fairly small, with only one nave, it is nevertheless a magnificent example of provincial colonial art. Huge **Cusqueña canvases** decorate the upper walls, while below are some unusual murals, slightly faded over the centuries; the ceiling, painted with Spanish flower designs, contrasts strikingly with the great Baroque altar.

To the south, the road leaves the Río Huatanay and enters the Vilcanota Valley. **HUARO**, crouched at the foot of a steep bend in the road 3km from Andahuaylillas, has a much smaller **church** whose interior is completely covered with colourful **murals** of religious iconography, angels and saints; the massive gold-leaf altarpiece dominates the entire place as you enter.

Urcos

Climbing over the hill from Huaro (see above) to Urcos, you can see **boulders** which have been gathered together in mounds, to clear the ground for the simple ox-pulled ploughs which are still used here. The road descends to cruise past **Lake Urcos** before reaching the town that shares the lake's name. According to legend, the Inca Huascar threw his heavy gold chain into these waters after learning that strange bearded aliens – Pizarro and his crew – had arrived in Peru. Between lake and town, a simple **chapel** now stands poised at the top of a small hillock: if you find it open, go inside to see several excellent Cusqueña paintings.

The town of **URCOS**, resting on the valley floor and surrounded by weirdly sculpted hills, is centred on the **Plaza de Armas**, where a number of huge old trees give shade to Indians selling bread, soup, oranges and vegetables. On one side of the plaza, which is particularly busy during the town's excellent, traditional **Sunday market**, there's a large, crumbling old church; on the other, low adobe buildings.

4

ARRIVAL AND DEPARTURE — URCOS

By bus Buses to and from Cusco, Puno, Paucartambo and Puerto Maldonado drop off and pick up passengers within two blocks of the Plaza de Armas.

ACCOMMODATION AND EATING

There are no quality **hotels** here, but you can usually find a room around the Plaza de Armas. All are very basic, crumbling old buildings with communal bathrooms. Although Urcos is not really a tourist town, the occasional traveller is made welcome; in the backstreets you can stop off at one of the **tiendas** (advertised by a pole with a blob of red plastic on the end) for a glass of *chicha* beer and some friendly conversation.

Alojamiento Municipal Jr Vallejo 137; no phone. Next to the telephones, this offers basic lodgings. **S/60**

El Cisne Azul Plaza de Armas. A simple restaurant on the main plaza. Daily 7am–9pm.

Hostal Luvic Belaunde 196; no phone. A basic place with rooms just to the right of the church. **S/60**

Templo de Raqchi

Daily 9am–5.30pm • Entrance by Cusco Tourist Ticket (see box, p.222) • Buses between Cusco and Urcos pass within a few hundred metres of the temple entrance

Between Urcos and Sicuani the road passes through **San Pedro de Cacha**, the nearest village (4km) to the imposing ruins of the **TEMPLO DE RAQCHI**, built in honour of Viracocha, the Inca creator-god (see box opposite). The temple was supposedly built to appease the god after he had caused the nearby volcano of Quimsa Chata to spew out fiery boulders in a rage of anger, and even now massive **volcanic boulders** and ancient lava flows scar the landscape in constant reminder.

With its adobe walls still standing over 12m high on top of polished stone foundations, and the **site** scattered with numerous other buildings and plazas, such as barracks, cylindrical warehouses, a palace, baths and aqueducts, Raqchi was clearly an important **religious centre**. Today the only ritual left is the annual **Raqchi Festival**

VIRACOCHA'S HUACA

One of the unusually shaped hills surrounding Urcos is named after the creator-god **Viracocha**, as he is said to have stood on its summit and ordered beings to emerge from the hill, thus creating the town's first inhabitants. In tribute, an ornate **huaca**, with a gold bench, was constructed to house a statue to the god, and it was here that the eighth Inca emperor received a divinatory vision in which Viracocha appeared to him to announce that "great good fortune awaited him and his descendants". In this way the emperor obtained his imperial name, **Viracocha Inca**, and also supposedly his first inspiration to conquer non-Inca territory, though it was his son, Pachacuti, who carried the empire to its greatest heights.

(usually June 16–22), a dramatic, untouristy fiesta comprising three to four days of folkloric music and dance – performed by groups congregating here from as far away as Bolivia to compete on the central stage. The performances are well stage managed, but the site, in a boggy field, can be mayhem, with hundreds of food stalls, a funfair, Quechua women selling *chicha* maize beer – and their drunken customers staggering through the tightly knit crowds.

The Puente Colgante

Get off a bus or combi at Combapata, about 30km before Sicuani and 10km further south than Checacupe; from Combapata it's another 31km (45min more by car) to the suspension bridge

Accessible from the Urcos-to-Sicuani road, the **PUENTE COLGANTE** is a hanging or suspension rope bridge that has been rebuilt almost ceremonially every year since before the Spanish Conquest. Annually, up to a thousand locals gather on the **second Sunday in June** to rebuild the bridge using traditional techniques and materials, including *ichu* grasses, to make ropes for the 33-metre span. The building and celebrations generally take three or four days and conclude with ceremony and dancing between the area's principal *ayllus*, or clans.

4

Sicuani

About 20km from Raqchi, **SICUANI** is capital of the province of Canchis and quite a thriving agricultural and market town, not entirely typical of the settlements in the Vilcanota Valley. Its busy **Sunday market** is renowned for cheap and excellent woollen goods, which you may also be offered on the train if you pass through Sicuani between Puno and Cusco. Although not a particularly exciting place in itself – with too many tin roofs and an austere atmosphere – the people are friendly and it makes an excellent **base for trekking** into snowcapped mountain terrain, being close to the vast Nevada Vilcanota mountain range which separates the Titicaca Basin from the Cusco Valley.

The train journey south continues towards Puno and Lake Titicaca (see p.184), with the Vilcanota Valley beginning to close in around the line as the tracks climb **La Raya Pass** (4300m), before dropping down into the desolate *pampa* that covers much of inland southern Peru.

ARRIVAL AND DEPARTURE — SICUANI

By bus Bus is the main way to get here, either from Cusco or Puno. There are several buses daily between Sicuani and Cusco (3hr) as well as Puno (4–5hr).

By train The train is the slowest and most expensive option and although it stops briefly at Sicuani, few if any tourists get off here, since they are obliged to buy a ticket all the way to Puno (see p.186).

ACCOMMODATION

Hostal Tairo C Mejia 120 ⓣ351297. A reasonable accommodation, if very basic. Alternatively, if you ask around it's possible to find a spot to pitch your tent overnight. **S/30**

The Central Sierra

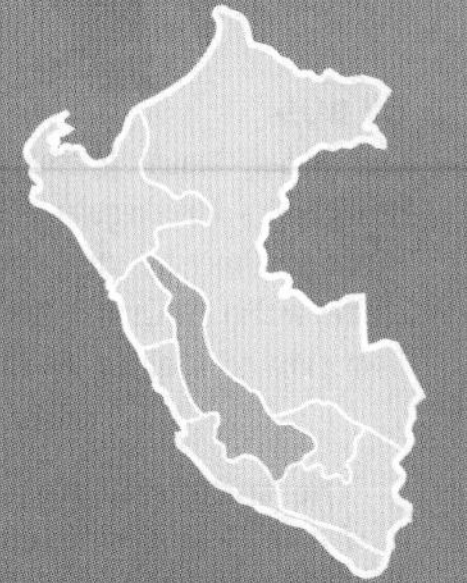

PLAZA DE ARMAS, HUANCAVELICA

5

The Central Sierra

Peppered with traditional towns and cities sitting in remote valleys, the green and mountainous Central Sierra region boasts some of Peru's finest archeological sites and colonial buildings. Although significantly fewer travellers make it here, compared with hotspots like Cusco and Machu Picchu, anyone with the time to spare will find this region a worthwhile destination in its own right, rather than just somewhere to stop en route to the Central Selva (see p.453). As well as fantastic mountain scenery, this amalgam of regions in the central Peruvian Andes offer endless walking country, a caving opportunity and a gateway into the country's Amazon rainforest.

Almost all travellers from Lima enter the Central Sierra by road, along the much-improved **Carretera Central**. The road passes close to the enigmatic rock formations centring on **Marcahuasi** and the village of **San Pedro de Casta** before climbing over the high pass at Ticlio. The old train – the "Tren de la Sierra" – now only rarely takes passengers up to the city of Huancayo.

The most attractive hub in the Sierra Central is the laidback town of **Tarma**, which has a relatively pleasant climate influenced by the cloud forest to the east, and is a major nodal point for pioneers from the jungle, traders and, to a lesser extent, tourists. To the north, pleasant **Huánuco** serves as a good base for exploring some of Peru's most interesting archeological remains, and **Tingo María**, the gateway to the jungle port of Pucallpa. To the southwest of Tarma lies the largest city in the northern half of the Central Sierra, **Huancayo**, high up in the Andes. South of Huancayo are the two most traditional of all the Central Sierra's towns: **Ayacucho** – one of the cultural jewels of the Andes, replete with colonial churches and some of Peru's finest artesan crafts – and **Huancavelica**. Immediately north of Huancayo lies the astonishing **Jauja Valley**, which has beautiful scenery, striped by fabulous coloured furls of mountain.

GETTING AROUND — THE CENTRAL SIERRA

Most people will travel this region by bus. Bar unpredictable events like landslides in the rainy season (Dec–March) or miners' union strikes, a car or bus will get over the Andes faster than the train (see p.284). All buses from Lima have to travel by the often-congested Carretera Central, up past some large mines and over the high pass at Ticlio before descending to La Oroya. The train follows the same route. Once up in the Sierra Central, apart from the Huancayo-to-Huancavelica railway, the only option for travel is by road. The area is well served by regular bus companies and most of the larger towns have colectivo cars or minibuses connecting them with a more informal service and without fixed departure times.

BY BUS

Cruz del Sur, Ormeño, Internacional, PerúBus and Expreso Huancavelica run regular buses between Lima and Huancayo. Other bus companies connect between main centres within the Central Sierra: Expreso Huamanga runs from Lima to Abancay via Huanta and Ayacucho; San Jerónimo connects Andahuaylas with Cusco, via Abancay; Turismo Central joins Huánayo with Huánuco; Palomino links Lima with Andahuaylas, Abancay and Ayacucho; and Expreso Nacional Cerro de Pasco runs between Huancayo and Cerro de Pasco.

ARTESANÍA IN AYACUCHO

Highlights

❶ **Marcahuasi** This high plateau covered in unusual rock formations and reports of UFO sightings makes for out-of-this-world weekend camping. **See p.285**

❷ **Tarma** An attractive little colonial town, known as La Perla de los Andes, is famous for its fantastic Easter Sunday procession and associated flower "paintings" that carpet the roads. **See p.286**

❸ **San Pedro de Cajas** This scenic and remote village is home to many craftspeople who produce some of Peru's superb modern weavings. **See p.287**

❹ **Huancayo–Huancavelica train** The last remaining working railroad in the region, this breathtaking high-altitude train journey is one of the finest in the world. **See p.290**

❺ **Ayacucho** One of the most traditional and architecturally fascinating cities in the Peruvian Andes – renowned for around forty impressive churches as well as boisterous religious fiestas. **See p.296**

❻ **Temple of Kotosh** Over 4000 years old, this impressive site's massive stone constructions suggest that complicated stonework began here centuries before anywhere else in the Americas. **See p.305**

HIGHLIGHTS ARE MARKED ON THE MAP ON P.284

5

BY CAR/TAXI

There are colectivo services between most neighbouring major towns and cities in the Central Sierra, but they are harder to find and without regular departure times. In Huancayo they tend to leave from Calle Real, a little beyond the centre of town; in Lima they start and end at Yerbadero. Hourly taxi rates are S/20–50 depending on the quality of car and how much fuel will be used (or how much waiting time).

BY TRAIN

The world-famous Lima-to-Huancayo railway line ("El Tren

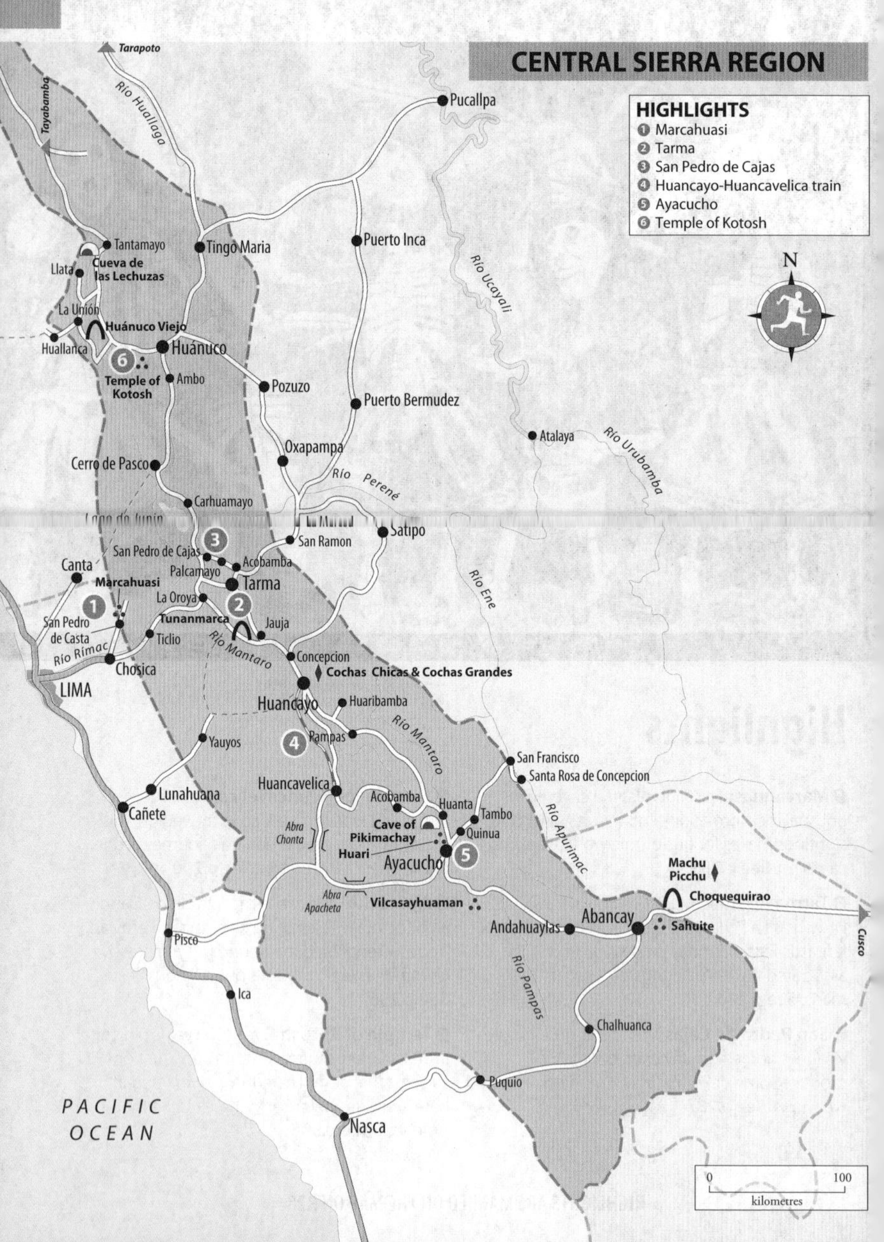

THE ANDES RAIL LINE

The original opening of the Lima-to-Huancayo **railway line** into the Andes in the late nineteenth century had a huge impact on the region and was a major feat of engineering. For President Balta of Peru and many of his contemporaries in 1868, the iron fingers of a railway, "if attached to the hand of Lima would instantly squeeze out all the wealth of the Andes, and the whistle of the locomotives would awaken the Indian race from its centuries-old lethargy". Consequently, when the American rail entrepreneur **Henry Meiggs** (aptly called the "Yankee Pizarro") arrived on the scene, it was decided that coastal guano deposits would be sold off to finance a new rail line, one that faced technical problems (ie, the peaks and troughs of the Andes) never previously encountered by engineers. The man really responsible for the success of this massive project was the Polish engineer, Ernest Malinowski. Utilizing timber from Oregon and the labour of thousands of Chinese workers (the basis of Peru's present Chinese communities), Malinowski's skill and determination finished Meiggs' railway over a 30-year period. An extraordinary accomplishment, it nevertheless produced a mountain of debt that bound Peru more closely to the New York and London banking worlds than to its own hinterland and peasant population.

de la Sierra") currently runs trains from Lima to Huancayo about twice a month (usually leaving Lima Fri or Sat) between April and September for this breathtaking 11hr journey.

Information Precise itineraries, up-to-date prices and tickets can be obtained from FCCA (Ferrocarril Central Andino) by phone or online (☎ 01 226 6363 ext 222 or 235, ⓦ ferrocarrilcentral.com.pe) or in person at the Lima office (Av José Galvez Barrenechea 566, 5th floor, San Isidro).

Mountain sickness You're more likely to suffer from *soroche* – mountain sickness (see p.45) – if you enter the Central Sierra by train, due to the relatively slow climb through the high Ticlio Pass (over 4800m). To avoid breathlessness and headaches, or the even worse effects of *soroche*, it's advisable to take the first few days over 3000m pretty easy before doing any hiking or other strenuous activities.

Tickets There are two classes of ticket: Touristic (S/350 return; S/235 one way) and Classic (S/195 return; S/120 one way).

Lima to Tarma

Vehicles take four to six hours to cross the high pass at Ticlio, after which they drop in less than an hour to the unsightly and mining-contaminated town and pit-stop of **La Oroya**. Just beyond here the road splits three ways: north to **Cerro de Pasco** and **Huánuco**; south to **Huancayo**, **Huancavelica** and, for the travel hardened, **Ayacucho**; or, eastwards towards **Tarma**, which is just another hour or two further.

Marcahuasi

S/10 entrance fee

MARCAHUASI (4100m) is a high plateau that makes a fantastic weekend camping jaunt and is one of the more adventurous but popular excursions from Lima. Its main attractions are incredible, mysterious **rock formations**, which, particularly by moonlight, take on weird shapes – llamas, human faces, turtles, even a hippopotamus. Located 90km east of Lima (40km beyond Chosica), the easiest way to visit this amazing site in the hard-to-access Santa Eulalia Valley is on a day-trip from Lima (see p.81). The annual **Festival de Aventura** takes place in Marcahuasi in early November, incorporating live music with outward-bound activities such as mountain biking, marathon running and motocross. Visitors at the end of July may well come across the **annual village festival** involving three days of ceremony, music, dance and festivities.

5

San Pedro de Casta

Located only a few kilometres from Marcahuasi (2–3hr trek), **San Pedro de Casta** makes a good overnight stop – unless you choose to camp at Marcahuasi. It's a small and simple Andean village, quaint but without much choice in its limited range of facilities.

ARRIVAL AND INFORMATION

LIMA TO TARMA

By bus There are no direct buses from Lima to Marcahuasi/San Pedro. Instead, take a colectivo to Chosica, where there are buses departing for San Pedro from the town's Parque Echinique. Empresa Santa Maria buses usually have signs reading "San Pedro" or "Marcahuasi". If your bus or truck terminates at Las Cruces, you'll have a 30min walk to San Pedro.

Tourist information There's an Oficina de Información (Mon–Fri 9am–6pm, Sat 9am–1pm; ⓣ 01 297 2344) on the main plaza in San Pedro de Casta, where there are also contacts for local guides and *arrieros* with mules (from around $10 a day, plus about $3 per mule).

Tour operators Peru Inka Adventures, Jr Diego de Almagro 535, Jesús María, Lima (ⓣ 01 995 117026 or 01 462 1581, ⓦ inkasadventures.com), organize two-day trips to Marcahuasi for around $170 (minimum 2 people). TEBAC (Trekking and Backpacking Club), Jr Huascar 1152, Jesús María, Lima (ⓣ 01 997 731959, ⓔ tebac@yahoo.com), also take tours.

ACCOMMODATION

Hostal Marcahuasi Plaza de Armas, San Pedro de Casta. Located close to the main square, this place has no working phone so it is impossible to book in advance; with this in mind, a tent is advisable as back-up. The staff are helpful and run a small restaurant-café; though the place is quite basic and has shared bathrooms only. **S/20**

La Oroya

Not a particularly inviting place, **LA OROYA** is a small, desolate mining town that gets fiercely cold at night. Located in a dreary spot above the treeline, some four hours or so by steep uphill road from Lima, La Oroya is some 50km beyond the highest point, the pass or *abra* of Ticlio (4758m). The only possible reason to stop here is to have lunch in one of the many roadside cafés.

Tarma and around

Known locally as "La Perla de los Andes", **TARMA** is by far the nicest mountain town in this part of Peru, with warm temperatures and an abundance of wild and farmed flowers, sitting on the edge of the Andes almost within spitting distance of the Amazon forest. The town makes a good living from its traditional textile and leather industries, and from growing flowers for export as well as for its own use. Although connected with the **Juan Santos Atahualpas rebellion** in the 1740s and 1750s, today Tarma is a quiet place, disturbed only by the flow of trucks climbing up from the Amazon Basin loaded with timber, coffee, chocolate or oranges. The town is particularly famous for an Easter Sunday procession, starting from the main plaza; the streets are covered by carpets of dazzling flowers depicting various local, religious or mythic themes.

The scenary **around Tarma** consitutes one of Peru's most beautiful Andean regions, with green rather than snow-capped mountains stretching down from high, craggy limestone outcrops into steep canyons forged by Amazon tributaries powering their way down to the Atlantic. It's nevertheless always a good idea to check with your embassy in Lima for up-to-the-minute intelligence on this area, since the occasional terrorist column has been known to be active in its remoter sectors.

Palcamayo to San Pedro de Cajas

45min by colectivo from Calle Paucartambo y Otero in Tarma

The rural village of **Palcamayo** makes an interesting day-trip from Tarma, though it's better appreciated if you camp overnight. From here it's an hour's climb to **La Gruta**

de Huagapo, which are the country's deepest explored **caves**; if dry they are generally accessible for about 180m without specialized equipment, or up to 1.8km with a guide and full speleological kit. If you've got your own transport, continue 20km along the same road (the only road in the valley) west to the beautiful village of **San Pedro de Cajas**, where craftspeople produce superb-quality weavings. As an example of how landscapes can influence local art forms, the village lies in a valley neatly divided into patchwork field-systems – an exact model of the local textile style.

Acobamba

Church Daily 7am–7pm • Free • Colectivo from Jr Huánuco in Tarma

Within day-tripping distance from Tarma (12km) is the small settlement of **Acobamba**, home of the **Sanctuary of the Lord of Muruhuay**, a small church built in 1972 around a rock painting where a vision of Christ on the cross led to this site becoming a major centre of pilgrimage. The chapel has an altar with weavings representing the Resurrection and the Last Supper. Some of the restaurants by the church serve excellent *cuy* and *pachamanca*.

ARRIVAL AND INFORMATION — TARMA AND AROUND

BY BUS

You'll most likely arrive and depart at one of the bus offices clustered on Callao and Castilla near the petrol station.

Bus companies Transportes Junín (Amazonas 669; ☎064 321234) stop briefly at their depot en route to Lima. Transportes Junín also serve La Merced and Satipo. To get to Chanchamayo, pick up a bus by the stadium on the exit for San Ramon and La Merced.

Destinations La Merced (several daily; 1–2hr); Lima (several daily; 5–7hr); Satipo (several daily; 3–5hr).

BY COLECTIVO

Colectivo offices are on Callao and Castilla, near the petrol station, and the drivers are usually parked up in and around here.

INFORMATION

Tourist information Municipal office on the plaza at Jr Dos de Mayo 773 (Mon–Fri 9am–5pm; ☎064 321010).

Tours Taruma Tours, Dos de Mayo 658, Tarma (☎064 322310, ⓦtaruma-tours.es.tl).

ACCOMMODATION

TARMA

Hospedaje El Dorado Jr Huánuco 488 ☎064 321914, ⓦhospedajeeldoradotarma.com. Great value and very clean, located in a colourful and stylish corner building and with its own inner courtyard where breakfast is served; all rooms have private bath, cable TV and wi-fi. S/70

Hostal Central Huánuco 614 ☎064 322625. Smallish rooms with shared or private bathrooms; there's a laundry and, unusually, its own observatory that non-guests can use on clear Friday nights. S/55

Hostal Internacional Dos de Mayo 307 ☎064 321830. A modern building with comfy rooms all equipped with hot running water and private bathrooms; service is reasonable, as is the price. S/90

Hotel Galaxia Calle Lima 262 ☎064 321449. Located on the Plaza de Armas, this is good value with private bathrooms, carpeted suites, 24hr room service and a car park. S/160

Hotel Los Portales Av Castilla 512 ☎064 321411, ⓦlosportaleshoteles.com. A hacienda-style entrance and building built in the 1950s just 2min drive from the Plaza de Armas; all 45 of its suites and rooms are very comfortable and the restaurant is highly thought of. S/210

AROUND TARMA

Hacienda Santa María Sacsamarca, 1.2km from Tarma ☎01 4451214 (contact in Lima) or ☎064 321232 (local contact), ⓦhaciendasantamaria.com. A very comfortable old hacienda, owned by the Santa María family for two centuries, this place offers first-floor rooms with private bath as well as a great restaurant. They also run excellent tours, to the Gruta de Huagapo caves (see opposite) and the Sanctuary of the Lord of Muruhuay (see above). S/280

Hospedaje Ecológica–Casa-Hacienda La Florida Km 39, Carretera Central ☎01 3441358 or ☎064 321041, ⓦhaciendalaflorida.com). Some 6km from Tarma on the Acobamba road (20min by taxi) this place is based on a dairy farm; it has very comfortable rooms of all shapes and sizes, home-cooked meals and campfires. Breakfast is included and there's a kitchen and room for camping (which has a shower and toilet facilities attached). Doubles S/184, camping S/25

EATING

Check out the food market on Dos de Mayo, just two blocks from the plaza. There are many *chifa* restaurants or *pollerías* located within a couple of blocks' radius of the Plaza de Armas.

Señorial Huánuco 138. In the centre of town, this place serves good, standard Peruvian cuisine and has good set-menu lunches. Daily 11am–3pm & 5–9pm.

DIRECTORY

Health Av Pacheco 362.

Money and exchange Money can be changed and there's an ATM at the Banco de Credito, Lima 407, on the main plaza; money can also be changed in one or two shops on Jirón Moquegua, just by the same plaza.

Post office Callao, within two blocks of the main plaza.

Telephones Plaza de Armas, first two blocks of Jr Lima.

South of Tarma

The bustling city of **Huancayo** is the natural hub of the mountainous and remote region **south of Tarma**. Nearby **Jauja Valley** is significantly more beautiful, less polluted and friendlier. Further afield, **Ayacucho** is a must for anyone interested in colonial architecture, particularly fine churches; while **Huancavelica** offers a slightly darker history lesson – the area has suffered from extreme exploitation both in colonial times, with the mines, as well as in the 1980s and 90s when terrorism was at a peak. The area is still occasionally visited by remnants of the Shining Path terrorist group (see box, p.498), but there have been no related problems for tourists in recent years. The trip out here by train (some 130km south of Huancayo), one of the world's highest railway journeys, passes through some stark yet stunning landscapes.

Huancayo

A large commercial city with over 350,000 inhabitants, **HUANCAYO** is the capital of the Junín *departamento*. An important market centre thriving on agricultural produce and dealing in vast quantities of wheat, the city makes a good base for exploring the Mantaro Valley and experiencing the region's distinct culture. While the area is rich in pre-Columbian remains, and the cereal and textile potential of the region has long been exploited, the city itself is mostly relatively modern, with very little of architectural or historical interest. It is still a lively enough place with a busy market and even some nightlife at weekends. It's also worth trying to coincide a trip with the splendid **Fiesta de las Cruces** each May, when Huancayo erupts in a succession of boisterous processions, parties and festivities.

Brief history

The region around Huancayo was dominated by the Huanca tribe from around 1200 AD, and the Huari culture before that, though it wasn't until Pachacuti's forces arrived in the fifteenth century that the Inca Empire took control. Occupied by the Spanish from 1537, Huancayo was formally founded in 1572 by Jeronimo de Silva, next to the older and these days relatively small town of Jauja (see p.293). In 1824, the **Battle of Junín** was fought close to Huancayo, when patriotic revolutionaries overcame royalist and Spanish forces. Apart from the comings and goings of the Catholic Church, Huancayo remained little more than a staging point until the rail line arrived in 1909, transforming it slowly but surely during the twentieth century into a city whose economy was based on the export of agrarian foodstuffs and craft goods.

More so than any other Peruvian city – except perhaps Ayacucho – Huancayo was paralyzed in the years of **terror during the 1980s and 1990s**. As home to a major army base, it became the heart of operations in what was then a military emergency zone. In

1999, an extensive army operation captured the then leader of **Sendero Luminoso**, Oscar Ramírez Durand, who had taken over from Abimael Guzmán in 1992.

Plaza de la Constitución

Plaza de la Constitución – named in honour of the 1812 Liberal Constitution of Cádiz – is where you'll find monuments in honour of Mariscal Ramón Castilla (who abolished slavery in Huancayo in 1854), surrounded by ornamental plants of local origin, like *quishuar* and *retama*. The plaza is the site where Huancayo was founded in 1572. Surrounded by the Neoclassical **Catedral de la Ciudad de Huancayo** (daily 7.30–9.30am & 5–7.30pm; free) and some of the town's major public buildings and offices, it was once home to the Feria Dominical market (see p.290), which was shifted in the mid-1990s to alleviate traffic problems.

Calle Real

Calle Real is the main drag running on the western edge of Plaza de la Constitución; it's here you'll find the **Capilla La Merced** (daily 9am–noon & 3–6.30pm; free), a colonial church, once the site for the preparation and signing of the 1839 Peruvian Constitution, and now designated a historic monument.

Plaza Huamanmarca

Plaza Huamanmarca sits at the heart of the city and is the oldest plaza, founded with

the town back in 1572. On April 22, 1882, three local heroes – Enrique Rosado Zárate, Vicente Samaniego Vivas and Tomás Gutarra – were shot here by the Chilean army. Today the square is surrounded by public buildings, the Municipality, the central post office and the old *Hotel de Turismo*.

Museo del Colegio Salesiano

Prolongación Arequipa 10 • Mon–Fri 8am–noon & 3–6pm • S/5 • ⓣ 064 247763

Museo del Colegio Salesiano, in the residential northern district of El Tambo, is an excellent natural history museum with almost a thousand exhibits of local flora and fauna as well as archeological objects, hundreds of fossils, paintings, sculptures, and a selection of interesting rocks and minerals.

Feria Dominical market

Blocks 2–12, Av Huancavelica • Daily (busiest Sun)

Established in 1572 to assist the commerce of the local population, the market still sells fruit and vegetables, as well as a good selection of woollen and alpaca clothes and blankets, superb weavings and some silver jewellery. Like most Peruvian city markets, it is the hub of activity early in the morning, and the wealth of tropical and Andean produce makes it exotic and satisfying to see and sense.

Parque de la Identidad de Huancayo

Taxi S/10 each way – more with a wait

Just 5km northeast from the city centre, in the Urb. San Antonio, the **Parque de la Identidad de Huancayo** covers nearly 6000 hectares, much of it green space open for public enjoyment. The main entrance is in the form of a giant gourd, one of the typical regional artesanía products, and inside there's a *mirador* (viewing platform), some shady pergolas, cacti and the Laguna de Amalu. The entire park was created in honour of the local *wanka* style of music and the musicians themselves.

Huari-Huilca archeological remains

Museum Daily 8am–6pm • S/5 • Taxi from Huancayo S/15–25

Some 7km west of Huancayo near the present-day pueblo of **Huari**, stand the **Huari-Huilca archeological remains** (800–1200 AD), the sacred complex of the Huanca tribe who dominated this region for over two hundred years before the arrival of the Inca. At the site is a small museum showing collections of ceramic fragments, bones and stone weapons.

ARRIVAL AND DEPARTURE — HUANCAYO

BY BUS

Bus companies Cruz del Sur (ⓣ 064 235650 or ⓣ 064 223367), Jr Ayacucho 287, serve Lima, via Jauja. Turismo Central (ⓣ 064 223128, ⓦ cruzdelsur.com.pe), same block as Cruz del Sur at Jr Ayacucho 274, serves Lima, Huánuco, Tingo María, La Merced and Satipo. Other buses tend to arrive at their respective company offices, with most of these located on Av Mariátegui blocks 10–12 in the Tambo district. Expreso Nacional Cerro de Pasco (Jr José Carlos Mariátegui 574 ⓣ 064 252822) for destinations north as far as Cerro de Pasco and Huánuco; Expreso Huancavelica (Av Tarapaca 391 ⓣ 064 213321) for Lima and Huancavelica; and PerúBus (Jr Paseo de la Breña 233 ⓣ 064 808053) for Lima.

Destinations Ayacucho (several daily; 8–9hr); Huancavelica (several daily; 2–3hr); Huánuco (several daily; 5–6hr); Jauja (several daily; 30–40min); La Merced (several daily; 3–4hr); Lima via Jauja (several daily; 6–7hr); Satipo (several daily; 8hr); Tingo María (1 or 2 daily; 8–10hr).

BY COLECTIVO

Colectivos start and finish their runs from Calle Loreto (7am–6pm) and serve Cerro de Pasco (several daily; 3–4hr); Lima (several daily; 5–6hr); Tarma (several daily; 1–2hr).

BY TRAIN

Train tickets are best bought online (ⓦ ferrocarrilcentral .com.pe).

Trains to and from Lima Serve the train station (ⓣ 064 217724 or ⓣ 064 215387) on Av Ferrocarril 461, within walking distance of the city centre.

Destinations Lima (twice monthly April–Sept; 12hr).

Trains to and from Huancavelica Serve a small station

in Chilca suburb (take a taxi from the city centre; 20min; $2–3), at the point where Avenida Ferrocarril crosses Avenida Junín. The journey takes 5–6hr.

Destinations Huancavelica (2 daily; 5–6hr).

BY PLANE

Flights from Lima to Huancayo land at Francisco Carle airport in Jauja. Cars are usually available (sometimes courtesy) from Jauja to Huancayo. LC Busre, Av Ayacucho 322, Huancayo (T 064 214514, W lcbusre.com.pe), and Star Perú, Jr Ancash 367, Plaza Constitución, Huancayo (T 064 233827, W starperu.com), are the carriers.

Destinations Huancayo (2 flights per day; 1hr).

GETTING AROUND, INFORMATION AND TOURS

Bicycle rental Huancayo Tours, C Real 543.

Tourist information Casa del Artesano (Mon–Fri 9am–2pm & 4–8pm; T 064 211799), C Real 481, just on the Plaza de la Constitución where the street meets Paseo La Breña.

Tour operators and guides Incas del Perú, Av Giraldez 658 (T 064 223303, W incasdelperu.com); Perú Profundo, Calle Real 261, Upstairs Office 18 (T 064 200099); and Dargui Tours, Jr Ancash 367, Plaza Constitución (T 064 233705), all offer trips throughout the region. These agencies also organize car rental. Lucho Hurtado, operating out of the *Casa de la Abuela* hostel in Huancayo (T 064 222395, W incasdelperu .org), is a recommended, local tour guide whose organization offers travel services and language lessons as well as cultural opportunities.

ACCOMMODATION

The best Huancayo offers in accommodation is its choice between rambling old or modern traditional city-centre hotels and a more familial setting in smaller outlying hostels. It doesn't offer anything spectacular in terms of rooms with views; for that you need to get out of town.

La Casa de la Abuela Av Giraldez 691 T 064 223303 or T 064 234383, W incasdelperu.org. Basic accommodation, with some private rooms available albeit all with shared bath. Otherwise, this hotel has good facilities including table tennis and a dartboard. S/18

Casa Alojamiento de Aldo y Soledad Bonilla Huánuco 332 T 064 232103. Located some eight blocks from the city centre, this friendly, family-run hostel has constant hot water and some of the staff speak English. S/50

Hostal El Marquéz Jr Puno 294 T 064 219026, W elmarquezhuancayo.com. A modernized and plush hotel with comfy large beds, nicely decorated rooms and a large restaurant with café-bar area. S/20

Hostal Plaza Ancash 171 T 064 23858 or T 064 210509. Good-value rooms with private bath, if fairly basic funishings; go for the rooms at the front as they have most light and best views. S/40

Hotel Baldeon Amazonas 543 T 064 231634. Affordable, family-run accommodation, with hot showers available on request, and use of the kitchen facilities; close to the colectivos for Jauja and located only a few blocks from the Plaza de la Constitución. S/20

Hotel Kiya Av Giraldez 107 T 064 214955, W hotelkiya .com. A centrally located and refurbished hotel, this is actually one of the first Huancayo buildings that still survives; there's a luggage deposit and laundry, plus all rooms have private bath, cable TV and wi-fi. S/60

★ **Hotel Presidente** C Real 1138 T 064 231275. Quite luxurious for Huancayo, with clean rooms and good, friendly service and a conference centre; *Hotel Presidente* is located close to the buses and only a few blocks from the heart of the city. S/180

Turismo Hotel Ancash 729 T 064 231072, W hotelpresidente.com.pe. One of the town's best hotels, with comfortable rooms and private bath, though its elegance has faded somewhat. The restaurant is generally fine, serving good local food, but its pisco sour drinks aren't always what they should be. S/280

EATING

Chifa Rapido Arequipa 511. This is arguably the best *chifa* restaurant in town, serving good-quality and inexpensive noodles, duck and *wonton* dishes, in a typical Peruvian-Chinese environment. Daily 10am–9pm.

Coqui Café Jr Puno 296 & Centro Comercial Real Plaza. With one branch located centrally, next to the *Hostal El Marquéz*, and another based out near the Lima-Huancayo railway station in the Centro Comercial Real Plaza, this is a popular pastry bakery that serves great snacks, small meals, local breads and sandwiches, plus good coffee. Daily 10am–9pm.

El Padrino Av Giraldez 133. Local dishes are on offer here, including *papas a la Huancaina*, a delicious local speciality of potatoes in a mildly spicy cheese sauce, topped with sliced egg, a black olive and some green salad. Daily 11am–10pm.

El Parque Southwest corner of Avenida Giraldez, Plaza de la Constitución. Especially recommended for its regional juices made from the wide variety of local and available tropical fruits; they also offer great pastries and other snacks. Mon–Sat 10.30am–9pm.

Restaurant La Cabaña Av Giraldez 652 ⊙ 064 223303. Pizzas, grills and trout in an agreeable ambience with occasional live folklore music and dance shows at weekends after 9pm. Mon–Fri 8am–11pm, later at weekends.

Rinconcito Oxapampino Jr Cuzco 840. Serves traditional foods from the central jungle region – plenty of salted meats and tropical juices – where the cooking is much influenced by Austro-German immigrants. Mon–Sat 11am–10pm.

DRINKING AND NIGHTLIFE

Taka Wasi Calle Huancavelica. Good criolla and folklore *peña*, but only really gets going between 9pm and midnight on Fridays and Saturdays. Fri & Sat 7pm–3am.

El Tayta Av Huancavelica 859 ⊙ 064 217357. This is the best-known and most popular bar-cum-disco; it plays good music and serves beer as well as cocktails. Daily 6pm till late.

DIRECTORY

Health Daniel Carrion 1552 ⊙ 064 222157.

Language schools Incas del Perú, Av Giraldez 652 (⊙ 064 223303, ⊚ incasdelperu.org); and also Katy Cerna (⊙ 064 201959, ⊜ katiacerna@hotmail.com).

Money and exchange Banco de Credito, C Real 1039, is best. To change dollars cash, try your hotel or the street *cambistas* along C Real.

Police Nacional, Av Ferrocarril 555 ⊙ 064 211653; Turismo, Av Ferrocarril 556 ⊙ 064 219851.

Post office Centro Cívico Foco 2 (Mon–Sat 8am–7pm).

Convento de Santa Rosa de Ocopa

Convent Wed–Mon 9am–1pm & 3–6pm • S/5 • **Museum** Daily except Tues 9am–noon & 3–6pm • Free • Catch a microbus from outside the Catedral de la Ciudad de Huancayo on Plaza de la Constitución (see p.290) to Concepción, then a bus or colectivo from Plaza de Armas to reach the convent (6km)

The **Convento de Santa Rosa de Ocopa** is reached from Huancayo via the town of Concepción, 22km from Huancayo; in the Plaza de Armas here you'll find a small seventeenth-century *pileta* and the square itself fronts both the Neoclassical Iglesia Matriz and the fine, colonial Casona Ugarte León.

Founded in 1724, and having taken some twenty years to build, the church was the centre of the Franciscan mission into the Amazon, until their work was halted by the Wars of Independence (see p.494), after which the mission villages in the jungle disintegrated and most of the natives returned to the forest. The cloisters are more interesting than the church, though both are set in a peaceful environment, and there's an excellent library with chronicles from the sixteenth century onwards, plus a **Museum of Natural History and Ethnology** containing lots of stuffed animals and native artefacts from the jungle.

A trip to the *convento* can be conveniently combined with a visit to the nearby village of **San Jerónimo**, about 12km west, well known for its Wednesday market of fine silver jewellery.

Cochas Chicas and Cochas Grandes

30min by frequent bus from outside the church of the Immaculate Conception, Huancayo

A good day-trip from Huancayo is to the local villages of **Cochas Chicas and Cochas Grandes**, whose speciality is crafted, carved gourds. Strangely, Cochas Grandes is the smaller of the two villages, and you have to ask around if you want to buy gourds here. You can buy straight from cooperatives or from individual artisans; expect to pay anything from $3 up to $150 for the finer gourds, and if you are ordering some to be made, you'll have to pay half the money in advance. The etchings and craftsmanship on the more detailed gourds is incredible in its microscopic depth, creativity and artistic skill. On some, whole rural scenes, like the harvest, marriage and shamanic healing are represented in tiny storyboard format. The less expensive, simpler gourds have fairly common geometric designs, or bird, animal and flower forms etched boldly across their curvaceous surfaces.

ANDES TRAVEL WARNING

It's best to travel through the Andes by day, although if you're confined to night-time travel choose your transport wisely: it's possible to hitch rides on trucks or take cheap local buses, but these are more at risk of being stopped and robbed during night journeys.

Jauja

Catch a bus or colectivo from Huancayo (1hr) from Calle Amazonas

Forty kilometres from Huancayo is **JAUJA**, a little colonial town that was the capital of Peru before the founding of Lima. Surrounded by some gorgeous countryside, Jauja is a likeable place, whose past is reflected in its unspoiled architecture, with many of the colonial-style buildings painted light blue. A much smaller and more languid town than Huancayo, its streets are narrow and picturesque, and the people friendly. Today, Jauja is more renowned for its traditional and well-stocked Sunday and Wednesday markets.

Capilla de Cristo Pobre

Between Calles San Martín and Colina • Daily 7–9am & 3–6pm • $1

The **Capilla de Cristo Pobre** shares some similarities with Notre Dame de Paris and, perhaps a tenuous claim to fame: Gothic in style, it was also the first concrete religious construction in the Central Sierra.

Laguna de Paca

10–15min by colectivo (S/2) from Jauja • Boats S/5/hr

If you fancy exploring the landscape around Jauja, it's possible to rent boats on the nearby **Laguna de Paca** and row out to the Isla de Amor; according to local legend, this lake is the home of a mermaid who lures men to their deaths. The lake is surrounded by *totora* reeds and brimming with birdlife. The shoreline is lined with cafés serving decent trout meals, and, at weekends, *pachamanca* (meat and vegetables placed in a hole in the earth on preheated hot rocks and covered with soil for slow cooking) is served.

Tunanmarca

30min by taxi from Jauja (S/25 return)

Just 15km from Jauja, there are some Huanca-tribe archeological remains at **Tunanmarca**; the ancient settlement here was occupied between 1200 and 1400 AD and boasts circular constructions as well as aqueducts and other pre-Inca water works. Located on a mountain pass, Tunanmarca is a pre-Inca defensive construction with a complex system of aquaducts, some of these subterranean. It is thought to have been the main base for the Wanka-Sausa culture and was originally called Siquillapucara.

ARRIVAL, GETTING AROUND AND INFORMATION — JAUJA

By colectivo Colectivos from Huancayo to Jauja leave hourly from the market or from the corner where Amazonas crosses Avenida Giraldez; they drop off and pick up from the corner of 25 de Abril with Jr Ricardo Palma in Jauja.

By bus A through-bus from Lima stops two or three times daily in Jauja's Plaza de Armas on its way to Huancayo.

Destinations Cerro de Pasco (several daily; 5hr); Huancayo (several daily; 30–40min); Lima (several daily; 5–7hr).

By taxi Local transport is mostly by mototaxi (from S/1.50 for trips around town).

Tourist information Dircetur Junín at Av Grau 528 (Mon–Sat 9am–6pm; ☎064 362897) and also the Municipality at Jr Ayacucho 856 (☎064 362017).

ACCOMMODATION AND EATING

Hostal Manco Capac Manco Capac 575 ☎064 361620, hostal-mancocapac.com. This is the best lower-end option in Jauja, with a lovely garden and hot water; rooms are very pleasant and the building has some style. **S/80**

Hotel Ganso de Oro Ricardo Palma 249 ☎064 362166.

This is a more basic option but nevertheless friendly and clean; double rooms have own baths. S/50

Restaurante Ganso de Oro *Hotel Ganso de Oro* (see above). Probably the best restaurant in town, offering some traditional local dishes like *patasca* (from about S/26) which is a maize-based soup dish containing beef (can be a head), onion and yellow chillies. Daily 8am–9pm.

Huancavelica

Remote **HUANCAVELICA**, at 3676m, is almost purely Indian in its ethnic make-up, which is surprising considering its long colonial history and a fairly impressive array of Spanish-style architecture. There's little of specific interest in the town itself, except the Sunday market, which sells local food, jungle fruits and carved gourds. A couple of pleasant walks from town will bring you to the natural hot springs on the hill north of the river, or the weaving cooperative, 4km away at Totoral. Local mines (see below) are an attraction, too.

Brief history

Originally occupied by hunter-gatherers from about 5000 years ago, the area then turned to sedentary cultivation as the local population was, initially, taken over by the Huari tribe around 1100 AD, a highly organized culture which reached here from the Ayacucho Valley. The Huanca tribe arrived on the scene in the fifteenth century, providing fierce resistance when they were attacked and finally conquered by the Inca. The weight of its colonial past, however, lies more heavily on its shoulders.

After mercury deposits were discovered here in 1563, the town began producing **ore** for the silver mines of Peru, replacing expensive imports previously used in the mining process. In just over a hundred years, so many indigenous labourers had died of mercury poisoning that the pits could hardly keep going; after the generations of locals bound to serve by the *mitayo* system of virtual slavery had been literally used up and thrown away, the salaries required to attract new workers made many of the mines unprofitable.

Today the mines are working again and the ore is taken by truck to Pisco on the coast. The Mina de la Muerte, as the **Santa Barbara mines** tend to be called around Huancavelica, are also an attraction in their own right, located several kilometres

southeast of town (about 1hr 30min by foot); the shield of the Spanish Crown sits unashamedly engraved in stone over the main entrance to this ghostly settlement. There's plenty to explore, but as with all mines, some sections are dangerous and not visitor-friendly, and it's best to ask local advice before setting off.

Plaza de Armas

Huancavelica's main sights are around the **Plaza de Armas**, where you'll find the two-storey Cabildo buildings, the **Capilla de la Virgen de los Dolores** and, at the heart of the square, a stone *pileta* in octagonal form incorporating two waterspouts, each portraying an Indian face, water gushing from their respective mouths.

Iglesia Catedral de San Antonio

Plaza de Armas • Mon–Sat 7am–5.15pm, or for Mass on Sun at 5.30am, 8am, 9.30am & 5.15pm

The seventeenth-century **Iglesia Catedral de San Antonio** features a fine altar and pulpit and some excellent paintings. Construction started in 1673, and it took a hundred years to complete. These days it's home to the sacred image of the city's patron – Nuestra Señora de las Mercedes. The elaborate gold-leaf altar was carved from wood, and the silver sheets on display beside it are from the Cusqueña and Huamanguina schools (see box, p.213). There is a distinct Baroque style in the volcanic stone craftsmanship, and religious paintings decorate the interior representing Heaven, Purgatory, Hell, the Last Supper and the Crucifixion.

Iglesia de San Francisco

Plaza Bolognesi

San Francisco, which along with Santo Domingo (see below) are connected to the cathedral via an underground passage, was built on the Plaza Bolognesi in 1774 by the Franciscan Order. Posessing a single nave and some fancy Baroque and Churrigueresque *retablos* of wood and gold leaf, it has just about survived some major earthquakes. During the nineteenth-century war with Chile, this church was commandeered by the Peruvian army, who sold its fine collection of musical instruments to finance the war effort. Today, the steps of San Francisco are the site, on December 24 and 25, of the awe-inspiring, traditional scissor-dancing performances (*danza tijera*) generally done by men wielding two long machete-like swords.

Iglesia de Santo Domingo

Calle Toledo

Santo Domingo is a church and convent complex, connected to the cathedral via an underground passage and founded in 1601, just thirty years after the city was established. The entrance is made from red stone brought from the Pucarumi quarry. Inside there are fine paintings, brought from Rome, of the Virgen del Rosario and the patron St Dominic, as well as a fine Baroque altar with some gold-leaf adornment; in the sacristy you can find a painting dating from 1666 representing *El Señor de la Sentencia y Resurrección*.

Museo Regional Daniel Hernández Morillo

Plazuela San Juan de Dios • Mon–Fri 9am–1pm & 4–6pm • 80¢ • ⓣ 067 753420

The small **Museo Regional Daniel Hernández Morillo** sits in the Instituto Nacional de Cultura building one block from the Plaza de Armas, and contains archeological exhibits, fossils from the Tertiary period, petrified marine species and displays on pre-Inca Andean cultures. As well as the archeology and anthropology section, this museum also boasts a room of popular art, showing paintings and objects depicting local culture.

5

ARRIVAL AND INFORMATION — HUANCAVELICA

By train All trains (Huancayo–Huancavelica and vice versa) leave from and arrive to Huancavelica twice daily (see p.290) from the station at Avenida Augusto Leguia (T 067 752898).
Destinations Huancayo (2 daily; 6–8hr).
By bus Accessible from Lima and Huancayo by bus with Libertadores whose depot is at Av Manchego Muñoz 755 T 01 4268067), there are also daily buses to Ayacucho, leaving at 5am with Expreso Huancavelica from Av Manchego Muñoz 516 (T 067 752964). For Pisco and Ica (6–10hr depending on condition of road) on the coast, Empresa Oropesa buses leave around 5.30pm from their office on the Plaza Santa Ana.
Destinations Ayacucho (1 weekly; 7–9hr); Huancayo (several daily; 5hr); Lima (several daily; 12hr).
Tourist information Dircetur, V. Garma 444 (T 067 452938, W regionhuancavelica.com).
Tours Turismo Andino on block 2 of Barranca (T 067 454190 or T 067 064 224419, W turismoandino.com).
Useful websites W huancavelicaperu.com and W huancavelica.com.

ACCOMMODATION

Hostal Camacho Carabaya 481 T 067 453298. This traditional old place offers excellent value in a clean and friendly atmosphere; there are only communal bathrooms and basic showers available, but they are well looked after. S/35

Hostal Tahuantinsuyo Carabaya 999 T 067 452968. Located at the corner of Manchego Muñoz, this is a little dingy but at least has good and reliable hot water, though rooms are all shared. S/35

Hotel Presidente Plaza de Armas T 067 452760, W huancavelicaes.hotelpresidente.com.pe. This is a clean and well-established place with large modern-styled rooms all with wi-fi, cable TV and private bathrooms. Room service and mini bar are available. S/180

EATING

Café Fuente de Soda 2nd block of Manchego Muñoz. Serves juices, sandwiches and other snacks; economic and fast service in a reasonably pleasant space. Daily 8am–8pm.

Mochica Sachun Jr Virrey Toledo 302. Does a great set lunch for around S/6 plus a range of meals, including the ubiquitous *lomo saltado*, and some Andean stews. Mon–Sat 11am–7pm.

Restaurant Olla Avenida Gamarra 305 T 067 752593. Dishes up reasonably priced international and Peruvian meals, including pasta and rice dishes plus stews and puddings, in a friendly atmosphere. Daily 9am–9pm.

DIRECTORY

Money and exchange The Banco de Credito is on Jr Virrey Toledo.

Post office Serpost (Mon–Sat 8am–8pm), Av Pasaje Ferrua.

Shopping The most traditional products made by local artisans include ceramics and weavings; for the best prices the Mercado Central on Jirón Victor Garma is your best bet.

Ayacucho

Roughly halfway between Cusco and Lima, **AYACUCHO** ("Purple Soul", in the Quechua language) sits in the Andes around 2800m high in one of Peru's most archeologically important valleys, with evidence such as ancient stone tools found in nearby caves at Pikimachay, which suggest that the region has been occupied for over 20,000 years. Its **climate**, despite the altitude, is pleasant all year round – dry and temperate with blue skies nearly every day – and temperatures average 16ºC (60ºF). The surrounding hills are covered with cacti, broom bushes and agave plants, adding a distinctive atmosphere to the city.

Despite the political problems of the last few years, most people on the streets of Ayacucho, although quiet and reserved (seemingly saving their energy for the city's boisterous **fiestas**), are helpful, friendly and kind. You'll find few people speak any English; Quechua is the city's first language, though most of the town's inhabitants can also speak some Spanish.

Brief history

Ayacucho was the centre of the Huari culture, which emerged in the region around 700 AD and spread its powerful and evocative religious symbolism throughout most of Peru over the next three or four hundred years. After the demise of the Huari, the

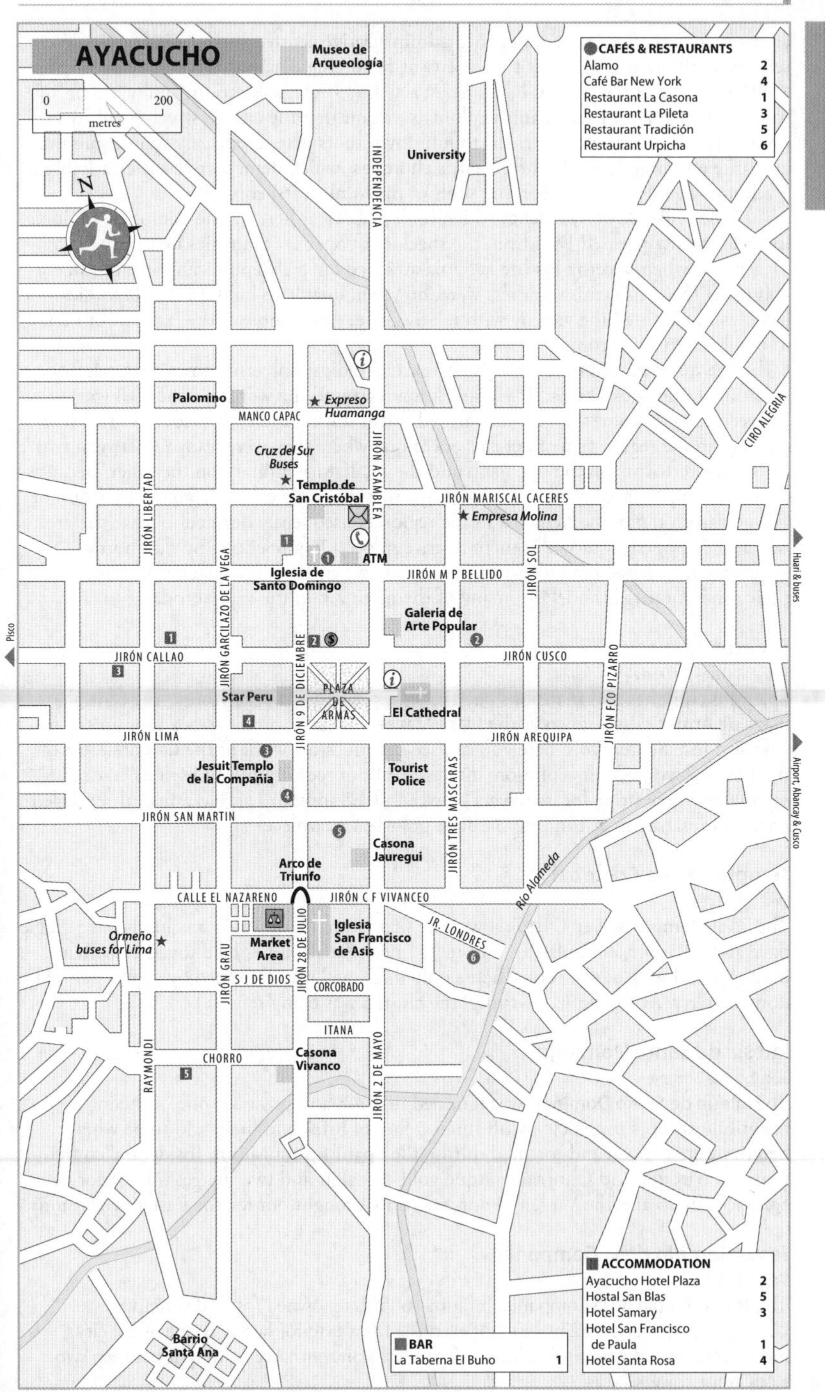
AYACUCHO
0
200
metres
N
CAFÉS & RESTAURANTS
Alamo 2
Café Bar New York 4
Restaurant La Casona 1
Restaurant La Pileta 3
Restaurant Tradición 5
Restaurant Urpicha 6
ACCOMMODATION
Ayacucho Hotel Plaza 2
Hostal San Blas 5
Hotel Samary 3
Hotel San Francisco de Paula 1
Hotel Santa Rosa 4
BAR
La Taberna El Buho 1
Museo de Arqueología
University
INDEPENDENCIA
Palomino
Expreso Huamanga
MANCO CAPAC
Cruz del Sur Buses
Templo de San Cristóbal
JIRÓN ASAMBLEA
JIRÓN MARISCAL CACERES
Empresa Molina
CIRO ALEGRIA
JIRÓN LIBERTAD
ATM
Iglesia de Santo Domingo
JIRÓN M P BELLIDO
JIRÓN SOL
Huari & buses
Galeria de Arte Popular
Pisco
JIRÓN CALLAO
JIRÓN GARCILAZO DE LA VEGA
JIRÓN 9 DE DICIEMBRE
PLAZA DE ARMAS
JIRÓN CUSCO
JIRÓN FCO PIZARRO
Star Peru
El Cathedral
JIRÓN LIMA
JIRÓN AREQUIPA
Airport, Abancay & Cusco
Jesuit Templo de la Compañia
Tourist Police
JIRÓN TRES MASCARAS
JIRÓN SAN MARTIN
Casona Jauregui
Arco de Triunfo
Río Alameda
CALLE EL NAZARENO
JIRÓN C F VIVANCEO
JR. LONDRES
Ormeño buses for Lima
Market Area
Iglesia San Francisco de Asis
JIRÓN GRAU
JIRÓN 28 DE JULIO
S J DE DIOS
CORCOBADO
ITANA
RAYMONDI
CHORRO
Casona Vivanco
JIRÓN 2 DE MAYO
Barrio Santa Ana

ancient city later became a major Inca administrative centre. The Spanish originally selected a different nearby site for the city at Huamanguilla; but this was abandoned in 1540 in favour of the present location. Ayacucho's strategic location, vitally important to both the Incas and the Spanish colonials, meant that the city grew very wealthy as miners and administrators decided to put down roots here, eventually sponsoring the exquisite and unique wealth of the city's **churches**, which demonstrate the clearly high level of masonic and woodworking skills of the local craftspeople.

The bloody **Battle of Ayacucho**, which took place near here on the Pampa de Quinoa in 1824, finally released Peru from the shackles of Spain. The armies met early in December, when Viceroy José de la Serna attacked Sucre's Republican force in three columns. The pro-Spanish soldiers were, however, unable to hold off the Republican forces who captured the viceroy with relative ease. Ayacucho was the last part of Peru to be liberated from colonial power.

Though quiet these days, Ayacucho was also a radical university town with a left-wing tradition going back at least fifty years, known around the world for the civil war between terrorists and the Peruvian armed forces during the 1980s (see p.495). Most civilians in the region remember this era as one where they were trapped between two evils – the terrorists on the one hand and the retaliatory military on the other. Because of this, several villages were annihilated by one side or the other. A large proportion of villagers from remote settlements in the region consequently decided to leave the area, which they hoped would offer them relative safety. Despite efforts by Fujimori's government to rehabilitate these communities and entice people back from Lima to their rural homes in the 1990s, many of them remain in the capital today.

El Catedral

Mon–Sat 11am–3pm • Free

Splendid churches and mansions pack together in dense blocks around the central **Plaza de Armas** (also known as the **Plaza Mayor**) at whose centre rests a monument to Mariscal José Sucre. From here you can see the fine stonework of the **Catedral**, just off the Plaza Mayor, which is of more interest. Built of red or pink stone in its central section and grey stone for its towers between 1612 and 1671, it has a fine, three-aisled nave culminating in a stunning Baroque gold-leaf altarpiece.

Templo de San Cristóbal

Block 7, Jr 28 de Julio

The 1540 **Templo de San Cristóbal** was the first church built in Ayacucho; it has a single nave and only one altar, plus an unusually fine or small stones held together with a lime mix and with adobe roof. There's only one small tower, topped by a gold-painted domed belfry. At the time of writing, the church was being restored.

Iglesia de Santo Domingo

Block 2, Jr 9 de Diciembre

The **Iglesia de Santo Domingo** was founded in 1548 and possesses one of the most beautiful exteriors in the city, with three arches of brick and lime, said to be where heretics were hanged and tortured during the Spanish Inquisition. Inside, the church houses a Baroque and Churrigueresque gold-leaf altar and two images – El Señor del Santo Sepulcro and the Virgen Dolorosa – only brought out for the Easter processions.

Jesuit Templo de la Compañía

Block 1, Jr 28 de Julio

The **Jesuit Templo de la Compañía**, built in 1605, is renowned for its distinctive Churrigueresque-style main altar, but even the front exterior facade is one of the city's most complex and colourful, with a red-painted stone entrance held tight between two stout stone towers.

Casona Jauregui

Block 2, Jr Dos de Mayo 210 • Mon–Fri 8.30am–4pm • Free

The **Casona Jauregui** is a lovely seventeenth-century mansion built by Don Cayetano Ruiz de Ochon; it has a superb patio and balcony with two lion statues and a stone shield of Indian influence displaying a two-headed eagle. Its main door is totally unique even within its own genre due to the architectonic elements incorporated, some in animal form supporting the balcony and a crown with a two-headed eagle within one of the arches.

Art galleries

Casona Vivanco Jr 28 de Julio 518 • Mon–Sat 10am–1pm & 3–6pm • 50¢ **Galería de Arte Popular** Jr Asamblea 138 • Mon–Sat 9am–6.30pm • Free

There are a couple of **art galleries** in town: the **Casona Vivanco**, with a particularly good collection of colonial art, and the **Galería de Arte Popular**, specializing in regional art. The latter – located near the Plaza de Armas next to the Banco de Credito – features an impressive collection of paintings, many created by acclaimed Peruvian artist, Joaquín López Antay (1897–1981) who was born in Ayacucho and awarded the National Prize of Culture in 1974, shortly before his death.

Museo de Arqueología

Av Independencia 502 • Mon–Fri 8am–1pm & 3–5pm, Sat 9am–1pm • 80¢ • ☎ 066 912056 • 30min walk or 5min taxi ride from the old centre

The **Museo de Arqueología** (also known as Museo Hipolito Unanue) is located in the university's botanical gardens. It's a small museum stuffed full of local archeological finds, mainly ceramics, dating from several millennia ago, plus exhibits from the Chavín, Huarpa, Nasca and Inca eras.

ARTS AND CRAFTS

Many visitors come for Ayacucho's thriving **craft industry**, mainly woven rugs and *retablos* (finely worked little wooden boxes containing intricate three-dimensional religious scenes made mainly from papier-mâché). If you've got the time to spare, however, it's more interesting and less expensive to visit some of the actual **craft workshops** and buy from the artisans themselves. Most of these workshops are found in the barrio of **Santa Ana**, just uphill from the Plaza de Armas: locals are always happy to guide visitors in the right direction. Some of the best-quality retablos are not all that expensive, but if you want one of their more complicated modern pieces it could cost as much as $300, and take up to three months to complete.

RUGS

Edwin Sulca – arguably the best known weaver here – lives opposite the church on the Plaza Santa Ana; his work sells from around $100 (almost double in Lima's shops), and many of his designs graphically depict the recent political horrors around Ayacucho.

Gerado Fernandez Palomino is another excellent weaver who has a store in his house and workshop located on Jr Paris 600, also in Santa Ana.

ALABASTER CARVINGS

Alabaster carvings – known in Peru as **Huamanga stone carvings** – are another speciality of Ayacucho. Try Señor Pizarro, Jr San Cristoval 215, who has a reputation as one of the best carvers in town. The craft cooperative Ahuaccllacta, Huanca Solar 130, is also worth checking out.

ARTESANÍA MARKETS

Head to the following: Plazoleta María Pardo de Bellido, and Jirón Libertad, blocks 7–9; the first block of Jirón Paris; second block of Pasaje Bolognesi; and the first two of Jirón Asamblea.

ARRIVAL AND GETTING AROUND — AYACUCHUO

BY PLANE

Most overseas visitors arrive in Ayacucho by plane from Lima. The airport is 4km from town; a taxi into town costs S/20–25; buses cost S/3 and leave from just outside the terminal.

Airline offices StarPerú, Portal Constitución 17, Plaza de Armas (T 066 316660); LC Busre, 9 de Diciembre 160 (T 066 316012).

Destinations Lima (daily; 35min).

BY BUS

Bus companies serving Huancayo, Huancavelica, Cusco or Lima mostly have their depots along Jirón 3 Mascaras or Avenida Mariscal Cáceres, both within a few blocks of the Plaza de Armas.

Bus companies Cruz del Sur, 9 de Diciembre, block 4, for Lima; Ormeño, Jr Libertad 257 (T 066 812495), for Lima; Palomino, Manco Capac 255 (T 066 316906), for Lima, Andahuaylas, Abancay and Cusco; Empresa Molina, Jr 3 Mascaras 551 (T 066 811623), for Huancayo; and Expreso Huamanga at Jr Mariscal Cáceres 828 (T 066 816972) for Lima, Huanta and Abancay.

Destinations Abancay (daily; 15–17hr); Andahuaylas (daily; 10–12hr); Cusco (daily; 18–22hr); Huancayo (several daily; 10hr); Huanta (daily; 3–4hr); Lima (several daily; 8–9hr).

BY CAR

Car rental Maurelio Services, Jr Pokras 119, Urb. Santa Rosa, San Juan Bautista, Ayacucho T 066 408424 or T 966 889450.

INFORMATION AND TOURS

Tourist information Municipalidad building, Portal Municipal 45, Plaza de Armas (Mon–Sat 9am–7pm; T 066 318305, W regionayacucho.gob.pe), has helpful staff who can arrange guides and trips in the area; there's also a tourist information kiosk at the airport (Mon–Sat 8am–8pm). Carlos Manco, contactable at *Hotel Crillonesa*, is another useful source.

Tour operators One of the easiest ways to visit the sites around Ayacucho is to take a guided tour. All the following companies offer half-day tours to Pikimachay (see p.302) for S/25–35 and half-day tours to Huari (see p.302) for a similar price. Full-day trips to Huari and Quinua (see p.302) will set you back around S/60. Operators include: Urpillay Tours, Portal Constitución 4 (Office 5), Plaza de Armas (T 066 315074, W ayacuchoviajes.com); Wari Tours, Jr Lima 138 (T 066 311415, W aritoursayacucho.blogspot.com); and Willy Tours, Jr 9 de Diciembre 209, Parque Luís Carranza, Huamanga, Ayacucho (T 066 314075, W wilytours.com). For adventure tourism, Warpa Picchu Eco-Aventura, Portal Independencia 65, Plaza de Armas (T 066 315191, E verbist@terra.com.pe), has a good reputation; Pierre Verbist is a Belgian guide who organizes mountain biking, horseriding and other adventures.

ACCOMMODATION

Finding a room in Ayacucho is easy enough outside of the Easter period when, because of the colourful religious festivals (see box below), the town is bursting at the seams with visitors from Lima and elsewhere. Most of the hotels are set in interesting old properties – many of which have been tastefully modernized – and service is of a high standard.

★ **Ayacucho Hotel Plaza** Jr 9 de Diciembre 184 T 066 312202. Easily the most luxurious hotel in town, set in a fine, stylish colonial mansion, with TVs in every room, private baths and a reasonable restaurant, though service can be slow. Centrally located on the Plaza de Armas. S/215

Hostal San Blas Jr Chorro 167 T 066 312712. A great budget option with friendly service and pleasant, fairly spacious and comfortable rooms with private bath. There's also the benefit of a laundry, communal cooking facilities and a reliable hot-water system. S/35

Hotel Samary Jr Callao 329-335 T 066 312442. A fine, welcoming place to relax for a few days, just a block east of

FESTIVALS AND MUSIC IN AYACUCHO

If you can be in Ayacucho for **Semana Santa**, the Holy Week beginning the Friday before Easter, you'll see fabulous daily processions, pageants and nightly candlelit processions centred on the Catedral. But beware of the beautiful procession of the **Virgen Dolores** (Our Lady of Sorrows), which takes place the Friday before Palm Sunday: pebbles are fired at the crowd (particularly at children and foreigners) by expert slingers so that onlookers take on the pain of La Madre de Dios, and so supposedly reduce her suffering. Around May 23, there is the elaborate religious procession of the **Fiesta de las Cruces**, when festivities often involve the local "scissors" folkdance performed by two men, each wielding a rather dangerous pair of cutlasses.

the Plaza de Armas; rooms are large and spacious and those on the top floor have brilliant views over the city. **S/40**

★ **Hotel San Francisco de Paula** Jr Callao 290 ⓣ066 312353, ⓦhotelsanfranciscodepaula.com. Every room in this high-quality hotel has a TV and private shower. There's also nice café on the roof with great views overlooking town. Breakfast is included. **S/160**

Hotel Santa Rosa Jr Lima 166 ⓣ066 314614. Only half a block from the Plaza de Armas, based in a stylish old mansion with fine courtyard and a decent restaurant; friendly service, too. **S/180**

EATING

Food and nightlife are both surprisingly good in Ayacucho, with the city's distinctive cuisine including *puca picante*, made from pork and potatoes seasoned with yellow chilli peppers and ground toasted peanuts, and the local *chorizo*, which is prepared with ground pork soaked with yellow chilli and vinegar, then fried in butter and served with diced fried potatoes. The courtyard complex of cafés and shops – Complejo Turístico San Cristóbal – at Jr 28 de Julio 178, offers a popular place for eating out.

Alamo Jr Cusco 215. This is certainly one of the best restaurants in the city and the best place to savour a range of the local dishes. Mon–Sat 11am–10pm.

Café Bar New York Complejo Turístico San Cristóbal. A popular spot serving burgers, pizzas, breakfasts, espresso and cocktails, among other delights. Mon–Sat 10.30am–9pm.

Restaurant La Casona Jr M. P. Bellido 463. This place offers excellent Andean criolla dishes; the set menus provide very reasonable meals with a local flavour. Daily noon–9.30pm.

Restaurant La Pileta Jr Lima 166. Excellent for dinner, preparing typical mountain dishes such as *sopa de quinoa* (around S/13) or roast guinea pig; service is good. Daily 9am–9pm.

Restaurant Tradición Jr San Martín 406 ⓣ066 312595. Offers a wide range of Peruvian and international dishes in a sophisticated but relaxed atmosphere; they prepare good home-cooked meals and also great coca-leaf teas. Daily 8am–9.30pm.

Restaurant Urpicha Londres 272 ⓣ/ⓕ066 813905). This is great for local specialities and comida criolla in general, although it gets pretty busy between noon and 2.30pm. Daily 11am–7pm.

DRINKING AND NIGHTLIFE

La Taberna El Buho 9 de Diciembre 288. Just two blocks from the main plaza and located upstairs, this is a disco and live music venue, including folklore *peña* combined, with various musical styles – even karaoke – alternating on different nights. Thurs–Sat 9pm–late.

DIRECTORY

Health Hospital Huamanga, Av Venezuela in Canan Alto ⓣ066 312180.

Internet Jr Asamblea close to the Plaza de Armas.

Money and exchange There's an ATM at the Banco de Credito on the Plaza Mayor (Mon–Fri 9am–6pm) and Interbanc, also with ATM, at Jr 9 de Diciembre 189, just half a block away from the plaza. Several shops on the Plaza de Armas will change dollars and euros.

Post office Jr Asamblea 295, two blocks from the plaza (Mon–Sat 8am–8pm).

Telephones Jr Asamblea 293 (daily 8am–8pm).

Tourist police Arequipa, 1st block (ⓣ066 312055), right on the plaza and close to the cathedral.

Around Ayacucho

Although the city itself is certainly the main pull, there are some quite fascinating places **near Ayacucho** that are possible to visit. Having said that, it's always a good idea to check with the tourist office (see opposite) beforehand on whether or not it's safe to travel in the rural environs of Ayacucho. At the time of writing, the region had been politically stable for over twelve years, but the situation is open to change and some villages are more sensitive than others.

GETTING AROUND — AROUND AYACUCHO

By organized tour The best way to travel in the area around Ayacucho is with one of the local tour companies and a guide (see opposite).

By car If you have your own transport or rent a vehicle (see opposite), you'll need good maps.

By taxi Taxis cost S/20–30/hr.

Pikimachay and Huari

Huari museum Daily 8am–4.30pm • S/5

The cave of **Pikimachay**, 24km northwest of Ayacucho, on the road to Huanta, where archeologists have found human (dated to 15,000 BC) and gigantic animal remains, is best visited on a guided tour with one of the tour companies (see p.300). This is also true of the ancient city of **Huari** (sometimes written "Wari"), about 20km north of Ayacucho on the road to Huancayo. Historians claim that this site, which covers about 2000 hectares, used to house some 50,000 people just over a thousand years ago. You can still make out the ancient streets, plazas, some reservoirs, canals and large structures. The small site **museum** displays skulls and stone weapons found here in the 1960s.

Quinua

Located about 37km northeast of Ayacucho, the charming and sleepy village of **QUINUA** is a bus ride (1hr) away, through acres of tuna cactus, which is abundantly farmed here for both its delicious fruit (prickly pear) and the red dye (cochineal) extracted from the *cochamilla* larvae that thrive at the base of the cactus leaves. The site of the historic nineteenth-century **Battle of Ayacucho**, just outside town on the pampa, is marked by a striking obelisk, unmistakeable at 44m tall. There are still some **artisans** working in Quinua: at San Pedro Ceramics (at the foot of the hill leading to the obelisk) it's often possible to look round the workshops, or try Mamerto Sánchez's workshop on Jirón Sucre.

Vilcasayhuamán and Intihuatana

About 120km from Quinua, some 4hr by road, is **Vilcasayhuamán**, a pre-Conquest construction with a Temple of the Sun, Temple of the Moon and a ceremonial pyramid. Vilcasayhuamán was an Inca administrative centre once home to 10,000 people. The central plaza was the focus for ceremonies and two very important buildings stood round it: the Sun Temple (Templo del Sol) and the Ushnu, a truncated pyramid. On the upper platform of this pyramid there's a large stone with unique carvings, thought once to have been covered with gold leaf. Originally, the city was constructed in the form of a falcon with the Ushnu located at the head. Another 25km on from Vilcasayhuamán, at a site called **Intihuatana**, there's another archeological complex, with a palace, artificial lake and a stone bath. This site reveals very fine Inca stonework in terracing and palatial doorways.

East to Cusco

It takes 20 to 28 hours to travel from Ayacucho to Cusco via **Andahuaylas** and **Abancay**, a distance of almost 600km. From Abancay, the rest of the journey to Cusco is a little less than 200km, usually taking five or six hours and passing through archeologically interesting terrain en route: shortly before crossing into the *departamento* of Cusco the road goes through the village of **Carahuasi** where the community of Concacha (3500m) is home to the archeological complex of Sahuite, comprising three massive, beautifully worked granite boulders, the best of which graphically depict an Inca village (though they have been partially defaced in recent years). Nearby at Conoc, meanwhile, there are hot medicinal springs.

Andahuaylas

It's a 270km (10hr) haul from Ayacucho across mountain passes and through several valleys to **ANDAHUAYLAS**, a lovely town which serves as airport for the larger Abancay. There's little to see or do here, despite the backdrop of splendid highland scenery. The main church here, **Catedral de San Pedro**, reflects a plain colonial style and the nearby plaza possesses a *pileta* cut from a solid piece of stone. Another fine example of *sillar* stone construction, the **Puente Colonial El Chumbao** road bridge gives access to the Nasca road and the airport (see p.304).

Sondor

45min by bus from Andahuaylas

Some 21km from Andahuaylas, the archeological remains of **Sondor** lie in the mountains about 2km beyond Laguna Pacucha at 3200m. This region – the province of Cotabambas and specifically at the village of Ccoyllurqui – is also home to the Yawar Fiesta, a dramatic festival that takes place every July, usually near the end of the month. The mythic re-enaction and community event involves capturing a live condor and tying it to the back of a bull, the latter representing the conquistadors and the condor being indigenous to Peru; usually the condor kills the bull.

Abancay and around

About 136 kilometres stretch between **ABANCAY** and Andahuaylas, usually covered in five to seven hours. Abancay is a large, bustling town, at 2378m above sea level, and sitting in a beautiful area. Despite few sights or tourist facilities (with Cusco so close, the town hosts relatively few tourists), it's nevertheless worth a stop as it's within striking range of a number of stunning sites, not least Choquequirau.

Choquequirau

The superb Inca ruins of **Choquequirau** overlook the Apurimac Canyon and provide a fantastic trek with archeological interest, one which competes well as an alternative to the Inca Trail (see p.252). Choquequirao is best approached with a planned expedition, hiring local guides and mules, or through one of the Cusco tour operators (see p.222).

Santuario Nacional de Ampay

Take a taxi from Abancay (30–45min/S/25 or hop off the Cusco–Abancay bus as it crosses the pass, beyond the Cachora turn-off • Free

The **Santuario Nacional de Ampay** can be accessed from a track about 5 or 6km north from Abancay (30–45min by car or bus) and is a protected area boasting forests, orchids and bromeliads, as well as foxes, deer, spectacled bears, *viscachas*, falcons and owls. The forest here is almost 4000 hectares of protected land mostly covered in endangered *intimpa* trees. It also contains waterfalls, glaciers and swampy areas. The Nevado Ampay, the glacial peak which dominates the landscape here, stands at 5235m tall. There's a small **interpretive centre** at the entrance, which is accessed via a track signposted to the left on the main road between Abancay and Sayhuite.

West of Abancay

Cusco is four or five hours east of Abancay; travelling west it's a relatively short hop to Puquio and from there down to Nasca on the coast, or even direct to Lima. The small town of Chalhaunca sits beside a popular thermal bath at a crossroads below Abancay, just before the serious mountainclimbs start on the route to Puquio.

Chalhuanca

Regular colectivos from Abancay (2hr; S/10)

CHALHUANCA is a small town in a deep valley a couple of hours downhill from Abancay en route towards Puquio and Nasca. Its claim as a stopping point rests mainly in the clean, and reputedly healing, hot thermal springs that can be visited just 2km from the town itself (taxi from the main plaza S/5–8).

Puquio

PUQUIO lies 180km west, over the Andes, from Chalhaunca. It is a base for exploring alpaca and *vicuña* land – particularly Pampas Galeras (see box, p.38). With the many

5

surrounding mines, the area is rich in treasures but, more importantly, great varieties of fruits and vegetables in different valleys of the region. There are also small volcanoes and even condor viewing points within a day or so of the town.

ARRIVAL AND INFORMATION

ANDAHUAYLAS

By plane The airport has flights to Arequipa, Cusco and Lima; LC Busre's offices are at Jr Bolívar 109 (T 083 421591); StarPerú is at Jr Ricardo Palma 324, Plaza de Armas (T 083 421979).

Destinations Arequipa (irregularly; 1hr); Cusco (weekly; 1hr); Lima (weekly; 1hr).

By bus The bus terminal is located on the first block of Avenida Lazaro Carillo. Buses travel to Lima and Cusco with Palomino, Av José María Arguedas 504 (T 054 722429), and San Jerónimo, Av Andahuaylas 188 (T 083 721400).

Destinations Cusco (daily; 10–12hr); Lima (daily; 16–18hr).

ABANCAY

By bus Cruz del Sur (Días Barcenas 1151 T 083 323028) and Palomino (Av Arenas 200 T 054 322932) run to Lima and Cusco. Cruz del Sur pass through Puquio and Nasca en route to Lima, while Palomino also connects with Ayacucho and Andahuaylas.

Destinations Cusco (several daily; 4–5hr); Lima (several daily; 15–17hr); Nasca (several daily; 12–14hr); Puquio (several daily; 9–10hr).

WEST TO NASCA

INFORMATION

Tourist information Regional government offices at Jr Puno 107 and Dircetur, Av Arenas 121, 1st floor T 083 3216654.

Useful websites W regionapurimac.gob.pe and W andahuaylas.com.

ACCOMMODATION

ANDAHUAYLAS

El Encanto de Oro Pedro Casafranca 424 T/F 083 723066. Easily the best choice in town, located between the main plaza and the market, it has a range of rooms at varying prices. S/120

ABANCAY

Hotel de Turistas Av Díaz Barcenas 500 T/F 083 321017. This is by far the most comfortable hotel in town and also has one of the best restaurants around, with great set menus at very good prices. S/150

Villa Los Lorros Huanipaca, Abancay, Carretera a Carmen Km 17.5 T 083 816052 or T 084 244552, W choquequiraobesttreks.com. Located strategically at the entrance to (or exit from) the trail to Choquequirao (see p.267), this superb lodge has well-appointed bungalows and a lovely dining room and lounge area where they serve very good Italian and Peruvian cuisine. Staff will arrange pick-up from Abancay or Cusco, but only by prior arrangement. S/250

DIRECTORY

ANDAHUAYLAS

Money and exchange The Banco de Credito can be found on the Plaza de Armas.

Post office The Serpost office can be found at Av Perú 243 (Mon–Sat 8am–8pm & Sun 8am–3pm).

ABANCAY

Money and exchange Banco de Credito, Jr Arequipa 218.

Post office Serpost, corner of Arequipa with Junín (Mon–Sat 8am–7pm, Sun 8am–3pm).

North of Tarma

North of Tarma there are two main routes: closest is the steep road which heads northeast down from the Andes into the Central Selva of Chanchamayo and beyond to a large region with its own possible but adventurous overland routes. The other goes back up to the crossroads just before La Oroya and then heads north to cerros de Pasco and Huánuco, interesting for its nearby archeological remains, such as Tantamayo, and itself another important gateway to the jungle region (see p.308).

Reserva Nacional de Junín

The **Reserva Nacional de Junín** is located some 85km northwest of Tarma on the La Oroya-to-Cerro de Pasco road; this is an excellent trip if you can afford the time and car rental or tour (see p.287). Located at around 4100m above sea level on the Pampa de Junín, it's packed with aquatic birds around the lakes as well as being home to plenty of *viscachas* in its 5300 hectares. It's possible to **wild camp** here (always asking local permission first), but there are no facilities at all.

Huánuco and around

The charming modern city of **HUÁNUCO**, more than 100km east of the deserted Inca town of the same name, and around 400km from Lima, sits nestled in a beautiful Andean valley some 1900m above sea level. It's a relatively peaceful place, located on the left bank of the sparkling Río Huallaga, and depending for its livelihood on forestry, tea and coca, along with a little low-key tourism. Founded by the Spaniard Gómez de Alvarado in August 1539, the city contains no real sights, save the usual handful of fine old churches and a small natural history museum. There are plenty of fascinating excursions in the area – notably, the 4000-year-old **Temple of Kotosh**.

Iglesia de San Francisco

Plaza de Armas • Daily 6–10am & 5–8pm

The sixteenth-century **Iglesia de San Francisco** houses the tomb of the town's founder and shows a strong indigenous influence, its altars featuring richly carved native fruits – avocados, papayas and pomegranates. It also displays a small collection of sixteenth-century paintings. Externally, it is not as impressive and doesn't look as old as it is, with a plain facade, painted mustard right up to its two towers.

Iglesia de la Merced

Calle Hermilio Valdizan • Daily 6–10am & 5–8pm • Free

The **Iglesia de la Merced** lies some three blocks south and west from the Plaza de Armas. It was built in 1566, in the Romantic style, and it's worth a look around if only for its spectacular Neoclassical gold-leaf altarpiece; there are also two notable Cusqueña-style (see box, p.213) religious paintings on display. From the outside the church is small and simple, painted cream.

Iglesia de San Cristóbal

Calle Damaso Beraun • Daily hours of Mass only • Free

The **Iglesia de San Cristóbal**, three blocks west of Plaza de Armas, has some fine gold-leaf altarpieces, and is said to be built on the site where the chief of the Chupacos tribe once lived and where Portuguese priest Pablo Coimbra celebrated the first Mass in the region. The first-ever Mass to be said in Huánuco was on this site on August 15, 1539, just seven years after the conquest of Peru. Some of the interior wood work depicts faces and hands.

Museo de Ciencias

Jr General Prado 495 • Mon–Sat 8am–noon & 3–7pm • S/5

The natural history museum, **Museo de Ciencias** houses regional archeological finds, mainly pottery, as well as a small display of Andean flora and fauna including some dried and some stuffed animals from the region. Established with the help of expert taxidermists back in 1947, there are brilliant examples of stuffed condors, eagles, sloths and armadillos, and also butterfly collections.

The Temple of Kotosh

Walk, or take the La Unión bus (see p.306) from Huánuco and ask the driver to drop you off at the path to Kotos • Guided tour from Huánuco will cost around S/30–50 per person, with a taxi from the Plaza de Armas costing about the same

Only 6km from Huánuco along the La Unión road, the fascinating, though poorly maintained, **TEMPLE OF KOTOSH** lies in ruins on the banks of the Río Tingo. At more

5

FIESTAS IN HUÁNUCO

If you can, you should aim to be in Huánuco around August 15, when **carnival week** begins and the city's normal tranquillity explodes into a wild fiesta binge. **Peruvian Independence Day** (July 28) is also a good time to be here, when traditional dances like the *chunco* take place throughout the streets. On January 1, 6 and 18, you can witness the **Dance of the Blacks** (El Baile de los Negritos) in which various local dance groups, dressed in colourful costumes with black masks (representing the slaves brought to work in the area's mines) run and dance throughout the main streets of the city; food stalls stay open and drinking continues all day and most of the night.

than 4000 years old, this site predates the Chavín era by more than a thousand years. A more or less permanent settlement existed here throughout the Chavín era (though without the monumental masonry and sculpture of that period) and Inca occupation, right up to the Conquest. The most remarkable feature of the Kotosh complex is the **crossed-hands symbol** carved prominently onto a stone – the gracefully executed insignia of a very early culture about which archeologists know next to nothing – which now lies in the **Museo de Arqueología** in Lima (see p.76). The site today consists of three sacred stone-built enclosures in generally poor condition; but with a little imagination and/or a good local guide, it is both atmospheric and fascinating to explore one of the most ancient temple sites in Peru.

ARRIVAL AND DEPARTURE — HUÁNUCO AND AROUND

By plane Aeropuerto Alférez FAP David Figueroa Fernandini (062 513066) is 6km out of town, and served by LC Busre, Jr Dos de Mayo 1321 (062 518113).
Destinations Lima (weekly; 1hr).

By bus Turismo Central, Tarapaca 552 (usually only a night bus), also serves Tingo María and Pucallpa. Cruz del Sur, 28 de Julio 341, and Internacional from 28 de Julio 1160 (062 519770) serve Lima, via the Central Highway and La Oroya. Turismo Unión, Jr Tarapaca 449, go to and from Tantamayo and La Unión.
Destinations La Unión (daily; 5–6hr; 7.30am); Lima (daily; 8–10hr); Pulcallpa (daily; 11hr; recommended to travel in daylight hours only, due to frequent night robberies in recent years); Tantamayo (daily; 7–10hr; leave around 7.15am); Tingo María (daily; 2–3hr).

By colectivo Colectivos are the best way to get from Huánuco to Tingo María; they leave and drop off from first block of C Prado. There are more bus options to Pucallpa from Tingo María, so it may be worth hopping onto a colectivo to Tingo and finding a bus there.

INFORMATION AND TOURS

Tourist information Casa de Aretano, Jr General Prado 718, right by the Plaza de Armas (Mon–Fri 9am–1pm & 4–6pm).

Useful website huanucoperu.com.

Tour operators Adventure and Expeditions, Jr Los Nogales Mz. N L. 33 Amarilis, Huánuco (062 512826); Mya Tours, General Prado 815, 2nd floor (062 799066, myatours-peru.com).

ACCOMMODATION

Gran Hotel Huánuco Jirón Damaso Beraun 062 512410, grandhotelhuanuco.com. This is a most comfortable hotel, right on the Plaza de Armas in the shade of some beautiful old trees. There's a pool, sauna, wi-fi and a reasonable restaurant. S/350

Hostal Las Vegas 28 de Julio 936 062 512315. Best of the budget options, right on the Plaza de Armas, this place has clean rooms and is well-run but basic. S/40

Hostal Residencial Huánuco Jirón Huánuco 861 062 515123. This is an attractive colonial building that's close to the plaza; service is passable and the rooms are spacious as well as comfortable and clean. S/45

EATING

El Café Plaza de Armas. This is the best restaurant for international cuisine, as well as a variety of criolla dishes. It's often quite busy, but the service is good. Daily 10am–9pm.

La Olla de Barro General Prado 852. Located right on the Plaza de Armas, you don't have far to go to try the local speciality, *picante de queso* – a spicy sauce made from yellow chillies and onions, poured over cold cheese and potatoes; great service in a traditional ambience. Daily noon–10.30pm.

Restaurant Vegetariano Dos de Mayo 1044. This has nice (vegetarian, unsurprisingly) dishes, particularly handy if you're looking for something lighter or simply different. Mon–Sat 11.30am–6pm.

DIRECTORY

Internet Internet cafés in and around the main plaza.

Money and exchange You can change money with the *cambistas* on the corner of Dos de Mayo and the Plaza de Armas, or at the Banco de Credito (with ATM), on Dos de Mayo, or the Banco Continental (also has ATM) on the plaza.

Post office Plaza de Armas (Mon–Sat 8am–7pm).

Shopping Artesanía is sold along blocks 7 and 8 of Jr General Prado and also blocks 11 of Dos de Mayo and 7 of Jr Huánuco.

Telephones Two blocks from the main plaza along 28 de Julio (daily 8am–9pm).

La Unión

A small market town high up on a cold and bleak pampa, **LA UNIÓN** is a base for visiting the Inca ruins of Huánuco Viejo; they are a tough – and not recommended due to preciptious mountain roads – 3 to 4hr hike away. La Unión has a few cafés and a couple of hostels.

Huánuco Viejo

Take a taxi from Plaza de Armas, La Unión (S/15–20) • Daily 8am–6pm • Free

Huánuco Viejo sits high up on the edge of a desolate pampa and is one of the most complete existing examples of an Inca provincial capital and administrative centre. The site gives a powerful impression of a once-thriving city – even though it's been a ghost town for four hundred years. The grey stone houses and **platform temples** are set out in a roughly circular pattern radiating from a gigantic *unsu* (Inca throne) in the middle of a plaza. To the north are the **military barracks** and beyond that the remains of suburban dwellings. Directly east of the plaza is the palace and temple known as Incahuasi, and next to this is the Acllahuasi, a separate enclosure devoted to the Chosen Women, or Virgins of the Sun. Behind this, and running straight through the Incahuasi, is a man-made water channel diverted from the small Río Huachac. On the opposite side of the plaza you can make out the extensive administrative quarters.

Poised on the southern hillside above the main complex are over five hundred **storehouses** where all sorts of produce and treasure were kept as tribute for the emperor and sacrifices to the sun. Well away from the damp of the valley floor, and separated from each other by a few metres to minimize the risk of fire, they also command impressive views across the plain.

Brief history

Virtually untouched by the Spanish conquistadors, the city became a centre of native dissent. Illa Tupac, a relative of the rebel Inca Manco and one of the unsung heroes of the indigenous resistance, maintained clandestine Inca rule around Huánuco Viejo until at least 1545. The Spanish built their own colonial administrative centre – modern Huánuco – at a much lower altitude, more suitable for their unacclimatized lungs and with slightly easier access to Cusco and Lima. Huánuco grew thoroughly rich, but was nevertheless regarded by the colonial Peruvians as one of those remote outposts (like Chile) where criminals, or anyone unpopular with officialdom, would be sent into lengthy exile.

ARRIVAL AND DEPARTURE — LA UNIÓN

By bus Buses link with La Unión daily; all arrive at the same terminal on Jr Comercio in La Unión.

By colectivo Colectivos arrive at the same terminal on Jr Comercio.

5

ACCOMMODATION

Hostal Gran Abilia Alvarado Comercio 1196. Quite comfortable and in a pleasant semi-rural setting; the rooms are spacious but some have shared bathrooms. Staff can, helpfully, point visitors in the direction of local guides. S/45

Tantamayo

About 150km north of Huánuco, poised in the mountainous region above the higher reaches of the Río Marañón, lies the small village of **TANTAMAYO**, with its extensive ruins nearby.

The precise age of the remote **ruins of Tantamayo** is unknown. Its buildings appear to fit into the Tiahuanaco-Huari phase, which would make them some 1200 years old, but physically they form no part of this widespread cultural movement, and the site is considered to have developed separately, probably originating from tribes migrating to the Andes from the jungle and adapting to a new environment over a long period of time. It is also thought that the ruins might reveal archeological links to Chavín de Huantar (see p.337) and Kotosh.

The architectural development of some four centuries can be clearly seen – growing from the simplest of structures to complex edifices. The thirty separate, massive constructions make an impressive scene, offset by the cloud forest and jungle flourishing along the banks of the Marañón just a little further to the north. Tall buildings dot the entire area – some clearly **watchtowers** looking over the Marañón, one of Peru's most important rivers and a major headwater of the Amazon, others with less obvious functions, built for religious reasons as temple-palaces, perhaps, or as storehouses and fortresses. One of the major constructions, just across the Tantamayo stream on a hill facing the village, was named **Pirira** by the Incas who conquered the area in the fifteenth century. At its heart there are concentric circles of carved stone, while the walls and surrounding houses are all grouped in a circular formation – clearly this was once an important centre for religious ritual. The **main building** rises some 10m on three levels, its bluff facade broken only by large window niches and by centuries of weathering.

ARRIVAL AND DEPARTURE — TANTAMAYO

By bus Buses leave daily from Huánuco to Tantamayo (8hr; S/18) with Turismo Bella from their depot at San Martín 571, Huánuco.

By combi Several combi-colectivos and buses run daily from La Unión to Tantamayo (6–7hr; S/15) which pick up and drop off from the main terminal on Jr Comercio in La Unión.

Into the jungle

The Amazon is the obvious place to move on to from Huánuco and the surrounding area, unless you're heading back to Lima and the coast. The spiralling descent north is stunning, with views across the jungle, as thrilling as if from a small plane. By the time the bus reaches the town of **Tingo María**, a possible stopover en route to Pucallpa (see p.461), the Río Huallaga has become a broad tropical river, navigable downstream in shallow canoes or by balsa raft. And the tropical atmosphere, in the shadow of the forested ridges and limestone crags of the **Bella Durmiente** mountain, is delightful. From Tingo María you can continue the 260km directly northeast on the dirt road through virgin forest, going through the **Pass of Padre Abad**, with its glorious waterfalls, along the way to Pucallpa, jumping-off point for expeditions deep into the seemingly limitless wilderness of tropical jungle (see Chapter Eight).

Tingo María

Once known as the "Garden City", because of the ease with which gardens, tropical fruit, vegetables and wild flora grow in such abundance, the ramshackle settlement of **TINGO MARÍA**, 130km north of Huánuco, lies at the foot of the Bella Durmiente

(Sleeping Beauty) mountain. According to legend, this is the place where the lovesick Princess Nunash awaits the waking kiss of Kunyaq, the sorcerer. These days the town welcomes more travellers than ever due to the decreased activity in the region's cocaine trade. However, that said, even the road on to Pucallpa from Tingo still sees the occasional armed robbery of buses travelling by night.

Despite Tingo María's striking setting, it is a tatty, ugly town, on which the ravages of Western civilization have left their mark. Dominated by sawmills and plywood factories financed by multinational corporations, with its forest of TV aerials sticking out from the rooftops, the town displays symbols of relative affluence, but the tin roofs and crumbling walls across the township betray the poverty of the majority of its inhabitants. There's little for visitors to see, other than the **Cueva de las Lechuzas** (Owls' Cave), the vast, picturesque home to a flock of rare nocturnal parrots (you'll need a torch), 14km out of town. Tingo María's major **fiesta** period is the last week of July – a lively and fun time to be in town, but on no account leave your baggage unattended.

ARRIVAL AND TOURS — TINGO MARÍA

By bus Be aware that buses travelling at night are frequently robbed at gunpoint, which is at the very least an unpleasant experience. Selva Express runs daily buses from Tingo María to Pucallpa from their depot at Av Tito Jaime 218 (T 062 562380).
Destinations Pucallpa (several daily; 7–9hr); Tarapoto (several daily; 20hr).

By colectivo Colectivos leave and arrive at all times of day and night connecting Tingo María with both Pucallpa and Huánuco from the corner of Callao with Raymondi, about five blocks from the Plaza de Armas. They also leave from here to Tarapoto and towns along the road that follows the Huallaga Valley north via Juanjui (16hr); this route is not recommended for travellers due to the traditionally high level of cocaine smuggling, terrorist activity and armed robbery. The new president Ollanta Humala is making a strong bid to eliminate these antisocial factors in this region, so one should also expect a high army presence.

Tour For tours to archeological sites and waterfalls in the region, try Silvia Silva Zamora, Av Raymondi 604 (T 062 406659, E 644@hotmail.com).

ACCOMMODATION

Hostal La Cabaña Av Raymondi 342 T 062 562146 and T 062 562178. Simple but excellent value; here all rooms are small and all bathrooms shared. It has a good associated restaurant of the same name. S/30

Hotel Viena Lamas 245 T 062 562194. Although inexpensive and clearly basic, *Hotel Viena* is surprisingly comfortable; rooms are clean and spacious, service friendly. S/35

Madera Verde Hotel 2km south of Tingo María T 062 562047 and T 062 561608. Upmarket option 2km south of town, with its own pool (open to non-residents for around S/5), and clean, comfortable bungalow-style rooms, most with private bath. S/220

Villa Jennifer Eco-lodge Carretera Castillo Grande Km 3.4 T 062 794714, W villajennifer.com. A short distance from the town centre, this ecological *albergue* has lovely rooms – white, simple and tasteful – plus fantastic gardens, a pool, bar and restaurant. S/100

Huaraz, the cordilleras and the Ancash coast

MOUNTAINS OF THE CORDILLERA BLANCA

6

Huaraz, the cordilleras and the Ancash coast

It is the majestic snow-capped peaks of the Cordillera Blanca that draw most visitors to this region – many of them to follow the area's awesome trekking trails and some to experience mountaineering in the high Andes (or "Andinismo"). The mountains are accessed via an immense desert coastline, where pyramids and ancient fortresses are scattered within easy reach of several small resorts linked by vast, empty beaches. Between the coast and the Cordillera Blanca, sits the barren, dry and dark Cordillera Negra. Sliced north to south by these parallel ranges, the centre of Ancash is focused on the Huaraz Valley, known locally as the Callejón de Huaylas. The city of Huaraz offers most of the facilities required for exploring the valley and surrounding mountains, though there are more rural alternatives.

The *departamento* of Ancash was a rural backwater when it was created in 1839. These days, the main industries are fishing (mainly restricted to Chimbote, Peru's largest fishing port), tourism (everywhere but Chimbote), mining (gold, silver, copper and zinc) and agriculture (primarily the cultivation of wheat, potatoes, maize corn and pulses, but also over forty percent of Peru's commercial marigold flowers). The region has a population of just over one million, with 250,000 of these people living in or around **Chimbote**.

For Peruvian and overseas visitors alike, Ancash offers more in terms of **trekking** and **climbing**, beautiful snowcapped scenery, "alpine" flora and fauna and glaciated valleys than anywhere else in the country. It is also extremely rich in history and **pre-Colombian remains** as well as possessing a truly traditional living culture. Given the severe earthquake damage this area has suffered throughout the twentieth century, it may lack some of the colonial charm seen in Cusco, Arequipa, Cajamarca and Ayacucho, yet more than makes up for it with the majesty and scale of its scenery. At around 3000m above sea level, it is important to acclimatize to the **altitude** before undertaking any major hikes.

Nestling in the valleys, the *departamento*'s capital, **Huaraz** – a six- or seven-hour drive north from Lima – makes an ideal base for exploring the region. It's the place to stock up, hire guides and mules, or relax after a breathtaking expedition. Besides being close to scores of exhilarating mountain trails, the city is also near the ancient Andean treasure, **Chavín de Huantar**, an impressive stone temple complex that was at the centre of a culturally significant puma-worshipping religious movement just over 2500 years ago.

MOUNTAIN BIKING NEAR HUARAZ

Highlights

❶ **Monterrey and Chancos** Relaxing in either of these two natural thermal baths is both a healthy and a hedonistic experience to remember. **See p.323**

❷ **Cordillera Blanca** Hiking or climbing in this mountainous region is as scenic an adventure as you could hope to find anywhere outside of the Himalayas. **See p.325**

❸ **Las Lagunas de Llanganuco** These calm, turquoise-coloured, glacial lakes sit 3850m above sea level, dramatically surrounded by Peru's highest peaks. **See p.330**

❹ **Huascarán** Dividing the Amazon Basin from the Pacific watershed, this mountain is the highest peak in Peru. **See p.330**

❺ **Caraz** A quaint, attractive town known for its honey and milk products, quietly settled below the enormous Huandoy Glacier and close to the little-visited ruins of Tumshucaico. **See p.333**

❻ **Chavín de Huantar** One of the most important ancient temple sites in the Andes – associated with a cult dedicated primarily to a terrifying feline god. **See p.337**

❼ **The Sechin ruins** A unique temple site whose outer wall is clad with some of the most gruesome ancient artwork to be found anywhere in South America. **See p.344**

HIGHLIGHTS ARE MARKED ON THE MAP ON P.314

6

Huaraz

Situated in the perfectly steep-sided Callejón de Huaylas valley, **HUARAZ** – 400km from Lima – is the focal point of inland Ancash. Only a day's bus ride from either Lima or Trujillo, it's one of the best places in Peru to base yourself if you have any interest in **outdoor adventure** or just sightseeing. As a market town and magnet for hikers, bikers, canoeists and climbers, the city centre has a naturally lively atmosphere, making it the ideal springboard for exploring the surrounding mountainous region; besides the stunning mountain scenery, the area boasts spectacular ruins, natural thermal baths and beautiful glacial lakes. The valley is dominated by the **Cordillera Blanca**, the world's highest tropical mountain range, and **Huascarán**, Peru's highest peak. The region is best experienced between May and September when the skies are nearly always blue and it rains very little. Between October and April, however, it's often cloudy and most afternoons you can expect some rain.

Brief history

Occupied since at least 12,000 years ago, the area around Huaraz was responsible for significant cultural development during the Chavín era (particularly 1500–500 BC), although the Incas didn't arrive here until the middle of the fifteenth century. Following the **Spanish conquest** of Peru, and up until less than a century ago, Huaraz remained a fairly isolated community, barricaded to the east by the dazzling snowcapped peaks of the Cordillera Blanca and separated from the coast by the dry, dark Cordillera Negra. Between these two mountain chains the powerful Río Santa

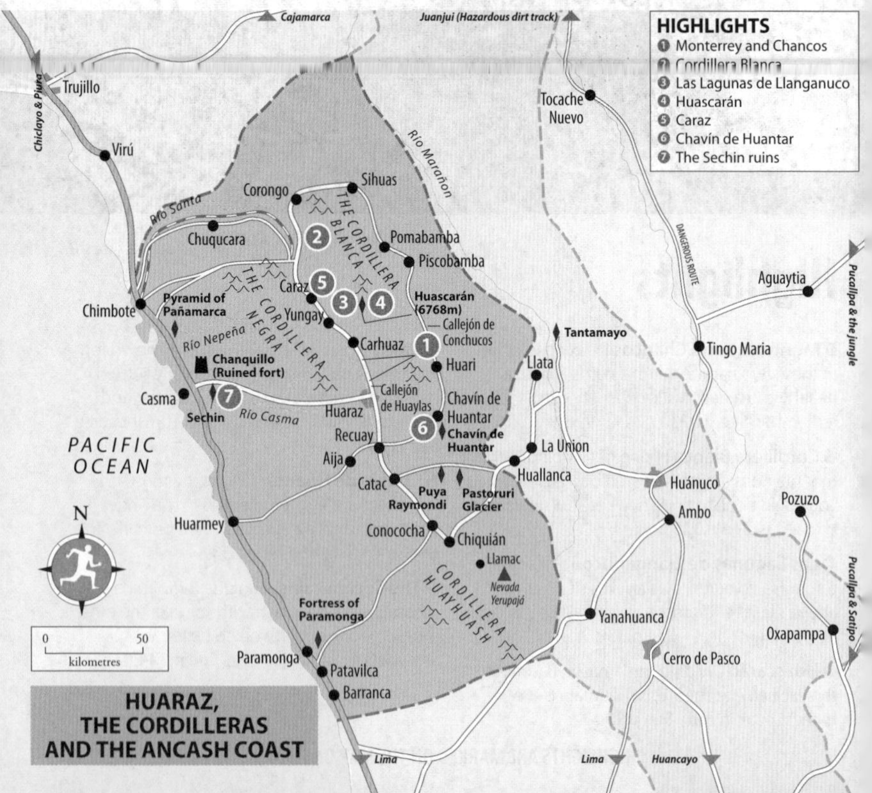

valley, known as the Callejón de Huaylas, is a region with strong traditions of local independence.

For several months in 1885, the people of the Callejón waged a **guerrilla war** against the Lima authorities, during which the whole valley fell into rebel hands. The revolt was sparked by a native leader, the charismatic **Pedro Pablo Atusparia**, and thirteen other village mayors, who protested against excessive taxation and labour abuses. After they were sent to prison and humiliated by having their braided hair (a traditional sign of status) cut off, the local peasants overran Huaraz, freeing their chieftains, expelling all officials and looting the mansions of wealthy landlords and merchants (many of them expatriate Englishmen who had been here since the Wars of Independence). The rebellion was eventually quashed by an army battalion from the coast, which recaptured the city while the Indians were celebrating their annual fiesta. Even today, Atusparia's memory survives close to local hearts, and inhabitants of the area's remote villages remain unimpressed by the central government's attempts to control the region.

Downtown Huaraz

Although well over 3000m above sea level, Huaraz has a somewhat cosmopolitan, and very busy, city centre. It has developed rapidly in terms of tourism and commerce since the completion of the highway through the river basin from Paramonga, and the opening of mainly US- and Canadian-owned zinc, silver and gold mines in both the Cordillera Negra and the Callejón de Conchucos. Even so, most tourism activity is geared towards goings-on out of town, like trips to Chavín de Huantar or mountaineering expeditions to the glaciated peaks and trekking country that surrounds Huaraz.

Avenida Luzuriaga is the town centre's north–south axis, where most of the restaurants, nightlife and tour agencies are based. The Parque Ginebra is set just behind Luzuriaga and the **Plaza de Armas**; the plaza is pleasant but something of an afterthought in terms of city planning and not yet fully integrated into the network of roads.

Virtually the entire city was levelled by the **earthquake** of 1970, and the old houses have been replaced with single-storey modern structures topped with gleaming tin roofs. Surrounded by eucalyptus groves and fields, it's still not quite the vision it once was, but it's a decent enough place in which to recuperate from the rigours of hard travel. There are many easy **walks** just outside of town, and if you fancy an afternoon's stroll you can simply go out to the eastern edge and follow one of the paths or streams uphill.

Museo Arqueológico de Ancash

Av Luzuriaga 762 • Mon–Sat 9am–5pm, Sun 9am–2pm • S/5 • Ⓣ 043 421551

Huaraz's major cultural attraction is the **Museo Arqueológico de Ancash**, facing the modern Plaza de Armas. Fronting attractive, landscaped gardens that are full of stones removed from Recuay tombs and temples, this small but interesting museum contains a superb collection of Chavín, Chimu, Wari, Mochica and Recuay **ceramics**, as well as some expertly trepanned skulls. It also displays an abundance of the finely chiselled stone monoliths typical of this mountain region, most of them products of the Recuay and Chavín cultures. There's also a model of the Guitarrero Cave, a local site showing evidence of human occupation around 10,000 BC. One of its most curious exhibits is a *goniometro*, an early version of the surveyor's theodolite, probably over a thousand years old and used for finding alignments and exact ninety-degree angles in building construction.

La Catedral

Plaza de Armas • Daily 7am–7pm • Free

On the other side of the Plaza de Armas from the museum stands the **Catedral**. Completely rebuilt after being destroyed in the 1970 earthquake, it has nothing special to see inside, but its vast blue-tiled roof makes a good landmark and, if you look closely, appears to mirror one of the glaciated mountain peaks, the Nevado Huanstán (6395m), behind it.

Museo de Miniaturas del Peru

Block 7 of Av Centenario, in grounds of Gran Hotel Huascarán • Mon–Fri 8am–1pm & 3–6pm • $1

The second of the town's museums to merit a visit is the **Museo de Miniaturas del Peru**, in the gardens of the *Gran Hotel Huascarán*, close to the town exit en route down the valley along Avenida Fitzcarrald. The museum contains an interesting collection of pre-Hispanic art from the Huaraz region and a range of local folk art and crafts, including fine red Callejón de Huaylas ceramics. It also displays a small model of Yungay (see p.328) prior to the entire town being buried under a mudslide as a result of the 1970 earthquake.

Santuario del Señor de la Soledad

Plazuela del Señor de la Soledad • Mon–Sun 8am–1pm & 3–6pm • Free • 043 728878

Uphill in the eastern part of town, at the Parque de la Soledad, the **Santuario del Señor de la Soledad** can be visited. It is another church built since the 1970 earthquake and houses the powerful sixteenth-century religious image of *El Señor de la Soledad.*

Trout Farm

Av Confraternidad Internacional Oeste • Daily 8am–5pm • 25¢, includes guided tour • A 15min walk up Av Raimondi then across the Río Quillcay bridge and down Av Confraternidad Internacional Oeste

It is worth the stroll to the regional **Trout Farm** (or Estación Pesquería), run by the Ministerio de Pesquería. It breeds thousands of rainbow trout every year and you can observe the process from beginning to end (more interesting than you might think); much of the excellent trout available in the restaurants of Huaraz comes from here.

Mirador de Rataquenua

Follow Av Villón out beyond the cemetery and up through the woods to the cross. Taxis (S/10–20 one way) will also take you there and back, which is safer than walking if you're on your own

There are one or two vantage points on the hills around the city of Huaraz, but the best and most accessible is the **Mirador de Rataquenua**, about a two-hour walk each way. It is not advisable to walk alone since there have been muggings reported on this route. Notwithstanding, it commands a splendid location, high above the town to the southeast, and looks out over the Callejón de Huaylas.

ARRIVAL AND DEPARTURE — HUARAZ

BY PLANE

There are now daily flights from Lima to Huaraz with LC Busre (Av Pablo Carriquiry 857, San Isidro, Lima; 01/2041313, lcperu.pe). The flight lands at a small airstrip close to the village of Anta, some 23km north of Huaraz; from here it's 30min into the city by colectivo or bus, both of which leave from the main road outside the airstrip, or 20–25min by taxi (S/20).

BY BUS

Most people arrive by bus from Lima or Trujillo. The most comfortable bus service is offered by Cruz del Sur; Movil Tours and Expreso Ancash also offer day and night buses and a range of services. All long-range buses come in at and leave from (or close to) their company's offices (see opposite). Local buses connect Huaraz with other towns along the valley – Carhuaz, Yungay and Caraz. These can be caught from just over the main river bridge from the town centre, on either side of the main road (Av Fitzcarrald), beside the Río Quillcay. Buses to Chiquián are run by Chiquián Tours from block 1 of C Huascarán, near the market, and leave every hour or so.

Destinations Caraz (6–8hr; S/15–20); Casma (4–5hr; S/15–20); Chimbote (5–7hr; S/20–35); Lima (8hr; S/40–80); Trujillo (8–10hr; S/35–70); Carhuaz (hourly; 45min); Catac (hourly; 80min); Chavín (daily; 2–3hr); Chiquián (daily; 3–4hr); Huánuco (daily; 12–14hr); Huari (daily; 4hr); La Unión (daily; 8hr); Pomabamba (daily; 8–10hr); Piscobamba (daily; 8–10hr); Pomacha (daily; 3hr 40min); Sihuas (daily; 10hr); Yungay (hourly; 1hr).

BUS OPERATORS

Chavín Express Jr Mariscal Cáceres 328 (043 424652). Services to Sihuas, Chavín and Huari.

CIVA Morales 650 (043 429253). Services to Lima.

Colectivos Comité 14 Av Fitzcarrald 216 (043 421202 or 043 421739). Services to Lima and Trujillo.

Cruz del Sur Jr Lucar y Torré 585 (043 428726). The best services for Lima and Trujillo.

Empresa Condor de Chavín Jr Tarapaca 312 (043 422039). Services to Chavín and Lima.

Empresa Huandoy Av Fitzcarrald 261 (043 727507). Services to Chimbote and Caraz.

Empresa Moreno Av Raimondi 858 (043 721590). Services to Casma.

Empresa Rapido Cáceres 380 (043 422887). Services to Chiquián, Huallanca and La Unión.

Empresa Rosario Jr Caraz 605. Services to Pomabamba, La Unión and Huánuco.

Empresa Sandoval Tarapaca 582 (043 426930). Services to Catac, Chavín, Pomacha and Huari.

Expresso Ancash/Ormeño Av Raimondi 853 (043 421102). Services to Lima and Caraz.

Movil Tours Av Raimondi 730 (043 422555). Services to Lima, Chimbote and Trujillo.

Rodríguez Services to Chimbote and Caraz.

Turismo Chimbote Services to Trujillo, Caraz and Chimbote.
Turismo Huaraz Jr Caraz 605. Services to Caraz, Piscobamba, Pomabamba and Chimbote.

BY COLECTIVO

Colectivos Comité 14 run daily services here from Jirón Leticia in Lima Centro and also to and from Trujillo. Colectivos also connect all the main towns and villages to the north – Carhuaz, Yungay and Caraz – at very reasonable rates (up to 2hr; up to S/10); these can be caught from just over the main river bridge from the town centre, on either side of the main road (Avenida Fitzcarrald), beside the Río Quillcay. Just before the same bridge, colectivos heading south to Catac (80min; S/4) and Olleros (20–30min; S/8) can be caught daily every 30min from the end of Jirón Cáceres, just below the market area.

GETTING AROUND

On foot Much of Huaraz Town can be easily negotiated on foot once you've acclimatized to the altitude (3091m); however, some of the more remote sectors should not be walked alone at night since incidents of mugging and rape have, albeit rarely, been reported here.
By colectivo For short journeys within the city, the best option is one of the regular colectivos, which run on fixed routes along avenidas Luzuriaga and Centenario (S/1).
By taxi Using taxis in and around the city costs around S/3–5. A long-distance taxi ride, say from Huaraz to Caraz, would cost at least S/50–70 during daylight, and taxis are also available by the day from around S/100 upwards.

TOURS AND ADVENTURE ACTIVITIES AROUND HUARAZ

The most popular **tours** around Huaraz are to the Llanganuco Lakes (8hr; $10–15/person), Chavín de Huantar (9–11hr; $10–15/person, including lunch in Chavín) and to the **thermal baths** at Chancos (4hr; from $8) and Caraz (6hr; from $10). You can also take a rather commercialized tour to the Pastoruri Glacier, 70km from Huaraz at 5240m (6–8hr return; from $10/person). Sadly, the glacier's ice is actually retreating these days, so although worth a visit, it's not as spectacular as it used to be. A new route around Pastoruri known as the **Ruta del Cambio Climatico** (Climate Change Route) was partially reopened in April 2011; you can get to the edge of the glacier now, but you can't touch it. There are mules available ([illegible]) to help visitors along the route. It's worth remembering that Pastoruri is very high and can be bitterly cold, so make sure you're well acclimatized to the altitude, and take warm clothing with you.

The Pastoruri tour usually includes a visit to see **Puya raimondii** plants (see box, p.332) as well.

ADVENTURE ACTIVITIES

In a region as exciting as this in terms of **outdoor adventure**, most people come for something active, namely trekking, climbing (see box, p.326), mountain biking, canoeing or even parapenting. Adventure activities should really be done in association with reputable **local tour agencies** and/or local guides. Always check on **inclusive costs** (and whether these include entry fees, food, porters etc) and if the guide leading your tour speaks English or another language you understand. Some companies may charge more if they consider their service superior. There's greater price variation in the more adventurous tours, treks, biking, mountaineering, canoeing and river-rafting trips, though tariffs generally start at around $40–60 per half-day.
Canoeing For canoeing, the most popular section of the Río Santa, which runs along the valley separating the two massive cordilleras, lies between the villages of Jangas and Caraz, navigable between May and October most years with rapids class 2 and 3.
Llama-packing If a three-day trek with llamas carrying your camping equipment appeals to you, then check out Peru Llama Trek at Pasaje Huaullac, Nueva Florida ((Ⓣ043 425661, Ⓦperullamatrek.com), a llama-packing initiative designed to promote ecotourism in the region; you can also ask for details in the Casa de Guías, Parque Ginebra 28-G (Ⓣ043 421811).
Mountain biking The Callejón de Huaylas offers one of Peru's most scenic bike rides, with most routes here going over 3500m; Llanganuco (3800m) from Yungay is popular, as is Carhuaz to the Abra de Punta Olímpica (4800m). The sun is very hot here, so always use good sunglasses and sun block.
Parapenting If you fancy parapenting, the Huaraz region is an ideal place (mostly around Caraz and Yungay, particularly around the Pan de Azúcar); the best local contact is Alberto Sotelo, contactable through Monttrek (see opposite).

INFORMATION AND TOURS

INFORMATION

Tourist information Plaza de Armas (Mon–Sat 8am–6.30pm, Sun 8am–2pm; ☎043 428812, regionancash.gob.pe). The staff are usually helpful and stock photocopies of trekking maps. The Tourist Police (☎043 421341) also have maps and information at the back of the same building by the plaza.

National Institute of Culture Office responsible for ancient monuments, Av Luzuriaga 766 (☎043 421829). Provides information about remote ruins.

TOUR OPERATORS

There are many tour operators in Huaraz who can assist with tours and treks around the city; Pony's Expeditions in Caraz (see p.325) is one of the best such operators.

Caillou Aventure Parque Ginebra ☎043 421214. Rock climbing, trekking, Andinismo (high Andes trekking and climbing) and mountain biking.

Monttrek Av Luzuriaga 646 (upstairs) ☎043 421124, monttrek.com.pe. Offers professional climbing, guides, treks, horseriding, river-rafting and snowboarding in the region. They also have a climbing wall, stock new and used camping and climbing equipment, and the office is a great place to meet other trekkers.

Mountain Bike Adventures Jr Lucre y Torre 530 ☎043 424259, chakinaniperu.com. Organizes bike tours with mountain bikes to rent as well as a variety of alternative routes for cyclists with particular interests, including cross-country, single track and up- or downhill options. English-speaking guides are available and there's the bonus of a book exchange in their office.

Pablo Tours Av Luzuriaga 501 ☎043 421145, pablotours.com. One of the best agencies for standard tours, Pablo Tours is particularly good for organized treks and canoeing, but also offers local cultural and city tours. Note that they get booked up very quickly.

Peruvian Andes Adventures Jr José Olaya 532 ☎043 421864, peruvianandes.com. This outfit offers a combination of trekking, climbing and day-trips to sites around the region, plus flights and bus tickets.

ACCOMMODATION

Even in the high season, around August, it's rarely difficult to find accommodation at a reasonable price, though rates do rise during the **Semana Turística** (or Semana del Andinismo) in June and between November and January when many Peruvians tend to visit. There are really three main areas providing accommodation in the urban area: west of the main streets avenidas Fitzcarrald and Luzuriaga; east of these streets; and another sector, away from the centre, up the Jirón José de Sucre hill to the east. From the Plaza de Armas along Avenida Luzuriaga there are countless hostels and many smaller places renting out rooms; outside of high season it is definitely worth bargaining. There are some peaceful places to choose from out of town, too, some with a garden or **thermal springs**, particularly those around Monterrey.

WEST OF FITZCARRALD AND LUZURIAGA

Alojamiento Quintana Mariscal Cáceres 411 ☎043 426060, hostal-quintana.com. An increasingly popular backpacker joint, less than three blocks from the Plaza de Armas. It is clean, comfortable and well managed, and most rooms have a private bathroom. S/90

B and B Mi Casa Av Tarapaca (also known as 27 de Noviembre) 773 ☎043 43375, micasahuaraz.jimdo.com. Just three blocks west of the Plaza de Armas, this place is distinguished by very friendly owners who provide excellent service and have expert cartographical information as well as general tourist info. There's also free wi-fi in rooms and a dining room serving breakfasts (included in price), as well as 24hr hot water and private bathrooms. S/50

Casablanca Hotel Av Tarapaca 138 ☎043 422602, huaraz.com/casablanca. A quite comfortable and upmarket hotel with fine wood-beamed ceilings. Used by a lot of tour groups, it actually seems quite out of place on this downmarket street. All rooms have a private bathroom and there's a good restaurant with inclusive breakfast. S/350

★ **Edward's Inn** Av Bolognesi 121 ☎043 422692, edwardsinn.com. One of the most popular trekkers' hostels, located just below the market area and offering all sorts of services, including up-to-the-minute tourist information, in a very convivial atmosphere. Rooms come with or without private bathroom, and hot water is almost always available. The owner, who speaks English, is a highly experienced trekker, climber and mountain rescuer. S/240

EAST OF FITZCARRALD AND LUZURIAGA

Alojamiento Alpes Andes and Casa das Guías Parque Ginebra 28-G ☎043 421811, casadeguias.com.pe. Located on a quiet little plaza in the streets behind Av Luzuriaga, this is a centre for local guides and mountaineers and also includes a hostel. It's very clean, with communal rooms and showers at reasonable rates, and you can safely leave baggage here while out of town on trekking expeditions. S/35

Hostal Gyula Inn Parque Ginebra 632 ☎043 421567. Located above an internet office, this hostel is relatively plain but excellent value with great views, private bathrooms and access to kitchen facilities; staff are cheerful to boot. S/45

Hostal Landauro Jr José de Sucre 109 ☎043 421212, willemml@yahoo.es, huaraz.info/hostallandauro. A popular place right on the Plaza de Armas, with small but

6

well-decorated rooms (with or without bathroom) set along narrow balconies boasting views over the town towards the Cordillera Blanca. S/40

Hostal Los Portales Av Raimondi 903 ⓣ043 428184. A spacious, if often dimly lit, hotel, well situated for most bus terminals. Rooms are clean with private bathrooms, and large, well-sprung beds and there's also a large, safe luggage store for trekkers, as well as a restaurant. S/90

Hostal Raymondi Av Raimondi 820 ⓣ043 721082. This hostel is large, clean and full of character, with a spacious, old-fashioned lobby. Rooms themselves are well-appointed if a little dark, with private bathrooms. S/75

Hostal Schatzi Jr Simón Bolívar 419 ⓣ043 423074, ⓔschatzihs@yahoo.com, ⓦwww.hostalschatzi.com. A lovely, very friendly little place set around a lush garden patio with small but tidy and nicely furnished rooms; those on the second floor are located on a wraparound wooden balcony with two floors and some views across the garden, town and valley. S/80

Jo's Place Jr Daniel Villarzan 276 ⓣ043 425505, ⓦjosplacehuaraz.com. Located 10min from the town centre – over the river bridge, on the fourth street on the right – *Jo's Place* is very relaxed, with comfortable rooms and a secure atmosphere making for great value, as well as popularity with backpackers. The staff can help organize tours and there is a large garden, a terrace and views across to the Cordillera Blanca. English newspapers and breakfasts are available. Dorms S/25; doubles S/50

EAST OF AVENIDA GAMARRA

Albergue Churup Jr Amadeo Figueroa 1257, La Soledad ⓣ043 424200, ⓦchurup.com. Just 5min walk from Plaza de Armas, this great-value establishment has a family atmosphere, a garden, lovely wood-burning stove, laundry, kitchen and left-luggage facilities as well as panoramic views. They also have lots of info on local trekking. S/55

★ **Casa Alojamiento La Cabaña** Jr José de Sucre 1224 ⓣ043 423428, ⓔedgon175@hotmail.com. A popular and very friendly *pensión* with safe, comfortable accommodation, a dining room and hot water all day. Rooms have private bathrooms and TV, while guests also have access to kitchen and laundry facilities, plus a dining room. S/40

★ **Hotel Andino** Jr Pedro Cochachín 357 ⓣ043 421662, ⓦhotelandino.com. An uphill hike away from the centre of town, albeit with the reward of beautiful views over the Cordillera Blanca and plush quarters in the best hotel in town. There are a variety of rooms to choose from, with or without terraces and fireplaces, and there's also a gourmet restaurant serving delicious food with a Swiss influence. S/340

Olaza Guest House Jr Julio Arguedas 1242, La Soledad ⓣ043 422529, ⓦolazas.com. Nice, large rooms here – very clean and with private bathrooms as well as access to the kitchen and laundry. This place is also a good source of local information, enjoys a roaring fire in the communal living space and has a roof terrace that is great for enjoying the spectacular views and mixing with fellow travellers over tea or breakfast. S/70

Steel Guest House C Alejandro Manguina 1467, in front of Hotel Andino ⓣ043 429709, ⓦsteelguest.com. A five-storey building with a pleasant communal area on the second floor offering a TV, small library and a billiard table. Rooms have private bathrooms, 24hr hot water and there's a laundry available. S/140

EATING

Café Andino Lucar y Torre 530 ⓣ043 421203. A popular upstairs café with library and games, serving breakfasts, good coffee, juices and Mexican food. A good place to meet other travellers, trekkers and climbers. Daily 8am–8pm.

★ **California Café** 28 de Julio 562 ⓣ043 428354. A good place for wi-fi and mingling with other travellers; the coffee is excellent, there's trekking information on offer and a relaxed atmosphere. Try the all-day American breakfast or waffles, especially if you've worked up an appetite after a few days' hiking. Daily 7.30am–7pm.

Chifa Yat Sen Av Raimondi and Av Comercio. A pleasant little Chinese restaurant, offering amazing-value three-course set lunches with a Peruvian twist, as well as a range of standard Chinese dishes available most evenings from around 6pm. Daily11am–10pm.

Crêperie Patrick Av Luzuriaga 422. A centrally located establishment close to the corner with Av Raimondi, *Crêperie Patrick* serves guinea pig, rabbit *al vino* and fondues in addition to excellent crêpes, salads and sandwiches. Daily 10.30am–9.30pm.

Fuente de Salud Jr José de la Mar 562. A vegetarian restaurant with an excellent reputation; the best and cheapest offering is the superb set menu at lunchtime. Tables outside make for a pleasant change when eating in the sunshine. Mon–Sat 11am–6pm.

Huaraz Querido Jr Simón Bolívar 981. Easily the best spot in town for fresh fish and seafood. The ceviche is generally delicious, but there's a wide range of other sea, lake and farmed fish options (starting at around S/15 a main dish). Daily 9am–10pm.

Limón Leña y Carbón Av Luzuriaga 1002. Out on a limb at the southern end of the main drag, this is another really good seafood restaurant that serves fresh fish delivered from Chimbote; the menu also includes local trout, meat dishes and pizzas in the evening. Daily 11am–9pm.

★ **Monttrek Pizza-Pub** Av Luzuriaga 646 ⓣ043 421124. A spacious place, very popular with trekkers and one of the town's top tour and climbing operators (see p.319). It also boasts a useful notice-board for contacting like-minded backpackers, as well as maps and aerial photos of the region. The food is delicious and the music good, and there's even a climbing wall. Daily 8am–10pm.

Pachamama Av San José de San Martín 687 ⊕043 421834. A fine café-bar, with a spacious and attractive environment, serving good wines and a range of other drinks, fish, chicken, meats and pastas. There's also good music and games, and even temporary exhibitions and silver craft work on display. Daily early afternoon to 10pm.

Restaurant Bistro de los Andes Jr Julian de Morales 823 ⊕043 426249. A great place for breakfast, with seats outside, good yoghurt, coffee and pancakes; also popular during the evening. Features a book exchange too. Daily 7.30am to around 9pm, closed Sun mornings.

Siam de los Andes Av Gamarra and Av Julian de Morales. Excellent Thai stir-fries and curries in a warm and welcoming ambience with great service and nice decor. Daily 6.30am–10pm.

6

DRINKING AND NIGHTLIFE

There's a lively nightlife scene in Huaraz, with several **peñas** hosting traditional Andean music, as well as a few **clubs** where locals and tourists can relax, keep warm and unwind during the evenings or at weekends. Nightlife joints start to open from 7pm and can go on until 3am.

Centro Folklórico Cultural Waracushun Jr Bolívar 1101, Belén, Huaraz. The folklore centre in Huaraz helps make local and regional music and dance culture more accessible. It generally has live music and dance shows at weekends, and most days serves reasonable meals and snacks. Daily 11am–11pm.

Tambo Taverna Jr José de la Mar 776. A restaurant-*peña* serving good drinks, with a great party spirit, a mix of popular sounds and occasional live music – a mix of Latin, rock and pop. Daily 6pm–midnight.

★ **Vagamundo Travel Bar** Jr Julian de Morales 753. Arguably the most trendy and popular bar in Huaraz these days, *Vagamundo* serves great sandwiches as well as a wide range of cocktails. Daily 7pm–late.

X-treme Bar Av Uribe and Av Luzuriaga. A popular cocktail lounge and dancefloor spinning everything from rock and pop to jazz, blues and Latin – one of Huaraz's best bars. Daily 8pm–2am.

SHOPPING

Huaraz is a noted **crafts centre**, producing, in particular, very reasonably priced, handmade leather goods (custom made if you've got a few days to wait around). Other bargains include woollen hats, scarves and jumpers, embroidered blankets, and interesting replicas of the Chavín stone carvings. Most of these items can be bought from the stalls in the small **artesanía market** in covered walkways set back off Av Luzuriaga (daily 2pm–dusk) or, for more choice, in the **Mercado Modelo** two blocks down Av Raimondi from Av Luzuriaga. Huaraz is also renowned for its **food**, in particular its excellent local cheese, honey and *manjar blanco* (a traditional sweet made out of condensed milk). These can all be bought in the **food market**, in the backstreets around Av José de San Martín (daily 6am–6pm).

FIESTAS IN AND AROUND HUARAZ

Throughout the year various **fiestas** take place in the city and its surrounding villages and hamlets. They are always bright, energetic occasions, with *chicha* and *aguardiente* flowing freely, as well as roast pig, bullfights and vigorous communal dancing, with the townfolk dressed in outrageous masks and costumes. The main festival in the city of Huaraz is usually in the first week of February and celebrates **Carnival**. In June (dates vary, so check with the tourist office for exact dates), Huaraz hosts the **Semana del Andinismo** (Andean Mountaineering and Skiing Week), which includes trekking, climbing, and national and international ski competitions, on the Pastoruri Glacier.

Caraz has its own Semana Turística, usually in the third week of June. Note that during this month accommodation and restaurant prices in Huaraz and Caraz increase considerably. Other festivals include the **Aniversario de Huaraz**, in July (usually on the 25th), when there are a multitude of civic and cultural events in the city, plus the annual folklore celebrations in the first week of August for Coyllur–Huaraz. The fiesta for the **Virgen de la Asunción** in Huata and Chancas takes place during mid-August. Late September sees the festival of the **Virgen de las Mercedes**, celebrated in Carhuaz, as well as other rural get-togethers you'll often come across en route to sites and ruins in the Callejón de Huaylas.

Centro Artesanal Next to the post office on the plaza. Sells textiles, ceramics, jewellery, stone- and leather-work – most of it made locally in the valley. Mon–Sat 10am–6pm.

Centro Naturista Fitzcarrald 356. Good for natural medicines, yoghurt, herbs and ecofriendly soaps and cosmetics; some of these products are locally manufactured using plant combinations based on traditional remedies. Mon–Fri 9am–7pm.

Market Ortiz Av Luzuriaga 401. One of the best supermarkets in town with everything from wine to trail mix on sale. Daily 8am–9pm.

Tierras Andinas Parque Ginebra. Has some fine handicrafts and local artwork. Mon–Sat 10am–5pm.

DIRECTORY

Health For emergencies, go to the hospital on Av Luzuriaga, block 8 (T 043 421861 or T 043 421290); San Pedro Clinic, Huaylas 172 (T 043 428811). For non-urgent medical treatment try Dr Simon Komori, Jr 28 de Julio 602 (24hr), or try the surgery at Av Luzuriaga 618 (Mon–Fri 9am–5pm). For dental treatment there's the Centro Odontologico Olident, Av Luzuriaga 410-204 (T 043 424918).

High Altitude Rescue Call T 043 493327 or T 044 93291 in an emergency. Yungay branch T 043 493333.

Internet Wi-Fi California Café, 28 de Julio 562, offers local, national and international phone calling at very reasonable prices. There are several other internet cafés along Av Luzuriaga and also at Parque Ginebra.

Laundry Lavandería BB, Jr la Mar 674, is the best; otherwise, try Lavandería Huaraz, Av Fitzcarrald, close to the bridge, or Lavandería El Amigo, on the corner of Jr Simón Bolívar and Jr José de Sucre.

Money and exchange Banco Wiese, Jr José de Sucre 766; Interbanc, on Plaza de Armas; Banco de Credito, Av Luzuriaga 691; Banco de la Nación, Av Luzuriaga. All banks open Mon–Fri 9am–6pm. *Cambistas* gather where Morales and Luzuriaga meet, or try the casa de cambio at Luzuriaga

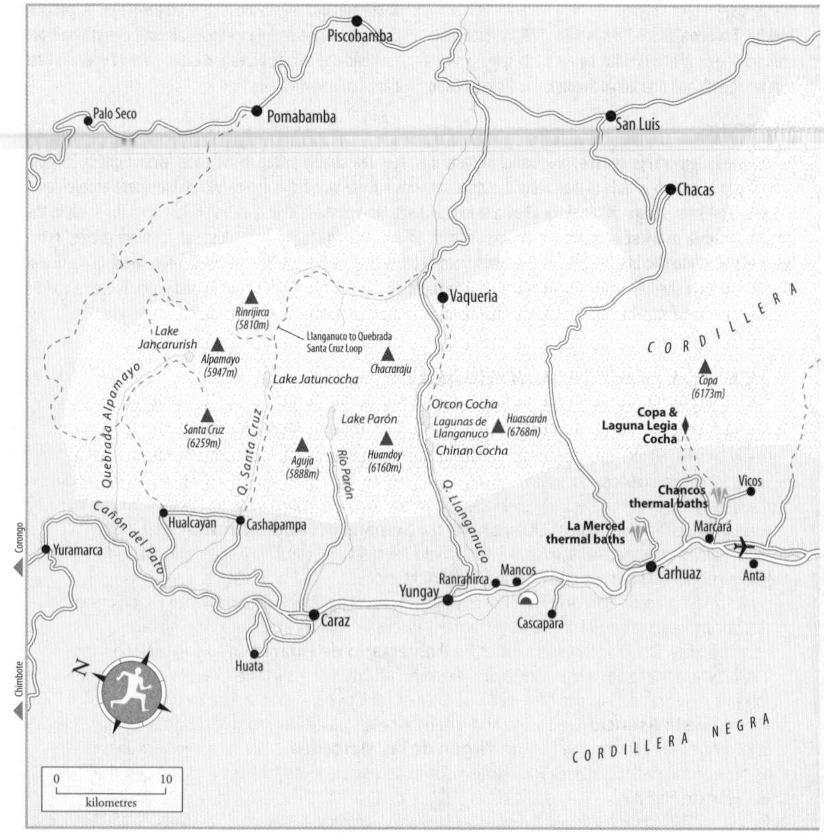

614 for good rates on dollars.

Police The Tourist Police are on the Plaza de Armas at Jr Larrea y Loredo 716 (043 421341 ext 315); National Police are at Jr José de Sucre, block 2 (043 421330).

Post office Plaza de Armas, Av Luzuriaga 702 (Mon–Sat 8am–8pm).

Telephones Locutorio Emtelser, Jr José de Sucre 797 (daily 7am–11pm).

6

Around Huaraz

There are a number of worthwhile sights within easy reach of Huaraz. Only 7km north are the natural thermal baths of **Monterrey**; higher into the hills, you can explore the inner labyrinths of the dramatic **Wilkawain temple.** On the other side of the valley, **Punta Callan** offers magnificent views over the Cordillera Blanca, while to the south of the city you can see the intriguing, cactus-like **Puya rayimondii**.

Monterrey

There's no town in **Monterrey** as such, just a street of a few properties, some of which have been converted or purpose-built as hostels or restaurants. At the top end of this street are the **thermal baths**, the reason there's any settlement here at all.

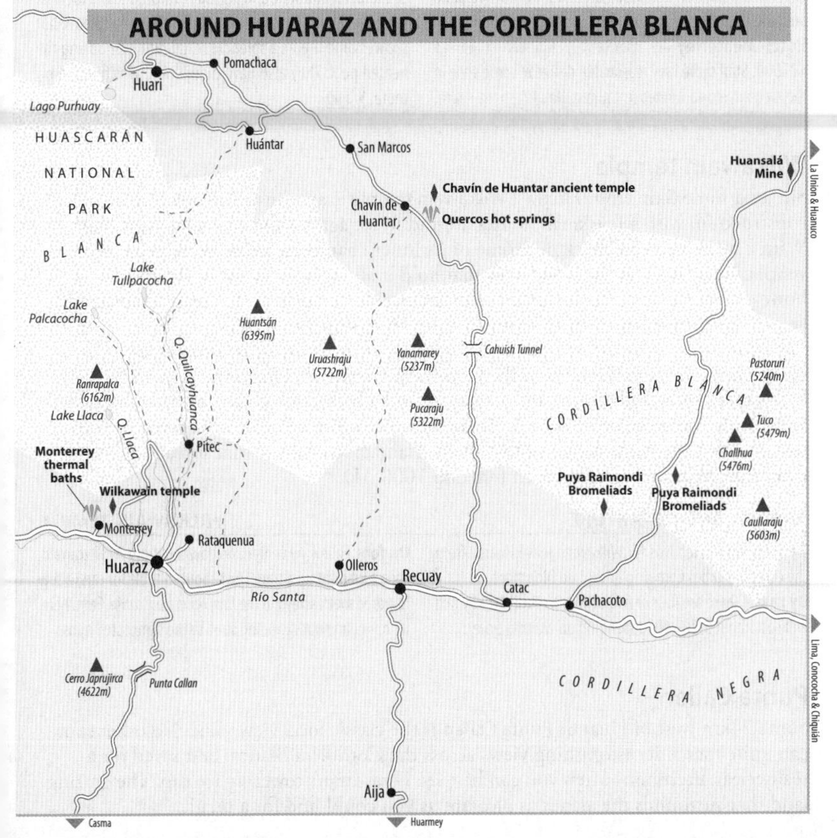

6

Monterrey thermal baths

Central Monterrey • Daily 7am–6pm • From around S/5

The vast **Monterrey thermal baths** include two natural swimming pools and a number of individual and family bathing rooms. Luxuriating in these slightly sulphurous hot springs can be the ideal way to recover from an arduous mountain-trekking expedition, but make sure you are fully acclimatized, otherwise the effect on your blood pressure can worsen any altitude sickness. If you're staying at the wonderful old *Real Hotel Baños Termales Monterrey* (see below), the baths are free. There's also an impressive waterfall just ten minutes' walk behind the hotel and baths.

ARRIVAL AND DEPARTURE — MONTERREY

By colectivo Monterrey is 15min by colectivo (S/1.5) from the centre of Huaraz; every 10min or so from the corner of avenidas Fitzcarrald and Raimondi.

ACCOMMODATION AND EATING

★ **Hostal El Patio de Monterrey** Av Monterrey, Monterrey ⊕043 424965, ⓦelpatio.com.pe; reservations ⊕01/4480254. Just a couple of hundred metres from Monterrey's thermal baths and only a few kilometres from Huaraz, this luxurious neo-colonial complex of clean, attractive rooms with iron bedsteads and more expensive bungalows, is based around an attractive patio and lovely gardens. Bungalows S/360; doubles S/220

Hotel Monterrey Av Monterrey, Monterrey ⊕043 427690. Staff serve very reasonable dishes in some style in this elegant, old-fashioned restaurant. Daily 7.30am–9pm.

El Monte Rey Opposite Artesanía Johao (the ceramic workshop on the main access lane to the baths). Arguably the best restaurant in town, this welcoming place serves great local food at excellent prices. Daily 9am–7pm.

Real Hotel Baños Termales Monterrey Av Monterrey, Monterrey ⊕043 427690. An old hotel full of character and style and actually attached to the thermal baths (residents have free access). The fine rooms have hot showers and there's a splendid restaurant overlooking the heated pool. They also have bungalows, which cost a bit more. S/160

Wilkawain temple

Situated some 8km from Huaraz, **Wilkawain temple** is an unusual two-storey construction, with a few small houses around it, set against the edge of a great bluff. With a torch you can check out some of its inner chambers, where you'll see ramps, ventilation shafts and the stone nails that hold it all together. Most of the rooms, however, are still inaccessible, filled with the rubble and debris of at least a thousand years. The temple base is only about 11m by 16m, sloping up to large, slanted roof slabs, long since covered with earth and rocks to form an irregular domed top. The construction is a small replica of the Castillo at Chavín de Huantar (see p.337), with four superimposed platforms and stairways, and a projecting course of stones near the apex, with a recessed one below it. There was once a row of cat heads carved beneath this, which is a typical design of the Huari-Tiahuanaco culture that spread up here from the coast sometime between 600 and 1000 AD.

ARRIVAL AND DEPARTURE — WILKAWAIN TEMPLE

By colectivo Colectivos for Wilkawain leave Huaraz from the corner of calles Comercio and 13 de Diciembre.

By taxi If there are four or five of you, a round-trip by taxi will cost about S/20–40 (depending on waiting time).

On foot Follow Av Centenario downhill from Av Fitzcarrald, then turn right up a track (just about suitable for cars) a few hundred metres beyond the *Real Hotel Huascarán*. From here, it's about an hour's winding stroll to the signposted ruins.

Punta Callan

Some 24km west of Huaraz, **Punta Callan** is the classic local viewpoint. No other spot can quite match its astonishing views across the Cordillera Blanca, best saved for a really clear afternoon, when you can best see Huascarán's towering ice cap. The grazing land that surrounds the area is as pleasant as you could find for a picnic.

ARRIVAL AND DEPARTURE **PUNTA CALLAN**

By bus Punta Callan can be reached in about two hours on the Casma bus (S/8) from Av Raimondi 336. Ask the driver to drop you off at Callan, shortly before the village of Pira along the road to Casma; from here it's a 20min walk up the path to the promontory. It's a relatively easy walk of a few hours back down the main road to Huaraz. Passing trucks or buses will usually pick up anyone who waves them down en route. Go early in the day, if you want to be sure you can get a bus back.

Cordillera Blanca

The **Cordillera Blanca** extends its icy chain of summits for 140 to 160km north of Huaraz. The highest range in the tropical world, the Cordillera consists of around 35 peaks poking their snowy heads over the 6000m mark, and until early this century, when the glaciers began to recede, this white crest could be seen from the Pacific. The **Callejón de Huaylas** is the valley that sits between the Cordillera Blanca and the Cordillera Negra mountain ranges. Under the western shadow of the Cordillera Blanca lie the northern valley Callejón towns, including **Carhauz**, **Yungay** and **Caraz**. Small and rustic, these towns generally boast attractive accommodation and busy little markets, and provide access to ten snow-free passes in the Cordillera Blanca; combining any two of these passes makes for a superb week's trekking. Yungay and Caraz in particular are both popular bases for trekkers.

Of the many mountain lakes in the Cordillera Blanca, **Lake Parón**, above Caraz, is renowned as the most beautiful. Above Yungay, and against the sensational backdrop of Peru's highest peak, **Huascarán** (6768m), are the equally magnificent **Lagunas de Llanganuco**, whose waters change colour according to the time of year and the sun's daily movements, and are among the most accessible of the Cordillera Blanca's three hundred or so glacial lakes.

The number of possible **hikes** into the Cordillera depends mostly on your own initiative and resourcefulness. There are several common routes, some of which are outlined below; anything more adventurous requires a local guide or a tour with one of the local operators. **Maps** of the area, published by the Instituto Geográfico Militar, are good enough to allow you to plot your own routes. The most popular hike is the **Llanganuco-to-Santa Cruz Loop** (see p.332), which begins at Yungay and ends at Caraz.

Chancos thermal baths

Chancos, Marcará • Daily 8am–6pm • S/2–5 • Take a bus or colectivo from the first block of Av Fitzcarrald or the market in Huaraz, along the valley towards Yungay or Caraz; get off at the village of Marcará and follow the rough road uphill for about 4km, passing several small peasant settlements en route, until you reach the baths

Known traditionally as the Fuente de Juventud (Fountain of Youth), the **Chancos thermal baths**, 30km north of Huaraz, consist of a series of natural saunas inside caves, with great pools gushing hot water in a beautiful stream. It is claimed that the thermal waters are excellent for respiratory problems, but you don't have to be ill to enjoy them, and they make an ideal end to a day's strenuous trekking.

Laguna Legia Cocha

From Chancos a small track leads off to the hamlet of Ullmey, following the contours of the Legiamayo stream to the upper limit of cultivation and beyond into the barren zone directly below the glaciers. Keeping about 500m to the right of the stream, it takes ninety minutes to two hours to reach **Laguna Legia Cocha**. Hung between two vast glaciers at 4706m above sea level and fed by their icy melted water, the lake is an exhilarating spot, with the added bonus of amazing views across the Santa Valley to Carhuaz in the north, Huaraz in the south and Chancos directly below. If you leave Huaraz early in the morning, you can enjoy a fine day-trip, stopping at Chancos for a picnic lunch, after walking an hour from Marcará, then returning again the same way.

6

TREKKING AND CLIMBING ROUTES IN THE CORDILLERAS

In 1932, when a German expedition became the first group to successfully scale Huascarán (see p.330), the concept of **Andinismo** – Andean mountaineering – was born. You don't have to be a mountaineer to enjoy the high Andes of Ancash, however, and there is plenty of scope for trekking and climbing in the two major mountain chains accessible from Huaraz as well; the closest is the **Cordillera Blanca** (see p.325). The **Cordillerra Huayhuash** (see p.341), about 50km south of that range, is still relatively off the beaten tourist trail and *andinistas* claim it to be one of the most spectacular trekking routes in the world. In order to hike in the Parque Nacional Huascarán, you need to get **permission** first from the park office (Parque Nacional Huascarán, Jr Federico Sal y Rosas 555) and the Casa de Guías in Huaraz (see box, p.318); both can also provide maps and information.

If you intend to hike at all, it's essential to spend at least a couple of days acclimatizing to the **altitude** beforehand; for high mountain climbing, this should be extended to at least five days. Although Huaraz itself is 3060m above sea level, most of the Cordilleras' more impressive peaks are over 6000m.

TREKKING ROUTES

One of the most popular trekking routes, the **Llanganuco-to-Santa Cruz loop** (see p.332), is a well-trodden trail offering spectacular scenery, some fine places to camp and a relatively easy walk that can be done in under a week, even by inexperienced hikers. The **Hualcayan-to-Pomabamba hike** (see p.333) offers a much longer alternative and is equally rewarding. There are shorter walks, such as the trails around the **Pitec Quebrada**, within easy distance of Huaraz, and a number of other loops like the **Llanganuco-to-Chancos** trek. Experienced hikers could also tackle the circular **Cordillera Huayhuash** route. Detailed information on all these walks is available from the South American Explorers' Club in Lima (see p.81) or, in Huaraz itself, from the Casa de Guías (see p.329), the tourist office (see p.319) or tour companies (see p.319).

CLIMBING ROUTES

To give a flavour of what you may expect from mountain climbing in the Cordillera Blanca, the expeditions below are some of the most popular among serious mountaineers. Remember to take a **local guide** (see box, p.329) if you do any of these; they're listed in increasing order of difficulty.

Pisco One of the easier climbs, up to 5752m, this is a good way to cut your teeth in the Cordillera Blanca. Little more than a hard trek, really, with access via the Llanganuco Valley (3800m), with a duration of only three days. Rated easy to moderate.

Urus A two-day climb reaching heights of around 5500m; access is via Collon to Quebrada de Ishinca and it takes only two days. Rated easy to moderate for the peaks Ishinca and Urus; or moderate to difficult if you tackle Tocllaraju (6034m).

Alpamayo A serious and quite technical mountain rising to 5947m, and requiring good acclimatization on an easier climb first. Access is from Cashapampa (accessible by bus from Caraz), and it usually takes around eight or nine days. Rated as difficult.

Huascarán The south summit at 6768m is the classic route and really requires thorough acclimatization. Access is via Mancos (from where it's an hour by bus to the village of Musho), and it normally demands a good week to tackle effectively. Rated, not surprisingly, as difficult.

ACCOMMODATION AND EATING — CHANCOS THERMAL BATHS

Camping There's no accommodation in Chancos, but the valley bus service is good enough to get you back to Huaraz within an hour or so, or you could camp (ask permission to camp on one of the grassy patches up- or downhill from the baths).

Restaurants There are a couple of basic restaurants on hand that are famous for their strong *chicha*, and are particularly popular with locals on Sunday afternoons.

Carhuaz and around

One of the major towns along the Callejón de Huaylas, **CARHUAZ**, some 30km from both Huaraz and Yungay, has an attractive, central Plaza de Armas, adorned with palm trees, roses and labyrinths of low-cut hedges and dominated by the solid, concrete Iglesia de San Pedro on its south side.

The market

On Sundays the streets to the north and west of the plaza are home to a thriving traditional **market**, where Andean and tropical foodstuffs, herbs and craft (in particular, gourd bowls) can be bought very cheaply. The colourfully dressed women here often sell live guinea pigs from small nets at their feet, and wear a variety of wide-brimmed hats – ones with blue bands indicate that they are married, ones with red bands show that they are single. Many also wear glass beads, on their hats or around their necks, as a sign of wealth.

Cave of Hombre Guitarrero

In the 1980s, a cave was discovered a few kilometres north of Carhuaz, on the other side of the Río Santa in the Cordillera Negra. Containing the bones of mastodons and llamas and suggesting human occupation dating from as far back as 12,000 BC, it is situated close to a natural rock formation that looks vaguely like a guitar, and the site is now known as the **cave of Hombre Guitarrero** (Guitar Man).

Mancos

Some 9km further north of Carhuaz, over a river, the road comes to the village of **MANCOS**. The village has an unusually attractive plaza, with palm trees and a quaint, modern church with twin belfries sitting under the watchful eye of the glistening glacier of Huascarán. The village's main **fiesta** (August 12–16) is in honour of its patron, San Royal de Mancos, and the plaza becomes the focus of highly colourful religious processions, dancing and, later, bullfighting.

ARRIVAL AND DEPARTURE — CARHUAZ AND AROUND

CARHUAZ

By colectivo Combi colectivos to Huaraz (S/2), Chancos (S/1.80) and Caraz (S/2) arrive at, and depart from, a stop one block west beyond the market side of the plaza.

By bus Buses to Lima, Huaraz and Caraz leave from a terminal on block 2 of Av La Merced, which is a continuation of the road from the market side of the plaza to the main highway.

CAVE OF HOMBRE GUITARRERA

On foot This archeological site can be accessed in just over an hour's walk, beyond the sports stadium in Carhuaz and up the stream past the unusual church, which sits beside the road from Carhuaz to Yungay.

MANCOS

By bus/colectivo Located on the main valley road between Carhuaz and Yungay, you'll need to ask your bus or colectivo driver to drop you in the village.

ACCOMMODATION AND EATING

CARHUAZ

El Abuelo Jr 9 de Diciembre 257, by the plaza ⊕043 394456, ⊕elabuelohostal.com. This is a modern, two-storey building with a dining room, comfortable beds and good hot-water supplies. Rooms are stylish without going over the top and service is attentive as well as friendly. **S/130**

Café Heladería El Abuelo On the plaza. This is the best eating place in Carhuaz; it shares the same owner as *El Abuelo* nearby and serves ice cream, snacks and full meals (ask for the local delicacy of beanshoots). Daily 9am–7pm.

Casa de Pocha Located at the foot of Hualcan mountain, about 1.5km above Carhuaz ⊕043 943613058, ⊕lacasadepocha@yahoo.com. This is a lovely eco-ranch offering accommodation in a traditional adobe lodge with eight spacious rooms under red-tiled roofs. There's a sauna, 12m swimming pool, solar cookers, horseriding and the hot springs of La Merced are nearby. The owner speaks Spanish, English, French and Italian. **S/120**

Hostal La Merced Jr Ucayali 724 ⊕043 394241. This centrally located place has commodious rooms with or without private bathrooms. Rooms are plain and service is good, with a locked room to leave bags in while trekking. **S/55**

MANCOS

Casa Alojamiento On the plaza. Offers clean, comfortable rooms and shared bathrooms. Though there are several restaurants around, none are especially good. **S/35**

Yungay

Fifty-eight kilometres up the Callejón de Huaylas from Huaraz, and just past Mancos, **YUNGAY** was an attractive, traditional small town until it was obliterated in seconds on May 31, 1970, during a massive earthquake. This was not the first catastrophe to assault the so-called "Pearl of the Huaylas Corridor"; in 1872 it was almost completely wiped out by an avalanche, and on a fiesta day in 1962 another avalanche buried some five thousand people in the neighbouring village of Ranrahirca. The 1970 quake arrived in the midst of a festival and also caused a landslide, and although casualties proved impossible to calculate with any real accuracy, it's thought that over 70,000 people died. Almost the entire population of Yungay, around 26,000, disappeared almost instantaneously, though a few of the town's children survived because they were at a circus located just above the town, which fortunately escaped the landslide. Almost eighty percent of the buildings in neighbouring Huaraz and much of Carhuaz were also razed to the ground by the earthquake.

The new town, an uninviting conglomeration of modern buildings – including some ninety prefabricated cabins sent as relief aid from the former Soviet Union – has been built around a concrete Plaza de Armas a few kilometres from the original site. Yungay still cowers beneath the peak of Huascarán, but it is hoped that its new location is more sheltered from further dangers than its predecessor. The best reason for staying here is to make the trip up to the **Las Lagunas de Llanganuco** and **Parque Nacional Huascarán**.

Old town of Yungay

Visible from the main road, before arriving at the new town of Yungay • Daily 8am–6pm • S/2

On the way into town from Carhuaz, a car park and memorial monument mark the entrance to the site of the buried **old town of Yungay**, which has developed into one of the region's major tourist attractions. The site, entered through a large, blue concrete archway, is covered with a grey flow of mud and moraine, now dry and solid, with a few stunted palm trees to mark where the old Plaza de Armas once stood. Thousands of rose bushes have been planted over the site – a gift of the Japanese government. Local guidebooks show before-and-after photos of the scene, but it doesn't take a lot of imagination to reconstruct the horror. You can still see a few things like an upside-down, partially destroyed school bus, stuck in the mud. The graveyard of Campo Santo, above the site, which predates the 1970 quake, gives the best vantage point over the devastation. A tall statue of Christ holds out its arms from the graveyard towards the deadly peak of Huascarán itself, as if pleading for no further horrors.

ARRIVAL AND DEPARTURE — YUNGAY

By bus/colectivo Buses and colectivos all stop and pick up passengers on 28 de Julio en route between Huaraz and Caraz. Colectivos for the Las Lagunas de Llanganuco (55min; S/5) leave from the same spot, or the Plaza de Armas, usually between 7 and 8.30am.

ACCOMMODATION AND EATING

Café Pilar On the plaza. This large space is good for breakfast and snacks like sandwiches, tamales (maize cakes) and cakes. Daily 8am–6pm.

Hostal Gledel Av Arias Graziani T 043 393048. A very friendly budget hostel at the northern end of town. Upstairs rooms are best, and though all rooms share toilet facilities, the hostel is spotlessly clean and a good place to meet trekkers and climbers. S/30

Hostal Yungay Jr Santo Domingo 1, on the Plaza de Armas T 043 393053. Well located and with private bathrooms, hot water, colour TV and laundry service, they have decent-quality rooms and a terrace with clotheslines for hanging your wet garments. It also gives out free maps and information on the area. S/45

Restaurant Alpamayo Av Arias Graziani in the Caraz end of town. This place has excellent fish meals including fried trout from local fish farms, but also serves other standard mains. Daily 10am–5pm.

6

ORGANIZING A TREK IN THE CORDILLERAS

People die and get lost on these mountains regularly, so ideally you'll be trekking with a **local guide**, perhaps with a tour group, who will ensure you have the right equipment for the terrain and local climatic conditions. If this is not the case, then you need to take responsibility for having good boots, appropriate clothing (including waterproofs), a warm sleeping bag, good mountain tent and other equipment (eg crampons and ice axe).

Wherever you end up, be sure to pay heed to the rules of **responsible trekking**: carry away your **waste**, particularly above the snow line. Note too that you should always use a **camping stove** – campfires are strictly prohibited in Parque Nacional Huascarán, and wood is scarce anyway. Just as important, though, is to realize that the **solar irradiation** in this part of the Andes is stronger than that found in the North American Rockies, European Alps or even the Himalayas. This creates unique glacier conditions, making the ice here less stable and necessitating an **experienced local guide** for the safety of any serious climbing or ice-walking expedition. It's also vital to **be fit**, particularly if you are going it alone.

COSTS

There are three levels of **guide** available: certified mountain guides, who cost upwards of $80/day; mountain guides undergoing the one-year trial period after training, from $50/day; and trekking guides, who cost from $35/day. Note that these costs don't include your transport or accommodation. **Porters** cost between $20 and $35/day, depending on whether they are leaders or assistants, and are not supposed to climb over 6000m, while **mule drivers** (*arrieros*) charge from $18/$25 a day, plus around $10/day per animal. Expedition **cooks** usually charge the same as *arrieros*.

INFORMATION

Both the Casa de Guías (see below) and the Parque Nacional Huascarán office (see p.333) can give you advice on the best and safest areas for trekking, since this region is not without its **political danger zones**; you also need to obtain permission from them before trekking in the national park. Tour operators offering guided treks can be found in the Huaraz section (see p.319).

Ideally you should have detailed maps – available from the Casa de Guías (see below) – and one or other of the following excellent guidebooks: *Trails of the Cordillera Blanca and Huayhuash*, *Classic Climbs of the Cordillera Blanca* or *The High Andes: A Guide for Climbers* (see p.532).

Casa de Guías (Mountain Guides) Parque Ginebra 28-G, Huaraz ☎043 421811. The best-organized association of mountain guides in Peru offering plenty of local expertise and the Andean Mountain Rescue Corps on hand. They also offer accommodation (see p.319).

AOTUM (the Asociación Peruana de Operadores de Turismo de Montaña) Based in the *Hotel Andino* (see p.320), in Huaraz. Offers very useful assistance to climbers. Other Peruvian mountaineering associations are all based in Lima (see box, p.82).

Mountain Institute Ricardo Palma 100, Pedregal district of Huaraz, south of Av Villón ☎043 423446. A mainly conservation-based organization whose focus is the Peruvian Andes and the Cordillera Blanca in particular.

Trekking and Backpacking Club Jr Los Libertadores 134, Independencia, Huaraz ☎01 9978 4193. Provides information for independent travellers interested in the region's archeology, trekking, backpacking and climbing.

TREKKING GUIDES

Alberto Cafferata Trekking guide contactable through Pony's Expeditions in Caraz (see p.335).

Oscar Ciccomi Based in Lima and contactable through Viajes Vivencial, Los Cerezos 480, Chaclacayo, Lima (☎01 4972394).

Eduardo Figueroa Contactable via *Edward's Inn*, Huaraz (see p.319).

David Gonzáles Castromonte, Pasaje Coral Vega 354, Huarupampa, Huaraz (☎043 422213).

HIGH MOUNTAIN GUIDES

High Mountain Guides (members of UIAGM – Unión Internacional de Asociaciones de Guías de Montaña), contactable through the Casa de Guías (see above), include:

Selio Billón One of the founders of La Asociación de Guías and the Casa de Guías, with 25 years' experience.

Michel Burger Owner of the *Bistro de los Andes* restaurant in Huaraz; offers trekking and fishing.

Arista Monasterio Provides customized guiding services.

Parque Nacional Huascarán

Daily 6am–6pm • $1.50 for day-visitors, $20 for trekkers or mountaineers • Permission must be obtained from the park office (see p.333) and Casa de Guías in Huaraz before trekking or climbing here

Parque Nacional Huascarán is home to the Lagunas de Llanganuco, two stunning, deep-blue lakes, as well as perhaps Peru's most awe-inspiring peak, glaciated Huascarán. On the way up to the level of the lakes you get a dramatic view across the valley and can clearly make out the path of devastation from the 1970 earthquake. The last part of the drive – starkly beautiful but no fun for vertigo sufferers – slices through rocky crevices, and snakes around breathtaking precipices surrounded by small, wind-bent *quenual* trees and orchid bromeliads known locally as *weclla*. Well before reaching the lakes, at Km 19 you pass through the entrance to the national park itself, located over 600m below the level of the lakes; from here it's another thirty minutes or so by bus or truck to the lakes.

Las Lagunas de Llanganuco

At 3850m above sea level, the **Lagunas de Llanganuco** are only 26km northeast of Yungay (83km from Huaraz), but take a good ninety minutes to reach by bus or truck, on a road that crawls up beside a canyon that is the result of thousands of years of Huascarán's meltwater.

The first lake you come to after the park entrance is **Chinan Cocha**, named after a legendary princess. You can rent **rowing boats** by the car park here to venture onto the blue waters (80¢ for 15min), and, if you're hungry, take a picnic from the **food stalls** at the lakeside nearby. The road continues around Chinan Cocha's left bank and for a couple of kilometres on to the second lake, **Orcon Cocha**, named after a prince who fell in love with Chinan. The road ends here and a **loop trail** begins (see p.332). A third, much smaller, lake was created between the two big ones, as a result of an avalanche caused by the 1970 earthquake, which also killed a group of hikers who were camped between the two lakes.

Huascarán

Immediately to the south of the lakes is the unmistakeable sight of **Huascarán**, whose imposing ice-cap tempts many people to make the difficult climb of 3km to the top. Surrounding Huascarán are scores of lesser, glaciated mountains that stretch for almost 200km and divide the Amazon Basin from the Pacific watershed.

LODGES IN THE CORDILLERA BLANCA

The two **lodges** listed below both offer an exciting opportunity to stay in relative comfort right on the edge of the Cordillera Blanca's wilderness. *Lazy Dog Inn* is the closest to Huaraz and is right on the edge of Parque Nacional Huascarán. *LLanganuco Lodge* is also on the edge of the national park, but is much closer to the Lagunas de Llanganuco and Huascarán.

Lazy Dog Inn ⊕043 943789330, ⓦthelazydoginn.com. Some 10km east of Huaraz, transport from the city is offered or you can take a taxi here(S/20–30); there's a sign at Km 12, a few kilometres beyond Wilkawain temple. Their cabins are comfortable but you can also stay inside the main adobe-built lodge. The service is excellent and the setting fantastic – it borders the Huascarán National Park (30min from Huaraz). S/280

★ **Llanganuco Lodge** Keushu Lake, Huandoy ⊕043 943669580, ⓦllanganucolodge.com. A fantastic new lodge catering to everyone who wants to stay in comfort by the lake, *Llanganuco Lodge* is located just underneath the Huascarán and Huandoy glaciers (contact in advance for transport or take a taxi). Accommodation is available in suites, rooms and dorms, and the lodge also offers great food, value and service (the restaurant is excellent) plus a library, games, DVDs and outward-bound activities including adventure trails organized on demand. Dorms S/35; camping S/15/person; doubles S/280

6

The Llanganuco-to-Santa Cruz Loop

The **Llanganuco to Quebrada Santa Cruz Loop** starts at the clearly marked track leading off from the end of the road along the left bank of Orcon Cocha (see p.330). The entire trek shouldn't take more than about five days for a healthy (and acclimatized) backpacker, but it's a perfect hike to take at your own pace. It's essential to carry all your food, camping equipment and, ideally, a medical kit and emergency survival bag. Along the route there are hundreds of potential campsites. The best time to attempt this trek is in the dry season, between April and October, unless you enjoy getting stuck in mud and being soaked to the skin.

From **Orcon Cocha** the main path climbs the Portachuelo de Llanganuco pass (4767m), before dropping to the enchanting beauty of the Quebrada Morococha (a *quebrada* is a river gully) through the tiny settlement of **Vaqueria**. From here you can go on to Colcabamba and Pomabamba (but only by diverting from the main loop trail), which are settlements located in the Callejón de Conchucos – though not in the rainy season, when you may well find yourself stranded. Most people prefer to continue on the loop back to the Callejón de Huaylas via Santa Cruz.

Continuing from Vaqueria the main loop trail subsequently heads north from Vaqueria up the Quebrada Huaripampa, where you'll probably camp the first night. From here it goes around the icecap of **Chacraraju** (6000m) and along a stupendous rocky canyon with a marshy bottom, snowy mountain peaks to the west and Cerro Mellairca to the east.

On the third or fourth day, following the stream uphill, with the lakes of Morococha and Huiscash on your left, you pass down into the **Pacific watershed** along the **Quebrada Santa Cruz**, eventually emerging, after perhaps another night's rest, beside the calm waters of Lake Grande (Lake Jatuncocha). Tracing the left bank and continuing down this perfect glacial valley for about another eight hours, you'll come to the village of **Cashapampa**, which has very basic accommodation, but don't bank on this since it

THE PUYA RAYIMONDII

The gigantic and relatively rare **Puya rayimondii** plant, reaching up to 12m in height and with a lifespan of around forty years, is found in Parque Nacional Huascarán. Most people assume the *Puya rayimondii* is a type of cactus, but it is, in fact, the world's largest **bromeliad**, or member of the pineapple family. Known as *cuncush* or *cunco* to locals (and *Pourretia gigantea* to botanists), it only grows between altitudes of 3700m and 4200m, and is unique to this region. May is the best month to see them, when they are in full bloom and average 8000 flowers and six million seeds per plant. Dotted about the **Quebrada Pachacoto** slopes (some 50km southeast of Huaraz) like candles on an altar, the plants look rather like upside-down trees, with the bushy part as a base and a phallic flowering stem pointing to the sky. Outside of late April, May and early June, the plants can prove disappointing, often looking like burned-out stumps after dropping their flowers and seeds, but the surrounding scenery remains sensational, boasting grasses, rocks, lakes, llamas and the odd hummingbird.

TOURS

By far the easiest way to see the Puya rayimondii is on an **organized tour** with one of the companies listed (see p.319). Alternatively, you could take a combi colectivo to Catac, leaving daily every thirty minutes from the end of Jirón Cáceres in Huaraz (roughly S/3.50). From Catac, 45km south of Huaraz, there are a few buses and trucks each day down the **La Unión** road, which passes right by the plants. Alternatively, it's possible to get off the combi colectivo 5km beyond Catac at Pachacoto (where there are a couple of cafés often used as pit stops by truck drivers) and hitch from here along the dirt track that leads off the main road across barren grasslands. This track is well travelled by trucks on their way to the mining settlement of Huansala, and after about 15–20km – roughly an hour's drive – into this isolated region, you'll be surrounded by the giant bromeliads. From here, you can either continue on to La Unión (see p.307), via the Pastoruri Glacier, or return to Huaraz by hitching back to the main road.

can't be booked before walking there. From here it's just a short step (about 2km) to the inviting and very hot (but temperature-controllable) thermal baths of **Huancarhuaz** (daily 8am–5pm; S/3), and there's a road or a more direct three-hour path across the low hills south to Caraz.

The Hualcayan-to-Pomabamba hike

The **Hualcayan-to-Pomabamba hike** is one of the longest in the Cordillera Blanca and requires good acclimatization as well as fitness. It takes about a week to cover the route's total distance of around 78km – altitudes vary between 3100 and 4850m. Starting at Cashapampa, near Hualcayan (with an archeological complex at 3140m), the route takes seven to ten days, taking in great views of the Cordillera Negra on the first day's uphill, zigzag, hiking, passing turquoise lakes and with views over the Santa Cruz glacier (6259m). The trail terminates at the village of Pomabamba, where there are thermal baths, a basic hotel and a road.

6

ARRIVAL AND INFORMATION — PARQUE NACIONAL HUASCARÁN

Parque Nacional Huascarán office Jr Federico Sal y Rosas 555, by corner with Belén, Huaraz ☎ 043 722086. If you're going to trek in Parque Nacional Huascarán, you'll need to register here and at the Casa de Guías in Huaraz (see box, p.329) beforehand.

THE HUALCAYAN-TO-POMABAMBA HIKE

By bus You can get to Hualcayan (3100m) and Cashapampa from Caraz by bus (1hr 45min), leaving from the corner of Grau with Santa Cruz, two or three times every morning. Pomabamba is connected by Los Andes bus with Yungay (daily; 4–6hr; S/18); there are sometimes colectivos, too.

ACCOMMODATION

THE HUALCAYAN-TO-POMABAMBA HIKE

Camping Campsites (free) along the way include: *Jamacuna* (4050m), *Osoruri* (4550m), *Jancanrurish* (4200m), *Huillca* (4000m) and *Yanacollpa* (3850m).

Caraz and around

The attractive town of **CARAZ**, less than 20km down the Santa Valley from Yungay, sits at an altitude of 2285m, well below the enormous Huandoy Glacier. Mainly visited for the access it gives to a fantastic hiking hinterland, it is also well known throughout Peru for its honey and milk products. Palm trees and flowers adorn a colonial-looking **Plaza de Armas**, which has survived well from the ravages of several major earthquakes. A small daily **market** (6.30am–noon), three blocks north of the plaza, is usually vibrant with activity, good for fresh food, colourful basketry, traditional gourd bowls, religious candles and hats.

Tumshucaico

A couple of kilometres northeast of Caraz along 28 de Julio, close to the Laguna Parón turn-off, lie the weathered ruins of **Tumshucaico**, probably the largest ruins in the Callejón de Hualyas. A possible ceremonial centre, dating from the formative period of 1800 BC, replete with galleries and worked stone walls, it may well also have had a defensive function given its dominating position overlooking the valley. These days its edges have been eaten away by the peri-urban growth of Caraz and the extension of local cultivated land.

Huata

Nine kilometres across the Río Santa from Caraz, set on the lower slopes of the Cordillera Negra, the small settlement of **HUATA** is a typical rural village with regular truck connections from the market area in Caraz. It serves as a good starting point for a number of easy walks, such as the 8km stroll up to the unassuming lakes of Yanacocha and Huaytacocha or, perhaps more interestingly, north about 5km along a path up Cerro Muchanacoc to the small Inca ruins of Cantu.

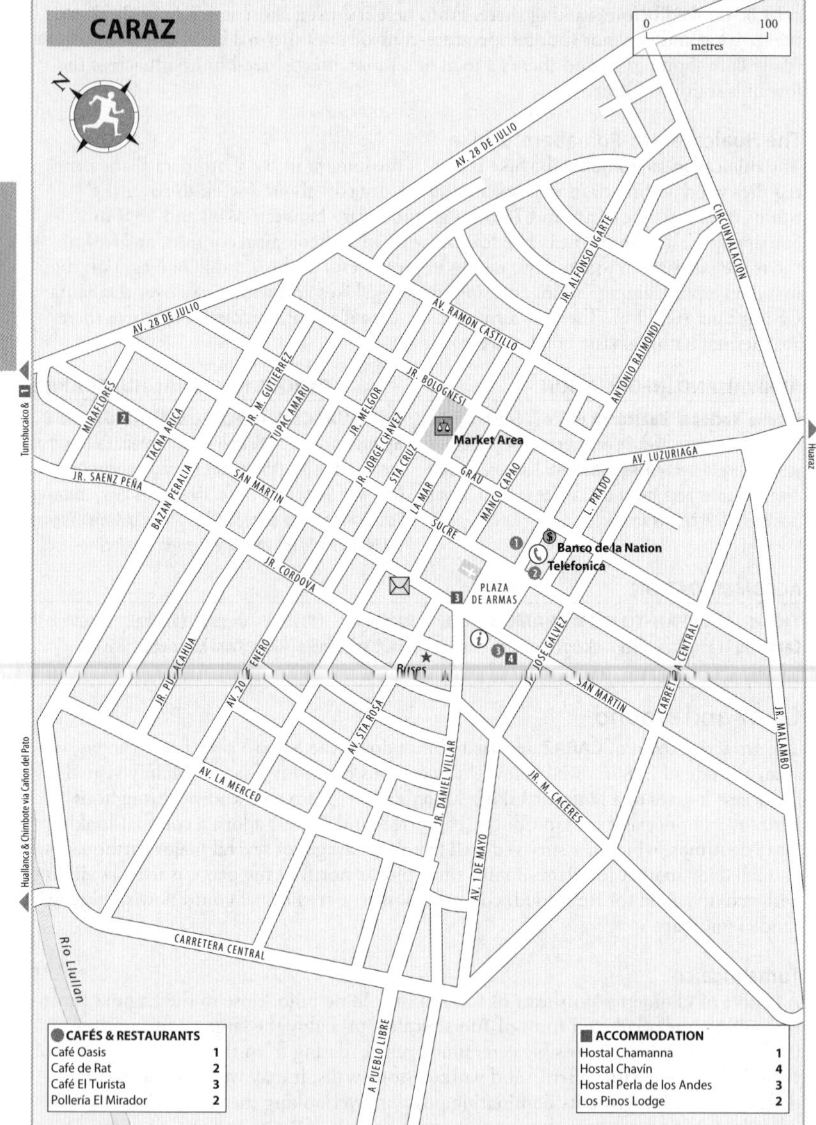

Laguna Parón

Some 30km, more or less, east of Caraz, the deep-blue **Laguna Parón** (4185m) is sunk resplendently into a gigantic glacial cirque, hemmed in on three sides by some of the Cordillera Blanca's highest icecaps.

ARRIVAL AND DEPARTURE — CARAZ AND AROUND

By bus Most of the bus offices are along jirones Daniel Villar and Cordova, within a block or two of the Plaza de Armas: Chinachasuyo serve Trujillo; Empresa Turismo go to Lima and Chimbote; Ancash to Lima; Movil Tours to Huraz and Lima; Region Norte runs buses to Yungay, Huaraz and Recuay; and Transporte Moreno to Chimbote.

By colectivo Colectivos for Huaraz leave from just behind the market roughly every thirty minutes.

TUMSHUCAICO

By taxi Tumshucaico is just a 15min drive from Caraz plaza. If you aren't with a tour bus and don't have your own transport the best option is a taxi (S/5–8 one way, more for waiting).

HUATA

By taxi Huata is a 20min drive from Caraz (S/8–10 one way).

LAGUNA PARÓN

By bus/colectivo Buses and colectivos (4.30–5.30am, returning from around 12.30pm; S/5 one way) travel from Caraz market up to Pueblo Parón, from where it's a hike of 9km (3hr) up to the lake. The last transport back from Pueblo Parón to Caraz is usually at 2.30pm.

By taxi Taxis to the lake (about S/20–30/person) can be found most days from the Plaza de Armas in Caraz.

6

INFORMATION AND TOURS

INFORMATION

Tourist information Plaza de Armas (Mon–Sat 7.45am–1pm & 2.30–5.30pm). Offers maps and brochures covering local attractions and some of the hikes (including the relatively demanding 6–8hr Patapata walk).

TOUR OPERATORS

For trekking guides, local information or help organizing and fitting out an expedition, there are two excellent local options with a wealth of expert local knowledge.

Pony's Expeditions Sucre 1266, Plaza de Armas ⓣ043 391642, ⓦponyexpeditions.com. A very professional organization that both fits out, and guides, climbing, trekking and mountain-biking expeditions in the area. An excellent source of local trekking and climbing information, they also run treks in other regions, such as the Cordillera Huayhuash, the Inca Trail and Ausangate.

Apu Aventura Parque San Martín 103 ⓣ043 391130 or 01 9683 2740, ⓦapuaventura.pe. Another excellent local option, Apu Aventura organize guides, porters, cooks and equipment for expeditions in the Cordillera Blanca and elsewhere in Peru.

ACCOMMODATION

★ **Hostal Chamanna** A little out of town down Av 28 de Julio, at Av Nueva Victoria 185 ⓣ043 9435 95343, ⓦchamanna.com. A rather different place, set in a lovely labyrinth of gardens, streams and patios. Not all rooms have a private bathroom but they are very stylish, adorned by ethnic murals; great meals available by prior arrangement. S/75

Hostal Chavín Jr San Martín 1135 ⓣ043 39117. Close to the plaza, clean and well organized, this hostel is good value and some rooms have a private bathroom. Breakfasts and travel assistance also available. S/55

Hostal Perla de los Andes Jirón Daniel Villar 179, Plaza de Armas ⓣ043 392007, ⓔhostalperladelosandes@hotmail.com. A modern and essentially good choice, it has a marbled lobby completely out of character with the laidback, quite rustic flavour of the rest of Caraz, and comfortable rooms with hot water, private bathrooms and TV. It also boasts a very nice restaurant. S/90

Los Pinos Lodge Parque San Martín 103 ⓣ043 39113. One of the least expensive options in town, *Los Pinos Lodge* is a youth hostel that also offers camping spaces and has internet facilities. There are shared rooms and also private. Camping S/7/person, dorms S/20, doubles S/55

EATING

Café Oasis Jr Antonio Raimondi 425 ⓣ043 391785. Just a small stone's throw from the plaza, this café is good for snacks and also has four rooms that they rent out (price on enquiry). Daily 8am–9pm.

Café de Rat Sucre 1266. Just down at the bottom southwestern edge of the Plaza de Armas, this café serves decent pasta, pizza, pancakes and vegetarian food, as well as having a dartboard, maps, guidebooks, music and internet access. Daily 8am–8pm.

Café El Turista Jr San Martín 1117. A great place for early morning hot snacks, full breakfasts and coffee. The staff are friendly and the service is good. Daily 7.30am–noon and 6–9pm.

Pollería El Mirador Sucre 1202. Right on the Plaza de Armas, this fried-chicken joint serves reasonably priced lunches and evening meals from a menu of Peruvian and international food. Daily 11am–9pm.

DIRECTORY

Money and exchange For money exchange there's a Banco de Credito at Jr Daniel Villar 217 or there's the Banco de la Nación on Jirón Antonio Raimondi, half a block from the Plaza de Armas.

Post office The post office can be found on Jr San Martín 909 (Mon–Sat 8.30am–6pm).

Telephones The telephone office is at Jr Antonio Raimondi 410.

Cañon del Pato

The first canyon village is Huallanca, reached by daily buses (see p.317) from Huaraz; from here, it's 8km on to Yuramarca where the road divides: one route branches off west along a rough road to Chimbote (another 140km) on the coast, or you can continue along the valley to Corongo and the Callejón de Conchucos

6

One of Peru's most exciting roads runs north from Caraz to Huallanca, squeezing through the spectacular **Cañon del Pato** (Duck's Canyon). An enormous rocky gorge cut from solid rock, its impressive path curves around the Cordillera Negra for most of the 50km between Caraz and Huallanca. Sheer cliff-faces rise thousands of metres on either side while the road passes through some 39 tunnels – an average of one every kilometre. Situated within the canyon is one of Peru's most important hydroelectric power plants; the heart of these works, invisible from the road, is buried 600m deep in the cliff wall. Unfortunately, the road is often closed for a number of reasons – causes include terrorists, bandits, landslides in the rainy season or just the sheer poor quality of the road surface. Much of the first section has been improved in recent years, but from Huallanca to Chimbote it's more like a dry riverbed than a dirt track. Check with the tourist office in Huaraz and local bus companies (see p.317) about the physical and political condition of the road before attempting this journey.

Callejón de Conchucos

To the east of the Cordillera Blanca, roughly parallel to the Callejón de Huaylas, runs another long natural corridor, the **Callejón de Conchucos**. Virtually inaccessible in the wet season, and off the beaten track even for the most hardened of backpackers, the valley represents quite a challenge, and while it features the town of **Pomabamba** in the north and the spectacular ruins at **Chavín de Huantar** just beyond its southern limit, there's little of interest between the two. The villages of **Piscobamba** (Valley or Plain of the Birds) and **Huari** are likely to appeal only as food stops on the long haul (141km) through barren mountains between Pomabamba and Chavín.

Brief history

The Callejón de Conchucos was out of bounds to travellers between 1988 and 1993, when it was under almost complete Sendero Luminoso **terrorist control**; many of the locals were forced to flee the valley after actual or threatened violence from the terrorists. The region's more distant history was equally turbulent and cut off from the rest of Peru, particularly from the seat of colonial and Republican power on the coast. Until the Conquest, this region was home to one of the fiercest ancient tribes – the **Conchucos** – who surged down the Santa Valley and besieged the Spanish city of Trujillo in 1536. By the end of the sixteenth century, however, even the fearless Conchuco warriors had been reduced to virtual slavery by the colonial *encomendero* system.

Pomabamba

The small town of **POMABAMBA**, 3000m up in dauntingly hilly countryside, is surrounded by little-known archeological remains that display common roots with Chavín de Huantar; try Pony's Expeditions in Caraz (see p.335) for further information on these, as well as maps, equipment and advice on trekking in this region. Today the town makes an excellent trekking base; from here you can connect with the **Llanganuco-to-Santa Cruz Loop** (see p.332) by following tracks southwest to either Colcabamba or Punta Unión. Alternatively, for a hard day's hike above Pomabamba, you can walk up to the stone remains of **Yaino**, an immense fortress of megalithic rock. On a clear day you can just about make out this site from the Plaza de Armas in Pomabamba; it appears as a tiny rocky outcrop high on the distant horizon. The climb takes longer than you may imagine, but locals will point out short cuts along the way.

ARRIVAL AND DEPARTURE — POMABAMBA

By bus Direct Empresa Los Andes buses to Pomabamba leave from the Plaza de Armas in Yungay at 8.30–9am, while Turismo Huaraz in Huaraz (see p.318) go to Piscobamba and Pomabamba. Alternatively, you can get here from Huaraz via Chavín, on a bus from Lima that comes north up the Callejón de Conchucos more or less every other day.

ACCOMMODATION

If **camping** then it's always best to consult with the locals to find a good, safe spot.

Hostal Estrada Vidal C Huaraz 209 ☎ 043 804615 or ☎ 043 751048. Located just one block from the small main plaza, this place is basic, but pleasant and clean. S/20

Hostal Pomabamba Huamachuco 338 ☎ 043 751276. Just off the Plaza de Armas, *Hostal Pomabamba* offers simple accommodation, with clean double and single rooms. S/40

6

Chavín de Huantar

Chavín • Daily 8am–5pm • S/10 • ☎ 043 754042

A three- to four-hour journey from Huaraz, and only 30km southeast of Huari (see p.341), the magnificent temple complex of **CHAVÍN DE HUANTAR** is the most important Peruvian site associated with the Chavín cult (see box, p.340). Although partially destroyed by earthquakes, floods and erosion from the Río Mosna, enough of the ruins survive to make them a fascinating sight and one of the most important ones in Peru's pre-history. Though the on-site **Sala de Exposición** features ceramics, textiles and stone pieces relating to the cultural influences of the Chavín, Huaras, Recuay and Huari, it is the **Chavín** culture that evolved and elaborated its own brand of religious cultism on and around this magnificent site during the first millennium BC. This religious cult also influenced subsequent cultural development throughout Peru, right up until the Spanish Conquest some 2500 years later (see p.490).

GETTING TO CHAVÍN DE HUANTAR

If you have the time, the journey to **Chavín de Huantar** is almost as rewarding as exploring the archeological site itself; the road has to climb out of the Huaraz Valley and cross over the mountains before dropping quite steeply to the modern-day village and remains of Chavín. There is also the option of reaching the ruins on foot from Olleros.

THE ROAD FROM HUARAZ

The vast majority of people approach the temple complex from **Huaraz**; buses (see p.317) turn off the main Huaraz-to-Lima road at the town of Catac. From here they take a poorly maintained road that crosses over the small Río Yana Yacu (Black Water River) and then starts climbing to the beautiful lake of **Querococha** (*quero* is Quechua for "teeth", and relates to the teeth-like rock formation visible nearby), which looks towards two prominent mountain peaks – Yanamarey and Pucaraju ("Red Glacier" in Quechua). From here the road, little more than a track now, climbs further before passing through the **Tunél de Cahuish**, which cuts through the solid rock of a mountain to emerge in the Callejón de Conchucos, to some spectacular but quite terrifying views. A couple of the more dangerous and precipitous curves in the road are known as the Curva del Diablo and Salvate Si Puedes ("Save yourself if you can"), from which you can deduce that this journey isn't for the squeamish or for vertigo sufferers.

OLLEROS-TO-CHAVÍN DE HUANTAR TREK

If you are feeling adventurous there is a two- to four-day trail over the hills from **Olleros** to Chavín. It follows the Río Negro up to Punta Yanashallash (4700m), cuts down into the Marañón watershed along the Quebrada Shongopampa, and where this meets the Jato stream coming from the north, the route follows the combined waters (from here known as the Río Huachesca) straight down, southwest to the Chavín ruins another 1500m below. It's quite a **hike**, so take maps and ideally a guide and pack-llamas (see box, p.329). A good account of this walk is given in Hilary Bradt's *Backpacking and Trekking in Peru and Bolivia* (see p.532).

The pretty **village** of Chavín de Huantar, with its whitewashed walls and traditional tiled roofs, is just a couple of hundred metres from the ruins and has a reasonable supply of basic amenities.

Brief history

The original temple was built here around 900 BC, though it was not until around 400 BC that the complex was substantially enlarged and its cultural style fixed. Some archeologists claim that the specific layout of the temple, a U-shaped ceremonial courtyard facing east and based around a raised stone platform, was directly influenced by what was, in 1200 BC, the largest architectural monument in the New World, at Sechin Alto (see p.344). By 300 BC, Sechin Alto had been abandoned and Chavín was at the height of its power and one of the world's largest religious centres, with about three thousand resident priests and temple attendants. The U-shaped temples were probably dedicated to powerful mountain spirits or deities, who controlled meteorological phenomena, in particular rainfall, vital to the survival and wealth of the people.

The temple area

The complex's main temple building consists of a central rectangular block with two wings projecting out to the east. The large, southern wing, known as the **Castillo**, is the most conspicuous feature of the site: massive, almost pyramid shaped, the platform was built of dressed stone with gargoyles attached, though few remain now.

Some way in front of the Castillo, down three main flights of steps, the **Plaza Hundida**, or "sunken plaza", covers about 250 square metres with a rectangular, stepped platform to either side. Here, the thousands of pilgrims thought to have worshipped at Chavín would gather during the appropriate fiestas. And it was here that the famous Tello Obelisk, now in the Museo de Arqueología, Antropología e Historia in Lima (see p.76), was found, next to an altar in the shape of a jaguar and bedecked with seven cavities forming a pattern similar to that of the Orion constellation.

Standing in the Plaza Hundida, facing towards the Castillo, you'll see on your right the **original temple**, now just a palatial ruin dwarfed by the neighbouring Castillo. It was first examined by Julio Tello in 1919 when it was still buried under cultivated fields; during 1945 a vast flood reburied most of it and the place was damaged again by the 1970 earthquake and the rains of 1983. Among the fascinating recent finds from the area are bone snuff tubes, beads, pendants, needles, ceremonial shells (imported from Ecuador) and some quartz crystals associated with ritual sites. One quartz crystal covered in red pigment was found in a grave, placed after death in the mouth of the deceased.

The subterranean chambers

Behind the original temple, two entrances lead to a series of underground passages and

subterranean chambers. The passage on the right leads down to an underground chamber, containing the awe-inspiring Lanzon, a prism-shaped 4.5m block of carved white granite that tapers down from a broad feline head to a point stuck in the ground. The entrance on the left takes you into the labyrinthine inner chambers, which run underneath the Castillo on several levels connected by ramps and steps. In the seven major subterranean rooms, you'll need a torch to get a decent look at the carvings and the granite sculptures (even when the electric lighting is switched on), while all around you can hear the sound of water dripping.

Another large stone slab that was originally discovered at Chavín in 1873 – the Estela Raymondi – is now in the Museo Nacional de Arqueología, Antropología e Historia in Lima; this was the first and most spectacular of all the impressive carved stones to be found. The most vivid of the carvings remaining at the site are the **gargoyles** (known as Cabeza Clavos) along the outer stone walls of the Castillo sector, guardians of the temple, which again display feline and bird-like characteristics.

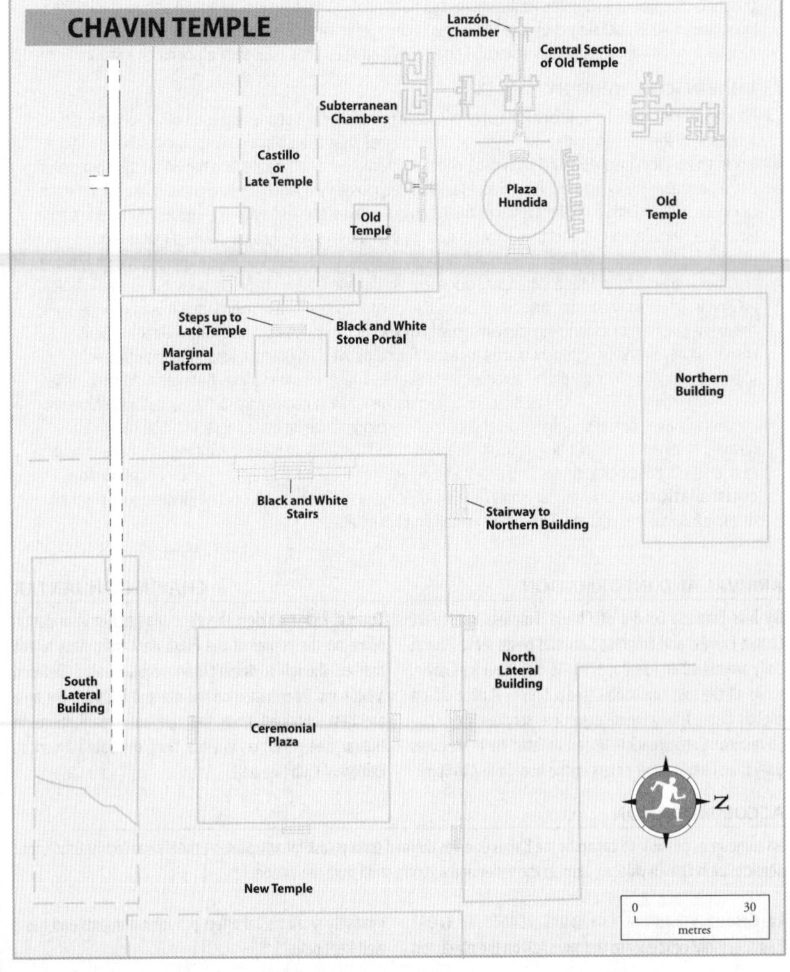

6

THE CHAVÍN CULT

The **Chavín cult**, whose iconography spread across much of Peru, was not a coherent pan-Peruvian religion, but more of a widespread – and unevenly interpreted – cult of the feline god. Chavín had a strong impact on the Paracas culture and later on the Nasca and Mochica civilizations. Theories as to the origin of its inspiration range from extraterrestrial intervention to the more likely infiltration of ideas and individuals or entire tribes from Central America. There is a resemblance between the ceramics found at Chavín and those of a similar date from Tlatilco in **Mexico**, yet there are no comparable Mexican stone constructions as ancient as these Peruvian wonders. More probable, and the theory expounded by medical doctor and Peruvian archeologist Julio Tello (1880 to 1947), is that the cult initially came up into the Andes (then down to the coast) from the Amazon Basin via the Marañón Valley. The inspiration for the beliefs themselves, which appear to be in the power of totemic or animistic gods and demons, may well have come from visionary experiences sparked by the ingestion of **hallucinogens**: one of the stone reliefs at Chavín portrays a feline deity or fanged warrior holding a section of the psychotropic mescalin cactus San Pedro (see p.507), still used by *curanderos* today for the invocation of the spirit world. This feline deity was almost certainly associated with the shamanic practice of visionary transformation from human into animal form for magical and healing purposes, usually achieved by the use of hallucinogenic brews (see p.507); the most powerful animal form that could be assumed, of course, was the big cat, whether a puma or a jaguar.

CHAVÍN ICONOGRAPHY

Most theories about the **iconography** of Chavín de Huantar's stone slabs, all of which are very intricate, distinctive in style and highly abstract, agree that the Chavíns worshipped three major gods: the moon (represented by a fish), the sun (depicted as an eagle or a hawk) and an overlord, or creator divinity, normally shown as a fanged cat, possibly a jaguar. It seems very likely that each god was linked with a distinct level of the Chavín cosmos: the fish with the underworld, the eagle with the celestial forces and the cat with earthly power. This is only a calculated guess, and ethnographic evidence from the Amazon Basin suggests that each of these main gods may have also been associated with a different subgroup within the Chavín tribe or priesthood as a whole.

Chavín itself may or may not have been the centre of the movement, but it was obviously at the very least an outstanding **ceremonial focus** for what was an early agricultural society, thriving on relatively recently domesticated foods as well as cotton, and well-positioned topographically to control the exchange of plants, materials and ideas between communities in the Amazon, Andes and Pacific coast. The name Chavín comes from the Quechua *chaupin*, meaning navel or focal point, and the complex might have been a sacred shrine to which natives flocked in pilgrimage during festivals, much as they do today, visiting important *huacas* in the sierra at specific times in the annual agricultural cycle. The appearance of the **Orion constellation** on Chavín carvings fits this theory, since it appears on the skyline just prior to the traditional harvest period in the Peruvian mountains.

ARRIVAL AND INFORMATION — CHAVÍN DE HUANTAR

By bus Empresa Condor de Chavín, Empresa Huascarán, Chavín Express and Empresa Sandoval buses leave Huaraz daily around 10am (3–4hr; S/10–15 one way) for Chavín, while all the tour companies (see p.319) in Huaraz offer a slightly faster, though more expensive, service (3hr; S/35–50 /return). Getting back to Huaraz or Catac, there are buses daily from Chavín, more or less on the hour from 3 to 6pm.

Tourist information There's a small tourist information office on the corner of the Plaza de Armas, next to the market, though it doesn't have regular hours. Detailed advice and information on the site and hiking in the area are best obtained from the relevant organizations in Huaraz (see p.319) or, in Lima, from the South American Explorers' Club (see p.81).

ACCOMMODATION

It's sometimes possible to **camp** by the Baños Quercos thermal springs (ask for an update at the Huaraz Tourist Office, tour agencies or in Chavín village), 2km up the valley and a 20min stroll from the village.

La Casona Wiracocha 130 ☎043 754048 or ☎043 754020. Right next door to the town hall on the plaza, this relatively small hostel offers private bathrooms and has a well-kept patio. **S/55**

Hostal Chavín Jr San Martín (previously Inca Roca) 141 ☎043 454055. Not all that comfortable, but popular and friendly with some shared spaces and a courtyard at its heart. S/60

Hotel Inca Wiracocha 170 ☎043 454021 or Lima ☎01 5742735. A pleasant place with small well-kept gardens and a very friendly atmosphere; some rooms have private showers. S/60

Konchukos Tambo Lodge San Marcos ☎043 454631, ⓦkonchukostambo.com. Some 10km from Chavín and a further 2km from the village of San Marcos, this Conchucos-based trekking lodge offers archeological and educational tours as well as day-hikes. Contact in advance for help with transfers. Online discounts also available. S/240

EATING

La Portada C 17 de Enero Sur 311. Based in an ageing mansion, *La Portada* offers good, simple, local food including soups, meat and rice. The service is very welcoming and there are some tables in the courtyard. Mon–Sat 10.30am–5.30pm.

Restaurant Chavín Turístico C 17 de Enero Sur 439. As the name suggests, it has a menu geared towards visitors to town. There is a small central patio garden, service is swift and the ambience pleasant. Daily7.30am–8pm.

Restaurant La Ramada C 17 de Enero Sur 577. Centrally located and popular with locals and tourists alike, with fresh trout served most days. Daily 8am–8pm.

North from Chavín

There are buses every hour from Chavín to San Marcos (20min; S/4) and Huari (1hr; S/8), or you can walk there in well under 2hr; to continue on to Pomabamba from Huari, there are buses every other day, usually leaving at 9pm (7hr; S/18)

Some 8km north of Chavín is the lovely village of **San Marcos**, a good base for mountain hiking. From San Marcos you can climb up another 300m in altitude to the smaller community of **Carhuayoc**, a hundred-year-old village whose population specialize in the production of fine textiles – mainly blankets and rugs (it's a 9hr return journey). About 35km from San Marcos, the town of **Huari** is a good base for a short trek to the scenic Lago Purhuay; it's only 8km from the town and a climb of some 400m, but it usually takes between five and six hours to get there and back.

Cordillera Huayhuash

To the south of Huaraz, the **Cordillera Huayhuash** offers much less frequented but just as stunning trekking trails as those in the Cordillera Blanca. Most treks start in the small town of **Chiquián**, 2400m above sea level. The most popular trek hereabouts is the **Chiquián Loop** (see box, p.342), which leaves Chiquián heading for Llamac and the entire Cordillera loop. There is also an alternative trek from Chiquián that is much easier (see below).

The mountains here, although slightly lower than the Cordillera Blanca and covering a much smaller area, nevertheless rise breathtakingly to 6634m at the **Nevada Yerupajá**, some 50km southeast of Chiquián as the crow flies. Yerupajá actually forms the watershed between the Cordillera Huayhuash to the north and the lower-altitude Cordillera Raura to the south. Large and stunning lakes, flocks of alpaca, herds of cattle and some sheep can be seen along the way. High levels of fitness and some experience are required for hiking or climbing in this region and it's always best to tackle it as part of a team, or at least to have a **local guide** along. The guide will help to avoid the rather irritating dogs that look after the animals in these remote hills and his presence will also provide protection against the possible, but unlikely, threat of robbery.

Chiquián

A very small and traditional Andean town, **CHIQUIÁN** is quiet (except during the town's festivals), reserved and very pretty. One popular Huayhuash trek from Chiquián follows a route from **Llamac** to Pampa de Llamac (via a very difficult pass), then on to the lake of **Jahuacocha**, where trout fishing is possible. Taking about five days, the scenery on the

6

THE CHIQUIÁN LOOP

One of the least-visited and most difficult trails, the **Chiquián Loop** lies at altitudes between 2750m and 5000m. It covers a distance of 164–186km and takes some fourteen days to hike (give or take a few, depending on your fitness, walking ability and desire). Rated as Class 4 (difficult), as the name suggests, the route starts and finishes in Chiquián. Note that maps are essential and local guides with mules advisable. It is also possible to do the trek in 16 days if you'd like to take things a little easier.

Day 1: Chiquián to Llamac This is an easy first-day walk. The wide and clearly marked path takes hikers to the far end of the valley. After crossing three times from one valley to the other, a short way up will lead walkers to Llamac, a typical highland village.

Day 2: Llamac to Matacancha A two-hour descent leads to another little Andean village called Pocpa, from where walkers must take the left bank of the river and start climbing to the campsite. The first mountain that appears is the Ninashanca at 5607m (18,391ft). The camping spot is at the far end of this dry and treeless valley.

Day 3: Matacancha to Janca The first ascent to the Cacananpunta Pass (La Abra Cacananpunta) at 4880m (16,006ft) is difficult and best reached before noon; descent to the camp does not require a major effort.

Day 4: Janca to Carhuacocha This day involves significant trekking up and back down, offering views of almost the entire scenery of the Cordillera Huayhuash. Arriving at the lakeside camp beside Carhuacocha, the Cordillera is clearly visible.

Day 5: Carhuacocha to Carnicero and Rinconada Leaving the lake at Carhuacocha in the morning, the next pass opens out to the Valle Carnicero. A not very steep, and beautiful, climb takes the hiker to the low Rinconada pass that forms visually spectacular rocky scenery.

Day 6: Carnicero to Huayhuash and Altuspata The descent continues to the next valley via the pass of Punta Carnicero (4600m), passing several small lakes and rivers along the way to the village of Huayhuash (4350m) and continuing to Altuspata, which has good camping.

Day 7: Altuspata to Lago Viconga Leaving the Altuspata campsite first thing, the ascent continues towards one of the highest passes on the route, which leads the way to the Lago Viconga. Walking around the lake through the narrow valley one reaches the next camping spot.

Day 8: Lago Viconga to Valle Huanacpatay A very long way and one of the toughest hikes on the route, this is where one crosses the Abra de Cuyoc pass at 5100m (16,728ft) next to the mountain of Nevado Cuyoc and close to Puscanturpa at 5442m (17,854ft). Descending from the pass, a small, steep and difficult corridor leads to the Valle Huanacpatay.

Days 9 and 10: Abra del Diablo Mudo Two days must be set aside for climbing two of the peaks around the Abra del Diablo Mudo pass to reach Huanacpatay (4500m).

Day 11: Huanacpatay to Huatiac Another long trekking day, but downhill overall, takes you from the high Valle Huanacpatay to a lower one at Huatiac (3800m). After a deep descent into the endless valley of the Huallapa River one starts seeing trees and plants, with the trail passing close by Huallapa village.

Day 12: Huatiac to Jahuacocha Leaving the pleasant Huatiac campsite, the trail continues upwards again to the Abra del Diablo Mudo pass at 5000m (16,400ft), an area bereft of plant life. Everything is downhill from the pass until the lake at Jahuacocha and past it, to camp.

Day 13: Lago Jahuacocha to Llamac After almost two weeks the path crosses again into Llamac village. There are two paths from Jahuacocha which lead back to Llamac's campsite: one is direct and very steep and is done in a shorter time, while the second one is longer but with no major or sudden descents.

Day 14: Llamac to Chiquián and Huaraz A repeated stretch, which also formed the first day's hike: a tough but marvellous trek through the Cordillera Huayhuash.

trek can only be described as breathtaking, the hiking itself as quite hard. The only downside is that you have to walk Chiquián–Llamac twice, and between Rondoy and Llamac a mining company has destroyed much of the beautiful countryside, apparently also polluting the river as well as building a rather ugly road. More information can be obtained from the Casa de Guías in Huaraz (see box, p.329). Most people who come this far, though, prefer to do the **Chiquián Loop** (see box above), which entails a tough couple of weeks, though the really fit might manage it in ten days at a push.

ARRIVAL AND DEPARTURE **CHIQUIÁN**

By bus Chiquián is easily reached by bus with Empresa Rapido, at Mariscal Cáceres 312 in Huaraz (6 daily; 3hr; 044 426437).

ACCOMMODATION AND EATING

After the town of Chiquián, it's virtually impossible to buy food, so it's a good idea to get most of this in **Huaraz** or in **Lima**, before arriving, supplementing when you arrive here with extras such as bread, dry biscuits, dairy products (including good local cheeses), rice and pasta.

Hotel Los Nogales Jr Comercio 1301 043 447121, hotel_nogales_chiquian@yahoo.com.pe. Friendly and safe, this is a good alternative to *San Miguel*, with a choice of rooms with TV, and with or without private bathroom. S/35

El Refugio de Bolognesi Tarapaca 471. This is the best of a limited set of small restaurants, offering perhaps the nicest set-lunch menus. Daily 7am–7pm.

San Miguel Jr Comercio 233 043 747001. Arranged around a patio, this rustic place has reasonably clean and comfortable beds and a nice little garden. S/40

6

The Ancash coast

The **Ancash coast** is a largely barren desert strip that quickly rises into Andean foothills when you head east and away from the ocean. Most people going this way will be travelling between Lima and either Huaraz (6–7hr) or Trujillo (8hr). Huaraz is reached by a turn-off from the Panamerican Highway following a well-maintained road that climbs furiously to the breathless heights of the Callejón de Huaylas. There is a small beach resort near **Barranca**, and **Casma** and **Chimbote** have some intriguing archeological sites nearby, and offer alternative routes up to Huaraz.

Barranca and around

The only likely reason to stop off at **BARRANCA** is as part of a visit to the nearby **Fortress of Paramonga**, the best preserved of all Peru's coastal outposts, built originally to guard the southern limit of the powerful Chimu Empire. To explore the ruins, it's best to base yourself in the town, where there are a few simple hotels and two or three places to eat.

Five kilometres north of Barranca is the smaller town of **PATAVILCA**, where Bolívar planned his campaign to liberate Peru. The main paved road to Huaraz and the Cordillera Blanca leaves the Panamerican Highway here and heads up into the Andes.

Fortress of Paramonga

7km north of Barranca • Daily: Fortress 8am–5.30pm; Museum 8am–5pm • S/8 • To get from Barranca to Paramonga, take the efficient local bus service, which leaves from the garage at the northern end of town, every hour or so (10–15min; S/1.5)

The **FORTRESS OF PARAMONGA** sits less than 1km from the ocean and looks in many ways like a feudal castle. Constructed entirely from adobe, its walls within walls run around the contours of a natural hillock and are similar in style and situation to the Sun Temple of Pachacamac (see p.97). As you climb up from the road, you'll see the main entrance to the fortress on the right by the site's small **museum** and ticket office.

CHIQUIÁN FIESTAS

In late August and early September there are some colourful fiestas in the town, for the **Virgen de Santa Rosa**, during the last day of which there is always a **bullfight**, with the local football stadium being transformed into an arena. The aim of the game is, as with most rural Peruvian bullfights, just to play with the bull (without hurting him) and this is done not only by the *toreador*, but by anyone who feels the urge to get involved (local youth, drunk men); they can challenge the bull with their poncho, which guarantees a lot of excitement and fun, with the public scattering when the irritated bull comes too close.

Heading into the labyrinthine **ruins**, you'll find the rooms and sections get smaller and narrower the closer you get to the top – and the original **palace-temple**. From here there are commanding views across the desert coast and across vast sugar-cane fields, formerly belonging to the US-owned Grace Corporation, once owners of nearly a third of Peru's sugar production. In contrast to the verdant verdure of these fields, irrigated by the Río Fortaleza, the fortress stands out in the landscape like a huge, dusty yellow pyramid.

There are differences of opinion as to whether the fort had a military function or was purely a ritual centre, but as most pre-Conquest cultures built their places of worship around the natural personality of the landscape (rocks, water, geomorphic features and so on), it seems likely that the Chimu built it on an older *huaca* (ancient sacred site), both as a fortified ritual shrine and to mark the southern boundary of their empire. In the late fifteenth century, it was conquered by the **Incas**, who built a road down from the Callejón de Huaylas. Arriving in 1533 en route from Cajamarca to Pachacamac, Hernando Pizarro, the first Spaniard to see Paramonga, described it as "a strong fort with seven encircling walls painted with many forms both inside and outside, with portals well built like those of Spain and two tigers painted at the principal doorways". There are still red- and yellow-based geometric murals visible on some of the walls in the upper sector, as well as some chessboard-style patterns.

ARRIVAL AND ACCOMMODATION — BARRANCA AND AROUND

By bus/colectivo Nearly all buses and colectivos on their way between Lima and Trujillo or Huaraz stop at Barranca. There are several buses daily to Casma (2hr), Chimbote (3hr), Huaraz (4–5hr) and Lima (3hr) from here.

Hotel Jefferson Jr Lima 946 ☎ 01 2352184. An inexpensive establishment with quite comfortable rooms. S/65

Casma and around

The town of **CASMA**, 170km north of Barranca, marks the mouth of the well-irrigated Sechin River Valley. Surrounded by corn and cotton fields, this small settlement is peculiar in that most of its buildings are just one storey high and all are modern. Formerly the port for the Callejón de Huaylas, the town was razed by the 1970 earthquake, whose epicentre was just offshore. There's not a lot of interest here and little reason to break your journey, other than to try the local speciality of duck ceviche (flakes of duck meat soaked deliciously in lime and orange juice) or to explore the nearby ruins, such as the temple complex of Sechin, the ancient fort of Chanquillo and the Pañamarca pyramid, 20km north.

The Sechin ruins

5km southeast from Casma • Daily: Ruins 8am–5pm; Museo de Sitio Max Uhle 8am–5.30pm • S/5

A partially reconstructed temple complex, the main section of the **Sechin ruins** is unusually stuck at the bottom of a hill, and consists of an outer wall clad with around ninety monolithic slabs engraved with sometimes monstrous representations of particularly nasty and bellicose warriors, along with their mutilated sacrificial victims or prisoners of war. Some of these stones, dating from between 1800 and 800 BC, stand 4m high. Hidden behind the standing stones is an interesting inner sanctuary – a rectangular building consisting of a series of superimposed platforms with a central stairway on either side. The site also contains the small **Museo de Sitio Max Uhle**, which displays photographs of the complex plus some of the artefacts uncovered here, as well as information and exhibits on Moche, Huari, Chimu, Casma and Inca cultures.

Some of the ceremonial centres at Sechin were built before 1400 BC, including the massive, U-shaped **Sechin Alto complex** (21km away near Buena Vista Alta; not accessible via public transport), at the time the largest construction in the entire Americas. Ancient coastal constructions usually favoured adobe as a building material, making this site rare in its extensive use of granite stone. Around 300m long by 250m wide, the massive stone-faced platform predates the similar ceremonial centre at Chavín de Huantar (see p.337), possibly by as much as four hundred years. This means that Chavín could not have been the original source of the temple architectural style, and that much of the iconography and legends associated with what is known as the Chavín cultural phase of Peruvian prehistory actually began 3500 years ago down here on the desert coast.

Pampa de Llamas

Several lesser-known archeological sites dot the Sechin Valley, whose maze of ancient sandy roadways constituted an important pre-Inca junction. The remains of a huge complex of dwellings can be found on the **Pampa de Llamas**, though all you will see nowadays are the walls of adobe huts, deserted more than a thousand years ago. At **Mojeque**, you can see a terraced pyramid with stone stairs and feline and snake designs.

Fort of Chanquillo

Some 12km southeast of Casma lies the ruined, possibly pre-Mochica fort of **Chanquillo**, around which you can wander freely. It's an amazing ruin set in a commanding position on a barren hill, with four walls in concentric rings and watchtowers in the middle, keeping an eye over the desert below. Less than one kilometre below the fort stand thirteen towers in a long line.

Pañamarca pyramid

At Km 395 of the Panamerican Highway, a turn-off on the right leads 11km to the ruined adobe pyramid of **Pañamarca**, an impressive monument to the Mochica culture, dating from around 500 AD. Three large painted panels can be seen here, and on a nearby wall a long procession of warriors has been painted – but all this artwork has been badly damaged by rain.

ARRIVAL AND DEPARTURE — CASMA AND AROUND

CASMA

By bus Turismo Chimbote buses, at block 1, Av Luís Ormeño, run at least every hour to Lima (6hr) and Chimbote (40min); for Huaraz, Huandoy buses, Av Luís Ormeño 158 (T 043 712336), take the fastest normal route, finishing at Caraz; while Empresa Moreno buses serve Huaraz three times a week via the scenic but dusty track over the Cordillera Negra via the Callan Pass (6–8hr).

THE SECHIN RUINS

On foot Walk south along the Panamerican Highway for 3km, then up the signposted side road to Huaraz for about the same distance; the walk should take just over an hour.
By taxi If you're not up to the walk here, your best option is to take a motorcycle taxi from Casma, (S/5 one way). Alternatively, there are taxis from the Plaza de Armas, for around $10–15 return, including a wait of an hour or so.
By colectivo There are no buses, but some local colectivos come here in the mornings from the market area of Casma.

PAMPA DE LLAMAS AND MOJEQUE

By taxi Both Mojeque and Pampa de Llamas are best visited from Casma by taxi; expect to pay around S/30 (return).

CHANQUILLO

By truck Trucks leave for Chanquillo every morning at around 9am from the Petro Perú filling station in Casma – ask the driver to drop you off at "El Castillo", from where it's a 30min walk uphill to the fort.

FORT OF CHANQUILLO

By taxi From Casma your taxi should take the turning east from the Panamerican Highway at Km 361; the driver will have to wait since it is unlikely there will be others at the site (S/15 one way, plus S/5–10 for the wait)).

PAÑAMARCA PYRAMID

By taxi This is not an easy site to visit; it is best to get a taxi from the Plaza de Armas in Casma for around S/15–20.

ACCOMMODATION

CASMA

Hospedaje Las Dunas Ormeno 505 T 043 711057. On the route to the Sechin ruins this place is well run with a good restaurant, and is only 10min from town by car or taxi. S/70
Hostal Las Aldas Panamericana Norte Km 347 T 01 4428523. Some 30km from Casma, this fun hostel is located near a pleasant beach at Playa Las Aldas (turn off the Panamericana Norte at Km 345); some of the bungalows face the ocean and are right on the beach. S/60
Hostal Gregori C Luís Ormeño 530 T 043 711073. Very

clean and quiet hostel with comfortable rooms in a modern building with an airy and pleasant lobby; service is good too. S/55

Hotel El Farol Tupac Amaru 450 043 711064, hostalfarol@yahoo.com. Just two blocks from the Plaza de Armas, this hotel is friendly and clean, with TVs and private bathrooms, a pool and a decent restaurant which sometimes serves *ceviche de pato* (see p.344). S/60

Chimbote

6

Elderly locals say that **CHIMBOTE** – another 25km beyond the turn-off to the Pañamarca pyramid – was once a beautiful coastal bay, with a rustic fishing port and fine extensive beach. You can still get a sense of this on the southern Panamericana approach, but the smell and industrial sprawl created by the unplanned fishing boom over thirty years ago undeniably dominates the senses. Chimbote has more than thirty **fish-packing factories**, which explains the rather unbearable stench of stale fish. Despite the crisis in the fishing industry since the early 1970s – overfishing and El Niño have led to bans and strict catch limits for the fishermen – Chimbote accounts for more than 75 percent of Peru's fishing-related activity. Most travellers stay in Chimbote one night at most; the town can be smelly and offers little of interest to visitors, apart perhaps from some attractive **marble sculptures** which adorn the central Boulevard Isla Blanca.

Chimbote's development constitutes the country's most spectacular **urban growth** outside Lima. Initially stimulated by the Chimbote–Huallanca rail line (built in 1922), a nearby hydroelectric plant and government planning for an anticipated rise in the anchovy- and tuna-fishing industry, the population grew rapidly from 5000 in 1940 to 60,000 in 1961 (swollen by squatter settlers from the mountains). Yet even Chimbote was virtually razed to the ground during the 1970 earthquake (see p.328).

ARRIVAL AND INFORMATION — CHIMBOTE

By plane The airport, where you can get daily flights to (or from) Lima and Trujillo can be found at Km 421 (043 311844 or 043 311062).

By bus Most important is knowing how to get out of town. Most buses call at and leave from the Terminal Terrestre El Chimbador, a few kilometres south of the city centre on Av de los Pescadores on the Carretera Panamericana. All the coastal buses travelling north to Trujillo (3hr north) and south to Lima along the Panamerican Highway stop here; it can be very busy. Turismo Huaraz run direct Chimbote–Huaraz buses, twice daily (one daytime, one at night) from Av Pardo 1713 (043 321235). Movil Tours, Turismo Chimbote, Expresso Huandoy and Trans Moreno all run daily buses to Huaraz via Pativilca and Casma, as well as (mostly nightly) services to Caraz via Huallanca and the Cañon del Pato, a very rough road) from Jirón Pardo, between Jirón José Galvez and Manuel Ruiz.

By colectivo Colectivos to Trujillo (2–3hr away) leave regularly from Calle Enrique Palacios, near the Plaza de Armas, while colectivos to Lima hang around on Manuel Ruiz, one block towards the sea off Av Prado.

Tourist information Bolognesi 421 (Mon–Sat 9am–5.30pm). Can advise on transport to nearby sites and sometimes stocks town and regional maps. Limited information can also be found at chimboteonline.com.

ACCOMMODATION

Gran Chimú Jr José Galvez 109m 043 321741. Dominating the Plaza 28 de Julio, this large hotel is reasonably priced, offering comfortable rooms and mod cons, and its restaurant, though not cheap, serves some of the best food found along this part of the coast; try the ceviche or the criolla dishes such as *aji de gallina*. S/180

Hostal El Ruedo Lote 15, Urbino Los Pinos 043 335560. Located a little way from the noisy town centre, this basic establishment is usually relatively free of fishy smells. S/65

Hotel La Casona Av San Pedro 246 043 322655. Located in the suburb of Miramar Bajo, this stylish and very comfortable hotel offers all modern conveniences. S/120

The Santa and Viru valleys

The valleys formed by the rivers **Santa** and **Viru** provide relief against the sun-blasted desert on the road north between Chimbote and Trujillo. Despite the bleak terrain and climate the roadside towards Trujillo is fast filling up with new settlements – a kind of ribbon development between two busy markets and population centres. The desert itself, beyond the road, is rarely visited, yet littered with **archeological remains**.

Great Wall of Peru

Twenty kilometres north of Chimbote, the Panamerican Highway crosses a rocky outcrop into the Santa Valley, where an enormous defensive wall known as the **Great Wall of Peru** – a stone and adobe structure more than 50km long and thought to be over a thousand years old – rises from the sands of the desert. The enormous structure was first noticed in 1931 by the Shippee-Johnson Aerial Photographic Expedition, and there are many theories about its construction and purpose. Archeologist Julio Tello thought it was pre-Chimu, since it seems unlikely that the Chimu would have built such a lengthy defensive wall so far inside the limits of their empire. It may also, as the historian Garcilaso de la Vega believed, have been built by the Spaniards as a defence against the threat of Inca invasion from the coast or from the Callejón de Huaylas. The wall stretches from Tambo Real near the Río Santa estuary in the west up to Chuqucara in the east, where there are scattered remains of pyramids, fortresses, temples and stone houses.

Further up the valley – albeit far off the beaten track, with no tourism infrastructure whatsoever – lies a double-walled **construction** with outer turrets, discovered by Gene Savoy's aerial expedition in the late 1950s. Savoy reported finding 42 stone-built strongholds in the higher Santa Valley in only two days' flying, evidence that supports historians' claims that this was the most populated valley on the coast prior to the Spanish Conquest. Hard to believe today, it seems more probable if you bear in mind that this desert region, still alive with wildlife such as desert foxes and condors, is fed by the largest and most reliable of the coastal rivers.

Viru

The Viru Valley's main town is the eponymous **VIRU**, a small place at Km 515 of the Panamerican Highway, with a bridge over the riverbed, which in the dry season looks as though it has never seen rain. The name Viru is believed by many to be the original source of the modern name Peru. According to the chroniclers, the Spanish conquistadors met a raft of fishermen out on the sea here, before landing in Peru. When the Spanish tried to find out from the fishermen where they came from, apparently they said "Viru, Viru".

An impressive cultural centre around 300 AD, when it was occupied by the Gallinazo or Viru people, today the town offers very little to the tourist. The most interesting ruin in the area is the **Grupo Gallinazo** near Tomabal, 24km east of Viru up a side road just north of the town's bridge. Here in the valley you can see the dwellings, murals and pyramids of a significant religious and administrative centre, its internal layout derived from kinship networks (with different clans responsible for different sectors of the settlement). The site covers an area of four square kilometres and archeologists estimate that over ten thousand people sometimes lived here at the same time. You can also make out the adobe walls and ceremonial platform of a Gallinazo temple, on one of the hilltops at Tomabal.

ARRIVAL AND DEPARTURE — THE SANTA AND VIRU VALLEYS

GREAT WALL OF PERU

By bus To see the wall, take any Trujillo bus north from Chimbote (see opposite) along the Panamerican Highway, and get off when you see a bridge over the Río Santa. From here, head upstream for three or four hours and you'll arrive at the best surviving section of the wall, just to the west of the Hacienda Tanguche farm, where the piled stone is cemented with mud to more than 4m high in places.

VIRU

By bus The road between Chimbote and Trujillo runs straight through Viru, so just take any bus and get off there.

Trujillo and the north

CHAN CHAN

Trujillo and the north

Northern Peru is packed with unique treasures – cultural, archeological and natural. Blessed with fewer tourists and better coastal weather than either Lima or the south (particularly in the high season – May to September), the area encompasses city oases along the coast, secluded villages in the Andes – where you may well be the first foreigner to pass through for years – and is brimming over with imposing and important pre-Inca sites, some of them only discovered in the last decade or two. For many, the biggest attraction will be the beautiful and trendy beaches. For others, it's the scenery, archeology, and the opportunity to get off the beaten tourist trail.

Trujillo is located on the seaward edge of the vast desert plain at the mouth of the Moche Valley. Its attraction lies mainly in its nearby ruins – notably **Chan Chan** and the huge, sacred pyramids of the **Huaca del Sol** and **Huaca de la Luna** – but also partly in the city itself, and some excellent, laidback outlying beach communities. **Huanchaco**, only 12km from Trujillo, is a good case in point, essentially a fishing village and a likeable resort within walking distance of sandy beaches and massive ancient ruins.

There are established bus **touring routes** through the Andean region above Trujillo, all of which present the option of winding through the beautifully situated mountain town of **Cajamarca**. It was here that Pizarro first encountered and captured the Inca Emperor Atahualpa, beginning the Spanish conquest of Peru. Cajamarca is also a springboard for visiting the smaller town of **Chachapoyas** and the ruined citadel complex of **Kuelap**, arguably the single most overwhelming pre-Columbian site in Peru. Beyond, there are possible routes down to Amazon headwaters and the jungle towns of **Tarapoto** and even **Iquitos** – long and arduous journeys.

The coastal strip north of Trujillo, up to **Tumbes** by the Ecuadorian border, is for the most part a seemingly endless **desert** plain, interrupted by isolated villages and new squatter settlements, but only two substantial towns, **Chiclayo** and **Piura**. Newly discovered archeological sites around Chiclayo possess some of the coast's most important temple ruins, pyramids and nobles' tombs, the latter containing a wealth of precious-metal ceremonial items, and there are some excellent regional museums such as the Museo de las Tumbas, based near Chiclayo. Northern Peru hosts a number of great beach resorts, such as **Chicama** and the warm seas of the hottest surf and beach scene in Peru at **Máncora**, located between Cabo Blanco and the border with Ecuador.

SURFING AT MÁNCORA BEACH

Highlights

❶ **Chan Chan** Located by the ocean near the city of Trujillo, this massive adobe city was built by the Chimu culture in the thirteenth century. **See p.367**

❷ **Kuelap** Way off the beaten track, this majestic mountaintop citadel rivals Machu Picchu for its setting and archeological interest. **See p.389**

❸ **Museo de las Tumbas** An excellent museum whose exhibits include precious objects of gold and silver, as well as a replica of the royal tomb of the Lord of Sipán. **See p.400**

❹ **Batán Grande** On the eastern edge of the Americas' largest dry forest, and right next to the beautiful Río de la Leche, ancient pyramids stand as an impressive monument to the ceremonial heart of Sicán culture. **See p.403**

❺ **Valley of the Pyramids** Standing in the hot dry desert of northern Peru is this magnificent collection of adobe pyramids from the Sicán culture, dating around 1100 AD. **See p.404**

❻ **Máncora beach** Peru's trendiest beach and surf resort, Máncora has warm water, strong sunshine and hot nightlife. **See p.414**

HIGHLIGHTS ARE MARKED ON THE MAP ON PP.352–353

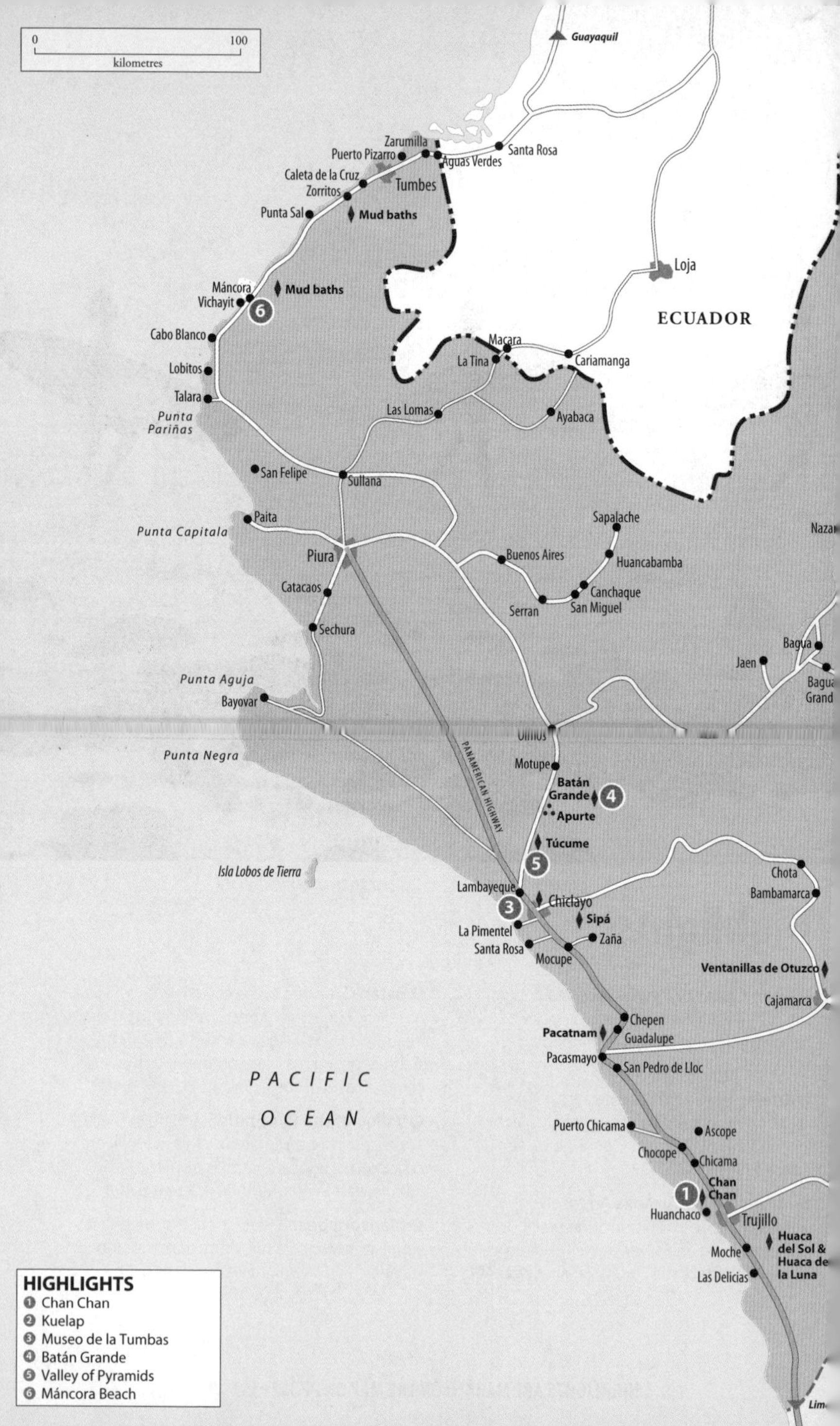

0
100
kilometres
Guayaquil
Zarumilla
Puerto Pizarro
Aguas Verdes
Santa Rosa
Caleta de la Cruz
Zorritos
Tumbes
Punta Sal
Mud baths
Loja
Máncora
Vichayit
Mud baths
ECUADOR
Cabo Blanco
Macara
La Tina
Cariamanga
Lobitos
Talara
Punta Pariñas
Las Lomas
Ayabaca
San Felipe
Sullana
Paita
Punta Capitala
Sapalache
Piura
Buenos Aires
Huancabamba
Catacaos
Canchaque
Serran
San Miguel
Sechura
Bagua
Jaen
Punta Aguja
Bayovar
Punta Negra
Motupe
Batán Grande
Apurte
PANAMERICAN HIGHWAY
Túcume
Isla Lobos de Tierra
Chota
Lambayeque
Chiclayo
Bambamarca
Sipá
La Pimentel
Santa Rosa
Zaña
Mocupe
Ventanillas de Otuzco
Cajamarca
Chepen
Pacatnam
Guadalupe
Pacasmayo
San Pedro de Lloc
PACIFIC
OCEAN
Puerto Chicama
Ascope
Chocope
Chicama
Chan Chan
Huanchaco
Trujillo
Moche
Huaca del Sol & Huaca de la Luna
Las Delicias
HIGHLIGHTS
1 Chan Chan
2 Kuelap
3 Museo de la Tumbas
4 Batán Grande
5 Valley of Pyramids
6 Máncora Beach

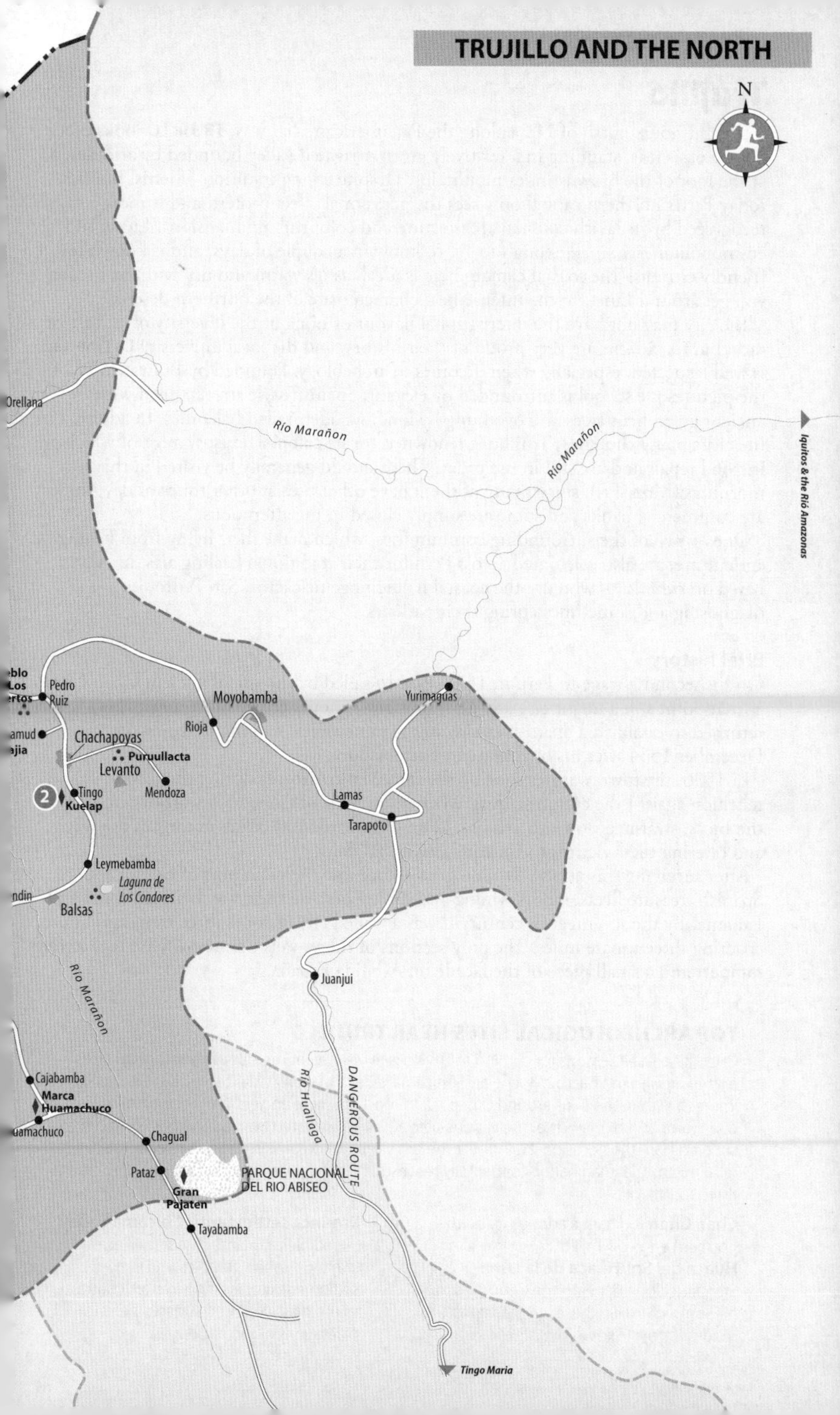
TRUJILLO AND THE NORTH
N
Orellana
Río Marañon
Río Marañon
Iquitos & the Río Amazonas
Pedro Ruiz
Moyobamba
Yurimaguas
Rioja
Chachapoyas
Puruullacta
Levanto
Mendoza
2
Tingo
Kuelap
Lamas
Tarapoto
Leymebamba
Laguna de Los Condores
Balsas
Juanjui
Río Marañon
Río Huallaga
DANGEROUS ROUTE
Cajabamba
Marca Huamachuco
Chagual
Pataz
PARQUE NACIONAL DEL RIO ABISEO
Gran Pajaten
Tayabamba
Tingo Maria

Trujillo

Just eight hours north of Lima along the Panamerican Highway, **TRUJILLO** looks every bit the oasis it is, standing in a relatively green, irrigated valley bounded by arid desert at the foot of the brown Andes mountains. Despite a long tradition of leftist politics, today Peru's northern capital only sees the occasional street protest, and is more recognized by its lavish colonial architecture and colourful old mansions. Lively and cosmopolitan, it's small enough to get to know in a couple of days, and is known for its friendly citizens. The coastal **climate** here is ideal, as it's warm and dry without the fog you get around Lima, or the intense heat characteristic of the northern deserts.

The city may not have the international flavour of Lima or the diversity of culture or race, but its citizens are very proud of their history, and the local university **La Libertad** is well respected, especially when it comes to archeology. Founded by Bolívar in 1824, the picturesque school is surrounded by elegant, Spanish-style streets, lined with ancient green ficus trees and overhung by long, wooden-railed balconies. In addition to the city's many **churches**, Trujillo is renowned for its **colonial houses**, most of which are in good repair and are still in use today. These should generally be visited in the mornings (Mon–Fri), since many of them have other uses at other times of day; some are commercial banks and some are simply closed in the afternoons.

One or two of the surrounding communities, which make their living from fishing or agriculture, are also celebrated across Peru for their traditional healing arts, usually based on *curanderos* who use the coastal hallucinogenic cactus, San Pedro, for diagnosing and sometimes curing their patients.

Brief history

On his second voyage to Peru in 1528, **Pizarro** sailed by the site of ancient Chan Chan, at that point still a major city and an important regional centre of Inca rule. He returned to establish a Spanish colony in the same valley, naming it Trujillo in December 1534 after his birthplace in Extremadura.

In 1536, the town was besieged by the Inca Manco's forces during the second rebellion against the conquistadors. Many thousands of Conchuco warriors, allied with the Incas, swarmed down to Trujillo, killing Spaniards and collaborators on the way and offering their victims to Catequil, the tribal deity.

After surviving this attack, Trujillo grew to become the main port of call for the Spanish treasure fleets, sailors wining and dining here on their way between Lima and Panama. By the seventeenth century it was a walled city of some three thousand houses covering three square miles. The only sections of those walls that remain are the **Herrera rampart** and a small piece of the facade on Avenida España.

TOP ARCHEOLOGICAL SITES NEAR TRUJILLO

One of the main reasons for coming to Trujillo is to visit the numerous **archeological sites** dotted around the nearby Moche and Chicama valleys. In many ways these sites are more impressive than the ruins around Cusco – and most are more ancient too. The pyramids, courtyards and high walls of the various sites are all constructed from adobe bricks which have suffered from the occasional rains over the last eight hundred years or so, consequently requiring a little imagination to mentally reconstruct them as you wander around. Here are the three to aim for:

Chan Chan A gigantic adobe city on the northern edge of Trujillo.

Huaca del Sol/Huaca de la Luna Standing alone beneath the Cerro Blanco hill south of Trujillo these are the largest mud-brick pyramids in the Americas.

Pre-Inca settlements, Chicama Valley Incredible remnants of vast pre-Inca irrigation canals, temples and early settlement sites existing in stark contrast to the massive, green sugar-cane plantations of the haciendas.

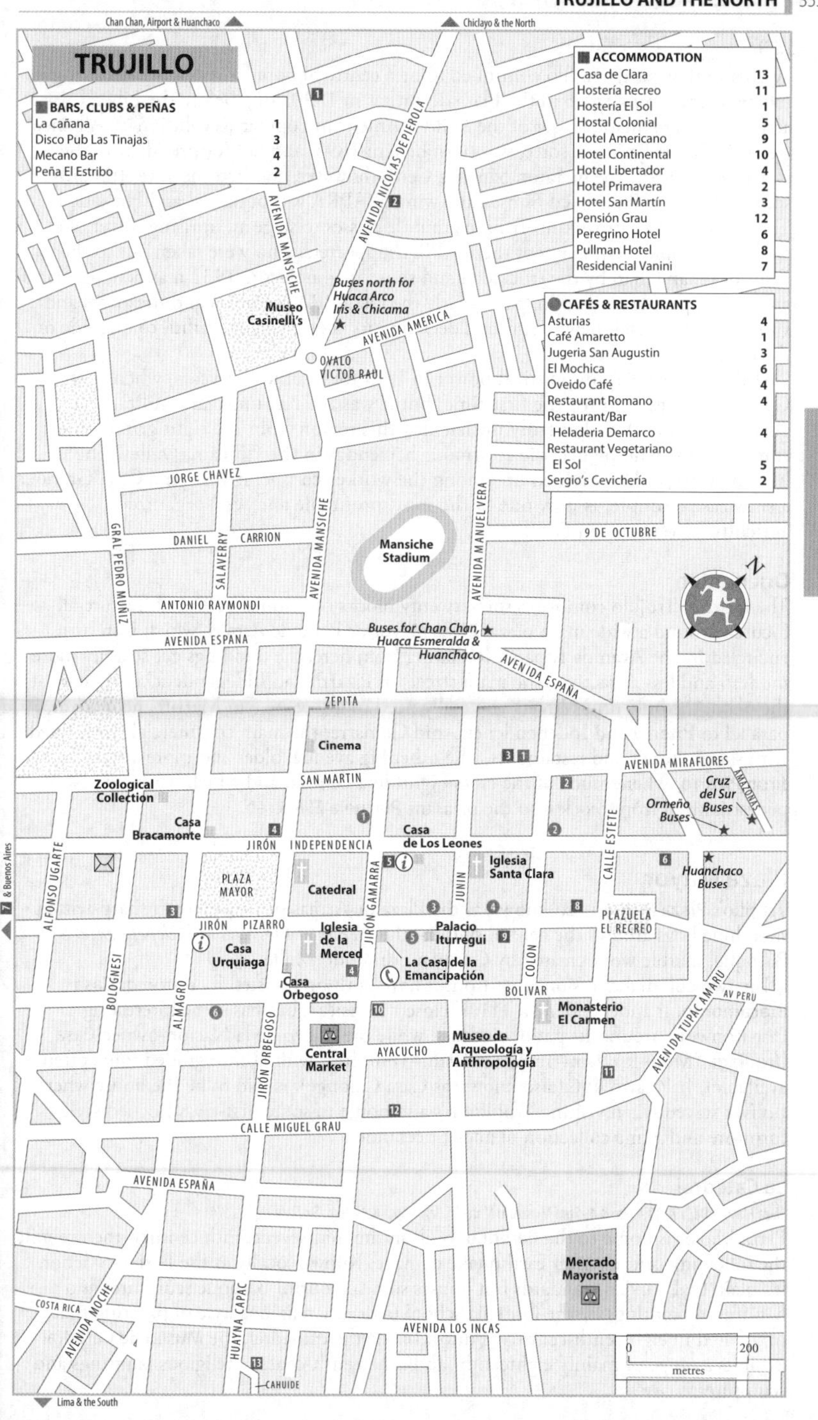
TRUJILLO
BARS, CLUBS & PEÑAS
La Cañana 1
Disco Pub Las Tinajas 3
Mecano Bar 4
Peña El Estribo 2
ACCOMMODATION
Casa de Clara 13
Hostería Recreo 11
Hostería El Sol 1
Hostal Colonial 5
Hotel Americano 9
Hotel Continental 10
Hotel Libertador 4
Hotel Primavera 2
Hotel San Martín 3
Pensión Grau 12
Peregrino Hotel 6
Pullman Hotel 8
Residencial Vanini 7
CAFÉS & RESTAURANTS
Asturias 4
Café Amaretto 1
Jugeria San Augustin 3
El Mochica 6
Oveido Café 4
Restaurant Romano 4
Restaurant/Bar Heladeria Demarco 4
Restaurant Vegetariano El Sol 5
Sergio's Cevichería 2
Chan Chan, Airport & Huanchaco
Chiclayo & the North
Lima & the South
7 & Buenos Aires
AVENIDA MANSICHE
AVENIDA NICOLAS DE PIEROLA
Buses north for Huaca Arco Iris & Chicama
Museo Casinelli's
AVENIDA AMERICA
OVALO VICTOR RAUL
JORGE CHAVEZ
DANIEL CARRION
GRAL PEDRO MUÑIZ
SALAVERRY
ANTONIO RAYMONDI
AVENIDA ESPANA
Mansiche Stadium
AVENIDA MANUEL VERA
9 DE OCTUBRE
Buses for Chan Chan, Huaca Esmeralda & Huanchaco
AVENIDA ESPAÑA
ZEPITA
Cinema
AVENIDA MIRAFLORES
AMAZONAS
Cruz del Sur Buses
Ormeño Buses
SAN MARTIN
Zoological Collection
Casa Bracamonte
JIRÓN INDEPENDENCIA
Casa de Los Leones
Iglesia Santa Clara
CALLE ESTETE
Huanchaco Buses
ALFONSO UGARTE
PLAZA MAYOR
Catedral
JIRÓN GAMARRA
JUNIN
PLAZUELA EL RECREO
JIRÓN PIZARRO
Casa Urquiaga
Iglesia de la Merced
Palacio Iturregui
La Casa de la Emancipación
COLON
BOLOGNESI
ALMAGRO
Casa Orbegoso
BOLIVAR
Monasterio El Carmen
AV PERU
AVENIDA TUPAC AMARU
JIRÓN ORBEGOSO
Central Market
AYACUCHO
Museo de Arqueología y Anthropología
CALLE MIGUEL GRAU
AVENIDA ESPAÑA
Mercado Mayorista
COSTA RICA
AVENIDA MOCHE
HUAYNA CAPAC
AVENIDA LOS INCAS
CAHUIDE
0
200
metres
7

APRA

With a restless past, Trujillo continued to be a centre of popular rebellion, declaring its independence from Spain in the Plaza de Armas in 1820, long before the Liberators arrived. The enigmatic leader of the **APRA** – American Popular Revolutionary Alliance (see p.497) – Haya de la Torre, was born here in 1895, and ran for president in the elections of 1931. The dictator, Sánchez Cerro, however, counted the votes (unfairly, some believe), and declared himself the winner. APRA was outlawed and Haya de la Torre imprisoned, provoking Trujillo's middle classes to stage an uprising. Over one thousand people died, many of them APRA supporters, who were taken out to the fields of Chan Chan by the truckload and shot. Even now, the 1932 massacre resonates among the people of Trujillo, particularly the old APRA members and the army, and you can still see each neighbourhood declaring its allegiance, in graffiti, to one side or the other.

APRA failed to attain political power in Peru for another 54 years, when Alan García was president for the first time; but it was the revolutionary military government in 1969 that truly unshackled this region from the tight grip of a few **sugar barons**, who owned the enormous haciendas in the Chicama Valley. The haciendas were then divided up among the worker co-operatives – the Casa Grande, a showcase example, is now one of the most profitable and well-organized agricultural ventures in Peru.

Orientation

The heart of Trujillo comprises some twenty blocks of colonial-style architecture all focused around a wide main plaza, **Plaza Mayor** or Plaza de Armas, which is in turn encircled by the Avenida España. Radiating from here, the buildings get steadily more modern and less attractive. The main streets of Pizarro and Independencia originate at the plaza; the only other streets you really need to know are San Martín and Bolívar, parallel to Pizarro and Independencia, and Gamarra, the main commercial street lined with shops, hotels and restaurants. The other big avenue, older and more attractive, is **Jirón Pizarro**, where much of the city's nightlife is centred and which has been pedestrianized from block 8 to the pleasant **Plazuela El Recreo**.

Plaza Mayor

Trujillo's **Plaza Mayor** (also known as the Plaza de Armas) is packed with sharp-witted shoeshine boys around the central statue – the *Heroes of the Wars of Independence*, a Baroque, marble work created by German Edmundo Muller.

The two colonial mansions that front it have both been tastefully restored: **Casa Bracamonte**, Jr Independencia 441, is closed to visitors but has some interesting cast-ironwork around its patio windows, while the Banco de la Nación-owned **Casa Urquiaga** (Mon–Fri 9am–3pm, Sat 10am–1pm; free, with 30min guided tours often available), Jr Pizarro 446 (also known as Casa Calonge), is said to be the house where Bolívar stayed when visiting Trujillo; it's also home to some first-class Rococo-style furniture and a fine collection of ancient ceramics.

La Catedral

Plaza Mayor • Daily 7–11.45am & 4–7pm **Museum** Mon–Fri 9am–1pm & 4–7pm, Sat 9am–1pm • S/4

Plaza Mayor is home to the **Catedral**, built in the mid-seventeenth century, then rebuilt the following century after earthquake damage. Known locally as the Basílica Menor, it's plain by Peruvian standards but houses some colourful Baroque sculptures and a handful of paintings by the Quiteña school (a deeply religious style of painting that originated in eighteenth-century Quito). Inside the cathedral, the **Museo de Catedral** exhibits a range of mainly eighteenth- and nineteenth-century religious paintings and sculptures.

Iglesia de La Merced

Jr Pizarro 550 • Daily 8am–noon & 4–8pm • Free

Just off the main plaza, the **Iglesia de La Merced**, first built in 1536, destroyed by a major earthquake in 1619, then rebuilt in 1634, is worth a look for its unique, priceless Rococo **organ**, plus its attractive gardens. The facade is fairly simple, a combination of Baroque upper section with Neoclassical entrance, painted subtly in white and earthenware orange.

Casa Orbegoso

Jr Orbegoso 553 • Daily 9.30am–8pm • Free

Between Plaza Major and the Central Market stands the most impressive of Trujillo's colonial houses – the **Casa Orbegoso**. This old mansion was the home of **Luís José Orbegoso**, former president of Peru, and houses displays of period furniture, glass and silverware amid very refined decor. Born into one of Trujillo's wealthiest founding families, Orbegoso fought for independence and became president of the republic in 1833 with the support of the liberal faction. However, he proved to be the most ineffective of all Peruvian leaders, resented for his aristocratic bearing by the *mestizo* generals, and from 1833 to 1839, although still officially president, he lost control of the country – first in civil war, then to the Bolivian army, and finally to a combined rebel and Chilean force. Today, even his family home has been invaded – although it's still in perfect condition and maintains the outstanding colonial elegance, there are temporary art exhibition spaces, and the main rooms around the courtyard have been converted into offices.

Mercado Central and Mercado Mayorista

Cnr of Ayacucho and Gamarra • Mon–Sat 7am–5pm

Trujillo's main market, the **Mercado Central** (known locally as the Mercado de los Brujos: the Witches' Market) is only two blocks east of the Plaza Mayor. As well as selling most essentials, such as juices, food and clothing, it has an interesting line in **herbal stalls** and healing or magical items, not to mention unionized shoe-cleaners. There's a second, much busier market, the **Mercado Mayorista**, further out, on Avenida Costa Rica in the southeast corner of town.

Museo de Arqueología y Antropología

Jr Junín 682 • Mon 9.30am–2pm, Tues–Fri 9.15am–1pm & 3–7pm, Sat & Sun 9.30am–4pm • $1.50, including optional 30min guided tour in Spanish • ☎ 044 474850

From the Central Market, head east along Ayacucho until you reach the corner of Junín, where you'll find the University's **Museo de Arqueología y Antropología**, which specializes in ceramics, early metallurgy, textiles and feather work. It is located in Casa Risco, a colonial mansion donated by the Peruvian government to the University of Trujillo in 1995. The whole place is laid out in chronological order, from 10,000 BC to the arrival of the Spanish in 1532.

La Casa de la Emancipación

Jr Pizarro 610 • Mon–Sat 9.15am–12.30pm & 4–6.30pm • Free

East of the main plaza, on the corner of jirones Pizarro and Gamarra, stands an impressive mansion, **La Casa de la Emancipación.** The building was remodelled in the mid-nineteenth century by the priest Pedro Madalengoitia (the reason it's also sometimes known as the Casa Madalengoitia), and is now head office of the Banco Continental. The main courtyard and entrance demonstrate a symmetrical and austere design, while the wide gallery has some impressive marble flooring. Inside are a couple of interesting, late eighteenth-century murals depicting peasant life, and paintings or historical photographs are usually exhibited in at least one of its rooms.

Palacio Iturregui

Jr Pizarro 688 • Daily 11am–6pm • S/5

Two blocks east of the Plaza Mayor is the **Palacio Iturregui**, a striking mid-nineteenth-century mansion. Built by the army general Don Juan Manuel de Iturregui y Aguilarte, the house is used today by the city's Central Club, which allow visitors to look round some of the rooms. The highlight of the building is its pseudo-classical courtyard, encircled by superb galleries, with tall columns and an open roof, which provides a wonderful view of the blue desert sky. The courtyard can be seen at any time of the day, by just popping your head inside.

7

Plazuela El Recreo

Eastern end of Jirón Pizarro

Five blocks from the Plaza Mayor, there's a small, attractive square known as the **Plazuela El Recreo** where, under the shade of some vast 130-year-old ficus trees, a number of **bars** and food stalls act like a magnet for young couples in the evenings. This little plaza was, and still is, an *estanque de agua* – a water distribution point – built during colonial days, but tapping into even more ancient irrigation works.

Monasterio El Carmen

C Colón and C Bolívar • Mon–Sat 9am–1pm • S/4 • ☎ 044 241823

A couple of minutes' walk south from Plazuela El Recreo stands the most stunning of the city's religious buildings, the **Monasterio El Carmen**, considered by many to be the most superb religious building in the north of Peru. Built in 1759 but damaged by an earthquake in the same year, its two brick towers were then rebuilt using bamboo for safety in case they toppled again. The church was also built above ground level to save it from El Niño's periodic flooding. Inside you can see the single domed nave, with exquisite altars and a fine gold-leaf pulpit. The processional and recreational cloisters, both boasting fine vaulted arches and painted wooden columns, give access to the **Pinacoteca** (picture gallery), where you can see Flemish works including *Last Supper* (1625) by Otto van Veen, one of Rubens' teachers. There are also some interesting figures carved from *huamanga* stone and a room showing oil paintings.

Casa de los Leones

Jirón Independencia 628 • Mon–Fri 9.15am–12.20pm & 3–6pm • Free

Jirón Independencia runs northeast from the Plaza Mayor and has a couple of minor attractions. Just one block from the plaza stands the **Casa de los Leones**, a colonial mansion also known as the Casa Ganoza Chopitea, which is larger and more labyrinthine than it looks from the outside. The building also holds exhibitions of photos, art, culture, crafts and wildlife, mostly of local historical or environmental interest.

Iglesia Santa Clara

Corner of Junín • Sun only 8am–6pm • Free

Along Jirón Independencia, you'll find the **Iglesia Santa Clara**, which contains fine religious paintings and examples of Baroque architecture. If you go in, be sure to check inside its chapel to see the altar covered with gold leaf and the pulpit with high-relief carvings.

FIESTAS IN TRUJILLO

Trujillo's main **fiestas** turn the town into even more of a relaxed playground than it is normally, with the **marinera** dance featuring prominently in most celebrations. This regional dance originated in Trujillo and is accompanied by a combination of Andalucian, African and Aboriginal music played on the *cajón* (rhythm box) and guitar. Energetic and very sexual – this traditional dance represents the seduction of an elegant, upper-class woman by a male servant – the *marinera* involves dancers holding handkerchiefs above their heads and skillfully prancing around each other. You'll see it performed in *peñas* all over the country but rarely with the same spirit and conviction as here in Trujillo. The last week in January, sometimes running into February (check with the tourist information office in Trujillo, for any particular year), is the main **Festival de la Marinera**. During this time there's a National Marinera Competition – el Concurso Nacional de Marinera – taking place in the city over several weeks, with dance academies from all over Peru.

The main **religious fiestas** are in October and December, with October 17 seeing the procession of El Señor de los Milagros, and the first two weeks of December being devoted to the patron saint of Huanchaco – another good excuse for wild parties in this beach resort. February, as everywhere, is **Carnival** time, with even more *marinera* dancing evenings taking place throughout Trujillo.

7

Museo Casinelli

Nicolás de Pierola 601 • Daily 9.30am–1pm & 3–7pm • S/7

The most curious museum in Trujillo is set in the middle of the road, in the basement of the Mobil petrol station on the Ovalo Victor Raul, just north of the large Mansiche Stadium. **Museo Casinelli** is simply stuffed with pottery and artefacts spanning thousands of years, collected from local *huaqueros*. The Salinar, Viru, Mochica, Chimu, Nasca, Huari, Recuay and Inca cultures are all represented, with highlights including **Mochica pots** with graphic images of daily life, people, animals and anthropomorphic deities. Señor Casinelli sometimes shows his visitors around personally and will point out his exquisite range of **Chimu silver artefacts**, including a tiny set of panpipes.

ARRIVAL AND DEPARTURE — TRUJILLO

BY PLANE

Aeropuerto Carlos Martínez de Pinillos (T 044 464013; daily 7am–9pm) is about 10km from Trujillo, near Huanchaco. Airlines include: LAN (Diego de Almagro 490; T 044 221469; Mon–Fri 9am–7pm & Sat 9am–1pm) and StarPerú (Independencia 463; T 044 226948). Taxis into the city will cost around S/15–20, or you can get a bus, which leaves every 20min (approx 6am–7pm) daily from the roundabout just outside the airport gates (S/1.50).

Destinations Chiclayo (daily; 45min); Lima (daily; 1hr 40min); Piura (daily; 1hr).

BY BUS

Most bus companies have terminals close to the centre of town near the Mansiche Stadium, on avenidas Daniel Carrion or España to the southwest, or east of it along avenidas America Norte or Ejercito. On the southern edge of town, between Ovalo Grau and Av La Marina, many bus companies drop off and pick up passengers en route to and from the south. You need to check with the bus company when buying tickets whether it's best to pick up the bus at the depot or at the terminal south of town.

Bus companies Cruz del Sur, Amazonas 437 (T 044 261801), and Ormeño, Av Ejercito 233 (T 044 259782) serve the coastal destinations and also Cajamarca. Others include: Alto Chicama, José Sabogal 305, Urbino Palermo (T 044 203659), for Chicama; Emtrafesa, Av Tupac Amaru 185 (T 044 471521), for Chiclayo; Linea, Av America Sur 2857 (T 044 297000) for Cajamarca and Huaraz; Trans Horna, Av Vallejo 1390 (T 044 210725), for Huamachuco; Tepsa, Diego de Almagro 849 (T 044 205017), for the north and south coasts; Transportes Guadalupe, Av Mansiche 331 (T 044 246019), or Tarapoto Tours, Av Nicolás de Pierola 1239 (T 044 470318), for Tarapoto, Yurimaguas and Juanjui; Turismo Chimbote, Jr Nicaragua 194–198 (T 044 245546), for Chimbote, Casma, Huaraz and Caraz.

Destinations Cajamarca (several daily; 6–8hr); Chiclayo (12 daily; 3hr); Lima (12 daily; 7–9hr); Piura, via Chiclayo (8 daily; 6hr).

BY COLECTIVO

Colectivos connecting with towns to the north mostly leave from and end up on Avenida España. If you're arriving by day it's fine to walk to the city centre, though at night it's best to take a taxi (S/5–8).

INFORMATION AND TOURS

Tourist information i-Peru office at Jr Diego de Almagro 420 (Mon–Sat 8am–7pm, Sun 8am–2pm; 044 294561, iperutrujillo@promperu.gob.pe) on the Plaza Mayor. The Tourist Police is at POLTUR, Jr Independencia 630 (Mon–Fri 8am–7pm; 044 291705). The official Camara Regional de Turismo (044 203718; Mon–Fri 9am–1pm & 4–8pm, Sat 9am–1pm) is next door to the Tourist Police at Independencia 628.

Tour operators and guides Most companies offer 3hr tours to Chan Chan and Huanchaco from around S/20–25 per person (including the site museum, Huaca Arco Iris and Huaca Esmeralda), and to huacas del Sol and Luna from S/25–30. For Chicama sites, expect to pay S/50 plus. Recommended operators include: America Tours, Jr Pizarro 476 (044 235182); Clara Brava's Tours at *Casa de Clara* (see below); Guía Tours, Independencia 580 (044 234856); and Peru Routes, Av San Martín 455, Office 5 (044 250000, peruroutes.com).

GETTING AROUND

7

By colectivo Colectivos are abundant for journeys in and around the city (flat rates around S/1.50); going north towards Huanchaco and Chan Chan, the best places to catch colectivos are beside the stalls near the Mansiche Stadium (see p.359). Going south, towards the Huaca de la Luna and the Huaca del Sol, colectivos can be picked up at the big service station at the junction where the Panamerican Highway heads towards Moche and Chimbote (see p.346).

By taxi Taxis cost less than S/6 for rides within Trujillo and can be hailed anywhere, but if you need to call one, Taxi Seguro (044 253473) is best.

By car Car rental is available at Jr Ayacucho 414, Oficina 11 (T/F 044 234985).

ACCOMMODATION

The majority of Trujillo's most interesting hotels are within a few blocks of the central Plaza Mayor: most of them are to the south, but a number of reasonable ones are along Jirón Pizarro, Independencia and San Martín. However, many people prefer to stay out of the city centre, at the nearby beach resort of Huanchaco (see p.365).

CENTRAL TRUJILLO

Hostal Colonial Jr Independencia 610 044 260261, hostalcolonial.com.pe. An attractive, centrally located place with some English-speaking staff members. Rooms are fine but for guaranteed peace and quiet get a room at the back; all have TVs, plus there's a patio, small library and cafetería. S/120

Hotel Americano Jr Pizarro 764 044 241361. Plenty of character but a bit shabby; the rooms, like everything else in this grand old hotel, are spacious but not spotless, and only some come with private bath. It's nevertheless a favourite with budget travellers, not least for the friendly service and great prices. S/35

★ **Hotel Continental** Jr Gamarra 663 044 241607, hotelcontinentaltrujillo.com. Plain but centrally located and popular with Peruvian business types. Rooms are clean with private bath, TV and reliable hot water. Breakfast is included. S/140

Hotel Libertador Jr Independencia 485 044 232741, or for reservations 01 518 6500, libertador.com.pe. This place is particularly grand, with excellent service and a superb restaurant renowned for its criolla dishes. The large, plush rooms have all modern conveniences. S/350

Hotel San Martín San Martín 743–749 044 252311. Lots of decent rooms in a large, rather tired-looking concrete building. Good service, and all rooms have private bath and TV. Often busy with conference goers. S/90

Pensión Grau C Miguel Grau 631 044 231022. Good central location, but can be busy and a bit noisy; rooms are nevertheless clean if very basic with little more than a bed. Only some rooms with private bath. S/30

Peregrino Hotel Av Independencia 978 044 203989. While primarily a place that specializes in events and weddings, both the service and the rooms are of quite a high standard, but not cheap. There's a good bar plus restaurant and internet access available. S/120

Pullman Hotel Jr Pizarro 879 044 223589, pullmanhoteltrujillo.com.pe One of the city centre's nicest hotels, the *Pullman* is cool and plush with solar water heating, good restaurant and bar plus all modern conveniences. S/100

Residencial Vanini Larco 237 044 200878, enriqueva@hotmail.com. A little outside the downtown area, but a very good value, family-run hostel. There's a choice of private bath, while the cheapest rooms are actually small rooms on the roof terrace. S/40

FURTHER AFIELD

★ **Casa de Clara** Cahuide 495, Santa María, Trujillo 044 299997 243347, casadeclara.xanga.com. Located near Huayna Capac 542, this is very nice bargain accommodation, with private bath, breakfast and internet available. The staff are very well informed about local places of interest, and will help organize reliable and affordable tours in the region. S/30

Hostería Recreo C Estete 647 044 220055, hotelrecreo.com. Away from the centre but still within easy walking distance of the Plaza Mayor, this is a very comfortable hotel with friendly service and its own restaurant. S/165

Hostería El Sol Los Brillantes 224, off block 12 of Av Mansiche in Santa Ines 044 231933, hosteriaelsol-trujillo.blogspot.com. Built in the shape of a Bavarian castle, *El Sol* is slightly out of the way, with dark but comfortable rooms, all with private bath. S/30

Hotel Primavera Av Nicolás de Pierola 872, Primavera district 044 231915. Located close to the Panamerican Highway, this concrete building lacks style but offers large, clean rooms with a/c comfort and private bath. There's also a small swimming pool, and the service is good. S/40

EATING AND DRINKING

Some of the liveliest restaurants and bars are along jirones Independencia, Pizarro, Bolívar and Ayacucho, to the east of Plaza Mayor. A speciality of the city is tasty, reasonably priced **seafood**, particularly ceviche, which is probably best appreciated on the beach at the nearby resorts of Buenos Aires or Huanchaco (see p.365). Goat and beans is a local speciality, too; if you get the chance try *cabrito con frijoles*, a truly traditional dish of goat marinated in *chicha* beer and vinegar and served with beans cooked with onions and garlic. There's a good supermarket for general provisions at Junín 372.

7

Asturias Jr Pizarro 739. Delicious fruit juices plus alcoholic drinks, lunchtime meals and snacks at this busy coffee bar. Mon–Sat 7am–7pm.

Café Amaretto Jr Gamarra 368. Great coffee and cakes, breakfast and snacks; smallish space but fast and friendly service. Daily 8am–9pm.

Jugería San Agustín Jr Pizarro 691 044 259591. An excellent juice bar, very popular with Trujillo's youth, and offering an enormous choice of tropical drinks, beers, sandwiches and snacks in a friendly environment. Will take phone orders and deliver to your door. Daily 8am–7pm.

El Mochica Bolívar 462. A superb, smart restaurant serving exquisite criolla dishes and local cuisine (if you're in luck they'll have *cabrito con frijoles*); sometimes local bands play here live. Daily 11am–9pm.

Oveido Café Jr Pizarro 737. Stuck between *Restaurant Romano* (see below) and *Restaurant/Bar Heladería Demarco*, this is a quality café that dishes out (pricey) breakfasts. Service is excellent and the clientele mostly Trujillo's well-to-do or businessmen. Mon–Sat 7.30am–7pm.

Restaurant/Bar Heladería Demarco Jr Pizarro 725 044 234251. A posh, Italian-style ice cream parlour-cum-bar and restaurant serving international and Peruvian dishes. Mon–Sat 11am–8pm.

Restaurant Romano Jr Pizarro 747 044 252251. Small, friendly restaurant with internet access specializing in good Peruvian and Italian dishes. Decent-sized portions, and exceptional value with its *económico familia* or *turístico* set menus, although it gets very crowded in the evenings, and reservations are advised. Daily noon–10pm.

Restaurant Vegetariano El Sol Jr Pizarro 660. Open for lunches and evening meals, *El Sol* serves simple, reasonably priced vegetarian food (the best in town), mostly based on rice, alfalfa, soya, maize and fresh vegetables. It's particularly popular with locals at lunchtime. Mon–Sat 9am–6pm.

Sergio's Cevichería Independencia 925. A small and surprisingly cheap seafood restaurant that serves very fresh food, cooked fish and squid as well as ceviche; excellent value for lunch. Tues–Sun 10.30am–5pm.

NIGHTLIFE AND ENTERTAINMENT

Trujillo has a fairly active nightlife, with several *peñas* and nightclubs celebrating local culture, dance and music, as well as Latin rhythms and the latest global popular sounds. The city is also well known worldwide for its January *marinera* dance fiesta (see box, p.359) and occasional international dance jamborees.

★ **La Cañana** San Martín 791 044 232503. A highly popular restaurant-*peña* (as well as a discotheque) that does excellent meals; it has a great atmosphere and good, danceable shows that generally start after 10pm and carry on into the early hours. Best Wed–Sat. Mon–Sat 8pm–2am.

Disco Pub Las Tinajas Pizarro 389 corner with Almagro. Very central and lively at weekends; plays rock and pop mostly but with a mix of Latin and Peruvian pop, too. Tues–Sat 8pm–3am.

Mecano Bar Jr Gamarra 574 044 201652. A great bar with mainly Latin, rock, pop, merengue, bachata and salsa music that keeps the crowd dancing all night. Best on Thursday nights when it's a little quieter. Thurs–Sat from 9pm.

Peña El Estribo San Martín 809 044 204053. A large and very popular dance and music venue with great weekend shows of coastal folklore and *música negra*. Thurs–Sun from 9pm.

DIRECTORY

Consulates UK, Av Jesús de Nazareth 312 ⓣ044 94971 1275 (Mon–Fri 9am–5pm).

Health Hospital Belén de Trujillo, Bolívar 350 ⓣ044 245281 (24 hr); Hospital Regional Docente de Trujillo, Av Manseriche 795 ⓣ044 231581 (24hr).

Immigration Av Larco 1220, Urb. Los Pinos, for visa renewals.

Internet There are several internet cafés along Pizarro between the Plaza Mayor and Gamarra. A 24hr service is available at Interc@ll, Zepita 728.

Language school Trujillo Language School ⓦperu-language-school.com. Based on the main square, they specialize in teaching Spanish for visitors to Peru.

Laundry Luxor, Jr Grau 637, and Lavandería El Carmen, Jr Pizarro 759.

Money and exchange Banco de Credito, Jr Gamarra 562; Banco Wiese, Jr Pizarro 314; Banco Latino, Jr Gamarra 574; Banco de la Nación, Jr Almagro 297. The Casa de Cambios Martelli, Jr Bolívar 665, give the best rates in town for dollars cash, or try the *cambistas* (though be very careful, especially after dark) on the corner of Jr Pizarro and Gamarra, or on the Plaza Mayor. A safer bet are the numerous casas de cambio on block 6 of Pizarro.

Post office Serpost (Mon–Sat 8am–7pm), Jr Independencia 286, a block and a half southwest of the plaza.

Shopping The following specialize in local crafts: Trama Perú, Jr Pizarro 754 (Mon–Sat 10am–10pm, Sun 10am–2pm); Liga de Artesanos, Jr Colón 423 (Mon–Sat 9am–noon & 3–7pm); and the Asociación de Pequeños Industriales y Artesanatos de Trujillo, located at Av España, block 18 (Mon–Sat 9am–8pm, Sun 9am–4pm).

Around Trujillo

The closest of the coastal resorts to Trujillo is the beachfront barrio of **Buenos Aires**, a five-kilometre stretch of sand southwest of Trujillo that's very popular with locals and constantly pounded by surf. Like other coastal resorts, its seafood restaurants are an attraction, though it doesn't have as much style or life as **Huanchaco**. For those in search of sand and seafood out of the city, the villages of **Moche** and **Las Delicias** are within easy reach.

Moche and Las Delicias

From Trujillo (20min), catch the direct bus (hourly) marked "Delicias" from the corner of avenidas Moche and Los Incas

After crossing the Río Moche's estuary, 2km south of Trujillo, you'll come across the settlements of **MOCHE** and **LAS DELICIAS**, both within an easy bus ride of the Huaca del Sol and Huaca de la Luna (see below). Moche is a small village some 4km south of the city, slightly inland from the ocean, blessed with several **restaurants** serving freshly prepared seafood. Close by, Las Delicias, 5km south of Trujillo, has a beautiful, long **beach** and a handful of reasonable restaurants. Las Delicias's main claim to fame is that the *curandero* El Tuno once lived at Lambayeque 18, right on the beach. By arrangement with his family there you can sometimes witness the fascinating diagnostic healing sessions that are now practised by El Tuno's apprentices, often involving rubbing a live guinea pig over the patient's body, then splitting the animal open and removing its innards for inspection while the heart is still pumping. It is believed to reveal the patient's problems – one of which may be nausea after viewing the event – after which he or she is sent away with a mix of healing herbs.

Huacas del Moche

Colectivos (S/1.50) leave from the south side of Ovalo Grau (every 10–15min) which is at the southern entrance of the Panamerican Highway into Trujillo city. Some go all the way to the Huaca de la Luna, but many prefer to drop you off on the road, within sight, but still a ten- to fifteen-minute walk away

Five kilometres south of Trujillo, in a barren desert landscape beside the Río Moche, two temples really bring ancient Peru to life. Collectively known as the **Huacas del Moche**, these sites make a fine day's outing and shouldn't be missed even if you only have a passing interest in archeology or the ancient civilizations of Peru. The stunning **Huaca del Sol** (Temple of the Sun) is the largest adobe structure in the Americas, and easily the most impressive of the many pyramids on the Peruvian coast. Its twin, the **Huaca de la Luna** (Temple of the Moon), is smaller, but more complex and brilliantly frescoed.

Brief history

After more than 18 years of excavation, the Huaca de la Luna is now believed to have been developed in two main phases: platform I and three plazas (know collectively as the old temple) around 600AD; platform III by around 900AD.

The complex is believed to have been the capital, or most important ceremonial and urban centre, for the Moche culture, at its peak between 400 and 600 AD. Although very much associated with the Moche culture and nation (100–600 AD), however, there is evidence of earlier occupation at these sites, dating back two thousand years to

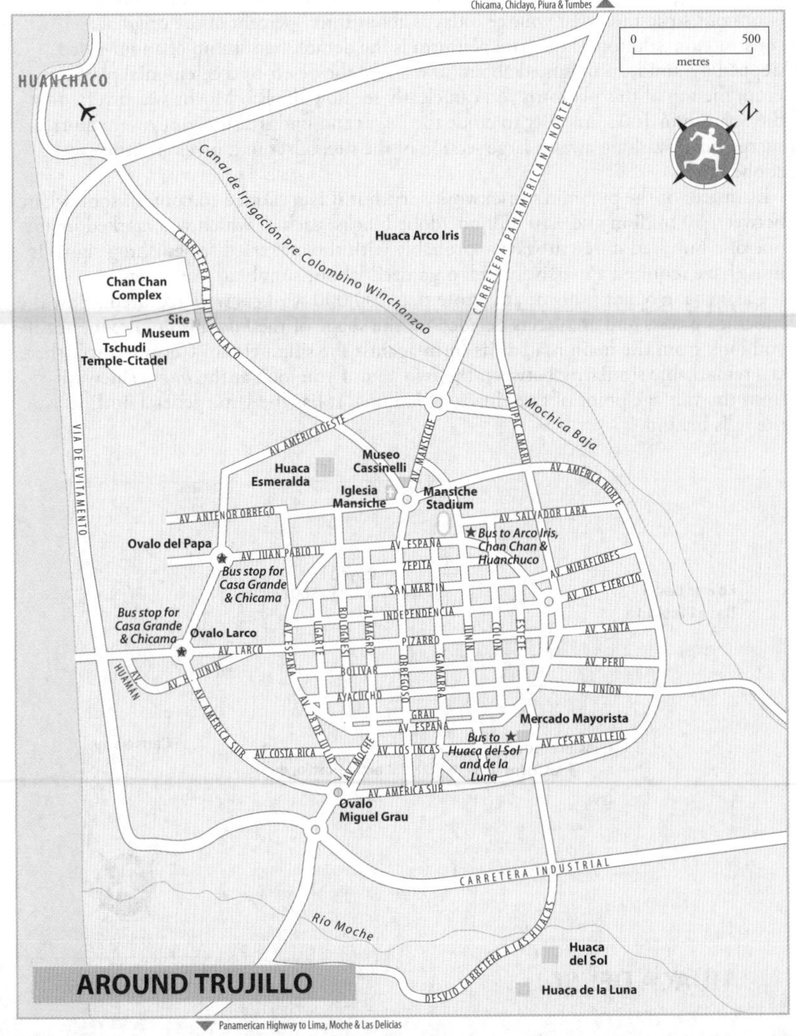

the Salinar and Gallinazo cultures, indicated by constructions underlying the *huacas*. The area continued to be held in high regard after the collapse of the Moche culture, with signs of Wari, Chimu and Inca offerings here demonstrating a continued importance. The latest theory suggests that these *huacas* were mainly ceremonial centres, separated physically by a large graveyard and an associated urban settlement. Finds in this intermediate zone have so far revealed some fine structures, plus pottery workshops and storehouses.

Huaca del Sol

Closed at the time of writing

7

The **Huaca del Sol** is presently off limits to visitors, but it's an amazing sight from the grounds below or even in the distance from the Huaca de la Luna, which is very much open to the public. Built by the Mochica around 500 AD, and extremely weathered, its pyramid edges still slope at a sharp 77 degrees to the horizon. Although still an enormous structure, what you see today is about thirty percent of the original construction. On top of the base platform is the demolished stump of a four-sided, stepped pyramid, surmounted about 50m above the desert by a ceremonial platform. From the top of this platform you can clearly see how the Río Moche was diverted by the Spanish in 1602, in order to erode the *huaca* and find treasure. They were quite successful at washing away a large section of the site, but found precious little except adobe bricks.

Estimates of the pyramid's brickwork vary, but it is reckoned to contain somewhere between 50 million and 140 million adobe blocks, each of which was marked in any one of a hundred different ways – probably with the maker's distinguishing signs. It must have required a massively well organized labour supply to put together – Calancha, a Spanish historian, wrote that 200,000 workers were required. How the Mochica priests and architects decided on the shape of the *huaca* is unknown, but if you look from the main road at its form against the silhouette of Cerro Blanco, there is a remarkable similarity between the two, and if you look at the *huaca* sideways from the vantage point of the Huaca de la Luna, it has the same general outline as the hills behind.

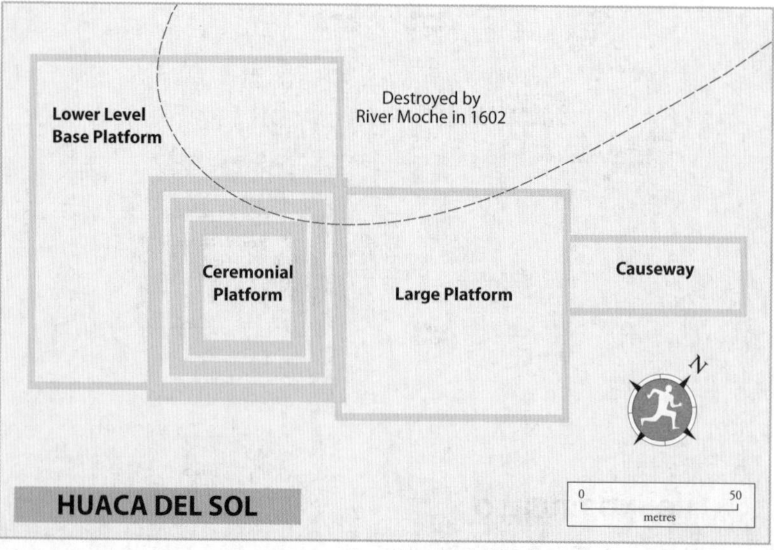

Huaca de la Luna

Daily 9am–4pm • $3.50, includes a 45min guided tour • T 044 291894

Clinging to the bottom of Cerro Blanco, just 500m from Huaca del Sol (see opposite), is **Huaca de la Luna**, a ritual and ceremonial centre that was built around the same time as its neighbour. What you see today is only part of an older complex of interior rooms built over six centuries that included a maze of interconnected patios, some covered and lavishly adorned with painted friezes. The **friezes** are still the most striking feature of the site, rhomboid in shape and dominated by an anthropomorphic face surrounded by symbols representing nature spirits, such as the ray fish (symbol of water), pelicans (symbol of air) and serpent (symbol of earth). Its feline fangs and boggle-eyes are stylizations dating back to the early Chavín cult and it's similar to an image known to the Moche as **Ai-Apaec**, master of life and death. The god that kept the human world in order, he has been frequently linked with human sacrifice, and in 1995, archeologists found 42 skeletons of sacrificial victims here. Sediment found in their graves indicates that these sacrifices took place during an El Niño weather phenomenon, something that would have threatened the economic and political stability of the nation. Ceramics dug up from the vast graveyard that extends between the two *huacas* and around the base of Cerro Blanco suggest that this might have also been a site for a cult of the dead. Cerro Blanco itself may have been considered a link to deity.

Behind the *huaca* are some frescoed rooms, discovered in the early 1990s, displaying multicoloured murals (mostly reds and blues). The most famous of these paintings has been called *The Rebellion of the Artefacts* because, as is fairly common on Mochica ceramics, all sorts of objects are depicted attacking human beings, getting their revenge, or rebelling. Over 6000 square metres of polychrome reliefs have been uncovered.

Museo Huacas de Moche

Close to the Huaca de la Luna • Daily 9am–4pm • S/3 • W huacasdemoche.pe

The new **Museo Huacas de Moche**, built in a pyramid style to look like Moche architecture, displays some fine ceramics – check out the warrior duck and the blind shaman – as well as a feline cat-cloak of gold and feathers. The museum combines exhibition rooms with an investigations centre, communal space and a theatre.

Huanchaco

Although no longer exactly a tropical paradise, **HUANCHACO**, 12km west of Trujillo, is still a beautiful and relatively peaceful resort, though there is a thriving scene geared toward surfers and young travellers. Until the 1970s, Huanchaco was a tiny fishing village, quiet and little known to tourists. Today it consists of half-finished adobe houses, concrete hotels and streets slowly spreading back towards Trujillo, and makes an excellent base for visiting many of the sites around the region, in particular the nearby ruins of **Chan Chan**. While development keeps on going strong, its intrinsic fishing-village appeal hasn't entirely diminished.

A good time to visit Huanchaco is during its June **fiesta** week, at the end of the month, when a large *totora* raft comes ashore accompanied by a smaller flotilla of *caballitos* (see p.366). But the best weather here is arguably between December and March. The town is always lively, with people on the beach, some surfers, fishermen and a few travellers hanging around the restaurants.

Iglesia Soroco

A 15min walk uphill from the seafront • Mon–Sat 8am–6pm

The town's only historical sight is the old, square **Iglesia Soroco**, perched high on the coastal cliffs. The second church in Peru to be built by the Spanish, it sprang up in 1540 on top of a pre-Inca temple dedicated to the idol of the Golden Fish, and was rebuilt after its destruction during the earthquakes of 1619–70.

The waterfront

Jetty S/1; boat trips S/10

Huanchaco hasn't entirely lost its intrinsic fishing-village appeal. There is a long jetty, where you can jostle with fishermen for the best **fishing** positions; just at the entry to the pier is a small artesanía **market**. Stacked along the beach, the rows of *caballitos del mar* – the ancient seagoing rafts designed by the Mochica – are still used by locals today. They are constructed out of four cigar-shaped bundles of *totora* reeds, tied together into an arc tapering at each end. The fishermen kneel or sit at the stern and paddle, using the surf for occasional bursts of motion. The local boat-builders here are the last who know the craft of making *caballitos* to the original design of the Mochica. Some of the fishermen offer ten- to fifteen-minute trips on the back of their *caballitos*.

ARRIVAL AND DEPARTURE — HUANCHACO

Be aware that due to the quite rapid growth of the pueblo, street and block numbers are in a state of transition, so it's quite easy to get confused by Huanchaco addresses.

By bus It's easy enough to take the frequent orange and yellow microbus from block 13 of Avenida España (on the far side of the road from the town centre), by the corner with Independencia, or pick up a bus or one of the white colectivos marked Empresa Caballitos de Tortora (S/2) from the Mobil or Shell petrol stations at Ovalo Victor Raul. On the way out to Huanchaco the bus travels the whole length of Calle Estete (returning via Colón); to get back into the city there's normally a line of buses picking up passengers from the waterfront.

By colectivo Colectivos for Huanchaco from Trujillo follow the same route; and start/stop in same locations as buses; but on the way back, it's best to check with the driver that the colectivos are going all the way back into Trujillo, because some of them turn left at the Ovalo Victor Raul and head towards Esperanza instead.

By taxi From Trujillo, taxis are around S/20–25.

ACCOMMODATION

The town is well served by the kind of accommodation range you'd normally expect at a popular beach resort. Many families also put people up in private rooms; these can be identified by the signs reading "Alquila Cuarto" on houses, particularly in the summer (Dec–Feb).

★ **Hospedaje Familiar La Casa Suiza** Los Pinos 308 044 461285, casasuiza.com. One of the best, friendliest budget places in Huanchaco, with a range of different rooms (some with bath), a rooftop terrace and a book exchange. There are laundry and internet facilities, they rent out body boards and surfboards, and the staff speak English. **S/75**

Hospedaje Nirvana Av Ricardo Palma 425 044 462502, nirvanahospedaje.com. Located next door to the *Big Ben* restaurant and just half a block from the sea, rooms here are small but comfortable enough, all with cable TV and hot water. Internet access and café bar available. **S/65**

Hospedaje Sunset Ribera 600 044 461863. Where many of the visiting surfers hang out; there's no hot water, but great views of the sea and hammocks on the balcony, plus a small restaurant. **S/50**

Hostal Ancla La Ribera 198 044 461030. Overlooking the beach, this well-established lodging has an interesting collection of old photos and memorabilia in its bar and cafetería. Rooms at the front can be noisy, though. **S/55**

Hostal Caballito de Totora La Ribera 348 044 461265, hotelcaballitodetotora.com.pe. Right on the seafront, this place offers rooms with ocean views plus cheaper, less panoramic options. There's also a small pool, garden, cafetería and sun terraces; some members of staff speak English. Price includes breakfast, and rates are cheaper in low season. **S/160**

Hostal Los Esteros Larco 618 044 461300, losesteroshuanchaco.com. An attractive option with sea views, where the tidy rooms all come with private bath and hot water. **S/100**

Hostal Solange Los Ficus 258 044 461410. This is a small, very comfortable, easy-going and friendly family-run hostel situated just two blocks from the beach, where you can do your own cooking if you wish, though there is a small café. Breakfast is extra. **S/20**

★ **Hotel Bracamonte** Los Olivos 160 044 461162, hotelbracamonte.com.pe. A lovely complex of different-sized chalets with solar-heated showers. Very welcoming for children, it has a pool, a games room, internet access, laundry facilities, a good restaurant and terraces with views over the ocean. You can camp in the grounds for from $5 per person or $15 including tent rental. **S/150**

Huanchaco Hostal Jr Victor Larco 185 044 461272, huanchacohostal.com. Good-value, comfortable hostel with pleasant gardens, a cafetería and a small pool. The service is excellent and most rooms have TV and private bath. There's also a dorm, pool room and parking. One of the entrances faces the sea, and the other opens onto the tiny but attractive Plaza de Armas. **S/120**

EATING, DRINKING AND NIGHTLIFE

There are seafood restaurants all along the front in Huanchaco, one or two of them with verandas extending to the beach. Not surprisingly, seafood is the local speciality, including excellent crab, and you can often see women and children up to their waists in the sea collecting shellfish. The fishermen can also usually return around 3–4pm on their *caballitos*, but the catches these days aren't huge. Anyone looking for nightlife should check out the small bars on La Ribera, just a few blocks south from the pier.

Chocolate Av Rivera 752 ⓣ044 462420. A small but very friendly café, they serve great snacks and breakfasts, good coffee, and the staff are a mine of local information; sometimes some B&B rooms available. Daily 7.30am–6pm.

Club Colonial Grau 272 ⓣ044 461015. A beautifully restored colonial house adorned with paintings, old photos and fine stained-glass work. The food is sumptuous, with an extensive menu of traditional dishes, but it's not cheap. The garden is the residence of some penguins and a couple of rare Tumbes crocodiles. Daily 11am–10.30pm.

Huanchaco Beach Restaurant Malecón Larco 602 ⓣ044 461484. Very tasty fish dishes, and excellent views across the ocean and up to the clifftop Iglesia Soroco. Daily 11am–7pm.

Restaurant Big Ben Av Larco 836. Serves probably the best and certainly the most expensive seafood dishes in Huanchaco, including excellent crab and sea urchin if you're lucky. Daily 11am–5pm.

Restaurant El Caribe Atahualpa 100. Just around the corner from the seafront to the north of the pier, this restaurant has great ceviche and is very popular with locals. Mon–Sat 10am–6pm.

Restaurant Don Pepe Malecón Larco 502. Among the best-positioned seafront restaurants, with a balcony overlooking the *caballitos del mar* and the fishermen mending their nets; it's not cheap, but the food, especially their selection of seafood dishes, is quite good. Daily 11am–6.30pm.

Restaurant Marimar Av Victor Larco 525. Just north of the pier, this is another good spot for seafood and great views of the pier and ocean; try the *sudado de pescado* or the *langostino al ajo* for full-flavour dishes. Daily 11am–7pm.

7

The Chan Chan complex

Daily 9am–4pm • Taxis from Trujillo are cheap and reliable; a half-day with one taxi can cost as little as S/75

The ruined city of **CHAN CHAN** stretches across a large sector of the Moche Valley, beginning almost as soon as you leave Trujillo northwards on the Huanchaco road, and ending just a couple of kilometres from Huanchaco. A huge complex even today, its main focus and museum site is the **Tschudi** sector (see p.369), which needs only a little imagination to raise its weathered mud walls to their original grandeur. Not far from Tschudi, **Huaca La Esmeralda** displays different features, being a ceremonial or ritual pyramid rather than a citadel. The third sector, the **Huaca Arco Iris** (or **El Dragón**), on the other side of this enormous ruined city, was similar in function to Esmeralda but has a unique design which has been restored with relish, if not historical perfection.

CHAN CHAN ESSENTIALS

Facilities There's a small interpretive centre at the Tschudi complex entrance, as well as toilets, a cafetería and souvenirs, plus a life-size model of a Chimu warrior in full regalia.

Guided tours Easily arranged (around S/10 for the museum); guides for the Tschudi complex (S/20 an hour) usually hang around at the Tschudi entrance, and, if you want, will also take you round the *huacas*.

Tickets Entrance to the three archeological sites of the wider Chan Chan complex and the Museo de Sitio is included on the same ticket (S/11), called the Talon Visitante, which is valid for only two days (but you can try asking for an extension if you need more time). Although you can visit each sector separately, there are only two ticket offices, at the entrance to the Museo de Sitio, and at the entrance to the Tschudi temple-citadel.

Brief history

Chan Chan was the capital city of the **Chimu Empire**, an urban civilization that appeared on the Peruvian coast around 1100 AD. Chimu cities and towns throughout the region stretched from Tumbes in the north to as far south as Paramonga. Their cities were always elaborately planned, with large, flat-topped buildings for the nobility and intricately decorated adobe pyramids serving as temples. Recognized as fine

Trujillo & Huanchaco

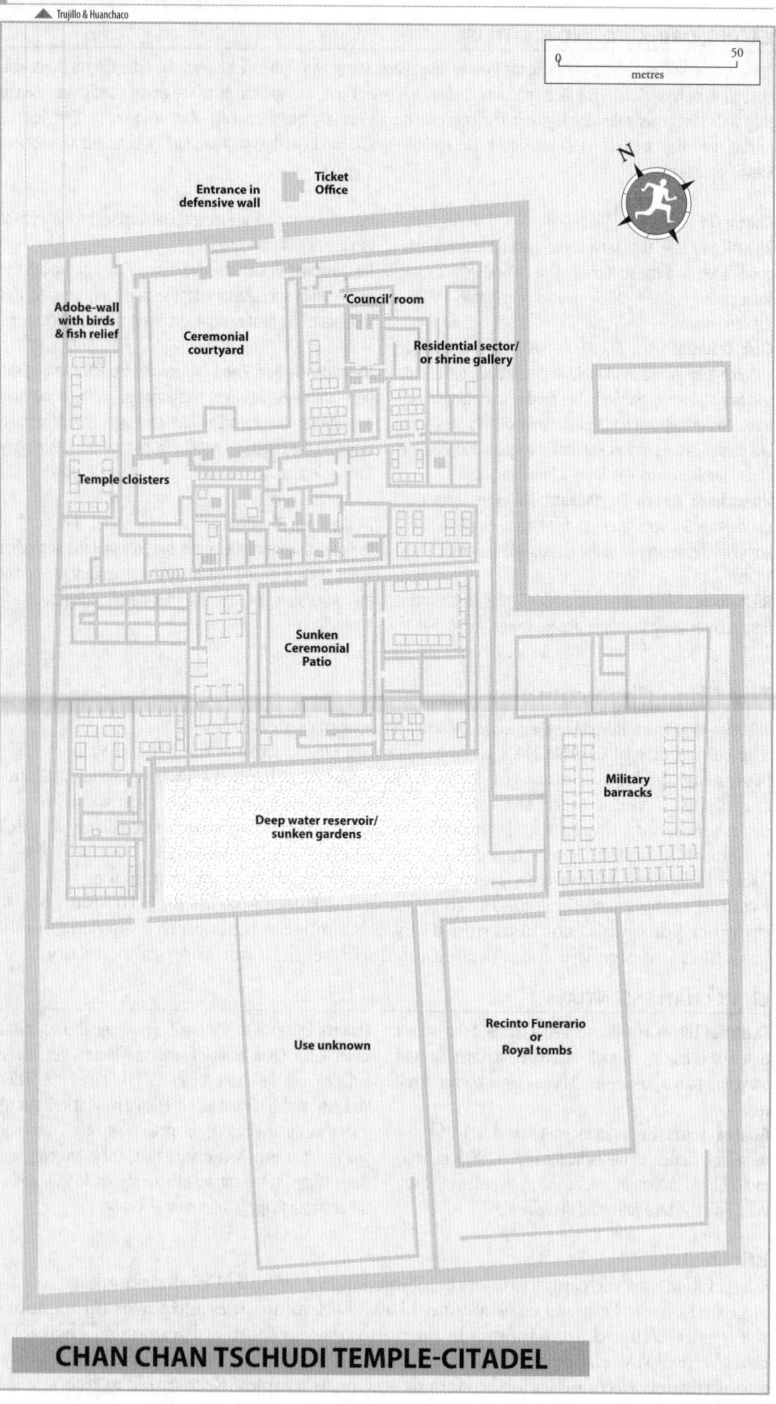

CHAN CHAN TSCHUDI TEMPLE-CITADEL

goldsmiths by the Incas, the Chimu panelled their temples with gold and cultivated palace gardens where even the plants and animals were made from precious metals. The city walls were brightly painted, and the style of architecture and relief decoration is sometimes ascribed to the fact that the Mochica (who predated the Chimu in this valley by several centuries) migrated from Central America into this area, bringing with them knowledge and ideas from a more advanced civilization, like the Maya.

Birth of a city

According to one legend, the city was founded by **Taycanamu**, who arrived by boat with his royal fleet; after establishing an empire, he left his son, Si-Um, in command and then disappeared over the western horizon. Another legend has it that Chan Chan's construction was inspired by an original creator-deity of the same name, a dragon who made the sun and the moon and whose earthly manifestation is a rainbow. Whatever the impulse behind Chan Chan, it remains one of the world's marvels and, in its heyday, was one of the largest pre-Columbian cities in the Americas.

The Chimu inherited ideas and techniques from a host of previous cultures along the coast, including the Mochica, and, most importantly, adapted the techniques from many generations of trial and error in irrigating the Moche Valley. In the desert, access to a regular water supply was critical in the development of an urban civilization like that of Chan Chan, whose very existence depended on extracting water not only from the Río Moche but also, via a complicated system of canals and aqueducts, from the neighbouring Chicama Valley.

By 1450, when the Chimu Empire stretched from the Río Zarumilla in the north to the Río Chancay in the south and covered around 40,000 square kilometres, Chan Chan was the centre of a chain of provincial capitals. These were gradually incorporated into the Inca Empire between 1460 and 1480.

Death of a city

The events leading to the city's demise are better documented than those of its birth: in the 1470s **Tupac Yupanqui** led the Inca armies down from the mountains in the east and cut off the aqueducts supplying Chan Chan with its vital water supply. After lengthy discussions, the Chimu council managed to persuade its leader against going out to fight the Incas, knowing full well that resistance would be met with brutality, and surrender with peaceful takeover. The Chimu were quickly deprived of their chieftains, many of them taken to Cusco (along with the highly skilled metallurgists) to be indoctrinated into Inca ways. Sixty years later when the first Spaniards rode through Chan Chan they found only a ghost town full of dust and legend.

Museo di Sitio

A few hundred metres before the entrance to the Tschudi temple-citadel • Take the orange-and-yellow Huanchaco-bound microbus from Avenida España in Trujillo and make sure you get off well before the junction where the road divides (one way leads to Huanchaco and the other to the airport); the museum is easy to spot, but it's best to play it safe by asking the driver to drop you at the Museo de Sitio when you jump on board

The **Museo de Sitio** is a good place to start your visit to Chan Chan. It offers an interesting eight-minute multimedia show in Spanish, and uses scale replica models, ceramics and other archeological finds to reconstruct life in the hot but irrigated desert before modern Trujillo was built.

The Tschudi temple-citadel

Take the orange-and-yellow Huanchaco-bound microbus from Avenida España in Trujillo and get off at the concrete Tschudi/Chan Chan signpost about 2km beyond the outer suburbs. From here, follow the track to the left of the road for 10–15min until you see the ticket office (on the left), next to the high defensive walls around the inner temple-citadel

The best place to get an idea of what Chan Chan must have been like is the **Tschudi temple-citadel**, even though it's now stuck out in the desert among high ruined walls, dusty streets, gateways, decrepit dwellings and open graves.

Following the marked route around the citadel through a maze of corridors, chambers, and amazingly large plazas, you will begin to form your own picture of this highly organized, ancient civilization. For example, in the courtyard just past the entrance gateway, some twenty-five seats are set into niches at regular intervals along the walls. By sitting in one niche and whispering to someone in another, you can witness an unusual acoustic effect: how this simply designed **council room** amplifies all sounds, making the niches seem like they're connected by adobe intercoms.

Fishing-net motifs are repeated throughout the citadel's design, particularly in the **sunken ceremonial patio** (an antechamber before the entrance to the *audiencias*, or little temples area), and show how important the sea was to the Chimu people, both mythologically and as a major resource. Dedicated to divinities and designed to hold offerings and tributes, the **audiencias** lead to the **main ceremonial courtyard** and also to the corridor of fish and bird designs.

The westernmost open point of the site is the burial area, known as the **Recinto Funerario**, and was the most sacred part of Tschudi, where the tomb of El Señor Chimo and his wives was located. Beyond the citadel extend acres of untended ruins that are dangerous for foreigners – some, certainly, have been robbed after wandering off alone.

Huaca La Esmeralda

Take the orange-and-yellow Huanchaco-bound microbus from Trujillo and get off at the colonial church of San Salvador de Mansiche, at blocks 14 and 15 of Avenida Mansiche, then follow the path along the right-hand side of the church for three blocks (through the modern barrio of Mansiche), until you reach the huaca

One of the most beautiful, and possibly the most venerated of Chimu temples, **Huaca La Esmeralda** (The Emerald Temple) lies in ruins a couple of kilometres before Tschudi, just off the main Trujillo to Huanchaco road. Unlike Tschudi, the *huaca*, or sacred temple, is on the very edge of town, stuck between the outer suburbs and the first cornfields. It was built in the twelfth or early thirteenth century – at about the same time as the Tschudi temple-citadel – and is one of the most important of the *huacas* scattered around Trujillo. Uncovered only in 1923, its adobe walls and decorations had already been severely damaged in the freak rains of 1925 and 1983. Now you can only just make out what must have been an impressive multicoloured **facade**. All the relief work on the adobe walls is original, and shows marine-related motifs including friezes of fishing nets containing fish, waves, a flying pelican, a sea otter, and frequent repetitive patterns of geometrical arabesques.

The *huaca* has an unusually complex structure, with two main platforms, a number of surrounding walls and several sloping pathways giving access to each section. From the top platform, which was obviously a place of worship and possibly the cover to a royal tomb, you can see west across the valley to the graveyards of Chan Chan, out to sea, over the cultivated fields around the site and into the primitive brick factory next door. Only some shells and *chaquiras* (stone and coral necklaces) were found when the *huaca* was officially dug out some years ago, long after centuries of *huaqueros* (treasure hunters) had exhausted its more valuable goods. These grave robbers nearly always precede the archeologists. In fact, archeologists are often drawn to the sites they eventually excavate by the trail of treasures that flow from the grave robbers through dealers' hands into the market in Lima and beyond.

Huaca Arco Iris

Take the regular Comité 19 red-and-blue microbus from the centre of Trujillo. Get off the bus at the blue concrete sign on the side of the main road; the huaca is to the west of the highway, surrounded by a tall wall and set back 100m or so, but largely hidden

The **Huaca Arco Iris** (Rainbow Temple) is the most fully restored ruin of the Chan Chan complex and one of the oldest sectors at 1100 years old, located just to the left of the Panamerican Highway, about 4km north of Trujillo in the middle of the urban district of La Esperanza. The *huaca* consists of two tiers: the **first tier** is made up of fourteen rectangular chambers, possibly used for storing corn and precious metals for ritual purposes, while a path slopes up to the **second tier**, a flat-topped platform used as a ceremonial area where sacrifices were held and the gods apparently spoke. From here, there is a wide view over the valley, towards the ocean, Trujillo, and the city of Chan Chan.

Several interpretations have been made of the **central motif**, which is repeated throughout the *huaca* – some consider it a dragon, some a centipede and some a rainbow. Most of the main **temple inner walls** have been restored, and they are covered with the re-created central motif. The outer walls are decorated in the same way, with identical friezes cut into the adobe, in a design that looks like a multi-legged serpent arching over two lizard-type beings.

Chicama Valley

The Chicama Valley, north of the Río Moche and about 35km from Trujillo, is full of **huacas** and ancient sites, the most famous being the **Huaca El Brujo**. The valley is also home to the remains of fortresses and an irrigation system that dates back nearly 6000 years when the Río Chicama was once connected to the fields of Chan Chan by a vast system of canals and aqueducts over 90km long. Today, however, the region looks like a single enormous sugar-cane field, although in fact it's divided among a number of large sugar-producing co-operatives, originally family-owned **haciendas** that were redistributed during the military government's agrarian reforms in 1969. Even more laidback, the isolated seaside village of **Puerto Chicama**, 65km north of Trujillo, offers excellent surfing opportunities.

Huaca El Brujo complex

50km north of Trujillo • Mon–Sat 9am–4pm; museum Mon–Sat 9am–4pm, entry included in site ticket • S/10 • From Trujillo, take a bus to Chocope from the Chicago bus terminal on Avenida America Sur, then pick up a colectivo from Chocope. For El Brujo, you need a colectivo to Magdalena de Cao, about 5km from the site and the nearest place that local colectivos actually pass through. Cars run every 30min to Magdalena (S/1.50) from Chocope

The **Huaca El Brujo**, whose name means "Temple of the Wizard", is a Mochica-built complex of associated adobe temple ruins incorporating the Huaca Cao Viejo to the south, plus the huacas Cortada and Prieto, slightly to the north. Most of the recent discoveries have been made in Huaca Cao Viejo, some 60km from Trujillo. In recent years a female mummy was excavated at the Huaca Cao Viejo; clearly a powerful shamanic leader, her face, hands and legs were tattooed with spiders and snakes. This is now on display in a small onsite **museum** (Museo Cao).

To get to the *huaca*, you have to pass through the nearby village of **Magdalena de Cao** – the ideal place to sample *chicha del año*, an extra-strong form of **maize beer** brewed in the valley.

SUGAR AND THE TRUJILLO REGION

Sugar cane was first brought to Peru from India by the Spaniards in the seventeenth century and quickly took root as the region's main crop. Until early in the twentieth century, the haciendas were connected with Trujillo by a British-operated rail line, whose lumbering old wagons used to rumble down to Trujillo full of molasses and return loaded with crude oil; they were, incidentally, never washed between loads. Although the region still produces nearly half of Peru's sugar, it has diversified as well. These days, Chicama is also well-known for the fine Cascas semi-seco **wine** it produces. The haciendas are also renowned for the breeding of *caballos de paso* – **horses** reared to compete in dressage and trotting contests – a long-established sport that's still popular with Peruvian high society.

The huacas

Three main ceremonial *huacas* make up the Huaca El Brujo site: Cortada, Cao Viejo and Prieta. Some of the walls on these *huacas* are adorned with figures in high relief and painted murals, discovered here as recently as 1990. On the top, third layer of the **Huaca Cortada**, there's a painted character with startled eyes, a sacrificial knife in one hand and a decapitated head in the other (decapitation apparently being common practice among the Mochica). The **Huaca Cao Viejo** is a larger pyramid, topped by a ceremonial platform some 30m high, and clearly of great significance to the Mochica ceremonial world and religious hierarchy.

Quite literally a heap of rubbish, **La Huaca Prieta** sits at the edge of the ocean, ten minutes' walk west of the main Huaca El Brujo site. It may be a dump, but it is one that has been accumulating rubbish for some 6500 years, and is crowded with evidence and clues about the evolution of culture and human activity on this coast. This small, dark hill is about 12m high and owes its discolouration to thousands of years of decomposing organic remains. On the top, there are signs of subterranean dwellings, long since excavated by archeologists Larco Hoyle and Junius Bird.

Puerto Chicama

PUERTO CHICAMA (also known as **Puerto Malabrigo**), 13km northwest of Paijan and 74km north of Trujillo, is a small fishing village that once served as a port for the sugar haciendas (see box, p.371), but is now much better known as a **surfers**' centre, offering some of the best surfing waves on Peru's Pacific coast. The place has a real lack of facilities, though, and there are seldom any boards to hire locally – which won't affect serious surfers, who generally bring their own. The surf here is said to have "the longest left-hand breaking surf in the world", often reaching heights of over 2m and running for over 2km at times. Novice surfers may want to check out the gentler waters of Máncora (see p.414).

GETTING AROUND — THE CHICAMA VALLEY

While there are buses and colectivos serving the Chicama Valley, it is a good day-trip from Trujillo and many people prefer to go on a guided tour (see p.360) or to hire a taxi with driver and guide for the day ($25–35).

By bus From Trujillo, catch one of the buses marked "Puerto Chicama", "Paijan" or "Chicama", which leave every 30min from opposite Museo Casinelli (see p.359).

By colectivo Plentiful, although they have no fixed timetables; it's quite easy to get to Puerto Chicama and even from one village to another.

By taxi You can usually find taxis in Chicama or Chocope who'll take you to the sites for around S/20 an hour. It might cost more per hour from Trujillo.

ACCOMMODATION

Chicama Surf Hotel and Spa Chicama ⊕044 576206, ⓦchicamasurf.com. A beach resort with 18 rooms and a pool; relatively upmarket for Chicama. It has wi-fi and a decent restaurant. Some surfing teaching assistance offered. S/160

Hostal Los Delfines Chicama ⊕044 576103. Good sea views and friendly service; relatively comfortable for a beach hostel with jacuzzis in some rooms and a swimming pool. S/100

Hostal El Hombre Chicama ⊕044 576077. Managed by local surfer "El Hombre", this was the first surfer's lodgings in Chicama; it is still basic but quite comfortable and the service good. Great sea views from some rooms. Singles S/40

Cajamarca

A grand Andean town, **CAJAMARCA** is second only to Cusco in the grace of its architecture and the soft drama of its mountain scenery. The city's stone-based architecture reflects the cold nights up here – charming as it all is, with elaborate stone

CLOCKWISE FROM TOP LEFT DETAIL OF WALL IN TÚCUME MUSEO, VALLEY OF THE PYRAMIDS (P.407); DANCING AT A LOCAL FESTIVAL (P.359); TRADITIONAL ARCHITECTURE IN TRUJILLO (P.354) >

filigree mansions, churches and old Baroque facades. Almost Mediterranean in appearance, Cajamarca, at 2720m above sea level, squats below high mountains in a neat valley. The climate is surprisingly pleasant, with daytime temperatures ranging from 6 to 23°C (43–75°F); the rainy season hits between the months of December and March.

Proud and historic Cajamarca has intrinsic interest as the place where Pizarro captured and ransomed the Inca Emperor, Atahualpa, for gold, before killing him anyway. Gold has been an issue here since Pizarro arrived. Today the operations of massive **gold mines** in the region are generating protest; there are grave concerns in the area that the gold industry is polluting the land and groundwater.

There are two main routes into this mountain valley from Trujillo, each exciting and spectacular. The speediest way is to head up the coast via **Pacasmayo**, then turn inland along a paved road which follows the wide Río Jequetepeque Valley in about eight hours. A slower route (usually two days) is by bus along the old road, currently in a poor state of repair, from Trujillo through **Huamachuco** and **Cajabamba**.

Brief history

As far back as 1000 BC the fertile Cajamarca Basin was occupied by well-organized tribal cultures, the earliest sign of the Chavín culture's influence on the northern mountains. The existing sites, scattered all about this region, are evidence of advanced civilizations capable of producing elaborate stone constructions without hard metal

PIZARRO IN CAJAMARCA

Atahualpa, the last Inca lord, was in Cajamarca in late 1532, relaxing at the hot springs, when news came of **Pizarro** dragging his 62 horsemen and 106 foot soldiers high up into the mountains. Atahualpa's spies and runners kept him well-informed of the Spaniards' movements, and he could quite easily have destroyed the small band of weary aliens in one of the rocky passes to the west of Cajamarca. Instead he waited patiently until Friday, November 15, when a dishevelled group entered the silent streets of the deserted Inca city.

For the first time, Pizarro saw Atahualpa's camp, with its sea of cotton tents, and an army of men and long spears. Estimates varied, but there were between 30,000 and 80,000 Inca warriors, outnumbering the Spaniards by at least two hundred to one.

Pizarro was planning his coup along the same lines that had been so successful for Cortés in Mexico: he would capture Atahualpa and use him to control the realm. The plaza in Cajamarca was perfect, as it was surrounded by long, low buildings on three sides, so Pizarro stationed his men there. Leaving most of his troops outside on the plain, Atahualpa entered the plaza with some five thousand men, unarmed except for small battle-axes, slings and pebble pouches. He was carried into the city by eighty noblemen in an ornate carriage – its wooden poles covered in silver, the floor and walls with gold and brilliantly coloured parrot feathers. The emperor himself was poised on a small stool, richly dressed with a crown placed upon his head and a thick string of magnificent emeralds around his aristocratic neck. Understandably bewildered to see no bearded men and not one horse in sight he shouted, "Where are they?"

A moment later, the Dominican friar, **Vicente de Valverde**, came out into the plaza; with a great lack of reverence to a man he considered a heathen in league with the devil, he invited Atahualpa to dine at Pizarro's table. The Lord Inca declined the offer, saying that he wouldn't move until the Spanish returned all the objects they had already stolen from his people. The friar handed Atahualpa his Bible and began preaching unintelligibly to the Inca. After examining this strange object Atahualpa threw it angrily to the floor. As Vicente de Valverde moved away, screaming – "Come out, Christians! Come at these enemy dogs who reject the things of God." – two cannons signalled the start of what quickly became a **massacre**. The Spanish horsemen hacked their way through flesh to overturn the litter and capture the emperor. Knocking down a two-metre-thick wall, many of the Inca troops fled onto the surrounding plain with the cavalry at their heels. Spanish foot soldiers set about killing those left in the square with speed and ferocity. Not one Inca raised a weapon against the Spaniards. Atahualpa, apparently an experienced warrior-leader, had badly underestimated his opponents' crazy ambitions and technological superiority – steel swords, muskets, cannons and horsepower.

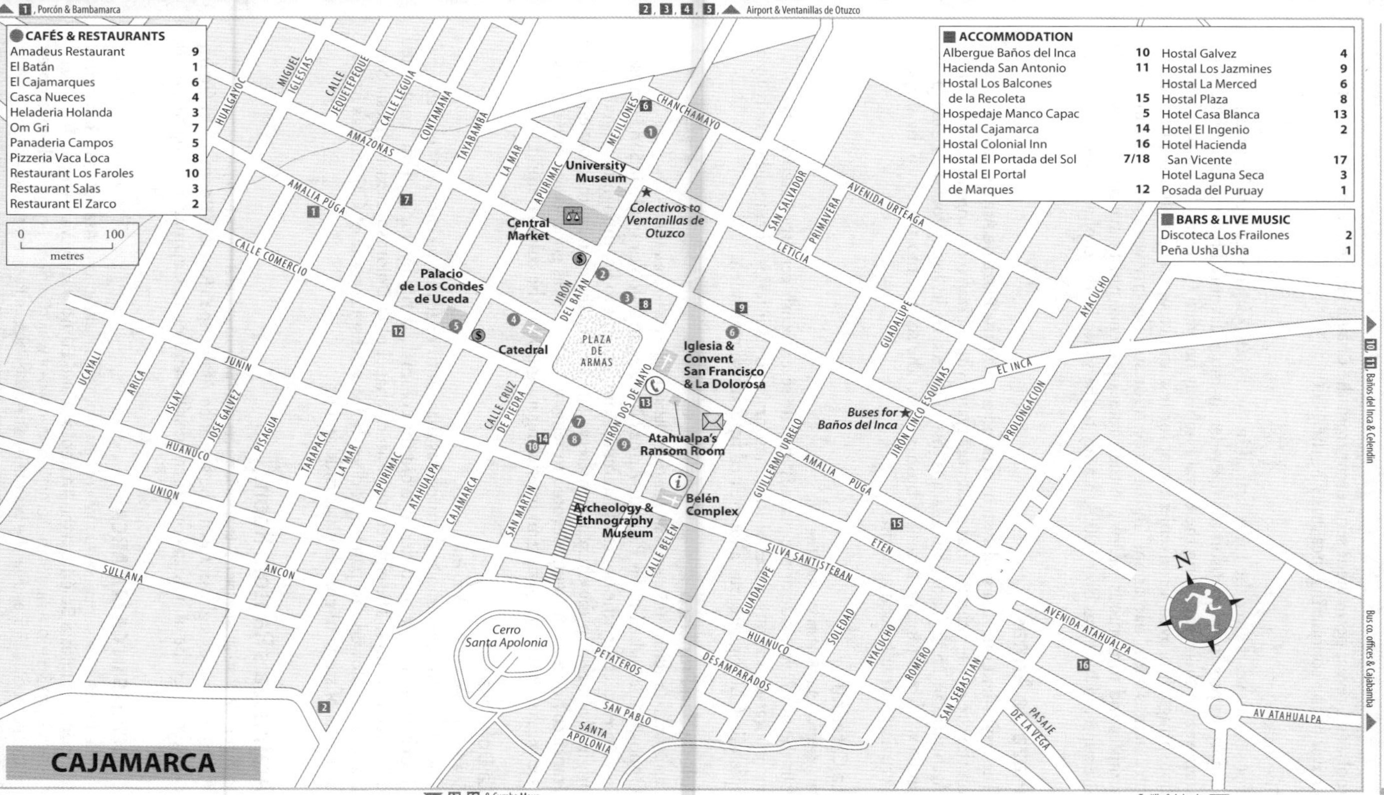
CAJAMARCA
CAFÉS & RESTAURANTS
Amadeus Restaurant 9
El Batán 1
El Cajamarques 6
Casca Nueces 4
Heladeria Holanda 3
Om Gri 7
Panaderia Campos 5
Pizzeria Vaca Loca 8
Restaurant Los Faroles 10
Restaurant Salas 3
Restaurant El Zarco 2
ACCOMMODATION
Albergue Baños del Inca 10
Hacienda San Antonio 11
Hostal Los Balcones de la Recoleta 15
Hospedaje Manco Capac 5
Hostal Cajamarca 14
Hostal Colonial Inn 16
Hostal El Portada del Sol 7/18
Hostal El Portal de Marques 12
Hostal Galvez 4
Hostal Los Jazmines 9
Hostal La Merced 6
Hostal Plaza 8
Hotel Casa Blanca 13
Hotel El Ingenio 2
Hotel Hacienda San Vicente 17
Hotel Laguna Seca 3
Posada del Puruay 1
BARS & LIVE MUSIC
Discoteca Los Frailones 2
Peña Usha Usha 1
0 100 metres
N
1, Porcón & Bambamarca
2, 3, 4, 5, Airport & Ventanillas de Otuzco
10, 11, Baños del Inca & Celendin
Bus co. offices & Cajabamba
Trujillo & Aylambo
17, 18 & Cumbe Mayo
University Museum
Colectivos to Ventanillas de Otuzco
Central Market
Catedral
Palacio de Los Condes de Uceda
Plaza de Armas
Iglesia & Convent San Francisco & La Dolorosa
Atahualpa's Ransom Room
Belén Complex
Archeology & Ethnography Museum
Buses for Baños del Inca
Cerro Santa Apolonia
Avenida Urteaga
Avenida Atahualpa
Av Atahualpa
Ayacucho
Prolongacion
El Inca
Jiron Cinco Esquinas
Guadalupe
Primavera
San Salvador
Leticia
Chanchamayo
Mejillones
Apurimac
La Mar
Tayabamba
Contamana
Calle Leguia
Amazonas
Calle Jequetepeque
Miguel Iglesias
Hualgayoc
Amalia Puga
Calle Comercio
Jirón del Batan
Calle Cruz de Piedra
Jirón Dos de Mayo
San Martin
Cajamarca
Atahualpa
Tarapaca
Pisagua
Jose Galvez
Junin
Islay
Arica
Ucayali
Huanuco
Union
Sullana
Ancon
Guillermo Urrelo
Eten
Silva Santisteban
Calle Belen
Desamparados
Petateros
San Pablo
Santa Apolonia
Soledad
Romero
San Sebastian
Pasaje de la Vega

7

tools, and reveal permanent settlement from the **Chavín** era right through until the arrival of the conquering **Inca** army in the 1460s.

The Incas

For seventy years after the Incas' arrival in the 1460s, Cajamarca developed into an important provincial garrison town, evidently much favoured by Inca emperors as a stopover on their way along the Royal Highway between Cusco and Quito. With its hot springs, it proved a convenient spot for rest and recuperation after the frequent Inca battles with "barbarians" in the eastern forests. The city was endowed with sun temples and sumptuous palaces, so their ruler's presence must have been felt even when the supreme Inca was over 1000km away to the south in the capital of his empire.

Plaza de Armas

The city is laid out in a grid system centred around the **Plaza de Armas**, which was built on the site of the original triangular courtyard where Pizarro captured the Inca leader Atahualpa in 1532. Today the plaza is distinguished by its lovely low trees, fine grass and a wealth of topiary: trimmed bushes adorn the square, most cut into the shapes of Peruvian animals, such as llamas.

La Catedral

Plaza de Armas • Daily 8–11am & 6–9pm • Free

On the northwest side of the plaza is the late seventeenth-century **Catedral**, its walls incorporating various pieces of Inca masonry, and its interior distinguished only by a splendid Churrigueresque altar created by Spanish craftsmen.

Iglesia San Francisco

Plaza de Armas • **Church** Mon–Fri 9am–noon & 4–6pm • Free • **Museum** Mon–Fri 9am–noon & 4–6pm • S/3

Opposite the cathedral on Plaza de Armas is the strange-looking **Iglesia San Francisco**, in whose sanctuary the bones of Atahualpa are thought to lie, though they were originally buried in the church's cemetery. Attached to the church, the **Convento de San Francisco** houses a **museum** devoted to religious art – not as good as the one in Cusco (see p.226), but still offering an interesting insight into the colonial mind.

La Dolorosa

Plaza de Armas • Mon–Fri 10am–5pm • Free

One of Cajamarca's unique features was that, until relatively recently, none of the churches had towers, in order to avoid the colonial tax rigidly imposed on "completed" religious buildings. The eighteenth-century chapel of **La Dolorosa**, next to Iglesia San Francisco, followed this pattern; it does, however, display some of Cajamarca's finest examples of stone filigree, both outside and in.

Atahualpa's Ransom Room

Amalia Puga 722 • Mon–Sat 9am–1pm & 3–6pm, Sun 9am–1pm, closed Wed • S/5 joint ticket (see box below)

The most famous sight in town, the so-called **Atahualpa's Ransom Room**, or El Cuarto del Rescate, is the only Inca construction still standing in Cajamarca. Lying just off the

TICKETS IN CAJAMARCA

One **ticket** allows entrance to three of Cajamarca's main attractions, **Atahualpa's Ransom Room**, the **Iglesia Belén** and the **Archeology and Ethnography Museum** (all Tues–Sat 9am–1pm & 3–6pm, Sun 9am–1pm) the latter two of which form part of the **Belén Complex**. The ticket costs S/5, and can be bought at either the Ransom Room or the complex.

Plaza de Armas, across the road from the Iglesia San Francisco, the Ransom Room can, however, be a little disappointing, especially if you've been waiting a long time, as it is simply a small rectangular room with Inca stonework in the backyard of a colonial building. It has long been claimed that this is the room which Atahualpa, as Pizarro's prisoner, promised to fill with gold in return for his freedom, but historians are still in disagreement about whether this was just Atahualpa's prison cell, rather than the actual Ransom Room. There is, however, a line drawn on the wall at the height to which it was supposed to be filled with treasure, and you can also see the stone on which Atahualpa is thought to have been executed. The room's bare Inca masonry is notably poorer than that which you find around Cusco, and the trapezoidal doorway is a post-Conquest construction – probably Spanish rather than native.

Mercado Central

In the streets around Apurimac, Amazonas, Arequipa and Leticia • Daily 6am–5pm

A block north of the Plaza de Armas, you'll find Cajamarca's **Mercado Central**. Because the town is the regional centre for a vast area, its street market is one of the largest and most intriguing in Peru – you can find almost anything here from slingshots, herbs and jungle medicines to exotic fruit and vegetables, as well as the usual cheap plastic imports. It is generally a busy, friendly place, but beware of **pickpockets**.

University Museum

Arequipa 269 • Mon–Fri 8am–2pm • S/2

North of the Central Market along Arequipa is the **University Museum** (note that entry is not included in the Cajamarca ticket mentioned in the box, opposite). As well as having a good range of informative tourism leaflets and brochures, it has fascinating collections of ceramics, textiles and other objects spanning some three thousand years of culture in the Cajamarca Basin; the museum also includes mummies, carved stones, drawings of the Cumbe Mayo petroglyphs and some erotic pots. Look out for the work of Andres Zevallos, whose representations of local people are reminiscent of Ribera and whose landscapes are in the style of Matisse.

The Belén Complex

Calle Belén • Mon–Fri 8.30am–noon & 4–6pm, Sat & Sun 8.30am–noon • S/5 joint ticket (see box opposite)

The **Belén Complex** of buildings known as the **Conjunto Monumental de Belén**, just southeast of the plaza, houses a variety of institutions, including two hospitals (in the lower part, the Hospital de Hombres has an exceptionally attractive stone-faced patio with fountains), a small medical museum (part of the university administration, the Instituto Nacional de Cultura) and the **Iglesia Belén**, whose lavish interior boasts a tall cupola replete with oversized angels. However, the most interesting part of the complex is the **Archeology and Ethnography Museum** (free, even without the joint tourist ticket). Located in what used to be the Hospital de Mujeres, over the road from the main complex, the museum displays ceramics and weavings from the region, as well as one or two objects that have been brought here from the jungle tribes to the east. Look out for the elaborate stone carvings on the archway at the entrance to the museum, which depict a mythic woman with four breasts, symbolizing fertility, and date back to when the building was a women's hospital.

ARRIVAL AND DEPARTURE — CAJAMARCA

BY PLANE

The airport (**T** 076 822523) is 3km out of town, on Avenida Arequipa. It is served by LAN from Lima (4 weekly; 1hr 20min), Jr Comercio 832 (**T** 076 367441; Mon–Fri 9am–7pm, Sat 9am–1pm), or LC Busre (daily flights to Lima), Jr Comercio 1024 (**T** 076 361098; Mon–Sat

8am–6pm). Buses leave from just outside the airport every twenty minutes or so for the market area, a couple of blocks below the Plaza de Armas in the city (S/1.50). Alternatively, a motorcycle taxi there costs less than S/3, or a taxi will be around S/5.

Destinations Lima (daily; 1–2hr).

BY BUS/COLECTIVO

Most people arrive in Cajamarca by bus, at one of the main bus company offices, many of which are on the third block of Avenida Atahualpa, a major arterial route running almost directly east out of the city.

Bus companies Cruz del Sur, Av Atahualpa 600 (076 361737), for coastal destinations like Trujillo (7–8hr) and Lima 12hr); Entrafesa, Av Atahualpa 315 (076 369663) for Trujillo; Movil, Atahualpa 405 (076 340873), for Leymebamba (8–10hr) and Chachapoyas (10–12hr); Transportes CABA, Atahualpa 299 (076 366665), for Celendin (3–4hr); and Rojas, Atahualpa 309 (076 340548), for Trujillo, Celendin and Cajabamba (4hr).

BY TAXI

Taxi Seguro, Av Independencia 373 (076 365103), are the best. A taxi straight to the Inca Baths (see p.382) from the airport costs about S/10.

BY CAR

Car rental Cajamarca Tours, Jr Dos de Mayo 323 (076 362813), and Promotora Turística, Manco Capac 1098, Baños del Inca (076 363149).

7

INFORMATION AND TOURS

Tourist information ITINCI office in the Belén Complex, on block 6 of Calle Belén (Mon–Fri 7.30am–1pm & 2.15–5.30pm; 076 822903). Alternatively, the University Museum, Arequipa 269 (Mon–Fri 8am–2pm), has some leaflets and maps, as do many of the tour companies (see below). Free tourist information is also sometimes available from the university office at Batán 289, next door to the museum (see p.377).

Tour and travel agents Catequil Tours, Jr Amalia Puga 689 (076 363958), offer the standard local and regional tours plus some adventure and even eco tour packages; Cajamarca Tours, Jr Dos de Mayo 323 (076 365674), is one of the better travel agencies in town for sorting out flights and buying air tickets; Cumbe Mayo Tours, Amalia Puga 635 (076 362938), is one of the best for city tours and tours to sites in the region.

ACCOMMODATION

Most of Cajamarca's accommodation is in the centre of the city, around the Plaza de Armas, although there are also some interesting options slightly out of town.

IN CAJAMARCA

★ **Hostal Los Balcones de la Recoleta** Amalia Puga 1050 /076 363302. A beautifully restored, late nineteenth-century building wrapped around a courtyard full of flowers. All rooms have private bath and some have period furniture. Good service too. S/90

Hostal Cajamarca Jr Dos de Mayo 311 076 362532. A lovely colonial building set around an attractive courtyard with an excellent restaurant *Los Faroles*. Rooms are comfortable and make for reasonable value. S/100

Hostal Colonial Inn Los Heroes 350 /076 313551. Halfway between the town centre and the bus offices, in an old, brightly painted building. Rooms are without or with bath, plus it has its own good Chinese restaurant. Singles S/30, doubles S/50

Hostal Los Jazmines Amazonas 775 076 361812, hospedajelosjazmines.com.pe. A comfortable hostel with good conveniences in a converted colonial house plus a courtyard with cafetería serving great snacks. Rooms have private bath. This place is associated with a charity that supports less-able children. Singles S/50, doubles S/80

Hostal La Merced Chanchamayo 140 076 362171. A small, friendly hostel which offers good value. Rooms are clean, with TV and private bath. While there's access to laundry facilities, towels, soap and toilet paper are not generally provided. S/70

Hostal Plaza Amalia Puga 669 076 362058. Situated in a once-lovely building on the Plaza de Armas, this is a rambling old place with creaky wooden floors. It's still good value, though, and rooms come with or without private bath. Some rooms have views across the plaza. S/75

Hostal El Portada del Sol Pisagua 731 076 363395 or 01 2254306, hostalportadadelsol.com. A charming colonial house with well-kept wooden floors, ceiling beams and an attractive covered patio where visitors can enjoy breakfast. All rooms have private bath, and there's also good internet access. They have an associated rural hacienda lodging of same name (see below). S/125

★ **Hostal El Portal de Marqués** C Comercio 644 076 368464 or 076 343339, portaldelmarques.com. An attractive colonial house on two floors with a large courtyard, quite grand and spacious restaurant, plus very clean and tidy rooms with carpets, private baths and TVs. Extras include a good restaurant, bar and internet access. S/160

Hotel Casa Blanca Jr Dos de Mayo 446 076 362141. A fine old mansion tastefully modernized to produce a comfortable hotel and a couple of shared patios; the floors, however, are still rickety, wooden and full of character, and there's hot water and private baths and TVs in every room. **S/120**

Hotel El Ingenio Av Via de Evitamiento 1611–1709 ⓣ076 368733, ⓦelingenio.com. A rather plush hotel located in a wonderful, converted old mansion with a patio, gardens, good food and stylish bar; its target market is mainly mine engineers, who likewise frequent the fine bar and restaurant. **S/135**

OUT OF TOWN

★ **Albergue Baños del Inca** Located behind the thermal bath complex ⓣ076 348385, ⓦctbinca.com.pe. This place has a number of chalets, all very comfortable and with their own built-in thermal bathrooms, TV, minibar, bedroom and living room. Many of the chalets afford stunning views of, and direct access to, the complex of atmospheric steaming baths. Dormitories are also available for more budget-minded travellers. Dorms **S/35**

Hacienda San Antonio Km 5 on the Baños del Inca road, then 1 or 2km down a signposted driveway ⓣ076 360905, ⓦfundosanantonio.com. An old hacienda with about 150 beds, its own chapel, dairy and very attractive gardens, close to the Río Chonta. There are open fireplaces and all rooms have private bath and are finely decorated. Breakfast and a ride on their *caballos de paso* (horses) are included. **S/160**

Hospedaje Manco Capac Manco Capac 712. A very basic, inexpensive hostel run by the local parish, with shared bathrooms and minimal amenities. Located right in front of the entrance to the thermal baths, this place is really aimed at poorer Peruvians who need access to the baths, but is also a good budget option for travellers. **S/35**

Hostal Galvez Manco Capac 552 ⓣ076 348396. Right beside the Baños del Inca, some 6km from the city centre, this comfortable hotel has thermally heated water pumped straight to your room. **S/150**

Hostal El Portada del Sol At Km6 on road from Cajamarca to Cumbemayo ⓣ076 363395 or ⓣ01 2254306, ⓦhostalportadadelsol.com. Based in 8 hectares of partly wooded land, by the village of Cajamarquino, this charming *albergue* has been lovingly built with mainly local materials in traditional hacienda style with patio and wooden balconies. All rooms have private bath, and there's also good internet access. **S/120**

Hotel Hacienda San Vicente 2km west of the city centre towards Cumbe Mayo ⓣ076 362644, ⓦhaciendasanvicentelodge.com. A luxuriously renovated hacienda with the full range of facilities. Room designs have been strongly influenced by Gaudí's works. **S/160**

Hotel Laguna Seca Manco Capac 10988 ⓣ076 584311, ⓦlagunaseca.com.pe. Very close to the Inca Baths, this is a good place to rest up; there is thermal spring water in the rooms and also private access to some of the hot springs, an outdoor pool and natural-steam Turkish baths. Service is very good. **S/390**

Posada del Puruay 5km north of the city ⓣ076 367928, ⓦposadapuruay.com.pe. A country mansion converted into a luxury hotel-museum. All rooms have colonial furniture as well as all the modern conveniences, but the place is especially notable for its ecological approach and has an organic garden. **S/360**

7

EATING AND DRINKING

You can eat very well in Cajamarca. There are some sophisticated restaurants specializing in the local, meat-based cuisine, but there are also lots of smaller speciality shops worth visiting to try out their pastries or fresh fruit ice creams.

Amadeus Restaurant Jr Dos de Mayo 930 ⓣ076 329815. A rather elegant restaurant just above the plaza serving pastas and pizzas as well as quality comida criolla and other dishes such as pasta, burgers and steak. Mon–Sat 11.30am–9pm.

El Batán Jr del Batán 369. Set in a converted colonial building, there's an art gallery on the first floor and other paintings adorn the dining room walls. The food's good, and includes local dishes that don't appear on the tourist menus; be sure to ask for *comida Cajamarqueña*. There's also live music on Fridays and Saturdays. Mon–Sat noon–11pm.

El Cajamarques Amazonas 770 ⓣ076 362128. An upmarket, traditional Cajamarca-cuisine restaurant decorated with colonial paintings, weapons and other artefacts. The cooking is excellent, and portions emphasize quality rather than quantity. Mon–Sat noon–10pm.

Casca Nueces Amalia Puga 554. Very popular with locals for its delicious *humitas* (sweet maize-meal pasties) and large slices of cream cake. Mon–Sat 8am–6pm.

Heladería Holanda Amalia Puga 657, on the plaza. There's a real artisan at work here preparing some excellent ice cream using local milk and fresh fruit. Try the unique coca flavour: it may even be good for the altitude. Daily 10am–8pm.

Om Gri San Martín 360. Not far from the plaza, this is an excellent spaghetti house serving a wide range of Italian dishes in a highly atmospheric ambience. Daily 11am–11pm.

Panadería Campos Comercio 661. Serves great pastries and cakes, as well as local cheeses and picture-postcards mostly taken by Sr Campos himself. Mon–Sat 7am–6pm.

Pizzeria Vaca Loca San Martín 330. If you can set aside any associations the name (Mad Cow) may bring, you'll enjoy the town's best pizzas at this busy spot. Daily 11.30am–9pm.

Restaurant Los Faroles Hostal Cajamarca, Jr Dos de Mayo 311. One of the best restaurants in town for criolla dishes, served in a quiet, plush atmosphere. If you like well-flavoured potatoes ask for the dish *caldo verde*, a potato soup made with local green herbs; otherwise, for a starter, you could try the *humitas*, made from maize meal. Mon–Sat 9am–7pm.

Restaurant Salas Jr Amalia Puga 637, Plaza de Armas. A small restaurant with an old-fashioned atmosphere and good service. The menu's similar to *El Zarco*'s (see below), if slightly more upmarket with better food, particularly the breakfasts – though the portions are smaller. Mon–Sat 8am–8pm.

Restaurant El Zarco Jr del Batán 170. One of the few local cafés to stand out in Cajamarca, *El Zarco* is always packed with locals. It plays a wide range of mostly Latin music and offers an enormous variety of tasty, large-portioned dishes, including excellent trout. It's by no means upmarket, even if a plethora of friendly red-coated waiters lend a refined, 1920s atmosphere. Mon–Sat 7.30am–8pm.

NIGHTLIFE AND ENTERTAINMENT

Nightlife isn't really Cajamarca's strong point, with the odd bar or café playing host to occasional local music, often incorporating violins as well as the more usual Andean instruments and guitars. During fiesta times at least, you should have no trouble finding traditional music and dancing. At weekends, many of the *peñas* host good live music, and the clubbier video-pub or disco scene is at its liveliest.

Discoteca Los Frailones Av Perú 701, Cnr Cruz de la Piedra ☎076 344272. Six blocks up Santa Apolonia from the plaza, this place plays all kinds of music and has fantastic views over the city from the dancefloor. Daily 9pm–2am.

Peña Usha Usha Amalia Puga 320. This is the best venue in town for live Peruvian, especially *criolla* music, as well as Cuban troubador-style performances. A small space particularly busy at weekends but also entertaining during the week when owner Jaime Valera inspires locals and tourists alike with his incredibly talented and versatile guitar playing and singing. Often lit only by candle, this bar has a cosy and inviting atmosphere. Wed–Sat 8pm–2am.

SHOPPING

For leathercraft, ceramics, woollens, jewellery and local hats (*sombreros de paja*) famous throughout Peru for their quality, try the inexpensive artesanía stalls lining the steps up to the sanctuary on Cerro Santa Apolonia and also in block 7 of Calle Belén.

Casa Luna Jr 2 de Mayo 334. This shop not only sells good artesanía and exhibits and sells a range of local artwork and crafts, but also has a cafetería and sometimes does storytelling for children. Daily 10.30am–7.30pm.

Quinde Jr Dos de Mayo 264 ☎076 361031. One of the best artesanía shops in town, this shouldn't be missed. Daily 10am–8pm.

DIRECTORY

Health Mario Urteaga 500 ☎076 362414.

Money and exchange Banco Continental, Jr Tarapacá 725; Banco de Credito, C Comercio 679; Banco de la Nación, Jr Tarapacá 647; and Interbanc, Plaza de Armas. *Cambistas* hang out along Jr del Batán, between *Restaurant El Zarco* and the Plaza de Armas. There's a good casa de cambio at Jr Arequipa 724 (Mon–Fri 9am–1.45pm & 3.30–7pm) opposite the Banco de Credito.

Police Plaza Amalia Puga 807 ☎076 365572.

Post office Amalia Puga 778 (Mon–Sat 8am–9pm).

FIESTAS IN CAJAMARCA

The best time to visit Cajamarca is during May or June for the **Festival of Corpus Christi**. Until the early twentieth century this was the country's premier festival, before it was superseded by the traditional Inca sun festival, Inti Raymi, held at Sacsayhuaman in Cusco. Corpus Christi nevertheless actually coincided with the sun festival and is traditionally led by the elders of the Canachin family, who, in the Cajamarca area, were directly descended from local pre-Inca chieftains. The procession here still attracts locals from all around, but increasing commercialism is eating away at its traditional roots. Nevertheless it's fun, and visited by relatively few non-Peruvian tourists, with plenty of parties, bullfights, *caballos de paso* meetings and an interesting trade fair. The city's other main fiesta is **Día de Cajamarca** (Cajamarca Day), usually around February 11, which is celebrated with music, dancing, processions and fireworks.

Around Cajamarca

Within a short distance of Cajamarca are several attractions that can easily be visited on a day-trip from the city. The closest is the **Cerro Santa Apolonia**, with its pre-Inca carved rocks, though these are not nearly as spectacular as the impressive aqueduct at **Cumbe Mayo**, or the ancient temple at **Kuntur Huasi**. However, the most popular trip from Cajamarca is to the steaming-hot thermal baths of **Baños del Inca**, just 5km from the city centre. A four-kilometre walk from Cajamarca lies the small village of **Aylambo**, known for its ceramics workshops, where you can try your hand at making your own pots.

Cerro Santa Apolonia

Parque Ecología • Daily 7am–6pm • S/1

A short stroll southeast from Cajamarca's Plaza de Armas, two blocks along Jirón Dos de Mayo, brings you to a path up the **CERRO SANTA APOLONIA**, a hill that overlooks the city and offers great views across the valley. At the top of the hill are the sensitively landscaped and terraced gardens known as the **Parque Ecología**, whose entrance is beside the Iglesia Santisima Virgen de Fatima, a small chapel at the top of the steps as you walk up from town. At the highest point in the park, you'll find what is thought to have been a sacrificial stone dating from around 1000 BC. It is popularly known as the Inca's Throne, and offers a great overview of the valley.

7

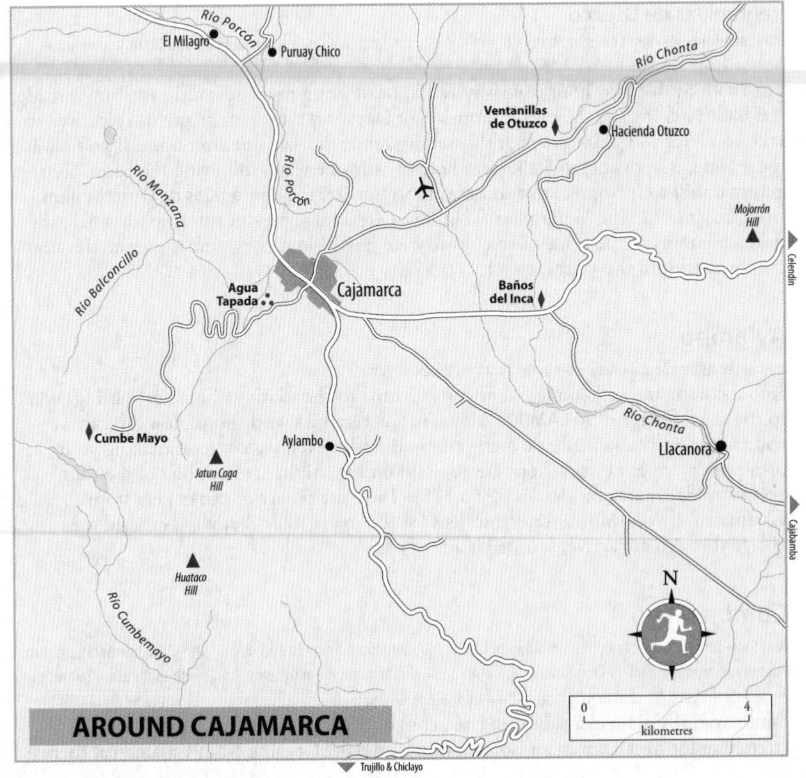

Agua Tapada

Just 2km southwest of the Cerro Santa Apolonia, along the road to Cumbe Mayo, is a further group of ruins – prominent among them an old pyramid, known to the Spanish as a temple of the sun, but now called by the locals **Agua Tapada** (Covered Water). Quite possibly, there is a subterranean well below the site – they're not uncommon around here and it might initially have been a temple related to some form of water cult.

Baños del Inca and around

5km east of Cajamarca • **Baths** Daily 6am–6.30pm; outdoor pool daily 6am–6.45pm, with sessions of up to 1hr 45min • S/3–8 **Sauna** Women only: daily 8–10.45am & 2–4.45pm; mixed 5–7.45am, 11am–1.45pm & 5–7.45pm • S/8–10 • 15min bus ride from block 10 of Amazonas; local buses and colectivos leave when full, usually every 10min or so (S/1–1.50)

Many of the ruins around Cajamarca are related to water, in a way that seems to both honour it in a religious sense and use it in a practical way. A prime example of this is the **BAÑOS DEL INCA**. As you approach the baths you can see the steam rising from a low-lying set of buildings and hot pools. The baths, which date from pre-Inca times, have long been popular with locals, though the whole place could do with a bit of a face-lift. Having said that, wallowing in the thermal waters is a glorious way to spend an afternoon. There's a restored Inca bath within the complex, but the stonework, though very good, is not original. It was from here that the Inca army marched to their doom against Pizarro and co.

The actual price of your dip depends on the type and grade of bath – the quality ranges from the Imperial, which is the best, through to the Turistas, followed by the standard Pavilions A, B and C. There is also an excellent sauna.

Ventanillas de Otuzco

Daily 9am–5pm • S/3 • Direct colectivos from Cajamarca to the Ventanillas (S/1.50) leave every 20min from Del Batán, just below the Mercado Central

For an enjoyable two-hour (one way) walk, head along the road southeast from outside the Baños del Inca to the pleasant pueblo of **Llacanora**; there are frequent colectivos to take you back to Cajamarca, but this service tends to fizzle out after 6pm. If you have more time, it's possible to **walk** from here (3–4hr one way), following the Río Chonta gently uphill to its source, to another important site, the **Ventanillas de Otuzco**, 8km from Cajamarca. The Ventanillas (Windows) are a huge pre-Inca necropolis where the dead chieftains of the Cajamarca culture were buried in niches, sometimes metres deep, cut by hand into the volcanic rock.

Aylambo

Frequent buses from Avenida Independencia in Cajamarca (15min; S/1.50)

A four-kilometre walk along Avenida R. Castilla to the south of Cajamarca brings you to the small village of **AYLAMBO**, known for its ceramics workshops. You can buy a wide range of locally made earthenware products or even have a go at making your own pottery. Special workshops are also laid on for children; ask at one of the tour agents in Cajamarca for details (see p.378). There are plenty of **buses** here from Cajamarca, if you want to save your legs for the many trails that wind around the village through attractive, forested land.

Cumbe Mayo

Daily 9am–5pm • S/3 • Best to visit with your own transport or go with a tour operator (see p.378; daily 9am–2pm; from S/25 per person). You can walk the 20km from the Cerro Santa Apolonia (see p.381) here in maybe five or six hours, though with an altitude of 3600m, it's not an easy stroll and you need to acclimatize to the altitude before starting

Southwest of Cajamarca stands the ancient aqueduct and canal of **CUMBE MAYO**, stretching for over 1km in an isolated highland dale. Coming from Cajamarca, there's an odd natural **rock formation**, the Bosque de Piedras (Forest of Stones), where clumps of eroded limestone taper into thin, human figure-like shapes – known locally as *los frailones* (the friars) because of their resemblance to robed monks. A little further on, you'll see the well-preserved and skillfully constructed **canal**, built almost 1200 years before the Incas arrived here. Dotted along the canal there are some interesting **petroglyphs** attributed to the early Cajamarca culture. The amount of meticulous effort which must have gone into crafting the aqueduct, cut as it is from solid rock with perfect right angles and precise geometric lines, suggests that it served a more ritual or religious function rather than being simply for irrigation purposes. In some places along the canal, the rocks have been cut into rectangular shapes. According to archeologists, these are remains left by the quarrying of stones for the construction of the canal. Cumbe Mayo originally carried water from the Atlantic to the Pacific watershed (from the eastern to the western slopes of the Andes) via a complex system of canals and tunnels, many of which are still visible and in some cases operational. To the right-hand side of the aqueduct (with your back to Cajamarca) there is a large face-like rock on the hillside, with a man-made **cave** cut into it. This contains some 3000-year-old petroglyphs etched in typical Chavín style (you'll need a torch to see them) and dominated by the ever-present feline features. There's a small but interesting site **museum** (S/5) with maps and a few archeological objects, but, more importantly perhaps, toilets at the entrance. Further on, past the first small hill, the guardian has a hut; if he doesn't catch visitors for payment at the museum he usually finds them here.

Kuntur Huasi

Daily 9am–5pm • S/5 • Visit using your own tranport or full-day tour (see p.378)

Largely destroyed by the ravages of time and weather, **KUNTUR HUASI**, 93km from Cajamarca, was clearly once a magnificent temple. You can still make out a variation on Chavín designs carved onto its four stone monoliths. Apart from Chavín itself, this is the most important site in the northern Andes relating to the feline cult; golden ornaments and turquoise were found in graves here, but so far not enough work has been done to give a precise date to the site. The anthropomorphic carvings indicate differences in time, suggesting Kuntur Huasi was built during the late Chavín era, around 400 BC. Whatever its age, the pyramid is an imposing ruin amid quite exhilarating countryside. There's a small site museum displaying mostly replicas of pieces uncovered here by archeologists plus maps of the site and photographs of the Japanese dig.

ARRIVAL AND DEPARTURE — KUNTUR HUASI

By bus From Avenida Atahualpa in Cajamarca, take the Trujillo bus to Chilete, a small mining town about 50km along the paved road to Pacasmayo. Here, you need to change to a local bus (leaving hourly or so) to the village of San Pablo, from where it's just a short downhill walk to the ruins. The journey can take around 5 hours.

By tour An organized tour from Cajamarca is the easiest option for visiting the ruins; around S/50 per person (see p.378).

On foot It's possible to walk the 90km from Cumbe Mayo to Kuntur Huasi, in the upper part of the Jequetepeque Valley, to the east of the Cajamarca Basin. This trek, however, takes three or four days, so you'll need a tent and food.

South from Cajamarca

It's a long, rough, but rewarding journey south from Cajamarca to the small town of **Huamachuco**, jumping-off point for visiting the archeological site of **Marca Huamachuco** as well as the fabulous, rarely visited and very remote ruins of **Gran Pajaten**. The whole journey from Cajamarca to the ruins takes at least five days, and involves a combination of bus and hiking. Cajabamba is the only other town of significance en route from Cajamarca to Huamachuco but its main interest is a place to change buses.

FIESTAS IN HUAMACHUCO

On the first weekend in August the **Fiesta de Waman Raymi** is held at nearby Wiracochapampa, bringing many people from the town and countryside to the Inti Raymi-style celebrations. Other festivals in the region include the **Fiesta de Huamachuco** (celebrating the founding of the city) on August 13–20, a week of festivities including a superb firework display on August 14 and aggressive male *turcos* dancers during the procession.

7

Huamachuco

Infamous in Peru as the site of the Peruvian army's last-ditch stand against the Chilean conquerors back in 1879, **HUAMACHUCO**, at 3180m, is a fairly typical Andean market town, surrounded by partly forested hills and a patchwork of fields on steep slopes. The site of the battle is now largely covered by the small airport, while the large Plaza de Armas in the centre of town possesses an interesting colonial archway in one corner, which the Liberator Símon Bolívar once rode through. Now, however, it's flanked by the modern, and less visually appealing, cathedral. Another lively part of town, the colourful rural **market** is on block 9 of Balta.

Marca Huamachuco

Daily 6am–6pm • Free; S/5 suggested tip for the guardian to the convento buildings • The 6km walk from the plaza takes 3hr; it's hard to get a taxi to take you there, although Alosio Rebaza, at D. Nicolau 100 (☎ 076 441488) will transport people in his 4WD vehicle (S/40 for up to 4, more if you want him to wait)

Take a walk from Plaza de Armas to the dramatic circular pre-Inca fort of **Marca Huamachuco**, located on top of one of several mountains dominating the town and the main reason most travellers end up in this neck of the woods. Some 3km long, the **ruins** date back to around 300 BC, when they probably began life as an important ceremonial centre, with additions dating from between 600 and 900 AD. The fort was adopted possibly as an administrative outpost during the Huari-Tiahuanaco era (600–1100 AD), although it evidently maintained its independence from the powerful Chachapoyas nation, who lived in the high forested regions to the north and east of here (see p.386). An impressive, commanding and easily defended position, Marca Huamachuco is also protected by a massive eight-metre-high wall surrounding its more vulnerable approaches. The *convento* complex, which consists of five circular buildings of varying sizes towards the northern end of the hill, is a later construction and was possibly home to a pre-Inca elite ruler and his selected concubines; the largest building has been partially reconstructed. An information sheet providing a **plan** of the site and some brief details is available from the Municipalidad in Huamachuco.

ARRIVAL AND DEPARTURE — HUAMACHUCO

By bus Take the Rojas bus from Cajamarca, which leaves daily from Avenida Atahualpa 309 (☎ 076 340548). It is 5hr to Cajabamba, where you need to change to a more local bus for the 3hr journey on to Huamachuco.

ACCOMMODATION AND EATING

Bar Michi Wasi San Ramón 461. On the plaza, this is a small and trendy spot with a nice atmosphere, and definitely the place to press locals for information about nearby attractions. Nightly 6–10pm.

Café Venezia San Martín 780. A café that rustles up great desserts and has excellent coffee made from beans fresh from the Marañón Valley. Daily 8am–8pm.

Casa de Hospedaje Las Hortencias Castilla 130 ☎ 076 441049. This has fairly basic rooms with bath in a friendly house and a nice courtyard where you can lounge around. Gets full during festival times, when you should try to book in advance. S/30

Hostal Huamachuco Castilla 354 ☎ 076 441393. Close to the Plaza de Armas, for rooms with or without bath in a rather old building; plenty of hot water available and there's a TV. S/25

El Karibe Plaza de Armas. Right at the heart of town, this very popular restaurant serves crispy cuy (guinea pig) and tasty goat as well as beef meals, soups and snacks. Mon–Sat 8am–7pm.

Gran Pajaten

To visit the extremely remote, highly regarded ruins of the sacred city of **GRAN PAJATEN**, **permission** must first be obtained from the Instituto Nacional de Cultura (see p.50); and this is generally only given to those who can demonstrate a serious and specific interest and reason for visiting this special site.

The main archeological site at Gran Pajaten is known as **Ruinas de la Playa.** Discovered in 1973, they cover some four hectares, with around 25 buildings, both round and square, built mainly of a slate-type stone (sometimes called *piedra pizarra*). One of the round structures is thought to have been a temple, another living quarters. Many of the walls have typical Chachapoyan (similar to those found around Kuelap; see p.389) geometric and anthropomorphic figures that have been created by the way in which these frequently thin stones are placed in the walls.

ARRIVAL AND DEPARTURE — GRAN PAJATEN

By bus and mule Agreda buses connect Huamachuco twice weekly (Wed & Sat) with the village of Chagual (around 12 very bumpy hours) where you can hire mules and guides (from S/25–30 a day per mule). It's a four- or five-day trek via the settlements of Pataz (20km; a 6hr walk from Chagual) and Los Alisos (another 8km or 3hr walk) to the true trailhead for Gran Pajaten – a further 3 or 4 days' walk. Occasional mining vehicles also go from Chagual to Pataz.

Chachapoyas and around

The small, modern town of **CHACHAPOYAS**, at 2334m high up in the Andes, is first and foremost a springboard for a wealth of nearby pre-Columbian remains. With the opening up of the road networks in these parts, Chachapoyas has developed into a thriving little market town (with a wide range of fruits and veggies, some craft goods, and some smaller woollen accessories such as straps and belts), supporting a mostly indigenous population of around ten thousand, themselves with a reputation for being among the most friendly and hospitable people in Peru.

The nearest ruins to Chachapoyas include the ruined city of **Purunllacta** – 40km south of the city and one of the likely capitals of the Chachapoyas people – while west are **Pueblo de los Muertos** and **Carajía**, two impressive cliff-face burial centres for the elite of this quite sophisticated culture. However, most famous and most worthwhile of all the Chachapoyan archeological remains is **Kuelap**, a fabulous, huge citadel complex. South of here lie **Balsas** and **Leymebamba.** To some extent, the ancient culture lives on in some of the remote, traditional communities like **La Jalca**, 76km south of Chachapoyas.

Much of the land in the Chachapoyas region is full of ravines and very steep sided valleys. All land over 3500m is considered *jalca*, or wild, and should be approached

THE ROAD TO CHACHAPOYAS

There are two routes up to Chachapoyas from the south; the best, and by far the fastest, is the road leaving the coast from Chiclayo and Piura via Olmos, Jaen and Bagua; this route has fewer and lower passes.

But a fascinating **alternative route to Chachapoyas**, though much more arduous and significantly longer (deceptively so, when you look at the map), winds its way up and down several massive valleys and passes. The route winds through green mountain scenery, past dairy herds and small houses in a variety of earthy colours. Passing via the market town of Celendin, the road descends into the Marañón Valley and the smaller town of Balsas. Climbing again, the bus comes through Leymebamba and reaches heights of almost 4000m before descending to the town of Chachapoyas. The whole trip from Cajamarca to Chachapoyas takes around 12 hours and can be done in a single bus ride with the bus company Movil (Atahualpa 409, Cajamarca ☎ 076 363374), in either direction.

only with a guide. Spectacled bear, puma and white-tailed deer roam while hummingbirds flutter about in the remote highland plains. Less than 30km north of Chachapoyas Town gush the fabulous **Cataratas de Gocta**, reputedly the tallest in Peru.

Brief history

In Aymara, Chachapoyas means "the cloud people", perhaps a description of the fair-skinned tribes who used to dominate this region, living in one of at least seven major cities (like Kuelap, Magdalena and Purunllacta), each one located high up above the Utcubamba Valley or a tributary of this, on prominent, dramatic peaks and ridges. Many of the local inhabitants still have light-coloured hair and remarkably pale faces. The Chachapoyas people, despite building great fortifications, were eventually subdued by the empire-building Incas. **Chachapoyas** was once a colonial possession rich with gold and silver mines as well as extremely fertile alluvial soil, before falling into decline during the Republican era.

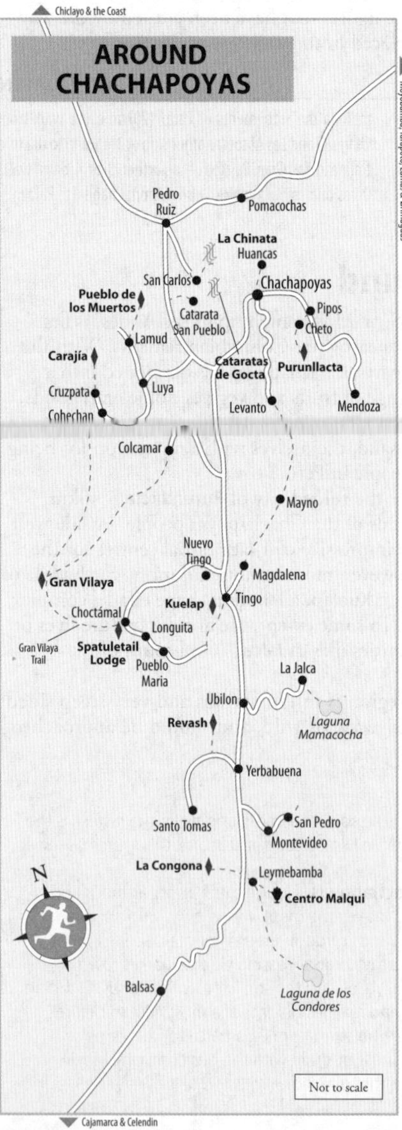

Plaza de Armas

As well as the cathedral and the municipal buildings, the tranquil **Plaza de Armas** contains a colonial bronze fountain, a monument to Toribio Rodríguez de Mendoza. Born here in 1750, he is considered the main source of Peru's own ideological inspiration behind independence from the mother country Spain. There's a small **museum** (Tues–Sat 8.30am–12.30pm & 2–5.30pm; S/5) on the plaza, featuring ceramics, some mummies, stone axes and ancient bone needles used for sewing, among other ancient objects.

Chachapoyas's churches

The town has a couple of churches of some interest, notably the **Iglesia de Santa Ana**, Jr Santa Ana 1056, the first church built here in 1569 by the Spanish and also home to a small religious art and archeology museum. This temple, built in 1569 to serve Chachapoyas's indigenous population until the mid-twentieth century, has a museum (Mon–Fri 8am–6pm, Sat & Sun 9am–1pm & 3–6pm; S/8)

TOUR OPERATORS IN CHACHAPOYAS

Andes Tours ⓣ041 477391, ⓦchachapoyaskuelap.com.pe/andestours. Run by the *Hotel Revash* (see below), this company is well organized and well equipped, able to take visitors to all the main sites and also off the beaten track, including Gran Vilaya on request.

Vilaya Tours Jr Amazonas 261 ⓣ041 477506, ⓦvilayatours.com. Has a good reputation, and offers a variety of tours including one to the fabulous Gocta Waterfalls, Peru's highest.

Chachapoyas Tours Grau 534 ⓣ041 478078 and 24hr line ⓣ051 941963327, ⓦchachapoyastours.com. Experienced, competent and has links with accommodation lodges in the Choctamal and Levanto areas. They also offer tours to Kuelap and Carajía.

Independent guides Martín Chumbe, Jr Piura 909, is contactable through the *Gran Hotel Vilaya* (see below) and is a well-known local guide who speaks some English and charges from around S/100 /day for tours of sites in the region, including Kuelap. Other recommended guides include Julio Soto Valle, Jr Libertad 812 (ⓣ041 477498), and Oscar Arce Cáceres, from the *Hostal Estancia Chillo*, some 4 or 5km south of Tingo at the base of the Kuelap ruins.

7

displaying items used in the old church, as well as archeological bits and bobs and an ecological display. The fabulous **Iglesia del Señor de Burgos**, on the Plaza Independencia some seven blocks east of the Plaza de Armas, is well known for its attractive colonial imagery.

ARRIVAL AND GETTING AROUND — CHACHAPOYAS

By bus Movil buses arrive at Libertad 464 (ⓣ041 478545). Buses from the coast (including Chiclayo and Piura) pass the Chachapoyas turn-off at the small settlement and army camp of Pedro Ruiz en route to Moyobamba and Tarapoto. You can hop off the bus here and take a local colectivo (usually waiting by the corner outside the *Hotel Casa Blanca*) or bus on to Chachapoyas. Other buses and colectivos arrive within a couple of blocks of the Plaza de Armas on block 3 of Grau (for Kuelap), along blocks 3/4 of Jirón Ortiz Arrieta, or around the corner on Jirón Salamanca, blocks 7/8.

Destinations Cajamarca (2 weekly via Celendin; 15hr); Chiclayo (several daily; 10–12hr); Kuelap (several daily; 3hr); Rioja/Moyobamba (3 daily; 9–12hr).

By rickshaw Transport around town tends to be by motorcycle rickshaw, with a flat rate of S/1.

INFORMATION

Tourist information i-Peru's office, Jr Ortiz Arrieta 590 (Mon–Sat 8am–1pm & 3–7pm; ⓣ041 477292 and ⓣ041 477292, ⓔiperuchachapoyas@promperu.gob.pe); or Dirección Subregional de Industria y Turismo ITINCI, C Chincha Alta 445 (Mon–Fri 9am–5.30pm; ⓣ041 457047), just a block from the plaza. For advice on archeological sites, try the Instituto Nacional de Cultura, Jr Junín 817 (Mon–Fri 9am–6pm).

Useful website ⓦcamayocperu.com, run by the Camayoc Foundation.

ACCOMMODATION

There aren't many hotels to choose from here and certainly nothing particularly plush, though rumour has it that this may soon change. Most of those listed, however, are friendly and do their best to keep you warm and comfortable, in most cases providing hot water and private bathrooms, but are rather stark and offer little in the way of luxury.

Gran Hotel Vilaya Jr Ayacucho 755 ⓣ041 477664. Located on the Plaza de Armas, this is a relatively comfortable, quality hotel, with its own restaurant. All rooms have private bath and hot water. S/70

Hotel Amazonas Jr Grau 565 ⓣ041 477199. A popular budget place on the Plaza de Armas, with an attractive, traditional patio. Rooms are available with or without private bath. S/25–35

★ **Hotel Revash** Plaza de Armas, Grau 517 ⓣ041 477391. Stylish rooms, mostly with private bath, and some with good views over the plaza. There's hot water, laundry facilities and the management (as Andes Tours) also run tours to Kuelap, Levanto and the Revash Circuit, among other sites. S/90

EATING AND DRINKING

While wining and dining isn't Chachapoyas's forte, there are nevertheless some surprising culinary delights. Places tend to close early (around 10pm); none of them are expensive.

Cuyería, Pollería y Panadería Virgen Asunta Jr Puno 401. *The* place to go for roast *cuy*, though you have to order it a couple of hours in advance. Mon–Sat 10.30am–6pm.

Restaurant Vegetariano El Eden Jr Grau. Situated half a block down from the plaza towards the market, this is a superb and very accommodating vegetarian restaurant serving brilliant breakfasts, snacks, lunches and juices; try the mixed juice with *maca* herb. Sun–Fri 7am–6pm.

Las Rocas Jr Ayacucho 932. A friendly little café where typical local food is served, including staple mountain meals such as rice and potato dishes and soups, which are usually made with chicken, *quinoa* and potato. A popular lunchtime place. Mon–Sat 10am–8pm.

El Tejado Santo Domingo 424 041 477592. Really good traditional Peruvian and local cuisine served in a warm and friendly ambience around a patio. Popular with locals, it can get busy at lunchtime. Mon–Sat noon–4pm, plus Mon–Fri 7–9pm.

La Tushpa Jr Ortiz Arrieta 753 041 777198. A great restaurant for meat dishes, particularly *cuy*, *chicharones* (deep-fried pork pieces) and burgers; also serves pizzas and tamales. Mon–Sat 1–10pm.

DIRECTORY

7

Internet Plenty of access on and around the Plaza de Armas.

Money and exchange The Banco de Credito, on the Plaza de Armas, will change dollars and can sometimes advance cash against Visa cards.

Post office Grau 561, on the plaza (Mon–Sat 8am–7pm).

Telephones The Telefónica office is at Jr Triunfo 851.

Purunllacta

Free • Daily bus from Grau street, Chachapoyas, to Pipos on the Mendoza road. Get off here and walk to the village of Cheto (40km from Chachapoyas), from where it's a short climb to the ruined city

PURUNLLACTA was one of the seven major cities of the Chachapoyas culture – and probably the capital – before they were all conquered by the Inca Tupac Yupanqui in the 1470s. The **site** consists of numerous groups of buildings scattered around the hilltops, all interconnected by ancient roads and each one surrounded by elegant agricultural terraces. At the centre of the ruined city you can clearly make out rectangular stone buildings, plazas, stairways and platforms. The most striking are two storeys high, and made of carved limestone blocks.

Carajía

Free • Catch an early morning colectivo or pick-up headed for Luya from Grau and Salamanca streets in Chachapoyas, then follow the walk described below

A characteristic of the Chachapoyas region is its **sarcophagi**, elaborately moulded, earthenware coffins, often stuck inaccessibly into horizontal crevices high up along cliff faces and painted in vivid colours. These were built by the Chachapoyas people in the twelfth and thirteenth centuries. A fine example – and a rewarding excursion, 46km southwest from Chachapoyas – are the sarcophagi at **Carajía**. Getting here involves a spectacular **walk** from Luya. Ask a local for directions to **Shipata**, where the path to the sarcophagi begins. From Shipata, walk down one side of the valley, over a bridge and then up the other side for about five minutes before taking a less clearly marked path to your right. The entire walk from Luya takes about four hours.

Pueblo de los Muertos

Free • Take the daily Chachapoyas–Chiclayo bus (from Chachapoyas market) and get off at Puente Tingobamba bridge. From here there's a track to the settlement of Lamud, close to the site (3–4hr walk)

The **PUEBLO DE LOS MUERTOS** (City of the Dead), located some 30km to the north of Chachapoyas and about 10km from Luya, is where you'll find overgrown roundhouse foundations plus **sarcophagi**, some up to 2m high and carved with human faces. Six were originally found here and three have been put back in their previous sites to stare blankly across the valley from a natural fault in the rock face. Each one has been carefully moulded into an elongated egg-like shape from a mixture of mud and vegetable fibres, then painted purple and white with geometric zigzags and other superimposed designs.

Cataratas de Gocta and La Chinata

Free • Reached via Pedro Ruiz by colectivo (S/10) or taxi (S/30; significantly more if you want them to wait)

Cataratas de Gocta (771m) claim to be the third tallest falls in the world. Only revealed to the outside world in 2002, local legend says that it is protected by an immense siren-like serpent. Getting to a good viewpoint – from where you can make out the main two tiers of the falls (231m above and another 540m below) – requires some hiking. The walk starts in the hamlet of Cocachimba, Bongará province; from here it's a 2km stroll to the base of the falls, but if you want to explore higher or return via San Pablo de Valera hamlet on the other side of the valley, you will need at least 4 to 6 hours. The hike goes through attractive cloud-forest terrain where Gallitos de la Roca (Peru's emblematic bird) and many other feathered species flit about. Also in the Bongará province, but reached via a different hike, the **La Chinata Waterfalls** (580m) are almost as magnificent, located in an area full of orchids and ferns at 1300m above sea level.

Kuelap

Daily 8am–5pm • S/15 • Organized day-tours from Chachapoyas with a guide cost from S/50 per person (see box, p.387)

The main attraction for most travellers in the Chachapoyas region is the unrestored ruin of **KUELAP**, one of the most overwhelming pre-Inca sites in Peru. Just 40km south of Chachapoyas (along the Cajamarca road), the ruins were discovered in 1843, above the tiny village of **Tingo** in the remote and verdant Utcubamba Valley. In 1993, Tingo was partly destroyed by flash floods, when more than a hundred homes were washed away, yet the village is still inhabited and remains an important point of access for visiting the ruins. A new village, Nuevo Tingo, has been built higher up above the valley.

Occupied from about 600 AD, Kuelap was the strongest, most easily defended of all Peruvian fortress cities, something that can be seen in the narrowing defensive form of the main entry passageways. This is thought to be the site which the rebel Inca Manco considered using for his last-ditch stand against the conquistadors in the late 1530s. He never made it here, ending up instead in the equally breathtaking Vilcabamba (see p.274), northeast of Cusco.

The site

It has been calculated that some forty million cubic feet of building material was used at Kuelap, three times the volume needed to construct the Great Pyramid of Egypt. An estimated three thousand people would have lived here at its height, working mainly as farmers, builders and artisans and living in little, round stone houses.

The site's enormous **walls** thrust 20m high, and are constructed from gigantic limestone slabs arranged in geometric patterns, with some sections faced with rectangular granite blocks over forty layers high. The average wall thickness is around 80cm and the largest stone 2m thick.

Inside the ruins lie the remains of some two hundred round stone **houses**, many still decorated with a distinctive zigzag pattern (like the modern ceramics produced by the locals), small, carved animal heads, condor designs, deer-eye symbols and intricate serpent figures. These are similar in style to the better-known Kogi villages of today's northern Colombia; and, indeed, there are thought to be linguistic connections between the Kogi and the Chachapoyas peoples, and possible links to a Caribbean or even Maya influence. There are a few rectangular buildings, too, which are associated with the later Inca occupation of Kuelap. Some of the structures in the central area have been recognized as kitchens because of their hearths, and there are a few that still have ancient pestles. The higher part of the site was restricted to the most privileged ranks in Chachapoyas society, and one of the buildings there, with fine, curved outer walls, is believed to have been a temple, or at least to have had a ceremonial function.

The site is overgrown to some extent with old trees laden with epiphytes. Even though it's high, this is still considered to be cloud forest. There are also various enclosures and huge crumbling watchtowers partly covered in wild subtropical vegetation, shrubs and even trees. One of these towers is an inverted, truncated cone containing a large, bottle-shaped cavity (known as the *tintero* or ink well), possibly a place of sacrifice, since archeologists have found human bones there, though these could date from after the original inhabitants of Kuelap had abandoned the citadel.

Revash

Accessed via trails from the village of Choctamal (see below)

7

The guardian at the site can also give information about the other, smaller ruins in the immediate vicinity such as **Revash**, a thirteenth-century burial site, built by the Revash culture (contemporaneous with the Chachapoyas people), where mummies and rock paintings are on view. The remains here consist mainly of limestone-built tombs and are within three to four hours' hike from the village of Santo Tomás.

ARRIVAL AND DEPARTURE — KUELAP

By colectivo Colectivo minibuses from the corner of Grau and Salamanca in Chachapoyas (usually leaving between 6 and 11am) pass through Nuevo Tingo and continue their winding, precipitous way on a circular anticlockwise route via the village of Choctamal to Pueblo María.

By bus If you're coming from Cajamarca and Celendin, the bus passes right through Tingo. Colectivos go from Tingo to the Kuelap car park (3hr).

FROM PUEBLO MARÍA

On foot Pueblo María is within two to three hours hike of Kuelap itself – a fairly level and easy-going walk along dirt roads and tracks. En route, you'll pass through Cuchapampa, Quisango and Malcapampa hamlets.

On horseback Having arrived in Pueblo María by colectivo (see above), it's possible to hire a horse for you and/or your bags (just ask the hospedaje owner; see below). Unlike the Tingo route, there's very little climbing involved and you'll arrive at Kuelap with more energy to enjoy this archeological marvel.

FROM TINGO

On foot If you're approaching Kuelap via Tingo it's a hard but hugely rewarding 1500-metre climb (around 4hr up and about 2hr back down) from the west bank of the Río Utcubamba. Leave early to avoid the mid-morning sun, and remember to carry all the water you'll need with you.

On horseback Mules or horses are usually available for hire from the hostel (S/20–30 per day) in Tingo (see below), or at El Chillo (S/20–35 per day), on the road to Tingo.

ACCOMMODATION AND EATING

PUEBLO MARÍA

Hospedajes ☎041 813088. Some families in the community offer bed and breakfast to visitors via an informal co-operative. They are usually very good, with plenty of blankets and quite comfortable beds in traditional wooden buildings. S/25

KM 20 GATEWAY TO GRAN VILAYA

Spatuletail Lodge Kuelap road Km 20 ☎041 478838 or ☎9419 63327 or ☎1 866 396 9582 (US), marvelousspatuletail.com. A great lodge with seven bedrooms, toilets and even a hot tub. An impressive, quite ornate building, it's also well located within a day's walk or horse ride of both Kuelap (40min by car) and Gran Vilaya, and in fact this is the start of the great Gran Vilaya trail, which follows ancient Inca stone roads. S/100

TINGO

Hospedaje Tingo Just outside Tingo ☎041 9417 32251. A pretty basic hostel but it has hot water, private baths in some rooms and reasonably good cafetería. S/30

KUELAP

Rooms No phone. Two rooms with enough space for twelve people with sleeping bags and a shared toilet facility, managed by the INC guardian at the entrance to Kuelap site (it is often booked, so best to have a tent for back-up). If these rooms are full, then the guardian can usually advise on space within households of neighbouring hamlets. Camping is usually free, just ask the INC guardian. S/5 per person

HIKING TO GRAN VILAYA

The best way to reach Gran Vilaya's remote, largely unexplored and hard-to-find sites is with a decent **guide** and some mules (see opposite) who could also take you to see the impressive network of Chachapoyan ruins spread out across an area about thirty miles (east to west) and fifteen miles (south to north), all requiring demanding hiking through stunning cloud forest. Don't forget **camping equipment and food**. Also, note that once you get beyond Choctamal and Pueblo María, it's often hard to use money, and it can prove handy to have some **trade goods** with you – pencils, fruit, chocolate, bread, canned fish or biscuits – and, of course, camping gear, unless you want to be completely dependent on the local hospitality.

Gran Vilaya

Free • Colectivos drop you off at the village of Choctamal. From here it is expedition-style trekking into the Gran Vilaya area, with or without mules but always best with guides through a local tour company or established local family (for example, in Pueblo María)

7

Less accessible (at least two days' walk) than Kuelap, but accessed via the same road, is the collection of ruins known as **GRAN VILAYA**. The name refers to a superb complex of almost entirely unexcavated ruins scattered over a wide area. Explorer Gene Savoy claimed to have "discovered" them in 1985, though travellers have been hiking into this area for years and there were several sketch maps of the ruins in existence years before he arrived. Despite Savoy's claim to have found thousands of buildings, a more conservative estimate puts the record at some 150 sites divided into three main political sections. About thirty of these sites are of note, and about fifteen of these are of real archeological importance. If you intend to venture beyond Kuelap to Gran Vilaya, note that you must first obtain **permission** from the Instituto Nacional de Cultura in Chachapoyas (see p.387).

La Jalca

Almost three hours south by road from Chachapoyas, the traditional village of **La Jalca** is within walking distance of a number of ruins. The folklore capital of the region, La Jalca also lays claim to some amazing fourteenth-century stone walls and a seventeenth-century stone-built **church**, with characteristic Chachapoyan zigzags. The houses in the village, built in typical Chachapoyas fashion along the ridge, are lovely, conical thatched-roofed constructions with walls of *tapial*-type mudwork.

ARRIVAL AND DEPARTURE — LA JALCA

By bus La Jalca is a stop on the Chachapoyas–Leymebamba bus.

Destinations Chachapoyas (daily; 2hr); Leymebamba (daily; 1hr).

ACCOMMODATION

Hospedaje Comunitario Just beyond the church. No phone. A good little hostel within easy walking distance of the plaza; service is good and it's communally run; good local breakfasts provided at extra cost. S/25–30

Leymebamba

The superb **Museo de Leymebamba** (Mon–Sat 8.30am–4.30pm; S/4) is the one real draw to the little village of **LEYMBEBAMBA**, some 80km (3–4hr) by road from Chachapoyas and another 8 to 10 hours from Cajamarca. The museum houses around 150 mummies from the Chachapoyas culture's mausoleum of the not-too-distant **Laguna de los Condores**, where the dead were placed in cliff-face niches and venerated. The building itself is the product of local labour and skills, using traditional materials and construction techniques including stonework, timber and *tapial*.

ARRIVAL AND DEPARTURE — LEYMEBAMBA

By bus Buses from Chachapoyas or Cajamarca generally stop close to the market in Leymebamba; it's a small town, so everything is easy to find.

Destinations Cajamarca (daily; 8–10hr); Chachapoyas (daily; 2–3hr).

ACCOMMODATION

Hostal La Petaca Jr Amazonas 426 ⓣ041 830105. Right on the town's main plaza, this is arguably the most comfortable place in town; rooms have private showers with 24hr hot water. Great service. S/35

Tarapoto

TARAPOTO, known as the "City of Palms", is a well-developed jungle settlement, with surfaced roads, fairly good hotels, a large market and an unexpectedly high proportion of young professionals and business people. It is also a good base from which to explore this part of Peru, visit the folkloric locus of Lamas (see opposite), prepare for a jungle trip, or do some whitewater rafting on the Río Mayo. It's also the start point for one of Peru's best Amazon river trips: by road to Yurimaguas, then by riverboat following the Río Huallaga further into the jungle, along the edge of one of Peru's best and least-visited protected lowland forests, the remote rainforest haven of **Reserva Nacional de Pacaya-Samiria** (see p.476).

The town, founded in 1772, lies just 420m above sea level and has an agreeable temperature range of 29–37°C (85–99°F). The Río Huallaga flows on from here, via the Amazon, until it finally empties into the Atlantic Ocean many thousands of kilometres away. A strange sort of place, Tarapoto has a large **prison** and a big drug-smuggling problem, with people flying coca paste from here to Colombia, where it is processed into cocaine for the US market (see box opposite). Nevertheless, the locals tend to be friendly and pleased to see tourists, themselves still few and far between.

This newly opened up jungle region around Tarapoto is full of quite astonishing natural treasures, many yet to be revealed to the travelling public. The **Cataratas de Ahuashiyacu** is a popular and scenic local swimming spot, with small but very pretty waterfalls; they are situated along the road east towards Yurimagua, and you can take a taxi here (30min; S/15). The falls are one of several ecotourist destinations around Tarapoto. Other contenders, all within easy taxi reach, include the **waterfalls of Huacamaillo** and also those of Shapaja (21km), the village of **Chazuta** with its fine ceramic tradition, the stunning **Laguna Azul** (50km from town) and the wild rainforest of the valley of **Shilcayo**.

ARRIVAL AND INFORMATION — TARAPOTO

By plane Tarapoto airport is 5km from the centre of town. If you need a taxi, call Taxi Expreso (ⓣ042 524962).

Destinations Iquitos (6 weekly; 1hr 30min); Lima (1 or 2 daily; 1hr 30min); Yurimaguas (1–2 weekly; 25min).

By bus The daily buses from Chiclayo to Tarapoto mostly arrive at, and leave from, blocks 6 to 8 of Avenida Salaverry. Probably the best bus for Chiclayo, Trujillo or Lima is Movil Tours, Av Salaverry 858. Paredes Estrellas, next door, is the next best bus for the coastal destinations.

Destinations Chiclayo (daily; 15–18hr); Lima (daily; 25–30hr); Trujillo (daily; 18–22hr).

Tourist information Oficina Zonal de Industria y Turismo (ⓣ042 522567, ⓔitatpto@viaexpresa.com.pe, ⓦregionsanmartin.gob.pe), Jr Angel Delgado, block 1.

THE JOURNEY INTO THE JUNGLE

You can head into the **jungle** for a day or two from Chachapoyas, Piura or Chiclayo by crossing the Andes in a **bus** or **flying** to Tarapoto (see above). If you're particularly adventurous and/or have lots of time, a **journey by land and river** could take you all the way from Chachapoyas via Tarapoto and Yurimaguas to the Peruvian jungle capital of **Iquitos** (see p.466) on the Amazon, not far from the Brazilian border.

It's difficult to estimate the duration of this trip – there are always long waits for connections and embarkations – but it's unlikely to take much less than a week's hard travelling.

THE ROAD SOUTH FROM TARAPOTO: A TRAVELLERS' WARNING

The route **south from Tarapoto** via Juanjui (150km) and Tingo María (a further 350km) through wild frontier jungle territory is not currently recommended for travellers. It passes through one of the most dangerous areas in Peru, dominated by the illegal **coca-growing industry**, and the army have been present in the region for years. Now and again there are confrontations and shoot-outs, and the region remains pretty well beyond the control of law and order. On some parts of the road from here to Tingo María, buses suffer regular armed **robberies**, some involving fatalities. It's simply not worth the risk of travelling here at the moment.

ACCOMMODATION AND EATING

Hotel Nilas Jr Moyobamba 173 ⓣ042 527321, ⓦhotelnilas.com. The best accommodation in Tarapoto, this relatively modern building stretching to several floors has a reasonably large rooftop pool with waiter service, large rooms, cable TV, wi-fi, private baths, a/c and room service. S/140

El Manguare Jr Moyobamba 161 ⓣ042 530342. On the main plaza, this café offers a good, cheap lunch menu and some interesting local dishes. Daily 9am–9pm.

La Mansion Jr Maynas 280 ⓣ042 530471, ⓔinfo@altamirahotel.com.pe. This is a very clean and comfortable mid-range option based around an old house with a swimming pool, central garden, private baths and TVs. S/75

Real Grill Jr Moyobamba 131 ⓣ042 522714. Superb evening meals including a mix of standard Peruvian dishes augmented with jungle produce such as *yuca* and plantains. Daily 8.30am–10.30pm, sometimes later.

7

DIRECTORY

Internet The best is probably Mundonet, one block from the Plaza Mayor at Jr San Martín 205 (ⓣ042 528531).

Money and exchange Banco de Credito has an ATM on Jr Maynas.

Post office Jr San Martín 482 (Mon–Sat 8am–7pm).

Lamas

An obvious and pleasant day-trip from Tarapoto is **LAMAS**, a small village 20km up into the forested hills and surrounded by large pineapple plantations. The village is based around three interconnected levels or plateaux; the lower level is mainly living spaces, while most commerce is on the second level. Not surprisingly, the best views are from the third. The inhabitants of Barrio Huayco are reputed to be direct descendants of the Chanca tribe, who escaped from the Andes to this region in the fifteenth century, fleeing the conquering Inca army. The people keep very much to themselves, carrying on a highly distinctive lifestyle which combines jungle and mountain cultures – the women wear long blue skirts and colourfully embroidered blouses, and the men adorn themselves on ceremonial occasions with strings of brightly plumed, stuffed macaws. Everyone speaks a curious mixture of Quechua and Cahuapana and the town is traditionally renowned for its *brujos* (wizards). The best month to visit is August when the village **festival** is in full swing. The days are spent dancing and drinking, and most of the tribe's weddings occur at this time.

ARRIVAL AND INFORMATION — LAMAS

By colectivo Colectivos to Lamas leave every hour or so from the Plaza de Armas in Tarapoto (S/4; 30min; taxis S/40 return, 20min).

Tourist information On the small Plaza de Armas, Lamas (ⓣ042 543013; Mon–Sat 7am–2.30pm).

ACCOMMODATION, EATING AND SHOPPING

Albergue Los Girasoles Jr Chancas ⓣ042 543439, ⓔstegmaiert@yahoo.de. Opposite the Mirador Los Chancas, a smart hostel at the very top level of the Lamas hills with great views and interestingly built along ecological lines; the operators also run a café and serve pizzas here (alternatively, the best restaurants are on the main street at the second level), as well as organize interesting eco-adventure treks through local communities

DOWNRIVER TO IQUITOS

From Yurimaguas, you can travel all the way to **Iquitos** by river (roughly S/60 on deck or S/110 for cabins, a three- to five-day trip). As soon as you arrive in Yurimaguas, head straight to La Boca port to look for boats, since they get booked up in advance. Boats leave regularly though not at any set times; it's simply a matter of finding a reliable captain (preferably the one with the biggest, newest or fastest-looking boat) and arranging details with him. The price isn't bad and includes food, but you should bring your own hammock if you're sleeping on deck, and bring clean bottled water, as well as any extra treats, like canned fish, and a line and hooks (sold in the town's *ferreterías*) if you want to try fishing.

The scenery en route is electric: the river gets steadily wider and slower, and the vegetation on the riverbanks more and more dense. Remember, though, that during the day the sun beats down intensely and a sunhat is essential to avoid **river fever** – cold sweats (and diarrhoea) caused by exposure to the constant strong light reflected off the water. On this journey the boats pass through many interesting settlements, including Santa Cruz and Lagunas, starting point for trips into the huge Pacaya-Samiria National Reserve (see p.476).

7

of the remote Lamas-controlled hills. S/50

Shopping There are at least two good artesanía shops: Amachay, a museum-cum-shop which sells inexpensive Lamas artesanía, from gourds and baskets to fossils as well as the local Lamas organic coffee (Oro Verde); and Artesanía Tropical, Jr San Martín 1203. Down on the lower level of the village, the Cachique family sell eco-artesanía.

Yurimaguas

From Tarapoto it's another 140km north along pretty but rough jungle tracks to the frontier town of **YURIMAGUAS**. This bustling market town has little to recommend it, other than its **three ports**, giving access to the Río Huallaga. The most important is the downriver port of **La Boca**, where all the larger boats leave from, including those to Iquitos. The port is located some fifteen to twenty minutes' walk from the town centre, or a $1 ride in a motorcycle rickshaw. The second, middle port, known as **Puerto Garcilaso**, is closer to the heart of Yurimaguas and mainly used by farmers bringing their produce into town from the nearby farms in smaller boats. Fishermen primarily use the third, upper port, called **Puerto Malecón Shanus**.

ARRIVAL AND INFORMATION — YURIMAGUAS

By bus/colectivo In the dry season (June–Sept) frequent colectivos (S/30) and buses depart from the Shilcayo barrio market area in Tarapoto (3–4hr; Nov–March a little longer) and once in Yurimaguas they drop off within a block or so of the Parque la Unión. Travel this route by day if possible, because there's less risk of being robbed or encountering trouble on the road.

Tourist information There are photos and interesting if sparse information on Yurimaguas at yurimaguasperu.com and yurimaguas.net.

The northern desert

The **northern desert** remains one of the least-visited areas of Peru, mainly because of its distance from Lima and Cusco, the traditional hubs of Peru's tourist trail, but it is still an invaluable destination for its distinctive landscape, wildlife, archeology and history.

Northern Peru has some excellent **museums**, besides the breathtaking coastal beauty of its desert environment, which itself contains the largest dry forest in the Americas, almost entirely consisting of *algarrobo* (carob) trees. The main cities of **Chiclayo** and **Piura** (the first Spanish settlement in Peru) are lively commercial centres, serving not only the desert coast but large areas of the Andes as well. If, like a lot of travellers, you decide to bus straight through from Trujillo to the Ecuadorian border beyond **Tumbes** (or vice versa) in a single journey, you'll be missing out on some unique attractions.

The coastal resorts, such as the very trendy **Máncora** and **Punta Sal**, but also **Cabo Blanco** and, further south **La Pimentel**, the beach serving Chiclayo's population, are among the best reasons for stopping: though small, they usually have at least basic facilities for travellers, and, most importantly, the ocean is warmer here than anywhere else in the country. The real jewels of the region, however, are the archeological remains, particularly the **Valley of the Pyramids** at **Túcume** and the older pyramid complex of **Batán Grande**, two immense pre-Inca ceremonial centres within easy reach of Chiclayo. Equally alluring is the **Temple of Sipán**, where some of Peru's finest gold and silver grave-goods were found within the last fifteen years.

Pacasmayo and around

Some 10km north of the town of San Pedro de Lloc, which is famous for its stuffed lizards, the Panamerican Highway passes by the growing port town of **Pacasmayo**; many buses pull in here to pick up passengers and it is a possible stopoff en route between Trujillo and Chiclayo. If you have your own car, it's a good place to stop for a meal or a drink and take twenty minutes to explore the seafront promenade. However, there are few hotels here, if you decide to spend the night. Despite the town's grim initial appearance, the area around the old jetty, thought to be the largest and most attractive surviving pier on the coast of Peru, possesses some dilapidated colonial mansions.

7

Pakatnamu

Free • Take a colectivo or bus from Pacasmayo, then 6km walk from the main highway to the site or take a taxi (S/20–30 with short wait)

A few kilometres north of Pacasmayo, just before the village of Guadalupe, a track leads off left to the well-preserved ruins of **Pakatnamu** (The City of Sanctuaries), overlooking the mouth of the Río Jequetepeque. Being off the main road and far from any major towns, the ruins of this abandoned city have survived relatively untouched by treasure hunters or curious browsers. The remains include pyramids, palaces, storehouses and dwellings. The place was first occupied during the Gallinazo period (around 350 AD), then was subsequently conquered by the Mochica and Chimu cultures. It gets very hot around midday, and there's little shade and **no food** or drink available at the site, so bring your own.

ARRIVAL AND DEPARTURE — PACASMAYO AND AROUND

by bus Buses pick up and drop off passengers where Leoncito Prado crosses the Av 28 de Julio at the centre of Pacasmayo, just a couple of blocks from the ocean.

Bus companies Most buses stop in or close to the main street, Leoncito Prado. Emtrafesa's depot is at Av 28 de Julio 104, just around the corner; while Cruz del Sur are at Jr Espinar C-7/90.

Destinations Cajamarca (6–7hr); Chiclayo (1–2hr); Lima (10–12hr); Trujillo (2–3hr).

ACCOMMODATION AND EATING

El Encuentro de Ignacio El Malecón. A pleasant seafront restaurant serving good fish dishes at lunchtime with tables inside and out. Daily 10.30am–7.30pm.

Hotel Pakatnamu Malecón Grau 103 ⊕044 52352. This hotel has an attractive wooden veranda and sea views; rooms are comfortable but simple, with plenty of carpet cover plus cable TV and private hot showers. S/75

Chiclayo

The commercial centre of northern Peru, **CHICLAYO** is better famed for its banks than its heritage. Nevertheless it has its own attractions, even if most of the city is an urban sprawl modernizing and growing rapidly. The city has an incredibly busy feel to it, with people and traffic moving fast and noisily everywhere during daylight hours. Tourists tend to attract attention in the main streets, not least because they aren't seen very often.

Parque Principal and around

The city's heart is known as the **Parque Principal**, where there is a futuristic fountain that's elegantly lit at night. You'll also find the Neoclassical **Catedral** here, built in 1869 and with its main doorway supported by Doric columns, and the **Palacio Municipal**, a Republican edifice built in 1919. Along Calle San José, you'll find the **Convento Franciscano Santa María**, built in the early seventeenth century but destroyed, apart from the second cloister, by El Niño rains in 1961.

La Verónica and the Plazuela Elías Aguirre

Six blocks directly west of the Parque Principal, there's the small, attractive chapel of **La Verónica** (daily 9am–4pm; free), Calle Torres Paz. Built at the end of the nineteenth century, its most notable feature is the altarpiece of silver- and gold leaf. In the **Plazuela Elías Aguirre**, just around the corner, there's a statue in honour of the *comandante* of this name, who was a local hero serving the Republicans in the Battle of Angamos during the War of the Pacific.

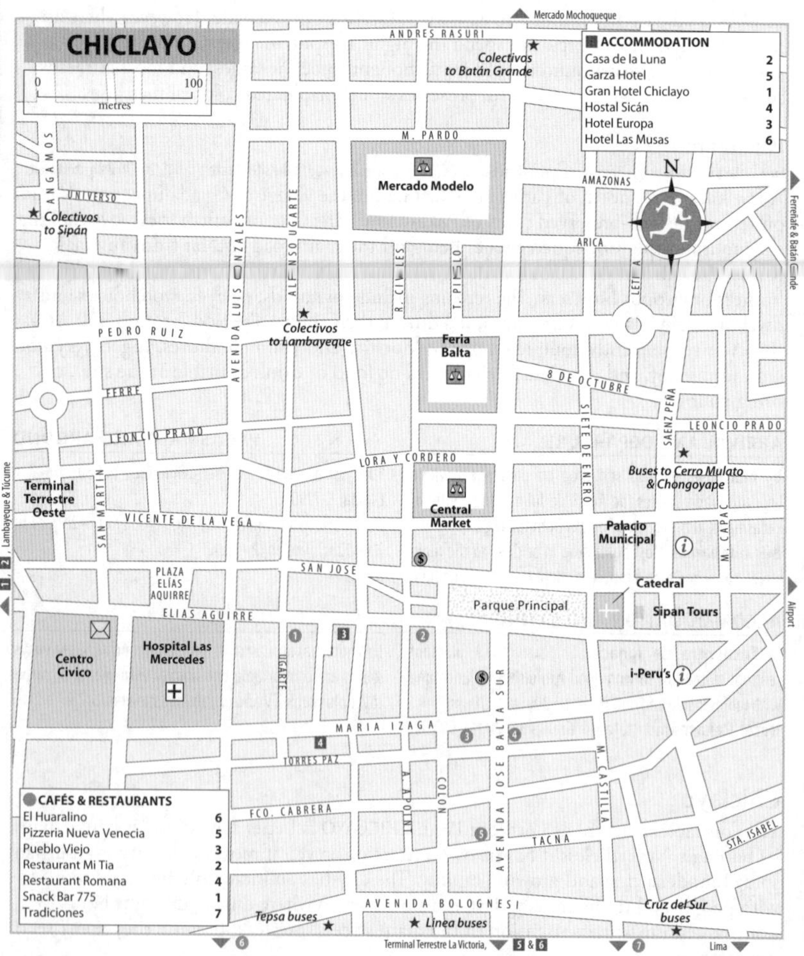

ATTRACTIONS AROUND CHICLAYO

Most places of interest in the region can be reached independently by taking a **colectivo** from the market area of Chiclayo, but you'll find it much easier to see all the archeological sites if you've got your own transport. You'll probably get the most out of these, however, by going with a knowledgeable local **guide** on an organized tour from Chiclayo. **Taxi** drivers can also be hired by the day or half-day (usually around S/60 for half-day and S/150 full day, but it depends on negotiation and, in particular, how much actual driving time).

LAMBAYEQUE TOURIST TICKET

Although tickets to most sites and museums can still be bought independently, it's possible to buy a general **Lambayeque Tourist Ticket** ($5), available from the Instituto Nacional de Cultura, Av González 375 (T 074 237261) in Chiclayo, and sometimes also available from the main local archeological museums; the ticket covers the main museums and sites in the region, including those at Túcume, Sipán, Lambayeque, Ferreñafe and Batán Grande.

7

ARRIVAL AND DEPARTURE — CHICLAYO

BY PLANE

José Abelado Quiñones González Airport is 2km east of town on Av Bolognesi (T 074 233192; 24hr), and easily reached by taxi for S/15–20. Flights are with LAN Perú, C Manuel María Izaga 770 (Mon–Fri 9am–7pm, Sat 9am–1pm; T 074 274875), and StarPerú, C Manuel María Izaga (Mon–Fri 9am–7pm, Sat 9am–1pm; T 074 225204).

Destinations Iquitos (several weekly; 2hr); Lima (daily; 2hr); Piura (daily; 30min); Tarapoto (several weekly; 90min); Trujillo (daily; 45min).

BY BUS

Buses connecting Chiclayo with La Pimentel and Lambayeque use the Terminal Terrestre Oeste, on the first block of Angamos, just off block 1 of San José. Services for all the southern cities – Trujillo, Lima and so on – use the Terminal Terrestre La Victoria on Calle Mochica, where it meets the Panamericana Sur, which has a waiting area, a left-luggage deposit and a hostel.

Bus companies Civa, Bolognesi 714 (T 074 223434), for Chachapoyas and Lima; Cruz del Sur, Bolognesi 888 (T 074 225508), for Trujillo, Lima and Tumbes or Máncora; Tepsa, Bolognesi 504, at Colón (T 074 224448), for Cajamarca; Movil, Bolognesi 195 (T 074 271940), for Chachapoyas, Bagua, Moyobamba and Tarapoto; and Turismo Kuelap, Bolognesi 504 (same depot and phone as Tepsa, above), for nightly buses to Chachapoyas.

Destinations Cajamarca (10 daily; 7–9hr); Chachapoyas (several daily; 10–12hr); Ferreñafe (several daily; 30min); Huancabamba (2 weekly; 15hr); La Pimentel (several daily; 25min); Lambayeque (several daily; 20min); Lima (8–10 daily; 14hr); Piura (12 daily; 4hr); Trujillo (12 daily; 3hr); Tumbes (8 daily; 10hr).

INFORMATION AND TOURS

Tourist information The main Regional Tourist Office is a couple of blocks from the Parque Principal on Av Sáenz Peña 839 (Mon–Fri 9am–5.30pm, Sat 9am–1pm; T 074 205703, 233132 or 238112, W regionlambayeque .gob.pe). i-Peru have an office at Siete de Enero 579 (Mon–Fri 9am–7pm, Sat 9am–2pm; T 074 205703). There are kiosks in the Parque Principal and nearby just a block down Balta Sur. You can also try the *Garza Hotel* (see p.398). Alternatively, contact the Tourist Police (see p.399).

Tour operators Tours around the area include trips to Túcume, Batán Grande and the local museums, and last 4–8hr; costs are from S/35–75 per person. The best tours are offered by Sipán Tours, 7 de Enero 772 (T 074 229053, W sipantours.com), and InkaNatura Travel, in the lobby of the *Gran Hotel Chiclayo* (T 074 209948, E opcix @inkanatura.com), or in Lima (T 01 4402022). Other companies include Indiana Tours, Colón 556 (T 074 222991), who also have a kiosk at the airport (T 074 238750), and Lizu Tours, Elías Aguirre 418, second floor (T 074 228871, E lizu_tours@latinmail.com).

GETTING AROUND

By bus Local buses depart from Terminal Terrestre.

By car Mines Rent-a-Car are inside the *Gran Hotel Chiclayo* (T 074 237512).

By taxi If you need a taxi try Chiclayo Rent-a-Car, Av Grau 520, Santa Victoria (T 074 229390, F 237512), which also has offices at the *Gran Hotel Chiclayo* (see p.398) and the airport (T 074 244291), or Robert Huima Suloeta, C Leticia 566 (T 074 498439).

CHICLAYO'S MARKETS

Central Market Daily 7am–6pm. Along with the massive semi-covered market lanes – part of which is called the Feria Balta – this is the main focus of activity in town. Known as the Mercado Modelo, the main part of the Central Market is packed with food vendors at the centre, and other stalls around the outside. This is one of the best markets in the north – and a revelation if you've just arrived in the country. There's a whole section of live animals, including wild fox cubs, canaries and even the occasional condor chick, and you can't miss the ray fish, known as *la guitarra*, hanging up to dry in the sun before being made into a local speciality, *pescado seco*. But the most compelling displays are the herbalists' shops, or *mercado de brujos* (witches' market), selling everything from herbs and charms to whale bones and hallucinogenic cacti.

Mercado Mochoqueque Daily 5am–11am. Further out on the eastern edge of town. Huge, cheap wholesale market and a fascinating window into life in this part of the world; it's best to come early on Tuesday or Friday, but if you stray here, beware – there are a lot of pickpockets.

7

ACCOMMODATION

Finding a place to stay is relatively simple in Chiclayo; but if you want peace and quiet, or to camp, you may prefer one of the out-of-town options like the beautiful *Hospedaje Rural Los Horcones* (see p.408). In Chiclayo itself, most of the reasonably priced hotels are clustered around the Plaza de Armas.

Casa de la Luna José Bernado Alcedo 250 ⊤074 270156, ⓦhotelcasadelaluna.com.pe. This is a very reasonable mid-range hotel, located several blocks from the centre of town. Rooms are adequate and modern with great bathrooms, TVs and some have wi-fi. There's a small pool, laundry and parking. S/140

Garza Hotel Bolognesi 756 ⊤074 228172, ⓦgarzahotel.com. Very central and pretty comfortable, with a pool and sauna, good food and staff who provide useful tourist information. They also rent out cars and jeeps. S/295

★ **Gran Hotel Chiclayo** Av Federico Villareal 115 ⊤074 234911, ⓦgranhotelchiclayo.com.pe. The best, most luxurious hotel in town, even if it is a little way from the centre. You get spacious, very comfortable rooms, excellent showers, a fine restaurant, decent swimming pool, wi-fi in rooms, a business centre and even a hot little casino-bar. S/350

Hostal Sicán Av María Izaga 356 ⊤074 208741 and ⊤074 237618. Nicely decorated, central, friendly and has TVs in rooms and communal internet access. The quietest beds are at the top, and the price includes breakfast. S/60

Hotel Europa Elías Aguirre ⊤074 237919, ⓔhoteleuropachiclayo@terra.com.pe. A very clean hotel with extremely friendly service and a small bar space with cafetería. All rooms have private TVs plus bath and there is internet access. S/75

★ **Hotel Las Musas** Los Faiques 101, Urb. Santa Victoria ⊤074 239884 or ⊤074 239885. Upmarket lodgings that are a little less expensive than you'd expect, with excellent service, nice rooms, a cool lobby and casino. S/200

EATING, DRINKING AND NIGHTLIFE

Eating out in or near Chiclayo offers quite a lot of variety. Being close to the ocean, seafood is the most common local dish, but the city also enjoys *criolla* meat dishes, such as *lomo saltado,* and Italian food – particularly pizza. One local speciality is rehydrated dried fish (*pescado seco*), often prepared from flat ray fish with potatoes.

El Huaralino La Libertad 155, Urb. Santa Victoria. Offers *tortilla de raya and pato a la Nortena* (duck with rice and vegetables Northern Peru style). Come early for a tasty set breakfast. Mon–Sat 8.30am–9.30pm.

Pizzeria Nueva Venecia Av Balta 365. Just a few blocks down from the Parque Principal, this is the best of Chiclayo's numerous pizza parlours; cosy in the evenings with small wooden tables and a large pizza oven. Efficient service and a choice of wines and other drinks. Daily noon–11pm.

Pueblo Viejo Maria Izaga 900 ⊤074 229863. The best of Chiclayo's restaurants with top *criolla* cooking, this place is excellent though it's better still when there's live music on Fridays. It has a wide ranging menu which varies over time. Best to book in advance. Tues–Sat 7–11pm.

Restaurant Mi Tía Elías Aguirre 698. A small but friendly place with a wide-range of traditional snacks and cakes along with pasta and goat dishes at very reasonable prices. Mon–Sat 10am–6pm.

Restaurant Romana Av José Balta Sur 512 ⊤074 223598. Great and quite spacious café and restaurant which is a popular meeting place for middle-class Chiclayanos. Typical Chiclayana food is at low prices, and the restaurant itself is open and pretty busy all day long. Good juices and sandwiches. Daily 7.30am–9pm.

Snack Bar 775 Ugarte 775. Great-value snacks that are limited to sandwiches, cakes and burgers. Daily noon–10pm.

Tradiciones 7 de Enero Sur 105 ⓣ 074 221192. Good for local dishes and also a popular meeting place offering very reasonable menus at lunchtime and quality à la carte at other times. Delicious juices, tamales and other snacks, too. Daily 8am–8pm.

DIRECTORY

Health The hospital is at C Hipolito Unanue 180 ⓣ 074 237776 (24hr).

Internet Click-Click, close to the plaza at San José 604, upstairs; and at San José 104.

Money and exchange The main banks are concentrated around the Parque Principal. *Cambistas* are on the corners of the Parque Principal, particularly Av José Balta, or there's the casa de cambio Hugo Barandiaran at Av Balta 641A (Mon–Fri 9.30am–5pm) next to the Banco Continental.

Post office Elías Aguirre 140, seven blocks west of the plaza (Mon–Sat 8am–8pm, Sun 8am–2pm).

Telephones Telefónica del Perú, Av José Balta 815; there's also a Locutorio Público at both Av José Balta 827 and Elías Aguirre 631, the latter within a stone's throw of the plaza.

Tourist police Sáenz Peña 830 ⓣ 074 236700 ext 311 (Mon–Sat 8am–6pm); also on call 24hr.

7

La Pimentel and around

An attractive beach resort just 14km southwest of Chiclayo, **La Pimentel** is a pleasant settlement with an attractive colonial-style centre around the **Plaza Diego Ferre**. More importantly, though, it offers a decent **beach** for swimming and **surfing** (competitions take place in Dec & Jan). The town is known for its small-scale fishing industry, much of it using the traditional *caballitos del mar* (made from *totora* reeds). For a small fee (25¢) you can access the long pier that divides the seafront *malecón* in two, where you can watch the fishermen.

More picturesque is the small fishing village of **La Caleta Santa Rosa**, about 5km south of La Pimentel. Here the beach is crowded with colourful boats and fishermen mending nets; the best and freshest **ceviche** in the Chiclayo area is served in the restaurants on the seafront here.

The area known as **El Faro** (The Lighthouse), slightly to the south of La Caleta Santa Rosa, is the best location for surfing. Continuing from here along the road inland for

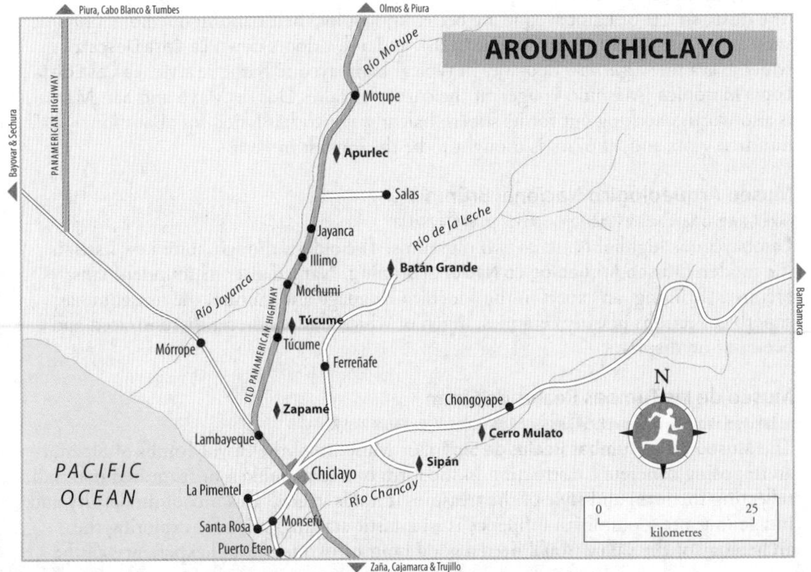

about 5km, you come to the small town of **Monsefú**, known as the "city of flowers" because of the local cottage industry that supplies blooms to the area. It's also known for its fine straw hats, straw-rolled cigarettes and the quality of its cotton, all of which you can buy at the daily **market**.

About 4km south from Monsefú you come to the colonial village of **Etén** and its nearby ruined church, the Capilla del Milagro, built following a local's vision of the Christ child in 1649. Southwest, towards the sea, lie the wide avenues of largely derelict **Puerto Etén**, just another 4km away, where there are abandoned nineteenth-century train carriages.

ARRIVAL AND DEPARTURE — LA PIMENTEL AND AROUND

By bus Buses depart from block 5 of Vicente da la Vega in Chiclayo and connect to La Pimentel (every 30min; 25min).

By colectivo Regular colectivos leave from Avenida Ugarte in Chiclayo and serve La Pimentel, Santa Rosa, Monsefú and Puerto Etén (50¢).

ACCOMMODATION AND EATING

Garnola Hostal Jr Quiñones 109, La Pimentel ⓣ 074 4529. Offering a selection of rooms, some with fine sea views, a laundry area on the roof and parking next door. S/45

Restaurant Las Gaviotas La Pimentel ⓣ 074 452808. As good as any of the seafood restaurants at the south end of the promenade, this spot is close to where the *caballitos del mar* are stacked on the beach; there are great, far-reaching views from upstairs. Daily 10.30am–6.30pm.

Lambayeque

The old colonial town of **LAMBAYEQUE**, 12km from Chiclayo city, must have been a grand place before it fell into decay last century; fortunately, it seems on the road to recovery, helped by its popular museums and vibrant Sunday **markets**. **Buildings** worth seeing here include the early eighteenth-century **Iglesia de San Pedro**, parallel to the main square between de Mayo and 8 de Octubre, which is still holding up and is the most impressive edifice in the town, with two attractive front towers and fourteen balconies.

Lambayeque's casonas

The dusty streets of Lambayeque are better known for their handful of colonial *casonas*, such as **La Casa Cúneo** (8 de Octubre 328), and a few doors down **La Casa Descalzi**, which has a fine *algarrobo* doorway in typical Lambayeque Baroque style. **La Casa de la Logia Masónica** (Masonic Lodge), at the corner of calles Dos de Mayo and San Martín, is also worth checking out for its superb balcony, which has lasted for about four hundred years and, at 67m, is thought to be the longest in Peru.

Museo Arqueológico Nacional Brüning

Block 7, Avenida Huamachuco • Daily 9am–5pm • S/10 • ⓣ 074 282110

Lambayeque's highlights are its two museums. The oldest, though quite new itself, is the modern **Museo Arqueológico Nacional Brüning**. Named after its founder Hans Heinrich Brüning, an expert in the Mochica language and culture, the museum has superb collections of early ceramics, much of which has only recently resurfaced and been put on display.

Museo de las Tumbas Reales de Sipán

Av Juan Pablo Vizcardo y Guzmán 895 • Tues–Sun 9am–5pm • S/10 • ⓣ 074 283978

The **Museo de las Tumbas Reales de Sipán**, or Museum of the Royal Tombs of Sipán, is an imposing concrete construction in the form of a semi-sunken or truncated pyramid, reflecting the form and style of the treasures it holds inside. This mix of modernity and indigenous pre-Columbian influence is a fantastic starting-point for exploring the archeology of the valley. You'll need a good hour or two to see and experience all the exhibits, which include a large collection of gold, silver and copper objects from the tomb of **El Señor de Sipán** (see below), including his main emblem, a staff known as **El Cetro Cuchillo**, found stuck to the bones of his right hand in his tomb. The tomb itself is also reproduced as one of the museum's centrepieces down on the bottom of the three floors. The top floor mainly exhibits ceramics, while the second floor is dedicated to El Señor de Sipán's ornaments and treasures. Background music accompanies you around the museum circuit using instruments and sounds associated with pre-Hispanic cultures of the region. A musical finale can usually be caught on the ground floor.

The Lambayeque Valley has long been renowned for turning up pre-Columbian metallurgy – particularly gold pieces from the neighbouring hill graveyard of **Zacamé** – and local treasure-hunters have sometimes gone so far as to use bulldozers to dig them out; but it's the addition of the Sipán treasures that's given the biggest boost to Lambayeque's reputation, and the museum is now one of the finest in South America.

ARRIVAL AND DEPARTURE — LAMBAYEQUE

7

By colectivo Take the short colectivo ride (10–15min) north from the street Pedro Ruiz close to the main Chiclayo market areas.

EATING

Lambayeque is also known for its sweet pastry cakes – filled with *manjar blanca* (a very popular condensed-milk product) and touted under the unlikely name of *King-Kongs*. In any of the town's streets, you'll be bombarded by street vendors pushing out piles of the cake, shouting "King-Kong! King-Kong!"

El Cantaro C Dos de Mayo 180 ⓣ074 282196. An excellent lunchtime restaurant whether you go for the set menus or à la carte; known by most taxi drivers, this is one of the most traditional restaurants in the region, serving ceviche, duck, goat and other local specialities. Daily 11am–5pm.

Zaña

Free • Buses leave from 7 de Enero 1349 in Chiclayo (hourly; 45min–1hr) • It is possible to get one of the Chiclayo tour companies (see p.397) to include Zaña on a local itinerary, but there are none specifically arranged on a regular basis

The ruined colonial settlement of **ZAÑA** sits in the desert about 12km away from the modern town of Mocupe, itself 38km south of Chiclayo along the Panamerican Highway. Elaborate arches, columns and sections of old churches, such as the once elegant **Convento de San Agustín**, stand partly overgrown by shrubs, giving evidence of what was once an opulent city. Founded in 1553, it became a centre for meting out justice to thieves, witches and errant slaves, but its wealth actually originated from the nearby port of Cherrepe, from where it controlled the passage of vessels along the coast between Lima and Panama. Zaña rapidly grew rich, and its subsequent excesses were soon notorious, attracting the attention of **pirates**, including a band led by one **Edward Davis**, who sacked the place in 1668. The city subsequently lost much of its prestige and most of the important families moved out, the rest following a few years later when news arrived of another English pirate off the Peruvian coast – Francis Drake. The final blow came in 1720, when the waters of the Río Zaña swept through the streets, causing such damage that the settlement was abandoned. Today, all you can see are some ruined buildings.

The Temple of Sipán

Tues–Sun 9am–5pm • S/8 • Combi colectivos (50min; S/3) leave Chiclayo every morning from the Plaza Elías Aguirre, just 6 or 7 blocks west of the Plaza de Armas

The **TEMPLE OF SIPÁN**, 33km southeast of Chiclayo, discovered in 1987 by archeologist Walter Alva has proved to be one of the richest **tombs** in the entire Americas. Every important individual buried here, mostly Mochica nobles from around 200–600 AD, was interred prostrate with his or her own precious-metal grave objects, such as gold and silver goblets, headdresses, breastplates and jewellery including turquoise and lapis lazuli, themselves now on show in the **Museo de las Tumbas Reales de Sipán** (see p.400). The most important grave uncovered was that of a noble known today as **El Señor de Sipán**, the Lord of Sipán. He was buried along with a great many fine gold and silver decorative objects adorned with semi precious stones and shells from the Ecuadorian coast.

There are two large adobe **pyramids**, including the Huaca Rajada, in front of which there was once a royal tomb; the place certainly gives you a feel for the people who lived here almost two millennia ago, and it's one of the few sites in Peru whose treasures were not entirely plundered by either the conquistadors or more recent grave robbers. There's also a **site museum**, displaying photos and illustrations of the excavation work plus replicas of some of the discoveries.

Pampagrande and around

Free • Buses to Chongoyape leave every hour from Avenida Saenz Peña in Chiclayo, by the corner with L. Prado in Chiclayo (S/4; 1hr 20min)

7

Pampagrande is, amazingly, a rarely visited site even though it was one of the largest and most active Mochica administrative and ceremonial centres in the region and was populated by thousands. Located in the desert some 20km (more or less) west of the Temple of Sipán (see p.401), it can be reached along dusty tracks, but you'll need a local driver to find it. Also worth a visit is the site of **Cerro Mulato**, near the hill town of **Chongoyape**, 80km out of Chiclayo along the attractive Chancay Valley.

THE SICÁN CULTURE

The **Sicán culture**, thought to descend from the Mochica (see p.489), is associated with the Naymlap dynasty, based on a wide-reaching political confederacy emanating from the Lambayeque Valley between around 800 and 1300 AD. These people produced alloys of gold, silver and arsenic-copper in unprecedented scales in pre-Hispanic America. The name Sicán actually means "House of the Moon" in the Mochica language. Legend has it that a leader called **Naymlap** arrived by sea with a fleet of balsa boats, his own royal retinue and a green female stone idol. Naymlap set about building temples and palaces near the sea in the Lambayeque Valley. The region was then successfully governed by Naymlap's twelve grandsons, until one of them was tempted by a witch to move the green stone idol. Legend has it that this provoked a month of heavy rains and flash floods, rather like the effects of El Niño today, bringing great disease and death in its wake. Indeed, glacial ice cores analyzed in the Andes above here have indicated the likelihood of a powerful El Niño current around 1100 AD.

The Sicán civilization, like the Mochica, depended on a high level of **irrigation technology**. The civilization also had its own copper money and sophisticated ceramics, many of which featured an image of the flying **Lord of Sicán**. The main thrust of the Lord of Sicán designs is a well-dressed man, possibly Naymlap himself, with small wings, a nose like a bird's beak and, sometimes, talons rather than feet. The Sicán culture showed a marked change in its burial practices from that of the Mochica, almost certainly signifying a change in the prevalent belief in an afterlife. While the Mochica people were buried in a lying position – like the Mochica warrior in his splendid tomb at Sipán (see p.401) – the new Sicán style was to inter its dead in a sitting position. Excavations of Sicán sites in the last decade have also revealed such rare artefacts as 22 "tumis" (semicircular bladed ceremonial knives with an anthropomorphic figure stabbing where a handle should be).

The Sicán monetary system, the flying Lord of Sicán image and much of the culture's religious and political infrastructures were all abandoned after the dramatic environmental disasters caused by El Niño in 1100 AD. **Batán Grande**, the culture's largest and most impressive city, was partly washed away and a fabulous new centre, a massive city of over twenty adobe pyramids at **Túcume** (see p.404), was constructed in the Leche Valley. This relatively short-lived culture was taken over by Chimu warriors from the south around 1370 AD, who absorbed the Lambayeque Valley, some of the Piura Valley area and about two-thirds of the Peruvian desert coast into their empire.

From Chongoyape, another dirt road traces an alternative route through the desert to Cerro Mulato. Here you can see some impressive Chavín **petroglyphs**, and in the surrounding region, a number of Chavín graves dating from the fifth century BC. There's also a conservation area at **Chaparri** (turn left at the entrance to Chongoyape for the Cruz de Mira Costa).

Ferreñafe and around

Buses to Ferreñafe leave Chiclayo from José Balta Norte at the corner with Andrés Rasuri (hourly; 30min)

Founded in 1550 by Captain Alfonso de Osorio, **FERREÑAFE**, 18km northeast of Chiclayo, was once known as the "land of two faiths" because of the local tradition of believing first in the power of spirits and second in the Catholic Church. Curiously, Ferreñafe is also home to more Miss Peru winners than any other town in the country.

Museo Nacional de Sicán

Tues–Sun 9am–5pm • S/8 • ⓣ 074 286469

Ferreñafe is best known for its excellent **Museo Nacional de Sicán**, which has an audiovisual introduction and a large collection of exhibits, mostly models depicting daily life and burials of the Sicán people (see box opposite), a great way to get a visual concept before or after visiting the local archeological sites themselves. One central room is full of genuine treasures, including the famous ceremonial headdresses and masks.

7

Batán Grande

Daily 9am–5pm • Free • Interpretative centre ⓣ 074 9746 32390

The site at **BATÁN GRANDE**, 57km northeast of Chiclayo, incorporates over twenty pre-Inca temple pyramids within one corner of what extends to the largest dry forest in the Americas, the **Bosque de Pomac**. There's an **interpretative centre** at the main entrance, which has a small archeological museum with a scale model of the site.

Part of the beauty of this site comes from its sitting at the heart of an ancient forest, dominated by *algarrobo* trees, spreading out over some 13,400 hectares, a veritable oasis in the middle of the desert landscape. Over ninety percent of Peru's ancient gold artefacts are estimated to have come from here – you'll notice there are thousands of holes, dug over the centuries by treasure hunters. Batán Grande is also known to have developed its own copper-smelting works, which produced large quantities of flat copper plates – *naipes* – that were between 5 and 10cm long. These were believed to have been used and exported to Ecuador as a kind of monetary system.

Brief history

The **Sicán culture** arose to fill the void left by the demise of the Mochica culture around 700 AD (see box opposite), and were the driving force in the region from 800 to 1100 AD, based here at Batán Grande. Known to archeologists as the Initial Lambayeque Period, judging by the beauty and extent of the pyramids here, this era was clearly a flourishing one. Nevertheless, Batán Grande was abandoned in the twelfth century and the Sicán moved across the valley to Túcume (see p.404), probably following a deluge of rains (El Niño) causing devastation, epidemics and a lack of faith in the power of the ruling elite. This fits neatly with the legend of the Sicán leader Naymlap's descendants, who evidently brought this on themselves by sacrilegious behaviour. There is also some evidence that the pyramids were deliberately burnt, supporting the latter theory.

The site

The main part of the **site** that you visit today was mostly built between 750 and 1250 AD, and comprises the Huaca del Oro, Huaca Rodillona, Huaca Corte and the Huaca Las Ventanas, where the famous **Tumi de Oro** was uncovered in 1936. The tomb of

El Señor de Sicán (not to be confused with the tomb of El Señor de Sipán; see p.401), on the north side of the Huaca El Loro, contained a noble with two women, two children and five golden crowns; these are exhibited in the excellent **museum** (see p.403) in Ferreñafe. From the top of these pyramids you can just about make out the form of the ancient ceremonial plaza on the ground below.

Bosque de Pomac

The **National Sanctuary of the Pomac Forest** is the largest dry forest in western South America. A kilometre or so in from the interpretative centre you'll find the oldest *algarrobo* tree in the forest, the **árbol milenario**; over a thousand years old, its spreading, gnarled mass is still the site for pagan rituals, judging from the offerings hanging from its twisted boughs, but it's also the focus of the **Fiesta de las Cruces** on May 3. In the heart of the reserve lies the *Bosque de Pomac*, where over forty species of bird such as mockingbirds, cardinals, burrowing owls and hummingbirds have been identified, and most visitors at least see some iguanas and lizards scuttling into the undergrowth. Rarer, but still present, are wild foxes, deer and anteaters. There's also a **mirador** (viewing platform) in the heart of the forest, from where it's possible to make out many of the larger *huacas*. Although there is hostel accommodation at the interpretative centre, it's rarely available or open: you'll have to turn up and chance it; there is a camping area outside, however. The café here, selling basic snacks, is not always functioning, so bring a picnic.

7

ARRIVAL AND TOURS — BATÁN GRANDE

By car If you're in your own transport, take the new northern road from Ferreñafe to reach Batán Grande; it's a 15–20min drive. There are two routes into the forest; one passes the interpretative centre, while another goes via Huaca El Loro and comes from the nearby village of Illimo, the next settlement north of Túcume. You'll need a decent car, preferably but not essentially 4WD, and a local driver or good map. If you take this route you'll be rewarded by close contact with small, scattered desert communities, mainly goat herders and peasant farmers, many of whose houses are still built out of adobe and lath.

By colectivo Colectivos to Batán Grande pueblo (10km beyond the site) leave each morning from block 16 of 7 de Enero in Chiclayo – go as early as possible and ask to be dropped at the interpretative centre (2hr; check with the driver for return journey times).

Tours To visit the site in just one day, it's best to take a guided tour from Chiclayo or Ferreñafe. There are sometimes guides with motorbikes or horses at the interpretative centre. Guide and ride costs from around S/20–25 per person.

Túcume and around

Daily 9am–5pm, though in reality the site is not fenced off and so accessible 24hr • S/10; guides sometimes available from S/10

The site of **TÚCUME**, also known as the **Valley of the Pyramids**, contains 26 adobe pyramids, many clustered around the hill of **El Purgatorio** (197m), also known as Cerro La Raya (after a ray fish that lives within it, according to legend), and is located some 33km north from Chiclayo. Although the ticket office closes at 4.30pm and the museum shortly after this, the site is accessible after these hours (being part of the local landscape and dissected by small paths connecting villages and homesteads), with the main sectors clearly marked by good interpretative signs.

Túcume's modern settlement, based alongside the old Panamerican Highway, lies just a couple of kilometres west of the Valley of the Pyramids, and doesn't have much to offer visitors except a handful of accommodation and eating options (see p.408).

Brief history

Covering more than two hundred hectares, Túcume was occupied initially by the **Sicán culture**, which began building here around 1100 AD after abandoning Batán Grande (see p.403). During this time, known as the Second Lambayeque Period, the focus of construction moved to Túcume where an elite controlled a complex administrative

system and cleared large areas of *algarrobo* forest (as is still the case today in the immediate vicinity of the Valley of the Pyramids and Cerro El Purgatorio at Túcume). Reed seafaring vessels were also essential for the development of this new, powerful elite. The Sicán people were clearly expert **seamen** and traded along the coast as far as Ecuador, Colombia and quite probably Central America; to the east, they traded with the sierra and the jungle regions beyond. They were also expert **metallurgists** working with gold, silver, copper and precious stones, and their elaborate funerary masks are astonishingly vivid and beautiful.

At Túcume's peak, in the thirteenth and early fourteenth centuries, it was probably a focus of annual pilgrimage for a large section of the coastal population, whose Sicán

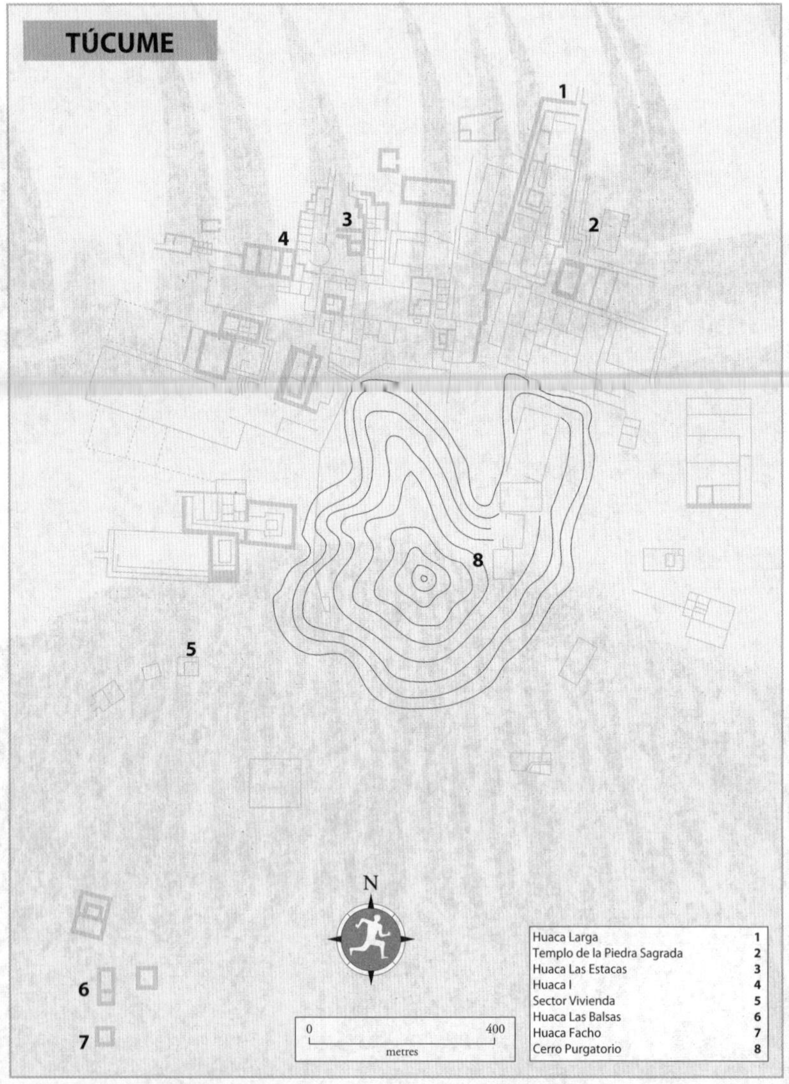

leaders were high priests with great agro-astrological understanding, adept administrators, a warrior elite, and expert artisans.

It wasn't long, however, before things changed, and around 1375 AD the **Chimu** invaded from the south. Within another hundred years the **Inca** had arrived, though they took some twenty years to conquer the Chimu, during which time it appears that Túcume played an important role in the ensuing military, magical and diplomatic intrigues. Afterwards, the Inca transported many Chimu warriors to remote outposts in the Andes, in order to maximize the Incas' political control and minimize the chances of rebellion. By the time the **Spanish** arrived, just over half a century later, Túcume's time had already passed. When the Spanish chronicler, Pedro Cieza de León, stopped by here in 1547, it was already in ruins and abandoned.

The site

From Túcume's plaza, follow the right-hand road to the site; it's a dusty 2km walk. Alternatively, take a mototaxi or combi colectivo for less than $1. At the end of the fields, the road divides: right leads to the museum and ticket office

Today, Túcume remains an extensive site with the labyrinthine ruins of walls and courtyards still quite visible, if slightly rain-washed by the impact of heavy El Niño weather cycles, and you can easily spend two or three hours exploring. The site has two clearly defined sectors: North is characterized by the large monumental structures; while the South has predominantly simpler structures and common graveyards. The adobe bricks utilized were loaf-shaped, each with their maker's mark, indicating control and accounting for labour and tribute to the elite. Some of the pyramids have up to seven phases of construction, showing that building went on more or less continuously.

El Purgatorio hill

There's a **viewing point**, reached by a twisting path that leads up **El Purgatorio hill**, from where you can get a good view of the whole city. This hill, circular and cone-shaped, at the very centre of the occupied area, was and still is considered by locals to be a sacred mountain. Access to it was restricted originally, though there is evidence of later Inca constructions, for example an altar site. It is still visited these days by the local *curanderos*, healing wizards who utilize shamanic techniques and the psychoactive San Pedro cactus in their weekly rituals, which researchers believe are similar to those of their ancestors and which could be one possible explanation for the name El Purgatorio (the place of the purge).

Museo di Sitio

Daily 9am–5pm

The **Museo de Sitio**, at the entrance to the site, has exhibits relating to the work of **Thor Heyerdahl**, who found in Túcume the inspiration for his *Kon Tiki* expedition in 1946 when he sailed a raft built in the style of ancient Peruvian boats from Callao, near Lima, right across the Pacific Ocean to Polynesia, as he tried to prove a link between civilizations on either side of the Pacific. The museum also covers the work of archeologist Wendell Bennett, who in the late 1930s was the first person to scientifically excavate at the site. More esoterically, Túcume has a local reputation for **magical power**, and a section of the museum has been devoted to a display of local *curanderismo*. There's also an attractive picnic area, and a ceramic workshop where they use 2500-year-old techniques. The museum was constructed to reflect the style – known as *la ramada* – of colonial chapels in this region, built by local indigenous craftsmen centuries ago and using much the same materials.

ARRIVAL AND INFORMATION — TÚCUME

By colectivo From Chiclayo, take one of the colectivos marked "Túcume" (S/5; a 40min trip), which leave every 30min or so from a yard on Las Amapolas, just off block 13 of Avenida Leguía (they can also be picked up on the main road leaving Chiclayo or as they pass through Lambayeque. You could also pick one up from the corner of Pedro Ruiz and

Avenida Ugarte, close to the Mercado Modelo in Chiclayo.

Tourist information Well-signposted tourist information centre (daily 8am–5pm) on the main road, Avenida Federico Villareal, just before the turn-off to the plaza.

Tours Complejo Turistíco Las Piramide (see below) organize excursions to local sites and ruins as well as horseriding tours.

ACCOMMODATION AND EATING

Complejo Turistico Las Piramides 074 995959 or Trujillo 044 370178, laspiramidestucume@terra.com. A nice campsite (price includes breakfast) with showers, campfire and *parillada* (grilling) facilities, as well as a restaurant which is fully open at holiday times and a refreshment kiosk almost always open during daylight hours. S/25

Hospedaje Acafala Federico Villareal 074 422029. Located about one block before the tourist office as you come into town, this is cheap and cheerful with shared bathrooms. S/30

Hospedaje Rural Los Horcones North of Túcume archeological site 074 2243401 or Lima 01 2640968, loshorconesdetucume.com. Luxurious rooms plus camping sites, shower blocks and local home-cooked food available here; buildings are constructed with traditional materials in a style reflecting that of the pyramid site next door. A very good breakfast is included. S/150, camping S/25

Restaurant La Sabrosa Block 3 of Calle Federico Villareal. Small restaurant serving reasonably tasty and cheap set-menus at lunchtime. Mon–Sat 8am–7pm.

7

DIRECTORY

Money and exchange The only places to change money in town are the Banco de la Nación, half a block south of the plaza, and the Ferretería Don José, just before the police station and petrol garage at the northern end of town.

Shamanic healing This is a strong local tradition and one renowned healer, Don Victor Bravo, who helped to design the shamanic section of the museum's exhibits (see p.407), lives very close to the ruins of Túcume; anyone seriously interested in participating in one of his *mesa* ceremonies (see below) could try asking for an introduction through the *Hospedaje Rural Los Horcones* (see above).

Túcume Viejo

Turn left along the sand track at the fork in the road just before you get to Túcume's site [illegible] (30min walk)

Although there are no tourist facilities as such, the Túcume ruins in the village of **Túcume Viejo**, less than 2km from Lambayeque, make for an interesting walk. Although an ancient site, check out the crumbling colonial adobe walls and a once-painted adobe brick gateway as well as the church, all of which have an elegant and rather grandiose feel, suggesting perhaps that the early colonists were trying to compete for attention with the Valley of the Pyramids.

Piura

The city of **PIURA** feels very distinct from the rest of the country, cut off to the south by the formidable Sechura Desert, and to the east by the Huancabamba mountains.

HEALING SESSIONS IN SALAS

Salas is known locally as the capital of folklore medicine on the coast of Peru. Here the ancient traditions of **curanderismo** are so strong that it's the major source of income for the village. Most nights of the week, but especially Tuesdays and Fridays, there'll be healing sessions going on in at least one of the houses in the village, generally starting around 10pm and ending at roughly 4am. The sessions, or *mesas*, are based on the ingestion of the hallucinogenic **San Pedro cactus** and other natural plants or herbs, and they do cost money (anything up to $200 a night, though the amount is usually fixed and can be divided between as many as five to ten participants). Combining healing with divination, the *curanderos* utilize techniques and traditions handed down from generation to generation from the ancient Sicán culture.

Salas is 20min by car from Túcume; take a back road for 17km off the old Panamerican Highway at Km 47 (27km north of Túcume). To contact a *curandero* about participating in a session, the best bet is to ask a local tour operator, or a trustworthy taxi driver from Túcume, to take you to the village one afternoon to see what can be arranged.

Francisco Pizarro spent ten days in Piura in 1532 en route to his fateful meeting with the Inca overlord, Atahualpa, at Cajamarca (see box, p.374). By 1534 the city, then known as **San Miguel de Piura**, had well over two hundred Spanish inhabitants, including the first Spanish women to arrive in Peru. As early as the 1560s, there was a flourishing trade in the excellent indigenous **Tanguis cotton**, and Piura today still produces a third of the nation's cotton.

The city has a strong oasis atmosphere, entirely dependent on the vagaries of the **Río Piura** – known colloquially since Pizarro's time as the Río Loco, or Crazy River. At only 29m above sea level, modern **Piura** is divided by a sometimes dry riverbed. Most of the action and all the main sights are on the west bank. With temperatures of up to 38°C (100°F) from January to March, the region is known for its particularly wide-brimmed straw sombreros, worn by everyone from the mayor to local goat-herders. You'll have plenty of opportunities to see these in **Semana de Piura** (first two weeks of Oct), when the town is in high spirits.

Plaza de Armas

The spacious and attractive **Plaza de Armas** is shaded by tall tamarind trees planted well over a hundred years ago. On the plaza you'll find a "Statue of Liberty", also known as *La Pola* (The Pole), and the **Catedral de Piura** (Mon–Fri 7am–8pm, Sat & Sun 8am–noon; free), where the town's poorest folk tend to beg. Though not especially beautiful, the cathedral boasts impressive bronze nails decorating its main doors, and inside, the spectacularly tasteless gilt altars and intricate wooden pulpit are worth a look. Surrounding the plaza, you'll see some pastel-coloured, low, colonial buildings that clash madly with the tall, modern glass-and-concrete office buildings nearby.

Plaza Pizarro and around

One block towards the river from the Plaza de Armas, along Jirón Ayacucho, a delightful elongated square, called **Plaza Pizarro**, is also known as the Plaza de Tres Culturas. Every evening the Piurans promenade up and down here, chatting beside elegant modern fountains and beneath tall shady trees. One block east of here is the Río Piura, usually little more than a trickle of water with a few piles of rubbish plus white egrets, gulls and terns searching for food. The riverbed is large, however, indicating that when Piura's rare rains arrive, the river rises dramatically; people who build their homes too close to the dry bed regularly have them washed away. Puente Piura bridge connects central Piura with the less aesthetic east-bank quarter of **Tacala**, renowned principally for the quality and strength of its fermented *chicha* beer.

7

Museo Casa Grau

Tacna 662 • Mon–Sat 9am–1pm & 3–6pm • Free • 073 326541

A block south of the Plaza de Armas, you'll find the **Museo Casa Grau**, nineteenth-century home of **Admiral Miguel Grau**, one of the heroes of the War of the Pacific (1879–80), in which Chile took control of Peru's valuable nitrate fields in the south and cut Bolivia's access to the Pacific. The museum includes a model of the British-built ship, the *Huascar*, Peru's only successful blockade runner, as well as various military artefacts.

Museo Complejo Cultural

Av Sullana and Jr Huánuco • Tues–Fri 9am–5pm • S/4

An array of the region's archeological treasures, and in particular the ceramics from Cerro Vicus, is displayed at the **Museo Complejo**, one block west of Avenida Loreto. One of the rooms has artefacts uncovered at the necropolis Vicús at Chulucanas, another is dedicated to the archeology of metallurgy, and another to 64 ancient gold objects, including jewellery, cups and pincers.

The market

One block north of Av Sánchez Cerro • Best between Mon–Sat 6.30–11am

The town's daily **market**, in the north of the city, is worth a visit for its straw hats (see p.409), well-made in Santo Domingo, ceramics from the villages of Chulucanas and Simbila, plus a variety of leather crafts.

ARRIVAL AND DEPARTURE — PIURA

BY PLANE

Piura airport (073 344503) is 2km east of the city. The LAN Perú office is at C Libertad 875 (073 302145). A taxi into the centre costs S/10–15.

Destinations Lima, via Chiclayo (2 daily; 2hr); Trujillo (1 daily; 1hr); Tumbes (daily; 30min).

BY BUS

El Dorado buses from Trujillo and Tumbes, Dorado Express buses from Tumbes, Sullana and Aguas Verdes, buses from Chiclayo, and EPPO buses from Talara and Máncora all arrive around blocks 11 and 12 of Avenida Sánchez Cerro. All other buses arrive at their companies' offices (see below).

Bus companies CIAL, Bolognesi 817 (073 304250), for Huaraz, Lima and Tumbes; Cruz del Sur, Circumvalación 160, with an office at corner of Bolognesi with Lima (bus passes both on way through town), just a few blocks south of the Plaza de Armas in the centre (073 337094), for Lima and the coast; Emtrafesa, Los Naranjos 255, Urb. Club Grau (073 337093), for Chiclayo, Trujillo and Tumbes; Linea, Av Sánchez Cerro 1215 (073 327821), for Chiclayo and Tumbes; Tepsa, Av Loreto 1195 (073 306345), for Trujillo and Tumbes; and EPPO, Sánchez Cerro 1141 (073 304543), for Talara and Máncora.

Destinations Chiclayo (12 daily; 2–3hr); Huancabamba (2–3 daily; 12hr); La Tina and Loja (4 daily; 10–12hr); Lima (8 daily; 13–15hr); Talara and Máncora (several daily; 1hr 30min–3hr); Trujillo (several daily; 5–7hr); Tumbes (8 daily; 4–6hr).

BY COLECTIVO

Colectivos, mainly from Tumbes and Talara, arrive and depart from the middle of the road at block 11 of Avenida Sánchez Cerro, ten minutes' stroll from the centre of town.

GETTING AROUND AND INFORMATION

By mototaxi The quickest way of getting around the city is by the ubiquitous mototaxi (motorcycle rickshaw), which you can hail just about anywhere for 50¢.

By taxi In-town taxi rides are set at around S/3.

Tourist information The Municipal building at Ayacucho 337, Plaza de Armas (Mon–Fri 9am–1pm & 4–8pm, Sat 9am–1pm; T 073 320249), or the Ministry of Tourism, Jr Lima 775 (Mon–Fri 9am–1pm & 4–6pm; T 073 327013, W regionpiura.gob.pe). Try a local tour operator (see below) if the above are not available.

Tour operators Piura Tours, Ayacucho 585 (T 073 328873); Tallan Tours, Tacna 258 (T 073 334647).

ACCOMMODATION

7

A wide range of hotels and hostels are spread throughout the town, with most of the cheaper ones on or around Avenida Loreto or within a few blocks of Avenida Grau and the Plaza de Armas.

Hospedaje California Junín 835 T 073 328789. A family-run establishment, brightly painted and decorated with plastic flowers, giving it a somewhat kitschy feel. It's good value and popular with backpackers, and while there are no private baths, rooms are usually equipped with fans. S/25

Hospedaje Terraza Av Loreto 530 T 073 310001. Cleaner and a much more pleasant option than some of the affordable lodgings in this area, but still pretty basic; rooms have fans, but baths are shared. S/35

Hostal La Capullana Junín 925 T 073 321239. Cleanish place with a welcoming atmosphere. All doubles have private bath, plus there are some cheaper singles. S/30

Hostal Moon Night Junín 899 T 073 336174. Hotels with this kind of name in Peru are generally aiming for the lovers' market, but it's still comfortable and pretty central, offering more than average modern conveniences and clean, spacious rooms with private bath and TV. S/40

Hotel Costa del Sol Av Loreto 649 T 073 302864, W costadelsolperu.com. A luxurious hotel with pool, casino, internet facilities, car park and restaurant. S/200

Hotel Latino Huancavelica 720 T 073 335114, E hoslatino@hotmail.com. A large, fairly modern establishment aimed primarily at Peruvian business travellers, *Latino* is centrally located with all the usual facilities, including TV and internet access. S/90

Hotel Perú Arequipa 476 T 073 333919. Good-value hotel with a spacious lobby and good restaurant/bar; its smart if small rooms have TV, telephone, fan and private bath. S/55

Hotel Los Portales C Libertad 875 T 073 321161, W hotelportalespiura.com. A luxury hotel set in a lovely old building with a pool; the rooms are full of character and very clean, if slightly overpriced. S/220

Hotel San Miguel Lima 1007, at Apurimac on the Plaza Pizarro T 073 305122. A decently priced, unstylish but comfortable hotel with some rooms overlooking the plaza. There's also a cafetería and all rooms have private baths with good hot water and TVs. S/80

EATING AND DRINKING

Most of Piura's restaurants and cafés are centred around Plaza de Armas, with many of the cafés specializing in delicious ice cream. Piura's speciality is a very sweet toffee-like delicacy, called *natilla*, bought from street stalls around the city. There's a supermarket, good for general provisions, by the Grau monument. In the evenings, you'll find most Piurans strolling around the main streets, mingling in the plazas, and drinking in the cheap bars along the roads around Junín.

Alex Chopp Huancavelica 538. A popular venue with a friendly atmosphere, serving good draught beers and fine seafood in the evenings. Daily 10am–10pm.

Café d'Pauli Lima 541 T 073 322210. A small but smart café serving pricey but delicious ice creams, cakes, teas and coffee. Daily 9am–8pm.

Cafetería Rosita Av Grau 223. Dishes up heavenly sandwiches and green tamales, and has a few veggie options as well as great breakfasts. Daily 7.30am–9pm.

Canimedes Café Lima 440. Open in daytime only, offering healthy foods including good breakfasts, yogurt and fig breads. Daily 9am–8pm.

Dulcinea C La Libertad 597. A small bar and mini-supermarket, very central and well stocked with breads, pies, pasties and sweet pastries. Daily 8am–8pm.

Heladería El Chalan Plaza de Armas. Excellent service in a bright and busy atmosphere; enjoy their sandwiches, juices, cakes and wonderful ice creams. They also have a newer place behind the cathedral. Daily 10am–9pm.

Heladería Venecia C La Libertad 1007. Choose your ice cream from a wide variety of flavours and savour it on the cool and elegant patio. Daily 9am–8.30pm.

Picantería La Santitos C La Libertad 1014. This place serves a good choice of traditional criolla dishes such *as majado de yuca* (mashed *yuca* with pieces of pork) and *seco de chavelo* (mashed plantain with pieces of beef), in a renovated colonial house. Daily 11am–3pm.

Restaurante Ganímedes Lima 440 ⓣ073 329176. The best restaurant in town for vegetarian meals; try the stuffed avocados or the Loco de Zapallo dishes. Friendly service, but cash only. Mon–Sat 10.30am–5pm.

Restaurante Romano Jr Ayacucho 580. A popular and quite large local backstreet eating-house cooking up a host of reasonably priced dishes, from burgers and sandwiches to the usual Peruvian cuisine such as *lomo saltado*. Mon–Sat 8am–10pm.

DIRECTORY

Internet There's a large, busy internet café at Sánchez Cerro 265 (daily 9am–11pm).

Money and exchange The Banco Continental is on the Plaza de Armas, at the corner of Ayacucho and Tacna. *Cambistas* are at block 7 of Av Arequipa, near the corner of Av Grau; but by far the safest and quickest casa de cambio is Piura Dolar by block 6 of Av Arequipa.

Post office Plaza de Armas, on the corner of C Libertad and Ayacucho (Mon–Sat 8am–4pm).

Catacaos

Just 12km south of Piura is the friendly, dusty little town of **CATACAOS**, worth a visit principally for its excellent, vast **market** (there's something here most days, but it's best at weekends 10am–4pm). Just off the main plaza, the market sells everything from food to crafts, even filigree gold and silver work, with the colourful hammocks hanging about the square being a particularly good buy. The town is renowned locally for its **picanterías** (spicy food restaurants), which serve all sorts of local delicacies, such as *tamalitos verdes* (little green-corn pancakes), fish-balls, *chifles* (fresh banana or sweet potato chips), goat (*seco de cabrito*) and the local *chicha* beer. While you're here you could also try the sweet medicinal drink *algarrobina*, made from the berries of a desert tree, and available from bars and street stalls.

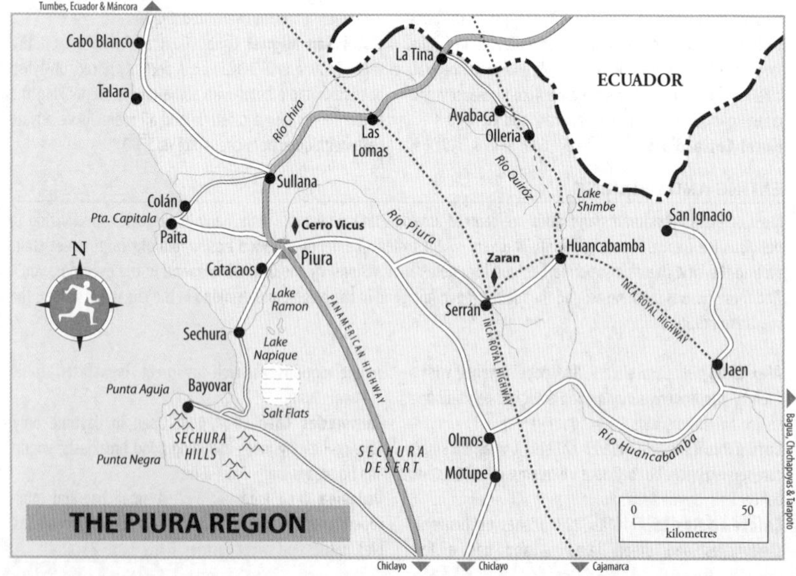

HOW PIZARRO FOUND ATAHUALPA

It was at Serran, then a small Inca administrative centre in the hills above Piura, that Francisco **Pizarro** waited in 1532 for the return of a small troop of soldiers he had sent up the Inca Royal Highway on a discovery mission. It took the soldiers, led by **Hernando de Soto**, just two days and a night to reach the town of Cajas, now lost in the region around Huancabamba and Lake Shimbe.

At Cajas, the Spaniards gained their first insight into the grandeur and power of the Inca Empire, although, under orders from Atahualpa, the town's 2000-warrior Inca garrison had slunk away into the mountains. The Spaniards were not slow to discover the most impressive Inca buildings – a sacred convent of over five hundred virgins who had been chosen at an early age to dedicate their lives to the Inca religion. The soldiers raped at will, provoking the Inca diplomat who was accompanying De Soto to threaten the troops with death for such sacrilege, telling them they were only 300km from Atahualpa's camp at Cajamarca. This information about Atahualpa's whereabouts was exactly what De Soto had been seeking. After a brief visit to the adjacent, even more impressive, Inca town of Huancabamba – where a tollgate collected duties along the Royal Highway – he returned with the Inca diplomat to rejoin Pizarro. Realizing that he had provided the Spanish with vital information, the Inca diplomat agreed to take them to Atahualpa's camp – a disastrous decision resulting in the massacre at Cajamarca (see box, p.374).

7

ARRIVAL AND DEPARTURE — CATACAOS

By colectivo Regular combi colectivos for Catacaos leave Piura when full, usually every 20min or so (S/1.50; 20min), from block 12 of Sánchez Cerro, or from the far side of Puente Piura.

EATING

La Chayo San Francisco 493 ⓣ073 370121. This place serves huge portions of tasty food, while there's *chicha* on offer, too. Daily 10am–6 or 7pm.

Sullana

Leaving Piura, the Panamerican Highway heads directly north, passing through the large town of **SULLANA** after 40km. This major transport junction has little of interest to travellers, except perhaps as a rest before or after taking the inland route to Ecuador. If you do stop, take a quick look at the **Plaza de Armas**, which boasts fine views over the Río Chira, and is the location for the old church of La Santísima Trinidad.

Talara

TALARA, 70km further north, would be more attractive if it wasn't for the entrance to the city being strewn with plastic rubbish. Until 1940, it was no more than a small fishing hamlet, though its deep-water harbour and tar pits had been used since Pizarro's time for caulking wooden ships – Pizarro had chosen the site for the first Spanish settlement in Peru, but it proved too unhealthy and he was forced to look elsewhere, eventually hitting on Piura (see p.408). Today the town is highly industrialized, with several fertilizer plants as well as the oil business (although you can find an unpolluted **beach** at La Pena, 2km away). Talara's **oil reserves** were actually directly responsible for Peru's last military coup in 1968. President Belaunde, then in his first term of office, had given subsoil concessions to the multinational company IPC, declaring that "if this is foreign imperialism what we need is more, not less of it". A curious logic, it led to the accusation that he had signed an agreement "unacceptable to true Peruvians". Within two months of the affair, and as a direct consequence, he was deposed and exiled. One of the initial acts of the new revolutionary government was to nationalize IPC and declare the Act of Talara null and void.

ARRIVAL AND DEPARTURE — SULLANA AND TALARA

SULLANA

By bus Most bus companies have their offices on or just off Avenida Lama. EPPO (eppo.com.pe) run buses twice daily to Talara and Máncora, while Emtrafesa serves Tumbes and Chiclayo.

By colectivo There are regular combis from Avenida Lama to Piura, while the faster colectivos cost slightly more. Combis for the inland border crossing with Ecuador (see p.423) at La Tina or close by at Ayabaca leave in the morning from Avenida Buenos Aires, close to the main market (3 daily; 2hr).

TALARA

Take the *Eppo* bus from Piura or Sullana to Talara (1hr 40min from Piura; 1hr 10min from Sullana).

Cabo Blanco

7

Thirty kilometres or so north of Talara, there's a turning off the highway to the old fishing hotspot of **CABO BLANCO**. Thomas Stokes, a British resident and fanatical fisherman, discovered the place in 1935, and it was a very popular resort in the postwar years. **Hemingway** stayed for some months in 1951, while two years later the largest fish ever caught with a rod was landed here – a 710-kilo black marlin. International fishing competitions still take place, and the area is much reputed for swordfish.

From here to Tumbes the Panamerican Highway cuts across a further stretch of desert, for the most part keeping tightly to the Pacific coastline. It's a straight road, except for the occasional detour around bridges destroyed by the 1998 El Niño. To the right of the road looms a long hill, the **Cerros de Amotape**, named after a local chief whom Pizarro had killed in 1532 as an example to potential rebels.

ARRIVAL AND DEPARTURE — CABO BLANCO

Located just over halfway between Talara and Máncora at Km 1137 of the Panamerican Norte, take the EPPO or Cruz del Sur bus from Piura to get to Cabo Blanco (3–4hr).

ACCOMMODATION AND EATING

Hotel El Merlin Km 1136.5, Cabo Blanco 073 256188, elmerlin.webs.com. A really nice place right on the beach, with stone floors, bamboo and *estera* (reeds) for the nine rooms overlooking the ocean. There's wi-fi and cable TV, kayaks available for use and excellent boat-based fishing trips arranged. S/100

Restaurante Cabo Blanco Km 1136.5, Cabo Blanco. Just 50m from *Hotel El Merlin* (see above), this place has the best reputation locally for seafood; try the superb ceviches. Daily, lunch only.

Máncora

vivamancora.com

Once just an attractive roadside fishing port, **MÁNCORA** is now the most fashionable beach in Peru, attracting a surf crowd from Ecuador and Brazil. It's a highly welcome and very enjoyable stopover when travelling along the north coast, well served by public transport, and spread out along the Panamerican Highway, parallel to a beautiful sandy beach.

At the north end of the main drag, there's a plaza and just beyond this there's sometimes a street market, though only the usual clothing, shoes and food. Between here and the south end you'll find most of the town's hotels and restaurants, and a promenade with hippie **artesanía** stalls, selling sea-inspired crafts and jewellery.

ARRIVAL AND DEPARTURE — MÁNCORA

BY BUS

Comng from the south – Lima, Chiclayo or Piura – there are several buses daily. Cruz del Sur are presently the best operator in terms of comfort, safety and reliability; their buses pull in and depart at Máncora from their offices on the second block of Av Grau. From Tumbes, buses and colectivos to Máncora leave daily from the main market, on Ramón Castillo, but return buses aren't frequent.

ACTIVITIES IN MÁNCORA

Máncora enjoys warm waters and its position is blessed as the place where northern tropical currents meet with the much, much cooler southern one: at Lobitos, the next beach down the coast from Cabo Blanco (30km south of Máncora), the sea is cold. This geographical position gives Máncora near perfect surf conditions at times, with barrel waves achieving up to 4m in height. Although fairly safe, there are offshore currents which surfing novices are advised to watch out for (ask one of the surf teachers before venturing out). **Kite-surfing** is an increasingly popular sport, too, along with **skateboarding**. The half-pipe (daily 3–6.30pm) offers skateboarding facilities and lessons; you can find it on the hill, by taking the road up behind *Restaurant Ramjosy* (road to the lighthouse); it's behind the *Hospedaje Salvalito*. You can hire gear, find surf tours or get surf lessons from several places, including:

Del Wawa (see below) Offers surf lessons from around S/50 an hour (board rentals S/15–20hr). There's also a notice board advertising surfing lessons in the Locutorio Público telephone office (see opposite).

Máncora Kitesurf ⓣ01 981167745, ⓦmancorakitesurf.com. Sells surf and kite-surfing equipment as well as operates surfing and kiting tours, plus visits to the local zip-line out in the desert, whale-watching, offshore snorkling and even yoga to complete the day.

Michel Expediciones Peru ⓣ01 9983 75051, ⓦvivamancora.com/michelexp/surf.html. Surf lessons and tours, including guided tours to see local flora and fauna.

Octopus Surf Tours ⓣ01 9940 05518, ⓦoctopussurftours.com. Operated by experienced Peruvian surfer Marco Antonio Ravizza, aka "Octopus"; they tend to offer surfing packages including food and accommodation.

Bus companies The bus companies are all in the main street, Avenida Piura, where you can buy tickets for their selection of daily and nightly services up or down the coast, connecting Tumbes with Lima and the major cities in between. Transportes EPPO run to Piura from their office just north of the plaza, towards the northern end of Máncora at Grau 468 (ⓣ073 258027). Cruz del Sur, Av Grau 208 (ⓣ073 258232), and Civa, Av Piura 704 (ⓣ073 258524), go to Piura and Chiclayo. Oltursa, Av Piura 509 (ⓣ073 258212) connect with Tumbes, Piura, Chiclayo and Lima. Tepsa, Av Grau 113 (ⓣ073 258672), cover the Panamericana up to Tumbes and down south to Lima. Colectivos depart from near the EPPO office for Los Organos (S/2; 30min), from where there are other combis to Talara (S/4; 1hr).

Destinations Chiclayo (several daily; 5–7hr); Lima (several daily; 15–16hr); Los Organos (several daily; 30min); Piura (several daily; 3–4hr); Talara (approx hourly; 1hr); Tumbes (several daily; 1hr 30min–2hr).

BY COLECTIVO

It's fairly easy to get south as far as Máncora in two colectivo rides; the first from block 1 of Avenida Tumbes Norte as far as Los Organos (1hr 10min; $1.25); change here for another car to Máncora (30min; $70c).

ACCOMMODATION

All the main hotels are located between the bridge at the south entrance to town and the plaza towards the north end, though there are several cheaper basic hostels strung out along the southern end of the Panamerican Highway and some more remote and upmarket options on Vichayito beach, beyond the southern entrance to Máncora. There's a notice board advertising rooms and bungalows for rent in the Locutorio Público telephone office (see opposite).

Del Wawa Avenida Piura, Frente al Point ⓣ073 258427, ⓦdelwawa.com. In many ways the hub of the local surf scene, *Del Wawa* is a small beachside hotel with colourful buildings, cool rooms, hammocks and a great restaurant. *Wawa* means baby in the Quechua language. S/180

Hostal Sol y Mar ⓣ073 258106, ⓦsolymarmancora.com. Very popular with the surfing crowd, this hotel right on the beach has a good swimming pool and games courts, plus a decent restaurant and bar, private baths and its own little shop, disco and internet café. S/20

Hotel Las Garzas Av Piura 262 ⓣ074 258110. With thirteen rooms, a restaurant and parking facilities plus a nice garden with hammocks, *Hotel Las Garzas* is quite peaceful for this town. They also offer surf lessons for kids and adults. S/65

Hotel Sunset Avenida Antigua Panamericana Norte 196 ⓣ073 258111, ⓦsunsetmancora.com. This is a stylish boutique hotel on a secluded beach with a good clifftop restaurant and bar terrace with a small pool and very fine service. Wi-fi is standard and they also offer tours and airport pick-up. S/170

Point Hostel Playa El Amor ⓣ073 258290, ⓦthepointhostels.com. Groovy and right on the beach, this place offers surf gear plus other rentals, has a games room and outside volleyball area, plus it runs one of the town's best bars. Bunk rooms and private spaces available. Bunk S/22, doubles S/80

EATING, DRINKING AND NIGHTLIFE

Comercial Marlon II, next to the ATM and Municipal building, has a superb range of groceries, including wholemeal bread, local honey and wines. For eating out, there's a surplus of restaurants in the centre of town, mainly along the Panamerican Highway.

There is a hectic nightlife scene based in the bars, beachside hotels and on the beach itself, especially during Peruvian holiday times. It's easy to find – just follow the sounds after dark.

The Bird House Beachfront just south of the *Hostal Sol y Mar*. This extremely popular spot is divided into shops, bars and cafés, mostly franchised out, which offer a wide range of international dishes (including burgers, ham and eggs) as well as local cuisine (try the fish and seafood at *Willka* up on the first floor); there's also a surf shop, cocktail bar, ice cream parlour and a pleasant beachside, shaded lounge area. Daily 8am–10pm.

De Angela Av Piura 396 ⓣ073 258603. A vegetarian restaurant set up by a young Austrian woman, who started over 12 years ago by selling her dark bread to people on the beach; now she runs a delivery and restaurant business serving delicious meals like avocado sandwiches, falafel, curries and, for the sweet toothed, a great *Apfelstrudel*. Daily 8am–11pm.

Iguana's Place Bar Av Piura 245. This place supplies a mix of services, doing tourism in the morning, lunchtime meals and then, after dark, it comes truly alive as it transforms into a busy bar with canned music. Daily11am–midnight.

Papa Mo's Milk Bar Av Piura 326. Located inside the commercial complex at this address, but with a good ocean view from the patio, you'll find this often lively bar which serves only beer, liquor and wine plus a few tapas like brochettes. Daily 10am–late.

El Tuno Av Piura 233 ⓣ01 994082410. Right on the main Panamerican road, this colourful Italian-Peruvian restaurant claims to offer a fusion of Peruvian and international cuisine; they serve very fresh octopus, prawns and tuna. There's usually a reasonable selection of wines, too. Daily10.30am–11pm.

DIRECTORY

Internet Cabinas Internet Máncora is at Av Piura 605 (daily 9am–9pm).

Money and exchange Banco de la Nacion, block 5 of Av Piura (Mon–Fri 8am–6pm); there are at least five ATMs scattered about Máncora.

Telephones The Locutorio Público telephone office (daily 8am–10pm) and shop is on block 5 of Avenida Piura opposite the small church.

Vichayito

Take the rough (old Panamerican) highway on the right just as you leave Máncora; it's a 15min, bumpy journey by mototaxi (S/3); alternatively, you could walk from Máncora along the coast (about 1hr), but make sure you take water with you

VICHAYITO, a stupendous and largely empty beach, is the continuation south from Máncora's less extensive (but closer to the road) strip of sand. It makes for a relaxing alternative, with good swimming, some surf and lovely coastal scenery – though the village is developing rather quickly.

Poza de Barro (mud baths)

Open access daily 24hr • S/3 • Take a taxi from Máncora or ride a horse (the latter through a local tour company; see box opposite). The entry road to the mud baths is off the Panamericana, just north of Máncora next to the "Comunidad Máncora Campesino" sign by the bridge

If the beach isn't relaxing enough, you can always head to the local **mud baths**. Set 11km from the main road and surrounded by hills and *algarrobo* trees, the warm natural bath appeared in the shaft following oil extraction in the 1980s. It's now visited for its cleansing subterranean waters (no sign of oil today). It has basic toilets and a changing hut.

Tumbes and around

About 30km from the Ecuadorian border and 287km north of Piura, **TUMBES** is usually considered a mere pit-stop for overland travellers, offering decent restaurants and better money-changing options than at the Ecuadorian frontier. However, the city has a significant history and, unlike most border settlements, is a surprisingly warm and friendly place. On top of that, it's close to many of Peru's finest **beaches** (see box, p.422)

7

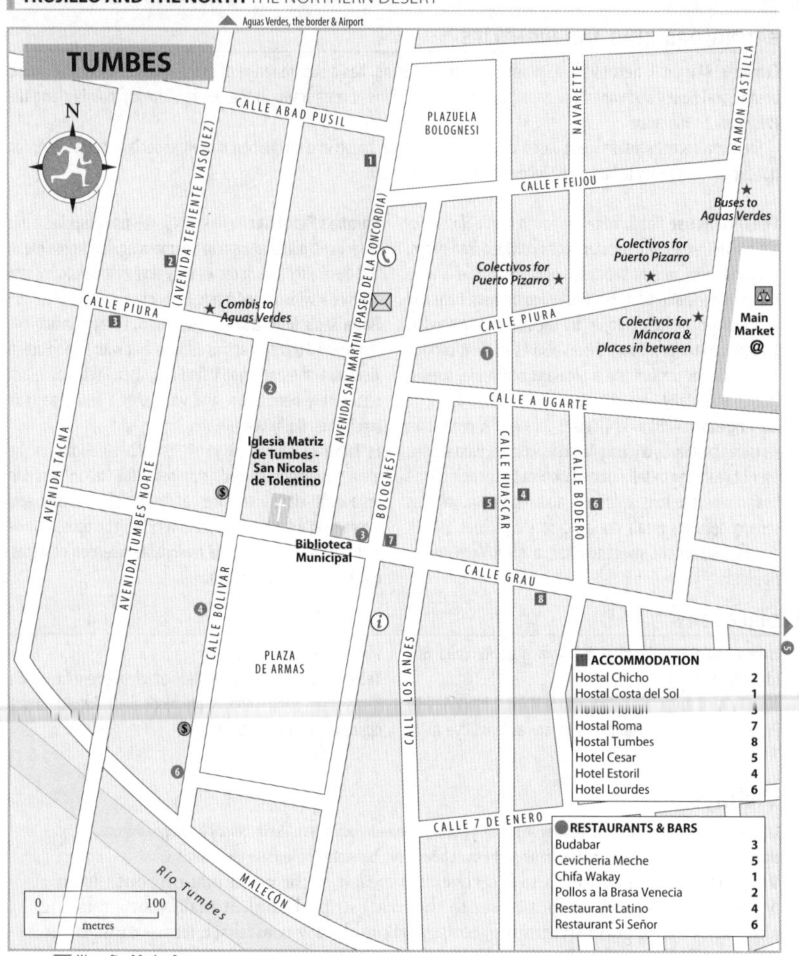

and two very distinct and unique forests and protected areas: the **Santuario Nacional los Manglares de Tumbes** and the **Zona Reservado de Tumbes**. The settlement of Zorritos is strung out along the seafront and Panamerican Highway some 28km south of Tumbes; as well as a long beach, this town is the point of access to some ancient, still-working natural mud baths.

The area can get very hot and humid between December and March, while the rest of the year it offers a pleasant heat, compared with much of Peru's southern coast. The sea is warm and while mosquitoes can be bothersome between September and January, they rarely make their presence felt on the beaches. Locals tend to be laidback and spontaneous, a trait reflected in the local traditions such as **las cumananas**, an expression in popular verse, often by song with a guitar. The verse is expected to be sparky, romantic, comical and even sad, but most importantly, spur of the moment and rap-like.

Brief history

Pizarro didn't actually set foot in Tumbes when it was first discovered by the Spanish in 1527. He preferred to cast his eyes along the Inca city's adobe walls, its carefully

BORDER RELATIONS WITH ECUADOR

Tumbes was the first town to be "conquered" by the Spanish and has maintained its importance ever since – originally as the gateway to the Inca Empire and more recently through its strategic position on the contentious **frontier with Ecuador**. Despite three regional wars (in 1859, 1941–42 and 1997–98) the exact line of the border remains a source of controversy. Maps of the frontier vary depending on which country you buy them in, with the two countries claiming a disparity of up to 150km in some places along the border. The traditional enmity between Peru and Ecuador and the continuing dispute over the border mean that Tumbes has a strong Peruvian army presence and a consequent strict **ban on photography** anywhere near military or frontier installations. Most of the city's hundred thousand people are engaged in either transport or petty trading across the frontier – huge numbers of Peruvians cross the border every day to buy cheaper Ecuadorian products – and are quite cut off from mainstream Peru, being much nearer to Quito than Lima, 1268km to the south.

irrigated fields and its shining temple, from the comfort and safety of his ship. However, with the help of translators he set about learning as much as he could about Peru and the Incas during this initial contact.

The Spaniards who did go ashore made reports of such grandeur that Pizarro at first refused to believe them, sending instead the more reliable Greek cavalier, **Pedro de Candia**. Dubious descriptions of the temple, lined with gold and silver sheets, were confirmed by Candia, who also gave the people of Tumbes their first taste of European technological might – firing his musket to smash a wooden board to pieces. Pizarro had all the evidence he needed; he returned to Spain to obtain royal consent and support for his projected conquest.

The Tumbes people hadn't always been controlled by the Incas. The area was originally inhabited by the **Tallanes**, related to coastal tribes from Ecuador who are still known for their unusual lip and nose ornaments. In 1450 they were conquered for the first time – by the **Chimu**. Thirteen years later came the **Incas**, organized by Tupac Inca, who bulldozed the locals into religious, economic and even architectural conformity in order to create their most northerly coastal terminus. A fortress, temple and sun convent were built, and the town was colonized with loyal subjects from other regions – a typical Inca ploy, which they called the *mitimaes* system. The valley had an efficient irrigation programme, allowing them to grow, among other things, bananas, corn and squash.

Pizarro longed to add his name to the list of Tumbes' conquerors, yet after landing on the coast of Ecuador in 1532 with a royal warrant to conquer and convert, and despite the previous friendly contact, some of the Spanish were killed by natives as they tried to beach. Moreover, when they reached the city it was completely deserted with many buildings destroyed, and, more painfully for Pizarro, no sign of gold. It seems likely that Tumbes' destruction prior to Pizarro's arrival was the result of inter-tribal warfare directly related to the **Inca Civil War**. This, a war of succession between Atahualpa and his half-brother, the legitimate heir, Huascar, was to make Pizarro's role as conqueror a great deal easier, and he took the town of Tumbes without a struggle.

Plaza de Armas and around

Although it has very few real sights, Tumbes is a surprisingly elegant city, at least around the broad **Plaza de Armas**, which is bounded by large trees, and beyond which sit the **Biblioteca Municipal** and the rather plain **Iglesia Matriz de Tumbes–San Nicolás de Tolentino**, built in the seventeenth century but restored in 1995, making it now one of the most modernized churches in northern Peru. It has an understated Baroque facade and both cupolas are covered in mosaics.

Located in the amphitheatre or stage at the southern end on the main plaza, the **municipal mural** entitled *Encuentro de Dos Mundos* (Encounter of Two Worlds) depicts a bold and vivid jungle, conquistador- and Inca-inspired scene symbolizing the influence of Spain on ancient Peru and in particular the Battle of the Mangroves. Leading off eastwards from the northern edge of the plaza is Calle Grau, an attractive old-fashioned hotchpotch of a street, lined with wooden colonial buildings.

Paseo de la Concordia

An attractive pedestrian precinct located in the first two blocks of Calle San Martín, the **Paseo de la Concordia**, decorated with colourful tiles and several large sculptures and statues, leads off the plaza between the cathedral and the *biblioteca* to the Plazuela Bolognesi. Here you'll find some small theatre areas and a couple of exhibition rooms with changing themes mainly represented in photos and art. There's also a sculpture with a llama (representing Peru) and an eagle (representing Ecuador).

Malecón

The slightly grubby **Malecón** promenade runs along the high riverbanks of the Río Tumbes, a block beyond the southern end of the Plaza de Armas. At the western end of the Malecón, you can see a massive Modernist **sculpture**, *Tumbes Paraiso del Amor y el Eterno Verano* (Tumbes Paradise of Love and Eternal Summer), depicting a pair of lovers kissing.

ARRIVAL AND GETTING AROUND

BY PLANE

Aeropuerto Pedro Canga Rodríguez, Av Panamericana Norte 1276 (T 072 521688 or T 072 525102), is just north of the city limits. LAN Perú, Jr Bolognesi 250 (T 072 521228), presently fly here from Lima and Piura. A taxi into town (10min) should cost around S/15. Taxis will happily take passengers directly from the town centre or airport to the main beaches: to Punta Sal, for instance, costs around S/75 and takes about an hour.

Destinations Lima (4 flights weekly; 2hr 30min); Piura (daily; 30min).

BY BUS

Most buses coming to Tumbes arrive at offices along Avenida Tumbes Norte (also known as Avenida Teniente Vásquez), or along Piura, although a new Terminal Terrestre is planned for the near future. Ormeño buses from Ecuador stop at Av Tumbes Norte 216 (T 072 522228).

Bus companies CIAL, Av Tumbes Norte 556 (T 072 526350), for Lima; CIVA, Av Tumbes Norte 518 (T 072 525120), for south down the coast; Cruz del Sur, Av Tumbes Norte 319 (T 072 522350 or T 072 896163), for Lima and the coast; El Dorado, Piura 459 (T 072 523480), for Máncora; Emtrafesa, Av Tumbes Norte 596 (T 072 522894), for Chiclayo and Trujillo; Oltursa, Av Tumbes Norte 307 (T 072 523048), for Lima; Ormeño, Av Tumbes (one block beyond CIAL [illegible]), for Trujillo.

Destinations Aguas Verdes (hourly; 20min); Chiclayo (8 daily; 10hr); Lima (8 daily; 23hr); Máncora (several daily; 1–2hr); Puerto Pizarro (hourly; 25min); Trujillo (4 daily; 12hr); Piura (6 daily; 5hr).

BY COLECTIVO

Comite colectivos pull in at Tumbes Norte 308 (T 072 525977).

BY MOTOTAXI

You can hail one of the many mototaxis (motorcycle rickshaws), which will take you anywhere in the city for around S/2.

INFORMATION AND TOURS

Tourist information i-Peru have an office on the 3rd floor in the Malecón III Milenio (E iperutumbes@promperu.gob.pe) and the local regional tourism office is at Jr Bolognesi 194, the first floor of the Centro Cívico, on the Plaza de Armas (Mon–Sat 8am–1pm & 2–6pm; T 072 524940, W regiontumbes.gob.pe).

Tour operators Tumbes Tours, Av Tumbes Norte 351 (T 072 524837, W tumbestours.com), run a number of tours including a 4-day/3-night trip exploring the nearby Puerto Pizarro mangrove swamp (see p.422), as well as local beaches from S/55 per person per day, depending on size of group. Preference Tours, Grau 427 T 072 525518), are good for general tourist information and tickets, and organize most standard local tour packages.

ACCOMMODATION

Central Tumbes has plenty of places to stay. Some of the better budget options are strung out from the Plaza de Armas along Calle Grau.

CENTRAL TUMBES

Hostal Chicho Av Tumbes Norte 327 ⓣ074 522282 & ⓣ074 523696. New and good value; some rooms come with private bath and TV, and the ones at the back are quieter with individual mosquito netting. S55

Hostal Costa del Sol Av San Martín 275 ⓣ072 523991, ⓦcostadelsolperu.com. Located close to the Plaza de Armas, the *Costa del Sol* offers very comfortable rooms with a/c, private baths and cable TV, as well as a nice pool. S/280

Hostal Florian C Piura 400 ⓣ072 522464. A large hotel, slightly down-at-heel, but with comfortable beds at reasonable rates. Rooms have a private bath. S/40

★ **Hostal Roma** Bolognesi 425 ⓣ072 522494 and 524137. Right on the Plaza de Armas, this is a popular travellers stopoff and a good place to pick up information on frontier crossing, local attractions and tourist services. There are decent showers in all the rooms, which themselves are large and have comfortable beds; no a/c but there are fans. S/50

Hostal Tumbes C Grau 614 ⓣ072 522203. Very pleasant rooms all with their own showers, the best-value of which are upstairs, affording better light; service is adequate for the price. S/40

★ **Hotel César** C Huascar 313 ⓣ072 522883. Small, very friendly and good value, offering plain but nicely decorated spaces, all with private bath and fans (rather than a/c) and most with TV. S/40

Hotel Estoril C Huascar 317 ⓣ072 524906. Small, comfortable and exceptionally good value, if undistinguished. All rooms with private bath. S/35

Hotel Lourdes C Mayor Bodero 118 ⓣ072 522126. Located in a quiet side-street, *Lourdes* is notably clean and well looked after; rooms are rather small but impeccable and with private bathrooms. Very helpful staff. S/40

ZORRITOS

Arrecife Hotel Fausino Piaggio 158, Zorritos ⓣ072 544462, ⓦarrecifehotel.com. Located over 30km south of the city in Zorritos, almost all the way to Punta Sal, this place is right on the beach and set among pretty gardens and patios; rooms are clean and simple with attractive bare stone walls. Great service. S/80

La Casa del Grillo Av Los Pinos 563, Zorritos ⓣ072 544222, ⓦcasagrillo.net. A fine choice if you're after cheap and cheerful hostel accommodation outside the city; on the main road in Zorritos (30km south of Tumbes) very close to the beach. S/40

7

EATING AND DRINKING

Tumbes has some excellent restaurants and is the best place in Peru to try *conchas negras* – the black clams found only in these coastal waters, where they grow on the roots of mangroves.

Budabar C Grau 309 ⓣ072 504216. A trendy lounge-bar right on the Plaza de Armas; serves great food and decently priced drinks. A good place to meet fellow travellers. Occasional live music events at weekends. Daily 8am–late.

Cevichería Meche C Lobitos 160 ⓣ072 858412. The best place in town for seafood; try a ceviche with *conchas negras* or a huge steaming dish of *sudado de pescado* (usually a whole fish steamed and served with a mildly sweet sauce). Tues–Sun 11am–5pm.

Chifa Wakay C Huascar 415 ⓣ072 522829. Dishes up well-priced, tasty Chinese food in a well-cared-for ambience; fantastic seafood is on offer, as well as the usual Chino-Peruvian delights such as *cien flores* and *wantan kamlu*. Daily 6–10pm.

Pollos a la Brasa Venecia C Bolívar 237. Does exactly what it says in its name – this is the best place in town for chicken and chips, but they are still a touch greasy. Daily 10.30am–11pm.

Restaurant Latino C Bolívar 163 ⓣ072 523198. Right on the Plaza de Armas, this old-fashioned spot offers a full à la carte range of local and international cuisine as well as specializing in excellent Continental and American breakfasts. Daily 7.30am–9pm.

Restaurant Si Señor C Bolívar 115 ⓣ072 521937. Serves mostly beer and seafood, right on the Plaza de Armas; the food is tasty, but it's best to make sure you're getting something made fresh if you go for the seafood. Daily 9am–10pm.

DIRECTORY

Consulate C Bolívar 155, Plaza de Armas ⓣ072 523022 (Mon–Fri 9am–4pm).

Internet Vernet, Jr Bolognesi 242.

Money and exchange Banco de Credito, C Bolívar 135, and Banco de la Nación, on the corner of C Grau and C Bolívar, by the Plaza de Armas; Banco Continental is at Bolívar 129. *Cambistas* are at the corner of Bolívar with Piura.

Police Av Mayor Novoa and C Zarumilla ⓣ072 522525.

Post office Av San Martín 208 (Mon–Sat 8am–8pm).

Telephones The Telefónica del Perú office is on Avenida San Martín in the same block as the post office.

BEST NORTHERN BEACHES

The area around Tumbes boasts some of the best **beaches** in the whole of the country. Along with Máncora (see p.414), here are some of the best:

Caleta de la Cruz 16–21km southwest (30min) of Tumbes. Reputed to be the bay where Pizarro first landed, Caleta de la Cruz is a very popular bay these days with Tumbes locals, particularly around Km19; the bay is half-moon-shaped and stretches over 4km. It offers good swimming in tranquil, relatively shallow, but warm water.

Punta Sal 50km southwest (1–2hr) of Tumbes, at Km 1119 of the Panamericana. Punta Sal is a very beautiful and long stretch of beach with rock pools and great sands; the water is warm, often peaceful and noted as excellent both for scuba diving and merlin or swordfish fishing.

Zorritos 34km southwest (1hr) of Tumbes. This is a long, narrow beach with fine sand and warm sea; while not always tranquil, the ocean offers great sole and bass fishing.

GETTING THERE

Buses and colectivos to Caleta de la Cruz, Punta Sal and Zorritos leave daily from the main market in Tumbes, on Ramón Castillo, but return buses aren't that frequent, so check return times with the driver before you leave Tumbes. Every day colectivos and combis patrol up and down the Panamerican Highway around all the beaches looking for passengers for Tumbes (1hr 30min–2hr; S/8). For transport to Máncora, see p.414.

7

Puerto Pizarro

If you've never seen a mangrove swamp, **PUERTO PIZARRO**, 13km northeast of Tumbes, is perhaps worth a visit, though it has no specific link with the conquistador it's named after, and the waterfront today is full of rubbish; better to plough on to Los Bosques de Manglares de Tumbes (see box, p.424).

An ancient fishing port, Puerto Pizarro was a commercial harbour until swamps grew out to sea over the last few centuries, making it inaccessible for large boats and permanently disconnecting Tumbes from the Pacific.

ARRIVAL AND DEPARTURE — PUERTO PIZARRO

Colectivos leave regularly for Puerto Pizarro (S/1.50; 20 min) from calles Piura and Navarette in Tumbes. Taxis cost around S/10–15 from Tumbes.

ACCOMMODATION AND EATING

Hospedaje Bayside Malecón, overlooking Puerto Pizarro port. This hotel is right on the waterfront; it has a pool, private bathrooms, palm trees and a restaurant-café. They can advise on fishing and boat excursions. S/40

Isla de Amor

Boats run to Isla de Amor from Puerto Pizarro; buy tickets ($15 per person) from the information and ticket booth on the seafront

From Puerto Pizarro you can take slow but pleasant **boat trips** out to the **ISLA DE AMOR**, where there's a bathing beach and a café. The boat operators will inform you of the history of the area and the mangroves themselves, as well as point out wildlife like the magnificant frigate bird (also called scissor-tail) and the occasional white iguana languishing among the mangroves. The tour will also take you through **mangrove creeks** where you'll see the *rhizopora* tree's dense root system. Perhaps the highlight of the boat trip is a tour around the centre for the protection of Peru's only indigenous, and **endangered, crocodile** (*Crocodylus acutus americano)* run by FONDERES, funded by the Peruvian government. There are only forty of these crocodiles left in the wild (where they can live for a hundred years), having been hunted in the past for their skin, and the centre has bred around 225 in captivity. It's possible to see the crocodiles at most life stages, with the largest growing to around 3m.

Baños de Barro Medicinal Hervideros (Medicinal Mud Baths)

Technically open from 6am–6pm, often unattended • S/3 (or free) • Turn off at Bocapan, Km 1214; signpost reads "Parque Nacional Cerros de Amotape"; the baths are about 4km down ths road. Walking, taxi or mototaxi from Zorritos are the only alternatives apart from going with a tour group from Trujillo or Máncora

Located 40km south of Tumbes, these amazing, little-visited **mud baths** are reputedly very good for your skin. Surrounded by hills and *algarrobo* trees, this is a really peaceful and relaxing spot. The *pozos de barro* (mud baths) were discovered by the archeologist Raymondi in 1882, though were almost certainly used for centuries before that. There are several mud baths, with a lower pool for washing down. Temperatures and health effects vary pool by pool; some of this is noted on small wooden signs, with analysis of the mud detecting iron oxides, calcium chloride, sodium chloride, aluminium chloride and magnesium chloride, among other chemical components.

Punta Sal

7

Located some 2km along a track from Km 1187 of the Panamerican Highway – also known in the north as the Panamericana Norte – **PUNTA SAL**, considered by many to be the best **beach** in Peru, has extensive sands and attractive rocky outcrops, swarming with crabs at low tide. It's a safe place to swim and a heavenly spot for diving in warm, clear waters.

In the low season you'll probably have the beautiful beach pretty much to yourself; in high season it's a good idea to book your accommodation (see below) in advance.

Fishing trips from here, famous for the high concentration of striped and black marlin, cost from around $230 for a half-day (you can take up to six people for this, double the price for a full day).

ACCOMMODATION AND EATING — PUNTA SAL

There are a couple of small bodegas in Punta Sal, so drinks and general groceries can be bought without leaving the beach area and travelling to one of the towns up or down the Panamericana.

Hospedaje Hua Punta Sal ⓣ072 540043, ⓦhua-puntasal.com. Located towards the middle of the beach, *Hua* is a rustic choice, with a main wooden building; some rooms have ocean views. Service is very good, plus there's a restaurant (camping only for pre-arranged tour groups). S120

Hotel Caballito del Mar ⓣ072 540058 or from Lima 01 2414455, ⓦhotelcaballitodemar.com. Plush, comfortable and overlooking the sea at the southern end of the beach, this place has its own swimming pool right by the exquisite ocean (very peaceful in low season), a restaurant, sun terraces and really comfortable rooms; a quality place, they offer massage and inclusive breakfast, although local tours and fishing trips cost extra. S/200

Punta Sal Club Hotel Km 1192, Punta Sal ⓣ072 596700, ⓦpuntasal.com.pe. At the northern end of the point, this rather exclusive place offers comfortable cabin-style accommodation right on the beach, a pool, a fantastic bar and restaurant facilities; it also offers fishing, horseriding and snorkelling. Bungalows S/120, doubles S/240

The Peru–Ecuador border

Crossing the **Peru–Ecuador border** is relatively simple in either direction. You have the choice of crossing at the busy frontier settlement of **Aguas Verdes** or at the crossing between **La Tina** and **Macará**, which is a very pleasant alternative, its main advantage being the scenery en route to Loja.

CROSSING THE BORDER

AT AGUAS VERDES

By bus Some long-distance buses enter Ecuador; these stop to give time for border processing of passengers at Peru's customs and immigration centre, before crossing the bridge by foot, going through Ecuadorian border formalities and walking into Huaquillas. From here, there are frequent buses for most major destinations in Ecuador. The best bet is to go on to Cuenca (5hr), a small, attractive

7

TUMBES PROTECTED AREAS

The Tumbes region is well endowed with natural resources, not least the three major **protected areas** of the Santuario Nacional los Manglares de Tumbes, the Parque Nacional Cerros Amotape and the Zona Reservada de Tumbes. These, plus the El Angulo Hunting Reserve, encompass many habitats only found in this small corner of the country. If you're short of time, it is just about possible to travel between these in just a day, but contact the local conservation organization – Pronaturaleza, Av Tarapacá 4–16, Urbino Fonavi (☎072 523412), on the outskirts of Tumbes – beforehand for impartial, expert advice. **Permission** from INRENA, opposite Pronaturaleza's office, is needed to enter all of these areas, though this is a formality for which no fees are payable.

THE SANTUARIO NACIONAL LOS MANGLARES DE TUMBES

The **Santuario Nacional los Manglares de Tumbes** comprises most of the remaining **mangrove swamps** left in Peru, which are under serious threat from fishing and farming (shrimp farming in particular). The best way to visit the sanctuary is via the Pronaturaleza centre near Zarumilla, here called CECODEM (Centro de Conservación para el Desarrollo de los Manglares). The centre also presents a lot of interpretative material about the mangroves, of which there are five species here. Red mangrove is the most common and this is where the *conchas negras* thrive, although the 1998 El Niño weather introduced large amounts of fresh water into the shell beds here, causing significant damage. The mangroves also contain over two hundred bird species, including eight endemic species, notably the rather splendid mangrove eagle.

Combis run from Tumbes market to Zarumilla regularly (S/2.50; 20min), from where it's only 7km down a track to CECODEM; a motorcycle taxi will cost S/5, and you can arrange for the driver to return to pick you up. If arranged in advance with Pronaturaleza in Tumbes (at least one day before), CECODEM offer a walking **tour** (2–3hr) following a raised walkway through the mangroves and a **canoe trip** with a guide (S/50 for up to six people).

ZONA RESERVADA DE TUMBES

This reserve extends right up to the Ecuadorian border and covers over 75,000 hectares of mainly tropical forest. The best route is inland, due south from Tumbes via Pampas de Hospital and El Caucho to El Narranjo and Figueroa on the border, but transport from Tumbes is only regular as far as Pampas de Hospital, and only occasionally further on to El Caucho, which is where the best forest is. Potential sightings include monkeys, many bird species, small cats and snakes, though the **Río Tumbes crocodile** is a highly endangered species, found only at two sites along this river. There is some small hope for this unique creature in the form of a local breeding programme, but the whole area is under threat from gold mining, mainly from across the border in Ecuador at the headwaters of the river. Pollution, too, from Tumbes is generating further disturbance.

PARQUE NACIONAL CERROS DE AMOTAPE

Home to the best-preserved region of dry forest anywhere along the Pacific coast of South America, the **Parque Nacional Cerros de Amotape** contains six other distinct habitats that cover over 90,000 hectares. Access is via Corrales, 5km south of Máncora, or via Chillo, just north of Sullana; you'll need permission from INRENA to visit (see above, or if coming via Chillo you can visit them en route at Encuentro de los Pilares). Animals here include the black parrot, desert foxes, deer, white-backed squirrel, *tigrillos* (ocelots), puma and white-winged turkeys. Remember to take all your drinking and other **water** needs with you when entering this zone.

Ecuadorian city and a major cultural centre, although Machala is nearer (75km; 2hr) and has some accommodation and other facilities.

By colectivo Combis (S/4) for the border leave Tumbes for the new Peruvian customs and immigrations centre right beside the international bridge (30min) from block 3 of Tumbes Norte every 20min or so between 7am and 7pm.

By taxi A taxi from Tumbes to the border bridge (taxis are not allowed over the 2 bridges into Huaquillas, Ecuador) costs S/25.

Entry/exit stamps Peruvian customs and immigrations centre at the international bridge (daily 24hr) is where you will have to hand in your tourist card and get an exit stamp in your passport before crossing over the bridge and then going through the Ecuadorian customs and immigration procedures (24hr). There are reports of pick pocketing, con artists and money-change cheaters based on both the Peruvian and the Ecuadorian side of this border.

Customs The main Peruvian customs point is actually a concrete complex in the middle of the desert between the villages of Cancas and Máncora, more than 50km south of the border. When it is operating buses are pulled over and passengers have to get out, often having to show documents to the customs police, while the bus and selected items of luggage are searched for contraband goods. This rarely takes more than twenty minutes.

Money and exchange In both directions the authorities occasionally require that you show an onward ticket out of their respective countries. Unless you intend to recross the border inside a week or two, it's not worth taking out any local currency: changing Peruvian nuevo soles in Ecuador or Ecuadorian sucres in Peru usually involves a substantial loss, and inflation is such that even two weeks can make quite a difference. The area of no-man's-land between the two countries' posts is basically a street market where everyone gets hassled to change money – grab a taxi to ease the passage. The best policy is to change as little money as possible (because of the poor exchange rates mentioned above) and, if you take a taxi, be firm on the price in advance.

VIA LA TINA AND MACARÁ

By colectivo The crossing is most conveniently approached by combi from Sullana, leaving from the Terminal Terrestre in Avenida Buenos Aires, not far from the main market, departing every 30 minutes or so between 6am and 6pm (128km; almost 2hr; S/15). A short mototaxi ride (S/1; 5min) connects small La Tina with the international bridge and immigration facilities.

Macará Macará is located some 4km from the border; motorcycle taxis (10min; 70¢) take people into town. Buses on to Loja (5hr) depart from Macará. Alternatively, there are also buses direct to Loja from Piura with Transportes Loja (Sánchez Cerro 1480 ⓣ 073 30940; daily; 10–12hr; S/30). The journey between the border and Macará is extremely hot – it's only a few kilometres, but if the sun's out, take water to drink. There are a couple of hostels in Macará.

Entry/exit stamps The Peruvian and Ecuadorian immigration offices are open 24hr; the frontier is based on a river bridge with the Peruvian immigration on the Peruvian end of the bridge. Hand in your tourist card and get an exit stamp in your passport here, then walk over the bridge to the Ecuadorian immigration facility. Coming into Peru you may have to have your completed tourist card stamped by the national police.

Money and exchange You can change money (dollars, sucres or soles) in Macará, and in La Tina at the bank (Mon–Fri 9am–4pm).

7

The jungle

MACAWS AT A CLAY LICK, MADRE DE DIOS

The jungle

The Amazon, the rainforest, the selva, the jungle, the green hell (*el infierno verde*): all attempt to name this huge, vibrant swathe of Peru. Whether you explore it up close, from the ground or a boat, or fly over it in a plane, the Peruvian jungle seems endless. Well over half of the country is covered by dense tropical rainforest, and this jungle region, sharing the western edge of the Amazon with Colombia, Ecuador and Brazil, forms part of what is probably the most biodiverse region on Earth. Jaguars, anteaters and tapirs still roam the forests, huge anacondas lurk in the swamps, toothy caimans sunbathe along riverbanks, and trees rise like giants from the forest floor. Many indigenous tribes still live scattered throughout the Peruvian section of the Amazon, surviving primarily by hunting and fishing.

8

The jungle of southeastern Peru is plentifully supplied with lodges, guides, boats and flights. Cusco is arguably the best departure point for trips into the **southern selva**, with air and road access to the frontier town of **Puerto Maldonado** – a great base for visiting the nearby forests of **Madre de Dios**, which boast the **Reserva Nacional Tambopata** and the **Parque Nacional Bahuaja-Sonene**, an enormous tract of virgin rainforest close to the Bolivian border. Many naturalists believe that this region is the most biodiverse on Earth, and thus the best place to head for wildlife. Reachable overland from Cusco, the **Manu Biosphere Reserve and National Park** runs from cloud forest on the slopes of the Andes down to relative lowland forest. For a quicker and cheaper taste of the jungle, you can travel by bus from Cusco via Ollantaytambo to **Quillabamba**, on the **Río Urubamba**, which flows north along the foot of the Andes, through the dangerous but unforgettable whitewater rapids of the **Pongo de Mainique**.

North of here lies **Pucallpa**, a rapidly growing, industrialized jungle town in the **central selva**, best reached by scheduled flights or the largely paved road from Lima. Another sector of this stunning central jungle region – **Chanchamayo** – is only eight to twelve hours by road from Lima, and is blessed with crystalline rivers, numerous protected areas for birdwatching, and good road links. Winding fast but precariously down from the Andean heights of Tarma, the Carretera Central is now paved all the way to **Satipo**, a jungle frontier town, relatively close to the **Río Ene**. En route, the road passes through the cloud forest via **La Merced**, from where there are buses to quasi-European **Oxapampa** and the fascinating Tyrolean settlement of **Pozuzo**.

RÍO TAMBOPATA

Highlights

❶ **Río Tambopata** You'll be hard-pushed to find anywhere as rich in flora and fauna as the rainforest around some of the lodges on this stunning Amazonian river. **See p.445**

❷ **Manu Biosphere Reserve** An excellent place to experience a truly pristine rainforest and spot plenty of jungle wildlife – from giant otters in secluded lakes to caiman littering the riverbanks. **See p.446**

❸ **Pampa Hermosa Lodge** Just eight hours' drive from Lima, this sumptuous cloud-forest lodge, one of the jewels of Peru, offers access to a cock-of-the-rock refuge, where Peru's national birds dance every evening. **See p.455**

❹ **Iquitos** A fun, vivacious city, ridiculously hot during the day, with an equally sizzling bar and club scene when the sun goes down. **See p.466**

❺ **Dolphin-watching** Quite common in the rivers around Iquitos, pink river dolphins and blue dolphins are a fantastic sight as they leap around your canoe. **See p.478**

❻ **Ayahuasca healing** Witnessing a shaman's ancient chants waft under the moonlit jungle canopy feels like a hallucinatory experience. **See p.479**

HIGHLIGHTS ARE MARKED ON THE MAP ON P.430

The main access point to the **northern selva** is the city of **Iquitos**, at the heart of the largest chunk of lowland jungle with no road connections to the outside world, just riverboat and plane. The northern selva can also be reached from the northern Peruvian coast via an increasingly popular but still adventurous route that takes the Río Huallaga from Yurimaguas (see p.394), a three- to four-day boat journey that can be broken by a visit to the immense **Reserva Nacional Pacaya Samiria** at the heart of the upper Amazon, a little-visited wildlife haven. The northern selva is also the most organized and established of the Peruvian Amazon's tourist destinations, with many reputable companies offering a range of jungle visits, from luxury lodges and cruises (see p.475) to no-frills survival expeditions.

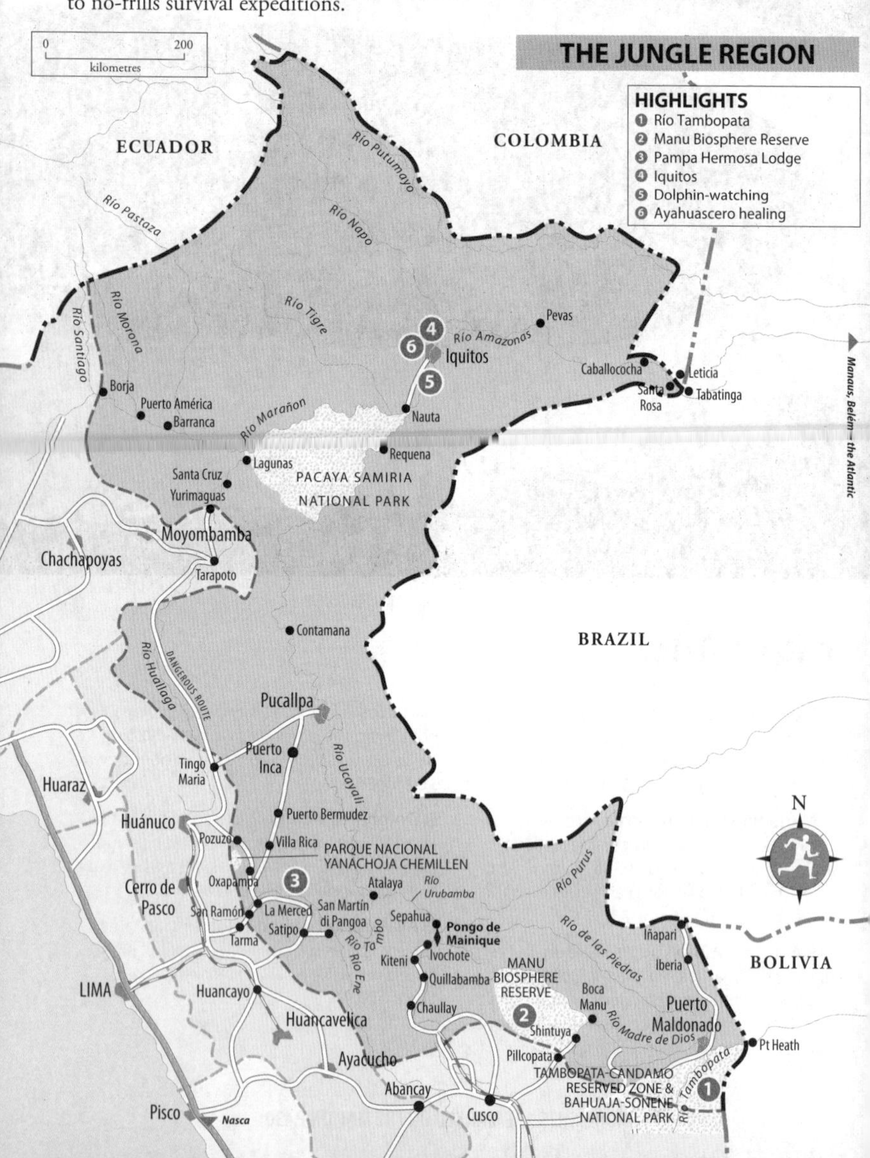

BEST OF THE JUNGLE

Given the breadth of options, it's not easy to decide which bit of the jungle to head for. Your three main criteria will probably be budget, ease of access (see p.433) and the nature of jungle experience you're after, whether it's a few days in a luxury lodge, exploring the rivers by boat or a back-to-nature week of wildlife-spotting. Below are the best places for…

Cash-strapped travellers Satipo or Puerto Maldonado; both can be reached with ease by bus. p.456 & p.435.

Trips of three days or less Puerto Maldonado or Iquitos. p.435 & p.466.

Off-the-beaten-track adventure Pucallpa, Iquitos and Puerto Maldonado are the best starting points; book through an established tour company. p.461, p.466 & p.435.

Wonderful wildlife The Manu Biosphere Reserve, Reserva Nacional Tambopata or Reserva Nacional Pacaya Samiria. p.446, p.445 & p.476.

Blow-the-budget luxury Iquitos and Puerto Maldonado/Tambopata are great for top-flight jungle tours. p.466 & p.435.

Brief history

Many archeologists believe that the initial spark for the evolution of Peru's high cultures came from the jungle. Evidence from **Chavín**, **Chachapoyas** and **Tantamayo** cultures seems to back up such a theory – ancient Andean people certainly had continuous contact with the jungle areas – and the **Incas** were unable to dominate the tribes, their main contact being peaceful trade in treasured items such as feathers, gold, medicinal plants and the sacred coca leaf. At the time of the **Spanish Conquest**, long-term settlements existed along all the major jungle rivers, with people living in large groups to farm the rich alluvial soils.

8

Early colonization

For centuries, the Peruvian jungle resisted major colonization. **Alonso de Alvarado** successfully led the first Spanish expedition, cutting a trail through from Chachapoyas to Moyobamba in 1537, but most incursions ended in utter disaster, defeated by disease, the ferocity of the tribes, the danger of the rivers, climate and wild animals. Ultimately, apart from white-man's epidemics (which spread much faster than the men themselves), the early conquistadors had relatively little impact on the populations of the Peruvian Amazon. Only **Orellana**, one of the first Spaniards to lead exploratory expeditions into the Peruvian Amazon, managed to glimpse the reality of the rainforest, though even he seemed to misunderstand it when he was attacked by a tribe of blonde women, one of whom managed to hit him in the eye with a blow-gun dart. These "women" are now thought to be the men of the Yagua tribe (from near Iquitos), who wear straw-coloured, grass-like skirts and headdresses.

The impact of the Church

By the early eighteenth century the **Catholic Church** had made deep but vulnerable inroads into the rainforest regions. Resistance to this culminated in 1742 with an **indigenous uprising** in the central selva led by an enigmatic character from the Andes calling himself **Juan Santos Atahualpa**. Missions were destroyed, missionaries and colonists killed, and Spanish military expeditions defeated. The result was that the central rainforest remained under the control of the indigenous population for nearly a century more.

The rubber boom

As "white-man's" technology advanced, so too did the possibilities of conquering Amazonia. The 1830s saw the beginning of a century of massive and painful exploitation of the forest and its population by **rubber barons**. Many of these wealthy men were European, eager to gain control of the raw material desperately needed following the

AMAZON ECOLOGY: THE BASICS

At about six times the size of England, or approximately the size of California, the tangled, sweltering **Amazon Basin** rarely fails to capture the imagination of anyone who ventures beneath its dense canopy. In the **lowland areas**, away from the seasonally flooded riverbanks, the landscape is dominated by red, loamy soil, which can reach depths of 50m. Reaching upwards from this, the **primary forest** – mostly comprising a huge array of tropical palms, with scatterings of larger, emergent tree species – regularly achieves evergreen canopy heights of 50m. At ground level the vegetation is relatively open (mostly saplings, herbs and woody shrubs), since the trees tend to branch high up, restricting the amount of light available. At marginally **higher altitudes**, a large belt of **cloud forest** (*ceja de selva*) sweeps the eastern edges of the Andes, stunningly beautiful and the most biodiverse of the rainforest zones.

discovery of the vulcanization process. Moreover, during this era the jungle regions of Peru were better connected to Brazil, Bolivia, the Atlantic, and ultimately Europe, than they were to Lima or the Pacific coast. The peak of the boom, from the 1880s to just before World War I, had a prolonged effect. Treating the natives as little more than slaves, men like the notorious **Fitzcarrald** (see box, p.440) made overnight fortunes.

Modern colonization

Nineteenth-century colonialism also saw the progression of the **extractive frontier** along the navigable rivers, which involved short-term economic exploitation based on the extraction of other natural materials, such as timber and animal skins; coupled to this was the advance of the **agricultural frontier** down from the Andes. Both kinds of expansion assumed that Amazonia was a limitless source of natural resources and an empty wilderness – misapprehensions that still exist today.

8

Coca barons

When the Peruvian economy began to suffer in the mid-1980s, foreign credit ended, and those with substantial private capital fled, mainly to the US. The government, then

INDIGENOUS JUNGLE TRIBES

Outside the few main towns of the Peruvian jungle, there are few sizeable settlements, and the population remains dominated by about fifty **indigenous tribes**. For most, the jungle offers a **semi-nomadic** existence, and in terms of material possessions, they have, need and want very little. Communities are scattered, with groups of between ten and two hundred people, and their sites shift every few years. For **subsistence** they depend on small, cultivated plots, fish from the rivers and game from the forest, including wild pigs, deer, monkeys and a great range of edible birds. The main species of edible jungle fish are *sabalo* or doncella (oversized catfish), *carachama* (an armoured walking catfish), the feisty piranha (generally not quite as dangerous as Hollywood depicts) and the giant *zungaro* and *paiche* – the latter, at up to 200kg, being the world's largest freshwater fish. In fact, food is so abundant that jungle-dwellers generally spend no more than three to four days a week engaged in subsistence activities, which, as some anthropologists like to point out, makes them "relatively affluent".

After centuries of **external influence** (missionaries, gold-seekers, rubber barons, cash-crop colonists, cocaine smugglers, soldiers, oil companies, illegal loggers, documentary makers, anthropologists and now tourists), many jungle Indians speak Spanish and live fairly conventional, westernized lives, preferring shorts, football shirts and fizzy drinks to their more traditional clothing and manioc beer. While many are being sucked into the money-based labour market, however, others, increasingly under threat, have struggled for cultural integrity and **territorial rights**; some – voluntarily isolated or uncontacted – have retreated as far as they are able beyond the world's enclosing frontier. Today they are struggling as their traditional and last remaining hunting grounds are infiltrated by oil companies and loggers.

JUNGLE ESSENTIALS

FOR ALL VISITS

- Certificate of inoculation against yellow fever (check with your embassy for prevailing health requirements)
- Malaria pills (start course in advance as directed by your doctor)
- Roll-on insect repellent containing DEET
- Suitable clothing (socks, trousers and long sleeves in the evenings)
- Toilet paper
- Waterproof poncho, cagoule (hooded nylon pack-away raincoat) or overclothes
- Whistle

FOR STAYS OF 3 DAYS OR MORE

The above plus…

- Anti-diarrhoea medicine (such as Lomotil or Imodium)
- Multipurpose knife (with can and bottle opener)
- Plastic bags for packing and lining your bags (a watertight box is best for camera equipment and other delicate valuables). Note that cardboard boxes dissolve on contact with the Amazon River or rain shower.
- Sunhat (especially for river travel)
- Torch and spare batteries
- Waterproof matches and a back-up gas lighter
- Gifts for people you might encounter (batteries, knives, fish-hooks and line, camera film, and so on)
- Insect-bite ointment (antihistamines, tiger balm or *mentol china*; toothpaste as a last resort)
- Running shoes; sandals (ideally plastic or rubber); rubber boots or strong walking boots if you're going hiking.

led by the young Alan García, was forced to abandon the jungle region, and both its colonist and indigenous inhabitants were left to survive by themselves. This effectively opened the doors for the **coca barons**, who had already established themselves during the 1970s in the Huallaga Valley, and who moved into the gap left by government aid in the other valleys of the *ceja de selva* (edge of the jungle) – notably the Pichis-Palcazu and the Apurimac-Ene. Over the subsequent decade, illicit coca production was responsible for some ten percent of the deforestation that occurred in the Peruvian Amazon during the entire twentieth century; furthermore, trade of this lucrative crop led to significant corruption and supported the rise of **terrorism**.

The twenty-first century

Clearing the forest for agriculture continues, and in Madre de Dios **gold mining** ravages the jungle. By the turn of the century, a massive desert had appeared around Huaypetue, previously a small-time, frontier mining town. The neighbouring communities of Amarakaeri (who have been panning for gold in a small-scale, sustainable fashion for some thirty years) are in danger of losing their land and natural resources. Attempts by NGOs and pro-Indian lawyers to maintain the boundaries of reserves and communities are constantly thwarted by colonists, who are supported by local government.

GETTING TO THE JUNGLE

By plane Flying to the main jungle towns – Iquitos (2hr), Puerto Maldonado (2hr), Tarapoto (2hr) and Pucallpa (1hr 30min) – from Lima or Cusco generally costs over $60 each way, but can save an arduous journey overland.

By bus or colectivo The southern and central selva are relatively easy to get to overland by bus, the former from Cusco or Puno in 12–20hr and the latter in 7–10hr (to La Merced) via a scenic route directly east from Lima. The closest you can get to Iquitos by bus or colectivo is to Tarapoto and Yurimaguas, both within a 20hr bus journey from Chiclayo.

By boat You can reach Iquitos relatively easy by boat from the frontier with Brazil and Colombia (see p.488).

TOP 5 ECO-LODGES

Amazon Explorama Ceiba Tops Near Iquitos, northern selva. p.478
Inkaterra Reserva Amazónica Near Puerto Maldonado, southern selva. p.445
Muyuna Near Iquitos, northern selva. p.479
Pampa Hermosa Near San Ramón, central selva. p.455
Refugio Amazonas Río Tambopata, southern selva. p.445

GETTING AROUND THE JUNGLE

BY BOAT

The three most common forms of river transport are canoes (*canoas*), speedboats (*deslizadoras*) and larger riverboats (*lanchas*). Whichever method you choose, it's a good idea to make sure you can get along with the boatman (*piloto*) or captain, and that he really does know the rivers.

By canoe Canoes can be anything from a small dugout with a paddle, useful for moving along small creeks and rivers, to a large 18m canoe with panelled sides and a *peque-peque* (on-board engine) or a more powerful outboard motor. Travelling in a smaller canoe isn't advisable without the help of reliable local expertise; this inevitably means a good tour company with professional guides, or reliable local guides.

By speedboat Speedboats tend to have lightweight metal hulls and are obviously faster and more manoeuvrable than canoes, but also more expensive.

By riverboat Riverboats come in a range of sizes and vary considerably in their river-worthiness: always have a good look at the boat before buying a ticket or embarking on a journey, and note that the smaller one- or two-deck riverboats are frequently in worse condition (and noisier) than larger ones. The best are the Iquitos-based tour boats, with cabins for up to thirty passengers, dining rooms, bars, sun lounges and even jacuzzis on board. Next best are the larger vessels with up to three decks that can carry two hundred passengers, with hammock spaces and a few cabins (for which you pay two to three times as much); if you're over 1.8m tall, it's best to take a hammock as the bunks may be too small. Always try to get a berth as close as possible to the front of the boat, away from the noise of the motor. On the larger riverboats (especially between Pucallpa and Iquitos, or Tabatinga and Iquitos) you can save money on hotels by hanging around in your hammock, as most captains allow passengers to sling one up and sleep on board for a few days before departure.

ON FOOT

Walking is slow and difficult in the forest, and should only be attempted with an experienced tour guide or local person willing to guide you. People rarely get from A to B on foot, since river travel is the fastest and safest route in much of the rainforest.

Getting lost Losing your bearings on walking trails in the forest is a genuine danger, even for locals. By straying less than a hundred metres from your lodge, camp, the river or your guide, you can find yourself completely surrounded by a seemingly impenetrable tangle of undergrowth. If there are any, one trail looks very much like the next to the unaccustomed eye. If you're with a group who will look for you when they realize you are lost, a sensible strategy is to shout, blow a whistle (always carry one!) or bang the base of big buttress-root trees as Indians do when they get lost on hunting forages. If no one is likely to come looking for you, find moving water and follow it downstream to the main river, where there's more probability of finding a settlement or passing boat. If you get caught out overnight, the best places to sleep are: beside a fire on the river bank; in a nest you could make for yourself in between the buttress roots of a large tree; higher up in a tree that isn't crawling with biting ants; in a hammock.

The southern selva

A large, forested region, with a manic climate (usually searingly hot and humid, but with sudden cold spells – *friajes* – between June and August, due to icy winds coming down from the Andean glaciers), the **southern selva** has only been systematically explored since the 1950s.

Named after the broad river that flows through the heart of the southern jungle, the still relatively wild *departamento* of **MADRE DE DIOS** is centred on the fast-growing river town of **Puerto Maldonado**, near the Bolivian border and just 180m above sea level. The town extends a tenuous political and economic hold over the vast *departamento* and has a fast-growing population of over 40,000, but most visitors come for the nearby **wildlife**, either in the strictly protected **Manu Biosphere**

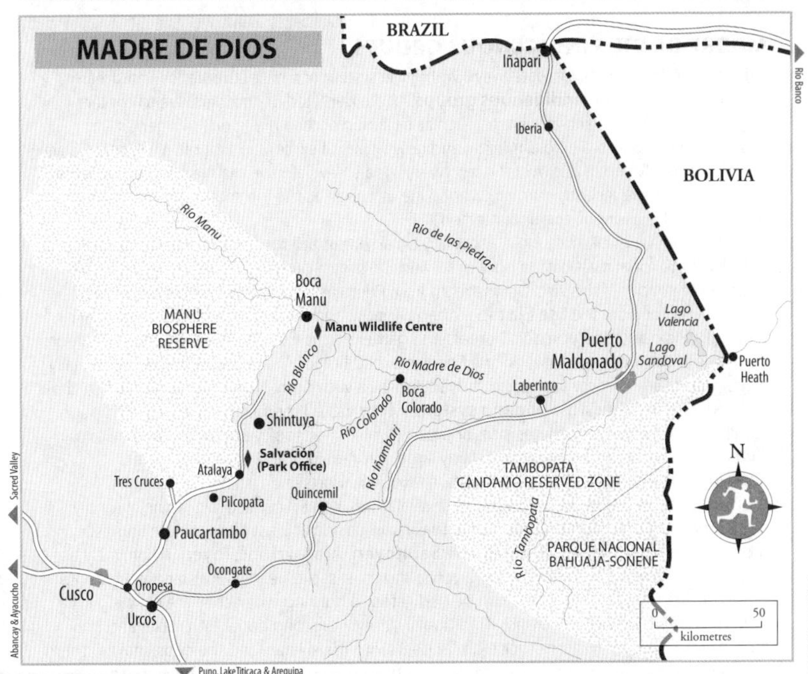

8

Reserve – still essentially an expedition zone – and the cheaper and easy-to-access **Reserva Nacional Tambopata**, chiefly visited by groups staying at lodges. Both offer some of the most luxuriant jungle and richest flora and fauna in the world. Another massive protected area, the **Parque Nacional Bahuaja-Sonene**, is adjacent to Tambopata.

Less accessible than the protected zones, but nevertheless offering travellers staying in Puerto Maldonado a taste of the rainforest, are **Lago Sandoval** and the huge expanse of **Lago Valencia**, both great wildlife spots east along the Río Madre de Dios and close to the Bolivian border. At the least, you're likely to spot a few caimans and the strange hoatzin bird, and if you're very lucky, larger mammals such as capybara, tapir or, less likely, jaguar – and at Valencia, you can fish for piranha. A little further southeast lies the **Pampas del Heath**, the only tropical grassland within Peru.

The Río Madre de Dios itself is fed by two main tributaries, the **Río Manu** and the **Río Alto Madre de Dios**, which roll off the Paucartambo Ridge just north of Cusco. West of this ridge, the **Río Urubamba** watershed starts and its river flows on past Machu Picchu and down to the jungle area around the town of **Quillabamba**, before entering lowland Amazon beyond the rapids of **Pongo de Mainique**.

Puerto Maldonado

A remote settlement even for Peru, **PUERTO MALDONADO** is a frontier colonist town with strong links to the Cusco region and a fervour for bubbly jungle *chicha* music. With an economy based on unsustainable lumber and gold extraction, and highly sustainable brazil-nut gathering from the rivers and forests of Madre de Dios, Puerto Maldonado has grown enormously over the last twenty years from a small, laidback outpost of civilization to a busy market town. Today, swollen by the arrival of businesses expecting a boom now that the road to Brazil is open, it's the thriving, safe

MADRE DE DIOS INDIGENOUS GROUPS

Off the main Madre de Dios waterways, within the system of smaller tributaries and streams, live a variety of different **indigenous groups**. All are depleted in numbers due to contact with Western diseases and influences, such as pollution of their rivers, environmental destruction by large-scale gold-mining, and new waves of exploration for oil. While some have been completely wiped out over the last twenty years, several have maintained their isolation. These groups have recently come to worldwide attention as the international press have highlighted the plight of "the uncontacted".

If you go anywhere in the jungle, especially on an organized tour, you're likely to stop off at a **tribal village** for at least half an hour or so, and the more you know about the people, the more you'll get out of the visit. Downstream from Puerto Maldonado, the most populous indigenous group are the **Ese Eja** tribe (often wrongly, and derogatorily, called "Huarayos" by *colonos*). Originally semi-nomadic hunters and gatherers, the Ese Eja were well-known warriors who fought the Incas and, later on, the Spanish expedition of Alvarez Maldonado – eventually establishing fairly friendly and respectful relationships with both. Under Fitzcarrald's reign, they suffered greatly through the **engaño system**, which tricked them into slave labour through credit offers on knives, machetes, pots and pans, which then took years, or in some cases a lifetime, to work off. Today they live in fairly large communities and have more or less abandoned their original bark-cloth robes in favour of shorts and T-shirts.

Upstream from Puerto Maldonado live several tribes, known collectively (again, wrongly and derogatorily) as the "Mashcos" but actually comprising at least five separate linguistic groups – the **Huachipaeri**, **Amarakaeri**, **Sapitoyeri**, **Arasayri** and **Toyeri**. All typically use long bows – over 1.5m – and lengthy arrows, and most settlements will also have a shotgun or two these days, since less time can be dedicated to hunting when they are panning for gold or working timber for *colonos*. Traditionally, they wore long bark-cloth robes and had long hair, and the men often stuck eight feathers into the skin around their lips, making them look distinctively fierce and cat-like. Many Huachipaeri and Amarakaeri groups are now actively engaging with the outside world on their own terms, and some of their young men and women have gone through university education and subsequently returned to their native villages.

8

(and fairly expensive) capital of a region that feels very much on the threshold of major upheavals. Where, only thirty years ago, there were hardly any four-wheeled vehicles and the town's only TV was set up outside the municipal building for the locals to watch football, these days enormous Brazilian trucks thunder past and satellite TV dishes have sprouted all over town.

While the busy city centre combines the usual bars and restaurants with pool halls, hammock shops and offices, there isn't much in the way of specific attractions, and most visitors come here primarily to enter the forest and stay in a **lodge** (see p.439).

Brief history

While gold mining and logging – both mostly illegal frontier businesses – keep Puerto Maldonado buzzing today, it was **rubber** that established the town at the beginning of the twentieth century. During the 1920s, **game hunters** dominated the economy of the region, and after them, mainly in the 1960s, the exploiters of mahogany and cedar trees arrived – leading to the construction of Boca Manu airstrip, just before the oil companies moved in during the 1970s. Most of the townspeople, riding coolly around on Honda motorbikes, are second-generation *colonos*, but there's a constant stream of new and hopeful arrivals, both rich and poor, from all parts of South America. The lure, inevitably, is **gold** (see box, p.438).

Plaza de Armas

The **Plaza de Armas**, with its bizarre, pagoda-style clock tower at the centre, is unusual in that it's not central to the city's street grid pattern; instead, the streets stretch out

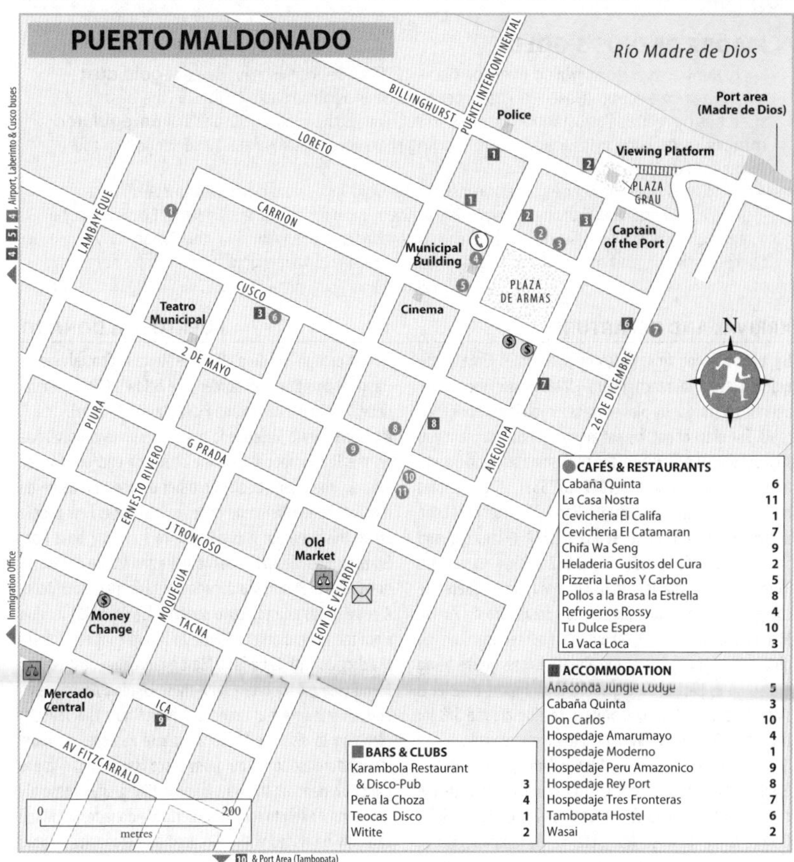

from the port, Tambopata riverfront and the Plaza de Armas – all bounded by rivers – towards the airport and forest. An important link in the creation of a fast land route from western Brazil to Lima and the Atlantic coast, a new transoceanic **suspension bridge** (Puente Intercontinental) spans the river to arrive at the Plaza de Armas, and is starting to transform the city at an alarming rate.

The port

Follow Jirón Billinghurst one block towards the river from the main plaza, and head down the steep steps to the main **port** area, situated on the **Río Madre de Dios**, and offering an otherwise rare glimpse of the river, which is largely shielded from view by the ever-growing rows of wooden houses and lumber yards; here you can see boat-builders and loggers, and even take a ferry over to the other side of the river and see the town from a different perspective.

Mercado Central

Block 4 of Jirón Ica • Daily 6.30am–4pm

The **Mercado Central**, just eight short blocks from the Plaza de Armas, is large, busy and brimming over with jungle produce, including Brazil nuts; it also has a couple of rainforest medicine practitioners.

MADRE DE DIOS'S GOLD

Every rainy season the swollen rivers of Madre de Dios deposit a heavy layer of **gold dust** along their banks, and those who have been quick enough to stake claims on the best stretches have made substantial fortunes. In such areas there are thousands of **unregulated miners**, using large front-loader earth-moving machines, destroying a large section of the forest, and doing so very quickly.

Gold lust is not a new phenomenon here – the gold-rich rivers have brought Andean Indians and occasional European explorers to the region for centuries. The Inca Emperor Tupac Yupanqui is known to have discovered the Río Madre de Dios, naming it the Amarymayo ("serpent river"), and may well have sourced some of the Empire's gold from around here.

ARRIVAL AND DEPARTURE — PUERTO MALDONADO

8

By plane Flying from Cusco or direct from Lima is the quickest way to reach Puerto Maldonado; most tour agencies will organize plane tickets for you if you book their tours. The blast of hot, humid air you get the moment you step out onto the runway of the city's small but modern and air-conditioned airport (☎082 571533) is an instant reminder that this is the Amazon Basin. Lan (corner of León de Velarde and 2 de Mayo; ☎082 573677, Ⓦlan.com) and StarPerú (León de Velarde 151; ☎082 573564, Ⓦstarperu.com) both operate jets from Lima via Cusco. There are currently no regular flights to Brazil from Puerto Maldonado, but details about ad hoc services can be obtained from officials at the airport. Unless you're being picked up as part of an organized tour, airport transfer is simplest and coolest by mototaxi, costing around S/8 for the otherwise impossibly hot eight-kilometre walk.

Destinations Cusco (2 daily; 40min); Lima (2 daily; 2hr).

By bus Most buses from Cusco – principally with the companies Movil Tours (Av Tambopata 428; ☎082 573567); CIVA (C Jaime Troncoso Mz. C Lte. 12, Av Tambopa; ☎082 9827 20884) and Huareño (Av Tambopata 602; ☎082 503580) – arrive at Puerto Maldonado's Av Tambopata; buses to and from Juliaca finish and start from the Mercado Central area. A large-span bridge over the Río Madre de Dios connects the Plaza de Armas in downtown Puerto Maldonado with the Brazilian border. Buses from Brazil or colectivos from the Iñapari border crossing (see below) tend to pick up and drop off in the Mercado Central area.

Destinations Brazilian border (see below); Cusco (several daily; 15–20hr); Juliaca and Puno (daily; 16–20hr).

By boat Puerto Maldonado has two main river ports, one on the Río Tambopata, at the southern end of León de Velarde, the main street; the other on the Río Madre de Dios, at the northern end of León de Velarde. Few people arrive this way, but it is possible to travel by boat from Brazil and Bolivia up the ríos Madeira and Madre de Dios, or downriver to Puerto Maldonado from Pilcopata and Manu. A regular bus and colectivo service (45min; S/15) leaving from the main market on Ernesto Rivero connects Puerto Maldonado with Laberinto. Most boats going upstream to Manu (see p.116) begin (and those coming downstream end) their journeys at Laberinto, though note that if you're planning to visit the Manu Biosphere Reserve, it's more straightforward to set out from Cusco (see p.220) if you're going overland all the way. If you're flying, then presently you're most likely to come via Puerto Maldonado, but Manu can only be visited with a licenced tour company, so your boat upriver will be organized for you.

Destinations Boca Colorado (several daily; 2–6hr); Boca Manu (6–10hr).

By car The new Interoceanic Highway heads to Brazil, with the border less than 3 hours' drive away. On occasion, visitors arriving here (by road or air) have to go through a yellow-fever vaccination checkpoint.

CROSSING INTO BRAZIL AND BOLIVIA

INTO BRAZIL

From Puerto Maldonado to the border It's easy to take a colectivo or bus to the border town of Iñapari, around 2hr 30min from Puerto Maldonado, where the Peruvian police and immigration offices are based. It's best to book colectivos at least a day in advance (S/40) and they will pick you up from your hotel: try Nuevo Perú, Jr Piura 790 (☎082 574235), or Iñapari Tours, Jr Piura 768 (☎082 793574). Make sure you get your exit or entry stamp from the Peruvian border post at Iñapari (Mon–Fri 8.30am–noon & 2.30–7pm, Sat & Sun 9am–noon & 2.30–6pm). It's only 2km from Iñapari to the Brazilian Federal Police and customs (colectivos available from the main plaza in Iñapari).

Hostal Milagros Iñapari; no phone. It's better to stay in Iñapari, on the Peruvian side; this is the best of the basic hostels. The settlement of Assis Brasil on the Brazilian side of the border has some cafés and hostels but is a bit of a dump. S/50

From the border to Brazil The best option for onward travel from the border into Brazil is to take a car from Assis Brasil (the closest settlement to the border on the Brazilian side) with Brazilian Drivers ($10/person, $40/car). Brazilian's office is just a couple of kilometres into Brazil over the Río Acre bridge. It's 112km to Brasiléia, a much larger town that also connects via a walkable bridge with the Bolivian free-trade-zone town of Cobija. From Brasiléia, colectivos and buses for Río Branco leave regularly from near the *Ponte Augusto do Araujó*.

Destinations Iñapari and the border (several colectivos daily from 4am; 2hr 30min).

INTO BOLIVIA

By boat Though not commonly done, it's possible to travel into Bolivia on one of the cargo boats that leave more or less every week from Puerto Maldonado. Before embarking on this, however, you'll have to clear your passport and visa with the Puerto Maldonado police and Migraciones offices (see p.441). Puerto Pardo is the last Peruvian frontier settlement (Bolivian formalities can usually be dealt with at the frontier post of Puerto Heath, from where you continue by river to Riberalta). Be aware that the journey from Puerto Maldonado to Riberalta is rough and usually takes 10–14 days; always make sure that the boat is going all the way or you might get stuck at the border, which, by all accounts, is not much fun, and you might have to wait days for another boat. From Riberalta there are land and air connections to the rest of Bolivia, as well as river or road access into Brazil via the Río Madeira or Guajará-Mirim.

GETTING AROUND AND INFORMATION

By mototaxi/motorbike The quickest way of getting around Puerto Maldonado and its immediate environs is to hail a mototaxi (S/2–3 in town, but check before getting in) or passenger-carrying motorbikes (S/1 flat rate).

Tourist information The airport has a tourist information kiosk (T 082 571164, W regionmadrededios.gob.pe), though it's rarely staffed. For permits to travel by river into the jungle call at the Captain's office on León de Velarde, between Av González Prada and Dos de Mayo (Mon–Sat 8am–6pm).

National park information The Manu National Park Office is at Av Bastidas 310, Cusco (T 084 240898). The local SERNANP office (dealing with national protected areas) is at Dirección Sub-regional Agraria Madre de Dios, Av 28 de Julio 482. Entry to the national parks of this region is either organized by your tour company or paid for at the relevant river entry points.

8

ACCOMMODATION

Anaconda Jungle Lodge Airport road T 082 571029, W anacondajunglelodge.com. Within ten minutes' walk of the airport (and about 6km from Puerto Maldonado's centre), *Anaconda Jungle Lodge* accommodates its visitors in attractive traditional palm-roofed bungalows set on stilts above the ground within pleasant jungle gardens. They have a swimming pool and a smart wooden restaurant that serves Thai cuisine among other delicious dishes. S/80

Cabaña Quinta Cusco 535 T 082 571045, W hotelcabanaquinta.com.pe. Close to the port and town centre, this is one of the more popular hotels in town. Rooms are comfortable, some have fans – the more expensive ones a/c – and all are complemented by a small attractive garden. There's also an excellent bar-restaurant, wi-fi and a small pool. S/160

Don Carlos León de Velarde 1271 T 082 571029, W hotelesdoncarlos.com. This well-run place overlooks the Río Tambopata in a pretty spot, within walking distance of the centre, but just beyond the heart of town. It has a swimming pool and a good restaurant, and most rooms come with fans and TVs, some with a/c; all have private bathroom. S/210

Hospedaje Amarumayo Libertad 433 T 082 573860, E residenciaamarumayo@hotmail.com. Located some 6km northwest of the town centre but only five minutes from the airport, this place has a small pool. Staff are friendly and rooms have fans and private bathrooms. S/60

Hospedaje Moderno Jr Billinghurst 359 T 082 300043, E hospedaje_moderno@hotmail.com. A brightly painted, very friendly and well-kept hostel, with something of a frontier-town character, not least by the nature of its clientele, who are mainly river traders. The rooms here are small with shared bathroom, but do come with TV. S/40

Hospedaje Peru Amazónico Jr Ica 269 T 082 571799, E peruamazonico@hotmail.com. Bright and clean, this small place has ample rooms around a little courtyard, all with cable TV and wi-fi access. The spacious lobby area is always quite cool. S/80

Hospedaje Rey Port León de Velarde 457 T 082 572685. Friendly but sometimes noisy; the beds are basic and rooms are small, though fans are provided and most are private rooms with bath. S/55

Hospedaje Tres Fronteras Jr Arequipa 357 T 082 300011. Less than a block from the main plaza, *Tres Fronteras* is housed in a modern concrete building with a cool, tiled interior, and plain but comfortable small rooms, each with TV, fan and good bathroom. The beds come with orthopedic mattresses. S/70

★ **Tambopata Hostel** Av 26 de Diciembre 234 T 082 574201, W tambopatahostel.com. A great-value pad for budget travellers in a very central cedarwood-built house with dorms, private rooms and hammock areas. There's free internet access, a communal kitchen, shared cable TV and an outside terrace. Airport transfers and breakfasts are included in the price, and tours to Lago Sandoval and Colorado clay lick are organized. Hammocks S/15, dorms S/30, doubles S/80

THE SAGA OF FITZCARRALD

While the infamous rubber baron, **Fitzcarrald** (often mistakenly called Fitzcarraldo), is associated with the founding of Puerto Maldonado, he actually died some twelve years before the event; his story is, however, relevant to the development of this region. While working rubber on the Río Urubamba, Fitzcarrald caught the gold bug after hearing rumours from local Ashaninka and Machiguenga Indians of an **Inca fort** protecting vast treasures, possibly around the Río Purus. Setting out along the Mishagua, a tributary of the Río Urubamba, he managed to reach its source, and from there walked over the ridge to a new watershed which he took to be the Purus, though it was in fact the Río Cashpajali, a tributary of the Río Manu. Leaving men to clear a path, he returned to Iquitos, and in 1884 came back to the region on a boat called *La Contamana*. He took the boat apart, and, with the aid of over a thousand Ashaninka and other Indians, carried it across to the "Purus". But, as he cruised down, attacked by tribes at several points, Fitzcarrald slowly began to realize that the river was not the Purus – a fact confirmed when he eventually bumped into a Bolivian rubber collector.

Though he'd ended up on the wrong river, Fitzcarrald had discovered a link connecting the two great Amazonian watersheds. In Europe, the discovery was heralded as a great step forward in the exploration of South America, but for Peru it meant more **rubber**, a quicker route for its export and the beginning of the end for Madre de Dios' indigenous tribes. Puerto Maldonado was founded in 1902, and as exploitation of the region's rubber peaked, so too was there an increase in population of workers and merchants, with Madre de Dios ultimately becoming a *departamento* of Peru in 1912. German director **Werner Herzog** thought this historical episode a fitting subject for celluloid, and in 1982 directed the epic *Fitzcarraldo*.

8

★ **Wasai** Parque Grau on Billinghurst ☎ 082 572290; in Cusco ☎ 082 221826; in Lima ☎ 01 436 8792; ⓦ wasai.com. The best of the higher-end options, offering fine views over the Río Madre de Dios, and a swimming pool with a waterfall and bar set among trees, overlooking a canoe-builder's yard. All rooms are cabin-style with TV and shower, and staff here also organize local tours and run the *Wasai Lodge* (see p.446). S/150

EATING

You should have no problem finding something delicious to eat in Puerto Maldonado. Manioc and fish are staple foods in the town's **restaurants**. A variety of river fish is always available, even in ceviche form, though there is some concern in the region about river pollution from the unofficial gold mining. Venison (try *estofado de venado*) and wild boar fresh from the forest are often on the menu too. Along León de Velarde are a number of **cafés** and bars, one or two of which have walls covered in typical *selvatico*-style paintings, developed to represent and romanticize the dreamlike features of the jungle – looming jaguars, brightly plumed macaws in the treetops and deer drinking water from a still lake.

CAFÉS AND SNACKS

La Casa Nostra León de Velarde 515 ☎ 082 573833. A popular little café with sandwiches, a range of tasty cakes, tropical fruit juices (including mango, passionfruit, pineapple and *carambola* – a local favourite – for around S/3 a glass), as well as tamales and *papas rellenas* (stuffed potatoes). It also serves pretty good coffee and Peruvian breakfasts. Daily 8am–10pm.

Heladería Gusitos del Cura Plaza de Armas. Great for cold drinks, ice creams and snacks, this is a large space with big wooden windows that open out onto the main plaza. Daily 8am–8pm.

Refrigerios Rossy Plaza de Armas. This small, basic café is good for sandwiches and morning coffee; located close to the municipal building on the Plaza de Armas. Mon–Sat 7.30am–9pm.

Tu Dulce Espera Velarde 505. A small café-shop selling a wide range of sweets and cakes, many made with tropical fruits from the region. Daily 9am–9pm.

La Vaca Loca Loreto 224. This swish, trendy place serves tasty steaks and great salads. Daily 8.30am–7pm.

RESTAURANTS

Cabaña Quinta Cusco 535 ☎ 082 571045. Based in the hotel of the same name, this restaurant is hard to beat for its excellent three-course set lunches (S/18), often including fresh river fish and fried manioc. Daily noon–3pm & 6–9pm.

Cevichería El Califa Jr Piura 266 ☎ 082 571119. A popular local lunchtime spot, *El Califa* is a garden-based restaurant, slightly hidden away, serving a variety of national and international dishes (from around S/22), including riverfish ceviche, palm heart, pigs-head soup and a range of *refresco* drinks made from tropical fruits. Mon–Sat 11am–5pm.

Cevichería El Catamaran 26 de Diciembre 241. Just

one block from the Plaza de Armas, this restaurant serves fantastic fish dishes from an airy wooden room with panoramic views and a balcony over looking the lower port suburbs and down the Río Madre de Díos towards Bolivia and Brazil. Daily 10.30am–4pm.

Chifa Wa Seng Dos de Mayo 253. Successfully combines traditional Chinese meals with an abundance of jungle foodstuffs. Daily 11.30am–9pm.

Pizzeria Leños y Carbón Carrion 105. Just off the Plaza de Armas, this place is modern and a little plastic in style, but has fast service and is very popular with locals. As well as pizza, it serves up great chicken and chips. Daily noon–10pm.

Pollos a la Brasa La Estrella Velarde 474 ⓣ 082 573107. This place offers grilled chicken and chips, as well as rather feeble salads. Daily noon–9.30pm.

DRINKING AND NIGHTLIFE

There's a surprisingly busy **nightlife** in this laidback town, especially at weekends. In the early evenings, most people just stroll around, stopping occasionally to sit and chat in the Plaza de Armas or in bars along the main street. At weekends and fiesta times, however, it's possible to sample rock, reggae, *chicha, cumbia or* Latin pop at one of the town's venues. Places get packed by 10pm on Friday and Saturday nights, with revellers moving from one club to another.

Karambola Restaurant and Disco-Pub Jr Arequipa 162. Offers decent grub and live music shows, sometimes with Brazilian-style dancing girls, at weekends. Wed–Sun 7pm–2am.

Peña La Choza Av Andrés Avelino Cáceres ⓣ 082 572872. A couple of kilometres out of town, on the airport road (take a *mototaxi*; S/5–6), this place has a massive, heaving dance area, plus cheap food and beer every Saturday night. Thurs–Sat 7pm–3am.

Teocas Disco Loreto. Close to the Plaza de Armas, this place has a large dancefloor that blasts out a mix of music, from jungle *cumbia* to europop. Tues–Sat 7pm–2am.

Witite León de Velarde 151. The best club in town, with Shipibo designs adorning the walls and a surprisingly advanced sound system playing the whole range of Latino music. Entry is usually free. Fri & Sat 7pm–5/6am.

8

DIRECTORY

Consulates Bolivia, Jr Loreto 272 (upstairs), on the Plaza de Armas (ⓣ 082 571290); Mon–Fri 8am–3.30pm).

Immigration Jr Ica 727, second floor (ⓣ 082 571069).

Money and exchange There are two banks on the plaza: Banco Credito, Arequipa 334; and Banco de la Nación, Jr Daniel Carrion 233 (both Mon–Fri 9am–1pm & 5–7pm). *Cambistas* usually hang out on the corner of Prada and Puno. Your hotel may also change dollars.

Police The National Police are one block from the Plaza de Armas on Billinghurst, more or less opposite the Hospedaje Moderno.

Post office León de Velarde 675, opposite the corner of Jr Jaime Troncoso (Mon–Sat 8am–8pm, Sun 8am–3pm).

Telephones There are public phones in most parts of town, many located outside shops and bars.

Around Puerto Maldonado

Madre de Dios boasts spectacular virgin **lowland rainforest** and exceptional **wildlife.** Brazil-nut tree trails, a range of lodges, some excellent local guides and ecologists, plus indigenous and colonist cultures are all within a few hours of Puerto Maldonado. Serious **jungle trips** can be made here with relative ease and without too much expense, and this part of the Amazon offers easy and uniquely rewarding access to rainforest that is much less disturbed than that around Iquitos, for example.

Lago Sandoval

1hr downriver from Puerto Maldonado (1hr 30min on the return), plus 20–30min walk

A short way downriver from Puerto Maldonado is **Lago Sandoval**, a large lake where the Ministry of Agriculture have introduced the large *paiche* fish. You can walk here from the drop-off point on the Río Madre de Dios. On arrival at the lake, boatmen and canoes can usually be obtained by your guide for a couple of hours, as can food and drink. At its best on weekday mornings (it gets quite crowded at other times), the lake offers decent opportunities for spotting wildlife, in particular **birds** similar to those at Lago Valencia, such as hoatzins and the occasional toucan. You may even spot a **giant otter**.

Incidentally, if you're travelling to the lake by river, most guides will show you the ruined hulk of an old boat lying close to the riverbank. If they claim it had anything to

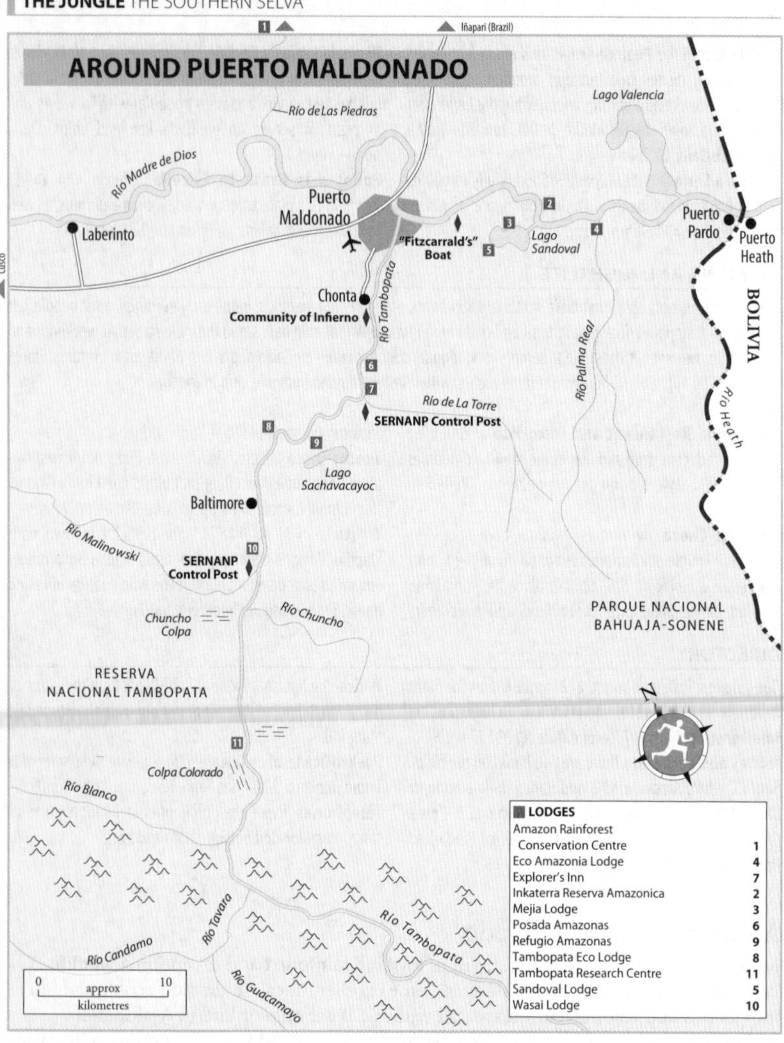

do with Fitzcarrald (see box, p.440), don't believe them; it may be similar in style to Fitzcarrald's, but in fact it's smaller and is a far more recent arrival – it's a hospital boat that was in use until two or three decades ago.

Along the river to Lago Valencia

From Puerto Maldonado it takes 6–8hr by canoe with a *peque-peque*, or around 2hr in a *lancha* with an outboard

Travelling by boat from Puerto Maldonado to the huge lake of **Lago Valencia**, you can stop off to watch some gold-panners on the Río Madre de Dios and visit a small settlement of **Ese Eja**; about thirty minutes beyond, you turn off the main river into a narrow channel that connects with the lake.

Easing onto the lake itself, the sounds of the canoe engine are totally silenced by the weight and expanse of water. Towards sunset it's quite common to see caimans basking on the muddy banks, an occasional **puma** or the largest rodent in the world, a **capybara**, scuttling away into the forest. Up in the trees around the channel lie hundreds of **hoatzin** birds, or *gallos* as they are called locally – large, ungainly creatures with orange and brown plumage, long wings and distinctive spiky crests. The strangest feature of the hoatzin is the claws at the end of their wings, which they use to help them climb up into overhanging branches beside rivers and lakes; they have almost lost the power of flight.

The settlement and around

An easy walk (20min) from the main Río Madre de Dios river bank brings you to the lake's one real **settlement**, a cluster of thatched huts around a slightly larger schoolhouse. Fewer than seventy people live here – a schoolteacher, a lay priest, the shop owner and a few fishing families. Some tour groups stay in a small camp further down, a seasonal nut-collectors' *campamento*, comprising just one cooking hut with an adjacent sleeping platform, though there is also a lodge and a hospedaje.

By day most people go for a **walk in the forest** – something that's safer and more interesting with a guide, though whichever way you do it you'll immediately sense the energy and abundance of life. Quinine trees tower above all the trails, surpassed only by the Tahuari hardwoods. Around their trunks you'll often see *pega-pega*, a parasitic, ivy-like plant that the shamans mix with ayahuasca into an intense aphrodisiac. Perhaps more useful are the liana vines; one thin species dangling above the paths can be used to take away the pain from a *shushupe* snake bite. Another, the *maravilla* or *palo de agua*, issues a cool stream of fresh water if you chop a section, about half a metre long, and put it to your lips. You may come upon another vine, too – the sinister *matapalo* (or *renaco*), sucking the sap from up to a square kilometre of jungle.

Río Heath

Less than 2hr from Lago Valencia in a motorized *lancha*

A good trip deeper into the forest from Lago Valencia is up to the **Río Heath**, a national rainforest sanctuary, though while the **Pampas del Heath** are excellent for watching macaws, they don't have the primary forest necessary for a great variety of wildlife. It now lies within the Parque Nacional Bahuaja-Sonene, and special permission is needed from the government protected-area agency SERNANP in Lima (see box, p.446) or, as a last resort, the SERNANP office in Puerto Maldonado (see p.439).

Reserva Nacional Tambopata

S/30 entry fee • Reached by 40min scheduled flight to Puerto Maldonado (or a 530km bus journey; 12–16hr), plus a few hours in a motorized canoe to get to lodges upriver • Ⓦ tambopata.com

Containing some of the world's finest and most biodiverse rainforest, the **RESERVA NACIONAL TAMBOPATA** is one of the most easily accessible parts of relatively pristine

WILDLIFE ON THE LAKES

Both Lago Valencia and Lago Sandoval are superbly endowed with **birdlife**. In addition to the hoatzin (see p.521) you might spot kingfishers, cormorants, herons, egrets, pink flamingoes, skimmers, macaws, toucans, parrots and gavilans.

Behind the wall of trees along the banks hide **deer**, **wild pigs** and **tapir**, all of them spotted occasionally. If you're lucky enough to catch a glimpse of a tapir you'll be seeing one of South America's strangest creatures – almost the size of a cow, with an elongated rubbery nose and spiky mane. In fact, the tapir is known in the jungle as a *sachavaca* ("forest cow" – *sacha* is Quechua for "forest" and *vaca* is Spanish for "cow").

There are caiman and larger fish in the lake, but the easiest fish to catch are **piranha** – all you need is some line, a hook, and a chunk of unsalted meat; throw this into the lake and you've got yourself a piranha.

Amazon rainforest. Described by *National Geographic* as one of the planet's seven "iconic natural sanctuaries", it is within easy reach of many of the lodges in the Puerto Maldonado region.

Transformed into a reserved zone mainly due to the scientific work of the adjacent *Explorer's Inn* lodge (see opposite), the area covers around 250,000 hectares, and is next to the **Parque Nacional Bahuaja-Sonene**, itself more than 1.5 million hectares. The expansion of the National Park is a major success for conservation in Peru, but despite this there are fears that the government has plans to open up the park in future to gas and oil exploitation.

It's only possible to visit the National Park on a **tour** with a licensed operator. Tours organized from Cusco or Puerto Maldonado can enter en route to one of the major macaw **salt licks** (*colpas*) in the region. The licks are the best places to see wildlife in the jungle, since their salts, minerals and clay are highly nutritious, attracting large numbers of wild birds and animals.

ARRIVAL AND DEPARTURE

By plane Flying from Cusco or direct from Lima is the quickest way to reach Puerto Maldonado (see p.438), and most tour agencies will organize plane tickets for you if you book their tours.

By boat Travelling independently from Puerto Maldonado can be rewarding, though note that most of the major river trips require visitors to obtain permission from the Captain's Office in Puerto Maldonado (see p.438) – though boatmen and guides generally do this for you and also organize payment of fees for you at entry to any protected areas.

By tour Compared with independent travel, an organized excursion saves time and generally offers reasonable, if not always luxurious, levels of comfort. It also ensures that you go with someone who knows the area, probably speaks English, and, if you choose well, can introduce you to the flora, fauna and culture of the region. Most people book a trip with a tour operator in Cusco (see p.222) before travelling to Puerto Maldonado, though it is possible to book in Puerto itself, either at the airport or through one of the offices (see below), or through the cafés on León de Velarde. It's worth noting that you are less likely to get ripped off with a registered company with a fixed office and contact details, especially if you should need redress afterwards.

TOURS

Explorandes Paseo Zarzuela Q-2 Huancaro, Cusco ☎084 238380; Arístides Aljovín 484, Miraflores, Lima ☎01 715 2323, ⓦexplorandes.com. A veteran company operating whitewater-rafting expeditions, including a twelve-day trip starting out from Puno by road, then travelling down through cloud forest, and finally rafting through class 3 to 5 rapids along the Río Tambopata to Puerto Maldonado, where the last night is spent in a lodge. They also offer cultural and adventure tours and tailor-made adventures. From $1500 per person, for a minimum of four.

Inotawa Expeditions Av Aeropuerto, Puerto Maldonado ☎082 572511; or in Lima ☎01 9971 49355, ⓦinotawaexpeditions.com. Located on the Río Tambopata quite close to the start of the Parque Nacional Bahuaja-Sonene, Inotawa operate a nice lodge in a good location, and offer expeditions to Colpa Colorado, the world's biggest macaw salt-lick a further 8hr into the forest from the lodge. Prices start at $240 per person for two nights, $310 for five nights, but the minimum group required is six.

Tambopata Tours León de Velarde 171, Puerto Maldonado ☎082 571320 and ☎082 9827 01779, ⓦtambopatatours.com. This company can customize trips, selecting lodges and guides to suit clients' pockets

CHOOSING A LODGE

The quality of the **jungle experience** varies from river to river and from lodge to lodge. Most companies offer full board and include transfers, though it is a good idea to verify the level of service and see photos before booking. You should also check what's included, and what **extra costs** you'll be liable for once you're there; complaints are common about the price of drinks. Remember, too, that conditions tend to be rustic and relatively open to the elements: **toilets** are generally fairly standard WCs, covered in mosquito netting, while **sleeping arrangements** range from bunk rooms to fairly comfortable doubles with doors and mosquito-net windows. **Food** is generally good, though you may want to take additional snacks.

and interests. They will also help organize jungle camping, birdwatching, fishing trips and visits to communities, the local canopy walkway and ayahuasca ceremonies. Prices depend on service level and lodge accommodation, but expect to pay $75–200 a day per person.

ACCOMMODATION

Amazon Rainforest Conservation Centre (ARCC) C Los Cedros B-17, Los Castaños, Puerto Maldonado 082 572961, laspiedrasamazontour.com. This lodge sits beside Lake Soledad, some 7hr (175km) by boat from Puerto Maldonado, in forest with several monkey species, giant otters, black caiman and macaw licks close by. The well-built lodge has eight comfortable hexagonal bungalows built from polished hardwood with palm roofs, set in a clearing surrounded by giant trees and illuminated by electric lighting (recharging point available). The same company also owns a camp at Tipishca, closer to Puerto Maldonado and en route to the *ARCC* lodge, and offers well-organized and adventurous tours. Three nights from **$300 per person**

Eco Amazonia Lodge Jr Lambayeque 774, Km 30 Bajo Río Madre de Dios, Puerto Maldonado 082 573491; C Garcilazo 210, Of. 206, Cusco 084 236159; C Enrique Palacios 292, Miraflores, Lima 01 2422708 ecoamazonia.com.pe. Less than 2hr downriver of Puerto Maldonado, this large establishment offers basic bungalows and dorms. The area abounds in stunning oxbow lakes, and while it can't claim the variety of flora and fauna of the Reserva Nacional Tambopata, it is recommended for birdwatching. With swamp-forest platforms, this is one of only two lodges in the area with tree-canopy access. Packages usually include visits to Lago Sandoval, about 30min upriver, and to the Palma Real community. Two nights from **$240 per person**

★ **Explorer's Inn** Plateros 365, Cusco 084 235342; or in the Peruvian Safaris (or Amazonia Tours) Lima office, Alcanfores 459, Miraflores 01 4478888, peruviansafaris.com; office in Puerto Maldonado at Av Fitzcarrald 136 082 572078. Located within the Reserva Nacional Tambopata, some 58km (about 3hr) in a motorized *canoa* upriver from Puerto Maldonado, this is a large, well-organized lodge that also conducts research, cataloguing species in the wild. Spanish- or English-speaking guides are available, and there are excellent displays, mostly in English, about rainforest ecology. The food is good, and accommodation is generally in twin rooms with private bath. The price includes full board, expeditions to a nearby macaw salt-lick and access to a superb network of jungle trails. Enquire about rates for special-interest visitors (eg ornithologists). Three nights from **$200 per person**

Inkaterra Reserva Amazónica Andalucía 174, Lima 01 6100404, inkaterra.com. One of the Peruvian jungle's most luxurious and stylish lodges, located an hour and a half downstream from Puerto Maldonado on the Río Madre de Dios, this is a great place for a gentle introduction to the wild in luxurious surroundings (Mick Jagger stayed here in 2011). The main lodge building is truly palatial, containing restaurant, bar and lounge areas. Most accommodation is in exceptionally comfortable bungalows. Half- and full-day excursions are on offer, including guided walking trails and night walks, plus visits to Lago Sandoval, a jungle farm and a native community, as well as fishing and birdwatching in the nearby Tambopata Reserve. The lodge is surrounded by its own protected rainforest area and boasts part of Peru's only canopy walkway. Two nights from **$400 per person**

Mejia Lodge León de Velarde 420, Puerto Maldonado 082 571428. Operated by Ceiba Tours, this is a rustic-style hostel (19 rooms) rather than a posh lodge on the side of Lago Sandoval; perfect for canoe exploration of the lake. It's rarely full, so it's fine to just turn up here by canoe from Puerto Maldonado without prior arrangement (get the boatman to drop you off on the trail from the Tambopata river bank). Per person, per night including food from **$20**

Posada Amazonas Contact through Rainforest Expeditions, Av Larco 1116, Dep 4, Miraflores, Lima 01 7196422, perunature.com. The nearest of Rainforest Expedition's lodges to Puerto Maldonado is now fully owned and managed by the Ese Eja indigenous community of Infierno. The accommodation maintains the company's excellent standards, bringing you into close contact with nature. Massage and other treatments are available, and it's also possible to organize trips combining this lodge with the more remote *Refugio Amazonas* (see below) and the most distant of all the region's lodges – the *Tambopata Research Centre* (see p.446). There is a series of forest trails and access to a nearby ethno-botanical garden, Centro Ñape (with overnight shelter for in-depth healing sessions). Two nights from **$355 per person**

Refugio Amazonas Contact through Rainforest Expeditions, Av Larco 1116, Dep 4, Miraflores, Lima 01 7196422, perunature.com. Run by Rainforest Expeditions, this is the most luxurious of the company's three lodges, located at different stages along the Río Tambopata, and is hard to better anywhere in the world for the quality of its facilities and guides. The lodge is a splendid mix of traditional hut design and extravagant architectural beauty, with 24 spacious rooms with large comfortable beds under mosquito nets opening out onto the forest, plus a great dining room and busy bar. A range of activities are on offer, including massage, photography expeditions, kayaking on the Tambopata River (no experience required), canopy climbing (training offered)

8

JUNGLE PERMITS

To enter some of the more remote and sensitive **protected areas**, such as the **Reserva Nacional Pacaya Samiria**, or the **Manu** and **Parque Nacional Bahuaja-Sonone**, official permission is essential, and a small daily **fee** (usually around S/30) payable either in advance or at entry points located on the main rivers. As a tourist, this will usually be handled for you by your **tour company**. Independent travel within these areas is discouraged, but if you want to enter for research purposes you will need to do this directly. For all Peruvian jungle protected areas contact SERNANP in Lima well in advance: C 17, 355 Urb El Palomar, San Isidro (T 01 225 2803 or T 01 224 3298, W sernanp.gob.pe).

and mountain-biking trails. The lodge is close to two lakes where otters are sometimes spotted, and also has an engaging educational trail for kids. Two nights from **$355 per person**

Tambopata Eco Lodge Jr González 269, Puerto Maldonado T 082 571397 and C Nueva Baja 432, Cusco T 084 245695, W tambopatalodge.com. Just over the river from the Reserva Nacional Tambopata, nearly 4hr from Puerto Maldonado and 12km upstream from the *Explorer's Inn*, this lodge has comfortable, individual cabin-style accommodation and offers tours of the forest in English. It's located quite close to a community of *colonos*, some of whom pan for gold. Trips include a visit to Lago Condenado and the Chuncho salt lick. Two nights from **$338 per person**

8

Tambopata Research Centre Contact through Rainforest Expeditions, Av Larco 1116, Dep 4, Miraflores, Lima T 01 7196422, W perunature.com. As an organizaton very hot on wildlife research and conservation across all its lodges, Rainforest Expeditions have combined, in *TRC*, a very comfortable lodge in an area of great bird diversity (including good populations of primates and large mammals), with serious and long-term research at the world's biggest macaw *colpa*, the Colpa Colorado. A minimum of six days is recommended, since it takes a full day by canoe both up and down river. Four nights from **$785 per person**

Sandoval Lodge InkaNatura, Manuel Bañon 461, San Isidro, Lima T 01 4402022, W inkanatura.com, or C Ricardo Palma, J1 Urb Santa Monica, Cusco T 084 255255. On the shores of Lago Sandoval, and usually accessed by canoe, this lodge offers a privileged location and gives you exclusive access to the lake in the early morning and late afternoon, best hours for wildlife viewing and photography. The lodge has one large communal building as a bar and dining room, plus electricity and hot water. Most groups spend time on the lake or explore the small, well-trodden surrounding trail system. Guides speak several languages, including English. Two nights from **$325 per person**

★ **Wasai Lodge** Contact through the Wasai hotel in Puerto Maldonado (see p.440). Four hours upriver from Puerto Maldonado, this smallish and relatively new lodge is set in the forest, with a pleasant jungle bar and dining area. Spanish- and English-speaking guides are available, with 15km of trails in the vicinity plus trips to the Chuncho *colpa* on request. Their programmes include a visit to Lago Sandoval, with the last night at the *Wasai* in Puerto Maldonado (to avoid a very early morning start). Discounts sometimes offered. Two nights from **$354 per person**

Manu Biosphere Reserve

Eco-tours in the **MANU BIOSPHERE RESERVE** are pricey, but represent good value when you consider its remoteness and the abundance of **wildlife** that thrives in its almost two million hectares of virgin cloud- and rainforest, a uniquely varied environment that ranges from crystalline cloud-forest streams and waterfalls down to slow-moving, chocolate-brown rivers in the dense lowland jungle. Created in 1973 as a national park, it was made a UNESCO World Heritage Site in 1987.

The only permanent residents within this vast area are the teeming forest wildlife; a few virtually uncontacted native groups who have split off from their major tribal units (Yaminahuas, Amahuacas and Machiguenga); the park guards; and the scientists at a biological research station just inside the park on the beautiful Lago Cocha Cashu.

The reserve is divided into three zones. By far the largest, **Zone A** is the core zone, the **Parque Nacional Manu**, which is strictly preserved in its natural state. **Zone B** is a Buffer Zone, generally known as the **Reserved Zone** and set aside mainly for controlled research and tourism. **Zone C** is the Transitional or **Cultural Zone**, an area of human settlement for controlled traditional use. Tourists are allowed into zones B and C only as part of organized visits with guides, following the basic rules of non-interference with human, animal or vegetable life. Zone A is restricted to the occasional scientist.

The interior of the protected area is only accessible by **boat**, so any expedition to Manu is very much in the hands of the gods, due to the temperamental jungle environment; the **rainy season** is from December to March, and visits are best organized between May and August when it's much drier, although at that time the temperatures often exceed 30°C (86°F).

The only way of visiting Manu is by joining an **organized tour** through one of the main Cusco agents (see p.223), which is safer and generally cheaper than doing it yourself. Most tours currently enter the area by fast boats (4–6hr) from Puerto Maldonado, since the **airstrip** at Boca Manu is not presently functioning (though efforts are underway to reopen it some time in 2012 or 2013). Until the closure of the airstrip, the reserve was more frequently reached from **Cusco** than from Puerto Maldonado; but with the airstrip closed, most tours choose instead to fly with

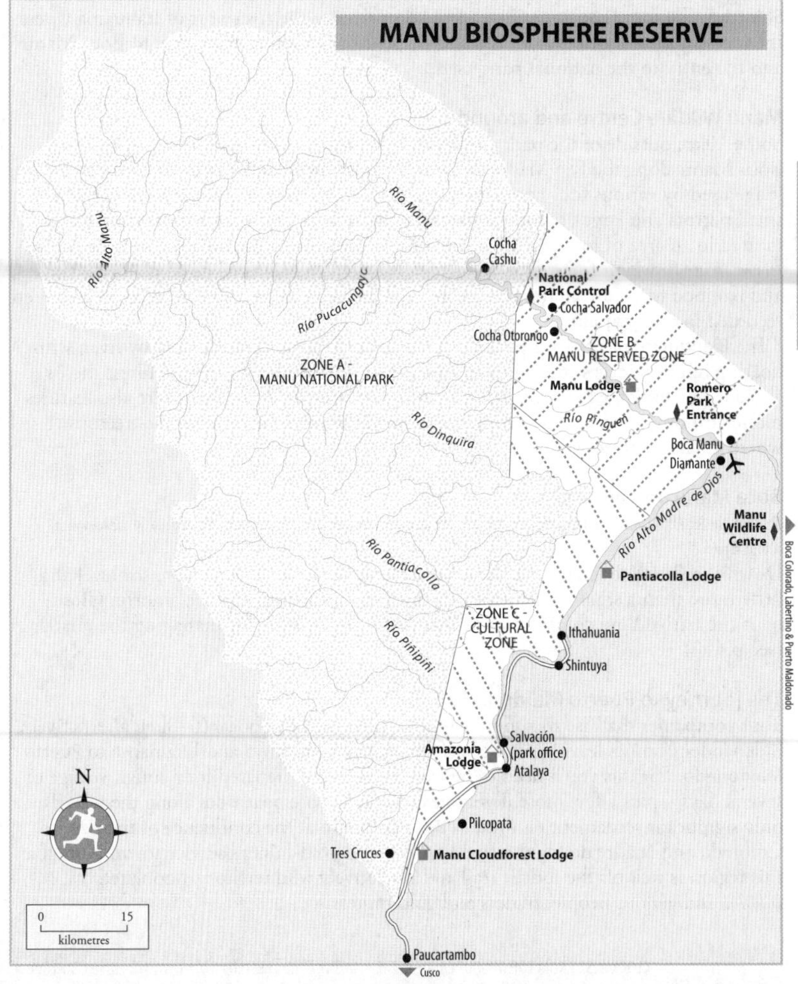

8

scheduled flights to **Puerto Maldonado**, then travel by boat upriver to Manu. Some tours, however, still incorporate a one-way overland entry from Cusco, returning by air (from Puerto Maldonado to either Cusco or Lima).

The overland route from Cusco

The road route to Manu from Cusco is highly scenic. The first four- to six-hour stage is by road to the attractive town of **Paucartambo** (see p.271), over stupendous narrow roads with fine panoramas of the region's largest glaciated mountain of Ausungate. From Paucartambo it's 25km to the **Tres Cruces** turn-off (see p.272), at the reserve's southern tip. The road drops steeply to the quiet jungle town of **Pilcopata**, a journey of around ten hours from Cusco. From here the terrain is fairly level as it skirts the Río Alto Madre de Dios, which eventually merges with the Río Manu to form the great Río Madre de Dios. A couple of hours beyond Pilcopata is the smaller riverside settlement of **Atalaya** (12hr from Cusco). Some twenty minutes down the road, at the pueblo of **Salvación**, 28km before Shintuya, the Manu Biosphere Reserve has an **office** where your guide will usually be expected to show his permits. Two hours beyond Atalaya, at **Shintuya**, the route continues just a few kilometres to the river port of Itahuania where the road finishes. From here all travel is by boat. It is another 55–60km to Boca Manu and the entry to the national park itself.

Manu Wildlife Centre and around

Some 10km outside of the park and further downstream (around 30min–1hr) from Boca Manu along the Río Madre de Dios is the **Manu Wildlife Centre**, a comfortable lodge used by various tour companies (see p.451). It's close to a superb **salt lick** where small **parrots** and larger, colourful **macaws** can be seen, and claims to be strategically located in an area of forest that has the highest diversity of microhabitats in the Manu: *tierra-firme* (lowland forest that doesn't get flooded), transitional flood plain, *varzea* and bamboo forest are all found close by, and an astounding 530 bird species have been recorded in one year alone.

The **Blanquillo** macaw-and-parrot salt lick is only thirty minutes away by river, with floating blinds to access the wildlife. About an hour's walk through the forest there's also a large salt lick where you can see tapirs and Brocket deer. The centre also features mobile canopy towers for watching the local wildlife right up among the treetops, where jungle creatures gather.

Boca Manu and around

4hr down the Río Alto Madre de Dios (from Shintuya) or 6–8hr up the Río Madre de Dios (from Puerto Maldonado) in a *lancha* with outboard motor

Down the Río Alto Madre de Dios, **Boca Manu** is a mere 300m above sea level and little more than a small settlement of a few families living near the airstrip. Close by is the native Yiné community of **Diamante**, responsible for managing the airstrip (see p.450).

The journey to Puerto Maldonado

Tour companies that use this route will have their own fast boats (6–8hr); alternatively, independent canoes leave most weeks from Atalaya, Shintuya and Diamante to **Puerto Maldonado**. For this you'll need to be well stocked and prepared for a rough voyage of several days – plus a few more if you have to hitch more boat rides along the way. The only significant settlement en route is **Boca Colorado** at the confluence of the ríos Colorado and Madre de Dios, a small rat-infested gold-miner's service town. Note that this region is well off the tourist trail and is relatively wild territory, populated by *colonos*, indigenous people, traders and gold miners.

CLOCKWISE FROM TOP DUGOUT CANOE IN THE AMAZON; CURL-CRESTED ARACARI; WHITE-LINED LEAF FROG >

MANU WILDLIFE AND FLORA

For **flora and fauna**, the Manu is pretty much unbeatable in South America, home to over 5000 flowering plants, 1200 species of butterfly, 1000 types of bird and 200 kinds of mammal. Rich in macaw salt-licks and otter lagoons, it's also home to prowling jaguars, thirteen species of monkey and seven species of macaw, and contains several species in danger of extinction, such as the giant otter and the black caiman. The highlight of most organized visits to Manu is the trail network and lakes of **Cocha Salvador** (the largest of Manu's oxbows, at 3.5km long) and **Cocha Otorongo**, both bountiful jungle areas rich in animal, water and birdlife.

OTORONGO OTTERS

The **Cocha Otorongo** lake is known for the **giant otters** that live there, one of the world's most endangered species. The otters are also bio-indicators of the environment, since they only live where there is clean, healthy water and a wide choice of fish. Only the oldest female of the group is mated with, so reproduction is very slow – the "queen" otters only have two or three cubs a year, usually around October, which can be expected to live for around thirty years. The top-ranking male otters are responsible for defending the group and do very little fishing, taking the catch from younger males instead.

Although they appear friendly as they play in their large family groups, the otters can be very aggressive, able to keep jaguars at bay and kill caimans that approach their lakeside nesting holes. Canoeing is not permitted, but there is a **floating platform** which can be manoeuvred to observe the otters fishing and playing from a safe distance (though your guide has to book a time for this): 30–50m is good enough to watch and take photos, though as this is Manu's most popular tourist area, you're likely to meet other groups and there can be severe competition for access to the platform.

OTHER WILDLIFE

Other wildlife to look out for includes the plentiful **caimans**, including the two- to three-metre white alligators and the rarer three- to five-metre black ones, and you can usually spot several species of **monkey** (including dusky titis, woolly monkeys, red howlers, brown capuchins and the larger spider monkeys known locally as *maquisapas*). Sometimes big mammals such as **capybara** or **white-lipped peccaries** (*sajinos*) also lurk in the undergrowth.

GIANT TREES

The flora of Manu is as outstanding as its fauna. Huge **cedar trees** can be seen along the trails, covered in hand-like vines climbing up their vast trunks (most of the cedars were removed between 1930 and 1963, before it became a protected area). The giant **catahua trees**, many over 150 years old, are traditionally the preferred choice for making dugout canoes – and some are large enough to make three or four; their bulbous white trunks seem to reach endlessly up to the rainforest canpoy.

ARRIVAL AND INFORMATION — MANU BIOSPHERE RESERVE

For the high biodiversity levels they offer, Manu is among the most easily reached parts of relatively pristine Amazon rainforest: from Cusco, Manu is either a day's journey by bus then a day more by canoe, or a thirty-minute flight and up to six hours in a speedboat.

By air Some tour companies transport their clients on scheduled flights from Cusco to Puerto Maldonado, then travel by river up the Madre de Dios; the airstrip at Boca Manu (see p.448), though not currently functioning, is expected to offer direct flights from the airport in Cusco some time in 2012 or 2013. Check with the tour companies or at Cusco airport (see p.220) for details.

By bus Most people travel on transport organized by their tour operators; otherwise, buses operated by Gallito de las Rocas (Av Manco Capac 105, Cusco; ☎ 084 277255) go to Pilcopata and usually beyond to Salvación at about 10am most Mondays and Fridays (S/25; a 10–14hr journey depending on road conditions).

By boat It is possible to travel independently on the rivers by picking up a boat at Shintuya or one of the other riverside towns. This won't allow you to enter the Manu National Park area, however, as you can only enter with a licensed tour company. If you hitch a ride with a boat already going downriver you can expect to pay around S/5–10 an hour. Hiring your own boat from Shintuya would cost from around S/500 a day, depending on distance and fuel consumption. Canoes go most weeks (cargo and river permitting) from Atalaya, Shintuya and Diamante downriver from Manu to Puerto Maldonado.

Tourist information The Manu National Park Office is at Av Bastidas 310, Cusco (T 084 240898). Entrance to the reserve is by organized tour, and it's virtually impossible to get permission to go it alone. If you're a naturalist, a photographer or can demonstrate a serious interest, then it is sometimes possible to gain a special permit for restricted areas; contact SERNANP in Lima (see box, p.446).

TOURS

There are quite a few **organized tours** competing for travellers who want to visit Manu. Many are keen to keep the impact of tourism to a minimum, which means **limiting the number of visits** per year (currently well into the thousands). However, companies do vary quite a bit in quality of guiding, level of comfort and price range. The options listed below have a good reputation both for the way they treat their tourists and the delicate ecology of the rainforest itself. Numbers are limited annually, so it's a good idea to book well in advance.

Caiman C Garcilaso 210, office 207, Cusco T 084 254041, W manucaiman.com. Caiman offers four days and three nights as their shortest Manu trip. Their six- to nine-day tours are better, since they include exploring within the Manu Reserve itself, including Lago Otorongo, with a chance of spotting the giant river otters (see box opposite). Four nights from $500 per person.

Expediciones Vilca Plateros 359, Cusco T 084 244751, W manuvilcaperu.com. Manu specialists Vilca have a good reputation and their guides are well informed, taking ecotourism seriously. Their eight-day tour includes camping in Zone B, plus a visit to the macaw lick at Blanquillo as well as three nights in lodges. Tour prices depend on route, days and whether you take a bus or plane. 7-night tours from $934 per person.

InkaNatura Travel Manuel Bañon 461, San Isidro, Lima T 01 2035000, W inkanatura.com. This outfit offers customized travel, from four to five days, operating from the Manu Wildlife Centre, where one of the nearby highlights is the world's largest tapir salt-lick. They also accommodate people at the *Cock of the Rock Lodge*, 6hr by road from Cusco, in one of the best cloud-forest locations for birdwatching. 6 nights deep in Manu National Park $1780 per person.

Manu Adventures Plateros 356, Cusco T 084 261640, W manuadventures.com. Jungle-trip specialists and one of the first operators to run trips into Manu, with their own vehicles, boats and multilingual guides. Their camping-based tours are cheaper than most, with the eight-day option travelling in and out by bus, but they also offer shorter options which travel in by bus and out by plane. Four nights from $415 per person.

Manu Expeditions C Jirón Clorinda Matto de Turner 330, Urbanización Magisterial Primero Etapa, Cusco T 084 239974, W manuexpeditions.com, W birding-In-peru.com. One of the best and the most responsible companies, run by a British ornithologist. They offer four- to nine-day lodge-based and tented camp expeditions into Zone B and to the Manu Wildlife Centre and *Romero Rainforest Lodge*, with solar-powered radio communications and audio visual interpretation, as well as top-quality service and English-speaking guides. They can also arrange a stay at the rustic *Casa Machiguenga* lodge in Manu, owned by the Machiguenga communities of Tayakome and Yombebato. They also organize air and overland transfers via Puerto Maldonado, and food, beds (or riverside campsite) and bird-blinds are all included. 5-night tour into the reserve from $1650 per person; 7 nights deep into the park costs $2445 per person.

Pantiacolla Tours C Sapphi 554, Cusco T 084 238323, W pantiacolla.com. A company with a growing reputation for serious eco-adventure tours. They organize short visits to the outskirts of Manu (such as a three-day trip to Pantiacolla in Zone C for $390), as well as longer options into Zone B (7 days $1275, 9 days $1395). They have an excellent lodge on the Río Alto Madre de Dios at Itahuania, and their tours into Zone B are based in tents at prepared campsites.

Río Urubamba and around

Traditionally the home of the Matsiguenga and Piro Indians, the **Río Urubamba** rolls down from the Incas' Sacred Valley to the humid lower Andean slopes around the town of **Quillabamba**. The river remains unnavigable for another 80km or so, with regular buses following a dirt road that continues deeper down into the jungle via the settlement of **Kiteni**, where the Río Urubamba becomes navigable again, to the even smaller frontier settlement of **Ivochote**. From here on, the river becomes the main means of transport, through the Amazon Basin right to the Atlantic, interrupted only by the impressive **Pongo de Mainique** whitewater rapids, just a few hours downstream from Ivochote. These rapids are generally too dangerous to pass between November and March.

Unlike the Manu Biosphere Reserve, most of the Urubamba has been colonized as far as the *pongo*, and much of it beyond has suffered more or less permanent exploitation of one sort or another – rubber, cattle or oil – for over a hundred years. In the last decade or so, the discovery and exploitation of a massive gas field is changing the river and communities fast, though this is still a relatively quiet and untouristed region compared with Manu or Madre de Dios.

Quillabamba

A rapidly expanding market town, growing fat on profits from coffee, tropical fruits, chocolate and, to a certain extent, the proceeds of cocaine production, **QUILLABAMBA** is the only Peruvian jungle town that's easily accessible by road from Cusco: the main attraction here is a quick look at the selva. Coming from Cusco, the initial section of road is a narrow gravel track along precipitous cliffs, notoriously dangerous in the rainy season, but after a few hours, having travelled over the magical Abra Malaga – the main pass on this road – the slow descent towards **Chaullay** starts. From here on, you'll see jungle vegetation beginning to cover the valley sides; the weather gets steadily warmer and the plant life thickens as you gradually descend into the Urubamba Valley.Your first sight of the town, which tops a high cliff, is of old tin roofs, adobe outskirts and coca leaves drying in the gardens. It's a pleasant enough place to relax, and you can get all the gear you need for going deeper into the jungle; the **market** sells all the necessities like machetes, fish-hooks, food and hats. Just ten minutes' walk from here, the **Plaza de Armas**, with its shady fountain statue of the town's little-known benefactor, Don Martín Pio Concha, is the other major landmark. The nearby waterfall of **Siete Tinjas** is a popular spot with locals during holidays, and a pleasant natural and peaceful setting in which to while away an afternoon.

8

ARRIVAL AND DEPARTURE — QUILLABAMBA

By bus or colectivo Buses from C Huascar in Cusco terminate by the market on the Plaza Grau side of town; colectivos from C General Buendio, by the San Pedro railway station in Cusco, or the plaza in Ollantaytambo, also finish their journeys near the market in Quillabamba, as do trucks and colectivos (best picked up from the plaza in Ollantaytambo). Buses back to Cusco leave Quillabamba from the market or block 5 of C San Martín, close to the market, several times a day.

Destinations Cusco (several daily; 8–10hr); Ollantaytambo (several daily; 5–8hr).

ACCOMMODATION AND EATING

Los Amantes First block of Jirón Cusco. A small restaurant serving decent set meals (from S/7) including the usual *estofado de res*, *caldo de gallina* (hen soup) or chicken and chips. Daily 8am–8pm.

Don Cebas Jr Espinar 235, on the Plaza de Armas. This place serves snacks and drinks, including coffee and cakes. Daily 7.30am–6pm.

Hostal Don Carlos Jr Libertad 556 ⓣ084 281150, ⓦhostaldoncarlosquillabamba.com. Just up from the Plaza de Armas, this is a cosy, friendly and popular place, especially with Peruvians. Rooms are smart and the place has a garden courtyard; it's also a good place to make connections for organized (though relatively costly) overland trips to Kiteni, and river trips onwards from there. S/90

Hostal Quillabamba Plaza Miguel Grau 590 ⓣ084 281369, ⓦhostalquillabamba.com. This hostel is very close to the market, offers modern, comfortable rooms and also has a swimming pool, hot water and a good restaurant. S/110

Venecia Jr Libertad 461 ⓣ084 281582. A reasonably good pizzeria right on the Plaza de Armas, with a pleasant atmosphere and piping-hot thin-crust pizzas. Mon–Sat 11am–10pm.

DIRECTORY

Internet More than one around town, but the best is Cobermaster on the Plaza de Armas.

Money and exchange The Banco de Credito, on C Libertad, is your best bet for changing dollars and travellers' cheques; there's also the Banco Continental, on the first block of Jr España. Sometimes *cambistas* will change dollars cash on the streets outside these banks.

Telephones Calls can be made from a Telefónica office, Bolognesi 237–249, or at Jr Cusco 242 (daily 7am–10pm).

Ivochote and around

The road continues down into the jungle from Quillabamba via Kiteni to the village of **Ivochote** (6hr), the staging point for the Pongo de Mainique; look for a boatman in the Ivochote port area. Boats to the *pongo* tend to set off early in the morning, following the bends in the river.

Travelling down the river from Ivochote, just before you reach the *pongo* there's a community at **San Idriato**. The people here, known as the Israelites, founded their village around a biblical sect; the men leave their hair long and, like Rastafarians, they twist it up under expandable peaked caps. Across the Urubamba from San Idriato the small community of **Shinguriato**, upstream from the Río Yuyato mouth, is the official entrance to the *pongo* itself.

Pongo de Mainique

The awe-inspiring **Pongo de Mainique rapids** – possibly the most **dangerous** 2km of (barely) navigable river in the entire Amazonian system – are hazardous at any time of year, and virtually impossible to pass during the rainy season (Nov–March).

As you approach, you'll see a forested mountain range directly in front of you; the river speeds up, and as you get closer, it's possible to make out the great cut made through the range over the millennia by the powerful Urubamba. Then, before you realize, the boat is whisked into a long **canyon** with soaring rocky cliffs on either side: gigantic volcanic boulders look like wet monsters of molten steel; imaginary stone faces can be seen shimmering under cascades; and the danger of the *pongo* slips by almost unnoticed, as the walls of the canyon will absorb all your attention. The main hazard is a drop of about 2m, which is seen and then crossed in a split second. Now and then boats are overturned at this dangerous drop, usually those that try the run in the rainy season – although even then locals somehow manage to come upstream in small, non-motorized dugouts.

8

ARRIVAL AND DEPARTURE — IVOCHOTE AND PONGO DE MAINIQUE

By organized tour If you want to take an organized tour or whitewater-rafting trip down through the *pongo*, it's best to do this in Cusco with one of the rafting companies (see box, p.224).

By bus or colectivo To get to Ivochote from Quillabamba, buses and colectivos (S/30 per person) leave from Quillabamba's northern bus depot, daily 8–10am.

By boat Boats regularly take goods and people from the river port at Ivochote to the gas operations and lower Urubamba communities through the *pongo* most days between May and October, and it's often possible to pay a small fee for a ride on one. However, this leaves you on your own and away from shops, towns and even roads. People may approach you in Quillabamba or Ivochote for a trip to the *pongo* and perhaps a little camping and fishing; the merits of these are entirely dependent upon the price you have to pay and the confidence you have in the guide.

The central selva

The obvious appeal of the central selva is its ease of overland access and proximity to Lima. Directly east of the capital, the region is endowed with an array of rainforest eco-niches. The large and modern jungle city of **Pucallpa** lies in lowland rainforest, while the nearby oxbow lake **Lago Yarinacocha** provides a fine spot to swim, rest up and watch schools of dolphins. Pucallpa is also a main point of departure for trips downriver to the larger destination of **Iquitos** (see p.466), a thousand-kilometre, four- to five-day journey.

Closer to Lima yet less explored by tourists, the **Chanchamayo** region – famous for its fantastic coffee – offers stunning forested mountain scenery, fast-running rivers, and trees dripping with epiphytes. A steep road descends from Tarma down to the jungle gateway towns of **San Ramón** and **La Merced**, separated by a twenty-minute drive. From here you can travel north, visiting the unique Austro-German settlements of **Pozuzo** and **Oxapampa**, both rich agricultural centres located within a mosaic of little-visited protected areas, including the stunningly beautiful **Parque Nacional Yanachaga-Chemillén**. Apart from Pozuzo, rough roads connect these towns to Pucallpa via Villa Rica, Puerto Bermudez and Puerto Inca.

East from San Ramón and La Merced, an easier paved road heads towards the lower forest region, focused on the frontier town of **Satipo**, where Ashaninka tribespeople often come to town in traditional robes to sell produce and buy supplies. Near Satipo are scores of native communities, mainly of the Ashaninka ethnic group, and some of South America's finest **waterfalls**.

The Chanchamayo Valley

The **CHANCHAMAYO VALLEY**, only 300km from Lima and 750m above sea level, marks the real beginning of the Central Selva directly east of the capital. Originally settled in 1635 by Franciscan monks on mules, the region was repeatedly reclaimed by the native tribes. These days access to the main towns of San Ramón and La Merced is easy and relatively safe, with much of the produce from the area's rich tropical-fruit plantations (oranges and pineapples) and productive *chacras* (gardens), transported over the Andes by road to Lima.

San Ramón

The settler town, **SAN RAMÓN**, is a more appealing place than its larger twin La Merced (see opposite), just 20 minutes further by bus down the Chanchamayo Valley – though the latter is the communications hub and is better for road connections deeper into the jungle.

Founded originally as a fort in 1849, to assist the colonization of the region in the face of fierce indigenous resistance, the town now has several good restaurants, decent accommodation and the leafy **Plaza Mayor**, as well as a couple of worthwhile attractions within easy reach, including the waterfalls of **El Tirol** (within an hour or two's walk of San Ramón) and the Ashaninka village of **Pampa Michi**, an hour's drive beyond La Merced.

ARRIVAL AND INFORMATION — SAN RAMÓN

By bus Direct buses run from Lima to San Ramón (Empresas Junín; ☎064 323494, and Turismo Central). Expreso San Ramón and Empresa Los Angelitos buses (first two blocks of Progreso) link the valley with Tarma and Huancayo in the Sierra.

Destinations Huancayo (several daily; 3hr); La Merced (many daily; 15–20min); Lima (several daily; 10–12hr); Tarma (several daily; 1–2hr).

By colectivo Colectivo cars link the twin towns of San Ramón and La Merced 24hr daily, leaving from within one block of each town's main plaza, and colectivo cars and slower combis also reach most regional destinations.

Tourist information Information is sometimes available from the municipal office at Jr Pardo 110 (☎064 331265). Failing that, try the tour companies based in La Merced (see p.456).

ACCOMMODATION

Hotel Conquistador Progreso 298 ☎064 331157, conquistador@viabcp.com. The best hotel in town, with lots of well-appointed rooms, great hot showers and a good breakfast option. Close to the Empresa Junín bus stop. S/90

El Rancho C Tulumayo s/n Playa Hermosa ☎064 331511, bungalowselrancho@yahoo.es. Five or six well-looked-after bungalows at very reasonable prices; all set in the delicious shade of avocado and mandarin trees beside the Río Tulumayo. S/70

El Refugio Av El Ejercito 490 ☎064 331082, hotelelrefugio.com.pe. A three-star hotel with lovely rooms, private bathrooms and fans provided. There's a good-sized pool and terrace with great views over the valley, as well as a decent restaurant, wi-fi and a tour service for groups. S/120

EATING AND DRINKING

Chanchamayo-Italia Ristorante Jr Tarma 592 ☎964 417217. Excellent for mainly homemade pastas and pizzas as well as good coffee and wine; the artichoke cannelloni are stupendous (S/26). Daily noon–3pm & 7–10pm.

Chifa Siu C Progreso 440 ☎064 331078. Based in an attractive, airy space on two storeys and overlooking a small jungle garden, this restaurant serves up superb Chinese food – probably unbeatable in the region. There are set meals at lunchtimes (around S12). Daily 11.30am–9.30pm.

Licoria Roma II Jr Progreso 185, on the main street. This is the place to enjoy a drink in the evenings; there's a wide range of wines, beer, coffee-based liqueurs and pisco. Daily 6–11pm.

El Tiroles C las Orchideas 128. A small, Germanic-influenced café and delicatessen, which serves excellent sandwiches, juices and full meals, mostly prepared with locally smoked meats. Daily 8.30am–5pm.

Catarata El Tirol

Walk from Playa Hermosa (5min from San Ramón by mototaxi or car), or take a mototaxi from San Ramón (around S/5)

About 5km from San Ramón, the **Catarata El Tirol** waterfalls enjoy a 35-metre drop into an attractive plunge pool. The falls are accessed by a pleasant 45-minute (2km) country walk from the riverside village of Playa Hermosa, along a dirt track surrounded by orchids and lianas.

Pampa Hermosa and around

About 20km (2–3hr) along a track from San Ramón there's the **Santuario Nacional de Pampa Hermosa**, an area of verdant virgin cloudforest. Covering some 11,000 hectares, this national forest sanctuary is blessed with a fabulous jungle-style **lodge** (see below). Several impressive waterfalls dissect the reserve's unusually rich vegetation, including orchids, royal palms, lianas and giant ferns, and the reserve also boasts what is considered to be the **oldest cedar tree** in South America, fondly known as *el abuelo* (the grandfather); a breathtaking sight, it's so wide at its base that it takes sixteen people to circle its circumference hand in hand.

Various **treks** using local hill paths can also be planned to start or finish at *Pampa Hermosa Lodge*, which is only a few hours' walk from the end of forest cover and the start of mountain scenery; the Andean community of Ninabamba is less than six hours' trek. Slightly nearer, a trek to the tiny settlement of Alto Perú offers possible glimpses of spectacled bears and access to pre-Columbian remains dating back over five thousand years.

8

ARRIVAL AND DEPARTURE — PAMPA HERMOSA AND AROUND

By 4WD Accessible by 4WD vehicles – the lodge (see below) can arrange transport – it takes around 2hr to reach Pampa Hermosa from San Ramón, crossing the Puente Victoria bridge and following first the Oxabamba River, then climbing up beside the bubbling Ulcumayo gorge.

By colectivo Local combi-colectivos only go to Pampa Hermosa (also known as Nueva Italia) on Thursday and Saturday mornings, leaving the Parque de los Enamorados in San Ramón around 5am (4–5hr).

ACCOMMODATION

Pampa Hermosa Lodge 2hr by track from San Ramón ☎01 225 1776 and ☎01 99 9876 310, ⓦpampahermosalodge.com. On the edge of the Santuario Nacional de Pampa Hermosa are these beautiful wooden bungalows set around a sumptuous pagoda-like restaurant, with great food, all in natural materials with palm-frond roofs. The lodge is secluded but within twenty minutes' walk, Peru's national bird – the vermillion cock-of-the rock – can be seen every afternoon. Abseiling down waterfalls and floating in huge tyres down the river is also possible. Guiding service and all meals are included in the price. Advanced bookings only. **S/560**

La Merced and around

The market town of **LA MERCED**, some 10km further down the Chanchamayo Valley, is larger and busier than San Ramón, with more than twelve thousand inhabitants, a thriving Saturday **market** a couple of blocks behind the main street, and several hectic restaurants and bars crowded around the Plaza de Armas.

Close to La Merced, the **Jardín Botánico El Perezoso** (daily 9am–5pm; S/15), 15km from town, boasts 10,000 species of plant, including the tall, red *bastones del emperador*; two hours is enough for a thorough visit. Other local attractions include native communities such as **Pampa Michi**, on the banks of the Perene River, less than an hour by road en route to Satipo; not to everyone's taste, because the experience lacks some authenticity, this Ashaninka village has opened its doors to tourists for a number of years now, performing dances and music to order, while selling handicrafts.

ARRIVAL AND GETTING AROUND

LA MERCED AND AROUND

By bus La Merced is accessible direct by bus from Lima (Empresas Junín ⓣ064 323494, and Turismo Central offer *bus-camas* – buses with comfortable reclining seats). Buses leave more or less constantly from the Terminal Terrestre in La Merced, and all have signs in the windscreens showing their destinations. You can head deeper into the lower Amazon Basin by bus or colectivo from the bus depot to the jungle town of Satipo. Other buses link La Merced with Oxapampa and Pozuzo; and dirt roads also link with Pucallpa via Puerto Inca (the final 298km from La Merced), along the corridor formed by the rivers Pichis and Pachitea.
Destinations Huancayo (several daily; 3hr); Lima (several daily; 10–12hr); Oxapampa (2–3 daily; 2–3hr); Pozuzo (1 weekly; 10–15hr); Pucallpa (1 weekly via Puerto Inca; 20–30hr); San Ramón (many daily; 15–20 min); Satipo (several daily; 2–3hr); Tarma (several daily; 1–2hr).

By colectivo Colectivo cars link the twin towns of San Ramón and La Merced 24hr daily, leaving from within one block of each town's main plaza, and colectivo cars and slower combis also reach most regional destinations. Colectivos leave from inside the Terminal Terrestre for Oxapampa, San Ramón, Satipo, Pozuzo and Pichanaki. All have signs in the windscreens and touts shouting out the destination.
Destinations Oxapampa (several daily; 2hr); Pichanaki (several daily; 1hr 30min), Pozuzo (daily; 10–15hr), Satipo (several daily; 2–3hr).

TOURS

Imagheren Peru Tours Jr Junín 512, La Merced ⓣ064 621608. This company offers local trips and packages to the main attractions, plus they can help with local transport and bus tickets.

Max Adventures Jr 2 de Mayo 682 ⓣ064 532175, ⓦmaxadventure.com.pe. The best of the local companies, with ten years' experience. All-inclusive packages or tours to Oxapampa, Villa Rica, Pozuzo, Tarma, the Huagapo cave and Satipo; excursions include visits to waterfalls, botanical and orchid gardens, native villages, coffee-processing plants and river rafting.

8

ACCOMMODATION

Fundo San José ⓣ064 531816, ⓦfundosanjose.com.pe. Located high up on the hillside to the left as you come into La Merced from San Ramón, this plush hotel offers quality bungalow accommodation with lovely views across the valley and a great swimming pool. S/450

Hostal El Eden Jr Ancash 342, on the main plaza ⓣ064 531183. A popular pad with clean bedrooms and friendly service, most with private bathroom. Downstairs there's a good restaurant overlooking the Plaza de Armas. S/75

Hostal Rey Jr Junín 103 ⓣ064 531185. A well-organized place with pleasant enough, if small, rooms; all have cable TV and private bathrooms. There's a restaurant and laundry, too. S/60

Hostal Los Victor Jr Tarma 373 ⓣ064 531026. Located on the Plaza de Armas, this hostel has rooms with or without private bathroom, and is one of the better budget options. S/50

EATING, DRINKING AND NIGHTLIFE

Broaster Chanchamayo Jr Junín 580. The best place in the valley for roast chicken and chips; the ambience is a bit white and clinical, but the food and service very good. Daily 10am–10pm.

Green Gold Av Pescheira ⓣ064 531493. A large café space that roasts and sells local Chanchamayo coffee by the cup and bag. Chocolates and local fruit preserves are also available, and it's within a stone's throw of the Terminal Terrestre, just over the river bridge. Daily 9am–6pm.

Kametsa Café Rock Av Puente Herreria 1 ⓣ064 532015 and ⓣ064 335265. This disco-style club overlooks the river; its large and lively dancefloor is best between 10pm and 3am. Wed–Sun 8pm–2am.

Shambari Campa Jr Tarma 383. Located on the Plaza de Armas, this is a large restaurant but always crowded. It serves some good traditional dishes, including venison and *zamaño* (a medium-sized forest rodent). Daily 8am–9pm.

Satipo

A real jungle frontier town, **SATIPO** is an ideal place in which to get kitted out for a jungle expedition, or just to sample the delights of the selva for a day or two. The settlement was first developed to service colonists and settlers in the 1940s, and continues in similar vein today, providing an economic and social centre for a widely scattered population of over forty thousand colonists, with supplies of tools and food, medical facilities and banks; the bustling daily **market** is best experienced at weekends.

In the 1940s, the first dirt road extended here from Huancayo, but it wasn't until the 1970s that a road was opened from Lima via La Merced; before this there were only mule trails from this direction. With the surfacing of the Carretera Marginal road all the way from Lima in the late 1990s – a veritable carpet unfurling through the jungle valleys – many more recent settlers have moved into the region, but the rate of development is putting significant pressure on the last surviving groups of traditional forest dwellers, mainly the **Ashaninka tribe**, who have mostly taken up plots of land and either begun to compete with the relative newcomer farmers or moved into one of the ever-shrinking zones out of contact with the rest of Peru. You can often see the tribespeople, in town to buy supplies and trade, unmistakeable in their reddish-brown or cream *cushma* robes.

ARRIVAL AND INFORMATION — SATIPO

By bus Satipo is accessible direct by bus from Lima (Empresas Junín; ⓣ064 323494, and Turismo Central both offer *bus-camas* – buses with comfortable reclining seats). Buses arrive in Satipo at various terminals, all within three or four blocks uphill of the Plaza de Armas.

Destinations Huancayo (daily; 6–8hr); La Merced (several daily; 2–3hr); Lima (several daily; 12–15hr).

By colectivo Colectivos arrive from La Merced, Pichanaki and Puerto Ocopa to one of the few small depots, all located in the first block downhill from the Plaza de Armas. The lowland jungle town of Atalaya, located where the Río Tambo meets the Río Urubamba, can be reached by colectivo from Satipo.

Destinations Atalaya (several daily; 6–8hr); La Merced (several daily; 2–3hr); Pichanaki (several daily; 1hr); Puerto Ocopa (several daily; 2hr).

Tourist information There's a small tourist office on the Plaza de Armas (Mon–Sat 9am–6pm), plus one or two kiosks selling local crafts on the plaza that can sometimes provide maps and flyers on local attractions.

ACCOMMODATION

Hostal Palmero C Manuel Prado 228 ⓣ064 545020. Slightly cramped and noisy, with over forty beds, but the family who run it are friendly and the location is fairly central, within half a block of the main plaza. S/60

Hotel Brassia Jr Los Incas 527 ⓣ064 545787, ⓦbrassiahotel.com. A relatively new hotel with a/c rooms, cable TV, hot water all day and good wi-fi. Service is excellent and there is a café next door. S/70

Hotel Majestic Jr Colonos Fundadores 408 ⓣ064 545762. Cool but sometimes airless rooms in a mid-twentieth-century style incorporating wood and stonework. The veranda overlooking the Plaza de Armas is a bonus. S/55

EATING AND DRINKING

Café Yoli Jr Augusto Leguía ⓣ064 333037. Located on the left in the first block from the Plaza de Armas, this small café is great for coffee, juices, snacks and breakfasts. Daily 8am–9pm.

Laguna Blanca In the Club Centro Social on the Avenida Marginal. Although difficult to find, most mototaxi drivers will know where this place is. It offers probably the best food in town, with good fish and *zamaño* forest meat as well as venison. To find it, head towards Río Negro, and the sign posted entrance is opposite the Medina petrol station. Daily lunchtimes only.

Recreo Turístico El Jaguar Fifth block of Jr Rubén Callegari ⓣ064 509948. A large, jungle-themed restaurant with dancefloor, bar and occasional live music, this place offers a range of tasty jungle cuisine, from river catfish to game animals. Daily noon–11pm.

DIRECTORY

Internet The best internet cafés are on Jr Colonos Fundadores.

Money and exchange For money-changing or ATMs, the Banco de Credito is opposite *Café Yoli* on Jr Manuel Prado.

Telephones There are several telephone offices, mainly around the Plaza de Armas and on the streets leading uphill from here.

Around Satipo

While Satipo sits in the middle of a beautiful valley, today the landscape around the town is more orange plantation than virgin forest; the best way to get a feel for the valley is by following a **footpath** from the other side of the suspension bridge, which leads over the river from behind the market area, to some of the plantations beyond town. Here you can see the local agriculture at closer quarters, as you pass some rustic dwellings.

Note that once you go beyond Satipo (except, arguably, by road to Atalaya), you are well beyond the tourist trail, with minimal if any facilities available.

San Martín de Pangoa

Colectivos run from Satipo to the end of the Carretera Marginal into relatively new settled areas such as that around **San Martín de Pangoa** – a frontier settlement that is growing fast on lumber, citrus and coca plantations. Instead of retracing your steps from Satipo via La Merced and San Ramón, you can follow a breathtaking direct road to **Huancayo**; the rough road passes Todopampa at 4200m, where there's an even rougher route (4WD only), which goes from the pueblo of Manzanilla to Concepción (4hr) via Lake Llangunchuco and the village of Comas.

Puerto Ocopa

Satipo is the southernmost large town on the jungle-bound Carretera Marginal, and a dirt road continues to **Puerto Ocopa** (a small river port originally founded by Franciscan missionaries in 1918), which makes a strategic location for travelling deeper into the forest along the rivers Tambo and Ene.

8

Atalaya

For the adventurous, a riverboat down the **Río Tambo** or the loggers' road from Satipo (not always passable) to **Atalaya**, deep into the central selva, is an exciting excursion, though this is way off the tourist trail: facilities are few and it's real jungle-frontier territory, largely beyond the arm of the law. Visits should only be made with local guides who know the current political situation; ask staff in the local hotels for recommendations.

Parque Nacional de Otishi and Cataratas de Parijaro

The mountain ranges south and east of the Tambo and Ene rivers, respectively, form the **Parque Nacional de Otishi**. On the Río Ene side of this new national park, the highest single-drop waterfall in Peru – the **Cataratas de Parijaro** – is a veritable jewel even among Peru's vast collection of impressive natural assets. The remote nature of this site and the total lack of infrastructure make it very difficult to reach as an independent traveller, and permission is required in advance from SERNANP, Peru's protected-area agency (see box, p.446).

ARRIVAL AND GETTING AROUND — AROUND SATIPO

SAN MARTÍN DE PANGOA AND HUANCAYO

By colectivo There are local colectivos from Satipo to San Martín (several daily; 2hr). For Huancayo, Los Andes buses do the 6–8hr journey (one daily between May and Oct).

PUERTO OCOPA

By colectivo Local colectivos run from Satipo to Puerto Ocopa (several daily; 2hr).

By boat Motorized **canoes** leave for the Tambo and Ene rivers from Puerto Ocopa.

ATALAYA

By colectivo There are local colectivos from Satipo to Atalaya (several daily; 8–9hr).

By boat Atalaya has boats arriving from and departing for Puerto Ocopa (to connect back with Satipo; 8hr on boat and 2hr more by car to Satipo), Pucallpa (2–3 days along the Ucayali river) and Sepahua (a small frontier settlement on the Urubamba river; roughly 6–8hr).

By air Atalaya has an airstrip on the edge of town with several unscheduled flights a week connecting with Lima and Pucallpa. There's no phone; you have to go to the airstrip by taxi and ask at the desk what flights are expected or available at the time.

Destinations Lima (usually at least 1 weekly; 1hr); Pucallpa (usually at least 1–2 weekly; 1hr).

Oxapampa

Slightly off the beaten track, some 78km by road (two hours) north of La Merced, and nearly 400km east of Lima, lies the small settlement of **OXAPAMPA**, a pleasant and well-organized frontier town strongly influenced culturally and architecturally by the nearby Tyrolean settlement of Pozuzo (see p.460). The town is also conspicuously clean, situated on the banks of the Río Chontabamba, some 1800m above sea level; the **Mercado Municipal**, one block from the main square, is probably the most orderly and most relaxed in all of Peru.

Oxapampa's main local **fiesta** takes place at the end of August; on the thirtieth, the town celebrates its founding, while on the following day the traditional **Torneo de Cintas** takes place, when local young men compete on horseback to collect ribbons from a post.

ARRIVAL AND GETTING AROUND — OXAPAMPA

By bus Oxapampa is reached by Transportes Junín and Oxabus buses from Lima or La Merced; all buses pull in at the Terminal Terrestre in Jr Loechle, one block off the main road that enters the town, Av San Martín, and a few long blocks from the Plaza de Armas.

Destinations La Merced (several daily; 2–3hr); Lima (daily; 13–16hr); Pozuzo (daily; 8–14hr, depending on weather and state of the road).

By colectivo Colectivos from La Merced and Pozuzo (via Yanachega Chemellin and the Cañon de Huancabamba) start and finish at the Terminal Terrestre (see above).

By mototaxi For getting around the town (to and from the Terminal Terrestre), mototaxis are everywhere (S/1–3).

INFORMATION AND TOURS

Tourist information For tourist information on Oxapampa and around, try the websites oxapampa.pe and oxapampaonline.com (in Spanish only).

Peru's protected-area agency SERNANP has a park office in Oxapampa, on the third block of Jr Pozuzo (063 462544, sernanp.gob.pe).

Tour operators Tourism infrastructure is in its early stages in Oxapampa, but there is one tour agency and some independent local guides: Ecotours Oxapampa (063 462659, ecotours_oxapampa@yahoo.com or tourisoxa@hotmail.com) and José Luís Zevallos Baldeom (963 697695, joseoxa@hotmail.com), who has his own inflatable raft for river-running and exploring some of the region's scenic areas.

8

ACCOMMODATION

Albergue Bottger Av Mariscal Castilla, block 6 063 762377, bottger_d@yahoo.com. Five blocks' walk from the plaza, this *albergue* is based in a luxurious modern mansion built and panelled largely from cedar and *diablo fuerte* wood; they serve brilliant breakfasts, rooms are spacious and super-clean, and there's a splendid suite above the bar. S/90

★ **Albergue Familiar Carolina Egg** Av San Martín 1085 063 462331 or 963 9691436, fraucarolinaegg.com. A lovely complex of independent rooms and bungalows, very close to the Terminal Terrestre, on the corner of Av Mullenbruc with C Loechle, where the colectivos stop. This is an exceptionally friendly and well-run place (managed by a family descended from the original nineteenth-century colonists), and the breakfasts are amazing. S/90

Eco-albergue Yanachaga Near Huancabamba, 24km along the road to Pozuzo 063 462506, isab58@yahoo.es. A rural retreat with stone-built rooms comprising private bathrooms with hot water, as well as a restaurant serving great home-grown food (breakfast included in price). S/80

Edelweiss Miraflores Km 53, Lote 58, just as you come into the entrance to town from the La Merced direction 063 762567, posadaedelweiss.com. A hundred-year-old cedar-wood house with forty beds based in chalets around a garden, with hammocks and a barbecue. No TV, but there is a shared kitchen and a spacious, stylish dining room. S/90

Loeckle Sinty Av San Martín, block 12, Pasaje San Alberto 063 462180 or 063 462615, sikels@yahoo.es. This wooden house was built seventy years ago to a similar specification as the large wooden church on Oxapampa's main plaza. Rooms are independent cabins opening out onto a pleasant garden, and there's also wi-fi and cable TV. S/90

Rocio Av San Martín. Located just off the plaza, this is one of the town's few cheaper options, offering TV and hot water in less than salubrious surroundings. S/45

El Trapiche Jr Mullembruck, first block 063 462551, trapichelodge.com. In countryside on the far edge of town, *El Trapiche* has several two-storey cypress-wood cabins and a fine restaurant; the management have good contacts with local tour guides and frequently organize typical Austro-German dances and fiestas. S/110

EATING AND DRINKING

Casa del Baco In the Miraflores suburb on the way into town at Km 2.5. Easily reached by mototaxi, this great garden restaurant dishes up tasty local beef and ham dishes. Thurs–Sun 11.30am–5.30pm.

Italos Prolongación San Martín ☎ 063 462367. A busy and popular garden-based restaurant specializing in fine beef cuts and grills; they also serve good salads and drinks. Daily at lunch.

Oasis Jr Bolognesi 363. This modern restaurant has a bit of a plastic interior, but it does serve superb set-menu lunches (from only S/12), as well as smoked pork and trout á la carte dishes (upstairs the speciality is roast chicken). Daily 10am–10pm.

Restaurante Típico Oxapampino First block of Mariscal Castillo. Traditional local meat dishes and superb breakfasts at very reasonable prices. Mon–Sat 7am–8pm.

Around Oxapampa

As a result of its economic dependence on timber, *rocoto* peppers, livestock and coffee, most of the forest immediately around Oxapampa has been cleared for cattle grazing, plantations and timber. There are nevertheless several sites of interest close to the town, which can be visited very easily with the help of the tour companies in Oxapampa (see p.459). These include a small bat cave, Tinicueva; a trout farm, El Wharapu; a sugar cane alcohol ranch and a suspension footbridge and old wooden church, the Iglesia Santa Rosa, around the nearby settlement of Chontabamba. Some forty minutes by taxi (S/50 return) from Oxapampa, the Catarata Anana waterfalls offer a pleasant half-day excursion, ideal for a picnic.

Parque Nacional Yanachaga-Chemillén

8

For access, permission and an advance payment of $2/day is needed from SERNANP, who have an office in Oxapampa (see p.459), or contact the Lima office (see box, p.446) • Best reached in 4WD vehicle with driver, organized through an Oxapampa tour company (see p.459), though you could also jump off a bus bound for Pozuzo from Oxapampa

Some 30km from Oxapampa lies the **Parque Nacional Yanachaga-Chemillén**, a 122,000-hectare reserve dominated by dark mountains and vivid landscapes, where grasslands and cloud forest merge and separate. Established as a protected area in 1986, it's accessed via the Cañon de Huancabamba. Best visited in the dry season (May–September), there are vast quantities of bromeliads, orchids and cedars, as well as dwarf brocket deer, giant rats and even the odd spectacled bear, some jaguar and around 427 bird species, including a significant variety of hummingbird. It's also home to around sixty Yanesha communities.

Villa Rica and Catarata El Encanto

Villa Rica is accessed by colectivo or bus from La Merced (1–2hr)

The town of **Villa Rica**, some 72km from Oxapampa, lying at 1480m in the *ceja de selva* (edge of the jungle), offers overland access to the Pichis and Palcazu valleys, the region's principal producers of coffee, pineapple and coca. Only 12km from town you'll find the **Catarata El Encanto** (the "Spell" or "Enchantment" Waterfall), which has three sets of falls; rainbows frequently appear here, and there are deep, dangerous plunge pools.

Pozuzo

Some 80km further down into the rainforest from Oxapampa at 823m above sea level, **POZUZO** is significantly smaller than Oxapampa. Reached via a very rough road that crosses over two dozen rivers and streams, the vista of wooden chalets with sloping Tyrolean roofs has endured ever since the first **Austrian and German colonists** arrived here in the mid-nineteenth century (see box opposite).

Pozuzo still receives relatively few tourist visitors, but is aware of its peculiar interest; places to check out include the fine **Iglesia San José**, built in stone and wood during 1875, the **Museo Schaffere** (displaying photos and curios of the indigenous tribes), the very Germanic **Casa Budweiser** with its stylish chimney, and the more recently built **Casa de Cultura de Pozuzo**. Among the most noteworthy of the **colonists' houses**, perhaps the Casa Típica Palmatambo and the Casa Típica Egg Vogt are among the

POZUZO'S TYROLEAN ROOTS

Back in the 1850s, Baron Schutz von Holzhausren of Germany and the then President of Peru, General Ramón Castilla, developed a grand plan to establish settlements deep in the jungle. The original **deal between Germany and Peru** required Peru to build roads, schools and churches; while the Austro-Germans needed to be of Catholic religion, have some kind of office and impeccable reputation.

The first group of three hundred, mainly **Tyrolean**, immigrants left Europe in 1857 on the British ship *Norton*, arriving in Lima on July 28. During the overland journey, cutting their way through jungle, almost half the colonists died of disease, accident or exhaustion. The town of **Pozuzo** was founded in 1859 when the area was ripe with virgin forest and crystalline rivers owned by the Yanesha tribe. Nine years later, a second group of immigrants arrived to reinforce the original population, which had been left, more or less abandoned, by the Peruvian authorities. The colonists began to expand their population and territory; first, **Oxapampa** was founded in 1891 by the Bottger family, then others went on to found **Villa Rica** in 1928.

Today the economy of Pozuzo is based on beef cattle; but **lederhosen** are worn for fiestas and **Tyrolean dances** are still performed, creating a peculiar combination of European rusticism (the local dance and music is still strongly influenced by the German colonial heritage) and native Peruvian culture. Moreoever, many of this unusual town's present inhabitants still speak German, eat *Schottsuppe*, waltz well and dance the polka.

most interesting, the latter with its own small family museum; on the edge of town, the **Casa de Zacarias Schuler** still operates a water-powered mill for crushing sugar cane to make the nonalcoholic drink *huarapo*.

8

ARRIVAL AND INFORMATION — POZUZO

By colectivo Colectivos leave for Pozuzo every day from the Terminal Terrestre in Oxapampa (8–12hr) or the bus depot in La Merced (10–14hr).

Tourist information For local information, call 063 287546, check out pozuzo.org, or call Prusia Tours in Lima (01 242 9876, prusiatours.com).

ACCOMMODATION AND EATING

Albergue Frau Maria Egg Av Los Colonos 01 444 9927 or 063 287559, pozuzo.com. Accommodation here is in attractive wooden chalets, with gardens and trees all around. The food served is exceptionally good, especially the hams and the wide range of fruity cakes. S/85

El Mango C Pacificación 185 063 287528, elmango_pozuzo@hotmail.com. This pleasant wood-built place offers excellent rooms and great smoked sausages. S/60

Around Pozuzo

En route to Pozuzo from La Merced, the road passes through the small town of **Huancabamba**, starting point for a four- or five-day trek up into the high Andes on an old Inca road crossing the Cordillera Huagurucho via the Abra Anilcocha pass (4500m) towards Lago Chinchaycocha and Cerro de Pasco. Out of town, the main attraction is the **Catarata Delfin**, which has an 80m drop and is an hour's walk from the Delfin hydroelectric plant by the Cañon de Huancabamba. At **Guacamayo**, beyond the Puente Prusia bridge and accessible only by 4WD vehicles, it's possible to visit a natural habitat for the cock-of-the rock bird which can be seen most afternoons following a thirty-minute stroll beyond the road. The area, which abounds in orchids, ancient ferns and palm trees, is also great for canoeing, trekking and mountain biking.

To visit these places you need a car, or contact the tour companies in Oxapampa (see p.459) to arrange activities locally.

Pucallpa

A sprawling, hot and dusty city with over 400,000 inhabitants, **PUCALLPA** holds little of interest to travellers, most of whom get straight into a mototaxi or a local bus for

Lago Yarinacocha (see p.464). If you stay a while, though, it's difficult not to appreciate Pucallpa's relaxed feel – or the entrepreneurial optimism of this burgeoning jungle frontier city.

Pucallpa's annual festival for visitors – the **Semana Turística de la Region Ucayali** – is usually held in the last week of September, offering mostly artesanía and forest-produce markets, as well as folklore, music and dance.

Brief history

Long an impenetrable refuge for **Cashibo** Indians, Pucallpa was developed as a camp for rubber gatherers at the beginning of the twentieth century. In 1930 the town was connected to Lima by road (850km of it), and since then its expansion has been intense and unstoppable. Sawmills surround the city and spread up the main highway towards Tingo María and the mountains, and there's an impressive floating harbour at the nearby port of **La Hoyada**, where larger commercial vessels land. In the twenty-first century, the city has been one of the main routes for lumber travelling from the Peruvian Amazon to Lima and the Pacific coast for export markets. Cattle-ranching is also big around here, putting increasing pressure on the rainforest's ecosystems and biodiversity.

Shops and markets

If you have an hour or so to while away in the town itself, both the downtown **food market** on Jirón Independencia and the older central **market** on Dos de Mayo are worth checking out; the latter in particular comprises varied stalls full of jungle produce. The port of **La Hoyada** and the older, nearby **Puerto Italia** are also bustling with activity by day. For **craft shopping**, artesanía can be found at Jirón Mariscal Cáceres block 5, Jirón Tarapacá block 8 and Jirón Tanca block 6.

Usko-Ayar Amazonia School of Painting

Jr Sánchez Cerro 467 • Mon–Fri 8am–5pm • Free

Among the few attractions in Pucallpa is the **Usko-Ayar Amazonia School of Painting**, also the home of the school's founding father, the self-taught artist **Pablo Amaringo**. Once an ayahuasca shaman (see box, p.479), Don Amaringo used the hallucinogenic ayahuasca, as do most Peruvian jungle healers, as an aid to divination and curing; his students' works, many of which are displayed at his house, display the same ayahuasca-inspired visions of the forest wilderness as his own paintings do.

Museo Regional de Historia Natural and around

The **Museo Regional de Historia Natural**, on Calle Inmaculada (Mon–Sat 9am–6pm; S/5), exhibits dried and stuffed Amazon insects, fish and animals, and has good displays of local crafts, including ceramics produced by the Shipibo Indians, plus other material objects such as clothing and jewellery from local tribes. There are also works by the Pucallpa-born wood sculptor **Agustín Rivas**; more of Rivas's work can be seen and bought at his house on Jirón Tarapacá 861 (Mon–Sat 10am–noon & 3–5pm).

ARRIVAL AND DEPARTURE — PUCALLPA

By air Pucallpa airport (☎ 061 572767) is only 5km west of town and is served by buses (20min; S/1), mototaxis (15min; S/4) and taxis (10min; S/18–20). LAN Perú, at the corner of Jr Tarapacá 805 (☎ 061 579840 and ☎ 061 594347), operate flights between Pucallpa, Lima and Iquitos, and StarPerú, Jr 7 de Junio 865 (☎ 061 590585), fly here from Tarapoto, Lima and Iquitos once a week. There are also irregular services run by Air Taxis (☎ 061 570059 and ☎ 061 575221), based at the airport, from Cruzeiro do Sul just over the Brazilian border.

Destinations Iquitos (1 weekly; 1hr 30min); Lima (1 daily; 1hr); Tarapoto (1 weekly; 1hr 20min).

By bus For speed and comfort, the best way to Pucallpa is direct from Lima on the sealed road via Huánuco and Tingo María. Several bus companies offer this service, all of which go via Huánuco (roughly the halfway point); the full journey is supposed to take 17–20hr but can be longer. All companies arrive at depots in Jr Raimondi: Transportes

Junín (Raimondi 897; 061 573963) and Transmar (Raimondi 770; 061 579778) are among the best. Take warm clothing for the high mountain sections, particularly if you'll be doing these overnight.
Destinations Lima (daily; 18–25hr); Tingo María (daily; 10–12hr).
By boat Boats arrive either at the floating port of La Hoyada on the eastern side of town, about 2km from the Plaza de Armas (S/5 by mototaxi, S/10 by taxi) or, much nearer to town, at the Malecón Grau. The operational port depends mostly on the height of the river. Boats upriver to Iquitos and Nauta leave most days (4–6 days). Their precise destinations can be identified directly in the port by notices on each boat: it's a matter of finding the right boat, then talking to the captain about prices and schedule.

GETTING AROUND AND INFORMATION

By colectivo Colectivos leave from near the food market on Avenida 7 de Junio.
By taxi and mototaxi Mototaxis and taxis can be picked up almost anywhere in town.
Tourist information Information is available at the regional office on Jr Dos de Mayo 111 (061 575110) and at pucallpa.com and hellopucallpa.com.
Tour operators Laser Viajes y Turismo, Jr Raimondi 399 (061 571120, laserviajesyturismo.com), at the corner with Jr Tarapacá, offer some of the best local tours, packages and travel tickets.

ACCOMMODATION

Grand Hotel Mercedes Jr Raimondi 610 061 571191, granhotelmercedes.com. This is one of Pucallpa's best hotels, which has a great swimming pool, lovely jungle gardens, a reasonable restaurant and bar. The rooms are comfortable and clean, but not large or luxurious. S/175
Hostal Sun Ucayali 380 061 598142. A pleasant budget option, reasonably central if a little down at heel. It has friendly service and small but clean rooms, with or without bath. S/45
★ **Sol del Oriente** Av San Martín 552 061 575154, soldelorientehoteles.com. Probably the best of all the hotels in Pucallpa, this place has a lovely pool, bar and restaurant. Airport pick-up available on request. S/285

EATING

Like all jungle cities, Pucallpa has developed a cuisine of its own; one of the unique dishes you can find in some of these restaurants is *inchicapi* – a chicken soup made with peanuts, manioc and coriander leaves. Try the local speciality *patarashca* (fresh fish cooked in *bijao* leaves), or the delicious *sarapatera* (soup in a turtle shell).

Restaurant El Golf Jr Huascar 545 061 574632. A family-run restaurant, this place serves up delicious local food, specializing in fish dishes. One of their must-try dishes is shrimps in passionfruit sauce (S/25). Daily 10.30am–9.30pm.
El Viajero Jr Libertad 374 061 575710. Offering great regional food and also comida criolla, this restaurant (which also offers delivery) has great set menus at lunchtime (from around S/10). Best to get there early since it gets busy 12.30–2pm. Daily 7.30am–9pm.

DIRECTORY

Internet Internet services can be found all over the centre of the town.
Money and exchange For exchange there's Banco de Credito, C Tarapacá, two blocks from the Plaza de Armas towards the main market by Parque San Martín, though for good rates on dollars cash try the *cambistas* on Calle Tarapacá, where it meets the Plaza de Armas.
Post office The post office is at Av San Martín 418 (Mon–Sat 8am–7pm).
Telephones Payphones are available at Telefónica del Perú, Ucayali 357, or on Jr Independencia.

8

Parque Natural y Museo Regional de Pucallpa

Barboncocha • Daily 8am–5pm • S/5 • Colectivos to Barboncocha can be picked up near the food market on Av 7 de Junio

Some 6km out of town, along the highway towards Lima, there's a small lakeside settlement and zoological park at Barboncocha. Known as the **Parque Natural y Museo Regional de Pucallpa**, it consists of almost two hundred hectares of lakeside reserve, with lots of alligators, birds (particularly parrots and macaws) and boa constrictors, as well as the usual caged monkeys and black jaguars.

BOAT TRIPS FROM PUERTO CALLAO

Various **excursions** to see wildlife, including dolphins, visit Indian villages or just to cross the lake are all touted along the waterfront. The standard day-trip goes to the Shipibo village of **San Francisco** ($20), sometimes continuing to the slightly remoter settlements of **Nuevo Destino** and **Santa Clara** (around S/50). San Francisco is now almost completely geared towards tourism, so for a more adventurous trip you'd do better to hire a *peque-peque* canoe and boatman on your own (from around S/150 a day); these canoes can take up to six or seven people and you can share costs, though if you want to go further afield (on a three-day excursion, say) expect prices to rise to $150 a day.

Yarinacocha

Some 9km from Pucallpa, beautiful **YARINACOCHA** is the most appealing place to stay near the town. The town is clustered around vast Lago Yarinacocha, which, apart from the tiny main port where buses drop off, is edged with secondary forest growth around most of its perimeter. **Dolphins** can usually be seen surfacing and diving into water, best witnessed by renting one of the rowing boats on the lakeside (about S/5 per hour). Around the port itself, and to a lesser extent, hidden behind the vegetation elsewhere, there is considerable settlement, but most of it is rustic. River channels lead off towards small villages of **Shipibo Indians** and a limited number of tourist lodges.

Puerto Callao

The port of **PUERTO CALLAO**, which is where most travellers stay, is known locally (and slightly ironically) as the "Shangri-la de la Selva", where the bars and wooden shacks are animated by an almost continuous blast of *chicha* music.

Moroti-Shobo Crafts Co-operative

Plaza Yarina, two blocks from Malecón Callao • Daily 9am–6pm • Free

The settlement boasts one of the best jungle Indian craft workshops in the Amazon, the **Moroti-Shobo Crafts Co-operative** – a project originally organized by Oxfam but now operated by the local Shipibo and Conibo Indians. Located on the main plaza, it sells some beautifully moulded ceramics, carved wood and dyed textiles, most of them very reasonably priced.

Jardín Botánico Chullachaqui

Daily 9am–5pm • Free • Take a *peque-peque* canoe from Puerto Callao (45min; S/8), then walk for a little over 30min down a clearly marked jungle trail

A pristine botanical garden, the **Jardín Botánico Chullachaqui** is on the far right-hand side of the lake. In a beautiful and exotic location, the garden boasts over 2300 medicinal plants, mostly native to the region.

ARRIVAL AND TOURS — YARINACOCHA

By bus or colectivo Buses and colectivos leave from the food market in Pucallpa on the corner of Jr Independencia and Ucayali (20min; S/2), and drop passengers off within a block of the lakeside Malecón Callao.

Tour operator A Lima-based operator, Runcato (T 01 4653018, W runcato.com), runs culturally authentic and responsible tours from Pucallpa to a more distant Shipibo-Conibo community and lodge at Puerto Nuevo, including options for ayahuasca ceremonies, natural herbal baths and wildlife-spotting (including pink dolphin); only one or two expeditions are run every year, so it's important to contact the company several months in advance.

ACCOMMODATION AND EATING

Albergue Amazónico Jana Shobo Yarinacocha, lakeside T 061 596943. This comfortable lodge has a restaurant, library and comfortable rooms, organizes bonfires and drum-dancing, and will pick up from Pucallpa airport; it also has boat transport for the lake and runs short local tours. S/300

Los Delfines Puerto Callao T 061 571129. Located on the lakeside, this hostel offers clean rooms and simple beds, but at a fair price; cold water only, but most rooms have private bathroom. S/50

La Maloka Malecón Yarinacocha. This bar and restaurant is associated with a hostel of the same name; it serves decent food, mainly local dishes, and cold beer. Daily 10am–10pm.

Pandisho Amazon Ecolodge On the shore of Lago Yarinacocha ⓣ061 596943, ⓦamazon-ecolodge.com. This lodge combines accommodation with interesting ecotoursim and treatments with rainforest medicines. They also offer canoe trips, jungle treks and visits to local communities. S/280

Peña La Catahua Malecón Callao. Most of the liveliest bars are along the waterfront in Puerto Callao; this is one of the best.

The northern selva

At the "island" city of Iquitos, by far the largest and most exciting of Peru's jungle towns, there are few sights as magnificent as the **Río Amazonas** (see box below). Its tributaries start well up in the Andes, and when they join together several hours upstream from the town, the river is already several kilometres wide. The town's location, only 104m above sea level yet thousands of miles from the ocean and surrounded in all directions by brilliant green forest and hemmed in by the maze of rivers, streams and lagoons, makes for a stunning entry to the **NORTHERN SELVA**.

Much of **Iquitos's** appeal derives from its being the starting point for excursions into the **rainforest** (see p.475), but the town is an interesting place in its own right, if only for the lively local people and magnificent architecture. It's a buzzing, cosmopolitan tourist town, connected to the rest of the world by river and air only: the kind of place that lives up to all your expectations of a jungle town, from its elegant reminders of the rubber-boom years to the atmospheric shantytown suburb of **Puerto Belén**, one of Werner Herzog's main locations for his 1982 film *Fitzcarraldo*, where you can buy almost anything, from fuel to ayahuasca medicines.

The town has a friendly café and club scene, interesting museums and beautiful, late nineteenth- and early twentieth-century buildings, and the surrounding region has some great island and lagoon **beaches**, a range of easy excursions into the rainforest and the possibility of continuing down the Amazon into **Colombia or Brazil**. The area has also become something of a **spiritual focus**, particularly for gringos seeking a visionary experience with one of the many local shamans who use the sacred and powerful hallucinogenic ayahuasca vine in their psycho-healing sessions (see box, p.479).

Unlike most of the Peruvian selva, the **climate** here is little affected by the Andean topography, so there is no rainy season as such; instead, the year is divided into "high water" (December–May) and "low water" (June–November) seasons. The upshot is that the weather is always hot and humid, with temperatures averaging 23–30°C (74–86°F) and with an annual rainfall of about 2600mm. Most visitors come between May and August, but the high-water months are perhaps the best time for seeing **wildlife**, because the animals are crowded into smaller areas of dry land.

THE AMAZON RIVER

The **Río Amazonas** lays claim to being the biggest river in the world. Originally it flowed east to west, before becoming an inland sea when the Andes began to rise along the Pacific edge of the continent around 100 million years ago. Another 40 million years of geological and climatic action later saw this "sea" break through into the Atlantic, which reversed the flow of water and gave birth to the mighty 6500-kilometre river. Starting in Peru as an insignificant glacial trickle on the Nevada Misma, northeast of the Colca Canyon, the waters swell as they move down through the Andes, passing Cusco before heading across the continent towards the Atlantic Ocean, still many thousands of miles away.

Iquitos

Self-confident and likeable, **IQUITOS** is for the most part a modern city, built on a wide, flat river plain. Only the heart of the city, around the main plaza, contains older, architecturally interesting buildings, but the river port and market area of **Belén** boasts rustic wooden huts on stilts – a classic image of Iquitos.

If it weren't for the abundant stalls and shops selling jungle craft goods it would be hard to know that this place was once dominated by hunter-gatherer **tribes** like the Iquito, Yaguar, Bora and Witito who initially defended their territory against the early Spanish missionaries and explorers. The townsfolk today, however, are warm and welcoming, wear as little clothing as possible and are out in numbers during the relative cool of the evening.

Brief history

Though founded in 1757 under the name of San Pablo de los Napeanos, the present centre of Iquitos was established in 1864. By the end of the nineteenth century Iquitos was, along with Manaus in Brazil, one of *the* great rubber towns. From that era of grandeur a number of structures survive, but during the last century the town veered

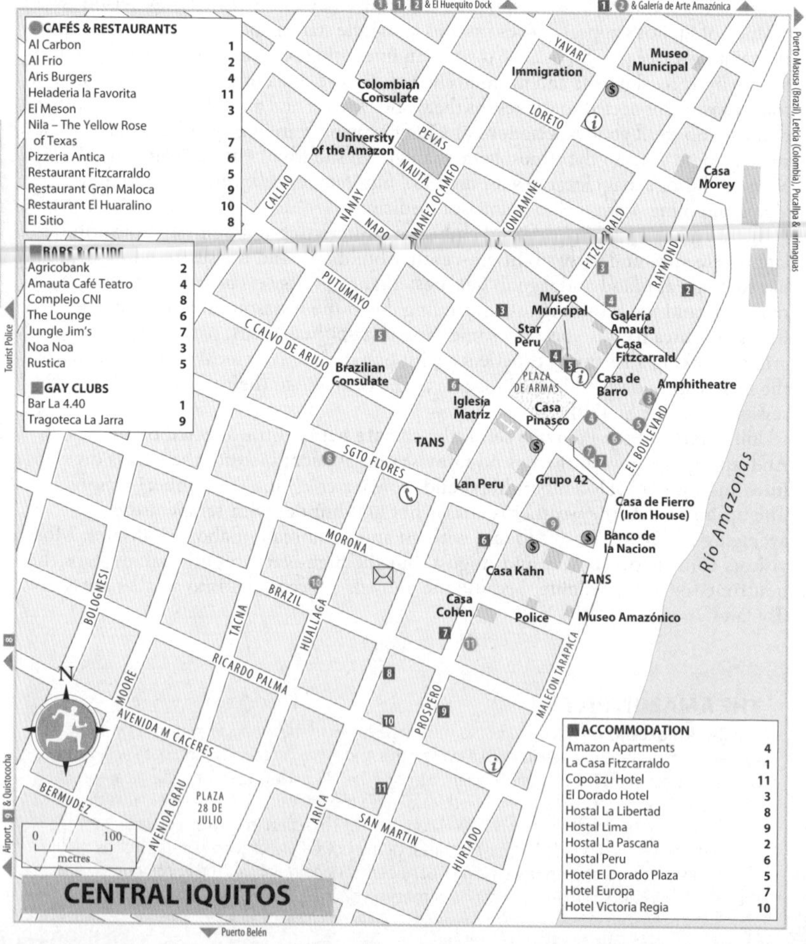

IQUITOS FIESTAS

Iquitos throws some good annual festivals. The carnival known as **Omagua** (local dialect for "lowland swamp") has grown vigorously over recent years and now involves not only townspeople, but hundreds of Indians as well, with plenty of chanting and dancing. The main thrust of activities is on the Friday, Saturday and Sunday before Ash Wednesday, and on Monday the town celebrates with the traditional Umisha dance around a sacred tree selected for the purpose. It's similar to maypole dancing in Britain, though in Iquitos the dancers strike the tree with machetes; when it eventually falls, children dive in to grab their share of the many gifts suspended from it.

Perhaps the best time to visit Iquitos, however, is at the end of June (supposedly June 23–24, but actually spread over three or four days), when the main **Fiesta de San Juan** takes place. The focus is on the small artesanía market of San Juan (the patron saint of Iquitos), some 4km from the city and quite close to the airport. It's the traditional time for partying and for eating *juanes*, delicious little balls of rice and chicken wrapped in jungle leaves; the best place for these is in San Juan itself. June is also the month for **Iquitos Week**: seven days of celebrations around the Fiesta de San Juan, though tending to spread right across the month.

In October the local tourist board organizes an **international rafting competition**, which draws enthusiasts from every continent for a five-hour, nineteen-kilometre river race, plus a longer six-day race. At the end of the month there's the **Espiritos de La Selva** (Spirits of the Jungle) festival, which coincides with Hallowe'en and All Souls, and involves street processions with costumes depicting mythological figures, plus the usual communal drinking and eating.

between prosperity (as far back as 1938, when the area was explored for oil) and the depths of economic depression. However, its strategic position on the Amazon, which makes it accessible to large ocean-going ships from the distant Atlantic, has ensured its continued importance. At present, still buoyed by the export of timber, petroleum, tobacco and Brazil nuts, and dabbling heavily in the trade of wild animals, tropical fish and birds, as well as an insecticide called *barbasco*, long used by natives as a fish poison, Iquitos is in a period of quite wealthy expansion.

Plaza de Armas

The central **Plaza de Armas** is still weirdly dominated by the towering presence of an abandoned and dilapidated high-rise **hotel**, built during the boom of the early 1980s, before the economy slumped and terrorism temporarily slowed tourism in the region. These days, it has little function other than as a foundation for antennas. The plaza's modern **fountain** attracts strolling townsfolk when illuminated at night, though its sound is generally drowned out by the mototaxis and cars whizzing around the square.

On the southwest side of the plaza, the **Iglesia Matriz** (daily 7am–5pm), the main Catholic church, houses paintings by the Loretano (Loreto is the *departamento* Iquitos is located in) artists Américo Pinasco and César Calvo de Araujo, depicting biblical scenes.

Museo Municipal

Plaza de Armas • Mon–Fri 8am–noon & 3–5pm • Free

The **Museo Municipal**, by the tourist office on the plaza, has an interesting, albeit a little half-baked, collection of exhibits featuring *manguare* drums, stuffed animals, information on tree and plant products from the forest, a large preserved *paiche* fish and some animal skulls.

Casa de Fierro

On the southeast corner of the plaza, you'll find the majestic **Casa de Fierro** (Iron House), which was restored just a few years ago and is hard to miss with its silvery sides glinting in the afternoon sunshine. Designed by Gustave Eiffel for the 1889 Paris exhibition and later shipped in pieces to Iquitos and reconstructed here in the 1890s by one of the local rubber barons, these days it's home to a quality restaurant located on the upper storey.

The riverfront

One block southeast of Plaza de Armas are the two best sections of the **old riverfront**, El Boulevard and Malecón Tarapacá, both of which have been recently restored to some of their former glory. **El Boulevard** is the busiest of the two areas, especially at night, full of bars and restaurants and with a small **amphitheatre** with live entertainment most nights, from mini-circuses to mime, comedy and music. The **Malecón Tarapacá** boasts some fine old mansions, one of which, at no. 262, with lovely nineteenth-century *azulejo* work, is now one of the town's better bakeries. On the corner with Putumayo stands the military-occupied building (no photos allowed) that was once the Art Nouveau **Hotel Palace**, no longer open to the public but one of the city's historical icons.

Museo Amazónico

Malecón Tarapacá • Mon–Fri 8am–1pm & 3–7pm, Sat 9am–1pm • S/5, students with ISIC card S/2.5

The municipal museum, **Museo Amazónico**, is devoted to the region's natural history and tribal cultures. Its collection includes some unusual life-sized human figures in traditional dress from different Amazon tribes; each fibreglass sculpture was made from a cast that had encapsulated the live subject for an hour or so. Also on display are some oil paintings, a few stuffed animals and a small military museum.

Casa Cohen

Cnr Próspero and Morona

8

The quaint, one-storey **Casa Cohen** is still a working shop, built in 1905 and beautifully adorned with iron work, colourful *azulejos* (tiles) and *pilastras* (mural-covered pillars) – all reflecting the past days of rubber-boom commerce and glory.

Casa Kahn

Block 1 of Sargento Lores

The **Casa Kahn** is a particularly fine example of the Portuguese tile decoration that adorns many of the late eighteenth- and early nineteenth-century buildings, some of which are brilliantly extravagant in their Moorish inspiration.

Casa Fitzcarrald

Napo 200–212

Once home to the legendary rubber baron of the same name, sadly the **Casa Fitzcarrald** is not open to the public. It was built of adobe and *quincha* (cane or bamboo plastered with mud) and has a central patio with arches, plus ceilings of roughly sawn wood.

Galería de Arte Amazónica

Trujillo 438 • Call for an appointment on ☎ 065 253120 • Free

In the Punchana sector of Iquitos, the **Galería de Arte Amazónica** exhibits the work of the Peruvian painter **Francisco Grippa**, as well as that of other national and local artists. Grippa, who lives and works mainly in Pevas (see p.477), arrived in the Amazon in the late 1970s after being educated in Europe and the US, and his work, described variously as figurative and expressionist, displays an obsession with light and colour, focusing on subjects such as Shipibo Indians, jungle birds and rainforest landscapes.

Galería Amauta

Nauta 248 • Mon–Sat 10am–6pm • Free

There's more art to be found at **Galería Amauta**, where there are exhibitions of oil paintings, caricatures and photographs, mostly by local artists including Francisco Grippa, whose work is large, colourful and almost absract.

CLOCKWISE FROM TOP LEFT CYCLISTS IN CENTRAL IQUITOS; NIGHT OWL MONKEY, RÍO MARANON, NEAR IQUITOS; BANANA MARKET, IQUITOS >

Puerto Belén

The most memorable part of town – best visited around 7am when it's most active – **Puerto Belén** looms out of the main town at a point where the Amazon, until recently, joined the Río Itaya inlet. Consisting almost entirely of **wooden huts** raised on stilts and, until a few years ago, also floating on rafts, the district has earned fame among travellers as the "Venice of the Peruvian Jungle". Actually more Far Eastern than European in appearance, with obvious poverty and little glamour, it has changed little over its hundred or so years, remaining a poor shanty settlement trading in basics like bananas, manioc, fish, turtle and crocodile meat. While filming *Fitzcarraldo* here, Werner Herzog merely had to make sure that no motorized canoes appeared on screen: virtually everything else, including the style of the *barriada* dwellings, looks exactly the way it did during the nineteenth century.

Pasaje Paquito

4–5min in a mototaxi (S/2)

Ask for directions to **Pasaje Paquito**, the busy herbalist alley in the heart of this frenetic community, synthesizing the rich flavour of the place. Here you'll find scores of competing stalls selling an enormous variety of natural jungle medicines, as well as some of the town's cheapest artesanía.

ARRIVAL AND DEPARTURE — IQUITOS

8

BY BOAT

If you've come by boat downstream from Yurimaguas (4–5 days) or Pucallpa (4–6 days) or upstream from Leticia or Tabatinga (3 days or 12hr, depending on type of boat), you'll arrive at Puerto Masusa, some eleven blocks northeast of the Plaza de Armas. Larger riverboats also go upstream from Puerto Masusa to Lagunas (3 days), or downstream to Pevas (about 1 day). Check with the commercial river transporters for a rough idea of departure dates and times. Speedboats go downstream to the three-way frontier (see p.480).

Boat companies The main companies have their offices on Av Raymondi, just a few blocks from the Plaza de Armas: Expreso Loreto, Raymondi 384 (065 238021); Transtur, Raymondi 328 (065 242367); and Transportes Rapido, Raymondi 346 (065 222147). Brastours, Jr Condamine 384 (065 223232), specialize in boats to Tabatinga, Brazil.

BY PLANE

Flights land at Iquitos airport (Aeropuerto Internacional Francisco Secada Vignetta; 065 260147), 6km southwest of town and connected by taxis (S/15) and cheaper mototaxis (S/8). Airline offices are mostly central: LAN Perú, Prospero 232 (next to Banco de Credito; 065 232421); StarPerú, Napo 260 (065 236208); StarPerú, Napo 298 (065 236208); Grupo 42, Prospero 215 (065 221071 or 233224), for reasonably priced flights to Requena, Angamos and Santa Rosa. For flights to Brazil, try Brastours, Jr Condamine 384 (065 223232).

Destinations Lima (several daily; 2hr); Pucallpa (daily; 1–2hr); Tarapoto (1 weekly; 1hr).

BY BUS

The furthest you can go by road from Iquitos is the town of Nauta, on the Río Maranon, close to the confluence with the Ucayali and Amazon rivers and relatively near to the Reserva Nacional Pacaya-Samiria. Several daily buses from Nauta (4hr) pull in on the Plaza de Armas and on C Huallaga and Jr Condamine.

GETTING AROUND

By mototaxi For getting around town you'll probably want to make use of the rattling mototaxis (most rides in town cost S/2–3).

By canoe If you want to get onto the river itself, canoes can be rented from the port at Bellavista (see p.474).

INFORMATION AND TOURS

Tourist information There's a helpful tourist information kiosk at the airport (daily 8am–9pm; 065 260251), and the main i-Peru PROMPERU tourist office is at C Loreto 201, (daily 8.30am–7.30pm; 065 236144, regionloreto.gob.pe). As well as stocking brochures and maps, helping with accommodation and keeping a list of registered tour operators and guides, the office also sells CDs of local music and DVDs of regional attractions. For more in-depth enquiries, the Dirección Regional de Turismo can be found at Av Ricardo Palma 113, 5th floor.

National park information The Reserva Nacional Pacaya-Samiria office is at Ricardo Palma 113, third floor (065 233980, rnps-zrg@aeci.org.pe). It's good for maps, information on the reserve and permission to enter it. SERNANP, the national body for protected areas, is at Jorge Chavez 930 (T 065 614216 or T 065 253555).

Tours City tours of Iquitos are offered by many of the tour companies (see box, p.475) and some hotels (try the *Hostal La Pascana* for tickets); they take about three hours, and usually leave daily at 9am and again at 2pm, costing around S/35.

Useful resources There's an online English-language newspaper for Iquitos (W iquitostimes.com), run by UK expat Mike Collis.

ACCOMMODATION

Like every other jungle town, Iquitos is a little expensive, but the standard of its hotels is very good and the range allows for different budgets. Even a room in an average place will include a shower and fan, and many others offer cable TV. Accommodation located **north of the plaza** offers closer access to the riverboat port and Río Nanay, while the area **south of the plaza** is nearer the main shops and Belén port and market.

NORTH OF PLAZA DE ARMAS

Amazon Apartments Napo 274, on the Plaza de Armas T 065 243088. Somewhere between an apartment building and hotel room, these suites are aimed mostly at the business traveller, although they do offer rooms as well, and there's also a small pool and jacuzzi. S/200

El Dorado Hotel Napo 362 T 065 232574, W grupo-dorado.com. Located less than a block from the Plaza de Armas, this is a reasonably good, if less than spacious, hotel with cable TV, restaurant and a small pool (also available to restaurant patrons). S/500

★ **Hostal La Pascana** Pevas 133 T 065 235581, W pascana.com. Popular *La Pascana* offers a ventilated, quiet haven from Iquitos' sometimes hectic street life, with appealing doubles arranged around a small courtyard close to the river, less than two blocks from the Plaza de Armas. It's clean and friendly, and there's also a book exchange and travel service. Best to book in advance. S/50

★ **Hotel El Dorado Plaza** Napo 258, Plaza de Armas T 065 222555, W eldoradoplazahotel.com. As well as being the first five-star in Iquitos, this is probably the best-quality hotel in the entire Peruvian Amazon. Rooms are large and spacious with excellent showers, a/c, cable TV and large beds, and the superbly cool lobby has a glass lift rising to all six floors. The service is as fine as you'd expect, and *El Dorado* boasts a nice pool, a *maloca*-style bar, a quality restaurant, as well as some fantastic rainforest-inspired paintings by local artist Francisco Grippa (see p.468). S/620

SOUTH OF PLAZA DE ARMAS

La Casa Fitzcarraldo Av La Marina 2153 T 065 601138, W lacasafitzcarraldo.com. Located in a large house on Av La Marina towards the port area of Bellavista, 5min from the Plaza de Armas in a mototaxi, this family-run B&B offers tastefully decorated and spacious accommodation with a naturally cool and very clean swimming pool (S/5 entry for non-residents), plus great food, drinks, lovely orchid-rich gardens and a three-level treehouse with panoramic views. S/280

Copoazu Hotel Prospero 644 T 065 232373, E hotel_copoazu@yahoo.com. A modern hotel with comfortable rooms and a quiet ambience; it also has a fairly central location and good facilities. S/110

Hostal La Libertad Arica 361 T/F 065 235763. A fine backpackers' place; rooms have private bath, hot water and cable TV, plus there's a restaurant and it's also home to a good tour company. S/50

Hostal Lima Prospero 549 T 065 221409. The place doesn't look like much from the outside but is surprisingly pleasant, possessing a certain jungle flavour, with parrots on the patio. Rooms come with private bath and fans. S/60

Hostal Perú Prospero 318 T 065 231531. Rather down-at-heel, though quite popular with Peruvians and travellers alike, perhaps because of its old-fashioned architecture and decor. It has shared bathrooms, fans in all rooms and some have cable TV. S/45

Hotel Europa Prospero 494 T 065 231123, W europahoteliquitos.net. Centrally located and six storeys high, this concrete hotel offers a stylish restaurant and small bar. All rooms have cable TV, a/c, minibar and private bath. S/120

★ **Hotel Victoria Regia** Ricardo Palma 252 T 065 231983 or Lima T 01 4424515, W victoriaregiahotel.com. Quite luxurious for Iquitos, the rooms here have been tastefully restored in recent years; there's also a small pool, good security and sterling service. Their award-winning restaurant serves delicious local specialities. S/231

8

EATING AND DRINKING

Food in Iquitos is exceptionally good for a jungle town, specializing in **fish dishes** but catering pretty well to any taste. Unfortunately, many of the **local delicacies** are now in danger of disappearing entirely from the rivers around Iquitos – notably, river turtle, alligator and the tasty *paiche* fish. Eating out is a popular pastime in the energetic evenings, which usually stretch well into the early hours, particularly at weekends. There are some good **bars and pubs** on the Boulevard and the first block of Putumayo, very close to the plaza, is known as "Little England" because of its legion of British- and US-run pubs and restaurants. This is always a busy spot at night and one of Iquitos' liveliest areas for a drink.

Al Carbon Condamina 115 T 065 223292. The most traditional of all restaurants in Iquitos, only open in the evenings and serving mostly meat dishes – try *cechina* (smoked pork) or *tacacho* (mashed bananas fried with bacon) – most of which are largely cooked over charcoals. Excellent salads are available, too. Daily 6pm–10pm.

★ **Al Frío y Al Fuego** Floating on the Río Itaya T 065 262721. This is a new and exceptionally good restaurant – and the only floating one in Iquitos; it serves the best presented and tastiest fish dishes in the city, with main dishes starting at around S/30. Get there on a mototaxi to El Huequito dock (5min) and the restaurant will provide a boat to take you there. Mon 6–9pm, Tues–Sat noon–3pm & 6–9pm, Sun noon–3pm.

★ **Aris Burgers** Prospero 127 T 065 231479. Actually serving more than burgers (though these are quite delicious), including dishes with a variety of river fish and even caiman meat, plus the best French fries in town. It's the most popular meeting spot in Iquitos and a bit of a landmark for taxi and mototaxi drivers. Daily 8am–midnight.

Heladería La Favorita Prospero 413. A roomy café specializing in juices and delicious jungle-fruit-flavoured ice creams. Daily 9am–9pm.

8

El Mesón El Boulevard T 065 231857. A popular restaurant serving a wide range of local dishes – try the *tacacho* (plantains and pork), or *pescado a la Loretano* (fish). It's not cheap though a good meal can be had for well under S/30 and the location is perfect, right at the heart of El Boulevard and with tables out front. Daily noon–11pm.

Nila – The Yellow Rose of Texas Putumayo 180 T 065 241010. *Nila*'s serves tasty local dishes from a reasonably priced menu at a handy location, near the plaza, with tables outside on the street. There's great coffee, friendly service and late hours. Daily 10am–1/2am.

★ **Pizzeria Antica** Napo, between the plaza and the Malecón T 065 241988. This Italian place has an extensive and delicious menu, including good vegetarian options and some dishes incorporating jungle ingredients, such as palm hearts. A large space with ceiling fans and driftwood decor, there's also a nice bar on the second level. Daily 11am–1am.

Restaurant Fitzcarraldo Napo 100 T 065 243434. A great place, close to the nightlife on the corner of the Malecón in the old headquarters of the once-successful Orton Bolivian Rubber Company. It isn't cheap but serves some of the best salads in town, plus good pastas, fish and comida criolla. Daily 10am–midnight.

★ **Restaurant Gran Maloca** Sargento Lores 170 T 065 233126, E maloca@tvs.com.pe. One of Iquitos' finest restaurants, lavishly decorated, with jungle paintings adorning the walls and a high-ceilinged, cool interior. Food is excellent, with some fantastic jungle-fruit-flavoured ice creams. Daily 11.30am–5pm.

Restaurant El Huaralino Huallaga 490 T 065 223300. Some of the best comida criolla in town, with great set-lunch menus; it's so popular with locals that it's often hard to get a table. Large and airy in a fairly central location. Daily 8am–8pm.

El Sitio Block 4 of Sargento Lores. A very creative snack bar/restaurant, inexpensive and with delicious *anticuchos*, *tamales*, *juanes* and fruit juices; best to get there before 9pm, or you'll miss out on the tastiest treats. Daily 10am–11pm.

NIGHTLIFE

While mainly an extension of eating out and meeting friends in the main streets, the **nightlife** in Iquitos is vibrant, and there are a number of discos, clubs and bars worth knowing about. They're quite easy to locate, especially if you are up and about after 11pm when things generally get going in the downtown areas, particularly around the Plaza de Armas and nearby Malecón Tarapacá. Iquitos has an unusually active **gay scene** for a Peruvian jungle town, and there are now a handful of dedicated gay clubs.

BARS AND CLUBS

Agricobank Pablo Rosel 300 T 065 236113. A smaller version of *Complejo CNI* and perhaps less vibrant, this is nonetheless a great and much more centrally located place to enjoy the local live music scene. S/3 entrance. Fri & Sat 10pm–late.

Amauta Café Teatro Nauta 250 T 065 233109. Different music – from jazzy jungle creole to folklore to romantic ballads – programmed from day to day, and there are tables outside and snacks available. Mon–Sat 10pm–2am.

★ **Complejo CNI** Mariscal Cáceres, block 13. More of a covered outdoor arena, this gives a flavour of what the Iquitos youth get up to at weekends, with over a thousand people dancing all night to mostly live salsa, *chicha* and *cumbia* bands, but with significant Brazilian influence creeping in. Take a mototaxi (S/3) or taxi (S/5). Thurs–Sat 8pm–3am.

Jungle Jim's Putumayo 168 T 065 235294. If you're still in the mood for alligator after your jungle trip, this is the place to get it. The newest English pub in town, *Jungle Jim's* serves a superb range of drinks as well as great regional cuisine. There are tables inside as well as on the street, and the place stays open as late as customers want. Daily 10am–1am.

★ **The Lounge** Putumayo 341. A very popular Australian-run lounge bar with great cocktails and up-to-the-minute rock, dance and trance sounds; some good inexpensive food too, including curries. Daily 10am–10pm.

Noa Noa Fitzcarrald 298 T 065 222993. Easily identified

after 11.30pm by the huge number of flashy motorbikes lined up outside, this is Iquitos's liveliest club, attracting young and old, gringo and *Iquiteño* alike. It has three bars and plays lots of Latino music, including the latest *technocumbia*. S/15 entrance. Mon–Sat 10pm–late.

Rústica Putumayo 467. Very central and pretty hectic, *Rústica* is one of the flashiest clubs in Iquitos, spinning good rock and Latin dance music and karaoke most nights, and serving cool drinks at several bars on different levels. There's also good a/c – a definite bonus in Iquitos. Wed–Sat 7pm–4am.

GAY CLUBS

Bar La 4.40 Opposite the Hospital Regional, in Punchana. With good music and a reasonable bar, this friendly place is not exclusively gay. Fri–Sun 8pm–3am.

Tragoteca La Jarra Av Quinones. A small but popular music bar. Thurs–Sun 10pm–late.

SHOPPING

ARTS AND CRAFTS

Artesanías La Jungla Prospero 483. Good for baskets, mats, hammocks, gourds, postcards and souvenirs. Daily 10am–8pm.

Artesanías Sudamerica Casa de Fierro, Plaza de Armas, Prospero 175. Sells hammocks and alpaca goods. Daily 9am–7pm.

Artesanías Todo Perú Prospero 685. A range of hammocks, hats, jewellery, musical instruments and souvenirs. Daily 9am–8pm.

Taller de Arte Prospero 593/595. Carved wooden sculptures and household goods. Daily 9am–7pm.

JUNGLE SUPPLIES

Bazar Daniela 9 de Diciembre 234. Useful trade items for visiting local villages, such as cloth, beads and coloured threads. Daily 9am–7pm.

Comercial Cardinal Prospero 300. Sells fishing tackle, compasses and knives. Daily 9am–6pm.

Mad Mick's Trading Post Putumayo 184b. This shop has been established to provide the basic essentials for a jungle trip, including rubber boots, rainproof ponchos, sunhats, fishing tackle, etc. They rent out rubber boots if you leave a deposit. Daily 9am–9pm.

8

DIRECTORY

Consulates Brazil, Morona 238 (T 065 232081); Colombia, corner of Nauta with Callao (T 094 231461); UK, Putumayo 182 (T 065 222732).

Health The nearest hospital is the Regional de Loreto, Av 28 de Julio, Punchana (T 065 252004). For pharmacies, try Botica Amazónicas, Prospero 699 (T 065 231832), or Botica Virgen de Chapi, Prospero 461.

Immigration Av Mariscal Cáceres, block 18 (T 065 235371). Come here to extend or renew your Peruvian tourist card or visa.

Internet Soho Internet, Putumayo 382, has fast computers and snacks; El Cyber, Arica 122 on the Plaza de Armas, is a large and popular internet facility (no drinks or food).

Laundry LavaCenter, Prospero 459 (T 065 242136); Lavandería Imperial, Putumayo 150; Lavandería Popular, C Loreto 640.

Money and exchange Banco de Credito, Putumayo 201; Banco Wiese, Prospero 282, for MasterCard; Banco de la Nación, block 4 Condamine; Banco Continental, Prospero Block 3, with a 24hr ATM, and also on Sargento Lores, block 1; and the Banco del Trabajo, block 1 of Prospero, has an ATM taking Visa. The only place that's reasonably safe for changing money with *cambistas* on the street is at the corner of Morona with Arica, by the post office (daytime only for safety). Otherwise, use one of the casas de cambio on Sargento Lores, or the banks.

Police Tourist Police, Sargento Lores 834 (T 065 242801); Guardia Nacional, Comisaría, C Morona 120 (T 065 231123).

Post office SERPOST, Arica 402 (Mon–Sat 7am–7.30pm).

Telephones Sargento Flores 321 (daily 7am–11pm); international phone calls at Napo 349, next to the Western Union office.

Around Iquitos

The massive river system around Iquitos offers some of the best access to **Indian villages**, **lodges** and **primary rainforest** in the entire Amazon. For those with ample time and money, the Reserva Nacional Pacaya-Samiria is one of the more distant but rewarding places for eco-safari tours; but there are also towns up and down the river, most notably Pevas, which is en route towards Brazil.

If you want to go it alone, colectivo boats run up and down the **Amazon River** more or less daily, and although you won't get deep into the forest without a **guide**, you can visit some of the larger river settlements on your own.

Hiring a **bike** can be an intriguing way to explore in and around Iquitos, but it's quicker to use **mototaxis**.

Padre Isla

Easily reached by canoe from Belén (30min each way) or the main waterfront in Iquitos

The closest place you can escape to without a guide or long river trip is **Padre Isla**, an island opposite Iquitos in the midst of the Amazon, over 14km long and with beautiful beaches during the dry season.

Bellavista and around

15min by mototaxi (S/3–4) from Plaza de Armas in Iquitos

Some 4km northeast of the centre of Iquitos, the suburb of **Bellavista**, on the Río Nanay, is the main access point for smaller boats to all the rivers. There's a small **market** selling jungle products, including local river fish, plus some bars and shops clustered around a port, where you can **rent canoes** for short trips at around S/15 an hour. Like Iquitos, Bellavista has recently been experiencing its highest and lowest recorded water levels, with all of the associated flooding and drying up; the bars sit on their stilts high above dried mud during the dry season, and the boats are moored some forty metres further out than they used to be.

From Bellavista you can set out by canoe ferry for **Playa Nanay**, the best beach around Iquitos, where **bars and cafés** are springing up to cater to the weekend crowds. Be aware that **currents** here are pretty strong, and although there are lifeguards, drownings have occurred.

EXPLORING THE JUNGLE AROUND IQUITOS

ORGANIZED TOURS

Short tours in the area (which can be arranged with most of the main hotels or lodge operators) include a boat trip that sets out from Bellavista and travels up the Río Momón to visit a community of **Yaguar or Bora Indians** at San Andrés, just beyond *Amazon Camp* (see p.478), then goes downriver to **Serpentario Las Boas**, an anaconda farm near the mouth of the Momón. Here you can see and touch anacondas and more (boas, sloths and monkeys, to name a few), slithering around in what is essentially someone's backyard. The whole trip lasts around 2hr and costs about $10 per person. A longer tour, lasting around 4hr and costing $15–20, includes the above but also takes you onto the Amazon River to visit an **alligator farm** at Barrio Florida and to watch dolphins playing in the river.

For **longer tours** beyond the limited network of roads around Iquitos, you'll have to take an organized trip with a lodge operator, a river cruise or hire a freelance guide. As a general rule of thumb, any expedition of **fewer than five days** is unlikely to offer more **wildlife** than a few birds, some monkeys and maybe a crocodile if you're lucky; any serious attempt to visit virgin forest and see wildlife in its natural habitat requires **a week or more**. The larger local entrepreneurs have quite a grip on the market, and even the few guides who remain more or less independent are hard to bargain with since so much of their work comes through the larger agents. That said, they mostly have well worked-out itineraries. Always deal with an established company or agent – check out which outfits are registered at the tourist office in Iquitos (see p.470) – and insist on a written contract and receipt. Be aware that there's no shortage of **con artists** among the many touts in Iquitos, some of whom brandish quality brochures which belong to companies they are not actually affiliated with. Under no circumstances should you hand money over until you are 100 percent certain of who you are dealing with. 8

If your jungle trip doesn't match what the agency led you to believe when selling you the tickets, it would help future visitors if you report this to the local tourist office and/or the 24-hour hotline of the **Tourist Protection Service** in Iquitos (T 065 233409, E postmaster@indecopi.gob.pe). Commercial tour operators with **riverboats** and services in the Iquitos area are listed below.

Amazon Explorama – Amazon Queen Ferryboat Av La Marina 340, Iquitos T 065 252530 or T 065 254428, toll-free in the US T 1 800 707 5275, W explorama.com. This superbly converted ferryboat now takes up to 180 passengers, mainly connecting Iquitos with Explorama's busiest lodge, *Ceiba Tops* (see p.478), and sometimes travelling down the Amazon and up the Río Napo. It arrives at *Ceiba Tops* in about 1hr 30min, while a large, comfortable lounge, card deck and carpeted bar on the second deck makes for a comfortable journey.

Amazon Tours and Cruises with Green Tracks W greentracks.com, W amazontours.net. Offers Amazon wildlife riverboat adventure cruises to the Reserva Nacional Pacaya-Samiria and other destinations.

Delfin Amazon Cruises Iquitos T 065 262721, Lima T 01 7190998, W delfinamazoncruises.com. With several extremely luxurious riverboats of varying sizes, possibly the fanciest on the Amazon, *Delfin* offer a variety of packages (mainly 3–6 nights visiting the Río Ucayali and Río Marañón). They also go to the Reserva Nacional Pacaya-Samiria.

INDEPENDENT TRAVEL

If Iquitos is your main contact with the Amazon and you're unlikely to return, you could **rent a boat** for an overnight trip from upwards of $60–70 per person. A group in low season may well be able to negotiate a three-day trip for as little as $40 per person per day, though there will be little guarantee of quality at this price. One or two of the smaller operators sometimes offer deals from as little as $30, but make sure they provide all the facilities you require.

There's an almost infinite amount of jungle to be rewardingly explored in any direction from Iquitos, and one of the less-visited but nevertheless interesting areas lies **east between Iquitos and the Brazilian border**. It's difficult to access this region without the help of a local guide and/or tour company; public boats plying this stretch of the Amazon River rarely stop and certainly don't allow any time for passengers to explore. But if you do want to stop off and spend some time here, **Pevas** (see p.477) is a possible base for making river trips more or less independently, at least without going through an Iquitos tour company, though it's always a good idea to make use of local guides.

Amazon Animal Orphanage and Pilpintuwasi Butterfly Farm

Near the village of Padre Cocha • Tues–Sun 9am–4pm • S/15, S/10 for students with ISIC card • 065 232665, amazonanimalorphanage.org • 20min by boat from Bellavista, involving a 15min walk from the beach village in the dry season, but accessible the entire way when the river is high

At the fascinating **Amazon Animal Orphanage and Pilpintuwasi Butterfly Farm** you can see a fantastic array of butterflies in a natural environment, plus a number of jungle animals, all rescued from certain death.

Quistococha

S/5 entry • Microbuses go to the lagoon at Quistococha (20–30min) from the corner of Bermudez and Moore, near Plaza 28 de Julio in Iquitos (around S/6)

A kilometre long and up to 8m deep, the waters of the **Quistococha lagoon** have been taken over by the Ministry of Fishing for the breeding of giant *paiche*. There's also a **zoo** of sorts with a small selection of forest birds, a few mammals and some snakes, plus an aviary, with a small **museum** of jungle natural history, as well as a small lakeside **beach**, restaurant and bar.

Moronacocha to Santa Clara

Take a mototaxi from Iquitos to Moronacocha (15min) or to Santa Clara (15–20min; S8–10)

On the western edge of Iquitos, a tributary of the Río Nanay forms a long lake called **Moronacocha**, a popular resort for swimming and waterskiing; some 5km further out (just before the airport), another lake, **Rumococha**, has facilities on the Río Nanay for fishing and hunting. Beyond this, still on the Río Nanay, but just beyond the airport and easier to access by mototaxi from central Iquitos, is the popular weekend white-sand **beach** of **Santa Clara**.

Santo Tomás and Lago Mapacocha

Well connected by local buses (30min) from Iquitos via Santa Clara

The agricultural and fishing village of **Santo Tomás**, 16km from central Iquitos and 2–3km from Santa Clara on the banks of the Río Nanay, is renowned for its jungle **artesanía**, and has another beach, on the **Lago Mapacocha**, where you can swim and canoe. There's also one really good fish restaurant here, on the riverfront, run by the Chrichigno family, best during the day, before the mosquitoes come out. If you get the chance, visit during **Santo Tomás's fiesta** (September 23–25), a huge party with dancing and *chicha* music.

Reserva Nacional Pacaya-Samiria

$30/5-day pass from SERNANP or the park office In Iquitos (see p.470)

The huge **RESERVA NACIONAL PACAYA-SAMIRIA** comprises around two million hectares of virgin rainforest (about 1.5 percent of the total landmass of Peru) leading up to the confluence between the ríos Marañón and the Huallaga, two of the largest Amazon headwaters and possessing between them the largest protected area of seasonally flooded jungle in the Peruvian Amazon.

Most people visit the Pacaya-Samiria for half a day as part of a tour package from Iquitos, but **Lagunas** is a good place to find a local guide and do a relatively indepenent safari, if you can afford it (expect to pay at least $75 a day without lodge accommodation). If you visit the park independently, allow a week or two for travel, and unavoidable hitches and delays en route. You will still need a local guide and a boat; the best bet to find these is to scout around the ports of Iquitos, Nauta or Lagunas. The reserve office in Iquitos (see p.470) provides maps and information on the region. You should come well prepared with mosquito nets, hammocks, insect repellent, and all the necessary food and medicines.

The reserve is a swampland during the **rainy season** (Dec–March), when the streams and rivers rise, and the rainforest becomes comparable to the Reserva Nacional Tambopata in southeastern Peru or the Pantanal swamps of southwestern

INDIGENOUS COMMUNITIES AROUND IQUITOS

With all organized visits to **Indian villages** in this area, you can expect the inhabitants to put on a quick show, with a few traditional dances and some singing, before they try to sell you their handicraft (sometimes overenthusiastically). Prices range from S/5 to S/35 for necklaces, feathered items (mostly illegal to take out of the country), bark-cloth drawings, string bags (often excellent value) and blowguns; most people buy something, since the Indians don't actually charge for the visit.

While the experience may leave you feeling somewhat ambivalent – the men, and particularly the women, only discard Western clothes for the performances – it's a preferable situation to the times when visits were imposed on communities by unscrupulous tour companies. Visitors are now these Indians' major source of income, and the Bora and Yaguar alike have found a niche within the local tourist industry. Some good independent contacts can help you find or organize the right trip: the Iquitos tourist office (see p.470) has a list of registered freelance **guides** and is usually helpful in providing up-to-date contacts.

Brazil in its astonishing density of visible **wildlife**. It is fine to visit in the dry season, but there are more insects, you'll see less wildlife, and the creeks and lakes are smaller.

This region is home to the **Cocoma tribe** whose main settlement is **Tipishca**, where the native community are now directly involved in ecotourism. They can be hired as guides and will provide rustic accommodation, but can only be contacted by asking on arrival. Visitors should be aware that around 100,000 people, mostly **indigenous communities**, still live in the reserve's forest; they are the local residents and their territory and customs should be respected. These tribal communities are also a source of detailed information on the sustainable management of **river turtles**: in recent years some of the communities have been collaborating on conservation projects.

8

ARRIVAL AND DEPARTURE — RESERVA PACAYA SAMIRIA

By organized tour Like most protected areas, to get the most from visiting the reserve your best bet is to go with a tour company – many of the Iquitos lodges located upriver from the city (see p.478) and most of the riverboat tour companies (see p.475) offer visits.

By bus and boat Take a bus from Iquitos as far as Nauta (2–3hr), which is located on the Río Marañón a little upstream from the confluence with the Río Ucayali, before it turns into the Amazon. From Nauta, it's 2–3 days by boat along the Río Marañón to Lagunas (S/30–80 hammock/shared cabin), a riverine settlement some 12hr downstream from Yurimaguas (see p.394), and accessible from there by colectivo boat (from S/25). Boats travelling between Nauta and Lagunas run along the western edge of the reserve for most of the route.

Pevas

The only way here is by riverboat (larger boats 12–15hr, speedboats 4–5hr), or with an organized tour from Iquitos (see p.475)

Downstream from Iquitos, some 190km to the east, lies attractive, palm-thatched **PEVAS**, the oldest town in the Peruvian Amazon and still a frontier settlement. The economy here is based primarily on fishing (visit the **market** where produce is brought in by boat every day), and dugout **canoes** are the main form of transport, propelled by characteristically ovoid-bladed and beautifully carved paddles, which are often sold as souvenirs, sometimes painted with designs. Artist **Francisco Grippa**, whose work is exhibited at the Amazon Art Gallery in Iquitos (see p.468), lives and has a gallery in Pevas.

The surrounding flood forest is home to hundreds of **caimans** and significant **birdlife**, including several types of parrots, eagles and kingfishers. The area is also good for **butterfly watching**, and November, in particular, is a great time to study orchids and bromeliads in bloom. Pevas is also noted for its **fishing** – piranha being one of the easiest kinds to catch.

WITOTO AND BORA INDIANS

The **Witoto and Bora Indians**, largely concentrated around Pevas, arrived here in the 1930s after being relocated from the Colombian Amazon. They are now virtually in everyday contact with the riverine society of Pevas, producing quality goods for sale to passers-by and yet retaining much of their traditional culture of songs, dances and legends, plus significant ethno-pharmacological practice in rainforest medicine. The nearby Bora village of **Puca Urquillo** is a good example, a large settlement based around a Baptist church and school, whose founders moved here from the Colombian side of the Río Putumayo during the hardships of the rubber era rather than be enslaved. A number of local Indian groups can be visited close to Pevas, including the Bora, the Witoto and the less-known Ocainas. **Costs** are from $60 per person per day, with extra for speedboat transport from Iquitos.

ACCOMMODATION — AROUND IQUITOS

Guided tours require some kind of camp setup or tourist **lodge** facilities. There are two main types of jungle experience available from Iquitos – what Peruvian tour operators describe as "**conventional**" (focusing on lodge stays) and what they describe as "**adventure trips**" (going deeper into the jungle).

Amazon Camp Amazon Tours and Cruises greentracks.com, amazontours.net. A pleasant, conventional lodge on the Río Momón between the Yaguar and Bora villages. This place can be visited in a day-trip, though it's more fun and a better deal if you stay longer. **$120 per person**

Amazon Explorama ACTS Field Station (Amazon Conservatory for Tropical Studies) Explorama, Av La Marina 340, Iquitos 065 252530 or 065 254428, toll-free in the US 1 800 707 5275, explorama.com. An hour's walk from the company's *ExplorNapo Lodge* (see opposite), this establishment owns some 750 hectares of primary forest and was designed for research, though it's available for short visits and is quite comfortable, with separate rooms and shared dining and bathroom facilities. There's a medicinal plant trail with an information booklet, but the really special feature is the well-maintained canopy walkway (the Amazon's longest), whose top most platform is 35m high. Can be visited in conjunction with other Explorama lodges; cost depends on size of group, length of trip and number of lodges visited. **$130 per person**

Amazon Explorama Ceiba Tops Contact Explorama, Av La Marina 340, Iquitos 065 252530 or 065 254428, toll-free in the US 1 800 707 5275, explorama.com. Explorama have over 38 years' experience and over five hundred beds across their various lodges and locations; they aren't cheap, but do offer great quality and their own very well-equipped riverboats. Some 40km from Iquitos, this is the most luxurious lodge in the Iquitos Amazon, with a fantastic jungle swimming pool, and proper bar and dining areas, surrounded by primary forest. Accommodation is in smart conventional bungalows with a/c and flushing toilets, or in simpler bungalow-huts. Phone and internet ($3/10min) available. Can be visited in conjunction with other Explorama lodges; price depends on size of group, length of trip and number of lodges visited. **$120 per person**

Amazon Explorama Lodge Contact Explorama, Av La Marina 340, Iquitos 065 252530 or 065 254428, toll-free in the US 1 800 707 5275, explorama.com. In a 195-hectare reserve 90km from Iquitos, this was Explorama's first lodge. Well equipped, it retains its rustic charm and acts as base camp for long-range programmes. Bora talking drums announce mealtimes in the dining room, and guides often play Peruvian music in the bar during the evenings. Bedrooms (no locks) are simple but attractive, with individual mosquito nets. They can arrange for you to swim with dolphins in the Amazon, plus there are night walks and visits to the nearby Yaguar Indians. Can be visited in conjunction with other Explorama lodges; price depends on size of group, length of trip and number of lodges visited. **$130 per person**

Amazon Rainforest Lodge Putumayo 159, Iquitos 065 233100 or 065 241628; in Lima: Av General Ernesto Montagne 685, 3rd floor, Of. 304, Aurora Miraflores 01 2663388; amazon-lodge.com. Up the Río Momón (1–3hr from Iquitos, depending on water levels), the heart of this large lodge, run by an English expat, is a stunning restaurant and bar with a large viewing-tower above. Accommodation is in 24 very comfortable new bungalows with private bathrooms, internet access, cable TV and hammocks out front for relaxing. It has the largest swimming pool in the Peruvian Amazon, with a 34m waterslide. There are trips to local Indian villages and lakes that include fishing, jungle walks and birdwatching, plus ayahuasca sessions with local healers. 7–17-yr-olds half-price. **$180 per person**

Amazon Refuge Nauta 242, Iquitos 065 965685002, amazonrefuge.com. A great lodge owned in collaboration with the San Juan de Yanayacu community, the *Amazon Refuge* is 1hr 30min by boat from Iquitos up the relatively remote Río Yanayacu. Based in 200 acres of primary rainforest and surrounded by a 2000-acre nature reserve, the lodge's buildings are constructed using naturally felled trees and thatched-palm roofs. Accommodation is in private bungalows, each with modern bathroom facilities. The English-speaking guides are top-rate and, not least because of the lodge's proximity to the park, wildlife and cultural treks into the Reserva Nacional Pacaya-Samiria are a speciality. 4-night wildlife ecotour based here from **$1045 per person**

Blue Morpho Av Guardia Civil 515, Iquitos ☎065 263454, ⓦbluemorphotours.com. *Blue Morpho* have two lodges: one, more of a camp, deep in the jungle on the Río Galvez, a tributary of the Río Aucayacu (accessed from the riverside town of Genaro Herrera); and a newer 180-acre site, much nearer at Km 53 of the Iquitos-to-Nauta road. They offer mid-priced adventure rather than luxury, and demand a minimum of five or six days' commitment; they also work with local shamans in ayahuasca ceremonies. 4-night wildlife ecotour based here from **$800 per person**

Cumaceba Lodge Putumayo 188, Iquitos ☎065 232229, ⓦcumaceba.com. A highly recommended budget option, with a lodge on the Amazon and also a camp on the more distant Río Yarapa. The lodge offers private rustic bungalows with individual bathrooms, as well as the usual communal dining area and hammock lounge, while lighting is by kerosene lamps. They visit local Yaguar villages and organize jungle walks; bird- and dolphin-watching also form part of their programmes. Optional extras include trips to the Reserva Nacional Pacaya-Samiria, water skiing (June–Nov) and ayahuasca sessions. Doubles **$158**

★ **ExplorNapo Lodge** Contact Explorama, Av La Marina 340, Iquitos ☎065 252530 or ☎065 254428, toll-free in the US ☎1 800 707 5275, ⓦexplorama.com. Over 145km from Iquitos, on the Río Sucusari (Orejon for "way in and out"). This lodge controls 3000 hectares of surrounding forest, the ExplorNapo Reserve, and its palm-roofed buildings, hammock areas and dining room/bar are linked by thatch-covered walkways; during full moons you can sometimes hear tropical screech owls and the common potoos. From here there's easy access (less than an hour's walk) to the canopy walkway at *Amazon Explorama ACTS Field Station* (see opposite); and a 2hr walk into the forest there is a jungle camp – *ExplorTambos* – where visitors can have a night out in the middle of the forest. This is in many ways the ultimate jungle experience: a small collection of open-sided *tambo*-style huts, offering a night close to the earth, the elements and the animals. Can be visited in conjunction with other Explorama lodges; price depends on size of group, length of trip and number of lodges visited. Doubles **$130**

Heliconia Amazon River Lodge Ricardo Palma 242, Iquitos ☎065 31959, or contact via the Hotel Victoria Regia (see p.471); ⓦamazonriverexpeditions.com. A pleasant lodge, 80km downriver from Iquitos, with accommodation in twin rooms with private bathrooms. They offer a basic three-day programme and also have their own fancy riverboats. Doubles **$120**

★ **Muyuna** Putumayo 163, Iquitos ☎065 242858, Lima ☎01 445 9441, ⓦmuyuna.com. 120km upriver from Iquitos, up a tributary called Yanayacu, this lodge is

SHAMANS AND AYAHUASCA SESSIONS

Ayahuasca sessions, or psychedelic tourism, have become a booming business in Iquitos. Ayahuasca is a jungle vine (*Banisteriopsis caapi*) that grows in the Western Amazon region and has been used for thousands of years as a "teacher plant", gaining a worldwide reputation for divination, inspiration and healing of physical, emotional and spiritual ailments (see p.507). The vine is generally mixed with other jungle plants to enhance its powers and transform it into a bitter-tasting hallucinogenic brew, usually taken in a public session with a shaman.

The **Temple of the Way of Light** (ⓦtempleofthewayoflight.org), out beyind Iquitos airport, has a good reputation for combining ayahuasca ceremonies with charitable and environmental work. There are also some well-known local ayahuasca guides, including **Francisco Montes** (Sachamama, 18km from Iquitos on the road to Nauta; try asking for him in hotels or the tourist office), who offers very traditional ceremonies with all the comforts of a lodge. Another popular shaman is **Agustín Rivas**, a famous sculptor who has dedicated over thirty years to working with ayahuasca; his sessions are run through *Yushintayta Lodge* on the Río Tamshiyacu, contactable via the *Hostal La Pascana*, Pevas 133 (☎065 231418). In addition, many if not most of the **jungle lodges and camps** around Iquitos regularly organize ayahuasca sessions.

This sacred business is currently not regulated at all and, given the extremely sensitive states of mind achieved by ingesting ayahuasca (which can be much more powerful than LSD), it's important not only to feel comfortable with the scene and setting, but also with the person leading it.

fairly close to the Reserva Nacional Pacaya-Samiria. Accommodation is in attractive cabins, with private mosquito-proofed rooms, en-suite bathrooms and tiled showers. They offer jungle walking, river safari trips in canoes, and other traditional excursions like piranha fishing, searching out giant lily plants and alligator-spotting. Most guides have university backgrounds, and the lodge works hard to distinguish itself from competitors, as protectors of wild animals' right to remain free rather than be kept in captivity. It's a stance that ensures their reputation as one of the greenest eco tour companies in the region. 2 nights from **$1025 per person**

Sinchicuy Lodge Pevas 246, Iquitos 065 231618. Reasonably priced, though a little too near a native village for there to be much wildlife in the immediate vicinity. Nevertheless, this lodge does offer a relatively cheap rural setting, making it an agreeable out-of-town option. Doubles **$75**

Zungarococha Resort Ricardo Palma 242, Iquitos 065 231959. A lodge offering the kind of comfortable rooms and bar associated with good middle-range conventional lodges, yet located only 14km from Iquitos on the Río Nanay. It offers jungle treks, nightwalks and canoe exploration. Doubles **$75**

The three-way frontier

Leaving or entering Peru via the Amazon River inevitably means crossing the **three-way frontier**, nearly 300km from Iquitos. Some boats from Iquitos go all the way to **Leticia (Colombia)** or **Tabatinga (Brazil)**, but many stop at one of the two small Peruvian frontier settlements of **Santa Rosa** or **Isla Islandia**. Generally, the big *lancha* boats pull in at Isla Islandia, opposite Benjamin Constante (which is on the Brazilian side of the frontier and just over the water) while the *rapido* speedboats from Iquitos finish their journeys at Santa Rosa. At Chimbote, a few hours before you get to Santa Rosa and on the right as you head towards the frontier, there's a small police post, the main **customs checkpoint** (*guarda costa*) for river traffic.

8

Leticia, Colombia

Having grown rich on tourism and contraband (mostly cocaine), **LETICIA** has more than a touch of the Wild West about it, but is still relatively safe.

If you do stay at one of the hotels here, be warned that it's a lively town, with *cumbia* and salsa music blasting out all over the place, and establishments remaining open until the wee hours of the morning. It's possible to arrange visits to some native communities from Leticia, and you can buy some of their excellent craftwork – mainly string bags and hammocks – from stores in the town.

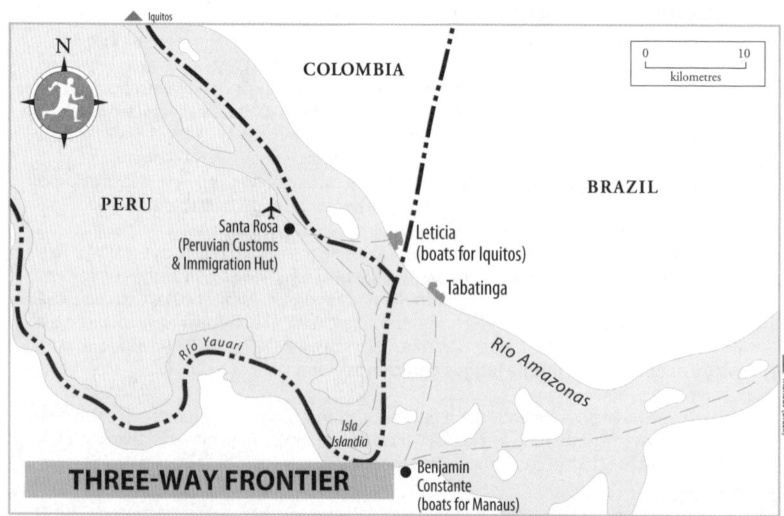

Tabatinga and Manaus, Brazil

Smaller than Leticia, and just a short stroll away, **TABATINGA** is hardly the most exciting place in South America, and many people stuck here waiting for a boat or plane to Manaus or Iquitos prefer to hop over the border to Leticia for the duration of their stay, even if they don't plan on going any further into Colombia. Boats leave from Tabatinga and from **Benjamin Constante**, on the other side of the Amazon, to **Manaus**. Bear in mind that it's virtually impossible to get from Isla Islandia to the federal police in Tabatinga and then back to Benjamin Constante in less than an hour and a half.

CROSSING THE BORDER INTO COLOMBIA AND BRAZIL

BY BOAT

The cheapest and most common route is by river from Iquitos to Isla Islandia, taking 3–4 days going downriver in a standard *lancha* riverboat which will usually have two or three decks, the middle one being for swinging your own hammock (S/50). The alternative journey ends at Santa Rosa (10hr downstream; 12hr going upriver against the current) in a *lancha rapida*, a big speedboat with two outboard motors running several times a week (S/150). Ferryboats connect Santa Rosa with Tabatinga and Leticia; most boats prefer to use Tabatinga, especially in low-water season.

Santa Rosa/Isla Islandia to Leticia (Colombia) There are speedboat ferries from Santa Rosa to Leticia (15–20min) and also from Isla Islandia to Leticia or Tabatinga (30–40min). It's a long, muddy hike from the quay to the surfaced streets of Leticia. If you want to go on into Colombia, the cheapest way is to take a canoe to Puerto Asis, where you can latch on to the bus transport system, but you'll need a tourist card to do this (see below).

Santa Rosa/Isla Islandia to Tabatinga (Brazil) There are two docks at Tabatinga, at both of which, the road goes right to the water's edge. At the smaller of the two, where smaller boats and canoes come and go with local produce and passengers, you'll encounter customs checks; Port Bras, the larger dock, is where you find the big *recreo* boats heading for Manaus.

Iquitos to Manaus (Brazil) If you're coming from Iquitos on a boat that's continuing all the way to Manaus, it's important to let the captain know whether or not you need to go into Tabatinga to quickly sort your visa business (use a taxi) and then meet the boat at Benjamin Constante (see below).

Tabatinga to Manaus (Brazil) Continuing downstream from Tabatinga to Manaus, a 4- to 7-day journey that is often very crowded, costs $80–250 depending on the size and condition of the boat, and whether or not you require a cabin. Pirarucu Turismo, Rúa Santos Dumont 2 (☎ 097 91515936) in Tabatinga, organize trips. Boats leave from Tabatinga in the early afternoon (frequently on Wed, but also less regularly on most other days), calling at Benjamin Constante on the other side of the Amazon an hour or so later. If there are no boats in Tabatinga, however, it may be worth taking a speedboat ferry (30min; $8) to Benjamin Constante to see if there are any departing from there.

BY AIR

The only other way of crossing these three borders is by flying – a much less interesting approach, but not necessarily a more expensive one.

Iquitos to Santa Rosa Flights from Iquitos to Santa Rosa are occasionally operated by Grupo 42 (Próspero 215, Iquitos; ☎ 065 221071 or ☎ 065 233224; in Santa Rosa take a mototaxi to the airstrip to see if there are any flights scheduled).

Tabatinga to Manaus Both Varig (Ⓦ varig.com) and Rico (Ⓦ voerico.com.br) fly to Manaus (2hr) from Tabatinga at least three times a week. Pirarucu Turismo, Rúa Santos Dumont 2, Tabatinga (☎ 097 91515936), can help organize flights from here downriver to Brazil or back up into Peru.

From Leticia (Colombia) From Leticia, Avianca (Ⓦ avianca.com) occasionally operate flights into other parts of Colombia.

CUSTOMS

Entry/exit stamps in Peru Santa Rosa is your last chance to complete formalities with Immigration if you haven't already done so at the Iquitos office (see p.473) – essentially obtaining an exit stamp from Peru, if you're leaving, or getting an entry stamp and tourist card if arriving, which can take up to an hour. On larger boats, you often don't have to disembark here, as the Immigration official may board the vessel and do the paperwork there and then.

Entry/exit stamps in Brazil Brazilian entry and exit formalities are processed at the Policia Federal office, Av da Amizade (☎ 097 34122180; daily 10am–8pm, 24hr for emergencies); if you're entering Brazil you'll usually be asked to show an exit ticket or prove that you have $500 in cash.

Customs checks in Colombia There's no physical border at the port or between Leticia and Tabatinga, though disembarking passengers sometimes have to go through a customs check, so carry your passport at all times. If you want to stay overnight or go on into Colombia via Puerto Asis, from where you can catch buses to the interior of Colombia, you'll need to get a Colombian tourist card from the DAS office (Departamento Administrativo de Seguridad, C 9, 9–62 ☎ 098 5927189 or ☎ 098 5924878; 24hr), just a few blocks from the port.

PIPE PLAYER, SACRED VALLEY

Contexts

History

The first Peruvians were descendants of the nomadic tribes who crossed into the Americas during the last Ice Age (40,000–15,000 BC), when a combination of ice packs and low sea levels exposed a neck of solid "land" that spanned what's now the Bering Strait. Following herds of game animals from Siberia into what must have been a relative paradise of fertile coast, wild forest, mountain and savanna, successive generations continued south through Central America. Some made their way down along the Andes, into the Amazon, and out onto the more fertile areas of the Peruvian and Ecuadorian coast, while others found their niches en route.

In a number of tribes there seem to be cultural memories of these long migrations, encapsulated in their traditional mythologies. There is archeological evidence of human occupation in Peru dating back to around 15,000–20,000 BC, concentrated in the **Ayacucho Valley** where these early Peruvians lived in caves or out in the open. Around 12,000 BC, slightly to the north in the **Chillon Valley** (just above modern Lima), comes the first evidence of significant craft skills – stone blades and knives for hunting. At this time there were probably similar groups of hunter tribes in the mountains and jungle too, but the climatic conditions of these zones make it unlikely that any significant remains will ever be found.

The difficulties of traversing the rugged terrain between the highlands and coast evidently proved little problem for the early Peruvians. From 8000 to 2000 BC, **migratory bands** of hunters and gatherers alternated between camps in the lowlands during the harsh mountain winters, and highland summer "resorts", their actual movements well synchronized with those of wild animal herds. One important mountain encampment from this **Incipient Era** has been discovered at **Lauricocha**, near Huánuco, at an altitude of over 4000m. Here the art of working stone – eventually producing very fine blades and arrow points – seems to have been sophisticated, while at the same time a growing cultural imagination found expression in cave paintings depicting animals, hunting scenes and even dances. Down on the coast at this time other groups were living on the greener *lomas* belts of the desert in places like **Chilca** to the south, and in the mangrove swamps around **Tumbes** to the north.

The emergence of cultism

An awareness of the potential uses of plants began to emerge around **5000 BC** with the **cultivation** of seeds and tubers (the potato being one of the most important "discoveries" later taken to Europe), to be followed over the next two millennia by the introduction, presumably from the Amazon, of gourds, Lima beans, then squashes, peanuts and eventually cotton. Towards the end of this period a climatic shift turned the coast into a

15,000–20,000 BC

The country's earliest archeological evidence of human occupation dates to this period.

12,000 BC

Significant craft skills develop in the Chillon Valley, not far from modern Lima.

8000 BC

A migratory population alternates between lowland camps during harsh mountain winters, and highland summer "resorts".

much more arid belt and forced those living there to try their hand at **agriculture** in the fertile riverbeds, a process to some extent paralleled in the mountains.

With a stable agricultural base, permanent settlements sprang up all along the coast, notably at **Chicama**, **Asia** and **Paracas**, and in the sierra at **Kotosh**. The population began to mushroom, and with it came a new consciousness, perhaps influenced by cultural developments within the Amazon Basin to the east: **cultism** – the burial of the dead in mummy form, the capturing of trophy heads and the building of grand religious structures – made its first appearance. At the same time there were also overwhelming technological advances in the spheres of weaving, tool-making and ornamental design.

The pyramids of Caral

Possibly the most important discovery since Machu Picchu, the **pyramids of Caral** were rediscovered in 1911 – this site represents human achievements that occurred four

THE CHAVÍN CULT

From around 1200 BC to 200 AD – the **Formative Era** – agriculture and village life was established in Peru. Ceramics were invented, and the slow disintegration of regional isolation began. This last factor was due mainly to the widespread dispersal of a religious movement, the **Chavín Cult**. Remarkable in that it seems to have spread without the use of military force, the cult was based on the worship of nature spirits, and an all-powerful **feline creator god**. This widespread feline image rapidly exerted its influence over the northern half of Peru and initiated a period of inter-relations between people in fertile basins in the Andes and some of the coastal valleys. How and where the cult originated is uncertain, though it seems probable that it began in the eastern jungles, possibly spreading to the Andes (and eventually the coast) along the upper Río Marañón. There may well have been a significant movement of people and trade goods between these areas and the rainforest regions, too, as evidenced by the many **jungle-bird feathers** incorporated into capes and headdresses found on the coast. More recent theories, however, suggest that the flow may have been in the opposite direction, starting on the coast. The stone and adobe temples, for instance, in the Sechin area, pre-date the Chavín era, yet seem to be culturally linked.

The Chavín Cult was responsible for excellent progress in **stone carving** and **metallurgy** (copper, gold and silver) and, significantly, a ubiquity of temples and pyramids emerged as religious and cultural centres. The most important known centre was the temple complex at **Chavín de Huantar** (see p.337) in Ancash, though a similar one was built at **Kotosh** (see p.305) near Huánuco; the cult's influence seems to have spread over the northern highlands and coast from Chiclayo down as far as the Paracas Peninsula (where it had a particularly strong impact). There were immense local variations in the expressions of the Chavín Cult: elaborate metallurgy in the far north; adobe buildings on stone platforms in the river valleys; excellent ceramics from Chicama; and the extravagant stone engravings from Chavín itself.

Towards the end of the Chavín phase, an experimental period saw new cultural centres attempting to establish themselves as independent powers with their own distinct cultures. This gave birth to Gallinazo settlements in the Viru Valley; the Paracas culture on the south coast (with its beautiful and highly advanced textile, technology based around a cult of the dead); and the early years of Tiahuanaco development in the Lake Titicaca region. These three cultural upsurges laid the necessary foundations for the flourishing civilizations of the subsequent Classical Era.

5000 BC	**2600 BC**	**1800 BC to 200 AD**
Plants like cotton are domesticated and stable settlements are characteristic.	Radiocarbon dating proves that the ancient pyramids of Caral were fully functioning for around five hundred years from this date.	The Chavín Cult is responsible for progress in stone carving and metallurgy. Temples and pyramids emerge as religious and cultural centres at Chavín de Huantar, Kotosh and Sechin.

thousand years earlier than the Incas appeared. These stone-built ceremonial structures were flourishing a hundred years before the Great Pyramid at Giza was built in Egypt.

Located in the Supe Valley 120km north of Lima, 22km inland from the ocean, radiocarbon dating proves that the site was fully functioning for approximately five hundred years, from around 2600 BC, complete with six stone platform mounds, with **ceremonial plazas** below and irrigation channels serving the surrounding fields. First discovered in 1905, Caral was then largely ignored by archeologists because, though large, no gold or even ceramics had ever been unearthed there. It was, in fact, a pre-ceramic site whose importance resided in another technology, that of the early **domestication of plants**, including cotton, squashes, beans and guava. Some of the best artefacts discovered here, in a ceremonial fire pit by the circular amphitheatre, include 32 flutes made from pelican and animal bones, and engraved with the figures of birds and monkeys, demonstrating a connection with the Amazon region even this long ago.

At its heyday it's thought that at least **three thousand people** were living in Caral. If the other seventeen so far unexcavated sites in the area had held similar-sized populations, then the total population living, working and worshipping in the Supe Valley around 4600 years ago might have been as high as 20,000 or even more. The complex appears to have been abandoned quite rapidly after about five hundred years of booming inhabitance; theories as to why include the possibility of drought, which would have forced them to move to another valley in search of available water and even more fertile soils.

The Classical Era

A diverse period – and one marked by intense development in almost every field – the **Classical Era** (200–1100) saw the emergence of numerous distinct cultures, both on the coast and in the sierra. The best-documented of these cultures, though not necessarily the most powerful, were the **Mochica and Nasca cultures** (see box, p.486) – both probably descendants of the coastal Paracas culture – and the **Tiahuanaco**, all forebears of the better-known Inca. In recent years, though, archeological discoveries in the Lambayeque Valley on the north coast have revealed important ceremonial centres – particularly the massive sacred complex of truncated pyramids at **Batán Grande** originating from the **Sicán culture** (see box, p.402).

In the north, the Valley of the Pyramids, or **Túcume** (see p.404), was a major ceremonial centre, covering more than two hundred hectares. Initially begun by the Sicán culture, who started building here around 1100 after abandoning their earlier centre at Batán Grande, it reached its peak in the thirteenth and early fourteenth centuries, during the power vacuum in the Mochica Valley, between the decline of the Mochica and the rise of the Chimu. Archeologists believe that this must have been a time of abundance and population growth in this desert region, with optimum weather conditions for agriculture, the improvement of irrigation techniques and plentiful seafood.

Intertribal warfare

An increasing prevalence of **intertribal warfare** characterized the era's later period, culminating in the erection of defensive forts and a multiplication of ceremonial sites, including over sixty large pyramids in the Lima area. The **Huaca Pucllana** (see p.69) is

200–1100

Classical cultures emerge throughout the land, including the Mochica and Tiahuanaco traditions. The Nasca Lines and Cahuachi complex are developed on the coast.

300

Technological advances in the Viru Valley and Paracas mean every known form of non-machine weaving is used in textiles that still rate among the world's finest.

CLASSICAL CULTURES

THE MOHICA CULTURE

The **Mochica culture** has left the fullest evidence of its social and domestic life, all aspects of which, including its work and religion, are vividly represented in highly realistic pottery. The peak of their influence came around 500 to 600 AD, when they had cultural and military control of the coast from Piura in the north to the Nepena Valley in the south. The first real urban culture in Peru, its members maintained a firm hierarchy, an elite group combining both secular and sacred power. Ordinary people cultivated land around clusters of dwelling sites, dominated by sacred pyramids – man-made *huacas* dedicated to the gods. The key to the elite's position was probably their organization of large **irrigation projects**, essential to the survival of relatively large population centres in the arid desert of the north coast. In the Mochica region, nature and the world of the ancestors seem the dominant cultural elements; occasional human sacrifices were offered and trophy heads were captured in battle.

THE NASCA CULTURE

More or less contemporaneous with the Mochica, the **Nasca culture** bloomed for several hundred years on the south coast. The Nasca are thought to be responsible for the astonishing lines and drawings etched into the Pampa de San José, though little is known for certain about their society or general way of life. The Nasca did, however, build an impressive temple complex in the desert at **Cahuachi**, and their burial sites have turned up thousands of beautiful ceramics whose abstract designs can be compared only to the quality and content of earlier Paracas textiles.

THE SICÁN CULTURE

Contemporaneous with the Mochica, to the south, there is also strong evidence that the **Sicán culture** revered the same demonic spirit or god, named **Ai-Apaec** in the Mochica language (the "Winged Decapitator"), who kept the world of human life and death in order. Ai-Apaec is also associated with the veritable treasure-trove found in the royal tombs at Sipán, just south of Lambayeque, and those of the **Vicus** culture, to the north, near Piura.

THE TIAHUANUCO CULTURE

Contemporaneous with the other classical cultures, but also pre-dating them, the **Tiahuanaco culture** was named after its sacred centre on the shore of Lake Titicaca. The Tiahuanaco culture, and in particular its central site of pilgrimage, was evidently active between 300 BC and 300 AD and then lasted for another 600 years. The last 500 years coincided with the classical Mochica period – with which, initially at least, it peacefully coexisted. Tiahuanaco textiles and pottery spread along the desert, modifying both Mochica and Nasca styles and bending them into more sophisticated shapes and abstract patterns. The main emphasis in Tiahuanaco pottery and stonework was on symbolic elements featuring condors, pumas and snakes – more than likely the culture's main **gods**, representing their respective spheres of the sky, earth and underworld. In this there seem obvious echoes of the deified natural phenomena of the earlier Chavín cult.

one of these pyramids, a vast pre-Inca adobe mound that can be visited in the suburb of Miraflores, in Lima. It has a hollow core running through its cross section and is thought to have been constructed in the shape of an enormous frog, a symbol of the rain god, who spoke to priests through a tube connected to the cavern.

1200

The Inca Empire is founded by the mysterious Manco Capac. An age of great city building begins.

1438–1532

Expansion of the Inca Empire from Cusco, north into Ecuador and south into Chile. Inca Highway constructed from Colombia to Chile, parts of which are still in existence.

1513

The Spaniard Francisco Pizarro stumbles upon and names the Pacific Ocean while on an exploratory expedition in Panama.

Although initially peaceable, the **Tiahuanaco** culture is associated in its decadent phase (900–1000 AD) with militarism. This seems most likely due to conflict with neighbouring powerful tribes, like the **Huari** who were based further north. The ruins at Huari cover some eight square kilometres and include high-walled enclosures of field stones laid and plastered with mud and decorated by just a few stone statues, suggesting that the Huari were warlike, or at least needed to defend their town.

The Chimu era

Eventually Huari-Tiahuanaco influence on the coast was uprooted and overturned by the emergence of three youthful mini-empires – the **Chimu**, the **Cuismancu** and the **Chincha**. In the mountains its influence mysteriously disappeared to pave the way for the separate growth of relatively large tribal units such as the **Colla** (around Titicaca), the **Inca** (around Cusco) and the **Chanca** (near Ayacucho).

Partly for defensive reasons, this period of isolated development sparked off a city-building urge which became almost compulsive by the Imperial Period in the thirteenth century. The most spectacular urban complex was **Chan Chan** (see p.367), near modern Trujillo, built by the Chimu on the side of the river opposite earlier Mochica temples. Indicating a much greater sophistication in social control, the internal structure of the culture's clan-based society was reflected in the complex's intricate layout. By now, with a working knowledge of bronze manufacture, the Chimu spread their domain from Chan Chan to Tumbes in the north and Paramonga in the south – dominating nearly half the Peruvian coastline. To the south they were bounded by the **Cuismancu**, less powerful, though capable of building similar citadels (such as Cajamarquilla near Lima) and of comparable attainment in craft industries. Further down the coastline, the **Chincha** – known also as the **Ica culture** – also produced fine monuments and administrative centres in the Chincha and Pisco valleys. The lower rainfall on the southern coast, however, didn't permit the Chincha state – or (to an extent) the Cuismancu – to create urban complexes anything near the size of Chan Chan.

The Incas

With the **Inca Empire** (1200–1532 AD) came the culmination of Peru's city-building phase and the beginnings of a kind of Peruvian unity, as the Incas, although originally a tribe of no more than around 40,000, gradually took over each of the separate coastal empires. One of the last to go – almost bloodlessly, and just sixty years before the Spanish conquest – was the Chimu, who for much of this **Imperial Period** were a powerful rival.

Based in the valleys around Cusco, the Incas were, for the first two centuries of their existence, much like any other of the larger mountain tribes. Fiercely protective of their independence, they maintained a somewhat feudal society, tightly controlled by rigid religious tenets, though often disrupted by inter-tribal conflict. The founder of the dynasty – around 1200 AD – was **Manco Capac**, who passed into Inca mythology as a cultural hero. Historically, however, little is known about Inca developments or achievements until the accession in 1438 AD of Pachacuti, and the onset of their great era of expansion.

1527	**1532**	**1533**
Huayna Capac dies of smallpox; civil war breaks out.	Spanish conquistadors, led by Pizarro, set foot on Peruvian soil for the first time and make their way overland to the Inca town of Cajamarca.	Pizarro brings Atahualpa to trial; the Spanish baptize and then kill him.

Inca expansion

Pachacuti, most innovative of all the Inca emperors, was the first to expand their traditional tribal territory. The beginnings of this expansion were in fact not of his making but the response to a threatened invasion by the powerful, neighbouring Chanca during the reign of his father, **Viracocha**. Viracocha, feeling the odds to be overwhelming, left Cusco in Pachacuti's control, withdrawing to the refuge of Calca along the Río Urubamba. Pachacuti, however, won a legendary victory – Inca chronicles record that the very stones of the battlefield rose up in his defence – and, having vanquished the most powerful force in the region, he shortly took the Inca crown for himself.

Within three decades Pachacuti had consolidated his power over the entire sierra region from Cajamarca to Titicaca, defeating in the process all main imperial rivals except for the Chimu. At the same time the empire's capital at **Cusco** was spectacularly developed, with the evacuation and destruction of all villages within a ten-kilometre radius, a massive programme of agricultural terracing (watched over by a skyline of agro-calendrical towers), and the construction of unrivalled palaces and temples. Shrewdly, Pachacuti turned his forcible evacuation of the Cusco villages to his advantage, relocating the Incas, his allies and ambassadors for the empire, in newly colonized areas. He also extended this practice towards his subjugated allies, conscripting them into the Inca armies while their chiefs remained as hostages and honoured guests at Cusco.

Inca territory expanded north into Ecuador, almost reaching Quito, under the next emperor – **Tupac Yupanqui** – who also took his troops down the coast, overwhelming the Chimu and capturing the holy shrine of Pachacamac. Not surprisingly the coastal cultures influenced the Incas perhaps as much as the Incas influenced them, particularly in the sphere of craft industries. Even compared to Pachacuti, Tupac Yupanqui was nevertheless an outstandingly imaginative and able ruler. During the 22 years of his reign (1471–93) he pushed Inca control southwards as far as the Río Maule in Chile; instigated the first proper census of the empire and set up the decimal-based administrative system; introduced the division of labour and land between the state, the gods and the local *ayllus*; invented the concept of "chosen women", or *mamaconas* (see p.504); inaugurated a new class of respected individuals (the *yanaconas*). An empire had been unified not just physically but also administratively and ideologically.

Huayna Capac and civil war

At the end of the fifteenth century the Inca Empire was thriving, as vital as any civilization before or since. Its politico-religious authority was finely tuned, extracting what it needed from its millions of subjects and giving what was necessary to maintain the status quo – be it brute force, protection or food. The only obvious problem inherent in the Inca system of unification and domination was one of over-extension. When **Huayna Capac** continued Tupac Yupanqui's expansion to the north he created a new Inca city at **Quito**, one which he personally preferred to Cusco and which laid the seed for a division of loyalties within Inca society. At this point in history, the Inca Empire was probably the largest in the world, even though it had neither horses nor wheel technology. The empire was over 5500km long, stretching from southern Colombia right down to northern Chile, with Inca highways covering distances of around 30,000km in all.

1535

Foundation of Lima – its colonial architecture draws heavily on Spanish influences, though native craftsmen also leave their mark.

1541

Pizarro is assassinated by displeased conquistadors; for the next seven years the country is rent by civil war.

1569

Francisco Toledo arrives in Peru as viceroy with a view to reforming the colonial system.

Almost as a natural progression from over-extending the empire in this way, divisions in Inca society came to a head even before Huayna Capac's death. Ruling the empire from Quito, along with his favourite son **Atahualpa**, Huayna Capac installed another son, **Huascar**, at Cusco. In the last year of his life he tried to formalize the division – ensuring an inheritance at Quito for Atahualpa – but this was fiercely resisted by Huascar, legitimate heir to the title of Lord Inca and the empire, and by many of the influential Cusco priests and nobles. In 1527, when Huayna Capac died of "the white man's disease", smallpox, which had swept down overland from Mexico in the previous seven years, killing over thirty percent of the indigenous population, civil war broke out. Atahualpa, backed by his father's army, was by far the stronger and immediately won a major victory at the Río Bamba – a battle that, it was said, left the plain littered with human bones for over a hundred years. A still bloodier battle, however, took place along the Río Apurimac at Cotabamba in 1532. This was the

THE INCA EMPERORS

Manco Capac (c.1200 AD) Legendary founder of the Incas and cultural hero, we have little actual information on him or his life.

Sinchi Roca (1230–60) His name means Magnificent Warrior; nevertheless, he was unable to expand the Inca territorial base.

Lloque Yupanqui (1260–90) This Inca failed to expand the Inca empire and also worsened relations with some of the neighbouring tribes.

Mayta Capac (1290–1320) Inheriting the imperial throne at a tender age, his uncle took command until he matured.

Capac Yupanqui (1320–50) Considered a Machiavellian Inca, since, as the son of Mayta Capac's sister, he was not in direct line to inherit the throne, but nevertheless took it by force.

Inca Roca (1350–80) The first to actually bear the title "Inca". Some of his palace still exists beside the modern Plaza de Armas in Cusco.

Yahuar Huaca (1380–1400) His claim to fame was crying tears of blood after being captured by a neighbouring tribe when he was 8 years old; he managed to escape but did little building in Cusco and was ultimately assassinated.

Viracocha Inca (1400–38) He took the sacred name of the Creator God Viracocha after having a dream. He had to escape Cusco when it was taken over briefly by the rival Chancas tribe from the Abancay region, and died in isolation.

Pachacuti (1438–71) Also called Pachacutec, he was the Inca who really created the empire; he expanded its territorial base from the Cusco Valley, began its true megalithic architectural heritage, and developed the social order required to take over and run other parts of Peru and beyond.

Tupac Yupanqui (1471–93) Pachacuti's son, he was responsible for extending the empire north into Ecuador and took over the Chimu dynasty on Peru's north coast.

Huayna Capac (1493–1525) Much of his reign focused on maintaining the northern end of the empire; in fact, he was in Quito when he first heard of strange sightings of white men in boats off the Peruvian shores. He died of smallpox before naming a successor.

Huascar (1525–32) Huascar was appointed Inca Emperor, but there were many other pretenders, including Atahualpa, who defeated him in battle just before Pizarro landed (see p.490).

Atahualpa (1532–33) The shortest reign of any Inca was terminated by the conquistadors in Cajamarca (see p.372).

1572

After fierce fighting and a near escape, Tupac Amaru is captured, brought to trial in Cusco and subsequently beheaded – an act by Toledo that was disavowed by the Spanish Crown.

1742

Juan Santos Atahualpa, a *mestizo* from Cusco who had travelled the world as a young man, rouses groups of forest Indians to rebellion.

decisive victory for Atahualpa, and with his army he retired to relax at the hot baths near Cajamarca. Here, informed of a strange-looking, alien band, successors of the bearded adventurers whose presence had been noted during the reign of Huayna Capac, he waited with his followers.

Francisco Pizarro arrives

Francisco Pizarro, along with two dozen soldiers, stumbled upon and named the Pacific Ocean in 1513 while on an exploratory expedition in Panama. From that moment his determination, fired by native tales of a fabulously rich land to the south, was set. Within eleven years he had found himself financial sponsors and set sail down the Pacific coast with the priest Hernando de Luque and Diego Almagro.

With remarkable determination, having survived several disastrous attempts, the three explorers eventually landed at **Tumbes** in 1532. A few months later a small, Pizarro-led band of Spaniards (less than two hundred men), arrived at the Inca city of **Cajamarca** to meet the leader of what they were rapidly realizing was a mighty empire. En route to Cajamarca, Pizarro had learned of the Inca civil wars and of Atahualpa's recent victory over his brother Huascar. This rift within the empire provided the key to success that Pizarro was looking for.

Pizarro seizes control

The day after their arrival, in what at first appeared to be a lunatic endeavour, Pizarro and his men massacred thousands of **Inca warriors** and captured Atahualpa. Although ridiculously outnumbered, the Spaniards had the advantages of surprise, steel, cannons, and, above all, mounted cavalry. The decisive battle was over in a matter of hours: with Atahualpa prisoner, Pizarro was effectively in control of the Inca Empire. Atahualpa was promised his freedom if he could fill the famous Ransom Room at Cajamarca with **gold**. Caravans overladen with the precious metal arrived from all over the land and within six months the room was filled: a treasure worth over 1.5 million pesos, which was already enough to make each of the conquerors extremely wealthy. Pizarro, however, chose to keep the Inca leader as a hostage in case of Indian revolt, amid growing suspicions that Atahualpa was inciting his generals to attack the Spanish. Atahualpa almost certainly did send messages to his chiefs in Cusco, including orders to execute his brother Huascar who was already in captivity there. Under pressure from his worried captains, Pizarro brought Atahualpa to trial in July 1533, a mockery of justice in which he was given a free choice: to be burned alive as a pagan or strangled as a Christian. They baptized him and then killed him.

With nothing left to keep him in Cajamarca, Pizarro made his way through the Andes to Cusco where he crowned a puppet emperor, **Manco Inca**, of royal Indian blood. After all the practice the Spaniards had in imposing their culture on the Aztecs in Mexico, it took them only a few years to replace the Inca Empire with a working colonial mechanism. Now that the Inca civil wars were over, the natives seemed happy to retire quietly into the hills and get back to the land. However, more than wars, **disease** was responsible for the almost total lack of initial reaction to the new conquerors. The native population of Peru had dropped from some 32 million in 1520 to only five million by 1548 – a decline due mainly to new European ailments such as smallpox, measles, bubonic plague, whooping cough and influenza.

1780

Another *mestizo*, José Gabriel Condorcanqui, leads a rebellion around Cusco – and a massacre of royalist troops – calling himself Tupac Amaru II. Within a year he is executed.

1819

The first rebel invaders – José de San Martén, chief of the army, aided by the Scotsman Lord Cochrane, admiral of the fleet – land at Paracas. Ica, Huánuco and then the north of Peru soon opt for independence, and the royalists retreat into the mountains.

Colonial Peru

Peru's vast wealth, of resources as well as treasure, was recognized early on by the Spanish. Between the sixteenth and seventeenth centuries Spain established only two Viceroyalties in the Americas: first in Mexico, then shortly afterwards in Peru. Queen Isabella indirectly laid the original foundations for the political administration of Peru in 1503 when she authorized the initiation of an **encomienda system**, which meant that successful Spanish conquerors could extract tribute for the Crown and personal service in return for converting the natives to Christianity. They were not, however, given the titles to the land itself. As governor of Peru, Pizarro used the *encomienda* system to grant large groups of Indians to his favourite soldier-companions. In this way, the basic colonial land-tenure structure was created in everything but name. "Personal service" rapidly came to mean subservient serfdom for the native population, many of whom were now expected to raise animals introduced from the Old World (cattle, hens, etc) on behalf of their new overlords.

Colonial city building

Many Inca cities were rebuilt as Spanish towns, although some, like Cusco, retained native masonry for their foundations and even walls. Other Inca sites, like Huánuco Viejo, were abandoned in favour of cities in more hospitable lower altitudes. The Spanish were drawn to the coast for strategic as well as climatic reasons – above all to maintain constant oceanic links with the homeland via Panama. The **foundation of Lima** in 1535 began a multilayered process of satellite dependency that continues even today. The fat of the land (originally gold and other treasures) was sucked in from regions all over Peru, processed in Lima, and sent on from there to Spain. Lima survived on the backs of Peru's municipal capitals which, in turn, extracted tribute from the scattered *encomenderos* (owners of huge tracts of land who were of Spanish descent, originally appointed by the King of Spain). The *encomenderos* depended on local chieftains (*curacas*) to rake in service and goods from even the most remote villages and hamlets. At the lowest level there was little difference between Inca imperial exploitation and the economic network of Spanish colonialism. Where they really varied was that under the Incas the surplus produce circulated among the elite within the country, while the Spaniards sent much of it to a monarch on the other side of the world.

In 1541 Pizarro was assassinated by a disgruntled faction among the conquistadors who looked to **Diego Almagro** as their leader, and for the next seven years the nascent colonial society was rent by civil war. In response, the first **viceroy** – Blasco Nuñez de Vela – was sent from Spain in 1544. His task was to act as royal commissioner and to secure the colony's loyalty to Spain; his fate was to be killed by Gonzalo Pizarro, brother of Francisco. But Royalist forces, now under Pedro de la Gasca, eventually prevailed – Gonzalo was captured and executed, and Crown control firmly re-established.

Colonial society

During the sixteenth and seventeenth centuries, **Peruvian society** was being transformed by the growth of new generations: creoles, descendants of Spaniards born in Peru, and *mestizos*, of mixed Spanish and native blood, created a new class structure. In the coastal valleys where populations had been ravaged by European diseases, slaves

1821

The great liberators – San Martín from the south and Bolívar from the north – enter the capital without a struggle. San Martín proclaims Peruvian independence on July 28.

1824

Spanish resistance to independence is extinguished at the battles of Junín and Ayacucho.

CATHOLIC CULTISM

Despite the evangelistic zeal of the Spanish, religion changed little for the majority of the native population. Although Inca ceremonies, pilgrimages and public rituals were outlawed, their mystical and magical base endured. Each region quickly reverted to the **pre-Inca cults** deep-rooted in their culture and cosmology. Over the centuries the people learned to absorb symbolic elements of the **Catholic faith** into their beliefs and rituals – allowing them, once again, to worship relatively freely. Magic, herbalism and divination have always managed to continue strongly at the village level, and have successfully pervaded modern Peruvian thought, language and practice (the Peruvian World Cup football squad in 1982 enlisted – in vain – the magical aid of a *curandero*). At the elite level, the Spanish continued their fervent attempts to convert the entire population to their own ritualistic religion. They were, however, more successful with the rapidly growing *mestizo* population, who shared the same cultural aspirations.

Miraculous occurrences became a conspicuous feature in the popular Peruvian Catholic Church, the greatest example being **Our Lord of Miracles**, a cult that originated among the black population of colonial Lima. In the devastating earthquake of 1665, an anonymous mural of the Crucifixion on the wall of a chapel in the poorest quarter was supposedly the only structure left standing. The belief that this was a direct sign from God took hold among the local populace, and Our Lord of Miracles remains the most revered image in Peru. Thousands of devotees process through the streets of Lima and other Peruvian towns every October, and even today many women dress in purple throughout the month to honour Our Lord of Miracles.

were imported from Africa. There were over 1500 black slaves in Lima alone by 1554. At the same time, as a result of the civil wars and periodic Indian revolts, over a third of the original conquerors had lost their lives by 1550. Nevertheless, effective power remained in the hands of the independent *encomenderos.*

In an attempt to dilute the influence of the *encomienda* system, the Royalists divided the existing twenty or so municipalities into **corregimientos**, smaller units headed by a *corregidor*, or royal administrator. They were given the power to control the activities of the *encomenderos* and exact tribute for the Crown – soon becoming the vital links in provincial government. The pattern of constant friction between *encomenderos* and *corregidores* was to continue for centuries, with only the priests to act as local mediators.

In return for the salvation of their souls, the native population were expected to surrender their bodies to the Spanish. Some forms of service (*mita*) were simply continuations of Inca tradition – from keeping the streets clean to working in textile mills. But the most feared was a new introduction, the *mita de minas* – **forced work in the mines**. With the discovery of the "mountain of silver" at Potosí (now Bolivia) in 1545, and of mercury deposits at Huancavelica in 1563, it reached new heights. Forced off their smallholdings, few Indians who left to work in the mines ever returned. Indeed, the mercury mines at Huancavelica were so dangerous that the quality of their toxic ore could be measured by the number of weekly deaths. Those who were taken to Potosí had to be chained together to stop them from escaping: if they were injured, their bodies were cut from the shackles by sword to save precious time. Around three million Indians worked in Potosí and Huancavelica alone; some had to walk over 1000km from Cusco to Potosí for the privilege of working themselves to death.

1826	1827	1845
Bolívar remains dictator of the Andean Confederation until 1826.	Within a year of Bolívar's withdrawal Peruvians vote for the liberal General La Mar as president.	Ramón Castilla is the first president to bring any real strength to his office. The country begins to develop on the rising wave of a booming export in guano fertilizer, made of bird droppings.

Francisco Toledo becomes viceroy

In 1569, **Francisco Toledo** arrived in Peru to become viceroy. His aim was to reform the colonial system so as to increase royal revenue while at the same time improving the lot of the native population. Before he could get on with that, however, he had to quash a rapidly developing threat to the colony – the appearance of a **neo-Inca state** (see box below). Toledo's next task was to firmly establish the viceregal position – something that outlasted him by some two centuries. He toured highland Peru seeking ways to improve Crown control, starting with an attempt to curb the excesses of the *encomenderos* and their tax-collecting *curacas* (hereditary native leaders) by implementing a programme of **reducciones** – the physical resettlement of Indians in new towns and villages. Hundreds of thousands of peasants – perhaps millions – were forced to move from remote hamlets into large conglomerations, or *reducciones*, in convenient locations. Priests, or *corregidores*, were placed in charge of them, undercutting the power of the *encomenderos*. Toledo also established a new elected position – the local mayor (or *varayoc*) – in an attempt to displace the *curacas* (local chieftains). The *varayoc*, however, was not necessarily a good colonial tool in that, even more than the *curacas*, his interests were rooted firmly in the *ayllu* (extended family or clan, usually village-based) and in his own neighbours, rather than in the wealth of some distant kingdom.

REBEL INCAS

After an unsuccessful uprising in 1536, **Manco Inca**, Pizarro's puppet emperor, had disappeared with a few thousand loyal subjects into the remote mountainous regions of Vilcabamba, northwest of Cusco. With the full regalia of high priests, virgins of the sun and the golden idol of Punchau (the sun god), he maintained a **rebel Inca state** and built himself impressive new palaces and fortresses between Vitcos and Espíritu Pampa – well beyond the reach of colonial power. Although not a substantial threat to the colony, Manco's forces repeatedly raided nearby settlements and robbed travellers on the roads between Cusco and Lima.

Manco himself died at the hands of a **Spanish outlaw**, a guest at Vilcabamba who hoped to win himself a pardon from the Crown. But the neo-Inca state continued under the leadership of Manco's son, **Sairi Tupac**, who assumed the imperial fringe at the age of ten. Tempted out of Vilcabamba in 1557, Sairi Tupac was offered a palace and a wealthy life by the Spanish in return for giving up his refuge and subversive aims. He died a young man, only three years after turning to Christianity and laying aside his father's cause. Meanwhile **Titu Cusi**, one of Manco's illegitimate sons, declared himself emperor and took control in Vilcabamba.

Eventually, Titu Cusi began to open his doors. First he allowed two Spanish friars to enter his camp, and then, in 1571, negotiations were opened for a return to Cusco when an emissary arrived from Viceroy Toledo. The talks broke down before the year was out and Toledo decided to send an army into Vilcabamba to rout the Incas. They arrived to find that Titu Cusi was already dead and his brother, **Tupac Amaru**, was the new emperor. After fierce fighting and a near escape, Tupac Amaru was captured and brought to trial in Cusco. Accused of plotting to overthrow the Spanish and of inciting his followers to raid towns, Tupac Amaru was **beheaded** as soon as possible – an act by Toledo that was disavowed by the Spanish Crown and which caused much distress in Peru.

1856

A new moderate constitution is approved. Castilla begins his second term of office.

1860

Sugar and cotton are exported from coastal plantations and guano exports are also substantial.

1870s

Construction of the high-altitude rail lines and other engineering projects. First exploitation of Amazonian rubber.

INDIGENOUS REBELLION IN THE EIGHTEENTH CENTURY

When the Habsburg monarchy gave way to the Bourbon kings in Spain at the beginning of the eighteenth century, shivers of protest seemed to reverberate deep in the Peruvian hinterland. There were a number of serious **native rebellions** against colonial rule during the next hundred years. One of the most important, though least known, was that led by **Juan Santos Atahualpa**, a *mestizo* from Cusco. Juan Santos had travelled to Spain, Africa and, some say, to England as a young man in the service of a wealthy Jesuit priest. Returning to Peru in 1740 he was imbued with revolutionary fervour and moved into the high jungle region between Tarma and the Río Ucayali where he roused the forest Indians to rebellion. Throwing out the whites, he established a millenarian cult and, with an Indian army recruited from several tribes, successfully repelled all attacks by the authorities. Although never extending his powers beyond Tarma, he lived a free man until his death in 1756. Twenty years later there were further violent native protests throughout the country against the enforcement of **repartimiento**. Under this new system the peasants were obliged to buy most of their essential goods from the *corregidor*, who, as monopoly supplier, sold poor-quality produce at grossly inflated prices.

In 1780, another *mestizo*, José Gabriel Condorcanqui, led a rebellion, calling himself **Tupac Amaru II**. Whipping up the already inflamed peasant opinion around Cusco into a revolutionary frenzy, he imprisoned a local *corregidor* before going on to massacre a troop of nearly six hundred royalist soldiers. Within a year Tupac Amaru II had been captured and executed but his rebellion had demonstrated both a definite weakness in colonial control and a high degree of popular unrest. Over the next decade several administrative reforms were to alter the situation, at least superficially: the *repartimiento* and the *corregimiento* systems were abolished. In 1784, Charles III appointed a French nobleman – Teodoro de Croix – as the new viceroy to Peru and divided the country into seven *intendencias* containing 52 provinces. This created tighter direct royal control, but also unwittingly provided the pattern for the republican state of federated *departamentos*.

Peruvian independence

The end of the eighteenth century saw profound changes throughout the world. The North American colonies had gained their independence from Britain; France had been rocked by a people's revolution; and liberal ideas were spreading everywhere. Inflammatory newspapers and periodicals began to appear on the streets of Lima, and discontent was expressed at all levels of society. A strong sense of **Peruvian nationalism** emerged in the pages of *Mercurio Peruano* (first printed in the 1790s), a concept that was vital to the coming changes. Even the architecture of Lima had changed in the mid-eighteenth century, as if to welcome the new era. Wide avenues suddenly appeared, public parks were opened, and palatial salons became the focus for the discourse of gentlemen. The philosophy of the Enlightenment was slowly but surely pervading attitudes even in remote Peru.

When, in 1808, Napoleon took control of Spain, the authorities and elites in all the Spanish colonies found themselves in a new and unprecedented position. Was their loyalty to Spain or to its rightful king? And just who was the rightful king now? Initially, there were a few unsuccessful, locally based protests in response both to this ambiguous situation and to the age-old agrarian problem, but it was only with the intervention of outside forces that **independence** was to become a serious concern in Peru. The

1872	1879	1879–83
Peru's first civilian president – Manuel Pardo – assumes power.	Peru cannot pay off its growing foreign debt.	Chile declares war on Bolivia and Peru as a result of arguments about nitrates mined in Bolivia.

American War of Independence, the French Revolution and Napoleon's invasion of Spain all pointed towards the opportunity of throwing off the shackles of colonialism, and by the time Ferdinand returned to the Spanish throne in 1814, royalist troops were struggling to maintain order throughout South America. Venezuela and Argentina had already declared their independence, and in 1817 San Martín liberated Chile by force. It was only a matter of time before one of the great liberators – **San Martín** in the south or **Bolívar** in the north – reached Peru.

San Martín was the first to do so. Having already liberated Argentina and Chile, he contracted an English naval officer, Lord Cochrane, to attack Lima. By September 1819 the first rebel invaders had landed at Paracas. Ica, Huánuco and then the north of Peru soon opted for independence, and the royalists, cut off in Lima, retreated into the mountains. Entering the capital without a struggle, San Martín proclaimed Peruvian **independence** on July 28, 1821.

The Republic

Once Peuvian independence had been declared, San Martín immediately assumed political control of the fledgling nation. With the title "Protector of Peru" he set about devising a workable **constitution** for the new nation – at one point even considering importing European royalty to establish a new monarchy. A libertarian as well as a liberator, San Martín declared freedom for slaves' children, abolished Indian service (*mita*) and even outlawed the term "Indian". But in practice, with royalist troops still controlling large sectors of the sierra, his approach did more to frighten the establishment than it did to help the slaves and peasants whose problems remain, even now, deeply rooted in their social and territorial inheritance.

The development of a relatively stable **political system** took virtually the rest of the nineteenth century, although Spanish resistance to independence was finally extinguished at the battles of Junín and Ayacucho in 1824. By this time, San Martín had given up the power game, handing political control over to **Simón Bolívar**, a man of enormous force with definite tendencies towards megalomania. Between them, Bolívar and his right-hand man, Sucre, divided Peru in half, with Sucre first president of the upper sector, renamed Bolivia. Bolívar himself remained dictator of a vast Andean Confederation – encompassing Colombia, Venezuela, Ecuador, Peru and Bolivia – until 1826. Within a year of his withdrawal, however, the Peruvians had torn up his controversial constitution and voted for the liberal **General La Mar** as president.

Political power games

On La Mar's heels raced a generation of *caudillos*, military men, often *mestizos* of middle-class origins who had achieved recognition (on either side) in the battles for independence. The history of the early republic consists almost entirely of internal disputes between the creole aristocracy and dictatorial *caudillos*. Peru was plunged deep into a period of domestic and foreign plotting and counterplotting, while the economy and some of the nation's finest natural resources withered away.

Generals **Santa Cruz** and **Gamarra** stand out as two of the most ruthless players in this high-stakes power game: overthrowing La Mar in 1829, Santa Cruz became president of Bolivia and Gamarra of Peru. Unable to sit on the sidelines and watch the increasing

1883	**1908**	**1890–1930**
The Treaty of Ancón brings the "War of the Pacific" to a close.	The powerful oligarch Augusto Leguía rises to power and is elected president.	Much modernization in Lima (including the building of the Presidential Palace), and grandiose public buildings are developed elsewhere.

pandemonium of Peruvian politics, Santa Cruz invaded Peru from Bolivia and installed himself as "Protector" in 1837. Very few South Americans were happy with this situation, least of all Gamarra, who joined with other exiles in Chile to plot revenge. After fierce fighting, Gamarra defeated Santa Cruz at Yungay, restored himself as president of Peru for two years, then died in 1841.

Ramón Castilla was the first president to bring any real strength to his office. After he assumed power in 1845 the country began to develop more positively on the rising wave of a booming export in guano fertilizer (made of bird droppings). In 1856, a new moderate constitution was approved and Castilla began his second term of office in an atmosphere of growth and hope – there were rail lines to be built and the Amazon waterways to be opened up. Sugar and cotton became important exports from coastal plantations and guano deposits alone yielded a revenue of $15 million in 1860. Castilla abolished Indian tribute and managed to emancipate slaves without social-economic disruption by buying them from their "owners"; guano income proved useful for this compensation.

His successors fared less happily. **President Balta** (1868–72) oversaw the construction of most of Peru's rail lines, but overspent so freely on these and a variety of other public and engineering works that it left the country on the brink of economic collapse. In the 1872 elections an attempted military coup was spontaneously crushed by a civilian mob, and Peru's first civilian president – the laissez-faire capitalist **Manuel Pardo** – assumed power.

The Peruvian Corporation

Modern Peru is generally considered to have been born in 1895 with the forced resignation of **General Cáceres**, who was twice President of Peru (1886–90 and 1894–95). However, the seeds of industrial development had been laid under his rule, albeit by foreigners. In 1890 an international plan was formulated to bail Peru out of its bankruptcy. The **Peruvian Corporation** was formed in London and assumed the $50 million national debt in return for "control of the national economy". Foreign

THE WAR OF THE PACIFIC

By the late nineteenth century Peru's **foreign debt**, particularly to England, had grown enormously. Even though interest could be paid in guano, there simply wasn't enough. To make matters considerably worse, Peru went to war with Chile in 1879. Lasting over four years, this "**War of the Pacific**" was basically a battle for the rich nitrate deposits located in Bolivian territory. Peru had pressured its ally Bolivia into imposing an export tax on nitrates mined by the Chilean-British Corporation. Chile's answer was to occupy the area and declare war on Peru and Bolivia. Victorious on land and at sea, Chilean forces had occupied Lima by the beginning of 1881 and the Peruvian president had fled to Europe. By 1883 Peru "lay helpless under the boots of its conquerors", and only a diplomatic rescue seemed possible.

The **Treaty of Ancón**, possibly Peru's greatest national humiliation, brought the war to a close in October 1883. Peru was forced to accept the cloistering of an independent Bolivia high up in the Andes, with no land link to the Pacific, and the even harder loss of the nitrate fields to Chile. The country seemed in ruins: with guano supplies virtually exhausted and the nitrates lost to Chile, the nation's coffers were empty and a new generation of *caudillos* prepared to resume the power struggle all over again.

1932

The Trujillo middle-class lead a violent uprising against the sugar barons and working conditions on the plantations.

1940s

Inflation is out of control; during the 1940s the cost of living in Peru rises by 262 percent.

1948

General Odría leads a coup d'état from Arequipa and forms a military junta.

companies took over the rail lines, navigation of Lake Titicaca, vast quantities of guano and were given free use of seven Peruvian ports for 66 years as well as the opportunity to start exploiting the rubber resources of the Amazon Basin. Under Nicolás de Piérola (president 1879–81 and 1895–99), some sort of stability had begun to return by the end of the nineteenth century.

The twentieth century

In the early years of the twentieth century, Peru was run by an **oligarchical clan** of big businessmen and great landowners. Fortunes were made in a wide range of enterprises, exploiting above all, sugar along the coast, minerals from the mountains, and rubber from the jungle. Meanwhile, the lot of the ordinary individual worsened dramatically. The lives of the mountain peasants became more difficult – the jungle Indians lived like slaves on the rubber plantations and the owners of sugar plantations were abusing their wealth and power on the coast. In 1932, the Trujillo middle-class led a **violent uprising** against the sugar barons and the primitive working conditions on the plantations. Suppressed by the army, nearly five thousand lives are thought to have been lost in the uprising.

The rise of the **APRA** – the American Popular Revolutionary Alliance – which had instigated the Trujillo uprising, and the growing popularity of its leader, **Haya de la Torre**, kept the nation occupied during World War II: the unholy alliance between the monied establishment and APRA has been known as the "marriage of convenience" ever since. More radical feeling was aroused in the provinces by **Hugo Blanco**, a charismatic *mestizo* from Cusco who had joined a Trotskyist group – the Workers Revolutionary Party – which was later to merge with the FIR – the Revolutionary Left's Front. In La Convención, within the *departamento* of Cusco, Blanco and his followers created nearly 150 syndicates, whose peasant members began to work their own individual plots while refusing to work for the hacienda owners. The second phase of Blanco's "reform" was to take physical control of the **haciendas**, mostly in areas so isolated that the authorities were powerless to intervene. Blanco was finally arrested in 1963 but the effects of his peasant revolt outlived him: in the future, Peruvian governments were to take agrarian reform far more seriously.

In Lima, the **elections** of 1962 had resulted in an interesting deadlock, with Haya de la Torre getting 33 percent of the votes, Belaunde 32 percent and Odría 28.5 percent. Almost inevitably, the army took control. Belaunde stood again in the 1963 elections and was in power until 1969.

Land reform and the military regime

By the mid-1960s, many intellectuals and government officials saw the agrarian situation as an urgent economic problem as well as a matter of social justice. Even the army believed that **land reform** was a prerequisite for the development of a larger market, without which any genuine industrial development would prove impossible. President Belaunde didn't agree. On October 3, 1968, tanks smashed through the gates into the courtyard of the Presidential Palace. General Velasco and the army seized power, deporting Belaunde and ensuring that Haya de la Torre could not even participate in the forthcoming elections.

1963

Revolutionary Hugo Blanco creates nearly 150 syndicates around Cusco, whose peasant members work their own individual plots.

1963

Organized shanty towns develop around Lima.

1968

On October 3, tanks smash into the Presidential Palace; General Velasco and the army seize power.

The new government, revolutionary for a **military regime**, gave the land back to the workers in 1969. The great plantations were turned virtually overnight into **cooperatives**, in an attempt to create a genuinely self-determining peasant class. At the same time guerrilla leaders were brought to trial, political activity was banned in the universities, indigenous banks were controlled, foreign banks nationalized and diplomatic relations established with East European countries. By the end of military rule, in 1980, the land-reform programme had done much to abolish the large capitalist landholding system.

SENDERO LUMINOSO

Sendero Luminoso (the Shining Path), founded in 1970, persistently discounted the possibility of change through the ballot box. In 1976 it adopted armed struggle as the only means to achieve its "anti-feudal, anti-imperial" revolution in Peru. Following the line of the Chinese Gang of Four, Sendero was led by **Abimael Guzmán** (alias Comrade Gonzalo), whose ideas it claimed to be in the direct lineage of Marx, Lenin and Chairman Mao. Originally a brilliant philosophy lecturer from Ayacucho (specializing in the Kantian theory of space), before his capture by the authorities in the early 1990s Gonzalo lived mainly underground, rarely seen even by Senderistas themselves.

Rejecting Belaunde's style of technological development as imperialist and the United Left as "parliamentary cretins", the group carried out attacks on business interests, local officials, police posts and anything regarded as outside interference with the self-determination of the peasantry. On the whole, members were recruited from the poorest areas of the country and from the **Quechua-speaking population**, coming together only for their paramilitary operations and melting back afterwards into the obscurity of their communities.

Although strategic points in **Lima** were frequently attacked – police stations, petrochemical plants and power lines – Sendero's main centre of activity was in the sierra around **Ayacucho** and **Huanta**, subsequently spreading into the remote regions around the central selva and a little further south in **Vilcabamba** – site of the last Inca resistance, a traditional hideout for rebels, and the centre of Hugo Blanco's activities in the 1960s. By remaining small and unpredictable, Sendero managed to wage its war on the Peruvian establishment with minimum risk of major confrontations with government forces.

Sendero was very active during the late 1980s and early 1990s, when it had some 10,000–15,000 **secret members**. Guzmán's success lay partly with his use of **Inca millennial mythology** and partly in the power vacuum left after the implementation of the agrarian reform and the resulting unrest and instability. The group's power and popular appeal advanced throughout the 1980s; in terms of territorial influence, it had spread its wings over most of central Peru, much of the jungle, and to a certain extent into many of the northern and southern provincial towns.

Much of Sendero's funding came from the **cocaine trade**. Vast quantities of coca leaves are grown and partially processed all along the margins of the Peruvian jungle. Much of this is flown clandestinely into Colombia where the processing is completed and the finished product exported to North America and Europe for consumption. The thousands of peasants who came down from the Andes to make a new life in the tropical forest throughout the 1980s found that **coca** was by far the most lucrative cash crop. The cocaine barons paid peasants more than they could earn elsewhere and at the same time bought protection from Sendero (some say at a rate of up to $10,000 per clandestine plane-load).

1969

The new government gives land back to the workers. Great plantations are turned into cooperatives virtually overnight.

1978

Peru knock Scotland out of the Argentine football World Cup by beating the boys in blue 3 to 1.

The 1970s and 1980s

After twelve years of military government the 1980 elections resulted in a centre-right alliance between Acción Popular and the Popular Christian Party. **Belaunde** resumed the presidency, having become an established celebrity during his years of exile and having built up, too, an impressive array of international contacts. The policy of his government was to increase the pace of development still further, and in particular to emulate Brazilian success in opening up the Amazon – building new roads and exploiting the untold wealth in terms of oil, minerals, timber and agriculture. But **inflation** continued as an apparently insuperable problem, and Belaunde fared little better in coming to terms with either the parliamentary Marxists of the United Left or the escalating guerrilla movement led by Sendero Luminoso (see box opposite).

The 1980s saw the growth of two major attacks on the political and moral backbone of the nation – one through **terrorism**, the other through the growth of the **cocaine industry**.

Belaunde lost the 1985 elections, with APRA (see p.497) taking power for the first time and the United Left also getting a large percentage of the votes. Led by a young, highly popular new president, **Alan García**, the APRA government took office riding a massive wave of hope. Sendero Luminoso, however, continued to step up its tactics of anti-democratic terrorism, and the isolation of Lima and the coast from much of the sierra and jungle regions became a very real threat. By 1985, new urban-based terrorist groups like the **Movimiento Revolucionario Tupac Amaru** (**MRTA**) began to make their presence felt in the shantytowns around Lima. The **MRTA** had less success than the Senderistas, losing several of their leaders to Lima's prison cells. Their military confidence and capacity were also devastated when a contingent of some 62 MRTA militants was caught in an army ambush in April 1988; only eight survived from among two truckloads. To make things worse, a right-wing death squad – the **Rodrigo Franco Commando** (**RFC**) – appeared on the scene in 1988, evidently made up of disaffected police officers, army personnel and even one or two Apristas (APRA members). Meanwhile, the once young and popular President García got himself into a financial mess and went into exile, having been accused by the Peruvian judiciary of high-level corruption and possibly even "misplacing" millions of dollars belonging to the people of Peru.

The 1990s

The year **1990** proved to be a turning point for Peru with the surprise electoral victory by an entirely new party – Cambio 90 (Change 90), formed only months before the election – led by a young college professor of Japanese descent, **Alberto Fujimori**. Fujimori implemented an economic shock strategy and the price of many basics such as flour and fuel trebled overnight. Fujimori did, however, manage to turn the nation around and gain an international confidence in Peru, reflected in the country's stock exchange – one of the fastest-growing and most active in the Americas.

However, the real turning point of the decade was the capture of Sendero's leader **Abimael Guzmán** in September 1992. Captured at his Lima hideout (a dance school) by General Vidal's secret anti-terrorist police, DINCOTE, even Fujimori didn't know about the raid until it had been successfully completed. With Guzmán in jail, and presented very publicly on TV as a defeated man, the political tide shifted. The

1980

After twelve years of military government, elections result in a centre-right alliance between Acción Popular and the Popular Christian Party. Abimael Guzmán launches the revolutionary wing of Peru's communist party – the Shining Path.

1982

Peru play in the World Cup finals in Spain, but despite having a normally exciting side, they play as if they have lead boots.

THE JAPANESE EMBASSY HOSTAGE CRISIS

The mid-1990s was also the time when the **MRTA** terrorists battled with Fujimori and his government. On December 17, 1996, the MRTA really hit the headlines when they infiltrated the **Japanese Ambassador's residence**, which they held under siege for 126 days, with over three hundred hostages. Some of these were released after negotiation, but Fujimori refused to give in to MRTA demands for the freedom of hundreds of their jailed comrades. Peruvian forces stormed the building in March 1997 as the terrorists were playing football inside the residence, massacring them all, with only one hostage perishing in the skirmish. Fujimori's reputation as a hard man and a successful leader shot to new heights.

international press no longer described Peru as a country where terrorists looked poised to take over, and Fujimori went from strength to strength, while Sendero's activities were reduced to little more than the occasional car bomb in Lima as they were hounded by the military in their remote hideouts along the eastern edges of the Peruvian Andes. A massive boost to Fujimori's popularity, in the elections of 1995 he gained over sixty percent of the vote. Perhaps it was also a recognition that his strong policies had paid off as far as the economy was concerned – inflation dipped from a record rate of 2777 percent in 1989 to 10 percent in 1996.

Fujimori continued to grow in popularity, despite Peru going to **war with Ecuador** briefly in January 1995, May 1997, and more seriously in 1998. The Ecuadorian army, which was accused of starting the fighting, imposed significant losses on the Peruvian forces. This dispute was inflamed by the presence of large **oilfields** in the region, currently on what the Peruvians claim is their side of the border, a claim the Ecuadorians bitterly dispute: Ecuadorian maps continue to show the border much further south than Peruvian maps. The two countries signed a formal peace treaty in 1998, although the dispute remains fresh in most people's minds.

The twenty-first century

The run-up to the **elections** of April 9, 2000, was marked by Fujimori's controversial decision to stand for a **third term** of office, despite constitutional term limits. He reasoned that the constitution was introduced during his second term, thus he was entitled to stand for one more. Even with his firm control of the media (especially TV), he encountered strong opposition in the person of **Alejandro Toledo**, a *serrano* (of mountain Indian blood) Perú Posible candidate representing the interests of Andean cities and communities. Toledo had worked his way up from humble beginnings to become a UN and World Bank economist before standing for president; such was the worry over his popularity that a smear campaign surfaced a few weeks before the voting, accusing him of shunning an illegitimate daughter and organizing a disastrous financial pyramid scheme in the early 1990s.

Fujimori polled 49.87 percent of the vote, missing outright victory by just 14,000 votes; Toledo followed behind with just over 40 percent. There were unproven allegations of **fraud** and **vote rigging**, and Toledo eventually withdrew from the contest. However, Fujimori was forced to resign in November 2000 following revelations that his head of intelligence, **Vladimiro Montesinos**, had been videotaped bribing politicians

1990

Fujimori gains a surprise victory over Mario Vargas LLosa in the presidential elections.

1990s

Fujimori improves roads and takes a firm hand with the terrorist groups Sendero Luminoso and MRTA.

1992

After twelve very bloody years Sendero's leader Abimael Guzmán is captured watching TV in his pyjamas, in a Lima hide-out.

before the last election and had also secreted away hundreds of millions of dollars (believed to be drug money) into Swiss and other bank accounts around the world. It quickly became clear that Montesinos had exerted almost complete control of the president, the army, the intelligence service and the cocaine mafia during the preceding few years. Soon after, Fujimori fled to Japan.

New elections were held in April 2001, which **Toledo** won easily, inheriting a cynical populace and a troubled domestic situation, with slow economic growth and deteriorating social conditions. His term of office, which ended in November 2006, was certainly a rocky one: in June 2002, riots broke out in Arequipa over Toledo's government's attempts to privatize the city's electric utility, followed a month later by paralyzing transport strikes and then furious demonstrations in the northern *ceja de selva* region. Despite lack of popular support and with little or no backing from Peru's powerful elite business classes, Toledo clung onto his office until 2006, when in a general election he was replaced, amazingly, by an older and much plumper **Alan García** – the very same man and ex-President who left Peru and his first term of office in disgrace back in 1988. Meanwhile, Fujimori returned to South America via Chile in late 2005, and was arrested on arrival. Charged with human rights abuses and corruption (including payments to members of Congress and illegal wiretapping), he was extradited to Peru in 2007; he was convicted and locked up despite being ill. Similarly, legal action was taken against his once right-hand man, Montesinos, who also remains locked up.

García's term of office is now over and in 2011 **Ollanta Humala** was elected President with a strong majority. The legacy of García's second term, at first view, a strong economy. However, beneath the growth figures are some less positive facts: Peru has taken over from Colombia as the main producer and trafficker of illegal cocaine (see box below); the massive inequality in incomes is growing; and Peru's mineral,

PERU'S WHITE GOLD

Coca, the plant from which cocaine is derived, has come a long way since the Incas distributed this "divine plant" across fourteenth-century Andean Peru. Presented as a gift from the gods, coca was also used to exploit slave labour under Spanish rule: without it the Indians would never have worked in the gruelling conditions of colonial mines such as Potosí.

The isolation of the active ingredient in coca, cocaine, in 1859, began an era of intense **medical experimentation**. Its numbing effects have been appreciated by dental patients around the world, and even Pope Leo XIII enjoyed a bottle of the coca wine produced by an Italian physician, who amassed a great fortune from its sale in the nineteenth century. On a more popular level, coca was one of the essential ingredients in Coca-Cola until 1906.

Today, **cocaine** is one of the most fashionable – and expensive – illegal drugs. From its humble origins cocaine has become very big business. Unofficially, it may well be the biggest export for countries like Peru and Bolivia, where coca grows best in the Andes and along the edge of the jungle. While most mountain peasants always cultivated a little for personal use, many have now become dependent on it for obvious economic reasons: coca is still the most profitable cash crop and is readily bought by middlemen operating for extremely wealthy cocaine barons. A constant flow of semi-refined coca paste leaves Peru aboard Amazon riverboats or ocean yachts bound for places like Panama and Mexico or in unmarked light aircraft heading for laboratories in Colombia. Seen by many peasants as a road to fortune and freedom, for others cocaine is a scourge, bringing violence, the mobsters and deforestation in its wake.

2000

The run-up to the April elections is marked by Fujimori's controversial decision to stand for a third term of office, despite constitutional term limits. By November, Fujimori is forced to resign following revelations of bribery and drug-money laundering.

2000–2003

Fujimori flees to Japan. The economy is unstable and there are protests over the country's coca eradication programme.

timber and petroleum assets are being sold off cheaply: over seventy percent of the Peruvian Amazon (most of which is actually indigenous community territory) had its assets put out to auction among multinational interests. The same happened to gold, copper and other mineral resources in the Peruvian Andes. Ollanta, with his socialist-nationalist tendencies, seems set to change things, at least a little. The worry is just how far he might go down the road taken by Hugo Chavez, the Venezuelan oil-rich President, and an ally of Ollanta's.

2006	2006 –2011	2011	2012
Political elections are held – ex-president Alan García wins, taking office for the second time.	President García is seen by many as putting Peru's natural resources out to auction and denies the existence of "uncontacted" Indians.	Ollanta Humala wins the presidential elections.	Peru has high hopes for its young national football team in the 2014 World Cup – watch out for Guerrero.

Inca life and achievement

In less than a century, the Incas developed and knitted together a vast empire peopled by something like twenty million Indians, that was to endure from 1200 to 1532. They established an imperial religion in relative harmony with those of their subject tribes; erected monolithic fortresses, salubrious palaces and temples; and, astonishingly, evolved a viable economy – strong enough to maintain a top-heavy elite in almost godlike grandeur. To understand these achievements and get some idea of what they must have meant in Peru five or six hundred years ago, you really have to see for yourself their surviving heritage: the stones of Inca ruins and roads; the cultural objects in the museums of Lima and Cusco; and their living descendants who still work the soil and speak Quechua – the language used by the Incas to unify their empire.

Inca society

The Inca Empire rapidly developed a **hierarchical structure**. At the highest level it was governed by the **Sapa Inca**, son of the sun and direct descendant of the god Viracocha. Under him were the priest-nobles – the royal ayllu or kin-group who filled most of the important administrative and religious posts – and, working for them, regional *ayllu* chiefs (*curacas* or *orejones*), responsible for controlling tribute from the peasant base. The Inca nobles were fond of relaxing in thermal baths, of hunting holidays and of conspicuous eating and drinking whenever the religious calendar permitted. *Ayllu* chiefs were often unrelated to the royal Inca lineage, but their position was normally hereditary. As lesser nobles (*curacas*) they were allowed to wear earplugs and special ornate headbands; their task was to both protect and exploit the commoners, and they themselves were free of labour service. One-third of the land belonged to the emperor and the state; another to the high priests, gods and the sun; the last third was for the *ayllu* themselves.

In their conquests the Incas absorbed **craftsmen** from every corner of the empire: goldsmiths, potters, carpenters, sculptors, masons and *quipumayocs* (accountants) were frequently removed from their homes to work directly for the emperor in Cusco. These skilled men lost no time in developing into a new and entirely separate class of citizen. The work of even the lowest servant in the palace was highly regulated by a rigid division of labour.

Special regulations affected both **senior citizens** and **people with disabilities**. Around the age of fifty, a man was likely to pass into the category of "old". He was no longer capable of undertaking a normal workload, he wasn't expected to pay taxes, and he could always depend on support from the official storehouses. Nevertheless, the community still made small demands by using him to collect firewood and other such tasks, in much the same way the kids were expected to help out around the house and in the fields. In fact, children and old people often worked together, the young learning directly from the old. Disabled people were obliged to work within their potential – the blind, for instance, might de-husk maize or clean cotton. Inca law also bound people with disabilities to marry those with similar disadvantages.

Inca women

Throughout the empire young girls, usually about 9 or 10 years old, were constantly selected for their beauty and serene intelligence. Those deemed perfect enough were taken to an *acclahuasi* – a special sanctuary for the "**chosen women**" – where they were trained in specific tasks, including the spinning and weaving of fine cloth, and the higher culinary arts. Most chosen women were destined ultimately to become *mamaconas* (Virgins of the Sun) or the concubines of either nobles or the Sapa Inca himself. Occasionally some of them were sacrificed by strangulation in order to appease the gods.

For most **Inca women** their allotted role was simply that of peasant/domestic work and rearing children. After giving birth a mother would wash her baby in a nearby stream to cleanse and purify it and return virtually immediately to normal daily activities, carrying the child in a cradle tied on her back with a shawl. As adults their particular role in society was dependent first on gender, then on hierarchical status. Women weren't counted in the census; for the Incas, a household was represented by the man and only he was obliged to fulfil tribute duties on behalf of the *ayllu*.

The Inca diet

The Inca diet was essentially **vegetarian**, based on the staple potato but encompassing a range of other foods like quinoa, beans, squash, sweet potatoes, avocados, tomatoes and manioc. In the highlands, emphasis was on root crops like potatoes, which have been known to survive in temperatures as low as 15°C (59°F) at over 5000m. On the valley floors and lower slopes of the Andes, maize cultivation predominated.

The importance of **maize** both as a food crop and for making *chicha* increased dramatically under the Incas; previously it had been grown for ceremony and ritual exchange, as a status rather than a staple crop. The use of **coca** was restricted to the priests and Inca elite. Coca is a mild narcotic stimulant which effectively dulls the body against cold, hunger and tiredness when the leaves are chewed in the mouth with a catalyst such as lime or calcium. The Incas believed its leaves possessed magical properties; they could be cast to divine future events, offered as a gift to the wind, the earth or the mountain *apu*, and they could be used in witchcraft. Today it's difficult to envisage the Incas' success in restricting coca growing and use; even with helicopters and machine guns the present-day authorities are unable to control its production.

Economy, agriculture and building

The main **resources** available to the Inca Empire were agricultural land and labour, mines (producing precious and prestigious metals such as gold, silver or copper) and fresh water, abundant everywhere except along the desert coast. With careful manipulation of these resources, the Incas managed to keep things moving the way they wanted. Tribute in the form of **service** (*mita*) played a crucial role in maintaining the empire and pressurizing its subjects into ambitious building and irrigation projects. Some of these projects were so grand that they would have been impossible without the demanding whip of a totalitarian state.

Although a certain degree of local barter was allowed, the state regulated the distribution of every important product. The astonishing Inca **highways** were one key to this economic success. Some of the tracks were nearly 8m wide and at the time of the Spanish Conquest the main Royal Highway ran some 5000km, from the Río Ancasmayo in Colombia down the backbone of the Andes to the coast, at a point south of the present-day Santiago in Chile. The Incas never used the wheel, but gigantic **llama caravans** were a common sight tramping along the roads, each animal carrying up to 50kg of cargo.

Every corner of the Inca domain was easily accessible via branch roads, all designed or taken over and unified with one intention – to dominate and administer an enormous empire. **Runners** were posted at *chasqui* stations and *tambo* rest-houses punctuated the road at intervals of between 2km and 15km. Fresh fish was relayed on foot from the coast and messages were sent with runners from Quito to Cusco (2000km) in less than six days. The more difficult mountain canyons were crossed on bridges suspended from cables braided out of jungle lianas (creeping vines) and high passes were – and still are – frequently reached by incredible stairways cut into solid rock cliffs.

Agricultural terracing

The primary sector in the economy was inevitably **agriculture** and in this the Incas made two major advances: large terracing projects created the opportunity for agricultural specialists to experiment with new crops and methods of cultivation, and the transport system allowed a revolution in distribution. Massive agricultural **terracing projects** were going on continuously in Inca-dominated mountain regions. The best examples of these are in the Cusco area at Tipón, Moray, Ollantaytambo, Pisac and Cusichaca. Beyond the aesthetic beauty of Inca stone terraces, they have distinct practical advantages. Terraced hillsides minimize erosion from landslides, and using well-engineered stone channels gives complete control over irrigation.

Inca masonry

Today, however, it is Inca construction that forms their lasting heritage: vast **building projects** masterminded by high-ranking nobles and architects, and supervised by expert masons with an almost limitless pool of peasant labour. Without paper, the architects resorted to imposing their imagination onto clay or stone, making miniature models of the more important constructions – good examples of these can be seen in Cusco museums. More importantly, **Inca masonry** survives throughout Peru, most spectacularly at the fortress of Sacsayhuaman above Cusco, and on the coast in the Achirana aqueduct, which even today still brings water down to the Ica Valley from high up in the Andes.

Arts and crafts

Surprisingly, Inca masonry was rarely carved or adorned in any way. Smaller stone items, however, were frequently ornate and beautiful. High technical standards were achieved, too, in **pottery**. Around Cusco especially, the art of creating and glazing ceramics was highly developed. They were not so advanced artistically, however; Inca designs generally lack imagination and variety, tending to have been mass-produced from models evolved by previous cultures. The most common pottery object was the *aryballus*, a large jar with a conical base and a wide neck, thought to have been used chiefly for storing *chicha*. Its decoration was usually geometric, often associated with the backbone of a fish: the central spine of the pattern was adorned with rows of spikes radiating from either side. Fine plates were made with anthropomorphic handles, and large numbers of cylindrically tapering goblets – *keros* – were manufactured, though these were often of cedar wood rather than pottery.

Refinements in **metallurgy**, like the ceramics industry, were mostly developed by craftsmen absorbed from different corners of the empire. The Chimu were particularly respected by the Incas for their superb metalwork. Within the empire, bronze and copper were used for axe-blades and tumi knives; gold and silver were restricted to ritual use and for nobles. The Incas smelted their metal ores in cylindrical terracotta and adobe furnaces, which made good use of prevailing breezes to fire large lumps of charcoal. Molten ores were pulled out from the base of the furnace.

Religion

The Inca **religion** was easily capable of incorporating the religious features of most subjugated regions. The Incas merely superimposed their variety of mystical, yet inherently practical, elements onto those they came across. At the very top of the **religio-social hierarchy** was the Villac Uma, the high priest of Cusco, usually a brother of the Sapa Inca himself. Under him were perhaps hundreds of high priests, all nobles of royal blood who were responsible for ceremonies, temples, shrines, divination, curing and sacrifice within the realm, and below them were the ordinary priests and chosen women. At the base of the hierarchy, and probably the most numerous of all religious personalities, were the **curanderos**, local healers practising herbal medicine and magic, and making sacrifices to small regional *huacas* (sacred sites or temples).

Most **religious festivals** were calendar-based and marked by processions, sacrifices and dances. The Incas were aware of lunar time and the solar year, although they generally used the blooming of a special cactus and the stars to gauge the correct time to begin planting. Sacrifices to the gods normally consisted of llamas, *cuys* or *chicha* – only occasionally were chosen women and other adults killed. Once every year, however, young children were apparently sacrificed in the most important sacred centres.

Divination was a vital role played by priests and *curanderos* at all levels of the religious hierarchy. Soothsayers were expected to talk with the spirits and often used a hallucinogenic snuff from the vilca plant to achieve a trance-like state. Everything from a crackling fire to the glance of a lizard was seen as a potential omen, and treated as such by making a little offering of coca leaves, coca spittle or *chicha*. There were specific problems which divination was considered particularly accurate in solving: retrieving lost things; predicting the outcome of certain events (including military escapades); and the diagnosis of illness.

Gods and symbols

The main religious novelty introduced with Inca domination was their demand to be recognized as direct descendants of the creator-god **Viracocha**. A claim to divine ancestry was, to the Incas, a valid excuse for military and cultural expansion. They felt no need to destroy the *huacas* and oracles of subjugated peoples; on the contrary, certain sacred sites were recognized as intrinsically holy, as powerful places for communication with the spirit world. When ancient shrines like Pachacamac, near Lima, were absorbed into the empire they were simply turned over to worship on imperial terms.

The **sun** is the most obvious symbol of Inca belief, a chief deity and the visible head of the state religion (Viracocha was a less direct, more ethereal, force). The sun's role was overt, as life-giver to an agriculturally based empire, and its cycle was intricately related to agrarian practice and annual ritual patterns. To think of the Inca religion as essentially sun worship, though, would be far too simplistic. There were distinct **layers** in Inca cosmology: the level of creation, the astral level and the earthly dimension. The first, highest, level corresponds to Viracocha as the creator-god who brought life to the world and society to mankind. Below this, on the astral level, are the celestial gods: the sun itself, the moon and certain stars (particularly the Pleiades, patrons of fertility). The earthly dimension, although that of man, was no less magical, endowed with important *huacas* and shrines which might take the form of unusual rocks or peaks, caves, tombs, mummies and natural springs.

Ancient wizardry in modern Peru

Bearing in mind the country's poverty and the fact that almost half the population is still pure Amerindian, it isn't altogether surprising to discover that the ancient shamanic healing arts are still flourishing in Peru. Evidence for this type of magical health therapy stretches back over three thousand years on the Peruvian coast, from the Chavín and Paracas to the Mochica and Chimu cultures. Today, healing wizards, or *curanderos* ("healers"), can be found in every large community, practising healing based on knowledge that has been passed down from master to apprentice over millennia. *Curanderos* offer an alternative to the expensive, sporadic and often unreliable service provided by scientific medics in a developing country like Peru. But as well as being a cheaper, more widely available option, *curanderismo* is also closer to the hearts and understanding of the average Peruvian.

Combine "holistic" health with psychotherapy, and add an underlying cultural vision of spiritual and magical influences, and you are some way towards getting a clearer picture of how **healing wizards** operate. The last four hundred years of Spanish domination have added a veneer of Catholic imagery and nomenclature to Peruvian beliefs. Nature spirits have become saints or demons, while ancient mountain spirits and their associated annual festivals continue disguised as Christian ceremonies.

Most *curanderos* use "teacher plants" (generally hallucinogenic); in almost every Peruvian Amazon tribe these traditions include the regular ingestion of **hallucinogenic brews** to give a visionary ecstatic experience. Sometimes just the shaman partakes, but more often the shaman and his patients, or entire communities, will indulge together, singing traditional spirit-songs that help control the visions. The visionary experience is the Peruvian forest Indian's way of getting in touch with the **ancestral world** or the world of spirit matter. Unlike the Western belief-system, the Andean-Amazon cosmology is based on reciprocity with nature rather than the exploitation of it. Healing wizards question the very foundations of our rational, scientific perception of the world.

Many coastal wizards get their most potent magic and powerful plants from a small zone in the **northern Andes**. The mountain area around Las Huaringas and Huancabamba, to the north of Chiclayo and east of Piura, is where a large number of the "great masters" are believed to live and work. But it is in the **Amazon Basin** of Peru that shamanism continues in its least-changed form.

San Pedro

Still commonly used by *curanderos* on the coast and in the mountains of Peru, the **San Pedro cactus** (*Trichocereus pachanoi*) is a potent hallucinogen based on active mescaline. Used for thousands of years, in one stone relief on the main temple at Chavín de Huantar a feline deity is depicted holding a large **San Pedro cactus** in his hand. A Chavín ceramic bottle has been discovered with a San Pedro cactus "growing" on it; and, on another pot, a feline sits surrounded by several San Pedros. Similar motifs and designs appear on the later Paracas and Mochica craftwork, but there is no real evidence for the ritual use of hallucinogens prior to Chavín. One impressive ceramic from the Mochica culture (500 AD) depicts an **owl-woman** – still symbolic of the female shaman in contemporary Peru – with a slice of San Pedro cactus in her hand. Another ceramic from the later Chimu culture (around 1100 AD) also shows a female healer holding a San Pedro.

A shaman, male or female, works by treating sick and worried people who may visit from hundreds of miles around, by utilizing a combination of herbalism, magical divination and a kind of psychic shock therapy involving the use of San Pedro. The *curandero* administers the hallucinogenic brew to his or her clients to bring about a period of revelation when questions are asked of the intoxicated person, who might also be asked to choose some object from among a range of magical curios that all have different meanings to the healer. Sometimes a *curandero* might imbibe San Pedro (or one of the many other indigenous hallucinogens) to see into the future, retrieve lost souls, divine causes of illness or discover the whereabouts of lost objects.

Ayahuasca

On the edges of most jungle towns there are *curanderos* healing local people by using a mixture of Indian jungle shamanism and the more Catholicized coastal form. These wizards generally use the most common tropical forest hallucinogen, *ayahuasca* (from the liana *Banisteriopsis caapi*). Away from the towns, among the more remote tribal people, *ayahuasca* is the key to understanding the native consciousness and perception of the world – which for them is the natural world of the elements and the forest plus their own social, economic and political setup within that dominant environment.

The **Shipibo tribe** from the central Peruvian Amazon are famous for their excellent ceramic and weaving designs: extremely complex geometric patterns usually in black on white or beige, though sometimes reds or yellows too. These designs were traditionally inspired by visions received while the shaman was under the influence of *ayahuasca*, whose effect is described as "the spirits coming down".

Vilca

As well as coca, their "divine plant", the **Incas** had their own special hallucinogen: **vilca** (meaning "sacred" in Quechua). The vilca tree (probably *Anadenanthera colubrina*) grows in the cloud-forest zones on the eastern slopes of the Peruvian Andes. The Incas used a snuff made from the seeds, which was generally blown up the nostrils of the participant by a helper. Evidently the Inca priests used vilca to bring on visions and make contact with the gods and spirit world.

Peruvian music

Latin America's oldest musical traditions are those of the Amerindians of the Andes. Their music is best known outside these countries through the characteristic panpipes of poncho-clad folklore groups. However, there's a multitude of rhythms and popular music alive in Peru that deserve a lot more recognition, including *huayno*, *chicha cumbia*, Afro-Peruvian and even reggaeton.

For most people outside Latin America the sound of the Andes is that of bamboo panpipes and *quena* flutes. What is most remarkable is that these instruments have been used to create music in various parts of this large area of mountains – which stretch 7200km from Venezuela down to southernmost Chile – since before the time of the Incas. Pre-Conquest Andean instruments – conch-shell trumpets, shakers which used nuts for rattles, ocarinas, wind instruments and drums – are ever-present in museum collections.

Andean music can be divided roughly into three types: firstly, that which is of **indigenous origin**, found mostly among rural Amerindian peoples still living very much by the seasons; secondly, music of **European origin**; and thirdly, **mestizo music**, which continues to fuse the indigenous with the European in a whole host of ways. In general, Quechua people have more vocal music than the Aymara.

Traditional music

Panpipes, known by the Aymara as *siku*, by the Quechua as *antara* and by the Spanish as *zampoña*, are ancient instruments, and archeologists have unearthed them tuned to a variety of scales. Simple **notched-end flutes**, or *quenas*, are another independent innovation of the Andean highlands found in both rural and urban areas. The most important pre-Hispanic instrument, they were traditionally made of fragile bamboo (though often these days from plumbers' PVC water pipes) and played in the dry season, with *tarkas* (vertical flutes – like a shrill recorder) taking over in the wet. *Quenas* are played solo or in ritual groups and remain tremendously popular today, with many virtuoso techniques.

MUSIC AT FESTIVALS

Peru's many **festivals** are a rewarding source of traditional music. One of the best takes place in January on the **Isla Amantani** in Lake Titicaca, its exact date, as is often the case in the Andean highlands, determined by astronomical events. The festival occurs during a period often called the "time of protection", when the rainy season has finally begun. It is related to the cleansing of the pasturage and water sources; stone fences are repaired, walking paths repaved, and the stone effigies and crosses that guard the planting fields replaced or repaired. A single-file "parade" of individuals covers the entire island, stopping to appease the deities and provide necessary maintenance at each site. At the front are local nonprofessional musicians, all male, playing drums and flutes of various types.

Some festivals are celebrated on a larger scale. On the day of the June solstice (midwinter in the Andes) the Inca would ceremonially tie the sun to a stone and coax it to return south, bringing warmer weather and the new planting season. **Inti Raymi**, the Festival of the Sun, is still observed in every nook and cranny in the Andean republics, from the capital city to the most isolated hamlet. The celebration, following a solemn ritual that may include a llama sacrifice, is more of a carnival than anything else. Parades of musicians, both professional bands and thrown-together collages of amateurs, fill the streets. You will be expected to drink and dance until you drop, or hide in your room. This kind of party can run for several days, so be prepared.

Large **marching bands** of drums and panpipes, playing in the co-operative "back and forth" leader/follower style that captivated the Spanish in the 1500s, can still be seen and heard today. The drums are deep-sounding, double-headed instruments known as *bombos* or *wankaras*. These bands exist for parades at life-cycle fiestas, weddings and dances in the regions surrounding the Peruvian–Bolivian frontier and around Lake Titicaca. Apart from their use at fiestas, panpipes are played mainly in the dry season, from April to October.

Folk music festivals to attract and entertain the tourist trade are a quite different experience to music in the village context. While positively disseminating the music, they have introduced the notion of judging and the concept of "best" musicianship – ideas totally at odds with rural community values of diversity in musical repertoire, style and dress.

Music explodes from every direction in the once Inca lands, but nowhere more so than in **Cusco**, a good first base for getting to grips with Andean music. Stay a week or two and you will hear just about every variety of Andean folk music that is still performed.

Charangos and mermaids

The **charango** is another major Andean instrument whose bright, zingy sounds are familiar worldwide. This small guitar – with five pairs of strings – was created in imitation of early guitars and lutes brought by the Spanish colonizers, which Amerindian musicians were taught to play in the churches. Its small size is due to its traditional manufacture from armadillo shells, while its sound quality comes from the indigenous aesthetic that has favoured high pitches from the pre-Columbian period through to the present.

In rural areas in southern Peru, particularly in the Titicaca region and province of Canas, the *charango* is the main instrument – used by young **single men** to woo and court the female of choice. Some villagers construct the sound box in the shape of a **mermaid**, including her head and fish tail, to invest their *charango* with supernatural power. When young men go courting at the weekly markets in larger villages they will not only dress in their finest clothes, but dress up their *charangos* in elaborate coloured ribbons.

Song and brass

Most **singing** in the Andes is done by women, and the preferred style is very high pitched – almost falsetto to Western ears. There are songs for potato-growing, reaping barley, threshing wheat, marking cattle, sheep and goats, for building houses, for traditional dances and funerals, and for many other ceremonies.

Huaynos and orquestas típicas

Visit the Peruvian central sierra and you find a music as lively and energetic as the busy market towns it comes from, and largely unknown outside the country. These songs and dances are **huaynos**, one of the few musical forms that reach back to pre-Conquest times, although the **orquestas típicas** that play them, from sierra towns like Huancayo, Ayacucho and Pucará, include saxophones, clarinets and trumpets alongside traditional

THE ANDEAN HARP: DON ANTONIO SULCA

Blind musician **Don Antonio Sulca**, of Ayacucho, is one of the great masters of the Andean harp – one of the mountains' most characteristic instruments. This huge harp has a sound box built like a boat and a mermaid's-head decoration (like many *charangos*). Its form is thought to have evolved from the harp brought from Spain in the sixteenth century and the Celtic harp brought by the Jesuits to the missions. It has 36 strings spanning five octaves and including resonant bass notes. In processions in the Andes, harpists often sling their instruments upside down across their shoulders, plucking with a remarkable backhanded technique.

instruments like violins, *charangos* and the large Amerindian harp. The music is spirited and infectious.

The buoyant, swinging rhythms of *huayno* songs are deceptive, for the lyrics fuse joy and sorrow. The musical style is regionally marked with typical *mestizo* instrumental ensembles of the region represented and musical features, such as specific guitar runs, identifying musicians with, for example, Ayacucho or Ancash. Sung in a mixture of Spanish and Quechua, they tell of unhappy love and betrayal, celebrate passion and often deliver homespun philosophy.

Afro-Peruvian music

Afro-Peruvian music has its roots in the communities of black slaves brought to work in the mines along the Peruvian coast. As such, it's a fair way from the Andes, culturally and geographically. However, as it developed, particularly in the twentieth century, it drew on Andean and Spanish, as well as African traditions, while its modern exponents also have affinities with Andean *nueva canción*. The music was little known even in Peru until the 1950s, when it was popularized by the seminal performer Nicomedes Santa Cruz, whose body of work was taken a step further in the 1970s by the group Perú Negro. Internationally, it has had a recent airing through David Byrne's Luaka Bop label, issuing the compilation, *Perú Negro*, and solo albums by the now world renowned **Susana Baca**.

Nicomedes Santa Cruz is the towering figure in the development of Afro-Peruvian music. A poet, musician and journalist, he was the first true musicologist to assert an Afro-Peruvian cultural identity through black music and dance, producing books and recordings of contemporary black music and culture in Peru. In 1964 he recorded a four-album set *Cumanana*, now regarded as the bible of Afro-Peruvian music. Santa Cruz himself followed in the footsteps of **Porfirio Vásquez**, who came to Lima in 1920 and was an early pioneer of the movement to regain the lost cultural identity of Afro-Peruvians. A composer of *décimas*, singer, guitarist, *cajonero* (box player) and *zapateador* (dancer), he founded the Academia Folklórica in Lima in 1949. Through Santa Cruz's work and that of the group **Perú Negro** and the singer and composer **Chabuca Granda**, Latin America came to know Afro-Peruvian dances, the names of which were given to their songs, such as *Toro Mata*, *Samba-malató*, *El Alcatraz* and *Festejo*.

Chicha and Cumbia

Chicha, the fermented maize beer, has given its name to a hugely popular brew of Andean tropical music, one which has recently spread to wider Anglophone world music circles. The music's origins lie in the rapidly urbanizing Amazon of the late 1960s, in places like Iquitos and Pucallpa, where bands such as **Los Mirlos** and **Juaneco y Su Combo** fused *cumbia* (local versions of the original Colombian dance), traditional

SUSANA BACA

Susana Baca, who was Peru's Minister for Culture for a few brief months in 2011, grew up in the black coastal neighbourhood of Chorrillos, near Lima, and has brought international acclaim to Afro-Peruvian music. Interviewed at WOMAD 1998, she recalled family traditions of getting together for a Sunday meal, and then making music, with her father playing guitar, her mother, aunts, uncles and friends singing and dancing. By the time she was a teenager and first heard the recordings of Nicomedes Santa Cruz, she realized she had absorbed quite a repertoire of the traditional songs black people had carried with them to Peru as slaves.

Baca's performing style is intimate and rooted in close contact with her **band**: "Nothing is written down, the musicians improvise and invent, so we need to be able to see each other's eyes to make a good performance, to share and enjoy and release the power of the music."

DISCOGRAPHY

COMPILATIONS

Afro-Peruvian Classics: The Soul of Black Peru (Luaka Bop, US). A unique blend of Spanish, Andean and African traditions, Afro-Peruvian music is different to Caribbean and other Latin black cultures. The compilation includes the definitive dance song *Toro Mata*, the first Afro-Peruvian success outside Peru, covered by the "queen of salsa", Celia Cruz. A fine collection intended to introduce the music to a wider audience outside Peru, it does a great job.

The Blind Street Musicians of Cusco: Peruvian Harp and Mandolin (Music of the World, US). Stirringly played *marineras*, *huaynos*, traditional tunes and instrumental solos exactly as heard on the streets of Cusco in 1984–85 from Leandro Apaza on a 33-stringed harp; Benjamin Clara Quispé and Carmen Apaza Roca on armadillo-shelled mandolins (not *charangos*); and Fidel Villacorte Tejada on *quena*. Excellent ambience recorded in musicians' homes and *chichería* bars.

Flutes and Strings of the Andes (Music of the World, US). The superbly atmospheric recordings of amateur musicians from Peru – harpists, *charanguistas*, fiddlers, flautists and percussionists, recorded in 1983–84 on the streets and at festivals – bring you as close to being there as you can get without strapping on your pack and striding uphill.

Huayno Music of Peru Vols 1 and 2 (Arhoolie, US). These excellent collections of *huayno* music from the 1950s to the 1980s focus on a slightly more local style. Vol 1 includes songs from the master, Jilguero del Huascarán, while Vol 2 is drawn from the recordings of Discos Smith, a small label that released *huayno* and criolla music in the late 1950s and 1960s.

Mountain Music of Peru (Smithsonian Folkways, US). John Cohen's selection, including a song that went up in the *Voyager* spacecraft, brings together compositions from remote corners of the mountains where music is integral to daily life, and urban songs telling of tragedies at football matches. Good sleeve notes, too.

The Rough Guide to Music of the Andes (World Music Network). A vigorous and broad range of Andean music from contemporary urban-based groups. Includes major 1960s musicians Los Kjarkas and Ernesto Cavou and their 1980s European travelling brethren Awatinas and Rumillajta; soloists Emma Junaro, Jenny Cardenas and Susana Baca, seminal Chilean group Inti Illimani and new song, or *nueva canción*, singer Victor Jara. Plus saxes and clarinets from Picaflor de los Andes.

Traditional Music of Peru: Vol 1 Festivals of Cusco; Vol 2 The Mantaro Valley; Vol 3 Cajamarca and the Colca Valley; Vol 4 Lambayeque (Smithsonian Folkways, US). A definitive series of field recordings from the 1980s and 1990s of music from specific areas. Includes the whole spectrum of music to be heard if you travelled around the whole of Peru. Excellent CD booklets, too.

highland *huayno* and Western rock and psychedelia. In the 1970s, mass migration carried *chicha* to Lima, and by the mid-1980s, it had become the most widespread urban music in Peru. Most bands have lead and rhythm guitars, electric bass, electric organ, a *timbales* and conga player, one or more vocalists (who may play percussion) and, if they can, a synthesizer.

While most lyrics are about love in all its aspects, nearly all songs actually reveal an aspect of the harshness of the Amerindian experience – displacement, hardship, loneliness and exploitation. Many songs relate to the great majority of people who have to make a living selling their labour and goods in the unofficial "informal economy", ever threatened by the police.

Chicha, and, more recently, the Peruvian version of *cumbia* (which is clearly more *cumbia* than *chicha*), has taken root and also achieved international acclaim. In Peru itself, this belated international recognition has witnessed a resurgence in interest in seminal artists like Juaneco y Su Combo, currently feted by the Lima cognoscenti and the subject of their own recent Barbès retrospective, *Juaneco y Su Combo: Masters of Chicha Volume 1*. The label even have their own in-house band, Chicha Libre, whose excellent debut, *!Sonido Amazonico!*, was released in early 2008. In the last few years,

ARTISTS AND ALBUMS

Ayllu Sulca

Blind harpist Don Antonio Sulca encapsulates everything that is *mestizo* music – the emergence of a hybrid blend of Amerindian and Spanish cultures. A virtuoso since early childhood, he plays as a soloist but mostly as part of his band – his *ayllu* – which includes three of his sons.

Music of the Incas (Lyrichord, US). Accompanied by violin, mandolin and *quenas*, Sulca plays ancient Inca melodies and more recent waltzes with pace and swing, including rustic versions of *salon* music.

Susana Baca

One of the few Afro-Peruvian artists touring worldwide, Susana Baca grew up in the coastal barrio of Chorrillos and learned traditional Afro-Peruvian songs from her family (see box, p.511).

Susana Baca (Luaka Bop/Warner Bros, US). Taking up the mantle of Chabuca Granda and Nicomedes Santa Cruz, these are fine versions of Afro-Peruvian and criolla classics sung with conscious emotion and passion.

Belem

Belem are one of the bands that have made *chicha* a force to be reckoned with in urban Peru.

Chicha (Tumi, UK). A pioneering release of Peru's hot fusion music. Belem's mix of *huayno*, salsa, *cumbia* and a touch of rock, deserves a listening. Andean pipe music, it ain't.

Arturo "Zambo" Cavero and Oscar Aviles

Arturo "Zambo" Cavero is one of the great male voices of black Peruvian music, as well as being an accomplished *cajón* player. During the 1980s he teamed up with Oscar Aviles to become a celebrated partnership, their music seen as reflecting the suffering, patriotism and passion of black people in Peru.

On the Wings of the Condor (Tumi, UK). One of the most popular Andean albums ever, but none the worse for that: the engaging sound of the panpipes and *charangos* is smoothly and beautifully arranged.

Hermanos Santa Cruz

Hermanos Santa Cruz are family members of Nicomedes Santa Cruz (see below).

Afro Peru (Discos Hispanos, Peru). Carrying on the tradition and heritage laid down by their forefathers, the Santa Cruz brothers present a 1990s version of Afro-Peruvian traditions.

Nicomedes Santa Cruz

The first true musicologist to assert Afro-Peruvian cultural identity through black music and dance.

Kumanana (Philips, Peru), *Socabon* (Virrey, Peru). Two albums showcasing Santa Cruz's majestic musicological studies of Afro-Peruvian music and culture.

Peruvian *cumbia* artists, like Barreto and also the Hermanos Yaipen, have become very popular.

Reggaeton

More rap than reggae, **reggaeton** is popular with the urban youth of Peru today. With Jamaican reggae roots, this sexually explicit and fairly macho genre began life in Panama and Puerto Rico in the late 1980s. Spreading slowly in underground fashion it gradually became popular all over Latin America until breaking through into radio and TV music channels in the twenty-first century. It hit the clubs of Lima between 2007 and 2011, scandalizing the Catholic establishment there with its sexually explicit *el perreo* dancing. If you sample the nightlife in Lima's clubs, you're bound to find this music style thriving in the early hours.

Original material written by Jan Fairley, with thanks to Thomas Turino and Raúl Romero, Gilka Wara Céspedes, Martín Morales and Margaret Bullen. Adapted from the *Rough Guide to World Music, Vol 2.* with additional contributions by Brendon Griffin. Re-edited by Claire Jenkins, 2012.

Wildlife and ecology

Peru's varied ecological niches span an incredible range of climate and terrain; the Amazon region covers 60 percent of Peru's land surface, yet has only 12 percent of its population; the highlands cover 28 percent of the land but are home to only 36 percent of the country's people; the desert coast, where 52 percent of Peruvians live, comprises a mere 12 percent of its land area. Between these three major zones, the ecological reality is continuous intergradation, encompassing literally dozens of unique habitats. Mankind has occupied Peru for perhaps twenty thousand years, but there has been less disturbance there, until relatively recently, than in most other parts of our planet, which makes it a top-class ecotourist and wildlife photo-safari destination.

The coast

Peru's **coast** is characterized by abundant sea life and by the contrasting scarcity of terrestrial plants and animals. The **Humboldt current** runs virtually the length of Peru, bringing cold water up from the depths of the Pacific Ocean and causing any moisture to condense out over the sea, depriving the mainland coastal strip and lower western mountain slopes of rainfall. Along with this cold water, large quantities of nutrients are carried up to the surface, helping to sustain a rich planktonic community able to support vast numbers of fish, preyed upon in their turn by a variety of coastal birds: gulls, terns, pelicans, boobies, cormorants and wading birds are always present along the beaches. One beautiful specimen, the **Inca tern**, although usually well camouflaged as it sits high up on inaccessible sea cliffs, is nevertheless very common in the Lima area. The **Humboldt penguin**, with grey rather than black features, is a rarer sight – shyer than its more southerly cousins, it is normally found in isolated rocky coves or on offshore islands. Competing with the birds for fish are schools of dolphins, sea lion colonies and the occasional coastal otter. Dolphins and sea lions are often spotted off even the most crowded of beaches or scavenging around the fishermen's jetty at Chorrillos, near Lima.

One of the most fascinating features of Peruvian birdlife is the number of vast, **high-density colonies**: although the number of species is quite small, their total population is enormous. Many thousands of birds can be seen nesting on islands like the Ballestas, off the Paracas Peninsula, or simply covering the ocean with a flapping, diving carpet of energetic feathers. This huge bird population, and the **Guanay cormorant** in particular, is responsible for depositing mountains of guano (bird droppings), which form a traditional and potent source of natural fertilizer.

The coastal desert

In contrast to these rich waters the **coastal desert** lies stark and barren. Here you find only a few trees and shrubs; you'll need endless patience to find wild animals other than birds. The most common animals are feral **goats**, once domesticated but now living wild, and **burros** (donkeys) introduced by the Spanish. A more exciting sight is the attractively coloured **coral snake** – shy but deadly and covered with black and orange hoops. Most animals are more active after sunset; when out in the desert you can hear the eerily plaintive call of the **huerequeque** (Peruvian thick-knee bird), and

EL NIÑO

In order to understand the Peruvian coastal desert you have to bear in mind the phenomenon of **El Niño**, a periodic climatic shift caused by the displacement of the cold Humboldt current by warmer equatorial waters; it last occurred in 1998. El Niño causes the plankton and fish communities either to disperse to other locations or to collapse entirely. At such a period the shore rapidly becomes littered with carrion, since many of the sea mammals and birds are unable to survive in the limited environment. Scavenging condors and vultures, on the other hand, thrive, as does the desert, where rain falls in deluges along the coast, with a consequent bloom of vegetation and rapid growth in animal populations. When the Humboldt current returns, the desert dries up and its animal populations decline to normal sizes (another temporary feast for the scavengers). While it used to be at least ten years before this cycle was repeated, global warming over the last two decades has witnessed the pattern becoming much more erratic. Generally considered a freak phenomenon, El Niño is probably better understood as an integral part of coastal ecology; without it the desert would be a far more barren and static environment, virtually incapable of supporting life.

the barking of the little **desert fox** – alarmingly similar to the sound of car tyres screeching to a halt. By day you might see several species of small birds, a favourite being the vermilion-headed **Peruvian flycatcher**. Near water – rivers, estuaries and lagoons – desert wildlife is at its most populous. In addition to residents such as **flamingoes**, **herons** and **egrets**, many migrant birds pause in these havens between October and March on their journeys south and then back north.

The mountains

In the **Peruvian Andes** there is an incredible variety of habitats. That this is a mountain area of true extremes becomes immediately obvious if you fly across, or along, the Andes towards Lima, the land below shifting from high *puna* to cloud forest to riparian valleys and eucalyptus tracts (introduced from Australia in the 1880s). The complexity of the whole makes it incredibly difficult to formulate any overall description that isn't essentially misleading: climate and vegetation vary according to altitude, latitude and local characteristics.

The Andes divides vertically into three main regions, identified by the Incas from top to bottom as the Puna, the Qeswa and the Yunka. The **Puna**, roughly 3800–4300m above sea level, has an average temperature of 3–6°C (37–43°F), and annual rainfall of 500–1000mm. Typical animals here include the main Peruvian cameloids – llamas, alpacas, *guanacos* and *vicuñas* – while crops that grow well here include the potato and quinoa grain. At 2500–3500m, the **Qeswa** has average temperatures of around 13°C (55°F), and a similar level of rainfall at 500–1200mm. The traditional forest here, including Andean pine, is not abundant and has been largely displaced by the imported Australian eucalyptus tree; the main cultivated crops include maize, potatoes and the nutritious *kiwicha* grain. The *ceja de selva* (cloud forest to high forest on the eastern side of the Andes) forms the lower-lying **Yunka**, at 1200–2500m, and has at least twice as much rain as the other two regions and abundant wildlife, including Peru's national bird, the red-crested *gallito de las rocas* (cock-of-the-rock). Plant life, too, is prolific, not least the region's orchids. On the western side of the Andes there is much less rainfall and it's not technically known as the Yunka, but it does share some characteristics: both sides have wild river canes (*caña brava*), and both are suitable for cultivating banana, pineapple, *yuca* and coca.

Mountain flora and fauna

Much of the Andes has been settled for over two thousand years – and hunter tribes go back another eight thousand years before this – so larger predators are rare, though still present in small numbers in the more remote regions. Among the most exciting you might actually see are the **mountain cats**, especially the **puma**, which lives at most altitudes and in a surprising number of habitats. Other more remote predators include the shaggy-looking **maned wolf** and the likeable **spectacled bear**, which inhabits the moister forested areas of the Andes and actually prefers eating vegetation to people.

The most visible animals in the mountains, besides sheep and cattle, are the cameloids – the wild **vicuña** and **guanaco**, and the domesticated **llama** and **alpaca**. Although these species are clearly related, zoologists disagree on whether or not the alpaca and llama are domesticated forms of their wild relatives. Domesticated they are, however, and have been so for thousands of years; studies reveal that cameloids appeared in North America some forty to fifty million years ago, crossing the Bering Straits long before any humans did. From these early forms the present species have evolved in Peru, Bolivia, Chile, Argentina and Ecuador, and there are now over three million llamas – 33 percent in Peru and a further 63 percent over the border in Bolivia. The alpaca population is just under four million, with 87 percent in Peru and only 11 percent in Bolivia. Of the two wild cameloids, the *vicuña* is the smaller and rarer, living only at the highest altitudes (up to 4500m) and with a population of just over 100,000. There are 4000 *guanaco* in Peru, compared to over 500,000 in Argentina alone.

Andean deer are quite common in the higher valleys and with luck you may even come across the rare **mountain tapir**. Smaller animals tend to be confined to particular habitats – rabbit-like **viscachas**, for example, to rocky outcrops; **squirrels** to wooded valleys; and **chinchillas** (Peruvian chipmunks) to higher altitudes.

Most birds also tend to restrict themselves to specific habitats. The **Andean goose** and **duck** are quite common in marshy areas, along with many species of wader and migratory waterfowl. A particular favourite is the elegant, very pink, **Andean flamingo**, which can usually be spotted from the road between Arequipa and Puno where they turn Lake Salinas into one great red mass. In addition, many species of passerine can be found alongside small streams. Perhaps the most striking of them is the **dipper**, which hunts underwater for larval insects along the stream bed, popping up to a rock every so often for air and a rest. At lower elevations, especially in and around cultivated areas, the **ovenbird** (or horneo) constructs its nest from mud and grasses in the shape of an old-fashioned oven; while in open spaces many birds of prey can be spotted, the comical **caracara**, **buzzard-eagle** and the magical **red-backed hawk** among them. The **Andean condor** (see p.520) is actually quite difficult to see up close as, although not especially rare, they tend to soar at tremendous heights for most of the day, landing only on high, inaccessible cliffs, or at carcasses after making sure that no one is around to disturb them. A glimpse of this magnificent bird soaring overhead will come only through frequent searching with binoculars, perhaps in relatively unpopulated areas or at one of the better-known sites such as the Cruz del Condor viewing platform in the Colca Canyon (see p.178).

Tropical rainforest

Descending the eastern edge of the Andes, you pass through the distinct habitats of the Puna, Qeswa and Yunka before reaching the lowland jungle or **rainforest**. In spite of its rich and luxuriant appearance, the rainforest is in fact extremely fragile. Almost all the nutrients are recycled by rapid decomposition (with the aid of the damp climate and a prodigious supply of insect labour) back into the vegetation, thereby creating a nutrient-poor soil that is highly susceptible to large-scale disturbance. When the forest is cleared, for example – usually in an attempt to colonize the area and turn it into viable farmland – there is not only heavy soil erosion to contend with but also a limited amount of nutrients in the earth (only enough for five years of good harvests and twenty years' poorer farming at the most). Natives of the rainforest have evolved cultural mechanisms by which, on the whole, these problems are avoided: they tend to live in small, dispersed groups, move their gardens every few years and obey sophisticated social controls to limit the chances of overhunting any one zone or any particular species.

Around eighty percent of the Amazon rainforest was still intact at the start of the twenty-first century, but for every **hardwood** logged in this forest, an average of 120 other trees are destroyed and left unused or simply burnt. Over an acre per second of this magnificent forest is burned or bulldozed, equating to an area the size of Great Britain, every year, even though this makes little economic sense in the long term. According to the late rainforest specialist Dr Alwyn Gentry, just 2.5 acres of primary rainforest could yield up to $9000 a year from sustainable harvesting of wild fruits, saps, resins and timber – yet the average income for the same area from ranching or plantations in the Amazon is a meagre $30 a year.

Amazon flora and fauna

The most distinctive attribute of the Amazon Basin is its overwhelming abundance of plant and animal species. Over six thousand species of plants have been reported in one small 250-acre tract of forest, and there are at least a thousand species of birds and dozens of types of monkeys and bats spread about the Peruvian Amazon. There are several reasons for this marvellous **natural diversity** of flora and fauna; most obviously, it is warm, there is abundant sunlight and large quantities of mineral nutrients are washed down from the Andes – ideal conditions for forest growth. Secondly, the rainforest has enormous structural diversity, with layers of vegetation from the forest floor to the canopy 30m above, providing a vast number of niches to fill. Thirdly, since there is such a variety of habitat as you descend the Andes, the changes in altitude mean a great diversity of localized ecosystems. With the rainforest being stable over longer periods of time than temperate areas (there was no Ice Age here, nor any prolonged periods of drought), the fauna has had the freedom to evolve, and to adapt to often very specialized local conditions.

But if the Amazon Basin is where most of the plant and animal species are in Peru, it is not easy to see them. Movement through the vegetation is limited to narrow trails and along the rivers in a boat. The river banks and flood plains are richly diverse areas: here you are likely to see **caimans**, **macaws**, **toucans**, **oropendulas**, **terns**, **horned screamers** and the primitive **hoatzins** – birds whose young are born with claws at the wrist to enable them to climb up from the water into the branches of overhanging trees. You should catch sight, too, of one of a variety of **hawks** and at least two or three species of **monkeys** (perhaps the **spider monkey**, the **howler** or the **capuchin**). With a lot of luck and more determined observation you may spot a rare **giant river otter**, **river dolphin**, **capybara**, or maybe even one of the **jungle cats.**

In the jungle proper you're more likely to find mammals such as the **peccary** (wild pig), **tapir**, **tamandua tree sloth** and the second largest cat in the world, the incredibly powerful **spotted jaguar**. Characteristic of the deeper forest zones, too, are many species of bird, including **hummingbirds** (more common in the forested Andean foothills), **manakins** and **trogons**, though the effects of widespread hunting make it difficult to see these around any of the larger settlements. Logging is proving to be another major problem for the forest fauna – since valuable trees are dispersed among vast areas of other species in the rainforest, a very large area must be disturbed to yield a relatively small amount of timber. Deeper into the forest, however, and the further you are from human habitation, a glimpse of any of these animals is quite possible. Most of the bird activity occurs in the canopy, 30 to 40m above the ground, but platforms such as the **canopy walkway** at the Amazon Explorama ACTS Field Station (see p.478) and another, newer one at Inkaterra's Reserva Amazonica (see p.445) on the Río Madre de Dios, make things a little easier.

AMAZON FLORA

Aguaje palm (*Mauritia flexuosa*) A tropical swamp plant, commonly growing up to 15m tall, with fan-shaped leaves that can be over 2m long, and barrel-shaped fruit (6–7cm long) with a purple, plastic-like skin; the thin layer of yellow pulp beneath the skin is consumed raw, made into a drink or used to flavour ice cream. The leaves can be used for roof-thatch or, more commonly, floor-matting. Younger leaves are utilized to make ropes, hammocks, net bags and sometimes baskets.

Ayahuasca (*Banisteriopsis caapi*) Interpreted from Quechua as "Vine of the Soul" or "Vine of the Dead", this is found exclusively in northwest Amazonia and is also called *yage* and *caap*. These names also refer to the hallucinogenic brew in which ayahuasca is the main ingredient, used widely in the Peruvian Amazon and by *curanderos*.

Brazil nut tree (*Bertholletia excelsa*) Up to 30m tall, these take over ten years to reach nut-bearing maturity, when a single specimen can produce over 450kg every year during the rainy season.

Breadfruit (*Artocarpus altilis*) This tree known locally as *pan del arbol*, related to the rubber tree, is cut open and dried so that the large brown beans can be taken and boiled for eating. Only in Central America are the whole fruits eaten and even in Peru, people only bother with these when they are out of bananas and *yuca* (manioc). The sap is a good medicine for hernias.

Caimotillo (*Manilkara bidentata*) Some spots in the primary forest are devoid of ground growth apart from this one species of small tree. Many Indians see these glades as *supay chacras* ("demons' gardens") and they keep away from them at night. The scientific explanation is that the azteca ant that lives on them has such acidic faeces that nothing else can grow where they live.

Capirona (*Calycophy spruceanum*) Related to the eucalyptus, this tree protects itself from insects by shedding its bark every two to three months. A fast grower, achieving 12m in just five years, it burns long and well and is consequently sold as firewood. Its sap can be applied to the throat for laryngitis, or mixed with lime and used as a gargle.

Catahua (*Eurocrypitan*) A large, hardwood tree reaching nearly 50m, this emergent tree depends on the Saki monkey for reproduction and seed dispersal. Its fruits are poisonous to most other animals.

Charapilla (*Dipteryx charapilla*) A gigantic tree, characterized by its six-metre base and a trunk over one metre in diameter. One of the hardest trees in the Iquitos region, it is rarely cut for timber because of its light yellowy colour. Young Conibo warriors were once tested for their strength and ability by how long they took to cut through the wood of ones that had already fallen. The fruit is eaten roasted, although the Achual of the Río Tigre prefer to eat them raw. The leaves are small and used for birth control by the Conibo.

Coca (*Erythroxylum coca*) Cocaine is just one of the alkaloids in coca leaves, which are traditionally sacred to Andeans. A vital aid in coping with the altitude, climate and rigours of the region, they help locals withstand low temperatures and act as a hunger depressant. Research also shows that they have a nutritional value, containing more calcium than any other edible plant, which is important in the Andes, an area with few dairy foods.

Epiphytes Often shrub-like plants, epiphytes live in the crowns or branching elbows of trees but are functionally independent of them. In the higher jungle areas, they are extremely common and diverse, encompassing various species of orchids, cacti, bromeliads and aroids. There are over five-hundred varieties of orchids recorded in the Amazon, many of them to be found in the *ceja de selva*.

Genipap (*Genipa americana*) Also called *huito*, this is related to coffee but is quite different. Growing up to 20m, it has small creamy flowers and fruit that's eaten ripe or used to make an alcoholic drink that alleviates arthritic pains and bronchial ailments. Unripe juice is taken for stomach ulcers. The sap turns from transparent to blue-black after exposure to the air and is used as a dye, or body and face paint.

Inga (*Inga edulis*) Belonging to the mimosa family and growing to over 35m, there are over 350 species in the *Inga* genus. Its most distinctive feature is its long bean pods containing sweet white pulp and large seeds, which some Indian groups use to treat dysentery.

Manioc (*Euphorbiaceae family*) The most important of cultivated plants in the Peruvian Amazon, and known in Peru as *yuca*, its most useful parts are the large, phallic-shaped tuber roots, the brunt of many indigenous jokes. High in carbohydrates and enzymes, which assist digestion of other foods, it is roasted (to get rid of the cyanide it contains) or brewed to make *masato* beer. It is also the basis of tapioca. As far as its medicinal functions go, the juice from the tubers is applied as a head wash for scabies or can be mixed with water to ease diarrhoea.

Monkey-ladder vine (*Leguminosae casalpinioideae*) Also known as the turtle-ladder vine, this unusual-looking vine spirals high up to blossom in the canopy of primary forests.

Peach palm (*Bactris gasipaes*) Also known as the *pihuayao*, and common in most areas of the Peruvian rainforest, its new shoots are the source for the Yaguar and Witoto Indians' "grass" skirts and headdresses. The bark of the stems is used for interior wall partitions in native houses. The cork-like insides of the stems are made into sleeping mats, a particularly important symbol of marriage among the Achual tribe along the Río Tigre. From its fallen trunks, the larvae of beetles are gathered as a delicacy by many indigenous groups.

Quinilla (*Manilkara bidentata*) This yellow flowering tree is easy to spot, not so much by its tall, straight forty-metre trunk, but by the sweetly scented carpet of flowers beneath it, or the yellow, cauliform patterns of its canopy, seen when flying over the forest.

Rubber tree (*Hevea brasiliensis*) Known as *jebe* in Peru and *seringuera* closer to the Brazilian border, as a valuable export these trees were the key to the Amazon's initial exploitation.

Sabre pentana (*Lupuna*) A softwood tree, mainly used as ply and now in danger of extinction, this is still one of the most impressive plants in the Peruvian Amazon, at nearly 50m tall. Harpy eagles nest in the same tree for life (if the tree is felled, the bird dies with it by refusing to eat again). The trees are scattered across the forest and are sometimes used by Indians as landmarks when travelling along the rivers.

Stilt palm (*Socratea exorrhiza*) Also abundant in the jungle, reaching heights of up to 15m, with a thin trunk and very thorny stilt roots that grow like a tepee above the ground. Its long thin leaves are used by some indigenous groups as a treatment for hepatitis. The most utilized part is the hard bark, which can be taken off in one piece for use as flooring or wall slats.

Thatch palm (*Lepidocaryum tenue*) A relatively thin plant growing to around 4m and with a noticeably ringed trunk. Its leaves are used as roof-thatch throughout the Peruvian Amazon.

Ungurahui palm (*Oenocarpus bataua*) The rotting trunks of this palm are home to the suri larvae of the rhinoceros beetle, a favoured food of local Indians. Its green fruits can also be squeezed for their oil, which is used to treat vomiting, diarrhoea and even malaria. The trunk and leaves are often used in house construction.

Walking palm (*Socratea exercisia*) The wood is often used for parquet flooring. Tradition has it that it developed spikes to protect itself against the now-extinct giant sloth, which used to push it over.

Wild mango (*Grias neuberthii*) The wild mango tree is frequently seen as an ornamental plant around rainforest lodges. A member of the Brazil nut family, it's actually unrelated to the true mango (*Mangifera indica*), but can grow up to 20m, with thin, spindly trunks and branches. Their delicate yellow flowers are odorous, but the fruit can be eaten raw, boiled or roasted and has a medicinal function as a purgative; the seed is grated to treat venereal tumours and associated fevers, as well as being used as an enema to cure dysentery. The bark can be used to induce vomiting.

AMAZON FAUNA

Anteaters There are four main types of anteater in Peru; all have powerful curved front claws but no teeth, instead using their long tongues to catch insects in holes and rotting vegetation, and share long, tube like snouts. They only have one baby at a time, which clings to the mother's back when she moves through the forest. Giant anteaters (*Myrmecophaga tridactyla*), which can be 2m long with hairy non-prehensile tails, are black, orange-brown and whiteish, with a diagonal black-and-white shoulder stripe. Solitary creatures, they can be seen day or night, and, while normally passive, can defend themselves easily with their powerful front legs. Collared anteaters, or southern tamandua (*Tamandua tetradactlya*), are smaller, at less than 1m long. Arboreal and terrestrial, they too are nocturnal and diurnal, though they move slowly as they have poor eyesight. Northern tamandua (*Tamandua mexicana*) are restricted to the northern jungles in Peru. The silky or pygmy anteater (*Cyclopes didactylus*) is quite small, rarely exceeding 25cm in length. It's a smoky-grey to golden colour on the upper parts, sometimes with dark-brown stripes from its shoulders to its rear. It's also distinguished by the soft whistling noise it makes.

Armadillos (*Dasypodidae* family) Of the giant armadillos and nine-banded long-nosed armadillos, the former are up to 1m long, the latter usually half this length. Both are covered in bony armour and have small heads with wide-set ears and grey-to-yellow colouring. Mostly nocturnal, they tend to feed on ants and termites, some fruit and even small prey. Giant armadillos are good diggers and live in burrows.

Bats Bat species comprise almost forty percent of all mammals in the Amazon, and all North, Central and South American bats belong to the suborder *Microchiroptera*. Vampire bats, which feed on the blood of mammals, are known to transmit rabies and are commonest in cattle-ranching areas rather than remote forest zones.

Brazilian tapir (*Tapirus terrestris*) Known as the *sachavaca* ("forest cow" in Quechua) in Peru, this is the largest forest land mammal at around 2m long, brown to dark grey in colour and with a large upper lip. Their tails are stumpy, their feet three-toed and their backs noticeably convex. Largely nocturnal, they browse swampy forests for fruit and grasses.

Capybara (*Hydrochaeris hydrochaeris*) The world's largest (friendly) rodent, the tan or grey capybara can be over 1m long and will give warning yelps to its family when scared. They eat aquatic vegetation and grasses, but are also known to fish and eat lizards when they come across them.

Dolphin The pink river dolphin (*Inia geoffrensis*) is about 2m long and has a noticeable dorsal fin. They feed exclusively on fish and will swim with or within a few metres of people. The smaller grey dolphin or tucuxi (*Sotalia fluviatilis*) achieves a maximum length of 1.5m, has a more prominent dorsal fin and usually jumps further and is more acrobatic than the pink dolphin.

Giant otter (*Pteronura brasiliensis*) Just over 1m long, ending in a thickish tail with a flattened tip. Their alarm call is a snort and they are very aggressive when in danger. They eat fish and move in extended family groups, with the males doing the least fishing but the most eating.

Manatee (*Trichechus inunguis*) Almost 3m in length, with a large tubular body, a flat tail, short front flippers and a whiskery face, this aquatic mammal is relatively common in the Iquitos area. They feed on water hyacinths and other aquatic vegetation, taking advantage of the high-water season to graze on the flooded riverside floor.

Paca (*Agouti paca*) Chestnut brown and white striped, this large, fat rat- and pig-like creature has plenty of flesh but a tiny tail, hardly visible beneath the rump hair. It's primarily nocturnal and feeds on roots and fallen fruit.

Peccary (*Tayassuidae*) Peccaries, or wild boar, are stocky with relatively spindly legs and biggish heads. The white-lipped peccary (*Tayassu pecari*) is up to 1m long and moves quickly in dangerous herds of fifty to a few hundred. Their diet is fruit and palm nuts, which they scour vast tracts of forest to find. The collared peccary (*Tayassu tajacu*) is smaller and moves in groups of five to twenty.

Red brocket deer (*Mazama americana*) Rarely much over 1m in length, these are mostly brown to grey, with large eyes, and the males have unbranched antlers which slope back. They are found in the forest or at waterholes, feeding on fruit and fungi.

Sloths The most common sloth in Peru is the brown-throated three-toed sloth (*Bradypus variegatus*). Up to 1m in length, they have small, round heads and whitish or brown faces with a short tail and long limbs. Their claws help them cling to branches, where they spend most of their time sleeping, but their slow movement makes them hard to spot (though you may see them around jungle lodges, where they are often kept as pets).

CATS

Jaguar (*Pantera onca*) Powerfully built, jaguars are almost 2m long, with black spots on silvery to tan fur; they hunt large mammals, though they fish too. Mainly rainforest dwellers, they are most frequently spotted sunning themselves on fallen trees. If you meet one, the best way to react is to make lots of noise.

Jaguarundi (*Felis* or *Puma yagouaroundi*) An unusual-looking wild cat, there are grey, black and red varieties, weighing up to 7kg and sometimes measuring up to 1.35m including tail. They once extended from Texas to Uruguay, but their last bastion is the Amazon.

Margay (*Felis wieldii*) Spotted and very slender, these cats are like skinny mini-ocelots or thin jaguars, found in many areas of the Peruvian Amazon.

Ocelot (*Felis pardalis*) Smallish with black spots and thin stripes on their torso, with a short tail and long slender legs, ocelots hunt rodents, lizards and birds, mostly in the rainforest.

Puma (*Felis concolor*) Brown to tan in colour, pumas hunt by day and night, preferring large mammals, but stooping to snakes, lizards and rats. They're most likely to be encountered in the Andes, and although wary of humans, can be dangerous; guides advise waving one's arms around and shouting in these situations.

PRIMATES

All South American primates are monkeys, which form a group of their own – *Platyrrhini* – subdividing into three main families: marmosets and tamarins (*Callitrichidae*); monkeys (*Cebidae*); and the Goeldi's monkey (*Callimiconidae*). Each of these has many types within it.

Capuchin monkey (*Cebus apella*) Reddish brown, with a black cap and paler shoulders, this noisy creature moves in groups of up to twenty while searching for fruit, palm nuts, birds' eggs and small lizards.

Dusky titi monkey (*Callicebus moloch*) The necks of these reddish-brown creatures are hidden by thick fur, giving them a stocky appearance belied by their hairless faces. Eating leaves and fruit, they are found in dense forest near swamps, or bamboo thickets beside rivers.

Pygmy marmoset (*Cebuella pygmaea*) These rarely achieve more than 15cm in length, and are distinguished by their tawny to golden-grey head and forequarters and mane of hair, plus slender tails. Found in the lower understorey of the trees in flood forests, they feed on tree sap, insects and fruit.

Saddle-backed tamarin (*Saguinus fuscicollis*) The most widespread species of tamarin in the forests of Manu and around Iquitos, though there are a further thirteen subspecies. Black to reddish brown, they are diurnal and arboreal, living under the tree canopy and eating nectar, fruit and insects.

Spider monkey (*Ateles paniscus*) These are entirely black, with a small head and long arms, legs and tail, and can be seen swinging through the primary forest in groups of up to twenty. Highly sociable, intelligent and noisy, they feed on fruit, flowers and leaves.

Woolly monkey (*Lagothrix lagothricha*) Mostly brown, they have a strong tail, which helps them travel through the upper and middle storeys of the forest in groups of up to sixty. They eat fruit, palm nuts, seeds and leaves and are found in primary forest, including wooded flood plains.

BIRDS

Andean condor (*Vultur gryphus*) Up to 1.3m long, with a wingspan of 3.5m and mostly black with a white neck ruff and white wing feathers, these are rarely seen in groups of more than two or three. Their habitat is mainly at 2000–5000m, but they are also seen on the coast of Peru, feeding off carrion.

Black-headed cotinga (*Cotingidae*) Related to flycatchers, they have a symbiotic relationship with a number of fruiting trees.

Curassow (*Crax mitu*) Their well-developed crests are mainly black, with a shiny blue mantle; both the bill and legs are red. Their booming song can be heard as they move in small flocks of two to five birds.

Cock-of-the-rock (*Rupicola peruvianus*) The national bird of Peru, the male of this species ranges from orange to deep red in plumage and can be spotted dancing in large groups – *Pampa Hermosa Lodge* (see p.455) is good for this – usually in a particular tree (*lek* or *danzadero*); the female is a duller brown in colour.

Fasciated tiger-heron (*Tigrisoma fasciatum*) Graceful river birds with short, dusky bills and a black crown, named for the stripy appearance of their rufous-and-white underparts.

Hoatzin (*Opisthocomus hoazin*) Their most distinctive features are long Mohican crests, and the hooks that the young have on their shoulders. Also, they haven't evolved full stomachs and their chromosomes are close to those of chickens. Usually spotted in sizeable and gregarious gangs, they are poor flyers and hide in swampy areas. Indians use hoatzins' feathers for arrow flights.

Hummingbird (*Trochilidae*) Distinguished by the fastest metabolisms and wing beats of any bird (up to eighty per second) and the ability to rotate their wings through 180 degrees, some varieties are the smallest birds in the world. Many tribes have a special place for hummingbirds in their religious beliefs.

Lawrence thrush (*Turdus lawrencii*). A species of bird in the *Turdidae* family, this clever bird is able to imitate other bird calls (over a hundred have been noted from one bird alone).

Macaw (*Psittacidae*) Noisy, talkative creatures with strong bills, macaws mate for life (which can be as long as a hundred years), and pairs fly among larger flocks. Common macaws in Peru include the blue and yellow macaw (*Ara ararauna*) which grows to almost 1m and has a very long pointed tail, the scarlet macaw (*Ara macao*) and the red and green macaw (*Ara cloroptera*).

Nunbird With slender red bills and mostly black plumage, black-fronted nunbirds (*Monasa nigrifrons*) are found in ones or twos at all levels of the rainforest and are noted for their noisy performance in the early evenings. White-fronted nunbirds (*Monasa morphoeus*) are slightly smaller and with a white forehead, but are similar in behaviour.

Oropendula (*Icteridae*) Related to the blackbird family, these like living near human habitations, their vibrant croaking making them unmistakeable. One of the commonest varieties is the large black oropendula (*Gymnostinaps guatimoziuus*), which has a long, brilliant lemon-yellow tail, with two black central tail feathers.

Roadside hawk (*Buteo magnirostris*) Grey to brown in colour, there are 12 subspecies of this hawk, sometimes known as the chicken hawk; these are not great flyers by hawk standards, and depend mainly on insects, vertebrates and small birds, like newly hatched domestic chicks.

Scaled fruiteater (*Ampelioden tschudii*) This bird is frequently seen in the upper canopy, usually alone but sometimes in pairs or, less frequently, in large mixed flocks.

Swainson's thrush (*Catharus ustulatus*) Small in stature but magnificent in voice, this timid, solitary bird lives mainly in lower primary forest.

Tinamou (*Tinamidae*) Rather like chickens with long beaks, the many varieties include the rare black tinamou (*Tinamus osgoodi*), the great tinamou (*Tinamus major*), noted for its tremulous whistling noises, and the grey tinamou (*Tinamus tao*), similar in behaviour to the great tinamou.

Toucan (*Ramphastidae*) Unmistakeable for their colourful plumage and large bill, there are many varieties. One of the more common is the white-throated toucan (*Ramphastos tucanus*) – also one of the largest, it is mainly black but with bursts of orange and red and a white throat and chest. Rarer and smaller is the yellow-ridged toucan (*Ramphastos culminatus*), with a distinctive yellow ridge across the top of its head and a yellow-and-blue band close to the eyes.

Trumpeter (*Psophiidae*) Common, largely terrestrial birds that eat vegetation, small lizards and shiny objects (including gold, silver and sometimes diamonds), they are often kept as pets in Indian and colonist settlements. The grey-winged trumpeter (*Psophia crepitans*) tends to be recognized by its nocturnal guttural sounds, which sound like the loud purring of a cat. Grey in the wild, its wings turn white in captivity.

Vulture (*Cathartidae*) Carrion-eaters, this family includes the Andean condor (see opposite) and the stunning king vulture (*Surcoramphus papa*), which has mainly white plumage with black rump, tail and flight feathers. It's mostly spotted in solitary flight and sometimes in pairs. Other vultures include the turkey vulture (*Cathartes aura*), the greater yellow-headed vulture (*Cathartes melambrotus*), the lesser yellow-headed vulture (*Cathartes burrovianus*) and the black vulture (*Coragyps atratus*), seen around every rubbish dump in Peru.

REPTILES AND AMPHIBIANS

Caiman (*Alligatoridae*) There are four types of caiman in Peru: the black caiman (*Melanosuchus niger*) is increasingly rare due to hunting, while the spectacled caiman (*Caiman crocodilus*) is usually found sunbathing along river beaches; the smaller musky caiman and smooth-fronted caiman are found in small tributaries and lakes.

Frog and toad Frogs grow to surprising sizes in Peru. Most are nocturnal and their chorus is heard along every Amazonian river after sunset. The most commonly spotted is the cane toad (*Bufo marinus*), which secretes toxins that protect it. More common still is the leaf-litter dweller (*Bufo typhonius*), but it's harder to spot as it imitates the colour and form of dead leaves.

Iguana (*Iguanidae* family) Often reaching up to a metre long and marked by a spiky crest along their backs, these are wholly vegetarian leaf-eaters that can be seen sleeping on high branches soaking up the sun. Less often they can

CONSERVATION AND ENVIRONMENTAL POLITICS IN PERU

Climate change is already having serious impacts on Peru's priceless environment and the country has been identified as a region which has the most to lose from global warming.

DIMINISHING GLACIERS

The glaciers are retreating fast. South America possesses more than 99 percent of the world's tropical glaciers, with over seventy percent of these located in Peru, where they act as a reservoir of meltwater which provides two very vital resources: on the one hand it gives the water for drinking, agriculture and hydroelectricity for urban areas, industry and agriculture in the Andes and the desert coast, even during the dry season; on other hand, and in the other direction, the glaciers feed the main headwaters of the Amazon basin. With the glaciers diminishing problems are beginning already in both directions – water shortages on the coast and very low dry-season river levels in the Amazon. The Peruvian glaciers, essential stores of the planet's most basic resource, have been described by Lonnie Thompson (an Ohio State University glaciologist) as the "water towers of the world". Nevertheless, Peru's most visited glacier – Pastoruri (see box, p.318), near the city of Huaraz – and previously the country's main ski resort, has finally split itself into two halves; retreating at an incredible 20m every year, it has lost more than half of its surface area since 1995 and will almost certainly vanish completely before 2020. CONAM, Peru's National Environment Agency, estimates that by 2025, Peru will be the first country in South America to experience "permanent water stress", principally, of course, along the urbanized coastal belt.

GROUND AND WATER POLLUTION

Ground and water **pollution**, among the worst in the world, has become a concern around some of Peru's Andean mining towns. La Oroya, just four hours by road from Lima, has been a major mining centre since 1922 when the US Cerro de Paso Corporation established its first smelter here. The three plants operating around La Oroya were once claimed by the Ministry of Energy and Mines to be producing around 1.5 tonnes of lead and over 800 tonnes of sulphur dioxide every day. These levels of pollution are significantly greater than is permitted under Peruvian law and blood samples from newborn babies in the town of La Oroya found over 8.8 micrograms of lead per 100 millilitres, very close to the maximum a baby can cope with without damaging its cognitive abilities. Other mines, mainly in the Mantaro river basin, close to La Oroya, pour contaminated waters downstream, affecting the health of indigenous and settler populations on the Amazon headwaters.

be seen swimming in rivers, mainly to get away from predators, such as hawks.

Snake Peru has the world's widest variety of snakes, but it's rare to meet anacondas, rainbow boas (*Epicrates cenchria*), fer-de-lances (*Bothrops atrox*) or bushmasters (*Lachesis muta*) in the Amazon. Anacondas kill mainly by twisting their tails around tree roots in lakes or riverbanks, then floating out from this before attacking. They also stun fish by violently expelling air from their coiled bodies. Smaller snakes tend to be scared of people and you're more likely to see them in retreat than heading for you.

Yellow-footed tortoise (*Geochelone denticulata*) The only land tortoise in the Amazon, it can grow up to around 1m long but is generally half this size. In prehistoric times, however, they reached the proportions of a Volkswagen Beetle.

Indigenous rights and the destruction of the rainforest

The indigenous people of the Peruvian jungles are being pushed off their land by an endless combination of slash-and-burn colonization, megadam builders, big oil companies, gold miners, timber extractors, coca farmers organized by drug-trafficking barons and, at times, "revolutionary" political groups. All along the main rivers and jungle roads, settlers are flooding into the area. In their wake, forcing land-title agreements to which they have no right, are the main timber companies and multinational oil corporations. In large tracts of the jungle the fragile selva ecology has already been destroyed; in others the tribes have been more subtly disrupted as they become dependent on outside consumer goods and trade, or by the imposition of evangelical proselytizing groups, and the Indian way of life is being destroyed.

In response to the dire situation of indigenous communities, self-determination groups sprang up throughout the 1970s and 1980s, such as AIDESEP (Inter-ethnic Association for the Development of the Peruvian Amazon) and CONAP (Coalition of Indigenous Nationalities of the Peruvian Amazon).

In May 2008, Alan García's government very publicly created Peru's first **Ministry of the Environment** during the Lima-based European Union–Latin America and the Caribbean Summit whose main focus was climate change. Cynics saw this as a direct attempt for Peru to access new and future global funds for conservation, rather than a serious effort to protect the country's rainforests and mega-biodiversity. Within weeks of the new ministry's creation, the government also announced plans to open up community-owned lands for commercial investment by making fundamental changes to the law of **land ownership** in the Andes and Amazon regions – a move which was integral to the new free-trade agreement between Peru and the US. The concept is straightforward: without long-term ownership of large areas of land, big corporations are simply unlikely to invest in massive agribusiness schemes such as soya production and the cultivation of crops for biofuels.

Deforestation

According to the UN Food and Agriculture Organization (FAO), 53.1 percent of Peru is forested. Of this, 88.5 percent is classified as **primary forest**, the most biodiverse and

MEGADAMS

The Brazilian electricity company Electrobras has an agreement with Peru to build at least six **megadams** to generate electricity in the Peruvian Amazon over the coming years. The plan is that eighty percent of the electricity produced, initially at least, be exported to Brazil to power **aluminium plants** in the western Brazilian Amazon. The dams are so big, however, that their social and environmental impact would be devastating, and the project is seen as another of ex-President García's big thumbs-down to the environment and indigenous Peruvian communities. More information on the most controversial of these megadam proposals can be found on these websites:

- internationalrivers.org
- latinamericacurrentevents.com
- rainforestfoundationuk.org
- indigenouspeoplesissues.com

carbon-dense form. **Deforestation** is responsible for nineteen percent of present global carbon dioxide emissions; alongside this there's the obvious travesty of concomitant destruction of forest habitats and biodiversity – Peru has some 2937 known species of amphibians, birds, mammals and reptiles – and the home of many indigenous peoples. Despite Peru's vested interest in mitigating climate change, logging of the Amazon region continues apace, up to eighty percent of it possibly illegal but whitewashed with official documents by the time the timber reaches Lima and the port of Callao for export. In total, between 1990 and 2010, Peru lost 3.1 percent of its forest cover. Combating these excesses may well be the biggest challenge for the present government.

Illegal gold mining

Peru's worst example of **illegal gold mining** is found in the southeastern jungles of Madre de Dios, home to the Amarakaeri people, where monster-sized machinery is transforming one of the Amazon's most biodiverse regions into a huge muddy scar. A number of gold miners have already moved into the unique Tambopata Reserved Zone, a protected jungle area where giant otters, howler monkeys, king vultures, anacondas and jaguars are regularly spotted. All plant life around each mine is turned into gravel, known in Peru as *cancha*, for just a few ounces of gold a day. Front-loading machines move up to about 30m depth of soil, which is then washed on a wooden sluice where high-pressure hoses separate the silt and gold from mud and gravel. **Mercury**, added at this stage to facilitate gold extraction, is later burnt off, causing river and air pollution. The mines are totally unregulated, and the richer, more established mining families tend to run the show, having the money to import large machines upriver from Brazil or by air from Chile.

The **indigenous tribes** are losing control of their territory to an ever-increasing stream of these miners and settlers coming down from the high Andes. As the mercury pollution and suspended mud from the mines upstream kill the life-giving rivers, they have to go deeper and deeper into the forest for fish, traditionally their main source of protein. Beatings and death threats from the miners and police are not uncommon.

There is a hope that improved **gold-mining technology** can stem the tide of destruction in these areas; mercury levels in Amazon rivers and their associated food chains are rising at an alarming rate. However, with raw mercury available for only $13 a kilo there is little obvious economic incentive to find ways of using less-hazardous materials. Cleaner gold-mining techniques have, however, been developed in **Brazil**. Astonishingly simple, the new method utilizes a wooden sluice with a gentler slope (instead of a steeper, ridged slope) to extract the gold from the washed river sediment and gravel. Trials have shown that this increases gold yields by up to forty percent, and the addition of a simple sluice box at the base of the slope has also led to the recovery of some 95 percent of the mercury used in the process. The same project has also developed a procedure of **test boring** to estimate quantities of gold in potential gravel deposits, which minimizes unnecessary and uneconomic earth-moving in search of gold. If taken on board by gold miners in the Amazon and elsewhere, these techniques should reduce environmental damage. However, the fact remains that pressure by international **environmental groups**, and the publicity they generate, continues to make a difference.

Voluntarily isolated tribes

Even now, in the twenty-first century, the largest of Peru's indigenous tribes or nations, like the **Ashaninka** and **Aguaruna-Huambisa**, stand firm against exploitation and invasion from outside influences. But more and more previously **uncontacted** or **voluntarily isolated** Indians are having their land invaded by loggers or oil companies. Ex-President García has disputed the very existence of these people, yet images of the tribes published in the media (see survivalinternational.org/tribes/isolatedperu) have recently brought them to worldwide attention.

Peruvian recipes

Peruvian cooking – even in small restaurants well away from the big cities – is appealing stuff. The nine recipes below are among the classics, fairly simple to prepare and found throughout the country (with a couple of coastal exceptions). You'll find all the ingredients listed readily available in local markets. All quantities given are sufficient for four people.

Ceviche

A cool, spicy dish, eaten on the Peruvian coast for at least the past thousand years.

1kg soft white fish (lemon sole and halibut are good, or you can mix half fish, half shellfish)
2 large onions, sliced
1 or 2 chillies, chopped
6 limes (or lemons, but these aren't as good)
1 tbsp olive oil
1 tbsp fresh coriander (or cilantro)
salt and pepper to taste

Wash and cut the fish into bite-sized pieces. Place in a dish with the sliced onions. Add the chopped chilli and coriander. Make a marinade using the lime juice, olive oil, salt and pepper. Pour over the fish and place in a cool spot until the fish is "soft cooked" (10min–1hr). Serve with boiled potatoes (preferably sweet) and corn on the cob.

Papas a la Huancaina

An excellent and ubiquitous snack – cold potatoes covered in a mildly *picante* cheese sauce.

1 kg potatoes, boiled
1 or 2 chillies, chopped
2 cloves of garlic, chopped
200g soft goat's cheese (feta or cottage cheese will work too)
6 crackers
1 hard-boiled egg
1 small can of evaporated milk

Chop very finely or liquidize all the above ingredients except for the potatoes. The mixture should be fairly thin but not too runny. Pour sauce over the thickly sliced potatoes. Arrange on a dish and serve garnished with lettuce and black olives. Best served chilled.

Palta Rellena

Stuffed avocados – another very popular snack.

2 avocados, soft but not ripe
1 onion, chopped
2 tomatoes, chopped
2 hard-boiled eggs, chopped
200g cooked chicken or tuna fish, cold and flaked
2 tbsp mayonnaise

Cut the avocados in half and remove the stones. Scoop out a little of the flesh around the hole. Gently combine all the other ingredients before piling into the centre of each avocado half.

Causa

About the easiest Peruvian dish to reproduce outside the country, though there are no real substitutes for Peruvian tuna and creamy Andean potatoes.

1kg potatoes
200g tuna fish
2 avocados, the riper the better
4 tomatoes
salt and black pepper to taste
1 lemon

Boil the potatoes and mash to a firm, smooth consistency. Flake the tuna fish and add a little lemon juice. Mash the avocados to a pulp, add the rest of the lemon juice, some salt and black pepper. Slice the tomatoes. Press one quarter of the tuna fish over an initial layer of mashed potato, then a quarter of the avocado mixture on top. Add a layer of sliced tomato. Continue the same layering process until you have four layers of each. Cut into rough slices. Serve (ideally chilled) with salad, or on its own as a starter.

Locro de Zapallo

A standard meal of vegetables in pumpkin sauce with rice, found on most set menus in the cheaper, working-class restaurants.

1kg pumpkin
1 large potato
2 cloves of garlic
1 tbsp oregano
1 cup of milk
2 corn on the cobs
1 onion
1 chilli, chopped
salt and pepper
200g cheese (mozzarella works well)

Fry the onion, chilli, garlic and oregano. Add half a cup of water. Mix in the pumpkin as large-cut lumps (they get very soft, very fast), slices of corn on the cob and finely chopped potato. Add the milk and cheese. Simmer until a soft, smooth consistency, and add a little more water if necessary. Serve with rice or over fish.

Pescado a la Chorillana

Probably the most popular way of cooking fish on the coast.

4 pieces of fish (cod or any other white fish will do)
2 large onions, chopped
4 large tomatoes, chopped
1 or 2 chillies, chopped into fairly large pieces
1 tbsp oil
half a cup of water

Grill or fry each portion of fish until done and keep hot. Fry separately the onions, tomatoes and chilli. Add the water to form a sauce. Pile the hot sauce over each portion of fish and serve with rice.

Asado

A roast – an expensive meal for Peruvians, though a big favourite for family gatherings, and only available in fancier restaurants.

1kg or less of lean beef
2 cloves of garlic
200g butter
1 tin of tomato purée
salt and pepper
1 tbsp soy sauce
2 tomatoes
1 chilli, chopped

Cover the beef with the premixed garlic and butter. Mix the tomato purée with salt, pepper and soy sauce. Liquidize the tomatoes with the chopped chilli. Spread both mixtures on the beef and cook slowly in a covered casserole dish for four or five hours. Traditionally the *asado* is served with *pure de papas*, which is simply a runny form of mashed potatoes whipped up with some butter and a lot of garlic: a very tasty combination.

Quinoa Vegetable Soup

Quinoa – known as "mother grain" in the Andes – is a natural whole grain with remarkable nutritional properties; it's simple and tasty to add to any soups or stews.

4 cups of water
quarter of a cup of quinoa
half a cup of diced carrots
quarter of a cup of diced celery
2 tbsp finely chopped onions
quarter of a green pepper
2 mashed cloves of garlic
1 tbsp vegetable oil
half a cup of chopped tomatoes
half a cup of finely chopped cabbage
1 tbsp salt
some chopped parsley

Gently fry the *quinoa* and all the vegetables (except the cabbage and tomatoes) in oil and garlic until browned. Then add the water, cabbage and tomatoes before bringing to the boil. Season with salt and garnish with parsley.

Aji de Gallina

Literally translated as "Chillied Chicken", this is not as spicy as it sounds and utilizes a delicious, cheesy yellow sauce.

1 chicken breast
1 cup of breadcrumbs
2 soup spoons of powdered yellow chilli
50g Parmesan cheese
50g peanuts

1 cup of evaporated milk (more if the sauce seems too dry)
1 sliced onion (red or white)

Boil the chicken breast, then strain and fry it for a bit. Mix the hot chicken water with the breadcrumbs. Meanwhile, in a pot, heat two tablespoons of olive oil and brown the onions. Mix in the yellow chilli powder. Mix in the breadcrumbs as liquidized as possible. After a few minutes still on the heat, add in the Parmesan cheese, the chicken, salt to taste and finally the peanuts. Boil for another ten minutes. Add the evaporated milk just before serving and stir in well. Decorate the plate with boiled potatoes, preferably of the Peruvian yellow variety (if not white will do), cut into cross-sectional slices about a centimetre or so thick. Add a sliced egg and black olives on top.

Thanks to Señora Delia Arvi Tarazona for this recipe

Books

There are few books published exclusively about Peru and very few works by Peruvian writers ever make it into English. Many of the classic works on Peruvian and Inca history are now out of date (o/p), though frequently one comes across them in libraries around the world or bookshops in Lima and Cusco. Travel books, coffee-table editions and country guides are also generally available in Lima bookshops. Others can be obtained through the South American Explorers' Club (see p.50), who also have specialist and out-of-publication articles, books, maps and documents. Titles marked ★ are especially recommended.

INCA AND ANCIENT HISTORY

Anthony Aveni *Nasca: Eighth Wonder of the World.* Contains much on the history of the Nasca people and explores the complex relationships between water, worship, social order and the environment. Written by a leading scholar who has spent twenty years excavating here.

Kathleen Berrin *The Spirit of Ancient Peru: Treasures from the Museo Arqueológico Rafael Larco Herrera* (o/p). Essentially a detailed exhibition catalogue with essays by reputable Andeanists with plenty of quality illustrations and photographs representing one of Peru's finest collections of mainly pre-Inca artefacts.

Hiram Bingham *Lost City of the Incas*. The classic introduction to Machu Picchu: the exploration accounts are interesting but many of the theories should be taken with a pinch of salt. Widely available in Peru.

Peter T. Bradley *The Lure of Peru: Maritime Intrusion into the South Sea 1598–1701* (o/p). A historical account of how the worldwide fame of the country's Inca treasures attracted Dutch, French and English would-be settlers, explorers, merchants and even pirates to the seas and shores of Peru. Includes descriptions of naval blockades of Lima and various waves of buccaneers and their adventures in search of Peru.

Richard Burger *Chavín and the Origins of Andean Civilisation*. A collection of erudite essays – essential reading for anyone seriously interested in Peruvian prehistory.

★ **Geoffrey Hext Sutherland Bushnell** *Peru* (o/p). A classic, concise introduction to the main social and technological developments in Peru from 2500 BC to 1500 AD; well illustrated, if dated in some aspects.

Pedro de Cieza de Leon *The Discovery and Conquest of Peru (Latin America in Transition)*. A new paperback version of the classic post-Conquest chronicler account.

Evan Hadingham *Lines to the Mountain Gods: Nasca and the Mysteries of Peru*. One of the more down-to-earth books on the Nasca Lines, including maps and illustrations.

★ **John Hemming** *The Conquest of the Incas*. The authoritative narrative tale of the Spanish Conquest, very readably brought to life from a mass of original sources.

Thor Heyerdahl, Daniel Sandweiss and Alfredo Navárez *Pyramids of Túcume*. A recently published description of the archeological site at Túcume plus the life and society of the civilization that created this important ceremonial and political centre around 1000 years ago. Widely available in Peruvian bookshops.

Richard Keatinge (ed) *Peruvian Prehistory*. One of the most up-to-date and reputable books on the ancient civilizations of Peru – a collection of serious academic essays on various cultures and cultural concepts through the millennia prior to the Inca era.

Ann Kendall *Everyday Life of the Incas* (o/p). Accessible, very general description of Peru under Inca domination.

Alfred L. Kroeber and Donald Collier *The Archeology and Pottery of Nasca, Peru: Alfred Kroeber's 1926 Expedition*. A historical perspective on the archeology of Peru.

Kim MacQuarrie *The Last Days of the Incas*. Available in both hardback and paperback, this is a thoroughly researched and highly dramatic account of Francisco Pizarro's conquest, depicting the Inca rebellion and subsequent guerrilla war. The book also covers the modern search for lost Inca cities.

J. Alden Mason *Ancient Civilisations of Peru*. Reprinted in 1991, an excellent summary of the country's history from the Stone Age through to the Inca Empire.

Michael E. Moseley *The Incas and Their Ancestors*. A fine overview of Peru before the Spanish Conquest, which makes full use of good maps, diagrams, sketches, motifs and photos.

Keith Muscutt *Warriors of the Clouds: A Lost Civilization in the Upper Amazon of Peru*. Some superb photos of the ruins and environment left behind by the amazing Chachapoyas culture of northern Peru.

William Hickling Prescott *History of the Conquest of Peru*. Hemming's main predecessor – a nineteenth-century classic that remains a good read, if you can find a copy.

Johan Reinhard *Nasca Lines: A New Perspective on Their Origin and Meaning*. Original theories about the Lines and ancient mountain gods. The same author also wrote *The Sacred Centre: Machu Picchu* (Nuevas Imagenes, Lima), a fascinating book, drawing on anthropology, archeology, geography and astronomy to reach highly probable conclusions about the sacred geology and topography of the Cusco region, and how this appears to have been related to Inca architecture, in particular Machu Picchu.

Gene Savoy *Antisuyo: The Search for the Lost Cities of the Amazon* (o/p). Exciting account of Savoy's important explorations, plus loads of historical detail.

★ **Garcilasco de la Vega** *The Royal Commentaries of the Incas* (2 vols; o/p). Many good libraries have a copy of this, the most readable and fascinating of contemporary historical sources. Written shortly after the Conquest, by a "Spaniard" of essentially Inca blood, this work is the best eyewitness account of life and beliefs among the Incas.

Oscar Medina Zevallos *The Enigma of Machu Picchu*. Written by a Peruvian explorer and historical writer, this book tries to answer some of the difficult questions posed by Machu Picchu.

MODERN HISTORY AND SOCIETY

Susan E. Benner and Kathy S. Leonard *Fire from the Andes: Short Fiction by Women from Bolivia, Ecuador, and Peru*. A fascinating read featuring unique and passionate writing.

Sally Bowen and Jane Holligan *The Imperfect Spy: the many lives of Vladimiro Montesinos*. Tracing the emergence of Montesinos, who virtually ran Peru throughout the 1990s, as head of SIN (Servicio de Inteligencia Nacional), this well-researched book covers his upbringing and career in a highly engaging and accessible style. It provides a fascinating insight into corruption and power in the CIA and the mafia, as manifested in Peru.

Eduardo Calderón *Eduardo El Curandero: The Words of a Peruvian Healer*. Peru's most famous shaman – El Tuno – outlines his teachings and beliefs in his own words.

Carlos Cumes and Romulo Lizarraga Valencia *Pachamamas Children: Mother Earth and Her Children of the Andes in Peru*. A New Age look at the culture, roots and shamanistic aspects of modern Peru.

Holligan de Díaz-Limaco *Peru in Focus*. A good (if short) general reader on Peru's history, politics, culture and environment.

James Higgins *Lima: a cultural and literary history*. A scholarly book showing great affection for Lima, carefully weaving together both its culture and social history. It guides the reader through Lima's historical sites with particular emphasis on the colonial era, and culminating with a section on modern-day culture.

★ **F. Bruce Lamb and Manuel Córdova-Rios** *The Wizard of the Upper Amazon*. Masterful reconstruction of the true story of Manuel Córdova-Rios – "Ino Moxo" – a famous herbal healer and *ayahuascero* from Iquitos who was kidnapped as a young boy and brought up by Indians in the early twentieth century. Offers significant insight into indigenous psychedelic healing traditions.

E. Luís Martín *The Kingdom of the Sun: A Short History of Peru* (o/p). The best general history of Peru, concentrating on the post-Conquest period until the 1980s.

Nicole Maxwell *Witch-Doctor's Apprentice* (o/p). A very personal and detailed account of the author's research into the healing plants used by Amazonian Peruvian tribes; a highly informative book on plant lore.

Sewell H. Menzel *Fire in the Andes: U.S. Foreign Policy and Cocaine Politics in Bolivia and Peru*. A good summary of US anti-cocaine activities in these two countries, written by credible academics.

David Scott Palmer (ed) *Shining Path of Peru*. A modern history compilation of meticulously detailed essays and articles by Latin American academics and journalists on the early and middle phases of Sendero Luminoso's civil war in Peru.

Michael Reid *Peru: Paths to Poverty* (o/p). A succinct analysis tracing Peru's economic and security crisis of the early 1980s back to the military government of General Velasco.

Orin Starn, Carlos Degregori and Robin Kirk (eds) *The Peru Reader: History, Culture, Politics*. One of the best overviews yet of Peruvian history and politics, with writing by characters as diverse as Mario Vargas Llosa and Abimael Guzmán (imprisoned ex-leader of Sendero Luminoso).

Americas Watch *Peru under Fire: Human Rights since the Return to Democracy*. A good summary of Peruvian politics in the 1980s.

FLORA AND FAUNA

Allen Altman and B. Swift *Checklist of the Birds of Peru*. A useful summary with photos of different habitats.

J.L. Castner, S.L. Timme and J.A. Duke *A Field Guide to Medicinal and Useful Plants of the Upper Amazon*. Of interest to enthusiasts and scientists alike, this book contains handy colour illustrations.

L.H. Emmons *Neotropical Rainforest Mammals: A Field Guide*. An excellent paperback with over 250 pages of authoritative text and illustrations.

★ **Steven L. Hilty and William L. Brown** *A Guide to the Birds of Colombia*. One of the few classic ornithology guides covering the fascinating and rich birdlife of Peru and its surrounding countries.

M. Koepke *The Birds of the Department of Lima*. A small but classic guide, for many years the only one available that covered many of Peru's species, and still good for its excellent illustrations.

★ **Richard E. Schultes and Robert F. Raffauf** *The Healing Forest*. An excellent and erudite large-format paperback on many of the Amazon's most interesting plants. It's well illustrated with exquisite photographs and is a relatively easy read.

Richard E. Schultes and Robert F. Raffauf *Vine of the Soul*. One of the best large-format books about the indigenous use of the hallucinogenic plant ayahuasca.

Thomas Valqui *Where to Watch Birds in Peru*. Divided into seven sections or regions of Peru, it covers 151 of the most important birding sites, featuring maps and details on how to reach the locations as well as where to stay nearby. Naturally, it also gives plenty of information on what books to look for and thorough descriptions of birds and their habitats. Incorporates an up-to-date Peru bird checklist.

Barry Walker and Jon Fjeldsa *Birds of Machu Picchu*. A splendid full-colour booklet focusing on the birdlife found in Peru's best-known National Sanctuary and the area within which the Inca Trail is located.

Walter Wust *Manu: el último refugio*. This is an excellent coffee-table book on the wildlife and flora of Manu National Park by one of Peru's foremost wildlife photographers. Available in most good bookshops in Lima and Cusco.

TRAVEL

Timothy E. Albright and Jeff Tenlow *Dancing Bears and the Pilgrims Progress in the Andes: Transformation on the Road to Qolloriti*. A slightly dry report on the Snow Star annual festival of Qoyllur Rit'i, which is attended by tens of thousands of Andean peasants at the start of every dry season.

Christopher Isherwood *The Condor and the Cows* (o/p). A diary of Isherwood's South American trip after World War II, most of which took place in Peru. Like Paul Theroux, Isherwood eventually arrives in Buenos Aires, to meet Jorge Luis Borges.

John Lane *A Very Peruvian Practice*. This comical and well-written autobiographical travel book about Lane's work as advisor to a new ladies' health clinic in Lima paints a colourful picture of life in Peru – from bullfights to funerals, and the rainforest to Andean mountaintops.

Patrick Leigh Fermor *Three Letters from the Andes*. Three long letters written from Peru in 1971, describing the experiences of a rather upper crust mountaineering expedition.

Dervla Murphy *Eight Feet in the Andes*. An enjoyable account of a rather adventurous journey Dervla Murphy made across the Andes with her young daughter and a mule. It can't compare with her India books, though.

Matthew Parris *Inca Kola, A Traveller's Tale of Peru*. Very amusing description of travelling in Peru, with a perspicacious look at Peruvian culture, past and present.

Tom Pow *In the Palace of Serpents: An Experience of Peru*. A well-written insight into travelling in Peru, spoilt only by the fact that Tom Pow was ripped off in Cusco and lost his original notes. Consequently he didn't have as wonderful a time as he might have and seems to miss the beauty of the Peruvian landscapes and the wealth of history and culture.

Paul Theroux *The Old Patagonian Express*. Theroux didn't much like Peru, nor Peruvians, but for all the self-obsessed pique and disgust for most of humanity, at his best – being sick in trains – he is highly entertaining.

★ **Hugh Thomson** *The White Rock*. One of the best travelogue books on Peru for some time, focusing mainly on the archeological explorations and theories of an English Peruvianist.

George Woodcock *Incas and Other Men* (o/p). An enjoyable, light-hearted tour, mixing modern and ancient history, and travel anecdotes. Still a good introduction to Peru over fifty years later.

★ **Ronald Wright** *Cut Stones and Crossroads: A Journey in the Two Worlds of Peru*. An enlightened travel book and probably the best general travelogue writing on Peru over the last few decades, largely due to the author's depth of knowledge of his subject.

PERUVIAN WRITERS

Martín Adán *The Cardboard House*. A poetic novel based in Lima and written by one of South America's best living poets.

Ciro Alegria *Broad and Alien is the World*. Another good book to travel with, this is a distinguished 1970s novel offering persuasive insight into life in the Peruvian highlands.

José María Arguedas *Deep Rivers* and *Yawar Fiesta*. Arguedas is an *indigenista* – writing for and about the native peoples. *Yawar Fiesta* focuses on one of the most impressive Andean peasant ceremonial cycles, involving the annual rite of pitching a live condor against a bull (the condor representing the indigenous Indians and the bull the Spanish conquistadors).

Cesar Vallejo *Collected Poems of Cesar Vallejo*. Peru's one internationally renowned poet – and deservedly so. Romantic but highly innovative in style, his writing translates beautifully.

Mario Vargas Llosa *Death in the Andes, A Fish in the Water, Aunt Julia and the Scriptwriter, The Time of the Hero, Captain Pantoja and the Special Service, The Green House, The Real Life of Alejandro Mayta, The War of the End of the World, Who Killed Palomino Molero?* The best-known and the most brilliant of contemporary Peruvian writers, Vargas Llosa is essentially a novelist but has also written on Peruvian society, run his own current-affairs TV programme in Lima and even made a (rather average) feature film. *Death in the Andes* deals with Sendero Luminoso and Peruvian politics in a style that goes quite a long way towards illuminating popular Peruvian thinking in the late 1980s and early 1990s. His ebullient memoir, *A Fish in the Water*, describes, among other things, Vargas Llosa's experience in unsuccessfully running for the Peruvian presidency. *Aunt Julia*, the best known of his novels to be translated into English, is a fabulous book, a grand and comic novel spiralling out from the stories and exploits of a Bolivian scriptwriter who arrives in Lima to work on Peruvian radio soap operas. In part, too, it is autobiographical, full of insights and goings-on in Miraflores society. Essential reading – and perfect for long Peruvian journeys. His latest novel – *The Way to Paradise* (*El Paraiso en la Otra Esquina)* – is a fictional re-creation of the life and times of Flora Tristan and Paul Gauguin.

NOVELS SET IN PERU

★ **Peter Mathiessen** *At Play in the Fields of the Lord*. A celebrated American novel, which catches the energy and magic of the Peruvian selva.

James Redfield *The Celestine Prophecy*. A best-selling novel that uses Peru as a backdrop. Despite not having much to say about Peru, it was a popular topic of conversation among travellers in the 1990s; some were actually inspired to visit Peru from having read this intriguing book, which expresses with some clarity many New Age concepts and beliefs. Unfortunately the book's descriptions of the Peruvian people, landscapes, forests and culture bear so little relationship to reality that it feels as though the author has never been anywhere near the country.

SPECIALIST GUIDES

John Biggar *The High Andes: A Guide for Climbers*. The first comprehensive climbing guide to the main peaks of the Andes, with a main focus on Peru but also covering Bolivia, Ecuador, Chile, Argentina, Colombia and Venezuela.

Ben Box *Cusco and the Inca Trail*. A good general guide to Peru's most popular destination.

Hilary and George Bradt *Backpacking and Trekking in Peru and Bolivia*. Detailed and excellent coverage of some of Peru's most rewarding hikes – worth taking if you're remotely interested in the idea, and good anyway for background on wildlife and flora.

Charles Brod *Apus and Incas: A Cultural Walking and Trekking Guide to Cusco*. An interesting selection of walks in the Cusco area.

CEV Collins *The Food and Cooking of Peru: traditions, ingredients, tastes & techniques*. A colourful book full of well-illustrated recipes, with alternative ingredients suggested for foods not readily available outside of Peru.

Richard Danbury *The Inca Trail: Cuzco and Machu Picchu*. Highly informative and smoothly written guide to this trekking destination, with fine contextual pieces. Also includes practical information for Lima.

★ **Peter Frost** *Exploring Cusco*. A very practical and stimulating site-by-site guide to the whole Cusco area (where it is widely available in bookstores). Unreservedly recommended if you're spending more than a few days in the region, and also for armchair archeologists back home.

Peter Frost and Jim Bartle *Machu Picchu Historic Sanctuary*. A well-written and beautifully photographed coffee-table book on South America's most alluring archeological site.

Bradley C. Johnson *Classic Climbs of the Cordillera Blanca*. Available in paperback only, this is a must for anyone seriously wanting to climb in Peru's most popular mountaineering destination.

Copeland Marks *Exotic Kitchens of Peru*. Takes a close look at Peruvian food, cooking and culture, and describes the variety of the country's kitchens.

David Mazel *Pure and Perpetual Snow: Two Climbs in the Andes*. Climbing reports on Ausangate and Alpamayo peaks. Available locally or from the South American Explorers' Club.

Lynn Meisch *A Traveller's Guide to El Dorado and the Incan Empire*. Huge paperback full of fascinating detail – well worth reading before visiting Peru.

Latin Works *Machu Picchu Guide*. A small booklet with accurate detail on the various compounds within the archeological site.

Language

Although Peru is officially a Spanish-speaking nation, a large proportion of its population, possibly more than half, regard Spanish as their second language. When the conquistadors arrived, Quechua, the official language of the Inca Empire, was widely spoken everywhere but the jungle. Originally known as Runasimi (from *runa*, "person", and *simis*, "mouth"), it was given the name Quechua – which means "high Andean valleys" – by the Spanish.

Quechua was not, however, the only pre-Columbian tongue. There were, and still are, well over **thirty languages** within the jungle area and, up until the late nineteenth century, **Mochica** had been widely spoken on the north coast for at least 1500 years.

With such a rich linguistic history it is not surprising to find non-European words intruding constantly into any Peruvian conversation. **Cancha**, for instance, the Inca word for "courtyard", is still commonly used to refer to most sporting areas – *la cancha de basketball*, for example. Other linguistic survivors have even reached the English language: **llama**, **condor**, **puma** and **pampa** among them. Perhaps more interesting is the great wealth of traditional **Creole slang** – utilized with equal vigour at all levels of society. This complex speech, much like Cockney rhyming slang, is difficult to catch without almost complete fluency in Spanish, though one phrase you may find useful for directing a taxi driver is *de fresa alfonso* – literally translatable as "of strawberry, Alfonso" but actually meaning "straight on" (*de frente al fondo*).

Once you get into it, **Spanish** is the easiest language there is – and in Peru people are eager to understand even the most faltering attempt. You'll be further helped by the fact that South Americans speak relatively slowly (at least compared with Spanish people in Spain) and that there's no need to get your tongue round the lisping pronunciation.

Pronunciation

The rules of **pronunciation** are pretty straightforward and, once you get to know them, strictly observed. Unless there's an accent, words ending in d, l, r and z are **stressed** on the last syllable, all others on the second last. All **vowels** are pure and short.

A somewhere between the "A" sound of b**a**ck and that of f**a**ther
E as in g**e**t
I as in pol**i**ce
O as in h**o**t
U as in r**u**le
C is soft before E and I, hard otherwise: **cerca** is pronounced "serka"
G works the same way, a guttural "H" sound (like the ch in loch) before E or I, a hard G elsewhere – **gigante** becomes "higante"
H is always silent
J is the same sound as a guttural G: **jamón** is pronounced "hamon"
LL sounds like an English Y: **tortilla** is pronounced "torteeya"
N is as in English unless it has a tilde (accent) over it, when it becomes NY: **mañana** sounds like "manyana"
QU is pronounced like an English K
R is rolled, RR doubly so
V sounds more like B, **vino** becoming "beano"
X is slightly softer than in English – sometimes almost SH – except between vowels in place names where it has an "H" sound – for example México (Meh-Hee-Ko) or Oaxaca
Z is the same as a soft C, so **cerveza** becomes "servesa"

Below is a list of a few essential words and phrases, though if you're travelling for any length of time a **dictionary** or phrase book is obviously a worthwhile investment – try the *Dictionary of Latin American Spanish* (University of Chicago Press). Bear in mind that in Spanish CH, LL and Ñ count as separate letters and are listed after the Cs, Ls and Ns respectively.

WORDS AND PHRASES

BASICS

Yes	Sí
No	No
Please	Por favor
Thank you	Gracias
Where…?	¿Dónde ?
When ?	¿Cuándo ?
What…?	¿Qué ?
How much…?	¿Cuánto ?
Do you have the time?	¿Tiene la hora?
Here	Aquí
There	Allí
This	Este
That	Eso
Now	Ahora
Later	Más tarde
Open	Abierto/a
Closed	Cerrado/a
With	Con
Without	Sin
Good	Buen(o)/a
Bad	Mal(o)/a
Big	Gran(de)
Small	Pequeño/a
More	Más
Less	Menos
Today	Hoy
Tomorrow	Mañana
Yesterday	Ayer

GREETINGS AND RESPONSES

Hello	Hola
Goodbye	Adiós
Good morning	Buenos días
Good afternoon/night	Buenas tardes/noches
See you later	Hasta luego
Sorry	Lo siento/discúlpeme
Excuse me	Con permiso/perdón
How are you?	¿Como está (usted)?
I (don't) understand	(No) Entiendo
Not at all	De nada
Do you speak English?	¿Habla (usted) inglés?
I don't speak Spanish	No hablo español
My name is …	Me llamo …
What's your name?	¿Como se llama usted?
I am English	Soy inglés(a)
… American	… americano/a
… Australian	… australiano/a
… Canadian	… canadiense
… Irish	… irlandés(a)
… New Zealander	… neozelandés(a)
… Scottish	… escocés(a)
… Welsh	… galés(a)

TRANSPORT AND DIRECTIONS

Do you know…?	¿Sabe…?
I don't know	No sé
How do I get to…?	Por dónde se va a…?
Left, right, straight on	Izquierda, derecha, derecho
Where is…?	¿Dónde está…?
…the bus station	…la estación de autobuses
…the train station	…la estación de ferrocarriles
…the nearest bank	…el banco más cercano
…the post office	…el correo
…the toilet	...el baño/sanitario
Where does the bus to… leave from?	¿De dónde sale el camión para…?
Is this the train for Lima?	¿Es éste el tren para Lima?
I'd like a (return) ticket to…	Querría un boleto (de ida y vuelta) para…
What time does it leave (arrive in…)?	¿A qué hora sale (llega en…)?

ACCOMMODATION, RESTAURANTS AND SHOPPING

I want	Quiero
I'd like	Querría
There is (is there)?	(¿)Hay(?)
Give me (one like that)	Deme (uno así)
Do you have…?	Tiene …?
…a room	…un cuarto
…with two beds/ double bed …	…con dos camas/ cama matrimonial
It's for one person (two people)	es para una persona (dos personas)
…for one night (one week)	…para una noche (una semana)
It's fine, how much is it?	¿Está bien, cuánto es?
It's too expensive	Es demasiado caro
Don't you have anything cheaper?	¿No tiene algo más barato?
Can one… ?	¿Se puede…?
…camp (near here?)	¿…acampar aquí (cerca)?
Is there a hotel nearby?	¿Hay un hotel aquí cerca?
What is there to eat?	¿Qué hay para comer?
What's that?	¿Qué es eso?
What's this called in Spanish?	¿Como se llama este en Castillano?

USEFUL ACCOMMODATION TERMS

Desk fan or ceiling fan	Ventilador
Air-conditioned	Aire-acondicionado
Baño colectivo/compartido	Shared bath
Hot water	Agua caliente

Cold water	Agua fría	**Single room**	Cuarto simple
Double bed	Cama matrimonial	**Taxes**	Impuestos
Single bed	Sencillo	**Check-out time**	Hora de salida

FOOD AND DRINK

BASICS

Arroz Rice
Avena Oats (porridge)
Galletas Biscuits
Harina Flour
Huevos Eggs
  fritos fried
  duros hard-boiled
  pasados lightly boiled
  revueltos scrambled
Mermelada Jam
Miel Honey
Mostaza Mustard
Pan (integral) Bread (brown)
Picante de… spicy dish of …
Queso Cheese

SOUP (SOPAS) AND STARTERS

Caldo Broth
Caldo de gallina Chicken broth
Causa Mashed potatoes and shrimp
Conchas a la parmesana Scallops with Parmesan
Huevos a la rusa Egg salad
Inchicapi Appetizing jungle soup made from chicken, peanuts, manioc (*yuca*) and fresh coriander herb
Palta Avocado
Palta rellena Stuffed avocado
Papa rellena Stuffed fried potato
Sopa a la criolla Noodles, vegetables and meat

SEAFOOD (MARISCOS) AND FISH (PESCADO)

Calamares Squid
Camarones Shrimp
Cangrejo Crab
Ceviche Marinated seafood
Chaufa de mariscos Chinese rice with seafood
  cojinova
Corvina Sea bass
Erizo Sea urchin
Jalea Large dish of fish with onion
Langosta Lobster
Langostino a lo macho Crayfish in spicy shellfish sauce
Lenguado Sole
Paiche Large jungle river fish
Tiradito Ceviche without onion or sweet potato
Tollo Small shark
Zungarro Large jungle fish

MEAT (CARNES)

Adobo Meat/fish in mild chilli sauce
Ají de gallina Chicken in chilli sauce
Anticuchos Skewered heart (usually lamb)
Bifstek (bistek) Steak
Cabrito Goat
Carapulcra Pork, chicken and potato casserole
Carne a lo pobre Steak, fries, egg and banana
Carne de res Beef
Chicharrones Deep-fried pork skins
Conejo Rabbit
Cordero Lamb
Cuy Guinea pig (a traditional dish)
Estofado Stewed meat (usually served with rice)
Higado Liver
Jamón Ham
Lechón Pork
Lomo asado Roast beef
Lomo saltado Sautéed beef
Mollejitos Gizzard
Pachamanca Meat and vegetables, cooked over hot, buried stones
Parillada Grilled meat
Pato Duck
Pavo Turkey
Pollo (a la brasa) Chicken (spit-roasted)
Tocino Bacon
Venado Venison

VEGETABLES (LEGUMBRES) AND SIDE DISHES

Ají Chilli
Camote Sweet potato
Cebolla Onion
Choclo Corn on the cob

Fideos	Noodles
Frijoles	Beans
Hongos	Mushrooms
Lechuga	Lettuce
Papa rellena	Fried potato balls, stuffed with olives, egg and mincemeat
Tallarines	Spaghetti noodles
Tomates	Tomatoes
Yuca a la Huancaina	Manioc (like a yam) in spicy cheese sauce

FRUIT

Chirimoya	Custard apple (green and fleshy outside, tastes like strawberries and cream)
Lucuma	Small nutty fruit (used in ice creams and cakes)
Maracuya	Passion fruit
Palta	Avocado
Piña	Pineapple
Tuna	Pear-like cactus fruit (refreshing but full of hard little seeds)

SWEETS (DULCES)

Barquillo	Ice cream cone
Flan	Crème caramel
Helado	Ice cream
Keke	Cake
Manjar blanco	Sweetened condensed milk
Mazamorra morada	Fruit/maize jelly
Panqueques	Pancakes
Picarones	Doughnuts with syrup

SNACKS (BOCADILLOS)

Castañas	Brazil nuts
Chifle	Fried banana slices
Empanada	Meat or cheese pie
Hamburguesa	Hamburger
Salchipapas	Potatoes, sliced frankfurter sausage and condiments
Sandwich de butifara	Ham and onion sandwich
Sandwich de lechón	Pork salad sandwich
Tamale	Maize-flour roll stuffed with olives, egg, meat and vegetables
Tortilla	Omelette-cum-pancake
Tostadas	Toast

FRUIT JUICES (JUGOS)

Especial	Fruit, milk, sometimes beer
Fresa	Strawberry
Higo	Fig
Manzana	Apple
Melón	Melon
Naranja	Orange
Papaya	Papaya
Piña	Pineapple
Platano	Banana
Surtido	Mixed
Toronja	Grapefruit
Zanahoria	Carrot

BEVERAGES (BEBIDAS)

Agua	Water
Agua mineral	Mineral water
Algarrobina	Algarroba-fruit drink
Café	Coffee
Cerveza	Beer
Chicha de jora	Fermented maize beer
Chicha morada	Maize soft drink
Chilcano de pisco	Pisco with lemonade
Chopp	Draught beer
Cuba libre	Rum and Coke
Gaseosa	Soft carbonated drink
Leche	Milk
Limonada	Real lemonade
Masato	Fermented manioc beer
Pisco	White-grape brandy
Ponche	Punch
Ron	Rum
Té	Tea
....con leche	....with milk
....de anis	....aniseed tea
....de limón	....lemon tea
....hierba luisa	....lemon-grass tea
....manzanilla	....camomile tea

NUMBERS AND DAYS

1	un/uno, una
2	dos
3	tres
4	cuatro
5	cinco
6	seis
7	siete
8	ocho
9	nueve
10	diez
11	once
12	doce
13	trece
14	catorce

15	quince	**500**	quinientos
16	dieciséis	**1000**	mil
20	veinte	**2000**	dos mil
21	veintiuno		
30	treinta	**first**	primero/a
40	cuarenta	**second**	segundo/a
50	cincuenta	**third**	tercero/a
60	sesenta		
70	setenta	**Monday**	lunes
80	ochenta	**Tuesday**	martes
90	noventa	**Wednesday**	miércoles
100	cien(to)	**Thursday**	jueves
101	ciento uno	**Friday**	viernes
200	doscientos	**Saturday**	sábado
201	doscientos uno	**Sunday**	domingo

GLOSSARY OF PERUVIAN TERMS

Aguajina Refreshing palm-fruit drink
Apu Mountain god
Arriero Muleteer
Ayllu Kinship group, or clan
Barrio Suburb, or sometimes shantytown
Bauda Curve in the river
Burro Donkey
Cacique Headman
Callejón Corridor, or narrow street
Campesino Peasant, country dweller, someone who works in the fields
Ceja de la selva Edge of the jungle
Chacra Cultivated garden or plot
Chaquiras Pre-Columbian stone or coral beads
Chicha Maize beer, or a form of Peruvian music
Chifa Peruvian-Chinese restaurant
Colectivo Collective taxi
Cordillera Mountain range
Curaca Chief
Curandero Healer
Empresa Company
Encomienda Colonial grant of land and native labour
Extranjero Foreigner
Farmacia Chemist
Flaco/a Skinny (common nickname)
Gordo/a Fat (common nickname)
Gringo A European or North American
Hacienda Estate
Huaca Sacred spot or object
Huaco Pre-Columbian artefact
Huaquero Someone who digs or looks for huacos
Jirón Road
Lomas Place where vegetation grows with moisture from the air rather than from rainfall or irrigation
Mamacona Inca Sun Virgin
Masato Manioc beer
El monte The forest
Paiche The world's largest freshwater fish, often found on jungle menus
Pakucho Jungle variant of "gringo"
Peña Nightclub with live music
Peque-peque Onomatopoeic word used for small-boat motor engines (usually a four or nine horsepower with the propeller on a long shaft which helps to steer the canoe and can be lifted easily out of the water in shallows)
Plata Silver; slang for "cash"
Poblado Settlement
Pongo Whitewater rapids
Pueblos jóvenes Shantytowns
Puna Barren Andean heights
Quebrada Stream
Remolino Whirlpool
Restinga Area of forest that lies above the river flood level on a permanent basis
Selva Jungle
Selvático Jungle dweller
Serrano Mountain dweller
Shushupero "Drunk" or inebriated individual, from the deadly *shushupe* snake
Sierra Mountains
Siete raices Strong medicinal drink, mixed from seven jungle plants and *aguardiente*
Soroche Altitude sickness
Tambo Inca Highway rest-house
Tienda Shop
Tipishca Oxbow lake
Tramites Red tape, bureaucracy
Unsu Throne, or platform
Varzea Forest which gets regularly flooded

Small print and index

A ROUGH GUIDE TO ROUGH GUIDES

Published in 1982, the first Rough Guide – to Greece – was a student scheme that became a publishing phenomenon. Mark Ellingham, a recent graduate in English from Bristol University, had been travelling in Greece the previous summer and couldn't find the right guidebook. With a small group of friends he wrote his own guide, combining a highly contemporary, journalistic style with a thoroughly practical approach to travellers' needs.

The immediate success of the book spawned a series that rapidly covered dozens of destinations. And, in addition to impecunious backpackers, Rough Guides soon acquired a much broader readership that relished the guides' wit and inquisitiveness as much as their enthusiastic, critical approach and value-for-money ethos.

These days, Rough Guides include recommendations from budget to luxury and cover more than 200 destinations around the globe, as well as producing an ever-growing range of eBooks and apps.

Visit **roughguides.com** to see our latest publications.

Rough Guide credits

Editors: Natasha Foges, Alison Roberts, Lucy White
Layout: Pradeep Thapliyal
Cartography: Swati Handoo
Picture editor: Rhiannon Furbear
Proofreader: Diane Margolis
Managing editor: Mani Ramaswamy
Assistant editor: Prema Dutta
Photographers: Tim Draper, Suzanne Porter
Production: Gemma Sharpe
Cover design: Nicole Newman, Tessa Bindloss, Pradeep Thapliyal
Editorial assistant: Eleanor Aldridge
Senior pre-press designer: Dan May
Design director: Scott Stickland
Travel publisher: Joanna Kirby
Digital travel publisher: Peter Buckley
Reference director: Andrew Lockett
Operations coordinator: Becky Doyle
Publishing director (Travel): Clare Currie
Commercial manager: Gino Magnotta
Managing director: John Duhigg

Publishing information

This eighth edition published October 2012 by
Rough Guides Ltd,
80 Strand, London WC2R 0RL
11, Community Centre, Panchsheel Park,
New Delhi 110017, India
Distributed by the Penguin Group
Penguin Books Ltd,
80 Strand, London WC2R 0RL
Penguin Group (USA)
375 Hudson Street, NY 10014, USA
Penguin Group (Australia)
250 Camberwell Road, Camberwell,
Victoria 3124, Australia
Penguin Group (NZ)
67 Apollo Drive, Mairangi Bay, Auckland 1310,
New Zealand
Penguin Group (South Africa)
Block D, Rosebank Office Park, 181 Jan Smuts Avenue,
Parktown North, Gauteng, South Africa 2193
Rough Guides is represented in Canada by Tourmaline Editions Inc. 662 King Street West, Suite 304, Toronto, Ontario M5V 1M7
Printed in Singapore by Toppan Security Printing Pte. Ltd.

552pp includes index
A catalogue record for this book is available from the British Library
ISBN: 978-1-40538-985-3

1 3 5 7 9 8 6 4 2

Help us update

We've gone to a lot of effort to ensure that the eighth edition of **The Rough Guide to Peru** is accurate and up-to-date. However, things change – places get "discovered", opening hours are notoriously fickle, restaurants and rooms raise prices or lower standards. If you feel we've got it wrong or left something out, we'd like to know, and if you can remember the address, the price, the hours, the phone number, so much the better.

Please send your comments with the subject line "**Rough Guide Peru Update**" to mail@uk.roughguides.com. We'll credit all contributions and send a copy of the next edition (or any other Rough Guide if you prefer) for the very best emails.

Find more travel information, connect with fellow travellers and book your trip on roughguides.com

ABOUT THE AUTHOR

Dilwyn Jenkins Based in rural Wales, Dilwyn Jenkins has been exploring Peru for over thirty years. With a background in social anthropology and renewable energy, he works on sustainable development, particularly in the Amazon region and with the Ashaninka tribe in Peru. Dilwyn's company, Ecotribal, offers indigenous communities alternative incomes from rainforest conservation, sustainably produced crafts, forest garden products and eco-cultural tourism. He also writes and works on TV documentaries, mainly on travel, tribal and environmental issues.

Acknowledgements

Thanks to Carlos, Maritza and Ignacio Montenegro, to Raphaelle and as always to all those who held the fort at home, particularly Tess, Bethan, Max, Teilo, TigerLilly, Tala Luna, Claire, Danny and Jenny.

Readers' letters

Thanks to all the readers who have taken the time to write in with comments and suggestions (and apologies if we've inadvertently omitted or misspelt anyone's name):

Tais Briceño; Carl Callaway; Peter Castro; Sue Conner; Maggie Dawson; Dan & Lois Easley; Denise Fussen; Sukhreet Ghuman; Kelly Grainger; Rand Hoffman; Ruth Horwitz; Kevin Hurley; Laura Joseph; Matthys Katrien; Michael Keating; Anita Kelles-Viitanen; Eyal Keshet; Kirsty Kothakota; Camden Luxford; Scott Mafater; Tom Nurick; Louis Otis; Amélie Ranger; Paul Rogers; Anna Sampy; Bill Scolding; Katy Shorthouse; Nicolas Vandenbroucque; Roy van der Meijs; Kelly Wiebe; Roland Zimmermann.

Photo credits

All photos © Rough Guides except the following:
(Key: t-top; c-centre; b-bottom; l-left; r-right)

p.1 Corbis/Pete Oxford/Minden Pictures
p.2 4Corners/Orient/SIME
p.4 Corbis/Robert Postma/First Light
p.5 SuperStock/MIVA Stock
p.9 Dorling Kindersley/Demetrio Carrasco (b)
p.11 Getty Images/David Tipling (t)
p.13 Corbis/AOLO AGUILAR/epa (c); Konrad Wothe (t); SuperStock/Eye Ubiquitous (b)
p.14 Alamy/Travel (b)
p.15 Alamy/neiljohn (bl)
p.16 Alamy/John Warburton-Lee Photography (tl); SuperStock/Jason Langley (br)
p.17 AWL Images/Nigel Pavitt (t)
p.18 Getty Images/Aurora Creative (t)
p.19 AWL Images/Paul Harris (b)
p.21 Corbis/Mike Theiss/National Geographic Society (b); Getty Images/Cuan Hansen/Gallo Images (tr)
p.22 Getty Images/Altrendo Travel
p.52 Getty Images/Juergen Ritterbach
p.73 Robert Harding Picture Library/Rodrigo Torres (b)
p.93 AWL Images/Danita Delimont (tr); Getty Images/Aurora Creative/Axel Fassio (b)
p.133 Dorling Kindersley/Linda Whitwam (t); NHPA/Photoshot/Kevin Schafer (b)
p.138 Dorling Kindersley/Linda Whitwam
p.150 Getty Images/Robert Harding World Imagery/Jane Sweeney
p.177 Corbis/Ed Kashi
p.227 Corbis/Hugh Sitton (b)
p.280 Dorling Kindersley/Demetrio Carrasco
p.313 Corbis/Marcos Ferro
p.331 Dorling Kindersley/Michel Burger (t, b)
p.348 4Corners/Stefano Torrione/SIME
p.351 AWL Images/Andrew Watson
p.373 Alamy/J.Enrique Molina (b); Corbis/Abraham Nowitz/National Geographic Society (tr)
p.405 Corbis/Andrew Watson/JAI (t)
p.415 Alamy/National Geographic Image Collection (tr); AWL Images/Andrew Watson (b)
p.426 AWL Images/Dennis Kirkland/Jaynes Gallery
p.429 NHPA/Photoshot/Andre Baertschi
p.449 Axiom Photographic Agency/Paul Miles (t); FLPA/David Tipling (br); Getty Images/Frans Lemmens (bl)
p.469 AWL Images/Aurora Photos (b); Paul Harris (tl); SuperStock/Wolfgang Kaehler (tr)

Front cover Machu Picchu © MIVA Stock/Superstock
Back cover Auto rickshaws in Iquitos © Altrendo/Getty Images (top); Mestiza Cuzquena dancer in motion, Cuzco © Gavin Hellier/Robert Harding World Imagery/Corbis (left); Red-eyed tree frog © iStock Photo (right)

Index

Maps are marked in **grey**

D

E

F

G

M

N

O

P

Q

R

S

T

Map symbols

The symbols below are used on maps throughout the book

- Airport
- Bus/taxi
- Parking
- Post office
- Information office
- Telephone office
- Internet access
- Hospital
- Bank
- Place of interest
- Campsite
- Beach
- Golf course
- Viewpoint
- Lodge
- Museum
- Fort
- Monument
- Pass
- Bridge
- Mountain range
- Mountain peak
- Spring
- Cave
- Ruins
- Cliff
- Arch
- Building
- Church (regional map)
- Church
- Stadium
- Market
- Park
- Saltpan
- Glacier

Listings key

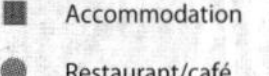
Accommodation
Restaurant/café

Bar/club & live music venue/ gay club/club & peña